CONTENTS

Company Histories

PREFACE

The St. James Press series *The International Directory of Company Histories (IDCH)* is intended for reference use by students, business people, librarians, historians, economists, investors, job candidates, and others who seek to learn more about the historical development of the world's most important companies. To date, *IDCH* has covered over 4,550 companies in 33 volumes.

Inclusion Criteria

Most companies chosen for inclusion in *IDCH* have achieved a minimum of US$50 million in annual sales and are leading influences in their industries or geographical locations. Companies may be publicly held, private, or nonprofit. State-owned companies that are important in their industries and that may operate much like public or private companies also are included. Wholly owned subsidiaries and divisions are profiled if they meet the requirements for inclusion. Entries on companies that have had major changes since they were last profiled may be selected for updating.

The *IDCH* series highlights 10% private and nonprofit companies, and features updated entries on approximately 45 companies per volume.

Entry Format

Each entry begins with the company's legal name, the address of its headquarters, its telephone, toll-free, and fax numbers, and its web site. A statement of public, private, state, or parent ownership follows. A company with a legal name in both English and the language of its headquarters country is listed by the English name, with the native-language name in parentheses.

The company's founding or earliest incorporation date, the number of employees, and the most recent available sales figures follow. Sales figures are given in local currencies with equivalents in U.S. dollars. For some private companies, sales figures are estimates and indicated by the abbreviation *est.* The entry lists the exchanges on which a company's stock is traded and its ticker symbol, as well as the company's NAIC codes.

Entries generally contain a *Company Perspectives* box which provides a short summary of the company's mission, goals, and ideals, a *Key Dates* box highlighting milestones in the company's history, lists of *Principal Subsidiaries, Principal Divisions, Principal Operating Units, Principal Competitors,* and articles for *Further Reading.*

American spelling is used throughout *IDCH*, and the word "billion" is used in its U.S. sense of one thousand million.

Sources

Entries have been compiled from publicly accessible sources both in print and on the Internet such as general and academic periodicals, books, annual reports, and material supplied by the companies themselves.

Cumulative Indexes

IDCH contains two indexes: the **Index to Companies**, which provides an alphabetical index to companies discussed in the text as well as to companies profiled, and the **Index to Industries**, which allows researchers to locate companies by their principal industry. Both indexes are cumulative and specific instructions for using them are found immediately preceding each index.

Suggestions Welcome

Comments and suggestions from users of *IDCH* on any aspect of the product as well as suggestions for companies to be included or updated are cordially invited. Please write:

The Editor
International Directory of Company Histories
St. James Press
27500 Drake Rd.
Farmington Hills, Michigan 48331-3535

STAFF

Tina Grant, *Editor*

Miranda H. Ferrara, *Project Manager*

Michelle Banks, Laura Standley Berger, Joann Cerrito, Jim Craddock, Steve Cusack, Kristin Hart,
Laura S. Kryhoski, Margaret Mazurkiewicz, Carol Schwartz, Christine Thomassini,
Michael J. Tyrkus, *St. James Press Editorial Staff*

Peter M. Gareffa, *Managing Editor, St. James Press*

Library of Congress Catalog Number: 89-190943

British Library Cataloguing in Publication Data

International directory of company histories. Vol. 33
I. Tina Grant
338.7409

ISBN 1-55862-392-2

Printed in the United States of America
Published simultaneously in the United Kingdom

St. James Press is an imprint of The Gale Group

Cover photograph: The Stock Exchange of Thailand building
(courtesy of The Stock Exchange of Thailand)

10 9 8 7 6 5 4 3 2 1

International Directory of
COMPANY
HISTORIES

VOLUME 33

Editor
Tina Grant

ST. JAMES PRESS

AN IMPRINT OF THE GALE GROUP

DETROIT • NEW YORK • SAN FRANCISCO
LONDON • BOSTON • WOODBRIDGE, CT

International Directory of
COMPANY HISTORIES

ABBREVIATIONS FOR FORMS OF COMPANY INCORPORATION

A.B.	Aktiebolaget (Sweden)
A.G.	Aktiengesellschaft (Germany, Switzerland)
A.S.	Atieselskab (Denmark)
A.S.	Aksjeselskap (Denmark, Norway)
A.Ş.	Anomin Şirket (Turkey)
B.V.	Besloten Vennootschap met beperkte, Aansprakelijkheid (The Netherlands)
Co.	Company (United Kingdom, United States)
Corp.	Corporation (United States)
G.I.E.	Groupement d'Intérêt Economique (France)
GmbH	Gesellschaft mit beschränkter Haftung (Germany)
H.B.	Handelsbolaget (Sweden)
Inc.	Incorporated (United States)
KGaA	Kommanditgesellschaft auf Aktien (Germany)
K.K.	Kabushiki Kaisha (Japan)
LLC	Limited Liability Company (Middle East)
Ltd.	Limited (Canada, Japan, United Kingdom, United States)
N.V.	Naamloze Vennootschap (The Netherlands)
OY	Osakeyhtiöt (Finland)
PLC	Public Limited Company (United Kingdom)
PTY.	Proprietary (Australia, Hong Kong, South Africa)
S.A.	Société Anonyme (Belgium, France, Switzerland)
SpA	Società per Azioni (Italy)

ABBREVIATIONS FOR CURRENCY

DA	Algerian dinar	Dfl	Netherlands florin
A$	Australian dollar	Nfl	Netherlands florin
Sch	Austrian schilling	NZ$	New Zealand dollar
BFr	Belgian franc	N	Nigerian naira
Cr	Brazilian cruzado	NKr	Norwegian krone
C$	Canadian dollar	RO	Omani rial
RMB	Chinese renminbi	P	Philippine peso
DKr	Danish krone	PLN	Polish Zloty
E£	Egyptian pound	Esc	Portuguese escudo
EUR	Euro Dollars	Ru	Russian ruble
Fmk	Finnish markka	SRls	Saudi Arabian riyal
FFr	French franc	S$	Singapore dollar
DM	German mark	R	South African rand
HK$	Hong Kong dollar	W	South Korean won
HUF	Hungarian forint	Pta	Spanish peseta
Rs	Indian rupee	SKr	Swedish krona
Rp	Indonesian rupiah	SFr	Swiss franc
IR£	Irish pound	NT$	Taiwanese dollar
L	Italian lira	B	Thai baht
¥	Japanese yen	£	United Kingdom pound
W	Korean won	$	United States dollar
KD	Kuwaiti dinar	B	Venezuelan bolivar
LuxFr	Luxembourgian franc	K	Zambian kwacha
M$	Malaysian ringgit		

International Directory of

COMPANY
HISTORIES

ACE Cash Express, Inc.

1231 Greenway Drive
Suite 800
Irving, Texas 75038
U.S.A.
Telephone: (972) 550-5000
Fax: (972) 550-5150
Web site: http://www.acecashexpress.com

Public Company
Incorporated: 1968 as MoneyMart
Employees: 1,731
Sales: $122.3 million (1999)
Stock Exchanges: NASDAQ
Ticker Symbol: AACE
NAIC: 522294 Secondary Market Financing; 52229 All
   Other Nondepository Credit Intermediation

ACE Cash Express, Inc. is the largest owner, operator, and franchiser of check-cashing stores in the United States. In addition to its booming check-cashing business, ACE offers a range of other services, such as small consumer loans, money orders, wire transfers, and electronic tax and bill payment. ACE also sells pre-paid phone cards, auto insurance (in conjunction with Instant Auto Insurance), and pre-paid Internet service (with ePOWER International). The company has grown considerably in recent years, doubling the number of its stores to 960 spread among 29 states between 1994 and 1999. A publicly traded company since 1993, ACE has labored to overcome the popular preconception that the check-cashing business is a sordid industry exploiting the poor and disadvantaged.

Early History of Check-Cashing Industry

Check-cashing stores existed long before ACE Cash Express, Inc. emerged as the industry's leader. The first such businesses sprang up in the 1920s when a number of companies began to pay their workers with checks instead of cash. Depression-era Americans were loathe to deposit their paychecks in the nation's failing banks, and instead opted to cash their checks in neighborhood outlets that charged a small fee for such services. After the Federal Deposit Insurance Corporation (FDIC) was created to place a safety net under individual bank depositors' assets, the average worker came to rely less on check-cashing businesses.

Adapting to this trend, check-cashing stores began to carve out a niche serving those who could not—or would not—obtain bank accounts. Often located in inner-city areas, these stores charged a fee to cash government or payroll checks for their clients. The entire industry was, in large part, unregulated, with some businesses exacting as much as 20 percent of the check's face value as a "service fee." Check-cashing stores typically conducted other transactions as well, including the sale of money orders, lottery tickets, and public transportation tokens.

ACE's Origins: 1968–85

ACE's roots stretch back to 1968 when MoneyMart was founded in Denver, Colorado. By the early 1980s, MoneyMart operated a sizable network of 70 check-cashing stores in Colorado and in Dallas and Houston, Texas. This degree of consolidation was rare in the check-cashing industry, as most businesses were owned individually. Yet more was to come. In 1984, Associates Corp. (a division of the financial services giant Gulf + Western Inc.), acquired the MoneyMart chain to complement its thriving money order business. After renaming the stores Associates Cash Express in 1984, Gulf + Western added 20 new stores to the chain by 1985. By 1986, Associates was by the far the biggest name in the industry.

That same year, two Gulf + Western executives recognized Associates Cash Express's prodigious revenue-generating potential. Wallace Swanson and Don Neustadt (then the president of Associates Corp.'s wider money-order operations) joine together with a group of private investors to acquire the e? Associates Cash Express division for approximately $5 lion. Rechristened ACE Cash Express, the now-ind? company concentrated on maintaining its sizable ' burgeoning check-cashing market.

Although still burdened by an unsavo? check-cashing industry was flourishing n? large part by the deregulation of the fin?

Company Perspectives:

Since beginning 32 years ago, ACE has followed the same disciplined practice of balanced growth through adding new stores, acquiring existing operations, expanding products, and enhancing services. Today, ACE serves more than two million customers each month.

in the early 1980s, check-cashing outlets laid claim to a growing number of customers. Deregulation had increased competition in the American banking industry, and as banks cast about for more profitable ways to do business, many began charging for basic services such as check cashing, thereby deterring many potential lower-income customers who could not or would not pay such fees. Exacerbating this trend was the fact that most banks went so far as to refuse to cash checks for those without an account at the bank (even for government-issued checks), and many raised the fees they charged to provide checking accounts, or levied penalties on accounts that dipped below a minimum balance. Moreover, as they sought further cost-cutting measures, banks closed less profitable branches in low-income neighborhoods, leaving whole classes of people without easy access to mainstream banks.

According to *US Banker,* the result of these industry shifts was a "service vacuum created by the banking industry itself." The Federal Reserve estimated that one-fifth of U.S. households did not have a checking account in 1983 and that 36 percent of those with annual incomes below $8,400 had neither a checking nor savings account. Check-cashing businesses filled this banking void by providing services for those who did not have a checking account at a bank. In addition to cashing checks for a fee, these stores sold money orders with which clients could pay bills.

Expansion: 1988–97

From its inception, ACE had to find its way in this shifting financial services landscape. Even more tumultuous was the fact that the company quickly had to fend off a 1987 takeover attempt by Cash America International Inc., a network of pawn shops eager to augment its operations. The publicly traded Cash America eventually abandoned the acquisition because of concerns on Wall Street that the company was venturing too far afield from its core pawn shop business. In the aftermath of Cash America's bid, ACE president Don Neustadt and chairman and CEO Ray Hemmig made expansion the company's top priority in an effort to maintain ACE's leading position in an increasingly competitive industry.

Consistent with its focus on growth, ACE opened 52 new stores between 1987 and 1989. By 1990, ACE reported revenue of $16.6 million. Although its operations were still highly concentrated in Texas and Colorado, the company also searched for opportunities to enter additional markets. To this end, ACE sought to acquire Check Express, another large check-cashing chain, in 1991. Strongly positioned in the southeast, Check Express offered ACE a foothold into new regions. The deal was rejected, however, by Check Express's board of directors in November 1991. ACE's sales for the year rose to $20 million nevertheless.

Spurned by Check Express, ACE opted to fuel its growth with a public stock offering instead. In December 1992 the company sold 1.5 million shares (earning $15.3 million in the process), and then launched an ambitious store-building plan early in 1993. Although it had been opening an impressive average of 30 new stores each year since 1987, the company planned to increase that number to 50. In fact, as Hemmig revealed to the *Wall Street Transcript* in 1993, "We hope to double the size of our company in the next five years." ACE's agenda was twofold. In addition to venturing into new regions, it sought to bolster its presence in its current markets. "Our game plan is to cover a market from north to south, from east to west," Hemmig told the *Dallas Morning News.* Moreover, despite the difficulties it had experienced with the Check Express deal, ACE did not forego acquisitions. In November 1993 ACE successfully purchased Mr. Money—a 23-store check-cashing chain well established in Georgia—for $4.1 million. By the year's end, ACE's roster of check cashers had grown to more than 300, and it had locations in ten states and the District of Columbia and was more than twice the size of its nearest competitor. Even more impressive were the company's soaring sales, which rose to $32.7 million in 1993, as well as its net income, which surged 62 percent the same year.

ACE's expansion strategy was not limited to opening new stores, though. The company also developed new services in an effort both to raise revenue and to win the repeat business of its clients. In 1990 ACE had introduced electronic tax filing, which proved popular among customers willing to pay a fee to receive quicker tax refunds. By 1993, tax filing had become ACE's third largest revenue source, trailing only check cashing and money order sales. Also in 1993, ACE entered the nascent pre-paid services market, when it began to offer pre-paid long distance phone cards at its check-cashing stores. Nevertheless, check cashing remained the staple of ACE's earnings, accounting for about 90 percent of its business. To minimize its risk from check fraud, ACE implemented a $2.5 million computer point-of-sale system in 1993, linking each store to the company's headquarters. The system also allowed ACE to track its consumers' transaction histories. "It gives us a greater control of the business and the ability to anticipate trends [in] customer behavior," Hemmig explained to the *Dallas Morning News.*

Despite its steady gains in sales and profits, ACE's stock prices had remained low as a result of the industry's negative reputation. As an anonymous check casher told the *Los Angeles Times,* the industry had a "bail bondsman image." To counter-balance the notion that check cashers gouged the poor to provide basic services, ACE took care to project a more positive image. Its green and white facade stores were clean and well lit, with the prices charged for various services prominently displayed, much like menus in fast food restaurants. Company officials stressed ACE's convenience and its array of services. ACE also emphasized its non-check-cashing services to help boost its image.

ACE's efforts to burnish its reputation were assisted by significant changes in the check-cashing industry as a whole. As the savings rate of the average American plummeted to an all time low, a greater number of families was saddled with hefty credit card debts. Increasingly, check cashers' prime customers were no

Key Dates:

1968: MoneyMart is founded in Denver, Colorado.
1984: Associates Corp. acquires MoneyMart and renames it Associates Express.
1986: Executives of Associates Express and some private investors purchase company and rename it ACE Cash Express.
1990: Company launches prepaid phone cards; begins offering electronic income tax filing.
1992: ACE makes initial public stock offering.
1993: ACE begins aggressive expansion plan; company purchases Mr. Money.
1995: Company acquires Check Express.
1996: ACE begins to franchise its check-cashing stores.
1999: ACE begins offering auto insurance and universal electronic bill-paying systems; ACE teams up with Goleta National Bank to provide ''payday'' loans.
2000: ACE joins with ePOWER International to provide prepaid Internet service.

longer the urban poor, but rather ''white-collar job holders who use their services to make ends meet,'' according to the *Cincinnati Enquirer*. So-called ''payday'' loans—in which check cashers allowed a customer to write a post-dated check and cash it on the spot for a fee—became an important aspect of the industry. As a result of the changing client base, check cashing outlets became more prevalent in suburban areas. Like its competitors, ACE reported that its most rapid growth by the mid-1990s occurred in suburban roadside shopping malls.

With its growing customer base, ACE was able to expand both its geographical presence and its range of services. In 1994 the company introduced ACE Bill Pay, which allowed ACE's walk-in customers to pay utility and other bills on the premises for a small fee (an arrangement not unlike the relationship between Mailboxes Etc. and the United States Postal Service, where the private company essentially acts as an intermediary and charges a premium for doing so). In December 1994 the company made two major acquisitions—of ChecksFirst Corp., a 19-store chain in Oklahoma, Arkansas, and Louisiana, as well as the four-store Check Cashers business. Sales in 1994 rose to $39.9 million. More acquisitions followed in 1995, when ACE purchased the 31-store Quick Cash Inc. chain. In October ACE finally added Check Express to its empire. The Check Express transaction proved especially important, since that firm had by then become the largest franchiser of check-cashing stores in the country. To augment its numerous acquisitions, ACE opened 117 new stores in 1995. Sales for the year topped $47 million. Guided by Check Express's expertise in franchising, ACE began to franchise the ACE name to check-cashing centers nationwide. A total of 105 new stores (including franchises) opened in 1996 and 120 opened in 1997. ACE reported a record-breaking $87.4 million in sales in 1997.

New Services: 1998 and Beyond

Despite its leading position in the check-cashing industry, ACE faced a number of challenges in the late 1990s. Its compet-

itors had taken note of ACE's accomplishments and adopted similar, expansion-focused strategies. By 1998, as a result, one-third of the nation's 6,000 check-cashers were owned by six companies. In addition to heated competition among businesses in the field, the industry was confronted by the rise of paperless transaction, which threatened to erode check-cashers' most important business—cashing checks. This new phenomenon was alarming to check-cashers because it threatened to do away with checks entirely, distributing funds through electronic transfers instead. But it also proved popular with the public: a number of U.S corporations implemented direct payroll deposits, and the federal government began to explore the possibility of implementing an Electronics Benefits Transfer system, whereby benefits such as Aid to Families with Dependent Children (AFDC) and social security would no longer be issued with checks but would instead be directly deposited into bank accounts.

As a result of these changes, ACE redoubled its efforts to develop non-check-cashing services, shore up its business with existing customers, and reach new customers. In a ploy to win customer loyalty, ACE issued the industry's first-ever frequent user card in 1998. The company hoped this would prove to be a popular feature since status ''isn't often conferred on our customers,'' an ACE executive told *Fortune* magazine. By June 1998, the company had issued more than four million of these Gold Cards. In 1998 ACE reached an agreement with retail giant Wal-Mart to open ACE outlets in 32 Wal-Mart stores.

The pace of ACE's diversification quickened in 1999 and 2000. That year, ACE linked its Gold Cards to check-cashing terminals that doubled as ATMs. Also in 1999, ACE teamed up with Instant Auto Insurance (IAI) to provide auto insurance to customers. Moreover, ACE forged an alliance with Travelers Express Company to expand on its Bill Pay system. Beginning in 1999, ACE offered its customers the ability to pay all their bills at a single store (including mortgages and car loans). The service was the first universal bill-paying system in the United States available to walk-in clients.

More important, ACE also joined forces in 1999 with Goleta National Bank (a unit of Community West Bancshares) to strengthen and safeguard its ''payday'' loan operations. Several states had passed legislation banning the practice of ''payday'' loans because they deemed the annual interest rates on these small, short-term loans (which often exceeded 400 percent) to be usurious. To circumvent these anti-usury laws, ACE would leverage its relationship with Goleta to provide such loans in states where they were outlawed. Under the terms of the agreement, ACE would merely process ''payday'' loan applications, but Goleta—headquartered in California where the practice was legal—would actually issue the loans. (ACE would later buy back a portion of the loans.) According to the *Wall Street Journal,* ACE's maneuver would most likely provide ''a big boost to the company's earnings and sales.''

As a result of its consistent attempt to increase its services at the same time that it continued to add to the number of outlets in its network, ACE ended the 20th century with excellent future prospects. Its sales had risen to $122.3 million in 1999, and its net income had climbed 35 percent. In addition to owning and operating 817 stores, ACE had added 147 franchised stores to its system. Its stock prices also had risen to all time highs. In

keeping with its goal of diversifying its operations, ACE could boast at the close of 1999 that it no longer relied exclusively on check cashing to sustain sales. Indeed, by the year's end, check cashing accounted for only 55.8 percent of sales (compared with 90.7 percent a decade earlier).

ACE continued to pursue new market niches. After Jay Shipowitz ascended to the position of president in 2000, the company announced that it had reached an agreement with ePOWER International (a privately held Internet technology company) to provide prepaid Internet service through ACE. ''Offering this service to our customers moves ACE closer to providing a complete line of financial-related services needed by every household,'' Shipowitz proclaimed in a press release.

Principal Competitors

Cash America International, Inc.; Check Into Cash, Inc.; EZCORP, Inc.; MFN Financial Corp.; FFP Marketing Company, Inc.; First Cash Financial Services Inc.

Further Reading

''ACE Cash Express and ePower to Offer Pre-Paid Internet,'' *PR Newswire,* January 5, 2000.

Berenson, Alex, ''Investors Could Cash in on Growth of Fringe Banks,'' *Denver Post,* May 5, 1996.

Branch, Shelly, ''Where Cash Is King,'' *Fortune,* June 8, 1998, pp. 201+.

Brooks, Nancy Rivera, ''Cashing in on Checks,'' *Los Angeles Times,* June 14, 1987, p. 1.

''CEO Interview'' (Ace Cash Express), *Wall Street Transcript,* August 2, 1993.

Hudson, Michael, ''The New Loan Sharks,'' *Dollars and Sense,* July 17, 1997, p. 14.

McKinney, Jeff, ''The Price of Convenience,'' *Cincinnati Enquirer,* July 14, 1996, p. E1.

Milligan, John, ''A Philosophical Reflection on the Metaphysical Natures and Existential Dilemma of Check Cashers,'' *US Banker,* July 1, 1996, p. 26.

Mitchell, Jim, ''No Deposits, Many Returns,'' *Dallas Morning News,* February 10, 1994, p. D1.

Palmeri, Christopher, ''Dialtones for Deadbeats,'' *Forbes,* November 3, 1997, p. 81.

Tippett, Karen, ''Ace Cash, a 'Shadow Bank,' Grows, But Expectations Outshine Results,'' *Wall Street Journal,* August 17, 1994.

Weil, Jonathan, ''ACE Cash Express May Be on Verge of Unchecked Growth, SatyBulls,'' *Wall Street Journal,* August 13, 1997.

——, ''Ace Cash's Payday-Loan Venture Could Be Catalyst for Stock Growth,'' *Wall Street Journal,* September 29, 1999, p. 2.

—Rebecca Stanfel

adidas-Salomon AG

Adi-Dassler-Strasse 1-2
91074 Herzogenaurach
Germany
Telephone: 49-9132-842471
Fax: 49-9132-843127
Web site: http://www.adidas.com

Public Company
Incorporated: 1949
Employees: 12,036
Sales: $5.94 billion (1999)
Stock Exchanges: Frankfurt
Ticker Symbol: ADDDY
NAIC: 315211 Men's and Boys' Cut and Sew Apparel
Contractors; 315212 Women's, Girls', and Infants'
Cut and Sew Apparel Contractors; 315299 All Other
Cut and Sew Apparel Manufacturing; 33992 Sporting
and Athletic Goods Manufacturing; 316211 Rubber
and Plastics Footwear Manufacturing; 316219 Other
Footwear Manufacturing

German-based adidas-Salomon AG is the second largest manufacturer of sporting goods in the world. Once the undisputed leader in the world athletic shoe market, the company faced fierce competition that left it nearly bankrupt in 1993. After cutting costs and transferring production to Asia, adidas returned to prominence. adidas expanded from an athletic shoe and apparel company into a major sporting goods manufacturer in 1997 with the acquisition of Salomon Worldwide, a French maker of ski, golf, and bicycle equipment. Among the brands in the adidas group are Taylor Made (golf equipment), Mavic (bicycle equipment), Erima (swimwear), and Salomon. In the late 1990s adidas focused on the U.S. market, the largest sporting goods market globally, and sponsored numerous sports teams, athletes, and high-visibility athletic events in an effort to boost brand recognition.

Humble Beginnings for the Athletic Shoe: 1920s–40s

adidas emanated from a bitter dispute between two brothers, Rudolph and Adi Dassler, in the small Bavarian mill town of Herzogenaurach. Rudi and Adi were born in 1898 and 1900, respectively, to Christolf and Pauline Dassler. Their hometown of Herzogenaurach was a regional textile manufacturing center at the time, but during the early 1900s most of the mills converted to shoemaking. Adi was trained to be a baker, but those skills offered him little hope of finding a job in the final years of World War I. Instead, the Dassler family started a tiny shoemaking business in the back of Pauline's laundry. Adi began making shoes using materials from old helmets, tires, rucksacks, and other refuse that he could scavenge. Adi's sister cut patterns out of canvas, and the always innovative Adi built a shoe trimmer that was powered by a bicycle.

The company's first shoes were bedroom slippers that sported soles made from used tires. Adi, who had a lifelong love of sports, converted those slippers into unique lightweight gymnastics and soccer shoes with nailed-on cleats. Demand for those shoes allowed the family to build a factory in 1926, when output rose to about 100 pairs per day. Adi's brother and father both quit their jobs to work in the company.

The Dassler family's company received a major boost when their shoes were worn by German athletes in the 1928 Olympics in Amsterdam. Four years later, moreover, athletes clad in Dassler shoes won medals in the Olympics in Los Angeles. Then, in the 1936 Games, the world-renowned American sprinter Jesse Owens raced to victory in Dassler shoes. Owens's shoes featured two widely spaced stripes that wrapped over the ball of the foot, a design that became increasingly commonplace on the feet of athletes around the world.

Demand for Dassler shoes mushroomed during the early 1930s and continued until the start of the German offensive that led to World War II. During the war, the Dassler factory was commandeered for the production of boots for German soldiers. Both Adi and Rudi were reportedly members of the Nazi party, but only Rudi was called to service. Adi stayed home and ran the factory. Allied forces occupied the region at the war's end, and American soldiers even moved into the Dassler home. Christolf Dassler died about that time. Adi made friends with some of the American soldiers, and even made a pair of track shoes for a U.S. soldier who eventually wore them in the 1946 Olympics.

After the soldiers left, Rudi returned to Herzogenaurach and rejoined his brother. He had spent several years fighting and one year interned in an American prisoner-of-war camp. Just as they had been forced to do after World War I, Adi and Rudi scavenged for shoemaking material to rebuild their business in wartorn Germany. They used army tents for canvas and old American tank materials for soles. They paid their 47 workers with such materials as firewood and yarn.

Sibling Rivalry and the Birth of adidas: Late 1940s

It was only a few years after Rudi's return that an infamous dispute broke out between the two brothers. Although the men kept the impetus for the fight a secret until their deaths, rumors swirled that the battle stemmed from disagreements related to the war. One story indicated that Rudi was upset that Adi had not used his connections with the Allies to get him out of the prison camp during the conflict. Whatever the reason for the feud, Rudi walked away from the family home and business forever in the spring of 1948, intent on starting his own shoe business. He took with him the company's sales force and control of a building that was to become a new factory. Adi kept most of the workforce and the original headquarters offices and factory. From that time forward, the brothers never spoke a word to one another except in court. The businesses that they created represented one of the most intense rivalries in all of Europe.

When they split, Rudi and Adi agreed that neither would be allowed to use the Dassler brand name on their shoes. Rudi named his new company and shoes Ruda, while Adi named his Addas. Shortly thereafter, Adi changed the name to adidas (emphasis on the last syllable) and Rudi, on the advice of an advertising agency, changed the name of his shoes to Puma. Adi altered the Dassler family trademark of two stripes by adding a third. He also adopted the slogan ''The Best for the Athlete'' as part of his marketing campaign. Rudi chose as his logo a cat's paw in motion.

For many years a signpost in the center of town had two arrows: one pointed to adidas and the other to Puma, which faced adidas on the opposite side of the River Aurach. Each company had its own soccer team, and employees from each company drank different beers. Enrollment at the two elementary schools in town was determined by the factory at which a child's father worked (adidas employees' children attended one school, while Puma employees' children attended the other), and children learned early in their lives to look down on the competing shoe company.

Each shoe company's culture bore the mark of its founder. It may have been for that reason that Adi came to dominate the global athletic shoe industry. Both Rudi and Adi were intelligent and able. Puma eventually became a venerable and established shoe company throughout the global industry. But under Adi Dassler's guiding hand, adidas grew during the mid-1900s to became the undisputed world shoe industry giant. Adi, considered shy but extremely bright, was respected in his village. A natural athlete, inventor, and craftsman, Adi combined his interests to produce a number of breakthrough innovations that catapulted the company to prominence. By the time Dassler died in 1978, in fact, adidas shoes were being worn throughout the world—more than any other sports shoe—by both professional and weekend athletes, and as casual footwear.

An Innovative Leader in Athletic Footwear: 1950s–70s

Adi was credited with numerous inventions during the late 1940s and 1950s, including the first shoes designed for ice and the first multi-studded shoes. adidas is also credited with pioneering the now commonplace practice among athletic shoe manufacturers of selling sports bags and athletic clothing bearing their brand name. Among Adi's most notable early contributions was his improvement of the soccer shoe. Prior to 1957, soccer shoes were designed as they had been for decades, with metal studs mounted in leather. These shoes were heavy, particularly when they got wet. Adi designed a new type of shoe that sported a nylon sole and molded rubber studs. The result was a more lightweight, durable shoe. Introduced in 1957, the revolutionary soccer shoe was eventually copied by other shoe companies, including chief rival Puma.

Another of Adi's pivotal innovations, and the one that helped most to thrust the company into the global limelight, was the screw-studded soccer shoe, which allowed worn cleats to be replaced. The cleats were introduced in 1954 at the World Soccer Championships in Bern, Switzerland. Heavy rains during the first half of an important game turned the soccer field to a muddy mess by half-time. The West German national team members went to their locker room, removed their standard cleats, and installed longer cleats to get a better grip in the field. Adi watched as the West German team captured a 3–2 victory over the favored Hungarians, a triumph that was viewed by the German people as a symbol of their return from the ashes of war. Soon after that event, adidas's shipments exploded from about 800 pairs to 2,000 pairs of shoes per day.

Two years later Adi started its successful and longstanding tradition of naming one of its shoes after the Olympics. The shoe introduced at the 1956 Olympics was the Melbourne—the Games were held in that Australian city that year—the first to offer multiple studs. Adi's son Horst handled the promotion with a marketing strategy that won accolades abroad. He simply gave the shoes away to Olympic athletes, who wore them for a global audience. Athletes wearing adidas shoes won a whopping 72 medals that year and set 33 records. After that, adidas scored another major marketing coup by signing agreements to supply entire sports teams with footwear, an agreement that ensured that adidas equipment would be worn by many of the world's greatest athletes on both sides of the Iron Curtain. Other shoe and sports equipment companies eventually followed the company's lead, and contracts to supply free equipment to such high-profile athletes became highly competitive.

Key Dates:

1926: Dassler family builds a factory to make athletic shoes.
1936: American runner Jesse Owens, wearing Dassler shoes, wins a gold medal in the 1936 Olympic Games.
1948: The Dassler brothers part ways, and Adi Dassler starts his own shoe company.
1949: adidas is registered as a company.
1957: adidas introduces a pioneering soccer shoe.
1978: Adi Dassler dies, and control of his company is handed to his family.
1990: French entrepreneur Bernard Tapie buys adidas.
1993: adidas acquires Sports Inc., a U.S. company. Tapie sells adidas to a group of European investors, and Robert Louis-Dreyfus joins adidas as CEO.
1995: adidas goes public.
1997: adidas acquires Salomon Worldwide and is renamed adidas-Salomon AG.

adidas initiated a number of savvy marketing programs during the 1950s, 1960s, and 1970s, but the Olympics remained the centerpiece of its marketing strategy for several years. In the 1964 Tokyo Games, medals won by adidas-shod competitors amounted to 80 percent of the total, as they captured all but 30 of the medals awarded. At the Montreal Olympics, adidas outfitted all of the winners in hockey, soccer, volleyball, and women's basketball. adidas shoes were worn by athletes who accounted for 83 percent of all medals awarded and a fat 95 percent of the track-and-field gold medals. adidas became virtually dominant in the athletic shoe industry. Aside from its clever marketing and winning designs, moreover, it was considered the quality leader. Indeed, other shoemakers considered adidas superior in machinery, craftsmanship, and materials.

adidas's most lucrative strategic maneuver was its entry into the giant and blossoming U.S. athletic shoe market in the late 1950s. adidas attacked that market at a good time. Its major competitors were manufacturers of canvas sneakers that bore names like Keds and P.F. Flyers. adidas's high quality, well-designed shoes became explosively popular, first with more serious athletes, but finally with the weekend athlete and casual footwear markets. Puma also made a run in the United States beginning in the 1950s. Its shoes sold relatively well, but ultimately came to be regarded as inferior to adidas in quality. In contrast, by the mid-1970s adidas had become nearly synonymous with quality athletic shoes in the United States.

adidas expanded globally during the 1960s and 1970s, maintaining its dominant position in the world sports shoe industry. By the late 1970s the company was churning out about 200,000 pairs per day and generating well over a half billion dollars in sales annually. (The company was still privately owned, so revenue figures are speculative.) adidas operated 24 factories in 17 countries and was selling a wide range of shoes in more than 150 nations. In addition, the company had moved by that time into diverse product lines including shorts, jerseys, balls and other equipment, track suits, and athletic bags. The company

had registered about 800 patents and was producing roughly 150 different styles of shoes. About 90 percent of all Formula 1 drivers, for example, raced in adidas.

Throughout the company's rampant growth, its founder continued to lead and innovate. In 1978 the 77-year-old president introduced what he considered to be his greatest contribution ever to his beloved game of soccer. In recognition of the fact that players spent about 90 percent of their time on the field running rather than kicking the ball, Adi designed an ultralight soccer shoe with a sole resembling a sprint shoe. The shoe also featured an orthopedic footbed, a wider positioning of the studs to give better traction and even a special impregnation treatment designed to counter the weight-increasing effect of the humid Argentinian climate. The shoes were first used in the World Cup in Argentina by almost every team in the competition.

Increased Competition and the Loss of Global Dominance: 1980s and Early 1990s

Adi Dassler died shortly after he introduced his landmark soccer shoe in 1978. He had run the company and its predecessor for about 60 years and built it into the unmitigated giant of the world shoe industry. His death marked the end of an era at the company. Indeed, adidas suffered a string of defeats in the late 1970s and 1980s that severely diminished its role in the world sports shoe industry. The company's loss of dominance was not solely attributable to Dassler's death, however. In fact, the athletic shoe industry became intensely competitive following his death, primarily as a result of aggressive U.S. entrants. The increased competition actually began after the 1972 Olympics in Munich, when a mob of companies decided to hop into the lucrative business. After having the industry mostly to themselves for years, adidas and Puma suddenly found themselves under attack from shoe manufacturers worldwide.

Dassler had carefully arranged a management succession before his death. Family members remained in key management positions, but several professional managers were also brought in to take over key functions like marketing, production, and public relations. Unfortunately, the effort failed to keep the company vibrant. adidas retained its lead in the global athletic shoe market for several years and remained dominant in its core European market into the 1990s. Importantly, though, it was soundly thrashed in the North American market by emerging athletic shoe contenders Nike Inc. and Reebok Inc. Those companies launched an almost militant marketing offensive on the North American sports shoe market during the 1980s that caught adidas completely off guard.

adidas, not used to such fierce competition, effectively ceded dominance of that important region. Incredibly, adidas's U.S. sales shrunk to a mere $200 million by the end of the decade, while Nike's grew to more than $2.4 billion. By that time, Reebok and Nike together claimed more than 50 percent of the U.S. athletic shoe market, compared to about three percent for adidas. The adidas brand name had become a fading memory in the minds of many aging baby boomers, and many younger U.S. buyers were virtually unaware of the brand. "This is a brand that has taken about five bullets to the head," said one observer in *Business Journal-Portland* in February 1993.

adidas managed to maintain its lead in the soccer shoe market and even to keep a healthy 26 percent of the European market for its products. However, the North American market became the core of the global athletic shoe industry, and adidas found itself scrambling to maintain respect worldwide. Moreover, besides increased competition, adidas suffered during the 1980s and early 1990s from relatively weak management. To make matters worse, members of the Dassler family and relatives that still owned adidas began fighting over control of the company. Amid increased competition and family squabbling, adidas's bottom line began to sag. The organization lost about $77 million in 1989 before the family sold the entire organization for only $289 million. The buyer was Frenchman Bernard Tapie, a 47-year-old entrepreneur and politician.

From the beginning, analysts doubted Tapie's ability to turn the ailing company around. A perpetual showman, Tapie purchased the company partly for the attention he would get from the French people for securing ownership of a renowned German institution. Tapie had already gained notoriety as an entrepreneur and as a parliamentary head of the ruling Socialist Party. Tapie's promotional skills did little for adidas. The company continued to lag and Tapie himself became embroiled in political and business scandals. Tapie stepped aside as chief of the company in 1992 and handed the reins to Gilbert Beaux. Tapie also started looking for a buyer for adidas.

Under new management, adidas looked as though it was beginning to turn the corner going into the mid-1990s. Of import was the company's 1993 purchase of U.S.-based Sports Inc., an enterprise that had been founded by Rob Strasser. Strasser was credited as the marketing genius that had helped to make Nike into the leading U.S. athletic shoe company. Strasser quit Nike in 1987 to form Sports Inc. When adidas bought out his 50-person marketing venture, it named Strasser head of the newly formed adidas America subsidiary. Strasser brought with him another former Nike executive, Peter Moore, with whom he hoped to regain some of adidas's lost glory. "We'll compete from day one," he said in the *Business Journal-Portland* in 1993, "but it won't happen overnight." Tapie finally found a buyer for adidas in 1993. The company was purchased by a group of European investors for $371 million. Unfortunately, Strasser died late in 1993. Moore took over as head of the U.S. subsidiary. adidas expected Moore to lead the company's turnaround on that continent and to help it eventually attain the kind of strength adidas International still exerted in Europe and some other parts of the world.

In 1993 the new owners of adidas hired Robert Louis-Dreyfus, a French businessman, to run the company. Though Louis-Dreyfus was unfamiliar with the athletic shoe business, he had a reputation for revitalizing failing companies; in fact, Louis-Dreyfus was credited with saving London advertising agency Saatchi and Saatchi. After joining adidas, Louis-Dreyfus implemented severe cost-cutting and reorganization strategies and moved production to Asia. He also increased the marketing budget, from 6 percent of sales to 11 percent, to increase brand visibility.

The Comeback of adidas in the Late 1990s

adidas reacted favorably to Louis-Dreyfus's changes, and profits rebounded, reaching DM 244.9 million in 1995, up from

DM 117.3 million in 1994. The company went public in 1995, and the relatively unathletic Louis-Dreyfus signaled his commitment to adidas and its athletic roots by running in the Boston Marathon. Also that year a new CEO, Steve Wynne, joined adidas's U.S. subsidiary. In 1996 apparel sales rose an impressive 50 percent, and brand visibility was enhanced by adidas's involvement with the 1996 Olympic Games—the company provided gear for about 6,000 competing athletes, representing 33 countries, and the Olympians sporting adidas's equipment won 220 medals.

In a significant move to strengthen its position in the global sporting goods category, adidas acquired French holding company Sport Developpement SCA in late 1997. Sport Developpement owned 38.87 percent of Salomon's shares and 56.12 percent of the voting rights. After sealing the deal with Sport Developpement, adidas acquired the outstanding shares of Salomon in a deal estimated to be worth $1.4 billion. The purchase, which included U.S.-based Taylor Made, manufacturer of premium golf clubs, and the French Mavic, maker of cycling equipment, positioned adidas in the number two position of sporting goods worldwide, behind Nike Inc. but ahead of Reebok International Ltd. Traditionally known as a manufacturer of ski equipment, Salomon had begun to branch out in the mid-1990s to shield itself from the declining winter sports and ski segments. The company placed a greater emphasis on Taylor Made and Mavic and also focused on hiking boots, inline skates, and snowboards. Salomon also changed its name to Salomon Worldwide in mid-1997 to signal its international diversification.

Though industry observers applauded adidas's purchase of Salomon and stated that consolidation within the sporting goods industry, particularly between equipment manufacturers and makers of apparel and shoes, was a growing trend, news of adidas's decision caused the share price to decline nearly four percent. Concerns that adidas's earnings would be adversely affected for several years by the debt-financed acquisition made many investors nervous. Still, many felt the adidas and Salomon merger was a positive move. Allan Raphael, president of Raphael, C.R.I. Global LP, said in the *Financial Post,* "adidas' goal is to be the No. 1 sports equipment company in the world and I think they're going to get there. . . . The key is that adidas' management has a very innovative sense of how to recreate a brand."

In 1998 adidas-Salomon turned toward the U.S. market while also focusing on integrating Salomon's operations. Though the global sporting goods market experienced flat growth that year, adidas managed to achieve extremely high sales growth. Overall net sales grew 48 percent in 1998 compared to 1997, and the company achieved record high net sales in both footwear and apparel. In the United States, the top market for sporting goods, adidas-Salomon achieved extraordinary growth rates. Net sales in the U.S. market alone rose 71 percent over 1997 results, and the brand's share of the U.S. footwear market reached 12 percent, thanks to the increase in footwear sales of 93 percent. Apparel sales also fared well in the United States, growing 48 percent. Sales in Europe, Asia, and Latin America also rose in 1998.

Despite strong growth rates in 1998, adidas-Salomon was not without difficulties. Integration of Salomon proved to be more time-consuming and challenging than had been anticipated, and the company's share prices fell 24 percent during the year. In addition, though some Asian countries experienced positive sales growth, overall sales in the Asian region fell more than 20 percent. The economic problems in Russia led to poor sales as well. The golf industry faced a difficult year in 1998, and this affected sales of Taylor Made, which declined by 15 percent.

adidas-Salomon concentrated on the positive rather than the negative, and although the company expected flat growth during 1999, the year of its 50th anniversary, the company endeavored to improve sales and strengthen operations. The company planned to construct a new world headquarters in Herzogenaurach and thus acquired a 90 percent interest in GEV Grundstücksgesellschaft mbH & Co. KG, a property investment firm that owned the property adidas selected for the building. adidas-Salomon also extended operations globally in the late 1990s, forming a subsidiary, adidas Japan K.K., to handle the distribution of adidas products in Japan, as well as ventures in the Netherlands and Turkey.

In terms of sports, adidas-Salomon had many winners in the late 1990s. adidas was the official sponsor of the 1998 Soccer World Cup, which had extremely high visibility and coverage, and in 1999 the company sponsored the Women's World Cup, which achieved strong popularity. The company also sponsored the New York Yankees baseball team beginning in late 1997. The Yankees won the World Series that season, and adidas-Salomon publicized its partnership with the team through award-winning advertising campaigns. Among the athletes signed by the company were cyclist Jan Ullrich, winner of the Tour de France in 1997 and runner-up in 1998, and National Basketball Association player Kobe Bryant.

For the first nine months of 1999, adidas-Salomon reported net sales of DM 8.14 billion, compared to DM 7.91 billion for the same period of 1998. Net income for the same period was down two percent. Sales improved during the course of the year, but the company maintained its forecast that annual sales would remain flat. At the beginning of 2000, Steve Wynne, president and CEO of adidas Salomon North America, announced his resignation. Wynne was credited with being a key figure in adidas's U.S. turnaround, and over the five-year period Wynne was with adidas, the subsidiary's sales grew from $450 million to $1.6 billion. Also early in 2000 adidas-Salomon announced a group restructuring designed to improve earnings and to facilitate quicker decision making. The company planned to develop innovative new products, increase its Internet presence, and increase the marketing and sales operations of Taylor Made and Salomon. Herbert Hainer, adidas-Salomon's chief operating officer, explained in a prepared statement, "In the year 2000, we will be laying the foundations for stronger growth in subsequent years." adidas-Salomon had been through many changes and faced many challenges over its 50-year history, but the company retained its desire to be the top sporting goods company in the world.

Principal Subsidiaries

adidas America Inc.; adidas-Salomon North America Inc.; adidas-Salomon USA, Inc.; Taylor Made Golf USA; adidas (Canada) Ltd.; Erima Sportbekleidungs GmbH (Germany); Sa-lomon GmbH (Germany); GEV Grundstücksgesellschaft Herzogenaurach mbH & Co. KG (Germany; 90%); adidas Sarragan France S.a.r.l.; adidas Espana SA (Spain); adidas Portugal Lda (Portugal); adidas Sport GmbH (Switzerland); Salomon SA (France); adidas Austria AG; adidas Benelux B.V. (Netherlands); adidas Belgium N.V.; adidas Budapest Kft. (Hungary); adidas (U.K.) Ltd.; adidas (Ireland) Ltd.; adidas Norge A/S (Norway); adidas Sverige AB (Sweden); adidas Poland Sp.z.o.o. (Poland); adidas Ltd. (Russia); adidas de Mexico S.A. de C.V.; adidas do Brasil Ltda. (Brazil); adidas Latin America S.A. (Panama); adidas Corporation de Venezuela, S.A.; adidas Japan K.K.; adidas Hong Kong Ltd.; adidas Singapore Pte Ltd.; adidas Asia/Pacific Ltd. (Hong Kong); adidas (Thailand) Co., Ltd.; adidas Australia Pty Ltd.; adidas New Zealand Pty Ltd.; adidas (South Africa) Pty Ltd.

Principal Competitors

Nike Inc.; Reebok International Ltd.; Fila Holding S.p.A.

Further Reading

Bates, Tom, "Adidas Names Moore to Replace Strasser," *Portland Oregonian,* November 10, 1993.

Carrel, Paul, "Adidas Shares Soar on Revamp Plan," *Reuters English News Service,* January 27, 2000.

Carter, Donna, "Mutombo's Shoes Take Off Worldwide," *Denver Post,* December 18, 1992, p. C1.

Colodny, Mark M., "Beaux Knows Adidas," *Fortune,* December 31, 1990, p. 111.

"Dreyfus Launches Adidas into Foot Race with Nike," *Financial Post,* September 17, 1997, p. 13.

Fallon, James, "Adidas Sold for $370.48 Million," *Footwear News,* February 22, 1993, p. 39.

Feitelberg, Rosemary, "Wynne to Exit Adidas," *WWD,* January 13, 2000, p. 16.

Francis, Mike, "Strasser Headed for Top of Adidas? One of the Founders of Sports Inc. May Become Head of adidas U.S.A.," *Portland Oregonian,* February 3, 1993.

Harnischfeger, Uta, "Flagging Golf Brand Hits Adidas Profits," *Financial Times London,* April 13, 1999, p. 28.

"How Adidas Ran Faster," *Management Today,* December 1979, pp. 58–61.

Manning, Jeff, "Adidas Slows Impressive Pace As Flat Sales Expected for 1999," *Portland Oregonian,* May 21, 1999.

——, "Adidas, Sports Inc. Join Forces, Strasser Heads U.S. Operation," *Business Journal-Portland,* February 8, 1993, p. 1.

Mitchener, Brandon, and Amy Barrett, "Adidas and Salomon Play by New Rules in $1.4 Billion Deal," *Wall Street Journal Europe,* September 17, 1997, p. 1.

Mulligan, Thomas S., "Adidas to Put U.S. Market in Hands of Ex-Nike Whiz," *Los Angeles Times,* February 5, 1993, p. D2.

Silverman, Edward R., "Foothold in Sneaker War," *New York Newsday,* July 8, 1992, p. 31.

Strasser, J.B., and Laurie Becklund, *Swoosh: The Unauthorized Story of Nike and the Men Who Played There,* New York: Harcourt Brace Jovanovich, 1991.

Wallace, Charles P., "Adidas Back in the Game," *Fortune,* August 18, 1997, p. 176+.

Waxman, Sharon, "Tapie: The Flashy Frenchman Behind the Adidas Acquisition," *Washington Post,* July 22, 1990, p. H1.

—Dave Mote

—updated by Mariko Fujinaka

Adobe Systems Inc.

345 Park Avenue
San Jose, California 95110-2704
U.S.A.
Telephone: (408) 536-6000
Fax: (408) 537-6000
Web site: http://www.adobe.com

Public Company
Incorporated: 1983
Employees: 2,800
Sales: $1.02 billion (1999)
Stock Exchanges: NASDAQ
Ticker Symbol: ADBE
NAIC: 51121 Software Publishers; 334611 Software
    Reproducing; 541511 Custom Computer Programming
    Services

Adobe Systems Inc. is a leading developer of desktop publishing software. Sales of three of the company's software products—Photoshop, Illustrator, and PageMaker—account for about 50 percent of Adobe's sales. Adobe also developed and distributes, free of charge, Acrobat Reader, which allows Internet users to view and print portable document format (PDF) files. The company has investments in about 20 technology companies and is involved in two venture capital partnerships. Adobe also sells print technology to original equipment manufacturers; the company's PostScript page description language became the industry standard for the imaging and printing of electronic documents.

Sparking the Desktop Publishing Revolution in the 1980s

Adobe was founded in 1982 by John Warnock and Charles Geschke, both former employees of Xerox Corp.'s Research Center in Palo Alto, California. At Xerox, Warnock conducted interactive graphics research, while Geschke directed computer science and graphics research as the manager of the company's Imaging Sciences Laboratory. In a 1989 interview with the *San Jose Business Journal,* Warnock recalled that he and Geschke were frustrated at Xerox "because of the difficulty in getting our products out of the research stage." Believing in the profitability of an independent venture, they left Xerox to establish their own business, which they named after a creek that ran by their homes in Los Altos, California.

Shortly after it was launched, Adobe introduced PostScript, a powerful computer language that essentially described to a printer or other output device the appearance of an electronic page, including the placement of characters, lines, or images. The introduction of PostScript proved integral to the desktop publishing revolution. With a personal computer and a laser printer equipped with PostScript, users could produce polished, professional-looking documents with high-quality graphics. An article in a 1989 issue of the *Los Angeles Times* stated that Adobe's PostScript "made desktop publishing possible by enabling laser printers, typesetting equipment and other such devices to produce pages integrating text and graphics." Advertising agencies, in particular, soon found the new technology indispensable.

Realizing the wealth of potential uses for the PostScript language, Adobe marketed and licensed PostScript to manufacturers of computers, printers, imagesetters, and film recorders. In 1985, Apple Computer, Inc., maker of the MacIntosh computer, incorporated PostScript for its LaserWriter printer. Shortly thereafter, Apple invested in a 19 percent stake in Adobe, which had reported revenues of $1.7 million the year before. Adobe's rapid growth led to an increase in staff from 27 in 1985 to 54 by 1986.

More than 5,000 PostScript applications were developed and made available for every operating system and hardware configuration. In 1986, Adobe signed an agreement to supply Texas Instruments Inc. with the software for two of its laser printers, producing the first PostScript-equipped printers made for use with IBM-compatible personal computers. In addition, PostScript soon became available for use with minicomputers and mainframes, and it remained the only page description language available for multiple-computer environments, such as corporate office networks. Independent software vendors marketed products that used PostScript to render images and text onto film, slides, and screens, for less money than traditional typesetting methods incurred. Used by corporations, professional publishers, and the U.S. government, PostScript rapidly became one of the most ubiquitous computer languages worldwide.

To supplement the PostScript language system, Adobe introduced a software technology known as Type 1, which provided digital type fonts that could be printed at any resolution. Vendors soon began developing different Type 1 typefaces until there were more than 15,000, including Japanese and Cyrillic character sets. By the end of 1986, Adobe reported sales of $16 million and income of $3.6 million. During this time, the company was taken public and began expanding its customer base to include IBM and Digital Equipment Corp.

The strategy of marketing and licensing technology to original equipment manufacturers (OEMs) such as Apple became the cornerstone of Adobe's success. In 1986 Apple accounted for 80 percent of Adobe's sales, and the other 20 percent was composed of retail sales, an area into which Adobe moved the following year.

In 1987 the company introduced the Adobe Illustrator, a design and illustration software program. Enabling users to create high-quality line drawings, the Illustrator became popular among graphic designers, desktop publishers, and technical illustrators. The company also released the Adobe Type Library, which contained a large selection of type fonts, many of which were original typefaces Adobe had created especially for the electronic medium. The Type Library eventually would become the most widely used collection in the industry.

As graphics became more widely used in business communications, Adobe was poised to offer new technologies. The company's introduction of a new version of the Illustrator, designed for use with Microsoft's Windows program, offered PC users an exciting array of graphics tools and helped pave the way for other PostScript language-based graphics packages. By 1988 many industries and universities had adopted the Illustrator standard. Moreover, the Type Library, with 300 typefaces, had become the world's largest collection of typefaces for personal computers.

Having successfully marketed its technology to both Macintosh and IBM, Adobe tackled a new project—developing the Illustrator and the Type Library for the NeXT computer system. Once this was accomplished, the NeXT computer system became the first to implement a new Adobe technology, Display PostScript. This adaptation of the original PostScript was unique in that it communicated directly with the computer's screen, rather than through the printer. Representing a breakthrough in the long struggle for what computer buffs called "WYSIWIG" (What You See Is What You Get), Display PostScript ensured users that images on the screen would be replicated exactly on paper through the printer. Display PostScript also allowed users to manipulate graphics on the screen; rotating, scaling, and skewing could all be performed to suit the user's needs. IBM and Digital Equipment Corp. soon followed NeXT's lead, licensing Display PostScript for their desktop systems.

In 1988 more than 25 PostScript printers and typesetters were on the market and 20 computer corporations had signed PostScript licensing agreements with Adobe. The company's revenues for 1988 were an impressive $83.5 million, representing a 112 percent increase over revenues of $39.3 million the year before. Moreover, net income for 1988 increased 137 percent, reaching $21 million. During this time, Apple Computer remained the company's biggest customer, accounting for 33 percent of Adobe's revenues. By the following year, Adobe's staff had increased to 300. As one of the fastest-growing software developers, Adobe sought to maintain its position in the industry and foil any potential competitors. Toward this end, Adobe kept its typeface strategies confidential, while continuing to expand into new areas.

At the 1989 MacWorld Exposition in San Francisco, Adobe introduced two new applications. Adobe Streamline software permitted users to reproduce hardcopy graphics onscreen, converting bit-mapped images into high-quality PostScript artwork. The second product, Collectors Edition II, could be used to set patterns. Adobe eventually adapted these technologies for IBM and IBM-compatible computers that used the Windows program.

Next on Adobe's agenda was international expansion. The company signed an agreement with Canon Inc. of Japan, under which Canon had full licensing rights to Adobe PostScript. The world's leading manufacturer of laser printers, Canon could bring the PostScript technology to international and multinational customers. To enhance its Type Library, Adobe signed agreements that permitted several companies to develop downloadable typefaces based on Adobe's proprietary technology.

Adobe ended the 1980s on a high note; revenues in 1989 were more than $121 million, and net income reached $33.7 million. That year, the company introduced Adobe Type Manager. This program used Adobe's outline fonts to generate scalable characters on screen, giving users greater flexibility and better WYSIWYG. The Type Manager also represented an expansion of the Adobe Type Library to 420 typefaces.

Also during this time, Adobe announced that it had acquired all rights to a software program called PhotoShop, an image editing application. PhotoShop, designed especially for artists and desktop publishers, was slated for market in conjunction with the Apple Macintosh. Designed to work with type, line art, and other images, PhotoShop provided users with a complete toolbox for editing, creating, and manipulating images. Other unique PhotoShop features included color correction, retouching, and color separation capabilities.

Continued Growth in the Early 1990s

By the end of the decade, the incredible boom in the computer business was showing signs of subsiding. In a 1989 *Los Angeles Times* interview, Adobe's president, John Warnock, suggested that "if you think you have a formula for success, you'd better figure out how to change it from year to year." Coming up with fresh formulas to ensure continued success was Adobe's focus as the company entered the 1990s. One of its strategies involved developing software that could operate platform-independent, allowing documents to be worked on and sent over many different computers and networks. In other words, Adobe envisioned a world in which a document could be produced on an IBM PC, for example, and sent directly to a MacIntosh.

On the way to realizing that goal, Adobe continued to set the pace for technological developments in the industry. In 1990 Adobe received what was believed to be the first copyright registration for a typeface program. The ITC Garamond font program was registered with the U.S. Copyright Office, a move that suggested that typeface programs could be considered creative works of authorship.

By this time, the Adobe Type Library had burgeoned from the original 12 type families to 134. The down-loadable type-faces were available for both IBM and Macintosh personal computers. The Type Manager, Adobe's scalable-font technology, was made available for IBM PCs, as well as UNIX, DOS, and OS/2 systems. Adobe launched PostScript Level 2, which enhanced the PostScript language with new features, such as improved forms handling, color support, and pattern manipulation, making PostScript a more practical and convenient language. One important feature of Level 2 was its use of data compression to reduced transmission times and save disk space by reducing the size of PostScript files on disk. Level 2 also boasted new screening and half-toning technology, better memory, and better printer support features, allowing users to specify color choices and receive those colors in their output.

Late in 1990, Adobe acquired BluePoint Technologies, a leading creator of chips for rendering type. Adobe also signed a new agreement with Apple Computer to work jointly on developing new products using Adobe's PostScript software and Apple's printer technology. Moreover, Adobe announced the creation of Adobe Illustrator for the NeXT system, providing NeXT users with the same powerful design and illustration tool used by owners of MacIntosh and IBM PCs.

Adobe's revenues continued to soar. In 1990 the company hit a new record of $168.7 million in revenues, with net income of $40 million. The following year, Adobe announced that it was developing a new type technology, multiple master typefaces, which would allow users to control the weight, width, visual scale, and style of a single typeface to produce endless variations.

Furthering its strategy of providing numerous licensing agreements throughout the early 1990s, Adobe signed contracts with Lotus Development Corp., Eastman Kodak, Tektronix, Inc., and others. In addition to its updated version of PhotoShop, Adobe also was responsible for another breakthrough in printing technology with the development of the Adobe Type 1 Coprocessor. The new device could render text 25 times faster than the fastest existing printers.

The company celebrated another year of record earnings in 1991. Revenues increased 36 percent to $229.7 million, and income shot up 29 percent to $51.6 million. Founders Charles Geschke and John Warnock received the *MacUser* magazine's John J. Anderson Distinguished Service Award, for "enduring achievement in the Macintosh industry."

Adobe's efforts to create a universal standard for viewing complex documents continued in 1992. That year, the company marked its tenth anniversary and branched out into new ventures. With Hayden, a division of Prentice Hall Computer Publishing, Adobe signed an agreement to create Adobe Press, a joint publishing venture for developing books about graphic arts, Adobe computer applications, and advanced technologies.

During this time, competition in the industry intensified, and Adobe sought new ways to maintain its lead in the industry. Adobe Carousel was the company's first foray into electronic transmission of newspapers, magazines, and other print media. Carousel would allow such materials to be displayed on screen complete with pictures, color, and multiple typefaces.

In June 1992, Adobe President and CEO Charles Geschke was kidnapped. Although he eventually was returned safely and began granting interviews two months after the incident, he refused to discuss details of the abduction. In an interview with the *San Jose Business Journal*, Geschke discussed Adobe's plans for the future. Maintaining that the company was beginning "a long journey down a digital highway," Geschke revealed that its primary mission was to make text, pictures, video, and, perhaps, sound computer-readable. Toward that end, Adobe acquired OCR Systems, an optical character recognition company that turned scanned documents into manipulatable text.

With the introduction of Adobe Premiere 3.0 for Macintosh in 1993, Adobe entered the fields of video and multimedia. The software enabled users to perform desktop video editing formerly achieved only with expensive equipment. Adobe Premiere featured nonlinear editing, graphics, and special effects.

In 1993 Adobe realized its goal of enabling incompatible computer systems to communicate. Adobe Acrobat software was designed to turn computers into information distributors that would allow Mac users to view a document in its original form, with formatting and graphics intact, even if the document had been created on an IBM. Analysts hailed Acrobat as a tool that could facilitate electronic distribution of everything from interoffice memos to training manuals to magazines. Adobe's revenues for the year rose to $313.4 million, up from $265.9 million in 1992, and net income was reported at $57 million.

Challenges and Diversification in the Mid to Late 1990s

Adobe solidified its position in the desktop publishing market in 1994 when it acquired Aldus, the maker of the industry-leading PageMaker desktop publishing software. Adobe and Aldus had worked in cooperation previously, and Adobe's font software was used in PageMaker. Also that year Adobe introduced After Effects, a program geared toward multimedia and film production efforts. After Effects provided tools for producing two-dimensional animation, as well as special effects and motion compositing. Adobe reported revenues of $676 million for fiscal 1994, up from $580 million the previous year.

In the mid-1990s Adobe continued to grow through acquisitions and worked to strengthen its position in the volatile software industry. The acquisition of Frame Technology Corporation, the developer of FrameMaker publishing software, proved to be an unfortunate purchase; after integrating Frame into the Adobe family of operations, Frame's sales declined heavily. Industry observers attributed the drop to Adobe's decision to get rid of Frame's technical support division. Also in 1995 Adobe bought Ceneca Communications, which developed tools for creating Web pages. The following year Adobe made additional acquisitions, including Ares Software, for about $15.5 million, and the research and development efforts of Swell Software, for about $6 million. The research project, however, was discontinued soon after the purchase. Also in 1996 Adobe spun off its pre-press division to Luminous Corporation for about $43.6 million and moved its headquarters from Mountain View to downtown San Jose. The following year Adobe divested its investment in Netscape Communications Corporation and separately acquired three software companies, spending a total of about $8.5 million.

On the software front, Adobe released PhotoDeluxe and PageMill in 1996. PhotoDeluxe, the first of its category, allowed consumers to manipulate and edit photographs on their computers. PageMill included tools for easily creating Web pages. In 1997 Adobe released upgrades of PageMaker, Illustrator, and FrameMaker. These releases, coupled with increased demand for Photoshop, PhotoDeluxe, and Acrobat products, led to total revenues of $912 million for fiscal 1997, up from $787 million the previous year. In addition, the company's balance of software revenues shifted from predominantly Macintosh-based software to Windows-based software.

Not everything was rosy at Adobe headquarters, however, and 1998 proved to be the most grueling in the company's history. In 1997 Hewlett-Packard chose to stop licensing Post-Script from Adobe when it developed its own clone version of the software. By the following year Adobe was feeling the effects of Hewlett-Packard's decision, and its licensing sales suffered. The decline in Macintosh software sales hurt Adobe as well, and competitors such as Microsoft Corporation took away precious market share. In addition, because of the economic recession in Asia, sales in Japan, one of Adobe's stronger markets, fell about 40 percent. Adobe's stock price fell as well, hitting a low that was less than half of its value. Industry observers noted that Adobe had not kept up with the pace of software introductions. As the *Wall Street Journal* reported in 1998, "In fast-moving industries, the quest for perfection can get in the way of cranking out good-enough products." Adobe's methodical approach to developing software had hindered its growth and success. Adobe also had grown its work force too enthusiastically, anticipating demand that failed to materialize.

In August 1998, Adobe indicated that third-quarter revenues would not meet expectations. For the nine months ended August 28, 1998, sales reached $101 million, down from $179 million for the same period in 1997. The company also announced a major restructuring designed to streamline operations and increase profitability. The firm planned to eliminate about 12 percent of the work force, about 300 people, including several top executives, and to concentrate more heavily on corporations and businesses, which represented a wider and more profitable niche than Adobe's traditional audience of designers and graphic artists. Just as Adobe announced its intentions, it received a hostile takeover bid from competitor Quark Inc., developer of the leading QuarkXPress professional publishing software. Adobe successfully fended off Quark's attempt and embarked on its restructuring journey. Despite the company's trials, CEO Warnock, for the most part, shrugged off Adobe's financial problems. "I don't think Adobe's struggling," Warnock told *Computer Reseller News*. "We're not a company that's in a turnaround situation. What we are is a company that was letting expenses get out of line."

The year 1999 proved to be busy for Adobe. Adobe sold off two noncore operations as part of its reorganization tactic—Adobe Enterprise Publishing Services, Inc., which offered services related to Adobe Acrobat products, and Image Club Graphics, which produced and marketed graphics products and typefaces. In addition, because Adobe wished to enhance its reputation as a provider of tools for Internet and Web applications, the company acquired GoLive Systems, which developed Web design software. Thanks in part to marketing efforts, an increasing number of consumers began to use existing Adobe products Photoshop and Illustrator to design Web pages. Adobe Acrobat, which had failed to catch on in the mid-1990s, was quickly becoming a ubiquitous presence on the Web in the late 1990s.

Adobe released a number of products in 1999, including a new version of Photoshop, GoLive, PressReady, ActiveShare, and InDesign. InDesign was Adobe's first offering in the high-end professional publishing segment, a segment dominated by Quark products. Called by many "Quark Killer," InDesign quickly created the largest backlog ever experienced by Adobe for a new product. In September 1999 Adobe reported record revenues of $260.9 million for the third quarter. Profit reached $72 million, up greatly compared with a loss of $6.1 million for the third quarter of 1998. Adobe's stock price more than tripled during the year. Bear, Stearns & Co. analyst Robert Fagin told the *Wall Street Journal,* "It's staggering. . . . In the space of one year, the company has been able to put together a true turnaround."

For the fiscal year ended December 3, 1999, Adobe reported revenues of more than $1 billion, the first time in the company's history that sales exceeded $1 billion. In January 2000 Adobe was named one of the 100 best companies to work for in America by *Fortune.* The company had successfully carried out its restructuring efforts and appeared ready to tackle new challenges. As Adobe approached a new era, it planned to increase profitability and continue developing cutting-edge technological solutions for publishers, graphic and Web designers, and businesses. President and co-founder Charles Geschke, who announced plans to retire effective March 2000, stated in a prepared statement, "Adobe enters the new millennium in its strongest position ever—in terms of the strength of its management team, its leadership market position, and the quality of its products."

Principal Subsidiaries

Adobe Systems Pty. Ltd. (Australia); Adobe Systems Europe Limited (United Kingdom); Adobe Systems Co., Ltd. (Japan).

Principal Competitors

Quark Inc.; Corel Corporation; Microsoft Corporation.

Further Reading

Chang, Greg, "Adobe Earnings Top Estimates Again; Cost-Cutting and Strong Web Demand Credited," *Seattle Post-Intelligencer,* December 18, 1999, p. B4.

Clark, Don, "Adobe Systems Beat Estimates for 3rd Quarter," *Wall Street Journal,* September 17, 1999, p. B11.

Collins, LaVon, "Adobe and IBM Sign Joint Marketing Agreement," *Business Wire,* November 16, 1988.

Darrow, Barbara, "Adobe Comes Out Swinging—What a Difference a Year Makes," *Computer Reseller News,* September 27, 1999, p. 190.

Downing, David, "Adobe Sets New Direction in Digital Type," *Business Wire,* March 5, 1991.

Goldman, James S., "Will Steve Jobs Buy Apple's Former Stake in Adobe Systems?," *Business Journal—San Jose,* July 10, 1989, p. 1.

Groves, Martha, "Adobe: Redesigning the Future," *Los Angeles Times,* April 30, 1989, p. 9.

Hansen, Brenda, "Adobe Announces Adobe Illustrator for the IBM Personal Computer," *Business Wire,* September 14, 1988.

Leone, Genevieve, "High-Flying Adobe Succeeds in Holding Off Clone Products," *Business Journal—San Jose,* January 23, 1989, p. 4.

Pender, Lee, "John Warnock: Adobe—The Developer Must Meet the New Challenges of Today's Publishing World," *Computer Reseller News,* November 9, 1998, p. 133.

Privett, Cyndi, "Adobe Supplies Software for New Laser Printers," *Business Journal—San Jose,* May 26, 1986, p. 15.

Prosser, Linda, "Adobe Previews PostScript Level 2," *Business Wire,* June 4, 1990.

Rensbarger, Fran, "Have Desk, Will Publish," *Washington Business Journal,* March 9, 1987, p. 9.

Rodriguez, Karen, "Adobe Plots Rebound Around Business, Corporate Market," *Business Journal,* September 28, 1998, p. 6.

Thurm, Scott, "Quark Tries To Catch a Fallen High-Tech Star," *Wall Street Journal,* August 27, 1998, p. B1.

Weber, Jonathan, "Adobe Software Could Start New Era in Computer Communication," *Los Angeles Times,* June 15, 1993, p. 1.

Weisman, Jonathan, "Adobe's Hopes Riding on Carousel," *Business Journal—San Jose,* August 24, 1992, p. 1.

Young, Margaret, "Adobe Expands Retail Role with Two Distribution Pacts," *Business Journal—San Jose,* October 19, 1987, p. 11.

—Marinell James
—updated by Mariko Fujinaka

Aerolíneas Argentinas S.A.

Bouchard 547
Buenos Aires 1106
Argentina
Telephone: (1) 4317-3000
Toll Free: (800) 333-0276; 0-810-222-VOLAR
Web Site: http://www.aerolineas.com.ar

Wholly Owned Subsidiary of Interinvest S.A.
Incorporated: 1949 as Aerolíneas Argentinas
Employees: 5,600
Sales: $949.5 million (1999)
NAIC: 481111 Scheduled Passenger Air Transportation

Aerolíneas Argentinas S.A. is the flagship airline of Argentina, with its hub in Buenos Aires and boasting an estimated 2,000 flights a day. Despite its size and strategic location (making it a key player in the world of global marketing alliances), the company's financial performance has been less than stellar. Decades of economic crisis and an extended, painful privatization have left the carrier still struggling. With years of losses, Iberia Airlines and other investors spent 1999 unsuccessfully trying to sell their stakes in the troubled carrier—not a terribly jubilant way to spend the company's 50th anniversary. However, a new infusion of management talent from American Airlines hoped to reverse the airline's disastrous path.

Origins

Argentine civil aviation has its roots in the French air mail line Aéropostale and its South American subsidiaries, one of which was Aeroposta Argentina. Aeroposta was established in 1927 primarily as a mail carrier. Early flights in this country were often perilous; rudimentary equipment, strong winds, and poor landing strips inspired flying adventures of the kind recounted by the famous French aviator and writer Antoine de Saint-Exupéry. Moreover, the company was battered by worldwide economic depression in the early 1930s, during which time the French government withdrew much of its financial support for parent company Aéropostale. In 1932, control of Aeroposta underwent several changes, including temporary

ownership by the Argentinian post office, but the company ultimately survived as Aeroposta Argentina, S.A., the national airline of Argentina. In 1937, Aeroposta's economic woes were somewhat allayed when Argentina's Pueyrredon financial group, a conglomerate of banks and insurance companies, bought out the remaining French interests in the line. Although Aeroposta came under the control of Ernesto Pueyrredon, it also continued to receive a subsidy from the Argentinian government.

Beginning in the late 1930s, other airlines were starting to crop up in Argentina. In 1946, the government of Argentina imposed some organization on the country's airlines (and fended off competition from foreign airlines, such as the U.S.-based PANAGRA), forming a system of mixed-stock companies. Besides Aeroposta, three new joint stock companies were created out of the airlines that had sprung up in the 1930s. The first was FAMA (Flota Aérea Mercante Argentina), which set the precedent for the nation's international air service. ALFA (Aviación del Litoral Fluvial Argentina) was formed by merging one private, one military, and one civil airline. ZONDA (Zonas Oeste y Norte de Aerolíneas Argentinas) took over PANAGRA's domestic trade network in the northwest.

1950s–70s: Striving to Stay Aloft Amidst Government Upheaval

On May 3, 1949, a new nationalistic government in Argentina, led by Juan Perón, merged the four joint-stock companies—Aeroposta Argentina, FAMA, ALFA, and ZONDA—into the new state airline, Aerolíneas Argentinas. This monopoly would last until 1956. After working to integrate the aircraft and routes of all four operations, Aerolíneas Argentinas achieved operating efficiencies and became a member of the International Air Transport Association (IATA).

However, when a military coup ousted Perón, a new provisional government liberalized the aviation market again. Competition ensued as Argentinian investors formed new airlines. Privately-backed Transcontinental, S.A., for example, provided six years of competition before financial woes resulted in its being taking over by Austral, another new private carrier.

Company Perspectives:

All the personnel at Aerolineas Argentinas are devoting all their efforts at satisfying your expectations when choosing us for your flights. We do our best to meet your needs and keep your trust. We know that you are aware of the incorporation of the latest technology in our modern aircraft, our in flight service improvements, the dependability on time performance, our favorable connections and competitive rates among other relevant aspects.

Aerolíneas Ini and Transatlántica were two other competitors for Aerolíneas Argentina's business during this period.

None of the new entrants had the experience or resources of Aerolíneas Argentinas (AR). AR was able to launch South America's first commercial jets in March 1959: six Comet IV's received to settle a bill for harboring British troops during World War II. Within a couple of years, however, half of these had crashed, and though no fatalities were reported the company's president was forced to resign. Under new leadership, AR continued to expand and modernize its fleet, retiring older aircraft and establishing service to popular resort destinations.

By the 1960s, AR was the leading South American airline, flying more than 600 million passenger-kilometers a year. However, financial and managerial woes were emerging. In 1963, the airline dropped out of the International Air Transport Association (IATA), a cartel of world airlines, when that organization denied AR the right to impose a surcharge for flights on jets. Both AR and its competitor Austral had been losing money on the regulated domestic fares and had been granted government subsidies to help offset the losses. A new board of directors took over AR in June 1964 amid charges of mismanagement and corruption at the airline. The next year, the new leaders set about improving the airline's fleet, establishing a relationship with Boeing, by ordering several of that company's 707s, that would last for many years. AR rejoined the IATA during this time; the year after that saw yet another change of administration.

In 1967, in order that AR and Austral might co-exist under government control, a new Argentinian president divvied up domestic air routes between Austral-A.L.A.(Aerotransportes Litoral Argentina, its new partner) and AR. By now, AR's Boeing 707s were flying the world's longest nonstop scheduled flight at the time: 5,700 miles from Rio de Janeiro to Rome. Service to New York had also begun, and by the end of the decade, AR had obtained clearance to open service to the west coast of the United States.

In 1972, Argentinian and U.S. authorities briefly locked horns over the rights of Pan American and Braniff airlines to serve Argentina. When Argentina officials denied these American airlines the right to expand their routes in Argentina, the U.S. government responded by attempting to curb AR's presence in the United States. Settlements over the routes were eventually made, and AR was able to add nonstop service to Miami and Cape Town in 1973, the latter in conjunction with South African Airways. In December, new management installed by the returning Juan Perón (the second executive shuf-

fle in a year) gave the airline a new emphasis on commercial viability in route selection and fare determination.

Although Perón died in 1974 and his wife, Isobel Perón, was overthrown in 1976, the structure of the airline remained relatively unchanged. The company continued to weather upheavals in management, intense competition from Austral, and ever-changing government policies. AR began operating massive Boeing 747 widebody jets to Madrid in January 1977, launching a period of expansion. After testing the route with charters, AR pioneered the first scheduled (monthly) service across Antarctica, to Auckland, New Zealand. AR began the 1980s as the third busiest airline in South America after VARIG and Mexicana, flying six billion passenger-kilometers a year.

The Path to Privatization in the 1980s

The disastrous Falklands War in April 1982 did not help Argentina's economy, which fell apart in the mid-1970s during Isobel Perón's rule. Inflation reached triple or quadruple digits, depending upon the estimate, and in 1986 the government of Argentina planned for the privatization of several large companies in order to satisfy its creditors. AR was to be one of the first.

In February 1988, the Directory of Public Enterprises (DEP) announced the sale of 40 percent of AR to SAS for $204 million. Cielos del Sur, which owned Austral, itself privatized in 1987, put forth an informal but well publicized counteroffer with the support of Swissair and Alitalia. SAS withdrew its bid in December 1988 after a highly politicized debate pitting President Raul Alfonsín against incumbent Carlos Menem. However, the Cielos del Sur group was not able to finalize its bid, due to a lack a financial disclosures from the government. Then, Swissair withdrew from the group, scuttling the offer. Menem renewed efforts to find a buyer after winning office in May 1989.

Menem's efforts were frustrated by the company's poor financial health; it was losing $10 million a month in 1990, which was a terrible year for the airline industry as a whole, with most of the world's major carriers posting losses. Nevertheless, a consortium led by Spain's carrier Iberia made a bid in June 1990, kicking off AR's tortuous, extended privatization process. In its initial offer, Iberia would control 30 percent; three Spanish banks another 19 percent; Argentinian investors 36 percent; employees ten percent; and the government, five percent; resulting in 51 percent Argentine ownership. Iberia and its partners agreed to pay more than $2 billion for their 85 percent share, including a $130 million initial cash payment. Not included in the new deal were AR's lucrative ramp service and duty-free businesses.

Several factors soured the deal for Iberia once it was committed to the buyout. When Enrique Pescarmon sold Cielos del Sur (and thus Austral) to Iberia in March 1991, leaving the partnership, his share was split between other Argentinian interests. Mounting losses through 1992 (when AR lost $189 million on revenues of $911 million) necessitated a capital infusion from the Spaniards and the Argentine government, diluting other shareholdings of the private local investors. However, the Spanish holdings remained the same. The government owned 43 percent, which it intended to reduce to ten percent once the

Key Dates:

1949: Aerolíneas Argentinas (AR) created by Juan Perón administration out of four existing airlines.
1959: AR launches South America's first commercial jets.
1967: AR's Boeing 707s operate world's longest nonstop scheduled flight.
1977: Widebody Boeing 747 service to Madrid begins; AR pioneers scheduled flights across Antarctica.
1982: Falklands War helps wreck Argentina's economy.
1988: SAS offers unsuccessful bid for 40 percent of AR.
1990: Group lead by Iberia agrees to pay $2 billion for 85 percent of AR.
1998: AMR Corp. buys ten percent of Interinvest, AR's holding company.
1999: Iberia-led group unsuccessfully tries to sell off its stake.

market allowed. In addition, $2.1 billion of foreign debt, part of Iberia's purchase requirement, ended up costing more than originally estimated. Finally, postponed layoffs of 775 workers incited labor protests. Moreover, Iberia suffered serious losses at home, $264 million on 1992 revenues of $3.6 billion.

New Investors in the 1990s

As costly as it proved to Iberia, AR still controlled one-third of South America's air traffic, making it a somewhat attractive investment to global competitors. Since Iberia needed government subsidies for its own survival, the European Commission mandated it reduce its holdings in AR. Merrill Lynch and Bankers Trust bought into the company in 1996, and American Airlines parent AMR Corp. beat out Continental to take a ten percent share of Interinvest, AR's holding company, in 1998.

The number-crunching methodology of American Airlines (AA) brought quite a culture change to the airline, accustomed to decidedly less formal decision-making. AA managers immediately set out to reduce short-term debt of about $700 million and slashed the payroll. They also used AA standards to improve customer service, starting out a process that could make AR eligible for membership in the OneWorld global alliance. Reducing the number of aircraft types was also a priority; still, the company ordered a dozen Airbus A340s, a type new to Latin America, for its long-haul needs.

AR faced stiff international competition from LAN Chile and VARIG. New open skies agreements cleared the way for Continental and Delta into the Argentine market as well. A recession at home compounded the carrier's difficulties in 1999, even as local cut-rate upstarts such as Southern Winds Líneas Aéreas plagued the airline. Losses for 1999 were expected to reach $125 million. AR's owners had failed to find a buyer—or a way out—by the end of December. Interinvest, which then owned 85 percent of AR, was in turn 80 percent owned by the Spanish government via SEPI, ten percent owned by Iberia, and ten percent by AA. Employees owned ten percent of AR and the Argentine government the remaining five percent. Nevertheless, company literature remained optimistic.

Principal Competitors

VARIG S.A.; LAN Chile S.A.

Further Reading

Cameron, Doug, ''Aerolineas Needs a Lift,'' *Airfinance Journal,* April 1996, p. 20.

Carey, Susan, ''Europe's Airlines Giving Up on Mergers in Favor of Other Forms of Cooperation,'' *Wall Street Journal,* April 6, 1988, p. 1.

Christian, Shirley, ''Argentina Closes Sale of Airline,'' *New York Times,* November 23, 1990, p. D1.

Davies, R.E.G., *Airlines of Latin America Since 1919,* Washington, D.C.: Smithsonian Institution, 1984.

Grosse, Robert, ''A Privatization Nightmare: Aerolíneas Argentinas,'' in *Privatizing Monopolies: Lessons from the Telecommunications and Transport Sectors in Latin America,* edited by Ravi Ramamurti, Baltimore: Johns Hopkins, 1996.

Forward, David C., ''Aerolíneas Argentinas Does the Tango with Toulouse,'' *Airways,* October 1999, pp. 20–27.

Kamm, Thomas, ''Privatization Campaign in Argentina Bogs Down,'' *Wall Street Journal,* October 25, 1990, p. A16.

Limo, Edvaldo Pereira, ''Tango American,'' *Air Transport World,* October 1999, pp. 96–99.

——, ''Tango Twosome,'' *Air Transport World,* December 1997, pp. 61–64.

Riding, Alan, ''Argentina's Privatization Battle,'' *New York Times,* November 28, 1988, p. D8.

Schumacher, Edward, ''Argentina's Chief Banker is Held; Pressure Grows to Renounce Debt,'' *New York Times,* October 4, 1983, p. A1.

Vitzhum, Carlta, and Craig Torres, ''Aerolineas Argentinas's Sale Deadline is Set to Expire with No Buyer in Sight,'' *Wall Street Journal,* December 30, 1999, p. A3.

—Frederick C. Ingram

Aéroports de Paris

291 Boulevard Raspail
75675 Paris Cedex 14
France
Telephone: (+33) 1 43 35 70 00
Fax: (+33) 1 43 35 71 17
Web site: http://www.adp.fr

Government-Owned Company
Incorporated: 1945
Employees: 7,779
Sales: FFr 7.94 billion ($1.41 billion) (1998)
NAIC: 48811 Airport Operations

Aéroports de Paris, a financially independent company owned by the French government, is responsible for the operations of all aviation field activity within a 50-mile radius of Paris, placing a total of 14 airfields under Aéroports de Paris's control, including international airports Charles de Gaulle-Roissy and Orly, the business class airport Le Bourget, 12 airfields serving light craft, and the Issy-les-Moulineaux heliport in Paris. Together Aéroports de Paris's properties are roughly two-thirds the size of Paris itself, making it Europe's largest airport body. It is also one of Europe's—and the world's—busiest airport operators. Serving nearly 64 million passengers in 1998, Aéroports de Paris boasts Europe's highest rate of continental air passenger traffic, and the second highest international passenger volume in the world, behind London. For total traffic volume, Aéroports de Paris ranks number eight in the world, behind London, New York, Chicago, Tokyo, Dallas, Los Angeles, and Atlanta. The company also ranks among the world's leading handlers of air freight, with more than 1.29 million tons of freight and mail handled in 1998. The opening of a terminal by Federal Express to handle all of its European shipping activity is expected to provide a substantial boost to Aéroports de Paris's freight operations. The company also has been expanding its airport consulting, construction, and management subsidiary, ADP Management, which has successfully competed for key airport contracts in China, among others. In 1998 Aéroports de Paris reported revenues of nearly FFr 8 billion.

Origins in World War II

Prior to the Second World War, passenger air travel remained rare, and flying in general was restricted to either the very daring or the very rich. At the turn of the century, however, Paris already boasted its own airfield, at Issy-les Moulineaux, near the Eiffel Tower. Many of France's pioneering heavier-than-air aviation efforts, including Ernest Archdeacon's test flight of a Wright-designed glider in 1905 and the first flight of the Trajan Vuia, took place at the Issy-les-Moulineaux site. Later, in 1924, the site served as the launching grounds for the first helicopter flight, piloted by the Marquis of Pescara.

By then, however, Paris was being served by a new airfield, at Le Bourget. Originally established as a camp to protect Paris from the German Zeppelins during the First World War, Le Bourget was soon after fitted with a runway; by the 1920s, Le Bourget was serving passengers and had its own air traffic control facility. By 1937, Le Bourget was serving more than 131,000 passengers and some 18,000 aircraft arrivals and departures per year.

During World War II, the Free French government, set up under Charles de Gaulle in London, began making plans for the postwar development of a civil aviation authority. In 1944, Alain Bozel, secretary general to the French ministry of war, submitted a proposal for the construction and operation of a major airport serving the Paris area. Dubbed the "Aéroport de Paris," the new body was to be placed under the supervision of the Ministry of Equipment, Housing and Transport, but controlled by the Ministry of Economy and Finance. Aéroports de Paris officially came into being in October 1945. Civilian aviation activities commenced in February 1946, when the Allied forces turned over the Le Bourget and Orly airfields to the new French government. In that year, Aéroports de Paris acted as host to the launch of Air France's Paris-New York flight. Passenger levels topped 300,000 in 1946.

The airfield at Orly had been in development since the 1920s and in service since the 1930s. Located less than 11 kilometers from Paris, it was to become the site of France's first major airport. Construction began on the North terminal at Orly, which was completed in 1948. Continued expansion soon led

Company Perspectives:

In order to assure its competitiveness in a highly contested environment, Aéroports de Paris has taken as its objectives to: respond to demands for capacity with an ambitious infrastructure development program; improve the quality of service; maintain a financial balance; successfully diversify its activities.

Air France to transfer its operations from Le Bourget to Orly, marking the latter's debut as France's primary airport. By then, passenger volumes at the Aéroports de Paris facilities topped one million per year.

Aéroports de Paris continued to expand during the 1950s. In 1954, with the opening of the first of the Orly South terminals, the company began offering commercial assistance services, including ticketing and check-in services for airline clients. The opening of Orly South also provided Paris with the infrastructure to receive the first jet plane arrivals. More than any other technological development, the use of the jet engine for aircraft signaled the start of the first real boom in civilian air travel. By 1957, Aéroports de Paris registered more than 2.5 million passengers per year, more than 42,000 tons of freight handled, and nearly 112,000 aircraft movements per year. These totals placed Aéroports de Paris as the world's second largest airport operator, behind London. That same year, the Issy-les-Moulineaux opened as an international heliport.

Expansion in the 1970s

The predicted rise in air passenger travel led Aéroports de Paris to begin searching for a site for a new airport as early as the late 1950s. By then, the company already had begun construction on the next phase of Orly, that of a second South terminal. In 1959, Aéroports de Paris also put into service a third runway, capable of receiving a new breed of four-engine jet craft serving the intercontinental market. The completion of the A6 highway, connecting Orly directly to Paris, marked the debut of a new boom in air travel that saw Aéroports de Paris quadruple its passenger traffic volume within ten years. In 1960, Aéroports de Paris, in addition to more than 60,000 tons of handled freight and 126,000 aircraft arrivals and departures, saw its passenger volume top 3.5 million.

The following year, Aéroports de Paris opened the new Orly South terminal. More than just a terminal, Orly South became France's most visited tourist attraction, receiving more than one million visitors per year, in addition to many of Aéroports de Paris's four million passengers per year. Serving as the launch pad for the sleek new rear-engined Caravelle jet, Orly South marked the debut of the modern era of passenger air travel. By 1964, more than five million passengers and 100,000 tons of freight passed through Aéroports de Paris's operations. In that year, the creation of a new airport to serve the Paris area was announced at the site of Roissy-en France. Work on the Roissy airport began in 1966. Meanwhile, infrastructure improvements continued to be made at Orly, including the opening of a new air traffic control tower in 1966, an airport washing facility, and the

debut of construction on what was to become the Orly South West terminal, opened in 1969. The following year, the Orly South East terminal began operations.

In 1970, more than 12 million passengers traveled through the Aéroports de Paris facilities. That year also saw the arrival of the first Boeing 747. The 747 proved to be something of a revolution to air travel and opened up a new era of less expensive air travel that was to make air travel, still rather restricted to wealthier passengers, a viable option for a vast new market of travelers. By the middle of the decade, Aéroports de Paris approached 20 million passengers per year; its freight activity had also expanded, reaching 400,000 tons. Helping to absorb the growing volume of activity was the inauguration of the first Roissy airport terminal, Charles de Gaulle 1, in 1974.

The Arab Oil Embargo and resulting economic crisis of the mid-1970s put a temporary stop to the work begun on the second Charles de Gaulle terminal. Work did not begin again until 1977. Construction on that terminal was completed in 1982. While Aéroports de Paris turned more and more toward a management and operations approach, rather than an airport builder, it began to take its expertise in all three areas overseas, winning airport construction contracts in such cities as Cairo and Abu Dhabi. Back in Paris, the completion of the de Gaulle airport allowed Aéroports de Paris to transform the small Le Bourget airport from a commercial airport to a business airport serving the high-end market.

After the heady growth of the 1970s, the beginning of the 1980s saw a slowdown in passenger growth. After several difficult years, which saw Aéroports de Paris losing passenger volume to the rapidly expanding ultrafast TGV train system, as well as facing increasing competition for the international and inter-European travel market from such cities as London, Brussels, and Amsterdam, Aéroports de Paris began to set new strategic objectives. With its vast real estate holdings, the company set out to recreate itself as an important hub for European transport, providing intermodal (air, rail, and road) services for both freight and passenger traffic. A major step toward achieving this objective was the commitment of the government-run railroad, the SNCF, to extend the TGV directly to the Charles de Gaulle 2 terminal.

Rebuilding Through the 1990s

The beginning of the 1990s, however, left the world air travel community in turmoil. The economic recession, and especially the outbreak of the Persian Gulf War and passenger fears for possible terrorist attack, caused a huge drop in air travel. The fall in passenger numbers continued to affect Aéroports de Paris into the middle of the decade.

By then, the Roissy-Charles de Gaulle airport had overtaken Orly as Paris's and France's primary airport facility, with more than 25 million passengers per year. The resulting strain on capacity was relieved, however, with the 1993 opening of a new terminal at Orly and the completion of a fourth wing at Charles de Gaulle 2, giving both Orly and Roissy the capacity to process 30 million passengers per year. The following year, the new TGV facility was put into service. In that year, Roissy's position as Aéroports de Paris's primary facility was reinforced when the

Key Dates:

1945: Creation by French government of Aéroports de Paris.
1946: Civilian air traffic returns to Orly and Le Bourget airports.
1948: Opening of North Terminal at Orly.
1953: Air France transfers to Orly from Le Bourget.
1954: Launch of commercial assistance operations; opening of South Terminal at Orly.
1957: Opening of heliport at Issy-les-Moulineaux.
1964: Creation of Roissy airport.
1974: Operations begin at Roissy-Charles de Gaulle airport.
1994: Opening of TGV station at Charles de Gaulle.
1997: Addition of two new runways at Charles de Gaulle.
1999: Opening of Federal Express cargo facility.
2000: Conversion of Cergy-Pontoise airport for international air traffic.

government, responding to residents' noise complaints, imposed new limits on the number of operating hours at Orly. On the bright side, Orly underwent a face lift, at a cost of some FFr 90 million, restoring much of the airport's former luster.

The end of the economic recession that had affected France for much of the first half of the 1990s brought renewed growth to Aéroports de Paris, which saw its passenger volume top 60 million in 1996. The following year, Roissy won the right to increase its aircraft traffic still further, with the addition of two new runways judged to be in the public interest by the Transport Minister. If Aéroports de Paris was nonetheless straining its passenger capacity, the opening of the fifth wing of Charles de Gaulle 2, the construction of a satellite wing for that terminal's Hall A, the placing into operation of an Arrivals Hall in the Charles de Gaulle T9 terminal, all in 1998, and the opening of the south tower of Charles de Gaulle 2 in 1999, added the infrastructure to meet projected passenger volume growth for

the near future. For the long term, however, Aéroports de Paris looked forward to converting its Cergy-Pontoise airport, some 38 miles from Paris, to an international flight facility.

Although passenger volume worldwide slowed in the late 1990s, due in large part to the economic crisis in Asia, Aéroports de Paris continued to mark increases in its passenger volume. The decision by Federal Express to open its new European service facility at Charles de Gaulle in May 1999, however, greatly enhanced Aéroports de Paris's position as a leading handler of air freight traffic. Although Aéroports de Paris remained committed to providing airport services to the Paris region, the company also began to look further afield. In February 2000, Aéroports de Paris was granted the right to acquire a ten percent stake in Beijing Capital International Airport, marking the company's first flight into the international scene.

Principal Subsidiaries

ADP Management (90%); Alyzia; Serta; France Handling (34%); Roissy SOGARIS SCI (40%).

Principal Competitors

Flughafen Frankfurt; Amsterdam-Schiphol; Alitalia-Linee Aeree Italiana, S.p.A.; BAA plc.

Further Reading

"Aéroports de Paris Wins Tunisian Airport Deal," *Reuters,* January 4, 2000.
"A Third Major Airport in the Wings for Paris," *World Airport Week,* January 5, 1999.
Fainsilber, Denis, "Aéroports de Paris et son partenaire GTM ont pris 10% du capital de l'aéroport de Pékin," *Les Echos,* February 4, 2000, p. 19.
Tiller, Alan, "Orly Travels Back in Time," *European,* August 29, 1996, p. 26.
"Turning Point in the Quest for Airport Growth," *World Airport Week,* October 21, 1998.

—M.L. Cohen

Akin, Gump, Strauss, Hauer & Feld, L.L.P.

1333 New Hampshire Avenue, N.W., Suite 400
Washington, D.C. 20036
U.S.A.
Telephone: (202) 887-4000
Fax: (202) 887-4288
Web site: http://www.akingump.com

Partnership
Founded: 1945
Employees: 1,800
Sales: $301 million (1998)
NAIC: 54111 Offices of Lawyers

Akin, Gump, Strauss, Hauer & Feld, L.L.P., is one of the world's largest law firms, with more than 870 lawyers based in Washington, D.C., Dallas, Houston, Austin, San Antonio, New York, Philadelphia, Los Angles, London, Brussels, and Moscow and an affiliate in Saudi Arabia. While the firm has a diversified practice in most aspects of modern corporate law, it is best known as one of the nation's top lobbying law firms. Its many prominent attorneys include founder Robert Strauss, a former chairman of the Democratic National Committee and U.S. ambassador to the Soviet Union; Vernon Jordan, a key member of the Clinton administration; former U.S. House of Representatives Speaker Thomas S. Foley; and Bill Paxon, a former member of the U.S. House of Representatives.

Origins and Early Years

Robert S. Strauss, one of the two founders of the firm, grew up in the small town of Stamford, Texas, and in 1941 graduated from the law school at the University of Texas in Austin. In college he met John Connally, whom he later helped become the governor of Texas. After law school, he joined the FBI as a special agent. In 1945 he and Richard Gump, a college friend who was also at the FBI, resigned to start a Dallas partnership known as Gump and Strauss. The firm's first big client was the Dallas Transit Company, a private firm being sold to the city government. That representation earned Gump and Strauss $450,000, and the firm was on its way.

In those early years, Gump and Strauss were heavily involved in politics and met many potential clients through their political activities. In the 1950s Strauss ran unsuccessfully for the Dallas City Council and secured an appointment as the chairman of the Texas State Banking Commission. Strauss raised money to help elect John F. Kennedy in 1960 and made the acquaintance of Lyndon Johnson before he became president in 1963.

The 1970s and 1980s

In 1971 the Washington, D.C., office of Akin Gump was established with two attorneys. By the late 1990s the former branch office included over 300 lawyers and served as the main office of the firm. Akin Gump opened a branch office in Austin in 1978 to serve clients in the oil industry.

In 1982 the law firm hired Vernon E. Jordan, Jr. Jordan was born and raised in Atlanta, graduated from Howard University Law School, worked as a civil rights lawyer, and served as the president of the National Urban League. Jordan had become acquainted with Robert Strauss when the two served as directors of the Xerox Corporation.

Like many other large law firms, Akin Gump expanded in the 1980s along with a booming American economy that added millions of new jobs. In 1984 the law firm opened an office in San Antonio, followed in 1988 by an office in Houston which grew to employ more than 75 lawyers by the late 1990s. In 1989 Akin Gump added an office in Brussels.

Practice in the 1990s

In 1991 President George Bush appointed Robert Strauss ambassador to the Soviet Union, which broke apart soon afterward. Although Strauss was no longer part of the firm, which changed its name to Akin, Gump, Hauer & Feld, the firm did benefit from his government service, as clients requested the firm's counsel in establishing business ventures in the region. In 1994 Akin, Gump joined the growing list of American law firms with branch offices in Moscow.

Company Perspectives:

We aspire, through dedicated effort, to become, and to be recognized as, a leading international law firm that excels at providing innovative legal services worldwide and thereby to be one of the major international law firms that will dominate the legal market for the twenty-first century. To fulfill our vision, we will position ourselves as a challenger to the firms that have dominated the market for services to corporate and financial America in the last half of the twentieth century by distinguishing ourselves through our ability to bring a new approach to the practice of the law that reflects our energy, creativity, skills–developed to serve the demands of the new economy–use of technology, and ability to affect the relationship of business and government worldwide.

Key Dates:

1945: Richard Gump and Robert Strauss leave the FBI to found the Gump and Strauss law firm in Dallas.
1950: The firm is renamed Goldberg, Fonville, Gump & Strauss.
1955: The Pipe Line Contractors Association becomes the firm's largest client.
1963: The firm becomes known as Goldberg, Fonville, Gump, Strauss & Hauer.
1966: Goldberg leaves to become a judge, and Henry Akin joins the firm.
1971: The firm opens its Washington, D.C., branch office.
1972: Founding partner Robert Strauss becomes Democratic National Committee chairman.
1978: An office is opened in Austin, Texas.
1982: Vernon Jordan joins the law firm.
1984: The firm establishes its San Antonio office.
1988: An office is opened in Houston.
1989: A branch office in Brussels is opened; firm includes 400 attorneys.
1991: The firm is renamed Akin, Gump, Hauer & Feld after Strauss becomes ambassador to the USSR.
1992: The firm becomes Akin, Gump, Strauss, Hauer & Feld after Strauss returns; Vernon Jordan is named chairman of President Clinton's transition team.
1993: The firm's New York City office is opened.
1994: An office is established in Moscow.
1996: An office is opened in Philadelphia.
1997: Offices in London and Los Angeles are opened.
1999: The firm acquires two intellectual property firms: Pravel Hewitt in Houston and Panitch Schwarze Jacobs & Nadel in Philadelphia; it also begins an affiliated practice in Saudi Arabia.

In 1992 Strauss rejoined the law firm, which again changed its name. At about the same time, several other attorneys joined or rejoined the firm after serving in government positions, including L. Kirk O'Donnell, general counsel to speaker of the House of Representatives from 1978 to 1986, and Stephen A. Wakefield, the Energy Department's general counsel from 1989 to 1991. Some have criticized this "revolving door" that enabled individuals to take advantage of their government service by returning to work in the private sector. When Vernon Jordan became the chairman of newly elected President Bill Clinton's transition team in 1992, he gained even more prominence as a key member of the new Democratic administration. Jordan was also a member of the board of directors of several corporations, including RJR/Nabisco.

In 1992 Akin Gump's clients included the People's Republic of China, the Korean Foreign Trade Association, the Chilean Exporter's Association, three Japanese companies, and the government of Colombia. The following year the firm opened a branch office in New York City with five attorneys. By the end of the decade more than 100 lawyers worked there, with many focusing on issues of international finance in cooperation with the firm's overseas branches. Akin Gump founded an office in Philadelphia in 1996 and offices in Los Angeles and London the following year.

In 1998 the U.S. military blew up the Al Shifa plant in Khartoum, Sudan, an action that was justified by the claim that the plant made chemical weapons for terrorist Osama bin Laden. However, the plant's owner maintained that the plant manufactured only pharmaceuticals, so it hired Akin Gump to sue the United States for $20 million to rebuild the plant. In June 1999 Akin Gump formed an affiliated practice with Abdulaziz Fahad of Saudi Arabia to better serve Akin Gump clients in the Middle East, including Salah Idris, the owner of the Sudan plant.

Akin Gump ranked number four among law firms serving as lobbyists, brining in $6.7 million and $9.7 million in lobbying fees in 1996 and 1997 from such clients as Mobil, Citizens Educational Foundation Inc., and Pacific Gas and Electric Company. Law firms donated to political parties to increase their influence in Washington and state capitals, and in 1998 the Center for Responsive Politics reported that Akin Gump had donated $674,000 by October 1st, with 53 percent of that amount to the Democratic Party and 47 percent to the Republican Party.

In the late 1990s Akin Gump served numerous companies and institutions, including the University of Texas, Samsung, 3M, American Physicians Service Group Inc., AT&T, Tivoli, Prime Medical Services Inc., Natural Gas Clearinghouse, and DeepTech International Inc. Akin Gump also represented Lukoil, Russia's largest oil company, when it signed an agreement to work with Houston-based Conoco to jointly develop oil fields in a 1.2 million acre area known as Russia's Northern Territories.

Some Akin Gump lawyers served as corporate directors, a practice that has raised questions about possible conflicts of interest. Vernon Jordan in the 1990s was a director of Ryder System, Union Carbide, Xerox, Sara Lee Corporation, J.C. Penney, and RJR/Nabisco, while Robert Strauss was a director of Archer-Daniels-Midland Company.

In 1999 Akin Gump merged with two smaller law firms, Pravel Hewitt of Houston and Panitch Schwarze Jacobs &

Nadel of Philadelphia. The latter arrangement gave the combined organization a total of more than 80 intellectual property lawyers, which was a large concentration for a general law firm. According to the magazine *IP Today,* Akin Gump and the Panitch law firm were two of the nation's largest filers of U.S. trademarks.

In July 1999 *The American Lawyer* ranked Akin Gump as number 20 in its annual listing of the nation's largest law firms based on annual revenue. Akin Gump reported $301 million in 1998 annual revenue, and was also listed as number 73 for revenue per lawyer ($405,000), number 56 for average compensation for all partners ($470,000), and number 63 for its pro bono work.

The International Financial Law Review in 1999 listed Akin Gump as the nineteenth-largest international law firm. However, it faced plenty of competition as many law firms expanded overseas. Consolidation and mergers were producing larger and larger law firms, while international accounting firms employed thousands of lawyers, posing another significant source of competition for the big law firms as they entered the new century.

Principal Competitors

Arnold & Porter; Covington & Burling; Hogan & Hartson.

Further Reading

"Akin Gump Becomes Number One in Trade Markets," *Managing Intellectual Property,* July/August 1999, p. 10.

Borrus, Amy, and Owen Ullmann, "Mugging on K Street: The GOP Assault on Business Lobbyists," *Business Week,* November 9, 1998, p. 59.

Brenner, Marie, "Mr. Ambassador! Bob Strauss Comes Home," *New Yorker,* December 28, 1992–January 4, 1993, pp. 146–156.

"Hired Guns Are Going Full Blast," *Legal Times,* May 25, 1998, pp. S30–S33.

Ivanovich, David, "Conoco, Russia's Lukoil Teaming Up," *Houston Chronicle,* March 12, 1998, pp. 1C, 3C.

Murray, Alan, "Private to Public: Robert Strauss Has Seen It All," *Wall Street Journal,* October 2, 1998, pp. A1, A6.

Piatt, Pearl J., "Akin Gump Taps Dealmakers to Lead L.A. Office," *Los Angeles Daily Journal,* August 1, 1997.

Rust, Michael and David Wagner, "Mount Vernon," *Insight on the News,* February 16, 1998, p. 40.

Standeford, Dugie, "The 3rd Wave: Case Management on the Computer," *Washington Lawyer,* January/February 1998, pp. 40–43.

Stone, Peter H., "Banking on Paxon's GOP Credentials," *National Journal,* October 2, 1999, pp. 2820–2821.

——, "The Firm," *National Journal,* November 27, 1993, pp. 2820–2826.

Taylor, Steven T., "Paralegal Hiring up to Satisfy Clients' Cost-Cutting Demands," *Of Counsel,* August 16, 1999, pp. 1, 6–9.

—David M. Walden

Allen Organ Company

150 Locust Street
Macungie, Pennsylvania 18062-0036
U.S.A.
Telephone: (610) 966-2200
Fax: (610) 965-3098
Web site: http://www.allenorgan.com

Public Company
Incorporated: 1961
Employees: 567
Sales: $58 million (1999)
Stock Exchanges: NASDAQ
Ticker Symbol: AORGB
NAIC: 339992 Musical Instrument Manufacturing

Allan Organ Company is the largest builder of church organs in the world. In addition to its popular organs, most notably the digital electronic church organ, the company operates subsidiaries involved in data communications, electronic assemblies, and audio equipment, all offshoots of technology used in the manufacture of the Allen Organ. The company was founded by the late Jerome Markowitz, who built his first experimental organ in 1936. The founder's son, Steven Markowitz, serves as CEO and president of the Allen Organ, and the Markowitz family owns 97 percent of the company's voting stock.

An Early Start

Jerome Markowitz, the founder of Allen Organ Company, became interested in technology at a very young age. By the time he was 13, Markowitz had built a battery-driven electric go-kart, and shortly thereafter, he became fascinated with radio, constructing his own ham radio station using a hand-made receiver and transmitter. Markowitz even built his own television set in his youth, on which he eventually managed to get a picture. News of Markowitz's technical abilities spread throughout his Jamaica, Long Island, neighborhood, and he became known as a technical whiz kid.

Markowitz's father owned a textile factory in Allentown, Pennsylvania, and Markowitz had originally planned to follow in his father's footsteps and join the family business after graduating from college. His parents sent him to Allentown Prep School and later to Muhlenberg College. However, Markowitz soon found that school took time away from his radio projects, and he pursued his education half-heartedly. In 1937, he suffered from an attack of appendix-related peritonitis, missed a month of college, and then left school all together.

The First Allen Organ in 1936

Also during his youth, Markowitz developed a passion for organ music; he had listened attentively to pipe organs in movie theaters and on the radio, and while in college had enjoyed listening to the chairman of the music department play the organ at mass. Markowitz decided his next project would be to build an organ. Markowitz's radio projects had taught him the fundamentals of electronics that he needed to build his organ. He built an oscillator—a frequency generator—similar to those he had built for his radio equipment and discovered he could connect oscillators to the keys of an organ keyboard. By doing this, he could build an organ without pipes, and he patented the technology that could create sound waves via an oscillator.

After researching other pipeless organs and organ-like instruments, he built his first experimental organ in 1936. Local organists encouraged him, noting that his organ produced a sound not unlike that of a pipe organ. However, Markowitz knew his organ needed more work. After his parents moved to Allentown in 1937, he set up a workshop in their basement. There he frequently visited the Masonic Temple, renting time on its pipe organ so he could master its sound.

Word of Markowitz's work in building a pipeless organ spread throughout town. In 1939, the *Allentown Evening Chronicle* referred to him as a "22-year-old Alexander Graham Bell." During this time, Markowitz moved his basement workshop to an empty section of his father's textile factory. There he met factory-maintenance man Norman Koons, who was an expert at mechanics and agreed to help Markowitz build a better pipeless organ. Together the men designed the organ on paper,

Company Perspective:

When a congregation expresses its faith through music, there is only one instrument equal to producing a sound as elemental, eternal, and exuberant as its celebration—the organ. The majestic sound of organ music will always be the sound of devotion. Sound that sweeps through the congregation in a wave of symphonic power. Sound you feel—in the soles of your feet and the depths of your heart. Sound that equals the spirit of your worship. The sound of an Allen. Quality, craftsmanship, technological superiority. . . . These are Allen hallmarks. With more than 20 diverse models to choose from and over 75,000 installations worldwide, Allen carries the banner of innovation into the 21st century. Our dedication to producing exceptional instruments is matched only by our commitment to providing unsurpassed customer service for the long term.

and Koons built the instrument. Markowitz and Koons named the organ after the city of Allentown, calling it the Allen Organ No. 1. Markowitz sold the Allen Organ No. 1 to the St. Catharine of Siena Roman Catholic Church in Allentown. His first sale marked the beginning of the Allen Organ Company. St. Catharine's used the organ until 1953, when they moved to a new cathedral.

By 1941, Markowitz had sold three more organs. He knew that his primary market would be the church, and this formed a commitment to building organs that would endure the tests of time. He later recalled in *Triumphs & Trials of an Organ Builder* that "Outside, the world appeared to be rather unpredictable with its many issues, events, and interests that emerged daily but quickly receded from relevance. But inside these churches there was a distinct ambiance of predictability, stability, and lasting values. I wanted Allen organs to fit comfortably into this ambiance of permanence. Therefore, I wanted Allen organs to be built to last."

Wartime Diversions and Postwar Struggles

Markowitz's business was put on hold after the Japanese bombed Pearl Harbor in 1941. The following year he enlisted and was employed by the military as a civilian electronics engineer. His military service would keep him away from organ-building until 1945, when he returned home. At that time, he decided to incorporate his business, a move that would allow him to solicit investment money through a sale of stock. In doing so, Markowitz raised enough capital, largely from family and friends, to lease factory space, buy equipment, and hire 15 employees. By 1946, he had sold ten organs locally, as the Allen organ proved less cumbersome and more affordable than traditional pipe organs.

Allen Organ soon needed more space. Markowitz leased 14,000 square feet of factory space at Eighth and Pittston Streets in Allentown and hired college chum Michale J. Mylymuk as shop manager. Getting Allen Organ off the ground was not an easy task, however, and the company struggled from 1946 to the early 1950s. During this time, Markowitz's cash flow was often not enough to cover his expenses. He was forced to lay off workers, a task that nagged at his conscience.

Despite these difficulties, Markowitz refused to compromise the design of his product. In 1949, his company developed and patented a Gyrophonic Projector. The "Gyro" was a rotating speaker system designed to add liveliness to the sound generated by the Allen organ. Organists could toggle the Gyro off an on as they played. Seeking to bolster sales, Markowitz decided to pursue customers outside of Allentown, and he quickly found them. By 1953, the company was back on track and earning a profit. The following year, Markowitz obtained more space and hired additional employees.

The 1960s: A Time of Growth

While the Allen Organ Company grew quickly over the next few years, the company was still a minor contender in the organ industry when compared to such giants as Hammond, Conn, Baldwin, and Wurlitzer. Amid such stiff competition, Markowitz strove to find a niche for his company. He set Allen Organ apart from competitors by tailoring his organ designs to meet the specific needs of each customer. Few competitors offered such a service, opting instead to produce a line of organs that they sold "off-the-shelf." Allen Organ also built a line of inexpensive organs for churches with limited funds.

In the 1960s, the company's products gained national attention, as customers and investors began to recognize the name of Allen Organ. In 1961, Lawrence Welk ordered an Allen electronic harpsichord to use on his popular television show. Also that year, the company made a public offering, attracting an additional 500 investors. At this time, the company had a workforce of over 600.

In 1966, Allen Organ established a subsidiary operation, Rocky Mount Instruments (RMI), in Rocky Mount, North Carolina. RMI produced portable keyboards, portable amplifiers, and other novelty instruments. Through RMI, the company established relationships with popular musicians of the time; the rock group the Doors used an RMI Rock-si-chord in their hit song "Hello, I Love You." Other musicians and bands such as Hank Williams, Jr., Deep Purple, the Association, Frank Zappa, and the Beach Boys used the Rock-si-chords' successor, the RMI Electra Piano and Harpsichord, in their music.

By 1970, Allen Organ had sold more than 30,000 organs, and their products were available on six continents. Moreover, the company distinguished itself by building the largest electronic organ in the world for the Tenth Presbyterian Church in Philadelphia. Virgil Fox, one of the world's top organists, played recitals on an Allen Organ.

The Advent of the Digital Organ: The 1970s

In 1969 Ralph Deutsch of North American Rockwell Corporation (later Rockwell International) in California, contacted Markowitz about entering into a partnership to develop the world's first digital organ. Rockwell had developed a new circuit technology called Metal-Oxide Semiconductor/Large-Scale Integrated, or MOS/LSI, for the aeronautics industry and felt that this technology could have many applications in more

Key Dates:

1936: Jerome Markowitz builds his first experimental pipeless organ.
1939: The Allen Organ No.1 is completed.
1945: Allen Organ Company is incorporated.
1949: The company introduces the Gyrophonic Projector.
1961: Allen Organ goes public.
1966: Rocky Mount Instruments is acquired.
1969: Markowitz signs a deal with North American Rockwell to produce the world's first digital organ.
1971: Markowitz approves the prototype of the digital organ and unveils the first Allen Computer Organ.
1990: Founder's son Steven Markowitz inherits leadership of the company.

commercial arenas. Under the proposed contract, Rockwell would adapt the digital technology, manufacture the circuitry, and provide technical support, while Allen Organ, which would gain exclusive rights to the new digital organ technology, would fund the project and provide Rockwell with their technical expertise in the fields of music and musical instruments. The partnership involved considerable financial risk to Allen Organ, requiring capital outlay of over $1.5 million, but the potential gains to be realized by the digital innovation were exciting for Markowitz and his team. The deal was signed in 1969, and the partnership was rocky from the start.

When Rockwell provided a working model of the first digital organ, Markowitz soon found that the musical integrity of the organ itself would be compromised to accommodate the circuitry. Deutsch and Markowitz would lock horns several times over the various issues, and Allen Organ's financial commitment to the project deepened. In 1970, right before the completion of an acceptable the prototype, Deutsch approached Markowitz about expanding the partnership to include the development of a smaller organ. Not wanting to commit further funds to the project, Markowitz refused, and the relationship between Rockwell and Allen Organ was further strained.

Nevertheless, Allen Organ approved the prototype of the world's first digital organ in 1971, and that year Allen Organ began marketing its Allen Computer Organ. Markowitz decided to call the instrument a computer organ rather than a digital organ because he thought the name would have more appeal to the public. The press hailed the Allen Computer Organ as "a major industry breakthrough." St. Mark's Evangelical Lutheran Church in Easton, Pennsylvania, became the first customer to purchase an Allen Computer Organ. In September 1972, the Allen Computer Organ was named by *Industrial Research* as one of the best 100 new products of the year, marking the first time a musical instrument had ever received such an award.

The strained relationship between Allen Organ and Rockwell would continue over the years, resulting in litigation, cases that were eventually settled out of court. Moreover, as Markowitz strove to defend his patent rights to the digital organ technology, a series of lawsuit with competitors ensued, including Yamaha, Klann Organ Company, and others.

Diversification in the 1980s and Beyond

While Jerome Markowitz moved gradually toward retirement, purchasing a farm and leaving day-to-day operations to an executive staff that included his son Steven Markowitz. During this time, the computerized organ, which mimicked the sound of traditional pipe organs better than the founder's analog organ had, became increasingly popular, and Allen Organ began a program of vertical integration, making its own circuit boards. The company also strove in the 1980s to automate its facilities, keeping up with new technologies that allowed for quicker production.

The production of circuit boards took on a life of its own, and in 1989, Allen Organ formed a subsidiary, Allen Integrated Assemblies(AIA), to oversee the sideline. By the mid-1990s, AIA was producing about 150,000 circuit boards annually, slightly less than half of which were sold to outside companies. The majority, however, were used in Allen organs and other musical instruments.

After Jerome Markowitz's death in 1990, his son took over the reins as CEO. Steven Markowitz had joined Allen Organ in 1975, after graduating from Penn State University, and had assumed the company's presidency in the 1980s. Under the younger Markowitz, Allen Organ continued to expand its size and scope. Several acquisitions were made and subsidiaries organized, as the company focused on keeping product costs low by manufacturing parts in-house. Among the new subsidiaries were Eastern Research, Inc., a manufacturer of digital components established in 1992, and Linear Switch Corporation, a manufacturer of matrix switches formed in 1993. Moreover, the company became involved in the manufacture of audio speaker cabinets for home theater systems through subsidiary Legacy Audio Inc. Nevertheless, the company continued to generate most of its sales from its digital organs, which had gained worldwide recognition.

By the late 1990s, Allen Organ was organized among four industry segments: musical instruments; electronic assemblies; data communications; and audio equipment. While sales continued to increase, profits were somewhat hampered by the costs incurred in investing in sales, marketing, and product development, particularly for the company's diversified subsidiaries. In February 2000, the company's stock soared to $82 per share, up 26 percent, on rumors that Allen Organ intended to jettison its Eastern Research data communications subsidiary.

In January 1999, several Allen Organs were used for major events associated with Pope John Paul II's visit to St. Louis, Missouri. An Allen Organ was installed in the Trans World Dome for the principal mass. A second Allen Organ was installed at the Kiel Center for the Youth Prayer Service. As it prepared to enter a new century, the Allen Organ Company maintained a dominant worldwide position as a manufacturer of church organs.

Principal Subsidiaries

Allen Audio, Inc.; Legacy Audio, Inc.; Linear Switch Corp.; Eastern Research Inc.

Principal Divisions

Allen Integrated Assemblies; VIR Linear Switches.

Principal Operating Units

Musical Instruments; Data Communications; Electronic Assemblies; Audio Equipment.

Principal Competitors

Casio Computer, Ltd.; Cisco Systems, Inc.; Yamaha Corporation.

Further Reading

Markowitz, Jerome, *Triumphs & Trials of an Organ Builder,* Macungie, Penn.: Allen Organ Co., 1989.

Orenstein, Beth W., ''Allen Organ Strikes Note of Success with Electronics,'' *Eastern Pennsylvania Business Journal,* June 5, 1995, p. 2.

Shope, Dan, ''Allen Organ May Sell Division,'' *Allentown (Penn.) Morning Call,* March 8, 2000, Bus. Sec.

—Tracey Vasil Biscontini

American Rice, Inc.

411 North Sam Houston Parkway East
Suite 600
Houston, Texas 77060
U.S.A.
Telephone: (281) 272-8800
Fax: (281) 272-9707
Web site: http://www.amrice.com

Private Company
Incorporated: 1987
Employees: 350
Sales: $515 million (1997)
NAIC: 311212 Rice Milling

One of the largest rice millers in the United States, American Rice, Inc. (ARI) produces, distributes, and markets worldwide white, brown, parboiled, and instant rice under a variety of brand names. The company's U.S. brands include Blue Ribbon, Adolphus, Comet, AA, and Wonder. ARI also operates in a number of international markets under its Abu Bint, Cinta Azul, 4-Star, and Blue Ribbon brands. Although Saudi Arabia is ARI's single largest export market, the company operates in other middle eastern countries, as well as in Africa, Asia, Europe, Latin America, the Caribbean, and Canada. Erly Industries Inc. had owned an 80 percent stake in the company since 1993, but after filing for bankruptcy protection in 1998, ARI emerged in 1999, controlled by its creditors.

Birth and Growth as Agricultural Cooperative

Rice is classified in three major categories—long, medium, and short grains. The shorter the grain, the stickier the rice will be when it is cooked. Until rice is milled it is inedible because it is encased in a hard shell called the "hull." Rice mills remove the hull and perform a variety of processes to produce the different varieties of rice found on supermarket shelves. If the rice is steamed within its hull before the hull is removed, the end result is termed "parboiled," which when cooked is firm and fluffy with grains that remain separate. Once the hull is removed, the rice kernel is brown. Although brown rice is high in vitamins, minerals, and fiber, many consumers prefer white rice, which is produced when mills polish the brown fiber layers off the rice kernel. Mills also are responsible for enriching white rice to restore its nutritional value.

American Rice, Inc. was founded as an agricultural cooperative by a group of Gulf Coast rice farmers in 1969. Initially, American Rice only graded rice and provided market information services for its rice growers, who were based in Texas, Louisiana, and Mississippi. In an effort to protect the interests of its members, however, the cooperative began selling unmilled rice to mills on behalf of its farmers in 1971. Although this diversification enabled ARI to negotiate better contracts from mills, the cooperative's farmers were, in large part, still at the mercy of the vicissitudes of the cyclical rice-growing market. But if the growers collaborated in the processing, packing, distribution, and sale of their rice, they would be in a more protected position. To this end, ARI bought what was then the Blue Ribbon rice mill, located in Houston, Texas, and began milling its farmers' rice in 1975.

ARI grew rapidly in its early years, increasing the number of farmers in the cooperative. With more than 1,500 rice growers included in its ranks by 1980, the cooperative was a formidable operation. As it grew, the company also launched or acquired a bevy of different brands, under which it sold different types of rice to distinct markets. For instance, when ARI purchased the Blue Ribbon operation, it gained the rights to the venerable Blue Ribbon brand, a long grain rice that dominated the market in the southeastern United States. Adolphus brand was particularly strong in the Houston area, where it had been sold since 1938, while Wonder rice had been popular in the southwestern United States since its inception in the 1940s. ARI also had a separate roster of international brands. Foremost among these was Abu Bint, a parboiled long grain rice that conformed to the tastes of Middle Eastern consumers. By 1986, ARI was one of the largest rice millers in the United States.

New Competitors in the 1980s

Despite its strength in the United States, ARI faced fierce competition from international rivals. In the early 1980s, new varieties of flood- and drought-resistant rice made it possible for countries that had once struggled to produce any rice at all to become self-sufficient. For example, South Korea had been one of the world's largest rice importers during the 1970s, but had freed itself from dependence on other countries by the mid-1980s. Moreover, U.S. rice growers had steadily lost share in global markets to Thailand. Due to less expensive production costs, Thai producers could sell rice for about $100 per ton less than their U.S. counterparts. As a result of these factors, U.S. growers were "taking a beating on world markets," according to the April 20, 1986 edition of the *Houston Chronicle*.

ARI addressed its shrinking global presence by banding together with other major rice producers and lobbying Congress for annual subsidies that would allow them to sell rice on world markets at deeply discounted prices. This strategy proved successful. The 1986 Farm Bill, for example, enabled U.S. rice growers to sell to international consumers for about $250 per ton, even though production costs actually ran between $400 and $500 per ton. Subsidies made up the difference.

In addition to meeting more vigorous competition abroad, ARI also had to ward off new domestic rivals. Since 1980, three large conglomerates—The Quaker Oats Company, Unilever, and Archer Daniels Midland Company—had begun marketing rice. Companies such as these had massive budgets for products development and promotion, as well as smooth distribution channels, and presented a formidable threat.

Alliance with Erly Industries: 1988–90

ARI recognized that to best these domestic competitors, it would have to bolster its own marketing and distribution presence. Lacking the resources to expand rapidly on its own, ARI joined forces with Comet Rice, Inc. in June 1986. This alliance was dubbed Comet American Marketing (CAM), a joint venture that sought to sell and market Comet and American brands more effectively in the United States, Canada, and the Caribbean. CAM's initial goal was a lofty one—to become the third largest supplier of dried rice to U.S. grocery stores by 1989.

Founded in 1903, Comet had existed since 1970 as a wholly owned subsidiary of Early California Industries. (Early was a diversified food products company that had been created through the merger of three California olive producers in 1964. After selecting Gerald Murphy to lead the venture, Early quickly branched into new sectors, acquiring Arizona Agrochemical—a forest fire retardant and agricultural consulting business—in 1968.) Upon adding Comet to its corporate fold,

Early made a spate of rice-related acquisitions, purchasing United Rice Growers and Millers of California as well as a major mill in Greenville, Mississippi. Early eventually folded all of its rice operations into the Comet subsidiary. Recognizing that its future lay in rice rather than olives, Early sold off its olive business in 1985, along with the Early name, to Specialty Brands, Inc., for $86 million. The erstwhile Early took a new name, Erly Industries, and continued to operate Comet. Soon after CAM was formed, Murphy's son, Douglas, was selected as CAM's president, and Gerald served as president and chief executive officer of Comet.

The year 1986 brought additional changes to ARI. After launching CAM, ARI opened a new milling and storage plant to facilitate international shipping. Operating out of its original Houston mill, ARI had needed to truck in its growers' rice from Louisiana, Mississippi, and elsewhere in Texas. After processing the rice, ARI again had to move it overland to a port, from which the milled rice could be shipped to international markets. The added costs were significant. Upon opening its new $30 million facility in Freeport, Texas, ARI moved its entire milling operation there. Unlike the Houston mill, Freeport was located on a deep water port, which made transporting raw and milled rice much more efficient.

But ARI was not finished revamping the way it did business. After incorporating itself in 1987, the cooperative opted to become a public company in 1988. At the same time, ARI solidified its relationship with Erly. In April 1988, Erly and ARI announced that Erly would acquired 48 percent of ARI. The $40 million deal consisted of two transactions. Erly purchased 3.9 million shares (about 24 percent) of ARI, while the Comet Rice unit acquired an additional 3.9 million shares of ARI. In return, Comet relinquished its 50 percent interest in CAM. With this exchange, ARI had access to the resources it needed to grow further.

Erly benefited from the 1988 transaction as well, by obtaining access to ARI's impressive distribution network. By 1987, ARI represented 2,300 farmers and realized sales of $194 million (up from $169 million in 1996). More important, ARI was a key player in global markets, particularly in Saudi Arabia (the largest market in the world for parboiled rice). ARI dominated the Saudi rice market, sending one-third of all of its rice to the Middle East kingdom. ARI's Abu Bint controlled about 70 percent of the Saudi rice market and was one of the most recognized brands in that country.

Merger and Expansion in 1990–97

Soon after ARI went public, the two companies announced plans for ARI and Comet to merge. As John Howland, ARI's president and chief executive officer, explained to the *Wall Street Journal* on March 19, 1990, a merger would enable both Comet and American Rice to "achieve operating efficiencies not otherwise available to each company individually." The proposed merger again involved two steps. First, Erly's Comet Rice subsidiary would give its 48 percent interest in ARI back to Erly. (Comet would receive cash from Erly in exchange, which would allow Comet to pay down its debt.) Second, ARI would acquire Comet from Erly for 17.2 million shares of ARI stock. The end result was that Erly controlled more than 75

Key Dates:

1964: Early California Industries is founded (later renamed Erly Industries).
1969: American Rice agricultural cooperative marketing association is founded.
1970: Erly acquires Comet Rice, Inc.
1975: American Rice purchases Blue Ribbon rice mill in Houston and begins milling its own rice.
1986: Comet Rice and American Rice form Comet American Marketing, a joint venture.
1987: American Rice is incorporated.
1988: American Rice becomes a public company.
1989: Erly combines Comet Rice with American Rice, giving Erly a majority ownership of American Rice.
1993: American Rice and Comet merge; Erly acquires 80 percent stake in American Rice.
1994: American Rice forms Vinafood, a joint venture with a Vietnamese state-owned rice processor.
1998: American Rice and Erly file for bankruptcy.
1999: American Rice emerges from bankruptcy proceedings.

percent of ARI. The transaction was delayed for two years while ARI struggled to secure adequate financing, but the merger was eventually concluded in June 1993. Douglas Murphy was installed as ARI's new president and CEO, and his father served as chairman. The resulting company was one of the United States' three largest millers and marketers of rice, with combined annual sales of more than $450 million.

After the merger was complete, ARI's sales soared as a result of favorable economic conditions. Japan's 1993 rice crop was severely damaged by weather. As a result, in 1994 the country had to import rice for the first time in more than 25 years. The boost in sales this gave ARI was only a prelude to 1995, when the terms of the General Agreement on Tariffs and Trade (GATT) were implemented. Because GATT required countries to import a small percentage of all products consumed annually, the treaty officially ended U.S. rice growers' long stalemate with Japan. (U.S. rice growers had been demanding since 1986 that the United States issue trade sanctions against Japan for its refusal to import U.S. rice). By the end of 1995, ARI accounted for more than 40 percent of total U.S. rice exports to Japan. ARI gained an additional platform to Asian markets in 1994, when the company formed a joint venture with Vietnam to produce rice and related products in Vietnam's Can Tho province.

In addition to attempting to grow by gaining access to broader geographical markets, ARI also strove to expand by entering new business sectors. In 1994 the company had founded Comet Ventures Inc., which specialized in rice by-product technology. In 1996 ARI reunited Erly with the olive business it had shed in 1985, when ARI acquired the Campbell Co.'s olive business for $38 million. (In 1987 Campbell had purchased Erly California Industries from Specialty Brands. In the intervening years, Campbell had built up other olive brands as well, all of which were included in the ARI purchase.) ARI

christened the new division Early California Foods and anticipated that its new unit would prove a boon in two ways: by diversifying ARI's revenue base, and by improving its marketing and distribution capabilities (because of the fact that many of ARI's rice markets were in olive-consuming countries, and others were in olive-producing ones). "[N]ot only do olives fit ARI," Douglas Murphy told the *Houston Chronicle* on June 14, 1986, "olives are something we understand and returning to the olive industry is like going home."

Troubled Times in the Late 1990s

ARI's good fortunes waned at the close of the 20th century, however, as the company was buffeted by legal troubles. In 1995 Kingwood Lakes South L.P. and the Tenzer Co. sued ARI, Erly, and Gerald and Douglas Murphy, alleging breach of contract and civil fraud and conspiracy claims stemming from a failed real estate venture. ARI lost the suit and was ordered to pay $7 million. In 1997 the Powell Group, which owned 14.9 percent of ARI's stock, sued the Murphys for breach of fiduciary duty, waste of corporate assets, and illegal corporate loans. Led by Nanette Kelley, the Powell Group claimed that the Murphys had squandered ARI's revenues by using corporate funds to pay for their personal legal problems (including the Lakes South/Tenzer suit).

In December 1997, ARI reported a third quarter loss of more than $5.2 million and a total loss of $10.9 for the first nine months of the fiscal year. ARI's problems stemmed in part from a packaging company in Saudi Arabia (Rice Milling and Trading Investments) that had breached its contract with ARI to distribute Abu Bint rice. Although ARI built an alternate distribution system as quickly as it could, Abu Bint shipments did not reach Saudi grocery stores for six weeks, costing ARI more than $15 million. At the same time, ARI's Early California olive business began losing about $1 million per month in 1997 and 1998 because of a global slump. In February 1998, ARI defaulted on loans worth more than $100 million, and Gerald and Douglas Murphy began to sell what would come to more than 700,000 shares of ARI stock in a six-month period.

ARI announced a massive restructuring plan in June 1998. In addition to reducing its global work force by one-third, the company pledged to refocus on its core rice milling operations. That summer, ARI sold Early California Foods to Musco Olive Products for $39 million and spun off Comet Ventures Inc. as well. Moreover, the Vietnamese government rescinded ARI's Vinafood license after four years of near-constant losses. Not surprisingly, Gerald Murphy abdicated his position as ARI's chairman (although his son remained as president and CEO).

In August 1998, American Rice filed for Chapter 11 bankruptcy protection. The following month, Erly did as well. In January 1999, ARI's creditors—which included the Internal Revenue Service and the Securities and Exchange Commission—filed a chapter 7 petition against the elder Murphy, which forced him into personal bankruptcy. During its restructuring in bankruptcy proceedings, ARI was separated from Erly, and Douglas Murphy resigned. Nanette Kelley was elected ARI's new president and CEO and Joseph Radecki the chairman. ARI emerged in October 1999 as a private company, closely held by its creditors. Its future remained uncertain, although Kelley and other ARI bondholders remained optimistic. "It's a very good business, a wonderful company," Radecki told the *Houston Business Journal.* Early in 2000, Steven Weinred was appointed ARI's interim CEO and president.

Principal Divisions

Comet American Marketing; International Marketing.

Principal Competitors

AWB Limited; Cargill, Inc.; Goya Foods, Inc.; Mars, Inc.; Riceland Foods, Inc.; Riviana Foods Inc.

Further Reading

"American Rice Abandons Plant Project Amid Row," *South China Morning Post,* December 20, 1999.

Antosh, Nelson, "ARI Plans Stock Sale to Erly," *Houston Chronicle,* April 7, 1988.

——, "Campbell Soup Sells Olive Brands to ARI," *Houston Chronicle,* June 14, 1986.

Antosh, Nelson, "Rice Farmers' Sales Up, But Future Still Unsure," *Houston Chronicle,* September 16, 1987.

Coclanis, Peter, "The Poetics of American Agriculture: The U.S. Rice Industry in International Perspective," *Agricultural History,* March 22, 1995.

Crowell, Todd, "New Rice Subsidy May Exceed All Other Crops," *Houston Chronicle,* April 20, 1986.

"Erly Agrees To Merge With American Rice," *Wall Street Journal,* March 19, 1990.

Moreno, Jenalia, "American Rice Seeks Chapter 11 Shield," *Houston Chronicle,* August 13, 1998.

Perin, Monica, "American Rice Cooking Again with Fresh Game Plan," *Houston Business Journal,* November 1, 1999.

Walsh, Jennifer, "Houston-Based American Rice Set for Bank Reorganization," *Houston Chronicle,* July 8, 1999.

—Rebecca Stanfel

American Tower Corporation

116 Huntington Avenue
Boston, Massachusetts 02116
U.S.A.
Telephone: (617) 375-7500
Toll Free: (877) 282-7483
Fax: (617) 375-7575
Web site: http://www.americantower.com

Public Company
Incorporated: 1995 as American Tower Systems
    Corporation
Employees: 975
Sales: $258 million (1999)
Stock Exchanges: New York
Ticker Symbol: AMT
NAIC: 513322 Cellular and Other Wireless
    Telecommunications

Boston, Massachusetts–based American Tower Corporation (ATC) is the leading independent owner, operator, and developer of broadcast and wireless communications sites in North America. The company operates a national network of over 10,000 sites in the United States and Mexico, including about 300 broadcast tower sites. ATC's primary business is the leasing of antennae sites. The company operates in three business segments: the TRM segment offers leasing and subleasing of antennae sites on multi-tenant towers for radio and television broadcasting and a wide range of wireless communication industries—such as cellular phone systems (computer-controlled systems that connect to a network of radiotelephones), personal communications services (PCS), and various mobile radio systems; the Services segment contributes network development, including network design, site acquisition and construction, zoning and other regulatory approvals, tower construction and antennae installation; the VVDI (video, voice, data, and Internet) segment provides transmission services in the New York City to Washington, D.C., corridor and in Texas. ATC Teleports, Inc.—an American Tower wholly owned subsidiary—is a leading provider of domestic and international satellite services. A teleport is the technical link for all video, voice, and data transmission to and from ground-based, terrestrial sources and satellites. ATC Teleports has Technical Operations Centers located in New York City, Dallas, and Alexandria, Virginia. The holding company's diversified base of customers includes most of the major wireless service providers—for example, AirTouch, Alltel, AT&T, AT&T Wireless, Bell Atlantic Mobile, Nextel, Omnipoint, PageNet, Sprint PCS, Teligent, WinStar—and a majority of radio and television broadcasters, such as ABC, CBS, Chancellor Media, Clear Channel, CNN, Fox, and NBC. ATC's net revenue rose from $17.5 million in fiscal 1997 to $200 million for the 12 months ending September 30, 1999.

1920–94: Genesis of Wireless Communications

The need for safety was the major catalyst for the growth of the wireless communications industry, according to AT&T's "Brief History of Wireless." In the 1920s, police departments in Michigan, New Jersey, and Connecticut wanted to equip their patrol cars with the radiotelephone technology that had improved the safety of oceangoing vessels. However, radiotelephone communication equipment that was easily housed on large ships was too large and unwieldy for installation in cars. Furthermore, bumpy streets, tall buildings, and uneven landscapes prevented successful transmission of radiotelephone signals on land. A major breakthrough occurred in 1935 when Edwin Howard Armstrong invented frequency modulation (FM) to improve radio broadcasting. This technology reduced the bulk of radio equipment and improved the quality of transmission.

During World War II the U.S. military used FM for efficient two-way mobile radio communications on the battlefield, and such companies as Motorola, AT&T, and General Electric began to focus on refining mobile and portable communications for commercial use. For example, Motorola's FM Handie-Talkie and Walkie-Talkie, products developed during the war years, carried over into peacetime use. By 1946 AT&T Bell Laboratories had created the Improved Mobile Telephone Service (IMTS), the first mobile telephone radio system to connect with the public telephone network.

Company Perspectives:

American Tower is a leading independent owner, operator and developer of broadcast and wireless communications sites in North America and Mexico. Headquartered in Boston, American Tower operates regional hub offices in Boston, Atlanta, Chicago, Houston, San Francisco and Mexico City. Our fully integrated areas of business—including site development, construction, components, monitoring, site management, and site leasing combine to form an indispensable resource center that serves the infrastructure needs of the wireless industry—everything from the ground up. As the burgeoning demand for wireless services continues to skyrocket, American Tower is committed to providing the most advanced technology, human support, and turnkey site solutions to meet these growing needs.

Development of this sophisticated technology, tests for its commercial applications, formulation of Federal Communications Commission (FCC) regulations, introduction of new radio frequencies for "land mobile communications," and the breakup of AT&T—among other events—delayed the construction of a pilot wireless systems until 1983 when Illinois Bell/AT&T began to operate a pilot wireless system in Chicago, and American Radio Telephone Service Inc. introduced a pilot system to serve Baltimore, Maryland, and Washington, D.C. The U.S. commercial mobile telephony service developed from these pilots. On December 5, 1994 the FCC, in an attempt to help national development of evolving telecommunication, began to auction national licenses for narrowband PCS, a family of mobile or portable radio services that later evolved into voice paging and data services that could be integrated with a variety of competing networks.

1993–97: Creating Aerial Real Estate

Meanwhile, in 1993 Steven B. Dodge had founded Boston-based American Radio Systems Corporation (ARS). By 1995 ARS operated 19 FM and nine AM radio stations in markets extending from Buffalo, New York, to West Palm Beach, Florida. Revenue had increased 55 percent from 1994, and operating income had grown by twice its 1994 figures. In July 1995 Chairman Dodge and his partners formed American Tower Systems Corporation (ATS) to operate as an ARS subsidiary, thereby positioning the parent company to meet its needs for broadcast towers in order to benefit from the opportunities created by the predicted explosive growth in wireless communications. Envisioning nationwide operation, ATS soon began to expand by acquiring close to 100 tower sites and/or locations.

In February 1996, ATS purchased Skyline Communications and acquired eight towers, six of which were in West Virginia and two in northern Virginia. With the purchase of Skyline Antennae Management, ATS gained management of over 200 antennae sites, primarily in the northeast region of the United States. The following April, the company acquired BDS Communications, Inc. and BRIDAN Communications Corporation. BDS Communications owned three towers in Pennsylvania; BRIDAN Communications managed or had sublease agree-

ments on approximately 40 tower sites located throughout the mid-Atlantic region. ATS also acquired ownership and operation of a tower site in Needham, Massachusetts, and several tower sites in Hampton, Virginia, and North Stonington, Connecticut. By year-end 1996, ATS had established itself in the Northeast, mid-Atlantic, and Florida regions of the United States.

Compared to what would happen in the future, ATS's 1996 acquisition program was modest, consisting of companies owning an aggregate of 15 communications sites and managing approximately 250 sites for others. During that year, however, the company entered into several other agreements that were consummated in 1997. For example, in May 1997 the company acquired 21 tower sites and a tower-site-management business operating in Georgia, North Carolina, and South Carolina and bought three other tower sites in Massachusetts. Other acquisitions included a tower site in Washington, D.C., six tower sites in Pennsylvania, and rights to build five tower sites in Maryland. July acquisitions included crossing the country for the purchase of a California-based tower-site-management business and 56 antennae sites located from the Mexican border to north of Santa Barbara. Then ATS acquired six tower sites in Connecticut and Rhode Island and another nine sites in Massachusetts, Rhode Island, and Oklahoma.

During October 1997 ATS acquired Jamieson, Pennsylvania-based MicroNet, Inc., one of the leading providers of antennae sites in densely populated areas of the mid-Atlantic states. MicroNet also owned 20 towers in California and 35 in Texas. Additionally, ATS bought MicroNet's transport operations, which included a teleport connecting New York City to Philadelphia and Washington, D.C., and a Dallas-based teleport that connected all the major cities in Texas. ATS further strengthened its position in California with the October purchase of Diablo Communications, Inc. Over and above 110 sites already in service and many others in various stages of development, Diablo operated a site-management business in California. Thus, in a few years ATS defined a national base to conduct business in the evolving field of telecommunication technologies: at the end of fiscal 1997, the company operated more than 1,775 towers in 44 states and the District of Columbia.

1998: Establishing a National Footprint

During the last years of the 20th century, according to ATC's *1998 Annual Report*, the growing mobility of the U.S. population, increased awareness of the benefits of mobile communications, technological advances in communications equipment, decreasing costs of wireless services, favorable changes in telecommunications regulations, and demand for higher-quality voice and data transmission were spurring the growth of the wireless industry, ATS's special field of interest. Growing demand for higher-frequency technologies (such as PCS and mobile radio) required a denser network of towers. Furthermore, the television broadcasting industry was planning a transition from analog to digital technology. ATS not only continued strategic acquisitions of additional towers but also deployed new towers for wireless carriers, created tower capacity designed to accommodate digital antennae for television broadcasters, and developed "build-to-suit" projects. The company also wanted to buy select site-acquisition companies, businesses

Key Dates:

1935: Edwin H. Armstrong invents frequency modulation (FM) technology.

1946: AT&T creates the first mobile telephoneradio system to connect with the public telephone network.

1983: Pilot commercial mobile telephone system operates in Chicago and Baltimore.

1993: Stephen B. Dodge founds American Radio Systems Corporation (ARS).

1994: Federal Communications Commission auctions national licenses for mobile radio systems.

1995: Dodge and partners form American Tower Systems Corporation (ATS) as an ARS subsidiary.

1998: ARS merges with CBS Corporation; ATS emerges as an independent company traded on the New York Stock Exchange and changes name to American Tower Corporation (ATC).

1999: Television industry plans transition from analog to digital technology.

engaged in tower fabrication, and providers of video, voice, and data transmission services.

Some of the significant activities by which ATS undertook to implement these plans in 1998 began when the company merged with OPM-USA, Inc., one of the fastest growing tower-construction companies in the southwestern United States. To provide non-broadcast wireless communication services, OPM had constructed 54 towers along major highways and had plans for an additional 160 towers. Next, ATS merged with Atlanta-based Gearon Communications. This company owned about 40 tower sites and was engaged in site acquisition, development, construction, and facility management of wireless network communication facilities. Gearon's customers included many of the larger providers of cellular and PCS services. ATS also purchased sites in Tucson Mountain, Indio Hill, and Montara Park in Arizona and 14 towers in Kansas. During April, in a build-to-suit project for Sprint, ATS completed construction of 27 towers in the Houston area and won a contract from Sprint PCS for 20 build-to-suit communications towers in the Chattanooga area. From BellSouth's Personal Communications Services Division, ATS won another build-to-suit contract to develop 200 towers in North Carolina. In May ATS acquired Washington International Teleport (WIT) and implemented a maintenance plan to upgrade all the WIT towers as well as those of MicroNet and Southwest MicroNet.

On June 4, 1998, CBS Corporation bought American Radio Systems Corporation and spun off American Tower Systems, which changed its name to American Tower Corporation (ATC) and began to operate under the ticker AMT as an independent, publicly traded company on the New York Stock Exchange.

In October ATC acquired a total of 322 towers in four transactions and a contract to build 100 towers in Michigan for NPI Wireless, a PCS provider. During November ATC purchased 15 sites in Oregon and Washington and won a contract to build 17 new sites for Central Wireless Partners. Then, in December, ATC contracted to build 115 tower sites in North Carolina, South Carolina, and Georgia for Triton PCS, which also contracted ATC's acquisition and zoning services for 175 sites in the same area. Furthermore, ATC completed contracts for the construction of 25 towers in the southwestern United States region and built 17 sites along the mobility corridors of Arizona and six new sites in northern California. The company also added a communication facility in West Tiger Mountain and another in Oklahoma. With these new components the company's net revenue for 1998 increased to $103.54 million from $17.5 million in 1997.

1999: Exponential Aerial and Terrestrial Expansion

During January 1999 ATC began what would prove to be a banner year. Among the first significant events of the year, ATC and American Electric Power (AES)—the second-largest utility company in the country—agreed on a co-development venture whereby AES would market its 175,000 transmission structures as telecommunications sites. A major development occurred in February when ATC merged with OmniAmerica, Inc. and with TeleCom Towers, L.L.C. OmniAmerica—a builder, owner, and operator of broadcast and wireless communications sites—also manufactured infrastructure components used in the construction and maintenance of wireless-communications transmitting and receiving facilities. TeleCom owned and operated national communications sites primarily serving wireless service providers. At the completion of these mergers, ATC owned and operated approximately 3,200 broadcast and wireless towers in 44 states and the District of Columbia.

In early March, ATC signed a contract with MariTEL Corporation—which provided VHF marine wireless-telecommunications services to the private- and commercial-boating industry. ATC agreed to develop a telecommunication-tower network of 250 to 300 sites along the coastal and inland waterways of the United States. MariTEL's subsidiary, MariNET, was to provide telecommunications services—including automated, encrypted, voice, fax, and data communications for up to 100 miles offshore. Then on March 16 ATC announced that it had begun construction of a broadcast tower in Missouri City, Texas, near Houston. The new state-of-the-art, multi-use facility was to support a maximum of seven television antennae, a master-panel FM antenna, auxiliary broadcast antennae, low-power television, a multitude of wireless and microwave gear—and accommodate television's transition to HDTV and other broadcast needs. ATC was in sync with the explosive growth of wireless telecommunications.

In April 1999, ATC's Broadcast Tower Group contracted with Sinclair Broadcast Group, a leading owner of television and radio stations in the United States, to develop broadcasting towers for Sinclair's digital transmission needs in 11 markets. ATC announced an agreement with Acrodyne Communications, Inc., a leading manufacturer and installer of television transmission systems, to offer television broadcasters the turnkey solutions required for analog and digital transmission.

In tune with its parent company's aggressive growth strategy, in May ATC Teleports signed a multi-year contract to provide U.S. teleport facilities and Internet backbone connectivity to Unitel, an Athens, Greece-based provider of satellite-communication services. Next, a 12-month contract with British Telecom North America Broadcast Services provided for bulk use of video services and of ATC Teleport's analog and digital services for coverage of the United States, Canada, and the Atlantic Ocean region. In accord with a three-year contract, ATC Teleport provided use of its facilities to DeTeSat Deutsche Telecom, a satellite communication company based in Germany. In May ATC also agreed to manage site acquisition and construction on some 80 communications sites in the Florida panhandle for Nextel Partners and won a contract from Tritel Communications—an AT&T affiliate based in Jackson, Mississippi—for 40 build-to-suit sites in Alabama.

In June ATC agreed to purchase close to 75 communications sites in central and southern Illinois from Illinois PCS (a Sprint PCS affiliate) and acquired a 1,151-foot broadcast communications tower in Philadelphia. ATC also agreed to merge with UNIsite, Inc., which owned and operated 600 wireless communication towers. UNIsite owned another 400 towers suited for co-location and held an exclusive build-to-suit contract with Omnipoint through the year 2012. In July came the completion of the ATC merger with Virginia-based CommSite International, Inc., an antenna-site development and site management company doing business primarily in Maryland, Virginia, Washington, D.C., and Florida. ATC also purchased Watson Communication Systems, Inc. This transaction included acquisition of 11 wireless and 10 broadcast communication towers in the San Francisco Bay area and a teleport for satellite transmission covering the full domestic arc and the Pacific international-service area. This transaction was followed by the acquisition of 108 wireless communication towers from Dobson Tower Company and a contract to build a minimum of 65 towers for Sygnet Communications, Inc.

On July 9, 1999, ATC Teleports signed a multi-year contract with a major telecommunications carrier, thereby enabling the U.S. military to obtain 24-hour-a-day surveillance of ongoing activities in the Middle East. ATC Teleports' next purchase of space-segment capacity on New Skies' satellite system made available greater international Internet connectivity via satellite to Africa, Eastern Europe, and the Middle East. Next came the acquisition of 192 wireless communication towers from Triton PCS (part of AT&T Wireless Network) and also a contract to develop a minimum of 100 build-to-suit towers and to provide turnkey services for co-location sites through 2001. On August 9, ATC signed an agreement with AirTouch Communications, Inc. (a unit of Vodafone AirTouch Plc, the world's largest wireless company). Through a master-lease agreement, ATC also acquired the rights to approximately 2,100 towers and an agreement for an exclusive three-year, build-to-suit project for 400 to 500 new communications towers. AirTouch served 9 million cellular and PCS customers residing in the top 30 U.S. markets of 25 states.

In early September ATC Teleports won a contract from Home Team Sports (HTS), a regional cable sports network serving the mid-Atlantic states. ATC Teleports agreed to execute HTS's complete transition to digital transmission. In mid-September ATC signed an agreement with AT&T, the world's premier provider of voice and data communications, to acquire approximately 1,942 microwave towers and to build 1,000 new wireless communications sites for AT&T Wireless Services

over the next five years. This transaction provided ATC with a nationwide network of tower facilities in 47 states. On September 20, ATC entered into an agreement with TV Azteca, S.A. de C.V., one of two broadcast television companies in Mexico, for building some 200 towers strategically located throughout Mexico. ATC agreed to loan up to $120 million to the television network in exchange for annual net payments of about $13.9 million, plus the rights to all existing and future third-party revenue on the towers.

During October, the Canadian Broadcasting Corporation renewed its contract with ATC Teleports for an analog uplink of uninterrupted news feeds over the ANIK-E2 satellite and agreed to provide broadcasting and satellite downlink transmission services to Virginia-based Netcast Incorporated for its Internet webcasts. Then ATC completed the acquisition of ICG Satellite Services, Inc.—a major 24x7 teleport facility in Holmdel, New Jersey—and bought Maritime Telecommunications Network, Inc., an ICGSS subsidiary which functioned as a Florida-based global maritime telecommunications network. The New Jersey teleport and operations center had major fiber connectivity to the Internet and 12 antennae that gave customers more choices in satellite coverage to the Atlantic Ocean region. MTN provided Internet, voice, and data services to major cruise lines, the U.S. military, Internet-related companies, and international telecommunication customers.

In late December ATC Teleports agreed to purchase the assets of U.S. Electrodynamics, Inc. The merger, scheduled to close in early 2000, included acquisition of 52 antennae with teleport facilities in Brewster, Washington; Whitinsville, Massachusetts; and Kingman, Arizona. ATC customers thereby gained immediate access to the Pacific Rim and India and enabled ATC to expand digital services to such high-growth areas as China, South East Asia, and Australia. At the end of the 20th century the American Tower portfolio spanned 48 states and the District of Columbia and had tower clusters in 43 of the largest U.S. metropolitan statistical areas. The majority of the 1,000 towers constructed in 1999 were built along major roadways; they were predominantly self-supporting monopoles and could accommodate multiple co-location tenants. Upon completion of all its pending acquisitions, ATC owned and operated more than 10,000 communications sites in the United States and Mexico. The company operated from regional hub offices in Boston, Atlanta, Chicago, Houston, San Francisco, and Mexico City.

2000: Transcending Limits

As January 2000 opened the door to a new millennium, ATC had gone beyond its projection for construction of towers in 1999 and was ready to let its tower power defy the bandwidth and geographic limits that could restrict its growth and success. A case in point was ATC Teleport's January 10 agreement with Pronto, a leading international wholesale carrier of voice and data services. Pronto provided termination services to some of the largest phone companies in the world through its gateways in Africa, Central America, South America, Canada, and the United States. With this agreement, ATC Teleports also provided uplink services and satellite space segment for duplex voice-over IP (Internet Protocol) service. The circuits originated from New York and were uplinked from ATC Teleports in Alexandria, Virginia, for termination in Senegal, Kenya, Guinea, Cameroon, Zambia, and the Ivory Coast using the New Skies 803 satellite located at 338.5 degrees east. ATC Teleports already provided Pronto with circuits to Central and South America on the SatMex 5 satellite located at 116.8 degrees west. As of 2000, ATC Teleports in New York also housed Pronto's switch at 60 Hudson Street in New York.

As ATC's towers reached up into the sky, the company was well on the way to encircling the world with wireless services. In fewer than five years the company had grown from a fledgling enterprise to national leadership as an owner and operator of wireless and broadcast towers. American Tower Corporation was poised to meet future competition.

Principal Subsidiaries

ATC Teleports, Inc.

Principal Competitors

Crown Castle International Corp.; Pinnacle Holdings Inc.; Spectra Site Holdings, Inc.

Further Reading

Bell, Robert, "Pioneers of a Weightless Cargo," *Telecommunications International,* July 1999.
Conlin, Michelle, "Tower Power," *Forbes,* March 22, 1999, p. 56.
O'Keefe, Sue, "Mixing up the Right Blend," *Telecommunications America,* January 2000.
Russo, Anthony, "Outsourcing: A Solution for Managing Network Evolution," *Telecommunications International,* December 1999.
Siwolop, Sana, "Buying the Backbones of the Wireless Age," *New York Times,* August 8, 1998, p. 10.

—Gloria A. Lemieux

Ameristar Casinos, Inc.

3773 Howard Hughes Parkway
Suite 490 South
Las Vegas, Nevada 89109
Telephone: (702) 567-7000
Fax: (702) 866-6397
Web site: http://www.ameristars.com

Public Company
Incorporated: 1993
Employees: 4,226
Sales: $264.4 million (1999)
Stock Exchanges: NASDAQ
Ticker Symbol: ASCA
NAIC: 713210 Casinos; 721120 Casino Hotels; 722110
     Full Service Restaurants

Ameristar Casinos, Inc. owns and operates five casinos with adjacent hotels, as well as related food, beverage, and entertainment services, in Nevada, Iowa, and Mississippi. On the high desert plateau of Jackpot, Nevada, the Horseshu Hotel and Casino provides gambling entertainment in a rustic, western setting, while Cactus Pete's Resort Casino offers a desert theme. The Ameristar Vicksburg is a dockside casino in the style of an 1870s riverboat located on the Mississippi River in Vicksburg, Mississippi. Ameristar also operates a riverboat casino from Council Bluffs, Iowa, across the Missouri River from Omaha. Land-based facilities at Council Bluffs include the Main Street Pavilion, with restaurants, hotels, family entertainment, and child care center. Ameristar's only Las Vegas area casino, The Reserve, provides gambling and entertainment in the exotic, colorful simulation of an African game reserve.

Small-Time Operation to Public Corporation

Before the town of Jackpot, Nevada, had a name, Don French and "Cactus Pete" Piersanti moved their slot machine gaming operations to the high desert plateau from Idaho. In 1954, French opened the Horseshu Casino, and Piersanti opened Cactus Pete's Desert Lodge; Cactus Pete's incorporated with three shareholders

in 1956. The two tiny casinos prospered on the "grind," casino lingo for obtaining small profits from a large volume of customers who play slot machines, rather than on high stakes gamblers. Located on Highway 93 at the border of Idaho, the Horseshu and Cactus Pete's thrived on visitors from Idaho, Oregon, Washington, Montana, northern California, and southwestern Canada, as well as on middle-income travelers driving to and from Las Vegas and other points in the southwestern United States. The two gambling sites slowly expanded over the years, beginning with the 15-room Desert Inn Motel at Cactus Pete's in 1958. Table games, such as poker, blackjack, craps, and roulette were added at both properties over the years. Then, in 1964, the Horseshu came under the direction of Cactus Pete's.

The death of one of Cactus Pete's shareholders led to a change in ownership in 1967, with the addition of three new shareholders. When one the new shareholders, Ray Neilsen, of Neilsen and Miller Construction, which had contracted work on the properties, died in 1971, his wife Gwen inherited Neilsen's shares, while his son Craig became involved in the daily operation of Cactus Pete's. Craig Neilsen became president in 1984, and became sole owner of the corporation in 1987, which included both properties by that time.

As the casino industry became more competitive and market-oriented in the 1980s, Craig Neilsen adapted. In an increasingly market-driven industry, free food and drink were no longer sufficient to attract customers. A new marketing strategy included "slot club cards" which strengthened Cactus Pete's repeat-customer base. The personalized cards, inserted into the slot machines, provided the casino with information as to which machines regular customers preferred, and the amount of time and money spent at each machine. The amount of a customer's game play determined what free gift a customer might acquire, such as a free meal, free t-shirt, or free hotel stay. Personal information obtained when players signed up for a club card allowed casino managers to add a personal touch to customer retention. When a computer has tracked a frequent player on a slot machine, the manager might send a casino employee over to offer a free meal or to send happy birthday wishes.

Neilsen initiated a $22 million expansion of Cactus Pete's in 1991, transforming it into a 25,000 square foot casino and destination resort for the northwestern United States. New amenities included a sports and keno lounge, the Bristlecone Emporium gift shop, the Ruby Mountain Ballroom, and an Olympic-sized swimming pool. In 1993 Cactus Pete's Resort Casino received a Four Diamond rating from the American Automobile Association, and would receive that designation annually.

With the proliferation of legalization gambling in the early 1990s, Neilsen sought to expand his casino operations outside of Nevada. A public offering of stock in Fall 1993 coincided with incorporation as Ameristar Casinos. Neilsen maintained 86.9 percent ownership of the casinos and became president and CEO of Ameristar. The stock offering funded final construction on the Ameristar Vicksburg casino which opened in February 1994 in Vicksburg, Mississippi. The 35,000 square foot dock-side casino, permanently anchored on the Mississippi River, 45 miles west of Jackson, included four bars, two restaurants, a cabaret, and a showroom, as well as a restaurant on the bluff overlooking the casino, the Delta Point River Restaurant. Gaming included poker, blackjack, roulette, craps, and over 1,000 slot machines. The tourist traffic in this area involved passers-by on Interstate 20 and visitors to Vicksburg National Military Park. Local residents and residents from eastern Louisiana provided a more regular customer base. The project included acquisition of 18 acres across from the dock for future development and a 20-acre mobile home park to provide housing rentals for employees and other local residents.

In 1995 Ameristar obtained one of three gaming licenses to operate a riverboat casino in Council Bluffs, Iowa, on the Missouri River. Ameristar planned a complete destination resort and entertainment center for the region, designed in the architecture of a late 1800s rivertown much like Council Bluffs itself. The 272 foot long and 98 foot wide riverboat casino encompassed 40,000 square feet on two levels, with high ceilings to create the grand, spacious atmosphere of a land-based casino. In addition to 1,098 slot machines, gaming activities included craps, blackjack, roulette, Caribbean stud, Spanish 21, Pai Gow, 21 Madness, and Let it Ride. A legal requirement for the riverboat casino involved two-hour cruises a minimum of 100 days during the excursion season, from April 1 to October 31. The Ameristar Council Bluffs casino opened for business in

January 1996, after a voyage along the Mississippi and Missouri Rivers from Jennings, Louisiana.

Ameristar opened the Main Street Pavilion on the land adjacent to the riverboat dock in June 1996. The 68,000 square foot Pavilion featured a main street designed in the style of the Victorian era, with restaurants and a variety of entertainment choices for children and adults. In a joint venture with New Horizon Kids Quest, the Pavilion included a 10,000 square foot activity center for children, which provided childcare on an hourly basis while parents gambled. The center accommodated 200 children for up to five days with hours of operation from 10:00 a.m. to 10:00 p.m. daily, and until midnight on Friday and Saturday nights. The Main Street Pavilion also included a 160-room hotel, with panoramic views of the Missouri River, which opened in November after a five-month delay. Visitors had access to the riverboat via an enclosed ramp from the Pavilion.

The proliferation of gambling casinos increased competition as well as opportunities for Ameristar. Specifically, the casinos in Jackpot experienced competition from Native American casinos which opened in Pocatello, Idaho, western Washington, and northeastern Oregon, as well as from casinos in Alberta, Canada, which sought to attract customers from the same geographical areas, the northwestern states and southwestern Canada. Ameristar responded by upgrading the slot machines to state-of-the-art equipment, with touch screens and color and sound effects, by remodeling the 3,500 square foot Horseshu casino, and by increasing its marketing efforts. The Ameristar Vicksburg faced competition from new casinos in Bossier City and Shreveport, Louisiana, as well as in Philadelphia, Mississippi.

Relocation to Las Vegas in 1996

Ameristar entered the casino market in the Las Vegas area through a merger with Gem Gaming, Inc. That company had begun construction on The Reserve casino in Henderson, Nevada, then a fast-growing suburb of Las Vegas and one of the fastest growing suburbs of the United States. Ameristar redesigned the project to elaborate on the African safari theme, to allow for more gambling space, and to enable possible expansion in the future. To oversee design of the new casino, Ameristar hired Henry Conversano, designer of the Mirage in Las Vegas and The Lost City at the Sun City Resort Hotel and Casino in Sun City, South Africa. The Reserve casino and hotel featured colorful murals, artificial aica trees, jungle sounds, and hand carved statues of large animals, such as elephants and giraffes, with some statues designed as encasements for slot machines. Exotic murals covered the exterior of the building, while monkey gargoyles perched on the hotel towers and replicas of elephant tusks bracketed the sign 120 feet tall.

The Reserve began as a $90 million project, but Ameristar's changes added $45 million in expenditures. The 42,000 square foot casino included 1,380 slot machines, sports book keno, a bingo hall with 300 seats, and 25 table games, for roulette, blackjack, poker, and craps. Amenities included four restaurants, including Congo Jack's, where the front of a small airplane has appeared to have crashed among the tables, three bars, and a 224-room, nine-story hotel, which offered an introductory rate of $19.95 per night. Future expansion on the 53-acre property would involve additional hotel towers, multi-level parking, and additional restaurants and bars. Credit problems related to the acquisition of Gem Gaming delayed the opening of The Reserve until February 1998, but thereafter, Ameristar relocated its corporate offices from Twin Falls, Idaho, to Las Vegas in conjunction with entry into the Las Vegas market.

For The Reserve's promotional campaign, Ameristar hired Seiniger Advertising, a specialist in the entertainment industry. Advertising for the The Reserve amplified the African safari theme. The main tagline for print, local television, bus wraps, and outdoor advertisements described The Reserve as "A whole new breed of casino." A print advertisement showed an orangutan with a stoic look and underlying text which stated, "We know a good poker face when we see one." The text under a picture of a cheetah advertised The Reserve's restaurants saying, "If the food were any fresher, you'd have to chase it." A 30-second television promotion showed elephants, giraffes, and other animals running across the African plains towards the casino.

Marketing targeted local residents of the Henderson-Green Valley suburbs. With 70 percent of The Reserve's customer base expected to come from within a ten-mile radius, Ameristar introduced the first "self-comping" players club in the Las Vegas area. Like Cactus Pete's slot club cards, The Reserve players club allowed regular customers to earn free meals and discounts. The casino and hotel also attracted travelers along Lake Mead Parkway, with new road construction expected to increase traffic near the casino.

For its first ten months of operation, February 1, 1998 to December 31, 1998, operations at The Reserve resulted in a loss of $16 million, including pre-opening costs of $10.6 million, and a loss of $12.7 million for the company overall in 1998. Ameristar intensified its marketing efforts, adding cash back opportunities for frequent players, and improved its operating margins, particularly in the area of food service.

Activities Outside Nevada in the Late 1990s

The controversy over legalized gambling had mixed effects on Ameristar. A 1998 Mississippi referendum to amend the state constitution to halt legalized gambling would have closed the Ameristar Vicksburg, but a state judge found the referendum invalid due to a mistake in its filing. Ameristar expected citizens to place a revised version of the referendum on the ballot in 2000. However, local concerns about gambling may have assisted the Ameristar Council Bluffs as the Iowa Racing and Gaming Commission regulated the number of gaming licenses to those already existing in 1998, thus eliminating any possibility of new competition without first overturning the regulation.

Ameristar maintained strong market positions at its casinos outside Nevada. Revenues at Council Bluffs increased steadily with growth in the gaming market there. Revenues increased 24.8 percent, from $70.3 million in 1996 to $87.8 million in 1997, followed by an additional 11 percent increase in 1998 with revenues of $97.7 million. At Vicksburg revenues declined from $66.2 million in 1996 to $64 million in 1997, largely attributed to a decline in the size of the gaming market there.

Ameristar maintained a leading position, however. Revenues increased to $68.5 million in 1998 with a new hotel and increased gambling revenues.

Ameristar expanded hotel facilities adjacent to its casinos in Mississippi and Iowa. In June 1998 the company completed a hotel in Vicksburg. The eight-story, 144-room hotel included a presidential suite, four luxury suites, and 16 king spa suites. Ameristar leased property at Council Bluffs to Kinseth Hotel Corporation to build a Holiday Inn Suites. The 140-room, limited service hotel opened in March 1999, with an enclosed, climate controlled walkway to the Main Street Pavilion.

In July 1999 the company began construction to add a third floor gaming deck to the Ameristar II riverboat at Council Bluffs, as well as land-based entertainment and parking facilities. The $41 million project involved the creation of the first shipyard in Iowa where Lee Vac Shipyards fabricated the ship's deck, which the company maneuvered as a whole onto the riverboat, allowing the casino to remain open throughout the new construction. The expansion increased the size of the riverboat casino to 37,000 square feet, with a capacity for 2,830 people, making it the largest riverboat casino in Iowa. Ameristar increased the number of slot machines to 1,446 and the number of game tables to 51, and added 18 state-of-the-art video poker and video reel slot machines. The Center Sports Bar featured 19 televisions with flat plasma screens, 40 inches by 20 inches, state-of-the-art technology for viewing sporting events as well as promotions. The grand opening celebration in November 1999 included a traditional boat launching ceremony, with a christening and champagne toast. In December 1999 Ameristar signed an agreement with Players Network to provide a closed circuit television network for its hotel patrons in Council Bluffs. The Players Network programs included instruction on casino gaming, sports and racing events, entertainment, and promotions and events at the casino-hotel property.

In fall 1999 Ameristar sought to revive a casino project in South St. Louis County, along the Mississippi River in Missouri. The company signed a letter of intent with Futuresouth Inc. to take over the lease for a potential casino site in Lemay, Missouri, on the Mississippi River. Ameristar expected the project to include restaurants, meeting facilities, ample parking; it would be structured to enable future expansion of the casino and additional amenities. As construction would take place on the site of an old lead plant, clean-up was estimated at $1 million. As part of the deal, Futuresouth, a local group of business people, maintained some interest in the casino project, giving Ameristar some initial political strength over its competitors.

Several factors added complexity to the case, however, as Isle of Capri's Lady Luck Gaming acquisition gave that company a financial edge in its endeavor to attain a potential casino site farther south. Moreover, a citizens organization opposed the casino in Lemay, speaking to the Missouri Gaming Commission of their concerns that gambling would be detrimental to local businesses and destroy the town's quaint atmosphere. Another citizens group formed in favor of a casino development in Lemay, citing the funds gambling taxes would generate for schools and senior citizens and noting Ameristar's donations to computer programs for schools in Iowa City.

Principal Subsidiaries

AC Food Services, Inc.; AC Hotel Corporation; Ameristar Casino Council Bluffs, Inc.; Ameristar Casino Las Vegas, Inc.; Ameristar Casino Vicksburg, Inc.; Cactus Pete's Inc.

Principal Competitors

Harrah's Entertainment, Inc.; Harveys Casino Resorts; Station Casinos, Inc.; Isle of Capri.

Further Reading

"Ameristar Breaks Ground For Hotel," *Biloxi Sun Herald,* April 13, 1997, p. G2.

"Ameristar Casinos Announces Settlement of Arbitration Proceedings with Former Gem Stockholders," *PR Newswire*, May 7, 1997.

"Ameristar Casinos, Inc. Responds to Jury Verdict in Pike County, Mississippi Litigation," *PR Newswire*, November 1, 1999, p. 3,259.

Dorr, Robert, "Ameristar Faces Credit Pinch," *Omaha World Herald*, March 28, 1997, p. 16.

——, "Ameristar Plans $41 Million Expansion of Facilities," *Omaha World Herald*, April 15, 1998, p. 17.

——, "Ameristar Says Hotel Delay Hurt Profits," *Omaha World Herald*, February 21, 1997, p. 16.

Berns, Dave, "At Last, The Reserve Opens," *Las Vegas Review-Journal*, February 12, 1998, p. 1D.

Buyikian, Teresa, "Seiniger's Wild West," *Adweek* (Western edition), February 23, 1998, p. 4.

Carroll, Chris, "Lady Luck Gaming's Sale Makes Casino More Likely, Leading Local Investor Says," *St. Louis Post-Dispatch,* October 25, 1999, p. 5.

"Casino to Provide Child Care," *Omaha World Herald*, June 11, 1996.

DeFrank, Sean, "King of the Jungle," *Las Vegas Review-Journal*, February 4, 1998, p. 1A.

Edwards, John G., "Earnings Rise for Casino Firms," *Las Vegas Review-Journal*, April 21, 1999, p. 1D.

Faust, Fred, "Company Proposes a New Casino South of Jefferson Barracks Bridge," *St. Louis Post-Dispatch*, August 25, 1999, p. C7.

——, "The Contest for the Next Casino License Gets an Interesting Twist," *St. Louis Post-Dispatch*, October 11, 1999, p. 2.

——, "Las Vegas Company May Seek to Revive Lemay Casino Plan," *St. Louis Post-Dispatch*, August 24, 1999, p. C7.

Little, Joan, "Lemay Residents' Group Opposes Proposed Casino," *St. Louis Post-Dispatch,* October 18, 1999, p. 2.

——, "New Group Forms to Defend Virtues of a Casino in Lemay," *St. Louis Post-Dispatch,* November 1, 1999, p. 1.

Langfitt, Frank, "Casinos Go from Sleazy to Slick—and They Want to Bring Their Act to Maryland," *Baltimore Morning Sun*, May 28, 1995, p. 1F.

"(No) Chance Encounters," *Advertising Age*, September 6, 1999, p. 42.

Palermo, Dave, "Rough Going Along the River: Casinos Stifle Heritage Tourism, History Buffs Say," *Biloxi Sun Herald*, November 16, 1997, p. A1.

"Players Network Announces First Affiliate Contract Outside of Nevada," *PR Newswire*, December 7, 1999, p. 6,334.

—Mary Tradii

ANALYTICAL SURVEYS
INCORPORATED

Analytical Surveys, Inc.

---

941 North Meridian Street
Indianapolis, Indiana 46204
U.S.A.
Telephone: (317) 634-1000
Fax: (317) 532-3440
Web site: http://www.anlt.com

Incorporated: 1981
Employees: 1,225
Sales: $113.5 million (1999)
Stock Exchanges: NASDAQ
Ticker Symbol: ANLT
NAIC: 54136 Geophysical Surveying & Mapping
    Services

Analytical Surveys, Inc. (ASI) is a provider of data conversion and computerized mapping services to the Geographic Information Systems (GIS) industry. The company gathers geographically related information, such as utility usage data, infrastructure patterns, aerial photographs, and tax records, and then converts that information into computerized, database format. This digitized information is then used to create a GIS: a high-resolution, computerized map that contains various "layers" of geographical data. The GIS also can incorporate database applications, such as query and statistical analysis.

ASI's customers are primarily large organizations that use extensive geographically-related information to manage their operations, such as municipalities, utilities, public works departments, and federal and state environmental agencies. The company has offices in Colorado, Wisconsin, North Carolina, Indiana, and Texas.

1980s: Laying a Foundation for Growth

Analytical Surveys, Inc. was founded in 1981 in Colorado Springs, Colorado by John Thorpe. Thorpe's educational background included a B.S. in geography and mathematics from Rhodes University in South Africa and an M.S in photogrammetric engineering from the International Training Center for Aerial Survey, in Holland. Prior to founding ASI, he had owned an aerial survey company in Johannesburg, South Africa, for 12 years.

ASI spent its first several years growing slowly, realizing steady gains in revenues, but experiencing fluctuations in net results. In 1984, the company went public, and by the end of the 1980s, began gearing up for a more rapid growth rate. The first order of business was to strengthen its infrastructure by investing in new equipment and additional employees. Toward this end, the company hired a new director of marketing and sales and expanded its research and development department. It also hired a new director for its GIS department.

These investments, mostly made in 1987, led the company to post a $183,796 loss for that year. "Even though we showed a loss, we felt good about 1987," explained ASI's vice-president of administration and finance, George Southard. "We had to build up the facility in order to win the work. We think that 1989 will be the year we begin to really reap the benefits of all the work we did in 1987," he observed. With the newly laid foundation for growth, the company planned to move forward rapidly; its goal was to increase sales by 50 percent annually for several years. ASI felt confident that the expanding digital mapping industry would easily support such a growth rate. With the use of GIS systems increasing rapidly, the industry was projected to grow from $390 million to $779 million within five years.

By 1988, ASI had returned to profitability, with sales of $5.3 million and earnings of $277,251. The company finished up the year by introducing a new service called digital orthophotography. Digital orthophotography was a method of converting aerial photographs into accurate, measurable digital images. To prepare a digital orthophotograph, ASI scanned an aerial photograph into a computer, using a high-resolution scanner. The company then used its own, proprietary software to remove the distortions that were caused by photography. The resulting orthophoto, which was delivered either as a computer data file or a printed image, was a true-to-scale depiction of surface features.

1990: Controlled Growth

In 1990 ASI appointed a new president and chief operating officer: Sidney Corder. Corder had served previously as president of Cubic Western Data, a San Diego-based subsidiary of

Cubic Corporation, and as general manager of manufacturing control for Rohr Industries, a company providing technology and manufacturing service to the aerospace industry. As ASI's new leader, the industry veteran was charged with managing the company's day-to-day operations and finances. Thorpe, who continued to hold the office of CEO, remained in charge of policy and strategic technical advancements. Shortly after hiring Corder, ASI initiated a new, controlled growth strategy that included improving and standardizing operating procedures and controls; upgrading its proprietary software; establishing capital sources; and making further investments in its infrastructure. Corder became the company's CEO in 1993.

By the early 1990s, the company's growth rate was, indeed, accelerating. In 1993 and 1994, the company's net earnings improved by 50 percent and 66 percent, respectively. Its average contract size had increased by 50 percent, and its backlog topped $10 million. In 1995, however, ASI decided to ratchet up the pace again. The company developed and implemented a much more aggressive growth strategy—one that had acquisition as its cornerstone.

Acquisition and Consolidation: 1995–96

In the mid-1990s, the GIS industry was highly fragmented. Its players included small regional firms, larger independent firms, major companies operating GIS divisions, and international providers of data conversion services. Many of the companies, however, specialized in only certain areas of data collection and conversion and, therefore, were unable to offer the full range of services necessary to complete large-scale projects. This being the case, ASI believed that the industry was ripe for consolidation—and it planned to lead the way. The company's newly minted growth strategy involved acquiring businesses that would broaden its geographic reach, capacity, customer base, product offerings, proprietary technology, and operational abilities.

ASI's first acquisition was Intelligraphics Inc., a utility mapping services company located in Waukesha, Wisconsin. The Intelligraphics purchase, which was completed in December of 1995, added 200 employees, 25 new customers, and $12.3 million in backlog to ASI's operation. More significantly, it gave the company entree into the utilities facility data conversion market, as well as establishing a presence in the Midwest.

A second acquisition followed within a few months. In July 1996, ASI purchased Westinghouse Landmark GIS, Inc. for $1.9 million. The North Carolina company, which was renamed ASI Landmark, specialized in land base and cadastral mapping. Cadastra maps, which indicated boundaries and property lines, were used for researching deeds or determining property areas

for tax purposes. Until acquiring Landmark, ASI had used outside subcontractors to perform this type of work; the acquisition, then, expanded the range of services the company could perform in-house. It also strengthened ASI's presence in the eastern and southeastern parts of the United States and provided it with approximately 20 new customers and 105 new employees.

By the end of 1996, less than two years into its new growth plan, ASI had revenues of $22.7 million—an increase of almost 70 percent from 1995. It posted earnings of $1.9 million. The company had grown from 119 employees to 377 during the same time span.

Industry Dominance: 1997–98

In 1997 ASI made its largest acquisition, purchasing MSE Corporation of Indianapolis, Indiana. With more than 200 customers, 335 employees, and annual sales of around $22 million, MSE was ASI's main competitor. By merging the two companies, ASI became the clear industry leader. The acquisition also gave ASI expertise in civil engineering, which it had previously had to contract out. "MSE fits well with our strategy of aggressively expanding our service base and geographic presence," ASI President Sidney Corder said in a July, 1997 interview with the *Indianapolis Business Journal*. "When we were bidding for jobs, we were always one, two or three with MSE, so it made sense. We are now the largest and most flexible company in our industry."

The acquisition led to some restructuring in the top echelons at ASI. MSE's previous owner, Sol Miller, joined ASI's board of directors. He also became the company's largest shareholder, holding approximately 14 percent of its stock. MSE's president, Randy Sage, became ASI's chief operating officer. John Thorpe retired as chairman of the board and was succeeded by Corder. Shortly after the acquisition, ASI moved its executive offices to Indianapolis, and its top managers—including Corder—relocated there.

Already the largest player in the GIS industry, ASI continued to bulk up. In June 1998, the company acquired the San Antonio-based Cartotech, Inc. Cartotech was a provider of GIS data conversion, digital mapping, and database construction services, with annual revenues around $15 million. The Cartotech acquisition gave ASI a stronger presence in both the utility market and in the southwestern part of the United States. It also added 50 new customers and 270 employees.

ASI made two smaller acquisitions in 1998 and 1999: Cartographic Sciences and Measurement Science, Inc. Cartographic Sciences was an India-based provider of data-conversion services. Measurement Science, based in Englewood, Colorado, was a provider of GIS-related engineering and surveying services with particular expertise in the use of Global Positioning System (GPS) technology for data collection. Prior to the acquisition, ASI had used both firms as outside contractors.

In addition to increasing production capability via acquisition, ASI also focused on using new technologies to improve its productivity. One such new technology was METRO—a new process for use in the production of orthophotographs. Whereas correcting distortions in an orthophoto had previously been a

Key Dates:

1981: John Thorpe founds Analytical Surveys, Inc.
1984: Company goes public.
1993: Sidney Corder becomes ASI's CEO.
1995: ASI embarks on aggressive growth plan, acquires Intelligraphics.
1996: Company acquires Westinghouse Landmark GIS, Inc.
1997: Company acquires MSE Corporation.
1998: Company acquires Cartotech, Inc.
2000: Sid Corder retires.

time-consuming, labor-intensive task, METRO made the corrections automatically—thereby greatly reducing the production hours and expense involved.

New Directions, New Alliances: 1999

ASI started 1999 with a commitment to and a strategy for expanding its field inventory services. Field inventory collection involved capturing positional and attribute data on fixed objects, such as utility poles and street signs. The data collected was ultimately used in the creation of a GIS. There was a growing demand for such collection services, particularly among utilities customers. To meet the demand, ASI invested more than $600,000 in capital equipment and software used for field inventory services and began increasing its staff of field inventory personnel.

The company also took a step that simultaneously extended its global reach and cut overhead when it formed a strategic alliance with Infotech Enterprises, Ltd., an India-based data conversion company. Under the terms of the partnership, Infotech agreed to provide ASI with data conversion services, using ASI's proprietary mapping software, at a cost that was considerably lower than ASI could obtain domestically. The partnership agreement also included the sale of the ASI-owned, India-based Cartographic Sciences to Infotech.

Corder explained the reasoning behind the Infotech alliance in a June 23, 1999 press release. "Increased worldwide demand for GIS services has prompted our efforts to increase the company's global capacity," he said, adding "We have taken several key steps to grow our domestic capacity in recent years, and those efforts will continue. This agreement allows us to expand our international presence in conjunction with our domestic growth programs." By January 2000, the Infotech partnership was proving so beneficial that ASI decided to move more of its data conversion work overseas.

The year 1999 also brought two small divestitures for ASI. The company sold two subsidiaries, Phillips Design Group and Mid-States Engineering, which had been acquired in 1997 as part of MSE. The company finished up 1999 with sales of $113,548—up 28.8 percent over 1998's $88.2. Net earnings showed a 117.1 percent improvement in 1999, jumping to $7.2 million from 1998's $3.3 million.

Mapping the Future: 2000 and Beyond

As the new millennium started, ASI found itself in a period of transition with regard to leadership. In late January 2000, company CEO and Chairman Sid Corder announced his retirement. Sol Miller, the former owner of MSE, was appointed interim CEO. James T. Rothe, a member of ASI's board since 1987, became chairman.

Leadership issues notwithstanding, the company's future was almost certain to include entry into several new markets where GIS technology was just beginning to be used. Target industries included wireless telecommunications, insurance, transportation, and financial services. The company believed that to effectively tap these new markets, it needed to help potential customers understand how GIS could benefit them. Toward this end, ASI planned to expand its consulting services, offering customers more complete guidance on how to design, use, and manage GIS.

Principal Subsidiaries

ASI Technologies, Inc.; ASI Landmark, Inc.; Intelligraphics International; MSE Corporation; Cartotech, Inc.; ids Digital Map Publishing Service; Phillips Design Group.

Principal Competitors

Bechtel Group, Inc.; Brown and Caldwell; Commodore Applied Technologies, Inc.; EA Engineering, Science, and Technology, Inc.; Ecology and Environment, Inc.; ECOS Group, Inc.; Harding Lawson Associates Group, Inc.; The Keith Companies, Inc.; Montgomery Watson; NSC Corporation; Sevenson Environmental Services, Inc.; Superior Services, Inc.; Tetra Tech, Inc.; TRC Companies, Inc.; United Water Resources; URS Corporation.

Further Reading

Arensman, Russ, "Analytical Surveys on Track: Firm Turns Around," *Gazette Telegraph,* December 10, 1988, p. C7.
Pletz, John, "MSE Scores in Buy Out: Analytical Surveys, Inc. Buys MSE Corp.," *Indianapolis Business Journal,* July 14, 1997, p. 1A.
Schoettle, Anthony, "ASI Becoming GIS Industry Kingpin," *Indianapolis Business Journal,* June 29, 1998, p. 9A.

—Shawna Brynildssen

Anaren Microwave, Inc.

6635 Kirkville Road
East Syracuse, New York 13057
U.S.A.
Telephone: (315) 432-8909
Fax: (315) 432-9121
Web site: http://www.anaren.com

Public Company
Incorporated: 1967 as Micronetics, Inc.
Employees: 290
Sales: $45.7 million (1999)
Stock Exchanges: NASDAQ
Ticker Symbol: ANEN
NAIC: 334220 Wireless Communication Equipment
Manufacturing; 334419 Other Electronic Component
Manufacturing; 334511 Search, Detection, Navigation,
Guidance, Aeronautical, and Nautical System and
Instrument Manufacturing

Anaren Microwave, Inc. operates in three business segments: wireless communications, satellite communications, and defense electronics. Its operations are organized in two groups, the Wireless Group and the Space and Defense Group. Founded in 1967, the company historically designed and manufactured microwave components and subsystems for the defense industry. In 1994–95 it began serving the emerging commercial wireless and satellite communications market. Its customers are the leading wireless, satellite, and defense OEMs (Original Equipment Manufacturers). By 1999 commercial applications accounted for about two-thirds of Anaren's sales.

Manufacture of Microwave Components and Subsystems for Defense: 1967–94

The company was incorporated in New York in 1967 as Micronetics, Inc., but the name was changed to Anaren Microwave, Inc. in that same year. The company designed and manufactured complex microwave subsystems for the defense market. These included microwave stripline components for wireless communications, including hybrid couplers, power dividers, mixers, modulators, attenuators, phase discriminators, and custom assemblies.

In 1981 Anaren moved to a new facility in East Syracuse, New York, which housed all of the company's marketing, manufacturing, administrative, research and development, systems design, and engineering experimentation activities. The facility was expanded in 1985 to 105,000 square feet. During the 1980s the company developed technology that was used for defense applications involving radar tracking, identification, and jamming.

Began Serving Commercial Wireless Communications Markets: 1994–95

It was in 1994 that Anaren, a pioneer in surface mount stripline passive components, became the first to introduce high power 90-degree surface mount stripline hybrid couplers for the wireless market. These devices were ideal for building amplifiers used in cellular and PCS base stations. They quickly became an industry standard, with their small size, high performance, and delivery in production-ready tape and reels. Anaren soon was delivering these products in high volume and at competitive prices.

In fiscal 1995 (ending June 30) Anaren expanded its capabilities to serve the emerging commercial wireless and satellite communications market. Between fiscal 1995 and 1999, commercial applications grew from five percent of sales to 66 percent of sales. During this period the wireless market showed remarkable growth that was forecast to continue well into the future. Anaren made signal distribution assemblies that were installed in cellular base stations. Between 1995 and 1999 the number of Anaren's cell site installations grew from 32,000 to 89,000 and was predicted to increase to 235,000 by 2003. Its customers included nearly all of the leading wireless companies, including, among others, Ericsson, Nortel Networks, Motorola, Nokia, Lucent Technologies, Siemens, and Alcatel Telecom. Wireless revenues grew from $300,000 in fiscal 1995 to $21.5 million in fiscal 1999.

In May 1995 Lawrence Sala was promoted to president after having served as vice-president of marketing. Co-founder Hugh A. Hair remained as chairman and CEO until September 1997, when he announced his planned retirement for June 30, 2000.

Company Perspectives:

We believe that the wireless market, fueled by the rapid growth of the Internet, will continue to accelerate—with customers demanding more and higher quality voice, video, and data services. This move (from narrowband, voice-only applications to broadband voice, video, and data applications) will require the significant technology advancements that Anaren is known for. Moreover, the shift from narrow- to broadband wireless will drive demand for network build-outs—and with them Anaren products—for many years to come.

Sala then became president and CEO, while Hair remained as chairman until 2000.

Sala's promotion to president was announced as an effort to strengthen Anaren's ability to penetrate developing commercial markets, and a new Commercial Division was established to pursue opportunities in the commercial wireless and satellite communications markets. Sala began his career at Anaren as an engineer responsible for design and testing of military electronics. As vice-president of marketing he was instrumental in the development of Anaren's Commercial Division.

Anaren had just won a $6 million contract to manufacture satellite antenna feed networks for global cellular telephone systems from an existing customer. To win the contract, Anaren had developed technology that compressed large, cased single-layer stripline components into a caseless multilayer unit that was 90 percent smaller, 90 percent lighter, and 20 percent less costly. It was this contract that led to the establishment of the company's Commercial Division, which would capitalize on the multilayer concept and design other products for the cellular industry's land-based applications.

Known as the "Anaren Solution," these proprietary processes known as Multi-Layer Stripline (MLS) technology enabled Anaren to deliver more compact and lightweight microwave signal distribution and interconnection networks for wireless and satellite communication systems. The MLS process integrated multiple layers of microwave circuitry, thus eliminating discrete components and discrete microwave cables. The result was a dramatic reduction in size, cost, and weight as well as improved performance. By combining MLS technology with its proprietary design libraries and turnkey capabilities, Anaren was able to provide custom solutions for original equipment manufacturers (OEMs).

Changes Brought by Shrinking Defense Budgets: 1996

In March 1996 Anaren divested its electronic warfare simulator manufacturing operation in Frimley, England. The maintenance and repair facility was closed, and the electronic warfare simulator operation was sold in a management buyout. Anaren Microwave Ltd., the company's wholly owned subsidiary in the United Kingdom, would remain as a sales and marketing center for Europe. These changes came about as a result of severe downsizing of military budgets in Europe. For the first nine months of fiscal 1996, the operation reported a substantial reduction in new orders and losses of $577,000. By divesting the operation, Anaren was able to focus on its domestic operations in defense and the expanding wireless communications business.

Anaren reported an increase in domestic orders for 1995–96, especially for new global satellite systems such as Motorola's Iridium and TRW's Odyssey, for which Anaren had become a critical supplier of antenna beamforming equipment. In August 1996 Anaren won a multimillion dollar contract from Martin Marietta Overseas Corp. (later Lockheed Martin) for the design and production of satellite antenna beamforming networks for its Asia Cellular Satellite System (ACeS). ACeS was a space-based cellular communications system serving Asia via two geosynchronous satellites.

To celebrate its 30th anniversary, Anaren issued a new full-line catalog of its standard components, including the Xinger brand of surface mount couplers and power dividers, which were available in all cellular and PCS frequency bands. Also listed were caseless couplers and connectorized components such as power dividers, couplers, butler matrices, attenuators, mixers, modulators, and phase discriminators.

Reorganization into Three Business Units: 1996–97

In fiscal 1997 the company reorganized into three business groups: the Wireless Group, the Satellite Communications Group, and the Defense Electronics Group. The Wireless Group supplied low cost surface mount components and custom subassemblies to manufacturers of cellular and PCS power amplifiers, receivers, and base station equipment. It also supplied beamformers for signal distribution networks for advanced base station designs.

In the Satellite Communications Group, the company's beamformer technology was used in satellite communications to improve system capacity by allocating capacity based on demand, or population density. The Defense Electronics Group provided the technology for airborne radar jamming and targeting. Space and defense customers included Hughes Space and Communications, Lockheed Martin, ITT Defense, TRW, Raytheon, and others. Between fiscal 1996 and 1999 Space and Defense revenues increased from $14.9 million to $24.3 million.

In fiscal 1997 ending June 30, net sales were $24.2 million, up 42 percent from $17.1 million in 1996. Net earnings were $2.1 million, compared with a net loss of $1.1 million in fiscal 1996. For the year 61 percent of revenues came from commercial contracts in satellite and ground-based wireless communications, compared with 39 percent in fiscal 1996. The company received follow-up orders for the manufacture of microwave signal distribution networks for use in wireless infrastructure equipment from Motorola and Northern Telecom. The Wireless Group reported $7.6 million in revenues, while the Satellite Communications Group had $8.5 million in revenues and more than $16.5 million in orders. Fueling the growth in satellite communications was progress on several commercial satellite programs, including Motorola's Iridium, Hughes Space and Communications Company's ICO, and Lockheed Martin's ACeS programs. New commercial satellite projects such as Teledisc, Cyberstar, Celestri, Astrolink, and others made the

Key Dates:

1967: Anaren Microwave is founded to design and manufacture complex microwave subsystems for the defense industry.
1995: Anaren expands its capabilities to serve the emerging commercial wireless and satellite communications market.
1997: Anaren reorganizes into three business units: the Wireless Group, the Satellite Communications Group, and the Defense Electronics Group.
1999: Anaren combines its Satellite Communications Group and its Defense Electronics Group into one new group called the Space and Defense Group.

future of this market very attractive. Applications included Internet access, interactive video, and other high-band uses.

On the other hand, the Defense Electronics Group reported a 14 percent decline in revenues to $8.1 million, while new orders exceeded $11 million. The group expected to return to revenue growth in fiscal 1998, when it would begin making shipments on the Airborne Self-Protection Jammer program (ASPJ) and the Integrated Defensive Electronic Countermeasures program (IDECM).

Strong Demand for Wireless Products: 1997–98

During fiscal 1998 sales of wireless products increased by 117 percent, while space and defense products increased by 26 percent. The wireless increase was attributed to continuing strong demand by the major wireless base station OEMs for Anaren's custom products and off-the-shelf surface mount components. Sales of space and defense products consisted of initial shipments of beamformers to Loral Space and Communications Ltd. as well as continued shipments to Lockheed Martin on the ACeS program and a program for Hughes. Sales of defense-oriented products rose by $4.2 million during fiscal 1998 as DRFMs (Digital Radio Frequency Memories) were shipped for foreign sales of the Airborne Self Protection Jammer (ASPJ) system, which entered full production in the second quarter.

Further Reorganization: 1999–2000

At the beginning of 1999 Anaren combined its Satellite Communications Group and its Defense Electronics Group into one new group called the Space and Defense Group. The combination allowed Anaren to more efficiently utilize its engineering, manufacturing, and marketing resources. The two groups had reached a level of sharing manufacturing processes and products that made it more economical to combine the two groups.

In the fourth quarter of fiscal 1999 the company dissolved its European subsidiary, Anaren Microwave Ltd., resulting in a $1 million tax benefit. In 1999 the company's major customers included the U.S. government, which accounted for 13 percent of sales; Motorola, Inc., with 18 percent of sales; and ITT Aerospace with 12 percent of sales. The company's sales were split 80–20 between U.S. and foreign shipments. Other major OEM customers included Raytheon, Lockheed Martin, and

Racal Ltd. Net sales for fiscal 1999 increased 22 percent to $45.7 million compared with $37.4 million for 1998. Shipments of wireless products rose 29 percent, while space and defense product shipments rose 16 percent.

In July 1999 Anaren announced a development partnership with Motorola's Semiconductor Products Sector. The two companies had developed cutting edge technology to produce a high-power/high-performance Universal Mobile Telecommunications System (UMTS) power amplifier. Anaren introduced the new AdrenaLine splitter/combiner networks designed to work with Motorola's latest RF LDMOS power devices. The launch of the new AdrenaLine product contributed to record growth of the company's Wireless Group. The AdrenaLine product line was being used by Motorola to meet the unique requirements of Third Generation (3G) wireless systems.

In December 1999 Anaren captured the Spaceway program contract, an advanced satellite subsystem contract involving high frequency broadband technology, which resulted in record new orders of $38 million. The contract was awarded by Hughes Space and Communications Company, which was developing the advanced Spaceway Global Broadband Satellite Network to provide high-bandwidth, high-speed communications for broadband and multimedia applications via geosynchronous satellites.

The company's Wireless Group posted a 57 percent increase in net sales for the quarter ending December 31, 1999, due to capturing increasing dollar content on wireless base stations and new technologies for third generation base station applications. The company also achieved record profitability through improvements in operating efficiency, with operating margins improving to 18.6 percent.

With its stock hitting a new 52-week high at the end of 1999, Anaren continued to pursue the strategy that had brought it success. It included five goals: to increase dollar content per platform, to further expand into commercial markets, to maintain leadership in microwave technology, to leverage and expand customer relationships, and to focus on operating performance.

Principal Divisions

Wireless Group; Space and Defense Group.

Principal Competitors

Electromagnetic Sciences, Inc.; S.T. Microwave, Inc.; M/A-Com division of AMP, Inc.; Mini Circuits Inc.; Filtronic Comtek, Inc.

Further Reading

Klass, Philip J., "Tests Show RWRs Can Locate, Identify Threats," *Aviation Week & Space Technology,* September 11, 1995, p. 52.
"Need to Detect Signals Instantly Spurs Call for Digital Components," *Aviation Week & Space Technology,* September 18, 1989, p. 104.
"Tracker Detects Low-Flying Missiles," *Design News,* March 27, 1989, p. 62.
Werner, Thomas, "Eye on the Pentagon: Anaren Microwave Would Benefit from Shift in Priorities," *Barron's,* August 24, 1987, p. 41.

—David P. Bianco

AUSTRIAN AIRLINES ➤

Austrian Airlines AG (Österreichische Luftverkehrs AG)

Fontanastrasse 1
A-1107 Vienna
Austria
Telephone: +43 (1) 1766 3334
Fax: +43 (1) 1766 3333
Web site: http://www.aua.com

Public Company
Incorporated: 1957
Employees: 4,700
Sales: EUR 1.38 billion (1998)
Stock Exchanges: Vienna
Ticker Symbol: AUAV.VI
NAIC: 481111 Scheduled Passenger Air Transportation;
481112 Scheduled Freight Air Transportation; 481211
Nonscheduled Chartered Passenger Air
Transportation; 56152 Tour Operators; 532411
Commercial Air, Rail, and Water Transportation
Equipment Rental and Leasing

Austrian Airlines AG (Österreichische Luftverkehrs AG) has traditionally been known as "little brother" to its German rival, Lufthansa. Its strategic location at the crossroads of East and West helped Austrian Airlines (AUA) attain early dominance in the Eastern European market and the uncongested hub at Vienna International Airport has allowed for ferocious growth. Strategic alliances, such as with long-time partner Swissair and, more recently, the Star Alliance, have extended AUA's reach to all corners of the world. Although it carries three million passengers a year, the company typically makes more money through its financial services companies.

Early 20th Century Origins

Austria was a pioneer in scheduled international air service, introducing a Vienna-Krakow-Lvov-Kiev route on April 1, 1918. Vienna-Budapest followed within a few months. The original Österreichische Luftverkehrs-AG (ÖLAG) operated three-engined transports between 1923 and 1938 and never lost a passenger in nearly five million miles. ÖLAG was the fourth busiest European airline in 1935 after Deutsche Lufthansa, KLM, and Air France. It became a part of Deutsche Lufthansa in 1938.

Civil aviation was banned by the Allies after World War II until the signing of the State Treaty in 1955. The new Austrian Airlines (AUA) was founded on September 30, 1957 as a government-owned company with a start-up capital of A$ 60 million. The next year, AUA began flying four chartered Vickers Viscount 779s. Vienna to London was its first scheduled route; soon AUA was flying to several capital cities across continental Europe, including Rome, Warsaw, and Paris, as well as a few important German-speaking destinations. The company carried more than 25,000 passengers and 186 tons of freight in its first year of operations.

AUA bought six Vickers Viscount 837s of its own in 1960. Domestic air service was launched with a DC-3 in January 1963. AUA's first jet, the Caravelle VI-R, began operations the next month. By the end of the decade, AUA had begun flying a Vienna-Brussels-New York route in conjunction with Belgian carrier Sabena, which supplied the Boeing 707 flown on it. AUA received its first DC-9 in June 1971.

AUA underwent an extensive reorganization in 1969. Thereafter, it focused on developing its role as the link between Eastern and Western Europe. In 1972, it entered into a technical cooperation agreement with Swissair, the beginning of a close, long-lasting alliance. AUA also posted its first annual profit: A$ 8.6 million. It would remain profitable for the next two decades. In fact, earnings grew markedly, reaching A$ 17 million in 1972 and A$ 20 million in 1973. In 1976, it began paying its first dividend based on 1975 earnings of A$ 22 million.

In 1974, the growing carrier set up its own maintenance facility. Later, with 1977 earnings of A$ 35 million, AUA acquired a 50 percent interest in WA-Wien Airport Restaurant und Hotelbetriebsges.m.b.H., a catering company. This later became Airest Restaurant und betriebsges m.b.H., expanding beyond Vienna to several airports. In 1981, the company bought 50 percent of Touropa Austria, the country's leading tour operator.

In 1977, it placed its first orders for the DC-9-80. Later known as the MD-80, this plane would become a workhorse of the AUA fleet. In 1980, AUA and Swissair became launch

---

Company Perspectives:

Forty successful years in aviation. As an Austrian aviation company, we have been providing services tailored to our customers on the global markets for 40 years now. As an Austrian aviation group, we work together with our partners Lauda Air and Tyrolean Airways to serve all segments of air transport, from scheduled and charter service to cargo service. To round out and optimize our range of services, the Austrian Airlines Group comprises numerous other companies associated with flight operations in the transportation, tourism, financing, IT and insurance sectors. We are the market leader in Austria, our home market. Our powerful domestic position provides a strong base for developing other expanding markets. At the center of these efforts is our further buildup of Vienna as a hub between West and East. Strategic alliances are the foundation upon which we are expanding our business. Through our close cooperation with other airlines, we offer our customer essential benefits while improving our own market position.

---

customers for the DC-9-81 variant. In 1984, along with Finnair, AUA was a launch customer for the MD-87. The next year, it ordered two Fokker 50s for shorter routes.

In the mid-1980s, AUA was carrying two million passengers a year and posting profits of A\$ 95 million. It started its own travel organizer, Austrian Holidays Ltd., London, in 1987. The next spring, AUA began listing shares on the Vienna stock exchange. Swissair acquired three percent, and the Republic of Austria remained the majority shareholder.

After the offering, AUA had cash and the newest planes kept arriving. Its first Airbus 310 was delivered in late December 1988 and an MD-83 was ordered the next year. Earnings remained robust, with profits of A\$ 154 million in 1989. That May, All Nippon Airways bought 3.5 percent of AUA's shares as Swissair raised its holdings to eight percent. A year later, both increased their holdings again, to nine percent and ten percent, respectively. AUA placed the largest aircraft order in Austria's history in October 1990. The 13 Airbus A320s and A321s, due for delivery in 1996, were valued at ATS 22 billion. However, with existing planes flying only half full, AUA was not quite prepared for the coming deregulation of European aviation.

Expanding Horizons in the 1990s

Profits slipped to A\$ 130 million in 1990. That year, AUA joined the European Quality Alliance (EQA), which then included SAS, Swissair, and Finnair. This extended AUA's long period of cooperation with Swissair. All four carriers operated the DC-9/MD-80 series of aircraft, making shared maintenance logical. This new teaming, however, extended into route selection and marketing as well. Together, the four airlines employed 80,000 people and carried 30 million passengers a year. They controlled 42 percent of the market for western-based carriers flying into Eastern Europe.

The dismantling of the Soviet Empire gave Austrian Airlines access to exciting new markets in Eastern Europe. With a strategy of connecting as many points as possible, AUA added frequent service to carefully selected destinations ranging across the Baltics, Ukraine, and Russia. It even fielded six flights a day to Prague and Budapest. By the mid-1990s, the Eastern European market was the world's second fastest growing after Southeast Asia, accounting for 40 percent of AUA's passenger load. Cooperation with local carriers extended AUA's reach further. These new routes provided the rationale for more larger, long-range aircraft.

In 1993, KLM, SAS, Swissair, and AUA discussed forming a new huge airline, named Alcazar after a Spanish fortress with four towers. It would have hubs devoted to specific regions: Copenhagen for northeast Asia; Amsterdam for the Americas; and Zurich for the southern hemisphere and southeast Asia. AUA would have held ten percent of the shares to the other carriers' 30 percent each. As Austria had not yet joined the European Union, Alcazar would have improved AUA's position with the coming liberalization of the aviation industry. Simultaneous talks with Air France, Lufthansa, and All Nippon Airways were revealed, however. Alcazar was to have been based at Amsterdam, with Swissair head Otto Loepfe as CEO. According to *Air Transport World,* it was KLM's insistence upon choosing Northwest Airlines as a U.S. partner that crumbled the concept. KLM owned 20 percent of Northwest. The other partners, however, preferred Delta Air Lines, feeling it to be more financially stable.

After Alcazar, AUA, Swissair, and SAS focused on their own existing EQA alliance. Each also looked for a partner among the European ''big three''—British Airways, Air France (which acquired 1.5 percent of AUA's equity), and Lufthansa (LH). Both LH and Swissair seemed likely merger possibilities for AUA. AUA promptly announced its own code-sharing link with Delta on the New York-Vienna route, whereupon Delta would rent seats on AUA's planes. The EQA was scuttled when SAS teamed up with Lufthansa, leaving AUA vying for a role in the Delta/Singapore Airlines/Swissair Global Excellence alliance.

AUA lost millions of schillings in 1993 and 1994 as the Alcazar drama played itself out. In addition to a global recession in the wake of the Persian Gulf war, the carrier faced relentless cost competition from Lufthansa and Lauda Air. A new dual presidency was appointed to meet the crisis. Marketing executive Dr. Herbert Bammer and Mario Rehulka, formerly chief of charter operations, took over in July 1993 and immediately set out upon a restructuring of the company. The two felt AUA had far too many vice-presidents. They cut 900 other jobs, leaving a work force of about 3,900. Since the company had so many new planes, heavy maintenance jobs were cut significantly. Some remaining employees worked longer hours.

In March 1994, AUA bought a 42.85 percent stake in Tyrolean Airways, into which it incorporated its subsidiary Austrian Air Services, Osterreichischer Inlands und Regionalflugdienst Gesellschaft m.b.H. This turned tiny Tyrolean, based in Innsbruck, into a serious regional airline, flying more than a million passengers a year. AUA enjoyed the benefits of a vigorous tourist market through its charter subsidiary Austrian Airtransport and Touropa Austria, wholly owned since December 1994. Charters accounted for half its European traffic.

Key Dates:

1923: Österreichische Luftverkehrs-AG (ÖLAG), precursor to the current Austrian Airlines, takes wing.
1938: Deutsche Lufthansa acquires ÖLAG.
1945: Allies ban civil aviation in Austria.
1957: State-owned Austrian Airlines (AUA) founded.
1963: AUA commences domestic service after years of international flights and receives first jets.
1969: Extensive reorganization focuses company on the East-West connection.
1972: AUA begins technical cooperation with Swissair.
1976: AUA pays first dividend.
1988: Initial public offering launched in Vienna.
1990: AUA joins European Quality Alliance with SAS, Swissair, and Finnair.
1993: New dual presidency begins cutting jobs and costs as proposed Alcazar alliance with Swissair, SAS, and KLM falls apart.
1996: AUA signs huge $1 billion Airbus order with Swissair and Sabena.
1998: AUA joins Qualiflyer Group with ten other European airlines.

AUA started service to Beijing, Tokyo, and Johannesburg with two Airbus A340s in early 1995. These long-range jets permitted the elimination of fueling stops on many routes. A new corporate identity appeared on new ''X-Large'' Fokker 70 Jets delivered in October 1995. New staff uniforms were unveiled with the January 1996 maiden flight of the new Airbus 321 from Vienna to Moscow. In the mid-1990s, AUA's network incorporated 80 cities in 46 countries on four continents—an impressive task for a fleet of just 29 planes, as *Air Transport World* noted. AUA turned a $5.3 million profit in 1995, reversing two years of losses. It had to contend, however, with a domestic challenger, Lauda Air, founded by champion race car driver Niki Lauda in 1979 and 39.7 percent owned by Lufthansa.

New Alliances at the End of the Millennium

Swissair's purchase of a 49.5 percent stake in Sabena brought its partner AUA closer to the Belgian flag carrier. In late 1995, AUA, Swissair, and Sabena pressed on with a concept similar to Alcazar. Joined by Delta, they asked for a U.S. antitrust exemption similar to the one that allowed KLM and Northwest to join forces. By this time, AUA also had agreements with EVA Air, Asiana, KLM, Alitalia, Air China, and Air Mauritius. Swissair, AUA, and Sabena placed a $1 billion order for new Airbus A330 widebody jets in December 1996. Their first joint procurement order also included the lease of eight more A330s. In February 1997, the trio's collaboration with Delta took wing under the ''Atlantic Excellence'' banner.

Lufthansa sold AUA a 19.7 percent stake in Lauda Air in April 1997. AUA had already acquired 9.7 percent from Niki Lauda and 5.9 percent from a private investor, giving it 36 percent control of voting capital. This kicked off consolidation among Austria's three carriers, AUA, Lauda Air, and Tyrolean. Lauda Air, a lean, stylish operator, specialized in leisure travel

to Asia and the Pacific. It had 1,270 employees to AUA's 4,040 and Tyrolean's 810. Joint sales and increased bookings were expected to save the three carriers as much as $200 million per year. A reduction of fees at Vienna International promised more savings. In fact, profits of ATS 189.4 million for 1998 were the best in AUA's history.

Many alliances shifted in the late 1990s. In July 1998, AUA joined the Qualiflyer Group with ten other European airlines including Swissair, Sabena, Air Portugal, Turkish Airlines, Air Littoral, and Air Europe. In May 1999, All Nippon Airways sold its shares to Australian investors. After a capital increase, the Republic of Austria was left with a 39.7 percent stake. Delta Air Lines dropped its Atlantic Excellence partners (AUA, Swissair, and Sabena) in October 1999 to concentrate on its relationship with the much larger Air France. Swissair and Sabena were themselves working more closely with American Airlines on trans-Atlantic code shares. AUA announced plans to join the massive Star Alliance in the summer of 2000. Its expansion plans for the first few years of the new millennium called for an investment of EUR 1.5 billion to bring its fleet to 100 aircraft.

Principal Subsidiaries

AUA Beteiligungen Gesellschaft m.b.H.; Austrian Airtransport, Österreichische Flugbetriebsgesellschaft m.b.H. (80%); Tyrolean Airways, Tiroler Luftfahrt-AG; Lauda Air Luftfahrt AG (35.9%); GULET TOUROPA Touristik (50%); Österreichische Verkehrsbüro AG (13.4%); TRAVIAUSTRIA Datenservice für Reise und Touristik Gesellschaft m.b.H. (61%); Austrian Airlines Lease and Finance Company Limited (Guernsey); AUA Versicherungs-Service AUA Versicherungs-Service Gesellschaft m.b.H.; Airest Restaurant- und Hotelbetriebsgesellschaft m.b.H. (35%); Austrian Aircraft Corporation, Österreichische Luftfahrzeug Gesellschaft m.b.H. (51%); AVICON Aviation Consult Gesellschaft m.b.H. (38%); ACS Aircontainer Services Gesellschaft m.b.H. (76%); Österreichische Luftfahrtschule Aviation Training Center Austria Gesellschaft m.b.H. (26%).

Principal Divisions

Airline Companies; Tourism/Sales; Financial and Insurance Services; Other Services.

Principal Competitors

Deutsche Lufthansa AG.

Further Reading

Adams, Jeremy, ''Hedging Secrets of Ambitious Austrian Airlines,'' *Corporate Finance,* February 1997, p. 29.
''Austrian Airlines Move to Closer Cooperation,'' *Airfinance Journal,* April 1997, p. 19.
Benisch, Reginald, ''Vienna: Austrian Airlines Compete,'' *Europe,* November 1997, pp. 39–40.
''Case Study: Austrian Airlines,'' *East European Markets,* August 2, 1996.
Feldman, Joan M., ''Strength in Numbers,'' *Air Transport World,* July 1997, pp. 161–63.

''Four-Airline European Cooperative Alliance Sets Its Sights on Eastern European Market,'' *Aviation Week & Space Technology,* May 14, 1990, pp. 95+.

Goldsmith, Charles, and Margaret Studer, ''Swissair, Sabena, Austrian Airlines Will Buy Jets—Joint-Fleet Purchase Marks Extensive Collaboration; Delta Will Participate,'' *Wall Street Journal,* December 20, 1996, p. 9A.

Hill, Leonard, '' 'Grand Prix' Airline,'' *Air Transport World,* July 1997, pp. 165–67.

——, ''Up from the Fiscal Brink,'' *Air Transport World,* February 1996, pp. 80+.

Norden, Walter, *Flieg mit uns: Reportage vom Werden und Wirkden der österreichischen Luftverkehrsgesellschaft Austrian Airlines,* Vienna and Munich: Verlag für Jugend und Volk, 1965.

O'Connor, Anthony, ''Austria's Airline Evolution,'' *Airfinance Journal,* October 1997, pp. 24–27.

Reed, Arthur, ''The Tumbling of Alcazar,'' *Air Transport World,* January 1994, pp. 33+.

—Frederick C. Ingram

AVA AG (Allgemeine Handelsgesellschaft der Verbraucher AG)

Fuggerstrasse 11
D-33689 Bielefeld
Germany
Telephone: (49)(5205) 94-01
Fax: (49)(5205) 94-1029
Web site: http://www.ava.de

Public Company
Incorporated: 1892
Employees: 27,704
Sales: DM 9.78 billion ($5.85 billion) (1998)
Stock Exchanges: Frankfurt/Main Düsseldorf
Ticker Symbol: AVA
NAIC: 5411 Grocery Stores; 5311 Department Stores;
    5231 Paint, Glass And Wallpaper Stores; 5995 Opti-
    cal Goods Stores; 5499 Miscellaneous Food Stores

Active throughout Germany and in the Netherlands, AVA AG (Allgemeine Handelsgesellschaft der Verbraucher AG) is one of Germany's leading retailers. Concentrating on large shopping facilities, AVA operates 110 Marktkauf discount department stores; 50 dixi hypermarket stores offering groceries, textiles, and other products; and 95 do-it-yourself outlets in Germany and nine in the Netherlands. AVA also holds a majority share in Delta Hauser Baumarkt GmbH & Co. KG, another do-it-yourself chain with 24 outlets. The company's Krane optical chain with 83 shops is Germany's third-largest optician in sales, while its real estate subsidiary, CEV, manages 14 large shopping centers under non-AVA brand names, four of which it owns. Since 1982, AVA has cooperated with the German Edeka Group, a food wholesaler and retailer, in purchasing. Their combined demand makes them Germany's largest food purchaser. With 49.9 percent of its stock, Edeka is also AVA's single largest shareholder.

Born Out of Hardship in 1892

The end of the war between Germany and France in 1870–71 brought about an economic boom, based on a united German Empire under chancellor Otto von Bismarck and fueled by French reparation payments in the billions. Bielefeld, a blue collar industrial town in the Ruhr, where many new enterprises of various kinds were founded, became a magnet for job-seekers. However, most of the workers were struggling at subsistence level. When a shortage of potato supplies in Bielefeld in 1891 pushed the price of 100 pounds to half a week's wages, a few workers collectively purchased the essential food for ''normal'' prices in Saxony. This endeavor was so successful that the workers soon included other foodstuffs into their combined orders. On January 17, 1892 a meeting was held to found the Bielefelder Konsum Verein, a limited liability cooperative. Each of the 35 founding members invested about a week's wages. The management board consisted mainly of locksmiths, carpenters, and foremen. The first warehouse was established in a former bowling alley, and the first piece of office furniture was a large crate.

Nine months later the Bielefelder Konsum Verein had 716 members, and management decided to establish six distribution centers, to hire a business manager, and to buy a cart. By 1893 the cooperative was renting a new warehouse and totaled 971 members. After a period of sluggish growth, sales increased three-fold between 1892 and 1896, and the cooperative was able to afford its own sleigh. In spring 1898 the Bielefelder Konsum Verein purchased a plot of land and moved into a newly built warehouse.

In 1903 the Bielefelder Konsum Verein passed the one million mark in sales mark. It purchased the neighboring plot of land and was able to afford the salary for a second manager. Over the next couple of years, other parcels of land were acquired to extend the business, and a third manager was added to the payroll. In 1909 the cooperative opened its own bakery and added production to its purchasing business. The new bakery was a hit and had to be enlarged after only a few weeks. A second large bakery was opened the following year.

Around 1900 consumption-cooperatives were on an upswing throughout Germany. They were organized under two umbrella organizations: the Zentralverband Deutscher Konsum-

Vereine and the Reichsverband Deutscher Konsum-Vereine. In addition to purchasing and distributing food and other products, their central purchasing organizations began in 1910 to offer their own products and services. They established bakeries, butcheries, and shoe repair workshops. They also produced pasta, canned foods, matches, soap, laundry detergent and cigars in their own factories. Moreover, they offered savings accounts and insurance contracts. The Bielefelder Konsum Verein even entered the real estate development market in 1913 when it started building two shops and 69 apartments for workers. In that year, the cooperative had 17,200 members and generated millions in sales.

Wars and Crises Bring More Hardship Until 1945

The outbreak of World War I in 1914 interrupted the economic upswing in Germany, and made day-to-day business increasingly difficult for the Bielefelder Konsum Verein. With prices going up and more and more products being rationed, a rising number of people joined the co-op, where only members were allowed to shop. At the same time, the operating environment for the organization became more restrictive. All wholesale was under government control, and the shops of the Bielefelder Konsum Verein were only able to sell what they received; private initiative was impossible. Margarine was scarce, there was only one kind of sausage available, and cheese was just a rumor. In 1918, the last year of the war, only a few products were freely available, and over the four previous years the price of basic foodstuffs had doubled. Between August and November 1918, the German authorities even decreed four meatless weeks. Moreover, the Bielefelder Konsum Verein's bakery had problems getting coal for their oven. Nevertheless, its membership reached 23,700 in the same year, up by more than one-third in comparison to the last prewar year.

The 1920s were even more challenging. The German government fought the heavy debt caused by the war and the reparations it was obliged to pay by printing new money. In 1920 the German currency was only worth one-tenth of the prewar value and by the summer of 1922 it was only worth one-hundredth. In 1923, the peak year of hyperinflation, an American dollar was worth 4.2 billion German Marks. A coachman of the Bielefelder Konsum Verein recalled that his coach was just as packed on his way back from the stores as it was before he had made his deliveries; instead of sugar, the sacks he carried contained bank notes. In order to bring all the money to the bank as soon as possible, he always pushed his horse to its limits. Even after the new Reichsmark replaced the old currency, customers continued to pay with the old money, while suppliers demanded the new currency. This resulted in losses of up to 50 percent for the Bielefelder Konsum Verein.

Membership of the consumer cooperatives jumped to new heights during these years. Although worker's wages were only two-thirds of the prewar level, and prices began rising again in October 1924, the Bielefelder Konsum Verein's bakery thrived. Fine baked goods for Sunday were the most sought after. Within one year the number of employees at the bakery jumped from six to 23. The cooperative also invested in better equipment for its coffee roaster and upgraded to a better quality of coffee. Despite another serious downturn in the local economy, the firm broadened its product line, including more household goods. It also invested heavily in store design to attract better clientele and opened a large store that successfully combined formerly separate stores, such as the bakery, the butcher shop, and the household store.

By 1930 consumer cooperatives accounted for 15 percent of the German food market. The Bielefelder Konsum Verein totaled 24,000 members that year. The depression following the 1929 crash of the stock market in New York created economic hardship in Germany. Moreover, there were other dark clouds onto the horizon as well. As mass unemployment rose, the Nazis began winning acceptance in Germany, and the party considered consumer cooperatives as Marxist, making it clear from the very beginning that there was no place for such organizations in their plans. Backed by small merchants who felt threatened by the new competitors, the Nazis, having gained political power in 1933, began to systematically destroy the Konsum system. The liquidation was executed in three steps. The Nazi threat began with anti-Konsum propaganda and violent terror; they distributed flyers requesting Konsum members to withdraw their memberships and savings, they arrested Konsum managers, and they vandalized stores. In the second step, they enacted new laws that merged the two umbrella organizations into one, forbade any promotional campaigns, and forbade the opening of any new stores. Finally, they enacted a law that obliged the Konsum cooperatives to pay all savings deposits back to their members by 1940. The Bielefelder Konsum Verein, like many other of its kind, went bankrupt, and its stores were privatized. Finally, in February 1941, a new law was enacted on the "adjustment of all Konsum cooperatives to war conditions" which served as the legal basis to abolish the surviving 1,200 cooperatives with their three million members and 12,000 stores.

Growth of Welfare Society Begins in 1948

After World War II was over the Konsum cooperatives once again emerged out of a hardship caused by postwar scarcity of literally everything, in particular food. As early as September 1946 the new Konsumgenossenschaft Bielefeld was officially registered. The newly founded business was able to attract 7,000 members by the end of 1947. Only five years later its number had again more than tripled. Almost ten years after the war ended, in 1954, the military government of the Western Allies gave the property that the Nazis had confiscated back to the Konsum cooperatives.

The beginning of the 1950s marked an unprecedented economic boom in Germany's history in which the Konsum cooperatives participated to a very great extent. Sales at the Bielefelder Konsumgenossenschaft increased almost ten-fold between 1947 and 1962. At the same time the cooperatives

Key Dates:

1892: 35 workers found the Bielefelder Konsum-Verein.
1909: Konsum Verein opens the first bakery of its own.
1930: Cooperative reaches a record 24,000 members.
1941: Konsum Verein goes bankrupt under Nazi pressure.
1946: Konsumgenossenschaft Bielefeld officially registered.
1954: Western Allies return property to the Konsum cooperatives; a new law allows co-ops to sell goods to non-members.
1965: Four Konsum cooperatives merge to become the Konsumgenossenschaft Ostwestfalen.
1975: The Allgemeine Handelsgesellschaft der Verbraucher AG (AVA) begins operations.
1986: AVA's stock trades on the Dusseldorf stock market.
1993: Edeka Zentrale AG becomes AVA's biggest shareholder.
1998: AVA sells all of its supermarket operations.

faced new challenges. While a new law enacted in 1954 allowed them to sell their goods to non-members, they found themselves competing for the same customers as the growing number of retail and food chains, department stores, and large supermarkets. Only consolidation enabled the cooperatives to survive. In 1956 the Bielefelder Konsumverein agreed to merge with the Bielefelder Haushaltsverein, another Bielefeld cooperative that was first founded in 1903.

In the mid-1950s, a novelty changed the retail business: self service. The idea, originating in the United States, soon won over German customers. The Bielefelder Konsumverein opened three self-service stores in 1957. Six years later these outnumbered the ''old-fashioned'' stores and were contributing 72 percent of all sales. Because the availability of goods at affordable prices was no longer an issue, another American concept— marketing—became more important. The central purchasing organization for all Konsum co-ops ventured into catalogue sales. In rural locations stores were enlarged and carried textiles and furniture. Beginning in 1962 the Bielefelder Konsumverein offered holidays trips to Italy, Spain, and other European countries. A member newsletter, fashion shows, and special events for homemakers or kids were organized to keep customers loyal and happy. Under a new cash-bonus system, members received bonus stamps with every purchase they made, put them in a booklet, and brought them to the Konsum store once a year to receive cash incentives. The same law that allowed the cooperatives to sell to non-members also restricted those reimbursements to three percent, so a Konsum member received between DM50 and DM200 on the average.

The Rise of Discounters Begins Around 1965

The advent of discount stores shook the German retail market in the mid-1960s. Offering a very narrow product line, discount markets lured customers with their extraordinarily low prices. Outside cities, but easy to reach by car, huge self-service outlets set up shop, offering a broad range of goods, including food, textiles, household goods, electric appliances, and auto-

mobile supplies at attractive prices. With competition becoming tougher, the Konsum cooperatives were under pressure to streamline their business. Smaller co-ops merged into bigger ones; smaller stores were closed, and new large stores opened.

In 1965 GEG, the Konsum's central purchasing organization, took over 56 supermarkets from the German retailer Eklöh GmbH. Eight of them were located in Bielefeld and the nearby cities Bunde-Lubbeke, Herford, and Guetersloh. The takeover caused major logistical problems for the Konsum cooperatives in those towns since none of them was able to keep their new stores stocked, and the new stores had begun to draw large numbers of shoppers. For this reason, the four Konsum cooperatives eventually merged into the Konsumgenossenschaft Ostwestfalen. The new company had almost 60,000 members, operated 209 stores and generated about DM 75 million in sales.

The new co-op Ostwestfalen invested heavily in building large supermarkets, streamlining purchasing, logistics, and marketing, as well as in a new central warehouse. In summer 1970 it merged with the co-op Lage into the co-op Ostwestfalen-Lippe eG. Between 1964 and 1974 the number of store locations shrunk from about 200 to 75, while sales skyrocketed to DM 250 million during the same period. This success was driven by the Marktkauf GmbH, a newly founded subsidiary of the co-op Ostwestfalen-Lippe, which specialized in large discount department stores. The six Marktkauf stores alone contributed almost 40 percent of total sales, while 78 co-op markets and another department store accounted for the other 60 percent.

In 1972 a new umbrella organization was founded. The co-op, Zentral AG aimed at merging all Konsum cooperatives into 20 large regional companies which were to go public by 1974. However, the representatives of the co-op Ostwestfalen-Lippe decided to remain independent and transformed their business into a public company.

A Modern National Retail Group Is Born in 1975

On January 4, 1975 the Allgemeine Handelsgesellschaft der Verbraucher (AVA) started operations. One quarter of the shares issued by the company were purchased by AVA employees. To ensure the company's independence, voting rights were limited to one-thousandth of the total share capital. The new player in the German retail market took off at an impressive speed. Only ten years after its founding, AVA's sales had grown fivefold and its profits six-fold. The company's workforce tripled, and the Verkaufsfläche was five times the size in 1985 as it had been ten years ealier. On August 21, 1986 the company's shares were for the first time publicly traded at the Dusseldorf stock market.

The fall of the Berlin Wall in 1989 and the introduction of the Deutschmark in East Germany in 1990 suddenly enlarged AVA's market. In September 1990 the first Marktkauf do-it-yourself outlet opened in the East German city of Greifswald. Two years later a brand-new logistics center was opened in the East German town Zarrentin. By 1992 the AVA was among the ten top German grocery chain operators, generating DM 320 million in sales. In 1993 one-fourth of AVA's sales floor space was located in the former East Germany.

The unexpected boom that the German reunification brought to German retailers faded away in the mid-1990s. Consumer spending dropped, caused by falling real wages, rising unemployment, and taxes, as well as by the Germans' rising skepticism about the future. Another factor that contributed to declining grocery sales was the growing concern about food quality in connection with several scandals including adulterating wines, hormones in meat and milk products, poisoning of certain brand products by blackmailers, and, more recently, dioxin-polluted chicken food and genetically engineered farm products. AVA fought falling sales by concentrating on large shopping facilities, strong communication concepts, and enlarging their network of shops. In October 1993 the company bought a 25 percent share in the Stuttgart-based Nanz Group with 11,000 employees and DM 2.8 billion in sales, as well as shares in two other former Konsum co-ops in western and southern Germany. In the same year the German grocery wholesaler and retailer Edeka Zentrale AG purchased 49.9 percent of AVA's share capital and became its single largest shareholder.

The late 1990s did not bring the awaited consumer upswing. Although better off than other retailers, AVAs shareholders did not receive any dividends between 1995 and 1997. In 1998 the AVA management decided to institute rigorous reorganization program. It refocused AVA on it's core business: large discount department stores, hypermarket stores, and 95 do-it-yourself outlets. It had sold all its supermarkets and shareholdings in other supermarket chains by mid-1998. It consolidated and integrated all large stores of the former Nanz group, and introduced its own brand for a line of 650 products, mainly food, in the lower price range. By the end of 1999 AVA took over the German do-it-yourself chain Delta Hauser Baumarkt GmbH & Co. KG from the Lidl & Schwarz group with 24 outlets and DM520 million in sales. In the same year company sold its nine do-it-yourself outlets in the Netherlands, but was planning to extend its activities in this market segment in the year 2000.

Principal Subsidiaries

Marktkauf Handelsgesellschaft mbH & Co. OHG; dixi Discount Handelsgesellschaft mbH; AVA-Baumarkt-Division; GHD GmbH; FG Frischwaren GmbH; Krane Optik und Akustik GmbH & Co. Betriebs KG (75%); Delta Hauser Baumarkt GmbH & Co. KG (51%); GDR Gesellschaft für Datenverarbeitung und Rechnungswesen mbH; CEV Center Entwicklungs- und Verwaltungs-GmbH; Marktkauf Süd GmbH & Co. Handelsgesellschaft OHG (59.5%); Marktkauf Süd-West Handels-GmbH + Co. Verbraucherhmärkte (59.9%); Marktkauf Ost Handelsgesellschaft mbH & Co. SB-Warenhaus OHG (59.9%); EZA Einkaufszentrum für Alle GmbH & Co. KG (59.9%); AVA Immobilien und Anlage GmbH Betriebs-KG (94%); KAUFMARKT Vermietungs- und Verpachtungsgesellschaft mbH; AVA-Beteiligungs-GmbH & Co. OHG.

Principal Competitors

ALDI Group; Metro AG; Tengelmann Group.

Further Reading

"AVA-Baumärkte expandieren," *Der Tagesspiegel*, December 28, 1999.
"AVA im Aufwind," *Westfalen-Blatt*, January 14, 2000.
"AVA kehrt zu früherer Ertragskraft zurück," *Frankfurter Allgemeine Zeitung*, January 14, 2000.
"AVA steuerte 1999 auf Wachstumskurs," *Handelsblatt*, January 14, 2000.
"AVA verleibt sich Hauser-Baumärkte ganz ein," *Lebensmittel-Zeitung*, December 30, 1999.
Wandel bedeutet Zukunft, Bielefeld, Germany: AVA Allgemeine Handelsgesellschaft der Verbraucher AG, 1992, 71 p.

—Evelyn Hauser

BAA plc

130 Wilton Road
London SW1V 1LQ
United Kingdom
Telephone: (44) 171-834-9449
Fax: (44) 171-932-6699
Web site: http://www.baa.co.uk

Public Company
Incorporated: 1987
Employees: 12,724
Sales: £2.01 billion ($3.16 billion) (1999)
Stock Exchanges: London
Ticker Symbol: BAAPY
NAIC: 488119 Other Airport Operations; 23311 Land
    Subdivision and Land Development; 485112
    Commuter Rail Systems; 45322 Gift, Novelty, and
    Souvenir Stores

BAA plc is a holding company for the world's largest organization of airports. BAA owns and operates seven major airports in the United Kingdom—Heathrow, Gatwick, Stansted, Glasgow, Edinburgh, Aberdeen, and Southampton. Originating as a government-owned enterprise known as the British Airports Authority, BAA became a private company in 1987 and has achieved a position of preeminence in airport development in the United Kingdom and around the world. BAA also provides management services for eight airports around the globe, including airports in the United States, Australia, Italy, and Mauritius. The company's retail services division, which includes restaurants and stores in airports, contributes more than half of BAA's annual revenues. BAA also is involved in property development.

Government Control: 1919–87

Great Britain's commercial airline industry began in 1919, when the Department of Civil Aviation was established as a division of the government's Air Ministry. When foreign competition nearly forced most British airlines out of business in 1921, the government provided temporary financial relief, and two years later, the Civil Air Transport Subsidies Committee was established to investigate long-term solutions to the airlines' economic struggles. The result was the 1924 formation of the government-owned and operated Imperial Airways, the first in a long line of British airlines under state ownership.

Although World War II brought a halt to commercial aviation, wartime aeronautical developments left the industry poised for advancement when hostilities ceased. Under the post-war Labour government, the expanding industry consisted of three state-run airways corporations: British Overseas Airways Corporation (serving the Commonwealth, North America, and the Far East), British European Airways (covering domestic and short European flights), and British South American Airways. Air traffic control facilities and the airports under development at this time also were run by the state.

Expansion in the industry was inevitable and remarkably swift during the 1950s, as air travel became a popular means of transportation. Faced with increasing numbers of passengers and technological developments in commercial aircraft, British airports strove to provide efficient, smoothly running, and attractive facilities that would lure the business of the country's most successful airlines.

As the boom in air transport continued into the 1960s, the burden of maintaining a network of state-of-the-art airports proved too complex and cumbersome a task for the government, and British airports began losing money. In 1965, the British government passed the Airports Authority Bill, which created a single statutory body to own and oversee operations of the country's airports while remaining answerable to Parliament. The following year, the new British Airports Authority officially took control of Heathrow, Gatwick, Stansted, and Prestwick. Under the direction of Chairperson Peter Masefield, the British Airports Authority transformed the industry from a bureaucratic operation, similar to that of a public utility, into a profitable semi-independent business.

Rapid Growth and New Challenges Following Privatization: Early 1990s

During the 1970s and early 1980s, airport profits rose dramatically and a program of expansion and refurbishment was undertaken. In fact, the industry's increasing success prompted the Conservative government to consider the Authority a prime candidate for a privatization program it was planning for some of the country's industries. Toward this end, the Airports Act of 1986 permitted the creation of a new company, BAA plc, a public holding company for airports. The ensuing advertising campaign for BAA stock was designed to appeal to a wide variety of investors. In one publicity stunt, the company hired people to dress up as Harry Heathrow—a teddy bear character created especially for the promotion—and carry placards around airport terminals advertising BAA's initial stock offering price of 245 pence per share. With nearly two and a half million applications, the stock was oversubscribed ten times and the flotation—on July 16, 1987—was a resounding success. BAA fared well since its public offering. From 1987 to 1993, passenger numbers increased by 42 percent, BAA's share price more than tripled, and profits increased by 130 percent.

Among BAA's established operations during this time, none rivaled the rapid growth and success of London's premier airport, Heathrow. Originally envisioned as a ring of city airports, the "London Airport—Heath Row" was planned during the war and opened in 1946. At that time, tents served as Heathrow's terminals, while its offices were set up in vans. Eventually a more substantial terminal, the North Side Terminal, was established and remained in use through the 1950s, when it was replaced by the Europa terminal, later known as Terminal 2. The Heathrow Oceanic terminal (which became Terminal 3) opened in 1961, followed by two more terminals in 1968 and 1986.

By the 1990s, Heathrow was the world's busiest international airport. During this time, BAA proposed construction of a third runway at Heathrow. Whereas airlines welcomed the idea of expanded facilities, local residents and environmental groups, including the Federation of Heathrow Anti-Noise Groups, were strongly opposed to the plan, which would have involved the demolition of some 3,500 homes in surrounding villages. In the face of such protests, BAA withdrew the proposal in May 1994. Similarly, BAA's plan to build a fifth terminal at Heathrow met with opposition. The terminal, expected to increase Heathrow's annual passenger capacity from 50 million in the early 1990s to 80 million by 2013, was criticized as involving further noise pollution and traffic jams in the area. BAA argued, however, that new aircraft technology, including the development of larger aircraft, would allow more passengers without necessitating more planes and increased noise levels.

Although some remained skeptical of BAA's promises, the company maintained that it was simply planning to ensure that London's airports remained adequately equipped to keep up with increasing demand. With 30 percent of Heathrow's business consisting of connecting flights, rather than final destina-

tions, BAA faced the potential threat of competition in this sector from airports in Amsterdam, Brussels, Paris, and Frankfurt, which were poised to accommodate customers. Public inquiry into the feasibility of BAA's fifth terminal was set to begin at the end of 1994; construction was not expected to be completed before the 21st century if at all. Nevertheless, BAA continued to expand services at Heathrow and worked on the construction of a new flight connection center in the mid-1990s.

The second largest BAA airport servicing the London area was Gatwick, located 27 miles south of the city. During the late 1940s and early 1950s, Gatwick was known primarily as an airport for charter flights or as an alternative in the event of bad weather at Heathrow. Major reconstruction completed in 1956, however, helped Gatwick develop into a popular international flight destination. Plans to purchase more land and add a second runway to Gatwick stalled in 1979, when the British Airports Authority agreed with the West Sussex County Council that it would not pursue expansion for 40 years.

When Stansted Airport, established in the London area in the 1940s, was designated for expansion in 1967, strong local opposition forced the Authority to relocate Stansted off the Essex coast, in Maplin Sands. In the early 1970s, plans for expansion at this site also were abandoned, when the oil crises and economic recession prompted predictions of declines in passenger volume. By the late 1970s, however, increasing air traffic was inevitable and the expansion of Stansted seemed imminent, particularly since competition from nearby foreign airports, especially in Amsterdam, had intensified.

Again, the Authority found itself embroiled in a lengthy public debate of the issue. In addition to environmentalist objections to the expansion, several airlines, including British Airways, protested the move, preferring their existing arrangements at Heathrow and Gatwick. Moreover, another interest group, the North of England Regional Consortium, representing northern regional airports and local authorities, lobbied to fill the growing market by developing provincial facilities rather than expanding Stansted. In 1985, a compromise was reached under which Stansted would undergo development in phases monitored by Parliament.

Despite its ambitious $400 million redevelopment program, which garnered numerous awards for architecture, environmental sensitivity, and marketing, Stansted did not meet expectations for increased capacity and profits. In fact, in 1993, American Airlines withdrew its services from Stansted, and the airport reported heavy losses. During this time, Stansted's direct competitor, Luton, claimed that BAA was unfairly subsidizing Stansted from profits derived from Heathrow, creating artificially low prices in an effort to attract customers.

In addition to its London airports, BAA also acquired facilities in Scotland, including airports at Prestwick, Edinburgh, Glasgow, and Aberdeen, during the 1960s and 1970s. Until 1990, Prestwick was the only Scottish airport allowed to accommodate transatlantic flights. Then, under the government's new "open skies" policy, several airlines began gravitating toward the more popular sites of Glasgow and Edinburgh, boosting profits at these airports and prompting BAA to sell the relatively unprofitable Prestwick airport. Although BAA's Scottish airports service significantly fewer passengers than its London airports, the growth rate for Scotland's air travel industry surpassed that of London in 1993. Thus BAA expected its Scottish airports to play an increasingly more prominent role in U.K. commercial aviation.

Although a healthy percentage of BAA's profits reflected fees levied on the airlines that used its airports, the bulk of BAA's profits during the early 1990s was generated from an auxiliary enterprise: retail sales. Attracting many large retailers and caterers, BAA established vast shopping complexes at its airports, which featured outlets for Harrods, Yves St. Laurent, Burberry's, The Body Shop, Cartier, McDonald's, Burger King, and several others. Retail profits also were bolstered by companies providing car rental and parking lot operations.

Unlike most commercial operations, BAA's retail sales were unaffected, in large part, by the economic recession of the early 1990s. In fact, while retail chains across the nation suffered losses, their airport branches reported healthy profits. Analysts suggested two reasons for this surprising statistic: many shoppers at airport stores were from foreign countries mostly unaffected by the recession, and air travelers on the whole were likely to have more disposable income than the average consumer. To offset expected retail losses beginning in 1999, when Europeans would no longer be able to purchase duty-free goods, BAA increased retail space in its London airports by 50 percent between 1992 and 1994. Restaurant operations at the airports also were expanded and diversified. The phenomenal success of BAA's airport shopping facilities prompted its mid-1990s joint venture with the U.S.-based McArthur Glen Realty to develop and operate outlet malls—where manufacturers sell directly to the public—in the United Kingdom and Europe.

An acknowledged expert in the industry, BAA increasingly put its experience to use in a variety of consultancy roles. In 1992 the company won a contract from the Greater Pittsburgh International Airport to develop and operate that airport's shops and restaurants. Moreover, as a designer of modern facilities known for their efficiency as well as their aesthetic merit, BAA secured several consulting contracts throughout the United Kingdom, Australia, Japan, Mexico, Hungary, St. Lucia, and the Bahamas and played a prominent role in the planning of new airports in Hong Kong and Kuala Lumpur. Forecasting, engineering, computing, and market research were among the other skills that BAA offered its clients.

In response to increasing public concern for the environment, BAA created an Environment Department to address issues surrounding the airline industry's role in noise pollution, air quality, water quality, and wildlife preservation. The company published a policy statement, affirming its commitment to environmental conservation, and began the annual publication of a report on its performance in these areas. In the mid-1990s, BAA explored options to acquire equity stakes in airports around the world. Despite the strength of its retail and consultancy operations, BAA's commitment to this core business was evidenced by its plans to continue refurbishing and upgrading its airport facilities.

International Expansion and a Changing European Climate: Late 1990s

To prepare for the impending end of duty-free shopping in Europe, BAA focused on expanding its international retail operations in the late 1990s. In 1996 the company acquired Allders International, the international duty- and tax-free business of Allders plc, for about £130 million. Allders International operated stores in the United States, Europe, Canada, and Australia. The majority of its shops were located at airports, on cruise ships and ferries, at border crossings, and in city centers. BAA added to its duty-free holdings in 1997 with the acquisition of Duty Free International, based in the United States. A year later the company integrated its international duty-free operations and formed World Duty Free plc, a holding company. Duty Free International was renamed World Duty Free Americas Inc., and the U.K. operations were renamed World Duty Free Europe Limited. A new World Duty Free flagship store was opened in Heathrow Airport's Terminal 3 in 1998, and the company continued to open new stores and introduce new concepts, including a specialty wine store, cigar store, and watch store. By the late 1990s World Duty Free was the global leader of the $20 billion duty-free market, with a five percent share. European operations consisted of more than 70 airport stores, U.S. operations had more than 160 stores at airports and border crossings, and World Duty Free Inflight offered duty-free products on 28 airlines.

The duty-free operations made up only a portion of BAA's retail activities, however, and the company strove to grow its commercial businesses around the world. In 1998 the company secured a new contract to operate the retail, food, and beverage operations in two terminals at Newark Airport in the United States. In March 1999 BAA signed a 15-year contract with Eurotunnel to operate the retail facilities in terminals at Folkestone and Calais/Coquelles. In 1998 about 13 million people traveled through these two terminals.

Not only did BAA operate retail concessions and duty-free shops, but the company also, through joint venture BAA McArthurGlen, developed and operated designer outlet centers in Europe. In fiscal 1999, which ended March 31, 1999, BAA opened four new centers to push its total number to seven. Plans to open an additional four centers in 2000 and 2001 were under way as well. The partnership also sold interests in three centers in 1998 and 1999. Total retail revenue, including duty-free operations and concession and retail elements, reached £1,033 million in fiscal 1999, an impressive 17.8 percent increase over 1998 sales, which were £877 million. Of the total, 43 percent came from airport retail operations and 47 percent from duty-free businesses.

First and foremost, BAA was known for its airports, and the company continued to strengthen its airport operations in the late 1990s. According to BAA, 112.5 million travelers passed through its U.K. airports during fiscal 1999, a 7.6 percent increase over the previous year. With traffic projected to continue increasing, BAA invested time and money into developing efficient, safe, and exciting facilities. During fiscal 1999 alone the company spent £512 million to improve and expand current facilities. Traffic at Stansted increased by 35.4 percent, making it the fourth busiest airport in Britain. BAA opened a new international satellite building at Stansted in early 1999 and planned to invest more than £200 million over a five-year period to increase the airport's capacity. BAA's other airports enjoyed increased traffic as well. Gatwick saw about 30 million passengers, an 8.1 percent rise over 1998, and BAA's three Scottish airports enjoyed an increase in traffic of six percent, to 13.8 million travelers. Heathrow also served more passengers—61 million, a rise of 4.9 percent. To accommodate more travelers, BAA sought to expand capacity at Heathrow. Its plans for Terminal 5 met with opposition from the middle to late 1990s, and in March 1999 the public inquiry ended. The fate of Terminal 5 then went into the hands of the British government, which was expected to provide a decision in 2000 or 2001.

BAA's airport operations were given a significant boost in June 1998 when the Heathrow Express was unveiled. Owned and operated by BAA, the Express provided rail service from London's Paddington Station to Heathrow Airport, offering a convenient alternative to road travel to Heathrow. The trains traveled at speeds of up to 100 miles per hour. In other airport matters, BAA's property development arm, BAA Lynton, chose to focus more closely on airport-related properties and thus planned to sell its nonairport-related investments by the end of fiscal 2000. BAA Lynton worked on three developments at Heathrow in 1998, constructed an office building at Stansted, and finished a cargo warehouse at Glasgow.

Despite healthy revenues and continued growth, BAA hit a snag when duty- and tax-free sales in the European Union ended on June 30, 1999. Although BAA was committed to maintaining the duty- and tax-free prices for European travelers, sales dropped more severely than expected; BAA attributed the decline to confusion about the new rules—although only tobacco and alcohol sales were affected, many travelers believed the rules applied to other products as well, thus impacting their shopping decisions. In addition, BAA's duty-free operations in the United States continued to underperform. BAA blamed the poor performance on major renovations of several large U.S. airports and the decline in the number of border crossings in North America. For the first half of fiscal 2000, BAA's duty-free operations reported a £1 million operating loss. The company also announced that overall pretax profit before exceptional items for fiscal 2000 would probably be at least £30 million below the market forecast of £505 million. As a result

of the October 1999 announcement, BAA shares fell more than 17 percent.

In October 1999 Sir John Egan, chief executive since 1990, retired and Mike Hodgkinson became the new CEO. Though BAA faced new challenges and difficult conditions, Hodgkinson remained optimistic about BAA's future. To educate travelers about the new duty-free rules, BAA launched a marketing campaign, coupled with sales campaigns at airports. Passenger traffic at BAA's airports increased 5.1 percent during the first half of fiscal 2000, and duty-free sales seemed to have slowed and reversed its downward spiral.

At the turn of the century, BAA remained committed as ever to the business of operating airports and specializing in travel retail operations. The company planned to continue growing its international presence and perhaps exploring new ventures— talk of privatizing Britain's air traffic control services led many to speculate on whether BAA would become involved. As a dominant force in worldwide airport operations, BAA worked to realize its avowed goal of becoming "the most successful airport company in the world."

Principal Subsidiaries

Heathrow Airport Limited; Aberdeen Airport Limited; Southampton International Airport Limited; Edinburgh Airport Limited; Gatwick Airport Limited; Glasgow Airport Limited; Stansted Airport Limited; World Duty Free plc; World Duty Free Europe Limited; World Duty Free Americas, Inc.; BAA Lynton; BAA McArthurGlen Europe Limited (50%); BAA McArthurGlen UK Holdings Limited (50%); Cheshire Oaks Limited (12.5%); BAA McArthurGlen Europe S.A. (50%; Belgium).

Principal Competitors

Lockheed Martin Corporation; National Express Group PLC; Serco Group plc.

Further Reading

"BAA Shares Dive 17% on Profit Warning," *Wall Street Journal Europe,* October 4, 1999, p. 7.

"Blue Skies Ahead for BAA," *Investors Chronicle,* March 12,1993.

Boschat, Nathalie, "BAA Shares Rise as Sales Stop Sliding," *Wall Street Journal Europe,* November 2, 1999, p. 8.

Davies, Peter, "Letter to the Editor," *The Times,* May 19, 1994, p. 17.

Donne, Michael, *Above Us the Skies: The Story of BAA,* London: BAA plc, 1991.

"Duty Free Heads for the Stratosphere," *Evening Standard,* March 1, 1994.

Elliott, Harvey, "BAA Abandons Third Runway for Heathrow," *The Times,* May 16, 1994, pp. 1–2.

Gribben, Roland, "BAA Warns of Further 'Hit' on Duty-Free," *Daily Telegraph,* November 2, 1999.

Harper, Keith, "The Man of His People: Mike Hodgkinson, Chief Executive, BAA," *Guardian,* October 30, 1999.

Kay, William, "Ground Control Charts Way for Airport Boss" (interview with Sir John Egan), *Independent on Sunday,* November 21, 1993.

King, John, and Geoffrey Tait, *Golden Gatwick: 50 Years of Aviation,* London: The Royal Aeronautical Society Gatwick Branch and the British Airports Authority, 1980.

"Luton Accuses BAA of Predatory Airport Pricing," *Financial Times,* June 5, 1993.

"Nowhere To Land," *Economist,* August 14, 1993.

"Protests Greet Heathrow Scheme for Fifth Terminal," *Independent,* February 18, 1993.

"Special Report on Airports UK: Can the Plane Take the Strain?," *Evening Standard,* March 14, 1994.

"Special Report on Airports UK: Shops Strike it Rich," *Evening Standard,* March 14, 1994.

"Special Report on Airports UK: Why We Must Have Terminal Five," *Evening Standard,* March 14, 1994.

"The Terminal?," *Evening Standard,* June 21, 1993.

—Robin DuBlanc
—updated by Mariko Fujinaka

Bashas'

Bashas' Inc.

22402 South Basha Road
Chandler, Arizona 85248
U.S.A.
Telephone: (480) 895-9350
Fax: (480) 895-1206
Web site: http://www.bashas.com

Private Company
Incorporated: 1932
Employees: 7,600
Sales: $1 billion (1998 est.)
NAIC: 44511 Supermarkets and Other Grocery (Except Convenience) Stores; 45291 Warehouse Clubs and Superstores

Bashas' Inc. operates several chains of supermarkets and superstores under the banners Mercado, Food City, Bashas' Markets, AJ's Fines Foods, and Eddie's Country Stores. Bashas' stores are scattered throughout Arizona, California, and New Mexico, but the majority are located in Arizona, where one-third of the 100 stores operate in the Phoenix area. The company also has six supermarkets operating in the Navajo Nation. Two of the company's supermarket formats, Mercado and Food City, are geared for Hispanic communities. AJ's Fine Foods touts itself as gourmet and specialty supermarket, featuring extensive wine collections and prepared meals. Bashas' also operates an online grocery-shopping operation through its Groceries On The Go service. The Basha family, who founded the chain in 1932, own the company.

Origins: From Lebanon to Arizona

Owing to its standing as a family-run business, Bashas' corporate roots stretch back to the arrival of the first Basha family member to the United States in the 19th century. In 1884, Tanius Basha left Lebanon for New York City, where he opened an import and export wholesale store. Two years later, after his entrepreneurial efforts had shown promise, Tanius sent for his oldest son to come to New York to help him with his store. Najeeb Basha, 16 years old when he arrived in New York

to assist his father, made the city his new home and mercantilism his new profession. In 1901, he married a fellow Lebanese immigrant named Najeeby Srour, and together the pair began raising a family from whose ranks Bashas' would be founded. Najeeby gave birth to nine children, all girls except for two boys, Ike and Eddie: the founders of Bashas' Inc.

Ike and Eddie Basha spent their childhood surrounded by the mores of retail trade. Their father left New York in 1910 to join several members of the Srour family in Ray, Arizona. There, Najeeb assisted his in-laws in the operation of a mercantile business. After a stint working for his wife's family, Najeeb was joined by his wife and children in Arizona and opened his own store. The store later burned down, prompting Najeeb to open a second store during the 1920s, by which time his children, Ike and Eddie included, were old enough to lend a hand in the family business. The store, located in Chandler, Arizona, catered to the rural needs of its community, selling groceries, dry goods, and household goods such as furniture.

The Bashas' Chain Begins with One Store in 1932

Ike and Eddie Basha learned the retail trade from their parents at the Chandler store, eventually deciding to enter the business themselves when they were old enough to set out on their own. They opened their own store in 1932, marking the beginning of what would later become the Bashas' chain. For their first store, they drew on the model created by their parents and took it one step further by placing a greater emphasis on serving the specifically rural needs of their customers. Aside from its primary stock of groceries, the Basha brothers' store carried a range of goods, including blankets, axes, and gasoline, presenting itself as the quintessential country store. The format endured for the ensuing two decades.

Although the two Basha brothers demonstrated their independence by becoming entrepreneurs, they by no means cut themselves free from their strong familial bonds. All family members, with Najeeby Basha presiding as family matriarch, were involved in running the first and subsequent stores. The women in the family played crucial roles in the business, with one sister serving as a buyer for the stores, another responsible for administrative

Company Perspectives:

Thousands of Bashas' members have poured labor and love into the company since its founding. Like any family, the personality of Bashas' is a reflection of the quality of the people who work for and grow with the company. Bashas' has survived the ups and downs of the supermarket industry, increased competition and national economic fluctuations because its members are determined to work together to continually make the company better able to serve our customers. Many members choose to remain with Bashas' for decades, and we think that says a lot about Bashas', and a lot about the people who are at its heart, our members.

matters, and other sisters working in various capacities to ensure the operational success of the business. With the entire family working in support, the stores secured a lasting presence in Arizona, representing the pillars upon which a legacy of Basha involvement in the grocery business was built.

The success of the first store led to the establishment of additional stores in the Basha's home state of Arizona. For roughly 20 years, the stores were modeled after the first country store, but by the 1950s a new breed of grocery stores was attracting consumers. Supermarkets, larger and stocked with a more diverse range of merchandise than traditional grocery stores, emerged as the format of the future for grocery retailers, convincing the Basha brothers that the success of their chain called for a revamped merchandising approach. They gradually began replacing their grocery stores with supermarkets, effecting an important strategic transition that positioned their stores to take full advantage of the postwar economic boom period.

Eddie Basha, Jr., Takes Control in 1968

During the pivotal transition from country stores to supermarkets, Bashas' lost the leadership of one of its founders. In 1958, Ike Basha died after a quarter-century of stewarding the fortunes of the family business. His death left his brother Eddie in full control over the enterprise, and he was soon joined by the second generation of Bashas in the business, his son Eddie Basha, Jr. After graduating from Stanford University, the younger Basha joined Bashas', helping his father to lead the company during a period in which expansion of the chain became top priority. The partnership of father and son at the helm continued until 1968, when Eddie Basha, Sr., died. At the time of his death, the Bashas' chain comprised 17 retail outlets.

For a company whose affairs were governed by a tightly-knit family, the loss of the founding brothers could have marked the beginning of a difficult period, but Bashas' enjoyed a seamless transition from one generation to the next. The ease with which the company passed through this potential sticking point was attributable to the talents of Eddie Basha, Jr. In his early 30s when his father died and he assumed full control over the company, Basha developed into an influential business leader and into a much-admired civic leader. He became renowned for his elaborate pranks and gained widespread notoriety as Arizona's Democratic gubernatorial candidate in 1994, when he ran a "people not politics" campaign, deprecatorily referring to himself as the "chubby grocer."

Basha lost the race for the governor's seat, but he recorded stirring success in building Bashas' into one of the largest private companies in the United States. His talent for expansion, however, was not fully expressed until he entered his 50s. During the intervening years, as the company progressed through the 1970s and 1980s, methodical expansion took place, as Basha experimented with different merchandising mixtures. Like his father and uncle before him, Basha endeavored to create supermarkets that catered to the needs of individual communities, the tastes and desires of which often changed from one location to another. By searching for the most appropriate mixture of goods and services, he created stores specifically tailored to what the company called "demographic neighborhoods." The fine-tuning process was never ending, as was the expansion of the chain, which by the end of the 1980s comprised approximately 45 units.

The size of the company at this point represented a half-century of growth, the product of the combined efforts of Ike, Eddie, Sr., and Eddie, Jr. During the ensuing decade, expansion occurred at a dizzying pace. In ten years time, Basha more than doubled the size of the company, adding a stable of retail banners to the company's portfolio.

Aggressive Expansion during the 1990s

Before Basha began expanding in earnest, he built the infrastructure to support the company's imminent growth. In 1991, the company opened a 125,000 square foot perishables warehouse, built to store the chain's frozen food, meat, and produce. A year later, in December 1992, Bashas' opened a 325,000-square-foot dry grocery facility, replacing the use of a leased facility in Phoenix. The new facilities, located 11 miles from the company's 40-year-old main office, composed Bashas' new distribution operation, which was consolidated with the offices of the buying staff by early 1993. Concurrent with the establishment of a single distribution complex, Bashas' opened its own health- and beauty-care (HBC) depot. Previously, the company had purchased up to 80 percent of its HBC inventory from a distributor named Impact Distributing, but control over its own depot enabled Bashas' to purchase nearly all HBC items directly from manufacturers, giving the company greater control over inventory. In the wake of the March 1993 debut of the HBC depot, sales increased markedly, ignited by the advantages engendered by vertical integration.

Rising sales became the predominate theme at Bashas' during the 1990s, particularly after the company embarked on an acquisition campaign that added several new store banners to its portfolio. Coming off $475 million in sales in 1992, the company made quick use of its new HBC depot and distribution complex by acquiring AJ's Fine Foods, an upscale, specialty chain offering prepared gourmet meals, a large wine collection, and specialty baked goods. Also in 1993, the company acquired a single Food City store in Phoenix. For 50 years, Food City had distinguished itself as a supermarket that catered to the particular needs of the Hispanic community in Phoenix, a tradition that Bashas' continued to observe once it took control of the format.

```
┌─────────────────────────────────────────────┐
│                  Key Dates:                   │
│                                               │
│ 1884:  The first Basha family member arrives  │
│        in the United States.                  │
│ 1910:  The Basha family moves to Arizona.     │
│ 1932:  Ike and Eddie Basha, Sr., open their   │
│        first store.                           │
│ 1968:  The death of his father leaves Eddie   │
│        Basha, Jr., in charge of the company.  │
│ 1993:  AJ's Fine Foods and Food City join     │
│        the company's fold.                    │
│ 1996:  MegaFoods Stores, Inc. is acquired.    │
│ 1998:  Sales reach an estimated $1 billion.   │
└─────────────────────────────────────────────┘
```

Bashas' operated another format tailored for Hispanics, the company's Mercado store, which operated in southern Arizona.

As expansion moved forward, the company continued to experiment with merchandising mixtures and new services. In 1994, for instance, the company opened its first "live" video department in a Bashas' Markets—the word live designating that the actual video tapes were displayed on the shelves. Designed as a "theater-within-the-store," the video department housed 5,000 rental units, or more than twice the number of units available at the company's other stores. Also in 1994, the company began installing two-foot by two-foot floor tiles that bore advertisements from national-brand manufacturers, using a tile system called the In-Floor Advertising Unit, patented by Indoor Media Group. Bashas' units, which secured an added revenue stream by using the advertising tiles, were one of the first 100 supermarkets in the country to use the In-Floor Advertising Unit.

By late 1994, Bashas' operated 67 stores in Arizona, making it the third-largest grocery chain in the state. Within two years, the company completed its climb up the state's rankings by completing another acquisition. In October 1996, Bashas' reached an agreement to acquire MegaFoods Stores, Inc. Mega-Foods, with 16 discount stores in Arizona, was operating under Chapter 11 bankruptcy protection, having declared bankruptcy in August 1994. At the time of the acquisition announcement, Bashas' had 73 stores in operation, 63 of which operated under the Bashas' Market name. The company's other stores included one Mercado unit, two stores that operated as discount units under the Bargain Basket logo, three Food City units, and four AJ's Fine Foods specialty stores. The acquisition of Mega-Foods, completed for $22.6 million on the last day of 1996, lifted the number of the company's stores to 89, making it the largest grocery chain in the state.

Following the completion of the MegaFoods transaction, attention was focused on what to do with the addition of the chain. In March 1998, the company announced it was dropping the MegaFoods name and converting the units to either the Food City or Mercado format.

By 1999, the conversion work had been completed, marking the end of a fruitful decade for the company. Annual sales had reach an estimated $1 billion, representing a more than 100 percent increase from the total recorded seven years earlier. Expansion had taken the chain out of its home state and into New Mexico and California, elevating the company's stature to that of a regional force. For the future, Bashas' appeared well poised to continue its long record of success. Its close attention to the demands of the communities it served and its willingness to change with the times—the company embraced the lucrative prospects of electronic commerce by offering online grocery shopping through its Groceries On The Go Service—promised to produce positive results in the 21st century.

Principal Subsidiaries

AJ Fine Foods; National Grocery Co.

Principal Competitors

The Kroger Co.; Safeway Inc.; Wal-Mart Stores, Inc.; Albertson's Inc.

Further Reading

Alaimo, Dan, "Bashas' to Open First Live Video Department, " *Supermarket News,* November 14, 1994, p. 57.

"Arizona Business Hall of Fame Inducts Six Members," *Business Journal—Serving Phoenix & the Valley of the Sun,* May 25, 1992, p. 26.

"Bashas' Consolidates Its Buying, Distribution Staff in Single Facility," *Supermarket News,* March 22, 1993, p. 6.

"Chubby Grocer Bags 'Boss' Title," *Business Journal—Serving Phoenix & the Valley of the Sun,* October 21, 1994, p. 1.

"Detroit Free Press Michigan Metro Column," *Knight-Ridder/Tribune Business News,* March 10, 1998.

Elson, Joel, "Bashas' Art Sales Called Fine," *Supermarket News,* May 1, 1995, p. 57.

——, "Bashas' Finds Depot Benefits Sales of HBC," *Supermarket News,* June 7, 1993, p. 33.

Riddle, Judith S., "Sourdough Is Rising: The Bread that Began as a San Francisco Specialty Is Now in Demand in Other Parts of the Country," *Supermarket News,* February 8, 1993, p. 45.

Tibbitts, Lisa A., "Double Feature: With Both Sell Through and Rental Going for Them, Supermarkets Have Revenues on Upward Spiral," *Supermarket News,* October 17, 1994, p. 40.

Turcsik, Richard, "Floor-Tile Ads Found to Help Raise Volume," *Supermarket News,* July 18, 1994, p. 23.

Zweibach, Elliot, "MegaFoods Is Selling Its Arizona Units to Bashas'," *Supermarket News,* October 7, 1996, p. 1.

—Jeffrey L. Covell

BATESWORLDWIDE

Bates Worldwide, Inc.

498 Seventh Avenue
New York, New York 10018
U.S.A.
Telephone: (212) 297-7000
Fax: (212) 297-8888
Web site: http://www.batesww.com

*Wholly Owned Subsidiary of Cordiant Communications
  Group plc*
Incorporated: 1940 as Ted Bates & Company, Inc.
Employees: 7,000
Gross Billings: $7.7 billion (1998)
NAIC: 54181 Advertising Agencies; 54183 Media
  Buying Agencies; 54189 Other Services Related to
  Advertising

Bates Worldwide, Inc., the primary subsidiary of Cordiant Communications Group plc, is one of the leading advertising and integrated communications networking companies in the world, with more than 156 offices in more than 70 countries and annual billings in excess of $7.7 billion in 1998. Headquartered in New York City, the company provides its clients with a full range of marketing communications services. Among its largest clients in the late 1990s were British American Tobacco, Warner-Lambert, Estée Lauder, and Hyundai.

1940s Birth of the Unique Selling Proposition: 1940s

Both brand name and international marketing were traditions that went back to Bates agency founder Theodore L. Bates, who established Ted Bates & Company in 1940. A 1924 graduate of Yale University, Ted Bates worked in advertising for several years, serving as a vice-president and director at Benton & Bowles before forming his own agency. Ted Bates began with two clients, Colgate-Palmolive-Peet and Continental Baking, and four brands to advertise: Colgate Dental Cream, Palmolive Shaving Cream, Hostess Cup Cakes, and Wonder Bread. Within the agency's first six months, gross billings stood at $5 million, an accomplishment largely attributed to the Unique Selling Proposition (USP) developed by Ted Bates and Rosser Reeves, the agency's chief creative officer.

USP focused on identifying a unique feature of each product and connecting it in the minds of consumers with the brand name. Moreover, early USPs emphasized the potential health benefits of a product. One early company publication described how the agency contracted with five leading universities to undertake dental research in discovering some new quality in Colgate Dental Cream. Conducted by recognized authorities, the tests continued for many months and provided the medical proof for the USP message: The Colgate Way Stops Tooth Decay Best. That declaration, repeated thousands of times in every medium, sent Colgate sales soaring in the United States. In another example, an advertising campaign for Continental Baking told consumers that Wonder Bread Helps Build Strong Bodies 12 Ways. The USP principle would later be applied in Bates ads for Minute Maid Orange Juice (Better For Health Than Oranges Squeezed At Home) and Royal Puddings (Give More Food Energy Than Sweet, Fresh Milk).

After ten years and a world war, the agency was working with 41 of its clients' brands, its billings approached $28 million, and, by one estimate, sales of the four original brands promoted by Bates had increased by 368 percent. With the agency doing so well, Ted Bates surprised the advertising industry in 1948 by dissolving the incorporated firm and converting the business to a partnership. Fourteen senior officers became members with equal shares, equal rights, and equal responsibilities.

Continued Growth: 1950s–70s

During the 1950s, Bates and Reeves were the first to take advantage of the advertising potential of television. "Advertising," Reeves wrote, "is the art of getting a Unique Selling Proposition into the heads of the most people at the lowest cost," and television offered the best way to do that. While most of their competitors had announcers reading ad copy and holding up the product, Bates introduced unique spot commercials, such as one for Anacin that featured hammers pounding on the heads of headache sufferers. As Paul Foley, of the Interpublic Group of Companies, later told the *New York Times*, Bates's "use of television in the early days developed a whole new advertising form."

Always looking for new ways to get USPs to more people, Bates was also quick to realize the potential of overseas markets. Europe was beginning to recover from the economic devastation of World War II, and a few American companies began setting up overseas branches or entering joint ventures. In 1956, Bates set about building an international network. Three years of negotiations with Hobson & Partners., Ltd., one of England's most successful agencies, resulted in the establishment in London of Hobson, Bates & Partners, Ltd. in 1959. This arrangement provided Bates's American clients with a fully operative overseas office and gave British clients access to the American market. Within a single year, Hobson's billings leaped from $5.4 million to $14.2 million.

The Bates agency was growing as well, adding both M&M/Mars and Nabisco, Inc. to its client base in 1954. In 1959, when Chase Manhattan Bank became a client, the agency began moving beyond its traditional packaged consumer goods accounts into services.

Such growth prompted Ted Bates to change the company's ownership structure again. In 1955 he dissolved the partnership and reconverted the company to a corporation. With several hundred employees on the payroll, a corporate structure made it easier to create appropriate levels of responsibility. Ownership in the corporation's stock was limited to Bates employees, and Ted Bates became honorary chairman of the board as well as chairman of the executive committee. Rosser Reeves became vice-chairman and eventually chairman and CEO. Bates continued to direct the agency's expansion into Europe, Southeast Asia, and Australia. When Bates died in 1972, Ted Bates & Company was among the five largest agencies in the world.

New Management in the 1980s

The company continued to prosper, developing a huge network of global offices and promoting its products with USPs. A new slogan, "Think Global, Act Local," introduced in 1984, reflected the company's philosophy that local affiliated offices should take full advantage of the economies of scale and resources of a worldwide network while responding to the local culture and market to sell messages.

In 1986, Saatchi & Saatchi plc purchased the company, then called Ted Bates Worldwide, for $450 million and merged it the following year with another U.S. agency, Backer & Spielvogel Advertising, which it had acquired for $65 million. In the first years after the merger, Backer Spielvogel Bates Worldwide (BSB) prospered, winning such clients as Wendy's, CPC International, and Burroughs-Wellcome. In fact, in 1988 BSB was named the top ad agency in Europe. However, Saatchi & Saatchi required BSB to drop its large, longtime Colgate business to avoid potential conflicts of interest with the clients that Saatchi & Saatchi retained at the time.

Under new parentage, Bates's tradition of research continued. In a 1990 *American Demographics* article, Rebecca Piirto reported that the agency had invested more than $2 million in Global Scan, an annual worldwide customer lifestyle study that analyzed markets and consumer desires in 17 different countries. Identifying five global "psychographic" personality types—strivers, achievers, pressureds, adapters, and traditionals—Global Scan helped agencies like BSB recognize cultural and economic differences that could make or break an international ad campaign. The companies could therefore tailor their advertising strategies to suit consumer preferences and ideals.

The company had also developed several other proprietary systems, including Brand Essence, a study that identified and refined distinctive and competitive brand positionings; Ad Scan, a pre-testing method of the relevance of advertising before production; and Brand Scan, which evaluated advertising over time and provided information on its real effect and cost.

However, the late 1980s and early 1990s also brought severe challenges to BSB's parent, Saatchi & Saatchi, which was debt-laden following its acquisitions and began losing new business bids. While Saatchi & Saatchi worked to recover and underwent several management shake-ups, BSB remained a core asset for the company.

Focus on Renewed Globalization in the Early 1990s

In January 1993, CEO Carl Spielvogel named Michael Bungey president and chief operating officer of Bates Worldwide. The following year Bungey became CEO and assumed the position of worldwide chairman at the end of the year when Spielvogel retired. Bungey had been with BSB for several years, having served as chairman of BSB Europe as well as chairman and CEO of BSB Dorland in London; he had a reputation for winning new accounts. "I learned how to do new business because I started an agency and we didn't have any business," Bungey told Stuart Elliot in a 1993 *New York Times* article. He was referring to Michael Bungey & Partners, which he started in 1971 and which eventually became part of BSB Dorland. In 1987, Bungey set out to build a creative reputation for Dorland and to develop new international business. By 1992, the company finished first among 20 top British agencies ranked on net billings gains, despite the unexpected loss of its $35 million Rover car account.

Key Dates:

1940: Theodore L. Bates founds Ted Bates & Company, Inc.

1948: Ted Bates is converted to a partnership.

1955: Ted Bates is reconverted to a corporation.

1959: Ted Bates forms a venture to found Hobson, Bates & Partners, Ltd. in London.

1986: Saatchi & Saatchi plc acquires Ted Bates.

1987: Bates is merged with Backer & Spielvogel Advertising to form Backer Spielvogel Bates Worldwide.

1994: Company changes it name to Bates Worldwide.

1995: Parent company Saatchi & Saatchi changes its name to Cordiant plc.

1997: Cordiant spins off Saatchi & Saatchi and Bates Worldwide. Bates becomes a subsidiary of a newly formed holding company, Cordiant Communications Group plc.

As chairman of BSB Europe Bungey restructured the company's European network. The local offices, the former Ted Bates affiliates, "were a mass of unwieldy local agencies still largely controlled by their local manager-founders," according to Noreen O'Leary in *ADWEEK*. Tim Corrigan, a BSB colleague, told O'Leary, "Michael has successfully changed the management of every single agency and created a whole new culture and new ways of doing things."

In assuming the worldwide position, "Michael's challenge now is no less than to take an organization built around a cult of personality and make it into the integrated global marketing concern it was always envisioned as," a Saatchi colleague told O'Leary. After moving from London to New York City, Bungey spent much of 1993 meeting with key clients, familiarizing himself with the New York office, and mapping out plans for the company's future. He established an account planning department and promoted Frank Assumma to president of Bates USA.

Bungey also began a year-long survey of clients, prospective clients, and agency management regarding the company's brand identity, resulting in the name change to Bates Worldwide in 1994. Although Bates had strong local agencies throughout the world, it was known by different names in different countries. To enhance brand recognition, every agency within the Bates network was expected to include the name Bates in its name to adopt a single brand name on a global basis. "The name change signals that Bates is now a reconstituted agency. In the past few years, they haven't been top of mind when you think of major agencies. Now they're becoming a contender," said Arthur Anderson, managing partner of agency search consultancy Morgan, Anderson & Co. of New York, in a 1994 *Advertising Age* article.

With regard to new business, Bungey aimed at adding more global company accounts. He told Penny Warneford in the *Australian* that multinational advertisers "rather than local national advertisers represent the future for agencies as the number of advertiser companies shrinks worldwide and national companies are swallowed by multinationals." Moreover,

O'Leary reported that Bungey had targeted "clients that already worked with the company in one or more countries—brands like Mercedes, Avis, Chanel, Estée Lauder, Nissan, 3M, and Goodyear—as well as international business from marketers like Energizer, British American Tobacco, and Electrolux which have not already aligned themselves with agencies on a regional or global basis." Bungey also reemphasized the Bates Unique Selling Position, a strategy that had been downplayed somewhat under BSB. During 1994 key agencies, including AC&R, McCaffrey & McCall, and CME/Houston, became part of Bates Worldwide.

By the end of 1994, things had improved considerably at Bates USA. As reported in *ADWEEK*, the agency won a bid for Warner-Lambert business valued at $70 million as well as Miller's estimated $40 million Lite Ice beer account. The $60 million Texaco account was transferred to Bates, and Miller and North American Phillips made new media-buying assignments. As a result, Bates USA business increased by more than $200 million.

Bates Worldwide showed record growth in 1994 and was ranked seventh among the top 20 U.S.-based agency networks by *ADWEEK*, with total worldwide billings of $5 billion, an eight percent increase over 1993 billings. This figure included $850 million in new business, such as the Compaq business for Europe, Africa, and the Middle East awarded to Bates Europe and British American Tobacco Company's Lucky Strike account and global creative assignment.

With regard to creativity, in 1993 and 1994 Bates won over 400 creative advertising awards worldwide at the top ten regional competitions. At the International Advertising Festival at Cannes, Bates ranked number two in 1995, with ten awards. Furthermore, two Bates agencies, Bates Hong Kong and Delvico Bates, placed in the top ten overall standings.

Bungey continued to expand the company while restructuring its organization. During 1994, Bates added new agency affiliations to the network in Argentina, Bangladesh, Chile, Croatia, Fyrom (formerly Macedonia), India, Israel, Latvia, Mexico, Pakistan, Paraguay, Peru, Slovenia, Sri Lanka, Turkey, Costa Rica, El Salvador, and Panama. Structurally, each of the regional directors in the company's four regions reported directly to Michael Bungey.

Bates Americas, headquartered in New York, included Bates North America (United States and Canada) and Bates Latin America, and had 700 million consumers. With 38 offices in 13 countries and billings of $1.7 billion, it handled 333 brands and had nine clients in four or more countries. During this time, Bill Whitehead became chief operating officer of Bates North America, as well as president and chief operating officer of Bates USA. Dan Reid was named chairman of Bates Latin America.

Bates Asia-Pacific, headquartered in Sydney, had 31 offices in 14 countries, with 3.3 billion consumers. The region had $900 million in billings, advertising 762 brands. Nineteen of its clients were in four countries or more, and it had the most member agencies in a local country's list of top five agencies. The largest non-Japanese-based agency network in the Asia-Pacific region, Bates was the first international advertising agency to be granted a license in Vietnam. Alex Hamill was regional director of Bates Asia-Pacific and chairman of George Patterson Bates in Australia.

Bates Europe, headquartered in London, had 85 offices in 29 countries, including a growing network of 13 offices in Central Europe and Russia. It had 1.1 billion consumers and billings of $2.5 billion, advertising 1,373 brands. Twenty-three clients were in four or more countries. Jean de Yturbe was chairman of Bates Europe and chairman and CEO of Bates France.

By 1995, Bates Worldwide also included several specialty shops with particular areas of expertise: HealthCom, with offices in London, Milan, New York, Canada, Australia, and Spain; Bates Alliance, specializing in retail advertising; Bates Direct for direct marketing; BKS/Bates Entertainment, for TV programming development, production, marketing and distribution; Bates Manhattan, specializing in prestige, fashion and luxury advertising; and Decision Shop, a strategic research consultancy in London.

At the beginning of 1995, parent company Saatchi & Saatchi Company PLC changed its name to Cordiant plc following the departure of the Saatchi brothers, who had built the agency, and named Michael Bungey to its board of directors. Unfortunately, in February of that year, Bates Worldwide lost its 40-year-old account with Mars, Inc., a $360 million billing. That loss led to some reduction in staffing levels in Bates's offices around the world. By mid-1995, however, Bates Worldwide had already recorded nearly $500 million in new business for the year. This included the Coles Myer media buying account, the largest media win in the history of Australian advertising, as well as the Jamont pan-European advertising program, Eurocard, and Optus Vision. Despite the Mars loss, the benefits of Bungey's rebranding effort were evident in the new business won in 1994 and 1995, especially from multinational and global companies.

Significant Changes in the Late 1990s

Cordiant suffered through sagging profits in 1995 but managed to return to profitability the following year. Still, the company struggled to recover from the loss of some large clients that resulted when the Saatchi brothers left the company to form their own agency. Bates, too, continued to work to overcome the hole left by the loss of the Mars account. Though Bates won a number of new clients, including Bayerische Motoren Werke AG, Mattel Inc., and Deutsche Bank AG, it failed to secure new major assignments. In addition, Bates lost the Miller Genuine Draft account in late 1996, and in mid-1997 the company lost its Compaq account in Europe, as well as its Texaco account, valued at $35–$40 million. Bates was not discouraged by the account losses, however, stating that it had gained $350 million in new business during the first half of 1997. Among the new business won by Bates were Toyota in Greece, CVS, the second largest drugstore chain in the United States, the pan-European Energizer business, and Europcar, a rental car business.

In April 1997 Cordiant announced its intention to spin off Saatchi & Saatchi and Bates into two individual companies. Bates Worldwide would function within the newly formed holding company, Cordiant Communications Group plc (CCG),

along with German agency Scholz & Friends and other marketing communications operations. CCG and Saatchi & Saatchi would jointly own Zenith Media, which handled media buying and planning. The demerger was finalized on December 15, 1997, and CCG went public on the New York and London stock exchanges.

Bates viewed the split positively and was anxious to launch an expansion strategy after gaining its independence. Bungey, who became CEO of CCG after the demerger, discussed Bates's future in *Times of London* and said, "A wall of fire has been built up within the company. Everyone wants to get going." Bill Whitehead, CEO of Bates North America, agreed. Whitehead told Jennifer Comiteau of *ADWEEK,* "The agency is reinventing itself." Bungey also explained that Bates would expand internationally and that it hoped to establish agencies in at least six Latin American countries, including Brazil, Mexico, Colombia, Chile, Argentina, and Venezuela. Bates also planned to set up offices in eastern and central Europe and search for strategic acquisitions, primarily in the United States. Bates had already expanded its operations in Asia, acquiring a stake in Clarion Advertising Services, based in Calcutta, India, in mid-1997. Strengthening U.S. business was a key goal for Bates, where during the first half of 1997 revenues fell, mostly as a result of the loss of the Miller account.

In 1998, its first year as an independent company, Bates enjoyed a record year in terms of new business acquired, and CCG's revenues climbed five percent, to £301.8 million. In the spring of 1999 Bates won the pan-European SEAT car account, with billings of US$140 million. The account represented Bates's largest single win in its history. SEAT was the Spanish operation of Volkswagen AG. Other significant new business gained in 1999 included Hyundai's pan-European business; the Cervejarias Kaiser Beer account in Brazil, with estimated billings of US$70 million; and the Ballantine's whiskey brand, Allied Domecq's key global brand. Bates also secured additional business from existing clients, including the Kool and Capri cigarette brands of Brown & Williamson Tobacco Company and Warner-Lambert's Lipitor brand.

As promised, Bates implemented its acquisition strategy. In North America, Bates acquired Churchill Public Relations, based in Houston, Texas, and The Criterion Group of Atlanta, Georgia. Criterion was a marketing communications agency that focused on the hospitality and travel sectors. In Europe, Bates launched Bates Poland, and Bates Holland was combined with a new acquisition—a Dutch creative shop named Not Just Film. In Latin America, Bates purchased Fernando Fernandez, a creative agency in Argentina, and bought a stake in Newcomm Bates in Brazil.

Entering 1999, Bates faced rumors that CCG was a target for acquisition by a larger advertising agency conglomerate. Bates denied that it was for sale, but speculation fueled trading activity, and CCG's share price climbed 16 percent on the New York Stock Exchange. In March the company opened the doors to its new headquarters in New York City, and in August CCG announced promising first-half financial results. Revenues increased 8.9 percent, to £158.6 million, compared to £143.6 million for the first half of 1998. More than US$200 million in new business was generated, including such key wins as

DuPont Co., Mercedes-Benz, and British American Tobacco PLC. Michael Bungey stated in *Wall Street Journal Europe,* ''Everything we have been doing so far has been geared to proving to the world at large that we can deliver on our numbers. . . . Now we feel that we're going to make use of the newfound confidence of this company. . . .''

Bates planned to step up its acquisitions to grow more aggressively at the turn of the century, and it got an early start in late 1999 by acquiring Healthworld, a marketing communications company that specialized in the healthcare field, and Interactive Edge, Inc., another marketing communications company focused on the Internet. To further reinforce Bates's goal to be a dominant global player with a unified vision, in December 1999 Bill Whitehead became CEO of Bates North America; Ian Smith, president of Bates Worldwide; and Jean de Yturbe, group president. The trio would work together with Bungey to operate the company centrally.

Principal Divisions

Bates North America; Bates Latin America; Bates Europe; Bates Asia Pacific.

Principal Competitors

The Interpublic Group of Companies, Inc.; Omnicom Group Inc.; WPP Group plc; True North Communications, Inc.

Further Reading

''Backer Spielvogel Bates Worldwide Plans New Office in China,'' *Advertising Age,* February 24, 1992, p. 49.

Barrager, Dave, ''Global News: Shops Bet on Vietnam As Next Asian Boom,'' *ADWEEK Eastern Edition,* February 8, 1993, p. 17.

''BAT Strikes Bates Lucky,'' *ADWEEK Eastern Edition,* January 16, 1995, p. 5.

Beatty, Sally, ''Cordiant Shares Rocket on Takeover Talk,'' *Wall Street Journal,* January 12, 1999, p. B9.

Beck, Ernest, ''Cordiant Plans to Spin Off Bates and Saatchi,'' *Wall Street Journal Europe,* April 22, 1997, p. 4.

——, ''Cordiant Pretax Profit Rises, in First Results Since Saatchi Spinoff,'' *Asian Wall Street Journal,* March 11, 1999, p. 25.

Burrett, Tony, ''Patterson Is Now a Global Role Model,'' *AdNews,* November 11, 1994.

Comiteau, Jennifer, ''Freedom for Now,'' *ADWEEK Eastern Edition,* October 20, 1997, p. 52.

''Cordiant Explores Cuts in Operations,'' *New York Times,* June 12, 1995, p. D7.

Elliott, Stuart, ''The Media Business: Advertising, Wendy's Return to Britain Convinces Backer Spielvogel of the Importance of a Global Focus,'' *New York Times,* April 9, 1993.

Fahey, Alison, ''An Asian Addition, Bates Gains a Place on Coke's Roster,'' *ADWEEK Eastern Edition,* July 17, 1995.

Farrell, Greg, ''Corner Office: A Firm Hand,'' *ADWEEK Eastern Edition,* November 21, 1994, p. 21.

Garcia, Shelly, ''Bates Bites the Bullet,'' *ADWEEK Eastern Edition,* February 27, 1995, p. 5.

Goldsmith, Charles, ''Cordiant Aims to Increase Acquisitions of Agencies,'' *Wall Street Journal Europe,* August 11, 1999, p. 3.

Kim, Hank, and Cristina Merrill, ''Texaco to Move Account from Bates,'' *ADWEEK Eastern Edition,* June 9, 1997, p. 3.

O'Leary, Noreen, ''Bungey Jumping,'' *ADWEEK Eastern Edition,* September 27, 1993, pp. 30–40.

Piirto, Rebecca, ''Global Psychographics,'' *American Demographics,* December 1990, p. 8.

''Saatchi & Saatchi Advertising,'' *ADWEEK Eastern Edition,* January 25, 1993, p. 12.

Snoddy, Raymond, ''Expansion the Key for Turning Bates into a Global Player,'' *Times of London,* October 15, 1997, p. 31.

''Ted Bates, Ad Agency Founder, Dies,'' *New York Times,* June 1, 1972, p. 46.

Warneford, Penny, ''Bungey Jumps into the Hot Seat at BSB,'' *Australian,* December 30, 1993, p. 20.

Wells, Melanie, ''BSB Sharpens Its 'Global Focus','' *Advertising Age,* June 7, 1993.

——, ''Bungey Pushes BSB Ahead into Bates Worldwide Era,'' *Advertising Age,* May 30, 1994, p. 35.

——, ''Cordiant Looks to Trim Costs,'' *USA Today,* June 9, 1995, p. B2.

Wentz, Laurel, et al, ''Backer Takes Top Ad Agency Spot in Europe,'' *Advertising Age,* September 12, 1988.

——, ''Michael Bungey, Building Backer's Confidence As New President,'' *Advertising Age,* March 15, 1993, p. 42.

—Ellen D. Wernick
—updated by Mariko Fujinaka

Bowthorpe plc

Gatwick Road
Crawley, West Sussex RH10 2RZ
United Kingdom
Telephone: (+44) 1293 528-888
Fax: (+44) 1293 541-905
Web Site: http://www.bowthorpe-plc.com

Public Company
Incorporated: 1936 as Goodlife Electric Supplies
Employees: 8,611
Sales: £675 million ($1.07 billion) (1999)
Stock Exchanges: London
Ticker Symbol: BWTH.L
NAIC: 33531 Electrical Equipment Manufacturing; 33411
    Computer and Peripheral Equipment Manufacturing;
    3342 Communications Equipment Manufacturing

Bowthorpe plc is one of the United Kingdom's leading suppliers of diversified electronics products, with an increasing emphasis on high-technology products for the telecommunications and other industries. Bowthorpe operates through a network of approximately 50 subsidiary companies with operations in more than 30 countries. Since its purchase of Netcom Systems in 1999, Bowthorpe's largest single market has been the United States, which accounted for more than 41 percent of sales. Europe, including the United Kingdom, continues to account for about half of the company's total sales. After a restructuring of its business focus in the late 1990s, Bowthorpe has reorganized its subsidiary companies into five core operating divisions. For the telecommunications industry, Bowthorpe provides testing instruments and systems, including ATM test systems, channel emulators, noise and interference emulators, and testing equipment and products for such satellite navigation systems as the Global Positioning System (GPS). In January 2000, Bowthorpe reorganized this division under the name SPIRENT Communications. In the Power Management field, the company offers products in three key areas, those of power control, power conversion, and power quality. This division's products include such wide-ranging applications as power control devices for wheelchairs and power supplies to the

telecommunications, networking, medical, computer, and other industries, as well as power conversion systems, and surge and lightning arrest systems and products. The company also produces the so-called "black boxes" for the avionics industry. Led by its WAGO spring clamp system, the company's Interconnection division produces approximately 12,000 cabling, wiring, and related products. Network management has taken on a larger role for the company, particularly since its $400 million purchase of Netcom Systems; this division also produces a range of customized mice, trackballs, and keyboards. The last of the Bowthorpe divisions is involved in sensing equipment, including thermal sensing, and management systems, a segment the company expected to exit by early 2000. Led by chief executive Nicholas Brookes, Bowthorpe posted sales in excess of £608 million in 1998.

Founding an Electronics Conglomerate in the 1930s

Bowthorpe was founded as Goodlife Electric Supplies by Jack Bowthorpe in the mid-1930s, a period that saw England rapidly becoming dependent on electric power. Bowthorpe's father had worked for General Electric; Jack Bowthorpe stuck close to his father's line, launching his own company in 1936. Bowthorpe's first employee was Ray Parsons, then only 15 years old. Apart from becoming Bowthorpe's brother-in-law, Parsons was to play a key role in the company's later growth, especially after Bowthorpe's death in the late 1970s, when Parsons was named chairman.

Goodlife first produced connectors and other fittings for the country's electric lines, prompting the company to adopt as its first slogan: "Up the Pole." Over the next decades the company—which changed its name to Bowthorpe in 1949—developed a wider focus, providing products for the electrical and other industries.

After assuming leadership of the company in 1978, Parsons began transforming Bowthorpe into a diversified conglomerate with a focus on niche electrical products. In 1979 Parsons was joined by chief executive Dr. John Westhead, who had been working for General Electric. Westhead took over as non-executive chairman in 1992, when Parsons retired after 55 years with the company.

Company Perspectives:

We will be the global leader in selected markets by providing creative solutions which improve the performance of customers' complex electrical and electronic systems. We are working towards achieving our objective by focusing on six elements of our strategy: Focusing on high growth markets: *Bowthorpe is committed to serving the needs of the world's rapidly developing industries, such as telecoms, aerospace and medical. We will anticipate and respond to customers' requirements by focusing our investment on these areas to create world class solutions;* Becoming truly global as a company: *To be dependable partners to our customers, we will provide consistently high quality products and support across our operations throughout the Americas, Europe and Asia Pacific;* Continuing our entrepreneurial culture: *Bowthorpe's ability to remain close to customers and their markets rests in part from our long-established entrepreneurial culture. While the business has grown to become a major international provider of electronic solutions, our flat organisational structure enables our operations to remain fast-moving and responsive;* Driving innovation through market foresight: *Our five operating groups bring together successful businesses with related technology or shared customers. This enables them to pool expertise and market knowledge to create the most effective, timely and appropriate solutions;* Moving up the value chain: *We are committed to providing greater added value to our customers, by offering comprehensive system solutions to customers which draw together our expertise in hardware and software;* Investing in our people: *Attracting, retaining and developing the best team is critical to achieving Bowthorpe's Vision. We will continue to enhance our employee development programmes, which are benchmarked against those of other world class organisations, to ensure that we enable our people to reach their potential to the benefit of our customers.*

In the meantime, the pair transformed Bowthorpe into a diversified, international operation. The company's overseas arm, Bowthorpe International, was created in 1982 and took charge of the company's expansion, especially into the U.S. market, as well as across Europe. By the late 1980s, Bowthorpe's focus began to shift again, now looking toward the booming electronics industry for its future growth. During the remaining years of the decade, the company made more than 20 acquisitions, including Optim Electronics of the United States in 1987. The company quickly added expertise in thermal management through the acquisition of Thermalloy and its heat sink products in 1988; a year earlier the company had acquired a line of surge suppression devices through the purchase of Atlantic Scientific. In the process, the company built up a strong position as a military defense contractor. About 30 percent of the company's sales came from the defense sector.

Bowthorpe's acquisition drive continued into the 1990s, creating an international conglomerate of more than 50 fairly autonomous companies. While operations had extended to 20 countries, the company's largest single market was now the United States. The end of the Cold War, coupled with an extended recession, brought the company into difficulties. In order to boost slowing sales and sinking profits, Bowthorpe moved to decrease its reliance on defense sector contracts.

Reorganizing in the 1990s

After selling off its Hellerman Deutsch and McGeoch defense manufacturing wing in 1990, Bowthorpe began strengthening its electronics base. In 1992, the company acquired Avionics, a leading flight recorder ("black box") manufacturer. The company also acquired B&D Electronics, Penny & Giles, and Odessa Engineering then moved into environmental testing with the purchase of the emissions monitoring business of Lear Siegler, in 1993. Bowthorpe had successfully reduced its exposure to the shrinking defense industry, which accounted for just over six percent of the company's total sales of £334 million in 1994. As the company's European and U.S. operations were recovering from the extended economic difficulties of the early 1990s, the company continued its growth-through-acquisition drive, reportedly looking at some 300 acquisition candidates per year. While adding to its U.S. and European base, the company also announced its intention to expand operations into the Asian markets.

The year 1996 marked the beginning of a new era. After Westhead retired to the position of non-executive chairman, Bowthorpe hired Nicholas Brookes as its new chief executive. Brookes intended to lead Bowthorpe into a reorganization of its operations to concentrate its activities on high-growth, high-technology products. Brookes also moved to streamline the company's structure: by then, Bowthorpe had grown to more than 100 subsidiary companies, organized into 12 primary divisions. Brookes cut back on the number of its divisions, setting up just five core business areas, including the booming telecommunications market, as well as power supply and systems testing markets. The company began selling off its newly non-core operations while continuing to make strategic acquisitions to round out its new divisions.

By the late 1990s, Bowthorpe had reduced its number of subsidiary companies to just 50. Telecommunications, and especially advanced testing equipment for ATM (asynchronous transfer mode) switching equipment, modems, cellular, and other voice and data transmission systems became a top priority for the company. With network and communications systems seen as one of the major growth areas for the coming decades, and with the world coming more and more to rely on satellite, cellular, telephone, Internet, and network technologies, Bowthorpe had recognized the need for increasingly sophisticated testing and analysis products, systems, and procedures to ensure smooth communication systems operations. In the late 1990s, the company boosted this division to its single largest, adding Wireless Telecom Group and Consultronics in 1999. In that year, also, Bowthorpe made its largest acquisition to date, paying $463 million to buy Netcom Systems, Inc., of California. The Netcom Systems acquisition helped secure Bowthorpe's position as one of the world's leading manufacturers of telecommunications testing equipment.

In the late 1990s, Bowthorpe expanded its power supply and power conversion division, with the acquisition in 1998 of

Conversion Equipment, a manufacturer of power supplies for telecommunications and computer systems based in the United States. Meanwhile, Bowthorpe continued to shed operations no longer central to its future strategy. In 1997, for example, the company sold off its Starpoint subsidiary, a maker of parts for amusement machines. In late 1999, Bowthorpe also announced its intention to exit one of its five core areas, that of thermal management products, a move expected to take place early in 2000. The sale of its Optim subsidiary in December 1999 was part of Bowthorpe's disposal of its automotive industry operations.

By the beginning of the year 2000, Bowthorpe had completed roughly half of its reorganization program. The company took a new step toward its final form at the end of January of that year, when it announced its intention to merge several of its telecommunications testing companies, including Netcom Systems, Adtech, Telecom Analysis Systems, Global Simulation Systems, and DLS TestWorks into a single testing and measurement subsidiary, dubbed SPIRENT Communications. While the full benefits of its reorganization were not expected to be seen for another two years or more, Bowthorpe was already beginning to reap the rewards of becoming one of the world's leaders in its core sectors, with profit forecasts for the 1999 year expected to top £95 million.

Principal Subsidiaries

Adtech, Inc.; Atlantic Scientific Corporation; Autronics Corporation; Bowthorpe Australia Pty Ltd.; Bowthorpe Components Ltd.; Bowthorpe EMP Ltd.; Bowthorpe Holdings Corporation; Bowthorpe International Inc.; Bowthorpe plc; Bowthorpe-Hellermann (Pty) Ltd. (90%); Curamik Electronics GmbH (65%); Devlin Electronics Ltd.; Edgcumbe Instruments Ltd; El.Bo.Mec. Thermalloy Srl (Italy); The Flight Data Company Ltd.; General Eastern Instruments Inc. (U.S.); Global Simulation Systems Ltd.; Hellermann France SA; Holaday Industries Inc. (U.S., 95%); Kaye Instruments Inc. (U.S.); Keystone Thermometrics Corporation (U.S.); Monitor Labs, Inc. (U.S.); Monitor Products Company Inc. (U.S.); Paul Hellermann GmbH (Germany); Penny & Giles Aerospace Ltd.; Penny & Giles Controls Ltd.; Penny & Giles Drives Technology Ltd.; Protimeter plc; Redpoint Thermalloy Ltd.; Switching Systems International (U.S.); Telecom Analysis Systems Inc. (U.S.); Thermalloy Inc. (U.S.); Thermometrics Inc. (U.S.); TytonHellermann do Brasil Industria e Commercio Ltda.; WAGO Kontakttechnik GmbH (Germany; 50%); Western Pacific Data Systems Inc. (U.S.).

Principal Operating Units

Communications; Interconnection; Systems; Cable Management; Sensing.

Principal Competitors

Agilent Technologies; Danaher Corp.; Eaton Corp.; Emerson Electric Co.; General Electric Company, plc; Hadco Corp.; Honeywell Inc.; Hubbell Inc.; IMI plc; MicroTel International Ltd.; Molex Inc.; Pirelli S.p.A.; Teradyne, Inc.; Thomas & Betts Corp.; Union Carbide Corp.; Von Roll; Wavetek Wandel & Goltermann.

Further Reading

"Bowthorpe Buys Netcom Systems," *Reuters Business Report*, June 15, 1999.

"Bowthorpe Set to Expand," *Independent*, March 28, 1996, p. 22.

Cole, Robert, "Bowthorpe Surges through U.S. Deals," *Independent*, September 22, 1994, p. 22.

Farrand, Tim, "Bowthorpe's U.S. Buy Boosts Shares," *Reuters*, June 15, 1999.

"Gold Offers Riches for Bowthorpe," *Daily Telegraph*, February 11, 2000, p. 37.

"Reliable Bowthorpe," *Independent*, March 24, 1994, p. 38.

—M.L. Cohen

Brauerei Beck & Co.

Am Deich 18-19
28199 Bremen
Germany
Telephone: (49) 421-5094-0
Fax: (49) 421-5094-667
Web site: http://www.becks-beer.com

Private Company
Incorporated: 1873
Employees: 3,738
Sales: DM 1.61 billion (1999)
NAIC: 31212 Breweries

Brauerei Beck & Co. is the world's largest exporter of beer, accounting for more than one-third of the total exports of beer products from Germany. Sold in some 200 countries, Beck & Co.'s core markets include the United States, Germany, the United Kingdom, Italy, France, Spain, and China. In addition to Beck's beer, the company also brews such brands as Haake-Beck, Beck's Dark, Beck's for Oktoberfest, and Rostocker. Although Beck & Co. is primarily a beer company, the privately held firm also benefits from holdings of glass manufacturing concerns and a bottling concession with Coca-Cola Co.

Early Years in a Brewery Town: 1870s through Mid-1900s

The original breweries that today comprise the corporate entity of Beck & Co. have roots that reach back to medieval times in Bremen, a major port on the Weser River. The city-state of Bremen was an important member of the Hanseatic League, a powerful federation formed by German merchants in the Middle Ages for trading and defense. Bremen's merchant class tightly controlled Northern European shipping and commerce for two centuries and influenced it for many more.

One of the largest exports out of the Bremen harbor during the Middle Ages was beer from the city's breweries, of which there were more than 300. As early as the 13th century, this beer was exported to Scandinavia, England, and Holland, and in

1489 the city's breweries formed the Bremen Brewers' Society to regulate the production and export of the beverage. As foreign markets clamored for Bremen's beers in subsequent centuries, competition increased, and only the brewers whose products consistently withstood long sea journeys survived. By 1870 only 30 of the original 350 members of the Bremen Brewers' Society remained, including the Beck Brewery, which had altered the chemical formulation of its beer to produce a heavy barley ale that survived the rigors of the trade routes. Until modern brewing technology was developed in the 19th century, this type of ale was a standard Beck product.

In the late 19th century, prominent Bremen business leader Lueder Rutenberg incorporated the company that became known as Brauerei Beck & Co. after the Beck brewery was merged with two other local breweries, Bierbrauerei Wilhelm Remmer and Hemelinger Aktienbrauerei. In 1921 Beck & Co. formed a cooperative agreement with another Bremen brewery, the Brauerei C.H. Haake & Co. Control of the market was divided between Beck & Co. and Haake, with Brauerei Beck & Co. agreeing to produce beer for the export market under the brand name of Beck's, while Haake-Beck Brauerei AG would sell its products under the names Haake-Beck, Remmer, and Hemelinger in the domestic German market. Haake-Beck Brauerei was later made a subsidiary of Beck & Co., making Brauerei Beck the largest privately owned brewery in Germany.

The location of Beck & Co. in the port city of Bremen contributed to its success and played an influential role in many outward aspects of the firm. Bremen's status as a major player in North European commerce facilitated Beck's delivery to several foreign ports. The reputation of the Bremen brewers solidified the beer's potential to hold and maintain increasing shares of foreign markets. Although the beer was at first shipped in the traditional barrels, Beck & Co. began exporting bottles sheathed in straw and packed in weighty wooden crates to withstand high seas.

In its advertising Beck & Co. features an important aspect of its history—the Reinheitsgebot, or Purity Law, enacted by the Bavarian Court of Duke Wilhelm IV in 1516. The law specified that only malted barley, yeast, hops, and water could be used in beer brewed in Germany for the German market. German beer

Company Perspectives:

Beck & Co. is prepared for the challenges ahead: with top quality products, creative brand marketing as well as efficient and customer-oriented services. For it is our declared aim to remain one of the most successful companies of our sector in Germany—well into the next millennium.

exporters stressed this law in citing the long tradition of excellence of German beers, but not all brewed their export beer in compliance with the statute. All of Beck's beers, according to the company's literature, contained only hops grown in the nearby Tettnag and Hallertau regions, water from Geest-area springs and the reservoirs of the Harz mountains, and a particular strain of yeast cultivated for decades by the brew masters at the Bremen plant.

Each year the city of Bremen held the Schaffermahl, a formal dinner held in mid-February that dated back to the 16th century when the Haus Seefahrt Foundation established the gathering to raise money for needy sailors. Prominent guests gathered in the city hall, smoked traditional white clay pipes, and dined on a meal of dried fish and smoked pork. The most important part of the dinner, however, was the beer brewed by Beck & Co. especially for the occasion and drunk from pewter tankards. This was a version of the company's original Seefahrtsbier, the extremely strong quaff that could withstand long sea voyages.

The evolution of lager beers (''lager'' being German for ''to store'') was spurred by technological developments, including research into yeast cultures and fermentation as well as the invention of refrigeration. In bottom-fermented beer, the yeast sinks to the bottom, which makes a clearer beer that is less likely to sour, but which needs to be stored and cooled longer than top-fermented ales. Beck & Co., like the other major German breweries, began producing lager beers late in the 19th century.

Because of its chemistry, beer had a relatively short shelf life, until modern brewing and storing methods improved matters. Beck & Co. continually invested in state-of-the-art brewing facilities, applying technological innovations to improve product quality. For instance, Beck & Co. managed to greatly reduce the oxygen count of its product to give it a longer shelf life. Beck & Co. was also one of the first breweries to use the modern keg. These have been improved by using stainless steel containers as well as a hygienic tap system that helps lengthen the amount of time beer can be stored and reduces the risk of contamination involved in pouring draft beers.

Building an International Presence: 1960s–80s

In the mid-1900s, Beck & Co. was the last brewer remaining in the city of Bremen. The brand name of Beck's, however, was found only on bottles exported out of Germany; the company's Haake-Beck, Remmer, and Hemelinger lines were brewed specifically for domestic consumers. These three brands retained their vestigial names to help differentiate them in a large and diverse home market and remind drinkers of Bremen's long brewing history. Each of them, while targeting different domes-

tic markets, also represented a distinct product, reflecting the dissimilar tastes of Germans for their beer. Haake-Beck's beer was distributed throughout all of Germany, whereas the Hemelinger and Remmer brands were part of the tradition of local specialty beers found in and around Bremen. Also carrying the Remmer brand name was a light beer with a lower alcohol and calorie content that was distributed throughout Germany.

On the international market, Beck & Co. attempted to appeal to the widest range of tastes while still adhering to German brewing standards. The Beck's beer sold in North America, for instance, was a much lighter version of a traditional German brew. Here, the products found under the Beck's label, in addition to the flagship lager, included Beck's Dark, Beck's Light, and Haake-Beck. These were imported by Dribeck Importers Inc. of Greenwich, Connecticut, a subsidiary founded in 1964.

Although there were several thousand breweries producing regional beers, Beck & Co. was one of the few that distributed throughout all of reunified Germany. The fall of the Berlin Wall in 1989 opened up a huge new market of consumers for German companies. Beer brewed in the former East Germany by state-owned breweries was poor in quality because of a shortage of raw materials and antiquated machinery. Frequently adulterated with corn or rice, East German beer required additives to enhance shelf life and thus did not meet Reinheitsgebot standards.

Increasing Competition and Challenges in the 1990s

Shortly after trade between the two Germanies was fully reestablished, Beck & Co. began selling its products in the former East German states and achieved remarkable gains in sales, due in part to the novelty of West German beer among consumers there. In April of 1991 Beck & Co. acquired the Rostocker Brauerei VEB, formerly a state-owned company in Rostock, a port on the Baltic Sea. Although Beck & Co. had to invest heavily to upgrade the brewery's equipment, it gave the company an excellent position from which to target the East German market, brewing a new and improved Rostocker for East German consumers. In addition, the geographical location of the newly acquired brewery permitted easier access for exports of Beck's beer to areas within the former Soviet Union. By 1992 Beck's products were sold in most of the former Eastern Bloc countries.

As consumers around the globe were drawn to import beers for their sophisticated edge, Beck & Co. sought to position itself as part of a centuries-old tradition of German brewing excellence, stressing both the company's longevity and the quality of its product. In the 1980s, however, a North American trend toward moderation in alcohol consumption had a significant impact on import sales, while a weakened U.S. dollar also made it difficult for foreign companies such as Beck & Co. to keep prices low. Competition in the beer market became fierce as consumers' palates became more discriminating. The company's inroads into Eastern Europe did help offset the decrease in import sales by its Dribeck subsidiary in the United States.

Although Beck & Co. expected a unified Germany to provide great opportunity for expansion and profit, by the mid-1990s conditions were gloomy for the beer industry in

Key Dates:

1873: Brauerei Beck & Co. is formed in Bremen, Germany.
1921: Beck & Co. forms a partnership with distributor Brauerei C.H. Haake & Co.
1945: Beck brewery is destroyed during World War II and production ceases.
1948: Reconstruction of the brewery begins.
1964: Dribeck Importers Inc. is established to handle distribution of Beck's beer in the United States.
1968: The six-pack is introduced to the German market.
1975: A new brewing facility is constructed.
1992: Beck & Co. introduces a nonalcoholic pilsner. The company expands into China.
1998: U.S. subsidiary Dribeck is renamed Beck's North America.

Germany. The market suffered from oversaturation, and as economic conditions in Germany worsened, so did beer consumption. During the second half of the decade, German consumption of beer fell at an annual rate of about two percent, and the trend was expected to continue into the early 21st century. A number of factors contributed to the change in beer consumption habits. The German population was not growing significantly, which meant the pool of new beer drinkers was shrinking. In addition, fewer young people were drinking beer. According to Beck & Co., only about two-thirds of Germans over the age of 16 admitted to consuming beer on a regular basis. Many of these young people preferred to drink mixed drinks or nonalcoholic beverages. The drop in beer consumption also was attributed to the 1998 reduction in the legal blood-alcohol limit while driving.

The weak German economy also prompted beer drinkers to opt for lower priced and private label products. This hurt sales of Beck's medium-priced Pilsner products. Beck & Co. indicated that the combined market share for all medium-priced and regional Pilsner brands fell by more than ten percent between 1994 and 1999. Not only were medium-priced Pilsners affected by the low-priced products, but they also faced competition from the high-priced premium brands, which were gaining in popularity.

In contrast, as the German beer market began its decline, the U.S. market thrived. U.S. subsidiary Dribeck reported double-digit revenue increases in 1996 and 1997, thanks in part to the increased popularity of imported beers and microbrews, which Beck & Co. believed influenced consumers to become more adventurous and open to trying beers with different tastes. Beck & Co. focused its efforts on building the North American market in the late 1990s, and in 1998 it changed the name of Dribeck to Beck's North America, Inc. It also expanded the role of Beck's North America to encompass not only sales duties but also marketing. To enhance the brand recognition of Beck's, Bill Yetman, CEO of Beck's North America, assembled a team of young district managers who were directed to establish relationships with bartenders and pub owners in the company's core markets, which included San Francisco, Chicago, Boston,

New York, and Miami, and to keep their fingers on the pulse of the beer market.

Despite positive growth in the United States—revenues of the subsidiary reached US $138 million for the fiscal year ended June 1999, up 8.7 percent over fiscal 1998—the company still had a long way to go in the highly competitive U.S. beer market. To that end the company invested US $20 million in a U.S. advertising campaign in 1999. The budget, which was twice as large as any of Beck & Co.'s U.S. advertising campaigns, was about a third of the company's total worldwide advertising budget. The campaign, which included television and radio spots as well as a print effort, was designed to position Beck's beer as the premium German beer and to boost brand recognition. Rainer Meyrer, executive vice-president of marketing for Beck's North America, explained in an interview with *Modern Brewery Age* that market research had indicated that "56% of our sample are convinced that the best beer brewed outside the United States is made in Germany." Therefore, Meyrer continued, "Our new campaign will focus on that issue—that Beck's is a German beer."

In other markets around the world, Beck & Co. experienced ups and downs in the late 1990s. The company introduced its beer in India in the mid-1990s through a partnership with Him Neel Breweries Ltd. In 1999 Beck & Co. dissolved its license agreement with the Putian Jinse Brewery, which was responsible for brewing its premium Pilsner. Beck & Co. formed a new agreement with Lion Nathan Ltd., an Australasian brewery, to produce and market Beck's beer to the Chinese market. Also in the late 1990s Beck & Co. merged Stralauer Glashütte GmbH with its Nienburger Glas unit and consolidated subsidiaries Franz Mielke GmbH & Co. KG, Getränke Liebelt GmbH & Co. KG, and W.I.R.: Liebelt GmbH & Co. KG into Bremer Erfrischungsgetränke-GmbH.

Although revenues for fiscal 1999 declined slightly, from DM $1.62 billion in fiscal 1998 to DM $1.61 billion, gross profit increased. Beck & Co.'s domestic sales fell 1.7 percent, but total domestic beer sales declined 3.9 percent, somewhat easing the blow of the drop. The outlook was more promising for fiscal 2000, and during the first half of fiscal 2000 the company reported that sales of Beck's beer rose 7.4 percent. An increase in growth in beer sales of three to four percent was forecast for the full fiscal year. Beck & Co. worked to expand international operations in 1999 as the German market continued to slump. The company formed strategic partnerships with companies in Poland, China, and Australia, and in November 1999 Beck & Co. made its largest foreign investment to date when it formed an alliance with Namibia Breweries Ltd., which had enjoyed an average growth rate in beer sales of about 15 percent since 1995. In January 2000 the company announced plans to spin off Nienburger Glas to concentrate on growing its international business. Beck & Co. also planned to expand its beverage offerings to include more nonalcoholic drinks and premium beers, which were predicted to undergo healthy growth.

Principal Subsidiaries

Beck's North America, Inc. (U.S.); Rostocker Brauerei GmbH; Brauhaus Karlsburg GmbH; RB Getränke Vertriebsgesellschaft mbH; Bremer Erfrischungsgetränke GmbH & Co. KG; Haus

Union-Erfrischungsgetränke GmbH; Bistromat Pausenservice GmbH; Victoria Heil-und Mineralbrunnen GmbH; Nienburger Glas GmbH; Nienburger Spedition & Service GmbH (51%); Haake-Beck Brauerei GmbH (98.91%); Paul Klein GmbH; Roland Gastronomie Verwaltungsgesellschaft mbH; Roland Assekuranzvermittlung GmbH & Co. KG; Bierbrauerei Wilhelm Remmer GmbH; Bremer Möbelverleih GmbH; Kaiserbrauerei GmbH & Co. oHG; Kaiserbrauerei GmbH; Klosterbrauerei GmbH; Roland Brauereibedarf GmbH; Glasrecycling Leeseringen GmbH & Co. KG (33.33%); Schrader Glasformenbau GmbH & Co. KG (39%); The Bottle Company Glasvertrieb GmbH (50%); Kommanditgesellschaft Nord-Zentra Erfrischungsgetränke GmbH & Co. (33.5%); Nord-Zentra Erfrischungsgetränke GmbH (33.5%).

Principal Competitors

Heineken NV; Guinness Ltd.; Anheuser-Busch Companies, Inc.

Further Reading

Anderson, Will, *From Beer to Eternity: Everything You Always Wanted To Know About Beer*, Lexington, Mass.: Stephen Greene Press, 1987.

"Beck's Counts Itself Among German Gems," *New York Times,* November 21, 1992, p. D19.

"Beck's Ramps Up for 1999: Beck's Marketing Executives Discuss Aggressive New Plans for the Upcoming New Year," *Modern Brewery Age,* January 18, 1999.

"Bulging Beck's," *Food and Beverage Marketing,* April 1992, p. 43.

Dennis, Darienne L., "How About a Beer?," *Fortune,* August 1, 1988, p. 8.

Fahey, Alison, "Party Hardly," *Adweek's Brandweek,* October 26, 1992, pp. 24–25.

Finch, Christopher, *Beer: A Connoisseur's Guide to the World's Best,* New York: Abbeville Press, 1989.

Gorman, John, "Beer Lovers Spread the Word: Beck's," *Chicago Tribune,* May 17, 1985, Sec. 3, pp. 1–2.

Hemphill, Gary A., "Imports: A Taste of Reality," *Beverage Industry,* September 1989, pp. 1–26.

Jackson, Michael, ed., *The World Guide to Beer,* New York: Prentice-Hall, 1977.

Marchetti, Michele, "Brewing a Comeback," *Sales & Marketing Management,* February 1, 1999, p. 18.

Tucker, Neely, "German Small Beer Makers See a Lot of Trouble Brewing," *Seattle Times,* August 11, 1996, p. A19.

—Carol Brennan
—updated by Mariko Fujinaka

British Vita plc

Oldham Road
Middleton, Manchester M24 2DB
United Kingdom
Telephone: (44) 161-643-1133
Fax: (44) 161-653-5411
Web site: http://www.britishvita.com

Public Company
Incorporated: 1966 as British Vita Company Ltd.
Employees: 14,368
Sales: £921.4 million ($1.46 billion) (1999)
Stock Exchanges: London
Ticker Symbol: U.BVI
NAIC: 325212 Synthetic Rubber Manufacturing; 325221
    Cellulosic Organic Fiber Manufacturing; 32614
    Polystyrene Foam Product Manufacturing; 326113
    Unsupported Plastics Film & Sheet (except
    Packaging) Manufacturing

British Vita plc manufactures and processes a wide assortment of polymers, including cellular foams, synthetic fiber fillings, specialized and coated textiles, and polymer compounds and moldings. The company's products are used in furniture, carpet underlay, bedding, apparel, automobile seat cushions, and more. British Vita is made up of three divisions—the industrial group makes thermoplastic sheet goods, the fiber and fabric division makes products used in clothing and construction industries, and the foam group makes cellular polymer products that account for 55 percent of total company sales.

Early History: 1950s–70s

Founded with £100 by Norman Grimshaw in 1949, the company first began business as Vitafoam Ltd. in Oldham. Its primary business was the manufacture of foam cushions and mattresses. Vita's first regional foam conversion plant was opened at High Wycombe, approximately 30 miles northwest of London, in 1954. The main office was moved to Middleton in 1957, and the company acquired Liverpool Latex the same year.

By 1960 Vita established its first foreign division when operations commenced in Rhodesia (now Zimbabwe). Another plant opened in Nigeria in 1962.

Vita's history is one of aggressive mergers and acquisitions that have allowed the company to expand its product base and market. The company was incorporated as British Vita Company Ltd in 1966, the same year that J. Mandelberg, a maker of coated fabrics and flame laminating, was acquired. Throughout the 1960s, Vita worked to diversify its product line, adding polyether foam, pvc foam, carpet underlay, general rubber molding, and coated fabrics. In 1967 the company celebrated its listing on the London Stock Exchange.

By 1968 Vita had 15 operations throughout the United Kingdom involved in the manufacturing of latex, polyurethane and polyvinyl foams, precision mold and pattern making, footwear components, fabric coating, and laminating. Its foreign holdings were expanding as well, and in 1971 British Vita International Ltd was formed to supervise the overseas operations. During the 1970s, Vita began to decentralize its operations and adopted new methods to cut costs and increase efficiency. At the same time, the company was expanding its foreign holdings into Australia, Canada, Indonesia, New Zealand, Japan, and Egypt.

Vita's management team has been singled out for its longevity and stability. Fernley Parker joined the company in 1954 and rose steadily through the ranks as corporate secretary, finance director, and chief executive officer before serving as chairman for ten years. He retired from the board in 1987 but remained involved in the company as chairman of British Vita Pensions Trust Limited. Robert McGee succeeded Fernley Parker as chief executive officer in 1975 and again as chairman in 1988. McGee had spent virtually all of his business career with Vita. He was hired in 1955 and was appointed to the board in 1972. Rod Sellers, McGee's successor as chief executive officer, had been with the company since 1971. Vita's deputy chief executive officer, Frank Eaton, was likewise a long-term employee of the company. Eaton was hired in 1958, was appointed to the board in 1975, and would not retire until 1999.

Company Perspectives:

As ever, our overriding motivation is to capitalise on the organic growth potential in our businesses through innovation whilst pursuing our acquisitional strategy in product and geographical areas of interest to us. We remain optimistic for the outcome of the year and confident in the success of our long-term business growth strategy.

Continued Growth Through Acquisitions: 1980s to Early 1990s

In 1978 Vita acquired Libeltex and Portways, both fiber manufacturers, and Caligen, a foam manufacturer. For the next five years, the company concentrated on developing its fabric knitting and finishing operations. During the 1980s, Vita continued to acquire companies that allowed it to increase its holdings. The European market was expanded through the acquisition of Tramico in France, Isofel in Spain, and Koepp/Veenendaal in Germany and The Netherlands. A joint venture with Viktor Achter, an automotive fabric firm, resulted in the formation of Vita-Achter. The industrial products division was expanded with the acquisition of three firms: PEC Plastics, Inversale, and Rubber Latex Limited. The latter is now known as Vita Liquid Polymers in the United Kingdom and as RLA Polymers in Australia.

During 1987 Vita further expanded its operations through acquisitions, the building of new plants, and the implementation of innovative production procedures. The German-based Metzeler Schaum group and Royalite Plastics, with operations in Scotland and Italy, were added to the Vita conglomerate. The company formed a new division, Engineering Thermoplastics, enlarged its coated fabrics operation, and began to manufacture staple fibers.

Vitafoam introduced combustion-modified high resilience foams in 1988. That same year, ICOA group of Spain and the UK-based Rossendale Combining Company were acquired. Acquisitions in 1989 included Esbjerg Thermoplast in Denmark; Alpha Flock, a manufacturer of fiber for electrostatic spraying in the United Kingdom; and Ball & Young Adhesives, a U.K.-based maker of rubber carpet underlays. Vita also purchased one-third of the Spartech Corporation, a manufacturer of engineering thermoplastics in the United States. A series of smaller acquisitions the following year allowed Vita to further strengthen its fiber processing, thermoplastic engineering, laminating, and foam operations.

In 1991 Vita made more inroads in the U.S. marketplace with the acquisition of a portion of Leggett & Platt in Missouri, which became Vitafoam Incorporated, with foaming plants in High Point, North Carolina, and Tupelo, Mississippi. In 1992 the Libeltex subsidiary obtained Sporta Vadd and its two fiber-processing operations, and Norman BV, a 100-year-old foam mattress manufacturer in The Netherlands, became part of Vita Interfoam. Yet another foam mattress company, Oost BV and its subsidiary, Sanaform BV, were acquired later the same year.

Although the company continued to enjoy growth and prosperity, Vita faced many of the same problems other businesses endured in the early 1990s. The economic recession in the United Kingdom slowed production. Increased competition from Italy and the restructuring of the automotive industry in Germany also affected Vita's growth in France and Germany. In addition, environmental regulations placed new restrictions on manufacturers, requiring them to modify some equipment. In 1993 Vita was forced to dispose of ICOA in a management buyout. Further restructuring was planned for Metzeler Laminados, one of the two remaining Spanish operations. The prolonged drought in Africa affected profits in the Zimbabwe companies. The company, however, remained optimistic about its growth potential and credited improvements to its manufacturing and quality systems as well as innovative product development as reasons for its continued success.

Acquisitions continued in 1993 with the purchase of Pre-Fab Cushioning in Canada and Nabors Manufacturing in the United States. In France, Vita acquired Pullflex, specialist foam converters, and the Gaillon Group, a Lyon-based manufacturer of thermoplastics. A subsidiary was formed in Poland with construction under way on a new factory for foam manufacturing and converting.

International Expansion and New Challenges in the Late 1990s

Sagging profits in 1994 and 1995 led British Vita to restructure operations and focus attention on strengthening operations. Vita faced declining demand in the cellular polymers division as furniture and bedding sales in Vita's major markets fell in the mid-1990s. In addition, increases in the prices of raw materials in the division affected Vita's bottom line. The fibers and fabrics group also faced similar difficulties, but fortunately for Vita, the industrial polymers group enjoyed increased demand due to stronger industrial and transport markets.

With economic conditions in its home country remaining poor, Vita turned to regions across eastern Europe to boost sales. Its foam operations in Poland, which commenced in 1994, continued to perform well, and in 1996 the company announced plans to expand plant capacity at its Polish Brzeg Dolny facility by 40 percent. While the company searched for strategic investments in Europe, it also divested itself of some underperforming and nonstrategic operations. With negative market conditions in Germany, Vita announced it would shut down its block-making facility in Wega, Germany, in 1996. Vita also chose to divest its share of Vita-Achter, a joint venture with the Viktor Achter Group that produced automotive fabrics. The company sold its Norman and Beddington mattress manufacturing businesses and closed the Oost unit in The Netherlands. Vita also chose to discontinue business in the molded polyether foams segment.

In addition to European expansion, Vita sought to grow internationally in the late 1990s. In 1996 Vita added to its U.S. holdings when it acquired the Olympic Products Division of Cone Mills Corp. for about US $40 million. Olympic, a leading supplier of foam and fiber products for the automotive, home furnishings, and industrial industries in the United States, had four plants in the Greensboro, North Carolina area and a plant in Tupelo, Mississippi. The following year Vita purchased Crest Foam Industries, also based in the United States. The company also explored investing in Asia and became involved in a joint partnership with Inoac Corp. of Japan.

```
┌─────────────────────────────────────────────┐
│              Key Dates:                      │
│                                              │
│ 1949: Norman Grimshaw forms Vitafoam Ltd.    │
│ 1960: Vitafoam expands internationally.      │
│ 1966: Company incorporates as British Vita   │
│       Company Ltd.                           │
│ 1967: British Vita goes public.              │
│ 1999: Company celebrates its 50th anniversary.│
└─────────────────────────────────────────────┘
```

In 1998 British Vita invested a record £173.1 million in acquisitions. The company's industrial division was boosted by the acquisitions of Axipack, a French maker of polypropylene sheet, and Caleppio ILT Spa, a manufacturer of thermoplastic sheet based in Italy. Caleppio's products were geared toward the automotive and sanitaryware industries. Vita also added Hyperlast Ltd. and Doeflex PLC to its liquid polymer compounding division. Doeflex was the largest plastic sheet extruder in the United Kingdom and one of Vita's primary domestic competitors. The £65.9 million purchase included Doeflex's three facilities in England—Iridon Ltd., Plastech Extrusions Ltd., and Doeflex Sheet Ltd. Doeflex also owned the Belgian Horizon Industries NV and Perrite Plastic Compounds Ltd. Doeflex's compounding operations included Doeflex Vinyl Ltd. and Synlon Ltd. Among Vita's other 1998 acquisitions were JGP, a compounding company, and an additional 33.3 percent share of Spartech Corporation, which boosted Vita's stake to 44.3 percent. Thanks in large part to the aggressive acquisition strategy, Vita's 1998 sales rose six percent over 1997 to reach £853 million.

Vita spent 1999 integrating its numerous acquisitions into its extensive family of operations. Still, the company looked forward to further strategic acquisitions. Jim Mercer, Vita's chief executive since 1996, told *AFX News* in early 1999, "Over recent months, we have embarked on a major acquisitions programme—our biggest and most ambitious ever. Our initial position this year will be to bed them down. But our radar is still switched on." In September Vita acquired Elian SA, a supplier of color concentrates used in specialist polymer compounding, for about £16.9 million. The end markets served by Elian included cosmetics, automotive, toys, and packaging. Vita strengthened operations in its fiber division by first investing £5 million toward a new plant for its Libeltex subsidiary. The new facility was earmarked for producing hygiene products, a quickly growing segment involving such markets as incontinence, diaper, and feminine care. In early 2000 Vita purchased Texidel Group, a French company that manufactured technical nonwoven fibers for the automotive and technical industries.

Vita announced positive financial results for the first half of 1999. Overall sales grew 15 percent, buoyed by strong growth in France and the United States. The company appeared to have successfully refocused its operations and energies and looked toward the 21st century to continue its international expansion and sales growth. Vita planned to strengthen its three main divisions—foams, industrial, and fibers—to provide innovative and technologically advanced products found in everyday goods such as vacuum cleaners, surgical gloves, diapers, and seat cushions.

Principal Subsidiaries

British Vita Investments Limited; Doeflex Industries Limited; Hyperlast Limited; Vitacom Limited; Vitafoam Limited; Caligen Foam Limited; Doeflex PLC; JGP Limited; Kay-Metzeler Limited; H.E. Mowbray & Company Limited; Plastech Limited; Silvergate Plastics Limited; The Rossendale Combining Company Limited; Vitafibres Limited; Vitamol Limited; Vita Industrial Polymers Limited; Vita Liquid Polymers Limited; Vita International Limited; Vita International Investments Limited; Vita Services Limited; Vita Thermoplastic Compounds Limited; Vita Thermoplastic Sheet Limited (Scotland); Vita-tex Limited; Axipack SA (France); Caligen Europe BV (Netherlands); Carolex SA (France); Deutsche Vita Polymere GmbH (Germany); Draka Interfoam BV (Netherlands); Gaillon SA (France); Horizon NV (Belgium); ICOA France SA; SA Isofel (Spain; 78.4%); Jackdaw Polymeres SA (France); Koepp AG (Germany; 94.25%); Krojcig Mebel Sp.z o.o (Poland; 51%); Libeltex AB (Sweden); Libeltex NV (Belgium); Libeltex SA (France); Metzeler Mousse SA (France); Metzeler Plastics GmbH (Germany); Metzeler Schaum GmbH (Germany); Morard Europe SA (France); Participation Moulinage du Plouy SAS (France); Pullflex SA (France); Radium Foam BV (Netherlands); Australia Vita Pty. Limited (Australia); Crest Foam Industries Incorporated (U.S.A.; 80%); RLA Polymers Pty. Limited (Australia); Vitafoam CA (Private) Limited (Zimbabwe); Vitafoam Incorporated (U.S.A.); CRF Services Limited (50%); Vita Cortex Holdings Limited (Ireland; 50%); Spartech Corporation (U.S.A.; 44%); Taki-Vita SAE (Egypt; 40%); Vitafoam Nigeria PLC (31%); Vitafoam Products Canada Limited (50%); Radium Latex GmbH (Germany); Royalite Plastics SRL (Italy); Tramico SA (France); UAB Vita Baltic International (Lithuania; 80); Veenendaal Schaumstoffwerk GmbH (Germany); Vitafoam Europe BV (Netherlands); Vita Polymers Denmark A/S; Vita Polymers Europe BV (Netherlands); Vita Polymers France SA; Vita Polymers Poland Sp.z o.o.

Principal Competitors

Carpenter Co.; E.I. du Pont de Nemours and Company; Foamex International Inc.

Further Reading

"British Vita Rises Despite Setbacks," *Daily Telegraph London,* September 5, 1995, p. 25.

Higgs, Richard, "Britain's Vita Buying Doeflex for $110 Million," *Plastics News,* September 14, 1998, p. 42.

Kavanagh, Paul, "British Vita Looks Good for Growth," *Sunday Times-London,* October 3, 1999, p. 12.

Moore, Nadja, "Interview: British Vita To Bed Down Buys in H1, But Still on Acquisition Trail," *AFX News,* March 8, 1999.

Reed, David, "Vita Hit by Hostile Market," *Urethanes Technology,* April 1, 1996, p. 8.

——, "Vita Reacts to Squeeze," *Urethanes Technology,* February 1, 1996, p. 2.

"Vita Buoyed by U.S. Sales," *Urethanes Technology,* April 1, 1999, p. 4.

—Mary McNulty
—updated by Mariko Fujinaka

Brown & Williamson Tobacco Corporation

200 Brown & Williamson Tower
401 South Fourth Street
Louisville, Kentucky 40202
U.S.A.
Telephone: (502) 568-7000
Toll Free: (800) 341-5211
Fax: (502) 568-7107
Web site: http://www.bw.com

Wholly Owned Subsidiary of British American Tobacco plc
Incorporated: 1906 as Brown & Williamson Tobacco
    Company
Employees: 6,600
Sales: $4.54 billion (1998)
NAIC: 312221 Cigarette Manufacturing; 312229 Other
    Tobacco Product Manufacturing; 31221 Tobacco
    Stemming and Redrying

Brown & Williamson Tobacco Corporation, a subsidiary of British American Tobacco plc, is the third largest manufacturer of cigarettes in the United States. The company possesses about 16 percent of the U.S. cigarette market and sells an assortment of cigarette brands, including Kool, GPC, Carlton, Lucky Strike, and Viceroy, as well as loose and specialty tobacco products, such as Kite and Sir Walter Raleigh Bloodhound. Brown & Williamson has overseas operations in Japan and South Korea. The company battled smoking-related lawsuits and negative publicity in the late 1990s.

Popularizing Tobacco in the Late 1800s
and Early 1900s

Brown & Williamson (B&W) was founded in 1894 in the tobacco heartland of Winston-Salem, North Carolina. The business was started by George Brown and Robert Williamson, who formed a partnership before incorporating the company as Brown & Williamson Tobacco Company in 1906. In the beginning, B&W concentrated on specialty products including Bloodhound, Brown & Williamson's Sun Cured, and Red Juice chew-

ing tobaccos. After establishing those successful brands during the early 1900s, B&W assumed a leadership position in the pipe tobacco segment when it purchased the Sir Walter Raleigh brand. That brand had been marketed on a regional basis by the J.G. Flynt Tobacco Company since 1884. B&W purchased it in 1925 and began distributing it nationally. Sir Walter Raleigh eventually became one of B&W's hallmark brands.

About the same time that it began marketing Sir Walter Raleigh pipe tobacco, B&W moved into the burgeoning cigarette market. Cigarettes had been a relatively small segment of the tobacco market prior to the turn of the century. They had first become popular with women during the 1800s as an alternative to cigars and plug, twist, and pipe tobacco. After cigarettes were issued to U.S. soldiers during World War I, though, demand began to escalate. B&W launched an aggressive drive into the cigarette industry following the war. Strong sales of cigarettes and other tobacco products created healthy profit growth at B&W, which caught the eye of outside investors. In 1927, London-based B.A.T. Industries PLC purchased B&W to operate as one of its subsidiaries. B.A.T. expanded B&W's name to Brown and Williamson Tobacco Corporation in 1927, and in 1928 and 1929 added extensive manufacturing facilities in Louisville, Kentucky. At that time, B&W moved its headquarters from Winston-Salem to Louisville.

B&W made its mark on the cigarette industry during the 1930s with a number of brands and products. Importantly, B&W introduced Kool brand cigarettes, which were the first menthol cigarettes marketed nationally in the United States. B&W also began selling Viceroy cigarettes, which were eventually credited with popularizing the filter-tip. Both Viceroy and Kool became mainstay brands for B&W and helped to make it a growing force in U.S. tobacco. Besides those brands, B&W brought out Bugler and Kite cigarette tobacco in the mid-1930s. B&W's Bugler Thrift Kit was the first roll-your-own kit sold in the country. B&W achieved another first with the introduction of the economy-priced pack of cigarettes. Dubbed Wings, the brand sold for just ten cents per pack (compared to 15 cents for most other brands at the time), making it a big hit during the Great Depression. Wings was also the first cigarette package to utilize an outer wrap of moisture-proof cellophane.

Company Perspectives:

To be the world's number one tobacco group and to perform within the top tier of global companies in terms of sustainable, profitable growth over the long term.

Cigarette Dominance in the Mid-1900s

Innovation and market growth buoyed B&W throughout the 1930s and 1940s. In fact, the legion of smokers in the United States spiraled upward after World War II and during the 1950s. At the same time, new influences began to shape the tobacco industry. Reports citing potential health risks associated with smoking cast a shadow on the industry. The results of the reported health risks were that tobacco taxes were increased, advertising channels for cigarette marketers were reduced, and smokers' preferences began to change. Among the most notable changes in preferences during the 1950s and 1960s was the switch to filter-tipped cigarettes. B&W, a pioneer in the filter-tip segment, responded with filter-tip versions of most of its cigarettes. Furthermore, B&W introduced the first filter made of cellulose acetate, which became a feature of its Viceroy Kings brand.

Despite negative health reports, smoking increased throughout the 1950s and most of the 1960s. By the mid-1960s more than 40 percent of the entire U.S. population was smoking cigarettes regularly. B&W benefited not only from increased smoking, but also from market share gains. Its most successful brand was Kool, which had struck gold in certain market niches, becoming the "king" of the menthol market. Studies also indicated that Kool dominated the African American market, about 70 percent of which smoked menthol cigarettes. By the early 1970s, Kool was controlling a whopping ten percent of the entire U.S. cigarette market. Augmenting the highly successful Kool brand during the early 1970s was a lineup of new low-tar brands, including Kool Milds, Viceroy Extra Milds, and Raleigh Extra Milds. Those brand introductions helped B&W grab a 17 percent share of the entire U.S. cigarette market by the mid-1970s.

Although B&W enjoyed some significant successes during the late 1960s and early 1970s, it also began to face some serious internal and external challenges. Importantly, in the late 1960s the percentage of Americans who smoked began to decline. The descent was largely a corollary of a 1964 federal government mandate that required manufacturers to post health warnings on cigarette packages and advertisements. Subsequent government controls, most notably the 1971 ban on television advertising, exacerbated the dilemma and the share of smokers began to decline gradually; by the early 1990s, the percentage would fall to about 25 percent. Another blow came in 1983, when cigarette taxes vaulted 100 percent. That increase, moreover, was followed by a string of tax increases that devastated the domestic cigarette industry.

Although the share of the U.S. smoking population declined during the late 1960s and early 1970s, the actual number of cigarettes sold continued to grow at a heady clip. Total U.S. cigarette consumption grew from about 500 billion in 1965 to nearly 650 billion by 1980. Unfortunately, according to some critics, B&W failed to take full advantage of the increased

industry volume. The problem was largely attributable to stalled growth of its core Kool brand. In 1975 B&W's Kool began to lose market share to such rivals as Salem. Importantly, B&W had failed to translate its successful "Come to Kool" advertising campaign from television to print following the federal ban on cigarette television advertising. B&W tried during the early 1970s to attract younger smokers to Kool by associating the brand with jazz music, but kids were favoring rock 'n roll. Meanwhile, competing brands such as Newport employed more successful marketing tactics and managed to steal Kool market share.

Declining Domestic Demand and International Expansion in the Late 20th Century

Between 1975 and 1985, Kool's share of the total cigarette market plunged from 10.3 percent to less than 7 percent. B&W tried to supplant lost sales with other products, but it achieved only moderate success. In 1981, for example, B&W introduced a new low-tar cigarette called Barclay, investing $100 million in the product launch to get Barclay off to a good start. Unfortunately, B&W had understated Barclay's tar content, and the Federal Trade Commission forced the company to revise the ads. Barclay's growth stagnated following the ad change. B&W's successes during the early and mid-1980s included product introductions geared for the value segment of the cigarette market, which began surging following big tax increases in the early 1980s. But gains in that niche failed to generate growth. In fact, B&W's total share of the U.S. cigarette market toppled from 17 percent in 1976 to about 12 percent ten years later.

For the first time since the turn of the century, cigarette purchases began declining in the early 1980s. Indeed, sales volume in the United States slipped steadily during the 1980s from nearly 650 billion cigarettes in 1980 to about 500 billion in 1990. That trend, combined with lagging market share gains at B&W, mandated a new strategic direction for the company. To that end, B&W promoted Thomas E. Sandefur, Jr., to president of the company in 1984. The 45-year-old Sandefur was a tobacco industry veteran, having worked for R.J. Reynolds Tobacco Co. from 1963 to 1982. He joined B&W with the understanding that he would eventually become head of the company. From 1982 to 1984 Sandefur worked to grow B&W's international operations as senior vice-president of international marketing. Sandefur worked under CEO Raymond J. Pritchard (a native of Wales and a former B.A.T. Industries executive) but was a major influence on the company's strategic direction.

Sandefur was known as capable, demanding, and shrewd. He grew up in Perry, Georgia, and earned a business degree at Georgia Southern College. Recruited by R.J. Reynolds as a salesman, he moved quickly up the corporate ladder on the marketing side of the business. Among his successes at R.J. Reynolds was a line of hugely successful low-tar brands including NOW and Camel Lights. Impressed by his success at Reynolds, B&W lured Sandefur away in 1982 and began grooming him for the top spot. Sandefur was also known as a tobacco hard-liner who vehemently opposed government regulation of his trade. Yet he tried to keep a very low public profile, despite occasional appearances (in caricature) in the Doonesbury comic strip. Even in his work for civic organizations—he was active in a number of civic organizations, particularly the Boy Scouts—Sandefur tried to minimize his public exposure.

When Sandefur took the helm in 1984 he initiated his drive to turn the company around. Specifically, he launched an aggressive bid to increase B&W's shipments overseas, where cigarette sales were growing, and to boost B&W's efforts in the surging U.S. low-priced cigarette segment. Toward the latter goal, B&W began marketing as value-oriented brands Viceroy, GPC Approved (a plain label brand), Raleigh Extra, and Richland, among others. On the international front, B&W moved aggressively into cigarette markets in Asia, Africa, South America, the Middle East, Europe, Japan, and Puerto Rico. Meanwhile, Sandefur and other B&W executives continued to battle the army of federal bureaucrats assaulting the tobacco industry. In April 1994, Sandefur and other tobacco industry executives were brought in front of a Senate subcommittee, interrogated, and lambasted for their role in promoting smoking. Sandefur and other executives reportedly denied that cigarettes were addictive at the hearing.

Despite government entanglement, Sandefur managed to boost B&W's performance during the late 1980s and early 1990s. International sales, for example, bolted 150 percent between 1986 and 1991 and B&W's control of the U.S. cigarette export business surged to 20 percent. By 1991, in fact, B&W's international business represented a full 45 percent of the company's total sales volume. B&W also assumed a leading role in the value-priced cigarette segment, with 21.2 percent of the total market in 1991. Meanwhile, B&W continued to innovate by introducing the first super-slim cigarette—Capri—in 1988. Throughout the late 1980s and early 1990s, moreover, B&W restructured its operations and management as part of an overall effort to cut costs and streamline operations. The net result was that B&W managed to hoist revenues to about $3.5 billion by the early 1990s and to increase profit margins.

When CEO Pritchard retired in 1993, Sandefur assumed full leadership of the company. He continued to restructure, expand internationally, and chase the value market. In 1994, in a major industry merger, B.A.T. (B&W's parent company) acquired The American Tobacco Company and integrated its operations into those of B&W. American Tobacco, which was once the unmitigated behemoth of the U.S. tobacco industry, controlled about seven percent of the U.S. cigarette market. Thus, the acquisition gave B&W a total of more than 18 percent of the U.S. market in 1995, making it the third largest cigarette manufacturer and marketer in the United States. American Tobacco owned well-known brands including Lucky Strike, Pall Mall, Misty, Montclair, Tareyton, and Private Stock. Those bolstered B&W's successful brands, which in 1995 included Kool, GPC, Capri, and Viceroy. In addition to cigarettes, B&W marketed loose cigarette tobacco, pipe tobacco, plug chewing tobacco, and snuff.

Challenges Amid Increasing Litigation in the Late 1990s

The increasing anti-smoking climate of the 1990s affected B&W in a number of ways. Lawsuits grew in number in the late 1990s, and in 1996 a Florida jury awarded $750,000 to a former smoker who had filed a suit against B&W. B&W appealed the case, but it was one of many the company faced. Other cases included lawsuits filed by state governments to recover the costs of treating poor people with smoking-related health problems. In 1997 B&W joined with three other major tobacco companies to try and reach a national tobacco agreement. Negotiating with a group of state attorneys general and lawyers of plaintiffs, the purpose was to settle legal claims. After several failed attempts, the group finally reached an agreement, called the Master Settlement Agreement, with 46 states, the District of Columbia, and five U.S. territories and commonwealths in November 1998. Under terms of the settlement, the major tobacco companies agreed to pay more than $200 billion over a 25-year period to finance healthcare costs. The tobacco companies also became limited in the scope of advertising—billboard advertising of tobacco products was prohibited, the use of cartoon characters in marketing was not allowed, restrictions were placed on the distribution of free tobacco samples, and more. Also as part of the settlement, the involved states agreed to dismiss existing claims against the tobacco companies and not to refile the lawsuits.

Though B&W dedicated many resources to handling legal claims and negative publicity, the company continued to strengthen tobacco operations to secure its market leadership position. In 1997 the company reported revenues of $4.38 billion. U.S. sales accounted for the largest segment, reaching $3.11 billion. B&W's share of the U.S. market was a solid 16.1 percent, and international operations grew, particularly in Japan, where Kent cigarettes became the leading import brand in 1997. The following year, B&W faced a price increase of ¥20 per pack in the Japanese market. Still, market share for brands marketed in Japan—Kent, Lucky Strike, Kool—all increased in 1998. The brands were available in 84 percent of onsite vending machines in Japan, which numbered more than 420,000. About 67 percent of B&W's sales in Japan were attributed to vending sales.

In 1997 and 1998, B&W faced increasing competition and heavy discounting, which cut into the company's market share. To combat the stiff competition, B&W implemented repositioning and modernization strategies for the Kool and GPC brands, which were suffering from tired brand images. The efforts included new packaging, marketing campaigns, and brand extensions. B&W introduced Kool Natural, an all-natural menthol product, and three additional Kool products in order to attract Kool's target audience of adult smokers under the age of 30. In addition to new packaging and the ''B Kool'' advertising campaign, B&W sponsored a Kool Champ Car in the FedEx Championship Series, a race car series. According to B&W, Kool's market share in the U.S. increased from 3.39 percent to 3.43 percent in 1998.

B&W hoped to enhance the image of traditionally low-priced GPC. The company felt the mainstreaming of GPC would help boost sales, which were suffering as a result of heavy discounting by other tobacco companies. Lowering the price of GPC, B&W believed, would prove unprofitable, and thus the company resisted lowering the price, but the brand's market share began to decline as consumers opted for discounted brands perceived to be higher quality. B&W fought back by initiating a marketing campaign designed to position GPC as a high-quality brand that also happened to be a good value. GPC also became the sponsor of the George Strait Country Music Festival in 1998.

Another brand B&W sought to reposition in the late 1990s was Carlton, a brand B&W gained from the 1994 merger with The American Tobacco Company. Carlton was an ultra low-tar brand, and among brands with up to one milligram of tar, Carlton commanded a 78 percent market share. B&W created new packaging and advertising for Carlton, boldly pushing its ultra low-tar feature to attract the target age group of smokers between the ages of 35 and 50. Other brands promoted by B&W included Lucky Strike, which was promoted in metropolitan markets, the value-priced Misty, and Capri. Despite such efforts, B&W's share of the overall U.S. market dropped to 15 percent in 1998 from 16.1 percent in 1997.

At the beginning of 1999 British American Tobacco, B&W's parent and the second largest cigarette manufacturer in the world, and Rothmans International BV, the fourth-largest cigarette maker in the world, merged. Rothmans, based in the Netherlands, was a unit of the Swiss Compagnie Financiere Richemont AG. Among Rothmans' cigarette brands were such premium labels as Dunhill, Cartier, and Rothmans. The deal was valued at $8.67 billion and created a global cigarette giant second only to Philip Morris. In October B&W consolidated its specialty tobacco units with those of Rothmans, which were located in Georgia. The combined division would supply 42 percent of the U.S. pipe tobacco market and about 62 percent of the roll-your-own cigarette segment. B&W planned to close its specialty tobacco plant in Winston-Salem, North Carolina, in 2000 or 2001 as a result of the consolidation.

In November 1999 B&W faced some excitement when *The Insider,* a major motion picture, was released nationwide. The film, though fiction, was based upon the true story of a former B&W executive, Jeffrey Wigand, one of the most well-known

whistle-blowers of the tobacco industry. Wigand claimed that B&W withheld information from the public about the hazards of smoking. B&W sued Wigand in 1995 for violating confidentiality agreements but agreed to dismiss the lawsuit in 1997. The film chronicled the life of a tobacco industry whistle-blower, who was threatened by his former employer after publicizing his experiences.

The 1990s was a challenging era for B&W, one that forced the century-old company to reevaluate its traditional practices and adjust to new beliefs. The company withstood countless lawsuits and suffered through extremely negative publicity. For 1999, earnings in the United States were predicted to be six percent lower than 1998 revenues, and it was estimated that B&W's U.S. market share dropped another 1.5 percentage points during 1999. As B&W looked toward the next century, however, the company hoped to build its market share, both in the United States and abroad. To accomplish this, B&W planned to move away from value-priced cigarette brands and promote premium-priced brands more heavily.

Principal Competitors

Philip Morris Companies Inc.; R.J. Reynolds Tobacco Holdings Inc.; Lorillard Tobacco Company.

Further Reading

Beck, Ernest, ''Deal Would Create Tobacco Powerhouse, May Signal Consolidation Wave,'' *Asian Wall Street Journal,* January 12, 1999, p. 1.

Broder, John M., ''Tobacco Industry Makes a Deal the Deal: Money Will Be Earmarked for Anti-Smoking Campaigns, Health Care,'' *Portland Oregonian,* June 21, 1997, p. A1.

The Brown and Williamson Story: A Retrospective, Louisville: Brown and Williamson Tobacco Corporation, September 1995.

Fitzgerald, Tom, ''Brown & Williamson Announces Changes Relating to American Tobacco,'' *PR Newswire,* December 22, 1994.

Louis, Arthur M., ''The $150-Million Cigarette,'' *Fortune,* November 17, 1980, pp. 121–22.

Otolski, Greg, ''Sandefur to Succeed Pritchard As Chief of B&W Tobacco,'' *Courier-Journal,* January 13, 1993, p. B10.

——, ''The Tangled Trail of B&W's Documents,'' *Courier-Journal,* April 2, 1995, p. A1.

Pomice, Eve, ''Kooling Off,'' *Forbes,* November 17, 1986, p. 230.

Rhyne, Debbie, ''Brown & Williamson Official Says Movie Unfairly Trashes Tobacco Company,'' *Macon Telegraph,* November 11, 1999.

Ward, Joe, ''B&W Throws Monkey Wrench into Tobacco Negotiations,'' *Courier-Journal,* June 12, 1997, p. A1.

Wessel, Kim, ''B&W Dismisses Lawsuit Against Wigand,'' *Courier-Journal,* August 1, 1997, p. B3.

Wolfson, Andrew, ''B&W Chairman Little-Known, and Likes It That Way,'' *Courier-Journal,* June 19, 1994, p. A1.

—Dave Mote
—updated by Mariko Fujinaka

Calcot Ltd.

1601 East Brundage Lane
Bakersfield, California 93307
U.S.A.
Telephone: (661) 327-5961
Fax: (661) 861-9870
Web site: http://www.calcot.com

Cooperative
Incorporated: 1927
Employees: 96
Sales: $435 million (1999)
NAIC: 11192 Cotton Farming; 42259 Other Farm
 Product Raw Material Wholesalers

Calcot Ltd. is one of the largest cotton cooperatives in the United States, with average annual sales between $650 and $700 million. It is cooperatively owned by approximately 2,200 cotton farmers in California and Arizona, and it sells about 1.6 million bales of raw cotton annually. Calcot markets 40 percent of all the cotton grown in California and more than 60 percent of the cotton grown in Arizona. It sells its cotton to customers in approximately 40 countries, most of which are located in Asia. Since 1999, Calcot has also represented almond farmers.

Cotton farmer Frank Green, a former Army officer and lawyer, first had the idea of organizing a cooperative for cotton growers in California's San Joaquin valley in 1926, after the Capper-Volstead Act of 1922 gave farmers the right to band together without violating anti-trust laws. Cotton had been grown in California for many years, and the cooperative was seen as a way of alleviating a number of problems faced by the state's cotton farmers, including high labor costs, uncertain supplies of water, and, in particular, dependence on powerful cotton firms who controlled cotton prices. The cooperative, as Green proposed it, was to be a non-profit entity organized by and operated for the benefit of cotton growers themselves and would thus assure growers the best price possible for their crop.

In February 1927, 151 growers met in Delano, California, a farming community about 30 miles north of Bakersfield, and unanimously approved the terms for a co-op called the San Joaquin Cotton Growers Association. By late summer 1927, the Association had 500 members representing about 40,000 acres. An important incentive for growers to join the Association was its loan program, offering 6.5 percent interest instead of the eight percent demanded by banks. It also instituted a program whereby members could sell part of their crop in advance to raise money for growing and harvesting in the coming season. A major flaw in the early organization, however, was a loophole that allowed members to deliver as much or as little of their cotton crop as they wanted—or even none at all—to the Association, though the negative implications of this situation did not become apparent until years later. In its first year of existence the Association handled 10,000 bales of cotton.

Following a bad 1928–29 harvest, Association members voted to sever ties with a Los Angeles cottonseed company that had helped finance its loans. As a result the cooperative formed its own finance arm, the California Cotton Growers Finance Company, which was capitalized for $200,000, money advanced to farmers for the 1929 crop. At the same time, the Association changed its name to the California Cotton Growers Association.

Depression in Cotton Markets

The 1929 harvest was a good one. Unfortunately, in a market glutted with cotton, prices fell and were driven down even further by the onset of the Great Depression at the end of the year. As the Depression worsened, Association members became increasingly dissatisfied with Green's leadership. Although he initiated a plan for surviving the crisis, including partnering with the American Cotton Cooperative Association (ACCA) and adopting a new name: California Cotton Cooperative Association (CCCA) to emphasize their cooperative status. The plan was adopted, but members remained unhappy with Green's leadership, and in June 1930 a new president, J.W. Guiberson, was elected by the Association's board of directors. However, Guiberson refused to take office due to the disarray of the organization's finances. In September, C.O. Moser, of the ACCA in New Orleans, was brought in to lead the California cooperative. After studying the situation, Moser recommended

Company Perspectives:

Calcot has evolved as agriculture has evolved. We have fewer members today than we did in 1960, but we handle more cotton. There are fewer farms, but they are larger. That has made competition for marketing their production more intense and while it has not made cooperatives less important, it has changed the nature of the original idea— that of representing the small grower in a world dominated by a few buyers—to one of partnership, operating as the direct marketing arm of growers' individual operations, providing first rate service at the lowest possible cost, allowing the grower to keep more of the actual selling price of their cotton, rather than paying a middleman to handle the risk.

strengthening the membership agreement which, he said, would result in reasonable volumes of cotton reaching the Association.

Despite the bad economic time, the Association, now known as the CCCA, processed more than 40,000 bales and paid more than $2.4 million to its members in 1930. It also named a new president, Clarence Churchill Selden, a successful cotton merchant, who instituted a series of cost-cutting measures. He also persuaded the Board to move the Association's headquarters from Delano to Bakersfield, a move that finally took place in late 1931, a year of legal strife.

By 1933, the CCCA was handling 25,000 bales annually, about 20 percent of the San Joaquin valley's total production. It was debt free and had about $23,000 in the bank. The CCCA acquired member cotton through open bidding and advanced growers the price the ACCA was paying. Baled cotton was classed as soon as it arrived from the harvest. Previously farmers had been paid a standard price regardless of the quality of their cotton. Grading thus enabled farmers to get the best, fairest price possible.

As the Depression wore on cotton consumption declined while cotton availability increased. Prices plunged, eventually reaching five cents a pound in 1933. The same year cotton pickers went on strike for higher wages. Encouraged by Lloyd Frick of the San Joaquin Valley Labor Board, growers resisted. Violent clashes ensued, but eventually the pickers lowered their demands. So impressed was the CCCA with Frick's leadership, he was voted president, beginning an association that would last 38 years.

In 1935, CCCA initiated its own ginning program, which further eroded the control cotton companies had over growers. Unfortunately, the ACCA refused to extend loans for the program and the CCCA was forced to find its own financing. The following year relations between the two groups were further strained when the ACCA tried to block the CCCA from giving its manager C.C. Selden a $1,000 raise. By 1937, CCCA's situation had stabilized. It handled a record 130,000 bales and could offer members a complete package of services, including advances, hedges, ginning, and government loans. That year, the situation was reversed and the ACCA came to the CCCA for financial assistance. Its request was refused. Finally, in August

1939, CCCA's board resolved to create its own independent financial structure and separate itself completely from the national organization.

Struggling into the 1940s

During the 1939–1940 cotton season new procedures were put in place for purchasing cotton from CCCA members. Unfortunately they could not be fully implemented until the end of the summer, and by then it was late to start making sales arrangements. It soon became a disastrous situation for the Association. By November 1939, when mills had already purchased the cotton they needed through January from other sources, CCCA had sold only 700 bales. By January, they had sold only 4,200 of 32,000 bales they had on hand. Growers, angry because they had yet not received their promised advances, threatened to sue. In February business was so bad that Selden asked the board to consider disbanding the CCCA entirely, a move that was unanimously rejected.

The cotton economy turned around decisively when the United States entered World War II in late 1941. Enormous quantities of cotton were needed for the war effort, for uniforms, blankets, bags, and tents. The government called on cotton farmers to increase their production. Nonetheless, despite the good times, the CCCA continued to struggle. Although California cotton production reached about 600,000 bales in 1945, the CCCA never sold more than 30,000 bales any year during the war. One thing that hampered the Association was its inability to borrow enough money to purchase reasonable amounts of cotton from its members. There was also the perennial problem of members not delivering to the cooperative the portion of their crop they had contracted for. Yet another problem was low storage capacity. However, when members were polled whether the CCCA should obtain its own warehouse, the response was a resounding negative.

All was not well at the CCCA. In 1942, Selden announced significantly lower overhead and a $175,000 profit. Two years later, though, auditors discovered that the CCCA's bookkeeping was faulty, which resulted in a *loss* of $192,000 for the 1943–44 season. Selden died later that year after a prolonged illness and was replaced by J. Russell Kennedy. Kennedy proved to be a dynamic, innovative executive, who would put the CCCA firmly on its feet again. The son of Texas cotton farmers, he was sympathetic to the problems growers faced; as a former USDA cotton specialist he knew his way around government programs. His first act was to sell off all of CCCA's cotton inventory to pay off its debt and finance the coming cotton season.

Postwar Regrouping

California experienced a postwar boom that affected the entire agricultural sector. Expanded irrigation in the state was added to the changes cotton farming as a whole was undergoing with the introduction of advanced practices and such modern equipment as automatic harvesting machines. Cotton acreage in the state exploded. In 1944 Kennedy introduced a plan for the CCCA that was radical in its simplicity and returned the Association to its original purpose as a cooperative working for its members. Under the plan, the CCCA would no longer bid for member cotton like other cotton buyers. Instead the cooperative

---

Key Dates:

1927: Co-op organized by Frank Green in Delano, California.
1930: In a period of financial crisis, C.C. Selden becomes manager.
1931: Headquarters move to Bakersfield.
1936: CCCA initiates its own ginning program.
1939: CCCA severs ties with American Cotton Cooperative Association.
1945: CCCA begins marketing cotton for members instead of buying it outright from them.
1947: First CCCA warehouses built.
1950: CCCA offers first financing to co-op cotton gins.
1953: Board changes name to Calcot Ltd.
1955: Arizona farmers join Calcot.
1959: Calcot builds a new headquarters in Bakersfield.
1973: Calcot becomes first Western company to sell directly to China.
1989: ''Zero Contamination'' Program initiated; additional marketing options introduced for members.
1994: Calcot makes record sale of 233,000 bales to China.
1999: Calcot becomes involved in almond marketing.

---

would take member cotton, market it, and return the money to the growers. Growers would get payments when the cotton was ginned; that money would be an advance on the final income. Kennedy also cut the cooperative's staff and forged closer ties with cooperative gins in the San Joaquin valley, which strengthened the cooperative nature of the entire cotton industry there.

In 1947 the California cotton crop was worth $157 million. It had become the state's top income-producing crop, surpassing even citrus. Cotton's phenomenal expansion brought the CCCA a new set of problems. In particular, warehouse space was suddenly at a premium. Before the war, the CCCA had warehoused its inventory at sites throughout the United States; Kennedy had centralized them all in a warehouse in Galveston, Texas. Finally, in 1947, the CCCA built its first warehouse on land purchased near the Bakersfield headquarters. In 1948, when production expanded even more, six more storage facilities were built.

Expansion into Europe and Arizona

CCCA processed 13 percent of California's total production in 1949: 123,000 bales, up from only 30,000 five years earlier. Kennedy toured Western Europe that summer, touting the state's cotton and signing up new customers in Britain, France, Germany, the Netherlands, Belgium, and Switzerland. In 1952, despite the new warehouses added every year since 1947, space was still a problem. It was solved in an unexpected way when it was noticed that smaller bales processed in a new compress enabled the cooperative to store twice as much cotton in its existing space. Moreover, the new process made it possible to get cotton to market more quickly because it bypassed other compressing.

The board changed the cooperative's name to Calcot Ltd. in 1953, a change members formally approved in 1956. In April

1955 Lloyd Frick expressed the desire to retire from the presidency, an office he had held since 1933. Rather than lose his experience, Calcot created a new position for him, chairman of the board. At the same time, the manager title was changed to president and chief executive officer.

By the mid-1950s, Arizona cotton farmers had expressed an interest in forming their own cooperative based on the Calcot model. When they realized what it would take, financially and administratively, to start their own association from scratch, they asked to be allowed to join Calcot themselves. The Board agreed on the condition that Arizona farmers deliver at least 25,000 bales to the cooperative annually. Uncertain at first—until then they had never harvested more than 10,000 bales a year—Arizona agreed. They ended up sending 40,000 to Calcot, and the following year the cooperative built its first Arizona warehouses in Phoenix.

The cooperative was entering a period of prosperity. In 1956–57, Calcot handled a record 459,000 bales, nearly 25 percent of California's crop and 12 percent of Arizona's. In March 1959 the cooperative dedicated a new headquarters building in Bakersfield. By the 1960s, Calcot agents were active in 23 countries throughout the world. In 1963 it sold its largest single block to date, 60,000 bales that went to a U.S. mill. In 1965, the cooperative had 54 permanent employees, 148 warehouses and 4,000 members, who delivered a record 837,000 bales.

Threats and Advances during the 1960s

Synthetic fibers such as rayon had been on the rise since the mid-1950s and in the 1960s became a serious threat to cotton. As a result of the growing popularity of synthetics, the total U.S. cotton market experienced a decline of 300,000 bales in 1962. By 1964 the total pounds of synthetics and cotton used in the United States were equal, and the following year the amount of synthetics used by American textile mills surpassed cotton. To combat the ascendancy of synthetics, Calcot considered expanding its activities in the textile marketplace into spinning, weaving, and promotion to the retail level. Ultimately, however, the cooperative decided to remain within its core competencies.

Calcot continued to modernize its processes throughout the 1960s. In 1965 it introduced an automatic sampler which removed a small portion of lint from a bale for sampling. This did away with over-sampling, which the cooperative estimated accounted for thousands of dollars in losses by members every year. By 1968 cotton was analyzed by optical devices which fed their results to a small computer. Computers also expedited the handling of cotton in Calcot's warehouses. More and more often truck transport was used instead of rail, while foreign orders were containerized before being shipped.

A jump in cotton prices in the fall of 1967 caused many growers to sell cotton they had promised Calcot to outside buyers, and the cooperative realized it had to further tighten its marketing agreement with members. A five dollar penalty was established for every undelivered bale; in extreme cases, membership could also be terminated. At the same time, Calcot began developing alternative marketing options for its members. It resurrected the ''call pool'' which allowed growers to

anticipate price rises and determine their own prices instead of relying on Calcot's marketing department do it.

In 1972, following Russell Kennedy's retirement, Calcot made its first inroads into the Eastern European market, resulting in sizable purchases by both Romania and Poland. In 1973 Calcot was the first Western cotton company to sell directly to the People's Republic of China. It was a substantial sale of 45,600 bales. By the mid-1970s cotton had recovered much of the market share that synthetics had taken, and in 1975 Calcot announced it had handled a record 1.4 million bales from members. Ten new warehouses were built to accommodate the increased demand, and more were added in following years. By 1977, the year Tom W. Smith took over as president and the cooperative's 50th anniversary, gross sales had reached an all-time high of $516 million.

In 1978, however, Calcot entered another rocky period. Bad winter storms that caused growers to delay planting the new year's crop were followed by a lygus infestation. The result was the worst harvest in 25 years. Calcot responded by allowing growers to fill their contracts with cotton from the following year and extending special loans to get them going into the next growing season. That season turned out to be one of the best in history. Calcot, expecting prices to drop, hedged a larger portion of its cotton holdings than normal in futures markets. Unexpected purchases by China, though, abruptly made cotton futures volatile. Before the cooperative could respond July futures were trading below May contracts. Caught in this inverted market, Calcot found itself saddled with a $3.2 million loss. Competitors and the media zeroed in, claiming the cooperative was on the brink of collapse. The market recovered before the end of the year, but not before Calcot's reputation had been tarnished, and ill will had grown among many members.

In the mid-1980s, Calcot was the U.S.A.'s largest cotton shipper, sending over 30 containers a day to port. Sixty-five percent of all its cotton—about one million bales a year—was sold to overseas customers. Nineteen eighty-three was a particularly good year: The U.S.S.R. bought about one million bales from the United States, about half of that supplied by Calcot. The late 1980s were a time of continuing innovation for Calcot. It initiated its "Zero Contamination" Program when it was discovered that increased mechanization combined with less-frequent human supervision resulted in greater amounts of contamination in cotton bales. The program became imperative when important Japanese customers began shopping elsewhere for cleaner cotton. A large part of the program consisted of an awareness campaign targeted at growers and cotton gins. The first harvest of the program saw contamination reduced by as much as 50 percent. In another innovation, by the 1990s, most of the classing of cotton had been taken over by high tech equipment, processes Calcot believed would ultimately lead to better yarn and productivity. Bar code systems, portable scanners, and computers streamlined warehousing and shipping as well.

By the early 1990s Calcot had introduced three new options that gave growers even more latitude in determining the final price they received for their cotton. The "seller's call," the "minimum price program," and the "basis call," in addition to the more traditional marketing options, allowed growers to settle for a fixed but safe price at the beginning of the season or to take varying degrees of risk on prices determined by futures markets.

In March 1994 Calcot made a sale to China that broke all company records: 233,000 bales at a price of $90 million. In fact, by July 1994, it had sold 900,000 bales to the People's Republic and booked near record sales for the year of $818 million. The Far East remained Calcot's strongest market throughout the 1990s. In 1996 a group of cotton importers in Indonesia lodged a formal complaint against the cooperative, claiming some 5,000 tons of Calcot cotton was infected with a rare bacteria. No samples of the shipment were made available for independent analysis, however. A government spokesperson supported Calcot, speculating the Indonesians were, in essence, trying to renegotiate a contract following a drop in world prices.

Calcot's membership declined in the closing years of the 1990s, contributing to a 29 percent downturn in revenues—dropping from $685 million in fiscal year 1997 to $488.1 million for the twelve months ending in January 31, 1999. One reason for the decrease was a move by farmers away from cotton to more lucrative crops, including grapes and almonds. In response to the shift in California agriculture, in 1999 Calcot began marketing almonds in addition to cotton.

Principal Competitors

Plains Cotton Cooperative Association; Dunavant Enterprises Inc.; Staple Cotton Cooperative Association; Weil Brothers Cotton Inc.; Southwestern Irrigated Cotton Growers Association.

Further Reading

Bangsberg, P.T., "Indonesian Group Calls for Boycott of U.S. Cotton Firm," *Journal of Commerce and Commercial*, June 18, 1998, p. 1A.

"Calcot, Ltd. President to Head National Cotton Council," *Bakersfield Californian*, February 18, 1996.

Carnal, Jim, "Calcot, Jess Smith Executives Predict Rosy Future for Cotton," *Bakersfield Californian*, June 14, 1996.

Cook, Dan, "A Controversial Crop: California Cotton Cooperative Calcot Ltd. Has to Balance High Yields against Even Higher Water Consumption," *California Business*, June 1991, p. 51.

Merlo, Catherine M., *Legacy of a Shared Vision: The History of Calcot Ltd.*, Calcot Ltd., Bakersfield, California, 1995.

Owen, Wendy, "Bakersfield, Calif., Exporter to Market Almonds," *Knight-Ridder/Tribune Business News*, November 18, 1998.

—Gerald E. Brennan

GROUPE CARBONE LORRAINE

Carbone Lorraine S.A.

Immeuble La Fayette
La Défense 5
TSA 38001
F-92919 Paris La Défense Cedex
France
Telephone: (+33) 1 46 91 54 00
Fax: (+33) 1 46 91 54 01
Web site: http://www.carbonelorraine.com

Public Company
Incorporated: 1891 as Compagnie Générale Electrique de Nancy; 1892 as Compagnie Lorraine de Charbons pour l'Electricité
Employees: 6,911
Sales: EUR 690 million ($662.98 million)(1999)
Stock Exchanges: Paris
Ticker Symbol: CBLP.PA
NAIC: 335312 Motor and Generator Manufacturing; 334419 Other Electronic Component Manufacturing; 335991 Carbon and Graphite Product Manufacturing; 335314 Brakes, Electromagnetic, Manufacturing

Carbone Lorraine S.A. is a world-leading manufacturer of electrical components, especially brushes, brush holders, and related equipment and assemblies for electrical motors; permanent magnets, especially for the computer industry, where the company's products are used in the production of disk drives, and for the automotive industry. Carbone Lorraine is also a global leader in the production of high-performance carbon- and graphite-based materials and components, used for such purposes as high-temperature protection for the nuclear, space, and aeronautics industries, among others, and high-energy braking systems for aircraft, trains, motorcycles, and heavy machinery. Carbone Lorraine has long operated beyond its French home base, with an international presence in more than 44 countries. Some 85 percent of the company's sales are made outside of France; the company's U.S. activities alone account for more than 22 percent of total sales. Led by Chairman and CEO Michel Cocozza, Carbone Lorraine has pursued a steady

acquisition campaign in the late 1990s. These acquisitions and the company's internal growth have secured it the number one positions worldwide in the production of brushes for electric motors and thermal corrosion resistance applications; the number two position for electrical protection products for semiconductors; and the world's number three position for production of permanent magnets for the automotive industry. Carbone Lorraine trades on the Paris Stock Exchange.

Powering the Electric Motor Industry in the 19th Century

Carbone Lorraine was formed by the merger, in 1937, of two prominent French manufacturers, Compagnie Générale Electrique de Nancy, and Compagnie Lorraine de Charbons pour l'Electricité. The first of the two was founded in 1891, with a factory in Pagny sur Moselle producing electric motors, lighting equipment, and electric dynamos and generators. The second company was formed one year later, near Paris, and played a central role in the development of the electric motor. In 1893, one of Compagnie Lorraine de Charbons's engineers discovered a means of artificially creating graphite from amorphous carbon. The company quickly specialized in this process, and began producing graphite brushes for electric motors.

Graphite had numerous advantages as a material. A naturally occurring ''pure'' state of carbon, graphite offered extremely high heat resistance, a high degree of both electrical and thermal conductivity, self-lubricating properties, and a chemical stability enabling it to resist corrosion. While naturally occurring graphite, along with the other ''pure'' carbon form, diamond, were relatively rare, the availability of carbon in its amorphous state—one of the most abundant substances on Earth and present in the form of coal, peat, and other mixed forms— offered an opportunity for unlimited, low-cost quantities of artificially produced graphite. In 1893 Compagnie Lorraine was granted the patent for its process of generating graphite from amorphous carbon using an electric arc.

Industries quickly adopted electricity and electric motors. Quieter and less polluting than internal combustion and steam engines, electric motors could be built on extremely small

Company Perspectives:

Carbone Lorraine's industrial strategy is driven by its customer. The Group serves widely diversified industries, both in the electrical components and in the thermal applications markets. These industries operate in a context of increasing globalization, and have gained powerful international positions. Right from its beginnings Carbone Lorraine has implemented a policy of accompanying its customers as their business develops on an international scale, and to this end sets up facilities near to their production sites to facilitate their integration. The overall aim is to promote partnerships with industrial customers, to offer the best lead times and to provide high-performance, close-at-hand services. To keep pace with the increasing internationalization of its markets, Carbone Lorraine has had to continuously intensify its international, industrial and commercial developments. Along with this increasing internationalization, the Group has expanded the number of products and services it provides to industry. From products to systems, Carbone Lorraine's supply strategy is now based on a total service and preassembled product provision approach. Its "made-to-measure" and integrated partnership initiatives have been elaborated with a view to satisfying the expectations of customers demanding greater and greater functionality and proximity. With nearly 85% of its sales figure turned over outside France, and industrial and commercial presence in over 40 countries, international recognition of its industrial expertise and an international customer base, Carbone Lorraine has everything it needs to successfully implement its strategy: development in niche markets where it is committed to winning worldwide market leading positions.

scales—such as the tiny electric motors in an automobile's windshield wipers. The company's graphite brushes and seatings, as well as its later partner's electric motors, were fast to find international markets. By 1892, Compagnie Générale Electrique de Nancy had already begun to develop its business beyond France, opening the first of its branches in England. Both companies quickly built their international networks, expanding into Germany, Belgium, Italy, Sweden, and Switzerland, before opening operations in Latin America and North America.

By the mid-1930s, both companies had succeeded in establishing themselves as leaders in electric motor technology. The two companies merged in 1937, forming Carbone Lorraine S.A. The build-up toward World War II provided some of the impetus for the merger, as the company's products came into demand to support the new generation of military vehicles, including the tanks and aircraft that were to play an important role in warfare for the first time. Yet, the Nazi takeover of France in 1940 temporarily halted Carbone Lorraine's independent operations.

After the war Carbone Lorraine returned to its international growth. While rebuilding its European network, the company expanded further in western Europe, forming subsidiaries in Denmark, Norway, Austria, Spain, the Netherlands, Greece,

and Turkey. Carbone Lorraine also boosted its presence in the Americas, complementing its existing Brazilian, Argentinean, and American presence with operations in Mexico, Columbia, Venezuela, and Canada. The company also took its first steps into the Pacific region, opening a subsidiary in Australia. In 1961, the company stepped up its graphite brush production with the opening of a new dedicated facility in Amiens.

Acquisition Drive in the 1980s

For much of its history, Carbone Lorraine remained focused on its core graphic brush production. In the early 1980s, however, the company saw the opportunity to expand its business into new areas, while building up leading global positions in its specialty areas. Carbone Lorraine's long background in graphite production led it to step up its development of advanced graphite materials and their applications. The company's thermal corrosion and heat resistance technologies played essential roles in developments in the nuclear power industry, the space and aeronautics industries, but also in such diverse areas as motorcycle racing, where the company's graphite composites provided secure braking materials as racers neared the 200 mile per hour mark. Carbone Lorraine established itself as the world leader in advanced graphite materials and technology.

The company's participation in the electric motor industry, primarily through its graphite brushes, led it to develop its expertise in related fields. In 1985, Carbone Lorraine purchased Ferraz, one of the world's leading producers of industrial fuses and electrical protection components. Based in France, Ferraz had established a strong worldwide presence, particularly through its North American and Japanese subsidiaries. With the Ferraz acquisition, Carbone Lorraine expanded its electrical components complement to include products such as lightning and surge arresters; isolating switches and short-circuit equipment; current conductors and protectors for the railroad and other industries; industrial fuses; and fuses for the protection of semiconductors. By the 1990s, Carbone Lorraine would gain the world's number two position in this market.

Spurring the company's growth in the 1980s was the deep-pocket financial backing of Groupe Pechiney, which held more than 64 percent of Carbone Lorraine's stock into the early 1990s. A new acquisition in 1991 propelled the company still higher in the ranks of leading electrical components suppliers. Buying up the North American assets of the Stackpole company, Carbone Lorraine secured its leadership position as the world's top producer of brushes for the electrical motor market, as well as boosting its position as a leading developer of advanced materials for high-temperature applications. Meanwhile, Carbone Lorraine looked beyond electrical components, and into the sealants, especially waterproofing, market, where the company hoped to build a strong market position.

The recession of the early 1990s, and the extended economic crisis in its core European market, cut deeply into Carbone Lorraine's growth. As its key customers in the automotive industry and in the chemical engineering and other fields cut back on orders, the company saw its sales shrink and its profits dwindle. The company's heavy reliance on the European market, where it posted some two-thirds of its annual revenues, left it vulnerable to a recession that lasted until the middle of the

Key Dates:

1891: Compagnie Générale Electrique de Nancy is founded.
1892: Compagnie Lorraine de Charbons pour l'Electricité is founded.
1893: First international branch opens, in the United Kingdom.
1937: Companies merge to form Carbone Lorraine S.A.
1961: Factory in Amiens, France, opens.
1980s: Group Pechiney acquires a significant stake in Carbone Lorraine.
1985: Carbone Lorraine acquires Ferraz (France).
1991: Company acquires Stackpole (United States).
1995: 21 percent share of Carbone Lorraine is sold to Paribas Affaires Industrielles.
1997: Paribas sells its stake, and Carbone Lorraine is an independent company.

decade for most of its European customers. The company began losing money, a pattern that continued into early 1993. By then, with annual sales topping FFr 2 billion, the company was forced to streamline its operations, while seeking capital from new investors. Groupe Pechiney, at the same time, began looking to decrease its majority share position in Carbone Lorraine.

In April 1995, Groupe Pechiney announced its intention to sell a 21 percent share of Carbone Lorraine to Paribas Affaires Industrielles. By then, Carbone Lorraine had largely completed its recovery from the difficult early years of the decade—with sales rising to FFr 2.6 billion, with profits returning to FFr 87 million. In that year, the company stepped up its electrical components arm with two major acquisitions, those of UGIMAG, one of the world's leading manufacturers of permanent magnets, and Dietrich, of Germany, which held the leading European position in the market for brush holders for electric motors.

In the second half of the 1990s, Carbone Lorraine seemed to have found its stride, beginning a series of acquisitions that secured leadership positions for the company in its core businesses of electrical components, particularly graphite brushes, permanent magnets, and electrical protection products, and advanced graphite materials and technologies. Completing the acquisitions of the ferrite magnet divisions of Philips and ITT-Automotive in 1997 and 1998, Carbone Lorraine added to its automobile products range. In 1997, also, the company purchased Astrocosmos, of the United States. Despite difficulties in merging Astrocosmos into its existing operations, the acquisition gave Carbone Lorraine an added boost in the market for corrosion resistant materials, and extended expertise in such advanced materials categories as titanium, zirconium, and tantalum.

After Paribas sold the bulk of its ownership position, Carbone Lorraine found itself an independent company, with the majority of its stock available on the stock exchange. At the same time, the company exited the sealings business, selling off its assets. The boost in funds provided the fuel for the company's strongest acquisition drive yet. In 1998 and through 1999, Carbone Lorraine completed some ten major acquisitions, including those of Canada's Gle Noram (industrial fuses); Danks Electrical Industri, of Denmark (brushes); Midland Materials (graphite parts for the semiconductor industry) and Vitre-Cell's carbon composite activities, both based in the United States; Bert, of Germany, and Soulé, of France, both specializing in high-power disconnect systems; and Metaullics System of the United States (heat exchangers).

Carbone Lorraine showed no signs of slowing as it approached the 21st century. After completing the acquisitions of the cerberite division of the United Kingdom's Johnson Radley, boosting its expertise in the manufacture of carbon compositions, the company announced its intention to acquire the ferrite magnet activity of Tongkook, in Korea. Carbone Lorraine hoped that the Tongkook purchase would give it a stronger base from which to pursue its development in the Far Eastern market, which had suffered during the economic collapse of the late 1990s. Another key acquisition came in July 1999, with the purchase of the electrical fuse division of Gould Electronics, of the United States, formerly one of Carbone Lorraine's chief competitors in that market. The purchase consolidated Carbone Lorraine's position as the world's number two producer of electrical fuses, in line with the company's future plans to achieve leadership status in its chosen areas of operation in the new century.

Principal Operating Units

Ferraz; UGIMAG; Ferroxdure; Carlor Finland; Le Carbone Holland; Carbone Norge (Norway); Carbone Danmark (Denmark); Le Carbone S.A. Belge (Belgium); Deutsche Carbone (Germany); G. Dietrich (Germany); Cometec (Germany); Sofacel (Spain); Il Carbonio (Italy); Le Carbone (U.K.); Sofacel (Spain); Cabonne KK (Japan); Nihon Ferraz (Japan); Carbone-Lorraine Korea Co. Ltd.; Carbone Lorraine Sdn. Bhd. (Malaysia); Le Carbone-Lorraine Australia Pty. Ltd.; Carbone of America (U.S.); Carbone Lorena de Mexico; Carbono Lorena (Brazil).

Principal Competitors

Morgan Crucible; Hitachi Metals, Ltd.; Sumitomo Corporation; TDK Corporation; Bussmann; Toyo Tanso; Ibiden; SGL Carbon.

Further Reading

"Carbone Lorraine Acquires Canadian Group," *European Report*, January 5, 1996.
Debontride, Xavier, "Carbone Lorraine désormais indépendant poursuit son ascension financière," *Les Echos*, September 17, 1997, p. 12.
Fay, Pierrick, "Claude Cocozza, président de Carbone Lorraine," *La Journal des Finances*, August 5, 1999.
Jacquin, Jean-Baptiste, "Exercice 1991 difficile pour le Carbone Lorraine," *Les Echos*, September 19, 1991, p. 29.
Lebocq, Valérie, "Carbone Lorraine: cap sur la croissance interne," *Les Echos*, March 10, 1999, p. 18.

—M. L. Cohen

Charter Communications, Inc.

12444 Powerscourt Drive, Suite 100
St. Louis, Missouri 63131
U.S.A.
Telephone: (314) 965-0555
Fax: (314) 965-9745
Web site: http://www.chartercom.com

Public Company
Incorporated: 1993
Employees: 13,000
Sales: $2.92 billion (1999)
Stock Exchanges: NASDAQ
Ticker Symbol: CHTR
NAIC: 513220 Cable and Other Program Distribution

At the end of 1999 Charter Communications, Inc. operated cable systems with 6.2 million subscribers, making it the fourth largest multi-system operator (MSO) in the United States behind AT&T Corp., Time Warner Inc., and Comcast Corp. The company was founded in 1993 and grew through a series of acquisitions. In 1998 it was purchased for $4.5 billion by Microsoft cofounder Paul Allen, who merged it with Marcus Cable which he had previously acquired. With Allen providing much of the funding, Charter went on an aggressive acquisition drive in 1998 and 1999. The company made eleven major acquisitions in 1999, culminating in an initial public offering (IPO) in November that raised approximately $3.5 billion.

Charter Grows through Acquisitions: 1993–98

Charter Communications, Inc. was formed in January 1993 by three former executives of St. Louis-based Cencom Cable Associates, Inc. Howard Wood was the former president and chief executive officer (CEO) of Cencom; Barry Babcock was the former chief operating officer (COO) of Cencom; and Jerry Kent was Cencom's former chief financial officer (CFO). Cencom had been acquired in 1991 by Crown Media Inc., a Dallas-based subsidiary of Hallmark Cards Inc., for an estimated $1 billion. Crown subsequently made an initial

investment of several hundred thousand dollars in Charter, and in turn received a 51 percent non-voting stake in the company. The decision to form Charter was precipitated by Crown's plans to move Cencom's headquarters from St. Louis to Dallas. Babcock became Charter's chairman, Kent president, and Wood was management committee chairman.

At first Charter was based in Cencom's offices in west St. Louis County. The company expected to acquire cable properties and began looking around the country. It was also considering such cable-related businesses as telecommunications and video data systems. When Charter was first established, the regulatory environment for cable television was changing. Congress had just passed a new cable bill over President George Bush's veto, but the Federal Communications Commission (FCC) had not yet established all of the regulations to enforce the new legislation.

In February 1994 Charter announced its first acquisition. It would spend nearly $200 million to acquire ten cable systems in Louisiana, Georgia, and Alabama. The systems were acquired from the McDonald Group of Birmingham, Alabama, and served about 100,000 subscribers in the Southeast. Charter's strategy at this time was to acquire smaller systems throughout the Southeast and eventually go public.

The price for cable systems jumped dramatically after the regional Bell operating companies (RBOCs) such as Southwestern Bell began buying cable systems in 1993. Southwestern Bell paid about $2,888 per subscriber in a $650 million acquisition in February 1993. The cost of Charter's first acquisition was estimated at about $1,500 to $2,000 per subscriber.

In June 1994 Hallmark Cards sold its Crown Media cable subsidiary to Charter and Marcus Cable for $900 million. Charter purchased the Crown cable systems serving about 270,000 customers in Connecticut, Kentucky, Missouri, North Carolina, and South Carolina. Charter also assumed management of Crown-affiliated cable systems serving another 360,000 subscribers. Marcus acquired the remaining Crown Media cable properties. It was estimated that Charter and Marcus paid about $2,000 per subscriber.

91

In January 1995 Charter, in partnership with the money management firm Kelso & Co., announced it would acquire Nashville-based Gaylord Entertainment's cable systems serving 180,000 subscribers in California, North Carolina, and South Carolina, for about $370 million. Gaylord selected the Charter-Kelso partnership, CCT Holdings, over Century Communications, with whom it had also been negotiating. The agreement was finalized in April, increasing Charter's cable systems to 850,000 subscribers, and completed in October, by which time Charter had over 900,000 subscribers. The Gaylord family was one of the initial investors in Charter with a 20 percent stake in the company.

In mid-1995 Charter picked up another 29,000 subscribers in northern and central Alabama from CableSouth Inc. for about $50 million. It also acquired Peachtree Cable Systems with 13,000 subscribers in Georgia for $20 million. At the same time the company was bidding for a much larger cable property, Multimedia Inc., which had hired the investment banking firm Goldman Sachs & Co. to auction the company. Multimedia's cable holdings included 125 franchises with 450,000 subscribers, mainly in Kansas, North Carolina, and Oklahoma. Charter's partners in the bidding were Kelso & Co. and Ellis Communications. They were competing against a group led by the National Broadcasting Co. that included cable giant TCI and others, but Multimedia was sold in 1994 to Gannett Company Inc. for $1.7 billion. At the time Charter was the 15th largest MSO in the United States.

In March 1996 Charter acquired WIBV(AM) serving the St. Louis area for between $1 million and $1.5 million. It was the company's first radio station. In April the company purchased the cable systems it had been managing for Cencom for $211.1 million. The systems served 100,000 subscribers in eight states. In August Charter expanded its share of the Southern California cable market by acquiring CVI Cable for an undisclosed amount. CVI served 67,000 customers in Long Beach and Signal Hill, while Charter had more than 250,000 customers in other Southern California communities.

Charter's fourteenth acquisition—the 37,000-subscriber Price Cable of Hickory, North Carolina—put it over the one million subscriber mark in February 1997. Between 1993 and 1997 Charter raised more than $2 billion in equity and debt to fund its acquisitions. The company had three or four major financial investors and adopted a different clustering strategy

with each partner. The acquisitions involving Kelso & Co. followed an urban clustering strategy, resulting in 230,000 subscribers in St. Louis, 250,000 subscribers in the Los Angeles metropolitan area, and 100,000 subscribers in the Northeast, notably Hartford and New York. Another financial partner, Charterhouse Group International, was used to acquire more than 400,000 subscribers in the southeastern United States.

During 1997 Charter attempted to acquire US West Media Group's 230,000-subscriber cable systems in Minneapolis-St. Paul for $600 million. However, the deal fell through, and in April 1998 the renamed MediaOne Group, a subsidiary of US West, was required to pay Charter between $30 and $50 million to keep the cable systems.

During the second half of 1997 Charter added 70,000 subscribers in Long Beach, California, with the purchase of KC Cable Associates LP for $150 million. In September 1997 Charter announced it would acquire cable systems with 117,000 subscribers in California and Utah from Sonic Communications. The deal closed in May 1998, and Charter moved into the top ten among MSOs. Other negotiations failed to add to Charter's systems. Charter's bid for a 300,000-subscriber Las Vegas systems was topped by Cox Communications' $1.3 billion offer, and Dallas-based Marcus Cable went to the entrepreneur Paul Allen for $2.8 billion.

Paul Allen Moves into Cable in a Big Way: 1998–99

Following his purchase of Marcus Cable, Allen bought Charter for $4.5 billion, or about $3,800 per subscriber. Allen's interest in cable properties may have been spurred by Bill Gates's $1 billion investment in 1997 in Comcast. Both Gates and Allen had developed a vision of a ''wired world,'' when everyone would have a PC at home and at work and be connected by a global network. Cable was now perceived as the best way of implementing that vision by delivering high-speed services over the Internet into American homes.

Kent was named president and CEO of the new company, which combined Charter's 139 cable systems in 17 states with those of Marcus in six states. Babcock became vice-chairman, and Wood was named senior adviser. The company's headquarters remained in St. Louis. The combination of Marcus and Charter created the seventh-largest MSO in the United States, with 2.4 million customers. By the end of 1998 Jeffrey Marcus had left Charter to join Chancellor Media, and Babcock was named chairman. Two top Marcus Cable officials were also dismissed following service problems in Fort Worth and other North Texas cities that were blamed on poor management.

In September 1998 Charter reached an agreement with EarthLink, one of the largest independent Internet service providers (ISPs) in the United States, for EarthLink to offer Internet access over cable modems to Charter's cable customers. The Charter Pipeline service, as it was called, began in 1997 in Southern California. The new agreement would eventually cover Charter's 19-state operating area and give EarthLink a potential market of 1.8 million customers. For 1998, Charter reported a net loss of $535.4 million on revenues of $2.7 billion.

In January 1999 Charter added 68,000 subscribers in Southern California with the purchase of four cable systems from

<table>
<tr><td colspan="2" align="center">**Key Dates:**</td></tr>
<tr><td>**1993:**</td><td>Charter Communications, Inc. is formed by three former executives of Cencom Cable Associates, Inc., in St. Louis, Missouri.</td></tr>
<tr><td>**1994:**</td><td>Begins acquiring cable television systems.</td></tr>
<tr><td>**1997:**</td><td>Reaches one million subscribers.</td></tr>
<tr><td>**1998:**</td><td>Charter is acquired by Microsoft Corp. cofounder, Paul Allen, for $4.5 billion.</td></tr>
<tr><td>**1999:**</td><td>Charter goes public in November after making more than ten major acquisitions in one year.</td></tr>
</table>

American Cable Entertainment of Stamford, Connecticut. After the acquisition Charter would have more than 500,000 subscribers in the region.

Also in January Charter joined with cable giant TCI Inc. in a $2.4 billion deal to purchase 60 percent of the subscribers of InterMedia Partners, ranked as the tenth largest MSO. Charter would acquire 400,000 InterMedia subscribers, primarily in the Southeast, for an estimated $1.3 billion. As part of the deal Charter would turn over about 140,000 of its subscribers to TCI. At the time TCI was in the process of being acquired by AT&T.

During February 1999 Charter made several acquisitions and added one million subscribers. By the end of the month it had about 3.33 million subscribers after completing the announced transactions and merging with Marcus Cable. The acquisitions would make Charter the sixth-largest cable operator in the United States. Among the acquisitions were cable systems serving 460,000 subscribers from Rifkin Acquisition Partners and InterLink Communications purchased for an estimated $1.5 billion. Charter also picked up 173,000 subscribers, mostly in central Massachusetts, from New Jersey-based Greater Media Inc., which also sold its cable properties in Philadelphia serving 79,000 subscribers to Comcast. Charter increased its presence in the Southeast by acquiring Renaissance Media Group, a New York partnership serving 130,000 customers near New Orleans, western Mississippi, and Jackson, Tennessee. The price was estimated at $450 million, or about $3,500 per subscriber.

SEC filings that were required before selling $3 billion worth of bonds to pay off higher-interest debt revealed that Allen had personally invested about $4.6 billion to finance $10.6 billion worth of cable acquisitions, making cable Allen's single biggest investment. Allen's personal fortune at the time was estimated at about $22 billion.

In March 1999 Charter confirmed rumors that it was planning an initial public offering (IPO) for the second half of 1999. With 3.4 million subscribers, it was the seventh largest MSO in the United States. The IPO was expected to raise $2–$3 billion. That same month Charter bought a collection of cable systems in the Southeast and Northeast with the $550 million acquisition of New Jersey-based Helicon Cable Communications. The systems served about 171,000 customers in eight states. Charter paid about $3,200 per subscriber. Allen had invested $11.2 billion for cable properties over the past year, with more to follow.

In April the Dallas-Fort Worth cable franchises that had been under Marcus Cable began doing business under their new name, Charter Communications. In May Charter acquired Avalon Cable TV for $845 million, adding 260,000 subscribers at about $3,250 per subscriber. The acquisition gave Charter 3.9 million customers, taking into account all pending acquisitions. Avalon had acquired most of its subscribers in 1998 from Cable Michigan Inc. when it bought the 220,000-subscriber cable company for $473 million. Charter also acquired a Vista Communications cable system in Smyrna, Georgia, for $125 million.

In May Charter announced it would acquire Falcon Cable TV of Los Angeles for $3.6 billion. The deal would give Charter a total of about five million subscribers and move it up in the rankings from fifth to fourth largest MSO. Falcon was the eighth largest cable operator in the United States with about one million subscribers in 27 states in primarily non-urban areas. It was Charter's ninth acquisition of 1999, and certainly not its last.

Charter's tenth acquisition of 1999 involved Fanch Communications Inc. of Denver. Fanch had 547,000 subscribers, including 308,000 in West Virginia and Pennsylvania, 70,000 in Michigan, and 70,000 in Indiana, Kentucky, Louisiana, and Wisconsin. It was reported that Charter paid $2 billion, or $4,000 per subscriber. The acquisition gave Charter a total of 5.5 million subscribers. Following the acquisition, Charter was the fourth-largest MSO behind AT&T with 16 million subscribers, Time Warner with 12 million, and Comcast with 6.2 million. Adelphia and Cox each had about five million subscribers. Figures include acquisitions pending at the time.

In July Charter was the successful bidder to acquire New York-based Bresnan Communications after the firm began receiving unsolicited offers prior to going public. The company was founded by cable industry pioneer William J. Bresnan in 1984. It had rebuilt and upgraded most of its systems and offered high-speed Internet service in about half of its markets. Charter's offer of $3.1 billion gave it an additional 690,000 subscribers at a cost of about $4,500 per subscriber, including 298,000 in Michigan, 221,000 in Minnesota, 110,000 in Wisconsin, and 61,000 in Nebraska. The acquisition gave Charter a total of 6.2 million subscribers.

Charter Continues as a Public Company: Late 1999 and Beyond

It was the $3.2 billion Bresnan acquisition that fueled speculation that Charter was about to go public. Analysts believed that while Paul Allen had "deep pockets," Charter would need the equity financing that a public stock offering would provide to continue making acquisitions. At the end of July Charter filed documents with the SEC for one of the largest initial public offerings (IPO) ever. The company proposed selling $3.5 billion worth of stock. Up to this time Charter's acquisitions had been financed primarily by Allen borrowing against his $28 billion worth of Microsoft shares. It was estimated that he had committed $11 billion of his own money to finance acquisitions totaling $21.8 billion between March 1998 and mid-1999.

When Charter went public in November 1999, the company raised $3.2 billion by selling 170 million shares, or 60 percent of its equity, at $19 a share. Underwriters had an additional 25 million-share allotment to sell later, which could push Charter's gross to $3.7 billion. In addition to the IPO, Allen infused $750 million of his own money into the company. Following the IPO, Allen retained control of the company through his ownership of Class B securities, which had about 10 times the voting power of the Class A shares available to the public.

Charter's strategy following the IPO was to launch digital cable service in its systems and offer high-speed Internet access through cable modems. At the time of the IPO Charter was heavily leveraged, with its debt level at more than seven times its annual cash flow. The company had $9.4 billion worth of acquisitions pending, including major deals for Falcon Cable TV, Fanch Communications, and Avalon Cable. Once those deals were completed in November 1999, Charter would have to invest heavily in upgrading their systems.

To help develop and execute Allen's vision of a "wired world," he created a consortium called Broadband Partners, consisting of companies in which he had financial interests. In addition to Charter, the consortium included RCN, a company that was dedicated to overbuilding existing cable systems with its own high-speed cable network. Just prior to the Charter IPO, Allen had invested $1.65 billion in RCN. Also part of the consortium were High-Speed Access Corp. and Go2Net. Broadband Partners would work together to develop and deploy content and services to Charter's cable subscribers.

Charter also began swapping customers with other systems to improve the geographic clustering of its systems. In December 1999 it signed a letter of intent with AT&T to swap 1.3 million cable subscribers in St. Louis as well as in Alabama, Georgia, and Missouri. The exchange would make Charter the dominant MSO in its home market of St. Louis, with 500,000 subscribers there that would be combined with subscribers in nearby Illinois for an 800,000-subscriber cluster. Charter said that its St. Louis customers would be the first to be offered advanced services such as cable telephone service, interactive video, and high-speed Internet access. The deal called for Charter to receive a total of 704,000 subscribers from AT&T in exchange for 632,000 Charter customers in California, Connecticut, Kentucky, Massachusetts, Tennessee, and Fort Worth, Texas. Analysts expected more exchanges of customers to take place in the cable industry, since most of the desirable MSOs that were willing to sell had been acquired by the industry's major players.

Principal Competitors

AT&T Corp.; Time Warner Inc.; Comcast Corp.; Adelphia Communications Corp.; Cox Communications Inc.

Further Reading

Ahles, Andrea, "St. Louis-Based Cable TV Company to Sell 170 Million Shares of Stock," *Knight-Ridder/Tribune Business News,* September 30, 1999.

"Allen Buys More Cable Systems," *Television Digest,* August 3, 1998.

"Allen Watch," *Broadcasting & Cable,* May 1, 1999, p. 188.

"Barry Babcock, Howard Wood, and Jerald Kent," *St. Louis Business Journal,* June 23, 1997, p. 5B.

Bournellis, Cynthia, "Billionaire's Two-Way Cable Dream," *Electronic News* (1991), August 3, 1998, p. 1.

Brown, Rich, "Charter Subs Rack Up," *Broadcasting & Cable,* June 12, 1995, p. 29.

"Charter on the Rise," *Broadcasting & Cable,* June 16, 1997, p. 44.

"Charter Weighing $2–$3 Billion IPO," *Television Digest,* March 22, 1999.

Colman, Price, "Allen Money Gives Marcus Room to Grow," *Broadcasting & Cable,* April 13, 1998, p. 7.

——, "Charter Gets One in Win Column," *Broadcasting & Cable,* May 25, 1998, p. 50.

——, "Charter, MediaOne Settle Dispute," *Broadcasting & Cable,* April 6, 1998, p. 140.

——, "Sonic Adds to Charter Buying Boom," *Broadcasting & Cable,* September 1, 1997, p. 55.

Cooper, Jim, "Cable Assets Swapped by TCI, InterMedia, and Charter," *Mediaweek,* February 1, 1999, p. 4.

——, "Paul Allen's Charter Acquires Two More MSOs," *Mediaweek,* May 31, 1999, p. 4.

——, "Wire Woos 2nd Cyber Titan; Paul Allen Drops $2.7 Billion for Marcus to Gain Bigger Bandwidth," *Mediaweek,* April 13, 1998, p. 8.

Couch, Mark P., "Charter Blames Bad Management at Marcus Cable for Poor Service in North Texas," *Knight-Ridder/Tribune Business News,* November 12, 1998.

Desloge, Rick, "Babcock, Kent, Wood Charter a New Course," *St. Louis Business Journal,* August 10, 1998, p. 1.

——, "IPO Fever: Sharing Wealth: GenAmerica, Charter Prepare to Go Public," *St. Louis Business Journal,* March 22, 1999, p. 1A.

Dwyer, Joe, III, "Ex-Cencom Officials Make Cable Buy: Charter Spending about $200 Million for 10 Systems," *St. Louis Business Journal,* February 14, 1994, p. 1.

——, "Charter in Bid for KSDK Parent," *St. Louis Business Journal,* June 26, 1995, p. 1.

Grone, Jack, "Cencom Chiefs Form New Firm," *St. Louis Business Journal,* December 7, 1992, p. 1.

Higgins, John M., "Allen's Big Buy Not His Last," *Broadcasting & Cable,* August 3, 1998, p. 8.

——, "Allen's Big Stretch," *Broadcasting & Cable,* March 8, 1999, p. 42.

——, "Charter Pays $3.1B for Bresnan," *Broadcasting & Cable,* July 5, 1999, p. 10.

"InterMedia Sells Most Subs," *Television Digest,* February 1, 1999.

"Notebook," *Television Digest,* May 24, 1999.

"Paul Allen Gets a Little Respect," *Business Week,* August 16, 1999, p. 84.

Peers, Martin, "Charter Buys Falcon for $3.6 Bil.," *Variety,* May 31, 1999, p. 24.

Quinton, Brian, "Earthlink, Charter Partner on Modems," *Telephony,* September 28, 1998.

Rathbun, Elizabeth, "Cable-Radio Crossover," *Broadcasting & Cable,* March 18, 1996, p. 80.

"Relationship Troubles," *Broadcasting & Cable,* November 23, 1998, p. 18.

Rios, Brenda, "Microsoft Cofounder Proves to Be Big Spender with Cable Entry," *Knight-Ridder/Tribune Business News,* June 11, 1999.

"St. Louis, Mo.-Based Cable Company Buys New York Firm," *Knight-Ridder/Tribune Business News,* July 1, 1999.

"This Cable Tycoon Can't Stop Buying," *Business Week,* June 7, 1999, p. 42.

Torpey-Kemph, Anne, "Charter Buys More Systems," *Mediaweek,* February 22, 1999, p. 34.

—David P. Bianco

Chicago Bears Football Club, Inc.

1000 Football Drive
Lake Forest, Illinois 60045
U.S.A.
Telephone: (847) 295-6600
Fax: (847) 295-8986
Web site: http://www.chicagobears.com

Private Company
Founded: 1920 as the Decatur Staleys
Sales: $101 million (1999)
Employees: 130
NAIC: 711211 Sports Teams and Clubs

The Chicago Bears Football Club, Inc. has one of the most colorful histories of any sports franchise in the entire world. One of the first professional football teams in the United States, the Chicago Bears have won nine world championships, including Super Bowl XX in 1986. Men who have played for the team comprise a who's who list of the best football players of all time, including such greats as Harold ''Red'' Grange (the galloping ghost), Bronco Nagurski, Sid Luckman, Dick Butkus, Gale Sayers, and Walter Payton. The Chicago Bears have appeared in the playoffs 22 times and have more players inducted in the Football Hall of Fame than any other team. Yet, even with such a storied past, the franchise was not able to recapture its former greatness throughout the 1990s, when the team was plagued with poor management, poor draft choices, an unwillingness to pay high-caliber players, and a coach whose win-loss record went steadily from bad to worse. More recently, however, the franchise was making moves to redress these problems by replacing the president, reorganizing its management team, and hiring a more effective head coach.

Early 20th-Century History

The founder and impetus behind much of the success of the Chicago Bears franchise was George Halas. Halas grew up in Chicago, Illinois, in modest circumstances. Born into a middle-class family, Halas worked hard to save enough money in order to attend the University of Illinois in Champaign-Urbana. A handsome young man with a quick smile and good physique, Halas was a born athlete and won letters in three sports while an undergraduate at the University. After he graduated, Halas spent a few years in the Navy and later joined the New York Yankees. Playing briefly as the Yankees' right fielder, the young man saw his baseball career cut short by a hip injury that severely hampered his ability to swing a bat. Disappointed and despondent, Halas returned to his roots in the Midwest and relocated in Decatur, Illinois.

Not long after establishing himself in Decatur, Halas found a job in a corn products business owned and operated by A.E. Staley. Staley was also a sports enthusiast who sponsored his own semi-pro baseball team and, as a result of their mutual interest in sports, the two men became friends. Recognizing Halas's passion for football, Staley reached a deal with Halas to form and organize an independent football team called the Decatur Staleys. With Staley's backing, Halas not only organized his own team but arranged to meet in Canton, Ohio, with the representatives of 12 other football clubs. There, in Ralph Hay's Hupmobile showroom, Halas was the driving force behind the formation of the American Professional Football Association, which was comprised of the 12 clubs at the meeting who agreed to play one another during the autumn of each year. Each team paid $100 to be a member of the Association, and thus the forerunner of the National Football League was established.

In 1920, with George Halas acting as player-coach, the Decatur Staley's posted a record of ten wins, one loss, and two ties, during its first year in existence, losing only to the Chicago Cardinals by a score of 7-6 in Normal Park. The team played its games all over Chicago that first year, but attendance remained low and it was anyone's guess as to whether or not professional football would catch on with the American public. Collegiate football, on the other hand, was one of the most popular sports throughout the United States, with teams like Army, Navy, the University of Michigan, Notre Dame, and the University of Chicago attracting thousands of people to each of their games. Still, the American Professional Football Association (APFA, later known as the NFL) was able to survive its first year of existence, and Staley and Halas payed their players $1,900 for the season, a very good salary at the time.

```
┌─────────────────────────────────────────────────┐
```

Key Dates:

1920:   George Halas establishes the Decatur Staleys football club.
1921:   Team becomes known as the Chicago Staleys.
1922:   Team changes its name to Chicago Bears.
1925:   Red Grange joins the team; the popularity of the sport grows rapidly.
1940:   Chicago Bears introduce the ''T-formation'' offense to professional football.
1956:   Founder Halas retires as the Bears coach only to return two years later.
1968:   Halas retires as the Bears coach and eventually becomes president of the National Football Conference (NFC).
1970:   Team switches its home venue from Wrigley Field to Soldiers Field.
1982:   Coach Mike Ditka is hired.
1985:   Chicago Bears win Superbowl XX.
1999:   Management shake-up results in a new coach, Dick Jauron, and a new corporate CEO and president, Ted Phillips.

The following year, the team changed its name to the Chicago Staleys and played its first game in Wrigley Field, the home of the Chicago Cubs since 1914. Even though the team won its first APFA title with a record of 9-1-1, A.E. Staley was convinced that professional football was just a trend and would not last very long. Consequently, he decided to give the club to Halas with a subsidy of $5,000 on the condition that Halas retain the name Chicago Staleys for at least one year. Halas, ever the entrepreneur, accepted Staley's generous offer and found a new partner in Dutch Sternaman, whom he none too easily convinced of the viability of professional football. In 1922, Halas renamed the team the Chicago Bears and made the first player deal in the club's history by purchasing the contract of tackle Ed Healey from the Rock Island Independents for the total sum of $100. In spite of all his efforts, professional football just wasn't as popular as the college game, and by 1924 it looked as if the APFA was not going to survive much longer.

It is not an overstatement to say that Red Grange saved professional football. In 1925, Halas signed Grange to one of the most lucrative sports contracts of the pre-World War II era when he agreed to pay $100,000 for Grange to become a Chicago Bear. Grange had been known as the ''Galloping Ghost'' when he played football for the University of Illinois. In fact, it was Grange that captured the imagination of the American public and brought success to the collegiate game. Halas was counting on Grange to do the same thing for professional football. Halas took Grange on a barnstorming tour that including 16 games in nine weeks across the United States. In his first game, which was played before 36,000 in Wrigley Field, Grange was held to 36 yards rushing by the Chicago Cardinals, and the score ended in a scoreless tie. However, when the team reached the West Coast and played the Los Angeles Tigers in front of 75,000 people at the Los Angeles Coliseum, the ''Galloping Ghost'' ran for two touchdowns to post a win of 17–7. Halas had achieved exactly what he wanted: an impressive

performance by his star player that impressed thousands of people. The remainder of the trip was just as successful. By its end, the Bears had posted a 11-4-1 record and, even more importantly, the American public was now flocking to see its favorite college athlete play professional football.

The Great Depression and World War II

The Chicago Bears, with Grange as its star player and attraction, posted winning seasons for the rest of the decade except for one year. Attendance continued to rise while revenues continued to increase. After the 1929 season, however, Halas decided to hire Ralph Jones in place of himself as head coach. Even though the team won the majority of its games under the coaching of Jones, due to the economic depression which was affecting every business across the United States, the financial health of the franchise began to suffer. With many people out of work, fewer and fewer individuals could pay for the cost of a ticket to attend a Bears game. Consequently, even though the team won the league championship in 1932, by the end of the season the franchise had lost approximately $18,000. Dutch Sternaman unloaded his half of the team ownership onto Halas, and Halas was forced not only to resume coaching the team in order to save the cost of a head coach's salary, but to pay many of the team's expenditures out of his own pocket.

With the advent of the 1940s, the fortunes of the Chicago Bears franchise began to improve. In 1940, the team beat Washington by a score of 73–0, while introducing the T-formation offense which revolutionized the game. When the United States entered World War II after the bombing of Pearl Harbor by the Japanese, however, Halas once again set aside his coaching responsibilities and decided to join the U.S. Navy. For the duration of the war, Halas remained in the Navy while his team continued to play in the National Football League (NFL). When the war ended, Halas resumed his coaching duties with the Bears and rode the wave of popularity that the public felt for the game of football. Ever-larger crowds attended Bear games, with over 58,000 people watching in 1946 as Chicago defeated the New York Giants for the NFL championship.

The Modern Era

Halas had always been at the forefront of new and innovative techniques that could be adopted for use by his team on the playing field. The T-formation, split ends, and the forward pass were all strategies used by Halas to win football games. During the late 1940s and throughout the decade of the 1950s, the quarterbacks for the Chicago Bears played an aggressive offensive scheme with the forward pass as one of their most important weapons. Sid Luckman, Johnny Lujack, and Bobby Layne were some of the best quarterbacks in the history of professional football, and the Chicago Bears were lucky to have them as players. In 1949, Lujack set an NFL record with 468 passing yards against the Cardinals. With the popularity and continuity of the game ensured, Halas decided once again to retire. In 1956, he turned the coaching responsibilities over to Paddy Driscoll and devoted himself exclusively to the administrative, organizational, and financial duties of the franchise.

Yet Halas was too much of a hands-on owner to ignore the team's development and win-loss record. So he returned as head coach in 1958 for his final tour of duty. By 1963, the Chicago Bears had once again won a championship title by defeating the New York Giants, 14–10, on a blustery winter day at Wrigley Field in Chicago. In 1965, the Bears drafted two of the best players ever to set foot on the field, Dick Butkus and Gayle Sayers. Butkus developed into one of the most outstanding middle linebackers professional football has seen, while Sayers set an NFL record of scoring 22 touchdowns during his first year with the Bears. By 1968, Halas was ready to relinquish his position as head coach of the Bears for the last time. When he did so at the end of the season, he retired as the all-time winningest coach in the history of professional football, with a record of 324 wins, 151 loses, and 31 ties during 40 seasons.

The 1970s and 1980s

During the 1970s and 1980s, the Chicago Bears franchise underwent many changes. In 1970, the Bears made a major change and switched their playing venue from Wrigley Field to Soldiers Field in order to accommodate more fans. Another major change occurred when the NFL and AFL merged, and George Halas was elected president of the National Football Conference. With his advancing age, and the growth of football as big business, Halas was no longer able to manage all of the details necessary to run a professional football franchise. As a result, in 1974 he hired Jim Finks as general manager and continued to give his son George "Mugs" Halas, Jr., more and more administrative responsibility, having been appointed by his father to serve as president of the franchise in 1963. Under Jim Finks and Mugs Halas, the Chicago Bears began to draft players and hire coaches that once again brought them into prominence. However, the front office was hit hard when Mugs Halas unexpectedly died of a heart attack in 1979.

The Bears had reached the playoffs twice during the late 1970s, but even with players such as Walter Payton the team was unable to advance much further. In 1982, however, Halas and Finks decided to hire Mike Ditka as head coach of the team, a former tight end for the Bears from 1961 to 1968 and an assistant coach at the Dallas Cowboys. Ditka was a no-nonsense type of coach whose one goal was to win the Superbowl.

George Halas died in 1983, while Jim Finks resigned his position as general manager and was also to die soon from cancer. However, the groundwork had been laid, and during the 1983 and 1984 seasons the team gradually improved both on defense and offense. The loss in the 1984 NFL Conference title game to the San Francisco 49ers set the stage for the next season. The Chicago Bears posted an 18–1 season for 1985, beating each of their opponents with a strong offense and a relentless, punishing defense. The team shut out both of their playoff opponents, and then easily beat the New England Patriots 46–10 in the Superbowl XX game held in New Orleans. Richard Dent won the Most Valuable Player trophy for the game, and the Chicago Bears were clearly the team to beat during the following season. Unfortunately, the Bears failed to win an NFC title game during the next three seasons.

The 1990s and Beyond

The Bears were able to reach the playoffs during 1990 and 1991, and the team lost much of its talent as the players who appeared in Superbowl XX either retired or went to other teams. Unable to maintain the high level of intense play and tradition of winning, Coach Ditka grew more and more frustrated with both his players and with management. After George Halas, Sr., had died, the franchise was run by Michael McCaskey, the grandson of George Halas and a business school professor and consultant from Boston. As friction mounted between Ditka and McCaskey, McCaskey decided to fire Ditka and bring in his own choice as head coach. In 1993, McCaskey hired Dave Wannstedt as coach. Although the team posted winning seasons in both 1994 and 1995, the team began to flounder and both McCaskey and Wannstedt came under intense criticism from the press. Wannstedt was criticized for losing more and more games, and being seemingly unable to choose talented players, while McCaskey was criticized both for his apparent meddling in coaching affairs and for his focus on building a new Bears stadium over the team performance.

In 1999, Virginia McCaskey, George Halas's daughter, decided that the entire Chicago Bears needed new leadership and a more clearly defined vision. Consequently, she fired her own son, Michael McCaskey, and hired Ted Phillips as the new president and CEO of the Chicago Bears franchise. Dave Wannstedt was also replaced as head coach by Dick Jauron, completing the reorganization of the Bears front office. The shake-up led to a reinvigorated team and an improved record for the 1999 season, though the Chicago Bears had a long way to go before they recaptured the championship aura that typified the franchise throughout most of their early history.

Principal Competitors

The Green Bay Packers Inc.; Minnesota Vikings Football Club; The Detroit Lions.

Further Reading

Amidon, Carole, M., "A Chicago Dome: Economic Development or Empty Promise," *Illinois Business Review,* Fall 1996, p. 4.
Borden, Jeff, "Forget McDome: Buy The Bears," *Crain's Chicago Business,* March 24, 1997, p. 1.
——, "Life After Mike: More Tough Decisions Ahead For Bears," *Crain's Chicago Business,* February 15, 1999, p. 3.
Brockinton, Langdon, "Ad Sales Staff Bears the Burden of Losing Season," *Mediaweek,* April 13, 1998, p. 22.
"Daley Shouldn't Budge in His Bid to Keep Bears," *Crain's Chicago Business,* November 20, 1995, p. 14.
Dunn, Peter, "Gear Vendors Develop New Marketing Ploys," *Electronic News,* February 17, 1992, p. 1.
Fritz, Michael, "Bears Don't Slow M&A Juggernaut," *Crain's Chicago Business,* April 21, 1997, p. 17.
Wulf, Steve, "Bad Bounces for the NFL," *Time,* December 11, 1995, p. 64.

—Thomas Derdak

中国南方航空公司

CHINA SOUTHERN AIRLINES

China Southern Airlines Company Ltd.

Baiyun International Airport
Guangzhou, Guangdong Province 510406
China
Telephone: (020) 8612 3355
Fax: (020) 8664 4623; (020) 8665 8989
Web site: http://www.chinasouthernair.com

Public Company
Incorporated: 1988
Employees: 15,000
Sales: RMB 11.85 billion ($1.43 billion) (1998)
Stock Exchanges: New York Hong Kong
Ticker Symbol: ZNH
NAIC: 481111 Scheduled Passenger Air Transportation;
   481112 Scheduled Freight Air Transportation

China Southern Airlines Company Ltd. (CSA) has been China's top passenger carrier for two decades, propelled by the robust economy of Guangzhou, the country's commercial center. After gaining permission to fly abroad, China Southern has eclipsed rivals China Eastern and Air China in terms of international prestige. CSA boasts one of the world's youngest fleets and an above-average safety record among Chinese carriers. It offers Western-style passenger amenities such as Hollywood movies and an in-flight magazine. One of the top 25 carriers in the world, China Southern flies to more than 80 cities worldwide, including Los Angeles and Amsterdam. The carrier is also developing a cargo network.

Origins and Independence

China Southern Airlines was formed out of the China Civil Aviation Administration (CCAC), which itself had been created from the U.S.-led China National Aviation Corporation and other assets left behind by those fleeing the Communists in 1949. Five years later, CCAC merged with the Sino-Soviet Joint Stock Company, which had responsibility for air service in the north of China. This created the Chinese Civil Aviation Bureau (CAB), with divisions based in Peking, Shanghai,

Shenyang, Si'an, Wuhan, and Guangzhou—later the base for China Southern. In April 1962, the CAB became the Civil Aviation Administration of China (CAAC). Over the next 20 years, the CAAC gradually evolved from dependence on Soviet aviation technology to a customer-driven preference for British and American jets, culminating in orders for Boeing 747s and Concordes, although the latter were never delivered.

A reorganization of the CAAC in late 1984 produced the following four regional divisions: Eastern, Southern, Southwestern, and Northwestern. The liberalization of the domestic market soon produced other carriers such as Xiamen Airlines, which operated on China Southern's turf. Because of the commercial importance of Guangzhou (formerly Canton), China Southern was cleared for international flights, along with Shanghai-based China Eastern. Yu Yanen, an active pilot himself, was appointed president of the airline.

China Southern was granted its autonomy on July 1, 1988. However, the CAAC still controlled aircraft purchasing and worked very closely with its newly independent branches. The government also made its voice known to domestic passengers—an official letter of recommendation was a prerequisite for booking a flight until 1993.

In spite of the oversight from Beijing, the airline pursued partnerships with Western aviation companies to increase its expertise and revenue potential. In 1990, China Southern set up a maintenance joint venture with Hutchison Whampoa (Hong Kong; 25 percent) and Lockheed (United States; 25 percent) called Guangzhou Aircraft Maintenance Engineering Co. (GAMECO). The center specialized in Boeing 757 and 747 aircraft and boasted labor costs one-forth of those in the West. A flight simulator station was also under development.

China Southern carried nearly six million people in 1991, up more than sixfold from a decade earlier. Cargo traffic boomed as well. The carrier flew to 90 cities at home and 17 international destinations and operated a fleet of 38 Boeing jets. Employment was about 6,000. One of China Southern's 737s flew into a mountain in 1992, puzzling observers who had seen the vast improvements made by China's commercial airlines in the previous decade.

Company Perspectives:

Stringent administration; safe and punctual flight; smooth and efficient operation; warm and courteous services are the main objectives of China Southern Airlines.

With fleet expansion and further growth of our route network, China Southern Airlines enters a new milestone.

Key Dates:

1984: Civil Aviation Administration of China divides into five separate airlines.

1988: China Southern Airlines (CSA) is officially granted autonomy.

1992: Beijing grants CSA further financial independence.

1997: CSA goes public, listing on the Hong Kong and New York Stock Exchanges.

1998: Asian financial crisis leads to CSA's first ever annual loss.

CSA posted a profit of US$102 million on revenues of US$537 million in 1992. With Air China, China Eastern, and a few dozen companies in other industries, the carrier was given special financial independence. One drawback to this was the increased cost of buying fuel on the open market and paying airport fees. China Southern also had to compete vigorously to attract qualified pilots. However, the carrier was able to shed various general aviation activities such as forestry service inherited from the 1950s.

Demand for commercial aircraft softened in the wake of the Persian Gulf War, giving Yu an opportunity to acquire the Boeing 777s needed to establish China Southern as a long-haul international carrier. Boeing lowered its price and stepped up its delivery schedule; CSA was the first Asian airline to operate this state-of-the-art jet.

Letting in the Foreigners in the Mid-1990s

The Chinese government opened its airlines to the possibility of foreign investment in 1994. United Airlines and China Southern were early to the negotiating table. CSA also began to plan for a listing on the New York Stock Exchange. It needed the capital to distance itself from other smaller, largely unprofitable Chinese airlines, among the world's most dangerous to fly. CSA had already entered training and maintenance agreements with U.S. carriers. It contracted with American Airlines' sister company Sabre Decision Technologies to develop its operations control center.

Sales doubled in 1994, although profit fell due to increased costs associated with the company's growth. It added four international and 26 domestic routes in 1995. Passenger traffic exploded in the early 1990s; gross revenues reached $1.1 billion in 1996; the Xiamen Airlines unit contributed another $400 million. Net income was $1.4 billion (RMB 887 million). CSA and associated airlines were flying 15 million passengers a year. CSA's domestic subsidiaries covered 68 destinations within China.

Yu had resisted pressure to order Airbuses (and, earlier in the decade, MD-80s being manufactured in Shanghai), at least until April 1996, when the CAAC ordered 20 Airbus A320s for the company. CSA added a fifth Boeing 777 in 1997 as it expanded international services in a bid to usurp Air China's leading position. CSA had an advantage in the liberal, business-oriented climate of its southern home, compared to Air China's bureaucratic home base of Beijing. The carrier operated 63 jets (plus 15 through Xiamen Airlines and dozens more through other subsidiaries) to Air China's 50.

Even though the airline had invested heavily in bringing capacity to the international market, domestic flights accounted for almost 80 percent of its passenger revenues. The domestic carriers were an important source of feeder traffic; to keep passengers coming in from abroad, CSA signed a code sharing arrangement with Delta Air Lines. However, international flights brought in vitally needed hard currency. Cargo operations provided less than ten percent of the carrier's revenues.

In July 1997, China Southern finally made its initial public offering on the Hong Kong and New York Stock Exchanges, raising some $600 to $700 million. A strong local economy and hub in the gateway city of Guangzhou were two key selling points. The CAAC still owned about two-thirds of CSA after the IPO. CSA reported revenues of $1.5 billion) in 1997. The next year, the first loss in CSA's history, compounded by unfavorable exchange rates, amounted to RMB 544 million ($65 million) on revenues of RMB 10.6 billion. As a group, Chinese airlines lost US$775 million in 1998.

Even after the IPO, CSA and Xiamen Airlines together had nearly US$2 billion in debt. Within a few months, the Asian financial crisis soured investors on CSA's short-term prospects. A sharp decline in traffic manifested itself quickly. In the first half of 1998, CSA lost even more than was expected, RMB 72 million. Managers scrambled to contain costs but with already cheap land, cheap labor, and expensive new planes to maintain, their options were limited. About 600 workers were laid off and a couple of airplanes returned. The prospect of growth via teaming with Delta Air Lines in the U.S. market offered some hope; CSA offered special incentives to U.S. travel agents. The Chinese government reduced infrastructure taxes to help the struggling airlines, saving China Southern approximately RMB 500 million a year.

The domestic Chinese market showed some signs of improvement by early 1999, as the CAAC intervened to control pricing and capacity. CSA's cargo traffic improved by 12 percent in the first quarter. The CAAC also planned to merge all of China's 34 airlines into a handful of groups. A merger of China Southern with Air China was expected to lead the process. China Southern management was likely to take over the proposed entity—Air China's head had already been replaced by the leader of China Eastern Airlines due to poor financial performance. In fact, Air China was not yet strong enough to launch its own public offering, despite several years of trying. Air China would bring better U.S. destinations to the merger, a key to competing with major U.S. airlines. As of mid-1999, CSA operated 99 aircraft and Air China 60, together accounting for more than a third of China's total commercial airliners and half the country's air traffic.

Although susceptible to exchange rate fluctuations in the future, China Southern has long demonstrated an uncanny ability to navigate between bureaucratic demands of the socialist regime at home and the requirements of competition in the open market. China Southern President Yan Zhi Qing stated a goal of becoming the world's number one airline—not an altogether out of sight target, given the airline's phenomenal rate of growth and the impending merger.

Principal Subsidiaries

China Southern Henan Airlines; Hubei Airlines; Hunan Airlines; Shenzhen Airlines; Hainan Airlines; Zhuhai Helicopter Company; Xiamen Airlines (60%); Shantou Airlines (60%); Guangxi Airlines (60%); Zhuhai Airlines (60%); Guangzhou Aircraft Maintenance and Engineering Co. (50 %); Guangzhou Nanland Air Catering Co. (51%); Baiyun Xinhua (Guangzhou) Air Cargo Service (70%); China Southern West Australian Flying College (Australia; 65%); Hainan Phoenix Information Systems (45%); Southern Airlines Group Finance Co. (47%).

Principal Competitors

China Eastern Airlines; Cathay Pacific Airways Ltd.; Korean Air Lines Co. Ltd.

Further Reading

Carey, Susan, "Air Crash in China Proves Puzzling, Differing Greatly from Past Disasters," *Wall Street Journal*, November 30, 1992.

——, "China's Airlines Are Growing at Rapid Rate—Beijing Appears to Be Giving Approval and Is Limiting Amount of Interference," *Wall Street Journal*, April 13, 1992.

Davies, R.E.G., *Airlines of Asia Since 1920*, London: Putnam, 1997.

Feldman, Joan M., " 'Independence' . . . with Strings," *Air Transport World*, October 1993, p. 52.

Forestier, Katherine, "Gameco: International Ambitions," *Asian Business*, January 1992, p. 11.

Jones, Dominic, "Dragon to Get Bit in the Year of the Tiger," *Airfinance Journal*, February 1998, pp. 28–30.

——, "The Next Step for China's Big Two," *Airfinance Journal*, February 1998, pp. 24–27.

Kahn, Joseph, and Miriam Jordan, "China's Big State Airlines Are Flying in New Direction—They Seek Operating Accords, and Possibly Funds, from Foreign Lines," *Wall Street Journal*, November 1, 1994, p. B4.

Leary, William M., Jr., *The Dragon's Wings: The China National Aviation Corporation and the Development of Commercial Aviation in China*, Athens, Ga.: University of Georgia, 1976.

Mackey, Michael, "Mainland Powerhouse," *Air Transport World*, September 1997, pp. 26–32.

——, "The Right Place," *Air Transport World*, July 1996, p. 67.

Mecham, Michael, "China Southern Looks to U.S. Market for Relief," *Aviation Week and Space Technology*, March 29, 1999, p. 45.

O'Connor, Anthony, "Meet the Boss," *Airfinance Journal*, July/August 1996, pp. 22–23.

——, "The Tearaway," *Airfinance Journal*, July/August 1996, pp. 16–19.

Proctor, Paul, "China Southern Closes on Air China for Premier Spot," *Aviation Week and Space Technology*, March 31, 1997, p. 44.

Thomas, Geoffrey, "China Airline Merger Talks May Spark a Trend," *Aviation Week and Space Technology*, July 19, 1999, p. 36.

—Frederick C. Ingram

ClubCorp, Inc.

3030 LBJ Freeway, Suite 700
Dallas, Texas 75324
U.S.A.
Telephone: (972) 243-6191
Fax: (972) 888-7700
Web site: http://www.clubcorp.com

Private Company
Incorporated: 1957 as Country Clubs, Inc.
Employees: 23,000
Sales: $1.02 billion (1999)
NAIC: 71391 Golf Courses and Country Clubs; 71394
    Fitness and Recreational Sports Centers

ClubCorp, Inc. is the world's largest operator of private clubs and resorts. The company owns or manages about 230 country clubs, golf clubs, resorts, city clubs, and athletic clubs. ClubCorp's properties include North Carolina's Pinehurst Resort & Country Club (which hosted the 1999 U.S. Open golf championship) and the Mission Hills Country Club in California. ClubCorp's properties are found throughout the United States, as well as in more than a dozen foreign countries, including Vietnam, England, and Australia. In addition to owning a 25 percent stake in ClubLink Corporation—the largest operator of private clubs in Canada—ClubCorp controls a substantial portion of the PGA European Tour Courses. The company also is allied with famed golfer Jack Nicklaus to design and operate several golf courses. With more than 250,000 members worldwide, ClubCorp is focused on aggressively expanding its holdings; its sales rose an impressive 20 percent in 1999 to reach $1.2 billion.

Humble Beginnings

ClubCorp's founder Robert H. Dedman's personal background was one of poverty. Growing up in rural Arkansas, Dedman's family of six shared a two-room house without electricity. Dedman vowed as a teenager to transcend his circumstances, and he set the lofty of goal of earning $50 million by the time he was 50. In pursuit of success, he left home when he was 14 to live with relatives in Dallas, Texas, so that he could attend a well-regarded public high school. He graduated as his class valedictorian. During a stint in the Navy, he earned degrees in engineering and economics. After leaving the military, he obtained a masters of law degree from Southern Methodist University, whereupon he joined a powerful Dallas law firm. Although he worked closely in this capacity with oil baron H.L. Hunt, Dedman realized that he was still a long way from his childhood goal of tremendous wealth.

While vacationing in southern California in the 1950s, Dedman took note of the publicity surrounding the opening of the Thunderbird County Club in Palm Springs. It was at this time, as *Sports Illustrated* explained, that he "struck upon the idea that would rocket him to the kind of wealth even he didn't have the chutzpah to dream of." Instead of conforming to the typical country club formula of building one golf course and one clubhouse, Dedman conceived of constructing three golf courses around a single clubhouse. In this way, a country club could accommodate more members and thus charge each member less expensive dues. Convinced that by attracting a broader base of clients he could turn a handsome profit, Dedman launched his new company, Country Clubs, Incorporated. Rather than targeting solely the wealthiest one percent of a community's residents as country clubs usually did, Dedman aggressively sold memberships to what he termed the "top 10 percent." The fledgling company bought 400 acres of land in the Farmers Branch suburb of Dallas in 1957, and by 1959 Country Clubs, Incorporated announced the opening of its first club—Brookhaven Country Club. The company's next project was to develop property in Tarzana, California to form the Deauville Country Club.

Growth in the 1960s

By 1961, the *Wall Street Journal* praised Country Clubs, Incorporated for its creative business strategies. In addition to building more than one golf course per facility, Dedman introduced other innovations to the staid world of country clubs. According to the *Las Vegas Business Press,* Dedman "turned the management of country clubs into what General Motors did for the automobile industry—he brought in management skill

---

Company Perspectives:

We strive to create an exceptional experience for guests by providing unmatched personal service, a welcoming environment, fine dining, excellent meeting facilities and a myriad of recreation ranging from championship golf and tennis to deep-sea fishing and water sports.

---

and turned a tidy profit.'' Prior to Dedman's entry, most country clubs were typically run as nonprofits by volunteer boards of members. While these members certainly enjoyed their clubs, most had virtually no experience running a complex business. Country Clubs, Incorporated, by contrast, employed management experts, cut expenses, and instituted formal training programs for staff.

The company broadened its horizons even further in 1966 when it opened The Lancers Club—its first city club—atop the LTV Tower in downtown Dallas. Unlike suburban country clubs, where golf was the central activity, city clubs offered fine dining in a sophisticated urban setting where members could entertain friends, family, and business associates. To signify that it no longer focused exclusively on developing country clubs, the company changed its name to the Club Corporation of America.

Rapid Expansion: 1970–90

The young company continued to grow in the 1970s, as it acquired or built country, city, and athletic clubs throughout the United States. In 1975 alone, Club Corporation bought 13 clubs, bringing its total to 49. Of these, the Inverrary Country Club in Fort Lauderdale, Florida was the most important. ''That told the world we arrived,'' Dedman explained later to *Sports Illustrated,* since the club was the site of a Professional Golfers' Association (PGA) Tour event. As a further incentive to prospective members, Club Corporation offered reciprocal privileges at its many clubs. In 1976, the company launched Club Corporation Realty to develop residential communities around country clubs. By 1980, the company owned and operated some 87 country and city clubs, offered club management consulting services, and had seven land development projects under way.

Club Corporation's expansion continued in the early 1980s. In 1981, the company purchased the Firestone Country Club in Akron, Ohio, which added another prestigious golf course to Club Corporation's collection. Built in 1929, Firestone hosted the World Golf Championship NEC Invitational. In 1983, Club Corporation entered into the international arena when it opened its first club outside the United States—Banker's Club in Taipei, Taiwan. By 1983, Club Corporation owned or managed more than 100 clubs.

In 1984, Club Corporation expanded its operations yet again with the purchase of the venerable Pinehurst Resort & Country Club in the Village of Pinehurst, North Carolina. As Club Corporation's first resort property, Pinehurst brought the company new challenges and opportunities. Founded in 1895 by the Tufts family, Pinehurst had achieved the distinction of being ''one of the South's greatest resort properties,'' according to the

Dallas Morning News. By the 1970s, though, Pinehurst had fallen on hard times. After the resort was sold by the Tufts family in 1970, it changed hands several times. The various real estate developers and banks who subsequently operated the resort paid little attention to its care and maintenance. In fact, shortly after Club Corporation bought the resort for $15 million, a staff member fell through the rotted out kitchen floor into the basement.

Club Corporation pledged to revitalize Pinehurst. ''We had to fix and rebuild everything,'' a company spokesperson later told the *Dallas Morning News.* Over the next 15 years, Club Corporation invested approximately $100 million in Pinehurst, constructing two new golf courses at the resort and restoring the historical Carolina Hotel. After acquiring Pinehurst, Club Corporation launched a new subsidiary—ClubResorts—specifically to manage destination golf and conference resorts.

Club Corporation's rapid growth was spurred by a variety of factors. Perhaps the most significant of these was the fragmentation of the overall golf market. Unlike the hotel industry, which had undergone considerable consolidation and branding, the vast majority of private golf courses and clubs were individually owned and operated. (By as late as 1995, only about 20 companies were involved in golf club management, according to *Forbes.*) In this fragmented environment, an efficient and organized operation like Club Corporation was able to distinguish itself easily. The company was well equipped to provide the infrastructure to run clubs profitably and could exploit its size to purchase goods in bulk—ranging from turf equipment to food products—at considerable discounts. Moreover, Club Corporation could reduce labor costs by instituting efficiency techniques. As *Business Week* noted, for example, Club Corporation knew ''how many worker-hours [were] needed to prepare and serve a given number of meals.''

Club Corporation's success also was due in part to the soaring popularity of golf. According to *Business Week,* golf's growth ''creat[ed] strong demand for new courses and for skilled club management.'' The number of rounds of golf played in the United States rose 67 percent from 1983 to 1985, and by 1991, new golf courses were opening at a rate of more than one per week.

During the late 1980s, Club Corporation continued to extend its reach, adding clubs in Asia, Australia, and Europe. In 1986, Club Corporation acquired a majority interest in Silband Sports Corp., which was then the second largest manager of public courses. ''We are now trying to cover the full gamut of the business, from public courses to the fanciest resort,'' Dedman told *Business Week.* To ensure that his company continued to operate efficiently, Dedman led Club Corporation through a major restructuring in 1986. Club Corporation was reorganized as a holding company—named Club Corporation International—with ten independent subsidiaries. ''These different businesses have different characteristics, different marketing requirements and management skills that are necessary to fully apply those opportunities,'' a company spokesperson explained to the *Dallas Morning News.* In 1988, Club Corporation branched into the financial side of the business with its acquisition of Franklin Federal Bancorp, one of the largest savings and loan thrifts in Texas. (Franklin Federal was sold to Norwest in 1996.)

Key Dates:

1957: Robert H. Dedman, Sr. founds Country Clubs, Inc.
1958: Country Clubs, Inc. begins constructing its first club—Brookhaven Country Club.
1965: Company name is changed to Club Corporation of America.
1982: Club Corporation opens its first foreign property.
1984: Club Corporation acquires its first resort property, the venerable Pinehurst Resort & Country Club in North Carolina.
1989: Robert H. Dedman, Jr., is elected Club Corporation's president.
1998: Company is renamed ClubCorp International, Inc.; ClubCorp forms partnership with Jack Nicklaus.
1999: Pinehurst Resort & Country Club hosts the prestigious U.S. Open golf tournament; company changes name to ClubCorp, Inc.

Club Corporation also continued to develop its network of exclusive private clubs during this period. In 1985, the company opened the Center Club in Costa Mesa, California and purchased two Michigan resorts—Shanty Creek and Schuss Mountain. The following year, Club Corporation launched the Columbia Tower Club in downtown Seattle, and in 1988 opened the City Club of San Francisco, located in the Stock Exchange Tower. To better communicate with its far-flung members, Club Corporation also began publishing *Private Clubs,* a magazine targeting an affluent audience.

In 1989, Dedman's son, Robert H. Dedman, Jr., was elected president of Club Corporation. Although the senior Dedman remained active in plotting the company's strategic course, Robert Dedman, Jr. took increasing responsibility for managing day-to-day business. By the end of the year, Club Corporation ran about 200 clubs worldwide, 53 of which were country clubs.

New Development in the 1990s

The 1990s brought further changes to Club Corporation. In 1991, the company launched Pinehurst Championship Management (PCM), a sports marketing division, which marketed and operated major championship golf events at Club Corporation properties. PCM's initial goal was to bring championship golf tournaments back to the Pinehurst Resort.

The company also added important new properties in the 1990s. For example, in January 1990, Club Corporation acquired the 650-acre Shangri-La Resort in Oklahoma. This luxury golf club and resort had been built in the early 1960s, but had fallen into disrepair. Club Corporation pledged to devote more than $7 million to renovating Shangri-La. In 1993, Club Corporation assumed the management and co-ownership of another resort, The Homestead in Hot Spring, Virginia. Once again, the company planned a comprehensive restoration of the resort, which had been founded in 1766.

Club Corporation also purchased a number of country clubs during this period. In 1993, the company bought the Mission Hills Country Club in Palm Springs, California. Mission Hills,

which was home to the LPGA Nabisco Championships, featured a course designed by golf legend Arnold Palmer and was a highly regarded gold club. The following year, Club Corporation acquired the Indian Wells Country Club in Indian Wells, California, which hosted the Bob Hope Chrysler Classic golf championship. The Gainey Ranch Golf Club in Scottsdale, Arizona became the next Club Corporation acquisition in 1995.

Club Corporation continued its expansion into international markets during this period as well. In 1994, the company launched its first enterprise in China, with the opening of the Capital Club in Beijing, and took over management of the Hanoi Club in Vietnam in April 1996. This latter acquisition "not only shows our long-term commitment, but also presents us and our reputation to Vietnam for the first time," the younger Dedman told the *Vietnam Investment Review.* In 1997, Club Corporation made its first move into the United Kingdom with its purchase of the Drift Golf Club in Surrey, England. Club Corporation also launched the Tower Club in Singapore in 1997. The company's international clubs were intended not only to appeal to U.S. business travelers abroad, but also to the local elite.

The company's growth proceeded at an even more rapid clip in the final two years of the century. After rechristening itself ClubCorp International, Inc. in 1998, the company forged a partnership with famous golfer Jack Nicklaus's Golden Bear International to develop at least three dozen signature Jack Nicklaus golf courses. Also that year, ClubCorp acquired a 20 percent stake in ClubLink Corporation, Canada's largest golf club management company, as well as a 22.9 percent share in the PGA European Tour Courses.

These maneuvers were part of an overall strategy shift spearheaded by Robert H. Dedman, Jr., who assumed the position of CEO in 1998. For most of its history, ClubCorp strove to maintain a low profile, fearing that "a chain of golf facilities would conjure up the image of McDonald's," which would not be good for its upscale image, according to the *Dallas Morning News.* However, in 1998, ClubCorp sought more exposure in an effort to capitalize on its brand image. "Prestige names are worth a lot of money," the *Dallas Morning News* observed, adding "ClubCorp sees the advantage of making its name mean something in the marketplace."

ClubCorp's move into the spotlight culminated in 1999, when the company's Pinehurst Resort hosted the U.S. Open Golf Championship. In addition to cultivating an elite image, the U.S. Open received more than 28 hours of television coverage, providing ClubCorp with considerable exposure. To signify its new direction, the company once again changed its name—to ClubCorp, Inc.

The company continued to add to its roster of clubs in 1999, purchasing 22 properties from Meditrust Companies' Cobblestone Golf for $393 million (marking the largest transaction in the industry's history). In October 1999, ClubCorp entered into an agreement with the Cypress Group, a New York-based investment firm, to finance further expansion. Under the terms of the deal, Cypress would invest up to $300 million in ClubCorp and two Cypress representatives gained seats on the ClubCorp board.

ClubCorp's future prospects were bright. Golf's popularity soared, as aging baby boomers pursued the game for leisure and business people came to view it as an essential networking tool. Moreover, the success of young golfers such as Tiger Woods boosted golf's image. By the close of the century, ClubCorp operated more than 230 private clubs and had assets greater than $1.4 billion and revenue of $851 million. Further expansion was likely. As Robert H. Dedman asserted to *Sports Illustrated,* "We will never stop acquiring. In this business you acquire or perish."

Principal Subsidiaries

ClubCorp USA, Inc.; ClubCorp Resorts, Inc.; ClubCorp Realty, Inc.; ClubCorp International, Inc.; ClubCorp Publications, Inc.

Principal Competitors

American Golf Corporation; National Golf Properties, Inc.

Further Reading

Alm, Richard, "Open for Business. ClubCorp's Quaint Pinehurst Joins Big Leagues with Golf Event," *Dallas Morning News,* June 17, 1999.

Bartlett, James, "The Golf Bag: Golf Resorts Being Purchased by Corporations," *Forbes,* March 13, 1995, p. 61.

Dedman, Robert H., and DeLoach, Debbie, *King of Clubs,* Dallas: Taylor Publishing Company, 1998.

Dung, Hanh, "ClubCorp Makes a Play for New Leisure Club in the South," *Vietnam Investment Review,* November 4, 1996, p. 13.

"Lawyer Profiting in Country Club Business," *Las Vegas Business Press,* August 1, 1986, p. 14.

Shipnuck, Alan, "The Prince of Pinehurst," *Sports Illustrated,* June 14, 1999, pp. 34+.

Symonds, William, "Driving To Become the IBM of Golf," *Business Week,* June 19, 1989.

Vogel, Todd, "Club Corporation Announces Operations Restructuring," *Dallas Morning News,* February 11, 1986, p. 4D.

—Rebecca Stanfel

Collins Industries, Inc.

15 Compound Drive
Hutchinson, Kansas 67502
U.S.A.
Telephone: (316) 663-5551
Fax: (316) 663-1630
Web site: http://www.collinsind.com

Public Company
Incorporated: 1971
Employees: 1,000
Sales: $196.39 million (1999)
Stock Exchanges: NASDAQ
Ticker Symbol: COLL
NAIC: 336211 Motor Vehicle Body Manufacturing;
  335112 Light Truck and Utility Vehicle
  Manufacturing; 333924 Industrial Truck, Tractor,
  Trailer, and Stacker Machinery Manufacturing

Collins Industries, Inc. is a leading manufacturer of specialty vehicles, building most of its products to customer specifications. As a pioneer in the development of small school buses, Collins Industries controls approximately 50 percent of the "Type A," small school bus market in the United States. The company's school bus manufacturing operations are conducted through two wholly owned subsidiaries, Collins Bus Corporation and Mid Bus, Inc. A subsidiary of Collins Bus Corporation named World Trans, Inc. sells a line of small- to medium-sized commercial buses, which are used for transit, charter, airport, and shuttle applications. Collins Industries is also the largest ambulance manufacturer in the United States, manufacturing and selling such vehicles through a subsidiary named Wheeled Coach Industries, Inc. The company's Capacity of Texas, Inc. subsidiary ranks as the second largest terminal truck manufacturer in the country, selling vehicles and equipment used to transport semi-trailers from one point to another. Collins Industries operates seven manufacturing and distribution facilities located in Florida, Ohio, Texas, and Kansas. The company is led by the founder's son, Donald L. Collins, Jr.

Origins

Collins Industries was formed to meet a need no other company had attempted to address. The company and its signal product were the inspiration of Don L. Collins, who experienced his epiphanic moment during the 1960s when he was working as a distributor for a Kansas school bus dealer. Collins's revelation was sparked by the sweeping consolidation of the area's school districts, as the number of schools serving Kansas City's outlying regions was reduced by folding one into another. The concentration of schools made for considerably longer school bus routes, forcing 65-passenger buses on long treks to pick up and transport a handful of rurally based school children. To Collins, the sight of mostly empty, full-sized school buses traveling great distances was grossly inefficient. What was needed, he thought, were smaller buses better suited for transporting small groups of children. His vision soon led to the creation of the first under 10,000 Gross Vehicle Weight school bus.

Collins took initiative and fashioned a prototype school bus by converting a cargo van. He installed bus seats, special lights, a reticulating arm for the bus's stop sign, and other required equipment. The result was a school bus designed to carry between 16 and 20 passengers, tailored for the special needs of transporting small groups of children efficiently. Kansas school districts soon placed orders for Collins's modified cargo vans, creating a groundswell of interest that spread to other states. Convinced he had struck upon a marketable product, Collins incorporated his company in 1971 and began manufacturing small school buses in earnest.

The formal creation of Collins's company also marked its move to Hutchinson, Kansas. Collins needed a manufacturing facility capable of supporting his growing business, and he found one in Hutchinson when a suitable space became available after the closure of a motorhome plant. By the time Collins had settled into Hutchinson, he had already diversified his business by modifying cargo vans into ambulances, adding another facet to his specialty vehicle business that in the years to come would develop into a mainstay business for Collins Industries.

Supported by orders for school buses and ambulances, Collins gained his footing in Hutchinson during the early 1970s,

Company Perspectives:

Every city, town, village, and hamlet today is represented with the products that were innovated and manufactured by Collins Industries.

establishing a business foundation that was solidified quickly by the announcement of new regulatory requirements. In the mid-1970s, the federal government ordered school districts to provide transportation for disabled children. The edict created a new market for specialty vehicle manufacturers, and Collins was quick to join the fray. His company built one of the first wheelchair lifts used by small school buses, cementing his reputation in the industry niche. Buoyed by the increasing demand for specially tailored transportation vehicles, Collins Industries registered encouraging growth during the latter half of the 1970s. Then, in 1979, disaster struck the company, threatening to eradicate the success of the previous decade.

In April 1979, the company's 60,000-square-foot manufacturing plant in Hutchinson burned to the ground. Collins's company was crippled by the loss. Collins entertained only one response to the devastation that had beset his promising company. He decided to rebuild, and he enlisted the aid of his son, Donald L. Collins, Jr., to help him restore the company. Collins had worked for his father's company as a teenager. After attending college, Collins was hired by Arthur Anderson & Co., a job he gave up when he joined his father in Hutchinson in 1980. Collins was in his late 20s when he became a permanent employee of his father's company.

Public Offering of Stock in 1983 Spurs Expansion

With the help of $3.5 million in industrial revenue bonds issued through the city of Hutchinson, the Collins family was back in business. Having literally risen from the ashes, the company emerged from the 1979 fire exhibiting far more ambition than had characterized its first decade of existence. By 1983, the company had fully recovered, confident enough to offer investors a stake in its operations and its future through an initial public offering (IPO) of stock. With the proceeds raised from the IPO, Collins Industries gained the resources to launch an aggressive expansion program. The 1980s proved to be the company's defining decade, delivering the growth that landed the company on the national stage.

Following the 1983 IPO, Collins Industries completed two significant acquisitions that greatly increased its stature within the specialty vehicle industry. In 1984, the company acquired Capacity of Texas, Inc., a company that coincidentally was founded in 1971, the same year of Collins Industries' official formation, by a family named Collins, who were not related to the Collins family heading Collins Industries. The Capacity of Texas acquisition steered Collins Industries into a new segment of the specialty vehicle industry, providing entry into the market for terminal tractors. Capacity of Texas vehicles were used to move semi-trailer equipment through a hydraulically activated fifth wheel, a piece of equipment that Capacity of Texas sold under the "Trailer Jockey" brand. Based in Longview, Texas,

Capacity of Texas added a new dimension to Collins Industries' operations, while the company's next acquisition substantially strengthened an existing business. In 1985, Collins Industries acquired Wheeled Coach Industries, Inc., a purchase that immediately made the company the largest manufacturer of ambulances in the world.

With the addition of the 1984 and 1985 acquisitions, Collins Industries recorded prolific growth during the 1980s. Between 1971 and 1983, annual sales had grown to $10 million, a respectable, albeit modest, revenue volume that swelled exponentially following the company's IPO. By the end of the 1980s, Collins Industries was collecting more than $100 million in sales a year, having evolved from a regional force into a national contender. By the early 1990s, the company's sales total had reached $140 million, rising energetically despite a national economic recession. But there was little to celebrate in Hutchinson during the early years of the decade. The first half of the 1990s was marked by another disastrous event, but unlike the 1979 fire, the problems of the 1990s were entirely of the company's own making.

As reported in the November 11, 1994 issue of the *Orlando Business Journal,* scandal rocked Collins Industries in 1993 and 1994. The company's difficulties stemmed from an overstatement of profits in its 1992 financial statements, the same year it recorded $140 million in sales. Unreported expenses at the company's Wheeled Coach subsidiary had inflated profits, engulfing Collins Industries in controversy. In March 1993, five days after the company announced it would have to revise its 1992 fiscal statements, Chief Financial Officer Joseph Hebb resigned. But Hebb's departure did not resolve the matter. In November 1994, the Securities and Exchange Commission (SEC) leveled a civil suit and administrative action against Collins Industries. Collins Industries settled the lawsuit without admitting or denying the SEC's findings, but the company incurred more than $3 million in costs associated with the investigation.

Despite the setback, the company's difficulties with the SEC did not cause any long-term damage. Company officials emerged from the debacle, as they had following the 1979 fire, confident that future growth would lessen the sting of earlier problems. Between 1992 and 1996, Collins Industries focused on reducing its debt, while revenues climbed methodically upward, eclipsing $150 million during the company's 25th anniversary year. After getting its financial health in order, the company began preparing for another expansion period, intent on maintaining its leadership in its markets. The growth achieved during the late 1990s came through the expansion of production capacity and through acquisitions, the mode of expansion that had ignited the company's growth during the 1980s.

Late 1990s Expansion

The beginning of Collins Industries' expansion program was marked by a change in leadership. In 1998, Donald Collins, Jr. was named chief executive officer, replacing his father, who retained the title of chairman. Collins took charge of the company at a time when sales were flat and profits were on the decline, spurring his desire to implement a strategic plan to promote growth. Considering that Collins Industries maintained

Key Dates:

1971: Don Collins' entrepreneurial efforts lead to the incorporation of Collins Industries.

1979: The company's manufacturing facility is swept away by fire, forcing the Collins family to start anew.

1983: With its comeback complete, Collins Industries completes its initial public offering of stock.

1984: The acquisition of Capacity of Texas, Inc. marks the company's entry into the terminal tractor market.

1985: Ambulance manufacturing operations become the largest in the world after the purchase of Wheeled Coach Industries, Inc.

1992: Misreported earnings touch off investigation by the Securities and Exchange Commission.

1998: Founder's son, Donald Collins, Jr., is named chief executive officer.

1998: Company acquires Mid Bus, Inc., bolstering its Type A school bus operations.

a leading position in mature markets, stagnant financial figures did not cause undue concern at company headquarters. A large percentage of the company's sales depended on the demand for replacement vehicles, lending a certain cyclicality to the company's fortunes. Company officials were optimistic, however, that market conditions would swing in a positive direction. The sincerity of their optimism was demonstrated in late 1998, as the company completed several bold moves.

In the fall of 1998, Collins Industries completed a $1.1 million, 90,000-square-foot addition to its manufacturing facility in Hutchinson, substantially expanding the existing 160,000-square-foot plant. Further plant expansion was under way in Orlando, where the company was constructing a 100,000-square-foot plant that was scheduled to open in January 1999. The addition to the plant in Hutchinson, site of Collins Bus Corp.'s school bus manufacturing, and the Orlando facility, which was geared for manufacturing ambulances during the fall and winter and manufacturing school buses during the spring and summer, testified to the sanguine outlook for the company. "The primary reason for these changes was to accommodate more volume," Collins explained in a December 1998 press release, "especially with large contracts with stringent delivery deadlines."

Amid the expansion in Hutchinson and Orlando, Collins rounded out his first year as chief executive officer by completing a move that significantly bolstered the company's position in its original business. In November 1998, Collins Industries signed a definitive agreement to acquire Mid Bus Inc., a Bluff-

ton, Ohio-based manufacturer of Type A school buses. The acquisition, completed in December 1998, widened Collins Industries' lead over all rivals, giving the company an estimated 50 percent share of the domestic market.

As Collins Industries prepared for the 21st century, growth forecasts fueled confidence at company headquarters. *School Transportation News,* an industry publication, projected the sale of small buses would increase by 25,000 to 30,000 between 1999 and 2004. Collins was intent on positioning his company to capture the bulk of the new sales orders expected to materialize. "We will be expanding our employment force very quickly," he declared to *Knight-Ridder/Tribune Business News* on March 2, 1999, "because we've got a lot of school buses to build." Growth was expected to come from increased regulation on the use of vehicles that did not comply with federal standards governing the transportation of school children. Industry experts projected that churches, day care centers, nonprofit agencies, and other organizations would be prompted by heightened awareness of safety issues to begin replacing vans with small school buses. One industry observer, J. Curtis Brewer, expected Collins Industries to be the company to benefit from such demand, offering a glowing appraisal of the company and its prospects for the future. "It's a company that has lots of ideas," Brewer noted in a March 2, 1999 interview with *Knight-Ridder/Tribune Business News,* "and has the courage to spend the money to bring it to fruition."

Principal Subsidiaries

Capacity of Texas Inc.; Collins Bus Corporation; Wheeled Coach Industries Inc.; Mid Bus Corporation; World Trans, Inc.

Principal Competitors

Federal Signal Corporation; Blue Bird Corporation; Thor Industries, Inc.

Further Reading

Alm, Rick, "Hutchinson, Kan.-Based Bus Maker Reports Rise in Earnings, Orders," *Knight-Ridder/Tribune Business News,* March 1, 1999.

Beall, Pat, "Collins Execs Resolve SEC Investigation," *Orlando Business Journal,* November 11, 1994, p. 1.

——, "Collins in Driver's Seat Now at Wheeled Coach," *Orlando Business Journal,* February 10, 1995, p. 1.

"Collins Industries Inc.," *Kansas City Business Journal,* February 19, 1993, p. 33.

Martell, Lillian Zier, "Kansas-Based Collins Industries Serves Strong Niche of Small-Bus Buyers," *Knight-Ridder/Tribune Business News,* March 2, 1999.

—Jeffrey L. Covell

CONSECO®

Conseco, Inc.

11825 North Pennsylvania Street
Carmel, Indiana 46032
U.S.A.
Telephone: (317) 817-6100
Fax: (317) 817-2847
Web site: http://www.conseco.com

Public Company
Incorporated: 1979 as Security National of Indiana Corp.
Employees: 17,187
Total Assets: $98.4 billion (1999)
Stock Exchanges: New York
Ticker Symbol: CNC
NAIC: 524113 Direct Life Insurance Carriers; 524114
  Direct Health and Medical Insurance Carriers; 524126
  Direct Property and Casualty Insurance Carriers;
  551112 Offices of Other Holding Companies; 52222
  Sales Financing

Conseco, Inc. provides insurance, investment, and lending services to more than 12 million customers. Targeting "middle America," or U.S. households with annual incomes between $25,000 and $75,000, Conseco's insurance products range from medical to life. Conseco also offers mutual funds and annuities. The company grew quickly during the 1980s and 1990s through some 40 acquisitions. In 1998 Conseco diversified and moved into finance and lending by acquiring Green Tree Financial Corporation, the nation's leading lender of mobile home loans.

Innovative Beginnings in the Late 1970s and Early 1980s

Stephen C. Hilbert founded the company and guided its meteoric rise. Hilbert had an unusual background for a chairman of a major financial institution. He was raised in a small rural community near Terre Haute, Indiana, and attended nearby Indiana State University. After only two years of college, however, Hilbert became restless. "I dropped out to sell encyclopedias," Hilbert explained to *Barron's* in 1991. "After

I made $19,000 my first year as a 19-year-old, I knew I didn't need a college education to make a good living."

Hilbert drifted into the insurance business in the 1970s. After working for a small company for a few years, he got a taste of the corporate world at Aetna. Although Hilbert admired the muscle of Aetna and its corporate counterparts, he was frustrated by their lack of innovation. During this experience he conceived the idea for a new kind of enterprise—a life insurance company that would combine the flexibility and innovation of a small firm with the marketing savvy, financial strength, and computer systems of a big financial institution.

Just as he had done to sell encyclopedias in the mid-1960s, Hilbert started knocking on doors in the late 1970s. This time, however, he was looking for seed capital to fund his business startup, Security National of Indiana Corp. Although several regional securities firms laughed Hilbert and his five-page business plan back into the street, by the early 1980s he had raised $3 million in capital. In 1982, Hilbert acquired his first life insurance company, Executive Income Life Insurance Co., for $1.3 million. By slashing the fat and inefficiency out of his new purchase, Hilbert was able to return the ailing insurer to profitability after only one year.

True to his original concept of combining size with innovation, Hilbert established his enterprise in 1982 under two separate companies. Security National Corp. was formed to acquire and manage existing life insurance companies. To complement that holding company's subsidiaries, Security National of Indiana was established to develop and market new life insurance products and services. Although the two companies merged to form one holding company late in 1983, internal operations still reflected Hilbert's original concept.

Hilbert's company acquired Consolidated National Life Insurance Co. in August 1983. In December of that year Hilbert's two holding companies were merged under the name Conseco, Inc. With about 25 employees and assets worth $3 million, Conseco substantially improved the performance of its two acquisitions during 1983 and 1984. The company then purchased Lincoln American Life Insurance Co. early in 1985 for $25 million. It quickly moved Lincoln's headquarters from

Company Perspectives:

Conseco is dedicated to leading the process of change in the financial services industry by setting the standard for performance in all the markets we serve. We believe strongly that this dedication ensures the best products and services for our customers and distributors, the highest value for our shareholders and the most rewarding careers for our employee associates.

Memphis to Conseco's burgeoning offices in Carmel, Indiana. Hilbert, now with a few successful acquisitions under his belt, took Conseco public in 1985 in an effort to boost its investment capital. By the end of the year the company's asset base had increased to $102 million.

Rapid Growth: Mid-1980s Through the Early 1990s

Satisfied with its recipe for acquiring and improving insurance companies, Conseco stepped up its acquisition efforts in 1986. It purchased Lincoln Income Life Insurance Co. and Bankers National Life Insurance Co. for $32 million and $118 million, respectively. In 1987, it added Western National Life Insurance to its portfolio at a cost of $262 million. By the end of 1987, Conseco's assets had grown to a whopping $3.4 billion, and its workforce had grown almost twenty-fold since 1984, to nearly 500.

Conseco reorganized and caught its breath in 1988. It moved the balance of the operations from its largest purchase, Bankers National, to its ballooning Carmel headquarters. It also moved much of its Lincoln subsidiary from Kentucky. Although it increased the value of its holdings to more than $4 billion in 1988, Conseco was able to reduce its workforce by almost ten percent.

After nearly two years since its last acquisition, Hilbert raised $68 million in June 1989 to purchase National Fidelity Life Insurance Co. It moved that concern's headquarters from Dallas to Carmel. To house its expanding staff and operations in Carmel, Conseco built a 40,000-square-foot data processing center in 1990.

Throughout the 1980s Wall Street perceived Conseco as young and inexperienced. However, the company's rapid growth finally began to pique the interest of industry analysts and mainstream investors. Hilbert's strategy seemed relatively simple to most observers: purchase troubled insurance companies with potential and increase their value by turning them around. When Conseco went hunting for acquisition candidates, it looked for organizations with sound asset portfolios. For example, it avoided the many companies that in the 1980s had invested heavily in risky real estate and junk bonds. In addition, Hilbert sought firms that had developed unique insurance and annuity products or had devised innovative distribution systems for their offerings.

Importantly, though, Hilbert also searched for insurers that were inefficient and bloated with excess personnel. He slashed the aggregate workforce of the five companies he had purchased

between 1985 and 1989, for example, from 850 to 450 by 1993. Conseco's 1989 annual report boasted that it had eliminated 83 percent of the employees from one of its acquisitions. Many of the cutbacks were accomplished by integrating Conseco's consolidated marketing, investment, and product development operations into the companies that it purchased. In addition, Conseco typically achieved significant efficiency gains by implementing advanced information and data processing systems.

By 1989, Conseco's assets were valued at $5.2 billion. Although Conseco's rise was impressive, rampant acquisition and expansion had a downside for the holding company. By the late 1980s, Conseco had accumulated about twice as much debt as equity. In order to continue acquiring new companies, Hilbert knew that he would have to find a new source of funding that was not linked to debt-burdened Conseco. Therefore, in 1990 Hilbert organized Conseco Capital Partners (CCP), a limited partnership that included several well-financed companies. The company was intended to serve as the primary vehicle for new life insurance acquisitions. CCP's first acquisition was Great American Reserve Insurance Co. for $135 million. It also purchased Jefferson National Life Group in 1990 ($171 million) and Beneficial Standard Life in 1991 ($141 million).

Continued gains in the value of Conseco holdings combined with the success of CCP investments resulted in dynamic growth during 1990 and 1991. Although many insurers suffered severe setbacks during the U.S. recession and experienced staggering declines in the value of their portfolios, Conseco swelled its asset base to $11.8 billion and doubled its workforce to almost 1,100. Indeed, as the insurance industry weathered record insolvencies, Conseco expanded its headquarters and opened an entirely new hub, the Conseco Annuity Center, in Dallas. Entering 1992, the company was valued at over $800 million.

Because Conseco's performance contrasted so sharply with that of most of its competitors in the early 1990s, many analysts were skeptical. Critics charged that Conseco's amazing asset growth was largely the result of questionable accounting techniques. They pointed to the company's relatively low net worth, which was equal to only two percent of its total assets in 1991. Some analysts believed that it was just a matter of time before Conseco would fall prey to the asset devaluation that had plagued other fast-growing insurers of the 1980s.

Despite Hilbert's insistence that Conseco's success reflected a commitment to sound business practices, skepticism continued. Conseco endured a string of disparaging articles in major business journals in the early 1990s that questioned its integrity. Shortsellers—investors that had bet on Conseco's downfall—were enraged when its earnings continued to multiply. "This (criticism) goes back to instinct and gut feeling, and no hard facts," said money manager Martin Lizt in a January 1993 issue of *Financial World*. "You have to ask the question, 'Have they found a new way to make white bread?'"

As detractors waited for Conseco's money machine to disintegrate in the early 1990s, Hilbert clung to his original guiding principles. As stated in the company's 1993 annual report, "Our operating strategy is to consolidate and streamline the administrative functions of the acquired companies, to improve their investment yield through active asset management . . . and to eliminate unprofitable products and distribution channels.''

Indeed, analysts familiar with Conseco's portfolios attested that the company's investments were much more liquid, of higher quality, and more conservative than those of most insurers. In addition to avoiding real estate and junk bonds, Conseco's portfolio managers steered away from other risky and trendy investment vehicles of the 1980s, particularly Guaranteed Investment Contracts. A study of the top U.S. insurers in 1991 showed that only 48 percent of their investments were fixed maturities, whereas over 50 percent were tied up in real estate and other less dependable assets. In contrast, more than 80 percent of Conseco's portfolio comprised fixed maturities, and only two percent consisted of real estate holdings.

In 1992, Conseco founded Conseco Capital Management, Inc. (CCM) to capitalize on its investment expertise. CCM provided a variety of financial and investment advisory services on a fee basis to both affiliated and nonaffiliated insurers. CCM was managing about $19 billion worth of assets going into 1994. Also in 1992, CCP shelled out $600 million to acquire Bankers Life and Casualty Co., one of the nation's largest writers of individual health insurance policies. In early 1993, Conseco acquired a controlling interest in MDS/Bankmark, a major marketer of annuity and mutual fund products.

The Conseco organization continued to add value to its holdings in the early 1990s and to achieve success with both CCM and CCP. In fact, it experienced stellar growth during 1992 and 1993. The company's net income increased 46 percent in 1992 to $170 million, and 75 percent in 1993 to $297 million. During the same period, the value of Conseco's assets ballooned from $11.8 billion to $16.6 billion—a gain of about 30 percent. As Conseco increased its value and expanded its asset base, suspicions about its performance began to wane in 1993 and 1994. Importantly, the company had eliminated much of its debt burden by 1994.

From an encyclopedia salesman in eastern Indiana, Hilbert had successfully boosted his status to that of corporate multimillionaire. In 1992, just ten years after starting his business, Hilbert was one of the highest paid executives in the United States. He received $8.8 million in pay and exercised stock options worth almost $30 million. Although some critics derided his benefits package and called it exorbitant, Hilbert was quick to point out that his compensation was tied to the

company's performance. After all, a $100 investment in Conseco in 1988 would have returned $2,062 in 1993.

Continued Expansion and Growth Through Acquisitions: Mid- to Late 1990s

Entering the mid-1990s, Conseco was poised for continued growth. Its goals for 1994 included increasing its assets under management by 30 percent. To help achieve this objective, Conseco formed a new limited partnership in early 1994, Conseco Capital Partners II, L.P. CCP II included 36 limited partners who had a combined investment potential of $5 billion to $7 billion. In contrast to CCP, the new partnership was designed to focus on the acquisition and improvement of larger companies valued at $350 million to $1.5 billion. The original CCP partnership was changed to CCP Insurance, Inc., in 1993, and began acting as a holding company for its three subsidiaries.

In addition to its insurance and financial management divisions, which accounted for more than 85 percent of Conseco's operations in 1993, the company was broadening its scope to include some nontraditional ventures. Conseco was investing tens of millions of dollars into new entertainment-related projects late in 1993 and 1994, including some riverboat gambling proposals. In fact, in October 1993 Hilbert formed Conseco Entertainment Inc., a holding company for Conseco's future entertainment investments. Other ventures included outdoor and indoor theaters in Indiana and Ohio. In addition, in 1992 the company paid $15 million for a 31 percent share of Chicago-based Eagle Credit Corp., an organization formed to provide financing to Harley-Davidson dealers and their customers. It also agreed to commit $5 million in 1993 to Rick Galles Racing, an Indy Car racing team in which Conseco owned a 33 percent share.

To its investors' chagrin, however, several of Conseco's past forays into nontraditional investments had not performed as well as its core insurance and financial holdings. In 1989, for instance, Conseco invested in a powdered drink mix developed by an Indiana doctor. The venture failed. Similarly, an investment in a restaurant chain that featured buckets of spaghetti fizzled. ''You have to stay where your strengths are,'' acknowledged Ngaire E. Cuneo, executive vice-president of corporate development, in the October 25, 1993, issue of the *Indianapolis Business Journal.* ''We are going to stay away from food and beverage.'' Despite a few unwise choices, Conseco was recognized for its highly conservative approach to investing.

In May 1994, CCP II made the first in a series of expected acquisitions when it agreed to purchase Statesman Group, Inc. for $350 million. In September the company entered into a $344 million partnership with American Life Holdings, Inc., which included subsidiaries American Life and Casualty and Vulcan Life. Conseco acquired the remaining 63 percent interest in American Life in September 1996. Conseco planned to retain its proven strategy of using innovative management techniques to increase the value of acquired holdings. Hilbert moved his main personal office to New York, where he planned to direct Conseco's CCP II. However, Conseco's headquarters remained in Carmel, and Hilbert planned to sustain his active management role there. ''This is what I love to do,'' Hilbert proclaimed in the June 7, 1993, issue of the *Indianapolis Business Journal.* ''I think you'd hear the same thing if you were talking to

Bill Gates or anyone else who has achieved success. . . . It's their baby.''

Continuing on its acquisition splurge, Conseco entered into agreements to merge with Kemper Corporation, an insurance company much larger than Conseco, for about $2.6 billion. Conseco withdrew from the deal after deciding that the asking price would cause too much accumulation of debt. Termination of the agreement, however, created bank and accounting fees of about $36 million and spurred a Merrill Lynch analyst to downgrade the company's stock. Conseco subsequently severed its relationship with Merrill Lynch, which had handled Conseco's initial public offering.

In 1995 Conseco formed a new division, Conseco Global Investments, and purchased the remaining shares of CCP. CCP was then merged into Conseco, and Beneficial Standard Life Insurance and Great American Reserve Insurance, both subsidiaries of CCP, became subsidiaries of Conseco. The company also acquired additional shares of Bankers Life Holding Corp., a holding company for Bankers Life and Casualty, upping its stake to 81 percent in 1995. The following year Conseco increased its share to 90 percent.

Over the next two years Conseco continued to gobble up insurance companies—it acquired eight in 1996 and 1997. Conseco Risk Management acquired Wells & Company, which offered casualty and property insurance products. The purchase created the biggest independent casualty/property agency in the state of Indiana. In July 1996 Conseco bought Life Partners Group, Inc. for about $840 million. The purchase included Massachusetts General Life, Philadelphia Life, Lamar Life, and Wabash Life. At the end of 1996 Conseco made two more acquisitions—American Travellers Corp. for $880 million and Transport Holdings, Inc., for $228 million. American Travellers offered long term care insurance, and Transport provided cancer insurance. Another cancer insurance provider, Capitol American Financial Corp., was purchased by Conseco for $696 million in March 1997. Then, in May, Conseco paid $505 million to acquire Pioneer Financial Services, Inc., a provider of life and health insurance products. Conseco rounded out the year with two additional purchases—Colonial Penn Group, which sold life insurance to elderly American citizens, and Washington National Corp., a provider of life and health insurance and annuities.

As Conseco headed into 1998, the company had a number of accomplishments under its belt. In 1996 the company was named to the *Fortune* 500, and in 1997 Conseco was added to the S&P 500 Index. The company's stock had returned an average of 39 percent a year since becoming a public company in 1985. Total revenues, after dropping from $3 billion in 1993 to $2.36 billion in 1994, climbed steadily, rising to $3.56 billion in 1995 and $3.79 billion in 1996. In 1997, total revenues reached $6.85 billion, a significant increase over the previous year.

In 1998 Conseco hoped to continue its growth and strong financial performance. To meet these goals, Conseco in March agreed to acquire Green Tree Financial Corporation, a diversified financial services company that offered home equity and home improvement loans, financing packages for the purchases of recreational vehicles and equipment, and credit cards. Green Tree was best known, however, as the leading U.S. lender for mobile home purchases. Green Tree was Conseco's first acquisition not related to insurance, and it was also the largest of Conseco's acquisitions—Conseco reportedly paid about $6 billion in stock for Green Tree. Conseco claimed the acquisition was a perfect fit, as both companies served the same target market, but many industry observers were skeptical, and Conseco's stock took a plunge. Not only did the company's stock fall about 15 percent upon announcement of the acquisition agreement, but it continued to drop; from a high of $58.12 a share in April 1998, Conseco stock dropped to about $20 a share in late 1999.

The Green Tree acquisition stirred up numerous questions, including whether Conseco had too much debt and whether Green Tree, which had a past of dubious accounting practices, was growing too rapidly—25 to 30 percent a year—and providing loans to high-risk borrowers. The company's stock decline also led to a deficit of collateral on company-guaranteed loans used by Conseco executives to purchase Conseco stock. Questions persisted, and in late 1999 Conseco announced plans to pare debt and slow growth. The company said it would divest of non-core assets, and it sold seven percent of its stock to private investment firm Thomas H. Lee Company for $478 million.

Falling stock prices did not completely hinder Conseco, and in 1999 Conseco acquired three health insurance marketing companies with plans to form a new subsidiary dedicated to supplemental health insurance distribution. The companies were Consolidated Marketing Group, Inter-State Service, Inc., and TLC National Marketing Company, which sold products door-to-door. In 1998 Conseco placed additional effort on building brand awareness. Not only did Conseco launch a major advertising campaign pushing the company as the ''Wal-Mart of financial services,'' but it also sponsored the Indiana Pacers basketball team and the Conseco Fieldhouse, an 18,500-seat facility that opened in late 1999. In 1999 Conseco secured a marketing partnership with the National Association for Stock Car Auto Racing (NASCAR) to become the ''Official Financial Services Provider of NASCAR'' and entered the second phase of its marketing campaign. In 1998 Stephen Hilbert received about $69.7 million in compensation. Though this was significantly lower than his 1997 pay of $119 million, it was enough for Hilbert to retain his reputation as one of the highest-paid CEOs in the nation.

Conseco renamed Green Tree Conseco Finance Corp. in 1999 and moved toward the next century intent on strengthening operations. The company, after 20 years in business, had grown tremendously—Conseco's total managed financial assets expanded from $8.2 billion in 1988 to $87.2 billion a decade later. Moreover, despite the company's stock price troubles, total revenues continued to grow; for the nine months ended September 30, 1999, revenues reached $5.92 billion, up from $5.75 billion for the comparable period in 1998. Stephen Hilbert demonstrated his confidence in the company by acquiring more than 638,000 shares in October 1999, pushing his total stake in Conseco to 10.4 million shares. Hilbert could not understand why industry insiders continued to hold reservations about Conseco. Hilbert told the *Indianapolis Star and News,* ''Everything at Conseco is hitting on all cylinders except the stock price. . . . I hate where our stock price is, but I cannot control the market. What's somewhat baffling is we haven't missed a [earnings] number. But my net worth's in Conseco. All I can say is, I'm buying more.'' As the company approached its 21st year of operations, Conseco remained confident that it could successfully attain its goals—to provide middle America with a wide array of financial and insurance products and services.

Principal Subsidiaries

Bankers Life and Casualty Company; Conseco Annuity Assurance Company; Conseco Direct Life Insurance Company; Conseco Health Insurance Company; Conseco Life Insurance Company; Conseco Life Insurance Company of New York; Conseco Medical Insurance Company; Conseco Risk Management, Inc.; Conseco Senior Health Insurance Company; Manhattan National Life Insurance Company; Pioneer Life Insurance Company; United Presidential Life Insurance Company; Washington National Insurance Company; Conseco Capital Management, Inc.; Conseco Variable Insurance Company; Conseco Fund Group; Conseco Finance Corp.

Principal Competitors

Metropolitan Life Insurance Company; New York Life Insurance Company; The Prudential Insurance Company of America.

Further Reading

Ambrose, Eileen, ''Green Tree Is Deal of Different Color for Conseco,'' *Indianapolis Star,* April 12, 1998, p. E1.

Andrews, Greg, ''Conseco Move Marks Evolution,'' *Indianapolis Business Journal,* September 20,1993.

——, ''Conseco Pouring Millions into Entertainment Ventures,'' *Indianapolis Business Journal,* October 25, 1993.

——, ''Hilbert Takes a Bite of the Big Apple,'' *Indianapolis Business Journal,* November 15, 1993.

Bailey, Jeff, ''Conseco's Chief Takes in $69.7 Million, Remains One of the Highest-Paid CEOs,'' *Wall Street Journal,* April 22, 1999, p. A4.

''Buoyed by Their Biggest Year Ever, Hilbert and Conseco Aim Higher,'' *Indiana Business Journal,* June 7, 1993.

Feaver, Christopher, ''Conseco Rolls Dice Again on Riverboat Gambling,'' *Indianapolis Business Journal,* December 6, 1993.

——, ''Conseco's New Partnership Will Stall Large Companies,'' *Indianapolis Business Journal,* January 17, 1994.

——, ''Western National IPO Means More Big Bucks for Conseco,'' *Indianapolis Business Journal,* February 14, 1994.

Francis, Mary, ''Carmel, Ind.-Based Financial Firm's CEO Tries to Prove Wall Street Wrong,'' *Indianapolis Star and News,* November 14, 1999.

''Indiana's Highest Paid CEOs,'' *Indiana Business,* July 1993.

Laing, Jonathan R., ''Deferred Risk? A Hard Look at Conseco, a Fast-Growing Life Insurer,'' *Barron's,* February 11, 1991.

Miller, James, ''Conseco Partnership Agreement to Acquire Statesman for $350 Million,'' *Wall Street Journal,* May 3, 1994.

Norris, Floyd, ''Its Price Share Sagging, Conseco Refocuses on Its Balance Sheet and Gets an Immediate Response,'' *New York Times,* December 1, 1999, p. 18.

Panchapakesan, Meenakshi, and Michael K. Ozanian, ''Loaded for Bear: Why High-Flying Conseco Is Proving Its Numerous Detractors Wrong,'' *Financial World,* January 19, 1993.

Rosensteele, James W., ''Corporate Profile for Conseco, Inc.,'' *Business Wire,* January 21, 1994.

—Dave Mote
—updated by Mariko Fujinaka

Corel Corporation

1600 Carling Avenue
Ottawa, Ontario K1Z 8R7
Canada
Telephone: (613) 728-8200
Fax: (613) 761-9176
Web site: http://www.corel.com

Public Company
Incorporated: 1985 as Corel Systems Corporation
Employees: 1,300
Sales: $243.05 million (1999)
Stock Exchanges: NASDAQ Toronto
Ticker Symbol: CORL COR
NAIC: 51121 Software Publishers

Corel Corporation is one of the world's largest developers of business productivity, graphics, and operating systems solutions. Corel's signature product is CorelDRAW, a graphics software package with sales that reached ten million copies in 1999. Aside from its graphics software, the company also develops and markets WordPerfect business productivity software, having purchased the WordPerfect division from Novell Inc. in 1996, as well as Internet applications for home and business customers. Corel markets its products in more than 15 different languages in approximately 70 countries. The company is led by its founder, Dr. Michael C.J. Cowpland, and is seven percent owned by Novell.

Origins

Corel is the offspring of Michael Cowpland, a high-energy entrepreneur and Ottawa celebrity who is credited with founding two of Canada's most successful high-technology ventures: Corel and the earlier Mitel. Cowpland was born in Sussex, England, in 1943 and received his bachelor of engineering degree from Imperial College in London. In 1964 he emigrated to Canada. There, he earned a master's degree and finally a Ph.D. at Carleton University while working as a research and development engineer at the respected Bell-Northern Research Ltd.

Cowpland worked at Bell-Northern with Terry Matthews, a friend who also had emigrated from the United Kingdom. In 1973 the pair left Bell to form a new venture dubbed Mitel (an abbreviation for Mike and Terry Electronics). They launched the tiny company with the hope of creating a device that could translate the pulses generated by rotary dial telephones into the tones created by touch-tone phones. Laboring in Cowpland's garage in Ottawa, the pair achieved their goal and went on to build one of Canada's most successful private telecommunications products companies.

Cowpland and Matthews realized stunning success with Mitel during the 1970s and early 1980s, doubling sales of its advanced telephone switching equipment every year for ten straight years. The darlings of the Canadian investment community, Cowpland and Matthews grew rich. In the early 1980s they began to chase new markets by diversifying into various digital technologies, and the pair seemed to have the Midas touch when most of those projects took off.

All seemed to be going well until the mid-1980s. Mitel posted revenues of C $343 million in 1984, in fact, by which time the company was employing more than 5,000 workers in ten plants around the world. It was in 1984, though, that Mitel's diversification effort suddenly began to look like a miscalculation. Significantly, Cowpland and Matthews fell behind schedule on the development of a state-of-the-art phone switch called the SX-2000. When computer giant IBM tired of the delay and shopped elsewhere for the technology, Mitel was faced with plant overcapacity, cost overruns, and a C $50 million research-and-development tab. Mitel began losing money, and Cowpland and Matthews were compelled to sell the enterprise to British Telecom. Still, both founders walked away with millions in cash.

Undeterred, Cowpland viewed the sale of Mitel as an opportunity to pursue the development of technology that was of greater interest to him at the time and to escape a job that had become an administrative burden. In 1985 he dumped C$7 million of his own money into a new venture, which he named Corel. His initial goal was to develop a better laser printer that could be used with personal computers. He found that it was too difficult to compete in that market with low-cost Asian manufacturers, however, and quickly shifted his strategy. Corel soon

Company Perspectives:

Since its founding by Dr. Michael Cowpland in 1985, Corel Corporation has built a reputation as an innovator with its leading-edge business and graphics software. The Company's products, used by more than 50 million people worldwide, are recognized for their excellence and value through hundreds of industry awards. Corel is dedicated to delivering advanced technology with compatible and user-friendly products that are competitively priced. Development of its CorelDRAW line of graphics applications and Corel Word-Perfect family of business tools is continually evolving to meet the demands of the corporate, retail and academic markets. In recent years, the Company has expanded its graphics expertise into a new line of consumer products designed for the home and small office market.

became a value-added reseller of computers, selling complete systems geared for desktop publishing tasks.

Cowpland scrambled during his first few years to find a role for Corel in the marketplace. He eventually added optical diskdrives to his desktop publishing system lineup and then started marketing local area networks. Considering the hefty start-up investment, sales grew tepidly—to about C$6.6 million during 1988—and for a few years, Cowpland seemed the consummate fallen star. "The first couple of years were the most challenging as we were trying to find the right niche, but I think that is typical of any new company," Cowpland recalled in the June 1992 *Profit.* "It's almost impossible to come up with the ideal concept right out of the starting gate," he added.

Corel's Graphic Software Debuts in 1989

While he pushed his value-added hardware, Cowpland labored behind the scenes on what became a pet project: the creation of software that offered better design and layout capabilities than were offered by leading applications of the time. To that end, he hired a crack software development team that he allowed to work relatively autonomously. Before the end of the decade, the team had developed a graphic arts software package that would become the standard for the PC-based desktop publishing industry. In 1989 Corel unveiled its cutting-edge Corel-DRAW software program. CorelDRAW, significantly, was the first graphics application to incorporate into one package all of the major graphics functions: illustration, charting, editing, painting, and presentation.

CorelDRAW was an instant success, which was surprising given the fact that Corel had never mass-marketed anything, much less a software application. Cowpland's savvy marketing strategy, however, eventually earned him almost as much respect in the software community as did CorelDRAW. Cowpland plowed millions of dollars into an aggressive sales campaign. Specifically, he bucked the industry norm by marketing CorelDRAW heavily in Europe and Japan. Most software companies at the time started out focusing almost solely on English-speaking consumers. Furthermore, as CorelDRAW became more popular, Cowpland refused to adhere to the convention of

selling different versions of the program one after the other. Instead, Corel developed and simultaneously sold multiple versions of CorelDRAW, each of which was tailored for a select market niche.

Corel's rapid-fire product development and marketing effort quickly boosted its bottom line. Indeed, sales (roughly 80 percent of which were attributable to CorelDRAW) rose to C$36 million in 1990 and then to C$52 million in 1991, while net income increased to a solid C$7 million. Going into 1992, Corel was employing about 250 workers and had shipped nearly 300,000 of its CorelDRAW packages to more than 40 countries. CorelDRAW was becoming increasingly popular with such customer groups as children, artists, architects, and business owners, among others. In short, CorelDRAW allowed users to create anything from T-shirt designs to corporate logos and technical drawings. Using a computerized pencil, or drawing from 12,000 programmed images, users could create an endless array of color illustrations, designs, and drawings.

As Mitel had, Corel reflected the insatiable drive of its founder. Cowpland had established his name in the Canadian business scene with Mitel, but his remarkable success with Corel revived his fame in his home town, where he "replaced Pierre Trudeau as Ottawa's most-watched celebrity," according to *Canadian Business Magazine.* In Ottawa, Cowpland was known as much for his persona as his business success. He raced around the city in flashy sports cars and generally made no apologies for his wealth. He and his wife built a massive new home that included a ten-car underground garage and two squash courts and was designed to mimic the look of Corel's gold-colored headquarters.

Cowpland's no-holds-barred, unemotional business style was mirrored more clearly on the tennis court, where he was known as an aggressive contender driven to win at any cost. Evidencing that drive was Cowpland's relationship with long-time tennis partner Ed Hladkowicz, the tennis pro at a club that Cowpland bought during his Mitel days. Cowpland hired Hladkowicz to work for Corel, and Hladkowicz became a manager in the company's systems division. Meanwhile, the two friends continued what became a 20-year run of regular tennis matches. Then, one day in 1992, Cowpland coldly and abruptly eliminated the systems division and sent Hladkowicz packing. A week later he phoned the stunned Hladkowicz to arrange a time to play tennis (the two eventually did resume their association).

Although Cowpland was criticized for his callous treatment of employees, few could dispute the success of his philosophy in the business arena. Cowpland prided himself on making quick decisions and moving briskly to capitalize on new opportunities. During the early 1990s Corel introduced a string of CorelDRAW programs geared for entry-level users, intermediates, and advanced buyers. Those introductions helped Corel to capture a hefty 55 percent share of the global market for drawing and illustration software products. The resulting revenues rose to C$90 million in 1992, C$140 million in 1993, and then to C$226 million in 1994, while net income increased to nearly C$45 million.

<table>
<tr><td colspan="2">Key Dates:</td></tr>
<tr><td>1985:</td><td>Dr. Michael Cowpland founds Corel as a systems integration company.</td></tr>
<tr><td>1989:</td><td>CorelDraw is launched after two years of code development.</td></tr>
<tr><td>1991:</td><td>CorelSCSI is launched.</td></tr>
<tr><td>1992:</td><td>CorelDraw 3 debuts, representing the beginning of the modern full-featured graphics suite.</td></tr>
<tr><td>1995:</td><td>CorelDraw 6 is launched simultaneously with Windows 95, becoming the first major 32-bit application available for the new operating system.</td></tr>
<tr><td>1996:</td><td>Novell Inc.'s WordPerfect division is acquired.</td></tr>
<tr><td>1999:</td><td>WordPerfect Office 2000 is released; sales of CorelDraw reach ten million copies.</td></tr>
<tr><td>2000:</td><td>Corel announces definitive merger agreement with Inprise/Borland Corporation.</td></tr>
</table>

Corel's success in 1993 and 1994 blasted critics, who claimed that Cowpland's downfall was imminent. Based on what they believed was a saturated market as well as Cowpland's history at Mitel, a number of investors began shortselling (betting against) Corel stock in 1992 in anticipation of an earnings slide. Instead, the company's earnings climbed rapidly in the wake of new product introductions and an improved balance sheet. Impressively, Cowpland had managed to grow Corel without taking on any debt. By 1994, in fact, Corel had virtually no long term debt. Furthermore, Cowpland still owned an equity stake in the company of about 20 percent by 1995, giving him an estimated net worth of $200 million.

By 1994, though, it could be argued that Corel was relying too heavily on a single product line geared for a market niche that was becoming saturated. So, after shipping nearly one million CorelDRAW programs in 15 different languages, Cowpland began looking for a new avenue to growth. In 1994 the company launched an ambitious initiative to branch into four new markets: consumer CD-ROMs, office suites (or "bundles" of productivity software), video-conferencing, and computer-aided design (CAD). Production of CD-ROM games and educational products was a top priority—Corel planned to launch 30 titles in 1995 and an additional 50 each following year. Corel planned to tap its established network of distributors in 60 countries to vie with venerable Microsoft in the $1 billion CD-ROM consumer market.

Creating its CD-ROM products in cooperation with Artech Digital Entertainments, Inc., Corel launched several CD-ROM products in 1995, including an electronic coloring book called "Blue Tortoise," a Marilyn Monroe photo compilation, a movie database, and collections of card and board games. At the same time, it continued to enhance its CorelDRAW line and to chase the other market categories it had targeted in 1994. For example, it announced plans to begin shipping a CAD software application called CorelCAD, which was designed to help homebuilders and people doing home renovations. Cowpland expected that effort to generate sales of $50 million annually by 1998. Likewise, Corel introduced a video-conferencing system early in 1996 called CorelVideo that was designed to operate efficiently on local area network systems.

Acquisition of WordPerfect in 1996

Critics wondered why Cowpland would take on so much risk by simultaneously jumping into industries in which he had little or no prior experience. Their concern was no doubt heightened early in 1996, when Corel stunned the software community by agreeing to purchase Novell Inc.'s vaunted WordPerfect division in a transaction valued at $124 million. WordPerfect word processing software was a leader in the massive word processing market. The deal also included Quattro Pro, a leading spreadsheet software, and the PerfectOffice application suite of productivity software. The surprising purchase was expected to more than triple Corel's annual revenue base.

The WordPerfect purchase vaulted Corel from a major niche player to a software industry contender in a business dominated by operating system powerhouse Microsoft: "Corel Feels Bold with WordPerfect Deal; CEO Has Glass House, But He Throws the First Stone at Microsoft," read the headline in the February 11, 1996 *Wall Street Journal.* By purchasing WordPerfect, Cowpland threw down the proverbial gauntlet, positioning his company to go toe-to-toe with Bill Gates's behemoth Microsoft. The acquisition marked the beginning of a new era for Corel. From 1996 onward, Cowpland's success with Corel would be measured by his ability to beat Bill Gates at his own game.

In the wake of the signal WordPerfect acquisition, Corel braced itself for the intense media scrutiny fueled by Cowpland's bid to break Microsoft's hegemony. The company continued its practice of relaunching CorelDRAW approximately every 13 months, recording consistent market success with its tried and true graphics product. In 1999, when CorelDRAW 9 was released, sales of Corel's mainstay product line reached ten million copies, a milestone achieved during the tenth anniversary of the product's release that testified to the one enduring strength supporting Corel. The company's success in posing as a legitimate threat to Microsoft's formidable position in business productivity software, however, was considerably less certain.

Corel's Java-compatible version of WordPerfect was tailored for compatibility with a variety of platforms, including Windows 95 and 98, Windows NT, Windows 3.1x, Macintosh, Unix, and Linux. In 1998 the company released WordPerfect Suite 8 with Dragon NaturallySpeaking, giving users speech-enabled word processing. A year later, Corel released WordPerfect Office 2000, but neither version catapulted the company to the rarefied heights for which it clamored. Corel lost $30 million in 1998 on $246 million in revenues and posted a $16 million profit on declining revenues of $243 million in 1999. To be fair, the company was pursuing an ambitious goal, one that could not be realistically achieved by the decade's end.

The true measure of Cowpland's success remained to be determined in the inaugural decade of the 21st century. Corel made a positive start to its determinative decade by completing an important merger. In February 2000, the company announced that it had signed a definitive merger agreement with Inprise/Borland Corporation, a transaction valued at $2.44 billion. The union of Inprise/Borland, a leading provider of Internet access infrastructure and application development tools and services, and Corel represented a pivotal step toward reaching Cowpland's goal. In a February 7, 2000 Corel press release,

Cowpland stressed the importance of the merger's effect on Corel's advances with the Linux operating system, which was capable of running on a wide range of hardware. "With Inprise/Borland's leadership in the software development community and Corel's Linux desktop operating system and productivity applications," Cowpland said, "we have an extraordinary opportunity to reach all facets of the exploding Linux market."

Upon completion of the merger, Inprise/Borland was to be organized as a wholly owned subsidiary of Corel. Based on 1999 figures, the two companies would generate over $400 million in revenues. Although the company's graphics and business productivity software was developed for a variety of platforms, much of its future success—particularly its success in wresting market share from Microsoft—hinged on the popularity of the Linux operating system. Toward this end, Cowpland's hopes were buoyed by the announcement that the Linux operating environment was expected to grow at a compound annual rate of more than 25 percent through 2003, according to International Data Corporation, an industry research organization. Whether or not such growth could inject Corel with muscle it needed to combat Microsoft remained to be determined in the years ahead.

Principal Subsidiaries

Corel Corporate Limited (Ireland); Corel, Inc.; Corel International Corporation (Barbados).

Principal Competitors

Microsoft Corporation; Adobe Systems Incorporated; Quark, Inc.

Further Reading

Aragon, Lawrence, "Caution: Stories Graphic in Nature: CEO Mike Cowpland's Plan to Diversify into Publishing and Video-Conferencing Could Lead His Corel to the Heart of Palookaville," *PC Week,* September 4, 1995, p. A10.

Bagnall, James, "Corel Good Example of New Wave of Business," *Ottawa Citizen,* January 10, 1994, p. A9.

——, "Corel Marketing Machine Goes Formal; Software Star Offers Big Reward for Top Artist," *Ottawa Citizen,* August 10, 1995, p. C6.

"Corel Corporation Integrates Jabber Instant Messaging into Corel-City.com Application Platform," *PR Newswire,* December 16, 1999.

Hatter, David, "The Fastest Finalists: Drawing on Innovation," *Profit,* June 1992, p. 32.

Hladkowicz, John, "Corel Establishes International Headquarters in Dublin," *PR Newswire,* June 11, 1993.

Kainz, Alana, "Corel Decides To Spread Its Software Bets Around; Company Moves Aggressively into New Markets," *Ottawa Citizen,* October 8, 1994, p. E1.

——, "Corel's No. 2 Executive Abruptly Quits on High Note," *Ottawa Citizen,* December 21, 1993, p. C8.

——, "Corel Up, Up and Away; Firm To Unseat Cognos as No. 1 in Software," *Ottawa Citizen,* December 24, 1994, p. H12.

Oberbeck, Steven, "Novell Finally Gets Monkey Off Back," *Knight-Ridder/Tribune Business News,* February 1, 1996.

Scott, Cindy, "Corel Ships Wild Board Games," *PR Newswire,* August 31, 1995.

"Stitch in Time," *PC Week,* September 11, 1995, p. A5.

Sutcliffe, Mark, "Racquet Scientist," *Canadian Business,* June 1995, p. 62(5).

Tamburri, Rosanna, "Corel Feels Bold with WordPerfect Deal; CEO Has Glass House, But He Throws the First Stone at Microsoft," *Wall Street Journal,* February 11, 1996, Sec. 2, p. 2.

Tillson, Tamsen, "Corel Inside Out," *Canadian Business,* Spring 1997, p. 58.

Urlocker, Michael, "Corel Has Last Laugh," *Financial Post,* July 11, 1992, p. 10.

—Dave Mote
—updated by Jeffrey L. Covell

Crédit Lyonnais

19, boulevard des Italiens
75002 Paris
France
Telephone: (1) 42-95-70-00
Fax: (1) 42-95-94-37
Web site: http://www.creditlyonnais.com

Public Company
Incorporated: 1863
Employees: 40,550
Total Assets: EUR 1.72 billion ($1.63 billion) (1999)
Stock Exchanges: Paris
Ticker Symbol: 18420.PA
NAIC: 52211 Commercial Banking

As one of France's three largest banks with assets of EUR 200 billion, Crédit Lyonnais provides a full range of commercial banking and financial services domestically and worldwide. Active in 60 countries, Crédit Lyonnais was once the world's largest bank. It has earned a reputation for innovation since the 19th century and was a pioneer in automated teller machines (ATMs). Ambitious expansion in the 1980s, however, spawned the world's largest financial disaster, estimated to have cost the French government $25 billion. Nevertheless, Crédit Lyonnais's 1999 flotation has made it something of a privatization success story, however sullied by scandal.

Origins and "La Belle Époque"

Crédit Lyonnais was created to fulfill a need in France for a bank that would accept small deposits during the expansion of the Second Empire, when the country needed an infusion of capital. The city of Lyons, with its rich and long-established banking tradition and the residents' desire to become independent of Parisian tutelage, was favorably suited to the formation of such a bank. The legal pathways were made clear by a May 23, 1863 law permitting the establishment of businesses without governmental authorization. The active personality of 39-year-old Henri Germain was also an important element in the bank's foundation.

The son of a prosperous Lyons family, Germain had been a lawyer, stockbroker, silk merchant, and mine manager before launching Crédit Lyonnais and becoming its first president. Of the bank's 20 million francs of capital (40,000 shares at 500 francs each), he became the biggest shareholder with 2,150 shares. On July 6, 1863, 200 businessmen met in the presence of a notary in Lyons to finalize a charter for Crédit Lyonnais, and on July 26, the bank opened for business at the Palais du Commerce in Lyons.

In its first years, Crédit Lyonnais operated as a deposit bank and served the needs of local business. Sudden losses in a dye factory in Lyons, however, deterred further direct participation in businesses. Germain's edict that the amount of all deposits and current accounts be equaled by liquid capital for immediate reimbursement became not only the rule at Crédit Lyonnais, but at all deposit banks. Such policy became influential in the bank's increasing reputation for reliability and security, as it expanded both in France and abroad.

By 1865, Germain had married into a Paris family and assumed a seat in the French parliament. A newly established branch of Crédit Lyonnais in Paris became increasingly more important, and Germain traveled regularly between Lyons and Paris. With the beginning of the Franco-Prussian War in 1870, Germain moved some of the bank's assets to London, creating Crédit Lyonnais's first foreign branch. During the Commune of 1871, a provisory office was installed at Versailles. Germain's active participation in negotiations over the financial clauses of the Frankfort treaty, which ended the Franco-Prussian War, reflected his growing influence in the financial community and helped to assure that his business went on as usual after the war. As a parliamentarian, Germain was much in the public eye and was suggested as a candidate for Finance Minister, but his attentions remained fixed on Crédit Lyonnais.

During the 1870s, Germain acquired some capital for expansion in Paris, southeastern France, and abroad. The construction in 1878 of a new, ornate building on Boulevard des Italiens to house the central Paris branch, which became known as a "temple of finance," signaled the ultimate dominance of Paris over Lyons in the bank's future. (It was built by Gustave Eiffel.) Branches also were established in Aix-en-Provence, Nice, and

Company Perspectives:

Crédit Lyonnais Group has refocused on its three core businesses in retail financing services in France, corporate and institutional banking and international asset management, activities in which it has real competitive strengths. Through its extensive branch network, Crédit Lyonnais offers a full spectrum of banking products and services to personal, professional and business customers in France, placing a strong emphasis on customer service and satisfaction. Crédit Lyonnais also offers its major corporate and institutional customers an extensive choice of products and services, designed to meet their specific needs in terms of technical complexity, innovation and worldwide coverage. The Group also provides a global asset management offer encompassing both domestic and international fund management and private banking services. Crédit Lyonnais enjoys an excellent reputation and regularly receives awards for its fund performance and management quality.

Montpellier, among other cities in the southeast of France. The international network of branches, which would become fundamental in the history of the bank, began as offices added in Constantinople and Alexandria in 1875, Geneva and Madrid in 1876, and Vienna in 1877. The establishment of a branch in St. Petersburg represented the first instance in Russia of a bank operating under its foreign name. The New York branch opened in 1879 on Broadway, but subsequently closed its doors at a loss in 1882 because of high U.S. federal government taxes. By 1882, 30 offices had opened in Paris alone, as well as others in Bordeaux, Toulouse, and Reims.

The recession of 1882 and the loss of confidence in the Banque de l'Union Générale, due to speculation, put a halt to Crédit Lyonnais's expansion. The crisis of its fellow bank, however, helped establish Germain's policy of maximum reimbursement of deposits in the face of the numerous withdrawals that took place, and confidence in Crédit Lyonnais grew. In 1888 the bank's prestige suffered somewhat due to the failure of its investment in the Panama Canal project. Nevertheless, that year Crédit Lyonnais played a substantial role in the 500 million franc loan to Russia, and these foreign loans became a specialty of the bank, although they were sometimes criticized for diverting French capital abroad. Crédit Lyonnais's business showed no signs of slowing from the late 19th century to the First World War, a period that became known as the company's "Belle Époque." The bank invested in real estate during this time, notably in Paris and on the Côte d'Azur, while also taking part in loans to foreign governments after the liberation of territory in 1870. From 1882 to 1900, branches increased from 110 to 189 with offices added in Moscow, Jerusalem, Madrid, and Bombay.

From 1901 to 1913, total assets rose from 1,700 million to 2,830 million francs. Despite the suspension of Russian government loans at the onset of the Russo-Japanese War and the circulation of pamphlets by radicals claiming that Crédit Lyonnais's foreign branches were political centers of reactionary propaganda, the bank's prosperity did not wane. Germain died

in 1905, but not before witnessing Crédit Lyonnais overtake Lloyd's and Deutsche Bank as first in the world in total assets, a ranking it maintained until 1920. Even Vladimir Lenin deposited his money at Crédit Lyonnais while in exile in France. The central office in Paris, designed by the architect Bouwens and completed in 1913, symbolized the worldwide power and prosperity of Crédit Lyonnais, at a time when the Federal Reserve Act had only just allowed U.S. banks to expand overseas.

WWI and WWII

With the outbreak of World War I, Crédit Lyonnais's supremacy was threatened. The war years saw weaker bank leadership and declining public confidence, in light of the bank's limited liquidation of accounts. With the complete cancellation of the Russian debt, due to the revolution in that country, came strong discontent among Russian clientele whose deposits were lost. In Petrograd, the Bolsheviks liquidated all private banks, Crédit Lyonnais included, and replaced them with the Bank of the People. Elsewhere, some 135 branches, now located in occupied territory, had limited or stopped services. The bank evacuated assets from Paris upon the German advance in the spring of 1918.

The postwar period of 1920 to 1929 was one of economic difficulty for Crédit Lyonnais, which for the first time in 40 years lost its premier position in the world to Société Générale. Furthermore, the bank faced economic inflation, which depleted its assets as well as those of its clientele, and competition from new, smaller banking establishments. As a result of the low salaries it now offered, the bank experienced a massive employee strike in the summer of 1925, and, four years later, one fifth of Crédit Lyonnais was bought out by the Berlin bank Mendelssohn. By 1928, deposits at Crédit Lyonnais were increasing once again. Due to a refined strategy for its foreign branches, an increase in new branches in France, and stronger leadership, Crédit Lyonnais was able once again to overtake Société Générale as the bank with the most assets in France. The bank withstood the Great Depression despite closing a few foreign branches and the death of the Madrid director in the Spanish Civil War. The company had to cut 18 percent of its staff, however, in the face of a 20 percent drop in profits.

At the outbreak of World War II, a 32-car train was used to evacuate 500 tons of stocks, bonds, and securities from Paris for safekeeping. In much of France, with the exception of the Alsace and Moselle regions, normal operations continued against great odds. Many Crédit Lyonnais directors and employees were killed in bombings or in combat during the Liberation. By 1944, normal relations were reestablished in Africa, and the bank retook possession of its offices in the Alsace and Moselle areas. All overseas offices were entirely reunified the following year. Most important for Crédit Lyonnais and the three other largest French deposit banks, the banking industry in France was nationalized after the Liberation. On January 1, 1946, Crédit Lyonnais shares were taken over by the government, and the bank remained a commercial company subject to common regulations in force for all private banks. Eduard Escarra, the bank's former general manager, became president after several years of transition.

Key Dates:

1863: Crédit Lyonnais opens for business in Lyons.
1878: Bank's elegant Paris headquarters constructed by Gustave Eiffel.
1914: World War I ends the company's "Belle Époque."
1946: Crédit Lyonnais nationalized after World War II.
1988: Haberer directs the bank in aggressive expansion.
1990: Bank's Dutch subsidiary makes disastrous $1 billion MGM loan to Giancarlo Parretti.
1993: Haberer fired as Crédit Lyonnais posts a $1.2 billion loss.
1999: Bank is privatized.

Postwar Nationalization

Due to protective legislation and less competition, Crédit Lyonnais experienced a successful postwar period. Expansion occurred in Latin America and Africa, after decolonization, as well as in Iran and Lebanon. During this time, Crédit Lyonnais became one of the front-runners in the application of banking technology and was the first bank to install automatic teller machines in 1956 and to introduce the Carte Bleue credit card in 1967. From 1966 onward, the French government created favorable conditions for a new cycle of expansion and innovation in the banking industry. In 1967, legislation to institute a "mixed bank" was passed, which effectively allowed for the bringing together of business banks and deposit banks. In addition, certain regulations overseeing the opening of branches were revoked. The merger in 1966 of BBCI and CNEP, the third and fourth largest French banks, into the Banque Nationale de Paris (BNP), made Crédit Lyonnais second in France. This merger, however, stimulated a dynamic competition between BNP, Société Générale, and Crédit Lyonnais.

Favorable legislative conditions were accompanied by an increase in the number of Crédit Lyonnais branches, which rose from 828 to 1,905, as well as employees, which increased from 29,000 to 47,000, in the years 1967 to 1974. The central office in Paris was renovated, and a branch was opened in 1973 at La Défense, the business district on the west side of Paris, to help decongest operations downtown. Another period of internationalization began in the early 1970s, pushing Crédit Lyonnais back into the ranks of the world's ten largest banks. Branches were opened in Tokyo in 1970 and in Singapore, Sydney, and New York the following year. In South America, Crédit Lyonnais helped form Banco Frances e Brasileiro in Brazil. It formed a consortium during this time with Germany's Commerzbank, with Italy's Banco di Roma, and later with Spain's Banco Hispano Americano to offer medium-term Eurocurrency loans. Crédit Lyonnais became the first western bank to obtain representation in Moscow in 1972.

Such expansion proved difficult to direct at times, however, and social unrest proved detrimental to the bank. In 1968 a general strike led by a Trotskyist caused the central office to close for ten days. Another long strike occurred in 1974, expanding to include other banks in the industry. In 1976 the bank's president, Jacques Chaine, was shot to death near the central office by a suicidal labor movement fanatic.

Stumbling Toward Privatization in the 1980s and 1990s

In 1982 France's socialist president, François Mitterand, completed the steps that nationalized the country's banking industry. Crédit Lyonnais, however, had already been nationalized for 36 years, and when a more conservative government returned briefly to power between 1986 and 1988, the new president of Crédit Lyonnais, Jean-Maxime Léveque, began to prepare the bank for privatization. He guided Crédit Lyonnais into dealings in securities and helped create Clinvest, the bank's investment arm in 1987. Such measures were halted subsequently by the return of the socialists to power in 1988.

That year, Jean-Yves Haberer, the former head of the Paribas merchant bank, assumed the bank's presidency. His leadership of Crédit Lyonnais was based on a commitment to the development of marketing and automated banking, more active cooperation with businesses, the development of European and international network strategies, and a unified European market. The bank took an extremely aggressive approach to expansion under Haberer, buying brokerage firms, financial service companies, and other banks, as well as nonbank assets. In 1990 Crédit Lyonnais took control of Thomson-CSF's finance operations subsidiary, Altus Finance, thereby bolstering profits. In 1992 the bank increased its stake in the Irish leasing and banking company Woodchester Investments to 48 percent. Crédit Lyonnais also acquired 20 percent of Aerospatiale from the French government after providing money for the development of new aircraft and missiles.

The bank had implemented its aggressive strategy in an effort to position itself for the 1993 opening of a single European market. In fact, Jean-Yves Haberer's organization of Crédit Lyonnais was that of a pan-European bank. In 1989 the company had established Crédit Lyonnais Europe, a wholly owned subsidiary, to consolidate the company's various European commercial banking units. Crédit Lyonnais's acquisitions, including Germany's Bank fur Gemeinwirtschaft in December 1992 and several in Spain and Italy, increased the size of its operations beyond the minimum required to operate successfully in the European community. In November 1991, Crédit Lyonnais was the lead manager of Spain's 13-year FFr 6 billion issue, which underlined the growing importance of the French franc sector of the Eurobond market. The deal, and its outstanding size and maturity, made Crédit Lyonnais the lead bookrunner for French franc Eurobonds.

In addition to concerted efforts at European expansion, Crédit Lyonnais's policy included a program of international expansion to transform itself into a universal bank, along the German model. As of 1993, Crédit Lyonnais was close to opening offices in China and was one of only several foreign banks awarded licenses to operate branches in Vietnam. It planned to enter the market in eastern Europe when political conditions became more favorable.

By the early 1990s, Crédit Lyonnais had a domestic network of approximately 2,400 branches, more than 700 offices in Europe, and 800 across the rest of the world. Along with the aggressive policy of acquisition and expansion under Haberer, however, came several bad loans and growing debt. Whereas profits in 1990 had increased 20 percent from the previous year, Crédit Lyonnais's first half 1992 earnings fell by almost two-thirds, as bad loans forced the bank to nearly double its loan provisions.

It had abused "The Power to Say Yes," its motto in the 1980s. The bank had several high-profile debtors, including the late Robert Maxwell, the former Soviet Union, the developer Olympia & York, and Giancarlo Parretti, who borrowed $1 billion through the bank's Dutch branch to take over Metro-Goldwyn-Mayer (MGM) in 1990. Parretti's inability to turn MGM around led to a suit removing him from the board. A Delaware court found him guilty of breaking a government contract and ordered him to relinquish control of MGM-Pathe Communications to Crédit Lyonnais in 1992.

In May 1993, France's newly elected conservative government announced a sweeping privatization program, involving 21 large, state-controlled companies, including Air France, Renault, and Crédit Lyonnais. The sell-off was to take place in the fall of 1993 on a company-by-company basis. Unlike a similar program carried out between 1986 and 1988, no limit was placed on foreign acquisition of shares. Among those expected to look at Crédit Lyonnais were other large European institutions that wanted to create pan-European institutions.

Haberer was sacked by a new conservative administration in November 1993. After his ouster, he claimed that the government pressured the bank into investing in money-losing, state-owned enterprises like Aerospatiale and the steel company Usinor Acilor, which together cost Crédit Lyonnais FFr 1 billion in 1993. Crédit Lyonnais's FFr 6.9 billion ($1.2 billion) loss in 1993 prompted an investigation into the bank's lending methods.

French conservatives blamed socialist cronyism for the funding of Giancarlo Parretti's doomed takeover of MGM and the purchase of adidas, the athletic apparel company, from Bernard Tapie. These were just high-profile examples of FFr 60 billion of nonperforming loans. Crédit Lyonnais's U.S.-based corporate banking unit and Asian securities brokerage, however, stood out amid the bleakness. The acquisition of California-based Executive Life brought with it a junk-bond portfolio that paid off handsomely, although the question of whether it was illegal for state-owned Crédit Lyonnais to buy the company caught the attention of U.S. investigators (Department of Justice, FBI, Federal Reserve). Crédit Lyonnais had covered its tracks by buying the company in a secret pact with French insurer MAAF.

After Haberer, former insurance executive Jean Peyrelevade took the reins. Selling half the bank's $11 billion industrial holdings and cutting about 4,500 jobs in Europe while shuffling upper management were on his agenda. He dramatically seized $50 million of Tapie's assets, including his furniture, in May 1994. Still, Crédit Lyonnais lost FFr 4.5 billion in 1994. Real estate produced the biggest losses. The French government had to recapitalize Crédit Lyonnais in the amount of about FFr 5 billion, much to the chagrin of France's other banks. Crédit Lyonnais tempered the bad news with a new advertising campaign. "Votre banque vous doit des comptes," it said, inviting customers to share concerns during an all-day open house. "Your bank owes you (an accounting)."

The French government announced its five-year recovery plan for the bank in March 1995. Selling off assets, MGM in particular, was a key part of the plan. (It finally sold the studio for $1.6 billion in 1995–96.) There was also a four-year austerity program. Finally, Crédit Lyonnais promised to pay the government a 30 to 60 percent dividend once it managed a profit.

The government's own damage control was seen by the *Economist* as a scandal in itself. In April 1995, it created the Consortium de Realisation (CDR) to sell off Crédit Lyonnais's bad debts. The CDR was not truly independent, however, and ended up also acquiring some of Crédit Lyonnais's more valuable assets, which it purchased with cheap loans from Crédit Lyonnais itself. CDR effectively recapitalized the Société de Banque Occidentale, the subsidiary that made the infamous Tapie loans, and sold it back to Crédit Lyonnais at a bargain, much to the dismay of already-privatized competitors and the European Commission, which estimated the total cost of the bailout at FFr 150 billion.

Crédit Lyonnais's venerable "temple of finance" was set ablaze in 1996. The fire destroyed two-thirds of the structure. In 1997, U.S. prosecutors expanded their investigation of the MGM deal to include Crédit Lyonnais Bank Nederland (CLBN), the subsidiary that Parretti and his money-laundering accomplice Florio Fiorini bribed into making the MGM loan. Investigators in France and Italy approached the scandal from other angles.

A long-awaited flotation on the Paris bourse was postponed in 1998 because of low values for financial stocks. Other bad news came from a Russian default that caught Crédit Lyonnais along with several other lenders. Still, the bank posted a profit of EUR 165 million in 1998, up from 1997's EUR 54 million in 1997. *Forbes* reported that Crédit Lyonnais had dropped to the world's 39th largest bank by 1999, and *Fortune* noted the French government had spent $25 billion on its recovery—$7.5 billion more than the Marshall Plan when adjusted for inflation.

There were many enthusiastic investors for the flotation in the summer of 1999, which raised about FFr 45 billion for the government. It retained ten percent of the company and employees owned four percent. Crédit Agricole, AGF, Allianz, AXA, Commerzbank, BBV, CCF, and Intesta together owned about a third and were restricted from selling their shares for two years, protecting Crédit Lyonnais from takeover attempts, as the European Commission had limited the bank's expansion in approving the French government's bailout.

Principal Subsidiaries

CL Assurance, Réassurance, Courtage; CL Capital Markets International; CL Développement Economique; CL Eurofactors France; CL Eurofactors Participations; CL Europe SA; CL Global Banking; CL Leasing Europe; CL Leasing Overseas; CL Marchés de Capitaux; COGEFO; Compagnie Rhodanienne de Bestion; Consortium Rhodanien de Réalisations; Crédit Lyonnais Securities USA Inc.

Principal Divisions

Retail Financing Services; Corporate and Institutional Banking; International Asset Management.

Principal Competitors

Banque Nationale de Paris S.A.; Caisse Nationale de Crédit Agricole; Société Générale.

Further Reading

"Banking's Biggest Disaster," *Economist,* July 5, 1997, pp. 69–71.

Beckett, Paul, and Carol S. Remond, "Crédit Lyonnais Closer To Accepting Russian Debt Pact," *Wall Street Journal,* March 5, 1999, p. A11.

Beckett, Paul, and Charles Fleming, "Mellon Bank, Crédit Lyonnais Discuss Strategic Alliance, Equity Investment," *Wall Street Journal,* March 18, 1999, p. A4.

Bouvier, Jean, *Le Crédit Lyonnais de 1863 à 1882,* Paris: S.E.V.P.E.N., 1961.

"CL Pitched at Top Price as Buyers Sense Bargain," *Euroweek,* July 2, 1999, p. 20.

"Credit Crunch," *Economist,* December 13, 1997, pp. 67–68.

"Crédit Lyonnais Sale Revived Against Fluid Banking Picture," *Euroweek,* March 19, 1999, p. 11.

Dagneau, Jacques, *Les Agences Regionales du Crédit Lyonnais, Années 1870–1914,* New York: Arno Press, 1977.

De Quillacq, Leslie, "A Family Affair," *Banker,* May 1995, pp. 22–23.

——, "Tragedy Turned Farce," *Banker,* June 1994, pp. 25–29.

"Dismal Era Ends as CL Heads for Stockmarket," *Euroweek,* June 18, 1999, p. 6.

Faircloth, Anne, "Crédit Lyonnais Privatization Slated: Country To Take a $19 Billion Bath," *Fortune,* June 7, 1999, p. 44.

"France Proposes Bailout for Star-Crossed Crédit Lyonnais," *Los Angeles Times,* March 18, 1995, p. 1D.

Histoire du Crédit Lyonnais, New York: Crédit Lyonnais, 1993.

Jack, Andrew, "A Gloss on Bad News," *Financial Times,* October 26, 1995, p. 15.

Kamm, Thomas, "LVMH To Drop Bid for Crédit Lyonnais—Luxury Firm Isn't Interested in Stake in Bank, Plans To Unveil US Purchase," *Wall Street Journal,* May 12, 1999, p. A19.

——, "Rejection of Bid for French Banks Sets Stage for Protracted Battle," *Wall Street Journal,* March 15, 1999, p. A14.

Labasse, Jean, *Les Capitaux et la Région,* Paris: A. Colin, 1955.

"The Lesson of Crédit Lyonnais," *Economist,* July 5, 1997.

McClintick, David, "The Bank Scandal That Keeps Growing," *Fortune,* July 7, 1997, pp. 36–38.

——, "The Dirtiest Bank in the World," *Forbes,* December 13, 1999.

Montagu-Pollock, Matthew, and Daniel Yu, "How the French Plan To Conquer Asia," *Asiamoney,* November 1997, pp. 21ff.

Rademan, Chad, "Crédit Lyonnais Securities Punts on the Punters," *Institutional Investor,* July 1997, pp. 161–62.

Riding, Alan, "France Is Selling 21 Big Companies," *New York Times,* May 27, 1993, p. C1.

Rivoire, Jean, *Le Crédit Lyonnais,* Paris: Cherche midi, 1989.

Un Siècle d'Economie Française 1863–1963, Paris: Crédit Lyonnais, 1963.

Stevenson, Richard W., "Bailing Out France's Biggest Bank," *New York Times,* January 26, 1995, p. 1D.

Toy, Stewart, "A Trail of Red Ink at Crédit Lyonnais," *Business Week,* April 18, 1994, p. 59.

Toy, Stewart, Bill Javetski, and William Glasgall, "To the Rescue of Crédit Lyonnais," *Business Week,* June 20, 1994, pp. 112–16.

Woodruff, David, "Crédit Lyonnais Float Draws Huge Response—Despite the Success, Future Is Unclear," *Wall Street Journal,* July 9, 1999, p. A12.

—Jennifer Kerns
—updated by Frederick C. Ingram

Dallas Cowboys Football Club, Ltd.

One Cowboys Parkway
Irving, Texas 75063
U.S.A.
Telephone: (972) 556-9900
Fax: (972) 556-9970
Web site: http://www.dallascowboys.com

Private Company
Incorporated: 1960
Employees: 226
Sales: $161.7 million (1999)
NAIC: 711211 Sports Teams and Clubs

The Dallas Cowboys Football Club, Ltd. is the most profitable professional sports operation in the United States. Since entering the National Football League (NFL) as an expansion team in 1960, the franchise has appeared in more Super Bowls than any other team and is one of only two teams to have won five of them. Under the direction of owner Jerral (Jerry) W. Jones, the Cowboys have excelled off the field as well. Jones has run the team as a business, boosting revenue and profits through marketing deals, as well as the sales of stadium suites and tickets. While Jones's individualistic and sometimes iconoclastic ways have led him into disputes with the NFL's power structure, they have benefitted himself and his team handsomely.

Early Years: 1960–70

The Dallas Cowboys Football Club entered the NFL as an expansion team in 1960. The driving force behind the team was its first owner, Clint Murchison, Jr., who paid $600,000 for the franchise. Even before he was awarded the team, Murchison had settled on his coaching staff, hiring Tex Schramm, then a public relations employee with the Los Angeles Rams, to serve as the Cowboys' general manager, and tapping then-New York Giants defensive coordinator Tom Landry as head coach. Schramm and Landry would lead the team for the next 29 years.

The Cowboys' first years were difficult. With no permanent stadium or training facility, the young team finished the 1960 season winless. Although Dallas recorded its first victory in the 1961, it would not boast a winning season until 1966.

Despite its early on-field struggles, the team gained a great deal of exposure and a loyal fan base. With his marketing savvy, Schramm recognized the importance of image to the Cowboys' long term success—both on and off the field. When Dallas negotiated the terms of its entrance into the NFL, Schramm had lobbied hard for the Cowboys to be included in the league's eastern division, home to the New York Giants, who played in the single largest television market in the country. As a result, Cowboys games reached millions of television viewers. Schramm made sure the team capitalized on the opportunity. "We captured people's imagination because we had good looking uniforms . . . [and] a modest head coach that people respected. . . . We were just the underdog people would be attracted to," Schramm told the *Dallas Morning News* in 1999.

The Cowboys also benefitted from league-wide changes that began the same year Dallas joined the NFL. At the time, the NFL was under pressure from the American Football League (AFL), a rival association of teams founded in 1960. (In fact, the AFL created the Dallas Texans in 1960, which competed directly against the Cowboys, though in 1963, the Texans moved to Kansas City, becoming the Chiefs).

Pete Rozelle, who had been named NFL commissioner in 1960, strove to rally the league against this upstart. By the early 1960s, the NFL had begun to lose some of its luster due to a growing competitive imbalance among its franchises. This situation arose largely because of the fragmented television coverage arrangements the NFL's individual teams had made. Until this point, each team had been free to negotiate its own broadcast deals and to keep whatever revenues were generated (with the exception of the NFL championship game, the rights fees for which were shared equally). As more popular teams in larger markets commanded better deals, they received more money, which they used to sign better players. Rozelle was able to convince the owners of the danger posed by this situation; if two or three teams gained total hegemony, fan interest (and therefore the league as a whole) would falter. National television contracts were soon negotiated, the proceeds of which were split evenly among all teams. In a similar vein, Rozelle

Key Dates:

1960: Clint Murchison, Jr., and Bedford Wynne are awarded Dallas Cowboys expansion franchise and hire Tom Landry as head coach.

1971: Texas Stadium opens; Cowboys win first Super Bowl.

1977: Team captures second Super Bowl win.

1984: H.R. ''Bum'' Bright purchases Cowboys from Murchison.

1989: Jerry Jones acquires Cowboys and selects Jimmy Johnson as new head coach.

1992: Cowboys win third Super Bowl title.

1993: Dallas captures second straight Super Bowl victory, fourth overall.

1994: Barry Switzer is named head coach.

1995: Cowboys win fifth Super Bowl.

1998: Chan Gailey replaces Switzer as Cowboys' head coach.

2000: Jones fires Gailey, and hires Dave Campo as head coach.

launched NFL Properties in 1963 to promote the league as a whole. Under this arrangement, royalties from the sale of the merchandise of each NFL team were pooled, with all teams sharing equally in the profits. It was, according to the *Orange Country Register*, ''at that point that the league really took off.''

In 1966, Schramm joined with Lamar Hunt, the owner of the Chiefs, to negotiate a merger between the NFL and the AFL. The union was consummated in 1967, with the two league's 24 teams converging under the NFL's umbrella. All teams now shared a common draft, all national television resources, and a championship game known as the Super Bowl.

While the NFL adjusted to these changes, the Cowboys began steadily to improve their record on the field. In 1966, Dallas won its first Eastern Conference title, though it lost the NFL Championship Game later that year to the Green Bay Packers. In 1967, the Cowboys again traveled to Green Bay, this time for the NFC title. (The winner would then play the AFC champion in the first Super Bowl.) Although Dallas again lost, the game raised the team's profile further. Played in temperatures well below freezing, the game (known afterwards as the ''Ice Bowl'') was closely contested and became a symbol of pro football's gritty image. Dallas at last captured the NFC crown in 1970, though it lost to Baltimore in the Super Bowl.

America's Team: 1970–80

In an effort to boost the Cowboys' ticket sales (one revenue source teams were allowed to keep for themselves), Murchison oversaw the construction of a new stadium, which was completed in 1971. Located in Irving, Texas, a suburb of Dallas, Texas Stadium could hold over 58,000 fans. Even more noteworthy was Murchison's prescience in building 180 luxury suites in the stadium. Unlike standard seats, luxury suites offered spacious and comfortable accommodations with excellent views of the field. Air-conditioned and glassed-in, the suites

provided a more upscale environment from which to watch the game. The suites carried a hefty price tag, though, and were marketed to profitable corporations as an ideal spot to entertain clients or colleagues. The revenue generated by the sale of these suites helped not only the team's bottom line, but also positioned it to attract a bevy of talented athletes who would lead the team on a glorious run through the 1970s.

In 1971, the Cowboys beat the Miami Dolphins 24–3 to claim their first Super Bowl title. After achieving its tenth consecutive winning season in 1975, Dallas again reached the Super Bowl, losing that game to the Pittsburgh Steelers. However, Dallas rebounded in 1977 to claim its second Super Bowl, downing the Denver Broncos 27–10. The Cowboys returned to the Super Bowl again in 1978, and were edged out once again by the Steelers in what is largely regarded as one of the more exciting title games in NFL history.

The Cowboys success during this period earned it legions of supporters nationwide. The Ice Bowl had given the team an image as a scrappy underdog, and its 1970s roster of charismatic stars—including quarterback Roger Staubach, wide receiver Drew Pearson, and running back Tony Dorsett—captured the hearts and minds of fans around the country. A highlight film produced by the league in 1976 referred to the Cowboys as ''America's Team.'' The moniker both fit and stuck.

Tough Times: 1980–89

While President Reagan declared that 1980 marked a new morning in America, ''America's Team'' found the dawning decade to be a bleak one after the brilliance of the 1970s. Staubach retired in March 1980, and while the Cowboys would return to the NFC championship game in 1980, 1981, and 1982, they were unable to make it back to the Super Bowl. In 1984, Murchison sold the team for $60 million to an 11-member limited partnership headed by Dallas entrepreneur H.R. ''Bum'' Bright. Bright instituted few personnel changes; both Landry and Schramm remained in their positions. However, the Cowboys' decline accelerated as the team missed the playoffs entirely for the first time in a decade. In 1985, the team moved its headquarters and training facility to the newly-constructed Cowboys Center in Valley Ranch, but its on-field performance continued to flag. In 1986, the Cowboys had their first losing season in 20 years, and things turned ugly. Both Schramm and Bright publicly sniped at Landry, who had by then become a Dallas institution. In 1988, the team recorded an embarrassing record of three wins and 13 losses. The team's profits spiraled downward with its record. Between 1983 and 1987, attendance at Texas Stadium fell 24 percent. To compound the problem, television revenues had decreased in the wake of declining ratings caused by fan disgruntlement with the labor disputes that plagued the league throughout the 1980s.

Rebuilding: 1989–91

Despite these downturns, Arkansas oilman Jerry Jones bought the Cowboys and Texas Stadium in 1989 for $140 million, the most ever paid for an NFL franchise. Observers were amazed at the price. Their shock only grew when Jones implemented sweeping changes at the organization. Jones confidently pledged that the Cowboys would win the Super Bowl within five years and immediately set out to rebuild the team. In an act which brought him death threats, Jones fired Landry and replaced him with University of Miami coach Jimmy Johnson. Schramm resigned soon after, and Jones named himself general manager.

Jones was determined to return the Cowboys to profitability. To do so, he cut expenses—laying off two-thirds of administrative personnel—and simultaneously strove to boost revenues. His first priority was to reverse the exodus of fans from Texas Stadium. After lowering regular ticket prices, Jones aggressively marketed vacant luxury suites. By the end of 1989, he had filled 27 of them, raising a total of $27 million. Jones used this money to attract excellent players, knowing that fans—and thus ticket sales—would return to watch a winning team. In 1989, he paid a record $10.4 million to secure the services of rookie quarterback Troy Aikman and, in 1990, drafted running back Emmitt Smith who—along with Aikman and wide receiver Michael Irvin—would form the heart of the Cowboys' successful teams of the 1990s.

A New Dynasty: 1991–95

Jones was universally despised during his first season as owner. To make matters worse, the Cowboys finished the 1989 season with a pitiful record of 1–15. The community "judged this man to be a fast-talking, hot-dogging, publicity-hounding Arkansas hillbilly with more dollars than sense," observed the *Houston Chronicle*. Nevertheless, the Cowboys broke even in 1989 with revenues of $32 million. Good news in the accounting department was soon followed by good news on the field, as the Cowboys returned to the playoffs in 1991, posting the team's best record since 1983. In 1992, Jones made good on his promise, as the Cowboys won their third Super Bowl. Moreover, the next year, the Cowboys again claimed the Super Bowl title. By then, Jones had nearly tripled the value of the franchise. With its net income in 1993 estimated to be $10.7 million, the Cowboys were ranked among the top five profit-producers of all U.S. sport franchises. As agent Lee Steinberg explained to *U.S. News & World Report:* "from the beginning, [Jones] has seen that everything—from his players to his stadium—has value beyond just that of a football team. Everything is part of a business that cross-fertilizes other ventures in that business."

Jones's financial success continued in the mid-1990s. By the close of the 1994 season, he had increased the number of occupied luxury stadium suites from 100 to 300 and was planning to build more. Because NFL franchises could keep local television contracts, Jones renegotiated these deals, boosting them from $2.8 million to $6.2 million in 1994. Even more impressive was Jones's savvy in bringing in local advertising revenues. By aggressively selling stadium billboards and local corporate sponsorships, the Cowboys raised advertising sales from $400,000 to $8.5 million in 1994. In the process, Jones forged an impressive profit-making cycle. The team's success generated revenue, which paid for talented players, who won more games, which improved the team's reputation, which generated more revenue. *Financial World* named the Cowboys the most valuable franchise in sports in 1994 and 1995.

Despite the Cowboys' success on the field, Jones replaced Johnson as head coach with Barry Switzer in 1994. The move

was not entirely shocking, as both Jones and Johnson were exceptionally strong willed and had clashed repeatedly. Even with the coaching change, the Cowboys returned to the Super Bowl—and won—in 1995.

Jones continued to seek new ways to convert the team's on-field success into profit. He began to lobby the NFL to end the practice of pooling merchandise sales, since in 1994 and 1995, nearly one-third of all NFL paraphernalia purchased in the United States bore the Cowboy's logo. However, the league refused. In response, Jones forged independent marketing alliances with sponsors in 1995. Nike Inc., PepsiCo, and American Express all made special agreements with the Cowboys that excluded the rest of the NFL. (In fact, the NFL as a whole had sponsorship relationships with Reebok and Coca-Cola, which directly competed against Dallas' individual sponsors. Moreover, the revenues derived from the NFL's corporate sponsors were equally divided among all the teams, including the Cowboys.) Because Dallas's deals were struck formally between Texas Stadium and its various sponsors, the Cowboys were not technically breaking the NFL's resource-pooling policies. Nevertheless, the NFL was deeply threatened by Jones's actions. "The whole system is based on revenue sharing and access to players," league commissioner Paul Tagliabue told *USA Today*. In September 1995, the NFL filed a $300 million lawsuit against Jones; he responded with a countersuit for $750 million. In 1996, both parties agreed to drop their suits.

The Late 1990s

Despite its high profile status and considerable earnings—*Financial World* estimated that in 1998 the team netted $41.3 million on revenues of $413 million—the team did not return to the Super Bowl after 1995. In part this was due to the aging of Dallas's core players. It was also a result of changes in the league's collective bargaining agreement that made it easier for teams to sign free-agents away from their competitors. While the Cowboys invested heavily in their marquee athletes, the league's salary cap prevented them from locking up many of the key players who had quietly but crucially contributed to the team's success. In 1998, Jones fired Switzer and installed Chan Gailey as head coach. However, this change failed to right the listing ship, and Gailey was released after a disappointing 1999 campaign. Dave Campo was then chosen to lead the team into the new century.

Even with its on-field woes, though, Jones had placed the franchise in an enviable financial position. As one of the first owners to view the operation of an NFL team as a true business, he established a course that appears likely to alter the face of the league for years to come.

Principal Competitors

Washington Football Inc.; Tennessee Titans L.L.P.; Chicago Bears Football Club Inc.; Arizona Cardinals; New York Giants; Tampa Bay Buccaneers.

Further Reading

Brown, Ben, "NFL Sues to Save Itself," *USA Today*, September 20, 1995, p. C3.

Campbell, Bill, "Underdog Image Helps Club Become America's Team," *Dallas Morning News*, September 12, 1999.

"Cowboys 'Broke Even' in 1990, NFL Records Show," *Fort Worth Star-Telegram*, August 19, 1992, p. 7.

"Cowboys Lucky if They Show a Profit for '84," *Baton Rouge Advocate*, January 14, 1985, p. C7.

Cowlishaw, Tim, "Jones: Cowboys' Financial Footing on Firm Ground," *Dallas Morning News*, November 22, 1989, p. B1.

Freeman, Denne H., "With Free Agency, Cowboys Won't Be in Lone-Star State," *Seattle Post—Intelligencer*, January 9, 1993, p. D4.

Haman, John, "Jerry Jones Hits Pay Dirt," *Arkansas Business*, February 15, 1993, p. 1.

Kelly, Kevin, "Jerry Jones: The Man Who Fired Tom Landry," *Business Week*, April 24, 1989, p. 148.

Markiewicz, David A., "Texas Stadium Endures as a Financial Gold Mine," *Fort Worth Star-Telegram*, October 22, 1996, p. 1.

McGraw, Dan, "The Very Lonesome Cowboy Jerry Jones Refuses to Join the NFL's Corporate Huddle," *U.S. News & World Report*, September 26, 1994.

Oppel, Richard A., and Doug Bedell, "A Gem of an Investment," *Dallas Morning News*, January 30, 1994, p. A1.

Robertson, Dale, "Jerry Jones Personifies a Real Dallas Maverick," *Houston Chronicle*, January 28, 1994, p. 4.

Seeholzer, Don, "The Evolution of Pro Football," *Orange Country Register*, January 29, 1993.

Swift, E.M., "Another Gusher for Jones," *Sports Illustrated*, December 12, 1994, p. 44.

—Rebecca Stanfel

Dave & Buster's, Inc.

2481 Manana Drive
Dallas, Texas 75220
U.S.A.
Telephone: (214) 357-9588
Fax: (214) 350-0941
Web site: http://www.daveandbusters.com

Public Company
Incorporated: 1982
Employees: 5,000
Sales: $182.3 million (1999)
Stock Exchanges: New York
Ticker Symbol: DAB
NAIC: 722 Food Services and Drinking Places; 713
    Amusement, Gambling and Recreation Institutions

Dave & Buster's, Inc. is a nationwide chain of huge, adult-oriented complexes that combine restaurants and bars with dinner theater and games ranging from pocket billiards and shuffleboard to high-tech arcade games to simulated golf and virtual reality space combat. At the end of 1999, the company operated 23 locations in the United States. There were also two Dave & Buster restaurants in the United Kingdom and one in Taiwan, operated under licensing agreements.

Origins in Little Rock: Late 1970s

The story of Dave & Buster's was the story of David Corriveau and James "Buster" Corley and started in Little Rock, Arkansas. Corriveau, whose resumé included selling snow cones and cars, dealing blackjack in Las Vegas, and waiting tables, started a restaurant called Cash McCools in 1975. He sold that booming business a year later and in 1977 opened Slick Willy's World of Entertainment. The site for this 10,000-square-foot billiard and game house was in Little Rock's renovated train station.

Meanwhile, Corley had been working his way up the management ladder with T.G.I.Friday's, where he started as a waiter in 1972. By the mid-1970s he was in charge of opening new units, and he looked at the train station as a possible location. But he had always wanted to have his own place. He approached Corriveau and others for backing and opened his restaurant, Buster's, right next to Slick Willy's in the train station. The two men became good friends and soon noticed that their customers moved back and forth between their two establishments. They began thinking what might happen if they combined Dave's games and Buster's food under one roof and how big that roof might be. They spent about a year developing a rough design, then Corriveau sold Slick Willy's to raise seed money and they went looking for a location.

Developing a Concept: 1982–88

Carriveau and Corley moved to Dallas, and in December 1982 they opened the first Dave & Buster's, in a former warehouse. They spent $3 million to make the 35,000-square-foot space what they wanted and it was a hit from the beginning. The place was packed with people playing pool, cashless blackjack, and pinball or other arcade games, while drinking and eating (burgers, steaks, finger food, salads).

Over the next several years the partners refined their "fun and food" concept, expanding the site in the process with the addition of a nine-hole simulated golf range. In 1988, they opened a second location, also in Dallas, the same size as the first.

Dave & Buster's was aimed at adults. Games rented by the hour. Customers played billiards on $15,000 tables made of handcrafted mahogany and rosewood, and the shuffleboard tables met tournament quality specifications. Full menu and bar service was available in the play areas, which were spread among several dining rooms within the complex. There was also the Million Dollar Midway, with electronic, skill, and sports-themed arcade games.

A New Majority Owner: 1989–94

Now that they had the concept established, the partners were ready to open more units. But for that, they needed money. In the winter of 1989, Carriveau and Corley entered into a deal with Edison Brothers Stores, Inc., a $1 billion conglomerate operating some 2,700 retail stores, primarily in the shoe and apparel markets. St. Louis-based Edison Brothers was developing an entertainment division and invested sufficient capital in Dave & Buster's to end up owning about 80 percent of the company. Carriveau and Corley retained ownership of the rest.

With the financial backing available from Edison Brothers, the company began building. In 1991, Dave & Buster's opened its third location, in Houston. The new complex was 53,000 square feet, nearly 20,000 square feet larger than the first two. The following year, in 1992, Dave & Buster's opened in Atlanta. Two years later the company moved north, opening a 70,000-square-foot complex in Philadelphia.

Also in 1994, the company dodged a potential legal catastrophe in Texas. A State District judge found that under a new state gambling law arcade customers could accumulate their winnings (such as coupons at Dave & Buster's) from the arcade games they played and swap them for prizes worth more than $5.

A Spin-Off and Expansion: 1995–96

Each new Dave & Buster's cost about $10 million to build and furnish, and this was proving to be a drain on Edison Brothers. In 1995, the majority owner spun off its interest in Dave & Buster's to its shareholders. Following the spin-off, Dave & Buster's went public, selling nearly $30 million in stock on the NASDAQ under the symbol DANB. Andy Newman, who resigned as CEO of Edison Brothers, became chairman of the new company, with Corriveau and Corley as co-chief executives.

During the summer of 1995, Dave & Buster's announced that it had signed a licensing agreement with Bass plc to operate up to seven units in the United Kingdom. In addition to being the United Kingdom's largest brewer of beers, Bass operated Holiday Inn hotels, 4,000 pubs, and a network of bingo clubs, betting shops, and ten pin bowling centers throughout the country. Also that year, Dave & Buster's opened its first complex in Chicago, bringing the number of locations in the United States to six. Meanwhile, by the end of the year, Edison Brothers had filed for bankruptcy.

With money available from the Edison buyout, the stock offering, and a $28 million secondary offering late in the year, expansion picked up steam. Corriveau and Corbey opened three locations (Hollywood, Florida; Bethesda, Maryland; and a second unit in Chicago) in 1996, with each unit expected to generate annual sales of between $12 to $15 million. The company also entered a joint venture with Iwerks Entertainment Inc. to develop and operate Iwerks 16-seat Turbo RideTheatres at several Dave & Buster's locations. Customers would be able to watch major films while sitting in seats synchronized to the big-screen action.

The Eatertainment Niche in the Mid-1990s

But Dave & Buster's was not the only company taking advantage of the American public's hunger for fun. In addition to existing theme chains such as Hard Rock Cafe, Planet Hollywood, and Rainforest Cafe, newcomers were planning restaurant prototypes such as the $11 million Laugh Factory Funhouse with comedy memorabilia and databases of jokes, Steven Spielberg's submarine-themed Dive!, music theme eateries featuring country music or Motown, and various combinations of video arcades and virtual or real games. By mid-1996, analysts were beginning to predict oversaturation in the "eatertainment" niche and eventual consolidation.

The exception to their less than cheery forecast was Dave & Buster's, whose 1995 profits were up almost 27 percent. Although the company had a good reputation for its casual dining food, the winning factor was its amusements, which accounted for more than 44 percent of sales. Recognizing that, Dave & Buster's constantly updated its games. "We can give [game makers] a certain amount of exposure and have a kind of most-favored national status with them," a company spokesman told *Investor's Business Daily* in 1996, adding "We're one of the first places to get new machines."

Thus the possibility of too many giant complexes going after customers' leisure dollars did not faze Corley and Corriveau. "We were ten years ahead of 'eatertainment'," Corriveau told *Restaurant Hospitality* in 1998. "Our average customer visits ten times a year. That sets us apart from 'eatertainment,' which looks for tourists to give them a quick visit and a T-shirt sale. We set out to firmly establish and nourish a local clientele at each location."

Continued Growth: 1997–98

The year 1997 saw more big names, including Disney, Spielberg, and Sony, entering the eatertainment niche and following Dave & Buster's model of giant complexes offering food and games. Meanwhile, Dave & Buster's kept opening units—four units in 1997 (in Ontario, Canada; Birmingham, United Kingdom; Cincinnati, Ohio; and Denver, Colorado). Restaurant locations were usually in metropolitan areas with a population of at least one million within a ten-mile radius, in high-profile sites close to shopping, offices, tourist attractions, and residential areas. Often the units were located in megamalls. Opening costs now averaged about $11.5 million, of which 65 percent was related to the site's games areas.

To keep customers playing, the company introduced the Dave & Buster's Power Card to activate its arcade games. This was a declining balance card that could be recharged as many times as wanted at conveniently located "power stations" and that helped games revenue increase by ten percent.

In 1998, the company opened five more complexes, bringing its total U.S. locations to 17. One of these, in Columbus, Ohio, was in the company's new "intermediate" format of 40,000

Key Dates:

1982: Dave Corriveau and "Buster" Corley open Dave & Buster's in Dallas.
1988: Second location opens.
1989: Edison Brothers Stores, Inc. acquires majority interest in company.
1995: Edison Brothers spins off Dave & Buster's and new company goes public.
1996: Dave & Buster's accelerates expansion.
1998: Company signs licensing agreement for Taiwan, Hong Kong, and China.
1999: Company moves to New York Stock Exchange.

square feet aimed at metropolitan areas of less than one million people. The company also created an even smaller format, which at 30,000 to 35,000 square feet was about the size of the original Dave & Buster's. This model would be built in smaller markets, with the first expected to be completed in 1999. Bass plc had two locations operating, in Birmingham and Bristol, England, and Dave & Buster's signed additional licensing agreements, covering the Pacific Rim (Taiwan, Hong Kong, and China), western Europe (Austria, Germany, and Switzerland) and Canada. During the year, Dave & Buster's settled litigation related to the 1995 spin-off from Edison Brothers Stores, agreeing to pay $2.244 million against all claims.

While its competitors went after families and younger adults, Dave and Buster's continued to focus on the 24 to 44 age group. The company had always attracted some corporate business, primarily private parties. In 1998 it became more proactive in this area, instituting a "Big on Business" marketing campaign to increase sales from events ranging from conferences to product intros to office picnics. It also introduced the "Company Challenge," a team-building exercise complete with referees, team shirts, scoresheets, and awards. At the end of the year, about 13 percent of the company's business was from corporate-sponsored parties. That year amusement revenue topped 50 percent of sales, which increased 42 percent over 1997.

Dave & Buster's obviously had a popular concept. Company revenues had grown significantly each year. In fiscal 1996, with nine locations, revenues reached $88.8 million with $6.3 million in profits. In fiscal 1997, with three more sites, revenues rose to $128.5 million with $8.9 million in profits. In fiscal 1998, with 17 complexes, the company took in $182.3 million and profits of $13.6 million. Whereas the average Dave & Buster's location had a volume of $10.7 million in 1995, by 1998 the figure had moved up to $13.2 million, and sales for existing sites increased six percent in 1998.

It's the Food: 1999

During 1999, the company moved to the New York Stock Exchange, taking the stock symbol DNB, and announced plans to double the number of locations in the United States (to 40) by 2002. In December, the company opened the first Dave & Buster's in Asia, in Taipei, Taiwan, and its 23rd location in the United States, in Rhode Island.

However, 1999 was a bad year for theme restaurants. Planet Hollywood filed for bankruptcy and Landry's Seafood Restaurants bought Rainforest Cafe after comparable store sales dropped ten percent. At Dave & Buster's, same-store sales dropped 2.2 percent and in August 1999 lower-than-expected profits caused the company's stock to drop 45 percent in one day.

"For the most part, theme restaurants have paid very little attention to food," Michael Beyard of the Urban Land Institute told the *Denver Post.* "The prevailing thought has been that it's enough to provide entertainment that is fun and visually stimulating. But without the basics, restaurants are going to fail no matter how good the theme is," he noted.

Food was only part of the picture. People also had to keep coming back. While many of the theme and eatertainment restaurants had people flocking to their doors when they opened, if customers came only once to "check it out," or as out-of-town tourists, a location would not survive. Dave and Buster's prided itself on its food, the huge turnouts at new locations, and the repeat business their older complexes did.

After the third quarter, with a 92 percent drop in earnings and same-store sales down 6.2 percent, the company announced that it would cut back on its expansion plans and increase unit-level support. It also increased its marketing and advertising budget by $4 million, hoping to build sales that way rather than by expansion and "word of mouth." As Corriveau told *Nation's Restaurant News* in January 2000, "Our stores enjoy a great honeymoon period when they open, but after that—around 18 months to two years—they need continued attention."

2000 to the Present

In December 1999, British multibillionaire Joseph Lewis bought 1.1 million Dave & Buster's shares through his Mandarin, Inc. This brought Mandarin's ownership to 10.6 percent of the company. A month later, Texas investor Lacy Harber increased his holdings to 9.8 percent of Dave & Buster's. The company board as a whole owned about ten percent, as did Dresdner RCM Global Investors of San Francisco, the chain's biggest institutional investor.

"The people at Dave & Buster's have to be considering their own options right now, and I would think that means they have to be looking at a management-led buyout as one of those options," Bill Baldwin of Dallas investment firm Baldwin Anthony McIntyre & Boles said in the same *Nation's Restaurant News* article. Dave and Buster's had been around for nearly 18 years, and its concept was popular from the very beginning, as was the company's profitability. However, aside from adding new games and rides, the concept had not changed much since the first complex in Dallas. As one analyst told *Nation's Restaurant News,* "They might need to update and become more contemporary and hip with today rather than 1985."

Principal Competitors

Planet Hollywood International Inc.; Hard Rock Café International, Inc.

Further Reading

Alva, Marilyn, "Games Good Ol' Boys Play," *Restaurant Business,* May 1, 1996, p. 68.

"Bass Launches 'Dave & Buster's' in the UK," *Universal News Services,* August 21, 1995.

Battaglia, Andy, and Richard L. Papiernik, "The British Are Coming: Buyers Eye Dave & Buster's," *Nation's Restaurant News,* January 3, 2000, p. 1.

Donald, LeRoy, "LR-Rooted Restauranteurs Take Concept Public," *Arkansas Democrat-Gazette,* February 15, 1995, p. 1D.

Frumpkin, Paul, "Walt Disney To Unveil ESPN Zone Eatertainment Complex in NYC," *Nation's Restaurant News,* September 9, 1999, p. 4.

"Fun and Games," *Restaurant Hospitality,* September 1998, p. 60.

Garcia, Eric, "Restaurant Didn't Violate Gambling Law, Judge Rules," *Dallas Morning News,* February 26, 1994, p. 36A.

Gubernick, Lisa, and Daniel Roth, "Burp!," *Forbes,* August 12, 1996, p. 52.

Heller, Karen, " 'Semi-Bored' in Philadelphia? Not at Dave & Buster's High-Tech Palace," *Times Union* (Albany, N.Y.), August 7, 1994, p. H15.

"Iwerks, Dave & Buster's Team Up," *Business Wire,* May 3, 1996.

Jaffee, Thomas, "Arrogance Goeth Before a Fall," *Forbes,* October 23, 1995, p. 128.

Johnson, Greg, "Whoever Gets the Most Leisure Dollars Wins," *Los Angeles Times,* March 23, 1997, p. D1.

"Local and State Business Briefs," *San Antonio Express-News,* February 10, 2000, p. 2E.

Martin, Richard, "Eatertainment Concepts Crowding Theme Niche," *Nation's Restaurant News,* July 29, 1996, p. 1.

Mencke, Claire, "The New America: Dave & Buster's," *Investor's Business Daily,* September 12, 1996, p. A6.

Papiernik, Richard L., "Focus on Finance: At Dave & Buster's They Play with the Bears—That's No Bull," *Nation's Restaurant News,* October 7, 1996, p. 11.

Raabe, Steve, "Reality Bites: 'Eatertainment' Leaves Sour Taste for Shareholders," *Denver Post,* November 7, 1999, p. L1.

Ruggless, Ron, "Dave & Buster's Makes Its Play To Double Its Size Over Next Three Years," *Nation's Restaurant News,* June 28, 1999, p. 12.

Sandoval, Joe, "Dave & Busters—There Is No Place Like It," *La Prensa de San Antonio,* February 7, 1999, p. 1A.

Snyder, Beth, "That's Eatertainment! As Americans Hunger for More Entertainment Value in Their Brands, A New Breed of Restaurants Prospers," *Advertising Age,* September 27, 1999, p. 18.

—Ellen D. Wernick

David's Bridal, Inc.

44 West Lancaster Avenue, Suite 250
Ardmore, Pennsylvania 19003
U.S.A.
Telephone: (610) 896-2111
Fax: (610) 896-6131
Web site: http://www.davidsbridal.com

Public Company
Incorporated: 1990
Employees: 1,445
Sales: $132.7 million (1999)
Stock Exchanges: NASDAQ
Ticker Symbol: DABR
NAIC: 44812 Woman's Clothing Stores; 44815 Clothing
    Accessory Stores

David's Bridal, Inc. is the largest retail bridal chain in the country. Whereas the bulk of the company's sales come from off-the-rack bridal dresses, the company also sells accessories and special occasion dresses. David's Bridal sells gowns under private labels, such as Michelangelo, Lady Eleanor, St. Tropez, and Santa Monica, and it holds exclusive licenses for wedding gowns from popular designers Gloria Vanderbilt, Jessica McClintock, and Oleg Cassini. The company's 100-plus stores are bridal superstores, which differ from traditional bridal salons in that they stock thousands of gowns in sizes two through 26. At a bridal salon, the bride-to-be usually tries on a sample gown and then orders the gown in her size. Because her gown must be ordered, her fitting can take several months to complete. At David's Bridal stores, the bride-to-be can pick out a gown in her size and often can take it home the same day. David's Bridal is the only bridal superstore that has achieved a national presence. The company maintains a high profile via radio, television, and billboard advertising. Nearly all of the gowns sold at David's Bridal stores are foreign made, and the average gown costs $500. Investor Robert Calhoun owns about 25 percent of the company.

A 1950s Bridal Salon

David's Bridal started in 1950 as a small bridal salon in Fort Lauderdale, Florida. South Floridian entrepreneur Phil Youtie purchased the salon in 1972 and opened several others throughout the state. From 1973 to 1988 Youtie owned 18 salons, which he operated primarily as leased bridal boutiques in department stores under the David's banner.

Youtie's traditional bridal salons developed a strong presence throughout Florida, but Youtie believed that times were changing. He observed many future brides flocking around clearance racks. He believed that brides in the 1980s were different from brides in the past, who often spent a great deal of time and money selecting and purchasing a wedding gown. "I saw a busy, intelligent bride-to-be who didn't have the time, patience, or money to shop for a wedding gown the old way," Youtie explained in *Chain Store Age Executive with Shopping Center Age.*

Youtie was right. The late 1980s marked the beginning of many changes in the bridal industry—and in the country as a whole. The United States was at war in the Persian Gulf and in a recession. The lifestyle of contemporary women was changing. More brides were on a tight budget; they were planning weddings with shorter guest lists and fewer bridesmaids, and they were borrowing gowns instead of buying them. In the *Sun-Sentinel,* Youtie described the bridal market as being in terrible shape because brides wanted to do everything smaller. Youtie was determined to adapt his salons to meet these changes.

David's Bridal Wearhouse in 1990

In 1990 he teamed up with childhood friend Steven Erlbaum, who was the founder of the Philadelphia-based Mr. Good Buy chain. The two men incorporated the company and launched the first David's Bridal Wearhouse in Hallendale, Florida. The bridal warehouse was the first of its kind. Stores were larger than average—about 12,000 square feet as compared with the average 2,500-square-foot bridal salon—and carried a full selection of wedding gowns in many different sizes and special occasion dresses and accessories, including headpiece foundations, gloves, and shoes. Unlike traditional bridal salons with luxurious interiors and full-service sales associates, the Wearhouse had no frills; customers searched through racks and racks of wedding gowns with little help from sales associates. Signs were posted in the Wearhouse warning customers that sales were final and that there were no onsite alterations.

Although the Wearhouse offered little in terms of comfort, brides-to-be could expect a bargain. They could walk out with a designer replica costing only about $150 to $900. A bride could expect to pay about 35 percent less for a gown at a David's Bridal Wearhouse. "We offer substantial savings," Erlbaum said in the *Philadelphia Business Journal.* "Today's bride, more than ever, is price-conscious. She is older than ever before and more likely to be paying for the gown herself," he explained.

In the bridal industry, reactions to the Wearhouse were mixed. Many felt that the company's discount trend was cutting into the business of traditional bridal salons. They claimed that the bridal business was a service business and that Youtie was cutting out the service and offering much-too-low prices. Said designer Paula Varsalona in the *Sun-Sentinel,* "This is the most important day in your life. It is not a time to save money."

David's Bridal became known as the "Wal-Mart" of the wedding industry—a title the company rejected. "There is little brand name recognition apart from the very upper end of the price spectrum in the bridal business," Erlbaum explained in *Chain Store.* "We cover all price points and all segments of the market, from blue-collar to affluent," he claimed.

Youtie believed that the Wearhouse attracted customers other than those who shopped at traditional bridal salons and, therefore, did not take away their business. "We get people who would have never gone to a regular bridal shop in here," he said. "We get people who are getting married in two weeks and just don't have the time for all of that." He countered that the Wearhouse was not taking business away from several of his traditional bridal salons, which were operating in different parts of Florida. As the company expanded, however, its stores drove many bridal salons out of business. Although some smaller bridal salons, such as those found in department stores, found ways to adapt and compete with David's, most struggled. "If a store was teetering financially before David's Bridal opens, it probably won't survive," remarked Erlbaum in the *Philadelphia Business Journal.* Most bridal salons lacked the volume that would allow them to buy in bulk and offer discounts. So

many brides flocked to David's $99 sales that the sales attracted media attention. "Just like in any other business, people care about price," Youtie said in the *South Florida Business Journal,* adding, "We simply adjusted and it's paid off."

Change and Expansion in the Mid-1990s

In 1994 and 1995, David's Bridal grew from 14 to 36 stores. The company hired a new management team to better handle its new stores and upgraded its existing stores. The company decided to convert its warehouses to bridal superstores. A bridal superstore offered the wide selections of a bridal warehouse, but with nicer surroundings and better service. Many of the company's competitors were converting to superstores as a way to adapt to the changes in the market, such as a faster-paced lifestyle, a decline in department stores, and foreign manufacturers' willingness to do business with discount bridal stores. David's Bridal felt that superstores were the best way to go. "We found that the warehouse concept to many customers meant like Home Depot—a barebones operation with no service," Erlbaum said in the *Philadelphia Business Journal.* "When it comes to a wedding, it's the most important day of a woman's life. She likes to be pampered, and she wants all the fuzzies. She wants to shop in some place that's comfortable and not threatening."

David's Bridal believed that superior customer service was the key to the company's future success. Management knew that if a bride-to-be bought a dress at David's Bridal and was satisfied with the service, she was more likely to buy the bridesmaids' dresses there. If the bridesmaids liked their dresses, they were more likely to come back to David's Bridal when they were looking for their own bridal gowns. Erlbaum claimed that superior service was the best way to build market share.

The company's new and upgraded bridal superstores had better lighting, comfortable dressing rooms, stylish interiors, and onsite alterations. A bride-to-be was greeted by a personal sales consultant who would stay with the bride-to-be as long as she was needed. When they entered the store, brides-to-be were asked to complete a questionnaire that helped sales consultants find them the perfect gown. The company dropped the "Wearhouse" from its name.

In 1996 the company named Robert Hurth as president. Hurth was formerly the chief financial officer of Melville Corporation in Rye, New York. Youtie wanted Hurth to manage the financial side of the company, so he could concentrate on fashion. Youtie planned to work with buyers and vendors and travel the globe selecting fabrics. Paul E. Taub, vice-president of marketing, explained in the *Philadelphia Business Journal* that it was imperative that the company's bridal gowns be absolutely breathtaking. "One thing is certain," he said, "when the mother of the bride cries, the store has made a sale."

Going Public in 1999

David Bridal's quick expansion and store upgrades put a strain on its capital resources and inventory controls. Because of its expenses, the company posted a loss of $415,000 in

1996. The company lacked a distribution center, and most merchandise flowed directly to its stores. In time, the company had an excess inventory of bridal and special occasion gowns.

Even though the company's earnings rose to $2.6 million in 1997 and to $5.8 million in 1998, it planned to go public. Youtie and Erlbaum were the principal shareholders before the company's initial public offering (IPO).

With its IPO, David's Bridal raised $104 million by selling eight million shares, including 6.39 shares sold by existing stockholders such as Erlbaum, who sold 1.2 million shares. The company used the capital to reduce the debt it had incurred with its expansion and upgrades and to fund further expansion and a new distribution center.

Also in 1999, David's Bridal launched an e-commerce Web site. Realizing that its internal management team knew more about retail than technology, the company hired an outside web development firm to oversee the project. Customers could use the web sight to learn more about the different styles of gowns at the stores and to find a store closest to them.

A Bright Future

Although David's Bridal cannot create more weddings to boost its business, it can profit on the more than two million weddings in the United States each year. The company has succeeded in capturing a large portion of the industry's market share and should continue to grow in the future. In 1999 Erlbaum said that the company's biggest challenge was finding enough people to work in its stores. Youtie expected the company to continue to thrive and said that he still found the bridal business rewarding. "After all these years in the business, I still get a thrill out of seeing the look on a customer's face when she puts on her wedding dress. There is nothing quite like it," he noted in an article in *Chain Store Age Executive.*

Principal Competitors

Federated Department Stores, Inc.; The May Department Stores Company; Saks Incorporated.

Further Reading

Feinstein-Bartl, Beth, "They Say 'I Do' on a Budget," *South Florida Business Journal,* August 19, 1991, pp. 1, 11.

Hagwood, Rod Stafford, "For Richer or Poorer," *Sun-Sentinel,* February 3, 1991.

——, "Match Wedding Gowns to the Bride," *Sun-Sentinel,* March 19, 1995.

Hals, Tom, "Bridal Chain Courts Customers with Discount Prices," *Philadelphia Business Journal,* August 2, 1996, p. 3.

Kolody, Tracy, "Chain Unveils Discount Path Down the Aisle," *Sun-Sentinel,* January 14, 1991, p. 3.

Ryan, Thomas J., "David's Bridal IPO Sells 8M Shares," *WWD,* May 25, 1999, p. 10.

Wilson, Marianne, 'Wedding Stores Go Big: David's Bridal Succeeds with Off-the-Rack Wedding Gowns," *Chain Store Age Executive with Shopping Center Age,* October 1995, p. 31.

—Tracey Vasil Biscontini

Delta and Pine Land Company

One Cotton Row
Scott, Mississippi 38772
U.S.A.
Telephone: (662) 742-4500
Fax: (662) 742-4196
Web sites: http://www.deltaandpine.com; http://
www.deltapineseed.com

Public Company
Incorporated: 1978
Employees: 555
Sales: $260.5 million (1999)
Stock Exchanges: New York
Ticker Symbol: DPL
NAIC: 11511 Support Activities for Crop Production

The Delta and Pine Land Company (D&PL) is a leader in cottonseed production, best known for the Deltapine, Paymaster, and Sure-Grow brands of cotton seed. The company provides its crossbred and genetically engineered cotton seed, as well as soybean seed, to agricultural enterprises worldwide. Commanding more that 60 percent of the U.S. market for cotton seed, D&PL breeds for fiber quality and cultivation characteristics, as well as for durability with picker or stripper harvest equipment and machinery used to transform cotton to fabric. In 1995 the company began working with chemical giant Monsanto, using the latter's Bollgard and/or Roundup Ready genes in cotton and soybean varieties for purposes of pest and herbicide resistance. Worldwide seed research and distribution involves breeding, testing, seed conditioning, such as the application of pesticides or fungicides, and cotton delinting. D&PL's research facilities are located in the United States, China, Australia, South Africa, Argentina, Brazil, Greece, and Spain. Company headquarters are located in the delta region of Scott, Mississippi, 15 miles north of Greenville.

Cotton Farming in the Early 20th Century

The company's earliest origins may be traced to its founding as a land speculation corporation chartered in 1886. The owners of the property in Bolivar County in the Mississippi delta region sold their wooded lands to timber interests; interestingly, not a single pine tree existed on the land. D&PL as it came to be recognized originated in 1911 when British textile manufacturers acquired land near the Mississippi River to supply cotton to their mills in Manchester, England. (Their source of long fiber cotton from Egypt had experienced low crop yields, and pirates assailed many of the vessels carrying cotton from North Africa to England.) Directors of the Fine Cotton Spinners' and Doublers' Association, Ltd. (FSA) became interested in investing in a U.S. cotton plantation when they met J.W. Fox, director of the Mississippi Agricultural Experiment Station (MAES), at the World Cotton Conference in Brussels. After a visit to Bolivar County, FSA negotiated with L.K. Salsbury for the acquisition of an estimated 36,000 acres from over a dozen property owners, as well as from Salsbury, for approximately $3 million.

Because an 1890 federal law prohibited farming operations from owning more than 12,500 acres of land, the British capitalists initially formed three companies. FSA organized operations under the Mississippi Delta Planting Company, which leased land from the other two companies, the Triumph Planting Company and the Lake Vista Planting Company. Salsbury became president of Mississippi Delta Planting Company and Fox managed the land holdings. The three companies would consolidate under the charter of D&PL in 1919 with the acquisition of D&PL's nearly worthless stock. Since the charter dated to before the 1890 law, the company was exempt from the land ownership limitation.

FSA invested $1.5 million in their new cotton plantation with mixed results. D&PL cleared virgin land, drained the soil along the bayous, and constructed cabins for tenant farmers. The first year's yield was only 2,800 bales of cotton, 500 pounds per bale, using hand and mule labor. The land was unable to produce the long staple cotton to the standard that FSA required and the company never used cotton fiber from the U.S. plantation in its mills. Short staple cotton sold on the open market at a higher profit, however, and D&PL proved to be a valuable investment for FSA whose sources in Egypt rebounded before World War I.

D&PL faced many difficulties in the early years, including drought, heavy rains, and an infestation of boll weevils which fed on cotton. MAES had initially researched the boll weevil problem before it reached Bolivar County in 1911. Research involved cultivation techniques and the crossbreeding of new varieties of cotton to avoid the populous season of the pests. At the MAES Delta Branch Station, Early C. Ewing pioneered hybrid cotton varieties to produce fast-fruiting and early maturing varieties of cotton for that purpose. D&PL hired Ewing in 1915 for its Cotton Research and Improvement Program where Ewing continued his work on pest control and crossbred cotton varieties for fiber length, strength, uniformity, and high crop yield. D&PL adopted the name Deltapine for these new cotton varieties.

In the company's first decades D&PL also contended with heavy rains and high water levels on the Mississippi River. The levee broke in 1912 and 1913, but sharecroppers were soon able to plant at higher elevations. A bridge built over Lake Bolivar in 1914 allowed cultivation of land on the far side, after it had been cleared of virgin timber and thousands of rattlesnakes.

While the levees held during the floods of 1916 and 1922, during the flood of 1927 the Mississippi River overflowed as much as 100 miles inland. The $500,000 damage sustained by D&PL involved the loss of 100 homes, 200 mules by drowning, and, of course, their loss of arable land. Specifically, the river deposited a two- to six-foot layer of sand on 5,000 acres of land, making some the company's best land unfit for crops. With Oscar Johnston as president, D&PL responded by planting grasses and converting the land to cattle grazing. The river receded too late in 1927 to plant on most of the land, and D&PL sharecroppers produced only 40 bales that year.

D&PL Thrives through the Great Depression and World War II

Under Johnston's leadership D&PL became a thriving cotton plantation, even through the Great Depression. Prior to the Government Cotton Control Program, designed to limit market surplus in the early years of the Depression, D&PL planted 14,000 to 18,000 acres. Regarded as a highly efficient organization, the cotton plantation was divided into 11 units, each supervised by a unit manager. Sharecroppers included 1,400 workers and their families. In 1936 D&PL plantations yielded approximately 15,000 bales of cotton on 11,700 acres. Sharecroppers earned about $1,000 from their cotton crop and supplemented that income on the one-half acre provided to each family for gardening and personal use.

D&PL was the largest, most successful plantation in the country and attracted visitors from countries around the world, including Turkey, Australia, Egypt, France, China, and South Africa. D&PL's cotton plantation averaged 9,130 acres between 1933 and 1943 and produced an average yield of 653.3 pounds

of cotton fiber per acre and 980 pounds of seed. A new variety of cotton introduced in 1942, Deltapine 14, yielded 737 pounds per acre. Acreage for corn averaged 2,183 acres between 1933 and 1943, while 7,736 acres provided food, animal feed, and grazing lands.

D&PL gradually converted to mechanized methods of planting and cultivation during World War II. In 1945 6,300 acres of cotton were cultivated by 612 sharecropper families, involving 1,547 workers, averaging ten acres per family plus seasonal workers. Use of Deltapine cotton varieties spread across the southern cotton states from Texas to North Carolina. Experimental stations in South America allowed D&PL to test its seeds during the winter in the northern hemisphere, speeding the process of developing and testing new varieties from parent lines.

As clothing manufacturers changed to synthetic fibers, cotton began to lose some of its share of the fiber market, creating a cotton surplus in the late 1950s. The change was gradual, from a 88.3 percent share of the fiber market in 1920, cotton declined to a 80.6 percent share in 1940, and to 65 percent in 1956. Private and government efforts aimed to strengthen cotton's share of the fiber market by strengthening the quality of cotton fiber. With Charles R. Sayer as president, D&PL increased its research budget by 50 percent between 1951 and 1957. A new, smooth leaf variety developed by D&PL at this time improved the quality of cotton and reduced waste. At 1957 prices, a $150 bale of cotton would be valued $7 to $10 more per bale. Negative effects of the cotton surplus on D&PL were offset by federal farm supports, which gave D&PL nearly $1.2 million in 1957 and expansion of the cattle herd.

Product Development: 1960s–1980s

After several years of supplying cotton seed to western farmers, D&PL began to expand operations into the southwest and west. The company opened its Western Division Office in Brawley, California, providing a sales office and quality control station to the Imperial Valley, and also located a sales representative in Chandler, Arizona. D&PL eventually attained 98 percent of the seed market in the Imperial Valley and 95 percent of the market in Arizona. The Western Division added a complete research facility in Casa Grande, Arizona. In 1961 D&PL began to develop Deltapine cotton varieties for the dry conditions of Texas, New Mexico, and parts of Oklahoma. The research station in Lubbock, Texas, added a full-time plant breeder in 1966. After ten years of research, the Southwestern Research Program released two new varieties of Deltapine cotton in 1971, while another two varieties, introduced two years later, were bred for cotton farmers in Arizona.

In 1978 Courtaulds plc, which had absorbed FSA, sold D&PL to Southwide, Inc., a holding company based in Memphis. Southwide sold a majority of D&PL's acreage to Prudential Life Insurance, approximately 25,000 acres of crop land, 4,000 to 5,000 acres of woodlands, and the rest cattle grazing areas. Southwide kept 90 acres for research and office facilities and leased 8,000 acres from Prudential for cultivation. Assets included two cotton gins, a delinting plant, a cottonseed processing plant, rice processing and storage plant, and a soybean and small grains plant. Roger Malkin became chairman and CEO of D&PL.

In the early 1980s D&PL introduced several new cotton and soybean varieties which remained in use for several years. After ten years of research on soybeans D&PL began to market soybean seed in 1980. New cotton varieties included the high yield Deltapine Acala 90 which produced a premium quality fiber and proved adaptable to different geographic regions. D&PL introduced two Acala varieties of cotton specifically for the San Juaquin Valley; Deltapine 50 and Deltapine 20 provided good fiber quality, strong yield potential, and a short maturity rate. Short maturity reduced costs as farmers used less water and agricultural chemicals, while early harvest lowered risk due to potential poor weather in the fall. By 1985 D&PL was marketing ten varieties of cotton seed and six varieties of soybeans; approximately 20 percent of 11 million acres of cotton crops in the United States were planted with some variety of Deltapine. Deltapine 50 remained one of the company's most popular varieties, used in 12.3 percent of upland picker cotton crops in the United States in 1993.

D&PL focused operations on the cotton seed market as the company sold its corn and sorghum business to Mycogen Plant Science. The sale involved the exchange of a sorghum processing plant for a cotton seed delinting facility in Lubbock. Development of cotton varieties continued with Deltapine 51 which yielded a higher quantity of cotton lint per cotton boll. New varieties designed for specific cotton growing regions included two new varieties applied to the mid-south and semi-arid desert valleys, while another variety, launched in 1994, was designed for the high plains of Texas. D&PL also released five new soybean varieties in 1994.

International and Technological Growth in the 1990s

D&PL's international division was formed in 1988 with two employees; by 1996 it would employ a workforce of 45. Sales in 1988 realized $350,000 and reached $2.3 million in 1990. The company's first breakthrough in the international market came after poor weather conditions in Paraguay increased that country's need for cotton seed. D&PL exported $6 million worth of cottonseed to Paraguay in 1992 and $2.1 million in cottonseed the following year. Satisfaction with Deltapine varieties prompted a joint venture to breed and process cottonseed in Paraguay.

D&PL became a public company in 1993 raising $34 million for international business activities and development of genetically engineered seeds. D&PL entered into a joint venture with government agencies in Singapore, the Cotton Research Institute and the Chinese Academy of Agricultural Sciences, to research and market cotton varieties in China. China, the largest consumer and producer of cotton worldwide, was still importing some cotton. New cotton varieties developed there would by marketed within China by the venture, D&PL China, and outside China by D&PL.

By 1994 D&PL sold cottonseed in 13 countries, primarily in South America, through export and to local markets through its subsidiaries. D&PL captured an 80 percent share of the market for cottonseed in Mexico as well as large market shares in Greece and Spain. The company added cotton seed breeding facilities and processing plants in Australia and South Africa, while Deltapine cottons were tested for use in Bulgaria, Brazil, Ecuador, and several southern African countries. Turkey's Ministry of Agriculture approached D&PL to develop a program to privatize the government operated seed industry there.

A collaborative research agreement with chemicals giant Monsanto Company came to fruition in November 1995 when the Environmental Protection Agency (EPA) approved Monsanto's Bollgard (Bt) gene for use with certain cotton varieties for pest control. Bt was derived from Bacillus thuringiensis, a soil bacteria which produced a protein fatal to the bollworm and the tobacco budworm (but not to animal or human life), when ingested via the cotton. D&PL spliced the Bollgard gene into some of its Deltapine varieties. In anticipation that the technology would be approved, the EPA permitted D&PL to plant 28,000 acres of NuCOTN for seed inventory in 1995. D&PL and Monsanto also formed a new joint venture with Chinese agencies in late 1995 to produce and market the genetically altered cotton seeds.

D&PL introduced NuCOTN to farmers in 1996 and expected savings on the cost of insecticides to range from $30 to $80 per acre. Farmers in eastern Texas using D&PL's NuCOTN reported insect damage to cotton crops in July as the unusually hot summer swelled the bollworm population. Unwilling to risk crop loss, farmers sprayed insecticides on an estimated 450,000 acres of NuCOTN. Of the 1.8 million acres planted with the Bollgard cotton varieties, pest damage to the Texas crops resulted in an extremely poor cotton yield on 18,000 acres. Monsanto paid damages to 25 Texas farmers seeking remuneration for low crop yield. Though conflicting research emerged after the first harvest of NuCOTN, D&PL's own study showed an average increase yield of 8.6 percent. For the year ending August 30, 1996, D&PL revenues increased to $153.2 million, a 54.8 percent increase due to the sale and licensing of NuCOTN varieties.

D&PL expanded its market share for cottonseed in the United States in anticipation of combining biologically engineered properties with existing varieties of cotton. In 1994

D&PL acquired Paymaster Cottonseed from Cargill, Inc. for $14 million, obtaining the Paymaster and Lankart tradenames and trademarks as well as seed inventory and breeding stock. In 1996 the company acquired the Hartz Cotton from Monsanto for $6 million. Through a $70 million stock transaction D&PL merged with Sure-Grow Seed, Inc., a deal that included the acquisition of Ellis Brothers Seed, Inc. of Alabama; Mississippi Seed, Inc.; and Arizona Processing, Inc. D&PL planned to cross breed the Sure Grow brand of cotton with Monsanto's Bollgard and Roundup Ready technologies, the latter a gene resistant to a Monsanto's Roundup herbicide used to kill weeds.

D&PL and Monsanto formed international joint ventures as well to produce, condition, and market Bollgard and Roundup Ready cotton seed. In 1997 Hebei Ji Da Cotton Seed Technology Company Ltd. began construction on a cotton seed conditioning and storage facility in China's Hebei Province. The new joint venture constructed an acid delinting facility with the capacity to condition seed for up to two million acres. The delinting process removed lint left on cotton seeds after ginning by soaking seeds in a solution of ten percent sulfuric acid and 90 percent water, then heating. The conditioned seeds produced a better harvest because they were less vulnerable to disease. After three years of testing of D&PL's Bollgard varieties with excellent results, the venture produced and conditioned enough of the seed for 500,000 acres for the spring 1998 planting but sold enough for 200,000 acres in the Hebei province. Similar joint ventures were established in the Anhui province of China, in Argentina, and in Brazil.

D&PL introduced cotton and soybean seeds engineered with the Roundup Ready gene for the 1998 spring planting season. Of the 812,000 acres sown with Roundup Ready cotton seed, 30,000 acres of cotton crops experienced heavy losses when sprayed with the Roundup herbicide. D&PL blamed the losses on atypical weather conditions in the five counties of Mississippi where they occurred, but critics blamed insufficient testing. Roundup Ready soybeans also generated controversy due to concerns about contaminating the gene pool of the world's food supply.

The controversy over bioengineering did not stop cotton and soybean growers, however. D&PL's transgenic seed was sown in approximately 6.7 million acres in 1999, compared to 3.8 million acres in 1998. Transgenic seed varieties accounted for 80 percent of D&PL's total unit sales. With increased sales in Australia and China, revenue for the year ending August 30, 1999 reached $260.5 million, an increase of 35.5 percent from $192.3 million for 1998.

In March 1998 D&PL received approval of a patent for Control of Plant Gene Expression; this generated even greater controversy than had the Roundup Ready Soybeans. Jointly held with the U.S. Department of Agriculture, the patented gene was designed to protect proprietary rights to bioengineered seed varieties, as D&PL had been concerned about protecting intellectual property rights of its seed varieties abroad. Labeled the "terminator," the gene would kill the seed of its own plant after the crop matured, thus preventing farmers from saving and planting successive generations of seeds. Critics argued that the gene made farmers dependent on large companies for seed stock and potentially polluted the seed of conventional plants. More-

over, if the wind carried pollen with the terminator gene to a nearby farm, any contaminated seeds would not germinate. The American Corn Growers Association met with Department of Agriculture Secretary Dan Glickman to encourage him to abandon the technology.

Monsanto's disavowal of the terminator technology did not interfere with an agreement to merge with D&PL, announced in May 1998. Monsanto eventually dissolved the agreement, however, and withdrew its filing for approval from the Department of Justice (DOJ) in December 1999. Delays, caused by a DOJ antitrust investigation into whether Monsanto would unfairly dominate the bioengineered cotton seed market, prompted Monsanto to terminate the merger agreement late in 1999. Having bailed out of the agreement, Monsanto ended up having to pay D&PL an $81 million termination fee, according to their original contract, and dissatisfied D&PL shareholders sought to bring a suit for punitive damages. Despite these legal entanglements and the failed merger with Monsanto, D&PL remained a highly competitive force in its industry. While some analysts speculated that the company remained ripe for acquisition, company representatives maintained that D&PL was well positioned to remain an independent company.

Principal Subsidiaries

Arizona Processing Inc.; Greenfield Seed Co.; D&M International LLC (50%); D&M Partners (50%); D&PL Argentina, Inc.; D&PL China PTE, Inc.(40%); D&PL Mexico, Inc.; Deltapine Paraguay, Inc. (40%); D&PL South Africa, Inc.; D&PL International Technology Corp.; Delta Pine De Mexico, S.A.; DeltaPine Australia PTY, Limited; Hebei Ji Dai Cotton Seed Technology Company, Inc.(China; 40%); Paymaster Technology Corp.; Delta and Pine Land International, Ltd.; Turk DeltaPine, Inc.

Principal Competitors

Dow Chemical Company; Pioneer Hi-Bred International, Inc.; DeKalb Genetics Corporation.

Further Reading

Blake, Ed, "Delta Seed Plantation Has Colorful History," *Pontotoc Progress*, May 8, 1986, p. 8.

Brandfon, Robert L., *Cotton Kingdom of the New South: A History of the Yazoo Mississippi Delta from Reconstruction to the Twentieth Century*, Cambridge, Mass.: Harvard University Press, 1967.

Byrne, Harlan S., "Seeds of Success," *Barron's*, September 12, 1994, p. 24.

Cantrell, Wanda, "Delta and Pine Land Getting into Corn Seeds," *Clarion/Jackson Daily News*, January 19, 1986, p. H5.

Cohen, Judith Radler, "Monsanto Maintains Delta is on Track," *Mergers and Acquisitions Report*, July 19, 1999.

Connor, Charles, "Cotton Seed Company Stock Soars on Patent News," *Commercial Appeal*, March 12, 1999.

——, "Mississippi Timber and Land Firm to Consolidate Operations, Cut Jobs," *Commercial Appeal*, October 16, 1997.

"Delta & Pine Land Begins NYSE Trading After Stock Split," *PR Newswire*, December 18, 1995.

"Delta & Pine Land Company Files Lawsuit Against Monsanto," *PR Newswire*, January 18, 2000, p. 3,651.

"Delta & Pine Land Tackles Performance Issues," *Agri Marketing*, February 1998, p. 62.

"The Delta Blues?," *Agri Marketing*, November 1996, p. 22.

Dixon, Mary, "Seeds Spell Success for Delta Pine," *Clarion/Jackson Daily News*, October 20, 1985, p. I3.

Galarza, Pablo, "Delta & Pine Land Co. Scott, Miss. Cotton-Picking Problems Benefit Seed Producer," *Investor's Business Daily*, May 26, 1994, p. 1.

Hansen, Bruce, "Delta Pine Joins Fortune-Seekers in China," *Memphis Business Journal*, January 17, 1994, p. 1.

"Monsanto Pays Out $81 Million Break-Up Fee," *Marketletter*, January 3, 2000.

Myerson, Allen, R., "Breeding Seeds of Discontent; Cotton Growers Say Strain Cuts Yields," *New York Times*, November 19, 1997, p. 1D.

Myerson, Allen, R. "Monsanto Paying Delta Farmers to Settle Genetic Seed Complaints," *New York Times*, February 24, 1998, p. 9D.

Sewell, Tim, "Delta and Pine Land to Foster New Growth through Reorganization into Divisions," *Memphis Business Journal*, April 7, 1997, p. 8.

Stannard, Fred Jr., "Cotton Campaign: Growers, Government Push Drive to Regain Sales, Eliminate Glut," *Wall Street Journal*, April 1, 1957, p. 1.

"State Firm Gets Million," *Jackson Daily News*, February 24, 1959.

Steyer, Robert, "Cotton Firm Eying China; Monsanto a Part of One Venture," *St. Louis Post-Dispatch*, June 2, 1996, p. 1E.

Steyer, Robert, "Monsanto Makes Bid to Buy World's Largest Cotton-Seed Company," *St. Louis Post-Dispatch*, October 8, 1999.

——, "Monsanto Rumor Could Endanger Delta & Pine Deal; Merger Speculation Causes Cotton Seed Company's Stock to Fall," *St. Louis Post-Dispatch*, November 11, 1999, p. C1.

——, "Monsanto Sells Cotton Seed Unit to Mississippi's Delta and Pine Land Co," *St. Louis Post-Dispatch*, February 6, 1996.

Tansey, Geoff, "Bitter Battle of Terminator Seeds," *Financial Times*, June 17, 1999, p. 28.

Williams, Wirt A., ed., *History of Bolivar County, Mississippi*, Jackson, Miss.: Hederman Brothers, 1948.

—Mary Tradii

Eateries, Inc.

3240 West Britton Road, Suite 202
Oklahoma City, Oklahoma
U.S.A.
Telephone: (405) 755-3607
Fax: (405) 751-7348

Public Company
Incorporated: 1984
Employees: 3,361
Sales: $94.6 million (1999)
Stock Exchanges: NASDAQ
Ticker Symbol: EATS
NAIC: 72211 Full-Service Restaurants

Eateries, Inc. operates full-service restaurant chains in 26 states, relying primarily on the business generated by its two mainstay concepts, the 48-unit Garfield's Restaurant & Pub and the 13-unit Garcia's Mexican Restaurants. The defining characteristic of the company is found in its original restaurant concept, Garfield's Restaurant, the success of which is attributed to its location in small-town shopping malls, a market mostly ignored by Eateries' competitors. In addition to the Garcia's chain, acquired in 1997, Eateries operates two Pepperoni Grill restaurants and an urban version of its Garfield's Restaurant concept, a nine-unit chain that operates under the Garfield's Café banner.

Background of the Founder

The architect behind Eateries' creation was a Connecticut native who found a wealth of opportunity in Oklahoma. Throughout his life, Vincent F. Orza, Jr., demonstrated an irrepressible desire to do what others claimed he was incapable of achieving. As a teenager, his high school guidance counselor informed him that he lacked the qualities required of a prospective college student. Orza ignored the advice and won a scholarship to Oklahoma City University, graduating in two and one-half years. Having already proved his guidance counselor wrong, Orza cast further doubt as to the counselor's professional capabilities with his subsequent achievements. He took a job teaching school while he pursued his master's degree, which he earned in nine months. By the time he was 21 years old, Orza

had two degrees and a year of teaching experience to his credit, clearly thriving in the role of an academic. He decided to pursue a doctorate degree and enrolled at the University of Oklahoma, where he earned his Ph.D. in education by the time he was 25. From there, Orza's interests wandered, leading to an array of occupations before he decided to found Eateries.

During the early 1970s, Orza's adopted state of Oklahoma was beset by a pernicious economic crisis. While watching the news, Orza found exception in a local television station's coverage of the oil embargo that stripped the economic vitality of Oklahoma and neighboring states. He wrote a letter expressing his views, which ultimately steered him in a new professional direction. He was hired as a news anchor and a reporter, performing his duties during the night. During the day, he taught at the School of Business at Central State University. Between his two jobs, the indefatigable Orza found time for a third occupation. He worked as a consultant in marketing and economics, which introduced him to the restaurant business and supplied the kernel of inspiration for the creation of Eateries and its flagship chain, Garfield's Restaurant.

Orza's first connection with the restaurant business came through one of his consulting clients, Kelly-Johnston Enterprises, which operated franchised units of the Chi-Chi's restaurant chain. Orza was intrigued by the possibilities of a casual-theme restaurant concept, but the timing of his interest could not have been worse. While Orza was entertaining the thought of starting his own restaurant, Oklahoma was deep in an economic trough, caused by what was referred to as the "Oil Bust." Orza again received advice he ignored and resolved to open his first Garfield's Restaurant. Orza later reflected on his decision to abandon his numerous careers and to devote all his energies toward Eateries in a March 19, 1990 interview with *Nation's Restaurant News.* "I basically did it to prove people wrong," he explained, adding "People kept telling me I couldn't do it. But it was worth the opportunity and the risk. I built the company in spite of the recession."

First Garfield's Restaurant Opens in 1984

Orza opened the first Garfield's Restaurant in November 1984 in Oklahoma City. The restaurant was named after a

Key Dates:

1984: Vincent F. Orza, Jr., opens the first Garfield's Restaurant in Oklahoma City.
1986: Orza's restaurant holding company, Eateries, Inc., completes its initial public offering of stock.
1994: A secondary offering of stock provides Eateries with the resources to pursue expansion.
1995: Eateries acquires Pepperoni Grill.
1997: Famous Restaurants sells 17 restaurants to Eateries.
1998: Eateries focuses on Garfield's Restaurants and Garcia's as its major expansion vehicles.
1999: Eateries acquires Bellini's Ristorante & Grill and Tommy's Italian-American Grill.

fictional character created by the company named Casey Garfield, a 19th century explorer who traveled the world, sampling its cuisine. Supposedly, the restaurant was meant to pay tribute to Garfield's travels, both with its menu and its décor. Offering Chinese, Tex-Mex, Italian, and American cuisine, the restaurant featured equally eclectic trappings, centered around a turn-of-the-century theme and filled with international bric-a-brac. As the concept developed into a chain, Garfield's Restaurant became best known for the cups of crayons on each table, which customers were encouraged to use to doodle on the white, newsprint tablecloths.

Orza survived the recessive economic conditions and secured an appreciable presence in Oklahoma. Two years after its inception, Eateries operated six Garfield's Restaurants and another, more upscale concept called The Steak Joint. To further expand his chain of stores, which were located in Oklahoma City, Norman, Edmond, and Stillwater, Orza turned to the stock market for expansion capital, completing Eateries' initial public offering of stock in 1986. By the end of the decade, as the chain approached two dozen units, Orza's success with Garfield's Restaurants had earned his company national recognition. In 1989, *Inc.* magazine ranked the Eateries chain as the 19th fastest growing small public company in the United States, vindicating Orza's decision to start the company in an uncertain economic environment.

Recessive economic conditions again greeted Eateries as it entered the 1990s. The company shrugged off the affects of the nationwide economic downturn, however, and expanded beyond Oklahoma's borders into Texas, Kansas, and Missouri. Much of the company's ability to succeed was credited to Orza's policy of site selection for the Garfield's Restaurant chain. He chose secondary markets, preferring to establish units in high-traffic shopping malls in small towns, picking sites most of his larger competitors ignored. The strategy delivered steadily increasing sales and profits, as well as consistently rising business volumes for individual units. The company's market focus drew praise from industry pundits, typified in one restaurant stock analyst's assessment of Eateries in the May 10, 1993 issue of *Nation's Restaurant News.* "Not only are they growing with well-run units," the analyst noted, "but they are growing in areas with little competition. Many of their units are near high-traffic generators like cineplexes and other entertainment centers in the mall. These secondary markets, in a shopping mall, are the kinds of places the big players don't pay any attention to."

Once the early 1990s recession ended, Orza was ready to renew his expansion efforts. The company signaled its readiness to push ahead aggressively by turning to Wall Street again, completing a secondary offering in February 1994 that raised $7 million. At the time of the stock offering, the Garfield's Restaurant chain comprised 34 units, but with a fresh infusion of cash the total was expected to grow at a pace decidedly faster than in previous years. The company planned to establish ten new Garfield's Restaurant units in 1994 and another 15 restaurants in 1995.

Acquisitions Dominate the Late 1990s

As Eateries entered the mid-1990s, a new expansion strategy began to take shape. Since its inception, the company had achieved its growth through internal means, first by creating its own dinner-house concept and then by establishing its own stores. Beginning in 1994, however, the company showed its first signs of turning to external means to expand its scope of operations. Although Orza continued to add units to the Garfield's Restaurant chain from the mid-1990s forward, he accelerated the company's internal growth by expanding through acquisitions. Toward this end, Orza moved slowly at first, but by the late 1990s he had thoroughly been won over by the appeal of expanding by purchasing established restaurant chains.

Approximately 40 Garfield's Restaurants were in operation in 18 states when, in November 1994, the company announced it had agreed to acquire a 150-seat Italian restaurant named Pepperoni Grill from Val Gene Associates Restaurant Group. Located in Oklahoma City, the restaurant's menu featured a variety of Italian entrees and brick-oven baked pizzas in particular. The transaction closed in January 1995. At the time of the announcement, Orza remarked that the Pepperoni Grill and Garfield's Restaurant concepts were being considered for tandem mall sites, but the Pepperoni Grill concept was never treated as an expansion vehicle. One more restaurant was established, but after that the company announced it was no longer considering adding any more units.

The purchase of Pepperoni Grill was not an acquisition to excite Orza's passion for purchasing established restaurant companies, but Eateries' next acquisition spurred Orza to scour the country for suitable acquisition candidates. In August 1997, Eateries agreed to acquire 17 restaurants from Phoenix-based Famous Restaurants Inc. The transaction, which was completed in November 1997, significantly increased Eateries' revenue volume, adding the $32 million in sales the 17 restaurants collected in 1996 to Eateries' 1996 sales of $56 million. Included with the deal were 11 Garcia's Mexican Restaurants, five Casa Lupita Mexican Restaurants, and one Carlos Murphy's Restaurant, all of which were combined in a wholly owned subsidiary named Fiesta Restaurants Inc. To the 53 Garfield's Restaurants and two Pepperoni Grills situated across the Sunbelt and the North Central states, the company's geographic presence was augmented by five restaurants in Phoenix, two in northern California, two in Colorado, and eight units scattered among Florida, Idaho, Illinois, New Jersey, Oho, and Utah. The estimated price of the acquisition was $10.8 million.

In Orza's mind, the advantages Eateries gained from the Famous Restaurants acquisition provided a compelling argument for further acquisitions. He perceived the purchase of the 17 restaurants as "a safer bet than building from scratch," according to his interview with *Nation's Restaurant News* on December 15, 1997. His next statement suggested an acquisition campaign was in the making at company headquarters. "We think there are a lot of good small- to medium-sized companies, just like Famous," Orza said, "and they can be bought for less money than they can be built." Orza noted that the company was searching for 15- to 40-unit restaurant companies to acquire, declaring, "We're on the prowl."

Acquisitions provided an expedient, cost-efficient way for Eateries to fatten its portfolio of restaurant properties, but the company did not forsake internal measures as a way to promote growth. While eyes were drawn to the signal Famous Restaurants acquisition, Eateries begin experimenting with its mainstay Garfield's Restaurant concept, searching for alternative methods to increase revenues. In 1997, the company unveiled Garfield's Café, an urban version of the company's predominantly small-town, rurally based chain. Initially, the company tested the concept in six major urban markets, offering a menu that was smaller and less expensive than the selection provided at traditional Garfield's Restaurant units. Early performance results were encouraging, prompting the company to establish two additional Garfield's Cafés and to convert a traditional Garfield's Restaurant to the Café format in 1998. By the end of 1998, there were nine Café locations in operation. There were no plans to establish additional Café units in 1999.

In the wake of the Famous Restaurants acquisition, Orza showed a preference for the Garcia's format over the other units operated by the Fiesta Restaurants subsidiary. As part of Eateries' plan to concentrate expansion on the Garcia's chain, divestitures occupied the company's attention during the late 1990s. In February 1998, Eateries sold three of the Casa Lupita restaurants to Chevy's, Inc., which led to a second agreement, concluded in May 1998, that passed ownership of a fourth Casa Lupita unit to Chevy's. As these separate transactions were taking place, Eateries closed the remaining Casa Lupita unit under its control and converted its lone Carlos Murphy's unit into a Garcia's, leaving the company sharply focused on its two major restaurant chains, Garfield's Restaurant and Garcia's.

As Eateries entered the 21st century, its activity during the late 1990s served as a model for the expansion expected to occur in the decade ahead. In 1998, the company built and opened two new Garfield's Restaurant units in regional malls, staying true to the market focus that underpinned the chain's success throughout its history. The company also purchased three Garfield's Restaurant units in July 1998 that it had franchised previously, a move signaling that in the future the company would focus its expansion efforts on company-owned restaurants rather than franchised restaurants. A concession stand version of Garcia's also opened in 1998, debuting at BankOne Ball Park in Phoenix. In 1999, the company planned to open six Garfield's Restaurant outlets and Garcia's restaurants, as it pushed forward with expansion through internal means. The company also made progress on the acquisition front, signing agreements to purchase Bellini's Ristorante & Grill and Tommy's Italian-American Grill in May 1999. As Eateries exited the 1990s, its growth was expected to come from the continued expansion of its two primary chains and via acquisitions, an avenue of growth Orza planned to explore more fully in the future.

Principal Subsidiaries

Fiesta Restaurants Inc.; Roma Foods Inc.

Principal Competitors

Darden Restaurants, Inc.; Metromedia Company; Brinker International, Inc.

Further Reading

"Eateries' Financial Health Weathers Bad Food Impact," *Nation's Restaurant News,* January 4, 1999, p. 12.

"Eateries Inc. Buys Pepperoni Grill," *Nation's Restaurant News,* November 21, 1994, p. 2.

"Eateries To Buy 17 Units from Famous Restaurants Inc.," *Nation's Restaurant News,* August 25, 1997, p. 2.

"Garfield's Operator Eateries Inc. Raises $7M in Secondary Offering," *Nation's Restaurant News,* February 14, 1994, p. 16.

Papiernik, Richard L., "Eateries Reports Net Loss of $89,000 in First Half of '99," *Nation's Restaurant News,* September 20, 1999, p. 14.

Prewitt, Milford, "Garfield's Operator Eyes Growth in Small-Town Malls," *Nation's Restaurant News,* May 10, 1993, p. 14.

Romeo, Peter, "Garfield's Plans a New Holiday; Eateries Inc. Agrees To Install Five Restaurants in Hotel Chain," *Nation's Restaurant News,* November 24, 1986, p. 3.

Ruggless, Ron, "Mexican Acquisitions Heat Up Eateries' Growth Plans," *Nation's Restaurant News,* December 15, 1997, p. 6.

Woodard, Tracey Taylor, "Eateries' Orza Makes Run at Okla. Governor's Seat," *Nation's Restaurant News,* March 19, 1990, p. 3.

—Jeffrey L. Covell

Encompass Services Corporation

8 Greenway Plaza, Suite 1500
Houston, Texas 77046
U.S.A.
Telephone: (713) 860-0100
Toll Free: (888) 626-4984
Fax: (713) 626-4766
Web site: http://www.groupmac.com

Public Company
Incorporated: 1996
Employees: 30,000
Sales: $3.6 billion (2000)
Stock Exchanges: New York
Ticker Symbol: ESR
NAIC: 23531 Electrical Contractors; 23511 Plumbing,
   Heating, and Air-Conditioning Contractors; 333412
   Industrial and Commercial Fan and Blower
   Manufacturing

Encompass Services Corporation, known as Group Maintenance America Corp. (GroupMAC) until its February 2000
merger with Building One Services Corporation, is the leading
provider of mechanical, electrical, janitorial, and related services
to residential, commercial, and industrial markets in the United
States. Group Maintenance's formation in late 1996 marked the
beginning of an ambitious acquisition campaign, as it sought to
create a national network of plumbing, electrical, heating, ventilation, and air-conditioning service providers from a highly fragmented industry. In November 1999, the company announced a
merger agreement with Building One Services Corporation, a
Minneapolis-based consolidator in the facilities services industry
which had been formed in 1997. Combined pro forma revenues
for the newly named Encompass, which after the merger boasted
250 locations nationwide, were $3.6 billion.

GroupMAC's Origins

At its formation, GroupMAC latched onto a trend that was
beginning to sweep through the electrical and mechanical services industry, a burgeoning movement that drew its protago-
nists and, arguably, its inspiration from the waste management
industry. During the 1980s and early 1990s, the waste management industry was undergoing rapid consolidation, as larger
companies swallowed up smaller companies in an effort to
realize the benefits of economies of scale. Among the consolidators was Browning-Ferris Industries Inc. (BFI). Three BFI
executives who assisted in orchestrating the acquisition campaign later left the company, forming Houston-based American
Residential Services to do the same thing to the electrical and
mechanical industry. American Residential embarked on an
acquisition campaign, purchasing nine companies and completing an initial public offering (IPO) of stock in September 1996
that raised $50 million, which gave the company financial
resources to feed its acquisitive appetite. American Residential
soon had a crosstown rival.

GroupMAC was quick to join the fray following American
Residential's IPO, formally organizing a month later. Also
headquartered in Houston, GroupMAC gained its chief architect from the waste management industry as well, a veteran
businessman named Richard K. Reiling. In 1989, Reiling and
two Houston businessmen formed an investment banking firm
named First Financial Alliance Group, which was used to create
Republic Waste Industries Inc. Like his counterparts at BFI,
Reiling formed Republic Waste to consolidate smaller landfill
operators under one corporate banner, which he accomplished
in a frenetic rush. During the company's first 18 months of
operation, Reiling acquired 13 companies, lifting revenues from
nothing to more than $100 million. Not long after Republic
Waste's initial surge, Reiling found his opportunities for growth
diminishing, primarily because BFI had already consolidated
much of the industry, particularly the larger landfill operators.
Reiling sold Republic Waste in 1995 and began exploring the
possibilities of consolidating the plumbing industry. His research eventually led him in the same direction the former BFI
executives had followed, prompting him to form GroupMAC.

In a December 6, 1996 interview with the *Houston Business
Journal,* Reiling explained how his initial interest in the plumbing industry evolved into the more expansive strategy adopted
by GroupMAC. "A good percentage of those companies

Company Perspectives:

There's a new powerhouse in the facilities services industry–Encompass Services Corporation. Encompass Services Corporation ranks as the largest provider of facilities systems and solutions in the United States.

[plumbing contractors] are in the heating and electrical business as well,'' he said, ''so we began to broaden the types of companies we were interested in.'' Reiling, along with a group of Houston-based entrepreneurs, created GroupMAC to acquire heating, ventilation, and air-conditioning (HVAC), electrical, and plumbing companies that served residential and commercial markets, endeavoring to create a nationwide network of companies operating under one corporate umbrella. Some consolidation strategies hinged on acquiring financially ill companies, which could then be purchased for a reduced price, but Reiling focused exclusively on financially sound companies, only considering candidates with strong management, respectable profits, and a minimum of $3 million in annual revenues. Further, with each acquisition, Reiling insisted on the acquired company retaining its name and its current management. If a contractor decided to sell to GroupMAC as a way to cash out and exit the business, the owner was expected to sign a three- to five-year employment contract with GroupMAC to ensure there was adequate time to install successor management. Supported by a well-defined business plan, Reiling formally established GroupMAC on October 24, 1996. The staff of ten individuals began meeting with potential acquisition candidates the following week, armed with $30 million in capital earmarked for GroupMAC's first wave of acquisitions.

Of intrinsic importance to GroupMAC's business strategy was obtaining the financial resources to wage an acquisition campaign. Toward this end, Reiling triumphed by convincing a Houston businessman, Gordon A. Cain, chairman of Sterling Chemicals Inc., to become GroupMAC's lead investor and majority owner. With the capital provided by Cain, Reiling did not have to hurriedly file with the Securities and Exchange Commission (SEC) for GroupMAC's IPO; instead, Reiling planned to keep GroupMAC private initially so he could pique investor interest. His target date for the company's IPO was during the second half of 1997, by which time he hoped to build GroupMAC's revenues to at least $100 million. As the executor of his plan, Reiling selected J. Patrick Millinor, Jr., as Group-MAC's president and chief executive officer. Millinor had worked directly for Cain, helping him start two biotechnology companies.

Reiling expressed no concern about running into the same problem with GroupMAC as he had with Republic Waste. Despite the nearby, burgeoning strength of American Residential, whose ex-BFI executives threatened to steal the thunder of GroupMAC's acquisition program, Reiling did not fear a dearth of acquisition candidates. He estimated there were more than 180,000 companies that met GroupMAC's acquisition criteria, representing a national market of some $64 billion in annual revenues. There was ample room for both American Residential and GroupMAC, Reiling believed, but the bounty of companies

available in the highly fragmented electrical and mechanical services industry did not lull him into complacency. Group-MAC's management team began canvassing the country in November, searching for the independent contractors to swell the stature of the fledgling company.

1997 Airtron Purchase; Acquisition Spree

GroupMAC's first acquisition left little doubt as to the lofty goals of its management team. In late January 1997, the company announced it had agreed to purchase Dayton, Ohio-based Airtron, one of the country's largest privately owned residential and light commercial HVAC contractors. With more than $80 million in annual revenues, Airtron (which ranked as Group-MAC's largest acquisition during its formative years) boasted service offices at 14 locations in Florida, Texas, and the Midwest. The acquisition gave GroupMAC an immediate and appreciable market presence, one that promised to balloon in the subsequent months. At the time of the announcement, Group-MAC was in the midst of negotiations with between 15 and 20 other contractors whose combined revenues totaled approximately $200 million.

The Airtron acquisition was a prime example of the extent of GroupMAC's acquisitive might, but with the big came the small. Not long after the company acquired Airtron, it completed a deal whose magnitude fell at the other end of the scale. In May 1997, GroupMAC purchased Costner Brothers Air Conditioning, a Rock Hill, South Carolina, company owned by brothers Roger and Donald Costner with annual sales of $3 million. As the company's acquisition program unfolded, both the big contractors and small contractors were absorbed into the GroupMAC network, creating what the company referred to as a ''family of GroupMAC companies.''

The family adopted a new senior executive in June 1997, when Reiling relinquished his chairmanship to James P. Norris. Norris, executive vice-president of Air Conditioning Contractors of America prior to joining GroupMAC, was put in charge of developing and executing the company's long-range strategic plan, including the implementation of a plan to add more cohesion to the GroupMAC affiliate network. In the wake of the June 1997 executive changes, Reiling became vice-chairman, continuing to play an active role in acquisitions and market development, while Millinor exerted day-to-day control over the organization.

Norris fulfilled an important facet of his duties two months after his appointment as chairman. In August 1997, GroupMAC acquired two national HVAC consulting organizations whose addition to the company would be crucial to its acquisition program. Callahan Roach and United Service Alliance were acquired to help integrate contractors into the GroupMAC system, enabling the company to more easily digest the firms that were joining the fold at an average of two per month. Additionally, the two consulting firms provided internal training, advertising, marketing, and other management services to the subsidiary companies.

By the time the two consulting organizations were acquired, GroupMAC senior managers were ready to take the company public. The company had completed 11 acquisitions by the time it filed with the SEC for an IPO, having broadened its market presence to a five-state region and increased its revenues to $139 million. The company expected to gain roughly $100 million from the IPO, which would make it the seventh publicly held, HVAC company in the country. Concurrent with the IPO, GroupMAC was slated to acquire 13 companies, which would extend the company's presence into 37 cities in 21 states. The largest of the 13 companies, Seattle-based MacDonald-Miller Industries, Inc., generated $66 million in annual sales. According to the SEC filing, GroupMAC was focusing much of its growth on the maintenance, repair, and replacement business, which yielded higher profit margins than new equipment installation. The goal was to reach a revenue mix of 60 percent maintenance, repair, and replacement and 40 percent new equipment installation.

On November 6, 1997, GroupMAC made its debut in the public spotlight, issuing 7.5 million shares at $14 per share. Simultaneous with the closing of the IPO, the 13 companies were acquired, lifting annualized sales to $320 million. Counting its most recent additions, GroupMAC ranked as the second largest operating company in the electrical and mechanical services sector, having acquired 23 companies during the year. More was in store, with as many as 60 potential acquisitions waiting in the wings and $100 million set aside for acquisitions in 1998.

The pace of expansion accelerated in 1998, fueled by the proceeds from the IPO and by zeal of GroupMAC's management. The company acquired 39 electrical and mechanical contracting companies in 1998, giving it a total of 59 operating companies and pushing sales above $750 million. Significantly, the acquisitions completed in 1998 helped GroupMAC achieve its previously declared revenue mix, as the company focused its acquisitive efforts on absorbing contractors who specialized in maintenance, repair, and replacement services. At the end of 1997, such services accounted for 45 percent of GroupMAC's revenues. By the end of 1998, the portion had risen to 60 percent.

Merger Plans with Building One in 2000

GroupMAC's pace of expansion slowed somewhat in 1999, but its revenue growth did not. By September 1999, the company had completed its expansion for the year, having acquired 13 more contractors for a total of 72 operating companies that performed services in 64 cities and 28 states. Despite complet-

ing a smaller number of acquisitions than it had completed in previous years, GroupMAC realized $365 million in added revenue from the purchased companies, an increase that was consistent with its historical record of growth. The company spent approximately $160 million on acquisitions during the first nine months of 1999, which ignited a more than 100 percent increase in systemwide revenues to an impressive $1.54 billion. Standing firmly entrenched in 44 of the largest 100 markets in the country, GroupMAC next prepared for the beginning of a new era in its short corporate life. The GroupMAC name was set to disappear, its departure caused by a corporate transaction of mammoth proportions. Reiling, Norris, and Millinor were ready to take the family of GroupMAC companies to the next level.

On November 3, 1999, GroupMAC signed a definitive merger agreement with Building One Services Corporation. The merger, which would be completed by the end of February 2000, proposed combining GroupMAC's $1.5 billion in revenue with the $1.8 billion in 1999 revenue generated by Building One, which provided many of the products and services required for the routine operation and maintenance of buildings. From the merger of Building One, whose services included electrical, mechanical, janitorial, and maintenance functions, and GroupMAC, a new company was set to be created. Called Encompass Services Corporation, the new company loomed as a domineering force in the electrical and mechanical industry. With much of the consolidation yet to take place at the time of Encompass's formation, optimism pervaded the headquarters of both companies.

Principal Subsidiaries

A-1 Mechanical of Lansing, Inc.; A-abc Appliance & Air Conditioning; AAAdvance Air, Inc.; Air Conditioning, Plumbing & Heating Service Co., Inc.; Air Conditioning Engineers, Inc.; Air Systems, Inc.; Aircon Energy Incorporated; Airtron, Inc.; All-Service Electric, Inc.; Arkansas Mechanical Services, Inc.; Atlantic Industrial Constructors, Inc.; Barr Electric Corp.; Callahan/Roach Products & Publications, Inc.; Central Air Conditioning Contractors, Inc.; Central Carolina Air Conditioning; Charlie's Plumbing; Colonial Air Conditioning; Commercial Air, Power & Cable, Inc.; Continental Electrical Construction Co.; Clark Converse Electric Service, Inc.; Costner Brothers, Inc.; DIVCO, Inc.; Evans Services, Inc.; The Fairfield Company; Ferguson Electric Corporation; Gentzler Electrical Contractors, Inc.; Gilbert Mechanical Contractors, Inc.; HPS Plumbing Services, Inc.; Hallmark Air Conditioning, Inc.; Hungerford Mechanical Corporation; J.D. Steward Air Conditioning, Inc.; Jarrell Plumbing; K&N Plumbing, Heating & Air Conditioning, Inc.; Laney's, Inc.; Linford Service Company; MacDonald-Miller Industries, Inc.; Masters, Inc.; Mechanical Interiors, Inc.; Merritt Island Air & Heat, Inc.; New Construction Air Conditioning, Inc.; Noron, Inc.; Pacific Rim Mechanical Contractors, Inc.; Paul E. Smith Co., Inc.; Phoenix Electric Company; Ray's Plumbing; Reliable Mechanical, Inc.; Romanoff Electric Corp.; Sibley Services, Incorporated; Southeast Mechanical Service, Inc.; Statewide Heating & Cooling, Inc.; Stephen C. Pomeroy, Inc.; Sterling Air Conditioning, Inc.; Sun Plumbing, Inc.; Team Mechanical, Inc.; Trinity Contractors, Inc.; United Service Alliance; Valley Wide Plumbing & Heating, Inc.; Van's Comfortemp Air Conditioning, Inc.; Wade's Heating & Cooling, Inc.

Principal Operating Units

Mechanical; Electrical/Communications; Industrial; Residential; Janitorial and Maintenance Management; National Accounts.

Principal Competitors

American Residential Services, Inc.; Comfort Systems USA, Inc.; Lennox International Inc.

Further Reading

Antosh, Nelson, "Houston-Based Building Maintenance Company Buys Eight More Firms," *Knight-Ridder/Tribune Business News,* September 1, 1998, p. OKRB982440C3.

Beauprez, Jennifer, "Newly Formed Dynalink Swiftly Bought," *Crain's Cleveland Business,* July 5, 1999, p. 2.

"Building One Services Corporation Announces Meeting to Approve Merger," *PR Newswire,* January 14, 2000, p. 1994.

"Excellence Alliance Acquires GroupMAC's United Service Alliance," *PR Newswire,* January 10, 2000, p. 7813.

Mader, Robert P., "Airtron Acquired by GroupMAC," *Contractor,* March 1997, p. 1.

——, "GroupMAC Adds Voice and Data," *Contractor,* October 1999, p. 5.

Mahoney, Thomas A., "Aggressive Acquisitions Help GroupMAC Get Closer to $1 Billion Sales Mark," *Air Conditioning, Heating & Refrigeration News,* November 2, 1998, p. 1.

Perin, Monica, "Collection of Roll-Up Consolidators Continues Acquisition Spree," *Houston Business Journal,* December 19, 1997, p. 8.

——, "Group Maintenance Follows Fellow HVAC Roll-Ups into Public Markets," *Houston Business Journal,* September 5, 1997, p. 6A.

Pletz, John, "Equipment Installers Newest Buyout Targets," *Indianapolis Business Journal,* June 7, 1999, p. 5.

—Jeffrey L. Covell

Enrich International, Inc.

748 North 1340 West
Orem, Utah 84057
U.S.A.
Telephone: (801) 226-2600
Toll Free: (800) 748-4334
Fax: (801) 226-6232
Web site: http://www.enrich.com

Wholly Owned Subsidiary of Royal Numico N.V.
Incorporated: 1985 as Nature's Labs, Inc.
Employees: 350
Sales: $200 million (1999 est.)
NAIC: 422210 Botanicals Wholesaling; 325412
   Pharmaceutical Preparations Manufacturing

Enrich International, Inc. produces and sells a variety of herbal and nutritional supplements, weight management items, and personal care products for healthy hair and skin. It is one of the increasing number of firms that sell such natural products to consumers interested in maintaining a healthy lifestyle and preventing illness. About 150,000 independent distributors use multilevel or network marketing to sell Enrich products in North America, Europe, Asia, and the Pacific islands. Enrich is one of the numerous supplement firms based in Utah, often considered the leading state in the supplement industry. With top managers drawn from rival firms and as a subsidiary of Royal Numico, a large Netherlands company, Enrich International seems well prepared for the future, even though some competitors are much larger.

Origins

In 1972 Eugene Hughes consumed powdered cayenne pepper (*Capsicum*) for his ulcer, but he was frustrated when he could not find capsules of that herb to avoid its strong taste. So the Hughes family, including Eugene's wife Kristine Hughes, five of Eugene's six brothers, and his brother-in-law Ken Brailsford, started a small herbal company to encapsulate herbs. Thus was born a company that became known later as Nature's Sunshine Products, a public corporation with its stock traded on the NASDAQ market.

Ken Brailsford was born in Niagara Falls, New York, grew up in Utah, earned an undergraduate degree from Brigham Young University in 1969, and served two years in the military before helping start Nature's Sunshine. He served as its president until 1979 and ran *Herbalist Magazine* until he sold it in 1981.

Those experiences prepared Brailsford to later found Enrich International. For a few years in the early 1980s Brailsford worked as a stockbroker, but then he decided to reenter the herbal industry after his noncompeting agreement with Nature's Sunshine had expired. On December 27, 1985 Kenneth E. Brailsford, his wife Linda Brailsford, and David T. Lisonbee incorporated Nature's Labs, Inc. under the laws of Utah and became its founding directors. The firm's original address was 1030 West 500 North, Lindon, Utah. On March 12, 1987 the name was changed to The Enrich Corporation, according to records at the Utah Division of Corporations.

To support Enrich, Nature's Sunshine Products, and other herbal corporations in Utah County, the R.P. Scherer Company in the 1980s began a plant in the Springville Industrial Park to produce gelatin capsules. Scherer's general manager claimed in the *Daily Herald* of Provo, Utah that his firm had "the world's largest plant that only produces capsules" and that it ran "365 days per year and 24 hours per day" to make some two billion capsules annually.

Growth in the 1990s

By November 1992 The Enrich Corporation was shipping between five and ten million capsules every month. Soon the firm moved to a much larger facility in Orem, Utah, formerly occupied by an educational software company called Wicat.

One popular Enrich product in the early 1990s was PerForm capsules. In 1992 the company sold $100,000 worth of PerForm, and in 1993 it planned to sell about twice that amount. Although PerForm was made with several herbs said to increase sexual drive, such as sarsaparilla root, Brazilian ginseng, and saw palmetto, Enrich marketed it as a nutritional supplement, not a love pill.

Company Perspectives:

The mission of Enrich International is to enhance the physical, mental, social, and financial well-being of our distributors, employees, families, and communities throughout the world. Enrich will continue to build on its foundation of vision, innovation, and integrity in order to offer an unparalleled opportunity for the entire Enrich family.

On May 27, 1994 Enrich International, Inc. was incorporated in Utah, with Kenneth E. Brailsford as its president. G. Paulo Bangerter served as the company's vice-president and general counsel. Effective May 31, 1994, The Enrich Corporation became a wholly owned subsidiary of Enrich International.

The following month, on June 30, 1994, a corporate reorganization resulted in four other companies becoming wholly owned Enrich International subsidiaries. The four were 1) Pharmatech Laboratories, Inc., a Utah corporation and manufacturing facility owned by Ken and Linda Brailsford, 2) Enrich International Industries, Ltd., a Canadian federal corporation, 3) Nature's Labs S.A. de C.V., a Mexican corporation, and 4) Enrich International S.A. de C.V., another Mexican corporation.

The vitamin and nutritional supplement industry received a major boost in 1994 when Congress passed the Dietary Supplement Health Education Act (DSHEA). Utah Senator Orrin Hatch sponsored that act in part because of Utah's leadership in the supplement industry. In addition to Enrich International, the following firms were headquartered in or had major facilities in Utah: Nu Skin Enterprises, Weider Nutrition International, Nature's Sunshine Products, Murdock Madaus Schwabe, E'ola, Solar Ray, New Ways, Cornerstone Nutritional Labs, Twinlab Corporation, Shaperite Concepts, T.J. Clark and Company, Morinda Inc., and Nutraceutical Corporation. The Utah Natural Products Alliance represented some of those firms when it lobbied for passage of the DSHEA.

That law helped improve the public image of the supplement business. "I think the industry is halfway out of quackery," said Luke Bucci, a biochemist and Weider Nutrition vice-president, in the October 12, 1997 *Deseret News*. "Many companies are conducting serious research now; many are hiring credible scientists who have doctorate degrees from major universities. And the industry is using pharmaceutical companies as models for how they conduct research and present that information to the public ... The public's attitude has changed since 1994. Instead of automatically assuming something is bogus, people are asking questions and asking if there are any studies to back up the claims. It is a much more positive environment than in the past when the industry was treated as a cult or simply ignored."

Four scientists led Enrich International's research and development in the late 1990s. Calvin W. McCausland, Ph.D., the firm's chief scientific officer, helped create more than 350 nutritional products and was "the first American to receive membership in the Russian Federation Academy of Medical Technical Science," according to a 1999 Enrich pamphlet. He also founded Trysan Research, which was acquired by Enrich in 1994. The three other scientists were Craig Stutz, Ph.D.;

Lincoln F. Berrio, Ph.D.; and Emma A. Oganova-Wilkinson, Ph.D., M.D.

By the late 1990s Enrich offered six categories of nutritional and personal care products. First, it sold more than 60 traditional herbal products, including single herbs, such as alfalfa, St. John's Wort, black walnut, and Norwegian kelp, and also various combined formulations like Enrich Packs for joint relief, female renewal, and cold and flu. Second, its Cleanse, Burn, Build line of weight management products featured such items as Enrich LifAloe, a drink with five forms of aloe; LiFiber supplements based on psyllium; and Bee Pollen capsules, Digestive Enzymes, and EnJuvenate supplements designed to help the body maintain an adequate level of human growth hormone. Enrich's Targeted Nutritionals included CardioHealth, Glucosamine AJF, and Enrich Ginkgo Complex. The company's Acorn Collection of four products, such as LifePath Chewies, was sold for children. Fifth, Enrich Home Basics included Australian Tea Tree Oil, Cold Plus, PMS Aid, and Cough-Eze, all made with natural products designed to replace over-the-counter medications made with chemicals and synthetic components. Finally, the firm's E International line of skin and hair products provided consumers with different kinds of shampoos, hair sprays, deodorants, conditioners, and cleansers.

Enrich purchased raw herbal materials from four continents, and then processed and manufactured its products in its own Pharmatech plant with six encapsulation machines. It was honored several times in the 1990s by being listed in *Inc.* magazine's annual listings of the fastest growing North American firms.

Independent Distributors and Multilevel Marketing in the 1990s

Independent distributors made Enrich successful. A good example was Seattle's Jimmy Kossert, who worked as a commercial fisherman, real estate agent, and network marketer for other firms before joining Enrich in 1991. Within three years Kossert built a sales organization of 50,000 Enrich associates and earned more than $140,000 every month.

Another Enrich distributor highlighted in the December 1996 issue of *Success*, a magazine that often wrote about multilevel marketing (MLM), was Marti Settle. In about 1990 she sold her small business and got a day job so she could work at night to build her new Enrich business. In December 1991 she began working full-time as an Enrich distributor. Within a year Settle received monthly checks for as much as $20,000. After joining Enrich, she said, "I found a new industry, a new company, and a new lease on life all at once—and I've never looked back."

In the December 1999 *Network Marketing Lifestyles,* Eric Lum of Malaysia said, "My electronics business was in such a terrible financial condition that I didn't know what to do." Then in 1997 Lum became a distributor for Enrich International. By 1999 he had paid off his debts and become prosperous from building a downline of nearly 30,000 distributors in Malaysia and opening branch offices in Japan and Taiwan.

Ken Pontius of Provo, Utah by 1995 had built a downline of more than 100,000 distributors. "When I started in network

Key Dates:

1985: Nature's Labs, Inc. is incorporated in Utah.
1987: Company name is changed to The Enrich Corporation.
1991: Company starts operations in Brunei and Malaysia.
1994: Company reorganized as Enrich International, Inc.
1995: Business begins in Russia and Kazakhstan, as well as in Trinidad.
1996: Enrich UK Holdings, Inc. is incorporated; company begins doing business in Latvia and Australia.
1997: Hunter Capital gains controlling interest in firm.
1998: Enrich Japan, Inc. is incorporated.
2000: Royal Numico N.V. completes its acquisition of Enrich International.

marketing 18 years ago, most of the distributors were working people. We didn't even try to approach professionals," said Pontius in the December 1995 *Success.* But times changed, so he recruited almost all professionals. "You don't have to babysit them. They're self-motivated," said Pontius.

Of course, relatively few distributors for Enrich or other MLM firms made as much money as the four distributors described here. Nonetheless, such success stories motivated others who were looking for alternatives to routine employment or other businesses.

Utah included numerous MLM firms such as Enrich. Bill Beadle, director of Utah's Better Business Bureau, said in the August 4, 1991 *Deseret News,* "It's either the first or second organized religion in the state." He felt that network marketers experienced almost a kind of religious conversion and then went out proselytizing their products and business opportunities.

"Network marketing is buzzing in the Beehive state [Utah] because it is a close-knit society," said writer Dennis Romboy in 1991. "Products are easily promoted by word of mouth through Utah's web of church, family and neighborhood connections."

New Managers and Owners in the Late 1990s

In the late 1990s Enrich International experienced several significant management and ownership changes. In December 1998 Enrich gained a new but very experienced leader when Richard Bizzaro became its president and chief executive officer. Bizzaro began his business career in New York City, where he worked for Kayser Roth and then teamed with his wife Wendy Gray to start and run their own clothing manufacturer, Wendy Gray Sports Editions. Then Bizarro began a 15-year stint at Weider Health & Fitness, including eight years as the president/CEO of its subsidiary Weider Nutrition International. He led a 650 percent expansion of Weider Nutrition and its transition from a private business to a public corporation.

David Mastroianni also moved from Weider Nutrition to Enrich International, where he became its executive vice-president and chief operating officer. He had worked with Rich-

ard Bizarro to build Weider Nutrition and brought several years of experience in the vitamin, herbal, sports nutrition, and weight management industries with him to Enrich.

On November 4, 1999 Enrich International announced its intent to be acquired by Royal Numico N.V., a leading developer, manufacturer, and seller of food items and nutritional supplements. Founded in 1896, Royal Numico (www.numico.com) was based in Zoetermeer, The Netherlands and sold its products in 95 nations. Earlier in 1999 Royal Numico purchased General Nutrition Companies (GNC), so it had already become a major player in the worldwide herbal and supplement industry before acquiring Enrich. After Royal Numico's acquisition was completed in early 2000, Enrich International retained its senior manager team.

"Joining the Royal Numico family of specialized nutrition companies," said Enrich International Chairman/CEO Richard Bizzaro in a press release November 4, 1999, "provides Enrich with financial strength, manufacturing capabilities, and research and development resources unmatched in the network marketing industry. We will leverage these resources to accelerate our expansion into new international markets while maximizing our growth in the United States, Canada, Japan, Malaysia, and our other established markets."

In 1999 Enrich officers announced plans to expand in 2000 into five new markets: Brazil, Venezuela, Singapore, Hong Kong, and Taiwan. Also significant were plans to expand the firm's efforts in the booming electronic commerce field. Thus on November 30, 1999 the firm announced that Richard C. Despain had joined the company as its vice-president of communications. His main responsibility was to help the corporation and its associates build their businesses using the World Wide Web. One of his tasks was to improve his firm's Web site, which in early 2000 had some inconsistent or inaccurate historical dates. A member of the Direct Selling Association's Internet Council, Despain came to Enrich from USANA, Inc., where he built and administered a 3,000-page Web site.

Many other multilevel marketing firms also enthusiastically embraced such new technology. Nu Skin in Provo, Utah spent $37 million to buy the Internet company Big Planet. Amway, the largest MLM firm, opened its Web site under the separate company name of Quixtar. Smaller MLM firms also used e-commerce, such as AllAdvantage, which in 1999 used the Internet to recruit 2.8 million individuals in just 180 days.

Writer Duncan Maxwell Anderson in 2000 described the potential of combining electronic commerce via the Internet with network marketing: "In a sense, the Internet will return us to pioneer days. Then, if you had dirt, water, and a gun, you could settle almost anywhere. In the Internet age, all you need is a phone line. The Internet will be part of the re-civilizing of America's heartland. Network marketers will grow their gardens, support their local Boy Scouts and county symphony, and swap stories at the general store . . . while building empires of residual income." That was the promise and the possibility, but exactly how well Enrich International fared in this new Information Age economy remained to be seen at the start of the new millennium.

Principal Competitors

General Nutrition Companies, Inc.; Herbalife International, Inc.; Mannatech Inc.; Amway Corporation; Nature's Sunshine Products; Nu Skin Enterprises, Inc.; Murdock Madaus Schwabe.

Further Reading

Anderson, Duncan Maxwell, "What the Internet Means to Network Marketing," *Network Marketing Lifestyles,* March 2000, pp. 56–57.

Anderson, Duncan M., and Michael Warshaw, "The New Elite," *Success,* December 1995, pp. 28–36, 38.

Boulton, Guy, "Orem Nutrition Products Company Is Being Sold," *Salt Lake Tribune,* November 5, 1999, p. E1.

Campbell, Joel, "Nature's Own," *Deseret News,* June 28, 1998, p. M1.

Forsythe, Jason, "The Internet Rules!," *Network Marketing Lifestyles,* March 2000, pp. 58–61.

Fue, Gale, "Malaysia The Wild, Wild East," *Network Marketing Lifestyles,* December 1999, p. 106.

Graham, Lamar, "Quick Hits: Love Potion in a Pill," *GC: Gentlemen's Quarterly,* February 1994, p. 110.

Hall, Norley, "County Home of 'World's Largest,' " *Daily Herald* (Provo, Utah), February 24, 1985, p. A6.

Moran, Tom, "A Business Maximized at Home," *Success,* December 1996, pp. 52–54, 56.

Poe, Richard, "Leverage for Success," *Success,* March 1995, p. 50.

——, "Wave 3," *Success,* June 1994, pp. 48–50, 52, 54.

Pusey, Roger, "Owner's Expertise Enriches Utah County Firm," *Deseret News,* November 16, 1992, p. B5.

Romboy, Dennis, "Scheme or Dream," *Deseret News,* August 4, 1991.

"Sale of Enrich Completed," *Salt Lake Tribune,* March 8, 2000, p. C5.

Spangler, Jerry, "From Quackery to Credibility," *Deseret News,* October 12, 1997, p. M1.

Walden, David M., "Utah Herbalism Since World War II," Chapter 5 in *Utah's Health Care Revolution: Pluralism and Professionalization Since World War II* (M.A. thesis), Provo, Utah: Brigham Young University, 1989, pp. 147–74.

—David M. Walden

Falcon Products, Inc.

9387 Dielman Industrial Drive
St. Louis, Missouri 63132
U.S.A.
Telephone: (314) 991-9200
Fax: (314) 991-9227
Web site: http://www.falconproducts.com

Public Company
Incorporated: 1957
Employees: 3,631
Sales: $222.5 million (1999)
Ticker Symbol: FCP
Stock Exchanges: New York
NAIC: 337127 Institutional Furniture Manufacturing;
   332332 Sheet Metal Work Manufacturing

Falcon Products, Inc., is a fast-growing international manufacturer of commercial furniture products with significant shares of the fast-food service and contract office markets. The company focuses on providing its customers with high-quality products that address a wide range of both functional and aesthetic needs. Falcon manufactures such items as conference and training tables, fast-food restaurant booths, table bases, wood and metal chairs and seats, bar stools, and many other items. The company's headquarters is located in St. Louis, Missouri, while its manufacturing facilities are spread across the states of Arkansas, California, Mississippi, and Tennessee. In addition, the company has large manufacturing operations in China, Denmark, Mexico, and the Czech Republic. Although overseas markets provide a small percentage of Falcon's annual revenues, company management is committed to increasing its volume of international sales significantly during the next ten years.

Early History

Falcon Products was founded in 1959 by Franklin A. Jacobs, a young man with an ambitious agenda. Jacobs had been schooled in the St. Louis area and worked a variety of odd jobs after graduating from college. He had always wanted to own and run his own firm, but had neither financial resources nor even an idea for establishing a business. After a number of years spent working in the retail furniture industry, however, Jacobs hit upon what he thought was a grand idea for a business. The young man decided to open a furniture sales organization with one product: table bases. Opening a sales organization didn't require the large amounts of investment capital normally needed for the construction of manufacturing plants, for example, and thus Jacobs was able to gather enough money from his own meager resources to underwrite his firm's start-up expenses. Jacobs's experience in the furniture industry had convinced him that success depended on meeting the needs of highly specialized markets. One of these niche markets was table bases for commercial use, and Jacobs's company began selling a wide variety of such items for businesses in the restaurant, hospital, and corporate sectors. Finally, Jacobs needed a name for his new company, and he settled on Falcon Products, Inc.

From the very first day the firm opened its doors for business, Jacobs realized that it was going to be a success. By focusing on a single product line of table bases, and by using his contacts already established in the retail furniture industry around the greater St. Louis metropolitan area, Falcon Products was soon receiving a small but steady stream of orders. For five years Jacobs worked tirelessly and patiently to build up his company's customer base. As the style of office furniture and restaurant decor began to change from old-fashioned, heavy, dark wood to the sleek, modern streamlined style that became phenomenally popular during the mid-1960s, Falcon Products was well positioned to take advantage of the trend. Table bases were seen as primarily functional rather than decorative, and the small product line that the company sold fit nicely into the modern, more functional, style.

By 1965 Falcon Products had grown large enough to begin considering additions to its product line. Revenue was increasing, and Jacobs confidently expected his company to expand. Adding new employees and moving to a more spacious location, Jacobs cautiously decided to enter into the design and manufacture of laminated tabletops and bases. Having been until this time a sales organization, Jacobs was very methodical in beginning to design his own products and developing the manufacturing facility to produce them on a tight schedule. Once again, however, Jacobs had enough savvy and experience in the furniture industry to recognize the need for and growing trend toward laminated tabletops and bases, and was one of the first entrepreneurs to take advantage of this market. Easy to clean, lightweight, and portable, laminated tabletops fit in well with the functional style that was at the height of its popularity.

Expansion, 1970s

The decade of the 1970s was one of the most important for the company. Always wary of expansion, Jacobs was cautious about designing and manufacturing an entirely new product, but in 1970 he gave the approval for Falcon Products to start making a line of wooden chairs, and, once again, he had correctly assessed the market demand for the products. Once he had three items in his product line, with each of them selling strongly, he began to seek further opportunities. At first he considered adding additional products by designing and manufacturing them in house; however, this was a lengthy process, and Jacobs was ready to make a major foray into the commercial furniture products industry.

After extended consultations with his board of directors, and after listening to industry experts about trends and growth areas within the industry, Jacobs and his management team laid out a detailed plan of strategic acquisitions for the entire decade. In a departure from his earlier, extremely cautious management style, Jacobs embarked on an aggressive strategy of growth through acquisitions. In 1971 Falcon Products made its first purchase, acquiring a small but well-known company called Duro-Chrome that specialized in the design and manufacture of metal stack chairs. The company had established a reputation for solid craftsmanship and the use of high-quality materials. Metal stack chairs fit in well with Jacobs's vision for his company's line of functional furniture.

Throughout the rest of the 1970s, Falcon Products continued to purchase other companies as a means of gaining market share. The acquisition of Duro-Chrome was followed by the

purchase of William Hodges & Company, a firm that manufactured wire shelving primarily for corporate offices. This acquisition, finalized in 1973, enabled Falcon Products to take advantage of the burgeoning need for office accessories, which was quickly developing into a multimillion-dollar market. Since Chicago served as the center of the commercial furniture products and accessories industry, Jacobs knew that Falcon Products would be best served by gaining some exposure in that city. As a result, the company opened a showroom in the Chicago Merchandise Mart, a prestigious location frequented by industry professionals.

In 1975 Falcon Products acquired the company's first overseas facility. Located in Juarez, Mexico, the facility produced iron castings, which were then made into table bases at Falcon's plants in the United States. One of the most important reasons for the acquisition of the facility in Juarez, besides the lower operating costs, was the availability of the raw materials in the Juarez area used in the manufacture of table bases. In 1980 the company acquired a manufacturing plant in Lewisville, Arkansas, in order to consolidate all of its wood chair manufacturing capabilities. Initially, Falcon made most of its wood chairs in house, but in time management discovered it could reduce costs by importing previously machined parts and then assembling them according to customer specifications.

During the 1980s Falcon expanded geographically as well as expanding its product line. Falcon's main manufacturing plant in Greenville, Tennessee, was relocated to a much larger space in Newport, Tennessee. After the move, the firm was able to increase its output in table bases, table tops, millwork, casegoods, and booths. The majority of the cast iron table bases made at the Juarez facility were shipped to the Newport plant and completed to customer specifications. Table tops, which sometimes were combined with table bases to make a complete product, were provided with a wood veneer or laminated surface, and painted and sealed with a durable topcoat. Casegood and millwork were produced from lumber purchased in large quantities, while booths were manufactured from the same rough lumber cut in the millroom of the Newport plant and then finished and colored according to customer specifications.

The 1990s and Beyond

While Falcon Products continued its acquisition program with the purchase of a domestic firm, Kaydee Metal Products, which manufactured metal chairs, Falcon's most significant acquisitions during the 1990s occurred overseas. One of the most important moves the company made was the purchase in 1994 of a controlling interest in Miton A.S., a firm located in the Czech Republic that produced wood chairs and wood chair parts for both domestic consumption and export. Under the leadership of Falcon Products, within two years the Miton plant was shipping nearly 50 percent of its wood chair parts to the Lewisville facility for assembly and distribution. Finished chairs and chair components were soon shipped to an ever-increasing customer base in Europe and on the Pacific Rim.

In addition to purchasing U.S.-based firms such as Charlotte Company and Decor Products, the company continued to expand overseas by opening a manufacturing facility in Shenzhen, in the People's Republic of China. Manufacturing table tops and millwork, the new plant was soon selling its product line to customers throughout the Pacific Rim. At approximately the same time, Falcon Products opened a new facility in Middelfart, Denmark, to assemble and market table tops and chairs specifically for the conferencing, training, and executive dining market in Europe. All of these acquisitions and facility expansions achieved a vertically integrated manufacturing process, which enabled Falcon Products to compete more readily and gain market share in an extremely competitive industry that was growing more intense with each passing year.

In 1998 Falcon Products made an acquisition with major implications for its future success. The company spent $18 million to acquire Johnson and Howe Furniture Corporation, one of the largest and best-known firms in the industry. Located in Trumbull, Connecticut, and selling its product line throughout the United States and Europe, Johnson and Howe specialized in manufacturing a wide variety of tables—including meeting, dining, training, conference, seminar, and banquet tables—for the hospitality, contract office, and institutional markets. Johnson and Howe, which had been in existence for more than 70 years, brought a new prestige to Falcon Products. Johnson and Howe had developed the folding table early in its history, and had recently introduced the 40/4 chair, which was purchased and used for major state occasions at St. Paul's Cathedral in London, England. In one swoop, Falcon Products increased its volume and reduced its operating costs. The result of the acquisitions and expansion strategy was impressive by any measure. From 1990 to 1998, revenues increased from $31 million to $143 million. Having acquired Johnson and Howe, consolidated and its domestic chair production facilities, restructured its sales and marketing operations, and vertically integrated its manufacturing, management believed that Falcon Products was moving forward with an enhanced position in a highly competitive marketplace.

Principal Subsidiaries

Shelby Williams Industries, Inc.; Johnson Tables St. Louis; Howe Furniture Corporation; Falcon Beky (Slovakian Republic); Falcon de Juarez S.A. de C.V. (Mexico).

Principal Divisions

Falcon Western Region; Falcon Midwest Region; Falcon Eastern Region; Falcon International; Falcon Government; KD/context; Decor Concepts.

Principal Competitors

Mity-Lite, Inc.; Virco Manufacturing Company.

Further Reading

"Advisors Hired to Examine Possible Sale of Company," *Wall Street Journal,* December 3, 1996, p. B4(E).

"Definitive Pact to Acquire Shelby Williams Is Struck," *Wall Street Journal,* May 7, 1999, p. A17(E).

"Falcon Building Stock Surges on Talk of Sale," *New York Times,* December 3, 1996, p. D4(L).

"Falcon Products Says It Will Acquire Shelby-Williams," *New York Times,* May 7, 1999, p. C4.

"Falcon to Acquire Shelby Williams," *Weekly Newspaper for the Home Furnishings Network,* May 17, 1999, p. 22.

"Leggett & Platt to Purchase Assets of Unit for $17 Million," *Wall Street Journal,* August 21, 1997, p. B2(E).

Shepley, Carol, "Falcon Products, Inc.," *St. Louis Business Journal,* September 22, 1997, p. 37A(11).

Vespereny, Cynthia, "Falcon Refocuses, Sinks Its Claws into Europe," *St. Louis Business Journal,* March 23, 1998, p.3A(1).

—Thomas Derdak

Firstar Corporation

777 East Wisconsin Avenue
Milwaukee, Wisconsin 53202
U.S.A.
Telephone: (414) 765-4321
Fax: (414) 287-3290
Web site: http://www.firstar.com

Public Company
Incorporated: 1853 as Farmers and Millers Bank
Employees: 12,700
Total Assets: $73 billion (1999)
Stock Exchanges: New York
Ticker Symbol: FSR
NAIC: 551111 Offices of Bank Holding Companies;
    52211 Commercial Banking; 52221 Credit Card
    Issuing

Firstar Corporation is among the leading bank corporations in the United States, with a particularly dominant market share in the Midwest. It oversees over 1,200 branch banks and in addition to its traditional consumer and business banking services offers a variety of financial services including trust and investment management, retail brokerage, and title and business insurance. Acquisitions and mergers with other banks, often resulting in name changes, have dominated much of Firstar's history. Founded in 1853 as a small, store-front operation called Farmers and Millers Bank, by 1919, it was known as First Wisconsin National Bank of Milwaukee, and in 1929 was placed administratively under the bank holding company Wisconsin Bankshares Corporation, which itself would be renamed First Wisconsin Bankshares Corporation in 1960, First Wisconsin Corporation in 1974, and Firstar Corporation in 1989. Aided by relaxed government regulations on interstate banking, Firstar had by 1994 become a regional power in the Midwest, boasting some 200 offices in Wisconsin, Illinois, Minnesota, and Iowa with a small number of offices in Arizona and Florida. In 1998 Firstar merged with the holding company Star Banc Corporation to create a new Firstar, a much larger concern with a stronger presence throughout the Midwest.

The First Half Century: 1853–1900

When Wisconsin achieved statehood in 1848, most of its settlers lived in the state's southwestern corner, where large deposits of lead had been discovered. In the southeast, however, settlers had formed a small village on Lake Michigan at the site of an Indian trading post. Called Milwaukee, the village experienced rapid population growth, expanding from fewer than a dozen settlers in the early 1830s to some 25,000 in 1853. New manufacturing concerns, including those for machinery, shoes, and beer, sprung up, and soon the city became a center for farm products, in particular wheat and hogs. A city bulletin during this time, however, pointed out that "our moneyed facilities are by no means commensurate with our needs."

During this period of great expansion and high hopes, Farmers and Millers Bank, the predecessor of Firstar, was organized. Founded by six stockholders and six bondsmen— led by Newcomb Cleveland, a Milwaukee businessman—the bank opened its doors for business on June 2, 1853. With total capital of $50,000, the bank initially operated out of a rented storefront located on East Water Street that was equipped with a newly installed "strong box." Four years later, the bank moved around the corner to a new location on Wisconsin Avenue.

With Cleveland as its first president, Farmers and Millers Bank helped provide financial stability for the new city. The 1850s were a difficult decade for banks, especially during the financial panic of 1857, which began after railroads defaulted on their bonds. Soon afterward, the Civil War brought great currency fluctuations, and, in 1861, bank riots occurred in Milwaukee. Despite these challenges, Farmers and Millers Bank, according to one history of the city, had quickly become "a power financially, as well as a general favorite with the public."

The bank underwent its first reorganization in 1863, when the federal government passed the National Bank Act. The Act provided for a national currency and implemented guidelines for establishing a network of federally supervised national banks, measures, it was hoped, that would calm the troubled financial times. Farmers and Millers, the first bank in Wisconsin to apply for a national charter, became a national bank on September 19th of that year and was renamed First National Bank of Milwaukee.

After the Civil War, Milwaukee became known increasingly as an industrial center. Its population also continued to grow rapidly, in part from an influx of Italian and Polish immigrants in the 1890s. With the growth in the city's industry and population came a corresponding rise in First National's assets, from just $1.5 million in 1873 to more than $29 million in 1913. Part of this increase was the result of its 1894 merger with Merchants Exchange Bank, which had been founded in 1870 as Home Savings Bank and had undergone two previous mergers before becoming part of First National. Growth also prompted First National to seek larger facilities. Construction began on a 16-story building on the corner of North Water Street and East Mason in 1912. Opened two years later, the new facility would house the bank's main office until 1973.

It was not long before the bank made another huge jump in assets, this time through a merger with Wisconsin National Bank, which had been formed in 1892. Effective on June 30, 1919, the merger created an immense new organization, First Wisconsin National Bank of Milwaukee, with assets surpassing $100 million. This new bank then set about expanding across the city, in part through opening up branch locations, and, in 1928, it merged with yet another institution, Second Ward Savings Bank, boosting assets to $177 million.

The following year, the directors of the bank founded Wisconsin Bankshares Corporation, a bank holding company (defined as a corporation owning at least two banks), which became the owner of First Wisconsin. This administrative change allowed for greater legal flexibility in acquisitions, and, by the end of 1930, Wisconsin Bankshares would acquire 23 additional Wisconsin financial institutions—such as Union National Bank in Eau Claire and First National Bank in Madison—giving the company a total of 16 national banks, 27 state banks, three trust companies, and seven other companies. All of Wisconsin Bankshares' acquisitions maintained their original officers and board of directors, and First Wisconsin remained the lead bank.

When the stock market crashed in 1929, sending the financial industry into a tailspin, Wisconsin Bankshares was in a strong position and, unlike many of its competitors, was able to maintain healthy growth throughout 1930 and 1931. As the Depression dragged on, however, the company would find its fortunes diminished. Many banks, in an effort to become more efficient and avoid closure, were merging, and Wisconsin Bankshares soon found itself forced down the same path. By the end of 1932, it had reduced the number of national banks under its control to 11 and the number of state banks to 25. One piece of good news came from Wisconsin's state government, which responded to the crisis by lifting the freeze on branch banking, in effect since 1909.

In the early months of 1933, the financial situation deteriorated even further as nervous depositors began to pull their money out of banks. On March 5, 1933, with financial collapse imminent, the newly elected U.S. President Franklin D. Roosevelt had little choice but to close all banks nationally for a "bank holiday." Lasting ten days, this cooling-off period gave federal officials time to investigate banks and helped restore some confidence among consumers. Wisconsin Bankshares, meanwhile, continued efforts toward greater efficiency. It transformed some of its banks into branches of First Wisconsin, for example, eliminating their boards and reducing the number of officers in the process. Bookkeeping was also consolidated. The company, moreover, began to sell off some of its financial institutions, and, by the end of 1944, with World War II nearing an end, Wisconsin Bankshares had been streamlined to just five national banks, in addition to First Wisconsin Trust Company (founded in 1894 and the oldest trust company in the state) and five other institutions. Overall, these moves resulted in a stronger, more financially sound company, which was able to boost its total assets from $301 million in 1931 to $666 million in 1944.

After World War II, Wisconsin Bankshares benefited from a robust economy. Also during this time, however, the state of Wisconsin decided to restore the freeze on branch banking. This move made it difficult for Wisconsin Bankshares to respond to a commercial trend in which shopping centers proliferated, drawing consumers away from the traditional shopping areas where most of the company's banks and branches were located. New regulations imposed by the Bank Holding Company Act of 1956, passed by Congress, also limited the company's flexibility. As a result, Wisconsin Bankshares, the largest bank holding company in the state, was prevented from both setting up branches and acquiring new banks, two of the most effective means of growth. It was, however, able to establish new banks (such as Southgate National Bank of Milwaukee in 1958), a slow and costly process, and to move some of its existing branches to more profitable locations.

In 1960, the company was renamed First Wisconsin Bankshares Corporation. Regulatory barriers, designed to protect small banks and to slow the consolidation of bank assets, would continue to frustrate the company until the late 1960s, when regulations began to be relaxed. In 1967, the company was allowed to acquire State Bank of Waunakee, and, in the next few years, it would start up new banks in such growing markets as Waukesha, West Green Bay, and Mequon. During the early 1970s, First Wisconsin became more involved in banking-related activities, forming, for example, First Wisconsin Financial Corporation (a commercial finance company) and First Wisconsin Mortgage Trust. It also established First Wisconsin International Bank, headquartered in New York. International

---

Key Dates:

1853: Farmers and Millers Bank is founded.

1863: The federal government passes the National Bank Act; the bank applies for a charter and is renamed First National Bank of Milwaukee.

1894: First National Bank of Milwaukee merges with Merchants Exchange Bank and founds First Wisconsin Trust Company.

1919: The bank merges with Wisconsin National Bank and changes its name to First Wisconsin National Bank of Milwaukee.

1929: First Wisconsin National is placed administratively under Wisconsin Bankshares Corporation.

1958: Wisconsin Bankshares establishes Southgate National Bank of Milwaukee.

1960: The bank is renamed First Wisconsin Bankshares Corporation.

1974: The bank is renamed First Wisconsin Corporation.

1987: First Wisconsin makes acquisitions in Illinois and Minnesota.

1989: The bank is renamed Firstar Corporation.

1995: Firstar undertakes its restructuring effort, Firstar Forward.

1998: Firstar merges with Star Banc.

---

loans would eventually produce a large percentage of its profits. In 1973, the company became even more prominent in Milwaukee with the completion of its new corporate headquarters, First Wisconsin Center, a 42-story facility near Lake Michigan and the tallest building in the state. The following year, because of its moves toward new types of services, the company decided to change its name to First Wisconsin Corporation.

In the late 1970s, Wisconsin's state government agreed to allow branch banking on a limited basis, giving First Wisconsin additional options for growth. The company quickly took advantage of its new freedom, and, by the mid-1980s, it had opened 19 new branches, expanding its total to 33. The company also continued to acquire existing banks across the state, helping to boost total assets to $4.75 billion in 1982 and $7.1 billion in 1986. During the same period, however, its profitable venture in international loans began to sour, resulting in large write-offs (especially for loans to developing countries) and in a net loss of $49 million in 1987.

Reset on a more conservative, steady course, First Wisconsin was given a boost by a new state law that took effect on January 1, 1987. Reflecting similar changes across the country, the law allowed Wisconsin banks to acquire or be acquired by other banks in eight neighboring states—Illinois, Minnesota, Ohio, Michigan, Iowa, Indiana, Missouri, and Kentucky—provided those states made similar laws themselves. First Wisconsin wasted little time in making its first out-of-state purchase, buying DuPage Bank & Trust Co. in Glen Ellyn, Illinois, on April 29, 1987. This was followed by additional purchases in Illinois, Iowa, and Minnesota (in the Twin Cities area), all states contiguous with Wisconsin. Among its most significant acquisitions were Naper Financial Corp. in Illinois (1987), Shelard Banc-

shares, Inc., in Minnesota (1987), and Banks of Iowa, Inc. (1991). By the end of 1993, total assets had reached $13.79 billion, $9.3 billion of which was generated in the company's home state of Wisconsin. The company's share of bank deposits was 15.6 percent in Wisconsin, 6.7 percent in Iowa, and two percent in Minnesota. In Illinois, where it had about $1 billion in bank deposits, all in the Chicago suburbs, its share was only .55 percent. The company also had three offices in Arizona and two in Florida.

The company became Firstar Corporation in 1989. For the first time neither banking nor Wisconsin was mentioned in its name, reflecting its status as a multistate, diversified financial corporation. The banks themselves were also renamed Firstar, though this did not occur in Wisconsin until 1992. Similarly, its corporate headquarters became Firstar Center.

By this time, Firstar had left its troubles of the mid-1980s far behind, and it was being widely praised for its sound management, led from 1991 by Roger L. Fitzsimonds, chairperson and chief executive officer. In particular, Firstar had made great gains in its fee-generating services—such as credit cards, brokerage, check collection, insurance, and investment management—which tended to be less vulnerable to economic downturns. These services were promoted not only through its numerous branches (some 200 by 1994), but also through more than 1,000 "correspondent banks," independent banks too small to offer their own fee-based services. At this time, CEO Fitzsimonds maintained in 1993, "Firstar is not in the banking business. We are in the financial services business. . . . We focus on the consumer, small business and commercial middle markets. We also provide operating services to the large corporate segment. There's nothing that we can't evolve to, acquire or change that won't meet these customers' needs."

On October 18, 1994, Firstar issued 1,801,577 shares of common stock to complete the acquisition of the $423 million First Southeast Banking Corp., a bank holding company for two banks with 23 offices in the Racine/Kenosha area. The company acquired several other banks during the next two years, including American Bancorporation of St. Paul in 1996. With the acquisitions came a management restructuring effort from late 1995 through 1997 that organized operations around business lines rather then geographic regions. This highly publicized effort, known as Firstar Forward, was later described in the press as a fatal step backward; despite its emphasis on efficiency and profitability and the elimination of one-fourth of the company's 10,000 employees, productivity sagged, revenue-growth slowed, and employee turnover increased.

A dynamic new leader for Firstar emerged in 1998, when Star Banc Corp., successor to the First National Bank of Cincinnati, agreed to acquire Firstar for $7.2 billion in stock. Jerry Grundhofer, chairman of Star Banc, was named president and chief executive of the newly merged banks, which opted to retain the Firstar name. Grundhofer, known in the industry as a fierce competitor and effective motivator, was also named to replace Fitzsimonds as chairman when the latter retired. In January 1999, soon after the merger was complete, *Forbes* named Grundhofer banker of the year for 1998, describing him as "not your genial sort of boss." The younger brother of Jack Grundhofer, chairman of U.S. Bancorp, he had taken the helm of Star Banc in 1993 where he instilled an aggressive incentive program that rewarded executives for their roles in increased revenues.

The merger more than doubled Firstar's assets to $38 billion and raised its national ranking to 21st in terms of size. The new Firstar had more than three million customers, 14,000 employees, and 720 branches in Ohio, Indiana, Kentucky, Tennessee, Illinois, Iowa, Wisconsin, Minnesota, Arizona, and Florida. Headquarters were consolidated in Milwaukee, while consumer banking operations remained in Star Banc's hometown of Cincinnati as did the hub of its finance company.

Under Grundhofer, Firstar set out to become a lean banking company that demanded and rewarded sales from employees, and expanded the parameters of traditional banking by installing more branches in supermarkets and corporate facilities, and offering more ATMs and kiosks. The new Firstar hoped to preserve the customer-friendly features of a small bank with the financial clout and convenience of a large bank. To achieve its goal, it implemented such unique policies as paying customers for having to spend too long a time in line. The holding company retained Star Banc's slogan—"a bank without boundaries"—as well as its "five star service guarantee."

The bank also centralized back-office functions such as mortgage and credit card processing, cutting the number of jobs by ten percent while significantly improving its efficiency ratio. Moreover, it peeled off layers of the old Firstar's hierarchical management; by 1999, Firstar had an entirely new management team. The bank also moved away from its old management structure based on geographic boundaries to one organized around its three areas of business: retail financial services, commercial financial services, and trust and investment management.

Analysts looked favorably on the revamped Firstar. In December 1998, Firstar moved into the Standard & Poor's 500-stock index, replacing Amoco; its stock hit an all-time high of $93 a share, a 60 percent appreciation for the year. The company experienced above average earnings growth of nearly 18 percent in an industry enjoying 12 percent overall, and Firstar announced a three-for-one stock split as well as its intention to buy back as many as five million pre-split shares. Firstar was named the top-performing bank in the country in 1998 by *American Banker Magazine* and the No.2 financial institution in the world in terms of shareholder performance by *The Economist*. The *Wall Street Journal* also cited Firstar as among the 32 companies posting best returns for shareholders.

As Firstar closed out the 20th century, it set itself the goal of becoming the preeminent financial service corporation in the Midwest. A major step in this direction occurred in 1999, when it again doubled its size, to 1,180 branches, and increased its assets to near $75 billion with the acquisition of the largest bank in Missouri, St. Louis Mercantile Bancorporation Inc. This purchase brought Firstar's total number of customers to five million, and put Firstar within competitive reach of Minneapolis-based U.S. Bancorp, run by Jack Grundhofer. Unfortunately, the merger announcement also prompted a 30 percent fall in its stock price. The drop, speculated analysts, may have been prompted by the fact that Mercantile was perceived as a subperforming company and that Firstar was perhaps becoming too acquisitive too quickly after the Star Banc merger. Neverthe-

less, management at Firstar continued to champion the merger, and analysts eventually had to agree. American Banker magazine named Jerry Grundhofer its "Banker of the Year" for 1999, citing his achievements in overseeing "two model deals in a single year." For Firstar, the nation's 12th largest bank and the second largest in the Midwest after the merger with Mercantile, continued growth seemed certain; in fact, analysts seemed to enjoy speculating on which bank Firstar would look to next.

Principal Subsidiaries

Elan Life Insurance Company; Firstar Finance, Inc.; Firstar Insurance Services, LLC; Firstar Investment Research & Management, LLC (FIRMCO); Firstar Title Corporation; Miami Valley Insurance Company; Mississippi Valley Life Insurance Co.

Principal Operating Units

Retail Financial Services; Commercial Financial Services; Trust and Investment Management; Insurance Services.

Principal Competitors

Bank One Corporation; Fifth Third Bancorp; First Bank System Inc.; U.S. Bancorp; Wells Fargo & Company.

Further Reading

Armstrong, Douglas, "Failed Restructuring Set Stage: Firstar Forward Plan Never Achieved Goals," *Milwaukee Journal Sentinel*, July 1, 1998, p. 1.

"Banking Brothers Area Study in Contrasts," *Columbus Dispatch*, July 12, 1998, p. 1H.

Byrne, Harlan S., "Firstar Corp.: Bank Company, Formerly First Wisconsin, Pushes Beyond State Lines," *Barron's*, January 16, 1989, pp. 39–40.

——, "Shining Brighter," *Barron's*, June 20, 1994, p. 19.

Causey, James E., and Kathleen Gallagher, "Firstar to Nearly Double in Size," *Milwaukee Journal Sentinel*, May 1, 1999, p. 1.

Causey, James E., "Analysts Muse About Bank Brothers Merger," *Milwaukee Journal Sentinel*, May 5, 1999, p. 1.

——, "Firstar Likely Looking to Branch Out in Other States," *Milwaukee Journal Sentinel*, May 9, 1999, p. 1.

Gallagher, Kathleen, "Bank on Change at New Firstar," *Milwaukee Journal Sentinel*, July 13, 1998, p. 6.

"Good Chemistry Helped Seal Firstar, Star Banc Deal," *Milwaukee Journal Sentinel*, July 3, 1998, p. 1.

Klinkerman, Steve, "Firstar's Chief Exec Says the Real Keys to Profits Are People, Not Technology," *American Banker*, January 13, 1994, p. 4.

Norman, Jack, "A Rising Star in the Midwest," *Milwaukee Journal*, September 13, 1992, pp. 1, 7.

"Peer Pressure (Interview with Firstar Chairman Roger Fitzsimonds)," *United States Banker*, September 1993, pp. 14–20.

Silverman, Gary, "Midwest Banks Left in Shadows by Their Own Caution," *Financial Times* (London), December 9, 1999, p. 34.

Weier, Anita, "Firstar Builds on Expansion Plan with Acquisition of Iowa Group," *Business Journal-Milwaukee*, August 13, 1990, p. 2.

——, "Firstar Consolidates Minnesota Banks," *Business Journal-Milwaukee*, February 11, 1991, p. 2.

—Thomas Riggs
—updated by Carrie Rothburd

Fiserv, Inc.

255 Fiserv Drive
Brookfield, Wisconsin 53045
U.S.A.
Telephone: (262) 879-5000
Toll free: (800) 425-FISV
Fax: (262) 879-5013
Web site: http://www.fiserv.com

Public Company
Incorporated: 1984
Employees: 12,500
Sales: $1.4 billion (1999)
Stock Exchanges: NASDAQ
Ticker Symbol: FISV
NAIC: 51421 Data Processing Services; 541611
   Administrative Management and General Management
   Consulting Services

Fiserv, Inc. is one of the three largest data processing firms in the United States and the nation's largest independent processor of checks. From its Brookfield, Wisconsin, base, the company offers a broad mix of integrated data processing and information management systems, including proprietary and off-the-shelf software solutions to approximately 10,000 financial institutions in more than 90 countries. The company continues to expand by providing alternative services to its customers in Australia, Canada, Indonesia, Poland, Singapore, and the United Kingdom.

Backgrounds of the Founders

Fiserv is the progeny of George Dalton and Leslie Muma, who together founded the company in 1984. Dalton and Muma, who each operated his own data processing company, had been trying to merge their operations since the late 1970s. The friends realized early on that to excel in their competitive industry they would need to form a large, national network of clients and service offerings. After purchasing their firms through management buyouts—Dalton and Muma had both been operating as subsidiaries of well-heeled parent companies—the partners joined forces in what would quickly become the fastest growing financial data processing firm in the country.

Dalton, who became CEO of the newly formed Fiserv, was experienced and well respected in the data processing industry. Although peers described him as a visionary, Dalton attributed much of his success to meticulous planning and old-fashioned hard work. One of Dalton's first jobs, for example, was at a Kroger grocery store. Between the ages of 14 and 16 he advanced from stock boy to butcher to journeyman, outpacing his peers. "I worked nights, weekends, and during the summers," recalled Dalton in a March 1993 issue of *Business Journal of Milwaukee,* he explained, adding, "The lesson I learned: Hard work produces results."

As evidence of his penchant for planning, Dalton began learning German as a junior in high school in 1944 in anticipation of serving his country in World War II; to his chagrin, he was sent to the Spanish-speaking Panama Canal Zone. It was also during his high school years, however, that Dalton "fell in love with data processing" and began preparing for his future career. After the war, he returned home and attended Northwestern University from 1947 to 1948. He then dropped out of college to accept a position with Bell & Howell Co.'s data processing department, or tabulating department, as it was called in those days.

Dalton's three eye-opening years at Bell and Howell confirmed his enthusiasm for data processing, which was evidenced by his quick mastery of the equipment with which he worked. Despite a dearth of banking knowledge, Dalton's enthusiasm helped him to land a position as head of Marine Bank's data processing division. It was during his 12 years at Marine that computers were introduced to the banking industry on a large scale. Dalton grasped the technology immediately.

Dalton's move to the head of Midland National Bank's data processing department in 1965 cemented the foundation for his future enterprise. Midland wanted Dalton to run the department as a separate profit center, a concept that remained untested. He quickly grew the business by expanding its services into non-banking areas, particularly retail, and establishing a healthy contracting business. When First Bank Systems Inc., of Minneapolis, acquired Midland in 1977 it was not sure how to treat Dalton's unique operation. It eventually established First Data Processing Inc. as a subsidiary in 1982, with Dalton at the helm.

Having established an in-depth understanding of the fledgling financial data processing industry, by the late 1970s Dalton was ready to branch out on his own and begin testing his new ideas about information processing. His ally would be Leslie Muma, of Freedom Savings and Loan in Tampa, Florida. Muma had befriended Dalton in the 1970s when Dalton was looking for fellow bank data processing department heads to share software development costs. By pooling their resources, Dalton reasoned, he and his industry cohorts could reduce data processing bills by as much as 60 percent. Muma was the only one who initially bought into the novel experiment.

Although Muma was only in his mid-30s when he and Dalton began working together, he was extremely knowledgeable of data processing systems and services. Before acquiring his master's degree in business administration from the University of South Florida, in fact, Muma had majored in theoretical mathematics. He worked as a data processing consultant at an accounting firm for a few years before joining Freedom Savings and Loan Association in Florida in 1971. Freedom developed a subsidiary, Sunshine State Systems, similar to that operated by Dalton, with Muma as president of that division in 1972.

Dalton and Muma Found Fiserv in 1984

By 1984, the subsidiaries headed by Dalton and Muma were serving more than 100 clients and generating annual revenues in excess of $22 million. Frustrated by their inability to get the two subsidiaries merged under one corporate umbrella, they struck out on their own in a risky venture. With venture capital backing, Muma and Dalton purchased their companies from their parent corporations and formed a single entity called Fiserv. To accomplish this feat, they were forced to surrender 89 percent of the equity in their venture to the financiers. "Eleven percent of something is worth more than 100 percent of nothing," noted Dalton in an April 1992 issue of *Forbes*.

Dalton and Muma, who was president of the start-up, planned to build a national data processing company based on the concept the two had been implementing since the late 1970s: increased efficiency through economies of scale. Up to that time, most companies developed and operated a separate data processing system in-house. They created their own software and managed their own systems, often at an enormous and constantly escalating cost. Fiserv would save money for these companies by contracting to handle some or most of their data processing activities. Because Fiserv could essentially use the same software and systems for its entire base of clients, it could significantly reduce their expenses. The partners planned to quickly grow their customer base by acquiring regional processing firms similar to Fiserv but smaller in size.

To finance Fiserv's strategy of purchasing companies with cash, rather than debt, the company began selling shares publicly in 1986. Although this strategy reduced the founder's ownership interest to only two percent each by the early 1990s, it allowed them to reduce their debt burden and sustain aggressive expansion efforts. As Dalton went searching for new acquisition candidates during the 1980s, Muma focused on developing a high-tech, efficient, customer-oriented operation that could smoothly integrate new acquisitions and the clients that accompanied them.

Rapid Growth Through Acquisition: 1984–89

Fiserv's success at purchasing good companies and providing top-notch service soon paid off. Between 1984 and 1989 Fiserv acquired 16 companies, boosting annual company sales more than 3,000 percent to $700 million. Likewise, Fiserv's work force swelled from just 300 in 1984 to a whopping 2,300 by 1989. Going into the 1990s, Fiserv was processing data in 36 states through 20 data centers. It served more than 800 financial institutions representing 19 million individual accounts. Furthermore, in the few years since its inception the company had expanded its operations internationally to include clients in Europe, Australia, and Canada.

Fiserv's rapid growth during the 1980s was largely a corollary of a metamorphosis of U.S. financial markets. Indeed, as a result new technologies, tax laws (such as the Tax Reform Act of 1986), increased competition, an easing of interstate banking regulations, and other factors, prospective Fiserv customers were increasingly seeking reduced costs associated with centralized, automated data processing. As a result, the data processing industry, in general, experienced growth and consolidation throughout the 1980s and early 1990s.

In addition to favorable industry trends, however, much of Fiserv's prosperity and dominance was attributable to its savvy management style. For example, Fiserv practiced extreme caution when it purchased new companies; of 600 acquisition candidates that it considered in 1992, it purchased only six. Besides examining a candidate's information systems, financial condition, and customer base, Dalton carefully considered the quality of its employees. When he finally decided to purchase a company, he did so with the intent of keeping the company's top management on board for at least three years. Furthermore, Dalton allowed the company's management to continue operating with a relatively high degree of autonomy.

Muma and other members of Fiserv's operations team complemented Dalton's prudent growth strategy with a near obsession with customer service. "Fiserv is very professional, very current, and up-to-date on all the new advances in the computer and financial services industry," extolled a Fiserv client in a November 1989 issue of *Business Journal of Milwaukee,* adding, "They are extremely responsive to our concerns and to incorporating our direction into the system." Indeed, Fiserv was credited with maintaining a range of specialized products and services unmatched in the industry.

Another element of Fiserv's quest for market share was flexibility. Unlike many of its competitors, for instance, Fiserv did not push its new customers to utilize its software. Instead, Fiserv adapted its services to work with the institution's existing systems. Fiserv also worked with a range of account sizes; whereas industry leaders Electronic Data Systems (EDS) and Systematics Inc. concentrated on larger customers, Fiserv was willing to work with credit unions and other small institutions.

Although EDS and Systematics both served a broader customer base than that assisted by Fiserv, the latter's focused management style allowed it to assume the leading growth position (among established competitors) in the data processing industry during the late 1980s and early 1990s. Of the three leaders, in fact, Fiserv was the only one that concentrated solely on serving financial institutions. "It's the best managed company of its kind because it's got a clear focus on what its business actually is," explained investment analyst Paul Shain in a July 1992 issue of *Business Journal of Milwaukee.* "It's a simple strategy of offering banks more sophisticated financial services and better customer service than they could otherwise afford," he maintained.

A Larger Client Base in the Early 1990s

Fiserv's strategy benefited shareholders during the early 1990s, as assets, revenues, and clients ballooned. Indeed, after ingesting its first 16 companies between 1984 and 1989, Fiserv stepped up its growth plans with 15 additional purchases during 1990 and 1991. New buys included a major acquisition of a Citicorp data processing division for $49 million; the new subsidiary brought an additional 400 clients to Fiserv.

The Citicorp purchase reflected the growing size of the companies in Fiserv's client base. Although the company had targeted smaller and mid-size companies prior to 1990, it began serving several customers with sales of $1 billion-plus in the early 1990s. By 1991, Fiserv was serving more than 1,400 banks, savings and loans, and credit unions of all sizes. Its sales, moreover, vaulted to a whopping $281 million, from which $18.3 million in profit was gleaned.

In addition to continued acquisition and client growth during 1992 and 1993, Fiserv also shifted its operational focus. It had previously served most of its customers via modem through mainframes connected to its clients' terminals. To serve its larger customers, however, Fiserv in the early 1990s began literally taking over entire data processing departments at large companies. It hired much of the existing staff and operated the data processing facility on-site using Fiserv technical know-how. This strategy, combined with continued increases in its number of smaller clients, helped the company to grow its customer base to more than 5,400 in 1992 as its workforce swelled to 4,800. Likewise, revenues shot up an impressive 15 percent to $332 million, and earnings grew 27 percent, to $23 million.

Fiserv sustained its aggressive growth tactics in 1993. Among its acquisitions early in that year were two data processing businesses owned by Mellon Bank. This purchase brought about 200 new clients to Fiserv worth an estimated $70 million per year in revenues. Furthermore, most of these new clients had assets of more than $300 million, much more than the average for Fiserv's existing client base. Most notable during 1993, however, was Fiserv's addition of its largest buyout ever, Basis Information Technologies, Inc., which added 1,000 new workers to Fiserv's payroll.

Although Dalton and Muma were aging going into the mid-1990s, their zeal for continued growth and innovation was reflected in pursuits outside their business. To prepare for his 12-hour workday that began at 6:30 a.m., Muma jogged six miles. An avid runner since the age of 32, he began competing in marathons to overcome a smoking habit. Also a hard worker, Dalton filled his free hours by cruising on his 1990 Harley-Davidson motorcycle. He was an avid automobile enthusiast, as well. Despite outside interests, however, both men were admitted workaholics. "We don't bowl on Saturdays," said Muma, in the April 27, 1992, issue of *Forbes,* "We come to work."

Fiserv posted record growth in 1993; sales ballooned an impressive 38 percent, as income spiraled to more than $30 million, and the company was poised for healthy expansion. Dalton and Muma reflected on the Fiserv's rampant rise in the company's 1993 annual report: "With the dedication and hard work of Fiserv people, we have grown this organization from two data processing centers in Milwaukee and Tampa employing less than 300 professionals to a company with locations in 61 cities supported by more than 6,300 industry professionals. We've grown from providing full-service processing for 170 clients in 1984 to over 2,500 clients in 1993. . . . We've built a strong foundation on which to base our future, and have in place a focused plan to direct that future."

Steady Growth Through the Late 1990s

Steady and impressive growth continued throughout the rest of the 1990s as continued downsizing, consolidation, and pressure to boost revenue prompted banks to hand over back-office functions to external providers. Bankers were beginning to "view their business not as transaction processing, but as information management and distribution," according to one consultant in the May 1996 issue of *ABA Banking*. "The third party performs processing, but channels the information back to the bank, so that the information becomes the primary currency," he noted. Fiserv, whose income was up another 25 percent to $51 million in 1994, was there to benefit from the intensified interest in outsourcing. By the end of 1995, the year in which Fiserv signed a multi-million dollar, 12-year strategic alliance with Chase Manhattan bank and a second alliance with State Street Bank in Boston, Fiserv was providing customer account processing to more than 3,000 financial institutions and had an annual income of almost $64 million. While the Chase contract ended when the bank merged a short while later with Chemical Bank, Fiserv rebounded by landing a ten-year $1.6 billion deal to handle back-office processing for two leading Canadian banks in 1996. Moreover, in 1998, it signed on to a five-year contract with First Federal of California.

From 1996 to 1998, Fiserv went from almost $900 million in sales to more than $1 billion and increased its customer base to 5,000, all the while maintaining its tried and true formula for success—choosing and integrating its acquisitions carefully, allowing them a large degree of autonomy, and solidly focusing on customer service. Company policy included surveying clients twice a year for feedback on their working relationship with Fiserv and tying the compensation of business-unit directors to customer satisfaction. At the same time, Fiserv was branching out into other areas of the financial information services processing sector. Six of the company's ten acquisitions in 1997 were related to the brokerage industry, ranging from a deep-discount brokerage house to a manufacturer of software that enabled customers to enter trade orders via the Internet or touch-tone phone. Fiserv also acquired businesses that provided marketing, seminar, and training materials for the financial industry. In 1998, it added a provider of administrative software systems to insurance companies and a provider of automotive leasing software. In all, Fiserv acquired 11 new businesses in 1998, bringing its total number of acquisitions since 1984 to 73.

In the late 1990s, Fiserv began a cross-selling strategy, lessening its dependence on acquisitions to stimulate growth in favor of adding new products that accommodated its customers' expansion into new markets. These included brokering, insurance, auto loan processing, and indirect lending. A Web product for banks, for example, allowed customers access to their bank-branded insurance accounts from the bank's home page. In 1999, Fiserv launched a subscription Internet service called ePrime@Fiserv, which bundled online banking, bill payment, investment and insurance products, cash management automation, back-office processing, and core-account processing into one solution. Fiserv also introduced TheLendingSite.com, which provided the technological backbone for Internet-based lending, such as loan approval and credit card authorization. To complement its new strategy, Fiserv implemented a national television advertising campaign, a branding effort making use of the tag line "Where money and technology meet." Another part of Fiserv's branding effort was its own company Web site launched in December 1998.

Overseas Expansion at the Turn of the Century

With 400 customers in 60 countries in late 1999, Fiserv began looking to expand overseas at the turn of the century. The domestic financial services market was still healthy with an annual growth of about 20 percent for the industry's top three competitors—Fiserv, M&I, and Deluxe—but bank mergers were drying up the pool of potential customers. In addition, the privatization of banks in foreign countries and the European Union's conversion to a single currency in 1999, had opened new doors for data processing companies. In some countries, such as Mexico, Brazil, and Argentina, growth for financial services providers was estimated at 30 to 35 percent in the coming years.

By the time George Dalton retired in 1999 and Leslie Muma took over as chief executive, Fiserv was averaging 28 percent annual growth in revenue, 20 percent growth in earnings per share, and 31 percent growth in net income. A share of Fiserv stock valued at $2.74 in 1986 had increased in value nearly 20 times to $52.68. Those who knew the hard-working Dalton were surprised by his decision to retire, but Muma expected to continue Fiserv's aggressive growth pace. As financial services increasingly converged under one umbrella, Fiserv intended to provide more and better services to customers, believing that continued growth through acquisitions, steady internal growth, and providing data services to financial institutions would carry it into the future.

Principal Subsidiaries

First Trust Corporation; Fiserv Correspondents Services Inc.; Fiserv Investor Services, Inc.; Fiserv LeMans, Inc.; Fiserv Solutions Inc.; Fiserv Securities Inc.; Information Technology, Inc.; The Freedom Group, Inc.

Principal Competitors

Affiliated Computer Services, Inc.; Alltel Information Services, Inc.; BISYS Group, Inc.; Computer Sciences Corporation; First Data Corporation; Deluxe Corporation; Electronic Data Systems Corporation; Integrated System Solutions Corp.; M&I Data Services.

Further Reading

Banker, John, "Big Competitors Can't Keep Pace with Fiserv," *Business Journal of Milwaukee,* August 7, 1993, p. 7.
Barthel, Matt, "Fiserv's Strategy for Rapid Growth," *American Banker,* August 27, 1993.
Causey, James E., "Fiserv, Dalton Setting Torrid Pace," *Milwaukee Journal* Sentinel, February 25, 1998, p. 1.
——, "New CEO to Keep Fiserv Growing," *Milwaukee Journal* Sentinel, March 29, 1999, p. 1.
——, "World Now the Arena for Local Data Processing Firms," *Milwaukee Journal Sentinel,* August 10, 1998, p. 12.
Cone, Edward, "Buy and Build—Fiserv's Two-Track Strategy Fuels 20 Percent Annual Growth," *Information Week,* October 5, 1998.

Dries, Michael, ''Shades of CEO: Heart and Soul—How Who They Are Plays a Role in How They Lead: George Dalton,'' *Business Journal of Milwaukee,* March 27, 1993, Sec. 3, p. 8.

——, ''Hot Shots—Wisconsin's Best-Performing Public Companies: Fiserv Inc.,'' *Business Journal of Milwaukee,* July 31, 1993, Sec. 3, p. 12.

Elliot, Suzanne, ''Fiserv Plans Move to Cheaper Offices for Ex-Mellon Subs,'' *Pittsburgh Business Times & Journal,* August 16, 1993, p. 1.

''Fiserv, Inc. and Mellon Bank Corp. Announce Agreement for Sale of Two Mellon Outsourcing Businesses for Bank Processing and Related Services,'' *Business Wire,* August 2, 1993.

Higgins, Terry, ''Fiserv Inc.,'' *Business Journal of Milwaukee,* July 25, 1992, Sec. 3, p. 12.

O'Heney, Sheila, ''Outsourcing is Hotter Than Ever,'' *ABA Banking Journal,* May 1996, p. 44.

Palmeri, Christopher, ''We Don't Bowl on Saturdays,'' *Forbes,* April 27, 1992, p. 104.

Snell, Ned, ''Fiserv Inc.,'' *Datamation,* June 15, 1993, p. 120.

''The CEOs of Wisconsin: George Dalton,'' *Business Journal of Milwaukee,* March 27, 1993, Sec. 3, p. 15.

Weier, Anita, ''Muma's Marathon Pace Keeps Fiserv on Growth Track,'' *Business Journal of Milwaukee,* November 20, 1989, Sec. 1, p. 10.

—Dave Mote
—updated by Carrie Rothburd

Fiskars Corporation

Mannerheimintie 14 A
P.O. Box 235
Helsinki
Finland 00101
Telephone: +358 9 618 861
Fax: +358 9 604 053
Web site: http://www.fiskars.fi

Public Company
Founded: 1649
Employees: 5,600
Sales: EUR 665 million ($637.69 million) (1999)
Stock Exchanges: Helsinki
Ticker Symbol: FIS
NAIC: 551112 Offices of Other Holding Companies;
332312 Fabricated Structural Metal Manufacturing;
326299 All Other Rubber Product Manufacturing;
326199 All Other Plastics Product Manufacturing;
332211 Cutlery and Flatware (Except Precious)
Manufacturing; 332212 Hand and Edge Tool
Manufacturing

Fiskars Corporation, headquartered in Helsinki, Finland, is one of the oldest companies in the western world, having been established as Fiskars Ironworks in 1649 and in continuous operation since then. Even during its involvement in several wars between Sweden and Russia, Fiskars gained a reputation as one of the finest iron and copperworks in the north. In the 1830s, the company expanded its knifeworks, manufactured forks and scissors, established Finland's first machine shop, and manufactured the first Finnish steam engine. After surviving the ravages of two World Wars, Fiskars gradually became the world's leading manufacturer of scissors and of other cutting products for home, school and office; produced lawn and garden accessories; and made products for craft and outdoor-recreation activities. The company's main focus is on the consumer products business that represents over 90 percent of corporate sales. Fiskars is organized into three business units, based on products: The Consumer Products Group, Inha Works, and The Real Estate Group. The Consumer Products Group is the largest business unit and is responsible for all the Fiskars' consumer products manufactured and sold throughout the world. Fiskars products are manufactured in 11 countries and marketed in 120 countries. Inha Works manufactures aluminum boats, building components, and rail fasteners, primarily for the Nordic markets. The Real Estate Group manages the corporation's properties and related services. Over the years, many of Fiskars' wide range of products have won prizes at international exhibits. Fiskars' consolidated net sales in 1998 amounted to US$ 626 million, of which 94 percent was generated outside Finland.

Industry Background

Finland's experience as an iron producing area dates back to the Iron Age (*circa* 600–800 BC). In the early Middle Ages, Finland was still a sparsely populated, remote country where the inhabitants farmed and also made pig iron from the ore gathered from their country's lakes and bogs. In the 12th century, Finland, which had remained relatively isolated from Western Europe, was annexed to Sweden and then began to evolve in the trading and the mining industries. During the reign of King Gustavus Vasa of Sweden-Finland, the first iron mine was opened at Ojamo in Lohja, Finland, in 1538–40. About 20 years later, the King set up a simple bar-iron shop which used ore from the Ojamo mine. Sweden had already become an important exporter of iron ore to Europe.

Early in the 17th century, under the reign of King Gustavus II Adolphus, Sweden-Finland became a great power and was a major producer of iron. However, Sweden's participation in the Thirty Years' War—fought on political and religious issues among the Germans, Swedish, French and Spanish, and ending in 1648—delved deeply into the Swedish kingdom's resources. The abundance of Finland's unharnessed water power and, especially, its immense forest resources for charcoal production (charcoal was made by burning wood in kilns) made it feasible to found ironworks in that country. Furthermore, private merchants, as well as the Crown, were allowed to develop the iron trade. Between 1616 and 1649, ironworks were established in Mustio, Antskog, Billnäs, Fagervik, and Fiskars—all located in, or close to, the parish of Pohja, which became the center of the Finnish iron industry. According to the Fiskars' company history *Fiskars 1649: 350 Years of Finnish Industrial History*, "the term *ironworks* referred to industrial establishments that had received official permits for such things as pig-iron works, blast furnaces and other installations which concentrated mainly on refining iron ore and processing iron."

In 1649 Peter Thorwöste, an immigrant from Holland, acquired Antskog ironworks. He received permission to mine iron ore from the Ojamo mine and to manufacture cast iron and forged products, with the exception of cannons. Thorwöste also gained a permit to set up a blast furnace and bar hammer in Fiskars Village, in Western Finland. Thus, Fiskars IronWorks came into being. Mining ore in Finland soon proved to be unprofitable; therefore iron ore was imported from the Utö mine in the Stockholm archipelago.

Among the items that Fiskars Ironworks produced were nails, wire, knives, hoes, reinforced wheels from pig iron, and cast-iron products—such as pots and frying pans. The finished products were sent via Pohjankuru either to Stockholm or to the southern provinces along the Gulf of Finland. Bar iron was exported to Sweden and sold at Stockholm's Iron Market. In 1656, according to *350 Years*, the Fiskars and Antskog ironworks had a workforce of 54, who were paid in cash and in goods. Employees included a master builder, a furnace supervisor, and 16 smiths. The peasants engaged by the ironworks worked 1.5 days a week.

1700–1900: Famine, Wars, Autonomy Under Russia, New Ideas

The last years of the 17th century brought famine to Sweden-Finland; the country was reduced to poverty and no longer enjoyed the unity brought about by King Gustavus Vasa. The famine claimed the lives of one-third of Finland's 500,000 inhabitants. The Russians began to ravage the Finnish coast in 1700, at the beginning of the Great Northern War that did not end until 1721. By that time, many Fiskars' workers were dead, and Sweden-Finland was no longer a powerful country. The new great power was in Russia and at St. Petersburg, the capital city. After the war, while the Finns could not finance the revival of their ironworks, wealthy men from Stockholm invested money in Finnish ironworks and recruited workers from abroad. In 1740, there were only 115 inhabitants in Fiskars Village.

As economic and cultural activity slowly revived, merchant shipping increased on the Baltic Sea and elsewhere. James Watts' invention of the steam engine offered new hope for industry, and coke could be used to replace the labor-intensive making of charcoal. Copper ore was discovered in the Orijärvi area, and Fiskars began to refine copper as well as iron. In 1783 Bengt Magnus Björkman acquired both the Fiskars and the Antskog ironworks. Fiskars' coppersmiths continued to forge artistically crafted utensils well into the 19th century.

In 1808 war broke out again between Russia and Sweden with the result that Finland was ceded to Russia and became an autonomous Grand Duchy with the status of a distinct nation. Bengt Ludvig Björkman, son of Bengt Magnus, moved to Finland and took over the management of the Fiskars, Antskog, and Doski ironworks. Problems with the availability of iron ore and with former trading relations, combined with Bengt Ludvig's option for a life of luxury, led to Fiskars being sold to Finnish Johan Jacob Julin. Fiskars had closed down its blast furnace in 1802, so what Johan Julin took over was really a copperworks rather than an ironworks.

Johan Julin sought knowledge not only for himself but for others. He had a school built so that all children, even those who were working, could be educated. He participated in founding the first savings bank in Finland and created a model farm in Fiskars Village, where crop rotation was practiced. Intending to shift the emphasis from refining of iron ore to the refining of iron, he travelled extensively in Sweden and Britain to gather information on fine iron forging, among other things. A forge was completed on the upper Fiskars River rapids in 1836. Although the ironworks used most of the forge's products, household utensils were also made at the forge. Furthermore, the Fiskars forge became famous for what was considered an extraordinary achievement at that time: 90 cast-iron columns and a large water-wheel were built for the Finlayson cotton mill in Tampere in 1837. The water-wheel's diameter measured more than six feet and did not have a match in all of Europe.

In 1837 Johan began construction of Finland's first machine workshop. The following year, the workshop produced the first steamship engine for the *SS Helsingfors*, the first Finnish steamship. In 1849 Johan was elevated to the rank of nobleman.

During the winter of 1851, the *SS Majava* ("the Beaver") was built on the ice in Pohjankuru harbor from finished components transported by horse and sleigh from the Fiskars machine shop. The ship was "automatically launched," so to speak, when the ice melted in the spring. Other products of the machine workshop included the iron gate and bridge structure for the Saimaa Canal; blowers; warm air generators; and agricultural equipment (such as ploughs, chaff rakes and sowing machinery).

The Industrial Revolution accelerated industrial and economic development in Europe; Fiskars' skilled workmen established the ironworks' reputation of being the finest iron and copperworks in the north. The ironworks not only expanded its manufacture of knives, forks, and scissors but also contributed to the development of Finnish agriculture. Various ploughs were imported for experiments, and then a plough especially suitable for Finnish soil was created. According to *350 Years*, "Ploughs became the ironworks' most important line of products. At the 1860 St. Petersburg exhibition, Fiskars' wooden plough won an award. By 1891 the ironworks was producing 11 different ploughs, and by the end of the century the range had been extended to 40 models. In all, over a million horse-drawn ploughs were made."

Johan Jacob von Julin died in 1853, and a guardianship administration, known as the "Ironworks Company John von Julin," was established to manage Fiskars Ironworks. However, power gradually became consolidated in the hands of Emil

Key Dates:

1649: Peter Thorwöste establishes the Fiskars Ironworks.

1783: Bengt Magnus Björkman acquires Fiskars Iron-works and Finland's first copper mine at Orijärvi.

1809: Finland is ceded to Russia and granted status as a distinct nation; Bengt Ludvig Björkman, son of Bengt Magnus, takes over the management of the Fiskars, Antskog, and Doski ironworks.

1822: Johan Jacob Julin buys Fiskars Ironworks and inaugurates one of the most progressive periods in the history of Finland's ironworks.

1837: J.J. Julin begins construction of Finland's first engineering workshop.

1883: Fiskars Ironworks becomes a joint-stock limited liability company and is renamed Fiskars Aktiebolag-osakeyhtiö.

1917: Finland declares its independence from Russia.

1920s: Fiskars expands and modernizes.

1960: Company manufactures the first Finnish microwave oven.

1967: The world's first scissors with plastic handles are introduced.

1978: Fiskars establishes scissors manufacturing in the United States.

1980: Company withdraws from the traditional iron and steel industry.

1999: Fiskars celebrates its 350th anniversary.

Lindsay von Julin. Furthermore, the company began experiencing financial problems, lacking adequate operating capital. As part of its recovery plan, Fiskars became a limited liability company, known as Fiskars Aktiebolag-osakeyhtiö, with a share capital of one million Finnish marks.

A railway line built between Helsinki and St. Petersburg offered additional opportunities for trade between Finland and Russia. In fact, Fiskars' continuing profitability was partly due to the fact that about half of the exports went to Russia. At the St. Petersburg's Exhibit in 1860, Fiskars received its first recorded recognition of a product: an award for a new horse-drawn plow. During the last decades of the 1800s the company invested in additional equipment for the ironworks. For example, Fiskars acquired the Åminnefors works and began to use a Siemens-Martin furnace built in 1887, the third of its kind in Finland. In a bankruptcy sale, Fiskars bought the Åminnefors rolling mill, which had four puddling furnaces, two welding furnaces, and a brick-built outdoor kiln for drying wood. In 1894 there were 250 employees working at the ironworks; the entire community consisted of about 1,050 inhabitants.

1900–97: Two World Wars, Independence, Strikes, Reorganization

Initially, World War I increased orders from Russia; however, when the Bolsheviks seized power, the upheaval had strong repercussions in Finland. In December 1917 Finland issued its Declaration of Independence, and the ensuing civil war and loss of the Russian market upset its economy. To compensate, Fiskars targeted the newly independent Baltic states and tried to win a larger share of the Western Europe market. After World War I, Fiskars began to expand and to modernize its operation. The rolling mill was renovated; better steel-refining methods were developed; and Fiskars founded Finland's first metal spring factory. The company acquired the Inha ironworks in Ähtäri, Oy Ferraria Ab with its plants in Jokioinen, Loimaa, and Pero on the Karalian Isthmus, and several other companies.

In 1930, worldwide economic depression halted Fiskars' expansion. Though an upward trend soon followed, involvement in World War II made Finland pay dearly in human lives, virtually wiped out trade, and stalled production for the domestic market until 1948. The end of the war and the signing of a peace treaty with the Soviet Union helped Finland on the road to recovery. Specifically, postwar demands by the Soviet Union generated much business for the metal industry. However, in 1956, as Finnish leader Urho Kekkonen began his 26-year presidency, a general strike practically paralyzed every field of industry; inflation and devaluations would continue into the early 1990s, while a strike in 1971 led to the closing of the Fiskars plant for several weeks.

During such challenging economic times, diversification seemed imperative. Fiskars at first had a moderate degree of success with new product exports and new designs. For example, the company was one of the first in Europe to produce the microwave oven in 1965, and the company also began a foray into plastic tableware in 1962.

Also during this time, a product was introduced for which Fiskars would gain its greatest notoriety, at least in the United States. Through experiments with strip stainless steel and injection-molded plastics, Fiskars engineer Olaf Backstrom reportedly designed the world's first light-weight "classic scissors" with orange plastic handles. The design was as artistic as it was functional. The scissors were later included in the Design Collection of the Museum of Modern Art in New York and in the Philadelphia Museum of Art. A few years after their introduction in the Finnish market, the scissors were spotted by representatives from Normark, a U.S. company that had distribution rights to Rapala lures, also manufactured in Finland. Normark obtained distribution rights to market the scissors in the United States, where they would quickly find an appreciative audience.

In the early 1960s Fiskars had set out to expand by means of takeovers. However, this expansion program, too broad in scope, was eroding the company's profits, and Fiskars soon found itself in need of focus and restructure. Toward that end, Fiskars sold some of its land and, more importantly, divested its original steel-making business, which it sold to Ovako Oy Ab, thereby safeguarding its supplies of raw materials and boosting Fiskars profits.

Under the tenure of Görman J. Ehrnrooth, chairman of the board, Fiskars completed its restructuring, with a strategy now based on new products, new markets, and acquisitions based on competencies. To assure its success as an international company, Fiskars focused on the United States, as it had the world's strongest economy and, according to *350 Years*, could provide "a foundation for internationalization, as well as a good location for expansion and also for gaining valuable experience."

1977–2000: Fiskars' Cutting Edge

In 1977 Fiskars established a scissors plant in Wausau, Wisconsin, and then acquired several consumer-oriented companies, such as Wallace Manufacturing Co., Gerber Legendary Blades, and Coltellerie Montana. Gradually, scissors became a profitable product line that appealed to consumers around the world. Over the next 20 years, Fiskars would come to function well as a business corporation structured in three business units—The Consumer Products Group (CPG), Inha Works Ltd., and the Real Estate Group—and made judicious acquisitions of companies that strengthened these units.

The Consumer Products Group (CPG), the largest business unit, was headquartered in Madison, Wisconsin, and managed the consumer business worldwide through offices in North America and most of the European countries, including an office and manufacturing facility in Fiskars Village. In 1996, CPG accounted for the largest share, about 89 percent, of the parent company's $461 million in revenues. This Group concentrated its activities on the manufacture, sale, and distribution of three primary families of products; scissors and other housewares products; outdoor-recreation products; and lawn and garden products. "We're very decentralized," CPG Vice-President Roy Prestage told Judy Newman of the *Wisconsin Business Journal*. "We keep decision-making close to the marketplace so we can respond quickly to its needs," Prestage explained. A case in point was Fiskars' Softouch Scissors, with their oversized, cushioned gray handles operated by squeezing the whole hand. The new scissors were developed when market studies showed that people with arthritis found regular scissors too painful to use. Moreover, the company applied the "whole hand" technology to a line of garden tools. "Ergonomics is what we're about," commented James Woodside, another CPG Vice-President.

Fiskars bolstered CPG operations in the late 1990s with the acquisitions: Aquapore Moisture Systems, Inc., which manufactured garden irrigation products; EnviroWorks, Inc. a manufacturer of portable shade structure and plastic-resin flower pots; Werga-Tools GmbH, a German distribution company in the lawn and garden products market; and Vikingate Ltd, a British company specializing in propagators and plastic flower pots. Research and development remained vital at CPG and in its new subsidiaries; Aquapore, for example, recycled automobile tires to make crushed-rubber mats, which were then used in gardens to prevent weed growth, as decorative garden stepping stones, and in rubber lawn edgings. In 1999 Fiskars acquired three additional companies that manufactured lawn and garden products: Richard Sankey & Sons Ltd., which made plastic pots similar to those made by EnviroWorks; American Designer Pottery L.P., which produced large decorative plastic pots; and Syroco Inc., a leading American manufacturer of resin outdoor furniture. As a result of all these acquisitions, the Lawn and Garden Group became the largest business category in the Fiskars CPG division.

The second product group at Fiskars was represented by Inha Works, Ltd., headquartered in Ähtäri, Finland, founded in 1841, and part of Fiskars since 1917. Inha was the leading manufacturer of aluminum boats for professional and leisure use in Northern Europe. The company also forged products and building components—such as hinges for the door and window industry and special-purpose radiators for humid rooms— distributed mainly to the Nordic market. Inha's principal forged products consisted of rail fasteners that were sold mainly to Finnish, Swedish, and Norwegian railways under long-term supply agreements. According to Fiskars' *1998 Annual Report*, Inha's "customer-driven product development, innovative models, and continuous improvement of production processes strengthened the position of the "Buster" [brand name] as the leading outboard boat in Scandinavia."

The Real Estate Group, headquartered in Fiskars, managed the corporation's 15,000 hectares (37,050 acres) of real estate properties and related properties. The land holdings, situated in Southwest Finland, were a valuable corporate asset that included some 100 lakes and 250 kilometers of shoreline. A 1998 agreement with the environmental authorities resulted in the designation of 100 hectares for the protection of the old-growth forest in this area. The major part (11,000 hectares) of the real estate was located in and around Fiskars Village. According to long-term plans, only environment-friendly forestry and farming were allowed; wood had to be harvested in a way that assured a good balance between the requirements of forest regeneration and the needs of the wood-processing industry. In order to preserve the Fiskars village as a lively historical industrial community, revenues from real-estate operations were applied to maintenance of the buildings and surrounding landscape.

Thus Fiskars approached a new millennium as a strong, international company based on providing innovative solutions to the needs of consumers. As its corporate vision statement intimated, the company remained "embedded in the soil of its old ironworks community" as it opened its strong business wings all over the world.

Principal Subsidiaries

Fiskars Oy Ab; Inha Works Ltd.; Ferraria Oy Ab; Fiskars Consumer Oy Ab; Fiskars Sverige AB (Sweden); Fiskars Norge A/S (Norway); Fiskars Danmark A/S (Denmark); Fiskars Deutschland GmbH (German); Fiskars Europe B.V. (Netherlands); Fiskars France S.A.R.L. (50%); Fiskars Montana S.r.l. (Italy); Fiskars Poland Ltd.; Fiskars Hungary Ltd.; Fiskars UK Ltd. (U.K.); Fiskars Canada Inc.; Fiskars de Mexico S.A. de C.V.; Fiskars Inc. (U.S.); Fiskars Pty Limited (Australia); American Designer Pottery, L.P. (U.S.); EnviroWorks, Inc.; Aquapore Moisture Systems, Inc. (U.S.); Richard Sankey & Sons Ltd. (U.K.); Vikingate Ltd. (U.K.); Werga-Tools GmbH (Germany); AO Baltic Tool (Russia).

Principal Operating Units

Consumer Products Group; Inha Works; The Real Estate Group.

Further Reading

"Fiskars: Finland's Gateway to the World," *Focus (Fiskars Corporation's Information Magazine)*, January 1999.
Fiskars 1649: 350 Years of Finnish Industrial History, Pohja, Finland: Fiskars Oyj Abp, 1999, 84 pp.
Newman, Judy, "Finnish Firm Fiskars Grows with Expanded Product Line, Acquisitions," *Wisconsin State Journal*, February 27, 1997.

—Gloria A. Lemieux

Flowserve Corporation

222 West Las Colinas Boulevard
Suite 1500
Irving, Texas 75039
U.S.A.
Telephone: (972) 443-6500
Fax: (972) 443-6800
Web site: http://www.flowserve.com

Public Company
Incorporated: 1997
Employees: 7,000
Sales: $1.06 billion (1999)
Stock Exchanges: New York
Ticker Symbol: FLS
NAIC: 333911 Pump and Pumping Equipment
   Manufacturing

Flowserve Corporation is a global leader in the design, manufacture, marketing, and maintenance of fluid-handling equipment. Formed in 1997 through the merger of Durco International and BW/IP, Inc., Flowserve operates in 29 countries through three distinct divisions. Flowserve sells its flow management equipment—which includes engineered pumps, precision mechanical seals, valves, and a range of services—primarily to the petroleum, chemical, and power industries. The company's growth strategy focuses mainly on acquisitions and alliances, although it faces formidable competitors as the industrial flow management industry undergoes a wave of consolidation. Flowserve's many brands include Durco (pumps), Valtek (valves), and GASPAC (seals).

Durco: 1913–97

Flowserve was created in July 1997 when two rival companies—Durco International and BW/IP, Inc.—merged to form a new corporate entity. At the time it joined forces with BW/IP, Ohio-based Durco International (which was known as the Duriron Company until shortly before the merger) had enjoyed ten years of record growth. Launched in 1913 as a foundry, Duriron had been producing chemical fluid handling equipment for more than 80 years. By the 1980s, the company had built a solid reputation for making the specialized equipment needed to move fluids in the chemical process market.

In the 1990s, Duriron embarked on a massive reorganizing effort. With more than 85 percent of its sales derived from the chemical industry, the company was buffeted by the "peaks and valleys" of that cyclical business, according to the *Plain Dealer*. Seeking to enter new segments of the fluid management industry, Duriron began to forge alliances and acquire companies that operated outside its chemical niche. This strategy proved successful, and by 1995, the chemical industry provided only about half of Duriron's business.

Equally important to Duriron's agenda in the 1990s was its expansion into international markets. Since most American industries were well established, few major chemical, petroleum, or other processors needed to invest significantly in costly new pumps and valves. But in less developed countries (and especially in the Middle East, Latin America, and Asia), the demand for flow management equipment was huge, as entire process industries were being created virtually from scratch. Recognizing that its future hinged on these new markets, Duriron embarked on another spate of acquisitions to gain entry. Duriron's strategy was successful. Between 1985 and 1995, international sales as a portion of the company's total revenue rose from 15 percent to about 33 percent.

Although Duriron's 1996 sales reached $605.5 million (a gain of nearly 13.7 percent from 1995), the company was falling behind in the rapidly consolidating flow management industry, as its competitors grew dramatically larger through mergers and takeovers. Duriron's ability to expand through further acquisitions of its own was particularly limited by its comparative lack of operating capital. To remain a major force in the industry, Durco (as Duriron had rechristened itself in 1997) would need to find new ways to grow.

BW/IP's Growth and Development
in the 1980s and 1990s

Like Durco, BW/IP was a leader in the manufacture of industrial pumps, although its strength was in the production of specialized pumps for the petroleum and power industries. But the petroleum industry—like the chemical process industry Durco served—was cyclical. In addition, because petroleum industry revenues had flattened in the late 1980s and early 1990s, BW/IP's growth had slowed as well. To protect itself from the vagaries of the petroleum industry, therefore, BW/IP sought to enter new markets.

Like Durco, BW/IP sought to use targeted acquisitions to achieve its goals. In 1996, for example, BW/IP acquired the Anchor/Darling Valve Company, which was an American manufacturer of high-specification, custom-engineered valves for the power and marine industries. A few months later, BW/IP purchased Stork Popmen B.V. This Dutch company manufactured pumps for the petroleum industry and offered BW/IP access to lucrative European markets. As a result of these efforts, BW/IP's sales rose nine percent in 1996, to $492 million. Nevertheless, again paralleling Durco, BW/IP was hindered by its lack of capital. Many of its key customers in the petroleum industry were true global companies, who required products and services across the world—a reach that BW/IP simply did not have.

Durco, too, was limited in its efforts to achieve a global presence. As Bernard Rethore, BW/IP's president, chairman, and chief executive officer (CEO), would later explain to the *Wall Street Transcript,* both companies "recognized that to serve our customers in the chemical, petroleum, and power markets on a world basis we needed to have a larger footprint, a greater scope as a company. As BW/IP and Durco, we couldn't do that because each company was too small." In late 1996, executives from the two companies began informal discussion about the potential for joining forces. The advantages of a merger became more apparent after ITT Industries Inc. paid $815 million to acquire Goulds Pumps Inc. in April 1997, thereby becoming the world's largest pump manufacturer. The industry "was consolidating and turning cut throat," an executive at another industrial pump company told *Business Week.* Faced with the prospect of being left hopelessly behind, BW/IP and Durco pledged to merge.

Flowserve Is Born in 1997

The union of the two companies was a merger of equals, effectuated by a stock-for-stock exchange in July 1997. BW/IP's Rethore was selected as the new company's chairman and chief executive, and William Jordan (the president, chairman, and CEO

of Durco) served as the president and chief operating officer (COO) of the new corporate entity. To reflect that the merger had created a new company with a broader range of products and services, BW/IP and Durco elected to take a new name. They settled on Flowserve because it "symbolizes the fact that . . . we will adopt an expanded vision of serving all the flow control needs of our customers in the 21st century," Rethore proclaimed in a press release. After closing BW/IP's headquarters in Long Beach, California, and Durco's in Cleveland, Ohio, Flowserve opened global corporate headquarters in Irving, Texas.

Almost immediately after the merger, Flowserve launched a $92 million integration program that consisted of 45 distinct projects. Although BW/IP and Durco each had carved out areas of focus in the wider flow management industry, there was a considerable degree of overlap. To eliminate these redundancies, Flowserve merged the two companies' pump, valve, and seal businesses into three streamlined divisions—the Rotating Equipment Division, the Flow Control Division, and the Fluid Sealing Division.

The new company also decided to focus on certain core areas, which necessitated shedding extraneous operations. To this end, Flowserve sold its Metal Fab Machine Corp. to Senior Engineering Group PLC for $19 million in November 1997. Moreover, as part of a cost-cutting program, Flowserve shuttered its high-cost pump manufacturing plant in Charleroi, Belgium and transferred production to two factories in The Netherlands. It also opened a valve production factory in 1997 in Bangalore, India, so that it could reduce labor and materials costs.

In addition to honing its existing operations, Flowserve also sought to enter a different—and lucrative—sector of the flow management industry: service and repair. Whereas the pump and valve business was subject to the cyclical downturns of the petroleum and chemical markets, the service and repair of existing equipment was not. In 1997, Flowserve formed the ServiceRepair Division, which focused on tending to the flow management equipment it had already installed. Flowserve would "go beyond just manufacturing," Rethore told the *Wall Street Transcript* and would provide "cradle-to-grave" service on its equipment.

By the close of 1997, the merger looked to be an unequivocal success. Sales for the year surpassed $1.15 billion, with nearly half of the total generated by operations outside the United States. With 44 manufacturing facilities and 88 service and quick response centers, the company was better positioned to provide a broader array of goods and services to a wide range of customers. Flowserve's net profit for 1997 was $51.6 million.

Investors and industry analysts had high expectations for Flowserve in 1998. The company's sales were balanced, with about one-third of total sales derived from the petroleum industry, one-third from the chemical sector, and one-third from power and other industries. As these markets tended to follow different cycles, Flowserve appeared to be less vulnerable to downturns than BW/IP and Durco had been on their own.

Troubles in 1998

In early 1998, however, both the petroleum and chemical markets softened simultaneously, as the Asian economic crisis

Key Dates:

1997: Two flow control companies merge to form a new company—Flowserve.

1998: Flowserve acquires Lokeren NV, ZAR Beheer, BTR Engineering Limited, and Valtek Engineering; company acquires remaining share of ownership of Durametallic Asia.

1999: Flowserve acquires Innovative Valve Technologies Inc.; company announces significant layoffs as part of a restructuring program.

2000: Flowserve announces acquisition of the Ingersoll Pump Unit of Ingersoll-Dressler; company receives contract to provide pumps to the Athabasca Oil Sands Project.

of 1997 spread around the globe. By the end of 1998, oil prices (when adjusted for inflation) were at their lowest level in the United States since the Great Depression of the 1930s. The chemical market was plagued by overcapacity, and prices there also dropped, reaching global all-time lows. As a result, the industries involved in these sectors postponed orders for new equipment.

Despite this untimely confluence of events, the company continued to integrate its operations. In 1998, Flowserve inaugurated its Flowserver initiative, a multiyear program intended to coordinate the myriad businesses within the company. Flowserver was predicted to have a $120 million price tag, with an expected completion date of 2001. The centerpiece of Flowserver was the establishment of an integrated information technology system that would consolidate computing and coordinate planning.

Flowserve also increased its efforts to enter new markets. The company made five important acquisitions in 1998, all of which expanded its global reach. In May, Flowserve purchased the Valtek Engineering Division of Roll-Royce plc. With annual sales of about $20 million, this unit was the British licensee for a number of Valtek control valve products. The acquisition strengthened Flowserve's position in Europe, the Middle East, and Africa. In October, Flowserve bought the remaining 49 percent ownership interest in Durametallic Asia, a fluid sealing manufacturer, from its joint venture partner, the Sanmar Group. In December, Flowserve purchased a mechanical seal business that operated in Australia and New Zealand from an Australian licensee and distributor, BTR Engineering Limited. During the year, Flowserve also acquired ARS Lokeren NV of Belgium and ZAR Beheer BV of The Netherlands. These European valve repair companies bolstered Flowserve's position in the profitable market for repairing flow management equipment.

Flowserve pursued the service end of the market in other ways in 1998 as well. Early in the year, the company consolidated its two most service-oriented divisions—ServiceRepair and Fluid Sealing—into a new division called Flow Solutions. This new unit was to be the centerpiece of Flowserve's drive to capture a greater share of the service market. As the company announced in a press release, "service and repair [will] be a

fundamental part of Flowserve's growth strategy." To improve on its network of service centers, the company built new facilities in locations such as Antwerp, Belgium, and Wilmington, North Carolina. By the end of 1998, Flowserve presided over 85 service centers in 23 countries.

Despite its many activities during 1998, however, Flowserve's sales and profits dropped as a result of the economic conditions afflicting its primary customers. Annual sales fell to $1.08 billion, while net earnings slid to $48.9 million. The company attributed the six percent drop in profits primarily to fallout from Asia's recession. Nevertheless, Rethore emphasized to the *Dayton Daily News* that the company had "dealt effectively with the negative impacts on [its] business of global economic turmoil, dramatically lower oil prices, and weakened chemical markets."

Retrenchment and Growth To Close Out the Century

In 1999 and 2000, Flowserve continued its two-pronged strategy of integrating the sprawling businesses of BW/IP and Durco into a cohesive framework on the one hand and gaining a larger presence in international markets on the other. Flowserve had new leadership to aid it in its mission. President and COO Jordan had left the company in October 1998 and was replaced by C. Scott Greer in July of the following year. Rethore remained chairman and CEO, although he planned to relinquish his duties as chief executive after Greer became more familiar with Flowserve's operations.

In November 1999, Flowserve made an important acquisition when it purchased Houston, Texas-based Innovative Valve Technologies Inc. for $15.7 million and the assumption of $84 million in debt. With 63 operating locations and annual revenues of more than $154 million, Innovative was a leader in maintenance, repair, and replacement services for valves, piping, and other flow management systems. "Through this acquisition, we will significantly expand our technical service and repair capabilities," Greer explained to *Petroleum Finance Week*. In addition to strengthening Flowserve's place in the service sector, the acquisition also positioned the company more strongly in critical emerging markets in the Middle East.

Flowserve also won two major contracts in 1999: one to provide flow management equipment to Suncor Energy's Millennium Project and one for AEC Pipelines' oil sands pipeline expansion. Although the petroleum industry had curtailed a number of projects, oil sands exploration (the extraction of oil from tar sands) continued because of the comparatively low costs involved and the high quality of the crude oil produced. The contracts were worth a total of $10 million.

Despite these considerable advances, Flowserve's 1999 sales were hindered by the continued overall weakness of the petroleum and chemical markets. Sales dropped two percent to $1.06 billion, and profit fell to $12.2 million. Faced with these difficulties, as well as with the continued need to eliminate certain redundancies that had persisted since the merger, Flowserve announced early in 2000 that it would close ten facilities and lay off nine percent of its work force (about 600 people).

Nevertheless, Flowserve continued to view expansion as the key to its future success. With the stated goal of becoming a

$2.5 billion company by 2004, Flowserve made the largest acquisition in its history to that point, when it agreed to buy the Ingersoll-Dressler pump unit of the Ingersoll-Rand Co. in February 2000. Once approved by federal regulators, the $775 million purchase would result in the second largest pump company in the world. "This type of acquisition has such a high level of hard synergies that we'll be able to take out excess capacity in the industry," Greer told the *Dow Jones News Service*. Also in February 2000, Flowserve announced that it had won a contract to provide $20 million worth of pumps for the Athabasca Oil Sands Project. One of its largest pump contracts ever, the deal held great promise for the company.

In light of developments such as these, Rethore was optimistic about Flowserve's future prospects. "As our markets recover, and they will, as we acquire successfully and well, and we will, and as we build further the internal operational excellence of this company, as we will, I believe our increasing success will be rewarded," he told the *Wall Street Transcript*.

Principal Operating Units

Cookeville Valve; Flow Control; Fluid Sealing; Rotating Equipment.

Principal Competitors

IDEX Corporation; Roper Industries, Inc.; ITEQ, Inc.

Further Reading

Bohman, Jim, "Dallas-Based Pump and Valve Maker To Eliminate 600 Jobs," *Dayton Daily News,* December 28, 1999.
——, "1998 Earnings; Flowserve Pins Drop on Industry," *Dayton, Daily News,* February 10, 1999.
Fletcher, Sam, "Flowserve To Take $27 Million Charge as Part of Restructuring Plan," *Oil Daily,* January 5, 2000.
"Flowserve Will Acquire Innovative Valve Technologies," *Petroleum Finance Week,* November 29, 1999.
"More Mergers in Valve Industry," *Water Technology,* June 1, 1997.
Murray, Matt, "Durco and BW/IP To Merge in Deal of $435.6 Million," *Wall Street Journal,* May 5, 1997.
Solov, Diane, "Duriron Co. Making the Most of Strong Markets," *Plain Dealer,* June 26, 1996.
Williams, Christopher, "Flowserve Backs 2001 EPS View 'In Neighborhood of $2,'" *Dow Jones News Service,* February 10, 2000.

—Rebecca Stanfel

Gardenburger, Inc.

Gardenburger, Inc.

1411 SW Morrison Street, Suite 400
Portland, Oregon 97205
U.S.A.
Telephone: (503) 205-1500
Fax: (503) 205-1650
Web site: http://www.gardenburger.com

Public Company
Employees: 320
Sales: $60.1 million (1999)
Stock Exchanges: NASDAQ
Ticker Symbol: GBUR
NAIC: 311412 Frozen Food Specialty Manufacturing;
422219 Other Grocery and Related Products
Wholesalers

Gardenburger, Inc., headquartered in Portland, Oregon, is the largest producer of meat-substitute burger patties in the country. It makes and distributes GardenProducts, ''meat analog'' foods which it wholesales to over 35,000 retail businesses, with markets in the United States, Canada, and Europe. Its chief customers are chain and independent grocers, club stores, restaurants, food-service cafeterias, and natural food stores. Its chain-restaurant customers include Applebee's, Back Yard Burgers, Denny's, Lyon's, Red Robin, Subway, and T.G.I. Friday's. Its club-store customers include Costo, Cost-U-Less, and Sam's Wholesale Club. The company's chief product, its signature Gardenburger, sold in eight flavors, is made from fresh vegetables and grains, soy beans, low-fat cheese and spices. The company also produces other natural, meatless foods, all manufactured at its plant in Clearfield, Utah, which it opened in 1998. Its research facility remains in Portland, its home base, but its production plant was closed there in 1999. In that same year, when Gardenburger's sales dropped to $60.1 million from the $100.1 million high from the previous year, there were speculations about a planned sale of Gardenburger, though company officials denied that any such sale was under consideration.

Wenner Founds Wholesome & Hearty Foods: 1981–85

The history of Gardenburger's meatless burger goes back to 1981, when the company's founder, Paul Wenner, created the first version of it at his Garden House Restaurant in Greshom, Oregon. As he explained in his cookbook, *Garden Cuisine*, Wenner became a dedicated advocate for meatless foods as a result of their beneficial effect on him. He suffered from asthma and tuberculosis in his youth, but his health began improving when he limited his diet to all natural, meatless foods, and initiated a program of vigorous exercise. Thereafter, when he was in his 20s, he started teaching cooking classes in college, focusing on health issues as well as methods of preparing foods. He subsequently opened both his Garden House Restaurant and his own cooking school.

At the Garden House Restaurant, with a fair amount of ingenuity and some leftover rice pilaf, Wenner patted together and grilled the veggie burger that would eventually become the signature product of Gardenburger, Inc., although with its ingredients much changed. Wenner's original version also used mushrooms, rice, onions, oats, and low-fat cheeses.

Despite the success of his burgers, Wenner could not keep his restaurant open. Oregon entered a recession soon after he started in operation, and the economic downturn forced him to close his doors in 1984. However, Wenner continued to make his patties, selling them to a widening circle of local stores. The growing demand for them encouraged him to found his wholesale business, Wholesome & Hearty Foods, Inc., which he incorporated in 1985.

Early Promise Gives Way to Bottom Line Difficulties: 1986–94:

Wenner gradually built his business up, creating other meat analog recipes and adding them to his line of foods. He was tapping into a fat-free, health food market that was rapidly growing as a health-conscious America was becoming increasingly receptive to low fat, low cholesterol foods. His prospective customers included reluctant vegetarians, people who had to give up eating meats not so much by choice as by dangerous

---

Company Perspectives:

Gardenburger, Inc. pursues visionary ideas that helping to sustain the health and integrity of our planet. We are committed to offering delicious and healthy whole-food choices to the world. Our objective is to develop products that are timely, yet futuristic; products that are made with compassion and a caring consciousness for the earth's fragile resources. We believe in the importance of producing only earth-wise products for all present and future generations.

---

cholesterol levels or other dietary concerns. The trick was to create passable look- and taste-alike substitutes for such old American favorites as hamburgers and hot dogs.

In 1986, to help publicize his foods, Wenner re-entered the retail market with a small cafeteria outlet at a natural foods trade convention, but he never again went into the restaurant business. He sought to extend his food line and customer base, which he managed to do with a fair degree of success, and in 1992 was confident enough to take the company public. At that time sales had reached $6.9 million, and the company was realizing a small net profit, but it soon became apparent that in its growth Wholesome & Hearty had hit a plateau. Although revenues were growing, their rate had slowed, and the company's earnings were stagnating. In particular, 1994 was a very disappointing year. The company's stock dropped to under $10 a share, down from as much as $14.50 in the previous year. Moreover, the company had a very low market profile and was simply limping along, generally outside much public notice. It was clear that Wholesome & Hearty needed some fresh thinking.

Expansion, Change, and Calculated Risks under Hubbard: 1995–98

Significant changes made in an effort to improve the company's image and to bolster sales and profits began in 1995, when Lyle Hubbard took the operating reins of the company as CEO. He came over from Quaker Foods, where he had worked for 15 years and had acquired a reputation as an imaginative innovator as head of Quaker's $500 million convenience-food division.

Hubbard was given carte blanche. Although founder Wenner stayed on as the senior chairman and as chief creative officer, a rather unique title, he stepped aside to give full operational control to Hubbard. It was a change that almost immediately brought positive results, for in 1996 revenues grew by ten percent, with sales of $39.63 million.

More of a business risk taker than Wenner, in that same year Hubbard began an expansion move with the acquisition of two companies: Gorilla Foods, Inc. and Whole Food Marketing, Inc. Wholesome & Hearty Foods purchased the former, a Southern California-based distributor of specialty foods, including Wholesome & Hearty Foods' products, for $350,000 in cash. Gorilla Foods was a manufacturer and distributer of wheat protein-based meatless foods, including a frankfurter called the GardenDog. Hubbard acquired it for 240,000 restricted shares of Wholesome & Hearty's common stock and $68,750 in cash.

At the time, the common stock, trading at $6.875 per share, was worth $1.65 million, but it was to be held in escrow before being distributed to Gorilla's stock holders if the sale of its gluten products met negotiated threshold targets.

The expansion was almost immediately complimented by moves to improve the company's efficiency. To reduce costs and boost sales, Hubbard and his staff decided to stop manufacturing a few products with a sluggish sales record, notably the company's breakfast sausage and faux hot dogs. These were dropped from its line in 1997. Steps were then taken to improve the sales volume of remaining line of foods.

The first was a move to refurbish the company's image. Hubbard oversaw the company's name change to Gardenburger in October 1997, a change designed to enhance the company's marketing profile. It brought no objections from stock holders, who saw the impact potential of the new name, one that could stick in customers' minds. It was a vital first step in achieving Hubbard's primary goal, to turn Gardenburger's signature burger into a household name, accepted not only as a health item but as a regular staple.

The second step was to launch a major advertising campaign, one that started with print but moved onto radio and television, most notably with a spot on the much-ballyhooed, final episode of *Seinfeld*, the very popular situation comedy, which aired in May 1998. The campaign was first designed and managed by a team at Hal Riney & Partners, a San Francisco firm with a very good reputation for producing creative ads that greatly improved brand-name recognition. The campaign involved putting $17 million into Gardenburger's 1998 advertising budget, an increase of 300 percent over the previous year. It was clearly a monumental risk for a company that in that in that previous year had only logged $56.8 million in sales. At a cost of $1.5 million, the *Seinfeld* spot alone ate up almost ten percent of that inflated budget. It seemed a justified expense, however, for sales immediately picked up, and by the end of its 1998 fiscal year, Gardenburger's volume of sales climbed to over $100 million, almost doubling. The campaign's success led Gardenburger to change its advertising account to Rubin Postaer & Associates after the three principal members of the original Riney team went to work for that firm.

By the end of 1998, the company had become the nation's leading wholesaler of vegetarian burgers, holding a 41 percent share of the marker in the frozen, meat-analog burger category, rated as a $132 million business. The company's chief competitor, Worthington Foods, a larger company with a more varied line of products, trailed behind Gardenburger at a 30 percent market share. The increased sales were very encouraging, and, among other things, prompted the company to add five new products to its growing line.

Gardenburger had to contend with some niggling problems, however. From 1996 to early 1999, the company faced some PR and marketing difficulties when it was subjected to a nationwide boycott instituted by PCUN (*Pineros y Campesinos Unidos del Noroeste*), Oregon's farm workers' union. In 1992, PCUN had begun a boycott of all NORPAC products, including FLAV-R-PAC and Westpac frozen fruits and vegetables, because of

Key Dates:

Key Dates:

1981: Paul Wenner creates his vegetarian burger at his Garden House Restaurant.
1984: Wenner closes his restaurant but continues selling veggie burgers to other outlets.
1985: Wenner founds Wholesome & Hearty Foods to wholesale vegetarian food.
1986: Wholesome & Hearty enters retail market at a natural foods trade convention.
1992: The company goes public.
1996: Wholesome acquires Gorilla Foods, Inc. and Whole Food Marketing, Inc.
1997: Company changes name to Gardenburger.
1998: Gardenburger becomes the nation's leading wholesaler of vegetarian hamburgers; begins production at new plant in Utah.
1999: Company closes its plant in Portland.

NORPAC's reputed and documented ill treatment of farm laborers. Since Gardenburger had been buying and continued to buy farm produce from NORPAC, in 1996 PCUN added Gardenburger's own products to its boycott list. Facing mounting pressure from advocacy groups that had taken up PCUN's cause, after three years Gardenburger was finally forced to terminate its contractual arrangements with NORPAC. It did so on April 23, 1999, and PCUN immediately suspended its boycott of the company's products.

More importantly, despite the great increase in sales in 1998, the company continued to suffer bottom line problems. These began in 1997. Although Gardenburger's sales volume in that year rose to $56.84 million, an increase of almost 45 percent over the previous year, its increased operating expenses produced a net loss of $2.06 million. In 1998, when, driven by the ad campaign, sales increased by almost 76 percent, the net loss ballooned to $14.35 million. Growing sales simply could not compensate for increasing costs, not in the short run at least. Hope still ran high for the long run, however, especially in light of the tremendous increase in volume in 1998.

Bottom Line Realities Leave Future Uncertain: 1999–2000

Yet the situation even worsened in 1999, when, alarmingly, sales dropped back down by 40 percent, to $60.11 million, and operating losses, more than doubling, rose close to $30 million. That was bad news in a year in which the company had taken measures to ensure that it could meet the projected sales volumes based on the figures from 1998. Its most important expansion step was to move its production base to a new facility in

Clearfield, Utah, a 120,000 square foot plant three times the size and product capacity of its old plant in Portland.

When it became obvious that the projected sales volume increase was not going to materialize, the company closed its old plant, leaving only its headquarters and research facility in Portland. It also began cutting back on some of its more aggressive expansion plans and marketing strategies.

By the second quarter of 1999, Gardenburger's net loss had already grown to $10.5 million. At that time, in July, Hubbard commented, ''We are changing our business model on a go-forward basis to emphasize near-term profitability over aggressive market growth.''

In September 1999, from change-of-control policy agreements filed with the Securities Exchange Commission (SEC), it appeared that Gardenburger might go on the auction block, but by the close of the year it had not been sold. At the time of the filing, Gardenburger's CFO Richard Dietz claimed that the company was not being prepared for sale, but, when asked, he also refused to divulge whether the company was pursuing a merger with another company. That led to speculation and rumor about Gardenburger's fate. Even so, the company had reason to hope that its future prospects might improve, thanks to such things as the FDA's October 1999 approval of claims that soy protein foods reduce the risk of coronary disease and the growing concern with obesity as a national and even a global problem, an issue widely publicized in the media in the early months of 2000.

Principal Competitors

Worthington Foods, Inc.; ConAgra, Inc.; Galaxy Foods Company; The Hain Food Group, Inc.; White Wave, Inc.

Further Reading

Dwyer, Steve, ''A Lean, Mean Meatless Machine,'' *Prepared Foods*, October 1998, p. 12.
''Gardenburger Cuts Ties to NORPAC,'' *Pineros y Campesinos Unidos del Noroeste* (Northwest Treeplanters and Farmworkers United), http://www.pcun.org/HTMLs/gbvictory.html.
Hill, Jim, '' 'Seinfeld' Finale Will Serve as Gardenburger's Entree,'' *Oregonian*, March 3, 1998.
Love, Jacqueline, ''Gardenburger's Coming Out Party,'' *Oregonian*, May 10, 1998.
Pollack, Judann, ''Gardenburger: Lyle Hubbard,'' *Advertising Age*, June 28, 1999, p. S2.
Rose, Michael, ''Gardenburger, Inc. Goes after Hamburger Lovers,'' *Business Journal-Portland*, October 24, 1997, p. 8.
——, ''Is Sale Next for Burger Boys?,'' *Business Journal-Portland*, September 10, 1999, p. 1.
Wenner, Paul, *Garden Cuisine*, New York: Simon & Shuster, 1997, 368 p.

—John W. Fiero

Golden State Vintners, Inc.

500 Drake's Landing Road
Greenbrae, California 94904
U.S.A.
Telephone: (415) 461-4400
Fax: (415) 461-4497

Public Company
Incorporated: 1934
Employees: 180
Sales: $107.8 million (1999)
Stock Exchanges: NASDAQ
Ticker Symbol: VINT
NAIC: 31213 Wineries; 31214 Distilleries

Located in northern California, Golden State Vintners, Inc. is one of the most successful makers of premium bulk wine products in the United States. The company, which began as a small vineyard in Cutler, California, in the mid-1930s, is involved in every aspect of the wine production industry, from the storage and fermentation process of various types of grapes to the marketing of its own private labels. Golden State receives the majority of its revenue from supplying well known labels with premium bulk wine, but the company is also the second largest producer of brandy in the United States, with brandy and grape sales comprising about 30 percent of Golden State's annual sales. The company, which has only been prominent nationally since the mid-1990s, includes among its customers such wineries as Gallo, Sutter Home, Sebastiani, and Heublein, and holds almost 10,000 acres of vineyard properties throughout central and northern California.

Golden State's Beginnings: A Small Winery in the 1930s

Golden State was founded by a businessman and eoniphile named Arpaxat "Sox" Setrakian in 1934. At that time, the wine industry was in its infancy in California, and consisted primarily of small, family-owned vineyards which produced a limited amount and type of grape. Having little chance of competing against the centuries old reputation and tradition of French and Italian wines, the inchoate California wine industry offered to American consumers what imported products could not: a good value.

The northern California climate proved to be particularly suitable for reliable harvesting of certain types of grape, especially the sort used in red wines, and within a couple of decades the industry took off, soon earning a reputation for its production of low-priced "jug" wines. Setrakian's Cutler vineyard, located in Tulare County in northern California, followed the trend of most regional wineries: it was small, consisting of only 120 acres, and until the 1980s remained a family-owned business which catered primarily to local consumers.

During the 1960s and 1970s, box, or jug, wines became increasingly popular, and the California wine industry firmly established itself as a leader among lower priced labels. Along with increased popularity among consumers, however, came increased competition, and companies like Gallo and Sutter Home began to gain ascendancy over small, regional vineyards. Though many of the smaller labels were bought out, Setrakian's company remained independent.

The late 1970s, however, brought a change to the industry which threatened both Golden State and the industry as a whole. As premium imported wine sales began to rise in the United States, domestic bulk wine revenue floundered, forcing California vineyards to revamp both their image and sales strategies.

1981–94: A Company Transformed

In 1981 Setrakian's grandson Jeffrey O'Neil joined Golden State, bringing to the ailing company some much needed energy and drive. After encouraging outside investors to fund the company's restructuring, O'Neil and his partners embarked on an aggressive campaign to transform Golden State from a small vineyard to a supplier of bulk wines of premium quality. Such a transition required not only a change in management, but increased vineyard acreage and fermentation facilities as well, and with the help of its investors Golden State began expanding its harvestable land.

As wine consumption and expertise became more and more fashionable in the 1980s, consumer taste changed drastically, becoming both more sophisticated in wine selection and more demanding over price. This shift in consumer preference offered Golden State an opportunity to mass-produce premium grapes at prices which, because of the quantity harvested, could be offered to customers on a wholesale level. In 1985 the company received its first real break on the wholesale end, when Gallo Wines contracted Golden State to provide several tons of bulk premium grape. The contract extended over a period of several years, and soon Golden State began earning a reputation within the wine industry for reliable wholesale production of high quality grape at a reasonable cost.

During this time Golden State began to look for ways in which to expand its role within the changing California wine market. Besides focusing on its wholesale sales, the company also began offering to large vineyards such services as storage and shipping, and in so doing performed necessary functions for companies which were increasingly undergoing rapid growth and consolidation. By evolving into a company more involved in the service and supply end of the wine market, Golden State was able to fill a unique role in the industry, and became partners with large companies which otherwise would have been competitors.

By 1987 large California vineyards had made a decided shift away from the type of inexpensive jug wines on which the industry had originally established itself. Because the companies did not have to pay import costs, California wineries were able to market wines of a quality equal to some higher priced European labels for substantially lower prices. The market's new, more sophisticated image payed off, and by the early 1990s the industry as a whole was generating sales into the billions of dollars.

The Expansion of Golden State: Mid-1990s to 1999

In the early 1990s Golden State began an ambitious campaign of expansion which would allow for the company's involvement in every segment of the winemaking industry. In just over three years, the company acquired five vineyards and winemaking facilities, bringing its production capacity to 9,600 acres of workable land.

Golden State's first major acquisition occurred in May 1994, when the company purchased Napa Valley Winery, a company which produced its own private label wine and operated a small bottling facility. A year later, in May 1995, Golden State acquired Lost Hills Vineyard, a winery which produced a variety of mainly premium quality grapes. That same month, the company bought what was to become one of its most important assets, the Reedley Facility. The Reedley Facility, located in central California, was Golden State's first entrance into brandy production, a small and for the most part untapped niche in the domestic wine industry.

In December 1996 Golden State continued its acquisition strategy, purchasing the Monterey Winery, a facility intended primarily for the processing and fermentation of grapes. Six months later, the company bought the Napa Warehouse, a large facility which allowed the company to greatly increase its barrel storage capacity. After this brief but intense period of expansion, Golden State was in a position to become one of the top wine suppliers and producers in the country. The company had increased its vineyards to 9,600 acres; it was also now capable of many more times the amount of storage and winemaking processes than it had been at the beginning of the decade; and, most importantly, by growing so drastically in size the company could serve the largest wineries in the industry. From growing various types and qualities of grape to storage and shipping, Golden State was by the middle of the decade a distinct presence in the industry.

Though the company continued to receive the majority of its income by acting as a supplier of premium bulk wine, Golden State also continued to develop its own private labels, which it marketed nationwide to grocery stores and chain stores such as Trader Joe's. Golden State's own brands specialized primarily in the production of Chardonnay wines, and the company's trademarks included such labels as Edgewood Estate, Summerfield, Summerfield Reserve, Monthaven, Cutler Creek, and Golden State Vintners, among others. The company's private labels were, with the exception of Monthaven and Summerfield Reserve, generally categorized as lower-priced premium wines—wines which sell for less than $10 a bottle but are made with high-quality grapes—and helped the company gain recognition among the broader consumer market.

After Golden State's expansion in the mid-1990s the company began to attract some of the most powerful players in the industry. Gallo remained one of the company's most important customers, and by 1997 the company had added such wineries as Sutter Home, Canandaigua, Sebastiani, and Vincor to its list of clientele. To these companies Golden State primarily provided wholesale wines; the company also, however, developed winemaking supply service relationships with such companies as Robert Mondavi, Beringer, and the Wine Group. By offering such an expansive array of services in wholesale wine production and storage, Golden State was able to remain flexible to any given client's needs, as well as be involved during any or all of a winery's production process.

By the middle of the decade Golden State had successfully defined itself as a company which worked ''behind the scenes'' of the domestic wine market: instead of focusing on its own brand and label recognition, the company operated support services for the biggest names in the business. When the company began its growth campaign at the end of the previous decade, its primary strategy was to become a bulk wine supplier. By 1997,

Key Dates:

1934: Arpaxat "Sox" Setrakian founds the original Golden State Vineyard in Tulare County, California.
1981: Jeffrey O'Neil, Setrakian's son, joins the company.
1985: Gallo becomes Golden State's first major customer for bulk premium wine.
1994: Golden State begins an aggressive acquisition campaign.
1998: Golden State goes public.

over 50 percent of Golden State's revenue came from its role as a premium supplier; the rest of the company's sales were accounted for in brandy production, grape sales, storage and case goods production, and the sale of its own labels. Although the company's brandy sales made up only about 12 percent of the company's revenue, Golden State by decade's end was the nation's second largest domestic producer of brandy.

Within two decades the California wine industry had undergone drastic changes, growing at an unprecedented rate. In 1987, about $932 million worth of California premium wine was sold. Ten years later, in 1997, about $3.8 billion worth of premium wine was bought by consumers. That year, higher quality wines accounted for almost 80 percent of the California wine market, with sales increasing throughout the previous decade at approximately 15 percent annually. Needless to say, the growth of both premium wines and the industry itself was beneficial, if not necessary, for Golden State, which relied on both quantity and quality for its financial well-being.

As wine consumption became more popular in the 1990s, particularly among the "baby-boomer" generation, competition became increasingly intense. It was not only domestic wineries which were competing in the low-end premium market: throughout the decade, South American wineries began to carve out a name for themselves through their high quality and low prices. With a climate conducive to efficient grape production and labor available at very little cost, South American vineyards proved to be tough competition to the California wine market, and forced companies like Golden State to keep their production costs down and their grape prices low.

By 1997 there were about 800 wineries in California. Out of that number, seven wineries made up for just over 75 percent of California's wine sales. With growing competition among domestic and international wineries the top California companies began to focus more than ever on advertising and high profile marketing campaigns. As such companies put more and more revenue into advertising, outsourcing became a lucrative and logical alternative to vineyard expansion. Golden State, along with only a small handful of other companies, was uniquely designed to answer such needs.

In 1998 Golden State, after being underwritten by J.P. Morgan and Goldman, Sachs, Hambrecht & Quist, went public on July 21. The company sold 2.15 million shares in its initial public offering (IPO), at a price of $17 each, which was slightly above what the company had originally predicted. Going public was a gamble for Golden State: there was no other bulk wine supplier being publicly traded, and the company's two main regional competitors, Delicato Family Vineyards and Bronco Wine Company, remained private.

At the end of the 1990s Golden State had not only penetrated the national wine market; the company had also begun exporting its products to European vineyards, and was by 1998 California's largest exporter of premium bulk wines. Golden State's own labels were gaining recognition as well, with three of the top selling "best-value" Chardonnays (bottles under $10) belonging to Golden State's vineyards. Though the company's stock had dipped a bit after its IPO, Golden State at decade's end had revenue of $112 million and was holding steady in growth and profitability.

Principal Competitors

Delicato Family Vineyards; Bronco Wine Company; The Wine Group.

Further Reading

Dutta, Mahua, "From the Valley to the Street," *IPO Reporter*, June 8, 1998.
Gannon, Michael, "Golden State Vintners," *Venture Capital Journal*, September 1, 1998.
"Golden State Vintners Announces Initial Public Offering," *Business Wire*, July 22, 1998.
"Golden State Vintners Reports First Quarter Fiscal Year 2000 Results," *Business Wire*, November 10, 1999.
Moore, Brenda, "Golden State Vintners Could Be Hot Seller As Wine Supply Tightens," *Wall Street Journal*, January 20, 1999, p. CA2.

—Rachel H. Martin

Groupe Lapeyre S.A.

2, rue Andre Karman
93300 Aubervilliers
France
Telephone: (+33) 1 48 11 74 00
Fax: (+33) 1 43 52 64 46
Web site: http://www.lapeyre-sa.fr

Public Subsidiary of Poliet S.A.
Incorporated: 1931 as SARL Lapeyre & ses Fils
Employees: 400
Sales: FFr 6.46 billion ($1.07 billion) (1998)
Stock Exchanges: Paris
Ticker Symbol: LAPGF
NAIC: 44411 Home Stores; 42139 Other Construction
 Material Wholesalers

Groupe Lapeyre S.A. is a leading European manufacturer and retailer of doors, windows, and other joinery products to the DIY consumer market and professional craftsman and construction industries. Since the late 1990s, Lapeyre also has added a service component, offering sales help and installation of products, as well as kitchens, staircases, and other products manufactured by its network of subsidiaries. Lapeyre's business has focused traditionally on its home French market, where it operates a nationwide chain of more than 75 Lapeyre warehouse stores, as well as a growing number of catalog-based sales outlets. Lapeyre-brand retail sales account for more than half of the company's FFr 6.5 billion in annual sales. The company also operates the GME-brand chain of bathroom and tile specialty warehouse stores. There are more than 50 GME stores, which generally operate alongside Lapeyre warehouse stores. In addition to offering services through the Lapeyre and GME retail chains, Lapeyre launched the K par K chain, targeting the consumer replacement window market. Featuring case-by-case consultation, sales, and installation services, the K par K chain, launched in the mid-1990s, has grown to a nationwide network of nearly 125 stores and sales agencies. On the manufacturing side, Lapeyre operates 12 plants in France, six plants in Germany, three facilities in Poland, and one in Belgium. In addition

to supplying the Lapeyre and GME stores, the company also markets to the professional building materials supply and construction markets under the OXXO and Les Zelles brand names. While continuing its expansion in France, Lapeyre has targeted European expansion for its continued growth, especially the German, Belgium, Swiss, and Spanish markets. Listed on the Paris Stock Exchange since 1992, Lapeyre has been a subsidiary of Poliet (itself a subsidiary of the French industrial giant Compagnie de Saint Gobain) since the mid-1970s.

Building a Demolition Business in the 19th Century

Groupe Lapeyre takes its name from its founding family. Natives of the Auvergne region, where the family was involved in the scrap iron business, the Lapeyres followed their fortunes to Paris. Family patriarch Pierre Lapeyre arrived in Paris in the 1850s, recuperating and reselling scrap iron. The demolition of a factory in Nevers gave Pierre Lapeyre the opportunity he needed. Lapeyre negotiated the contract for the factory's scrap metals, which he then sold in Paris for a profit. From there Lapeyre became one of the capital city's leading demolition and recuperation specialists at a time when, under the leadership of Napoleon III and Baron Haussmann, Paris was undergoing the transformation that brought the city into the modern era. Haussmann's plans called for the demolition of entire neighborhoods within the city. With Haussmann's backing, Lapeyre won more and more of these demolition contracts.

In the 1880s, Pierre Lapeyre's nephew, Jean-Baptiste, then aged 13, came to Paris and joined his uncle's business. By the age of 22, Jean-Baptiste had taken a leading role in the business, leading it into new areas, such as the recuperation and sale of marble, and from there to stone and marble chimneys. By the turn of the century, Lapeyre also had begun manufacturing iron gates. Lapeyre's oldest son, Martial Lapeyre, joined his father's business in 1926, at the age of 22. With an engineering degree from the Ecole de Travaux Publics in Paris, Martial Lapeyre became the architect of the Lapeyre company's modern success.

Martial Lapeyre was given the leadership of the family business in 1931, when the company formally adopted the name of Lapeyre et ses Fils. Much of the company's business in-

Company Perspectives:

International development is imperative and we are striving to achieve that goal. Although the Lapeyre Group ranked Number 1 in its sector in Europe, we were only strongly established in France. Now our objective is to adapt our retail networks in Spain, Belgium and Switzerland, and to federate the joinery product companies acquired in Germany and Poland, while leveraging shared expertise and skills. We are constantly looking for opportunities to develop marketing structures for retailing and for providing services to end users, while taking into account different situations and cultural diversity. In conclusion, Lapeyre Group has strong potential for growth in France and, thanks to its expanded scope, new prospects for business in other European countries. These factors will underpin sustained, profitable growth in future years.

volved the sale of antique doorways, gates, chimneys, and other joinery items recovered from demolition sites. Recognizing the strong demand for these antique styles, Martial Lapeyre turned the company to manufacturing new joinery products based on these antique designs. Lapeyre's products quickly found a strong market among Parisian craftsmen and consumers, who were happy to have the choice of these newly manufactured products to match the styles and dimensions of their homes. In this way, Lapeyre helped initiate the modern French home improvement and renovation market. One factor in the company's success was Lapeyre's decision to print up catalogs detailing his products. The first catalog was produced in 1932 and distributed free to customers. In 1931, the company had posted annual sales of 800,000 francs; by the end of that decade, the company's sales had grown to more than three million francs.

The Second World War and the German occupation put a temporary halt to Lapeyre's business. With the Liberation in 1945, however, Martial Lapeyre, who had returned to the Auvergne to avoid being drafted into the German forced labor program, returned to Paris and restarted the Lapeyre company's operations. The need to rebuild much of northern France and the resulting economic boom years saw Lapeyre become one of the Paris region's primary suppliers to the home improvement and renovation markets.

Building a National Network in the 1970s

In 1949 Lapeyre changed its corporate status and took on the name of Lapeyre et Cie. Martial Lapeyre also brought the company into the retail sphere. By then Lapeyre not only manufactured its own products, but also had begun contracting products from a growing network of manufacturers. Lapeyre opened the first of its "depots" on the rue de l'Abbé Groult in Paris's 15th arrondissement and operated as a cash and carry business, a novel feature at the time. Craftsmen and consumers were able to come to the depot, make their purchases, and leave with the products from the depot's stock without delay. As manufacturer of many of its products, Lapeyre was able in this way to save on distribution costs. The company passed these savings on to its customers,

in the form of highly competitive prices. These, in turn, were nonnegotiable, another new concept for the time.

More of a marketplace than a retail store, the first Lapeyre depot marked a grand success for the company. By the end of the 1950s, the company had grown to some 30 employees—still led by Martial Lapeyre—and had begun to take on the structure of a mature business, adding purchasing and marketing departments. In 1960 the company also began to expand, opening a second, larger depot store in Aubervilles, just outside of Paris. Lapeyre was expanding its manufacturing operations as well, buying up those of the Société Anonyme des Menuiseries du Centre, while also negotiating an exclusive contract with long-time supplier and friend Marcel Pasturel. Although Lapeyre continued to expand its own manufacturing capacity, such partnerships were essential to its growth during the 1960s, as Lapeyre expanded its product lines and materials offerings through contracts with such partners as Etablissements Roy and Etablissements Poreaux, both of which became exclusive suppliers to Lapeyre in the 1960s. In turn, Lapeyre invested heavily in its partners' operations, providing funds, materials, and facilities to expand production capacity. In many cases, Lapeyre's partners became Lapeyre subsidiaries, as was the case with Pasturel and Poreaux in the late 1970s.

At the same time that it expanded its retail distribution and manufacturing capacity, Lapeyre also began a mail order service. As customers in the French provinces sought the company's highly competitive prices, the company's mail order services were first operated informally out of its Abbé-Groult depot. By the late 1960s, the company decided to decentralize the mail order business, opening a facility in Châteauroux, in central France, marking the company's first foray beyond the Paris region.

Dubbed Lapeyre Correspondance, the service quickly revealed itself not only as expensive, but also as unable to match the growing demand. Lapeyre soon looked instead toward building a network of retail depots modeled on its original Parisian locations. Rather than operate its own stores, however, Lapeyre adopted an approach similar to a franchise concept. In 1967, the first two provincial Lapeyre depots opened, in Gamaches in the north and in Nimes in the south. Lapeyre owned the actual buildings and provided the store stock and signage, but the actual operation of each store was placed entirely in the hands of its manager, who was paid on commission. In this way, the Lapeyre depots functioned as independent businesses, yet joined together as a centralized network. By the mid-1970s, the company had added nine provincial Lapeyre depots. The company's operations included five factories and produced sales of FFr 115 million per year.

International Growth in the 1990s

In 1975, Martial Lapeyre, aged 71 years with no children, sold Lapeyre to French construction materials market leader Poliet. The sale, of 80 percent of Lapeyre for FFr 55 million, helped to secure Lapeyre's future and also complemented Poliet's own product range, which in large part had ignored the joinery sector. Martial Lapeyre turned over direction of the company he had built, yet remained actively involved in its operations until his death in 1984.

Key Dates:

1904: Birth of Martial Lapeyre.
1931: Formation of SARL Lapeyre & ses Fils.
1932: First Lapeyre catalog produced.
1942: Cessation of operations during German occupation.
1945: Production and sales restarted.
1949: Incorporated as Lapeyre et Cie. S.A.; first "depot" store opened in Paris.
1960: Second Paris store opened.
1967: Opening of first two stores outside of Paris.
1975: Acquisition by Poliet S.A.
1989: Opening of Barcelona store; launch of K par K subsidiary.
1991: Opening of stores in Switzerland and Italy.
1992: Public offering on Paris Stock Exchange.
1993: Restructuring of international operations.
1996: Exit from Italian market.

Under Poliet, Lapeyre greatly expanded its production capacity, buying up many of its longtime suppliers, while investing heavily in modernizing its facilities. In addition to adding computer-aided design and computer-aided manufacturing capabilities, Lapeyre adopted modern inventory and purchasing techniques, while streamlining its manufacturing. Meanwhile, the company's provincial expansion continued, with the number of depots growing to 18 by 1983. Beginning in 1984, however, the company determined to step up its expansion, devoting some two-thirds of its investments to new store openings. Seven more retail stores were added in that year. By then, also, the company had made its first international expansion, opening a store in Lieges, Belgium.

During the 1980s, Lapeyre, which continued to produce and distribute its ever-growing catalog, also began to invest in advertising for the first time. In addition to a print campaign, the company, as a manufacturer as well as retailer, was able to launch a successful television advertising campaign (French legislation barred retailers from television advertising). At the same time, Lapeyre expanded its retail operations, acquiring French retail bathroom and tiling specialist GME in 1982. With this purchase, the company's new store openings took on an expanded concept, featuring a GME retail center side by side with a Lapeyre store. By the mid-1990s, the company operations included more than 30 such double-signage locations.

The GME purchase marked the first of a number of acquisitions that transformed Lapeyre into Groupe Lapeyre. In 1987 Lapeyre added construction materials and PVC distribution specialists GIMM and SAFERM, later reformed as OXXO and Les Zelles. The addition of these two companies gave Lapeyre the lead in the French PVC-based joinery products manufacturing market. In that same year, Lapeyre also began to diversify into the services sector, with the opening of its first K par K ("case by case") replacement window center.

The Liege store remained the company's sole foray into the international market for most of the 1980s. In 1989 the company began to extend deeper into Belgium, opening stores in Brussels and in Antwerp. At the same time, the company determined to move into the Spanish market, in particular to take advantage of the coming Olympic Games in Barcelona in 1992. After opening in that city, the company added four more Spanish stores, enjoying success—up until the end of the Olympics, at which time the company's Spanish sales all but collapsed. Meanwhile, Lapeyre was having difficulties in Switzerland and Italy as well, where it had opened new stores in the beginning of the 1990s. Then Lapeyre's Belgian operations also failed to provide the desired success.

Lapeyre, which went public in 1992, yet remained more than 72 percent owned by Poliet, was forced to reconsider its international operations. The company quickly came to the conclusion that its attempt to reproduce its French success formula did not take into account the cultural particularities of its neighbor markets, and efforts were made to revamp its product lines and relaunch its international growth. Taking the decision to exit the Italian market, Lapeyre remained committed to the Spanish, Belgian, and Swiss markets. By the mid-1990s, the company's international operations were posting growth once again in both sales and profits.

The company's French market, however, remained its primary source of sales. For the beginning of the new century, Lapeyre began developing a third prong to its French business, adding a services component, including installation and other services. In the late 1990s, however, Lapeyre began to target international expansion for its future growth. The company began to make acquisitions of manufacturing operations, notably in Germany, where it acquired six wood and PVC factories in 1998, and in Poland, where it acquired that country's leading PVC window manufacturer Erg-Okfens, in January 1999. These acquisitions, as well as that of Sofiplas of Belgium, were expected to help the company boost its international sales from just 14 percent of total sales—which topped FFr 8 billion for the 1999 year—to more than 30 percent of sales in the early years of the 21st century.

Principal Subsidiaries

Lapeyre; GME; K par K; O'Carré; SGM; GIMM; OXXO; Les Zelles; Lapeyre International; Reckendrees (Germany); Bernsdorfer Bauelemente (Germany); Becher (Germany); Dahm (Germany); Kühn (Germany); Erg-Profil Ltd. (Poland); Okfens sp. Z.o.o (Poland); Sofiplas (Belgium).

Principal Competitors

Berisford International plc; Boral Ltd.; Royal Group Technologies; Groupe Castorama-Dubois Investissements; Mr. Bricolage.

Further Reading

Gay, Pierre-Angel, "En 1999, Lapeyre devrait pesait 1.22 milliard d'euros," *Les Echos,* April 13, 1999, p. 21.
Lapeyre: La passion d'entreprendre, Paris: Albin Michel, 1995.
"Lapeyre met l'accent à l'international," *Le Figaro,* April 13, 1999.

—M.L. Cohen

Havas SA

31, rue du Colisée
75383 Paris Cedex 08
France
Telephone: (33) 1 53 53 30 00
Fax: (33) 1 53 53 37 37
Web site: http://www.havas.fr

Wholly Owned Subsidiary of Vivendi SA
Incorporated: 1835 as Agence Havas
Employees: 18,600
Sales: FFr 18.9 billion ($2.74 billion) (1998)
NAIC: 51111 Newspaper Publishers; 51112 Periodical
    Publishers; 51113 Books Publishers; 54181
    Advertising Agencies

Havas SA, a wholly owned subsidiary of utilities and telecommunications giant Vivendi SA, is the largest publishing firm in France and a global media and communications company. Through an extensive network of subsidiaries, Havas publishes professional, reference, education, and consumer books in France, Italy, Spain, Latin America, and the United Kingdom. Havas also produces about 80 press titles, including professional, business, and general interest works, in Europe. Eager to strengthen operations in multimedia and electronic publishing, the company established Havas Interactive, a leading developer of education, entertainment, and information software with headquarters in the United States. Havas also organizes trade fairs and expositions. Havas has a 20 percent stake in Havas Advertising, one of the largest advertising networks in the world. About a third of the company's revenues are generated in France, but Havas plans to increase its international presence.

Roots in News Reporting: 1800s

The history of Havas may be traced to its founder, Charles Havas, a former supply officer in Nantes who, from a very early age, recognized the importance of information as a commodity. While working as a banker and importer in the international cotton trade, Havas gained exposure to the governmental business of translating foreign newspapers, becoming co-proprietor of the newspaper *Gazette de France* from 1813 to 1815. When Louis-Philippe proclaimed freedom of the press in 1830, Havas was convinced that the traffic of news could be organized and made public.

In 1832, Havas founded Bureau Havas in Paris to supply the rapidly growing number of French newspapers with translations of foreign publications. In 1835, he added the service of translating French publications for foreign newspapers, and the bureau was renamed Agence Havas, an international press agency. From the onset, the agency recognized the importance of being the quickest to supply news to the press and was constantly exploring new methods of transporting information, from carrier pigeons to the electric telegraph. Moreover, Havas founded his company with a belief in cooperating with the government to gain financial support, avoid conflicts, and have exclusive access to governmental information. This status as official government supplier of news both facilitated the company's enormous success over the following 150 years and caused much corruption, exploitation, and public mistrust of the media until the end of World War II.

In 1851, in addition to operating a successful press agency, Havas founded the first publicity agency in France. Despite the limits imposed upon the press under the Second Empire, Havas prospered during the great commercial and industrial expansion of the era. The company's success and power stemmed from the faith that the French government, business community, and press had in its services, as well as from its expansion into newspaper circulation, improvements in the telegraph, and the increasing importance of public opinion. When Charles Havas died in 1858, his sons assumed control of the business and inherited their father's belief in the need to be a loyal instrument of the state to retain the agency's monopoly on information. In 1862, Auguste Havas finalized an agreement with the Minister of the Interior to make Havas the exclusive diffuser of official news.

During this time, Paul-Julius Reuter, a former employee of Havas, opened a press agency in London, and another former Havas worker, Bernhard Wolf, opened a similar office in Berlin. By 1856, Havas, Reuter, and Wolf had signed an accord to exchange information and cooperate to exploit future markets, while still retaining monopolies in their respective regions.

Company Perspectives:

Our store of knowledge is growing every day. And at Havas we are committed to sharing it, giving people the keys they need for discovery, understanding, self-improvement and entertaining. We make knowledge available to an increasing number of people around the world, in every possible way, through all media—constantly striving to improve its quality. French author La Bruyère stated, "One writes only to be understood," then added: "but in writing, you must be sure that what is understood is appealing." The success of Havas is and will remain founded on the appeal that our group's many talents create.

Following attempts by German statesman Otto von Bismarck to retain control of the German-language press, Havas, Reuter, and Wolf signed a new agreement in 1869, establishing new geographic domains for each agency. Wolf controlled Austria, Scandinavia, and Russia, and Reuter covered England, Holland, and their dependencies. France, Italy, Spain, and Portugal became the domain of Havas. Reuter expanded into Australia, Egypt, the Antilles, and the Far East, while Havas established itself in South America and Indochina. Since 1867 when the transatlantic telegraph cable linked London and New York, the United States was declared neutral, with each agency establishing relationships with clients and collecting news independently. Each agency signed a separate accord with the American Associated Press. The three agencies retained close ties to one another to discourage the foundation of competition.

During the Franco-Prussian War, the exchange of news between Havas and Wolf took place through Reuter in London. With the siege of Paris by the Prussians, Auguste Havas installed himself in Tours, and Havas Paris depended upon Gambetta's hot air balloons to communicate the news of the besieged capital to the rest of France and abroad. The Prussians released falcons to intercept the messenger pigeons used by Havas Paris to get news from Tours. During the Paris Commune of 1871, the insurgents took control of the Havas dispatches. Auguste Havas returned to Paris immediately after the Commune fell. By this time, 24 of 164 parts of Havas's press agency division were controlled by Auguste Havas and his son. The remaining divisions were in the hands of industrialists, politicians, and businessmen, whose connections played a large role in Havas's success.

Auguste Havas sold the business to Emile d'Erlanger, an international financier, and in 1879 the company sold stocks to the public. The agency's international network expanded yearly and was enjoying exceptional prosperity by 1881. Havas's threefold function as press agency, publicity agency, and liaison between the government and the business community made the company very appealing to investors. The company was expanding in France, adding newspapers in Lyon, Lille, Marseilles, Toulouse, and Dijon. Havas's commercial activity increased tenfold, and its connections to influential financiers were augmented by its involvement with the Banque de Paris et des Pays-Bas (Paribas). This period in the company's history was marked by efforts at discretion in relation to its customers and at trying to follow government objectives without losing journalistic credibility, despite a climate of journalistic corruption.

During this time, the publicity division of Havas made an agreement with the Compagnie Générale de Publicité Étrangère, facilitated by an American, John Jones. Like the accord between Reuter and Wolf in 1856, the new agreement divided the publicity market geographically to avoid a price war. Havas won exclusive rights to publicity in Spanish, Portuguese, and Russian newspapers, while Jones retained rights in Dutch, Scandinavian, Danish, and Austrian journals. Hungarian, Swiss, and Belgian customers were shared equally so that competition remained only for British customers.

In the figure of Léon Rénier, Havas found a natural leader who played a major role in establishing the company as a powerful and diversified news monopoly. Under Rénier, Havas and Paribas invested in telegraph communications linking France with northern Europe, the Antilles, and the United States. Rénier played a large role in Havas's contract for exclusive advertising in the Parisian subway system and at kiosks in Paris. As the number of daily newspapers with large circulations increased and the business of publicity grew larger, Rénier made Havas a more dynamic enterprise and became one of the most powerful men in France.

The immense power Havas wielded in the media was evidenced by the fact that most newspapers depended so completely on Havas dispatches for national and international news that they did not maintain their own offices in Paris. The philosophy of efficiency and speed of dispatches upon which Havas was founded continued through the agency's progressive use of the telegraph and the telephone. One example of the company's commitment to efficiency involved the dispatching of news on the Dreyfus affair at Rennes in 1899. To obtain news about the trial of the alleged traitor, Alfred Dreyfus, Havas employed cyclists to pedal between the Palais de Justice and the central telegraph agency and maintained a telephone at the stock exchange, incurring costs of FFr 1 million.

Increasing Control Over the Media in the Early 1900s

Around the turn of the century, Havas became the privileged intermediary for financiers and foreign governments seeking to influence French public opinion discretely through the press. For example, after Russia borrowed money from French banks in the last years of the 19th century, the revolutionary events of 1905 in Russia were smoothed over by reassuring dispatches by Havas. The banks, including Paribas, made big profits by avoiding public anxiety about the loans, which amounted to 80 percent of Russia's public debt. Havas also received FFr 1.5 million from Banque Périer and Banque Impérial Ottomane to assure support in Parisian newspapers for loans to the Turkish government. According to Antoine Lefebure in *Havas, les arcanes du pouvoir*, Havas was one of the principal instigators of corruption of the French press by foreign governments. This corruption had limited political consequences during the time, but that was not to be the case in the next century.

In January 1914, Société Générale des Annonces, a joint stock publicity company, became part of Havas, which then came under the control of the Syndicat Central de Publicité, the sole purpose of which was to control the publicity of the four big Paris newspapers. In each of these four papers, *Le Journal, Le Matin, Le Petit Journal,* and *Le Petit Parisian,* the Syndicat Central de Publicité and Léon Rénier played major roles. With Rénier's election as head of both Havas Information and Société Générale des Annonces, press and publicity became even more united within the company. With the beginning of the war in 1914, the need to control public opinion became all the more important. Havas took part in propaganda campaigns against the Germans and received FFr 6 million from the French government for propaganda distribution. The agency received money from Greece in 1919 and from Yugoslavia in 1920 to influence the French press in their favor against Italy.

The postwar period was very profitable for Havas, despite the corruption scandals and the high amount of government involvement in the press. The agency added newspapers in Mulhouse, Nice, and Bordeaux to its publicity administration. Paribas increased its influence in Havas and took part in that company's move to increase capital by selling stocks. Although the agency did by no means have a monopoly on the publicity market, it did expand its business after the war by combating a general mistrust of advertising in France. In 1931, advertising budgets in France were eight times less than in the American market. Therefore, Havas took a more subtle approach with its clients by avoiding newer media, such as radio. Big businesses did not want to appear to be directly controlling the press, and so Havas played the role of intermediary between the press and the business community, protecting the anonymity of companies. The agency also influenced the contents of a newspaper to benefit such clients as the government, banks, and small companies. The French government, which relied on the press for its own electoral motives, did not intervene in these manipulations of publicity.

After World War I, Rénier convinced the publishers of the five largest Parisian dailies that competition for publicity could damage their profitability, and the five papers gave over to Havas their publicity offices, with a percentage of their capital being put aside for operations of common interest. As the meeting point of political groups and powerful financiers, Havas and this publicity consortium played a powerful role in French politics between the wars. One formidable competitor was François Coty, who had made a fortune in perfumes before he began to construct a newspaper empire. When Havas and its consortium refused to distribute, print, or sell any of Coty's

journals, it was forced to pay FFr 14 million in damages for unfair competition. By 1934, however, Coty's empire had disintegrated, and Havas bought him out.

The hegemony of this consortium limited the diversity of the press, which was controlled mostly by political conservatives. A Socialist movement, led by Léon Blum, who served as premier from 1936 to 1938, denounced Havas for its omnipotence, manipulation, and corruption. Citing the American example, Blum called for a separation of news and publicity and for the publication of newspaper budgets without secret financing by foreign governments. Rénier agreed to the latter regulation and agreed to cooperate with Blum's government if the agency was not dismantled. Blum accepted, and Havas received the contract for the publicity of the 1937 World Exposition.

Difficult Times and Significant Changes in the Mid-1900s

With the beginning of World War II, the accord between Havas, Wolf, Reuter, and Associated Press ended. Wolf became a propaganda office for the Nazi regime, and Havas's correspondent in Germany was expelled from the Reich by the Gestapo. Abroad, Havas's offices became press agencies for the French embassies. The consortium of five Parisian dailies was dismantled, and Havas came upon difficult financial times. By 1940, many of its former clients were no longer advertising; on June 9, 1940, the French government retreated to Tours, and the next day Havas suspended its news service.

The occupying German forces considered Havas an agent of French propaganda and forbade its operations in the occupied zone while taking over a large share of its stock. Moreover, Havas was forced to agree to the harsh regulations imposed upon it by the Vichy government in 1940. The agency was both careful not to offend Hitler or Mussolini and anxious to reinforce its ties to Vichy, creating an "official propaganda" service to run ministerial publicity. Despite the adverse conditions, Havas's capital increased from FFr 300 million in 1942 to FFr 400 million in 1943. The company's collaboration with the Vichy government and the Germans was an effort to protect the company's interests and investments, which had increased before the war. In the postwar movement of nationalization, however, Havas and Rénier were seen as open participants in economic collaboration with the occupiers, as well as instigators of corruption under the Third Republic. Called a traitor, Rénier was replaced by Jean Schloesing, who set about reestablishing Havas's reputation. In 1945 Havas was nationalized, with the French government controlling the stocks previously held by the Germans.

By 1947, the agency had a FFr 62 million deficit and was competing with Publicis for advertising clients. In these difficult years, Havas finally eliminated editorial work from its press agency and separated information activity from publicity. The final split between news and publicity came in 1959, when Jacques Douce was named commercial publicity director. Havas's president, Jean Chevalier, focused the agency's operations on private industry to offset the business it no longer conducted with the government. The company also invested in travel agencies, cinema, and radio.

By 1952, Havas's publicity contracts reached 1938 levels, and from then on, contracts doubled every ten years. By 1972, the publicity market in France was seven times larger than prewar levels, because of the explosive expansion in television, radio, news weeklies, and industrial investment in publicity. In 1974 Douce created Eurocom, a publicity subsidiary of Havas, and in 1978 Havas agreed to develop new media interests with its direct competitor, Publicis.

Renewed Growth in the Late 1900s

On November 4, 1984, Havas President André Rousselet launched Canal Plus, the first cable television station in France. Although some observers were surprised that the top publicity group in France would become involved in a medium that needed no outside publicity, Rousselet hoped that the innovative move would open up a potentially profitable market. In 1985, President François Mitterand announced the opening of private commercial television channels, and Canal Plus's subscription rate declined sharply. The channel continued in operation, however, and, with aggressive advertising and competent management, Canal Plus became one of the biggest French audiovisual successes of the 1980s.

In 1986, with French President Edouard Balladur's plans for massive privatization, publicity contracts poured into Eurocom. Havas itself was privatized in 1987, ending 40 years of government control. In 1988 American Robert Maxwell bought almost five percent of Havas in his quest for a French communications acquisition. Also that year, Rousselet left Havas to head Canal Plus, in which Havas had gained a 25 percent interest by 1992. Publicity skyrocketed for Havas in the 1980s, as revenues from television advertising doubled between 1983 and 1989. The company showed less expansion in areas in which it had traditionally been successful, such as information and newspaper publicity.

During this time, Havas made investments in cinema through Canal Plus and took part in several large acquisitions, including the publicity group RSCG (Roux, Séguéla, Cayzac, Goudard) in 1992, which made Euro-RSCG the seventh largest publicity group in the world. In the early 1990s, with the international recession, business slowed and the publicity market weakened because of depressed consumer spending.

Nevertheless, in 1992, Havas was France's largest media and communications group, comprising a wide range of business and investments, including local and audiovisual media, international multimedia sales, tourism, full-service advertising, and publishing. With the deregulation of European television markets, Havas emerged as one of the top four pan-European companies. Although Europe remained the company's first priority, Chairperson Paul Dauzier announced plans to expand aggressively outside of France. Euro-RSCG opened an office in Poland in 1992 and reorganized its offices in the United States. Havas's publicity department took part in a joint venture with Czechoslovak Television to bring Western commercials and programming to Czechoslovakia and made similar arrangements with Magyar Television in Hungary.

Major Changes in the Late 1990s

The flexibility and diversity that Havas exhibited in the second half of the 20th century were expected to help ensure its future success in the industry. Moreover, the company's position at the forefront of communications in France and throughout Europe seemed stable, due in large part to the wide range of business in which it was involved, the broad geographical spread of its activities, and its continual innovation in new media. In 1996 Havas's sales reached $8.1 billion and profit was $248 million. Despite Havas's strengths, however, industry analysts and investors accused the company of lacking a long-term business strategy. Analyst Pierre-Yves Gauthier of Cholet-Dupont, a Paris-based brokerage, told *Advertising Age International,* "In Havas, a lot of people see a holding [company] with relatively profitable diversity but not a great deal of big-picture strategy."

In February 1997 Havas's fate was irrevocably altered when Compagnie Générale des Eaux (CGE), a French utilities company, became the controlling shareholder of Havas with a 30 percent interest. Although CGE had long been France's national water utility, the firm began to diversify when a new chairman, Jean-Marie Messier, came on board in 1996. Messier hoped to turn CGE into a media conglomerate, and he expanded into telecommunications and media, while exiting from nonstrategic operations such as real estate and funeral services. With controlling interest Messier used his influence to redirect Havas's focus to emphasize electronic media and multimedia. Havas began to sell off noncore businesses, beginning with the news magazines *Le Point* and *L'Express* in October 1997. Havas chairman Pierre Dauzier stated in *Advertising Age International,* "Our aim is clear: to build an integrated multimedia group with the size and strength to meet the challenges ahead. We are now set to pool our know-how with Générale des Eaux in network technology to create a full-fledged multimedia division."

The following March CGE acquired full control of Havas for about FFr 40 billion, and Havas became a wholly owned subsidiary of CGE. Chairman Dauzier was replaced by Eric Licoys, an associate of CGE's Messier. A month later, in April 1998, CGE changed its name to Vivendi, shedding a name that had been part of the company since 1853. Vivendi's Messier told *Times of London,* "The name Vivendi is warm, full of life and it resembles what we do—local services which improve daily life.... It will give the group the international fame that it lacks today."

With Vivendi in control of Havas, the strategy to concentrate on building multimedia and specialized publishing operations was quickened. Havas sold Havas Voyages SA, the travel division, to American Express Co. in June 1998 for more than FFr 1 billion. Havas also divested of its Gault-Millau restaurant guides division and sold Oda, which specialized in media representation for telephone directories, to France Telecom. Just as quickly as Havas sold off noncore businesses, however, the company acquired new companies. In April 1998 Havas bought Quotidien Santé, the largest medical publication business in France. A few months later the firm purchased Ediciones Doyma SA, the largest medical publishing company in Spain, and in November Havas acquired OVP-Vidal group from Cofip-Didot-Bottin, a pharmaceutical information publisher. The acquisitions significantly boosted Havas's medical publishing operations, a division Havas intended to grow.

Havas also strengthened its educational offerings, acquiring Grupo Anaya, the second largest publisher of school and reference works in Spain, in late 1998. Havas also bought L'Etudiant, a media group specializing in information for high school and college students. L'Etudiant was involved not only in publishing and electronic information services but also in trade fairs. Havas launched Internet Ecoles, an online information site for teachers, students, and schools, with partner Cegetal in late 1998 as well.

Havas boosted its educational and electronic divisions significantly with the purchase of Cendant Software in November 1998. The U.S. company developed interactive products, including educational software and games. Cendant was the global sales leader in game software, the second largest in educational software, and the third largest company in lifestyle software. Cendant was renamed Havas Interactive, Inc.

In 1999 Havas continued to streamline operations and build its core businesses. In April the company sold its outdoor advertising business, which consisted of Avenir, HMC Transports, and Claude Publicité, to JCDecaux group for FFr 5.75 billion. Several months later Havas sold Havas Régies, a media representation business. Toward the end of the year Havas reduced its stake in Havas Advertising by selling nine percent of its interest. Despite the sale, Havas remained the principal shareholder of the subsidiary, with a 20.7 percent stake. Although industry analysts had speculated that Havas would divest itself of the advertising unit to focus on print and electronic media, Havas stated its intention to remain involved in advertising.

Among Havas's acquisitions and partnerships in 1999 were a joint venture with Bertelsmann to form BOL France, an Internet bookseller, and a partnership with Bernard Fixot to establish an international publishing house. Havas in March announced a takeover bid for Barbour Index, a U.K. trade information business focused primarily on the building industry.

To grow internationally and expand its presence in Spanish-speaking regions, Havas acquired Aique, the third largest schoolbook publisher in Argentina, in April. In August the company announced a joint venture with Abril, the leading publisher of magazines in Latin America, to acquire Atica and Scipione, schoolbook publishers in Brazil. Havas's Licoys said in a prepared statement, "Following the acquisitions of Anaya in Spain and Aique in Argentina, this investment further consolidates the international position of Havas, expanding its presence in schoolbook publishing in Latin America. . . . It is an outstanding opportunity for Havas . . . to move into Brazil, Latin America's largest market with a population of 160 million including nearly 60 million aged under 15 and 45 million pupils."

Continuing to expand its medical publishing unit, Havas acquired MediMedia in May 1999 for FFr 1.6 billion. MediMedia was a leading international health care information provider, distributing its products in 20 languages to 100 countries. MediMedia published journals and provided drug information and consumer health care media. More than half of MediMedia's revenues came from European sales, although sales in North America and Asia were on the rise. The acquisition succeeded in making Havas the fourth largest health care information specialist in the world and the world's leader in drug information systems.

Though more than a century old, Havas had managed to modernize with the times. Under new guidance as a subsidiary of Vivendi, Havas was prepared to face new challenges and extend its global reach as it neared the turn of the century. The company planned to continue building its operations in education, leisure, and information and to carve out a leadership position in electronic media and publishing. Havas appeared finally to have adopted a long-term business strategy that it could follow for years to come.

Principal Subsidiaries

Havas MediMedia International Group; Havas Business Information; Havas Interactive, Inc.; Groupe Expansion; Groupe L'Etudiant; Groupe Express; Comareg-Delta Diffusion; Havas Numerique; Havas Education et Reference; Laffont; Plon-Perrin; Les Presses-Solar-Belfond; Nouvelles Editions Havas; Hemma; Havas Poche; Sogedif; France Loisirs (50%); Bol France (50%); Havas Services; Havas Advertising (20.7%).

Principal Competitors

Bertelsmann AG; Lagardere SCA; Reed Elsevier plc.

Further Reading

Bruner, Richard W., "E. Europe Attracts Media Magnates," *Advertising Age,* July 16, 1990, p. 27.
Crumley, Bruce, "Havas Shareholder Forces Focus on Core Business: Ad Business Could Be Sold As French Giant Pins Its Hopes on New Media," *Advertising Age International,* November 10, 1997, p. 4.
Fleming, Charles, "Cie. Generale des Eaux Agrees To Buy Rest of Havas SA in a Stock-Cash Deal," *Wall Street Journal,* March 10, 1998, p. B10.
Goldsmith, Charles, "Vivendi Sells Havas Voyages to U.S. Firm," *Asian Wall Street Journal,* June 18, 1998, p. 9.
Kamm, Thomas, "Havas Purchase of Doyma Expands Publishing Role," *Wall Street Journal Europe,* June 25, 1998, p. 3.
Kasriel, Ken, "Feeling Heat in Hungary: Havas Unit's Media Venture Sucked into Power Struggle," *Advertising Age,* January 18, 1993, pp. 1–6.
Lefebure, Antoine, *Havas, Les arcanes du pouvoir,* Paris: Bernard Grasset, 1992.
Rosenbaum, Andrew, "Havas to Know No Boundaries," *Advertising Age,* June 25, 1990, p. 36.
Sage, Adam, "French Water Starts to Live," *Times of London,* April 4, 1998, p. 28.

—Jennifer Kerns
—updated by Mariko Fujinaka

HEALTHSOUTH®

HealthSouth Corporation

1 HealthSouth Parkway
Birmingham, Alabama 35243
U.S.A.
Telephone: (205) 967-7116
Fax: (205) 969-4719
Web site: http://www.HealthSouth.com

Public Company
Incorporated: 1984 as Amcare, Inc.
Employees: 51,901
Sales: $4.07 billion (1999)
Stock Exchanges: New York
Ticker Symbol: HRC
NAIC: 621493 Freestanding Ambulatory Surgical and
Emergency Centers; 621111 Offices of Physicians
(Except Mental Health Specialists); 62134 Offices of
Physical, Occupational and Speech Therapists, and
Audiologists; 621512 Diagnostic Imaging Centers;
621498 All Other Outpatient Care Centers; 621999
All Other Miscellaneous Ambulatory Health Care
Services

HealthSouth Corporation is the leading provider of medical rehabilitation health care and outpatient surgery services in the United States. With more than 1,900 locations in the United States, the United Kingdom, and Australia, HealthSouth provides physical and other therapy in its rehabilitation facilities, offers imaging services through its diagnostic centers, and provides nonemergency surgical services at its outpatient surgery centers. The company also has occupational medicine clinics that deal exclusively with patients suffering from work-related health conditions. HealthSouth has contracts with managed care plans, insurance companies, and major corporations, including Wal-Mart and Goodyear. HealthSouth also has alliances with professional sports associations and schools to supply rehabilitative and sports medicine services.

A New Twist on Rehabilitation Services: 1980s

HealthSouth was the brainchild of Richard Scrushy. Scrushy grew up in Selma, Alabama, and earned a degree in respiratory therapy from the University of Alabama, Birmingham. By the age of 30 he had advanced to vice-president at Lifemark Corp., a Houston-based health care management firm. At Lifemark, Scrushy witnessed firsthand the changes sweeping the health care industry. The dominant trend was toward a reduction in reimbursement dollars available to traditional medical practitioners. Corporations and insurance companies were trying to cut health care expenditures while, at the same time, costs in the medical field were rising. ''I saw the squeezing of reimbursement in the health care system and I wanted to take advantage of that change,'' Scrushy said in a June 1990 article in *Forbes*. ''My idea,'' he added, ''was to provide high-quality hospital-type rehabilitation services in a low-cost setting.''

Scrushy got his chance to start his rehabilitation company in 1984, when Lifemark Corp. was purchased by Los Angeles-based American Medical International. Armed with a plan, Scrushy lacked only the money to get started. His break came in a Houston restaurant, when a Citicorp venture capitalist overheard Scrushy outlining his business plan and eventually offered a $1 million grubstake, giving birth to what would become HealthSouth. Scrushy convinced four of his Lifemark associates to break ranks with him and move to Birmingham to build the company's first outpatient facility. Their company was incorporated in January 1984 as Amcare Inc. before its name was changed to HealthSouth Rehabilitation Corporation in May 1985.

Scrushy got into the rehabilitation industry at a good time. During the early 1980s people began to view rehabilitation as a means of reducing medical expenses. Specifically, rehabilitation could be used to minimize unnecessary, expensive surgeries. It also helped injured workers get back to their jobs more quickly, thus eliminating expensive worker's compensation and disability costs. As health and insurance professionals began to recognize those benefits, the use of rehabilitation services soared. Between 1982 and 1990, in fact, rehabilitation expenditures increased at an average annual rate of about 20 percent and the number of outpatient rehabilitation centers

Company Perspectives:

The fundamental human relationships involved in the delivery of quality healthcare services are the foundation of our way of doing business. Therefore, we place primary value upon our patients, their families and our employees. We are dedicated to providing superior care to those individuals whose lives are entrusted to us. Our primary focus is to respond to their needs. Our dealings with them will be professional, courteous, helpful and cooperative. Our employees are critical to our success as a corporation. We will respect their individuality, recognize and reward their good performance, provide opportunities for their growth and development and encourage their participation in the decision-making process. We consider respect, trust and integrity to be essential in all our dealings. We expect honest, ethical behavior from ourselves, and we encourage it in others. Our employees live and work in the larger context of society. Therefore, we value and encourage responsible individual and corporate citizenship. We recognize our obligation to be a positive influence in the communities in which we maintain a corporate presence. We are progressive in our response to the changing needs of our business and prudent in the management of our resources. We value superior, high-quality work at the individual, unit and corporate levels. Without apology, we are profit-oriented, for only profitable companies can adapt and survive to meet their long term commitments to patients, employees and stockholders.

soared. That industry growth contributed to healthy gains for HealthSouth throughout the decade.

Perhaps more important than general industry expansion for HealthSouth during the 1980s was Scrushy's and his fellow managers' unique operating strategy. When HealthSouth got started in 1984, rehabilitation centers were stereotyped as drab, institution-like facilities with, generally, mediocre staff. Scrushy wanted to change that image. Borrowing from health clubs, he designed his rehab centers as bright, open-spaced, mirrored rooms with trained physical therapists and sporty equipment. The centers more closely resembled high-priced health clubs than traditional hospital-styled rehab centers, and doctors became increasingly willing to send patients to a HealthSouth facility for treatment. Scrushy added a few more HealthSouth outlets and by 1985 was generating nearly $5 million in annual revenues.

HealthSouth added new rehab centers to its chain throughout the middle and late 1980s. Because of the company's unique recipe for success, its centers became known as effective and cost-efficient, and as models for other companies in the rehab industry. Rather than focusing on a specific rehab niche, such as head or spinal injuries, HealthSouth differed from many of its competitors in that it targeted the larger market for less expensive, general outpatient rehabilitation services. HealthSouth's facilities were built around a large gymnasium, in which some patients rode exercise bikes while listening to rock music. Old and young people worked out side by side, often with the help

of a therapist, while others enjoyed physical, occupational, or speech therapy in private treatment rooms. Some of the machines even were hooked to computers that fed reports to doctors about how patients were responding to treatment.

HealthSouth appealed to the medical community by offering a number of rehabilitation programs tailored for different ailments. At the urging of Dr. Scott Burke, a Denver spinal rehabilitations specialist, HealthSouth designed a program to treat back problems. Becoming widely used, the whole package—incorporating stretching, aerobic conditioning, anatomy education, and work simulation exercises—took about four weeks and cost a total of only $3,700, which was much less than the patient might otherwise spend on unnecessary surgeries and hospital costs. HealthSouth also began offering special services for the lucrative sports rehabilitation market. To that end, HealthSouth eventually launched an entire sports division with separate facilities and prominent doctors. Dr. Jim Andrews, one of HealthSouth's most renowned surgeons, treated such celebrities as Bo Jackson, Jane Fonda, and Charles Barkley, among others.

While HealthSouth kept the doctors and patients happy with state-of-the-art facilities, it stayed on the good side of the insurance companies by minimizing overhead and treatment costs. It saved money on construction, for example, by using the same basic floor plan and architecture for all of its outpatient centers, including the same carpeting, wallpaper, and furniture. Because the centers processed so many patients—about 15 to 20 per hour, or roughly 200 a day at many HealthSouth facilities—the average cost of a visit was kept at a low $50 to $90. Insurers did not blink at the cost, because it was much less expensive than traditional treatment. A study conducted by Northwestern National Life Insurance Co. estimated that every $1 spent on rehabilitation saved about $30 on disability benefits.

By 1988 HealthSouth was operating a network of 21 outpatient facilities, 11 inpatient facilities, and seven rehabilitation equipment centers in 15 states, making it a leader in the U.S. rehabilitation industry. Sales had spiraled upward at an average of more than 100 percent annually since 1984, peaking at $75 million in 1988. Revenues shot up to $114 million in 1989 and then to $181 million in 1990, about $13 million of which was netted as income. In fact, HealthSouth managed to post successive profits every year after 1985. Aside from increasing its customer base at existing centers, the company grew by purchasing other rehab and health care companies and restructuring them to fit into the HealthSouth organization. It was in December 1989, for example, that Scrushy jumped into the sports rehab business when he paid $21 million for a 219-bed general hospital in Birmingham that specialized in orthopedic surgery and sports medicine.

Rapid Growth Through Acquisitions in the Early 1990s

By the mid-1990s, HealthSouth was operating 14 inpatient and 31 freestanding outpatient rehabilitation centers in 21 states. The company continued to add new general rehabilitation centers to its chain in 1991 and 1992. Meanwhile, its specialized sports business flourished and it enjoyed success with its new orthopedic hospitals that featured leading surgeons. By 1992 HealthSouth had established itself as one of two leaders in the U.S. rehabilitation industry. Its chief nemesis was Continental Medical Systems Inc., of Pennsylvania. Continental, with $20 million in net earnings in 1991 compared with $22 million for HealthSouth, generated most of its profit from rehabilitation service contracts with hospitals, schools, and nursing homes. Like HealthSouth, it operated inpatient and outpatient rehab centers across the country.

Continental and HealthSouth nearly merged in 1992. The resulting company would have been a $2 billion concern had the deal not fallen through. Instead, HealthSouth remained independent and went on to become the largest provider of rehabilitative services in the nation. It attained that status through an aggressive merger and acquisition agenda advanced during the early and mid-1990s. Chief among its acquisitions was the purchase of National Medical Enterprises Inc. in December 1993. That pivotal buyout added 31 inpatient rehabilitation facilities and 12 outpatient rehabilitation centers to HealthSouth's portfolio, boosting the total number of outpatient centers in its chain from 126 at the end of 1992 to 171 going into 1994. Evidencing the effectiveness of HealthSouth's strategy was a substantial improvement in the performance of National Medical's facilities in the two years following the acquisition.

HealthSouth's revenues for 1993 surged impressively to $575 million and the company assumed the industry lead. HealthSouth achieved its dazzling gains during the early 1990s, in part, by focusing on rehabilitating people who were injured rather than chronically ill. That was the primary growth market, because employers and insurance companies were eager to get those people out of the health care system. HealthSouth's Workstart program was a good example of its core service. The Workstart plan was designed to get most workers back on the job after surgery or an injury within 30 days at an average cost of just $2,700. The program was ideal for employers because HealthSouth, using advanced testing and statistical analysis, was able to determine the extent of the patients' pain and injury. Among other benefits, that kind of analysis discouraged faking or exaggerating the extent of injuries to take advantage of disability payment programs.

HealthSouth stepped up its acquisition program in 1994 and 1995 by absorbing a number of new companies. Two major purchases included the September 1994 acquisition of ReLife Inc. and the February 1995 buyout of NovaCare, Inc.'s inpatient rehabilitation hospital division. ReLife brought 31 inpatient rehabilitation facilities and 12 outpatient centers that added roughly $119 million in annual revenues to HealthSouth's income statement. That and other acquisitions helped to push HealthSouth's sales past the $1 billion mark to $1.13 billion in 1994. Furthermore, net income vaulted to $53.23 million and the company's stock price raced to a record level. Following the NovaCare acquisition, the company's total network rose to more than 425 facilities located in 33 states.

HealthSouth sustained its aggressive growth drive throughout 1995, snapping up several smaller competitors. Significantly, in October 1995 HealthSouth announced that it had agreed to purchase the rehabilitation services operations of Caremark International for $127 million in cash. The Caremark operations consisted of 123 outpatient rehabilitation facilities that were generating about $80 million in annual revenues. That gave the company a total of about 440 outpatient facilities and about 40 percent of the total rehabilitation market. HealthSouth also bought Diagnostic Health Corporation, which offered outpatient imaging services. Perhaps most notable was the early 1995 acquisition of Surgical Health Corporation, which represented HealthSouth's diversification into an entirely new market: outpatient surgery services. The $1.1 billion acquisition, the company's largest to date, immediately catapulted HealthSouth into the lead as the top operator of outpatient surgery centers in the nation.

Continued Diversification and New Challenges in the Late 1990s

HealthSouth's steady string of acquisitions did not end as the company headed into the second half of the decade. Purchases in 1996 included Surgical Care Affiliates, Inc., which included 67 outpatient surgery centers in 24 states, for an estimated $1.4 billion; Advantage Health Corporation, which owned about 136 inpatient and outpatient rehabilitation centers in 11 states, for about $315 million; Professional Sports Care Management, Inc., which included 36 outpatient rehabilitation centers in New York, New Jersey, and Connecticut, for about $59 million; and ReadiCare, Inc., which operated 37 occupational health centers in Washington and California, for about $76 million.

The following year HealthSouth acquired Health Images, Inc., which owned 55 diagnostic imaging centers in the United Kingdom and 13 states in the United States; ASC Network Corporation, which operated 29 surgery centers in eight states; and National Imaging Affiliates, Inc., which ran eight diagnostic imaging centers in six states. The most significant acquisition, however, was the purchase of Horizon/CMS Healthcare, the largest provider of specialty health care services in the United States. The transaction included 30 inpatient rehabilitation centers and about 275 outpatient rehabilitation centers, in addition to other businesses. After completing the deal, HealthSouth sold Horizon's 139 long term care facilities, 12 specialty hospitals, 35 institutional pharmacies, and more than 1,000 rehabilitation therapy contracts to Integrated Health Services, Inc.

In 1998 HealthSouth made two major acquisitions. The firm purchased National Surgery Centers, Inc., which operated 40 surgical facilities in 14 states, and also acquired 34 surgery centers from Columbia/HCA Healthcare Corporation. To focus on its core operations, HealthSouth decided in 1998 to sell its nonstrategic businesses, including its home health operations. HealthSouth's numerous acquisitions had significantly strengthened and expanded its dominance and presence in rehabilitative and outpatient surgery services, and by the end of the year HealthSouth had nearly 1,900 centers in 50 states, the United Kingdom, and Australia.

Despite HealthSouth's leadership position and long history of steady earnings growth, the company faced new challenges in the late 1990s that cut into its profits. The federal government's Balanced Budget Act of 1997 placed new restrictions on Medicare, which resulted in lower reimbursements for some medical services. A significant portion of HealthSouth's revenues came from Medicare, and the new legislation led to decreasing reimbursements for HealthSouth. In addition, managed care companies and health maintenance organizations (HMOs) were growing in number and power, and their attempts to lower reimbursement costs to health care providers posed a serious threat to HealthSouth, which received about 60 percent of its total revenue from managed care. In October 1998 HealthSouth announced that earnings growth was slowing to about 15 to 20 percent from about 30 percent a year. As a result, the company's stock tumbled from a high of about $30 per share during the summer to less than $8. HealthSouth's founder and CEO was undaunted, however—Scrushy noted that growth of between 15 and 20 percent a year was quite acceptable and commented on the share price erosion in the *Wall Street Journal.* "It's all paper," Scrushy stated, adding "I'm very calm."

HealthSouth continued to face difficulties in 1999. In June the company announced plans to divide its inpatient and outpatient operations by spinning off the inpatient services into a new company, to be called HealthSouth Hospital Corporation. The strategy would have allowed HealthSouth to concentrate on its more profitable outpatient operations, but in September, the corporation decided to postpone its plans. HealthSouth also stated that it expected operating profit margins to fall lower than forecast during the third and fourth quarters of 1999. The company said it would take charges of between $250 and $300 million. As a result, share prices dropped to a low of $4.56 per share. For the third quarter of 1999 HealthSouth reported revenues of $993.3 million, down from $1.05 billion during the comparable period of 1998. The overall picture was not necessarily bleak, however, and for the nine months ended September 30, 1999, HealthSouth's revenues were $3.07 billion, up from $2.97 billion in the same period of 1998.

Hoping to rise above its recent problems, HealthSouth endeavored to strengthen and continue building its empire. The company acquired American Rehability Services, which operated outpatient rehabilitation centers in 18 states, from Mariner Post-Acute Network, Inc., in July 1999. HealthSouth also formed a partnership with WebMD, Inc., a provider of health care information on the Internet, and Healtheon Corporation, a provider of electronic commerce services related to the health care industry, to develop and operate a channel dedicated to sports medicine issues on the WebMD Web site. The channel, which was launched in early 2000, offered sports medicine information, links to HealthSouth centers, online chat events with physicians and celebrity athletes, and online communities. The venture extended HealthSouth's presence on the rapidly growing Internet medium and significantly raised its brand recognition.

HealthSouth had nearly 2,000 locations in 50 states, Puerto Rico, the United Kingdom, and Australia by the end of the decade. The company had enjoyed phenomenal growth since its inception in 1984 and believed it was poised to overcome the obstacles of the late 1990s as it prepared to greet a new century. With leadership positions in the rehabilitative health care, outpatient surgery, and diagnostic imaging markets, HealthSouth hoped to realize and maintain its standing as "the healthcare company of the 21st century."

Principal Subsidiaries

HealthSouth Medical Center, Inc.; HealthSouth Aviation, Inc.; HealthSouth Community Re-Entry Center of Dallas, Inc.; HealthSouth Doctors' Hospital, Inc.; HealthSouth IMC, Inc.; HealthSouth International, Inc.; HealthSouth Medical Clinic, Inc.; HealthSouth Network Services, Inc.; HealthSouth Orthopedic Services, Inc.; HealthSouth Specialty Hospital, Inc.; Advantage Health Corporation; ASC Network Corporation; CMS Capital Ventures, Inc. (15%); Diagnostic Health Corporation; Disability and Impairment Evaluation Centers of America, Inc.; Horizon/CMS Healthcare Corporation; National Imaging Affiliates, Inc.; National Surgery Centers, Inc.; Physical Therapeutix, Inc.; Physician Practice Management Corporation; Professional Sports Care Management, Inc.; ReadiCare, Inc.; Rehabilitation Hospital Corporation of America, Inc.; Surgery Center Holding Corporation; Surgical Care Affiliates, Inc.; Surgical Health Corporation; The Company Doctor.

Principal Competitors

Columbia/HCA Healthcare Corporation; NovaCare, Inc.; Tenet Healthcare Corporation.

Further Reading

Brown, Valerie D., "HealthSouth Corporation Acquires Therapy Group," *Springfield Business Journal,* July 24, 1995, p. 3.

Carrns, Ann, "HealthSouth Posts $4.3 Million Loss, Hurt by Bad-Debt Charge, Other Items," *Wall Street Journal,* November 4, 1999, p. A10.

——, "HealthSouth Shelves Plans To Spin Off In-Patient Centers, Sees Falling Margins," *Wall Street Journal,* September 10, 1999, p. B10.

Japsen, Bruce, "Chairman of Largest Health-Care Companies Thinks Rebound Is in Sight," *Chicago Tribune,* October 29, 1998.

Moss, Michael, "CEO Exposes, Sues Online Critics," *Wall Street Journal Europe,* July 8, 1999, p. 11.

Paris, Ellen, "Straighten That Back! Bend Those Knees!," *Forbes,* June 11, 1990, p. 92.

Sharpe, Anita, "HealthSouth Stock Plunges on Forecast," *Wall Street Journal,* October 1, 1998, p. A3.

Yardley, Jim, "The Road to Recovery," *Atlanta Constitution,* February 20, 1992, Sec. B.

Young, Randy, "HealthSouth Puts Injured Workers Back on Wellness Track," *San Antonio Business Journal,* June 26, 1989, Sec. 2, p. 17.

—Dave Mote
—updated by Mariko Fujinaka

Herley Industries, Inc.

10 Industry Drive
Lancaster, Pennsylvania 17603
U.S.A.
Telephone: (717) 397-2777
Fax: (717) 397-9503
Web site: http://www.herley.com

Public Company
Incorporated: 1965
Employees: 511
Sales: $61 million (1999)
Stock Exchanges: NASDAQ
Ticker Symbol: HRLY
NAIC: 334511 Search, Detection, Navigation, Guidance, Aeronautical, and Nautical System and Instrument Manufacturing; 334419 Other Electronic Component Manufacturing

Herley Industries, Inc. is a small but innovative firm that designs, develops, and manufactures flight instrumentation systems and their related components, as well as microwave products that are marketed to the U.S. government, many foreign governments, and a long list of aerospace companies around the world. Included in the company's list of flight instrumentation systems are command and control systems, transponders, flight termination receivers, telemetry transmitters and receivers, pulse code modulator encoders, and scoring systems. Herley's microwave products are sold primarily for application in the defense electronics industry and include systems and components for radar and defense electronic systems on tactical fighter aircraft, airborne and shipboard navigation and communications, missile guidance systems, satellite communications, and automatic test equipment. Organized into two product groups, the Space and Communications Product Group located in Lancaster, Pennsylvania, and the Microwave Products Group in Woburn, Massachusetts, the company has launched an aggressive acquisitions strategy that includes the purchase of firms to expand its market base, especially overseas. In fact, Herley has increased its revenues coming from overseas customers signifi-

cantly during the past five years, with nearly 29 percent of its total revenues in fiscal 1999 originating outside the United States. Early in the year 2000, Herley entered the wireless telecommunications market, establishing subsidiary Herley Wireless Technology Inc.

1960s Origins

Herley was founded by Lee N. Blatt and his partner Herman Kagan. Blatt, the driving force behind the company during the early years, was born and raised on the Eastern Seaboard of the United States, spending much of his youth in the state of New York. He attended Syracuse University in upstate New York, where he devoted himself to the study of engineering, and graduated with a Bachelors Degree in Electrical Engineering. He immediately sought a job in the burgeoning field of the electronics industry.

After working in a variety of jobs within the industry, Blatt began to work towards establishing his own business. With his background and contacts developed over the years, Blatt decided that he would design and manufacture products for military applications, specifically having to do with microwave devices. Yet the young man's ambition was mitigated by his realization that he had no formal training for starting a business venture of his own. As a result, Blatt decided to attend City College of New York in order to provide for himself the necessary skills to successfully launch his own firm. In a short span of time, with diligence and intense concentration, Blatt graduated with a Masters Degree in Business Administration. Now prepared with a suitable background, Lee Blatt founded an engineering firm with partner Herman Keegan, calling the company Herley (formed by a contraction of the partners' first names) and setting up headquarters in 1965 in Long Island, New York.

At the beginning, Blatt and his small team of electrical engineers focused on the design and manufacture of solid state microwave devices for use in tactical military programs. Specifically, the company produced lower power, broad band microwave integrated assemblies for the U.S. electronic defense business. The time was right for this business, as the United States was involved in the Vietnam War, and the company soon found that solid state microwave devices were highly lucrative products.

After the war, however, the demand for Herley microwave products declined. Seeking to diversify, the company began producing a sideline of decorative giftware. An odd departure for the electronics firm, the pewter giftware was manufactured by a central Pennsylvania foundry, and Herley eventually moved its headquarters to Lancaster, Pennsylvania, to be closer to its supplier.

Fortunately for the company, in the late 1970s when the market for its giftware sideline dried up, Herley found itself in a position to return to its defense work. During the Reagan administration, as U.S. defense spending increased dramatically, Herley focused again on designing and manufacturing high-tech electrical components for tactical U.S. military applications.

Growth and Expansion

For most of the 1980s, the company grew at a conservative pace. This, however, changed in the late 1980s, when a new presidential administration came into office, and defense spending was cut dramatically. Moreover, with larger corporations using strategies of vertical integration to achieve economies of scale, manufacturing themselves the same solid state microwave devices as Herley offered, the company's financial viability was threatened.

In response, Herley management decided to pursue a more aggressive expansion policy, looking to broaden its market share via acquisitions. Blatt, still very well informed about developments within the electronics industry, decided to make one of the most important strategic acquisitions ever made for the welfare of his company. With the acquisition of a relatively small and unknown firm that designed and manufactured range safety transponders for military aircraft, Herley immediately placed itself in a favorable position to take advantage of a burgeoning niche market.

Transponders are used for a variety of purposes having to do with aircraft, including range safety, the identification of friend or foe, scoring systems, and command and control. The transponder itself is a small self-contained electronic system which is made up of a transmitter, sensitive receiver, and internal signal processing equipment. The transponder is used in aircraft to receive signals from radar, change the amplification and frequency of those signals, and send back a reply on a different frequency and signal level if necessary. In this way, the tracking

radar locks onto the signal, a far superior method than tracking aircraft by employing the method of skin reflection, especially when adverse weather conditions are present.

Herley began to apply its recently acquired transponder business to the specific area of unmanned aerial vehicles. The company's transponders enabled the U.S. military and the National Aeronautical and Space Administration (NASA) to track space launches and unmanned aerial vehicles, missiles and target drones so that these objects wouldn't interfere with the flight path of any military or commercial manned aircraft. In addition, the company used the technology and engineering skills of its recent acquisition to design and develop a flight termination receiver, or FTR, that is installed in an unmanned missile, target drone, or space launch as a safety device. With a built-in decoder that enables it to receiver a series of highly complex audio tones, the FTR was then able to trigger an explosive charge that destroyed the unmanned vehicle.

Strategic Acquisitions During the 1990s

With the success of its first acquisition, management at the company began look seriously at the prospect of a growth through acquisition strategy. Blatt and his management team were convinced that, by using this as a method of operation, each carefully considered subsequent acquisition could place them in an more advantageous market position, and thereby increase revenues. Accordingly, Herley purchased all of the assets of Micro-Dynamics, Inc., a microwave subsystem designer and manufacturer located in Woburn, Massachusetts. Soon afterwards, management decided to consolidate all of its solid state microwave device design and manufacturing facilities at the Woburn site. In June 1993, the company purchased Vega Precision Laboratories, Inc., situated in Vienna, Virginia, and in October of the same year moved that company's operations to Lancaster. line. In March 1994, Herley entered into a strategic licensing agreement for the exclusive manufacture and sale of the Multiple Aircraft GPS Integrated Command & Control systems. In July 1995, management decided to make another purchase. This time it was the government systems business of Stewart Warner Electronics Corporation of Chicago, Illinois, a well-known and highly respected manufacturer of ''IFF'' (Identification Friend or Foe) interrogator systems and of high frequency radio.

The two most important acquisitions, however, included the purchase of Metraplex Corporation in August 1997 and the purchase of General Microwave Corporation in 1999. Since its inception in 1972, Metraplex Corporation had been providing a wide range of services and products to the commercial aerospace, defense, automotive, construction and mining industries. The company was the leading designer and manufacturer of pulse code modulation and frequency modulation systems used in the testing of space launch vehicle instrumentation, aircraft flight testing, and other types of vehicle testing, including industrial, amphibian, and automotive. Herley's acquisition of Metraplex enabled the company to develop a fully-integrated, and complete airborne data link system.

The acquisition of General Microwave Corporation was just as important. General Microwave Corporation was involved for years in the design, manufacture, and marketing of a wide variety of microwave components and subsystems, as well as electronic testing and measurement equipment. Although the firm's headquarters was located in Farmingdale, New York, General Microwave Corporation also operated facilities in Massachusetts and Israel. The acquisition was motivated by Herley's strategy to expand its product line in the field of microwave components and electronic systems, as well as expanding its client list in the commercial telecommunications industries. After its purchase, management at Herley quick incorporated the company's product line into its own operating facilities where appropriate, and relocated some of its other operations to smaller, more efficient and less expensive sites.

The 1990s and Beyond

In order to remain a viable firm in an extremely competitive industry, management was convinced that Herley's future growth depended largely on it ability to expand its technology, product line, and manufacturing processes in the most cost-effective manner. One area in which Herley's strategy was undoubtedly successful was in the high frequency communications equipment that it designed, manufactured and sold to the U.S. Navy. Products that the company developed, such as high frequency radio and IFF interrogators, were used by the U.S. Navy and foreign navies when they conducted joint military exercises. IFF interrogators were not only used as shipboard equipment by the U.S. Navy and its allies, but were also used along long stretches of isolated coastlines as a type of silent sentry. For years, Herley has provided this type of equipment to the Republic of Korea, and new contracts from that nation were imminent. In 1999, the company was listed by *Aviation Week & Space Technology* as one of the Top 20 Best Performing Suppliers in the industry.

During the late 1990s, company management made a concerted effort to expand its product line so that its reliance upon government contracts would diminish as its market for the commercial market expanded. Herley's strategic acquisitions were part of this effort and provided both the opportunity for growth and for expanding into the international marketplace. Toward that end, in early 2000, Herley formed a new subsidiary, Herley Wireless Technology Inc., which would be staffed largely by engineers who came to Herley via the General Microwave acquisition as well as the acquisition of Robinson Laboratories, completed in January 2000. The new concern would seek to compete in the rapidly expanding commercial wireless indus-

try. As the company prepared to enter a new century, Herley was fortunate to have an astute and far-sighted management team, still headed by Lee Blatt, with enough experience and prudence to forge its own way through a highly competitive industry.

Principal Subsidiaries

Herley Wireless Technology Inc.

Principal Divisions

Herley-MDI; Herley-Metraplex; Herley-Vega; Global Security Systems.

Principal Operating Units

Space and Communications Product Group; Microwave Product Group.

Principal Competitors

Signal Technology; L-3 Communications Corporation; Microsystems, Inc.; AMP, Inc.; Remec, Inc.; BAE Systems, Inc.; Racal Electronics, Inc.; Raytheon Corporation.

Further Reading

Covault, Craig, ''Radar Flight Meets Mapping Goals,'' *Aviation Week & Space Technology,* November 10, 1999, p. 36.

George, Fred, ''GPS Non-Precision Approach Planning,'' *Business & Commercial Aviation,* January 2000, p. 84.

——, ''UNS Super FMS,'' *Business & Commercial Aviation,* February 2000, p. 80.

''New Herley Subsidiary Enters Wireless Market,'' *Lancaster (Penn.) New Era,* February 25, 2000, Bus. Sec.

Rohland, Pamela, ''Top Fifty Fastest Growing Companies: Herley Industries Inc. #31,'' *Central Penn Business Journal,* October 9, 1998, p. S15.

Wall, Robert, and Geoffrey Thomas, ''South Korea Sets Ambitious Plans,'' *Aviation Week & Space Technology,* February 21, 2000, p. 91.

Wall, Robert, ''Prospects Mixed for UAVs in Asia,'' *Aviation Week & Space Technology,* March 6, 2000, p. 51.

''Who Needs to Ask Directions?,'' *Design News,* October 4, 1999, p. 19.

—Thomas Derdak

The Hertz Corporation

225 Brae Boulevard
Park Ridge, New Jersey 07656
U.S.A.
Telephone: (201) 307-2000
Toll free: (800) 654-3131
Fax: (201) 307-2644
Web site: http://www.hertz.com

Public Company
Incorporated: 1967
Employees: 26,700
Sales: $4.71 billion (1999)
Stock Exchanges: New York
Ticker Symbol: HRZ
NAIC: 532111 Automobile Rental; 53212 Truck Rental

The Hertz Corporation is the world's largest car rental company, handling more than 30 million rentals worldwide with approximately 6,500 locations in more than 140 countries and a fleet of 550,000 vehicles, including 300,000 vehicles in the United States. Through its subsidiary Hertz Equipment Rental Corporation, the company also rents construction and industrial equipment to contractors and industrial and government markets. Hertz's Claim Management Corporation subsidiary is a leading third-party administrator, while Hertz Technologies, Inc. provides telecommunications services to corporations. Hertz Local Edition specializes in providing vehicles to the insurance community and auto dealers. In addition to its diverse offerings, the company has focused on international expansion, and in the late 1990s Hertz rental cars were available in Russia and all Eastern European countries, as well as in Australia, Canada, Africa, Asia, the Middle East, and Latin America. The oldest company in the car rental industry, Hertz has experienced many changes in ownership since its founding, and was taken public in 1997.

Independent Venture to Corporation: 1918–53

The origins of the company date back to 1918, when Walter L. Jacobs, a 22-year-old car salesman with a fleet of a dozen Ford Model Ts, started a small car rental business in Chicago. Within five years, Jacobs had expanded his operations such that the business was generating annual revenues of about $1 million through a fleet of 600 cars. In 1923, Jacobs sold the company to John Hertz, the head of Yellow Cab and Yellow Truck, although Jacobs remained with the company, serving as its chief operating officer. Hertz held the DriveUrSelf System, to which he would add his name, for three years before including it as part of his deal to sell Yellow Truck to General Motors Corp.

General Motors kept the thriving business until 1953 when it was sold to the Omnibus Corporation. The following year Omnibus changed its name to The Hertz Corporation, and went public on the New York Stock Exchange, where the company's shares would remain until 1967. During this time, in 1954, the newly public Hertz acquired Metropolitan Distributors, a pioneer in New York truck leasing and the largest truck rental business at the time, with a fleet of 4,000 trucks. The purchase was made for $6.75 million in cash. Walter Jacobs, who was president of Hertz until his retirement in 1960, commented at the time that the acquisition "rounds out Hertz operations by providing in New York City the largest single truck rental operation in existence." Leon C. Greenbaum, the president of Metropolitan, became vice-chairman of the Hertz board of directors. The acquisition brought the total Hertz fleet to 15,500 trucks and 12,900 passenger cars.

By 1960, the market for rental cars was rapidly expanding, reflecting the expansion of air travel among the general consumer market and the rapid growth of the travel industry as a whole. Despite the influx of new firms into the industry, Hertz retained the number one position throughout the 1960s. Much of its success was attributed to the expertise and guidance of rental car veteran Walter Jacobs, who was recognized as being "the maven of the car rental business," knowing how to buy and sell cars expertly in order to build and maintain a profitable rental car fleet.

The RCA and UAL Years: 1967–87

In 1967, ownership of Hertz was again altered, this time in a merger/stock swap deal. The new association was with Radio

Corporation of America (RCA); while Hertz became a wholly owned subsidiary (though the company operated as a separate entity with its own management and board of directors), Hertz stockholders received RCA stock in return. Leon Greenbaum, who was chairman of Hertz by this time, became a director of RCA.

The relationship with RCA continued until 1985, when RCA decided to focus on its more traditional product lines and sold Hertz to UAL, Inc., owner of United Airlines, the largest airline in the country. UAL ostensibly planned to combine Hertz with its airline and its Westin Hotel Co. subsidiary in order to position itself as the most formidable travel corporation in the world. The deal was expected to face resistance from federal government antitrust scrutiny, but it did not, and once closed, Hertz joined the three leaders in their respective competitive industries. Since United Airlines also invested in travel agencies, UAL clearly meant to overlap nearly all travel services "from reservation to check-in to baggage handling," according to Richard J. Ferris, chairman of UAL. One unique aspect of the deal, according to some analysts, was that during a time of great leveraged buyouts, the acquisition of Hertz did not involve any investment bankers. In the meantime, UAL was concerned that it might find itself the target of a takeover.

In 1987, UAL changed its name to Allegis, Inc. Later that year, as suspected, Allegis was involved in hostile takeover attempts, as several investor groups believed that the conglomerate would be worth more if it were to be dissembled. Frank A. Olson, the chairman and CEO of Hertz, was named to those positions at Allegis. As part of a restructuring plan in which UAL (the Allegis name was dropped) divested itself of its non-airline holdings, Hertz was sold yet again. In a $1.3 billion deal that was completed in December 1987, Allegis sold Hertz to the Park Ridge Corporation, an investor group, made up of Ford Motor Co. executives as well as some from Hertz, formed expressly to acquire Hertz. In the buyout, Ford obtained 80 percent of the equity, and Hertz management received the remainder. Of the $1.3 billion in necessary capital, $520 million was provided by Ford while the balance was borrowed. Ford later sold 31 percent of its investment to Commerzbank of Germany and Volvo of Sweden. After UAL's transition, Frank Olson gave up the chairman and CEO positions of that company, although he remained a member of the board of directors.

Ownership Changes in the Late 1980s

After the sale, there was some speculation that Ford eventually might want to take Park Ridge public, a move that had proved profitable in other leveraged buyouts at the time. Buyout groups would make an acquisition and hold it for a short time then sell shares to the public at a sizable profit. More importantly for Ford, the buyout was undoubtedly good strategy. Hertz had been buying 65,000 vehicles a year from Ford domestically and 15,000 overseas. In fact, Ford's share of Hertz's vehicle orders, about 50 percent, would increase and thereby help Ford maintain its market share even though Hertz would still buy cars from other makers. Although auto sales to rental car companies were not particularly profitable (since rental cars generally had a low profit margin), Ford thought the move would allow it to keep rivals out and preserve its strong relationship with the rental companies. Put more pointedly by David Healy, an auto industry analyst at Drexel, Burnham, Lambert, "They bought it to keep Hertz out of the hands of Chrysler."

At the same time it was completing its takeover of Hertz via Park Ridge, Ford was also trying to keep a distance from some serious legal problems being faced by the car rental company. In August 1988, Hertz was involved in a dispute involving charges for repairs that resulted from collisions with Hertz vehicles. It was charged that Hertz, in some instances, had claimed for damages when repairs were not made and, in other instances, paid discounted wholesale rates for car repairs, while charging the retail rates to the parties involved. Although it was noted that such rental car companies as Avis, Budget, and Alamo also followed the practice of charging retail repair costs, according to *Business Week*, Hertz failed to disclose to those concerned that they would be billed for repairs at "prevailing retail rates." Hertz agreed to pay $13.7 million in restitution and $6.35 million in fines, "the largest fine ever imposed upon a corporation in a criminal consumer fraud case," according to Andrew J. Maloney, U.S. attorney for the Eastern District of New York.

In addition to this history-making legal settlement, Hertz's parent company, Park Ridge Corporation, faced change in 1988 as well. The Volvo North America Corporation, a subsidiary of AB Volvo of Sweden based in Rockleigh, New Jersey, became an investor in Park Ridge, paying $100 million in cash to Ford in exchange for a 20 percent interest in the joint venture. Park Ridge Corporation was then merged into The Hertz Corporation so that the investors, who retained their equity positions, owned the company directly.

Increased Competition in a Commodity-Based Market

Meanwhile, the competitive battle between the major car rental companies continued to rage. In January 1992, Hertz and Avis, Inc. reached a settlement after Hertz brought suit against its competitor, accusing them of false advertising. Avis had received the Alfred Award given to the "best car rental company" by Gralla Publications' *Corporate Travel*. Hertz's suit questioned the validity of the magazine's readers poll. In the settlement, Avis was enjoined from further advertising its receipt of the Alfred Award.

In another legal battle, a federal judge in New York City upheld a newly enacted city ordinance that prohibited all rental companies from imposing "resident-based" rates, but at the same time barred the city from putting the law into effect. Specifically, Hertz and others were charging residents of the

---

Key Dates:

1918: Walter L. Jacobs starts a car rental business in Chicago with a fleet of 12 cars.
1923: Jacobs sells the company to John Hertz, head of Yellow Cab and Yellow Truck.
1927: Jacobs sells his Hertz DriveUrSelf System, along with Yellow Truck, to General Motors.
1950: Hertz begins European operations.
1954: Omnibus Corporation acquires Hertz and takes it public on the New York Stock Exchange.
1960: Walter L. Jacobs retires.
1967: Hertz becomes a subsidiary of Radio Corporation of America (RCA).
1985: UAL, holding company of United Airlines, acquires Hertz.
1987: Hertz is sold to Park Ridge Corporation, an investor group affiliated with Ford Motor Co.
1988: Volvo North America Corporation becomes an investor in Park Ridge.
1991: Hertz Technologies subsidiary is established.
1994: Ford buys out the Park Ridge investors, and Hertz becomes a subsidiary of Ford.
1997: Hertz is spun off as a public company.

---

boroughs of Manhattan, the Bronx, Brooklyn, and Queens higher rates when cars were rented locally. The U.S. Court of Appeals later reversed the U.S. District Court ruling and remanded the case for trial. Later, in 1994, the state of New York sued Hertz and other rental car companies for refusing to rent vehicles to licensed drivers between the ages of 18 and 25. The judgment in this case eventually went against Hertz in 1997, the same year that Hertz agreed to pay somewhere between $4 million and $6 million in refunds to customers who had purchased their unregulated rental car insurance in Texas.

Competition remained fierce among the top five car rental companies in the early 1990s, and many analysts likened the ensuing price wars to those of the airline and hotel industries, whose markets complemented the rental car business. The car rental business was becoming increasingly a commodity market, meaning that there were more rental cars available than customers. In addition to price cutting, Hertz offered various promotional strategies to expand its product base. One strategy, for example, allowed customers to earn mileage in the frequent flyer programs of such airlines as American, Northwest, United, and U.S. Air, as well as to gain points in Mariott's Honored Guest program. Another involved removing mileage limits in the United States in 1995 and expanding its ''Rent It Here/ Leave it There'' program in Europe. In 1994, in the aftermath of the O.J. Simpson murder trial, Hertz abruptly cancelled Simpson's sponsorship, begun in 1975, in favor of its new ''Not Exactly'' campaign.

Improvements to the actual Hertz rental fleet were also focused on in the mid- and late 1990s. In 1995, Hertz introduced Rockwell-built vehicle navigation system units, a technology it named NeverLost, to many of its mid- and full-size cars. In 1996, it increased safety features–adding anti-lock brakes and

airbags in most of its cars—and teamed with Shared Technologies Cellular to offer cell phone rental.

Hertz also began to diversify; in 1991, for example, the company established Hertz Technologies, a wholly owned subsidiary involved in the telecommunications services business. Four years later, it launched Hertz Insurance Replacement Entity (HIRE), later renamed Hertz Local Edition, a subsidiary specializing in providing vehicles to insurance community and auto dealers. In 1996, the company expanded its used-car sales business, adding lots in almost 40 U.S. cities of 50 to 60 cars. The year also marked Hertz's foray onto the Internet, with the introduction of its informational Website located at www.hertz .com. By 1997, the site would become interactive, offering rate quotes and the possibility of checking on availability, and booking, confirming, and canceling reservations on-line.

Adding to the competition among rental car companies, the big three automakers raised their acquisition costs for cars, no longer subsidizing fleet purchases beginning in 1992. At the time, Hertz was purchasing approximately 70 percent of its domestic fleet and one-third of its European fleet from Ford. For three successive years, Hertz's holding costs rose about 30 percent per year, for a compounded impact in excess of 100 percent. The higher cost of cars meant that rental companies had to keep their vehicles longer (from three to six or nine months). Despite this hardship on revenue, the environment for rentals in the United States continued to improve steadily, a by-product of an American boom in travel; throughout most of the 1990s, the rental car industry averaged an 11 percent increase per year on rentals.

Eroding profits became a problem for Hertz and its competitors. Squeezed between spiraling car costs and competitive pricing, the industry as a whole showed losses of $150 million in 1995. Car rental companies, including Hertz, responded by raising rates several times beginning in 1993, and by cost-cutting, weeding out unprofitable locations, and limiting excess inventory. Yet Hertz managed to remain profitable throughout the early and mid-1990s. Its revenues for 1994 were $2.1 billion; in 1995, that figure rose to $2.27 billion.

Consolidation Trend in the Mid- to Late 1990s

By the mid- to late 1990s, the $14 billion-a-year car rental industry was undergoing a transition toward consolidation and public ownership. In 1994, Ford bought Commerzbank A.G.'s five percent stake in Hertz, thereby raising its own stake to 54 percent and acquiring control of Hertz. It then purchased the 46 percent of the company owned by Volvo and the company's management. In 1997, with Hertz enjoying 29 percent of the car rental market, Ford floated about one-fifth of its shares.

Although Hertz was eclipsed in 1995 by Enterprise as the rental car company enjoying the largest number of U.S.-based rentals, Hertz held its own through the remainder throughout the 1990s in terms of profit and kept its position as the largest car rental company worldwide. In fact, beginning in 1993, Hertz enjoyed a six-year string of record earnings. In 1999, it recorded revenues of $4.7 billion, an increase of more than 11 percent over the $4.2 billion garnered in 1998. Craig Koch, who became company president in 2000, attributed the 1999 record performance to strong demand, improved car rental pricing, and continuing cost efficiency.

Principal Subsidiaries

Hertz Claim Management Corporation; Hertz Equipment Rental Corporation (HERC); Hertz Local Edition; Hertz Technologies, Inc.

Principal Competitors

Alamo Rent A Car, Inc; Avis Rent A Car, Inc.; Budget Rent-A-Car Corporation; Enterprise Rent A Car, Inc.; National Car Rental System, Inc; Dollar Thrifty Automotive Group, Inc.

Further Reading

Buder, Leonard, "Hertz Admits Use of Fraud in Bills for Auto Repairs," *New York Times,* August 5, 1988.

Cano, Debra, and James F. Peltz, "The Siege of Alamo," *Los Angeles Times*, April 20, 1996, p. D1.

Cole, Robert J., "United Airlines Set to Buy Hertz from RCA in $587 Million Deal," *New York Times,* June 18, 1985.

Dickson, Martin, "Ford to Take Full Ownership of Hertz and Raise Payout," *Financial Times (London),* April 15, 1994, p. 23.

Flynn, George, "Jury Clears Hertz in Lawsuit Over Insurance Dispute," *Houston Chronicle,* February 19, 1998, p. A21.

"Ford to Raise Hertz Stake to Total 54 Percent," *New York Times,* February 15, 1994, p. D3.

Halper, Mark, "Hertz Mulls Outsourcing Rescue," *Computerworld,* June 22, 1992.

Harler, Curt, "How Hertz Makes Its Call Center #1," *Communications News,* November, 1992.

"The Hertz Corporation," Park Ridge, N.J.: Hertz Corporation, January 1993.

"Hertz Corp. Plans Acquisition Here," *New York Times,* December 4, 1954.

"Hertz Is Doing Some Body Work—On Itself," *Business Week,* February 15, 1988.

"Hertz Warns that Car Rental Fees Could Rise," *New York Times,* November 11, 1992.

"IBM Reaches Pact With Hertz," *Wall Street Journal,* March 31, 1993.

"Judge in New York Upholds Law Barring Surcharge by Hertz," *Wall Street Journal,* April 1, 1992.

Magenheim, Henry, "Car Rental Firms Expect a Boost from Air Fare Restructuring," *Travel Weekly,* May 11, 1992.

McDowell, Edwin, "Pricing Plans Shift at Hertz and Alamo," *Wall Street Journal,* May 5, 1992.

Miller, Lisa, "Rental Car Industry Merger Trend Could Hurt Consumers," *Kansas City Star*, January 19, 1997, p. F4.

Moskowitz, Milton, et. al., eds., *Everybody's Business: A Field Guide to the 400 Leading Companies in America,* New York: Doubleday, 1990.

Ross, Philip E., "Volvo to Get 20% of Hertz Parent," *New York Times,* June 23, 1988.

Ruggless, Ron, "Operators Woo Foreign Tourists With Hertz's Help," *Nation's Restaurant News,* April 12, 1993.

Salpukas, Agis, "Ford Leads Group Deal for Hertz," *New York Times,* October 3, 1987.

Sherefkin, Robert, "Hertz Rental Cars Getting Rockwell Navigational System," *Crain's Detroit Business,* August 28, 1995, p. 25.

Thomas, Charles M., "Hertz Pays Record Fine: Pleads Guilty to Defrauding Consumers," *Automotive News,* August 8, 1988.

Yung, Katherine, "Big Three Exiting Car Rental Business," *Detroit News,* January 15, 1997, p. B1.

—John A. Sarich
—updated by Carrie Rothburd

Hochtief AG

Opernplatz 2
Essen 45128
Germany
Telephone: (49)(201) 824-0
Fax: (49)(201) 824-2777
Web site: http://www.hochtief.de

Public Company
Incorporated: 1875 as Offene Handelsgesellschaft Gebr.
    Helfmann
Employees: 37,229
Sales: DM 4.41 billion ($2.64 billion) (1998)
Stock Exchanges: Frankfurt
Ticker Symbol: HOTG
NAIC: 23493 Industrial Nonbuilding Structure Construction; 23591 Structural Steel Erection Contractors;
    23331 Manufacturing and Industrial Building
    Construction; 23412 Bridge and Tunnel Construction;
    23411 Highway and Street Construction; 23491
    Water, Sewer, and Pipeline Construction; 23332
    Commercial and Institutional Building Construction;
    23571 Concrete Contractors; 23581 Water Well
    Drilling Contractors; 23593 Excavation Contractors;
    23594 Wrecking and Demolition Contractors

Hochtief AG is the German market leader in the construction industry and is among the world's leading international contractors with special expertise in dam, harbor, bridge, tunnel, nuclear power plant, pre-cast plant, and airport construction. The company has also gained a reputation in financing, promoting, and operating airports as well as developing special software for managing complex construction projects. Hochtief owns a wide network of subsidiaries and minority shareholdings worldwide, especially in the Netherlands, Brazil, Argentina, Australia, Hong Kong, South Africa, and the Middle East, as well as new subsidiaries in Poland, Russia, and the United States. Hochtief is majority owned by the German RWE Group (Rheinisch-Westfälische Elektrizitätswerk).

Two Ambitious Craftsmen Take a Chance in 1875

In the early 1870s Balthasar and Philipp Helfmann, two brothers from the small German town of Kelsterbach near Frankfurt, were struggling to make ends meet. They had learned the meaning of hard work as youths by helping their parents in their small brick-burning business. Despite the combined effort of all the family members, the family was poor, and Balthasar and Philipp Helfmann dreamed of a better life. Balthasar Helfmann became a trained locksmith, while Philipp Helfmann trained as a bricklayer. Before the French-Prussian war they muddled through with small transportation and wood trading jobs. However, after the war ended, they teamed up, bought a small brick-burning business and worked together on wrecking and demolition jobs. Finally, in 1875 they decided to found their own construction business in Frankfurt/Main, the Offene Handelsgesellschaft Gebr. Helfmann.

At that time, Germany was at the end of an unprecedented boom in business start-ups that followed the victory over France. A number of the businesses founded in the heat of the times went bankrupt. The Helfmann brothers, however, pursued a conservative strategy in order to survive in this environment. They started out with a lumberyard, a carpentry shop, a brick-oven, and 20 horses for transportation. First, they built houses as subcontractors, and later they began to built at their own risk. Philip Helfmann carefully studied the real estate markets in and around Frankfurt and specialized in estate development. Soon the two Frankfurt mayors Miquel and Franz Adickes hired him as a real estate broker in matters pertaining to property the city was planning to acquire.

Still, construction remained the Helfmann brothers main business, and their business philosophy was to complete all of their projects rapidly and with excellent quality. Three years after the business was founded it garnered its first large project: the complete construction of a university in the German city Giessen. Soon the company became involved in other projects in addition to dwelling construction, building sewer systems and sewer basins in Frankfurt and other cities, as well as sluices, harbor quays, and basins. By the late 1870s the Helfmann business had become one of the leading construction firms in the Frankfurt area.

Company Perspectives:

Behind every successful project there is a vision. Our engineers, businessmen, and craftspeople set them into practice with excitement and know-how—without long decision processes, but with a great deal of self-responsibility. They are masters of construction on whom we count as a system leader of the future.

The Helfmann brothers' success was based on hard work, calculation, and planning. Philipp Helfmann valued trade skills over academic titles, for himself as well as for employees. During this time, 12-hour days were normal for weekdays at the company; even on Saturday, construction workers were on the job from six o'clock in the morning until four in the afternoon. Philipp Helfmann was modest and hard-working himself. He reportedly preferred a sandwich to large meals and traveled by night so that he would not lose a work day.

Never had German citizens and politicians show off their wealth so openly in the form of magnificent buildings as during the era of the German Empire in the 1870s. The Helfmann brothers profited from this boom. Many public buildings such as schools, post offices, and courthouses were on the young firm's list of projects, as were Frankfurt's Hotel Continental, the Hotel Kaiserhof, and the Auguste-Victoria-Baths in Wiesbaden. Moreover, the construction boom was driven during the last two decades of the 19th century by the Industrial Revolution. During that period, railroad, tunnel and canal projects dominated the Helfmann brother's business.

A Public Company Replaces the Old Business in 1896

In 1896, Balthasar Helfmann died, and his widow resigned from the business. Philipp Helfmann then liquidated the old business and founded the Actien-Gesellschaft für Hoch- & Tiefbauten (AHT) in Frankfurt/Main; for legal reasons it was impossible to use the Helfmann name for a time. Philipp Helfmann owned 42.5 percent of the new joint stock company's shares, while two other major shareholders—the Frankfurt banks J. Dreyfus & Co. and E. Ladenburg—held each 20 percent of the share capital.

Helfmann continued to manage the business, often without consulting his new co-owners or Balthasar's son Fritz Helfmann, who joined the executive management board in 1897. Obviously concerned about their investment, the bankers visited Helfmann's office almost daily. They grew concerned about the capital involved in the company's larger projects, and Helfmann started ignoring their numerous invitations to business meetings.

In 1899, shortly before his death, Philipp Helfmann landed his first contract from abroad when AHT acquired a share of an Italian silo company located in the northern Italian harbor town Genoa. In an unusual move for the time, the construction firm took over the huge project as general contractor and guaranteed a fixed price (of SF 3.25 million, an amazingly high figure for that time). It was not at all common to give a single firm full

responsibility for such a complex project, which included the construction of large grain silos and the facilities necessary to run them. The project was carried out by AHT in cooperation with German and Italian subcontractors. Although it was a struggle, the company managed to finish this project without realizing any losses.

In the grain silo project in Genoa, AHT used a brand-new technique. Invented by a French gardener by the name Monier in 1867, this technique soon revolutionized construction technology. The gardener had begun to use iron cable to stabilize the planter boxes he built out of concrete. This process proved long-lasting and stable. Combining iron and concrete required a completely different technology. Instead of putting one brick over the other to build a wall, construction workers built forms which were filled with concrete. A wall could be made in one piece, and steel reinforced concrete became, of course, the material of choice.

AHT kept renewing its reputation for solid, quickly executed work. In 1903, for example, in just five months, the company built a hall for a festival in Frankfurt that was big enough to house over 9000 people. The company continued to expand up until World War I broke out in 1914. In addition to many railroad and train station construction projects, it built churches and army barracks. For clients from the Ruhr area, such as Krupp, Thyssen, and the Gelsenkirchener Bergwerks AG, it built harbor facilities and quays on rivers. One of the biggest projects during this time was the construction of a train station, Badischer Bahnhof, in Basel Switzerland between 1907 and 1912.

Turbulent Times Began in 1914

The majority of employees of AHT served on the front during World War I, and as a result civil construction projects became rare. After its defeat, Germany was obliged by the Versailles Peace Treaty to pay enormous reparations to the winners of the war. Hugo Stinnes, one of Germany's most powerful businessmen, was among the representatives who negotiated the agreement in 1920. One year later, when AHT raised their share capital, a Stinnes-owned company acquired almost all of the newly offered shares and thereby owned 50 percent of Hochtief's share capital. One of the projects Stinnes used Hochtief for after the war was to help built canals of the River Mosel in France. In the four offerings of the company's shares that occurred before 1923, Hugo Stinnes continued to acquire and soon became the majority shareholder. He then consolidated Hochtief into his empire, which included many coal and steel companies, and ships, as well as shares in banks, newspapers, and construction companies. Under Stinnes' influence Hochtief moved its headquarters from Frankfurt/Main to Essen, the center of the Stinnes realm of influence, where there was also more construction activity going on than in other parts of the country. Two years after Hugo Stinnes suddenly passed away in 1924, his empire broke apart. Due to the help of associated banks it was possible to keep Hochtief out of the turmoil and to preserve it as an independent enterprise.

In 1924 Hochtief's name was changed to Hochtief Aktiengesellschaft für Hoch- und Tiefbauten vorm. Gebr. Helfmann, Essen. In June 1926 the Rheinisch-Westfälische Elektrizitätswerk (RWE), one of Germany's largest electricity

Key Dates:

1875: Balthasar and Philipp Helfmann found their own construction business in Frankfurt/Main.
1896: The Actien-Gesellschaft für Hoch- & Tiefbauten in Frankfurt/Main replaces the old business.
1923: Hochtief is integrated into the Hugo Stinnes group of companies.
1926: The Rheinisch-Westfälische Elektrizitätswerk (RWE) become Hochtief's biggest shareholder.
1950: Hochtief begins building nuclear power plants.
1970: Hochtief becomes involved in airport construction.
1990: RWE becomes the majority shareholder in Hochtief.
1995: Hochtief wins the Athens International Airport project.
1999: Hochtief acquires Turner Corporation.

suppliers, acquired a significant share of Hochtief, 31 percent; this percentage would remain about the same for the following 20 years. After a period of hyperinflation ended, the construction sector began thriving again. A consequence of the reinforced concrete technology, construction sites looked more and more like mobile factories and the style of architecture focused on utility rather than aesthetics. Heavy investment in new office machines allowed Hochtief to install an up-to-date accounting and controlling system which enabled project managers at the Essen headquarters to monitor the progress of each construction project precisely and thereby keep financial losses at a very low level.

In 1927 a new CEO took office and laid the groundwork for Hochtief to become an internationally competitive company. Eugen Vögler, a civil engineer who started working for Hochtief in 1913 and whose father was CEO of a large steel company, had successfully set up the Hochtief offices in Essen and joined the executive management board in 1921. He set up a sustainable organizational structure with largely independent profit centers, moved the majority of the company's business activities to reinforced concrete construction, forced the company to move abroad, and founded an apprenticeship workshop to train qualified professionals—the first of its kind in the industry. One of the most prestigious projects during this period was construction of a large stretch of the Albert Canal in Belgium in 1929. The project's total value was equivalent to two years worth of total sales at Hochtief and was finished in less than five years—half of the time originally planned for the project—thanks to the creativity of Hochtief's civil engineers.

Unlike many other construction businesses, Hochtief was able to survive the Great Depression, due to its activities abroad and the great variety of its domestic projects. Surviving construction companies in an industry so sensitive to economic cycles cut back their staffs by up to 90 percent. In winter 1929 salaries of Hochtief employees were cut by one-third. However, after the company's recovery it established a highly competitive wage scale.

During the Nazi regime, between 1933 and 1945, Hochtief like all other big enterprises was in practice managed by the government bureaucracy. Until the early 1940s the number of employees increased fivefold to 10,000. Hochtief became involved in the Nazis' war projects such as the construction of the so-called "Westwall" along the French border and submarine bunkers. One of Hochtief's most famous civil projects of that time was the construction of Berlin's Olympia-Stadium where, in 1936, the last Olympic Games before World War II were held.

Building Nuclear Power Plants After World War II

During World War II many of Germany's cities were bombed into ruins, and it was expected to take a few decades to rebuild the country. However, Germans seemed energized by this challenge and worked passionately to rebuild their houses, factories, and streets, with the help of companies such as Hochtief. The 1950s also brought new technologies to the construction industry such as hydraulic drives, large cranes, and mechanized construction, all of which boosted productivity.

In the mid-1950s Hochtief expanded into a new field which would later become one if its main fields of expertise: the construction of nuclear power plants. With very strict regulations and safety requirements, such projects demanded special know-how that Hochtief was able to acquire over the years. The company pioneered methods for calculating the necessary strength of concrete containers under pressure in order to withstand earthquakes, airplane crashes, or gas explosions; their calculation methods were later incorporated into general safety laws. Between 1956 and 1986 Hochtief was heavily involved in more than 30 nuclear reactor construction projects, from research reactors to big power plants in Germany and later abroad.

Despite the domestic construction boom, Hochtief soon reactivated contacts with its international customers in Belgium, the Netherlands, France, Turkey, and Iran. The company also expanded into new markets such as Egypt, Australia, India, and some Latin American countries, and later in the 1970s into Arabic countries, particularly Saudi Arabia. In the 1960s more than half of all international construction carried out by German firms was done by Hochtief. Between 1971 and 1980 the company's sales abroad grew tenfold, reaching DM 3.3 billion at the end of this period. Hochtief had become one of the world's leading construction firms.

One of the company's most prestigious projects during this time was the "New Jeddah International Airport" in Saudi Arabia. Worth over DM 10 billion, this was the biggest construction contract ever given to a single company; it was begun in 1974 and finished ten years later. Other international Hochtief projects included the subway in Hong Kong; a water power station in Saryar, Turkey; the "Mossy-Marsh-Tunnel" in Tasmania, Australia; 23 hospitals in Peru; dams in Mozambique, Pakistan, and Irak; the relocation of the Temple of Abu Simbel; the Bosporus bridge in Turkey; and harbors all over the world.

1990s Bring New Challenges at Home and Abroad

The year 1990 brought two major changes for Hochtief: the RWE conglomerate became its majority shareholder, and Germany was reunited. Regarding the latter, Hochtief became involved in several projects in the former East Germany. A high percentage of the country's residential buildings were in bad condition, and modern, new production facilities, and transportation infrastructure were needed to make East German companies competitive. Hochtief focused on environmental projects such as landfill construction and reconstruction, a field in which it also conducted research on new technologies, as well as for cleaning the ground and ground water from pollution. However, Hochtief realized that the sudden boom in the German construction industry would not last forever and therefore focused on acquiring new business outside the country.

One of the main Hochtief hallmarks in the 1990s was airport construction. The company had already built the airports in Frankfurt/Main and Cologne as well as in Saudi Arabia, and the growth of international trade and travel resulted in a need for more modern airports worldwide. In the early 1990s Hochtief enlarged the airport facilities in Warsaw, Poland. In the mid-1990s the company helped modernize and enlarge the airport in Beirut, Lebanon, while it continued operation. The project included a new landing strip over two miles long that reached far out into the ocean, a 1.5 mile long breakwater, a new passenger terminal for six million people, and a new coastal highway. The company also acquired a 36 percent share in the Athens International Airport S.A. (AIA) and won the major contract for planning, financing, and building the new international airport in Athens in 1995. Two years later Hochtief founded the Hochtief AirPort GmbH subsidiary to focus on planning, financing, and operating airports worldwide, a field in which Hochtief was investing as a second focus for its business in addition to construction. In the same year the company acquired a share in the Flughafen Dusseldorf GmbH and won a contract to modernize and enlarge the Dusseldorf airport.

Hochtief's latest involvement with airports was its majority stake in a consortium that would plan, finance, and run the new Airport Berlin Brandenburg International with an annual capacity of 20 to 30 million passengers. However, one of its competitors in bidding on the project, IVG, went to court accusing Hochtief of corruption. A Berlin court ruled the deal void in September 1999, finding four violations in the bidding process. Hochtief AirPort CEO Wolfhard Leichnitz remained under investigation in the late 1990s.

The 1990s also intensified fundamental structural changes in the worldwide construction business. A growing number of complex international projects involved the collaboration of several companies. Global players with appropriate know-how emerged as the main planners and financiers who teamed up with national partners in public-private partnerships, while the actual construction was done by local mid-sized companies. In order to participate in all those markets Hochtief systematically extended and enhanced its network of international subsidiaries, even in traditional Hochtief markets such as the Netherlands, Brazil, Argentina, Australia, Hong Kong, South Africa, and the Middle East, and formed new subsidiaries in Poland and Russia.

Moreover, in the fall of 1999 Hochtief agreed to acquire Turner Corporation, the U.S. market leader in nonresidential construction. The deal was completed in September 1999, with Turner maintaining its autonomy, and Hochtief gaining a foothold in the U.S. construction market. As it moved toward a new century, Hochtief seemed well prepared to build on its success.

Principal Subsidiaries

Hochtief AirPort GmbH; Hochtief Verkehrswegebau GmbH; Hochtief Rohrleitung- und Kanalbau GmbH; Hochtief Umwelt GmbH; Streif AG; Streif Baulogistik GmbH; Hochtief Fertigteilbau GmbH; A.L.E.X. Bau GmbH; Hochtief Facility Management GmbH; Hochtief (U.K.) Construction CTD; Hochtief do Brasil S.A. (Brazil; 91.42%); Beta Acquisition Corporation (U.S.); Turner Corporation (U.S.); Kitchell Corporation (U.S.; 35.34%); PT Ballast Nedam Indonesia Construction (47.44%); Ballast Nedam N.V. (Netherlands; 48%); Hochtief Russia; Leighton Holdings Limited (Australia; 46.96%); Concor Limited (South Africa; 49.99%); Hochtief Polska Sp.z.o.o. (Poland); Garantie-Koza Insaat Sanayi ve Ticaret A.S. (Turkey; 41.93%); Hochtief Construcciones S.A. (Argentina); PT Ballast Nedam Indonesia Construction.

Principal Competitors

ABB Ltd.; Bechtel Group, Inc.; Philipp Holzmann AG.

Further Reading

Die Aufgabe Heisst Bauen, Essen, Germany: Hochtief AG, 1985, 37 pp.

Dubow Ben, "Berlin Airport," *Privatisation International*, September 1999.

"Turner, German Contractor to Merge," *Building Design & Construction*, October 1999, p. 9.

Reinke, Martha, "Germans Buy Share of Kitchell," *Business Journal—Serving Phoenix & the Valley of the Sun*, July 9, 1993, p. 1.

"Head of Hochtief AG under Investigation in Berlin Airport Privatisation Scandal Case," *Airline Industry Information*, November 1, 1999.

"Elefanten-Hochzeit geplatzt," *Die Welt* (online edition), June 4, 1997.

Parkes, Christopher, "Hochtief Builds Case for Holzmann," *Financial Times*, October 24, 1994, p. 27.

Lindemann, Michael, "Hochtief Determined to Swallow its Prey Whole," *Financial Times*, July 12, 1995, p. 24.

Hein, Christoph, "Hochtief kritisiert Bundeskartellamt, *Die Welt* (online edition), July 1, 1995.

"Kammergericht erlaubt Hochzeit der Bauriesen," *Die Welt* (online edition), March 19, 1998.

"Neue Attacke gegen Holzmann," *Die Welt* (online edition), March 24, 1997.

Exner, Thomas, "Absage von Hochtief lä*at* Holzmann-Aktie fallen," *Die Welt* (online edition), September 26, 1998.

—Evelyn Hauser

HomeBase, Inc.

HomeBase, Inc.

3345 Michelson Drive
Irvine, California 92612-0560
U.S.A.
Telephone: (949) 442-5000
Fax: (949) 442-5779
Web site: http://www.homebase.com

Public Company
Incorporated: 1985 as HomeClub, Inc.
Employees: 8,400
Sales: $1.52 billion (1999)
Stock Exchanges: New York
Ticker Symbol: HBI
NAIC: 42131 Lumber, Plywood, Millwork, and Wood
   Panel Wholesalers; 44419 Other Building Material
   Dealers; 44411 Home Centers; 44413 Hardware
   Stores; 44412 Paint and Wallpaper Stores

HomeBase, Inc. is one of the leading chain of home improvement stores in the western United States. From its base of operations in California, HomeBase has spread throughout the West. By early 1999, it had 47 warehouse stores in California and 37 in the states of Washington, Oregon, Idaho, Nevada, Arizona, New Mexico, Utah, Colorado, and Texas. The company planned to open an additional six stores later that year. Each HomeBase store averages over 103,000 square feet of space and carries a broad variety of building supplies and home improvement merchandise for the kitchen, bathroom, and remainder of the home. The central focus of each store is the Design Center, with a selection of home decor items. Stores also include nursery and gardening sections. In 1999 HomeBase reported net sales of over $1.44 billion, down slightly from the previous fiscal year.

The Birth of HomeClub to the Merger with Zayre: Mid-1980s

HomeBase Inc. has its origins in two HomeClub Stores which opened in southern California in 1983. The stores were part of the early boom in so-called warehouse stores, where shoppers who became members were entitled to discounts on purchases. In 1984, HomeClub obtained $5 million in venture capital which it used to build an additional five stores in California and to expand into Nevada. Only one year later, an October 1985 public offering brought HomeClub $30 million and the chain opened 12 new stores in California. In January 1986, flush with success, HomeClub merged with the Zayre Corporation, a department store chain headquartered in Framingham, Massachusetts. HomeClub became a wholly owned Zayre subsidiary and formed, with BJ's Wholesale Club, a Zayre's warehouse division. After the merger, HomeClub opened another ten stores in the western United States.

The Zayre discount department stores were entering a period of decline in the late 1980s, however. Zayre reported a loss of $69 million for the first half of 1988, and in September, Zayre cut its 392 department stores loose, selling them for $800 million to Ames Department Stores of Rocky Hill, Connecticut. Zayre was left with two healthy businesses, the home improvement chain HomeClub and BJ's Wholesale Club, a discount warehouse operation. In December 1988 Zayre announced it was planning a thoroughgoing restructuring. First, it spun off its two profitable subsidiaries, HomeClub and BJ's. What was left of Zayre was then merged into TJX Cos., a group of firms that included apparel chains Hit or Miss and T.J. Maxx, and the Chadwicks of Boston mail-order catalog.

New Life Under Waban: Late 1980s to Early 1990s

After the spinoff, HomeClub and BJ's became part of Waban Inc., a new company named for a small town near Zayre's old headquarters, with a management team made up primarily of former Zayre executives. Analysts saw a healthy future for the new company—one predicted 30 percent profit growth for several years' time—and maintained its stock was significantly undervalued considering the large, yet-unsatisfied market for warehouse stores which then was said to exist. Over the course of the next year or two events seemed to justify Wall Street's optimism—by early 1990, HomeClub operated 59 stores throughout the West.

Company Perspectives:

"The Base," as HomeBase has become known, distinguishes itself from other "big box" home improvement stores in three important ways: HomeBase services do-it-yourselfers and professional contractors by providing everyday low prices; our stores maintain an extensive merchandise selection that includes thousands of name brand and private label items; and our highly trained staff provides exceptional and timely customer service. Building relationships is what HomeBase is all about. It starts with our team members, the people who staff our stores everyday. Specially skilled tradespeople and support team members undergo constant training programs to better serve our customers, who range from the first time do-it-yourselfers to the seasoned contractor. HomeBase depends on strong relationships with vendors to maximize our product selection and maintain competitive pricing. Together, these relationships form HomeBase—a company focused on positive growth and committed to building long-term value for our stockholders.

Only six months later, however, HomeClub President John R. Chase resigned suddenly, an event some observers attributed to the climate in the home improvement market which had begun to turn turbulent. In particular, HomeClub found itself in fierce competition with the rapidly expanding Home Depot chain. James Halpin became HomeClub's president, its fifth in as many years. In March 1991, in an attempt to build the chain's customer base, Halpin introduced a major change in Home-Club's operation: henceforth its stores would no longer offer memberships. For the previous eight years, both members and nonmember could shop at HomeClub stores. The $10–$15 annual membership fee entitled shoppers to a five percent discount on their purchases. The membership plan, in addition to breeding customer loyalty, was designed to provide HomeClub with an up-to-date mailing list. However, company research discovered that the membership plan was keeping many potential customers away because the public in general believed that *only* members were allowed to shop at HomeClub.

The change had an immediate effect on Waban's bottom line. Member fees had to be refunded on a pro-rated basis. All customers were offered the five percent discount from then on. At the same time HomeClub lost the significant amount of income that the membership fees had brought each year. In the end, abandoning the membership plan forced Waban to take an $8.8 million charge against earnings in the fourth quarter of 1990. Part of the loss was offset by a public offering Waban Inc. made in November 1991, when four million shares of common stock were sold at $19 per share.

In an attempt to combat Home Depot's growing ascendancy in the home improvement market, Halpin also instituted other changes at HomeClub. He tried to extend the chain's appeal beyond its traditional clientele of contractors and hardcore do-it-yourselfers. Store layout and design were made more attractive in order to appeal to women, who decided how home decorating money was spent in most households. The chain

began stocking merchandise with more upscale appeal. The HomeClub advertising budget was shifted away from its primitive-looking direct mail flyers to four-color newspaper supplements. Some $20 million was spent on computers to track stock in stores and keep tabs on shipments. Additional warehouses were built to expedite order fulfillment. Departments in Home-Club stores which were not directly related to core business—photo-finishing, for example—were abolished. The strategy was initially successful. In the last quarter of 1990, sales increased by 7.4 percent to $279 million, and by 18 percent to $1.3 billion for all of 1990. HomeClub also added eight new stores that year. Sales rose again in 1992, to $2.8 billion, an increase of 15.5 percent for the year.

The Change to HomeBase: 1992

In February 1992, Waban announced that the name of all HomeClub stores would be changed to HomeBase. The change was meant to eliminate any remaining confusion in the mind of the public about the chain's lack of membership requirements. At the same time, HomeBase management began to stress quality customer service in stores; and the chain's motto was changed to reflect this, from "America's D-I-Y Warehouse"—do-it-yourself was seen as the antithesis of customer service—to "America's Best Home Improvement Warehouse." The new motto was also meant to better define exactly what HomeBase did.

Although the name change was expected to cost the company an additional $2.1 million, in the fall of 1991 Waban Inc. put into motion an ambitious plan for national expansion, opening a number of stores in the Midwest, in particular in Chicago. Besides kicking off the national expansion of HomeBase, the plan was intended to reduce the chain's dependence on changeable economic conditions in the home building and improvement market in California where 47 HomeBase stores—well over half of all its units—were located. In addition to Chicago, Washington state was a focus of expansion, and moves into Kansas City, Detroit, and Cleveland were rumored. All in all, by the end of 1992 Waban hoped to have 88 HomeBase stores in 12 states.

In November 1992 James Halpin resigned as HomeBase president and was succeeded by William Patterson, who came over from Sears, Roebuck. One of Patterson's first moves was to create a contractor services program made up of 120 installation sales representatives recently laid off by Sears. Under the program, the service reps would offer the full range of services they offered by Sears, but for HomeBase. Patterson saw the plan as a way to capture business that had not been tapped by competitors, especially Home Depot.

In May 1993, investors were shocked when John F. Levy, the CEO of Waban Inc. and the nephew of Waban Chairman Sumner L. Feldberg, stepped down, citing disappointing growth and earnings in previous years. Although Levy's public statements maintained that his departure was voluntary, speculation was rife that he had, in actuality, been forced to leave. What seemed clear was that Waban and HomeBase were not performing in the marketplace at the same level as companies like Home Depot. The shake-up continued in October when Patterson was replaced after less than a year as HomeBase president. One cause for the change was differences in management philosophy between Patterson and the new Waban CEO Herbert J.

Key Dates:

1983: HomeClub opens two membership stores in southern California.

1984–85: HomeClub opens 17 more California stores.

1985: HomeClub goes public.

1986: HomeClub becomes a wholly owned subsidiary of Zayre Corporation of Framingham, Massachusetts.

1989: Zayre spins off its warehouse division; HomeClub becomes part of Waban Inc.

1992: HomeClub drops membership discount and changes name to HomeBase.

1997: Waban Inc. spins off BJ's Wholesale Club subsidiary and becomes HomeBase, Inc.

Zarkin. On the other hand, Patterson's replacement, Allan Sherman, had already worked closely with Zarkin at BJ's Wholesale Club. Another cause for Patterson's ouster was Waban's continuing demand for higher profits from HomeBase. Its operating income rose slightly in 1992, but it was only 2.9 percent of sales, a percentage that was down from 3.2 percent the previous year. The drop in income was blamed partly on the cost of opening new stores and a recession in California. A cutback in HomeBase's ambitious expansion program was an austerity measure that was unveiled at the end of 1993, when Waban announced plans to close or sell 24 of its 90 HomeBase stores. At the same time, it decided to limit its business to states in the West. It pulled out of the Midwest completely, sold its seven Chicago-area stores, and tabled plans already underway for new stores in Illinois, Ohio, and Indiana. The change in those strategic plans cost HomeBase about $100 million.

By October 1996 HomeBase had 84 stores in its chain once again. That month Waban Inc.'s board of directors approved a proposal to spin off BJ's Wholesale Club. Under the plan, Waban would continue as a separate entity under the name HomeBase Inc. The rationale behind the change was to enable the management of each company, BJ's and HomeBase, to focus exclusively on its own goals and operations. Most analysts considered the move long overdue. A decade earlier the two companies had been too small to attract on their own financing adequate for growth. The year 1996 was seen as an optimal time for a split which would enable markets to better evaluate the strength and value of each company, which would then maximize the stock values of each. HomeBase was also considered a brake on the growth most investors felt BJ's was capable of.

Less than four months later, however, in February 1997, the spinoff was shelved indefinitely when Waban Inc., Kmart, and Leonard Green & Partners, a private merchant banking firm in Los Angeles that specialized in buyouts of established companies, announced a deal that would combine HomeBase and Kmart's troubled Builders Square chain. Under the terms of the proposed transaction, Leonard Green would be the majority shareholder of the new company, while Waban and Kmart would each retain 20 percent minority interests. With about 250 stores and annual revenues of approximately $4 billion, the chain would be the third largest home improvement company in the United States behind Home Depot and Lowe's Companies.

Just two months after the merger was announced, it was called off again though, apparently by Waban Inc., which in public statements simply said the parties had been unable to agree on terms. One analyst speculated that Waban may have started thinking more optimistically about HomeBase's future during its negotiations, and that Leonard Green failed to close the deal quickly enough. In the wake of the failed merger, Waban revived its earlier plan to spin off BJ's Wholesale Club.

The Spinoff of BJ's and the Renaming of Waban: Late 1990s

By mid-1997, when the spinoff was approved by shareholders, HomeBase—Waban Inc. had been renamed HomeBase Inc.—was struggling against Home Depot, even on its home turf in southern California. According to the *Orange County (California) Register,* almost 74 percent of consumers said they had shopped at Home Depot sometime in 1996, compared to only 46 percent for HomeBase. Compounding the problem was an aggressive program of expansion into southern California by Home Depot and Eagle Hardware & Garden, a chain based in Washington state. Part of HomeBase's problem was the look of many of its stores—about half had been remodeled, and the older ones had the dirty, bare-bones warehouse look of the early HomeClub concept. In December 1997, announced that it was accelerating its remodeling program; the 17 still slated for renovation would be completed within six months rather the two years originally planned. HomeBase also planned to build about 14 new stores over a three year period.

As the summer of 1998 rolled around, HomeBase's situation became more and more precarious. Its net income for 1997 took a nosedive to $1.5 million from $21.4 million in 1996. Sales at stores open a year or more fell by 1.7 percent. HomeBase Inc.'s stock price rose only 10.8 percent in 1997 compared to a 16.4 percent average for other companies in its sector.

In late 1998, however, HomeBase Inc. announced an unexpected profit of one cent per share, compared to its ten cents a share loss the previous year. When it announced the profit, however, the company also announced plans to increase sales staff and its advertising budget. Those changes, company officials warned, would probably depress 1999's profits.

In the spring of 1999, the board of directors approved a so-called shareholders' rights plan which was designed to forestall hostile takeover attempts. Under the plan, if an investor obtained more than 15 percent of HomeBase shares, the company's directors had ten days to determine whether the move constituted a takeover attempt. If so, other shareholders would be offered HomeBase stock at a discounted price.

As 1999 ended, HomeBase Inc. found itself the defendant in a lawsuit over one of its oldest stores. The owners of the Orangefair Marketplace, a mall in Orange County, California, sued the company for more than $100,000 in back rent on a store that had been part of the chain practically from the beginning. HomeBase closed the store at the end of September 1999, but refused to vacate the property on the grounds that its lease ran through 2002. HomeBase maintained it was not required to pay rent if mall occupancy fell below 62.5 percent; the mall argued that occupancy dropped that low only because Home-

Base closed. Just before Christmas 1999, a judge ordered HomeBase to pay $135,000 in back rent. The mall planned a further suit for losses it had incurred due to HomeBase's refusal to relinquish the property, a claim that could total more than $3 million.

Principal Competitors

Home Depot, Inc.; Eagle Hardware and Garden Inc.; Hechinger Stores Co.; Builders Square Inc.; Payless Cashways Inc.; Orchard Supply Hardware Corp.; Lumbermen's Building Centers.

Further Reading

Barron, Kelly, "Waban Inc. May Spin Off HomeBase, BJ's Warehouse Club," *Orange County Register*, June 20, 1997.

Biddle, Frederic M., "BJ's Chief Is Ousted by Parent Company; Results Short of Board's Goals," *Boston Globe*, May 26, 1993, p. 47.

——, "Waban Inc. to Take $100m Charge in Unit's Restructuring," *Boston Globe*, November 17, 1993, p. 61.

Brown, Corie, and Amy Dunkin, "Zayre Zooms—Downward," *Business Week,* August 29, 1988, p. 31.

Earnest, Leslie, "HomeBase to Increase Sales Force, Step Up Advertising; Retail: The $13-Million Plan Will Cut into Next Year's Profits. Store Inventories Are Expected to Rise 10%," *Los Angeles Times*, February 2, 1999, p. C14.

Earnest, Leslie, "HomeBase Updates Poison Pill," *Los Angeles Times*, April 7, 1999, p. C7.

Fitch, Ed, "HomeBase Puts the Pieces Together," *Building Supply Home Centers*, June 1992, p. 66.

Flagg, Michael, "HomeBase President Resigns, Is Replaced; Shake-Up: William Patterson Is Out, Allan Sherman Is In. Parent Firm Says It Expects More Profit from Chain," *Los Angeles Times*, October 1, 1993, p. D6.

Gendron, Marie, "Waban Inc. to Spin Off BJ's to Shareholders; Waban Inc. to Spin Off BJ's," *Boston Herald*, October 24, 1996, p. 28.

"HomeBase to Close Three Stores and Accelerate Remodeling," *Do-It-Yourself Retailing*, December 1997, p. 27.

"HomeBase to Phase Out by 2002 Sales of Endangered Wood," *Business Wire,* November 8, 1999.

Jones, John A., "Waban Rides Out California Slump In Shape for Rebound," *Investor's Business Daily*, June 8, 1992.

Mehegan, David, "Zayre Sells Its Discount Stores for $800m," *Boston Globe*, September 16, 1988.

Stanton, Russ, "HomeBase Chief Gets 13% Raise," *Los Angeles Times*, April 17, 1998, p. D7.

Woodyard, Chris, "HomeClub Drops Membership Plan; Retailing: The Home-Improvement Chain Is Abolishing Its Two-Tiered Pricing Structure in an Effort to Broaden Its Customer Base," *Los Angeles Times*, March 5, 1991, p. D5.

——, "New Name Gets HomeClub Back to the Base-Ics," *Los Angeles Times*, February 26, 1992, p. D5.

——, "President of HomeClub Steps Down," *Los Angeles Times*, May 15, 1990, p. D5.

—Gerald Brennan

Hot Topic, Inc.

18305 East San Jose Avenue
City of Industry, California 91748
U.S.A.
Telephone: (626) 839-4681
Fax: (626) 839-4686
Web site: http://www.hottopic.com

Public Company
Incorporated: 1989
Employees: 1,653
Sales: $103.4 million (1999)
Stock Exchanges: NASDAQ
Ticker Symbol: HOTT
NAIC: 44815 Clothing Accessories Stores; 44819 Other
Clothing Stores

Hot Topic, Inc., a retail chain operating almost 200 stores in malls nationwide, occupies a unique space within the apparel industry: it is the only large national chain that caters exclusively to the ''alternative'' lifestyle trends of teenagers and young adults. Specializing in such merchandise as body jewelry, artificial tattoos, multi-hued hair-dye, and unisex, music-influenced apparel, Hot Topic proves that shock value can lead to stock value, with the company generating revenue into the hundreds of millions of dollars after little more than a decade in business. The company occupies and has helped to create a singular, rapidly expanding niche market in the retail industry, and makes no secret of the fact that its targeted market is one usually shunned by more traditional merchants. Founded by retail veteran Orv Madden, Hot Topic devotes itself equally to the sale of trendy, MTV-influenced apparel and novelty items, some of which are marketed under the company's own label. The retailer went public in 1996 and has a goal of opening 500 stores before the year 2010.

The Founding of Hot Topic: 1989 to 1994

Hot Topic was founded by Orv Madden in 1989, after the executive became aware of the marketing opportunities which had been created by MTV and other popular forms of alternative youth culture. Previous to starting Hot Topic, Madden had spent the entirety of his working life in the retail industry. A native of Alton, Iowa, Madden earned his MBA from the prestigious University of Chicago and eventually earned a position as vice-president of the Federated Department Stores' Children's Place and Accessory Place divisions, a title he held for six years. While Madden's retail experience well prepared him to strike out on his own, it was his personal drive and lifelong devotion to contemporary music that allowed him to see the market niche Hot Topic would eventually fill.

During the 1980s, when MTV first made its presence felt in modern music and culture, Madden realized that there was a potentially huge consumer market for music-influenced apparel and accessories which, while being served by regional, independent stores and venues, was largely overlooked by national chains and outlets. In a 1997 interview, Madden said that in starting Hot Topic he ''saw an underserved market—music-related t-shirts and apparel—that traditional mall-based retailers were ignoring, and I decided to pursue it.''

And pursue it he did. At the end of the decade he and his wife put all of their savings into the opening of the first Hot Topic store, located in a mall in Montclair, California. The store sold t-shirts emblazoned with the logos of popular bands, music posters, and trendy costume jewelry. From the company's outset, it was overtly devoted to the sort of contemporary, edgy merchandise which could be associated with what came to be known as alternative culture, with even the shop's floor design and lighting being laid out more like a setting for a music video than a department store. Due to Madden's extensive experience in the industry, as well as his knack for keeping up with the whirlwind changes of teenage tastes, Hot Topic broke even in the 1980s, and the store's initial success paved the way for expansion during the next decade.

Madden's vision for Hot Topic was large in scope from the company's outset: he wanted Hot Topic to be a multi-chain operation, with stores located in upscale malls. Though Madden had to start small, with only one location, he had a good deal of pull within the industry, and after his first year as an independent entrepreneur he found no shortage of outside investors willing to aid him in making the company's growth a reality. In the next few years, Madden raised over $11 million for Hot Topic and began to open new stores at strategically located sites around the country. The stores all followed a pattern similar to the company's flagship location: they were lit with low, "Gothic"-style lighting, and carried inventory which shocked parents and delighted their kids. All the sites were approximately 1,500 square feet in space, and, despite their indoor mall locations, were constructed to look like a mix between a nightclub and a teenage fun house, with music played loud enough to match both environments.

To some in the industry Madden's company seemed a risky, perhaps flash-in-the-pan venture. What, after all, changes more quickly than the trends and tastes of punk or alternative teenagers? Hot Topic's sales, however, proved naysayers wrong: by the middle of the 1990s the company had opened dozens of locations, and all were pulling a profit.

1995–97: The Explosive Growth of Hot Topic

The key to Hot Topic's success, other than the obvious one of keeping up with music trends and styles, was the company's tremendous variety and scope of merchandise. No other apparel company which marketed itself to teens and young adults carried the amazing number of different logos, t-shirts, and novelty items carried by Hot Topic; and no company was as willing to so overtly appeal to a group which had traditionally defined itself through cultural alienation. Logos and apparel inspired by such controversial bands as Marilyn Manson and Nine Inch Nails were actively promoted by the company; cosmetics of strange hues and even more eccentric names were prominently displayed next to jewelry meant to go anywhere but one's ear lobes; and, most important, the displays and inventory changed faster than almost any other national chain. Madden, in speaking of his store lay-out, said in an interview that "Our target consumers are kids 12 to 22 years old. We want those kids to be totally overwhelmed with our merchandise mix when they first walk in the door."

To keep up with this ever-revolving, ever-shifting cache of merchandise, Madden bought a 45,000 square foot warehouse located in the City of Industry, California, where he headquartered his distribution space and his management team. There, the company employed dozens of buyers who were responsible for keeping up with music and teen fashion, and who aggressively canvassed merchants around the country. As head of the company, Madden kept the atmosphere at company headquarters pointedly open and the hierarchy to a minimum. The space was without cubicles; there was no dress code—indeed, piercings, baggy urbanwear, and varying hair colors were encouraged—and the entire area was covered with huge video screens which played the newest music videos throughout the day. The location was state-of-the-art in terms of technology, too, with a computer system tapped into every store's inventory, which was monitored and updated daily.

Hot Topic's policy of openness was part of the company's success and contributed a good deal to its rapid growth. Sales people were encouraged to take an active role in the development and introduction of new merchandising ideas for the company, and every buyer was required to respond personally to suggestions. Madden even developed a policy whereby the company would pay for the ticket to any concert a salesperson desired to attend if the employee agreed to write up a "fashion report" the following day. This was a direct and effective way of keeping up with the trends of teens and young adults in any region, and such a policy also allowed undiluted access to the tastes of the company's primary consumer market. In one case, a Hot Topic employee attended an all-night rave, and the next day he presented his company with an idea for creating special jeans pockets in which to store the popular see-in-the-dark glow sticks many ravers carried; within months the jeans had become a Hot Topic exclusive.

By 1996 Hot Topic had sales of over $44 million and had opened almost 80 locations nationwide. In the fall of that year, Hot Topic went public with an initial public offering of 1.3 million shares of stock. The stock, which initially sold at $18 a share, raised almost $24 million for the company. Madden retained a 30 percent ownership in the company, which only one year later was valued at over $100 million. Hot Topic had truly taken off and was helping to create a new and powerful niche market in the retail industry.

After going public in the autumn of 1996, Hot Topic's stock had by May of the following year skyrocketed in value, trading at almost double its initial price. However, despite the company's drastic increase in sales and steady expansion, it suffered a slight set back on the market during the summer of 1997. During that time, Hot Topic's stock fell sharply in a period of a few days, causing some analysts to question the wisdom of taking public a company that devoted itself exclusively to such an unpredictable consumer base. While reasons for the company's stumble were never made clear, some thought the rough luck of Hot Topic's competitor Gadzooks, which had suffered severely on the market, was rubbing off on the company, making investors worried. Despite this period of rockiness, however, Hot Topic soon recovered, and that year saw an 85 percent increase in its overall revenue compared to the company's previous year.

1997–99: Hot Topic Takes Off

The end of the 1990s saw Hot Topic only increase its sales and location sites, blossoming in just a period of months from a chain of 79 stores, in 1997, to a chain of 128 locations the following year. The company had also continued to expand its inventory, its apparel and novelty items growing into the thousands, and had undertaken the introduction of its own label as well. The company's line, which it called Morbid, produced everything from t-shirts to make-up. The line had sold well from its inception and eventually grew to make up for over 20 percent of company sales.

The majority of Hot Topic's sales consisted of the company's music-inspired products, from t-shirts with band logos to CDs. To keep up with customer demand, Hot Topic developed licensing agreements with such major distributors as Sony Music and Winterland which allowed the company quick access to popular product lines and logos. Particularly popular in 1998 were products featuring the bands Korn, Pantera, Marilyn Manson, and Metallica. That year, Hot Topic's sales were also aided by the huge popularity of the controversial animation sitcom "South Park." "South Park" t-shirts and logos had recently become a staple at Hot Topic locations, and, when the show took off, so did the company's "South Park"-inspired inventory. The company also continued expanding its general apparel lines, selling juniors, unisex, and men's clothing from small, trendy labels such as Kik Girl, Taffy, Caffeine, Lip Service, and Porn Star. Indeed, increased growth in every segment seemed the only strategy for Hot Topic, a fact reflected in the company's 1998 sales, which were almost 62 percent higher than those of 1997.

By the end of the decade Hot Topic had developed an ordering strategy which helped the company keep current on consumer trends despite the company's rapidly growing size: the buying team never ordered items any more than 60 days ahead of when the items were to be debuted; this way, a product or even an entire line of apparel could almost literally jump from the images of MTV to the consumer's wardrobe. Even though Hot Topic sought aggressively to become a staple in the traditional mall setting, non-traditional, fresh inventory remained the company's primary focus, and it was this mode of operation which attracted a loyal customer following. In a 1997 interview with *Chain Store Age,* the financial analyst Lauren Cooks Levitan said of Hot Topic that the company "has won the hearts of its customers by listening to them. The confidence and trust teens have in this company is amazing."

It was a trust—and loyal customer base—with the potential for a huge financial payoff. At the end of the 1990s it was estimated that the average teenager spent about $3,000 a year on recreation; not a great deal of money at first glance, until one multiplies that sum with the United States' expanding teenage population. Hot Topic aimed at nothing less than gaining the loyalty of every popular-music lover under the age of 25, and it appeared by decade's end that the company had just about succeeded in its aim. By 1999, the company's sales were up another 25 percent, and it had opened almost 200 stores in 35 states.

Principal Competitors

Claire's Stores, Inc.; Gadzooks, Inc.; Pacific Sunwear of California, Inc.; Urban Outfitters, Inc.

Further Reading

Ascenzi, Joseph, "Hot Topic Music Retail Chain Sounds Note of Success," *Knight-Ridder Tribune Business News*, May 27, 1997, p. 527.

Curan, Catherine, "South Park Fuels Big Gain for Hot Topic," *Women's Wear Daily*, March 18, 1998, p. 19.

——, "American Eagle, Hot Topic Pace Good Quarter at Junior Retailers," *Women's Wear Daily*, November 20, 1998, p. 2.

Grover, Beth, "Teenage Wasteland, *Forbes,* July 28, 1997, p. 44.

Howard, Bob, "California's Hot Topic Retailer, Analysts Puzzled by Stock Drop," *Knight-Ridder Tribune Business News*, July 14, 1997, p. 714.

Kletter, Melanie, "Profits Surge at Hot Topic, Wet Seal, Urban Outfitters," August 20, 1998, p. 4.

Williamson, Rusty, "Hot Topic Heats Up Teen Market," *Women's Wear Daily*, October 7, 1999, p. 25.

Wilson, Marianne, "Kids Shop Where It's Hot," *Chain Store Age*, June 1997, p. 31.

—Rachel H. Martin

Iceland Group plc

Second Avenue
Deeside Industrial Park
Deeside, Flintshire CH5 2NW
United Kingdom
Telephone: (+44) 1244 830-100
Fax: (+44) 1244 814-531
Web site: http://www.iceland.co.uk

Public Company
Incorporated: 1970
Employees: 20,618
Sales: £1.74 billion (US$2.89 billion) (1998)
Stock Exchanges: London
NAIC: 445110 Grocery Stores; 492210 Grocery Delivery
Services; 422420 Frozen Foods, Packaged (Except
Dairy Products), Wholesaling; 421620 Kitchen
Appliances, Household-Type, Electric, Wholesaling

"Revolutionary Family Food Company" Iceland Group plc is one of the United Kingdom's leading frozen food retailers, with more than 750 retail stores featuring both frozen and fresh foods under the Iceland and other brand names. Once considered a down-market grocer among the U.K.'s class-conscious consumers, Iceland continues to offer competitively priced foods while emphasizing a strong service component as well. In addition to traditional in-store shopping, Iceland customers can place orders by telephone or through the Internet and receive free home delivery. As the company has faced growing pressure from the U.K.'s giant supermarket chains, such as Tesco and Wal-Mart-owned ASDA, which began adding their own frozen foods while also entering the Internet and home delivery sector, Iceland has carved a new niche for itself as one of the U.K.'s foremost health-conscious grocers. In 1998, the company gained nationwide attention when it announced its intention to remove all genetically modified ingredients from its own-brand products—which account for the majority of products in its stores. In October 1999, the company went even further, guaranteeing that all of its products would be free from artificial colorings, and, where possible, preservatives as well. In keeping with its growing "green" image, Iceland also sells its own line of Kyoto refrigerators and freezers (named after the Kyoto environmental summit of 1997). Meanwhile, Iceland has begun to expand its store concept, rolling out a growing number of Iceland Extra stores, featuring a wider variety of traditional grocery and fresh foods items, in addition to its frozen foods selection. In January 2000, Iceland reached an agreement with Storehouse to sell Iceland food products in a number of Storehouse's BHS stores. While boosting its supermarket operations, Iceland has also been growing its food service component, Woodward Foodservice. Iceland continues to be led by co-founder, chairman, and CEO Malcolm Walker.

From Roadside to High Street in the 1970s

Malcolm Walker and Peter Hinchcliffe were in their 20s when they began selling strawberries from the North Wales roadside. Frustrated with their jobs as management trainees with retailer Woolworths, Walker and Hinchcliffe had begun looking toward starting their own business. Buying up the stock of strawberries from another roadside vendor, the pair set up a stall on the road near Llangollen, selling to passing tourists. While modestly successful, Walker and Hinchcliffe did not see their long-term future in roadside sales. Instead, the pair turned to retail, paying £60 for one month's rent of a storefront in Oswestry, North Wales. Walker and Hinchcliffe filled their small shop with freezers and stock bought on credit, and opened for business in November 1970.

Soon to become known as Iceland, the shop offered customers loose frozen foods, rather than packaged foods. The store's foods were displayed on freezer trays, and customers could take as much or as little as they wanted. The shop soon built up a steady clientele, attracted by the store's low prices. Walker's and Hinchcliffe's employers, however, were less impressed with their moonlighting activity and fired them both. The two had no choice but to decide to expand their store concept, creating the new retail food niche of loose frozen food.

From its first shop, Iceland began to expand to new locations, keeping to the North Wales region. After acquiring a second shop and a 20,000-square-foot cold storage facility in

Rhyl in 1973, Walker and Hinchcliffe put the Iceland concept into high gear. By 1975, the pair operated a chain of 18 stores, and had come a long way toward developing the Iceland look: clean, bright shops featuring a blue and white motif.

The next step in Iceland's evolution was the move away from loose foods to prepackaged frozen foods. As Iceland continued to make acquisitions of other frozen foods shops, struggling in the recession of the mid-1970s, the company also prepared the launch of the first "mature" Iceland shop, opened in Arndale Centre, in Manchester, England, in 1977. This was the first Iceland store to abandon loose foods altogether, in favor of prepackaged food items. By 1978, the company had begun to expand into a national food store chain, with 28 stores under the Iceland name. As its stores were also growing in size, ranging from 2,000 to 3,000 square feet, Iceland opened a 300,000-square-foot cold store facility in Deeside, Flintshire, in North Wales, where it also moved its headquarters.

Iceland was gaining a reputation among consumers as a low-priced alternative to the major supermarket chains. The company's low prices contributed to a somewhat down-market image, which dogged the company into the 1990s. Nevertheless, Iceland continued its rapid growth, boosting its number of stores to 42 by the beginning of the 1980s, while also introducing selected chilled and grocery items for the first time. In 1981, Walker and Hinchcliffe began preparing the next phase of expansion by selling a 16 percent share of the company to the British Rail Pension Fund, giving Iceland a £1.6 million war chest for further growth. The following year, Iceland rolled out its own brand label, the Iceland line of prepackaged frozen foods, which became the basis of the company's success in the 1980s. The large majority of frozen food items sold in the Iceland stores soon featured its own brand. In order to meet the rising demand for the highly successful Iceland brand, the company opened a new one million-square-foot cold store facility at its Deeside location.

Growth in the 1980s

In 1983, the company made its first major acquisition when it bought up the failing 18-store chain of St. Catherine frozen food centers. Iceland was able to turn around the St. Catherine stores and integrate them under the Iceland signage within months. At the same time, Iceland began converting its stores to a new image, abandoning the somewhat chilly blue-and-white color scheme for a warmer red-grey-beige combination. Iceland began looking for more shops to rent and other acquisitions.

Going public in 1984 provided the funding for stepped-up expansion. The company's listing was oversubscribed some 116 times—giving the company the momentum to develop into a nationwide chain. The increase in capital allowed Iceland to continue to expand its stores, and also develop its own label lines of chilled foods and grocery items. At the same time, Iceland found it easier to acquire leases for its stores, as landlords were more comfortable renting to a public company. Two years after its IPO, Iceland was able to complete its national expansion, moving into southern England with the acquisition of Orchard Frozen Foods. That acquisition had pitted Iceland against larger rival Bejam Group.

Bejam, two-and-a-half times larger than Iceland and in increasing competition as the two chain's operations began to overlap, became Walker and Hinchcliffe's next target. Joining the takeover wars that marked the mid-1980s, Iceland, which had seen its initial acquisition offers rebuffed, turned hostile and launched a takeover battle that lasted some three months. In the end, Iceland won, barely, gaining 50.09 percent of Bejam's shares in 1988. Integrating Bejam's stores, which doubled the Iceland chain to some 275 stores, proved as difficult as acquiring the larger company, especially due to management conflicts. Bejam's operations were moved to Iceland's headquarters, and Bejam storefronts were converted to the Iceland signage. By the start of the 1990s, the integration had largely been achieved. In addition to expanding Iceland's chain of stores, the Bejam purchase also brought the company into home appliance sales for the first time.

From Iceland to "Green"-land in the 1990s

The faltering economy, with consumers battered by a recession and soaring jobless rates, slowed Iceland's growth at the start of the 1990s. In 1993, however, the company returned to its expansion program, winning an agreement to take over the food halls of the Littlewoods department store chain. The first of the "Iceland at Littlewoods" stores was rolled out in 1993. At the same time, Iceland moved into the Irish market, opening its first stores in Northern Ireland. That year, Iceland attempted a European expansion, buying up the Au Gel chain of frozen foods retail shops in France. That purchase proved untimely, and the company was forced to shut down the Au Gel subsidiary within a year. Efforts to export the Iceland brand's frozen food products were more successful, and the company built a £30 million depot in Swindon to support its domestic business and growing export sales. In 1994, cofounder Hinchcliffe retired to a nonexecutive position with the company, and Walker took over as chairman and CEO.

After the collapse of the Au Gel subsidiary, Iceland refocused on its core U.K. market. During the mid-1990s, the company stepped up its store opening program, adding some 50 new stores—now with an average store size of more than 4,000 square feet—per year. Nevertheless, Iceland's per-store sales growth—and share price—were affected by the sluggish economy and increasing competition from the major, full-line supermarkets. Iceland turned to expanded services to make the difference. In 1996, the company added home telephone sales and home delivery; while only a small part of the company's sales, these new services nonetheless were quickly profitable.

Key Dates:

1970: Malcolm Walker and Peter Hinchcliffe open first frozen foods store.
1973: Second retail store opens; company purchases 20,000-square-foot cold storage facility.
1975: 15 Iceland stores are in operation.
1978: Company opens 300,000-square-foot cold store in Deeside.
1981: Company sells 16 percent share to British Rail Pension Fund for £1.6 million.
1982: Iceland brand frozen foods line rolls out.
1984: Company completes IPO on London Stock Exchange.
1988: Hostile takeover of Bejam Group is effected.
1993: Roll out of ''Iceland at Littlewoods'' takes place.
2000: Company reaches agreement with Storehouse to sell Iceland-brand food products in BHS department stores.

While the company rebuilt its retail sales momentum, it also began to diversify, purchasing Woodward Frozen Foods, the third largest foodservice provider to the U.K. catering and restaurant markets. Iceland quickly expanded its foodservice division, adding Cold Move, in 1997. In that year, the company renamed its Woodward operations as Wood Foodservice. Within two years, Iceland had built up its food service division to some £50 million in sales per year; Walker made no secret of his plans to extend Woodward's share of the U.K. foodservice market, and especially a targeted doubling of Woodward's sales by the end of 2000.

As Iceland faced ever-growing competition from the giant supermarket chains—which were rapidly introducing their own frozen food selections—Iceland sought new ways not only to differentiate itself from its competitors, but also to improve its image among consumers. In 1998, catching the spirit of growing public resistance to genetically modified foods (GM foods), Iceland announced its intention to remove all GM food products from its Iceland-branded foods. The move proved highly successful with British consumers, who were becoming more and more fearful of the possible harmful effects of the so-called ''Frankenstein foods.'' The company further boosted its new-found ''green'' image by introducing its own line of environmentally friendly refrigerators and freezers, replacing freon and other harmful cooling agents with hydrocarbon based systems. The new appliance line was named ''Kyoto'' after the 1997 environmental summit in Kyoto, Japan. Later that year, Iceland teamed up with U.K. retailer J. Sainsbury to offer home appliances through Sainsbury's DIY (do-it-yourself) superstore subsidiary, Homebase House & Garden Centre.

After boosting its foodservice division in 1999 with the acquisitions of Rossfish and Deep Freeze supplies, which strengthened Iceland's foodservice component in southwestern and northeastern England, and brought the company into Scotland, Iceland beefed up its service component, becoming one of the first U.K. grocers to offer free Internet shopping services. On the physical front, Iceland also rolled out a new store concept, Iceland Extra, which offered an extended range of fresh and grocery items, as well as convenience products such as tobacco and newspapers. By mid-1999, the Iceland Extra format began showing its promise—the first eight Extra stores, operating in the London area, had increased their sales by some 40 percent. Iceland began making plans to roll out an additional 20 Extra stores nationwide, and saw the potential to convert perhaps 70 more stores of the entire chain's more than 700 Iceland stores to the expanded format.

In 1999, Iceland found a new bandwagon from which to trumpet its health-conscious message. In October of that year, the company made headlines by promising to remove all artificial colors from its branded foods, as well as reducing where possible preservatives and other additives. With more and more studies linking food colorings and other additives to a series of health problems and disorders such as hyperactivity, Iceland's ''clean food'' image continued to impress the British consumer. Iceland had also impressed other retailers: in January 2000, Iceland announced its agreement with Storehouse to create a special line of Iceland products, particularly chilled and fresh food products, for the Storehouse BHS department store chain. The move by BHS to add food products was made to enable that chain to compete head-to-head with rival Marks and Spencer. After a successful prototype run in BHS's Birmingham store, the Iceland-Storehouse agreement called for a rollout of Iceland products in another ten BHS stores, with a possible extension to an additional 90 stores by the end of 2001.

From a roadside strawberries stand to a national chain of more than 750 retail stores, Iceland expected to continue its successful growth into the new century.

Principal Subsidiaries

Bejam Group PLC; Burgundy Limited; Iceland Foods (Ireland) Limited; Iceland Foodstores Limited; Iceland Frozen Foods plc; Trans European Insurance Limited; Woodward Foodservice Limited.

Principal Competitors

ALDI Group; Marks & Spencer p.l.c.; ASDA Group plc; Safeway plc; Booker PLC; Somerfield; Dixons Group plc; Tesco PLC; J Sainsbury plc; Wm. Morrison Supermarkets PLC; John Lewis Partnership plc.

Further Reading

Green, Matthew, ''Iceland Continues 10 Pct. Growth,'' *Reuters*, July 20, 1999.
''Iceland Beats Harrods in Online Shopping Table,'' *Financial Times*, December 1, 1999.
Merriman, Jane, ''UK's Iceland Profits from Food Scare,'' *Reuters*, March 23, 1999.
Rankine, Kate, ''Iceland to Drive up Sales Through Home Delivery,'' *Daily Telegraph*, September 2, 1997.
''Storehouse Expands Iceland Link,'' *Financial Times*, January 21, 2000.
''UK's Iceland Boosted by Anti-Modified Food Stance,'' *Reuters*, March 23, 1999.

—M.L. Cohen

Intuit Inc.

2535 Garcia Avenue
Mountain View, California 94043
U.S.A.
Telephone: (650) 944-6000
Toll Free: (800) 446-8848
Fax: (650) 944-3699
Web sites: http://www.intuit.com

Public Company
Incorporated: 1984
Employees: 4,025
Sales: $847.6 million (1999)
Stock Exchanges: NASDAQ
Ticker Symbol: INTU
NAIC: 51121 Software Publishers

Intuit Inc. is the leading U.S. developer of personal finance software. The company, though primarily known for such software packages as Quicken personal finance and TurboTax tax-preparation, attributes about half of its sales to QuickBooks, an accounting software program for small businesses, and tax-preparation software programs for businesses. Intuit, focused on increasing its Internet presence in the late 1990s, offers a range of financial services and information through its Quicken.com web site. The company's other Internet products include mortgage lending, auto and life insurance, and payroll processing.

Humble Beginnings in the Early 1980s

Intuit was the brainchild of entrepreneur Scott Cook, who cofounded the company with Tom Proulx in 1983. Cook, then only 23 years old, had moved to northern California in 1980 and was working in banking and technology assignments for the consulting firm Bain & Co. One night he and his wife, Signe, were sitting at their kitchen table in San Francisco paying their bills. It occurred to Scott that there must be a better way to manage their household finances and automate the hassle of bill paying. Inspired to start his own software company, he went to Stanford University to place an advertisement for a programmer.

When he got to the campus, he stopped a passing student, Tom Proulx, for help in locating a bulletin board. Proulx, it turned out, had done some programming and agreed to write a simple check-balancing program for Cook. In his dorm room he created the first Quicken program, which he and Scott used to launch Intuit.

Cook's idea for a check-balancing program was unique, but he was only one of many people trying to break into the burgeoning personal computer software market at the time. According to many of his associates, it was his background, intellect, and enthusiasm that separated him from the rest of the pack. Cook earned degrees in both math and economics at the University of Southern California (USC). (He credited summer internships with the federal government with encouraging him to go into business rather than the bureaucratic public sector.) Also at USC, Cook took it upon himself to resurrect the school's ailing ski club. He rented out a cabin at the nearest ski area and charged club members a mere $1 per night to stay. The club became one of the most successful organizations on campus and played an important role in getting him accepted into Harvard's graduate business school. Indeed, Cook was one of only a handful of students to enter Harvard straight out of undergraduate school and was the youngest member of his 800-member class. "When I look back, that ski club success, as much as anything, led me to believe that I could start a successful company," Cook explained in 1992 to the *Business Journal—San Jose*.

Cook was snatched up by the Cincinnati-based marketing giant Procter & Gamble immediately after he graduated from Harvard in 1976 and was placed in charge of the Crisco shortening brand. At Procter & Gamble he met coworker Signe Ostby, his future wife. In 1980 the couple moved to California for its climate, with Scott taking the consulting job with Bain and Signe becoming vice-president of marketing at Software Publishing Corp. During the next few years Scott gained important experience related to banking and technology while Signe learned about marketing software. Meanwhile, Tom Proulx labored in his dorm room creating the first version of Quicken. After polishing up the program the pair launched Intuit in 1983.

While Proulx contributed the technical expertise to the original Quicken program, Scott drew on his consumer marketing background to ensure that the program would meet a real need in the marketplace. He conducted numerous telephone interviews and focus groups, for example, in an effort to determine exactly what households needed financially and what features were most important to potential customers. Coworkers called his emphasis on customer input fanatical, and Cook's fixation eventually became well known within the software industry. The application resulting from this research allowed people to enter data on screens that looked much like a check and a checkbook. The data was automatically processed, thus eliminating much of the tedium of balancing a checkbook.

Cook and Proulx started Intuit in Proulx's basement with a single product and seven employees. Cook originally planned to sell the software through bank branches, a strategy that soured when he realized that banks were poorly equipped to sell prepackaged software. Moreover, because Intuit was just one of several companies trying to market a personal financial software program, Cook was unable to find a retail distributor that would take his unknown product. By 1985 the company was struggling to stay afloat. Three employees left when Cook and Proulx became unable to pay salaries. The other four, still believing in their product, kept working for six months without any pay.

Cook remained surprisingly upbeat and helped to buoy the Intuit team during their initial struggles. Whenever Proulx's wife would come down into the basement to see how things were going, Cook would tell her that they could not be better. "The truth is that things couldn't be worse," Proulx recalled in 1995 to the *San Francisco Business Times*. "Years later he told me that in 1985, when we were out of money, if someone had agreed to buy the company from him to pay off his loans, he would have done it." In fact, Cook was more than $300,000 in debt and was facing a long 30 years of trying to pay off those obligations if his venture failed. "I never had any doubt that he would eventually succeed," Proulx said. "A large part of my belief was from having been propagandized by Scott."

By 1986 Cook and Proulx were beginning to see some light at the end of the tunnel. Importantly, the Apple version of Quicken was getting positive attention in the trade press, and sales were slowly picking up. Recognizing the power of such trade articles to generate sales, they made a pivotal decision that turned the company around. Instead of selling the programs through banks, they would sell them directly to customers through advertisements. In a risky move that could have

quashed the entire venture, Proulx coaxed a reluctant Cook into placing $125,000 worth of advertisements, despite the fact that they had only $95,000 left in the bank. Cook wrote the ads himself, drawing on his marketing experience at Procter & Gamble. He emphasized the benefits of the program as opposed to its features, unlike most software ads of the time. "End financial hassles" was the key benefit touted in Cook's ads.

The advertising campaign was a success, and from that point forward Intuit's fortunes improved. Still, the company lacked a broad retail distribution channel and faced growing competition in the financial software market. In an effort to expand his advertising efforts and boost Quicken's exposure, Cook approached more than 30 venture capital firms during the mid-1980s. All of them turned him down, including one represented by his former Harvard roommate. Nevertheless, Cook and Proulx persisted. Cook determined that word-of-mouth critiques of his program and customer loyalty would become the most valuable advertising tools at his disposal. For that reason, he decided that customer service and input would take top priority throughout the entire company.

Stories of Cook's obsession with customer service abound. Once, while visiting the office of a software association, Cook walked by a clerk entering data on one of his programs. He immediately stopped to interview her about the application and later incorporated one of her suggestions into a version of the program. When Cook preached customer service to his employees at a meeting in 1988, he told them that he wanted Intuit's service to improve to the point where customers would become "apostles" for Quicken by purchasing other Intuit products and telling their friends about Intuit's offerings.

Rapid Growth in the Late 1980s and Early 1990s

By the late 1980s Intuit was clearly on the fast track to success. In just a few years sales of Quicken exploded, and the program became one of the best-selling personal financial applications. Intuit suddenly had little problem securing more financing. Several well-known venture capital companies, including Sierra, Technology Venture Investors, and Kleiner Perkins Caufield and Byers, were willing to back Intuit's efforts to expand its retail distribution. Thus, during the late 1980s and early 1990s Quicken became one of the top-selling software applications in the world, surpassed only by industry staples like WordPerfect and Lotus 1-2-3. Sales climbed to $55 million in 1991 from just $20 million three years earlier, and Intuit's workforce more than doubled in 1991 to about 425 employees.

Intuit broadened its scope in 1991 when it introduced QuickPay, a software program designed to help small businesses process their payroll. The $60 program, which was designed to work in conjunction with Quicken, was readily accepted by many users of Quicken. Intuit followed that introduction in 1992 with QuickBooks, a full-featured small-business bookkeeping program that provided an easier and less-expensive alternative to traditional accounting software. It was priced at about $140 and was also designed to work in cooperation with both Quicken and QuickPay. By 1992, Quicken (at a retail price of $70) was dominating the personal financial software market with a powerful 70 percent share. Much of that success was attributable to the company's emphasis on customer satisfaction: one 1992 survey showed that 85 percent of all Quicken users had recommended the program to at least one other person.

Having established its dominance in the market for stand-alone personal and small-business financial software, Quicken started looking at the much bigger picture. Indeed, Cook and his associates believed that Intuit's future was in providing a means of electronically linking customers with banks, brokers, and other businesses, and in providing various electronic financial services to the public. To that end, Intuit struck a deal with Visa that allowed Quicken users to download credit card statements directly onto their computers and into Quicken. In 1993 Intuit spent $243 million to purchase ChipSoft, which allowed customers to file tax returns electronically. Intuit scored again later that year when it bought out the National Payment Clearinghouse Inc., a processor of electronic transactions, for $7.6 million.

Cook realized in 1993 that Intuit was evolving from an entrepreneurial startup company to an established corporation. The company had even gone public by that time on the OTC market and was rapidly adding employees and facilities in the wake of ongoing acquisitions and surging sales. Early in 1994 Cook selected 53-year-old William V. Campbell to serve in the newly created post of president and chief executive officer. Campbell, a former Apple executive, was skilled in building organizations. In addition to his background in the computer industry, he had also served as the head football coach at his alma mater, Columbia University. Campbell would oversee the day-to-day operations at Intuit while Cook, as chairman of the board, would continue to spearhead the company's strategic plans.

By the mid-1990s Intuit was drawing attention from a much larger suitor, with software giant Microsoft eyeing Intuit as a possible takeover target. To Microsoft, Intuit represented an entry into the only major software category in which it did not have a significant presence. Microsoft was competing successfully with its own personal financial program, Microsoft Money. By 1994, though, that application was serving only 22 percent of the market, compared to Quicken's walloping 70 percent. Furthermore, Intuit owned other programs of interest to Microsoft, such as TurboTax, MacInTax, and ProSeries, all of which were geared for the personal and small-business tax-return-preparation market. Finally, Intuit had valuable experience related to conducting computerized transactions over telephone lines.

Microsoft, with Cook's cooperation, attempted a buyout of Intuit in 1995. Critics and Microsoft competitors balked, claim-

ing that the merger was anticompetitive and would give Microsoft too much power in the software industry. To Cook's dismay, the Justice Department tried to block the deal, which would have been the largest merger in the history of the software industry. Both Microsoft and Intuit fought the Department's efforts, and Microsoft even offered to sell off its Money program. Nevertheless, the $2 billion deal eventually collapsed. With that, Microsoft CEO Bill Gates renewed his efforts to make Microsoft Money a contender. Microsoft hired away a top Intuit salesman and launched a revamped version of Money to be used with Microsoft's long-awaited new operating system, Windows 95.

Like Microsoft, Intuit turned its attention back to its growing array of products following the failed merger. The company was still trying to digest the flurry of product and company acquisitions completed during the early 1990s. To that end, Intuit was working to consolidate and streamline its information systems and operational and financial controls. Intuit also began its online banking service in 1995 and acquired Japanese software company Milk Way KK. Even though the company's fiscal year was shortened by two months in 1994, revenues surged to about $194 million. In the long term, Intuit was positioning itself to become a leader in the burgeoning electronic banking and financial services industries.

Diversification and Expansion in the Late 1990s

The mid-1990s were a difficult period for Intuit. Not only was the company recovering from the disappointment from the failed Microsoft merger, but Intuit was also facing challenges in the software front. Overall sales of packaged software were declining as an increasing number of computers were sold with software installed, and Intuit's software sales were also affected by a saturated market—many in the target audience for personal finance software already owned Quicken. Another imposing threat to Intuit was the increasing presence of the Internet, which signaled the possibility of the demise of stand-alone software programs. Between November 1995, when Intuit's stock hit a high of $89 per share, and August 1997, the share price fell 72 percent, to $25 per share. The company racked up net losses of $44.3 million and $20.7 million for fiscal 1995 and 1996, respectively. The company was forced to eliminate nearly ten percent of its workforce in mid-1997. Analyst David Farina of William Blair declared in *Fortune*, "Quicken is over! . . . It's done. It's almost a nonfactor."

Intuit was not about to throw in the towel, however, and it worked to transform itself into a fast-moving Internet company, hoping to leverage its brand equity to attract consumers and gain credibility. "The Net was forcing us to learn fast, change fast, and even fail fast," Cook told *Fast Company*. "The only thing wrong with making mistakes would be not learning from them." Intuit decided to divest itself of non-core operations and sold Intuit Services Corporation, its online banking and electronic transaction processing subsidiary, to Checkfree in 1997. The company also sold its consumer software and direct marketing operations, Parsons, to Broderbund Software, Inc. Meanwhile, Intuit worked to increase its Internet presence. In 1996 Intuit acquired GALT Technologies, Inc., a provider of mutual fund information on the Web, for about $14.6 million. The following year the company invested about $40 million in

Excite Inc. Excite, one of the leading Internet search engines, boasted about 2.5 million users daily. Under terms of the agreement, Intuit would be the exclusive provider of financial information on the Excite web page. Early in 1998 Intuit inked a $30 million deal with America Online, Inc. (AOL), and Intuit became the exclusive provider of tax preparation services, life and auto insurance, and mortgage services for AOL members. Intuit launched a revamped version of Quicken.com in 1997 that offered a host of financial services and information, including QuickenMortgage, an online service that allowed customers to search for mortgages from a number of different lenders. Quicken.com quickly became the most popular personal finance site on the Web, and Intuit's stock price began to climb. Intuit's William Harris, who became CEO in 1998, asked in *Fast Company*, "Isn't it amazing, . . . how quickly you can become a company of the past—or a company of the future?"

Though Intuit focused its energies on the Internet, it did not neglect its core software operations. The company continued to enhance and improve its personal finance software and worked to bridge the gap between the Internet and packaged software by offering web versions and integrating web links. In fiscal 1999 Intuit introduced its QuickBooks Online Payroll service, which allowed QuickBooks users to connect with banks and tax agencies to facilitate payroll processing. By the end of the fiscal year, more than 6,000 businesses had signed up for the service. The company also offered WebTurboTax, which combined TurboTax features with electronic tax filing capabilities and allowed users to complete their tax returns and file them online. More than 240,000 1998 federal tax returns were completed and filed using WebTurboTax.

Intuit continued to make strategic acquisitions, and in 1997 it purchased Nihon Micom Co. Ltd. through its Japanese subsidiary. Nihon Micom developed accounting software for small businesses. The following year Intuit purchased Lacerte Software Corporation and Lacerte Educational Services Corporation for about $400 million. Lacerte developed professional tax preparation software. In 1999 Intuit bought the customer lists and intellectual property rights of TaxByte, Inc., a professional tax preparation software business, and Compucraft Tax Services, LLC, another professional tax preparation software company. Intuit also acquired Computing Resources, Inc., a payroll services provider, for about $200 million; Boston Light Software Corp., a developer of Web products and software geared toward small businesses; SecureTax.com, which developed online tax preparation services; and Hutchison Avenue Software Corporation, a developer of Web products and software. Intuit completed its acquisition of mortgage lender Rock Financial Corporation in December 1999.

In September 1999 William Harris stepped down as CEO. Former CEO William Campbell filled in as interim CEO as the search for a permanent replacement commenced. Intuit continued to add features to its Quicken.com web site, including the ability to view and pay bills, as well as view Discover credit card accounts. The company entered another agreement with AOL to be the exclusive provider of bill management services for AOL members, which numbered about 19 million in late 1999. Intuit also formed a number of partnerships with financial organizations, such as Fidelity Investments and Vanguard Group, to provide tax preparation software to online customers of those organizations. For fiscal 1999, Intuit reported total revenues of $847.6 million, up 43 percent from fiscal 1998. Net income reached $376.5 million, a significant improvement over a net loss of $12 million in 1998. The leader of personal finance software was quickly becoming the leader of e-finance as well, building upon its legacy as an innovator and provider of personal financial management solutions. With more than 15 million customers, Intuit was in a strong position as it approached a new decade. The company planned to continue dominating the personal finance segment by offering the latest and greatest finance solutions, both online and off.

Principal Subsidiaries

Intuit Insurance Services, Inc.; Boston Light Software Corp.; Computing Resources, Inc.; Intuit Lender Services, Inc.; Lacerte Software Corporation; Lacerte Educational Services, Inc.; Quicken Investment Services, Inc.; SecureTax.com, Inc.; Intuit Canada Limited; Intuit NS ULC (Canada); Intuit GmbH (Germany); Intuit KK (Japan); Intuit Ltd. (U.K.).

Principal Competitors

Sage Group PLC; H&R Block, Inc.; Automatic Data Processing, Inc.; Microsoft Corp.

Further Reading

Brown, Eryn, "Is Intuit Headed for a Meltdown?," *Fortune*, August 18, 1997, p. 200.

Buck, Richard, "Intuit Stock Tumbles on Microsoft Ruling," *Seattle Times*, February 16, 1995, p. C1.

Crosariol, Beppi, "US Fights Microsoft's Takeover of Intuit," *Boston Globe*, April 28, 1995, p. 1.

Dillon, Pat, "Conspiracy of Change: How Do You Overthrow a Successful Company?," *Fast Company*, October 1, 1998, p. 182.

Janah, Monua, "Mountain View, Calif.-Based Firm Plans Full-Service Financial Web Site," *San Jose Mercury News*, November 15, 1999.

Krey, Michael, "Scott Cook: Intuit Co-Founder Got up to Speed at USC Ski Club," *Business Journal-San Jose*, July 20, 1992, p. 13.

Levine, Daniel S., "Executive of the Year: After Bringing Bill Gates to His Knees, Scott Cook Plans to Revolutionize the Finance Industries," *San Francisco Business Times*, January 6, 1995, p. 1.

Swisher, Kara, "Intuit CEO Bill Harris Resigns; Bill Campbell to Be Interim Chief," *Wall Street Journal*, September 24, 1999, p. B3.

——, "Intuit to Integrate Web Links into Small-Business Software," *Wall Street Journal*, October 21, 1999, p. B15.

"Welcome Back to the Jungle, Intuit," *Business Week*, June 5, 1995, p. 4.

—Dave Mote
—updated by Mariko Fujinaka

Iron Mountain, Inc.

745 Atlantic Avenue
Boston, Massachusetts 02111
U.S.A.
Telephone: (617) 535-4766
Toll Free: (800) 883-8000
Fax: (617) 350-7881
Web site: http://www.ironmountain.com

Public Company
Incorporated: 1951
Employees: 8,600
Sales: $519.5 million (1999)
Stock Exchanges: New York
Ticker Symbol: IMTN
NAIC: 49311 4225 General Warehousing and Storage

Iron Mountain, Inc., is the largest records and information management company in the world. The company provides a full range of records storage and management services to the business sector, health care industry, law profession, and management consulting industry throughout the United States and the United Kingdom. The company can assist its customers with the storage of computer disks and tapes, microfilm and microfiche, audio and video tapes, x-rays and blueprints, film and optical disks and, of course, paper. The trend toward outsourcing records and information management has catapulted Iron Mountain to the top. In 1994, 1995, and 1996, company revenues increased at growth rates of 19, 33, and 50 percent respectively, and in 1998 the company reported that revenues increased a whopping 103 percent over the previous year. At the same time, Iron Mountain executed a comprehensive acquisitions strategy that led to the purchase of 15 firms noted for their strength and potential in records and information management. With the purchase of British Data Management, Ltd. in the same year, Iron Mountain took the worldwide leadership position in the industry, a position it cemented with the 1999 acquisition of competitor Pierce Leahy Corporation.

Early History

Iron Mountain was established in 1951 by a group of dedicated visionaries who understood the nature of the modern business era. Through the end of World War II, records for all types of business activities were recorded by hand. If the company was organized and prosperous enough, the records were later typed and then filed in a filing cabinet or appropriate container, often a heavy-duty cardboard box. As time passed, older records were then stored in a basement or warehouse, whichever was most convenient and least damp.

The entrepreneurs who decided to open a records management firm understood the old-fashioned methods and knew that these methods would not be able to keep pace with the burgeoning economy and the rise of the consumer product era in postwar America. How could a company that sold millions and millions of items keep records of all the transactions and inventory by hand? How could a firm with thousands of employees ensure that they received their paychecks in the exact amount at the right time? How could hospitals maintain patient information for rapid retrieval and analysis? As businesses expanded, how could management be sure that their ventures met with the regulatory standards set by state and federal government agencies?

As laborious and time-consuming in-house record keeping began to drain valuable resources away from the primary focus of a company, managers began to search for new ways to store and manage their records while retaining easy access to critical information. At first, Iron Mountain was contracted by large businesses within and around the Boston metropolitan area to provide consulting services for records management. Soon, however, the consulting services turned into an operational activity when Iron Mountain started its business records storage and management system. Iron Mountain assisted a company in gathering and organizing records; establishing a file system by date, product, or topic; and then providing a cost-effective method to manage the entire system that had been established. By the end of the 1950s, Iron Mountain had gained a reputation for providing reliable, efficient, highly organized, cost-effective solutions to the problems faced by both small and large companies in managing their records.

Company Perspectives:

Iron Mountain is proud of its dramatic growth of the past several years—growth that has further reinforced the Company's position as the recognized leader in the records management industry. Iron Mountain builds upon enduring customer relationships in records management while offering a range of related services and products. The Company aggressively invests in technology to improve customer access and information flows. And the Company sees continuing growth opportunities in the U.S. market along with largely untapped opportunities in the global marketplace. Against the backdrop of this growth, the business fundamentals remain constant. That is why the same themes reappear in Iron Mountain's annual report each year—themes of Growth, Stability, Leadership, and Technology. These central themes have sustained the Company's success over the past three decades. Continued execution along these themes will determine Iron Mountain's success for the foreseeable future.

Throughout the 1960s, management at Iron Mountain focused on providing high-quality consulting services, as well as assisting firms in the storage and management of business records. During this time, the company began to expand the range of its services. Active file management became one of the services that was most sought after, especially by larger firms, and Iron Mountain came up with the innovative idea to use customized retrieval labels so that any record could be routed from a manager's or supervisor's desk in the administrative office to the receiving dock with minimal effort and maximum efficiency. As management in larger firms began to realize the importance of controlling critical information and having access to it at a moment's notice, Iron Mountain began to develop new and even more efficient methods to meet customer needs, including such techniques as sealing files to protect their contents and a new way to re-file records quickly and accurately.

Expansion: 1970s–80s

During the 1970s and 1980s Iron Mountain expanded its operations across the United States and into Europe. Having already established the nation's first underground center for records storage in 1951, the year the company was founded, Iron Mountain was now inundated with requests from *Fortune 500* firms to assist them in their management and storage of an ever-increasing number of records. To meet this demand, the company embarked upon a comprehensive strategy to expand across the United States. While maintaining its headquarters in Boston, the company opened offices in New York City and throughout the state of New York, as well as in Ohio, California, Indiana, Florida, Pennsylvania, Delaware, Arizona, New Jersey, New Hampshire, Kentucky, Texas, Connecticut, Virginia, North Carolina, Rhode Island, and Nebraska. And this was only the first round of the company's expansion program. Additional offices followed in New Mexico, Michigan, Georgia, Maryland, Alabama, Louisiana, Colorado, Missouri, Nevada, Oregon, Minnesota, Maine, Utah, and Washington. By the end of the 1980s, Iron Mountain provided a wide variety of records storage and management services to nearly one-third of the companies on the *Fortune 500* list, as well as to a host of start-ups, small firms, and mid-sized companies.

During the 1980s Iron Mountain expanded its services dramatically in the field of medicine, becoming the nation's leading provider of records storage to a wide spectrum of doctors, hospitals, and insurance companies within the health care industry. The specialized services that the company provided involved open-shelf filing, on-site indexing projects, on-site purges, stat and regular schedule deliveries of patient records, and radiology file management. Iron Mountain worked with some of the country's busiest hospitals and largest research laboratories, as well as small clinics and group practices, to provide safe record storage and management. Perhaps the most innovative and useful of all the services provided by the company included the stat delivery of patient records. Iron Mountain operated and maintained its own storage facilities for hospitals that were able to deliver hundreds of medical files throughout the day and night at a moment's notice in the case of a life or death matter.

It was also during the 1980s that the company grew into the leading provider of records storage services for the legal profession. Although Iron Mountain had been providing such services to lawyers from its inception, during the 1980s the company developed customized searching, sorting, and selection criteria that enabled law professionals to either broaden or narrow the scope and range of their search for legal records and documents. Iron Mountain also developed a filing system for lawyers based on customer needs, including access to files by attorney, date, client, issue, or any other field that was requested. This aspect of the company's services grew rapidly throughout the decade, and most of the firm's offices around the United States were provided some sort of legal file storage and management. As the 1980s drew to a close, Iron Mountain was providing state-of-the art legal file storage and management services to some of the most prestigious law firms in the United States.

The 1990s and Beyond

By the early 1990s, Iron Mountain offered a full range of services, including business records storage and management, software escrow, healthcare records storage and management, active file management, vital records protection, data security services, records management consulting, facilities management, film and sound archive services, destruction services, disaster recovery support, and storage cartons and supplies. By the mid-1990s, Iron Mountain was clearly the dominant company within the industry, and continuing to grow at a record pace. The firm had 30 million square feet of storage space, and was providing its services to over 25,000 customers, including an ever-increasing number of *Fortune 500* firms.

Ambitious as ever, and ready to take an even larger share of the market, management at the company decided to implement one of the most aggressive growth through acquisitions strategies in modern corporate history. During four years beginning in 1994, Iron Mountain acquired no less than 62 companies, enabling the firm to establish a new presence in 46 markets. In 1998 alone the company made 12 purchases, some of the more

Key Dates:

1951: Iron Mountain opens for business in Boston.
1955: Company expands legal profession records storage and management services.
1960: Active file management services are expanded.
1970: Underground records storage facilities are enhanced.
1994: Major growth through acquisitions strategy begins.
1998: Company makes first oversees acquisition, British Data Management, Ltd., and reports revenues of $423 million at the end of the fiscal year.
1999: Iron Mountain acquires its top competitor Pierce Leahy.

notable including the Arcus Group, Inc., which expanded Iron Mountain's data security service business and propelled it to number one within the industry; National Underground Storage, located in Pennsylvania, which significantly enhanced and strengthened the company's vital records and film and sound archive storage services; and a number of companies in the Pacific Northwest, which resulted in Iron Mountain becoming the leader in the region. All of these acquisitions were reorganized and incorporated into Iron Mountain's administrative and regional operations. In addition, Iron Mountain made a foray into Europe, acquiring British Data Management, Ltd., one of the two leaders in providing records storage and management services throughout the United Kingdom. Although Europe remained behind the United States in outsourcing records storage and management services, Iron Mountain's management saw the market as having great potential for the future and viewed the acquisition of British Data Management as a step toward further expansion on the continent, including France, Germany, and the Netherlands.

By the end of fiscal 1998, Iron Mountain could justifiably lay claim to the title of ''The World's Largest Records Management Company.'' The company counted offices in nearly 70 cities across the United States, with additional offices planned due to the continuing acquisitions program. Most impressively, the company reported a 103 percent increase in revenues from 1997 to the end of 1998. Revenues for 1998 reached $423 million.

However, Iron Mountain did not stop there. In October 1999, the company announced a deal to merge with its chief rival, Pierce Leahy Corporation in a stock swap valued at around $1.1 billion. This ''reverse merger'' was completed in February 2000, with Pierce Leahy assuming the Iron Mountain name. Together, the two powerhouses boasted over 115,000 clients through their 77 facilities in the United States, nine Canadian operations, and joint ventures in Mexico, South America, and Europe. The new Iron Mountain assumed its former rival's debt of about $570 million as well as the costs incurred in the transaction, while Pierce Leahy shareholders acquired about 35 percent of the new entity's stock. Prospects for the year 2000 looked just as bright. Early in the year, the company announced yet another acquisition, that of Data Storage Centers, Inc., of Jacksonville, Florida, which would give the company a greater presence in the southeastern states, particularly Florida. With the global business sector generating ever-greater amounts of data and information, whether paper or electronic, the demand for Iron Mountain's services can only grow.

Principal Subsidiaries

Comac Inc.; Arcus Data Security Inc.; British Data Management, Ltd.(U.K.)

Principal Competitors

Lason, Inc.; Administaff, Inc.

Further Reading

Dillon, Paul, ''Iron Mountain Adds to Records Storage Empire,'' *Orlando Business Journal,* August 23, 1996, p. 4.
''Iron Mountain Buys Four Records-Management Companies,'' *New York Times,* April 14, 1999, p. C19(E).
''Iron Mountain, Inc.,'' *New York Times,* July 9, 1999, p. C4.
''Iron Mountain, Inc.,'' *New York Times,* May 10, 1999, p. C14.
''Iron Mountain Listing Change,'' *Wall Street Journal,* April 26, 1999, p. C19.

—Thomas Derdak

ITT Technical Institute **ITT**

ITT Educational Services, Inc.

5975 Castle Creek Parkway North Drive
Indianapolis, Indiana 46250
U.S.A.
Telephone: (317) 594-9499
Fax: (317) 594-4284
Web site: http://www.itttech.edu; http://
www.ittesi.com

Public Company
Incorporated: 1968
Employees: 3,120
Sales: $316.4 million (1999)
Stock Exchanges: New York
Ticker Symbol: ESI
NAIC: 61121 Junior Colleges

ITT Educational Services, Inc. is a private, postsecondary education provider, with 67 colleges operating in 28 states. The colleges, called ITT Technical Institutes, offer technology-focused, career-oriented programs that lead primarily to associate's and bachelor's degrees. ITT's total enrollment is approximately 25,000, and its students attend classes year-round.

1960s: Building the Business

The business that was eventually to become ITT Educational Services began as part of Howard W. Sams and Co. Inc., an Indianapolis-based publisher of technical training manuals and textbooks. Sams had been in the publishing business for almost 20 years when it decided to try its hand at running a private trade school. It established its first school—Sams Technical Institute—in Indianapolis in 1963. The institute, which taught electronics, consisted of 28 students. Sams acquired two more schools in 1965 and 1966: Teletronic Technical Institute, of Evansville, Indiana; and Acme Institute of Technology, Inc., in Dayton, Ohio. A fourth school was also opened in Fort Wayne, Indiana, during that time period.

In October of 1966, Howard W. Sams and Co. was purchased by ITT Corporation, a large, New York-based conglom-

erate. Two years later, ITT Corporation incorporated its private school subsidiary as "ITT Educational Services" and established its headquarters in Indianapolis. ITT's first president was William D. Renner, who had previously been the vice-president of training for Howard W. Sams.

In 1968, with the backing of its capital-rich parent, ITT Educational embarked upon an ambitious plan for expansion that led to a flurry of acquisitions. By the end of the year, the company had acquired seven new schools located in Chicago, St. Louis, Boston, New York City, and Hempstead, New York. This brought the total number of schools in the ITT system to ten. The company began working toward standardizing the materials and lesson plans used in the various schools' courses by establishing curricula committees.

In 1969 ITT Educational entered the foreign market when it acquired Ecole de Gaulle, a Paris-based system of five schools focusing on vocational, business, commercial, and trade training. To hold and manage its international operations, the company established the subsidiary ITT Educational Services-Europe. Meanwhile, ITT continued to add to its domestic school system at a breakneck pace. Between February and early September of 1969, it acquired ten business and technical schools, scattered through Ohio, Michigan, Washington, Idaho, Illinois, Minnesota, and Washington, D.C. It also opened two new schools in Bethesda and Annapolis, Maryland. Both the new schools operated under the name "ITT Business Institute."

1970s: Leadership Changes

ITT Educational started the new decade with a series of transitions in its leadership. Late in 1969, the company's first president, William Renner, relinquished the position he had assumed only the year before. He was replaced in 1970 by Burton Sheff. But in May of 1972, Sheff resigned, and ITT was once again leaderless. Sheff was replaced by Neil R. Cronin, who also stayed with the company for a short time.

In 1974, however, ITT found a leader with a greater staying power: Richard McClintock. McClintock, who had been employed by ITT Corporation and its subsidiaries since 1957, had served previously as the company's comptroller and treasurer.

215

Upon taking the helm in 1974, he immediately set about implementing new administrative structures and procedures. Two of his first initiatives were to establish an executive committee for the company and to begin establishing curriculum advisory committees for each region.

The year 1973 marked an important milestone in ITT's growth. That year, the company became a part of the Federal College-based tuition grant and loan programs, which had until then been reserved only for traditional colleges and universities. Acceptance into these programs allowed ITT to offer its students a full range of college loan and grant programs. This meant that attending an ITT school became a viable option for a new pool of students—those who needed federal financial aid to pay for schooling.

1980s: Adding New Divisions

After expanding its school system so rapidly in the late 1960s, ITT had spent much of the 1970s refining it. By the end of the 1970s, the company had significantly pared down the bulky system by selling or phasing out various schools, including ones in Boston, Akron, Toledo, New York, and Bethesda, Maryland. In 1980 the total number of schools was down to 21.

In 1981, however, the company began a period of controlled growth, implementing several new expansion initiatives. One of the first was the creation of a new division designed to target individuals who were already employed in the business world, but who wanted to improve existing or learn new skills. The new division, named the Business Division, opened its first school in Indianapolis in the spring of 1982. More schools of the same type followed—in Chicago, Los Angeles, Tampa, and Arlington, Texas.

Three years later, ITT created still another division: Employer Services. The Employer Services Division worked directly for businesses, training their employees in word processing. The division's services were offered originally at ITT locations in Indianapolis, Chicago, Houston, and El Segundo, California. Shortly after the division was formed, however, it expanded its services to temporary staffing by merging with a Los Angeles-based provider of interim personnel.

The company also grew via its old, tried-and-true method of adding new schools in new locations. Between 1981 and the end of 1985, more than a dozen new ITT facilities opened in Florida, California, Indiana, Texas, Tennessee, Utah, and Colorado.

In October 1984, ITT's ten-year leader, Richard McClintock, died. The company's executive committee took over day-to-day governance of the operation until a new president could be appointed, and in September of 1985, the position was filled by Rene Champagne. Champagne had spent 16 years in various high-level administrative positions with Kendall Company, a subsidiary of Colgate-Palmolive. Immediately prior to joining ITT Educational, he had served as the executive vice-president and chief operating officer of Continental Pharma Cryosan Inc., a health care company.

The mid-1980s brought changes to ITT's Employer Services Division. In 1985 the division announced that it was closing the training and temporary staffing operations in Indianapolis, Chicago, Houston, and Los Angeles. Two years later, the Employer Services Division broadened its services by offering both temporary and permanent technical staff placement. In 1988, however, the entire division was sold to Olsten Corporation.

In 1986 the company's Resident Division took steps to become more unified and standardized. The schools operating under the Resident Division—which were those that offered such technical programs as electronics and HVAC—were renamed ''ITT Technical Institutes.'' The Resident Division itself also was rechristened to correspond to the schools' new name, becoming the ITT Technical Institutes Division.

1990s: Ownership Changes and Rapid Growth

The early 1990s marked a turning point in ITT's evolution. In 1992 the company unveiled the Vision 2000 plan, a strategy for changing the way it was perceived. Since its formation in the 1960s, ITT institutes had been viewed primarily as ''trade schools.'' Under the Vision 2000 initiative, however, the company planned to make the institutes more like actual colleges by offering more bachelor's degrees. In addition to this repositioning, Vision 2000 called for aggressive geographic expansion and the addition of new curricula. ITT's new goal was to have a network of 80 technical colleges located across the country, serving more than 45,000 students, by the year 2000.

ITT immediately took steps toward achieving its newly articulated goals. By the end of 1993, four new schools had been opened and plans were under way for three more. The company also had added several new degree programs to its offerings, including a bachelor of applied science in hospitality management, a bachelor of applied science in industrial design, and a bachelor's degree in electronics engineering technology. By the end of 1994, ITT Educational was operating 54 schools in 25 states. Of the more than 20,000 students it served, approximately 70 percent were enrolled in electronics-engineering technology and related programs.

In December 1994, ITT's parent company, ITT Corporation, spun off 17 percent of ITT Educational in a $20 million initial public offering, still retaining majority ownership of 83 percent. The goal of the spin-off, according to ITT Educational President Rene Champagne, was to raise the company's visibility among investors. ''The main reason we decided to do the public stock offering was that we were a moderate sized company in a $23 billion-a-year corporation. We were getting lost in the corporate complex,'' he said in a June 1995 interview with the *Indianapo-*

Key Dates:

1963: Textbook publisher Howard W. Sams opens Sams Technical Institute in Indianapolis, Indiana.
1966: Sams is purchased by New York-based ITT Corp.
1968: ITT incorporates its education subsidiary as ITT Educational Services.
1981: ITT creates its new Business Division.
1984: Employer Services Division is created.
1992: ITT initiates Vision 2000, a growth strategy plan aimed at offering more degree programs and adding more colleges to the system.
1994: Parent company ITT Corp. spins off 17 percent of ITT Educational in a public offering.
1998: ITT Corp. is purchased by Starwood Hotels and Resorts Worldwide Inc.; ITT introduces its information technology program.
1999: Starwood sells off all remaining ITT Educational stock in a public offering.

lis Star. "Most people in the investment community were not aware of who we were." Less than a year after the spin-off, ITT Corporation itself announced a sweeping reorganization. During the restructuring, the giant conglomerate split into three publicly held companies. ITT Educational was a part of the new public company that continued to be called ITT Corporation.

In 1995, ITT took another step toward repositioning its "schools" as "colleges" when it established a Graduate Division at its Indianapolis ITT Technical Institute. The first degree offered by the Graduate Division was a master's in project management. The coursework and class schedules in the program were designed to appeal to adults who wanted to complete an advanced degree while working full-time.

Early 1998 brought yet another shift at the corporate level for ITT. In February, its parent company, ITT Corporation, was acquired by New York-based Starwood Hotels and Resorts Worldwide Inc. From the time of the acquisition, ITT Educational knew that change was in the offing. Starwood made it immediately clear that it had no interest in maintaining an educational subsidiary that did not fit with its core businesses of hotels and gaming. In June, Starwood sold 13 million shares of ITT Educational stock, reducing its ownership in the company from 83 to 35 percent. Then in an early 1999 public offering, the company sold the remainder of its ITT Educational stock, making ITT an independent, stand-alone company for the first time in its history.

Despite the ownership upheavals of the 1990s, ITT had continued to steadily add new colleges and new programs to its system. By spring of 1999, the company had 67 ITT Technical Institutes operating nationwide. It was also in the middle of rolling out an important new information technology program: Computer Network Systems Technology (CNST). ITT first introduced CNST at three locations in 1998, with plans to add it to 13 more schools in 1999. The program—which focused on

such areas as computer network systems, programming, and Web development—was so well received, however, that the company decided to introduce it at 27 locations, rather than the 13 originally planned.

ITT Educational finished up 1999 with record revenues of $316.4 million, an 8.6 percent increase over 1998. Student enrollment was up by approximately 3.2 percent over the previous year. Enrollment increases were particularly noticeable in the schools offering the company's new CNST program; schools offering that program increased their total student enrollment as of December 31, 1999 by 7.8 percent over December 31, 1998.

What's Ahead for ITT Educational

As ITT moved into the future, it was placing increasing emphasis on its information technology program. The rapidly growing IT industry was in dire need of qualified workers, and demand was expected to increase in the coming years. ITT planned to capitalize on that demand. "We are focused on repositioning our company to meet the demands of the 'new economy' for more graduates in information technology," Champagne said in a January 21, 2000 press release, adding "The IT program is serving an important catalyst for future growth."

The company planned to continue rapidly rolling out the IT program to the remainder of its schools in 2000. According to a January 21, 2000 press release, an additional 16 schools were expected to begin offering it during the first quarter of 2000. Additional schools were scheduled to begin offering the program in each of the three remaining quarters of 2000 to complete the roll-out by the end of the year. It was expected that with ITT's new focus on information technology and the continued roll-out of the CNST program to its schools, enrollment and revenues would increase in the coming years.

Principal Competitors

DeVry Inc; Computer Learning Centers, Inc.; Corinthian Colleges, Inc.; Apollo Group, Inc.; Learning Tree International, Inc.; Micro Electronics, Inc.; Quest Education Corporation; Strayer Education, Inc.; Whitman Education Group, Inc.

Further Reading

Andrews, Greg, "Fast-Growing School Biz Plans IPO, Faster Growth," *Indianapolis Business Journal,* December 5, 1994, p. 3.
——, "ITT Spin-Off at Top of Class," *Indianapolis Business Journal,* November 25, 1996, p. 1A.
Francis, Mary, "Tech Institute Places Itself on the Cutting Edge," *Indianapolis Star,* March 2, 1999, p. D1.
Lieber, Tammy, "ITT Looks to Future Despite New Ownership, Lawsuits," *Indianapolis Business Journal,* November 16, 1998, p. 9.
Smith, Bruce, "ITT Educational Services Is Ahead of the Pack," *Indianapolis Star,* June 14, 1995, p. F01.
Taylor, Jeffrey, "The New America: ITT Educational Services Inc.," *Investor's Business Daily,* April 7, 1995, p. A6.

—Shawna Brynildssen

Jenoptik AG

Carl-Zeiss-Strasse 1
D-07739 Jena
Germany
Telephone: (49)(3641) 65-0
Fax: (49)(3641) 42-4514
Web site: http://www.jenoptik.com

Public Company
Incorporated: 1846 as Carl Zeiss
Employees: 8,540
Sales: DM 3.12 billion ($1.87 billion) (1998)
Stock Exchanges: Frankfurt/Main
Ticker Symbol: JEN
NAIC: 333295 Semiconductor Machinery Manufacturing;
334413 Semiconductor and Related Device
Manufacturing; 339111 Laboratory Apparatus and
Furniture Manufacturing; 333314 Optical Instrument
and Lens Manufacturing

Jenoptik AG is a high-technology company, based in Jena, Germany, that specializes in the fields of systems engineering and photonics. A now-independent offspring of the renowned optical group Carl-Zeiss-Stiftung, it specializes in clean room systems for the semiconductor and other high-tech industries as well as industry applications of laser technology, optical inspection systems, and other electro-optical and electromechanical equipment. Jenoptik maintains a high level of in-house research and development, which resulted in 746 patent applications in 1998, and conducts research for third parties. The company's asset management subsidiary buys and sells shares in small high-tech companies. Through its subsidiary M + W Zander Holding GmbH, Jenoptik is active in Western Europe, South East Asia, the United States, Israel, and Hungary.

Jenoptik's Predecessor Founded in 1846

It was in the year 1846 when 30-year-old mechanic Carl Zeiss set up a mechanical workshop in the German town of Jena. One year later he sold the first 23 microscopes he had made. However,

he came to the realization that lens crafting was very time consuming and that his trial and error method would be inappropriate to scientific use and mass production. In 1866 Zeiss convinced German physicist Ernst Abbe to come to work for him. Abbe's task was to develop a scientific basis for lens construction. His research and theories became a fundamental part of modern optical science and enabled Zeiss to manufacture microscopes of a much higher quality. In order to become independent of foreign suppliers who delivered the special types of glass necessary, Abbe began working in cooperation with chemist Otto Schott who specialized in glass-making technologies. In 1882 Schott moved to Jena and two years later the three collaborators founded the Glaswerk Schott & Genossen, a glass making company.

In 1888 Zeiss died. Abbe, who had become a partner in Zeiss' business in 1875, thought that a foundation would be the best legal form to preserve the close relationship of scientific research and production, and in 1889 founded the Carl-Zeiss-Stiftung. According to its by-laws, the new organization had high social responsibilities to fulfill, which a private company would not be able to guarantee in the long run: to ensure close cooperation with the Jena University; to foster research in natural science and mathematics; to guarantee a highly qualified staff by offering extraordinary benefits; to provide jobs for the Jena region; to cooperate with local nonprofit organizations; and to contribute to cultural life and public education.

Around the turn of the century, natural sciences such as astronomy and biology made enormous progress. As a result, the demand for high-quality research microscopes grew rapidly as did requirements for their precision. At the same time, demand for eyeglasses, binoculars, and surveying equipment rose tremendously. Another driving force in the optical industry was the rising demand by the military for optical instruments. The Carl Zeiss enterprises thrived under those conditions and gained a worldwide reputation for its precision instruments. In 1914 the Zeiss factory employed 5,280 people who made microscopes, optical measuring instruments, camera lenses, binoculars and telescopes.

A New Beginning in 1948

World War II brought a sudden end to the company's bright future. The American troops, who were the first to enter Jena,

Key Dates:

1846: Mechanic Carl Zeiss starts building microscopes in his own workshop.

1875: Physicist Ernst Abbe becomes Zeiss's business partner.

1884: Chemist Otto Schott, Zeiss, and Abbe start their own optical glass making plant.

1889: Carl-Zeiss-Stiftung founded by Abbe.

1945: U.S. troops move patents and scientists to Oberkochen after World War II.

1948: The Carl-Zeiss Stiftung is expropriated by Soviet Allies.

1951: A new firm under the name of Carl Zeiss is registered in Heidenheim.

1950–80: Two companies, each with the name Carl Zeiss, exist in East and West Germany and fight for brand name rights.

1990: Former government-owned VEB Carl Zeiss Jena is privatized.

1991: Carl Zeiss Oberkochen-Heidenheim is granted all brand name rights; Jenoptik GmbH becomes legal successor of the VEB Carl Zeiss Jena owned by the state of Thuringia.

1996: Company is renamed to Jenoptik AG and goes public.

1998: Jenoptik's first public offering on the Frankfurt stock exchange.

took with them when they left the core of the Zeiss company: patents, construction drawings, and the most brilliant people. While they set up a new Zeiss company in their own zone of occupation in the Swabian town of Oberkochen, Thuringia and Jena came under Soviet control. In 1946 the Oberste Alliierten Kontrollrat decided to dismantle the Zeiss production facilities as war reparations—and that could have been the end of the company.

Just as Germany was divided into two separate states, so was the Zeiss enterprise divided into two separate companies. After the Soviets expropriated the Carl-Zeiss Stiftung in 1948, a new firm under the name of Carl Zeiss was officially registered in the West German town Heidenheim in 1951. Many of the key technical and managerial Carl Zeiss employees had moved to work in this new company in Germany's southwest region. However, most of the qualified staff and traditional ties remained in the Jena region. In an extraordinary endeavor, a new plant was established there during the 1950s. It started manufacturing products it had produced before the war and soon developed new versions, and eventually new instruments. By the mid-1950s the government-owned VEB Carl-Zeiss Jena was exporting its products to no less than 88 countries. The Carl-Zeiss-Stiftung was also re-established in Jena, resulting in a battle over brand name rights that went on for decades between the two foundations which had the same name.

The VEB Carl-Zeiss Jena soon became a showpiece of the newly-founded German Democratic Republic (GDR), where politicians, not business people, ruled the economy. While large

companies in the Western world started dismantling the huge, inflexible bureaucracies, the government in East Germany made a conscious decision to create them. In 1971 the VEB Carl Zeiss Jena became a so-called *Kombinat*, comparable to a holding company that managed a large number of subsidiaries in one industry. The chronic scarcity of raw material and other supplies in East Germany encouraged such conglomerates to produce themselves as many of the supplies needed as possible to ensure control over the whole chain of production. About 25 companies with 69,000 employees located all over the GDR—optical companies, engineering companies, foreign trade offices and research centers—were organized under the umbrella of the *Kombinat* Carl Zeiss Jena, which even included it's own power plant and a production facility for crates. More than 1,000 products, such as electronics, technical equipment for scientific laboratories, lasers, equipment for medical and astronomical research, technology for measurement and research, cameras, household glassware, as well as whole planetariums, observatories, and optical plants, were all made under the Carl Zeiss Jena label. Even under less than perfect conditions, Carl Zeiss Jena made some remarkable innovations, most notably the multiple spectrum camera, the MKF 6, which delivered detailed images of the earth's surface from the Soviet space stations Sojus 22 and Salut 6.

In the mid-1980s, when the semiconductor and computer industries were on the rise worldwide, the East German government decided that their leading companies in those industries, which were located primarily in Dresden, should be taken over by the *Kombinat* Carl Zeiss Jena. Some 60 percent of the net profits generated by the company were transferred to the government budget. In addition to that, the *Kombinat*'s three main subsidiaries—the VEB Carl Zeiss Jena, glass-maker VEB Jenaer Glaswerk, and the drug company VEB Jenapharm—transferred between 40 and 50 million East German Marks per year to the Carl Zeiss Jena foundation which helped finance scientific research at the Jena University, as well as a planetarium, a museum, a library, and other educational and healthcare institutions in town.

The Second New Beginning in 1990

The unexpected fall of the Berlin Wall marked the next turning point in Jenoptik's history. For the second time it appeared the East German company would be unable to survive. With the introduction of the West German currency in East Germany in the summer of 1990, the company suddenly lost most of its business, as Eastern European countries were no longer able to pay for Jenoptik's products in hard currency. At the same time, the government subsidies that had traditionally kept Jenoptik's prices low, were abolished, and it was no longer competitive on the world market. Finally, the profitable business relationship with the East German military abruptly ceased. The consequence was huge financial losses.

The legal situation following German reunification was complicated as well, especially in the case of the VEB Carl Zeiss Jena. According to the agreement between the East and West German governments, state-owned East German companies had to be privatized. This enormous task was taken over by a newly-established institution, the *Treuhandanstalt*, headquartered in Berlin. In July 1990, the *Treuhandanstalt* took over responsibility for the *Kombinat* Carl Zeiss Jena, which at that time consisted of 25 major subsidiaries at 11 locations with approximately 69,000 employees. They were split into several independent private companies. The core business was transformed into the Jenoptik Carl Zeiss Jena GmbH, which included 13 major subsidiaries and over 30,000 employees.

On June 16, 1991 a meeting held at the Berlin *Treuhandanstalt* determined the fate of the two Carl Zeiss foundations and the associated companies. It was decided that there should be only one Carl-Zeiss-Stiftung—the one in Heidenheim. The details were negotiated in a treaty between the German states of Baden-Würtemberg and Thuringia. The Carl-Zeiss Stiftung Jena transferred its brand name rights and licenses to the Heidenheim-based foundation. The core of the old Carl Zeiss production line, including about 3,000 employees with pension rights, was also taken over by Carl Zeiss Oberkochen-Heidenheim through its newly-founded subsidiary Carl Zeiss Jena GmbH. Anything that was not part of core business assets, such as the planetarium, optical museum, and other nonprofit institutions, became the property of a newly created foundation in Jena—the Ernst Abbe Stiftung. At the same time, Jenoptik, the successor of the *Kombinat* Carl Zeiss Jena, was determined to take over the rest of the business and to become a breeding ground for a new "high-tech valley."

On July 1, 1991 Lothar Späth, who had once been president of the German state of Baden-Würtemberg for more than a decade, took over the complicated task of restructuring what was left of the former East German *Kombinat* Carl Zeiss. In October 1991 the Jenoptik Carl Zeiss Jena GmbH was split into the Jenoptik GmbH and the Carl Zeiss Jena GmbH. Jenoptik GmbH became the property of the state government of Thuringia which together with the *Treuhandanstalt* paid out DM 1.7 billion, about half of which went to pay off Jenoptik's past debts while the other half went toward ongoing costs, including financial compensation for employees who lost their jobs at Jenoptik. However, a precondition of the deal was that Jenoptik preserve 10,000 jobs in Jena, and at the same time, the company was supposed to become profitable once again.

Within just a few months, a complex program of numerous buy-outs and split-ups created about 200 new companies which provided some 7,000 jobs for former Jenoptik employees. This gave the Jena region a boost as an industrial and scientific research center. In order to preserve the incredible potential of the 10,000 former Carl Zeiss Jena employees with college degrees, the German Ministry for Research and Technology funded over 100 research projects in basic physics, microbiology, optics, and glass making technology. The ministry also provided DM 14 million in subsidies for 14 Jenoptik research projects in 1991.

At the same time, Jenoptik attempted to sell many of its subsidiaries to private investors. In summer 1991, its optical chain was sold to the Nuremberg-based Apollo Optik GmbH. Other companies, including a foundry, plastics production facilities, leather making factories, and cable plants, were sold in the same year. In 1992 the Glaswerke Schott in Mainz took over the management of the former Jenaer Glaswerk. The promise to preserve 10,000 jobs was kept: 3,000 people were taken in by the Carl Zeiss Jena GmbH; 1,700 were employed by Jenoptik;

and the rest received jobs in one of the newly-founded start-up companies or in Jena's growing service sector.

Becoming a Global Player in the Mid-1990s

After the most important legal issues were finally resolved, the remainder of Jenoptik began a long and painful process of restructuring. Beginning in 1992, Jenoptik became a holding company with a great variety of shareholdings, real estate assets, and a group of manufacturing companies in the fields of opto-electronics, systems technology, precision measuring, and mechanical instruments. Joint ventures were set up with prominent partners such as Sandoz AG and the DASA. In mid-1992, CEO Späth declared international expansion to be Jenoptik's primary goal. One of Jenoptik's new fields of expertise was laser technology, an area in which the company had done a great deal of research.

By the end of 1992, Jenoptik had become the German market leader in light-exposure equipment for semiconductor production facilities. In order to get access to international markets Jenoptik began acquiring companies which were already established internationally. In 1994 Jenoptik purchased the Stuttgart-based semiconductor company Meissner + Wurst GmbH & Co.; in 1996 the Berliner telecommunication company Krone AG; and finally in 1997 ESW-Estel Systems Wedel, a supplier to the automobile and aerospace industries of technically complex and innovative products and services such as drive and stabilization technologies, measuring systems, and control systems. Other smaller acquisitions in the fields of laser technology, optics, and systems engineering followed. At the same time the legal structure of the company was also changed. On January 1, 1996 Jenoptik became a public company and changed its name to Jenoptik AG. The state of Thuringia retained a minority interest of 50 percent minus one share in the company's share capital.

The year 1998 marked the second phase of Jenoptik's restructuring. Beginning on June 16, 1998 Jenoptik shares were traded on the Frankfurt stock exchange for the first time. The state of Thuringia kept a minority share of 18.9 percent; 8.2 percent was held by a group of banks; 4.1 percent was purchased by Jenoptik employees; and 68.8 percent was sold to other investors. In mid-1999 the company announced that it would streamline its business and concentrate its efforts in just two high-growth markets: Clean Systems Technologies and Photonics Technologies. The telecommunication branch Krone AG, was sold to the American GenTek Inc. headquartered in Hampton, New Hampshire. A large percentage of Jenoptik's shares in Deutsche Effecten- und Wechselbeteiligungsgesellschaft AG (DEWB), its publicly traded asset management division, was offered to interested strategic partners. In order to strengthen the Clean Systems Technologies division, Jenoptik sold its subsidiaries Jenoptik Infab GmbH to Brooks Automation, Inc. in exchange for a minority share in the American company. Brooks was a manufacturer of handling robots used in super-clean areas of semiconductor and flat screen production plants. With this step Jenoptik was hoping to be able to extend its promising market position in the global semiconductor industry into new markets—as a supplier of special high-tech equipment to the pharmaceuticals, food, and biotechnology industries.

Principal Subsidiaries

M + W Zander Holding GmbH (72.14%); Jenoptik Extel AG; Deutsche Effecten- und Wechsel-Beteiligungsgesellschaft AG (99.32%); Jenoptik Bioinstruments GmbH; OPAL JENA Gesellschaft für optische Analytik und Labortechnik mbH; Jenoptik Mikrotechnik GmbH; Jenoptik Systemhaus GmbH; Jenoptik MedProjekt GmbH; 4 MBO International Electronic GmbH (44%); Jenoptik Camera Europe GmbH; Laser Imaging Systems GmbH & Co. KG (33.4%); UV Systec Gesellschaft für UV—Strahler und Systemtechnik mbH (Germany; 24.88%); Jenoptik (U.K.) Ltd.; HVB Beteiligungen GmbH; Aesculap-Medutec GmbH Jena; Ceram Holding GmbH (24.9%); Klaus Kleinmichel GmbH (49.9%).

Principal Competitors

ATS Automation Tooling Systems Inc.; Daw Technologies, Inc.; PRI Automation, Inc.

Further Reading

Blau, John, "Jenoptik Sparks Jena Tech/Innovation Park," *Research-Technology Management*, January-February 1999, p. 3.

"Furioser Börsenstart der Jenoptik," *Die Welt* (online edition), June 17, 1998.

"Jenoptik Anticipates Soaring Profits through 1999," *Colorado Springs Business Journal,* September 12, 1997, p. 1.

"Jenoptik hofft auf einen hoeheren Aktienkurs," *Frankfurter Allgemeine Zeitung*, January 25, 2000, p. 21.

"Jenoptik trennt sich von Verlustbringern," *Die Welt* (online edition), July 14, 1999.

Müller, Uwe, "In Jena steht und fällt alles mit Lothar Späth," *Die Welt* (online edition), September 9, 1996.

——, "Jenoptik profitiert von Chipboom in Südostasien," *Die Welt* (online edition), November 9, 1995.

Murphy, Cait, "Will the Future Belong to Germany?," Fortune, August 2, 1999, pp. 128+.

"Technologiekonzern Jenoptik beendet Verschlankungskurs," *Die Welt* (online edition), November 9, 1999.

Templeman, John, "Eastern German IPO," *Business Week,* June 15, 1998, p. 63.

"Vorstandschef Späth will Jenoptik-Konzern straffen," *Die Welt* (online edition), July 12, 1999.

"Wie Phoenix aus der Asche," *Die Welt* (online edition), June 4, 1998.

—Evelyn Hauser

VOITH

J.M. Voith AG

Sankt Pöltener Strasse 43
D-89522 Heidenheim
Germany
Telephone: (49)(7321) 37-0
Fax: (49)(7321) 37-7000
Web site: http://www.voith.de

Private Company
Incorporated: 1867 as Maschinenfabrik J.M. Voith
Employees: 12,650
Sales: DM 3.9 billion ($2.33 billion) (1999)
NAIC: 333291 Paper Industries Machinery
Manufacturing; 3511 333611 Turbine and Turbine
Generator Set Units Manufacturing; 333310 Other
Commercial and Service Industry machinery
Manufacturing

J.M. Voith AG, with headquarters in Heidenheim, Germany, is one of the world's leading producers of paper making machines and turbines for hydropower plants. Four independent divisions are organized under the umbrella of this holding company: Voith Sulzer Paper Technology, maker of machines and systems for the production of mechanical pulp, paper and paper finishing; Voith Turbo Power Transmission, a company that produces automatic transmissions for buses, coaches and trucks, drive systems for rail vehicles, and hydrodynamic couplings and drive systems for industrial use; Voith Fluid Machinery, maker of turbines, storage pumps, and control technology for hydro powerplants and marine technology; and Voith Appleton Paper Machine Clothing based in Appleton, Wisconsin, producer of forming fabrics, wet felts, dryer screens, and measuring technology for paper and board making machines. J.M. Voith is also actively involved in research and development in each of its fields. With production companies in Europe, North and South America, and Asia, as well as sales offices in more than 100 countries on all continents, J.M. Voith is a global player with about 80 percent of their sales generated from exports. As the company entered a new century, it remained a Voith family owned business.

1825–67: Foundations for Solid Engineering Business

When Johann Matthäus Voith took over the family locksmith shop in 1825, his hometown Heidenheim in the Swabian Alps was a rural community of 2,000, still suffering from the devastation of the Napoleonic Wars and as yet untouched by the coming industrial revolution. The local economy—consisting of some iron ore mines, ironworks, and textile factories—relied primarily on water power, as did the young craftsman Voith. While tending and repairing machinery at water powered mills such as paper mills and textile making machines, he moved his own business to a grinding mill where he set up a mechanical workshop with five hired helpers.

Soon thereafter, Voith became involved in developing a revolutionary technology for paper-making. Newspapers and books, as well as the growing needs of an emerging industrial bureaucracy caused the demand for paper to rise sharply. The supply lagged behind demand, since most paper at the time was made by hand in the German kingdom of Wuertemberg. While Voith was already involved in building a paper making machine in Heidenheim in 1830, it would take another 18 years to achieve a major breakthrough.

Beginning in 1848, Voith teamed up with Heinrich Voelter, Jr., a Heidenheim-based paper manufacturer, who owned the patent to a new invention first conceived by inventor Friedrich Gottlob Keller, on that made paper from wood. Until that time, paper was made out of cloth rags, an expensive process. The new technology, which transformed wood pulp into a paste, utilized a raw material that was available in abundance. Voith helped Voelter optimize the new technology. A visit at the Paris World Exhibition inspired and convinced him that only by innovation and developing technologies for niche markets would he be able to keep up with the tough international competition.

In 1859 Voith invented the pulp refiner, a grinder that made better quality paper by diminishing the splinter content of the rough pulp. Voelter became Voith's most important business partner, as together they built wood grinding machines for a growing market, which enabled Voith to enlarge his workshop and construct a brand-new foundry.

Company Perspectives:

We employ the tradition of the Voith corporate culture which is marked by mutual respect and trust. We strive to maintain an independent family-owned company. We actively contribute to social, economic and ecological issues. Our Commitment: Esprit. *Pioneering spirit and innovative strength determine our future.* Excellence. *Our activities are directed at producing superior quality for the benefit of our customers.* Efficiency. *Our success is governed by experience and achievement.*

When Friedrich Voith, the founder's son, entered the family business in 1864, it had grown into a 30-employee machine building factory powered by steam engines. Friedrich had studied engineering in Stuttgart and spent a few years working as an apprentice in other factories, before he officially took over the business in 1867.

Although his father had been a creative force, he had also been hesitant to make take risks with his business. In contrast, Friedrich Voith was a business visionary and willing to assume large risks in order to realize his ideas. He was reportedly a good organizer, open-minded, dedicated to translating technical ideas into marketable products of high quality, and proud that Voith products were made in Heidenheim. The year in which Friedrich Voith took over his father's flourishing business also marked it's official incorporation as Maschinenfabrik J.M. Voith.

1870–1913: Expansion under Friedrich Voith

Friedrich Voith took over the business at a prosperous time. Following the founding of the German Reich in 1871, fueled by the ongoing Industrial Revolution, the German economy began to take off. Heidenheim got a railroad connection in 1870 and thereafter developed into a rapidly growing industrial town. The demand for energy skyrocketed with the burgeoning use of machinery.

The Voith factory next started designing and building water turbines, a market that J.M. Voith was involved in right from the beginning, when he experimented with his own water turbines to power his mechanical workshop. Friedrich Voith did a great deal of research work as well, maintaining contacts with a professor from the Technical University of Stuttgart and keeping informed about state-of-the-art theoretical research. At the same time, he conducted his own experiments on pulverized coal engines with his friend Gottlieb Daimler at the Voith research laboratories. In 1870, Maschinenfabrik J.M. Voith started building 100 PS-Henschel-Jonval turbines. Two years later the company built the first Francis turbine, an American invention that was greatly improved in design and efficiency by Friedrich Voith, his engineers, and associates. Those improvements made possible a great variety of uses for this turbine type, and J.M. Voith acquired a reputation for his special expertise in turbine design and technology. All this was at a time when power plants were being built all over the world, and turbines to generate electricity were in high demand.

While J.M. Voith was able to equip paper factories with turbines, it also continued its involvement with paper-making technology. Friedrich Voith and his engineers developed large wood grinders, control systems for the grinding process, magazine grinders with automatic wood refilling and vibrating graders that produced the raw material for paper of better quality. The Voith factory also started building machines for processing the wood pulp. Finally, in 1881 the first complete paper machine left the Voith factory. Expanding the product range required expanding production facilities; the machine factory was enlarged, a new and much larger foundry was set up, and a plant for boiler making and an assembly workshop were added, as were numerous research sites for wood grinding system and turbine testing. A new building for administration and a family residence were also built, and the factory was equipped with a railroad connection.

In the late 1890s Friedrich Voith focused his efforts on international expansion, traveling to the United States where he made valuable business contacts at the Columbian Exhibition in Chicago. J.M. Voith was soon able to compete in the world market, but it was one single contract made the company an international brand name. Between 1903 and 1912 Voith delivered 12 of the world's most powerful Francis spiral turbines to the power stations at Niagara Falls, the combined power of which equaled 12,000 HP. The year 1903 also witnessed the establishment of Voith's first foreign subsidiary, in St. Pölten, Austria, from which paper making equipment was delivered to Austria-Hungary and Russia. When Friedrich Voith died in 1913, his company had an international reputation and employed about 3,000 people.

1914–60: Wars and Recovery under Hanns Voith

One year after Friedrich Voith's death, World War I broke out, and his three sons were confronted with a brand new political and economic environment. After the company lost 200 highly-qualified workers in the war, it struggled with hyperinflation, a disturbed economy, and international isolation. However, under the management of the third Voith generation the company managed to recover and even expand.

In 1922 J.M. Voith introduced a new product—the Kaplan turbine. Invented by professor Viktor Kaplan and further developed over many years by Voith engineers, it's economic efficiency for smaller water power plants such as those located on rivers was unprecedented. Other Voith innovations of the time included the "continuous pulper," a machine that made pulp production faster, as well as the "headbox," a device that enhanced the speed of paper machines.

Other companies gained world market share from Voith during World War I; building heavy machinery remained a risky business, depending much on economic stability that encouraged large investments. In order to gain some stability, J.M. Voith entered a new market in 1922 when it became involved in the mass production of power transmissions. Voith engineers had been working for a time on drives for water turbines and paper machines, which also functioned with cog-wheels so this field was not a completely new one. In 1929, when the world economy was shaken by the stock market crash on Wall Street, Voith's first hydro-dynamic couplings were developed and built

Key Dates:

1867: Maschinenfabrik J.M. Voith incorporated in Heidenheim, Germany.
1903: First foreign subsidiary is established in St. Pölten, Austria, and Voith delivers the world's most powerful twin water turbines to Niagara Falls power station.
1913: Third Voith generation takes over the family business.
1922: J.M. Voith introduces the Kaplan turbine and starts mass producing power transmissions.
1950: J.M. Voith GmbH is founded.
1961: J.M. Voith delivers the world's largest newspaper machine to Finland.
1965: Voith's paper machine division sets up a subsidiary in Sao Paulo, Brazil.
1977: Voith's paper machine division sets up a subsidiary in Appleton, Wisconsin.
1992: The family holdings are split between Voith heirs.
1994: Voith Sulzer Papiertechnik GmbH is founded.
1997: J.M. Voith reorganizes, with all stock held by the Voith family and German banks.

into pumped storage power stations. Other Voith products in this new field included drives for railway vehicles and buses, and hydrodynamic transmissions and couplings for industrial equipment. Another new area of expertise was the development of ship propulsion systems. J.M. Voith developed a ship drive based on a propeller invented by the Austrian Ernst Schneider. The new drive, called the Voith-Schneider Propeller, became famous for its steerability, stability, and ability to enable ships turn in place, features which were especially useful for tugs, floating cranes, car ferries, and passenger vessels. In 1941 a subsidiary for the repair of Voith-Schneider propellers was set up in the Northern German city of Bremen. During World War II, Voith propellers were intensively used by the fleet of the German Navy.

The end of World War II marked another serious interruption in Voith's history. Not only was 15 percent of the workforce dead or missing, but there was literally no demand for Voith paper machines, and the company found itself once more isolated from its international market. By 1947, of the three Voith brothers only Hanns Voith, the youngest, was still alive. He, along with his close friend Hugo Rupf, led the company out of the postwar dilemma. Fortunately, Heidenheim was not destroyed by bombs during the war. At first, the Voith company survived by repairing damaged bridges, locomotives, and American military vehicles, and even began a foray into the manufacture of saucepans. However, just one year after the war had ended, orders from abroad began rolling in again. Among them was an order from the Turkish government for a brand-new paper factory.

Hanns Voith was dedicated to supporting Voith employees, letting them grow with the firm and participate in its success. When food was in short supply in the years after the war, Voith employees were provided with donations from foreign cus-

tomers and paid extra money by the company. Other social benefits for J.M. Voith employees included emergency household assistance, a health center, a company healthcare plan, a housing program that sponsored the rebuilding of residential structures in Heidenheim, and the construction of well-equipped training facilities. When the company was transformed into J.M. Voith GmbH in 1950, its workforce was back at its prewar level of 4,000.

1961–90: Growth and Innovations

The three decades after reconstruction saw J.M. Voith expand its capacities and develop new innovative products. In the field of paper making, rising environmental concerns put pressure on paper producers to use less harmful technologies and to recycle. Voith developed a new de-inking technology that removed ink from waste paper, which was used in waste paper treatment and recycling. The company also made headlines when it delivered the world's largest newspaper machine, which was 8.5 meters wide, to a Finnish customer in 1961. Voith then broke its own record five years later with a paper machine of nine meters in lengths for a Swedish company. Moreover, in the late 1960s J.M. Voith brought the so-called Duoformer to the market, a sheet formation system that helped make the paper quality equal on both sides. For Voith's paper machine division, subsidiaries were set up in Sao Paulo, Brazil, in 1965 and in Appleton, Wisconsin, in 1977.

Voith's activities in water turbine building were just as successful. The company's most prestigious project was the world's largest hydroelectric power plant in Itapu, Brazil, which Voith engineers helped plan. Voith equipped it with Voith Francis turbines with a combined power of 13,000 megawatts (MW). During the 1970s and 1980s hydroelectric power plant projects became more complex, given rising safety standards and new control system technologies. Voith responded by expanding its product line, including start-up turbines, shut-off devices, synchronizing transformers and clutches, mechanical and hydraulic control devices, and control systems for whole power plants.

The market for Voith turbo transmissions and hydraulic couplings, which had thrived especially in the 1950s, had resulted in the establishment of a new production facility in Heidenheim and of the Voith Turbo KG subsidiary for transmissions in Crailsheim and other branch offices abroad. In 1961 another subsidiary for managing the couplings market, the Voith Getriebe KG, was set up. Another successful Voith invention was the retarder, a hydrodynamic brake that was nearly wear-free and therefore very reliable. Retarders were built into coaches, trucks, and rail vehicles, and in the 1960s they were used in the United States for diesel locomotives that hauled freight trains almost five kilometers in length through the Rocky Mountains. In the early 1980s J.M. Voith introduced electric speed control systems for mobile and stationary brakes and eventually whole drive systems.

Also during this time, Voith's marine technology division introduced a new kind of tug called the ''Voith water tractor.'' Equipped with the Voith-Schneider Propeller, it offered a great deal of safety and maneuverability. It was an instant hit, given its reliability, and it helped lower the number of tug accidents.

By the end of the 1980s there were almost 600 "Voith water tractors" in use in more than 100 ports around the world.

1992–99 Reorganization and New Ventures

In the 1990s J.M. Voith went through fundamental organizational changes and pursued rigorous globalization through joint ventures and acquisitions. Until 1992 J.M. Voith was managed jointly by the successors of Herman and Hanns Voith. In that year, the family holdings were divided between the two family groups. Herman Voith's heirs took over the machine tool construction sector and a large share of the company's financial holdings. Hanns Voith's successors, on the other hand, took over the production facilities. Beginning in 1994, Voith and the Swiss Sulzer Group merged their paper technology activities into Voith Sulzer Papiertechnik GmbH, an independent joint venture based in Heidenheim. In 1995 the other two corporate divisions—Voith Turbo and Voith Hydro—became legally independent. Two years later, in order to strengthen its capital base, the mother company J.M. Voith GmbH was transformed into a public company. The descendants of the Hanns Voith family took over 92.5 percent of all shares, while the remaining 7.5 percent of the company's share capital in the amount of DM 200 million—about $115 million—was held jointly by Deutsche Bank AG, Commerzbank AG, and Sal. Oppenheim & Cie., another German bank. None of the stock was offered to the public.

By the late 1990s, over one-third of all paper produced worldwide was processed with Voith-made machinery and 30 percent of all energy was derived from hydropower generated by Voith-made turbines. More strategic ventures followed. In 1998 Voith Turbo took over Scharfenbergkupplung GmbH, another German coupling-maker. In 1999, the Voith group acquired the paper machine and paper machine clothing businesses from the British Scapa Group. In the same year J.M. Voith AG and the renowned German Siemens AG announced a planned joint venture between their hydro power activities, with J.M. Voith holding a majority share of 65 percent. The main goal of this venture was to make Voith Siemens Hydro the global leader in its field, combining Voith's leadership in turbines with Siemens's strength in generators. In addition to their already existing joint venture in China with Shanghai Electric, Voith's access to the Japanese market through its cooperation with Fuji was well complemented by Siemens' strength in India.

The year 1999 also saw a major change in the upper management of the J.M. Voith group of companies. Dr. Michael Rogowski, who had represented J.M. Voith's management team since 1986, announced at his 60th birthday in 1999 that he would resign as CEO following the Annual General Meeting in 2000, making way for a new generation to lead J.M. Voith into a new millennium.

Principal Subsidiaries

Voith Sulzer Papiermaschinen GmbH; Voith Hydro Kraftwerkstechnik GmbH; Voith Sulzer Paper Technology North America Inc.(United States); Voith S.A.-Paper Technology Division (Brazil); Voith Sulzer Papiermaschinen AG (Austria); Shanghai Voith Paper Machinery Co. Ltd. (China); Voith Sulzer Stoffaufbereitung GmbH; Voith Sulzer Finishing GmbH; Voith Sulzer Papiertechnik Service GmbH; Lindsay Wire Inc. (United States); Appleton Mills Papermaking Supplies Industry Co. Ltd.(China); Voith Vertriebsgesellschaft Antriebstechnik GmbH; Scharfenbergkupplung GmbH; Voith Turbo GmbH (Austria); Voith India Private Ltd. (India); Voith Hydro GmbH (Austria); Voith Hydro Inc. (United States); Voith S.A.-Power Generation Division (Brazil); Shanghai Hydro-Power Equipment Co. Ltd. (China); Voith Dienstleistungen GmbH.

Principal Competitors

Harnischfeger Industries, Inc.; Metso Corporation; Parsons & Whittemore Inc.

Further Reading

From Craftsman's Workshop to Worldwide Company, Heidenheim, Germany: J.M. Voith, 1992, 20 p.

"J. M. Voith AG," *Pulp & Paper,* September 1999, p. 82.

"KNP Leykam," *Pulp & Paper,* March 1996, p. 31.

"Maschinenbauer Voith plant Personalabbau," *Die Welt* (online edition), November 25, 1998.

"Siemens und Voith bündeln Wasserkraft," *Die Welt* (online edition), July 22, 1999.

"Voith verhalten optimistisch," *Die Welt* (online edition), March 30, 1999.

—Evelyn Hauser

Jones, Day, Reavis & Pogue

North Point
901 Lakeside Avenue
Cleveland, Ohio 44114-1190
U.S.A.
Telephone: (216) 586-3939
Fax: (216) 579-0212
Web site: http://www.jonesday.com

Partnership
Founded: 1893 as Blandin & Rice
Employees: 3,200
Sales: $530 million (1998 est.)
NAIC: 54111 Offices of Lawyers

Jones, Day, Reavis & Pogue (Jones Day) is one of the world's major law firms, with numerous offices in the United States and overseas. Its clients include about half of the *Fortune* 500 corporations and several foreign companies, such as CBS, Bridgestone/Firestone, Ernst & Young, Goldman Sachs, Chemical Banking Corporation, Toyota, The Fuji Bank, and Honeywell. Clients from Europe, Asia, Latin America, the Middle East, and Australia call on Jones Day for legal advice. The firm's international business practice concentrates on mergers and acquisitions, joint ventures, financing issues, labor, environmental, tax, and other corporate concerns. Jones Day is well known for defending numerous companies in high-profile product liability lawsuits, the best known being its long-term representation of RJR Nabisco in hundreds of tobacco lawsuits. The firm is also well known for its antitrust practice.

Origin and Early Practice

In 1893, two experienced lawyers in Cleveland formed a new partnership that years later evolved into Jones, Day, Reavis & Pogue. Edwin J. Blandin, the older partner, was born in New York state in 1843, attended Hillsdale College and Commercial College of Cleveland, and in 1870 was admitted to the Ohio bar. He became a well-known judge and litigator before meeting the junior partner, William Lowe Rice, a native of Delaware. Rice studied civil engineering before serving an apprenticeship in a

law office and then being admitted to the bar in 1883. His practice centered on providing counsel to corporations facing increased laws and government regulations in the Progressive Era.

The new partnership played a key role in helping Cleveland and Ohio grow around the turn of the century. For example, the firm's clients included some of the area's major utilities, financial institutions, railroads, local interurban transit systems, manufacturing firms, and coal companies. Early partners acted not only as outside counsel, but sometimes served as corporate officers and directors. Companies such as Cleveland Trust Company, W.S. Tyler Company, and the Ohio & Pennsylvania Coal Company hired the firm. The founding partners were prominent citizens and leaders of the Cleveland Bar Association.

In the early 20th century firm attorneys helped write the Ohio Municipal Code and represented corporate clients, including the Lake Shore Electric Railway that connected Cleveland, Toledo, and other nearby communities, and the Baltimore & Ohio Railroad. The firm's continuing reputation for representations of utility and energy concerns was established with early work on behalf of the East Ohio Gas Company, Ohio Bell Telephone Company, and the Cleveland Electric Illuminating Company.

A 1913 merger with another partnership almost quadrupled the firm's annual sales, although it still was a relatively small firm with just 14 attorneys in 1918. From the end of World War I to the mid-1930s, the partnership represented O.P. and M.J. Van Sweringen, a local Cleveland family prominent in real estate and railroads. For example, the Van Sweringens purchased in 1916 the New York, Chicago, and St. Louis Railroad, often known as the Nickel Plate. The law firm defended the Nickel Plate against lawsuits and helped it acquire other lines.

In the late 1920s the law firm gained one of its historic victories when it represented the Nickel Plate in Snyder v. New York, Chicago, & St. Louis R.R. The Ohio Supreme Court ruled that the Nickel Plate's consolidation efforts did not violate the 1920 Federal Transportation Act and that no antitrust laws had been violated. The U.S. Supreme Court upheld the state court's decision.

Meanwhile, the partnership represented other Van Sweringen business interests, such as the Higbee Company, a major Cleveland department store, and also the family's construction of Cleveland's Union Station and Terminal Tower on Public Square. In addition, the firm represented two Cleveland firms started by local inventors: Thompson Products, Inc., which became TRW, and the Weatherhead Company, a diversified manufacturing company that remained a major client until 1983.

In the 1920s the firm began representing the steel companies owned or managed by Elroy J. Kulas, including Otis Steel Company and the Midland Steel Products Company that made car frames and brakes. About the same time firm attorneys developed the land trust certificate as a way to finance new commercial buildings without paying certain high Ohio taxes. Although significant, the land trust certificate was no longer needed after Ohio changed its tax code in the 1930s. Other significant clients developed during the period who would remain clients into the 1990s and beyond were North American Coal and M.A. Hanna Co.

When Cleveland's Union Trust Company opened on December 31, 1920, firm partner Frank Ginn served as its counsel. Formed from a merger of 29 banks and savings and trust companies, the Union Trust Company was the nation's fifth largest trust company. In 1924 the partnership moved its office to the newly constructed Union Trust Building, where it remained until 1987.

The Great Depression and World War II

After the stock market crashed in 1929, many businesses declared bankruptcy or were forced to reorganize or recapitalize. Although millions of Americans lost their jobs during the Great Depression, attorneys found new ways to serve clients during the crisis. The famous bank holiday in 1933 led to the law firm helping the Union Trust Company reorganize, while the federal government forced unsound banks to close their doors. The 1935 Wagner Act revitalized the labor movement and led to new work for many labor attorneys, including those at the Cleveland firm.

In November 1938, the partnership, then known as Tolles, Hogsett & Ginn, announced a merger effective January 1, 1939 with a smaller Cleveland law firm called Day, Young, Veach & LeFever. The merged firm named Jones, Day, Cockley & Reavis consisted of 22 partners and 20 associates. The Tolles partnership chose to merge with the Day law firm primarily because of its representation of the Republic Steel Corporation and the iron firm of Cleveland Cliffs Iron Co. In 1940 the merged firm for the first time since the 1929 stock market crash enjoyed cash revenues of over $1 million.

However, America's entry into World War II resulted in 15 Jones Day lawyers leaving for military service. The firm hired additional associates; some remained after the war ended. During the war the partnership continued its litigation practice, representing its corporate clients as they geared up to meet war demands. For example, about this time firm attorneys devised a way for mining companies to create what were known as ''cost companies'' as a way to decrease taxes, a mechanism that survived until 1977 as an accessible means of financing joint ventures.

In 1944, an explosion at the East Ohio Gas Company killed 130 people and destroyed about 680 homes. After immediate investigation, on the advice of Jones Day lawyers, the gas company admitted its liability in the *Cleveland Plain Dealer*. Thus, claims were settled without lawsuits for most victims within three months of the explosion.

Growth in the Early Post–World War II Period

In 1946 Jones Day opened its first branch office in Washington, D.C., based on one of its attorney's considerable experience in the government. That office in 1952 worked with Luther Day from the Cleveland office to fight President Truman's order that the federal government take control of most steel mills. Using his authority as commander-in-chief, the president intended to prevent a steelworkers' strike that would hurt the nation's military during the Korean War. However, the steel industry, including Republic Steel, which hired Jones Day, argued the president's order exceeded his constitutional authority. In 1952 the U.S. Supreme Court agreed with the steel industry, a ruling that helped Jones Day become a nationally recognized law firm.

In the postwar era, the firm represented two prominent financiers: Abe List, who organized the conglomerate Glen Alden Corporation that later purchased the RKO Theatres Corporation from Howard Hughes; and Cyrus Eaton and his securities firm Otis & Company.

In the 1950s Jones Day worked on securities financing for such clients as American Greetings Corporation, TRW, National City Bank of Cleveland, Sherwin-Williams Company, and the J.M. Smucker Company. It also assisted underwriters such as Smith Barney and Kidder Peabody.

The law firm in the 1960s and 1970s represented Midland-Ross Corporation in mergers with Industrial Rayon Corporation and the National Casting Company. Other corporate clients in that time period were Diamond Alkali Company, Clevite Corporation, Scott & Fetzer Company, Diamond Shamrock Corporation, and Mogul Corporation. In the 1960s, the firm's litigation practice took root with a number of significant representations, including that of General Motors in several lawsuits involving the much-maligned Corvair, as well as Firestone Tire & Rubber Co. in patent litigation involving oil-extended rubber.

Key Dates:

1893: Edwin J. Blandin and William Lowe Rice begin partnership in Cleveland.

1900: Firm name is changed to Blandin, Rice & Ginn with addition of partner Frank H. Ginn.

1912: Partnership becomes Blandin, Hogsett & Ginn after Thomas H. Hogsett joins firm.

1913: Firm is renamed Tolles, Hogsett, Ginn & Morley.

1927: Firm adopts name of Tolles, Hogsett & Ginn.

1939: Merger with another Cleveland firm leads to name Jones, Day, Cockley & Reavis.

1946: The firm's office in Washington, D.C., is opened with three lawyers.

1967: Washington, D.C. office merges with Pogue & Neal.

1974: Jones, Day, Reavis & Pogue is adopted as firmwide name.

1986: Firm merges with Surrey & Morse, adding offices in New York, London, Paris, and Riyadh.

1989: Brussels, Tokyo, and Pittsburgh offices are opened; merger with Atlanta's Hansell & Post.

1993: Firm celebrates its centennial by publishing its own history.

2000: Firm opens its office in Madrid.

In 1972 Jones Day won a case that allowed Ohio banks to start branches outside their home county.

Rapid Growth in the 1980s and 1990s

In 1980, differences in strategic goals resulted in a majority of the Washington, D.C., office splitting away from Jones Day to form Crowell & Moring. Both branches continued to grow and prosper, with the Crowell law firm expanding by the early 1990s to 200 lawyers in three offices. The re-established Washington office eventually grew to over 200 lawyers as well.

The 1980s at Jones Day can be described as a period of geographic expansion. The firm established many new offices during this time, both to serve its corporate clients that were expanding nationally and also to take advantage of new industries developing in different parts of the nation. In 1980 it opened an office in Columbus, Ohio, mostly with local attorneys. On January 1, 1981 it opened its new Dallas office following the acquisition of the 20-lawyer Dallas firm of Meyers, Miller, Middleton, Weiner & Warren that represented Crow businesses and was well-known in the local real estate and construction industries.

Although some native Texan lawyers called the newcomers from Ohio "corncobs from the Middle West," according to the Borowitz history of the firm, that did not stop Jones Day. They gained acceptance in Dallas and other new cities by participating in local bar associations and other civic causes. In 1984 Jones Day opened its second Texas office, this time in the state capital of Austin, a fast-growing city with more high-tech firms supported by research at the University of Texas.

Other new Jones Day offices were opened in Irvine, California; New York; Hong Kong; Chicago; Geneva; Brussels; Tokyo; Pittsburgh; Atlanta; Taipei; Frankfurt; Shanghai; and Madrid. Like many other law firms, Jones Day was responding to an increasingly globalized economy.

Jones Day's rapid growth in the 1980s was not unusual. Increased economic growth, new high-tech industries, new laws and regulations, and a litigation explosion led to more demands for legal services. Another major factor was the U.S. Supreme Court's 1977 decision in Bates v. Arizona that lawyers had the right to advertise as a form of free speech guaranteed by the First Amendment. That decision and new legal publications started in the late 1970s, such as the *National Law Journal* and the *American Lawyer* that printed data about law firm finances and management, led to increased competition for top partners, higher salaries, and generally an increased business orientation by most big law firms.

Jones Day attorneys played leading roles in the litigation explosion of the late 20th century. In 1980, for example, the firm sued one president and defended another. In cooperation with the Independent Gasoline Marketers Council, it sued President Jimmy Carter over his gasoline tax. Citing the firm's 1952 defense of the steel industry, the courts found that only Congress could impose such a tax for fuel conservation purposes.

Later that year, Jones Day defended Republican Ronald Reagan during the presidential campaign. The Carter team, represented by Cravath Swaine & Moore, wanted to hold up $29.4 million in federal elections funds while the courts determined the legality of certain independent Reagan committees. Jones Day won this case based on the argument that even a few days delay in distributing the federal funds could seriously damage a campaign.

Major product liability clients were represented by Jones Day in the 1980s and beyond. The firm represented Firestone for over 15 years when it was sued for accidents from multipiece truck rims and wheels. Many cases against Firestone were dismissed, and Jones Day helped dispose of over 100 other cases in ten states, Puerto Rico, and the District of Columbia. Starting in 1987, the law firm represented Sherwin-Williams in lawsuits claiming damages from lead in the company's paint.

In 1985 R.J. Reynolds (later RJR Nabisco Holdings Corporation) chose Jones Day to be its national coordinating counsel when it and other tobacco manufacturers were sued for health damages. The firm won a jury trial in the Galbraith case in California, a case extensively covered by the media, and by 1999 Jones Day had helped Reynolds win some 250 cases, but the antismoking forces also won their share. In 1997, 40 states reached a settlement with the tobacco industry that agreed to pay $368.5 billion over the next 25 years to compensate the states for healthcare costs, pay individuals suing for damages, conduct research, and fund programs to prevent juveniles from starting smoking.

In 1999 gun manufacturers faced lawsuits from at least 23 municipalities that blamed them as being at least partially responsible for violence in America. Colt Manufacturing Company chose Jones Day as its national coordinating counsel.

To serve clients such as RJR Nabisco and Colt and others involved in lawsuits, Jones Day by the late 1990s had over 500 lawyers involved in about 4,000 litigation cases in the United States and international settings.

Partners at Jones Day and other major law firms earned hundreds of dollars per billable hour, and Americans of modest means could not typically afford such legal services. In his 1994 book *The Betrayed Profession,* Sol Linowitz quoted Jones Day partner Erwin Griswold, a former Harvard Law School Dean, as recalling that ''some of his most depressing moments are when he has to tell people he knows who need the services of a lawyer that, except for truly pro bono work, of which his firm does a good deal, its managing committee can't even consider matters where the amount involved is less than $25,000.'' While Linowitz was lamenting the ways in which the legal profession had changed over the century, the example nevertheless pointed to the success of firms such as Jones Day.

During the 1990s, Jones Day built one of the nation's premier bankruptcy practices. It represented the debtor in matters for Federated Department Stores, TWA, Montgomery Ward, Morrison-Knudsen, and USG Corporation. It represented the creditor committees in bankruptcies involving Olympia & York, Drexel Burnham Lambert, Resorts International, and Allegheny Health, Education & Research Foundation.

Also during this time, Jones Day emerged as a leader in the mergers and acquisitions practice. Consistently ranked in the top five firms based on the number of transactions handled, the firm has represented clients across a broad spectrum of industries with particular concentration in the energy, media, telecommunications, and health care industries.

According to annual surveys by the *American Lawyer*, Jones Day ranked as the United States' third largest law firm based on its 1997 revenues of $490 million and its 1998 revenues of $530 million and its 1998 revenues of $530 million. With about 1,300 attorneys in 2000, Jones Day remained a major international law firm, but it faced plenty of competition and challenges. Several law firms merged, creating larger firms to serve clients growing in the globalized economy. For example, in 1999 London's Clifford Chance and New York City's Rogers & Wells announced the first merger of major British and American law firms. Moreover, top accounting firms employed thousands of lawyers, and one of the big issues that confronted Jones Day and other law firms in 2000 was the possibility of the American Bar Association allowing lawyers to work with other professionals such as accountants.

Principal Operating Units

Business Practice; Government Regulation; Litigation; Tax.

Principal Competitors

Baker & McKenzie; Clifford Chance; Skadden, Arps.

Further Reading

Barrett, Paul M., and Milo Geyelin, ''Big National Law Firms Leap to Help Gun Industry As It Fights Suits by Cities,'' *Wall Street Journal*, July 14, 1999, p. B7.

Borowitz, Albert, *Jones, Day, Reavis & Pogue: The First Century,* Cleveland: Jones, Day, Reavis & Pogue, 1993.

Dougan, Arthur L., *Jones, Day, Reavis & Pogue: A Slightly Irreverent History from the Beginning to 1975,* Cleveland: Jones, Day, Reavis & Pogue, 1985.

''Glass Ceilings Breaking. . . . At Last,'' *Georgia Trend*, December 1999.

Haberman, Ian, *The Van Sweringens of Cleveland: The Biography of an Empire,* Cleveland: Western Reserve Historical Society, 1979.

Jackson, Harvey H., *Hansell & Post: From King & Anderson to Jones Day Reavis & Pogue 1890–1990,* Atlanta: 1989.

''Jones, Day, Reavis & Pogue,'' in *Los Angeles: Realm of Possibility*, by A. Donald Anderson, et al., Chatsworth, Calif.: Windsor Publications, 1991, p. 320.

Linowitz, Sol M., with Martin Mayer, *The Betrayed Profession: Lawyering at the End of the Twentieth Century,* New York: Charles Scribner's Sons, 1994, p. 146.

Mahar, Maggie, ''Tobacco Showdown,'' *Barron's*, April 14, 1997, p. 15.

Smolowe, Jill, ''Sorry, Pardner,'' *Time*, June 30, 1997, pp. 24–29.

Steinberger, Mike, ''Is Clifford Chance/Rogers & Wells the Next Wave, or Simply Overkill? Big Transatlantic Legal Merger Sparks Fierce Debate on Global Strategy,'' *Investment Dealers' Digest*, August 9, 1999, pp. 12–13.

—David M. Walden

Kampgrounds of America, Inc.

550 North 31st Street
Billings, Montana 59101
U.S.A.
Telephone: (406) 248-7444
Fax: (406) 248-7414
Web site: http://www.koakampgrounds.com

Private Company
Incorporated: 1962
Employees: 190
Sales: $26.6 million (1998)
NAIC: 721211 RV (Recreational Vehicle) Parks and
Campgrounds; 71399 All Other Amusement and
Recreation Industries

Kampgrounds of America, Inc. (KOA) is the world's largest system of privately operated campgrounds. The company enjoys a reputation of consistently providing clean and conveniently located camping accommodations across the United States. Almost all of KOA's 500 campgrounds are independently owned and operated. Each campground pays KOA a franchise fee, as well as a yearly royalty. In return, they can use KOA's universally recognized logo, and can reap the benefits of belonging to a well-known and highly respected network. The pioneer of franchised campgrounds, KOA has had to evolve to keep up with changes in the camping industry. As tent camping has declined in popularity, KOA has built furnished cabins (Kamping Kabins and Kamping Kottages) to house visitors. Moreover, KOA caters to recreational vehicle (RV) travelers in a number of ways. Since 1992, KOA has expanded aggressively into international markets. The company is owned by the family of Oscar L. Tang.

The Early Years: 1962–75

In the early 1960s, Montana businessman Dave Drum took note of the abysmal condition of most American campgrounds. He observed that campgrounds across the country were owned and operated by a hodgepodge of entities, ranging from various branches of government to private individuals and companies,

and were "by and large pretty spartan and scruffy places," according to the *Billings Business Journal.* At the same time that the nation's campgrounds were often unsatisfactory, young Americans were taking to the roads in record numbers. These baby boomers sought affordable, decent accommodations, and liked the idea of sleeping outdoors.

Drum recognized an opportunity. The Billings, Montana-based entrepreneur had already revolutionized the Montana cattle industry by building two massive feedlots in the mid-1950s. However, one of the parcels of land he had earmarked for a feedlot lay vacant because a local farmer had cut off irrigation. Drum convinced Robert Boorman and two other Billings investors that his scenic property on the Yellowstone River nevertheless offered considerable profit-making potential. The 1962 World's Fair was scheduled to be held in Seattle, Washington, and Drum anticipated that a significant number of travelers would be passing through Montana on their way to the event and would desire affordable but pleasant accommodations. Drum and his partners built a new kind of campground that featured individual hot showers, clean restrooms, and a convenience store. They hung up a sign and watched with gratification as their site filled up with customers.

Rather than resting on the laurels of his initial success, Drum was sure that his concept had appeal beyond the local level. He quizzed campers and sent questionnaires to former campground guests and chambers of commerce in towns and cities of all sizes. The responses to these surveys "provided Drum with his customer demographics and with leads on locations with high campground demand," explained *Western Business.* Determined to build a franchised network of campgrounds, Drum bought out his original co-investors and found two more. The group cast about for a name for their endeavor and settled on Campgrounds of America. However, they could not obtain a copyright for this moniker because "Campground" was an everyday word. To circumvent this problem, Drum and his associates opted for the distinctive name "Kampgrounds of America." In 1962, they sold their first franchise in Burley, Idaho.

In the next few years, they rapidly expanded, selling franchises to campground owners across the United States. "It was Dave's idea, pure and simple," one-time investor Boorman told

Western Business. "Developing a directory of franchises put people in the campgrounds." To ensure that KOA's rapid growth did not compromise the quality of the company's product, Drum insisted that each campground maintain certain standards of cleanliness and service. Each franchise—whether an existing campground that had converted to KOA or a first-time enterprise—was expected to provide basic amenities. Hot showers and sanitary facilities were required of all franchisees. As a result, KOA quickly developed a reputation for offering a consistent level of accommodations. As the *Worcester Telegram & Gazette* explained, KOA "changed the way a lot of campers, accustomed to roughing it, felt about campgrounds."

In many ways, Drum's innovation of campground franchising mirrored the contemporary development of budget hotel chains. Like these motel franchises, KOAs cropped up at regular intervals along the nation's newly constructed interstate highway system, making them accessible and ubiquitous—a traveler could count on finding a KOA at virtually any point in his journey. Like the more successful of these motel chains, KOA's hallmark was cleanliness and consistency, not opulence.

Changes in Leadership: 1975–85

Drum left KOA in 1975. His role as president and chairman was assumed by Darrell R. Booth, who presided over KOA's continued growth and development. By 1980, 800 campgrounds had entered the KOA fold. Booth also oversaw KOA's acquisition of Sir Speedy, Inc. A leading copy and printing services chain that operated on a franchise basis similar to KOA's, Sir Speedy had suffered from mismanagement and was bankrupt. KOA purchased the ailing company to provide it with more balanced earnings throughout the year. Campgrounds were a cyclical business, booming with visitors during the summer and lying largely vacant during the long stretch between Labor Day and Memorial Day. Nevertheless, the acquisition surprised a number of analysts. "The only thing the two companies had in common [was] that they were both franchise operations," a KOA executive told the *Orange County Business Journal.*

KOA's leadership changed hands again, following Booth's death in 1980. In November of that year, Hong Kong businessman Oscar L. Tang purchased Booth's entire stake in the company and took the helm. Tang became the driving force behind

KOA, but preserved many of the strategies his predecessors had implemented. Like Drum and Booth, Tang initially focused on growth. Tang also recognized that the individual campground franchises were the key to the company's success. In the early 1980s, KOA franchisees had founded the KOA Kampground Owners Association. Rather than antagonize its franchisees by making significant management decisions from on high and then imposing them on the individual operators, as many other major franchisers had done, Tang and his management team sought to solicit input from the individual campground owners. KOA's relationship to its franchisees was unique in other ways as well. Rather than charge a hefty up-front fee, as was common in the franchising world, KOA looked for owners who were willing to devote what the *Billings Business Journal* termed "sweat equity."

In the early 1980s, Tang made another decision that was to have a significant impact on KOA's long-term success. In an effort to gain more control over the company's direction, Tang took KOA private, thereby freeing himself from accountability to shareholders. This was an important decision because shareholders tended to measure the company's success solely by its rate of expansion. In this new arrangement, however, Tang was able to refocus the company first and foremost on the quality of its campgrounds. As a result, Tang and company president Art Peterson began to cull some 200 campgrounds that had sunk below KOA's standards. Analysts and company executives praised Tang's move in later years, crediting KOA's privatization as having laid the foundation for its future success. Another result of this new decision-making latitude proved less salutary, however. In 1985, KOA chose to enter a new area of business when it purchased Mid Pacific Air Corp. and its Mid Pacific Airline unit. Unfortunately, the airline would eventually enter bankruptcy proceedings.

In any event, KOA's overall success during this period was aided by the flourishing of the entire camping industry during the late 1980s and early 1990s. The U.S. recession of this period contributed to a steep increase in the number of consumers who camped, as families eager to travel but who were constrained by tight budgets, flocked to KOA and its competitors. Indeed, two million more Americans took camping trips in 1990 than in 1989, according to the *Atlanta Journal-Constitution.* A 1991 survey conducted by KOA revealed that over one-third of Americans who planned vacations that year intended to stay overnight in a campground. People's passion for camping was also fueled by a surging awareness of environmental issues. Moreover, as baby boomers married and started families, they turned to camping as a pleasurable family activity. Just as they had embraced camping as traveling teenagers, baby boomers returned to camping as a way to be together as a family. "It's really just a change of values," a spokesperson for the Recreational Vehicle Industry Association told *USA Today.* "The baby boomers who strived to achieve so much, so fast now want to relax and enjoy it."

International Expansion in the Early 1990s

The United States was not the only nation experiencing an outdoor activities boom. While KOA had long eyed international markets, and had launched franchises in Canada as early as 1970 (45 KOA campgrounds operated in Canada by 1993), it had

---

Key Dates:

1962: Dave Drum founds KOA with three other investors.
1970: KOA franchise expands into Canada.
1975: Drum sells his share of company.
1977: KOA purchases Sir Speedy, Inc.
1980: Family of Oscar L. Tang acquires KOA.
1984: KOA introduces Kamping Kabins.
1993: First KOA franchise opens in Japan.
1996: First KOA franchise opens in Mexico.
1998: KOA introduces Kamping Kottages, as well as KOA RV and Boat Storage.

---

delayed extending its network beyond North American borders. In 1992, however, KOA signed a master franchise licensing agreement with investor Shinsuke Nikaido for the development of KOA campgrounds in Japan. American-style car camping had grown in popularity in Japan, and the Japanese were experiencing an increased sensitivity to environmental issues that paralleled developments in the United States. The number of campers in Japan nearly doubled between 1988 and 1992.

In September 1993, the first KOA in Japan opened in the Okayama Prefecture west of Kobe. Two dozen more Japanese KOA campgrounds were scheduled to be built by 1994. All would offer the same amenities as their U.S. counterparts. KOA's interest in international markets was twofold. The company naturally wanted to introduce other nations to the benefits of camping KOA-style, and also hoped to attract American tourists traveling abroad to foreign KOAs. More importantly, though, KOA sought to use its foreign campgrounds to promote its U.S. campgrounds among international travelers. As the *Billings Gazette* noted, "foreign visitors who become familiar with KOA in their homeland will feel more comfortable choosing KOA when they come to America." In keeping with this strategy, KOA joined international tourism organizations, forged alliances with foreign camping chains, and advertised in international markets.

In the wake of the North American Free Trade Agreement (NAFTA), which increased economic links between the United States and its North American neighbors, KOA accelerated its plans to expand into Mexico. In 1996, the company debuted Acapulco West KOA, the first in a series of KOAs planned for Mexico. Relying on U.S. consumers' familiarity with its brand, the campground particularly targeted Americans vacationing in Mexico. In 1998, the company also opened Mexican KOAs in Puerto Vallarta and Tecate.

A Changing Industry: The Mid-1990s and Beyond

Despite its success in both U.S. and international markets, KOA faced a rapidly changing camping industry in the mid-1990s. Tent camping's popularity declined during this period, as increasing numbers of campers elected to travel and sleep in RVs. A number of factors led to the boom in RV camping, the most important of which was demographics. The United States was an aging nation. Not only were the number of young families declining, but the number of retired and semi-

retired people was increasing, especially as the baby boom generation moved into its 50s. Buoyed by a strong economy, these older Americans frequently opted to purchase (or rent) RVs and to travel for extended periods of time. As a spokesperson for the recreational vehicle industry explained in a 1997 press release, the "vanguard of the great boomer generation [had] reach[ed] prime RV-buying age."

RV campers had a different set of needs and demands than the tent campers of the 1970s and 1980s. By 1998, about 60 percent of all KOA campers were in RVs, and with more luxurious RVs becoming the norm, KOA campground operators were often required to provide cable television and even Internet connections on top of the customary electrical, water, and plumbing hookups. Moreover, wider RVs necessitated that campground operators build larger sites for the bulky vehicles.

RV campers alone, however, were not the only force driving changes in the industry. Campers—both young and old, tent and RV—were increasingly less inclined to give up comfortable amenities when camping. In addition, more American families were headed by single parents, who wanted outdoor vacations that took less preparation, planning, and equipment. These trends led to the tremendous popularity of an older feature of some KOA campgrounds—Kamping Kabins. These rustic cabins, which provided beds, air conditioning, heat, and an eating space, had first been introduced by KOA in 1984, and the company rushed to add new ones to meet burgeoning consumer demand. By 1998, more KOA campers stayed in Kamping Kabins than in the traditional tents, and 90 percent of all KOA campgrounds contained Kamping Kabins.

Many guests wanted even more luxurious accommodations. To satisfy this demand, KOA debuted Kamping Kottages (units offering full kitchens, bathrooms, and dining areas) at select locations in 1998. KOA also introduced campgrounds that verged on resorts. For instance, the company's Saco/Portland South KOA in Maine touted whale watching excursions and deep sea fishing. Furthermore, in June 1996, the company debuted its first "family adventure ranch" near Butte, Montana. With a roster of activities ranging from horse-riding to cattle drives, this KOA represented a new breed of camping. No longer just an inexpensive method of travel, camping had become an end in itself. As the *Worcester Telegram & Gazette* explained, "what was once viewed as a rustic blue-jeans and hiking-boots experience has become more sophisticated."

Demand for more activities and amenities like these led to a change in the profile of the average KOA franchisee. Camping was an increasingly competitive industry, and the cost of building a "modern" campground soared. KOA's president, Art Peterson, told *RV Business* that constructing a campground in 1998 cost approximately $10,000 per campsite. The trend at the turn of the century was for professional investors—rather than the individual owner/managers who had long formed the core of campground operation nationwide—to launch KOA franchises. The company adjusted to this shift. Beginning in 1996, the company implemented "untraditional growth strategies to reach out to investment buyers," according to *RV Business*. Rather than waiting for individual owners to start campgrounds, KOA began to build more expensive campgrounds itself, which it then sold as turnkey operations to investors willing to put up money but not sweat equity.

KOA's capacity to adapt to consumers' changing demands kept the business successful in a shifting industry. Rather than rest on its laurels, though, the company continued to innovate. In 1998, for instance, KOA teamed up with the Disney Company to promote the entertainment titan's line of Goosebumps audio products. In exchange for selling the Disney audiotapes in its onsite convenience stores, KOA was given the right to use Disney characters on its signage.

Always seeking opportunities for growth, KOA also launched a new enterprise in 1998. Recognizing that many RV campers had no place to store their cumbersome vehicles for most of the year (especially since many neighborhood committees forbade the permanent parking of RVs or boats on the street), KOA created an independent company—KOA RV and Boat Storage—to cater to this segment. By March 1999, KOA had opened three boat and RV storage facilities. With its long track record of success, familiar brand, and willingness to innovate, KOA's future prospects appeared bright.

Principal Subsidiaries

Sir Speedy, Inc.

Principal Competitors

Affinity Group Holding, Inc.; Global Outdoors; International Leisure Hosts, Ltd.; Outdoor Resorts of America, Inc.; Thousand Trails, Inc.

Further Reading

''Five Regional Risks Pay Off,'' *Western Business,* November 1, 1985.

Glazner, Elizabeth, ''King of Copies,'' *Orange County Business Journal,* March 26, 1990, p. 13.

Goldenberg, Sherman, ''KOA's Art Peterson,'' *RV Business,* May 1, 1998, p. 17.

LaRocque, Ray, ''Montana Idea Grew and Put a 'K' into Campground,'' *Worcester Telegram & Gazette,* April 5, 1992.

''More Happy Campers Pitching in Across U.S.,'' *Atlanta Journal-Constitution,* May 19, 1991.

Nottingham, Nancy, ''Camping Worldwide,'' *Billings Gazette,* January 15, 1995, p. 1.

''Old Timer Celebrates Its 25th Year of Camping Out,'' *Billings Business Journal,* July 1, 1987, p. 19.

''RV Industry Is Riding High with Another Strong Season Forecast,'' *Business Wire,* March 26, 1997.

''This Year Is KOA's Silver Anniversary,'' *Billings Business Journal,* July 1, 1987, p. 1.

Tom, Denise, ''Boomer Families Go Camping,'' *USA Today,* July 25, 1991, p. C8.

—Rebecca Stanfel

KPMG International

Burgemeester Rijnderslaan 20
1185 MC Amstelveen
The Netherlands
Telephone: (20) 656-6700
Fax: (20) 656-6777
Web site: http://www.kpmg.com

Private Company
Incorporated: 1897 as Marwick, Mitchell & Company
Employees: 102,000
Sales: $12.2 billion (1999)
NAIC: 541211 Offices of Certified Public Accountants;
    541219 Other Accounting Services; 541618 Other
    Management Consulting Services

KPMG International is the third-largest accounting firm in the world. Headquartered in the Netherlands, KPMG provides accounting, consulting, tax and legal, financial advisory, and assurance services from more than 820 locations. KPMG's member firms are located in more than 159 countries across the globe. In the late 1990s, the company focused on unifying its historically loose federation of member firms to build a cohesive global image and offer a consistent array of products and services.

A Demanding and Rewarding
First Century: 1890s–1970s

KPMG got its start in 1897, just a few years after the first American accounting firm had been set up. The company was formed by James Marwick and Roger Mitchell, who had both immigrated to the new world from Scotland. They set up their new partnership, called Marwick, Mitchell & Company, in New York City. Eight years after its founding, Marwick, Mitchell & Company launched a banking practice, focusing its efforts on one industry for the first time. This effort proved so successful that the firm later went on to offer tailored services to companies in the insurance industry, the thrift field, and to mutual fund brokers.

In 1911 Marwick, Mitchell & Company merged with a British accounting firm headed by Sir William B. Peat. The new transatlantic company was called Peat, Marwick, Mitchell & Company. Through the merger, Marwick, Mitchell & Company strengthened its operations in Europe, while Peat gained greater access to the rapidly growing North American market. This configuration of the company remained in effect for the next three-quarters of a century.

During this time, Peat Marwick grew steadily, becoming one of the "Big Eight" major public accounting firms in the United States. In the late 1960s and early 1970s, Peat Marwick's business and revenues began to grow dramatically, as did those of their competitors. This boom in demand for accounting services came as a result of increasingly complex tax laws, securities laws, and industry regulations. Between 1973 and 1976, for example, the Securities and Exchange Commission (SEC) added 16 new disclosure requirements for publicly held companies. With the ever-increasing mandated need for accounting services, Peat Marwick's revenues grew steadily as demand outstripped supply.

In addition to the welter of new federal regulations, accounting industry standards became more exacting. The Accounting Principles Board and the Financial Accounting Standards Board issued a wide variety of directives to members of the industry in response to complaints that the accounting industry was not fulfilling its watchdog role in corporate America stringently enough. Like the rest of its peers in the industry, Peat Marwick was defendant in several lawsuits charging it with failing to prevent or expose financial malfeasance.

In the early 1970s, the legal entanglements continued. In May 1972, for example, the Raytheon Company sued the accounting firm over its audits of the Visual Electronics Corporation from 1968 to 1970, charging that its work failed to show how bad the company's financial straits were.

Nevertheless, by this time Peat Marwick had become the largest public accounting firm in the nation. The company had grown by providing services to corporations and also by winning government contracts. In 1972, for instance, it won a Department of Transportation contract to analyze the department's planning techniques.

Company Perspectives:

For decades, KPMG has been serving companies with international interests. We know it takes more than sheer numbers of people and offices to build a meaningful global capability that's responsive to the marketplace. It takes a sound strategy, implemented by highly skilled teams of professionals—individuals who are industry-smart, internationally savvy, and technically exceptional. It also takes ideas—grown in the right culture, nurtured with the proper investment, and matched with the necessary technology. And as markets and companies continue to globalize, KPMG will continue to serve them—anywhere.

In response to a general consensus that the financial industry was moving toward greater accountability, Peat Marwick took steps in 1975 to shore up the controls on its accounting practice. "We have a little bit of an image problem, and we'd better start doing something about it," Peat Marwick's senior partner told the *Wall Street Journal.* The firm was concerned that its recent bad publicity was causing local government units, highly sensitive to public opinion, to seek other firms for their auditing business.

Hoping to clear its name, Peat Marwick engaged another Big Eight accounting firm, Arthur Young & Company, to audit its quality control procedures and make the results available to its clients and staff. In taking this step, Peat Marwick became the first public accounting firm to inaugurate a peer review process. The audit was scheduled to begin in June, in place of an earlier planned process that would have been conducted by the American Institute of Certified Public Accountants. Peat Marwick abandoned its plan for this review because it wished to make the results of the audit public.

In November 1975, Peat Marwick released the study of its operations by Arthur Young & Company in an effort to bolster its reputation for reliability. The report, which cost the company more than half a million dollars, was favorable in its account of the company's activities. In April 1976, the company revised its audit manual to include more use of internal auditors.

Just two months after this report, Peat Marwick won a major new governmental client when it was selected to audit New York City, a job that brought with it an annual fee of nearly $1 million. In addition to its other big clients, the firm was engaged by the General Electric Company for an audit so broad in scope that it required 429 employees in 38 different offices.

In 1978 Peat Marwick formed Peat Marwick International to oversee the firm's activities outside the United States. With this change, the company set up a multinational umbrella partnership of different firms in locations around the world. By doing this, Peat Marwick hoped to prepare itself for further globalization of the world economy and financial markets by combining a single firm image with well-respected and established local accounting organizations.

In 1979 Peat Marwick reported record revenues from its worldwide operations, which yielded $673.8 million in reve-

nues over a 12-month period, an increase of 15 percent from the previous year. As Peat Marwick entered the 1980s with this strong financial performance behind it, the company began to face a maturing market for its services and growing competition from the other Big Eight firms. In addition, under pressure from the federal government, the accounting industry was forced to abandon its self-enforced prohibition on advertising. This resulted in a far more hotly contested market for accounting services.

Increasing Competition and New Ownership in the 1980s

Entering a new decade, Peat Marwick and the accounting business both appeared to be in solid positions. Though Peat Marwick was somewhat narrow in its focus, primarily handling auditing and accounting services in the early 1980s, the company's revenues for the year ended June 1981 reached $979 million, a 20 percent increase compared to fiscal 1980 results. Business seemed to be increasing as well; workload figures rose by more than eight percent over 1980. About 80 percent of the firm's revenues were generated from auditing and accounting, about 14 percent was attributed to tax advice, and the remainder came from management consultancy services. Peat Marwick earned more than half of its sales in North America. Among the firm's significant new clients were Vickers Ltd. of Britain, which included Rolls-Royce Motors, and the State of California, for which Peat Marwick was hired to develop and install a major accounting system.

Despite significant growth, competition in the accounting industry was heating up, and in 1981 Peat Marwick moved to counter rising competition by automating the audit process. As a first step in this process, Peat Marwick developed a program called SeaCas, an abbreviation for Systems Evaluation Approach-Computerized Audit Support. Three years later, the company switched to the Apple Macintosh for all its future computer applications. Also in 1984, Peat Marwick purchased another accounting firm, W.O. Daley & Company, based in Orlando, Florida. With this move, the company added eight new partners to its worldwide tally of 1,284.

Major diversification and expansion finally arrived at Peat Marwick in 1986, when the company agreed to merge with Klynveld Main Goerdeler (KMG), a Dutch accounting firm. KMG had been formed in the early 1980s through the merger of German company Deutsche Treuhand-Gesellschaft, Dutch firm Klynveld Kraayenhoff & Co., U.S. company Main Hurdman & Cranstoun, and several other European and Canadian accounting firms. The resultant international accounting federation, KMG, was based in the Netherlands, and the U.S. arm had become known as KMG Main Hurdman.

KMG was the ninth-largest accounting firm in the United States in 1986, while Peat Marwick was number two. The merger of KMG and Peat Marwick created the largest accounting firm in the world in terms of size and revenue. In its new configuration, Peat Marwick enhanced its ability to attract as audit clients large U.S. companies with multinational operations. After approval by Peat Marwick's 2,733 partners and KMG's 2,827 partners, the joined companies were to be known as Klynveld Peat Marwick Goerdeler, or KPMG, and were to be headquartered in Amsterdam. In September 1986, Peat Marwick announced that it had opened negotiations to buy a public relations company and a consulting business, both with ties to the high-tech industry. In the wake of its proposed merger with KMG, this move was seen as a bid by the company to enhance its profile in the consulting field.

On January 1, 1987, the merger between Peat Marwick and KMG was officially completed, capping the largest merger in the history of the accounting business. The new firm instantly inherited worldwide revenues of $2.7 billion, with $1.7 billion contributed by Peat Marwick. In the United States, the operations of both KMG, with 79 U.S. offices, and Peat Marwick, with 91, were combined into one organization, which was to be known as Peat Marwick. Peat Marwick was the more dominant of the two companies in the United States, with annual revenues of about $1.1 billion, compared to KMG's $249 million. In Europe, however, KMG was stronger than Peat Marwick. KMG had more than 13,000 European employees and just under 200 locations, while Peat Marwick had only 34 offices and about 2,000 employees. With combined power, KPMG hoped to hold a leadership position across the world.

The combining of two large firms with varying operating cultures and management styles proved difficult, and integration of the merger occurred slowly. Member firms in Australia and New Zealand, for example, opted not to join the new company. KMG Hungerfords, the Australian branch of KMG, began investigating merger deals with competing accounting firms after voting against the merger. Establishing agreements with other partners, including firms in West Germany, Switzerland, Spain, and France, lingered past the final merger date as questions regarding partnership details arose.

As the 1980s came to an end, the accounting business once again found itself in a period of transition. During the previous decade, booming business conditions had produced brisk growth for accounting firms, and KPMG had expanded rapidly along with the rest of the industry. By the end of the decade, the firm's client base had started to shrink as a result of changes in the financial world, such as the collapse of the savings and loan industry. Peat Marwick, which changed its name to KPMG Peat

Marwick in 1989, found itself the object of a sweeping inquiry into its audits of savings institutions by the Office of Thrift Supervision as a result of the firm's involvement with the San Francisco Savings and Loan Association. In addition, the wave of bankruptcies that followed the frenzy for mergers and leveraged buyouts in the 1980s resulted in a reduction in need for accounting services and also generated a large number of lawsuits for public accounting firms as a result of their participation in these activities.

These factors combined to flatten KPMG's revenues in 1988 and 1989. In late 1990 the partnership elected a new chairman, Jon C. Madonna, and KPMG Peat Marwick began to implement changes to improve its profitability. In February 1991, the company announced that 265 partners, or one in seven, would be laid off from the firm in a streamlining effort. KPMG Peat Marwick predicted that severance costs would amount to $52 million. Despite this drain on U.S. earnings, the company's worldwide returns remained strong, as it posted annual revenues of $6 billion.

Consolidation and International Growth in the 1990s

In March 1992, KPMG began to reorganize its operations under the aegis of a Future Directions Committee. Relying on input from the company's Client Service Measurement Process, a survey of customer satisfaction inaugurated in 1989, the firm chose six lines of business: financial services; government; health care and life sciences; information and communications; manufacturing, retailing, and distribution; and special markets and designated services. In addition, KPMG Peat Marwick divided the country into ten separate geographical practice areas. The company then organized accountants, tax specialists, and consultants into industry-specific teams. Within this framework, KPMG Peat Marwick sought to develop specialists with certain areas of expertise who would entice new clients and bring high-paying tax and consulting jobs.

In September 1993, as growth in the company's targeted industries remained sluggish, KPMG Peat Marwick launched an advertising campaign for the first time. Focusing on the company's international stature, the ads urged companies to "go global—but not without a map." KPMG Peat Marwick enjoyed increased revenues following its launch, recording revenue for 1996 of $2.53 billion, a rise of ten percent over 1995 revenues of $2.29 billion. Fiscal 1996 was the third year of revenue growth for KPMG Peat Marwick, a welcome relief after five years of little growth.

KPMG Peat Marwick also gained a new CEO and chairman in 1996 with the hiring of Stephen G. Butler, while Jon Madonna continued as chairman of KPMG International. Butler indicated the company would strengthen its consultancy services, a market with significant growth potential, and offer new services. Expanding existing services into new markets was another strategy for company growth. "Our plan is to increase revenue more than 10% a year," Butler stated confidently in the *Wall Street Journal*. "We have every expectation we'll be able to do that," he asserted.

KPMG's strategy proved successful, with the firm growing 11.1 percent in 1997 compared to 1996. In 1998, revenues grew

15.6 percent over 1997 to reach $10.4 billion. The firm launched an effort to unify its operations to form a more centralized operation and also attempted to boost brand recognition. To that end KPMG Peat Marwick initiated a $60 million global branding campaign. The campaign, which included television, radio, and print ads, adopted the tag line, "It's time for clarity." KPMG marketing officer Tim Pearson explained the tag line in a company statement, noting, "The emphasis on clarity–not simply knowledge management or insight—in our brand advertising campaign strongly differentiates KPMG in the increasingly crowded business advisory arena and articulates KPMG's business strategy." To further enhance the brand, KPMG Peat Marwick shortened its name to KPMG LLP at the end of 1998.

In the late 1990s the firm took additional action to strengthen and unify its core businesses of audit, tax, and consulting services. In August 1998 the U.S. arm announced plans to sell its compensation consulting practice to human resources consulting firm William M. Mercer, Inc. The decision marked KPMG's move away from non-core operations. In March 1999 KPMG restructured its operations to create global operating regions. The newly formed KPMG "Americas" group included 19 member firms in Mexico, Latin America, the Caribbean, Australia, and New Zealand. These partners combined operations with the U.S. firm of KPMG LLP. The "EMA" group covered Europe, the Middle East, and Africa and included member firms in such countries as France, the Netherlands, Germany, and the United Kingdom. The firm planned to form an Asia-Pacific group at a later date. In September 1999 Stephen Butler became the chairman of KPMG International, succeeding Colin Sharman, who had been the firm's chairman since 1997. Butler's new position was in addition to his continuing roles as chairman and CEO of KPMG LLP.

Despite KPMG's continued growth, the firm suffered a few setbacks in its expansion efforts. In late 1997 KPMG's Canadian arm announced plans to merge with accounting firm Ernst & Young. The deal, which fell through in early 1998, would have created the largest accounting and consulting firm in the world. The firms hoped their combined strength would help make inroads in the emerging markets of Latin America and China and enhance global opportunities. In 1999 KPMG Canada faced another failed merger attempt. On March 25 the firm declared its plans to separate from KPMG International and merge with Arthur Andersen, but the deal was called off just over a week later, on April 5. The soured deal left KPMG divided into opposing groups. Also that year KPMG's consulting practice in Belgium was acquired by rival PricewaterhouseCoopers.

The setbacks did little to slow the firm down, however, and KPMG made some acquisitions itself. In May 1999 the firm expanded its consulting business by acquiring Softline Consulting & Integrators, Inc., a firm based in San Jose, California. KPMG also added new partners, many of whom had defected from PricewaterhouseCoopers, in Taiwan, Israel, Indonesia, and the Philippines. In the United States, KPMG separated its consulting business from its accounting operations and planned to sell stock in the entity, if approved by the U.S. Securities and Exchange Commission. In August 1999 Cisco Systems Inc. agreed to purchase a 20 percent stake in the consulting business for about $1 billion. KPMG intended to use the funds to further invest in its expanding Internet services. The partnership provided Cisco with access to KPMG's international corporate clients, while KPMG gained access to Cisco's equipment and expertise in computer networking. David Crawford, chairman of KPMG Australia, commented on the deal in *The Age,* noting, "This is a very significant development. . . . It puts us at the forefront of e-commerce development and the exploitation of the Internet." In January 2000 KPMG Consulting, LLC was incorporated. The new business included KPMG's consulting operations in the United States and Mexico. KPMG expected to add additional firms, including those in Asia, Canada, and Latin America, during the course of the year.

As KPMG entered a new century, the company appeared headed for continued growth and success. The firm had expanded significantly in the late 1990s while also integrating operations into a more centrally run entity. KPMG reported record revenues of $12.2 billion for the year ended September 30, 1999, up 17 percent over fiscal 1998 revenues. All business areas enjoyed substantial growth during 1999: the consulting services division grew 32 percent to reach $3.5 billion, financial advisory services grew 39 percent, tax services increased 16.5 percent, and assurance services rose nine percent. The firm's geographic regions experienced growth as well, with the Americas group surging 19 percent, Asia Pacific growing 20 percent, and the EMA region expanding 15 percent. Chairman Stephen Butler looked forward to the continued globalization of KPMG and indicated that the firm would take advantage of opportunities for growth, particularly regarding the Internet. "I'm enthused about KPMG's future prospects," Butler stated in a prepared statement. He remarked: "We'll continue moving KPMG toward a vision that emphasizes a cohesive and capable firm that effectively serves multinational clients anywhere they operate."

Principal Subsidiaries

KPMG LLP (U.S.); KPMG Consulting, LLC (U.S.; 80.1 percent).

Principal Competitors

Andersen Worldwide; Ernst & Young International; PricewaterhouseCoopers.

Further Reading

"Accounting Business is Thriving," *Globe and Mail,* January 4, 1982, p. B5.

Andrews, Frederick, "Fraud Trial of Peat Marwick Attracts Anxious Attention of Other Accountants," *Wall Street Journal,* October 29, 1974.

——, "Peat Marwick Is the First Big CPA Firm to Submit to 'Quality Review' by Peers," *Wall Street Journal,* June 17, 1974.

——, "Two Auditors Are Convicted of Stock Fraud," *Wall Street Journal,* November 15, 1974.

Barker, Garry, "Cisco Buys into KPMG US," *The Age,* August 10, 1999, p. 1.

Berton, Lee, "Peat-KMG Merger Proposal Strained As Units in Some Countries Drop Off," *Wall Street Journal,* January 6, 1987.

——, "Peat-KMG Merger Will Form a Goliath," *Wall Street Journal,* September 12, 1986.

——, "Peat Marwick and KMG Main Agree to Merge," *Wall Street Journal,* September 4, 1986.

Bevan, Judi, "The 'Tough Nut' at Accountancy's Core," *Sunday Telegraph London,* July 23, 1995, p. 12.

Cowan, Alison Leigh, "Regulators Investigate Peat on Its Auditing of S.&L.'s," *New York Times,* May 23, 1991.

Gibb-Clark, Margot, "KPMG Suffers Internal Blows from Aborted Union," *Globe and Mail,* April 15, 1999, p. B13.

Heinzl, John, "Ernst & Young, KPMG to Create Global Giant," *Globe and Mail,* October 21, 1997, p. B6.

MacDonald, Elizabeth, "KPMG International Chooses Butler as Its Chairman, Succeeding Sharman," *Wall Street Journal,* July 1, 1999, p. B13.

Mann, Simon, "Peat and KMG Call Off Plans for Merger," *Sydney Morning Herald,* December 19, 1986, p. 13.

Minard, Lawrence, and Brian McGlynn, "The U.S.' Newest Glamour Job," *Forbes,* September 1, 1977.

Stodghill, Ron, "Who Says Accountants Can't Jump?," *Business Week,* October 26, 1992.

Tannenbaum, Jeffrey A., "Butler, Elected Peat Marwick CEO, Plans to Increase Revenue 10% a Year," *Wall Street Journal,* October 4, 1996, p. A3.

Weiss, Stuart, "Peat Marwick Merges Its Way to the Top," *Business Week,* September 15, 1986.

—Elizabeth Rourke
—updated by Mariko Fujinaka

The Krystal Company

I Union Square
Chattanooga, Tennessee 37402
U.S.A.
Telephone: (423) 757-1550
Toll Free: (800) 458-5841
Fax: (423) 757-5610
Web site: http://www.krystalco.com

Wholly Owned Subsidiary of Port Royal Holdings
Incorporated: 1932
Employees: 8,150
Sales: $257.4 million (1998)
NAIC: 722211 Limited-Service Restaurants

The Krystal Company develops, operates, and franchises a chain of fast-food hamburger restaurants in the southeastern United States. Founded in 1932, Krystal is the second-oldest fast-food chain in the country. The company's success stems in part from its continuity. Famous for its Krystal burger—an onion-flavored, steamed, square patty that is much smaller than other fast-food hamburgers—the company has created a niche for itself in the highly competitive fast-food sector. However, class action lawsuits forced Krystal into Chapter 11 bankruptcy protection in 1995. When the company emerged in 1997, it was acquired by Port Royal Holdings, a closely held investment company belonging to Philip Sanford. Now a wholly owned subsidiary of Port Royal, Krystal owns 241 restaurants, and its franchisees operate an additional 110 units.

The Early Years: 1932–60

The Krystal Company was founded in the midst of the Great Depression by textile businessman R.B. Davenport, Jr. Inspired by White Castle, a fast-food hamburger business that preceded Krystal by 11 years, Davenport opened the first Krystal in 1932 on a busy street in downtown Chattanooga, Tennessee. Davenport christened his venture Krystal because his wife admired how "crystal clean" the restaurant was. In an effort to distinguish his restaurant from others, Davenport chose its distinctive

spelling. The restaurant flourished, as value-conscious Chattanoogans flocked to Krystal for its five cent hamburger.

Buoyed by the success of his restaurant, Davenport opened new units in the 1930s and 1940s. Although the company grew rapidly throughout the Southeast, Krystal never sought to extend itself too far north because of an agreement it had reached with White Castle soon after Krystal debuted. Because the two companies offered such similar products, they pledged never to compete head-to-head in the same market. "The old Mason-Dixon line is the separation between Krystal and White Castle territory," a Krystal spokesperson later told the *Atlanta Journal-Constitution*. While White Castle proliferated in the Midwest and the Northeast, Krystal centered its empire in Tennessee, Georgia, and Alabama.

The pace of Krystal's expansion accelerated in the 1950s and 1960s, as hamburger chains became part of the American landscape. The rise of a car culture in post-World War II America did much to spur this growth. Fast-food chains such as Krystal and White Castle were eager to accommodate their customers' love of cars. Following the example of drive-in movie theaters, fast food purveyors built drive-through restaurants. By 1950, Krystal had stopped constructing restaurants with a seating area inside and opened only drive-throughs. Unlike the drive-up windows that became prevalent in the 1980s and 1990s, these early drive-throughs retained many aspects of a restaurant. Although customers ate in their cars, waiters took orders and brought the meals out.

Expansion and Brand-Building: 1960–90

In the 1960s and 1970s, fast-food restaurants began to occupy a new niche in American society and were no longer considered a novelty dining destination. Customers frequented fast-food restaurants to get an inexpensive, consistent meal quickly, and convenience became the new standard for fast-food chains. As women entered the workforce in record numbers, eating out became less of a luxury and more of a commonplace time-saver for families with two working parents. Fast-food restaurants again conformed to their customers' wishes and became even more efficient. Spearheading this

---

Company Perspectives:

While the rest of the world believes bigger is better, we at The Krystal Company proudly offer our customers a hamburger that is fresh, hot, small, and square. In a word, unique. And thanks to over 65 years of brand building upon that small, yet sturdy foundation, The Krystal Company is more than a success. It's a hamburger institution. So while other Quick Service Restaurants must now battle for position in the customer's mind, we inspire people to drive halfway across town because nothing else will do.

---

effort was the McDonald's Corporation, which eliminated waiters, streamlined food operations, and pared the standard fast-food menu. By 1970, the fast-food segment accounted for 25 percent of total restaurant spending.

Krystal continued to build its chain in the Southeast during this period, expanding into northern Florida and Mississippi. After drive-throughs fell out of favor, Krystal began building free-standing units offering both sit-down and takeout service, but the company kept its menu much the same, with its small, square hamburger accounting for over 70 percent of the company's sales. In fact, the company played up its distinctive burger and regional heritage to differentiate itself from its rivals. For example, while McDonald's boasted of being the largest fast-food chain in America, Krystal trumpeted the fact that its steamed burgers were a favorite of Elvis Presley and Dolly Parton, and that in 1967, country musician Crystal Gale (formerly Brenda Gail Webb) was inspired by Krystal to choose her stage name. Krystal's positioning was deliberate. As a privately held, family business, the company could not compete directly with the likes of McDonald's and the Burger King Corporation, so instead of trying to keep pace, Krystal kept its small-town southern image—and its small burgers.

Again unlike many of the company's rivals, Krystal did not fuel its growth by selling franchises. This was largely because franchising limited the amount of revenue the company could obtain from each store. (In the franchising system, a franchisee pays the company a set fee for rights to the name, as well as an annual percentage of sales. However, the franchisee keeps the remaining revenue). Eventually, though, the company recognized the benefits that franchising could bring. In an innovative departure, however, Krystal chose to become a franchis*ee* rather than a franchis*or*. In 1969, it created a division called DavCo Foods to procure franchises from other food chains. Most significantly, in 1976, DavCo reached an agreement with Wendy's International, Inc., a fast-food rival of Krystal, to become the exclusive operator of Wendy's franchises in Baltimore and Washington, D.C. (As Krystal did not compete directly in these markets, this arrangement did not risk cannibalizing business from the company's flagship restaurants.)

By 1979, DavCo oversaw more than 30 Wendy's franchises and was awarded the Wendy's franchise business in northern Virginia as well. However, DavCo's per unit operating costs ran above industry standards, casting doubt on the venture's long-term viability. Undaunted, DavCo bought the Po Folks restaurant chain in 1982. DavCo, however, proved unable to digest this new acquisition. As a result, Krystal spun off Po Folks as a public corporation the following year. The newly independent Po Folks promptly gobbled up DavCo itself.

After shedding DavCo, Krystal focused heavily on strengthening the Krystal brand. Carl Long—who became Krystal's president in 1981—recognized that the company's unique products and image were its two greatest assets. To underscore these things, Krystal launched a massive advertising campaign in 1983, featuring a hyperactive cowboy named Sid and a honking stick horse named Sheila who proclaimed that "When you've got to have a Krystal, you've got to have a Krystal." The campaign was an unequivocal success. As *Nation's Restaurant News* noted on September 17, 1990, during the hey-day of the Sid and Sheila campaign, the "Krystal chain was traditionally known for two things: square burgers and the zany TV commercial tandem."

Although Krystal bolstered its brand image during the early and mid-1980s, the company did not add many new restaurants to its chain. Even more problematic was the slowing service at its existing restaurants. Since the company's most rapid expansion had occurred prior to 1980, many Krystal units were beginning to show their age. Worse, Krystal's in-store technology lagged behind rivals'. With older kitchen equipment, many Krystal restaurants were more labor-intensive—and therefore much slower—than their competitors. The company lost sales.

As its customer base shrank, R.B. Davenport III took action to right the listing company. In 1985, he led a leveraged buyout of Krystal, which enabled the company's management to "refocus its energies on operating the core Krystal concept," according to the January 17, 1994 edition of the *Wall Street Transcript.* Together with Long, Davenport then invested in capital improvements. In addition to making Krystal units brighter and cleaner, he purchased new restaurant technology that speeded the cooking and serving processes. After hiring and training more qualified store managers, he charged them with improving restaurant staffs. The company also introduced new products during this period, such as the Sunriser breakfast sandwich, which debuted in 1989 and boosted Krystal's flagging breakfast sales by about 25 percent in a few months. Due to these efforts, Krystal's sales rose at an annual rate of about six percent in the late 1980s. However, the company's considerable capital outlays meant that profits did not keep pace with surging sales.

Changes in the 1990s

Satisfied with the improved quality of existing Krystals, Davenport next turned his attention to expanding the chain. Because the company did not have the resources to fund a building spree, Davenport finally decided to use franchises as the means of expansion, selling the first ever in 1990. While still not completely enamored with the prospect, Davenport recognized that franchising would allow Krystal to add to its empire—and thus build the power of its brand—in a less expensive way (franchisees paid the initial building and equipment costs, which were the most costly aspect of adding stores). During this early phase of franchising, Krystal only allowed franchisees to build drive-through restaurants. These new "Krystal Kwik" restaurants had more limited menus but were easier to open (in 1992 and 1993, Krystal began to permit full-

Key Dates:

1932: R.B. Davenport, Jr., opens the first Krystal restaurant in Chattanooga, Tennessee.
1969: DavCo Foods is founded by the Krystal family and operates as a Krystal division.
1976: DavCo opens its first Wendy's franchise.
1982: Krystal acquires the Po Folks restaurant chain.
1983: Po Folks becomes a public company and subsequently acquires DavCo; Krystal launches its famous Cowboy Sid and Sheila the Wonder Horse advertising campaign.
1990: Krystal begins franchising.
1992: Company makes initial public stock offering to fuel expansion.
1995: Krystal files for Chapter 11 bankruptcy protection.
1997: Port Royal Holdings acquires Krystal.
1998: Port Royal institutes expansion plan.

service Krystal franchises). By March of 1992, Krystal had 19 franchised restaurants in operation.

According to the *Wall Street Transcript*, the average Krystal restaurant reported a per-store profit gain of about 20 percent during this period, but to boost sales and profits further, the company needed to add to its store network. In order to raise funds to launch new, company-owned stores, as well as to institute a more aggressive franchising system, Krystal opted to go public in May of 1992. The company earned $24 million in its initial public offering and devised an expansion strategy whereby Krystal would launch new, company-owned stores in important urban markets where Krystal already had a presence, leaving smaller markets and rural areas to its franchisees. The company's plan was stalled until June 1993, however, because industry-wide price wars eroded profits. Despite the difficult climate, Krystal earned $7.5 million of income on total sales of $236.7 million in 1993.

With 240 company-owned Krystals and 44 franchises by early 1994, Krystal sought to advance into new markets (over 80 percent of its restaurants were then clustered in Georgia, Tennessee, and Alabama). After venturing into North Carolina and Missouri for the first time in November 1993, Krystal opened restaurants in Columbia, South Carolina, Owensboro, Kentucky, and Little Rock, Arkansas. Moreover, Long announced that Krystal's ultimate goal was to double the number of its restaurants by 1998 and to have franchises account for 40 percent of the system. "Translating these products into newer markets is part of our challenge," a company executive told *Nation's Restaurant News* on November 15, 1993. At the same time, Krystal did not plan to reach outside the Southeast or to abandon its position as a southern alternative with a unique product. "[We] must remain vigilant about protecting the company's niche as it expands," Long stressed to the *Wall Street Transcript*.

Legal Troubles: 1994–97

Although Krystal's sales rose in 1994 to more than $248 million, its profits dropped to $6.9 million. Several factors accounted for this decline. Fierce price-cutting swept the hamburger fast-food industry that year, adversely affecting the company's bottom line. The capital expenditures Krystal's expansion entailed diminished the company's profitability, but the most significant factor was a major class-action lawsuit filed against the company by several employees in July 1994. The suit claimed that Krystal restaurant managers had altered time cards to delete overtime work hours and had required employees to stay on call without pay after scheduled shifts had ended. Krystal settled the suit for $800,000, which led the company to take a $2 million charge in the fourth quarter of 1994 for legal costs.

The company's legal troubles did not end with this settlement. Employees from four other states filed lawsuits in early 1995. In an effort to restructure its finances and to guard against possible negative court judgments, Krystal filed for Chapter 11 bankruptcy protection in December of 1995, but the company remained upbeat. "We think the future looks very good," a spokesperson told the *Tampa Tribune* on February 5, 1996. "This is not a typical bankruptcy. The company has the financial resources to conduct business as it normally does," he maintained.

Acquisition and New Growth: 1997 and Beyond

Krystal emerged from Chapter 11 in April 1997. In September, the company along with its Krystal Aviation Co. and Krystal Aviation Management Co. subsidiaries, was acquired for $135 million by Port Royal Holdings, an investment company owned by Philip Sanford, a former Coca-Cola executive. (Frustrated by the poor maintenance service it was receiving for its corporate jets, Krystal had purchased a fixed base operation—essentially the aircraft equivalent of a gas station and a repair garage—at Chattanooga's Lovell Field in 1978. The company soon discovered that not only did this arrangement save it money and aggravation on its own planes, but that it could be quite profitable in its own right. In 1992, Krystal Aviation even purchased Signal Aviation Service, another Lovell Field-based maintenance outfit. By the time Krystal emerged from bankruptcy proceedings, its aviation operations accounted for roughly three percent of the company's total revenues.) Sanford, who had grown up in the South eating Krystal burgers, also purchased 53 percent of the stock owned by the Davenport family, and took the company private. In his new role as Krystal chairman, Sanford instituted an 18-month plan to "reenergize" the brand's identity. Sanford was confident that he could leverage the Krystal brand and return the company to profitability. "Krystal is a true southern icon," he noted to the September 8, 1999, edition of the *Tampa Tribune*. "It is part of the fabric of the South. I don't know anyone who has a Burger King story. I don't know anyone who has a Hardees story. But every Southerner has a Krystal story."

Sanford's approach was multi-faceted. He planned to double the number of Krystals in five years and to use the sale of franchises as the primary growth vehicle. He would not move outside the Southeast but would instead bolster Krystal's presence in key markets. "Krystal is underpenetrated in every single market," he told *Nation's Restaurant News* on March 29, 1999. "I like the idea of growth in concentric circles." Sanford also instituted a new store design late in 1999 that incorporated a more traditional look, and he simplified the menu. Moreover, he added new technology, such as Chicksaw Technology's IntelliKitchen Management System, to improve operational efficiency. After signing an agreement with Jimmy Dean Foods (a division of the Sara Lee Corp.) to distribute frozen microwaveable Krystal burgers to southern grocery stores, Sanford oversaw the release of the Krystal Chik, a small fried chicken sandwich. However, the centerpiece of Sanford's strategy was to focus on Krystal's unique core product, the Krystal burger. The company launched a new advertising campaign that used the slogan, "Fresh. Hot. Small. Square." to underscore the qualities that differentiated Krystal's products from its competitors. "The Krystal brand is a sleeping giant," a company spokesperson told *Nation's Restaurant News.* As a result of these changes, Krystal expected to achieve significant success as it entered the 21st century.

Principal Subsidiaries

Krystal Aviation Co.; Krystal Aviation Management Co.

Principal Competitors

Burger King Corporation; Jack in the Box Inc.; McDonald's Corporation; Sonic Corp.; Wendy's International, Inc.

Further Reading

Carlino, Bob, "Burger Chains Find It's a Hit to Be Square," *Nation's Restaurant News,* September 17, 1990.

——, "Krystal Gets A-Head with Offbeat Ad Campaign," *Nation's Restaurant News,* May 20, 1991.

Curriden, Mark, "True South: Classic Krystal," *Atlanta Journal-Constitution,* March 15, 1992.

Hayes, Jack, "Krystal Puts Growth beyond Home Base," *Nation's Restaurant News,* November 15, 1993.

——, "Krystal Co.'s New Owners Ready Revival of Regional Burger 'Icon,'" *Nation's Restaurant News,* March 29, 1999.

"The Krystal Company," *Wall Street Transcript,* January 17, 1994.

Power, Paul, Jr., "Bitty Burgers Big Business," *Tampa Tribune,* February 5, 1996.

Reinan, John, "Tennessee-Based Hamburger Chain Plans to Expand in Tampa, Fla., Area," *Tampa Tribune,* September 8, 1999.

—Rebecca Stanfel

K-Swiss, Inc.

31248 Oak Crest Drive
Westlake Village, California 91361
U.S.A.
Telephone: (818) 706-5100
Fax: (818) 706-5390
Web site: http://www.kswiss.com

Public Company
Incorporated: 1966
Employees: 283
Sales: $285.5 million (1999)
Stock Exchanges: NASDAQ
Ticker Symbol: KSWS
NAIC: 316219 Other Footwear Manufacturing

Founded in 1966, K-Swiss, Inc. is one of the fastest-growing athletic shoe companies in the footwear industry. Unlike its competitors, which include the retail giants Nike and Reebok, much of K-Swiss's success is due not to keeping up with constantly changing styles and trends but instead to the company's reliance on a single distinctive design in a type of shoe the company calls "the Classic." K-Swiss appeals directly to upscale consumers, and for the first two decades of its existence did not even advertise, preferring instead to gain its reputation through word of mouth. In the past few years, K-Swiss had changed its focus from the exclusive production of tennis shoes to a broader range of performance shoes, including footwear for technical climbing and aerobics. K-Swiss has about 3,000 retail accounts nationwide, including Footlocker and Nordstrom, as well as a large consumer base in Japan and Europe.

K-Swiss's Beginnings: 1966–86

K-Swiss was founded by two Swiss brothers, Art and Earnest Brunner, who moved to California in 1966 and promptly started their business venture. The Brunners were both avid skiers and tennis players, and together the two decided to design a shoe that would respond to and support the specific needs of the tennis player. The Brunners focused particularly on cushioning for the soles of the feet, as well as the construction of a firm upper that wouldn't easily give way to the pressure of forceful lateral movement.

Calling their shoe "the Classic," the Brunners introduced their design at Wimbledon in 1966 to instant success. The shoe's design was intended for intense use, but its appearance was pointedly austere: three sturdy leather pieces constituted the shoe's upper, which was held in place by five narrow leather strips. The shoe's sole was a thin but strong strip of lightly treaded rubber, which allowed it to be light and relatively frictionless. Outside of a small Swiss flag on the heel of the shoe, K-Swiss's design was entirely white in color, and thus gave the shoe a timeless, preppy appearance.

Tennis players and upscale consumers took to the shoe immediately, and soon K-Swiss was enjoying a small but growing popularity in the United States. Because K-Swiss was located in California, the company's products were particularly visible along the West Coast, an area that attracted a great number of Japanese residents and tourists. In the 1970s, K-Swiss's shoes began to gain an almost cult-like status in Japan, and during the course of that decade the company opened up dozens of accounts in that country. As the company's U.S. market grew, it began to have its shoes produced in Southeast Asia, where labor costs were low, thus making K-Swiss products even more readily available to Asian markets.

Much of K-Swiss's success was paradoxically based on what the company did *not* do: it didn't advertise on radio, in magazines, or on television; it didn't put out new styles of shoes every season, and it made no attempt to create consumer interest through eye-catching logos or colorful designs. The shoes were worn by athletes, and gained their popularity primarily through a reputation for durability and reliability. K-Swiss's quiet but steady presence kept the company small, but also allowed it to maintain a stable niche in the growing athletic footwear industry. Such a strategy held the young company in good stead throughout the 1970s, when athleticwear was reserved exclusively for the courts and the track, but when trends began to change in the next decade, K-Swiss found itself faltering.

In the 1980s the athletic apparel industry exploded, with companies such as Nike, Reebok, and Adidas popularizing

Company Perspectives:

A wise man once said, 'build a better mouse trap and the world will beat a path to your door.' However, nowadays, it seems that building a mediocre mouse trap and spending over a hundred million bucks on advertising will do the trick. Well, call us crazy, but we'd rather build better shoes. That's why we don't pay high ticket athletes to wear K-Swiss. That's why we don't change our color schemes every six weeks. And that's why we don't have a planet named after us. We have more important things to worry about. Like making athletic shoes that help you win. Help you excel. Help you get to that would-be ace and pound it back across the court. There's only one reason to wear K-Swiss. They're the best. If you don't believe us, just ask someone who wears them, or a try a pair on for yourself.

everything from sweatshirts to basketball shoes. Athletic gear was no longer just for working out: it became a fashion statement. The simple sneaker was no more, as footwear became increasingly specialized, as styles for cross-training, running, walking, basketball, and aerobics took the place of what was once a relatively generic design. Simplicity gave way to flashy and colorful styles, with companies like L.A. Gear becoming more popular than the staid lines offered by K-Swiss. By the mid-1980s, K-Swiss was still enjoying some success, particularly in Japan, but its sales had slowed.

The Renewal of K-Swiss, Mid-1980s to the Mid-1990s

In the mid-1980s a retail executive named Steven Nichols took an interest in K-Swiss that was to change the shape of the company's future. Nichols was aware that K-Swiss's sales were stumbling and thought the company's founders might be amenable to being bought out. At the time, Nichols was president of Stride Rite Corporation, maker of the famous Sperry Top-Sider, and as president he encouraged his company to buy K-Swiss. When Stride Rite refused, Nichols resigned, convinced that with the proper backing he could acquire K-Swiss himself and take advantage of the rapidly expanding athleticwear market.

Nichols's dramatic exit from Stride Rite was proof that risk takers are needed in the business world: within eight months, the executive had raised more than $116 million, and in January 1987 he purchased the company and assumed the role of CEO. Nichols thought that much of the company's success lay in its snob appeal. It was a popular label with wealthier consumers—the average price of a pair of K-Swiss shoes was well above that of many of its competitors—and in a sense its almost anonymous styling was what made the shoe so desirable. Year after year "the Classic" endured, while trends came and went. However, Nichols also knew that in the increasingly competitive arena of athletic footwear, K-Swiss needed more visibility in order to survive. The trick, then, was to maintain the label's "country club" appeal while simultaneously broadening its targeted market.

After Nichols took over at K-Swiss, the company began to advertise for the first time. Eschewing television ads as too mainstream and expensive, K-Swiss began a print campaign in

athletic magazines, utilized billboard space, and bought radio air time in select cities. The ads quietly emphasized quality, simplicity, and durability, and did not follow the trend set by Nike in which high-profile athletes donned company sweatshirts and shoes emblazoned with slick logos.

Nichols's strategy worked, and between 1988 and 1989 the company increased its revenues by a phenomenal 72 percent, bringing in over $60 million in sales. In addition, K-Swiss discontinued all of its Japanese accounts with the exception of certain exclusive department stores, and within a year revenue was up in Japan and comprised 31 percent of its sales. By 1990 K-Swiss shoes were selling for the U.S. equivalent of $100 in Japan, a price that made the shoe desirable as a "luxury" item.

In 1990 K-Swiss went public at $17.50 a share, and within a year its share price rose to $21. Nichols had gambled and won: in 1986, K-Swiss had sales of about $21 million; only three years later the company had almost tripled that number. In November 1991, K-Swiss opened a 251,000 square foot distribution center in Fontana, California, which allowed the company to keep up with its rapidly increasing pace. In 1991 K-Swiss began to cultivate a customer base in Europe, forming a partnership with the 175-year-old company C & J Clarks to distribute K-Swiss shoes to selected department stores in Britain and continental Europe.

The early 1990s brought other successes as well. In February 1992 K-Swiss was granted the patent to two designs, the Cushion Board sole construction and the D-R Cinch lacing system. The former patent was a design in which a shoe's padding was moved from the heel of the shoe and redistributed throughout the shoe's sole, allowing for more support and shock absorption in high-impact exercise. The D-R Cinch lacing system was a multi-ring design in which the shoe's laces were wrapped all along the upper of the shoe, which gave the wearer more support during lateral movement. Such a lacing structure had been used by K-Swiss since the company's inception, and after 1992 no other company could copy it.

Around this time K-Swiss began to expand its inventory and make overt attempts to compete—or at least keep up—with competitors such as Nike and Reebok. In 1993 the company introduced three new designs made specifically for basketball and made a foray into the crowded aerobics gear market, offering two styles, "the Belais" and "the Belais-LT," which at about $70 a pair were priced to compete with other upscale shoes. The early 1990s also saw K-Swiss make a transition from being an exclusively "indoor" footwear company—producing shoes intended only for the courts or the track—to being a producer of footwear for the trail as well. In the fall of 1994 K-Swiss premiered twelve new designs, most of which were intended for light hiking or walking. The company's "Davos" collection, consisting of five different styles, was intended for hard-core technical climbing. K-Swiss started advertising in magazines such as *Outside* and *Backpacker,* expanding its reach to different types of athletes.

Changing Image for Changing Times: The late 1990s

In 1996 K-Swiss began advertising on television for the first time, expanding its target market beyond its traditional upscale

Key Dates:

1966: K-Swiss is founded.
1986: The company is purchased by Steven Nichols.
1990: K-Swiss goes public.
1996: Television advertising dramatically increases sales.
1998: K-Swiss launches a $17 million ad campaign to update its image.

customer to a younger, more active market. By the next year K-Swiss, while not anywhere near such companies as Nike, Reebok, or Adidas in sales, was carving out a higher profile, with sales at $116 million and stock trading at $28 a share.

By the late 1990s K-Swiss had more than 2,000 accounts and was sold in such stores as Footlocker, Just for Feet, Footaction, Finish Line, Champs, Nordstrom, and Dillards. While it kept its products highly visible to the consumer, the company was methodical about limiting its inventory. By introducing certain styles for a limited amount of time, or making only a certain number of a particular design available, K-Swiss ensured its reputation for making quality shoes which weren't "mass produced." So even when K-Swiss began to advertise and expand, it sought to preserve its exclusive image. In a 1999 interview with *Sporting Goods Business,* Nichols stated, "Many of our shoes we introduce for a very short period of time and then at some future date we reintroduce it and we reintroduce it on allocation to make sure that nobody buys too many. . . . When a retailer sells out virtually to the last pair, that's when we're the happiest."

Selling to the last pair, however, took more than reputation in the highly competitive athleticwear environment of the 1990s. In 1998 K-Swiss launched a $17 million ad campaign which the company called "Club K-Swiss." In this campaign, the company utilized professional athletes as spokespersons for the company and produced commercials in which hip-hop music and fast, flashy images of sports events were interspersed with pictures of K-Swiss products. The revamping of the company's image worked, as 1998 sales soared to $162 million. K-Swiss stock continued to climb, prompting the magazine *Footwear News* to maintain that K-Swiss "epitomized the little athletic footwear company that could." At millennium's end, K-Swiss's future looked bright from every angle.

Principal Competitors

Nike; Reebok; adidas-Salomon, Inc.

Further Reading

Dutter, Greg, "K-Swiss Banking on New Hoop Styles," *Sporting Goods Business,* January 1993, p. 20.

Friedman, Wayne, "Casual K-Swiss Refocuses on Performance Footwear," *Advertising Age,* June 14, 1999, p. 8.

Plotkin, Amanda, "Rising Earnings Bring K-Swiss to Top of Game," *Footwear News,* August 2, 1999, p. 2.

Russell, Dianne, "K-Swiss Makes Outdoor Marquee," *Sporting Goods Business,* September 1994, p. 26.

Schlax, Julie, "The Shoe as Hero," *Forbes,* August 20, 1990, p. 7.

Solnik, Claude, "While Other Industry Heroes Struggle, K-Swiss Plays Hard to Get," *Footwear News,* December 7, 1998, p. 8.

Taub, Daniel, "No Bells and Whistles, but Big Profits for K-Swiss," *Los Angeles Business Journal,* June 28, 1999, p. 9.

Tedeschi, Mark, "Steven Nichols: President & CEO, K-Swiss," *Sporting Goods Business,* September 17, 1999, p. 24.

—Rachel H. Martin

Kulicke and Soffa Industries, Inc.

2101 Blair Mill Road
Willow Grove, Pennsylvania 19090
U.S.A.
Telephone: (215) 784-6000
Fax: (215) 659-7588
Web site: http://www.kns.com

Public Company
Incorporated: 1956
Employees: 2,200
Sales: $399 million (1999)
Ticker Symbol: KLIC
Stock Exchanges: NASDAQ
NAIC: 333295 Semiconductor Machinery Manufacturing

Kulicke & Soffa Industries, Inc. (K&S) is the world's largest manufacturer and supplier of semiconductor assembly equipment. The company offers comprehensive assembly solutions to its many customers worldwide, including chip and wire solutions of wire bonding, die bonding, wafer dicing equipment, and also factory automation. Flip chip solutions include flip chip bumping technology, die placement equipment, glob top and underfill materials, and thin film organic laminates. K&S has an extensive network of worldwide facilities which offer a wide range of sales, service and applications development. Although the company is headquartered in the sleepy town of Willow Grove, Pennsylvania, it has facilities in such highly diverse and far away locations as Israel, Hong Kong, and Switzerland. In fact, approximately 80 percent of the company's total sales volume is generated overseas.

Company Origins in 1951

Like many other firms, the history of Kulicke & Soffa Industries begins with the biography of its founders, Fred Kulicke and Albert Soffa. Kulicke and Soffa were both educated as engineers and started working as employees for Proctor Electric upon their graduation from college. Based in Philadelphia, Pennsylvania, Proctor Electric was a well-known company specializing in consumer electronics products. Ever since

the end of World War II, with the growing prosperity of the American economy, the general public had been clamoring for more sophisticated consumer electronics products in order to make their lives more convenient. In order to meet this burgeoning demand, engineers like Kulicke and Soffa were hired to design consumer products. Shortly after the two men became employees of Proctor Electric, they found themselves designing such products as cake mixers and electric irons. In fact, it was a project to design electric irons that brought Kulicke and Soffa together for the first time.

Kulicke and Soffa were extremely ambitious and entrepreneurial young men, not satisfied with designing electric irons for a large company not their own. As the two men became more acquainted with one another, and started discussing their dreams and ambitions for the future, not surprisingly they discovered they had much in common. A close friendship developed as the two men worked on various projects at Proctor Electric and, after a short time, Kulicke and Soffa decided to strike out on their own and establish a custom engineering business. In the steamy month of July 1951, Fred Kulicke and Albert Soffa put their ambitions on paper and formed a partnership that was destined to last until one of them died. Thus Kulicke and Soffa Industries was born.

There was only one problem, and not a small one at that. The two men didn't have much money to start their business with. So they did what they could to raise the necessary funding, including raising loans from friends and acquaintances and pooling their own meager resources to begin operations. They established themselves in a small one-room office and began designing solutions to manufacturing problems by automating processes, while at the same time repairing broken machinery in order to pay the monthly rent and phone bills.

With their combined energy and technical ingenuity, Kulicke and Soffa aggressively contracted numerous small businesses and manufacturing firms throughout the greater metropolitan area of Philadelphia. When a packing firm approached them to stuff their sausages, the two entrepreneurs devised a machine to standardize and stuff sausage into casings in mass quantities. When a retail manufacturer asked them to design a machine to stretch kidskin for ladies' gloves, Kulicke and Soffa were only too happy to

Company Perspectives:

The K&S mission is to maintain global leadership in semiconductor assembly by providing customers with high-quality, reliable and cost-effective systems and services. K&S specializes in applying advanced process technology to individual assembly problems and delivering solutions that add real value by helping customers meet their business objectives. K&S gives customers the highest quality hardware and software and the highest level of responsiveness in the way it engineers, manufactures, delivers and supports its equipment. Key K&S strengths are technological expertise, the ability to manufacture high-quality, reliable assembly systems, marketplace presence and long-standing relationships with many of our customers. These close working relationships, some of which involve sharing technology ''roadmaps'' and long-range strategic plans, provide important information for our development programs, help us enhance machine performance and help us develop process and equipment solutions for customers' future assembly problems.

oblige with an innovative machine resulting in a significant increase in productivity and thus higher sales. Additional designs during their first years of business including innovative machines for cleaning beer cases as well as machines made to standardize the size of hamburger patties. In just of few short years, K&S became known as one of the most innovative and reliable custom engineering firms on the East Coast.

By 1956, K&S had been in business for five years. What transpired that year was to change the direction of the company's endeavors forever. The Nobel Prize in Physics was given to three engineers working at Bell Labs for the development of a semiconductor chip. Before the Nobel winners even returned home from the award ceremony in Stockholm, Sweden, the manufacturing division of Bell Labs, Western Electric, had decided to contract Kulicke and Soffa Industries to develop the equipment necessary to efficiently manufacture these early versions of semiconductor chips. The two partners, thrilled with the contract, agreed to it almost without hesitation. Then reality started to sink in, and Kulicke and Soffa realized what they had agreed to, namely, accepting the challenge of connecting microscopic wires from the transistor die in the semiconductor chip to the leads on its package. Within a few months, to the surprise of the electronics industry, Kulicke and Soffa had met the challenge, designing and beginning to manufacture the world's first wire bonder. Thus the company became one of the world's first designers and manufacturers of semiconductor assembly equipment.

From the moment the company introduced its wire bonder, it took a leading role in the semiconductor assembly equipment industry. In 1961, the owners decided that it was time to take the company public, so K&S made an initial stock offering of 100,000 shares on the NASDAQ market. The company's shares were bought immediately and subsequent additional offerings were held throughout the decade. Fortunately, the partners had been at the right place at the right time and, as the semiconductor industry expanded by leaps and bounds throughout the 1960s,

demand from around the world for K&S equipment skyrocketed. In addition to its legendary series of wire bonders, the company began to diversify its product line to include such items as manual and semi-automatic equipment for wafer preparation, wafer fabrication, die bonding, and micro-tools.

Growth and Expansion: 1960s–80s

One of the most important strategic decisions that the two men made early on in the organization and administration of their firm was to forge a commitment to research and development. Both owners were willing to invest more capital in research and development than was available from annual net profits. Nothing could have been smarter, since from the early 1960s, K&S became synonymous with technological leadership in the semiconductor industry. By now, company operations had significantly outgrown the first machine shop where the two entrepreneurs spent many hours building their business, so K&S moved to larger facilities in Willow Grove, Pennsylvania, while opening sales and services offices at the same time throughout the United States. Expansion was not limited to the United States. Due to the increasing demand for its products from around the world, the company established facilities in such strategic locations as Hong Kong, Switzerland, and Israel.

The mid-1970s brought with it a severe economic recession, and the semiconductor industry was hard hit. K&S suffered as a result, and the company was forced to either sell off or shutter all of its product line, except those focusing on semiconductor assembly operations. Still maintaining the priority of research and development in that core area, however, the company's engineers were able to introduce the first digitally-controlled, fully automatic wire bonders in the industry. This product, designed to operate at extremely high speeds with more accuracy and greater yield than any previous wire bonders, provided the firm's clients with the advantage of meeting the growing demand for PCS. Due to the introduction of this innovative product in 1976, Kulicke and Soffa Industries was able to recover from the losses suffered earlier and re-establish itself as the pre-eminent leader in the semiconductor assembly equipment industry.

The 1980s started well enough for K&S, and the company celebrated its 30th anniversary with much fanfare and celebration. During the early 1980s, management at the firm changed hands, but stayed in firm control of the Kulicke family. Even with this transition of leadership from one generation to the next, the company's long-term strategic goals remained the same, namely, a clear priority to research and development and a firm commitment to expanding its overseas markets. To this end in 1981, management decided to develop a major presence in the Japanese semiconductor market, which was growing by leaps and bounds at the time. Kulicke and Soffa (Japan) Ltd. opened for business in Tokyo and was soon competing with other major semiconductor assembly firms on their own turf. By 1984, company sales had reached their highest level ever.

The mid-1980s were not as kind to the fortunes of the company. The ever-volatile semiconductor industry took another severe downturn, and the new leadership was confronted with its first major financial crisis. Astute and prudent decision-making by management, however, enabled K&S to weather the gyrations of the market and continue its leadership in the industry by introducing a host of new and cutting-edge products for die bonding, wire bonding, and dicing. Such focus paid off handsomely as time went on. By the end of the 1980s, K&S had recovered financially and had introduced numerous innovative products that assured its technological leadership for years to come in the semiconductor assembly industry.

The 1990s and Beyond

During the 1990s, the semiconductor industry grew in importance, with an accompanying worldwide dependence on K&S products. K&S profited immensely from the volume, complexity, and variety of semiconductor assembly equipment required by its ever-growing list of clients. With this explosion in the industry, the company expanded dramatically: technology centers were established in Willow Grove, Pennsylvania, Japan, Israel, and Singapore; customer resources centers were opened in Taiwan and The Philippines; Micro-Swiss facilities were constructed in Hong Kong, Singapore, and Israel; fine wire operations were built in Alabama, Singapore, and Switzerland; a new Semitic manufacturing plant was opened in California, while a state-of-the-art Flip Chip Technologies wafer bumping manufacturing center was established in Arizona; an X-LAM Technologies research and development laboratory was dedicated in California, and an Advanced Polymer Solutions manu-

facturing facility was built at the company's headquarters in Willow Grove, Pennsylvania. The company also completed a massive 214,000 square-foot administrative, design and manufacturing facility to serve as a new headquarters to direct worldwide operations.

By 1999, K&S employed more than 2,200 people and controlled more than 50 percent of the global wire bonding equipment market. The largest supplier of semiconductor assembly equipment in the world, K&S was well-positioned to continue its dominance of the market. More than twice the size of its nearest competitor, the company was searching for ways to expand its presence in Asia and Europe, while maintaining its position of strength in the United States. As long as management continued to focus on research and development and introduced innovative products, there was no end in sight for the company's continued growth and expansion.

Principal Subsidiaries

American Fine Wire, Inc.; Flip Chip Technologies, LLC; Semitic, Inc.

Principal Competitors

ESEC Holding, Inc.; Kaijo, Ltd.; Shinkawa Ltd.

Further Reading

Dorsch, Jeff, "Kulicke and Soffa Acquires Assembly Technologies," *Electronic News*, p. 2.
"Kulicke and Soffa Industries, Inc.," *Wall Street Journal*, August 22, 1996, p. B6(E).
"Kulicke and Soffa Revenues Dip In Quarter," *Electronic News*, April 27, 1998, p. 46.
Levine, Bernard, "Flip Chip Moves Accelerate," *Electronic News*, July 8, 1996, p. 8.
Levine, Bernard, "Kulicke and Soffa Wins Orders," *Electronic News*, August 16, 1999, p. 30.
Socolovsky, Alberto, "K&S Struggles To Make Money," *Electronic Business*, November 1992, p. 73.
"Tool Manufacturer Gets Key Benefits From Israeli Plant," *Industrial Engineering*, July 1992, p. 22.

—Thomas Derdak

La Madeleine French Bakery & Café

6060 North Central Expressway
Suite 100
Dallas, Texas 75206
U.S.A.
Telephone: (214) 696-6962
Toll Free: (800) 975-2623
Fax: (214) 696-0485
Web site: http://www.lamadeleine.com

Private Company
Incorporated: 1982
Employees: 2,500
Sales: $117 million (1999)
NAIC: 722211 Limited-Service Restaurants; 311812
  Commercial Bakeries; 72232 Caterers

La Madeleine French Bakery & Café, headquartered in Dallas, where it was founded by Patrick Esquerre in 1982, operates more than 60 neighborhood bakeries in nine carefully selected markets, including Dallas/Fort Worth (18), Houston (13), Austin (three), San Antonio (four), Baton Rouge (two), New Orleans (six), Atlanta (six), Phoenix (three), and Washington, D.C. (eight). Like an actual village café, each bakery features a cuisine and setting that is distinctly and authentically French, albeit with some concessions made to American tastes, including cafeteria-style dining and a growing takeout service for those who wish to dine at home. Menu offerings are diverse and include such dishes as creme brulee, quiche, Caesar salad, tomato-basil and French onion soups, grilled rosemary chicken, and various puff pastries and croissants—common enough fare in France, perhaps, but hardly ordinary chain restaurant offerings in the United States. La Madeleine bakeries prepare their foods daily, using fresh, natural ingredients containing no preservatives. They make their breads and pastries using traditional wood-burning ovens and serve them in a setting that features French antiques, warm woods, and hand-painted tiles, providing the atmosphere of a genuine French café. The bakeries also offer some charming and unusual features, including French lessons for their customers and a variety of gift items. In addition, la Madeleine markets some of its breads and dishes at select supermarkets in five cities, and in three of these—Dallas, Houston, and New Orleans—also provides catering services.

Origins and Early Expansion: 1982–92

Patrick Esquerre, a native of France, founded la Madeleine in 1982, opening the company's first bakery in the next year. He had grown up in a Loire Valley chateau on a farm. He later described his childhood in a cookbook, *From a French Country Kitchen,* that he wrote with his mother, Monique Esquerre, from whom he learned the cooking and baking skills he would eventually tap in creating his successful chain. In his early adult years, he developed other useful skills, working for Young & Rubicam, a Paris marketing and public relations firm, and eventually establishing his own company, Dialoguer. Although fascinated with his country's foods and traditions, he was too much involved in both the religious and political affairs of his country to develop what he had learned about his native cuisine from his mother into a business. When he emigrated to the United States to set down new business roots, however, he left many of his public concerns behind.

Initially, Esquerre's plan was to help book foreign rodeos in the United States, but when that did not work out he decided to try turning his entrepreneurial and culinary skills into another sort of business—an authentic French bakery. Encouraged by Dallas retail wizard Stanley Marcus, Esquerre built his first outlet on Mockingbird Lane in the Highland Park area of Dallas, near Southern Methodist University. Because it was Esquerre's idea to add new bakeries one at a time, Marcus encouraged him to select Dallas over Houston for his initial site and to select college students as his initial target base.

Esquerre built the first unit without using an architect, in a somewhat haphazard fashion that involved many changes, some of which came from suggestions made by casual observers who were merely passing by the site. Named for a Paris church, la Madeleine, Esquerre's eatery was almost exclusively a bakery at first, featuring various French breads and pastries, but its menu gradually evolved in a fashion similar to the building

---

Company Perspectives:

"La Douzaine" (the Baker's Dozen) is a guiding set of principles practiced by la Madeleine officers, directors, managers and associates in their daily interaction with each other and their guests: Joie—We create a feeling of joie de servir in all of our relationships; Food—We have an uncompromising commitment to the quality and uniqueness of our food; Surprise—We have a carte blanche to delight and surprise our guests; Community—We try to be a good neighbor; Listen—We create an open environment where we genuinely listen to and respect one another; Balance—We care for our associates and respect the balance between home and la Madeleine; Profitability—We make a profit for the benefit of all; Recognition—We seek ways to celebrate our successes "big & small"; Individuality—We value the individuality and unique contributions of each associate; Integrity—We act honestly, fairly & ethically; Improvement—We challenge ourselves to be better today than yesterday; Development—We support and develop our associates so that we may all succeed; Roots—We embrace the preserve the heart and spirit that is la Madeleine.

---

itself, especially after la Madeleine became a neighborhood gathering spot. At first, salads and sandwiches were offered, but Esquerre kept adding other authentic French foods to the growing menu, entrees that quickly attracted a widening circle of customers. He even took suggestions from some of them for a few of the menu additions, then saw to it that such newly adopted dishes had a genuine French taste. To make sure everything was authentic, Esquerre hired his bakers in France, bringing them to America and serving as their paternal guide, always referring to them as "associates" and treating them more like family members than employees. Esquerre also had a strong sense of a business's responsibility to its host community, and he is credited with having developed la Madeleine's *"menage a trois"* marketing concept, donating $1 in food to local food banks for each $2 pledged by viewers or listeners to public television or radio.

La Madeleine expanded quickly, tapping into urban markets that Esquerre and his managerial team believed would be ideal for the kind of cuisine it offered. In 1984, while also expanding in Dallas, it opened its first bakery in New Orleans, in the celebrated French Quarter. In the next year, the company also began preparing foods for wholesale distribution to restaurants, hotels, and grocery chains within some of its market areas, ultimately to include Dallas, Fort Worth, Houston, San Antonio, New Orleans, and Baton Rouge.

A key to its early and ongoing success was not just the authenticity of la Madeleine's foods but their increasing variety. For many holidays, Esquerre's associates prepared special dishes, such as *Bûche de Noël* (a traditional French dessert prepared at Christmas), Mardi Gras king cakes, and a two-portion version of *Sacher Torte* (an Austrian classic dessert) prepared for St. Valentine's day. These were part of the "surprise" the company has always stressed as a necessary strategy for renewal in what is an extremely tough market.

Growth Brings Changes in Management: 1992–97

By 1993, when Esquerre was named a finalist for the Ernst & Young's Entrepreneur of the Year award, the la Madeleine chain, a term Esquerre himself deplored, consisted of 16 bakery-cafés. All of them were in Texas except for those in New Orleans, but new outlets were planned for Washington, D.C. and Atlanta. Revenue from sales that year approached $36 million.

The Washington, D.C. market was added in 1994, as was a new Texas market in Austin. Openings followed the next year in Baton Rouge, Atlanta, and Phoenix, which, with other openings in established markets almost doubled the number of bakery-cafés in the chain. The rapid growth and success argued that a more scientific method of market analysis and operational planning would have to replace Esquerre's primarily intuitive entrepreneurial style of management, his paternal and familial approach, which clearly had diminishing relevance and suitability in the face of the wider distribution of la Madeleine's markets.

A smooth and amicable transition in operational control followed. It was one that began in 1992, when William Allen, formerly with Marriott, joined the management team and thereafter served as president and CEO until, in 1997, he was replaced by John Corcoran. Another key member was A. Guy Mercurio, vice-president of real estate development, appointed in 1996. In 1997, with 45 la Madeleine units open, Patrick Esquerre stepped down and severed his formal relationship with la Madeleine, selling his interest in the business to his partners and la Madeleine's chief executives.

The change of guard did not interfere with la Madeleine's basic commitment to providing both an authentic and varied cuisine. By the mid-1990s, menus were featuring new items on the average of two per year, providing customers with the chance to enjoy dishes from various French regions, such as Alsace, Provençe, and Burgundy. As with la Madeleine's recipes for its signature items, always offered, recipes for the new additions were developed by la Madeleine's French chefs through extensive research that required repeated trips to their homeland. The resulting dishes were then "field tested" by a tasting panel and on location with focus groups that included regular la Madeleine patrons. Once a recipe was accepted and was added to the master recipe book, the company used a "train the trainer" approach for teaching it to regional managers, who in turn trained bakers and chefs at each outlet.

New Directions and Management Transitions: 1998–2000

In 1997 la Madeleine began planning a new, smaller kind of unit to add to its chain. The first of these was scheduled for opening in an upscale section of Dallas in October, but unforeseen delays pushed the opening back to April 3 of the next year. At 2,400 square feet, the new outlet was just more than half the size of the regular 4,500-square-foot units. Dubbed "La Madeleine Cuisine," it featured a menu consisting of about 80 percent of the dishes at the larger la Madeleine restaurants, and included such standard signature dishes as rosemary chicken and tomato-basil soup plus a few new dishes. Although the new Cuisine could seat 50 customers, it was based on a "home-meal replacement concept" and was created to increase the com-

<table>
<tr><td colspan="2">**Key Dates:**</td></tr>
<tr><td>1983:</td><td>Patrick Esquerre opens the initial la Madeleine bakery in Dallas.</td></tr>
<tr><td>1984:</td><td>The first la Madeleine bakery outside Texas is opened in the French Quarter of New Orleans.</td></tr>
<tr><td>1985:</td><td>Company begins wholesaling goods to restaurants, hotels, and grocery stores; it also opens its first bakeries in Houston and Fort Worth.</td></tr>
<tr><td>1994:</td><td>The company taps into new markets with openings in Washington, D.C. and Austin, Texas.</td></tr>
<tr><td>1995:</td><td>La Madeleine adds three more market sites in Atlanta, Phoenix, and Baton Rouge.</td></tr>
<tr><td>1997:</td><td>Patrick Esquerre sells his interest in la Madeleine to his partners, and John Corcoran is appointed CEO; the company also begins catering services in Houston.</td></tr>
<tr><td>1998:</td><td>The company opens its first la Madeleine Cuisine, a home-meal replacement outlet.</td></tr>
</table>

pany's takeout customer base while not sacrificing la Madeleine's special ambiance. According to John Corcoran, la Madeleine's president, the new Cuisine's slogan was "Take home a little French dish." Plans called for new Cuisines to open at a rate of from two to five per year, starting with the next unit built in Houston.

As the century drew toward its turn, Corcoran continued building a management team to help with the streamlining of la Madeleine. Brought on board were Ole Jensen (vice-president of manufacturing and distribution) and Harry Martin (vice-president and general counsel), who joined in 1998; and Mark Menking (executive vice-president), Scott Gordon (vice-president of operations), and Mark Hudzel (vice-president of training), all of whom assumed their posts in 1999. The challenge was to preserve the charm and authenticity of la Madeleine bakery-cafés while steering the company along more profitable lines of development and continued expansion, to keep, in brief, the friendly environment and some of the personal feel that were Esquerre's trademarks while using more objective and impersonal methods of management and planning.

Many of la Madeleine's bakery-cafes still had bakers and chefs who had been brought from France by Esquerre, and, as previously noted, they would often return home to research and perfect authentic French dishes. For Americans hired as general managers, the company, as it had done from the outset, still provided a short training session in France, so that, despite some changes in its marketing dynamics, its restaurants could maintain their special French ambiance and authentic European cuisine.

La Madeleine's management has insisted that it is wholly committed to the company's founding principles and to retaining the unique, unpretentious atmosphere of each of its bakery-cafés as well as its community support of local charities, something that Esquerre had initiated early on in the company's development. Corcoran attributes the success of la Madeleine, twice named one of the top ten bakeries in the United States by *Bon Appétit* magazine, to his team's ability to balance the demands of growth and profitability with those founding principles, including its obligations to the host communities of its bakeries.

There has certainly been growth. In 1999 the company broke all its previous records. Its sales were especially strong over the year-end holiday season, between Thanksgiving and New Year's Day, when they totaled $12.1 million, up nine percent from the previous year. By then there were 62 units in operation, employing more than 2,500 "associates," as Patrick Esquerre always insisted on calling his staff members. Plans called for opening an additional two units by February of 2000, but none were projected beyond that point. According to Corcoran, to ensure successful future growth, for the time being the company was going to focus on operations in existing markets, concentrating on wholesale breads and salad dressings and on its catering services. Still, it remains to be seen whether the growth can continue indefinitely without drastically altering la Madeleine's unique image.

Principal Divisions

Bakery and Cafes; Wholesale; Catering; Retail and Catalog; Real Estate and Development.

Principal Competitors

Brinker International, Inc.; Darden Restaurants, Inc.; Starbucks Corporation.

Further Reading

Frye, Cathy, "French Baker's Merci Strategy Helps Profits Rise," *Dallas Business Journal,* June 25, 1993, p. S19.

Higham, Kathryn, "La Madeleine Chain Has the Flavor of France," *Baltimore Sun,* April 4, 1999, p. 15.

"La Madeleine Bakery Plans New Concept," *Nation's Restaurant News,* August 18, 1997, p. 136.

Malouf, Mary Brown, "Listen. Adapt. Surprise," *D-Dallas/Fort Worth,* November 1, 1998, p. 25.

Ruggless, Ron, "New, Smaller La Madeleine Offers Bigger-Sized Options," *Nation's Restaurant News,* April 13, 1998, p. 8.

——, "Patrick Esquerre," *Nation's Restaurant News,* January 1, 1997, p. 56+.

Stones, Lori, and Kelly O. Lynn, "Entrepreneurism + Customer Service = Success," *Management Review,* November, 1993, p. 38+.

—John W. Fiero

Latham & Watkins

633 West Fifth Street, Suite 4000
Los Angeles, California 90071-2007
U.S.A.
Telephone: (213) 485-1234
Fax: (213) 891-8763
Web site: http://www.lw.com

Partnership
Employees: 1,300
Sales: $502 million (1998)
NAIC: 54111 Offices of Lawyers

Latham & Watkins is one of the world's largest law firms, with about 1,000 attorneys practicing in 14 American and international offices. It represents business clients in many industries, including healthcare, software, and technology. From its historic foundation of tax and labor law, Latham & Watkins has diversified to provide counsel on virtually all aspects of modern business practice, including financing, bankruptcy, regulatory compliance, litigation, and intellectual property issues. Because of the firm's emphasis on teamwork and cooperation, it has often been cited as one of the nation's best-managed law firms.

The Depression and World War II

Dana Latham and Paul R. Watkins were both born in Illinois in the late 1890s. Latham graduated from Harvard Law School in 1922, and Watkins studied law at Illinois Wesleyan University. In January 1934 the partners founded a law firm in Los Angeles. Latham's expertise was in state and federal tax law, while Watkins, formerly the general counsel for Pacific Finance Corporation, built a strong practice in labor law.

In spite of the Great Depression, the new law firm prospered. Its first significant client was Consolidated Rock Products Company (which was still a client fifty years later). Within a year the partnership had gained clients including Pacific Finance Corporation; the Crushed Stone, Sand & Gravel Association (the predecessor of the Southern California Rock Products Association); West Shore Company; the Rule Company; Western Geophysical Company; and the London retailer Fortnum & Mason.

Soon after the United Geophysical Company was founded in 1937, it began using the services of Latham & Watkins. As United Geophysical was exploring for oil overseas, especially in Central and South America, the law firm gained its first experience in international law. When Consolidated Engineering Corporation was spun off from United Geophysical and became a public corporation, Latham & Watkins began its initial venture into securities law. Herbert Hoover, Jr., the son of President Herbert Hoover, played an important role in helping Latham & Watkins gain several early clients, including United Geophysical.

The partnership developed an emphasis on labor law after the passage of the National Labor Relations Act in 1935, which guaranteed collective bargaining. The firm represented employers in many union disputes, and major unions opposed the firm. By the time World War II began in 1939, Latham & Watkins had four attorneys. During the war, the company continued to prosper, in part because many new laws and regulations were enacted as part of the war effort.

In the early years of World War II, Latham began representing Major Corliss Champion Moseley, who ran aviation companies based in Southern California. During the war Moseley trained some 26,000 pilots and 13,000 mechanics at the Glendale, California, airport under a federal contract and was a key player in building up civilian and military aviation capabilities during the war and into the early 1950s.

Post-World War II Practice

In the early postwar period the firm grew as it recruited young attorneys and some of its veterans returned, and in 1949 Latham & Watkins established its first written partnership agreement. By 1954 the firm employed 14 attorneys and had begun to develop a litigation practice. In 1967 Latham & Watkins remained modest in size with just 30 attorneys, but rapid growth in the years ahead made it one of the nation's largest firms, surpassing many law firms that were much older.

Clinton R. Stevenson was chosen managing partner in 1967. Three years later Latham & Watkins installed a new computer system, "the first installation of its size and nature in a law firm west of the Mississippi," according to its corporate history,

252

Bold Beginnings. In 1972 two partners opened an office in Santa Ana, Orange County, in a building owned by one of the firm's clients, C.J. Segerstrom & Sons. By 1983 the Orange County office had moved to Newport Beach and employed 21 attorneys.

In 1978 the firm recruited its first experienced attorneys in order to open a branch office in Washington, D.C. Carla Hills, secretary of the Department of Housing and Urban Development (HUD) under President Gerald Ford, was hired to head the new office. This office developed new clients, such as Synfuels and Continental Wingate, and the location allowed the firm to better serve other clients, including Sears, Roebuck; The Signal Companies; Hughes Aircraft; and Mars, Inc.

Latham & Watkins established a San Diego office in 1980. In its early years this office handled real estate development for Torrey Enterprises and Mobil Land Development Company, conducted litigation in the AFTRA antitrust case, and represented National Semiconductor, Intermark, Oak Industries, Nucorp Energy, and other clients. In early 1982 extended negotiations resulted in a merger between Latham & Watkins and the Chicago firm Hedlund, Hunter, & Lynch, which employed 20 lawyers and specialized in litigation. This was the firm's first merger, a difficult but productive turning point in its history. By 1983 the firm had grown to 237 attorneys and added new specialties such as bankruptcy, commercial, and international law.

The growth of Latham & Watkins in the late 1970s and 1980s was part of a national trend as many law firms expanded rapidly, often by hiring experienced attorneys from rival law firms. In the late 1970s the nature of the law profession changed to become more competitive, especially after the U.S. Supreme Court ruled that professional restrictions against advertising were unconstitutional, and the *American Lawyer* and the *National Law Journal* were founded to provide information on law firm management and finances.

In 1985 David H. Maister, president of the Boston consulting firm Maister Associates, described Latham & Watkins as a prime example of a well-managed "one-firm firm" that emphasized institutional loyalty. "In contrast to many of their (often successful) competitors who emphasize individual entrepreneurialism, autonomous profit centers, internal competition and/or highly decentralized, independent activities, one-firm firms place great emphasis on firmwide coordination of decision making, group identity, cooperative teamwork, and institutional commitment." To promote that kind of corporate culture, Latham & Watkins discouraged individual stardom by having few status symbols for prominent partners, relied on training its own lawyers while recruiting few experienced lawyers from the outside, and seldom acquired other law firms. It also used its institutional history as a way of promoting long-term thinking and loyalty to the firm. Although many Latham & Watkins attorneys were specialists, Maister wrote, "What strikes any visitor to a one-firm firm is the deeply held mutual respect across departmental, geographic, and functional boundaries." While the law firm had a strong leader in Clinton Stevenson, it emphasized open communication and the participation of other partners and even junior associates in recruiting, selecting new partners, and compensation issues.

From 1978 to 1981 the firm devoted many of its resources to representing Gulf Oil Corporation in the so-called uranium cases, wherein Westinghouse Electric Company sued Gulf for alleged price fixing of uranium. Westinghouse had sold nuclear power plants to several electrical utilities and agreed to provide them with uranium fuel. This was a particularly important case, since in the mid-1960s the United States had placed an embargo on imported uranium as a way to aid domestic suppliers. In 1981 Gulf and Westinghouse settled a major part of their dispute out of court.

Practice in the 1990s

In 1990 the law firm founded a San Francisco branch in temporary offices at 580 California Street, and later that year signed a lease for up to 60,000 square feet at 505 Montgomery Street. The office's managing partner, Robert Dell, stated in the *San Francisco Business Times:* "We want to make it a full-service firm, so we'll start with a core group of finance and corporate attorneys and a litigation group with emphasis on securities litigation." Responding to an economic downturn, in 1991 Latham & Watkins assigned 20 attorneys to its Insolvency Project, which advised clients on how to handle bankruptcy and restructuring. In some cases, the law firm advised companies that it had helped expand through leveraged buy-outs and high-yield bonds. Other firms such as San Francisco's Brobeck, Phleger & Harrison also shifted some of their resources to meet the new demands.

In 1991 Latham & Watkins also released 43 junior associates, a drastic move in light of its commitment to retain attorneys from the time they were hired to the time they retired. This decision came as the firm's profits plummeted in the early 1990s, partly as a result of the bankruptcy of Drexel Burnham Lambert, the law firm's major investment banking client in the booming 1980s.

In 1993 the firm made a major change that rewarded individual efforts of those "rainmakers" who brought in more business, thus ending the seniority system that was part of the firm's team approach. Nevertheless, in a 1997 article in the *American Lawyer,* firm partners insisted that the Latham & Watkins emphasis on collegiality remained intact, although some outside observers had their doubts.

In any case, Latham & Watkins rebounded as the economy improved and its rainmakers brought in more business. In 1997 at least 100 partners brought in a minimum of $1 million each in billings. Profitable clients also improved the bottom line. For example, Latham & Watkins defended Navistar International Transportation Corporation, the owner of Denny's restaurants, when it was charged with racial discrimination lawsuits settled in 1996. It also represented Minnesota Mining and Manufacturing Company (3M) when it was sued for injuries caused by its breast implants.

Latham & Watkins and other firms like Netscape, Pacific Bell, Sun Microsystems, and Goldman Sachs backed the work of the Electronic Frontier Foundation to protect individual liberties in cyberspace while also promoting responsible use and regulation of such resources. "We need an appropriate balance," said EFF's Executive Director Lori Fena in an interview in the March/April 1998 *Online* to maximize First Amendment rights while also protecting minors from pornography. The foundation dealt with such issues as government regulation of electronic commerce, restrictions on encryption, and the growing volume of unwanted e-mail.

In late 1997 Latham & Watkins helped America Online in its opposition to junk e-mail, also known as spam. AOL gained a court injunction that barred Over the Air Equipment Inc., an advertiser of pornographic Web sites, from sending its unrequested messages to AOL subscribers. "The notion is to pursue them vigorously until the overall effect of deterring spam has been achieved. If you can do it with five suits, that's a good number. If it takes more than that, we'll file more," said Latham & Watkins partner Everett Johnson in the *Washington Post*.

In the late 1990s Latham & Watkins continued to be a leader for corporate financial transactions. In 1998 it participated in mergers and acquisitions worth almost $60 billion, over $36 billion in private and public financings, and over $30 billion in a private 144A placement. Its corporate clients included Amgen; Bear, Stearns & Company; Cedars-Sinai Medical Center; DreamWorks SKG; Harrah's Entertainment; Hilton Hotels; Hughes Communications; Kohlberg Kravis Roberts & Company; Nestle U.S.A.; Nintendo of America; Smith Barney; and Safeway.

To keep its clients informed using the Internet, Latham & Watkins created the International Environmental NetworkSM (IEN) as a full-text database with the latest government laws and regulations. The firm also established the Regulatory Flexibility Group, an extranet-based "advocacy consortium of Southern California companies working with regulators to find new ways to reduce emissions from manufacturing plants," according to the firm's Web site.

In July 1999 the *American Lawyer* ranked Latham & Watkins as the nation's fourth-largest law firm, with gross revenues of $502 million. The firm also ranked seventeenth in revenues per lawyer ($605,000) and fourteenth in average compensation for all partners ($870,000). Despite the firm's prosperity, it also confronted challenges from other large firms, some with as many as 2,000 lawyers, and big accounting firms that also employed hundreds or even thousands of lawyers.

Principal Competitors

Gibson, Dunn & Crutcher; O'Melveny & Myers; Skadden, Arps, Slate, Meagher & Flom.

Further Reading

Dewey, Katrina M., "How an Upstart L.A. Firm Made It to the Top," *California Law Business,* October 8, 1990, pp. 28–30.

Galanter, Marc, and Thomas Palay, *Tournament of Lawyers: The Transformation of the Big Law Firm,* Chicago: The University of Chicago Press, 1991.

Hidula, Scott, and Lisa Davis, "Major Law Firm Notes Intent on Large Lease Here," *San Francisco Business Times,* May 28, 1990, p. 3.

Hock, Sandy, "What Goes up and Comes Down May Be Restructured," *San Diego Business Journal,* August 12, 1991, p. 17.

Kizilos, Peter, "Interviews with Infopros: Lori Fena," *Online,* March/April 1998, pp. 35–38.

Leibowitz, Wendy R., "Lawyers Find Niches on the 'Net," *National Law Journal,* November 23, 1998, p. A1, 7.

Maister, David H., "The One-Firm Firm: What Makes It Successful," *Sloan Management Review,* Fall 1985, pp. 3–13.

Osborne, D.M., "Latham's Leap Forward," *American Lawyer,* April 1997, pp. 47+.

Peck, Austin H., Jr., *Bold Beginnings: A Story about the First 50 Years of Latham & Watkins,* Los Angeles: Latham & Watkins, 1984.

Pollock, Ellen Joan, "Singing the Latham Song," *American Lawyer,* October 1986, pp. 125–31.

"Washington Hearsay," *Washington Post,* December 22, 1997.

—David M. Walden

L.B. Foster Company

415 Holiday Drive
Pittsburgh, Pennsylvania 15220
U.S.A.
Telephone: (412) 928-3400
Toll Free: (800) 255-4500
Fax: (412) 928-7891
Web site: http://www.lbfoster.com

Public Company
Incorporated: 1902
Employees: 529
Sales: $241.92 million (1999)
Stock Exchanges: NASDAQ
Ticker Symbol: FSTR
NAIC: 331221 Rolled Steel Shape Manufacturing; 33121
  Iron & Steel Pipe and Tube Manufacturing from
  Purchased Steel; 327332 Concrete Pipe Manufacturing

L.B. Foster Company manufactures and distributes rail and trackwork, piling, highway products, earth wall systems, tubular products, and portable mass spectrometers. The company began as a distributor of recycled rail to coal miners, but it has diversified into other industrial segments to serve customers in construction, transit, chemical, utility, and agricultural markets. Approximately 55 percent of L.B. Foster's revenues are derived from rail products, which include a full line of new and used rail, trackwork, and accessories. The company operates nine manufacturing plants and 15 sales offices.

Origins

L.B. Foster Company was founded by Lee B. Foster, who in 1902 started the company to distribute steel rail. During its early years, the company used mules to pull track out of coal mines, operating as a railway track recycler that resold "relay" rail. Although L.B. Foster counted rail distribution as one of its business segments for the duration of the century, the company's diversification in later years added several new facets to its business that eventually overshadowed its original relay distribution business. As the company evolved, it diversified into the tubular and sheet products market, coupling its ventures into other realms of the steel business with geographic expansion. After more than a half century of business, the company's roots in the celebrated steel city of Pittsburgh were planted firmly, but longevity did not necessarily impart prolific growth. In terms of revenues, L.B. Foster's stature remained relatively diminutive until it struck upon a market that recorded explosive growth. The company's heyday arrived during the 1970s.

L.B. Foster latched onto the business that ignited its growth when it reached an agreement with Nippon Steel. The company agreed to take oil field pipe from Nippon Steel and process the pipe for use in oil rigs. L.B. Foster threaded the pipe and finished it, putting the company in a position to reap the benefits of a rapidly expanding oil exploration market. From 1973 to the early 1980s, the oil exploration market enjoyed astounding growth, creating a demand for finished pipe that exceeded supply. While other processors struggled to keep pace with the growth, L.B. Foster rose to the occasion, processing more than one million tons of pipe.

1977 Leveraged Buyout

Ironically, the decade that delivered the greatest growth to L.B. Foster also marked the beginning of troubled times, precipitating a protracted financial tailspin. The problems surfaced not long after the Foster family ceded ownership of the company. In 1977, Kohlberg Kravis Roberts & Co. (KKR) acquired L.B. Foster through a leveraged buyout (LBO), taking over the company that had evolved into a distributor and manufacturer of construction, rail, and tubular products. At the time, L.B. Foster was recording robust growth, exuding enviable financial health that KKR sought to cash in on four years later. In 1981, KKR and its backers sold 19 percent of L.B. Foster to the public, raising $31 million from the offering. The proceeds from the stock sale represented a financial boon for KKR considering that the company had paid $57 million for the 81 percent of L.B. Foster it controlled after the offering. It was not the last time L.B. Foster shareholders' loss would be KKR's gain.

Key Dates:

1902: L.B. Foster Company is formed to distribute used rail to coal mine.
1977: Kohlberg Kravis Roberts & Co. acquire L.B. Foster in a leveraged buyout.
1981: Public offering coincides with the collapse of the U.S. oil exploration market.
1986: Architectural hardware and banking equipment businesses are acquired.
1987: Acquisitions are sold to reduce soaring debt.
1990: Lee B. Foster II is appointed president.
1997: Company enters mass spectrometer market.
1999: CXT Inc. is acquired.

At the time of the public offering, L.B. Foster was saddled with $64 million in long-term debt, or more than one-third of the company's market value. Shareholders eagerly paid $17 per share for a piece of the debt-laden company, but their zeal quickly soured when market conditions placed a stranglehold on L.B. Foster. In December 1981, not long after KKR officials celebrated the successful offering of L.B. Foster stock, the oil services industry was beset by a depression. The market that had vaulted L.B. Foster toward unprecedented riches began to sputter, causing the U.S. oil rig count to diminish significantly. Consequently, the pipe finishing plants that had worked feverishly to keep pace with demand experienced an alarming respite, as production at L.B. Foster's pipe finishing plants fell below 70 percent of capacity. The company's chairman, Milton Porter, subsequently made a regrettable decision. Porter, who had married into the Foster family during the 1940s, saw the recessive conditions in the oil exploration market as an opportunity to expand. He attempted to double the company's production capacity, hoping to better position L.B. Foster for the eventual upswing in oil exploration activity. The strategy backfired. Losses escalated throughout the first half of the 1980s, as the company's revenues from tubular products sank precipitously, falling from $367 million in 1981 to $176 million by 1985.

The errant decision to double capacity in the face of plunging demand was the first in a series of imprudent decisions that stripped L.B. Foster of its vitality. Porter retired in 1984, leaving the company in a precarious state. He was replaced by a longtime business associate of KKR named Edward Mabbs, who joined L.B. Foster from Incom International, where he had served as chief executive officer for the previous decade. Mabbs assumed his new title with more than a modicum of anxiety. L.B. Foster was floundering and seemingly destined for more profound trouble. Robert Kanters, an analyst who closely followed L.B. Foster, visited Mabbs not long after the new chief executive officer moved into his new office. In a November 2, 1987 interview with *Forbes* magazine, Kanters offered some insight into Mabbs's mindset. "Mabbs had me in his office showing me all these graphs and charts and telling me why they had to do something other than oil tube threading," Kanters revealed. "He was saying the drill count is terrible, and we don't see this thing going anywhere for a long time. Mabbs said that we have to do something." What followed was another egregious mistake made by an L.B. Foster leader.

1986 Diversification

Reportedly, Mabbs was under pressure from L.B. Foster's three KKR board members to diversify. Their advice, for which they charged L.B. Foster a $2.5 million fee to provide, convinced Mabbs to complete two acquisitions that moved the company into businesses entirely distinct from its core businesses. In February 1986, Mabbs paid $302 million to Kidde, Inc. for five architectural hardware and banking equipment businesses, which immediately mired L.B. Foster in debt. Annual interest payments stemming from the acquisitions were more than $42 million, thrusting the company into an untenable position. Mabbs quit, moving on to retirement in Florida, which paved the way for another KKR-appointed chief executive officer, Jerry Goldress. Goldress, who had helped rescue other KKR companies, faced grimmer prospects than his predecessors had, inheriting a company that was teetering on the brink of bankruptcy. "We had too much debt," he was quoted as saying in the November 2, 1987 issue of *Forbes*. "Creditor pressure was being brought to bear, and we were in trouble with our suppliers."

Backed into a corner, Goldress chose the only option available for the beleaguered company. He decided to divest the ill-conceived acquisitions. The banking equipment group was sold in June 1987, followed by the sale of the architectural hardware group two months later. L.B. Foster obtained $337 million from the sale of the two divisions, which erased much of the company's debt but could do little to erase damage that had been done. L.B. Foster's stock, which had sold for $17 per share in 1981, had plummeted to barely more than $2 per share by 1987.

Shortly after completing the divestitures, Goldress stepped down as chief executive officer, having guided the company through its initial stage of restructuring. Goldress stayed on as chairman and relinquished his other title to Joseph H. Dugan, who became the fourth L.B. Foster chief executive officer in a three-year span. Unlike his predecessors, Dugan took control of a company without grave financial ills. Long-term debt had slipped below $10 million, and with finances under control, optimism—long absent from company headquarters—had returned. Company officials believed they could construct a sizable business around spiralweld pipe, used to transport water, as well as record appreciable growth in the company's traditional businesses in oil field pipe, rail products, and construction products. Along with the renewed optimism came an important change in the company's operating strategy. Roughly 65 percent of L.B. Foster's revenues were derived from the marketing products made by other companies, while the rest was collected from fabricating its own products. Dugan wanted more of a balance, announcing that in the future L.B. Foster would concentrate on manufacturing more of the products it marketed. Toward this end, the company committed to opening a new spiralweld pipe facility in Houston.

The restructuring process continued under Dugan's stewardship, nearing its end by the time Dugan resigned from the company to return to consulting work in 1990. Goldress resigned as chairman as well in 1990, replaced by James Wilcox. For Dugan's replacement, the board of directors returned the company to its roots. In May 1990, Lee B. Foster II was selected to head the company.

Foster Family Member Guides Company Through the 1990s

The founder's grandson, Foster gave the company what it had lacked throughout the 1980s: enduring leadership. Foster, who led the company throughout the 1990s, had been part of the family business for more than 15 years by the time he was appointed its leader. He had majored in engineering and anthropology at Cornell University and the University of Pittsburgh, forgoing a future in his academic disciplines to join L.B. Foster in 1974. Foster started as a clerk before joining the company's sales force, which took him to L.B. Foster offices in Orlando, Atlanta, and Houston. He took charge of the company's international sales program in 1980, and several years later he was selected to head the company's Southwest region. In his last post before completing his ascent of the company's managerial ladder, Foster was in charge of L.B. Foster's tubular products division, serving in such capacity from 1986 to 1989.

Foster, in his early 40s when he took command of the company, reiterated Dugan's commitment to the manufacturing side of L.B. Foster's business. By manufacturing more of the products it sold, the company could realize greater profit margins in value-added steel products such as threaded and coated pipe. Before the company could begin any significant investments in fabricating facilities, however, its core businesses needed to recover fully from the travesties of the 1980s. Much of L.B. Foster's business was dependent on federal government spending directed toward infrastructure projects, such as highways, bridges, and railways. Unfortunately for Foster, the first few years of his reign were pocked by a national recession, which hampered the company's recovery from its earlier miscues. In 1993 the federal government announced $30 billion in transportation and highway spending, giving the company "a significant shot in the arm," according to Foster's assessment in the March 8, 1993 issue of the *Pittsburgh Business Times*. The spending package provided a welcomed boost to the company's core businesses, but lackluster financial results continued to characterize L.B. Foster's performance during the decade. Foster's response, evident during the latter half of the decade, was to enter new markets through acquisitions and create more diverse distribution channels for the company's expertise in rail, construction, and tubular products.

Late 1990s Acquisitions

During the late 1990s, there were several significant deals completed by Foster that described his company's progress at the end of the century. In May 1997, the company acquired Monitor Group Inc. from Industrial Scientific Corp., organizing the acquisition into a separate L.B. Foster division. Monitor Group manufactured portable mass spectrometers used to measure gas compositions and concentrations, a new field of business for L.B. Foster. The applications for Monitor Group's spectrometers were varied, including monitoring air quality for the mining industry and as a process monitor and diagnostic tool in chemical manufacturing industries.

L.B. Foster's next acquisition represented less of a distant reach, strengthening one of the company's core competencies rather than moving it far afield. In November 1997, the company acquired Georgetown, Massachusetts-based Precise Fabrication Corporation. The addition of Precise, a steel fabricator, gave the company a regional manufacturing facility in the New England market and it enabled the company to offer a comprehensive selection of components to the highway, bridge, and transit markets. A similar advantage was gained from L.B. Foster's next acquisition, completed in December 1997. The company purchased Watson-Haas Lumber Company, a supplier of iron clad and steel ties to the mining industry. Like the purchase of Precise, Watson-Haas's inclusion within the company's fold enabled L.B. Foster to offer its customers a more complete package of products, specifically all the rail and track requirements demanded by the mining industry.

As the 1990s drew to a close, appreciable financial growth continued to elude L.B. Foster. Although the company was consistently profitable, its revenues were essentially flat, increasing a mere $8 million between 1994 and 1999. By the end of the decade, the Monitor Group had not yet generated any revenues, frustrating company officials who had miscalculated the acquisition's market readiness. L.B. Foster executives suffered through another delay, after operating without a domestic sheet piling supplier from March 1997 forward. In September 1997, the company reached an agreement with Chaparral Steel to become the firm's exclusive North American distributor of steel sheet piling and "H" bearing pile, but the agreement was pending the completion of Chaparral's new Richmond, Virginia facility. By the end of the decade, the Richmond facility had not been completed. Two acquisitions that the company hoped would produce more immediate results were completed in 1998 and 1999. In August 1998, L.B. Foster acquired the Geotechnical Division of VSL Corporation, giving the company a leading supplier of mechanically stabilized earth wall systems. In June 1999, the company purchased CXT Inc., a manufacturer of engineered prestressed and precast concrete products used in the railroad and transit industries. As L.B. Foster prepared for the 21st century, hopes were pinned on these new acquisitions to provide a spark to the company's financial totals.

Principal Subsidiaries

CXT Incorporated.

Principal Divisions

Foster Rail; Foster Piling; Foster Precise; Foster Fabricated Products; Foster Coated Pipe.

Principal Competitors

ABC-NACO Inc.; DaimlerChrysler Rail Systems; AMSTED Industries Incorporated.

Further Reading

Antonelli, Cesca, "L.B. Foster Could Pile on the Profits with Chaparral Distribution," *Pittsburgh Business Times,* September 12, 1997, p. 6.
Clements, Jonathan, "Thank You, Kohlberg Kravis," *Forbes,* November 2, 1987, p. 38.
Cotter, Wes, "Will Infrastructure Finally Rescue L.B. Foster?," *Pittsburgh Business Times,* March 8, 1993, p. 12.
"Foster Buys Fabricator," *American Metal Market,* November 20, 1997, p. 3.

Haflich, Frank, "Northwest Pipe Buying Foster Unit," *American Metal Market,* March 2, 1998, p. 3.

Kovatch, Karen, "Industrial Scientific Corp. Unloads Its Monitor Unit to Eager L.B. Foster," *Pittsburgh Business Times,* March 31, 1997, p. 2.

"L.B. Foster Acquires Midwest Rail Assets," *Railway Age,* July 1993, p. 22.

"L.B. Foster Ups Railroad Stake," *American Metal Market,* January 22, 1999, p. 4.

Petry, Corinna, "Chaparral, Foster Join Forces on Piling," *American Metal Market,* September 5, 1997, p. 2.

Teaff, Rick, "Foster Returns to Family Ties," *Pittsburgh Business Times,* May 14, 1990, p. 10.

——, "L.B. Foster Keeps Bonds with Its Railroading Past," *Pittsburgh Business Times,* May 22, 1989, p. 2S.

——, "L.B. Foster Leaves Restructure Year with Profits," *Pittsburgh Business Times,* February 15, 1988, p. 8.

—Jeffrey L. Covell

Legg Mason, Inc.

100 Light Street
Baltimore, Maryland 21202
U.S.A.
Telephone: (410) 539-0000
Toll Free: (800) 577-8589
Fax: (410) 454-4923
Web site: http://www.leggmason.com

Public Company
Incorporated: 1981
Employees: 4,350
Sales: $1.04 billion (1999)
Stock Exchanges: New York
Ticker Symbol: LM
NAIC: 55111 Offices of Other Holding Companies;
    52392 Portfolio Management; 52592 Trusts, Estates,
    and Agency Accounts

Legg Mason, Inc. is the holding company for several subsidiaries that provide a wide range of financial services for private, public, and corporate clients. The chief subsidiaries are Legg Mason Wood Walker, Inc.; Howard, Weil, Labouisee, Friedrichs; Gray, Siefert & Co.; and The Fairfield Group. Among other services, these and other companies owned by Legg Mason broker securities; manage assets; offer investment advising; broker public and corporate finance, insurance, and annuity product sales and purchases; and provide mortgage banking services for commercial interests. It is one of the most successful financial service holding companies in the United States and one of the few to remain independent through the 1990s, when many regional brokerages were absorbed by finance service industry giants. At the close of the century, the company operated more than 120 domestic and overseas offices, staffed by 1,200 financial advisors and more than 4,200 total employees, and was managing individual and institutional assets of $82 billion. Its revenue also had reached the $1 billion mark for the first time in its history.

A Complex History: 1899–1981

Although Legg Mason can trace its origins back to 1899, when its grandparent company, George Mackubin & Co. was founded in Baltimore, it began taking its present shape under the tutelage of its current CEO, Raymond A. (Chip) Mason, when, in 1981, it was incorporated as a holding company to manage a group of subsidiaries that had evolved through an intricate history of growth and changes in firm partnerships. Its most immediate predecessor was Legg Mason & Company, formed in 1970 through the merger of two brokerage firms—Mason & Company and Legg & Company.

Chip Mason and some associates had formed Mason & Company in 1962, in Newport News, when Mason was only 25. He had entered the world of securities in his hometown of Lynchburg, Virginia, where his great uncle and uncle ran Mason & Lee, a small brokerage firm. In 1959, after graduating from the College of William and Mary, he entered that family business as a trainee, but, anxious to start up his own firm, he left after two years. With $200,000 borrowed from local businesses and the help of close college friends, most of whom were his Sigma Alpha Epsilon fraternity brothers, Mason was able to open his own company. Among his friends was James Brinkley, who would later run Legg Mason's expansive retail brokerage operation.

Mason guided his young business through a successful beginning and healthy early growth. Among other things, the firm avoided the devastating "back-office crisis" that afflicted many other investment firms in the 1960s. By 1970, Mason & Co., with 60 brokers, was operating six offices, including four branch offices in Virginia and Washington, D.C. It also had drawn the attention of Legg & Co., which was looking to expand into the South, and the two firms negotiated a merger to establish Legg Mason Co.

It was Legg, a solidly capitalized, long-established company, that was the surviving successor to Mackubin & Goodrich, a firm with business roots set down in Baltimore in 1899. It had started as George Mackubin & Co., as a broker-dealer firm, but went through several permutations before emerging as Legg & Co. It became Mackubin & Goodrich within the first year, when Mackubin took on co-founder G. Clem Goodrich as a partner. In the next year it hired John Legg, whose first principal task was to chalk up stock prices on a blackboard. Five years later, in 1905, he became a partner.

The firm had to weather difficult years. First during World War I, when there was a moratorium on stock trading and the company's business was reduced to financing real estate mortgages. Then in the aftermath of the 1929 stock market debacle, when the partners had to keep the firm solvent by selling off their own stock. The company nearly floundered completely, in part as a result of the defection of T. Rowe Price, who, at the time, was a growth-stock portfolio manager for Mackubin & Goodrich. He left to form T. Rowe Price Associates, an industry giant that by the end of the 1990s had more than $140 billion in assets under its management.

In 1932, after Goodrich died, the firm became Mackubin, Legg & Co., and finally, in 1942, John C. Legg & Co., after Mackubin and Legg had a falling out and Mackubin left to join a competing firm. Under Legg's leadership, the firm prospered in the post-World War II boom and was in a favorable position to enter the new partnership with Chip Mason's company.

In 1973, three years after the merger, a second major change occurred when Legg Mason merged with Wood Walker & Co., a New York-based investment firm. The resulting company, Legg Mason Wood Walker, Inc., added a 20 percent growth in revenue in that year. With its headquarters in Baltimore, and Chip Mason as chairman, the company's rapid expansion continued. Over the 13-year period from 1970 to 1983, when the Legg Mason holding company went public, the firm acquired six brokerages, significantly increasing its volume.

In the same period, under Chip Mason's tutelage, Legg Mason Wood Walker & Co. was broadening its investment markets. A major step was taken in 1979, when the company set up its first mutual, money-market fund, the Legg Mason Cash Reserve Trust.

The growth also encouraged Legg Mason Wood Walker to create a new corporate entity as a holding company for its various subsidiaries. The company did so in 1981, forming Legg Mason, Inc. All the firms owned by Legg Mason Wood Walker, and the parent company itself, were at that time placed under the Legg Mason corporate umbrella.

Going Public and Rapid Growth Through Acquisitions: 1982–90

The year after it created the Legg Mason Fund Adviser, Inc., formed in 1982 to manage the retail funds of its growing family of subsidiaries, Legg Mason went public and was listed on the New York Stock Exchange. It was also in 1982 that Chip Mason convinced his research associates to set up an equity mutual fund to complement its existing mutual, money-market fund. The resulting Legg Mason Value Trust, having no front- or back-end sales load, was a slow starter, in part because of the sluggish economy, but by the end of 1985 the fund had drawn $422 million in investments.

Encouraged by its performance, Legg Mason thereafter inaugurated two additional mutual funds. These helped give Legg Mason a desired noncyclical revenue and encouraged Chip Mason and his associates to acquire asset-managing firms. In 1986, despite serious reservations voiced by his staff, and using Merrill Lynch & Co. as broker, Legg Mason acquired Western Asset, a California-based bond-managing firm that had been placed on the auction block by First Interstate Bancorp. Mason's colleagues were dubious, in part because the $20 million price tag represented about half of Legg Mason's liquid capital, and in part because fixed-income managers had performed badly during the previous two decades. In just more than a year, however, the bond manager increased its asset management load by $1 billion, and by 1988 it was providing most of a $10 million increase in Legg Mason's revenue from its investment advising services.

Although not always with the same success, Western's performance encouraged Chip Mason and his fellow executives to continue an aggressive expansion through acquisitions. One of these, the Howard Weil Financial Corp., a New Orleans-based broker-dealer specializing in the energy field, acquired in 1987, imposed considerable risk because the Tax Reform Act of 1986 had undermined its municipal bond underwriting business. In addition, Legg Mason subsidiaries took some bottom line setbacks in 1988 when post-Black Monday uncertainties depressed brokerage commissions by 13 percent.

Western's success compensated for these problems, however, and after a three-year cooling-off period, Legg Mason began to purchase and expand again, widening the circle of its subsidiaries, both in their kind and geographical reach. In 1990 it ventured into the commercial mortgage banking field, purchasing Latimer & Buck, the base company in what would become Legg Mason Real Estate Services, an operation run by Chip Mason's close friend, James Brinkley.

Continued Growth and Diversification: 1990–2000

By 1993, Legg Mason had 870 brokers in 83 offices, primarily located in middle-Atlantic and southern states. In that year it continued its acquisitions, buying Horsham, a Pennsylvania-based Fairfield Group, and in the next year, Gray, Siefert & Co., a New York-based, high-net-worth money manager. Its acquisitions continued in 1995, when it purchased Boston's Batterymarch Finan-

Key Dates:

1899: Forerunner to Legg & Co., George Mackubin & Co. is founded in Baltimore.

1962: Raymond A. Mason, a Virginia broker-dealer, incorporates Mason & Company, Inc. in Newport News.

1970: Mason & Company and Legg & Company merge to form Legg Mason & Company.

1973: Legg Mason acquires Wood & Walker Co., a New York broker-dealer, forming Legg Mason Wood Walker, Inc.

1979: Company introduces the Legg Mason Cash Reserve Trust, its first mutual, money-market fund.

1981: Legg Mason, Inc. is incorporated in Maryland as a holding company for its subsidiaries, including Legg Mason Wood Walker, Inc.

1982: Legg Mason Fund Adviser, Inc. is created to manage Legg Mason Funds and the Legg Mason Value Trust is introduced as the company's first equity mutual fund.

1983: Legg Mason, Inc. goes public and is listed on the New York Stock Exchange.

1990: Legg Mason enters the commercial mortgage banking field by buying Latimer & Buck, Inc.

1995: The company establishes an overseas office in London.

1996: Legg Mason acquires Bartlett & Co. and Lehman Brothers Global Asset Management Limited.

1998: Company moves headquarters to Light Street in downtown Baltimore.

cial Management, a company that specialized in equity management on a global scale. A year later it also bought Cincinnati-based Bartlett & Co., a domestic equity manager, and Lehman Brothers Global Asset Management's London-based international fund management branch. The latter was turned over to Western Asset and renamed Western Asset Global Management. Another major acquisition, Brandywine Asset Management, Inc., a "deep value" equity manager based in Wilmington, Delaware, was made in 1998, the year in which Legg Mason also moved its headquarters to 100 Light Street in downtown Baltimore.

Legg Mason's ability to compete successfully in the mergers and acquisitions arena, sometimes beating out higher bidders, is explained in large part by the fact that Chip Mason has consistently granted the firm's subsidiaries real operating independence, allowing them a latitude seldom permitted by larger money-managing firms. That can, of course, cause some problems, but of the acquisitions made in the 1990s, only Batterymarch proved troublesome. When Legg Mason bought it, the company's sole proprietor, Dean LeBaron, and his staff were offered earn-out incentives if they could meet certain revenue targets over a three-year period. These were not met, however, in part because the firm lost a lucrative subadvisory contract with the Vanguard Group. That loss alone was not enough to explain why, in 1997, Batterymarch managed only $4.3 billion in assets, $700 million less than it managed when acquired by Legg Mason.

Despite such occasional problems, Legg Mason has had a history of solid investments in its growth and has gained a reputation for stability in a volatile industry. One reason for this is its refusal to put its capital at risk. In 1993, for example, its debt was only 36 percent of its capital, whereas that of Merrill Lynch was 68 percent. It also has a history of conservative underwriting, preferring safer municipal financing to such risky investments as initial public offerings. In 1992 the company underwrote 263 municipal bond issues with a value of $11.7 billion. Still, it was through diversification that Legg Mason gained its solid performance record and continued growth. By broadening the scope of its services, especially by moving more deeply into asset management, Legg Mason was able to log impressive gains. At the end of 1999, the firm had $85 billion under management, an increase of $16 billion over 1994. Moreover, between 1994 and 1998, the company's investment advisory fees increased by nearly 300 percent, moving up from $91 million to $365 million. That sort of performance predictably led to much speculation about Legg Mason's inevitable absorption through the leverage of a larger firm, something that Chip Mason has deflected throughout his tenure as the firm's CEO. In 1998, however, Mason announced his plans to retire within five years, and that decision prompted some speculation that his successor might be less reluctant to guide Legg Mason into a larger corporate fold through the company's acquisition or merger.

Principal Subsidiaries

Legg Mason Wood Walker, Inc.; Legg Mason Capital Management, Inc.; Legg Mason Fund Advisor, Inc.; Legg Mason Real Estate Services, Inc.; Legg Mason Financial Services, Inc.; Legg Mason Merchant Banking, Inc.; Legg Mason Trust Co.; Howard, Weil, Labouisee, Friedrichs Inc.; Bartlett & Co.; Batterymarch Financial Management, Inc.; Brandywine Asset Management, Inc.; Gray, Siefert & Co., Inc.; Western Asset Global Management Ltd. (London); Western Asset Management Co.

Principal Competitors

The Charles Schwab Corporation; Citigroup Inc.; The Goldman Sachs Group, Inc.; J.P. Morgan & Co. Incorporated; Liberty Financial Companies, Inc.; Morgan Stanley Dean Witter & Co.; Paine Webber Group Inc.

Further Reading

Barrett, Amy, "Legg Up in Baltimore: Legg Mason Is a Successful Asset Manager Disguised As a Regional Broker," *Financial World,* August 7, 1990, p. 78.

De Lombaerde, Geert, and Joanna Sullivan, "Legg Mason Acquires U.K. Mutual Fund Co.," *Baltimore Business Journal,* October 22, 1999, p. 11.

Garmhausen, Stephen, "Legg Mason Is Preparing to Take On Bank Rivals," *American Banker,* September 10, 1999, p. 1.

Glenn, Karen A, "Two CEOs in Search of Successor," *Baltimore Business Journal,* December 18, 1998, p. 1.

James, Ellen, "At Third with Legg Mason," *Financial World,* October 16, 1985, p. 85.

Meeks, Fleming, "Bucking the Trends," *Forbes,* September 13, 1993, p. 202.

Phillip, Ben, ''Chip Mason's Stealth Strategy,'' *Institutional Investor,* May 1998, p. 71.

''Raymond A. 'Chip' Mason'' (Interview), *Baltimore Business Journal,* October 23, 1998, p. 18.

Santoli, Michael, ''A Legg Up; Diversification Keeps Chip Mason's Firm Ahead of Other Regional Brokers,'' *Barron's,* April 26, 1999, p. 21.

Sullivan, Joanna, ''Legg Fund Tries To Capitalize on Bank Takeovers,'' *Baltimore Business Journal,* May 12, 1995, p. 1.

—John W. Fiero

LEXIS-NEXIS Group

9393 Springboro Pike
Miamisburg, Ohio 45342
U.S.A.
Telephone: (937) 865-6800
Toll Free: (800) 227-9597
Fax: (937) 865-7476
Toll Free Fax: (800) 34-NEXIS
Web site: http://www.lexis-nexis.com/lncc
Wholly Owned Division of Reed Elsevier plc
Incorporated: 1994
Employees: 7,900
Sales: $1.23 billion (1998)
NAIC: 514191 On-Line Information Services

The LEXIS-NEXIS Group, a business division of Reed Elsevier plc, is a major electronic publisher and information provider. It serves customers in more than 60 countries, offering legal, business, government, academic, and financial information through the Web, dial-up online, CD-ROM, and books. LEXIS Publishing combines the company's legal brands: Lexis-Nexis, Matthew Bender, Shepard's, Martindale-Hubbell, and Michie. The NEXIS division consists of the NEXIS news and business information service and publisher Congressional Information Service Inc. The LEXIS-NEXIS database contains 2.5 billion searchable documents from nearly 25,000 news, business, and legal sources, with more than 14 million documents added each week.

From Defense Contracting
to Legal Research: 1955–67

LEXIS-NEXIS could trace its history to a defense contractor, Systems Development Corporation, which began operations in Dayton, Ohio in 1955. The company later changed its name to Data Corporation and made money primarily from sole source contract work for Wright-Patterson and Rome Air Force bases in Ohio. Its CEO was William L. Gorog.

Wright-Patterson was the Air Force's principal research center, and one of Data Corporation's projects there was the development of a program called Recon Central. This was a computer-based system for storing and retrieving information about procurement contracts and worldwide inventories of radar equipment, basically a database of the Air Force's optical and photographic equipment. Later, the system was used to retrieve aerial reconnaissance photos. Another project was the development of an ink jet printer.

In 1966 the company put the research software created for Recon Central to a civilian use. The Ohio State Bar Association, headed by James Preston, Jr., was looking for a more effective way for its members to conduct legal research. Preston asked Data Corporation to come up with a system that would allow attorneys to use computers to research case law and state statutes. The resulting system, using the Recon Central software, cut research time from days to hours.

A New Owner: 1968–70

While Ohio attorneys were finding citations more quickly, the Mead Corporation, a longtime paper-making company based in Dayton, was deciding that it needed to diversify to counter the cyclical ups and downs of the paper industry. Mead chose to move into high technology and in 1968 paid $6 million for Data Corporation, which it renamed Mead Technology Laboratories. Mead was particularly interested in Data Corporation's ink jet printer and the Recon Central photo retrieval and storage system.

Gorog stayed with the company, supervising research and development, including the Ohio Bar Association research project. Not knowing quite what to do with the tiny database of Ohio law, in 1969 Mead hired the consulting firm Arthur D. Little, Inc. to analyze the marketing potential of that system. On the consulting team were attorneys H. Donald Wilson and Jerome Rubin.

The team submitted its report to Mead in 1970, finding that existing electronic legal research systems, including the Recon Central system, were inadequate. The major problem was that these systems did not search the text of the documents themselves, but depended on abstracts, indices, and document summaries. The team also found that there was a definite market for a high-quality, national computerized system to store and retrieve legal information. It recommended that Mead invest $20 to $30 million to develop such a system. To the surprise of just about everyone, Mead approved the proposal.

Mead Data Central, Inc.: 1970–73

To undertake the project, in 1970 Mead created a new subsidiary, Mead Data Central, Inc. (MDC), and Wilson and Rubin formed a management partnership to head it. That partnership lasted until September 1971, when Wilson stepped down as president. Jerome Rubin then assumed full control.

As Mark Voorhees wrote in a December 1999 article in the *American Lawyer,* Rubin faced monumental challenges. "The goal was to launch the service with 2 billion characters of information. An interactive free-text system of that size had never been built. . . . The world of computing was far different then. One hundred megabytes of computer storage cost nearly $50,000. (Today, a typical personal computer hard drive stores 30 to 40 times that amount and costs less than $200.)"

Over the next 18 months, and after spending $14 million, Rubin and his crew of computer engineers and linguistic specialists found answers to those challenges, even though several of the staff were skeptical of the system's potential. "The question was whether you could build a service that could support hundreds or even thousands of simultaneous users," Edward Gottsman told Mark Voorhees. Gottsman, who was Rubin's chief strategist, also doubted that lawyers would use it.

Rubin addressed that particular issue by marketing the system to large law firms in New York City, where competition was fierce. On April 2, 1973, with four big firms as the first subscribers, MDC launched the LEXIS legal reference service. LEXIS provided a lawyer with the ability to search the full text of New York and Ohio codes and cases, the federal code, and a federal tax library.

LEXIS was what was known as a "dial up" system. To connect with MDC, a lawyer at a subscribing firm dialed a number and placed the telephone receiver into the cradle of a modem that converted the signals coming from Dayton. Then the lawyer only had to type a question into a custom-designed computer terminal and LEXIS would generate a listing of relevant case law from its database.

A Decade of Growth: 1974–83

Within four years, the LEXIS service was making a profit. In 1979 the company introduced a news and business research service called NEXIS and opened a new computer center to house MDC. Revenues that year reached $22.9 million. NEXIS was packaged free with the LEXIS service and provided law offices with general and business news and current information about companies.

Meanwhile, a competitor appeared on the scene (or screen). In 1975 West Publishing Company entered the electronic legal research business with its Westlaw service. By the late 1970s, recognizing that lawyers comfortable with researching online would be more likely to become customers, both LEXIS and Westlaw began making their online services available free to law students.

By 1983, the LEXIS database had 12.5 million pages, including the full text of federal and state laws, court decisions, and much of British and French law. NEXIS provided access to 160 major newspapers, magazines, newsletters, wire services, and the Encyclopedia Britannica. That year, the company signed a licensing agreement with the *New York Times* giving MDC exclusive right to the newspaper's electronic archives. MDC had revenues of approximately $100 million and LEXIS was used by nearly every large law firm, law school, court, and government agency.

In an important step to expand its markets, MDC began allowing access to its databases through personal computers. The company did this by putting the information on computer disks, which it sold in a package with documentation and keyboard templates. At the same time, it signed marketing agreements with IBM and AT&T.

Growth and Consolidation in Electronic Information: 1984–89

More and more entities were seeking ways to provide information electronically. In 1985 the Securities and Exchange Commission started automating the filing and retrieval of companies' reports through its EDGAR project (Electronic Data Gathering and Retrieval System). MDC performed much of the development work for EDGAR and then was involved in managing the filings and making copies available for dissemination.

During this period, MDC sued West Publishing, challenging West's system for copyrighting legal citations. The case was settled in 1988, when West agreed to license its citation system to LEXIS for about $3 million a year for ten years.

By 1988, the growth of the electronic information industry had lead to consolidation, with 20 major purchases during the year. A total of 40 percent of these involved foreign companies or their subsidiaries, including the purchase by Reed Publishing Ltd./U.K. of the Cahners publishing business. Maxwell Communication Corp, one of media magnate Robert Maxwell's companies, bought Macmillan for $2.5 billion and BRS Information Technologies, a bibliographic-based online service, for $25–$30 million, and Knight-Ridder bought Dialog from Lockheed for $353 million.

MDC was also making acquisitions. In December 1988, it completed the purchase of the Michie Company from Macmillan for $226.5 million. Michie published 22 annotated state codes and helped in building the LEXIS database to 50 state

Key Dates:

1966: Data Corporation contracts with Ohio Bar Association to create a computerized legal research system.
1968: The Mead Corporation buys Data Corporation.
1970: Mead creates Mead Data Central to develop a full-text, national legal research system.
1973: Four New York law firms are first subscribers to the LEXIS legal information service.
1979: NEXIS's news and business information service begins.
1994: Reed Elsevier plc purchases Mead Data Central and renames it LEXIS-NEXIS.
1999: Company forms LEXIS Publishing.

statutes. By 1989, MDC's revenues were expected to reach $400 million, up from $22.9 million in 1979.

Facing Growing Competition: 1990–93

LEXIS dominated the electronic legal information market through the 1980s, but in 1989 the service's growth began to slow. Initially this happened as a result of the recession, with layoffs and cost cutbacks in legal firms. Then, in the early 1990s, increased competition and changes in technology ate into its market share.

Among online (dial-up) competitors, West Publishing's Westlaw was gaining market share. While the two services were about equal in the legal information they offered, Westlaw's prices were lower, its natural language software was easier to use than that of LEXIS, and it offered gateways to Dialog and Dow Jones News/Retrieval services to provide current news and business information similar to that offered by NEXIS. According to a 1994 article in *Legal Publisher,* ''[LEXIS] has instituted interface and access enhancements only in response to competition and the whole computer system is in need of major upgrading and overhaul.'' The result, said Marcia Berss of *Forbes,* was that LEXIS's market share dropped from 95 percent in the early 1980s to 60 percent in 1992.

Computer disks (CD-ROMs) containing volumes of works from legal publishers such as Matthew Bender and Martindale-Hubbell were another source of competition. LEXIS offered CD-ROMs of legal information for selected states through the Michie Company, and Micromedex, another MDC subsidiary, used that format for drugs, toxicology, and other information for the health care industry.

Furthermore, desktop computers had become much more powerful and the information industry was trying to determine how to move from its mainframe environment to a client/server setting. In addition, the Internet made it possible for people to search for masses of information and anticipated drops in telecommunications costs would give more people access to that information. Players in the industry were busy developing methods to organize and package information in ways that would be helpful to the user.

As Rod Everhart, CEO of MDC, told Marydee Ojala of *Online,* ''There are oceans of data out there . . . and MDC is a data packager. We know how to collect it, and how to put it in a form that makes it productive and efficient and effective for the user, and that they will be willing to pay for. If we fail to do that, to add value in that data collection process, then we're going to have to change our business.''

To accomplish this, MDC grew the business through acquisitions, buying Jurisoft, a legal software publisher, Folio Corporation, a developer of infobase management software that was used by CD-ROMs, and LEXIS Document Services, a retrieval service of public records. The company also made software changes on its LEXIS-NEXIS database, including making it easier to deal with numbers in its company and financial data service, put more resources into NEXIS, and offered more connection options at different prices.

Internationally, consolidation within the information industry continued. In 1993, Reed International plc, a major British publisher with holdings in the United States, and Elsevier NV, a huge Dutch publisher, merged to create Reed Elsevier plc. The new entity became the third largest information company in the world, behind Time Warner Inc. and Bertelsmann A.G.

On the Sales Block: 1994

In May 1994, Mead Corporation announced that it was getting out of the electronic information business to concentrate on making paper and it put MDC on the market. In the previous year, the subsidiary had earnings of $50.4 million on sales of $551 million and accounted for 12 percent of Mead's total revenues. Analysts' estimates of the final sales price ranged from $750 million to $2 billion. At the time, LEXIS had 45 specialized libraries and NEXIS contained more than 2,400 full-text sources. By September, three companies were seriously considering the purchase, with bids up to $1 billion: Times Mirror Co. of Los Angeles, Canada's Thompson Corporation, and the newly formed Anglo-Dutch conglomerate, Reed Elsevier plc.

In October, Reed Elsevier announced that it was buying Mead Data for $1.5 billion. The next day, Reed Elsevier was listed on the New York Stock Exchange. The purchase of MDC signaled the company's intention to shift from dependence on hard copy publishing to increased use of online information, with electronic publishing expected to double to 20 percent in 1995.

Reed Elsevier was the publisher of more than 1,000 journals and magazines, including *Lancet,* the British medical journal, *Modern Bride, Variety,* and various science and computer magazines as well as books and newspapers. It owned the Martindale-Hubbell lawyer directory, British legal publishers Butterwork & Company Ltd., R.R. Bowker, a leading library publisher, and Reed Exhibitions.

In December, Reed Elsevier completed the transaction and announced that although their new holding would remain in Ohio, it would do so under a new name, LEXIS-NEXIS, to take advantage of the well-known brand names. The company also announced a new, ten-year agreement with the *New York Times* under which LEXIS-NEXIS would have immediate access to *Times* material but no longer would have exclusive license to the newspaper's archives.

The Internet and the Web: 1995–97

Reed Elsevier's purchase of MDC moved the publisher right into the online information business. But major technological changes were occurring that would greatly impact electronic publishing. The Internet and the World Wide Web became more important tools to both searchers for and deliverers of information. Weekly business and news magazines began appearing online. West Publishing put its *Legal Directory* on its web site. Search engines such as Yahoo, Infoseek, and Lycos made it easier to find sites on the Internet. As the industry continued to consolidate, in 1996 Canadian publisher Thompson Corporation bought West Publishing.

That same year, LEXIS-NEXIS introduced ReQUESTer, an Internet service offering small businesses access to major newspapers from around the world for $59 a month. A year later, LEXIS launched its legal Web service, Xchange. Whereas access to the legal database required a subscription account at costs similar to the company's traditional service, Xchange also offered current legal news free of charge.

Acquisitions and Competition: 1998–99

During 1998, Reed Elsevier bought legal publisher Matthew Bender and Shepard's, a legal citation service, from Times Mirror for $1.65 billion. On the news side of the LEXIS-NEXIS business, the company introduced its Web-based Universe service, providing access to a broad range of information at a flat rate rather than its traditional per-article fee. The new service was a big move on the part of the company to attract professional researchers who were not in the legal profession.

But despite these moves, LEXIS-NEXIS was having problems. Free Internet sites were providing stiff competition to NEXIS and other traditional information providers and Thompson's West Group continued cutting into LEXIS business. During the first half of 1999, LEXIS-NEXIS sales grew only one percent and operating profits dropped 17 percent, not counting acquisitions. Just under half of the sales came from online business and the rest from its Web-browser based products.

Two major shifts occurring in the electronic information industry were affecting LEXIS-NEXIS. One was the movement from proprietary telecommunications software connections to Web-based online searching. The second involved the growing demand for general and business information by an audience much wider than legal professionals.

1999 to the Present

By the end of 1999, LEXIS-NEXIS was moving to differentiate its two main businesses, beginning by calling itself the LEXIS-NEXIS Group. To strengthen its legal products and services, the company combined its five legal brands (LEXIS-NEXIS, Michie, Shepard's, Matthew Bender, and Martindale-Hubbell) into a separate business unit, called Lexis Publishing. It also introduced lexis.com, a new Web-based search system for legal information that added case synopses and a new, up-to-date legal classification system. In December, the company announced that select offerings, including state and federal court decisions, would be available on a pay-per-use basis on the Web through WinStar Telebase. In January 2000, it offered

journalists a "Meet the Experts" database of more than 100 legal authorities.

NEXIS also was undergoing a restructuring, even as it introduced a new product, Company Dossier, offered with Universe. In January, the LEXIS-NEXIS Group bought the Business Information Product unit of England's *Financial Times,* and a month later announced an agreement with e-solutions Software to develop a news and information service on the Web for sales professionals.

Crispin Davis, who took over as CEO of Reed Elsevier in September 1999, announced at the end of February 2000 that the company planned to greatly increase its research and development spending, investing $1.2 billion in online activities over the next three years. As he told Raymond Snoddy of *The Times* (London), the business would focus on providing "solutions, not just information." For the LEXIS-NEXIS Group, such solutions were expected to include responding to lawyers' verbal requests made through "a little machine." As the fight for the legal and business customer continued to intensify, the only sure prediction was that by 2002 the business would look very different.

Principal Operating Units

NEXIS; Martindale-Hubbell; LEXIS Publishing; Matthew Bender; Shepard's; Michie; Congressional Information Service Inc.

Principal Competitors

Thomson Corporation; Dialog Corporation; Dow Jones Reuters Business Interactive LLC.

Further Reading

Ambrogi, Robert J., "West and LEXIS Open Shop on Web," *Chicago Lawyer,* May 1998, p. 59.

Bates, Mary Ellen, "Accessing SEC Filings Via EDGAR," *Information Advisor,* December 1994, p. 1.

Berss, Marcia, "Logging Off Lexis," *Forbes,* January 4, 1993, p. 46.

Bischoff, Laura A., "LEXIS-NEXIS Laying Off Scores, Restructuring NEXIS," *Dayton Daily News,* November 21, 1999, p. 1F.

——, "LEXIS-NEXIS Parent Company Changes Course," *Dayton Daily News,* December 10, 1999, p. 1E.

Blake, Paul, "What European Ownership Will Mean for MDC," *Information Today,* December 1994, p. 15.

Burt, Tim, "North America Proves the Right Connection for an On-line Future," *Financial Times* (London), October 6, 1994, p. 23.

Dillon, Jim, "Mead Data Sale Due Soon," *Dayton Daily News,* September 21, 1994, p. 5B.

——, "Lexis-Nexis Is Born," *Dayton Daily News,* December 3, 1994, p. 1A.

Evans, Storm M., "Pay-Per-Use Access to Lexis-Nexis," *Law Practice Management,* November 1999/December 1999, p. 27.

Fabrikant, Geraldine, "Mead To Sell Its Data Base Unit," *New York Times,* May 17, 1994, p. D1.

Fox, Nicholas, "Reed Plugs into the Superhighway," *Sunday Telegraph,* October 9, 1994, p. 5.

Griffith, Cary, "Mead Data Central Acquires Folio Corporation," *Information Today,* March 1993, p. 26.

——, "Hunter Grant on Lexis/Nexis," *Information Today,* November 1991, p. 40.

Hane, Paula J., "Lexis-Nexis Consolidates Legal Brands, Introduces Research System," *Information Today,* September 1, 1999, p. 1.

Kaufman, Joshua J., ''A Computer Primer for Novices,'' *Texas Lawyer,* July 26, 1993, p. 26.

''LEXIS-NEXIS Completes Purchases of Matthew Bender and Shepard's,'' *Legal Publisher,* November 30, 1998, p. 3.

''Lexis-Nexis Counts Coup with Financial Times' BIP,'' *Min's B-to-B,* January 24, 2000.

''LEXIS-NEXIS Group Teams with e-solutions Software, Inc.,'' *Business Wire,* February 7, 2000.

''LEXIS' Service Going Back to Its Roots,'' *PR Newswire,* May 15, 1991.

Lubove, Seth, ''Dial-a-Mess,'' *Forbes,* January 24, 2000, p. 68.

Manville, Richard, ''Sorting Out Sources of Marketing Data; Choosing Correct Database for Your Needs,'' *Telephone Engineer & Management,* April 15, 1985, p. 116.

Marino, Jacqueline, ''New Ear for Mead Data Central,'' *Gannett News Service,* July 8, 1994.

''Mead Embracing High Technology,'' *New York Times,* September 20, 1980, p. B25.

Miller, Tim, ''Lexis, Nexis and PCs,'' *PC Magazine,* October 16, 1984, p. 149.

Ojala, Marydee, ''Business Databases, 1995: An Interesting Year,'' *Online,* December 1995, p. 68.

——, ''Rod Everhart, Change Agent at Mead Data Central,'' *Online,* September 1993, p. 16.

Pemberton, Jeff, ''Who Will Buy Mead Data Central . . . How Much Will They Pay?,'' *Online,* July, 1994, p. 13.

Phelps, John, ''Reed Soars After 200M Pound Pledge on Investment,'' *Scotsman,* December 10, 1999, p. 25.

''Reed Elsevier Purchase Equals Nearly Three Times MDC Sales,'' *Legal Publisher,* October 31, 1994.

Ruben, Richard C., ''Online Legal Publishing Gets DOJ Review,'' *ABA Journal,* December 1994.

Snoody, Raymond, ''The Man with a Blueprint for Recovery at Reed Elsevier,'' *Times* (London), February 25, 2000.

Urrows, Henry and Elizabeth, ''An Inside Look: Money Chasing Innovation,'' *Computerworld,* May 23, 1983.

Voohees, Mark, ''The Searcher,'' *American Lawyer,* December 1999.

Waltner, Charles, ''Internet Stirs Up Information Services,'' *Business Marketing,* September 1998, p. 10.

—Ellen D. Wernick

POLSKIE LINIE LOTNICZE•POLISH AIRLINES

S.A.

LOT Polish Airlines (Polskie Linie Lotnicze S.A.)

LOT Air Terminal
65/79 Jerozolimskie Avenue
00-697 Warszawa
Poland
Telephone: 952, 953
Toll Free: 0-800-225757
Fax: 630-55-03
Web site: http://www.lot.com

Joint Stock Company
Incorporated: 1929 as Linie Lotnicze
Employees: 4,200
Sales: PLN 2.14 billion ($517.97 million) (1998)
NAIC: 481111 Scheduled Passenger Air Transportation;
481112 Scheduled Freight Air Transportation; 481211
Nonscheduled Chartered Passenger Air
Transportation; 48819 Other Support Activities for
Air Transportation

Polskie Linie Lotnicze S.A., or LOT Polish Airlines, was the first airline in Eastern Europe to ditch its fleet of old Soviet jets in favor of a modern, all-western one. Customer service was also retooled. While deregulation has opened Poland's frontiers to aggressive international competitors like Lufthansa, LOT has aimed beyond its traditional captive audience to international business travelers and ethnic Poles abroad—ten million in North America alone. Alliances with top-flight competitors British Airways and American Airlines and a new strategic partnership with SAirGroup ensure LOT a place in the global market.

Origins

While many European countries sponsored state airlines after WWI, the Republic of Poland was only just establishing its own independence. Although the Austrian military did supply air mail service (possibly Europe's first) in 1918, Warsaw's first scheduled air service came from the Compagnie Franco-Roumaine de Navigation Aérienne (CFRNA) in April 1921. Poland subsidized this foreign-owned company with free fuel.

The next year, local oil interests joined the German Junkers industrial group in founding Aerolloyd Warszawa. Warsaw-Lvov and Warsaw-Gdansk service began in September 1922. Flights to Krakow and Vienna were added in subsequent years. Aerolloyd flew Junkers F-13 aircraft and three-engined, Fokker F.VII planes, although the company switched to Dutch-designed Fokkers exclusively after ending its relationship with Junkers. (Some of the Fokkers were made in Poland under license.)

Aerolloyd Warszawa became an entirely Polish-owned joint stock company in the spring of 1925. It was joined soon by a new competitor, Aero T.Z., operating routes between Warsaw, Poznan, and Berlin. In 1928 the newly created Civil Aviation Office fostered a merger between Aerolloyd Warszawa and Aero T.Z., creating Linie Lotnicze (LOT) on December 28. Only a couple of local governments were able to contribute to the company's PLZ 8 million ($1.2 million) capitalization. (Polish currency, the zloty, was designated as PLZ until 1995 when the country re-denominated its currency and changed the zloty symbol to PLN.) In the end, the Polish government owned 86 percent of the shares, Silesia owned ten percent, and the cities of Bydgoszcz and Poznan owned two percent each.

Bydgoszcz was rewarded for its investment by new air service after LOT commenced operations on January 2, 1929. So was Silesia, whose regional manufacturing center Katowice was connected to the existing network. At the end of 1929, a year that marked the signing of the historic Warsaw Convention on international air traffic, LOT prefixed its name with ''Polskie'' and adopted its crane logo.

In the 1930s, the new carrier became a conduit not so much between east and west as between north and south, connecting the Baltic with the Mediterranean. LOT's fleet reached 33 aircraft in 1934. By the end of the decade, it was operating an 18-strong fleet made up mostly of Lockheed Electras, and its network extended as far as Helsinki and Beirut. LOT also flight tested routes to the Americas and Africa.

LOT penetrated the Western European market modestly, operating flights to Berlin, Paris, and London in conjunction with Deutsche Lufthansa, Air France, and British Airways,

Company Perspectives:

Air carriers operate in a highly competitive environment, and the airline business has been largely deregulated. Like any other provider of services, an air carrier depends for its existence on the buyers of its services: passengers and cargo forwarders. It is the customer who chooses the carrier, and this choice is influenced mainly by the quality and pricing of the product. Quality means first of all safety, punctuality and efficient service. It also means comfort and a professional and friendly approach. Providing our customers with services of the highest quality is seen by the management of LOT Polish Airlines as our top priority. We shall pursue our quality enhancement policy to the best of our abilities, to ensure customer satisfaction, loyalty and trust, which will result in more and more people making LOT their carrier of choice.

respectively. LOT did not manage to turn a profit before World War I, however, and received $1 million (PLZ 6.5 million) worth of government subsidies in 1938 alone, when it had nearly 700 employees and carried 65,000 passengers a year between 25 cities. The airline's operations were stopped by the Nazi blitzkrieg that razed Poland in September 1939. Many personnel escaped to Great Britain where they joined the Royal Air Force.

Cold War Realities

Poland was left under Soviet control after World War II. The provisional government's first act on March 6, 1945 was to take over the airline. By the end of the month, LOT had acquired aircraft allowing it to resume service to some of the larger Polish cities. New territory ceded from Germany (Gdansk, Wroclaw) was also immediately incorporated into the network. Transporting government officials was one of the carrier's chief duties, and LOT cooperated closely with the Polish military. The airline received its first six-year plan in 1960. Like Aeroflot, LOT was given responsibility for domestic forestry and agricultural projects in addition to passenger services.

By 1946, the airline owned 39 planes, mostly Douglas C-47 transports and their Soviet-built copies (Lisunov Li-2s). In 1949 LOT acquired five of the slightly more refined Ilyushin Il-12s for high-profile international routes (such as Paris, Stockholm, and Prague). These planes replaced five obsolete French Sud-Est SE.161 Languedocs bought two years earlier. In 1955 the improved Il-14P replaced the older Ilyushins.

LOT and the Czech airline CSA were the only two Soviet bloc carriers regularly flying to the West in the 1950s. A rise in nationalist politics in the middle of the decade gave LOT more freedom to raise fares on domestic routes and to provide more links to western Europe. Poles themselves, however, had little freedom to choose airlines other than the official state carrier. In the last half of the 1950s, LOT had about 1,500 employees. It carried 200,000 passengers and 3,333 tons of cargo in 1956. By 1966, it was carrying nearly 500,000 passengers and ten tons of cargo a year.

The Jet Age

Unlike its Czechoslovakian counterpart, LOT was slow to invest in new jet aircraft. Instead, it used prop-driven planes bought secondhand from western airlines, such as Sabena and British United, to cover its bases until the introduction of Ilyushin's Il-18 turboprop. Turboprops, which use a jet turbine to drive a propeller, were more efficient to operate on shorter routes than pure jets. After two of its Viscounts crashed, LOT replaced them with Antonov An-24s, which became the mainstay of its fleet. LOT finally bought a jet, the Tupolev Tu-134, in 1966, and used a handful of them for medium-range routes.

A 1963 pricing agreement between Bulgaria, Czechoslovakia, the German Democratic Republic, Hungary, Romania, and Poland set air transport rates at half those of the International Air Transport Association, the western airline cartel. LOT could not recoup its costs under these low fares and posted a PLZ 271 million operational loss in 1966.

LOT's passenger count exceeded one million in 1971. Soon, a bilateral accord gave LOT access to the American market. It shared a Warsaw-New York route with Pan American Airways. LOT bought nine Il-62M jets within the decade for such long-range routes, which soon extended to Canada and Asia. International traffic grew by 30 percent a year. By 1976, LOT was carrying 1.5 million passengers a year and 22,000 tons of cargo.

In 1978 CSA gave LOT some serious competition from behind the Iron Curtain when it began operating a route between Warsaw and Bratislava, a $5 bus ride away from Austria, which LOT also served. CSA ended this controversial service, seen as a threat to socialist brotherhood, a few years later. LOT's passenger count stood at 1.7 million in 1981, although cargo tonnage had fallen to less than 12,000 tons. Revenues were PLZ 10,000 million.

Jerzy Slowinksi replaced the previous, politically appointed director in 1986 as LOT became more commercial in its focus. Although the company ordered 14 flexible, mixed-use Tupolev Tu-154M jets the same year (deliveries of which continued into 1991), it was aggressively pursuing opportunities to buy more efficient and reliable western-made aircraft. A disastrous series of crashes, including one of an Ilyushin Il-82 en route to New York that killed 183 people in 1987, reinforced the desire for modern western planes.

The defeat of the United Workers Party in the elections of 1989 by Solidarity was the first, and perhaps most significant, event leading toward LOT's privatization. The Sejm (Polish parliament) voted to allow LOT to become a joint stock company. That year, revenues at PLZ 454,400 million were up nearly fourfold from the year before, when they had doubled 1987's results.

In light of such promising performance, a complex financing arrangement among 17 banks (led by Citibank) allowed LOT to lease a couple of Boeing 767s beginning in 1989. The 767s were attractive, as they carried more payload while using 50 percent less fuel and offered better range than the Airbus A310 and McDonnell Douglas DC-10 also considered.

Key Dates:

1929: LOT, formed out of two existing airlines, makes its first flight.
1938: Prewar operations peak at 65,000 passengers a year.
1945: LOT comes under Soviet control.
1963: Six Eastern European nations set low air rates.
1973: LOT begins scheduled flights to New York.
1989: LOT begins expensive transition to all western-made fleet.
1999: SAirGroup picked as LOT's strategic partner.

After 1989, LOT began to westernize its fleet full-force. It chose Franco-Italian ATR-72 turboprops over the Canadian de Havilland Dash-8 in part because of reciprocal orders at Polish aviation plants. The relatively small amount of financing needed was arranged by just two Paris banks. With the help of American financiers, LOT also was able to lease a few Boeing 737s in the early 1990s, the biggest order in its history at $300 million. With debts of $500 million, LOT then unloaded as many Russian aircraft as it could on former Soviet republics.

A work force reduction plan began in 1991, reducing employment of 7,300 by 40 percent in three years. In December 1992 LOT was reorganized as PLL LOT SA, capitalized at PLZ 2 billion ($150 million). LOT's commercial director, Jan Litwinski, was subsequently named president and CEO. In the run-up to privatization, ground handling and other businesses were sold. LOT Ground Services became a wholly owned subsidiary in July 1992, and a 49 percent interest was sold to the national airport company, PPL (Przedsiebiorstwo Panstwowe Porty Lotnicze). American Airlines parent AMR Corp. was contracted to manage the new company through a joint venture known as AMR Polska. Similarly, LOT had SAS run its catering operation. Poor results among European airlines in the mid-1990s kept stock prices down and conspired to postpone LOT's privatization. Investments in tourism and petroleum kept LOT viable during this protracted process.

LOT lost PLZ 471 billion ($44.2 million) in 1991. LOT's new director, Bronislaw Klimaszewski, was able to guide the airline to a PLZ 63 billion ($3.4 million) profit in 1993 even as the value of Polish currency plunged. The company launched an unprecedented advertising campaign to identify itself as the Polish flyer's "home away from home" (*dom poza domem*). It launched a frequent flyer program in 1991, signing up 4,000 business-class members within three years. In 1992 LOT contracted with KLM's Pegasus Ltd. to train 1,400 employees how to deliver customer service with a human face.

Before the collapse of the Soviet Union, LOT had dominated traffic between Poland and the western Soviet republics, which had a sizable population of ethnic Poles. Although the business was wiped out when artificially low fares were removed, LOT was able to rebuild it quickly after Poland signed a series of cooperative agreements with several Baltic states. Still, the Russian market remained the most important part of its eastern network, accounting for 40 percent of income there.

LOT installed business class seating on its ATR-72 turboprops to capitalize upon the strength of the business segment in the Russian market. It faced serious competition, however, from the highly sophisticated operations of Lufthansa, Air France, and British Airways, each of which carried many more passengers in the eastern market. Lufthansa had five times LOT's passenger volume there. The resulting tension prompted quibbles over market access with Britain and The Netherlands. Nevertheless, LOT succeeded in rebuilding market share in the east. Profits from that market rose 50 percent in 1994.

A new passenger terminal at Okecie Airport allowed LOT to begin developing Warsaw as a hub between east and west. The company developed relationships with the newly created airlines of the Commonwealth of Independent States (CIS), which provided feeder traffic into Warsaw. It pooled equipment with Air Ukraine on flights to and from Kiev and Lvov; contractual capacity restrictions limited its growth, however. LOT entered other cooperative alliances with Tatra Air (Slovakia), CSA, Swissair, Austrian Airlines, and Lufthansa.

LOT sought to join one of the new mega-alliances both to gain access to a computerized reservations system and to attract potential investing partners. The coming liberalization (deregulation) of the European Community's civil aviation market made it all the more imperative for LOT to find strong partners. LOT signed an extensive code-sharing agreement with American Airlines in May 1994. The U.S. Congress refused to allow the alliance on antitrust grounds, however, until the Poles opened their home market more to outside competitors.

By 1995, LOT's annual passenger count had recovered at 1.8 million. Cargo tonnage was 17,000. Trade with the United States accounted for half of this volume and was growing at an incredible clip—50 percent a year. Shipments to France and other countries were also up. A new department was created to expedite these operations: the Office for Cargo and Mail. LOT's new Boeings could carry nine tons of cargo each in addition to their typical passenger loads, while the Soviet jets could carry only a tenth as much. LOT refinanced the 767s with five Japanese banks in 1995, reducing its interest payments by $5 million a year.

Late 1990s

Traffic did not quite meet projections in the late 1990s, leaving the carrier with excess capacity. LOT had spent about $1 billion on new planes, and interest payments wiped out profits in 1996 and 1997. Privatization, ardently desired, would allow LOT to pay off some of its debts. Government officials slowed the process, however, as CSA and the Hungarian carrier Malev saw their partnerships with western airlines (Air France and Alitalia) fizzle. LOT's own management sought an investor outside the airline industry, to reduce the potential for power struggles. In July 1998, LOT refinanced $100 million of its debt through a five-year Eurobond.

LOT created EuroLOT, a lean, low-cost domestic carrier in 1997. It also was planning to spin off its charter operations (mostly tourist flights to the Mediterranean). British Airways tapped LOT in early 1998 to help it compete with the United Airlines/Lufthansa/SAS-led STAR Alliance. (By 1999, LOT also would ink deals with Iberia and Finnair.) Traffic figures were up, and LOT showed a modest profit (PLN 2 million or $521,000) in 1998, albeit in large part due to a change to western accounting methods (changing the amortizing period from 12 years to an average of 22).

In 1999 the Polish government again asked for bids in another attempt to privatize LOT. The first stage would be the sale of ten percent of the company, with money going to the treasury. Next, the strategic investor would recapitalize LOT and increase its holdings to 38 percent. Finally, an IPO was planned for 2001. The list of potential investors was narrowed to British Airways, Lufthansa, and SwissAir by September.

Operationally, LOT brought in new Embraer ERJ 145 regional jets to increase the number of flights a day it could offer business passengers to western Europe. Poland's new membership in NATO increased business traffic to Brussels; joining the European Union would do the same for traffic to many other commercial centers.

In October 1999, Poland picked SAirGroup as LOT's strategic investor. The group, which had recently lost a long alliance with Austrian Airlines, offered up to $30 million for the initial ten percent stake. The Polish government planned to retain 51 percent of shares.

Principal Subsidiaries

LIM (50%); Casinos Poland; PetroLOT (49%); EuroLOT; Amadeus START Polska (25%).

Principal Competitors

Austrian Airlines; Malév Plc; Deutsche Lufthansa AG; Air France; CSA; Tarom; Scandinavian Airlines Systems.

Further Reading

Berniker, Mark D., ''Poland's LOT Shifts Plans To Expand into High Gear,'' *Journal of Commerce,* March 17, 1989, p. 5B.

Breskin, Ira, ''Boeing Sale to Poland Cracks Iron Curtain,'' *Journal of Commerce,* November 4, 1988, p. 9B.

Brzezinski, Matthew, ''Polish Airline Undergoes Metamorphosis To Survive: Planes Are New; So Are Clerks' Smiles,'' *Houston Chronicle,* Bus. Sec., May 8, 1994, p. 5.

Canning, Rachel, ''Single Minded,'' *Airfinance Journal,* September 1995, pp. 34ff.

Dwyer, Rob, ''The Next LOT for Sale Is. . . ,'' *Airfinance Journal,* September 1999, pp. 44–46.

Filipczyk, Joanna, ''LOT: Connecting East and West in Poland,'' in *Flying the Flag: European Commercial Air Transport Since 1945,* edited by Hans-Liudger Dienel and Peter Lyth, New York: St. Martin's Press, 1998.

Hill, Leonard, ''A LOT To Worry About,'' *Air Transport World,* January 1998, pp. 64–69.

Koening, Robert, ''SAirGroup Forms Alliance with LOT Polish Airlines,'' *Journal of Commerce,* November 2, 1999, p. 8.

Lenanne, Alexandra, ''Third Time Lucky? LOT for Sale Again,'' *Airfinance Journal,* September 1997, pp. 46–47.

''LOT Polish Builds Cargo Base,'' *American Shipper,* June 1996.

''LOT Zeroes in on Eastern Europe Air Freight Business,'' *AirCommerce,* February 26, 1996, p. 6A.

Michaels, Daniel, ''Poland Puts Its National Airline on the Runway to Privatization,'' *Wall Street Journal,* February 26, 1998, pp. A12ff.

——, ''Poland's Airline Expects To Attract Six Bidders,'' *Wall Street Journal,* July 26, 1999, pp. B8Eff.

''Passenger Airline Finds Success in Freight Shipping,'' *AirCommerce,* December 30, 1996, p. 40.

Selwitz, Robert, ''A LOT Going On in Poland,'' *Global Trade & Transportation,* November 1993, p. 40.

Skapinker, Michael, ''BA and LOT Set for Tie-Up To Fight Rival Alliance: Partnership Deal Due Today,'' *Financial Times,* Companies & Markets, January 15, 1998, p. 31.

Verchere, Ian, ''Not for Sale,'' *Airfinance Journal,* July/August 1996, pp. 26–27.

Widman, Miriam, ''Polish Airline Seeks Partner To Develop Freight Service,'' *Journal of Commerce,* January 2, 1991, p. 1A.

—Frederick C. Ingram

LVMH
MOËT HENNESSY • LOUIS VUITTON

LVMH Moët Hennessy Louis Vuitton SA

30 avenue Hoche
755008 Paris
France
Telephone: (33) 1 44 13 22 22
Fax: (33) 1 44 13 21 19
Web site: http://www.lvmh.com

Public Company
Incorporated: 1854 as Louis Vuitton SA and 1971 as
   Moët-Hennessy
Employees: 33,000
Sales: FFr 56 billion ($9.51 billion) (1999)
Stock Exchanges: NASDAQ Paris
Ticker Symbol: LVMHY
NAIC: 551112 Offices of Other Holding Companies;
   31213 Wineries; 31214 Distilleries; 316991 Luggage
   Manufacturing; 316992 Women's Handbag and Purse
   Manufacturing; 44819 Other Clothing Stores; 44815
   Clothing Accessories Store; 44612 Cosmetics, Beauty
   Supplies, and Perfume Stores

LVMH Moët Hennessy Louis Vuitton SA, created through a
$4 billion merger in 1987, is the world's leading luxury goods
vendor, providing products ranging from champagne to perfumes
to designer handbags. Its fashion and leather goods division includes such prominent brands as Louis Vuitton, Kenzo, Givenchy,
and Céline, while its fragrance and cosmetics group distributes
brands including Christian Dior, Givenchy, and Guerlain.
LVMH's wine and spirits group includes such premium brands as
Dom Pérignon, Hennessy, Krug, and Moët Chandon. The company also owns luxury retailers, including a majority stake in DFS
Group Ltd., a group of duty-free stores, and Sephora, a cosmetics
and perfume chain. The company sought to expand and diversify
in the late 1990s through a number of acquisitions.

The History of Louis Vuitton

Historically a supplier of luggage to the wealthy and powerful, Louis Vuitton is known for combining quality fabrication
with innovative designs to reflect the needs of customers and the
ever-changing modes of world travel. Louis Vuitton left
Anchay, his birthplace in the Jura, for Paris in 1835 at age 14.
After one year of traveling on foot, he reached the capital and
soon became an apprentice packer and trunkmaker. The son of a
carpenter, Vuitton mastered the skill of woodworking and designing trunks and, within ten years, had become an expert.
During his apprenticeship, Vuitton gained experience in packing by traveling to the homes of wealthy women, where he was
employed to pack their clothes before they embarked on long
voyages. With his master, Monsieur Maréchal, Vuitton went
regularly to the Tuileries Palace as the exclusive packers to the
Empress Eugénie and her ladies-in-waiting.

In 1854, Vuitton opened his own business at 4 rue Neuve des
Capucines, very close to the couture houses around Place
Vendôme. Due to his familiarity with wood, silk, and satin, he
became well respected by the couturiers, who hired him to pack
their creations. His invention of flat-topped trunks, which were
more easily stacked for travel than the traditional domed trunks,
established his reputation as a master luggage-maker. Vuitton
began covering his trunks in grey Trianon canvas, which was
both elegant and waterproof when varnished.

As the business grew increasingly successful, Vuitton built
workshops outside Paris in Asnières, where transportation of
wood from the south was convenient. When his original store
became too small, business was transferred to 1 Rue Scribe, and
Vuitton began focusing on trunk-making rather than packing.
Vuitton became the supplier of luggage to many of the most
famous people of the era, from King Alfonso XII of Spain to the
future Czar Nicholas II of Russia. He created special trunks for
Ismail Pacha, the viceroy of Egypt, for the inauguration of the
Suez Canal as well as a trunk-bed for Savorgnan de Brazza, who
discovered the source of the Congo in 1876. The quality of the
materials, the arrangement of interiors, and the finishings made
Vuitton's deluxe trunks far superior to anything that had previously been produced.

In an attempt to discourage copying of the Trianon grey
canvas in 1876, Vuitton introduced new designs featuring red
and beige stripes and brown and beige stripes to cover his
trunks. By 1888, these striped canvases were imitated, and a
patented checkered material was implemented. A large part of
the company's success was its ability to respond to the changing

modes of travel which emerged at an astonishing rate in the second half of the 19th century. Vuitton designed classic wardrobe trunks for sleeping cars and lighter versions of the suitcase traditionally used by the English aristocracy. His son Georges played an important role in the managing of the business, opening the first Vuitton branch abroad in London in 1885.

In 1890, Georges invented the theft-proof five tumbler lock, which provided each customer with a personal combination to secure all his luggage. Two years later, the company's first catalog presented a wide range of products, from very specialized trunks for transporting particular objects to simple bags with the typical traveler in mind. Four years after the death of Louis Vuitton in 1892, Georges introduced a new canvas design in another attempt to thwart counterfeiters. In memory of his father, Georges' new design featured Louis Vuitton's initials against a background of stars and flowers; it was patented and became an immediate success.

Traveling to America for the Chicago Exposition of 1893, Georges became convinced of the importance of a sales network abroad. By the end of the century, John Wanamaker began representing Louis Vuitton in New York and Philadelphia, and the London store was transferred to New Bond Street, in the heart of London's luxury commerce. The company also expanded its distribution to Boston, Chicago, San Francisco, Brussels, Buenos Aires, Nice, Bangkok, and Montreal in the early 20th century.

Georges also foresaw the importance of the automobile as a form of transport and began designing automobile trunks, which imitated the lines of the car, to protect travelers' effects from rain and dust. Contending that one should be able to take in a car what one could take on a boat or train, he created iceboxes, canteens, and light and flexible steamer bags. Other efforts to adapt to the changes in the travel industry included the manufacture of airplane and hot air balloon trunks and cases for spare tires. In 1914, the company erected a new building on the Champs-Elysées as the center for its growing network of distribution; this store became the world's largest retailer of travel goods.

During World War I, production was modified to the needs of the war effort, as simple and solid military trunks replaced delicate and luxurious models. Part of the factory in Asnières produced folding stretchers which were loaded directly into ambulances leaving for the front. With the 1918 German offensive 60

kilometers from Paris, Georges had difficulty supplying his factory with materials and assuring the safety of his workers. After the war, the Vuittons struggled to supply their stores with what remained of the factory. Although the company supplied Prince Youssoupov with a jewel case to transport precious stones to America before the Bolshevik revolution, such personal orders were less common after the war, and the factory devoted more time to producing showcases for traveling salesmen.

As economic times improved, and Louis Vuitton regained its stylish clientele, special orders increased. The workshop at Asnières worked to produce orders for Coco Chanel, the Aga Khan, Mary Pickford, the Vanderbilts, and the president of the French Republic, among others. Charles Lindbergh ordered two suitcases from Vuitton for his return trip to America after his famous flight to France. During this time, the company provided some packing services for foreigners who came to buy garments from the Paris couture collections. In the early 1930s, exoticism was in vogue, and Vuitton used tortoise shell, lizard skin, ebony, and unusual woods in its fabrications.

As economic conditions deteriorated worldwide, however, the Vuittons realized the necessity of increasing the company's profitability. Georges's son, Gaston, worked with his father to increase efficiency. An advertising agency was set up and a design office was created to make detailed sketches of products to show customers before fabrication. By the time Georges Vuitton died in 1936, special orders had dramatically declined, and the company's sales depended more than ever upon its catalog offerings, which were expanded to include trunks for typewriters, radios, books, rifles, and wine bottles.

During World War II, when delivery of Vuitton products was curtailed, overseas contracts were terminated, and the Vuitton factory and stores closed. The post-war period involved resupplying the stores, rebuilding business to pre-war levels, and restructuring operations. Three of Gaston's sons played important roles, Henry in commercial management, Jacques in financial administration, and Claude in factory management. The first important postwar order at the company was for the President of the Republic, Vincent Auriol, who made an official visit to the United States.

In 1954, the company's 100th anniversary, Louis Vuitton moved from the Champs-Elysées to Avenue Marceau. As travel times were cut with the development of trains, cars, and airplanes, the company created and improved its soft-sided luggage. In 1959, Gaston perfected a system of coating his motif canvases, making them more durable, waterproof, and suitable for shorter journeys. These lightweight, practical bags signified a new standard in luggage. Gaston invited well known artists to take part in the design of accessories. From 1959 to 1965, an average of 25 new models of Vuitton luggage were created each year.

With the company's success and reputation for luxury came a vast wave of counterfeit Louis Vuitton products. One year before his death in 1970, Gaston Vuitton decided to take action against the counterfeiters by opening a store in Tokyo; by offering the real Vuitton product in the Asian market, he hoped to better inform customers and discourage the purchase and manufacture of imitations. The company also undertook a successful advertising campaign to battle the increase in counterfeiting.

Key Dates:

1743: Claude Moët and his son, Claude-Louis, open Moët et Cie to sell wine.

1792: Claude Moët dies and leaves company to grandson Jean-Rémy.

1832: Jean-Rémy hands over control of the company to his son and son-in-law; business is renamed Moët et Chandon.

1854: Louis Vuitton opens his own packing and trunk-making business in Paris.

1885: Louis Vuitton expands internationally by opening a store in London.

1969: Louis Vuitton enters the Asian market with a store in Tokyo.

1971: Moët et Chandon merges with Jas. Hennessy & Company, the largest cognac producer in France, and is renamed Moët-Hennessy.

1984: Louis Vuitton goes public.

1987: Louis Vuitton and Moët-Hennessy merge in a $4 billion deal.

Henry Racamier, the husband of Gaston Vuitton's daughter Odile, took over management of the company in 1977. Racamier had founded Stinox, a steel manufacturing business, after the Second World War and had sold it at a huge profit before coming to Louis Vuitton. Under Racamier, the company's sales soared from $20 million in 1977 to nearly $1 billion in 1987. Racamier recognized that the major profits were in retail and that to succeed on an international level, Louis Vuitton had to expand its presence in stores and distributors in France. As a result, Louis Vuitton stores were opened all over the world between 1977 and 1987, and Asia became the company's principal export market. Moreover, product diversification ensued, and in 1984, at the urging of financial director Joseph Lafont, the company sold stock to the public through exchanges in Paris and New York.

The 1980s were profitable years for Louis Vuitton, as the Vuitton name was prodigiously promoted. In 1983, Louis Vuitton became the sponsor of the America's Cup preliminaries. Three years later, the company created the Louis Vuitton Foundation for opera and music. Also in 1986, the central Paris store moved from avenue Marceau to the posh avenue Montaigne. Production at the factory at Asnières incorporated the use of lasers and other modern technology during this time, and a distribution center was opened at Cergy-Pontoise, north of Paris. The company allocated two percent of annual sales revenue to the unending battle against counterfeiters.

Under Racamier, Louis Vuitton began to acquire companies with a reputation for high quality, purchasing interests in the couturier Givenchy and the champagne house Veuve Cliquot. Louis Vuitton's takeover philosophy was personal, courteous, and discreet, rather than systematically aggressive.

The History of Moët-Hennessy

Moët-Hennessy, whose product lines include Christian Dior perfume, Dom Pérignon champagne, and Hennessy X.O. co-gnac, is a well-established and extremely successful French enterprise. What began as the business of a talented French vintner around 250 years ago became a world leader in the production of wines, spirits, cosmetics, and perfumes.

Claude Moët considered the Champagne region east of Paris, in the Marne River valley, to be an ideal location for wine production. He established a vineyard near Epernay but became frustrated dealing with the *courtiers en vin*, or distributors, who took his wine to market. Instead of depending on them to sell his wine, Moët decided to buy one of the offices of *courtiers en vin* and sell the wine himself.

In 1743 Moët et Cie (Moët and Company) was formed. Joined by his son Claude-Louis, Moët quickly established customer accounts which included a number of landed gentry and nobles. In 1750 father and son established an account with Madame du Pompadour, who regularly ordered Moët champagne for the royal court at Compiègne. That same year Moët began selling champagne in Germany, Spain, Eastern Europe, and America.

Claude Moët died in 1792, leaving the company to his grandson Jean-Rémy, who laid the groundwork for the later success of Moët et Cie. He expanded the base of operations at Epernay by purchasing the vineyards of the Abbey of Hautvillers, where a century earlier the Benedictine monk Dom Pérignon perfected the double fermentation of wine to create champagne. However, it was Jean-Rémy's friendship with Napoleon that helped the company attract a loyal international following.

Jean-Rémy became mayor of Epernay in 1802 and first met Napoleon two years later. Napoleon and his entourage were lavishly wined and dined by Jean-Rémy in newly built guest houses at the firm's address, 20 avenue de Champagne. Champagne historian Patrick Forbes wrote of the period: "everybody who was anybody in Europe was passing through the Champagne district en route from Paris to the Congress of Vienna and they all wanted to visit the celebrated champagne maker. . . . His 10 years in the Napoleonic limelight had made him the most famous wine-maker in the world and orders for his champagne began pouring in with such profusion that he hardly knew how to fill them." Later, before abdicating, Napoleon rewarded Jean-Rémy for his generosity by giving him his own Officer's cross of the Legion of Honor. Moët later dedicated its Brut Imperial in Napoleon's honor.

Jean-Rémy's customer list in the early 19th century had grown to include such famous people as Czar Alexander of Russia, Emperor Francis II of Austria (Napoleon's father-in-law), the Duke of Wellington, Madame de Staël, Queen Victoria, and the Prince Royal of Russia (later to become emperor of Germany). In 1832 Jean-Rémy retired and relinquished direction of the company to his son Victor and son-in-law Pierre-Gabriel Chandon de Briailles. To reflect the new partnership, the company's name was changed to Moët et Chandon.

Victor and Pierre expanded the firm's operations, and by 1879 Moët et Chandon dominated the Marne Valley with its introduction of more flavorful grapes from Cramant, Le Mesnil, Bouzy, Ay, and Verzenay. At this time Moët et Chandon employed close to 2000 people working as cellarmen, cork cutters, clerks, vineyard farmers, tinsmiths, needlewomen, basketmarkers, firemen, packers, wheelwrights, and stableboys. The company had even established a social security system for employees, which included free medical attention, housing assistance, pensions, maternity benefits, sick pay, and free legal aid.

Moët's average annual sales were believed to have been about 20,000 bottles during the 1820s. By 1872 that figure had risen to two million, and by 1880 it had reached 2.5 million. At the turn of the 20th century, Moët et Chandon's clientele remained primarily within the upper echelons of society.

During World War I, bombs demolished the offices and guesthouses where Napoleon had dined. Despite the destruction, Moët et Chandon reaffirmed its place in the market in the late 1920s by creating the Dom Pérignon brand of vintage champagne. Described by connoisseurs as the most perfect champagne available, Dom Pérignon also became the most expensive. The introduction of Dom Pérignon initiated a trend other champagne houses later followed: that of creating a premium brand, which placed other regular vintages second in status. Dom Pérignon, however, emerged as the most successful premium champagne.

Despite interruptions in its business during World War II, Moët et Chandon recovered quickly after the war, as a result of its prompt modernization of facilities. From the installation of new wine presses to a comprehensive system of work incentives, the goals of fairness and efficiency were emphasized in all aspects of production. Count Robert-Jean de Vogüé, one of France's most important wine buyers in the mid-1950s, led the company to even greater success. Under de Vogüé, Moët et Chandon experienced its most rapid period of growth to date, marked by its transformation from a family-owned venture into a Société Anonyme, or corporation. A series of acquisitions, mergers, and diversifications expanded the company's product line.

Moët et Chandon gained control of Ruinart Père et Fils (France's oldest champagne house and Moët's chief competitor) in 1962. The company acquired Mercier, another rival champagne house, in 1970, and soon thereafter purchased an interest in Parfums Christian Dior, marking the company's first undertaking outside the champagne business. Moët et Chandon later completed its takeover of Dior, whose perfume products include Miss Dior, Dioressence, and Eau Savage.

Moët et Chandon merged with Jas. Hennessy & Company, France's second largest cognac producer, in 1971. The new company, called Moët-Hennessy, enjoyed a broader financial base and was better able to stimulate the growth of its interests abroad. The merger of Moët and Hennessy was brought about mainly as a result of a 1927 statute which limited the Champagne growing region to 34,000 hectares. (The statute was intended to protect the quality of French champagne by discouraging price competition). While less than 25,000 hectares were under cultivation in 1970, Robert-Jean de Vogüé believed that growing demand for champagne would exhaust the supply of land by the year 2000. Until other regions suitable for champagne production could be found, de Vogüé decided that diversification through a merger with Hennessy would insure a stable future for Moët.

Moët-Hennessy established a firmer presence in the United States in 1973 when it opened the Domaine Chandon winery in Napa Valley, California, a location which proved ideal for the production of sparkling wines. The production of sparkling wines at Domaine Chandon grew dramatically and enabled Moët-Hennessy to expand in one of its most important foreign markets. The winery also reduced, somewhat, demand in North America for French champagne, whose production was still restricted by law.

Alain Chevalier, a protegé of de Vogüé, was chiefly responsible for the success of Domaine Chandon. He was named chief executive officer in the mid-1970s and began transforming Moët-Hennessy into a less conservative company with more aggressive marketing strategies. After de Vogüé's death in 1976, Chevalier continued the diversification program started by his predecessor.

In 1977 Moët-Hennessy purchased the Rozes companies in Portugal and France in an effort to raise demand for champagne. The following year, the company purchased Roc, a French cosmetics firm specializing in hypoallergenic make-up. The company also acquired Delbard, a French rose company, which was unable to continue financing the development of special new rose hybrids. The company also purchased Armstrong Nurseries of Ontario, California, the largest farmer of rosebushes in America. Moët-Hennessy was trying to apply rosebush cloning techniques to grape vines in order to produce better hybrids. As a result of these acquisitions, Moët-Hennessy became the world's leading producer of roses. Chevalier, who became president of Moët-Hennessy in 1982, told *Business Week*, ''Roses are a commodity. We can make them a brand name like champagne.'' Losses incurred by both Roc and Armstrong, however, depressed Moët-Hennessy's earnings. The introduction of a popular new perfume from Dior called Poison, however, helped offset those losses.

Continuing its expansion in the United States, Moët Hennessy acquired its American sales agent, Schieffelin & Company, one of the oldest wine and spirit distributors in North America. Moët-Hennessy was one of the first French companies to use European Currency Units (or ECUs), more stable in value against the dollar and therefore preferable for funding investments in the United States. By the late 1980s, Moët-Hennessy had yet to realize fully an $11.7 million investment in research and development made during 1983 and 1984.

The 1987 Merger

In June 1987, a $4 billion merger was effected between Louis Vuitton with Möet-Hennessy, which allowed Louis Vuitton to expand its investments in the luxury business, while saving Möet-Hennessy from the threat of takeover. Moreover, the merger respected the autonomy of each company over its own management and subsidiaries. As Möet-Hennessy was three times the size of Louis Vuitton, its president, Alain Chevalier, was named chairperson of the new holding company, Möet-Hennessy Louis Vuitton (LVMH), and Racamier became executive vice-president. Massive disagreements and feuding followed, however, as management at Louis Vuitton believed that Möet-Hennessy was trying to absorb its operations. The 60 percent ownership that

Racamier and the Vuitton family had held in Louis Vuitton became a mere 17 percent share of LVMH.

After several disputes and legal battles between Racamier and Chevalier over the running of the conglomerate, Racamier invited the young property developer and financial engineer Bernard Arnault to acquire stock in the company. Hoping to consolidate his position within LVMH with the help of Arnault, Racamier soon saw, however, that Arnault had ambitions of his own. With the help of the French investment bank Lazard Frères and the British liquor giant Guinness plc, Arnault secured a 45 percent controlling interest of LVMH stock for himself.

An 18-month legal battle ensued between Racamier and Arnault, after Chevalier had stepped down. Despite Louis Vuitton's strong performance, accounting for 32 percent of LVMH sales, Racamier could not hold onto his stake in LVMH against Arnault, who had the support of the Möet and Hennessy families. The courts eventually favored Arnault, and Racamier stepped down to create another luxury goods conglomerate, Orcofi, with the backing of such French investors as Paribas and L'Oréal. Arnault weeded out Vuitton's top executives and began to bring together his fragmented luxury empire.

Guinness plc had originally been brought into LVMH by Alain Chevalier, who had hoped to find an ally in his feuding with Racamier, in a deal to exchange one-fifth of the two companies' equity capital. Guinness then united with Arnault to control LVMH. In 1990, when Racamier left, Arnault increased his interest in Guinness from 12 to 24 percent, fueling rumors that Guinness would be his next target. Takeover speculation was also encouraged by the fact that Guinness directors had little power in LVMH, while Arnault had by far the largest shareholder vote in Guinness. However, Arnault's percentage in Guinness was proportionately equal to the 24 percent Guinness controlled of LVMH. In the early 1990s, Arnault controlled the world's largest luxury empire, with about $5 billion in worldwide sales. His holdings were structured as a pyramid of interconnected companies with control of LVMH central to his power, as it had a market capitalization of $10 billion in 1990.

The ubiquity of the Louis Vuitton monogram in the mid-1980s had damaged its reputation as a status symbol, and both profits and sales declined in the early 1990s. However, demand for luxury goods was expected to rise again, especially in Japan, Korea, and China, where buying power was growing rapidly. Still, the American market, which accounted for 17 percent of LVMH sales, was not expected to remain strong as an upheaval in upscale retail outlets was hurting sales. Arnault planned to create data processing and advertising sharing among his luxury retailers, including Louis Vuitton, Dior, Givenchy, Lacroix, and Loewe. Also in the early 1990s, Yves Carcelle, a former textile executive, became president of Louis Vuitton and broadened the range of products distributed to the company's 150 stores in an attempt to increase sales. Rampant counterfeiting, a difficult world economy, and its own flagging image were Louis Vuitton's nemeses in the early 1990s.

Ups and Downs in the Late 1990s

LVMH focused on growth and expansion in the mid-1990s and spent more than $3 billion during 1996 and 1997 on acqui-

sitions. In 1996 Arnault invested $2.6 billion for a 61 percent interest in DFS Group Ltd., a specialty retailer that catered to international travelers. The purchase included 180 boutiques in Asia, DFS's largest market. LVMH also invested in winery Chateau D'Yquem and purchased the fashion companies Céline and Loewe. The following year LVMH acquired Sephora, the French retailer of perfumes and beauty products, for $267 million, and invested in Douglas International, a German retailer of cosmetics and beauty goods.

Though LVMH diversified and grew its operations, many challenges arose in 1997 and 1998, and the company suffered from sagging sales. LVMH was hit hard by the economic crisis in Asia, a market that accounted for about half of LVMH's total sales. The company's investment in DFS was initially a disappointment; during the first half of 1997, DFS profits declined 50 percent, and during the first nine months of 1998, group sales for the retailing division that included DFS and Sephora declined 22 percent. In addition, several markets in which LVMH operated experienced difficulties. Increased competition and shrinking margins in the perfume industry, for example, posed a threat to LVMH's perfume operations. In 1998, sales of LVMH's fragrance and cosmetics division declined three percent. The wine and spirits segment was a slow-growing business, and LVMH's sales of cognac had the most trouble, primarily due to a poor market in Japan, which accounted for about 20 percent of cognac sales. Cognac shipments to Japan fell from 6.2 million bottles in 1996 to 5.0 million in 1997. In 1998, shipments fell even further, to 4.3 million bottles, and total LVMH cognac sales fell 13 percent. LVMH also spent much time and money attempting to thwart the merger of drink rivals Guinness plc and Grand Metropolitan plc, and this, coupled with the financial situation in Asia, led to a 38 percent drop in LVMH's share price between July and November. For the year ended December 31, 1998, LVMH reported total net income of FFr 3.45 billion, down from Ffr 4.87 billion in 1997.

Despite LVMH's struggles in the late 1990s, the company remained confident that what was being experienced was only a temporary slump. In LVMH's 1998 annual report, in fact, Arnault stated that "1998 was a year of consolidation and restructuring, aimed at laying strong foundations for resumed growth in 1999." Many industry analysts appeared to agree. Merrill Lynch Global Securities analyst Edouard de Boisgelin predicted in *Business Week* in late 1997, "Asia will come back. It will be a phenomenal source of growth for years to come." To prepare for the renewal in growth, LVMH continued to seek acquisitions. In 1998 the company purchased Le Bon Marché, an exclusive specialty retailer in Paris. LVMH also bought Marie-Jeanne Godard, a leading distributor of fragrances and cosmetics in France. Marie-Jeanne Godard offered 77 shops in mostly medium-sized cities in France, and six stores in other European nations. LVMH felt the Marie-Jeanne Godard acquisition was a perfect supplement to its Sephora stores, and during 1998 LVMH managed to convert 18 Marie-Jeanne Godard stores to the Sephora format. LVMH added to its champagne division in 1998 by acquiring the premium champagne brand Krug from Rémy Cointreau. The firm also upped its interest in Gucci, from 4.8 percent to 34.4 percent in early 1999, with the hopes of acquiring the company. French retailer Pinault Printemps Redoute SA beat out LVMH in mid-1999, however, by gaining a majority stake in Gucci.

A return to success came quickly, and 1999 was a strong year for LVMH. Asian economies were on the mend, helping to boost LVMH's sales activity. Between January and August, the company's share price rose 77 percent. For the first half of 1999, LVMH reported sales of EURO 3.59 billion, a 16 percent increase over the first half of 1998. Though DFS continued to rack up losses, the amounts were shrinking, and the company felt strongly that DFS had hit a turning point. Though cognac and spirits also continued to struggle, other divisions made up for the loss—operating profits in champagnes and wines rose 39 percent, perfumes and cosmetics increased 45 percent, and fashion and leather goods climbed 15 percent.

As sales increased, so did LVMH's acquisitions. The year 1999, in fact, marked the company's busiest year in terms of acquisitions. To expand its fragrance and cosmetics holdings, particularly in the United States, the company invested in four American beauty products companies: Hard Candy, which targeted female youths, Bliss Spa, BeneFit Cosmetics, and Make Up For Ever. LVMH also established a new watch and jewelry division, which included Tag Heuer AG, a Swiss watch maker in which LVMH gained a majority interest in September 1999. LVMH also acquired luxury watch makers Zenith, Ebel, and Chaumet.

LVMH also entered into some strategic partnerships to remain competitive in the marketplace. In October LVMH partnered with Italian fashion company Prada, usually a competitor, to acquire a majority stake in fashion design house Fendi, an Italian company operated by five sisters. Among LVMH's other 1999 acquisitions were a majority interest in Thomas Pink, a British shirt maker, and the purchase of Phillips Auctioneers. The company also increased its stake in Inter Parfums Inc., a perfume manufacturer, from 6.3 percent to 20 percent.

LVMH sales in 1999 reached a record Ffr 56 billion, up 23 percent over the previous year. The company appeared to have recovered indisputably and solidified its position as the leader of the luxury goods market. Champagne sales rose by more than 21 percent, and cognac sales fared better for the full year, with sales up by seven percent. By the end of 1999, the fashion and leather goods division consisted of 261 boutiques and 15 global stores. Louis Vuitton sales, which had suffered during 1998, did much better in 1999, particularly in the fourth quarter, during which sales increased 45 percent. Fragrance and cosmetics sales rose 24 percent, and sales in the selective retailing division increased 21 percent, indicating a more positive situation with DFS. Sephora stores expanded aggressively during 1999, and 127 new stores were opened that year. By year's end, there were 253 Sephora stores in Europe and 50 in the United States. Sephora enjoyed its first store opening in Tokyo and began selling products via its Web site as well. LVMH opened its U.S. headquarters in New York City in December 1999 and seemed poised to enter the 21st century full steam ahead.

Principal Subsidiaries

Möet-Hennessy; Louis Vuitton; Champagne Möet & Chandon; Champagne Mercier; Krug, Vins fins de Champagne S.A.; JA Hennessy & Co.; Thomas Hine & Cie; Edward Dillon & Co. Ltd. (Ireland); Louis Vuitton Malletier; Belle Jardiniere; Loewe SA (Spain); Berluti; Celine; Parfums Celine SNC; Kenzo; Givenchy SA; Christian Lacroix SNC; Parfums Christian Dior; Guerlain SA; Parfums Givenchy S.A.; DFS Group Ltd. (U.S.A.); Sephora Holding; Sephora France; Le Bon Marche Rive Gauche; Franck & Fils.

Principal Competitors

Chanel S.A.; Pinault Printemps Redoute SA; Gucci Group N.V.; The Seagram Company Ltd.

Further Reading

Berman, Phyllis, and Zina Sawaya, "Life Begins at 77," *Forbes,* May 27, 1991, pp. 160–67.

Carreyrou, John, "LVMH Seen Enduring Asia Storm," *Wall Street Journal Europe,* November 28, 1997, p. 12.

——, "LVMH Shares Soar 5.2%, But Analysts' Doubts Grow," *Wall Street Journal Europe,* October 13, 1998, p. 6.

Carson-Parker, John, "Dese, Doms and Diors," *Chief Executive,* November/December 1989, pp. 34–7.

Caulkin, Simon, "A Case of Incompatibility," *Management Today,* February 1993, p. 88.

Edmondson, Gail, Sharon Reier, and Julia Flynn, "LVMH: Life Isn't All Champagne and Caviar," *Business Week,* November 10, 1997, p. 108.

"Fashionable Takeover," *Economist,* July 16, 1988, p. 66.

"French Capital Markets: Bags of Bubbly," *Euromoney,* January 1987, p. 40.

"Guinness: Stout Fellows," *Economist,* June 9, 1990, pp.66, 68.

Kamm, Thomas, and Deborah Ball, "LVMH, Prada Ready Joint Bid to Win Control of Designer Fendi," *Wall Street Journal,* September 30, 1999, p. A21.

Kamm, Thomas, "Global Corporate Report: LVMH Expects Profit Growth to Top 20%," *Wall Street Journal Europe,* September 20, 1999, p. 7.

Lloyd, Simon, "Louis Vuitton Breezes Along In An Expansive Mood," *Business Review Weekly,* October 29, 1999, p. 50.

"LVMH's Big Shopper," *Business Week,* January 10, 2000, p. 67.

Monnin, Philippe, and Claude Vincent, *Guerre du luxe—L'affaire LVMH,* Paris: François Bourin, 1990.

Sebag-Montefiore, Hugh, *Kings on the Catwalk: The Louis Vuitton and Möet-Hennessy Affair,* London: Chapmans, 1992.

Toy, Stewart, "Avant le Deluge at Möet Hennessy Louis Vuitton," *Business Week,* April 24, 1989, p. 16.

——, "Meet Monsieur Luxury," *Business Week,* July 30, 1990, pp. 36–40.

Vuitton, Henry L., *La malle aux souvenirs,* Paris: Editions Mengès, 1984.

—Jennifer Kerns
—updated by Mariko Fujinaka

Mackie Designs Inc.

16220 Wood-Red Road, N.E.
Woodinville, Washington 98072
U.S.A.
Telephone: (425) 487-4333
Fax: (425) 487-4337
Web site: http://www.mackie.com

Public Company
Incorporated: 1988
Employees: 946
Sales: $153.8 million (1999)
Stock Exchanges: NASDAQ
Ticker Symbol: MKIE
NAIC: 33431 Audio and Video Equipment
   Manufacturing

Mackie Designs Inc. is a leading developer and manufacturer of professional audio equipment, whose products are used in sound recordings, live presentations, and in an array of applications, such as CD-ROM authoring, video production, and public address systems. Mackie Designs established its reputation by producing high-quality, mid-priced audio mixers. After several years of record sales, the company expanded into new areas of the market with products such as amplifiers, professional audio speakers, and digital audio mixers. Mackie Designs' equipment has served a range of consumers—from enthusiastic amateur musicians in home studios to pop music superstar Madonna. Its products are sold in over 1,000 retail outlets in 100 countries.

The Genesis of Mackie Designs: 1969–88

Although the company was not founded until 1988, Mackie Designs' roots date back to 1969, when Greg Mackie founded Technical Audio Products (TAPCO) with his partner Martin Schneider. A musician in a Seattle rock band, Mackie was frustrated by the poor quality of most audio mixers. Mixers are used to adjust the tone, volume, and quality of the different sound sources that make up recordings and soundtracks, and that are fed into the speakers at live performances. For instance, audio mixers allow bands to adjust the pitch and volume of the different instruments and/or vocals before broadcasting the audio signal through the speakers; likewise movie production companies will use mixers to adjust the levels of background music and dialogue in the making of soundtracks.

TAPCO's first success occurred with the release of its Model 6000 audio mixer, which was the first mixer designed specifically for the louder volumes required by rock bands. Musicians quickly embraced the equipment. Not only were TAPCO's mixers inexpensive and effective, they were also durable. Within a few years the company had made millions of dollars. When the firm began implementing stringent cost-cutting measures, however, Mackie parted ways with TAPCO in 1977.

Mackie launched his second business venture, Audio-Control, that same year. This new company soon established itself as a leading producer of stereo equalizers and analyzers for home consumers. Despite his good fortunes at Audio-Control, though, Mackie left the business in 1985 to pursue a new endeavor. The music industry had changed radically in the early 1980s, and Mackie identified a niche market that he believed could be profitably captured. A wave of technology had led to the proliferation of high-tech music equipment, with polyphonic keyboards, tone modules, and outdoor processors becoming the norm throughout the industry. Audio mixers—Mackie's former area of expertise—had changed little, though. The market for mixers was effectively split between high-end units used by professional recording studios and cheap, mass-produced mixers intended for more recreational consumers. As Mackie would later tell the *Seattle Post-Intelligencer*, "nobody took mixers seriously."

Early Success: 1988–91

Mackie formed Mackie Designs in 1988 to fill this need for high-quality, reasonably priced compact mixers. He initially ran his eponymous business from his three bedroom condominium in Edmonds, Washington. Using a closetful of spare parts from his prior companies, Mackie was determined to produce an inexpensive mixer that performed well. He stripped down mixing boards

Company Perspectives:

Through aggressive advertising and fanatical attention to quality and reliability, Mackie has developed a loyal customer base and a very positive image in the market place. The Company believes it can leverage the Mackie brand name to introduce products at a wider variety of price points within the professional audio equipment market. Over the past several years, Mackie has continually expanded its product lines to address the need for professional audio systems in existing and new markets.

to determine which components were essential for excellent sound, and which could be eliminated. For instance, he found that he needed microphones on only six of the mixer's channels, rather than on 16, as most other models. His efforts were a resounding success. According to *Forbes*, ''the result of this tinkering was a mixing board that cost much less and sounded much better than similar models from big competitors.''

The company's first product offering—the LM-1602—was an instant hit. In addition to providing an excellent product, Mackie Designs reaped the rewards of fortuitous timing. Few in the industry realized how popular a mid-level mixing board would prove to be. Although most considered sophisticated equipment such as mixing boards to be solely the purview of professionals, an array of consumers bought Mackie's product. Amateur musicians who had long wanted to build home recording studios drove early sales, but corporate video departments, churches, and schools were important customers as well.

Rapid Growth in the Early 1990s

Buoyed by this early success, Mackie Designs moved from its founder's home to a factory. In 1991, the company released the CR-1604 audio mixer, which would revolutionize the industry. (The CR-1604's effect on the music business would later be equated with the impact the computer had on publishing). Despite his company's flourishing sales, though, Greg Mackie adhered to his original strategy. Instead of moving outside the niche he had identified, Mackie stuck to mixers—and he made them well. For the most part, his products contained no proprietary technology. His formula was simply that ''he made [them] better, cheaper, and easier to use,'' a company spokesperson told the *Post-Intelligencer*. He kept his product line small, and reinvested a hefty percentage of his profits into production, purchasing top-of-the-line manufacturing equipment.

The company continued to introduce audio mixers that won it the loyalty of consumers worldwide. In 1993, Mackie Designs debuted its 8-Bus mixer consoles, which were designed specifically for multi-track recording and live sounds. Still a privately owned enterprise, Mackie Designs' annual growth rate was spectacular throughout the early 1990s, averaging well over 100 percent each year. Nevertheless, the company remained focused on its targeted sector. Over 48 percent of its sales in the mid-1990s were derived from one product (the CR-1604), and it had not strayed beyond audio mixers. As *Music Trades* succinctly explained on April 1, 1995, what made ''Mackie's

runaway success particularly noteworthy [was] the fact it was all accomplished with narrow product offerings.'' Revenues for 1994 topped $35.5 million, and the company had over 250 employees.

A Public Company: 1995

The year 1995 would prove to be a momentous one for Mackie Designs. The company sold its 100,000th mixer and moved into a new 89,000-square-foot manufacturing facility that was equipped with state-of-the-art production machines. By pioneering the implementation of semi-automated manufacturing in the audio industry, Mackie Designs was able to boost its production. It launched important product lines that year as well. In May, the SR 32-4, a 32 channel mixer designed exclusively for live sound applications, debuted. Soon after, the company introduced the SR-24-4 and the UltraMix Universal Automation System. As Mackie Designs' first software-based mixer, the UltraMix allowed the consumer to automate, store, and replicate over 136 channels. Despite its innovative nature, the UltraMix retailed for $2,795, which was well within the company's average typical product price range of $399–$5,000.

Mackie Designs' success brought with it unique challenges, as the company's profitability awakened its once dormant rivals. According to the *Post-Intelligencer*, Mackie Designs had ''so thoroughly defined and dominated the market that competitors [could] now promote their products as 'Mackie-style' mixers.'' Moreover, as its operations expanded, Mackie Designs had difficulty finding enough employees to fulfill its needs. To surmount these hurdles and to fuel future growth, Greg Mackie opted to take his company public. In August 1995, Mackie Designs made an initial public stock offering in hopes of raising over $25 million in operating capital. Mackie would continue to serve as president and chief executive officer.

Despite the company's entrance onto Wall Street, it vowed to keep alive the spirit of daring and innovation that had characterized the enterprise since its founding. ''We're definitely not your average pro audio company,'' Mackie Designs would crow in press releases. Mackie himself touted the ''combination of intense professionalism and sheer silliness that sets us apart from the big conglomerate companies.'' Whatever its attitude, the company closed 1995 with record sales of $63.9 million, a 28 percent increase from 1994 and three times 1993's results. Its employee rolls had grown to 320, and international sales had swelled during the year to account for 34 percent of total sales. Reflecting for *Music Trades* on the year's many developments, Mackie encapsulated his company's position: ''Our challenge is to keep investing in new products, production technology, and services to maintain our current position and set the stage for future growth.''

Expansion into New Sectors and New Markets: 1996 and Beyond

In keeping with his commitment to remain on the cutting edge of manufacturing, Mackie oversaw an 81,000-square-foot addition to the company's recently completed headquarters in February 1996. The expansion housed an advanced silk screening facility, a metal shop, and a training center, and allowed Mackie Designs to perform inhouse many of the services it had

once contracted out. Mackie's emphasis on infrastructure was logical. By vertically integrating its operations, Mackie could stay ahead of its competitors. Although the audio mixer market had grown more crowded, Mackie Designs had a head start on its rivals. Because it had channeled its capital into factory technology, it could keep its prices down—thereby underselling newer entrants to the audio mixer sector.

Following on the heels of its public stock offering, Mackie Designs charted a new course in 1996. Its footing was solid in the mid-price audio mixer market. Drawn by the potential to access a market more than twice the size of the $735 million audio mixer sector, Mackie Designs planned to expand its product offerings. The company slated a line of studio monitors (high-end speakers used in recording studios), amplifiers, and public address systems for release that year. Moreover, Mackie Designs announced that it would venture into the realm of higher-tech audio mixers with the planned debuts of digital mixers and desk-top mixing systems.

At a National Association of Music Merchants (NAMM) convention in July 1996, the company previewed its first-ever non-mixer product—the M-1200 premium power amplifier designed for private studios, theater/cinema broadcasts, and disk jockeys—as well as the Mackie 8200 Accuracy Active Studio Reference Monitor professional speakers. At the same time that it strove to break into new product spheres, Mackie Designs also hoped to enter the high-end market for audio mixers. In keeping with this shift, the company also unveiled its SR40-8 large-format mixing console, which, at $8,995, was priced well above any other audio mixer it had ever sold.

Mackie Designs appeared to be unstoppable. Its bold expansion plan coupled with its stellar past performance was impressive. In May 1996, *Inc. Magazine* ranked the company 78th on its list of the fastest-growing American companies. The magazine cited as particularly impressive Mackie Designs' 1,583% growth from 1991 to 1995, during which time its sales had risen from $3.8 million to over $64 million. Nevertheless, the company faltered toward the end of 1996. Delays in shipping its new products caused its earnings—and thus its stock price—to sink. After finally sending out its large format mixer boards and the power amplifiers in December 1996, company officials vowed that Mackie Designs' troubles were over. Even with late shipments eroding its profits, though, 1996 sales rose 15 percent to $73.2 million.

Undeterred, the company continued to stress product launches in 1997, devoting its largest budget ever to research and development. That year, Mackie Designs launched additional new products, beginning in January when it debuted its first digital product—the Digital 8-Bus Recording Console. By year-end, five new Mackie product lines had shipped, including power amplifiers and a studio monitor. Its breakneck pace of expansion depleted the company's resources. Though its sales and income grew during the year, the rate of increase had slowed markedly. Sales for 1997 were $74.7 million.

In 1998, Mackie Designs ventured into new territory once again when it made international expansion its top priority. Although international sales had always played a significant role in the company's earnings, in 1998 Mackie Designs aggressively sought to enter the global market for a wide range of audio equipment—not just audio mixers. In keeping with this strategy, the company acquired an Italian company, Radio Cine Forniture (RCF) S.p.A., as well as Fussion Audio of California. Since both RCF and Fussion were well-established high performance speaker companies, Mackie Designs planned to use them as a springboard to establish itself in sound delivery system markets across the globe. RCF also provided the company with its first international manufacturing facility. Upon completing the acquisition, Mackie took over speaker production at RCF's plant in Reggio Emilia, Italy. Furthermore, Mackie Designs began construction on its first overseas reload center in 1998. Its goal was to establish closer contact with its international customer base.

The company's strategy was overseen by Roy Wemyss, who had been named Mackie's chief operating officer in November 1996, and assumed the helm of the company in April 1999. As Wemyss would later explain in a press release, he had presided over the company during a tumultuous period when it grew from an "entity serving a single niche in the music market" to a "full-line, pro-quality music equipment business with substantial operations in both the United States and Europe." Despite these achievements, Mackie Designs continued to be hindered by slow product shipments. Although its 1998 sales grew to over $100.97 million, the company's net profit had lagged. Following these revelations, Wemyss resigned in October 1999.

Mackie Designs' blistering pace of expansion did not slow, however, as over 20 new products were launched in 1999 alone. Among its other offerings that year, the company released the CFX Series Compact Mixers and the C300 Sound Reinforcement Loudspeakers. Mackie also stepped up production at the manufacturing facility in Reggio Emilia, Italy. In February 2000, Mackie Designs acquired Eastern Acoustic Works (EAW), a leading designer and manufacturer of high-end professional loudspeakers, based in Whitinsville, Massachusetts. EAW's 1999 sales exceeded $40 million.

Despite the difficulties Mackie Designs experienced in the late 1990s in integrating its acquisitions and adjusting to manufacturing new products, the company's outlook in the early 21st century looked bright.

Principal Subsidiaries

Radio Cine Forniture S.p.A.; Fussion Audio; Eastern Acoustic Works Inc.

Principal Competitors

Alesis; Harman International Industries, Inc.; Koninklijke Philip Electronics N.V.; Pioneer Corporation; Sony Corporation; TEAC Corporation; Telex Communications, Inc.; Yamaha Corporation.

Further Reading

Karabell, Shellie, "Greg Mackie, President and CEO of Mackie Designs," *Dow Jones Investor Network*, April 16, 1996.

La Franco, Robert, "Trampler, Tramplee (Mackie Designs Inc.)," *Forbes*, November 18, 1996.

"Mackie Designs Expands with New 81,000 Square Foot Plant," *Music Trades*, February 1, 1996.

"Noteworthy Achievements of 1994," *Music Trades*, April 1, 1995.

Virgin, Bill, "Mackie Designs Discovers the Right Mix for Success," *Seattle Post-Intelligencer*, February 23, 1995.

——, "Mackie Plans to Add to Its Mix," *Seattle Post-Intelligencer*, April 26, 1996.

—Rebecca Stanfel

Mannatech Inc.

600 South Royal Lane, Suite 200
Coppell, Texas 75019
U.S.A.
Telephone: (972) 471-7400
Fax: (972) 471-7260
Web site: http://www.mannatech-inc.com

Public Company
Incorporated: 1993 as Emprise International, Inc.
Employees: 294
Sales: $179.7 million (1999)
Stock Exchanges: NASDAQ
Ticker Symbol: MTEX
NAIC: 422210 Botanicals Wholesaling

Mannatech Inc. is a relatively new but rapidly growing firm that uses multilevel marketing (MLM) to sell a variety of nutritional supplements in the form of capsules, drink powders, bars, and chewable products. Its patent-pending and proprietary Ambrotose complex, made with Aloe Vera juice and other ingredients, is found in almost all of its various products. Mannatech leaders state that their company joined the supplement industry due in part to the U.S. Congress passing a 1994 law that prevented overregulation by the Food and Drug Administration (FDA). Mannatech thus is part of a growing industry fueled by favorable laws, increasing consumer demand for natural health products, and more acceptance by health care professionals who during much of the 20th century considered supplements a form of quackery. Mannatech operates in the United States, Canada, Australia, and the United Kingdom.

Getting Started

Mannatech began as Emprise International, Inc., incorporated on November 4, 1993 under Texas laws. William C. Fioretti was its first president/CEO. His cousin Charles E. Fioretti was a founding director and vice-president. Samuel L. Caster was Emprise's third founding director. Other original officers were Secretary Gary L. Watson and Treasurer/Chief Financial Officer Patrick D. Cobb.

Sam Caster, in an interview in the January 1998 *Success* magazine, explained some of the background that led to the start of Emprise. In the 1980s he used multilevel marketing to sell insulation through a company called Eagle Shield. Although that firm's gross sales reached $120 million in its third year, the firm's products lacked patent protection and were not consumable, and thus sales quickly declined.

Caster then teamed up with biochemist William (Bill) Fioretti. The two looked into nutritional products, but decided that the timing was not right. "Instead, we decided to go into the pharmaceuticals business and actually started making biotech products for the agriculture industry." But then a new federal law changed everything.

"We started the company," said Sam Caster in the *Mannatech Magazine* (1998, volume 3, number 1), "as a result of Congress' passage of the Dietary Supplement Health and Education Act." That 1994 law, sponsored by Utah Senator Orrin Hatch, prevented the FDA from closely regulating vitamins and nutritional supplements like it regulated drugs. Many supplement and natural products firms had lobbied for passage of that law, a major victory for the industry.

"The real key to this new law was that if you were willing to do research on a particular functioning component of any food product, that information could then be reported in what's known as a peer-review journal," said Caster in *Success*. "And that offered a huge, huge, opportunity to reenter the nutrition industry."

Caster and Fioretti hired scientists from three pharmaceutical firms, including Carrington Laboratories of Dallas. In 1994 Emprise began selling products made with Manapol, a patented stabilized form of Aloe Vera made by Carrington. Aloe Vera was well known for its healing and health benefits, but under most manufacturing conditions the fresh plant product lost its usefulness.

In 1994 Emprise introduced the following products: ManAloe, Plus caplets, MVP, Sport capsules, PhytAloe, Firm, and Naturalizer (later renamed Ambroderm). Based on the sale of those products, in 1994, the company's first full year in business, its net sales were $8.4 million, with a net loss of $342,000.

Expansion in the Mid-1990s

In 1995 the company introduced three new products: Emprizone, EmPact sports drink, and chewable PhytoBears, a more nutritious version of the popular Gummi Bears candy. A major step occurred in 1996 when the firm introduced its patent-pending product Ambrotose, described in company literature as "naturally occuring [sic] plant polysaccharides including freeze-dried Aloe Vera Gel Extract-Manapol powder." From that point, most company products contained Ambrotose. Other new products in 1996 were Profile 1, Profile 2, Profile 3 vitamins and minerals, Sport with Ambrotose, and Mannatonin tablets made with Manapol and melatonin.

Emprise officials in 1995 also began the process of changing the company's name to Mannatech Incorporated. By early 1996 the transition was completed.

With new products and more distributors signed up, the company's net sales in 1995 increased to $32.1 million, and Emprise gained a net income of $2.3 million. In 1996 sales jumped to $86.3 million with net income of $7.2 million. In 1996 the American Naturopathic Medical Association honored Mannatech with the Biochemistry Discovery of the Year Award, and the NBC *Today Show* highlighted the firm's PhytoBears chewable supplements as one of the top products of 1996. Other positive publicity came when USA Track & Field chose Mannatech to supply supplements to the American athletes participating in the 2000 Olympics.

In March 1997 Mannatech moved to its new 110,000-square-foot headquarters in Coppell, Texas, and the following January its new distribution center opened nearby, capable of shipping 40,000 orders daily. To plan for future growth, the company also teamed up with "an international distribution partner that has over 450 distribution centers worldwide," according to *Mannatech Magazine.*

Mannatech in 1997 introduced three new products (Bulk Ambrotose, Bulk EmPact, and MannaCleanse), and its net sales reached $150.6 million, with a net 1997 income of $10.6 million.

Leading Distributors in the Middle to Late 1990s

Mannatech's growth came not only from the corporation's efforts but also its independent self-employed distributors,

called "Associates" by the company. One leading associate was Vivian Saccucci, a homemaker and mother of four who daily milked 46 cows and helped her husband run a remote Canadian dairy farm before joining Mannatech. By 1997 she was one of the firm's top 100 income earners, which allowed her and her husband to sell their dairy in 1998.

Gene and Lora Enabnit owned four women's clothing stores in Iowa before becoming Mannatech associates. Although they earlier had a poor experience with another MLM firm, in 1995 they became Mannatech associates. By 1997 they had been honored as Mannatech's Distributor of the Year and had made almost $1 million in Mannatech, which allowed them to sell their stores and buy a farm. Their purpose was not to grow crops but to build memories and enjoy the rural lifestyle, including Gene's prized restored tractors and other farm equipment. "Mannatech has made it possible for us to spend so much time and share so much with our children and their families," said Gene in a 1997 *Mannatech Magazine,* adding "How can you put a price on that?"

A third Mannatech distributorship was started by Joyce Oliveto in 1996. She started distributing Mannatech products to clients at her Brighton, Michigan healing center called Health Horizons. By the end of her first year with Mannatech, Oliveto made $30,000 a month. In 1998 she and her new husband used Mannatech profits to buy an 80-acre children's camp to serve needy Detroit children.

To facilitate communication between the corporation and its distributors, in October 1996 Mannatech associates elected their first Associate Advisory Council, comprised of six women and six men. By that time the number of Associates had reached more than 152,000, so a formal structure was needed to build bridges and solve problems.

Growth and Challenges in the Late 1990s and Beyond

To expand internationally, in 1998 Mannatech installed a new mainframe computer system that was needed to create a seamless global commission system, in which distributors would be paid commissions for their integrated downlines, instead of being paid separate commissions for sales in different nations.

In fall 1998 Mannatech began recruiting new distributors and shipping products in Australia, its first market outside North America. The company's six-person staff worked in an office in Hombush, a Sydney suburb. The following spring, on April 30, 1999 Board Chairman Charles Fioretti and President Sam Caster wrote to Mannatech shareholders as follows: "Australia has responded enthusiastically to our products as well as to our Mannatech culture, as sales there have far exceeded our expectations."

New Mannatech products introduced in 1998 included protein and carbohydrate versions of its MannaBar nutritional bars, each with the company's recommended daily minimum amount of Ambrotose, PhytAloe, and Plus. A Canadian company headed by lawyer Saul Katz helped develop MannaBars and other nutrition bars in cooperation with the University of Alberta Hospital, which received royalties on the sale of MannaBars. Mannatech in 1998 also introduced Manna-C capsules

```
┌─────────────────────────────────────────────┐
│              Key Dates:                      │
│                                              │
│ 1993:  Emprise International, Inc. is incor- │
│        porated under Texas law on November 4.│
│ 1994:  Company begins selling products with  │
│        Manapol powder made by Carrington     │
│        Laboratories.                         │
│ 1996:  Emprise changes name to Mannatech     │
│        Incorporated; company's independent   │
│        associates elect the first Associate  │
│        Advisory Council; firm begins opera-  │
│        tions in Canada.                      │
│ 1998:  Mannatech's new distribution center   │
│        is opened in Coppell, Texas; company  │
│        begins Australian operations in the   │
│        fall.                                 │
│ 1999:  Mannatech goes public.                │
│ 2000:  Expansion into Japan is planned; firm │
│        renews its contract with Carrington   │
│        Laboratories, the producer of Manapol │
│        powder.                               │
└─────────────────────────────────────────────┘
```

with Ambrotose and herbs to provide Vitamin C and other nutrients, Bulk PhytAloe, and Ambrostart drink powder with Ambrotose and Bulk PhytAloe to start the day.

Mannatech in February 1999 became a public corporation with the initial public offering (IPO) of its common stock traded on the Nasdaq National Market. Underwriters for the Mannatech IPO were Hilliard Lyonds; NationsBanc Montgomery Securities; and Piper Jaffray. Mannatech stock prices increased 181 percent to close at $22.50 per share after its first day of trading. The next day the stock reached $44.50 per share.

Some analysts thought that part of that huge stock gain was probably due to Mannatech Associates investing in the company, but confusion accounted for the rest of the rapid gain. "I think people thought this was an Internet or a technology company: Mann-A-TECH," said Joe Hammer of Adams, Harkness & Hill in the February 22, 1999 issue of the *Investment Dealers' Digest.* In any case, Mannatech's stock performance declined during the rest of 1999 and early 2000, falling below $5 per share.

The firm's IPO raised funds needed for international expansion. In November 1999 Mannatech began operations in the United Kingdom by opening an office in the city of Basingstoke. In early 2000 President Mike Steinle and other leaders of Mannatech Limited, the U.K. subsidiary of Mannatech Incorporated, held meetings in England, Scotland, and Northern Ireland. The country's first national convention was held in Nottingham on February 5, 2000, featuring Mannatech Incorporated President Sam Caster.

To support such international expansion, in late 1999 Mannatech hired Prestige International to aid communication between Mannatech employees, sales associates, and customers. Prestige operated a "global call center network bridging the gap between companies and consumers," according to a December 22, 1999 *Business Wire.* Prestige staff used 13 languages and telephones, fax, mail, and e-mail to serve its clients such as Mannatech.

Mannatech faced various legal and public relations challenges in the late 1990s. In February 1997 it entered into a consent decree with the state of Michigan in which the company agreed to monitor product purchases by its associates to prevent any coerced sales or stockpiled inventories.

Stephen Barrett, M.D. and chairman of Quackwatch Inc., asked, "Why are they telling consumers one thing and investors another?" He was referring to Mannatech telling consumers that its supplements were safe and effective but also telling investors in a stock prospectus that it was not sure if its products were safe or effective, according to the May 1999 *National Council for Reliable Health Information Newsletter.* The National Council Against Health Fraud was critical of what it considered Mannatech's deceptive descriptions of Manapol.

Several newspaper articles in 1999 covered a serious problem involving Mannatech, the University of California at Irvine, and a researcher named Darryl See, M.D. who had joined the UC Irvine faculty in 1992. In 1997 See's wife became a Mannatech distributor, and the following year he began speaking at Mannatech sales meetings. Mannatech also paid him $10,000 a month as a nutritional consultant. In 1998 See resigned from UC Irvine after admitting not following university research rules. In 1999 he published an article in the *Journal of the American Nutraceutical Association,* however, that caused concern for both the university and Mannatech. UC Irvine said his research was not funded, as See claimed, by a grant from the National Institutes of Health (NIH).

In August 1999 Mannatech sued See in the U.S. District Court in Dallas, alleging that he misled the company when he claimed that the study had been funded by the NIH and conducted under the auspices of the UC Irvine. See's article claimed that Mannatech supplements ranked as one of the top five out of 196 tested supplements. He also claimed that Mannatech products were effective against AIDS and cancer. Mannatech distributors used See's research to support their sales efforts and illustrate the positive effects of its glyconutritional products. Mannatech thus sued See for fraud, misrepresentation, and breach of contract. This story was covered on the Web page of MLM Watch (www.mlmwatch.org).

The See brouhaha illustrated important issues involving scientific research and commercial interests. Perhaps most important was the issue of conflict-of-interest, since See had financial incentives to demonstrate the value of Mannatech supplements. In the 1990s many supplement firms used scientists to back their efforts. How unbiased were they? Scientific fraud in several fields, not just nutrition, received more press coverage in the 1990s, aiding those who questioned the limits of science. In any case, Mannatech in 2000 continued to operate from its Texas base as it weathered the storm over the research by its former consultant.

Principal Subsidiaries

Mannatech Limited; Mannatech Foreign Sales Corporation; Internet Health Group; Mannatech Australia Pty, Limited.

Principal Competitors

General Nutrition Companies, Inc.; Herbalife International, Inc.; Nu Skin Enterprises, Inc.; Rexall Showcase International;

Rexall Sundown; Solgar Vitamin and Herb Company, Inc.; Twinlab Corporation; Weider Nutrition International, Inc.; Amway Corporation; Body Wise International, Inc.; Enrich International, Inc.; ENVION International; Melaleuca, Inc.; Forever Living Products, Inc.

Further Reading

Alexander, Karen, "UCI Probes Research of Ex-Professor," *Los Angeles Times* (Orange County edition, Record edition), August 5, 1999, p. 1.

——, "Willing Subjects Donated Blood, Researcher Says; Medicine: Dr. Darryl See Reveals Source Amid a UCI Inquiry into Possible Breaches of Protocol in His Study," *Los Angeles Times* (Orange County edition, Record edition), September 6, 1999, p. 7.

"Carrington and Mannatech Sign Two-Year Extension of Manapol(R) Purchase Agreement," *PR Newswire,* February 10, 2000, p. 7384.

Evans, David, "Mannatech Tells Consumers & Investors Different Tales," *National Council for Reliable Health Information Newsletter,* May 1999, p. 3.

"Ex-UCI Professor Sued: Firm Alleges Data Falsified," *Los Angeles Times* (Orange County edition, Record edition), August 26, 1999, p. 7.

Fogg, John Milton, "Err Quality," *Success,* January 1998, pp. 72–74.

Jenkin, Denise, investigative series on supplements, alternative medicine, and Mannatech, *Oakland Press* (Pontiac, Mich.), January 10–13, 21, 1999 and June 13–15, 1999.

Lacey, Steve, and Brian Garrity, "In Mannatech IPO, Tech Craze Formally Surpasses Tulips," *Investment Dealers' Digest,* February 22, 1999, pp. 6–7.

"Mannatech," *National Council Against Health Fraud Newsletter,* May–June 1996, p. 2.

"Mannatech Ltd. Schedules Meetings in England, Scotland and Northern Ireland," *Business Wire,* January 20, 2000.

Ornstein, Charles, "Coppell, Texas, Nutritional Supplements Firm Sees Stock Soar Since IPO," *Knight-Ridder/Tribune Business News,* February 18, 1999, p. OKRB9904903F.

"'Outsource': Password to Global Consumer Marketplace; Prestige International Launches Worldwide Multilingual Customer Care Network," *Business Wire,* December 22, 1999.

Prial, Dunstan, "IPO Outlook: Stock Mixup Is Online Peril," *Wall Street Journal* (Eastern edition), February 22, 1999, p. C18.

Sayewitz, Ronni, "Mannatech Launching $110M IPO for Multilevel Marketing Business," *Dallas Business Journal,* April 17, 1998, p. 3.

"Science Versus Antiscience?," *Scientific American,* January 1997, pp. 96–97.

Verone, Peg, "Two Weeks To Change a Life," *Network Marketing Lifestyles,* December 1999, p. 117.

Weil, Jonathan, "Mannatech, A Hot IPO Last Week, Now Leaves Some Analysts Cold," *Wall Street Journal* (Eastern edition), February 24, 1999, p. T2.

—David M. Walden

Marconi plc

One Bruton Street
London W1X 8AQ
United Kingdom
Telephone: +44 (0) 20 7493 8484
Fax: +44 (0) 20 7493 1974
Web site: http://www.marconi.com

Public Company
Incorporated: 1886 as The General Electric Apparatus Co.
Employees: 84,000
Sales: £7.62 billion pounds ($12.29 billion) (1999)
Stock Exchanges: London
Ticker Symbol: MNI
NAIC: 334210 Telephone Apparatus Manufacturing;
    334220 Radio and Television Broadcasting and
    Wireless Equipment Manufacturing; 334419 Other
    Electronic Component Manufacturing; 513390 Other
    Telecommunications

The British company Marconi plc had been known as The General Electric Co. Ltd. (GEC) for more than 100 years before changing its name and focus in 1999. During the 20th century it grew through acquisitions to become England's leading electrical company and one of Europe's top defense electronics contractors. In the late 1990s the company divested many of its traditional businesses, culminating in the $12 billion sale of its defense electronics business to British Aerospace in 1999. At the same time it began redefining itself as an information technology (IT) company with two major acquisitions, Reltec and Fore Systems, that positioned the company to compete in the rapidly changing telecommunications industry.

19th-century Origins

Marconi's immediate predecessor, GEC, had its origins in G. Binswanger and Company, an electrical goods wholesaler established in London during the 1880s by a German immigrant named Gustav Binswanger (later changed to Byng). In 1886 Byng was joined by another German immigrant, Hugo Hirst (later Lord Hirst), who had experience with several applications of the new electrical power; he had driven an electrically powered boat on the River Thames, ridden on an electric cycle, and even developed an electric-powered dog cart for an Indian rajah. The men changed the company's name to The General Electric Apparatus Company and became wholesalers of electric products, with an eye toward someday becoming manufacturers of electric products. The following year, they issued the first electrical catalog of its kind.

In 1888 the firm acquired its first factory, in Manchester, to manufacture telephones, electric bells, ceiling roses, and switches. In 1889 The General Electric Co. Ltd. was formed as a private company with its main office in Queen Victoria Street, London. GEC developed the use of china as an insulating material in switches and began manufacturing light bulbs in 1893. Osram, a separate company, was set up in 1909 for the manufacture of lamps.

Expansion under Lord Hirst: 1900–40s

In 1900 GEC was incorporated as a public limited company. There was a growing demand for lamps and lighting equipment, and the company expanded in England and abroad, establishing branches in Europe, Japan, Australia, South Africa, and India, with substantial export trade to South America. In 1902 GEC built its first factory, the Witton Engineering Works, near Birmingham.

During this time, GEC operated with Byng as chairman and Hirst as managing director. When Byng died in 1910, Hirst took full control as chairman and managing director until his death in 1943. Under his direction GEC became one of the major companies in the United Kingdom.

During World War I GEC produced radios, signaling lamps, and arc lamp carbons for the war effort. As a result of the heightened demand, GEC's workforce swelled to over 15,000, and the company became a major player in the electrical industry. Between the two wars GEC expanded to become an international corporation as well as a national institution in England. In 1918 GEC took over Fraser & Chalmers, a heavy engineering firm, and the following year it established Britain's first separate

Company Perspectives:

If you could build a communications and data networking company with the ideal credentials for the Internet Age, what would it look like? It would be built on a solid foundation—a legacy of innovative thinking and individual accomplishment. It would lead the industry in Internet Age technology: optical networking, transmission and next-generation access for the New Public Network, and enterprise switching and e-commerce solutions for the Modern Enterprise. And it would have a service culture so strong that nothing would stand in the way of delivering on a commitment to a customer. It's here. Marconi plc. The legacy of Marconi, the father of modern communications. The power of Marconi Communications' and Fore Systems' technology. And the commitment to absolute reliability that thousands of customers worldwide already appreciate.

industrial research laboratories at Wembley, headed by Sir J.J. Thompson, a Nobel Prize-winning physicist. In 1921 the company moved its headquarters to Kingsway, London. The company kept busy during the decade supplying electrical equipment for use in Britain's National Grid, a network of power-generation stations built to meet the growing industrial and residential demand for electric power. In the 1930s, GEC began early research into television technology.

GEC grew through acquisitions, joint ventures, and expanding both its manufacturing operations overseas and its domestic branch network. The company was a major supplier of electrical and engineering products during World War II. Major contributions included the development of the cavity magnetron for radar, advances in communications technology, and the ongoing mass production of lamps and lighting equipment.

GEC's growth slowed following World War II. In spite of growing demand for electrical consumer goods and large investments in heavy engineering and nuclear power, GEC's profits began to fall for the first time, due to increasing competition and internal disorganization.

The Weinstock Era: 1960–90s

In 1961 GEC took over Radio and Allied Industries, which manufactured radio and television sets. The acquisition brought Arnold Weinstock to GEC, and he took over as managing director in 1963. GEC was having trouble meeting its payroll at the time, so Weinstock worked to reduce the firm's payroll and move the company's main office from Kingsway to smaller quarters at Stanhope Gate. While implementing this program of cutbacks, Weinstock also rejuvenated GEC through a series of mergers. In 1967 GEC acquired Associated Electrical Industries (AEI), which included Metropolitan-Vickers, BTH, Edison Swan, Siemens Bros., Hotpoint, and W.T. Henley. In 1968 GEC merged with English Electric, which included Elliott Bros., The Marconi Co., Ruston and Hornsby, Stephenson, Hawthorn & Vulcan Foundry, Willans and Robinson, and Dick Kerr. These companies were primarily electronics and electrical equipment manufacturers.

GEC continued to expand under Weinstock in the 1970s with the acquisition of Yarrow Shipbuilders in 1974 and Avery in 1979. In the late 1970s GEC won several major government contracts in defense and the public sector from the British Ministry of Defense, British Rail, the Central Electricity Generating Board, British Telecom, and local government. These defense, telecommunications, and power generation contracts helped keep GEC's plants running at full capacity and attracted investors.

In the mid-1980s GEC had annual sales equal to $8.7 billion, the equivalent of $2 billion in cash, and very little debt. All told, the company had about $7 billion in assets. GEC built up its cash reserve under Weinstock by keeping its dividend payouts low compared to other electrical companies. From 1975 to 1985 the company had a higher return on equity than the American General Electric Co. or Westinghouse. It also spent a greater percentage of its revenues on research and development.

For fiscal 1985 (ending March 31) GEC turned a profit worth $590 million. About half of the firm's revenues came from electronics, electrical equipment, and telecommunications. The other half came largely from power generation and automation equipment. With its huge cash reserves, the firm was positioned to make more acquisitions.

In 1985 GEC made a hostile $1.75 billion bid for Plessey Company, plc. Plessey resisted the takeover, claiming the merger would be anticompetitive. In August 1986 the British government's Monopolies and Mergers Commission ruled the takeover would be against public interest because it would reduce competition. Still, the two companies were both involved in System X public switches and had been amenable to the idea of combining these activities. Their main customer in this area was British Telecommunications plc. By 1988 the two companies had formed GPT, a joint venture the primary business of which was to supply British Telecom with System X switches.

GEC's Avionics subsidiary accounted for about 17 percent of the firm's revenues in the mid-1980s. In 1986 it lost a British government contract to Boeing for early-warning aircraft (AWAC) and had to terminate its nine-year, $1.33 billion Nimrod program.

In 1987 GEC and Simon Engineering plc entered into a joint venture to manufacture programmable logic controllers for industrial applications in the Soviet Union. Simon would build the plant in the Soviet Union, while GEC would provide technical expertise to product the controllers. The contract was valued at $480 million.

Also during this time, GEC formed a joint venture with two American companies—General Electric Co. and Bendix Corp.—to produce advanced turbines for aerospace engines and industrial machinery. GEC's Ruston Gas Turbines subsidiary had previously only manufactured turbines for industrial applications, notably for the North Sea oilfields.

GEC was broadly diversified in defense and non-defense markets, with defense accounting for 43 percent of the firm's 1987 revenues. The loss of the AWAC contract in 1986 to Boeing was a major blow to the firm, but GEC remained the largest supplier of defense electronics to the British Ministry of

Key Dates:

1886: The General Electric Apparatus Company is founded by Gustav Binswanger (later Byng) and Hugo Hirst.

1889: The General Electric Co. Ltd. (GEC) is formed as a private limited company in London.

1900: GEC is incorporated as a public limited company.

1910: Hugo Hirst, later Lord Hirst, takes control of the company as chairman and managing director, following Byng's death.

1919: GEC establishes Britain's first separate industrial research laboratories at Wembley.

1961: GEC takes over Radio and Allied Industries, which manufactures radio and television sets.

1963: Arnold Weinstock, later Lord Weinstock, becomes managing director.

1967: GEC acquires Associated Electrical Industries.

1968: GEC merges with English Electric.

1988: GEC and Plessey Co. plc form a telecommunications joint venture, GPT.

1989: GEC and Siemens jointly acquire the assets of Plessey Co.; GEC and France's Compagnie General D'Electricitie (CGE) form the joint venture GEC Alsthom.

1996: Lord Weinstock retires; George Simpson becomes managing director.

1999: GEC sells its defense electronics business to British Aerospace and acquires two U.S. telecommunications companies, changing its name to Marconi plc.

Defense in 1988. Most of the firm's defense operations were organized under a subsidiary called GEC Marconi Ltd. GEC also owned a controlling interest in Canadian Marconi, which made communications equipment, avionics, and microelectronic components. During 1988 GEC sold Cincinnati Electronics to Canadian Marconi to better integrate Marconi's North American operations. Cincinnati Electronic specialized in tactical communications systems and jammers and was a leading developer of manpack transceivers, antennae, and intercommunication sets. It also made the infrared receiving sets used on aircraft to warn of missile launches and to initiate appropriate countermeasures.

In the area of defense GEC was also a major developer and producer of air, naval, and surface radar. GEC Avionics was a leading supplier of various systems and displays, and in 1987 acquired the flight control division of Lear Siegler as well as Developmental Sciences Corp., which manufactured remotely piloted vehicles. Other units of GEC were actively involved in the European fighter aircraft program.

Toward the end of 1988 GEC teamed with Germany's Siemens AG to try to purchase Plessey for the equivalent of $3.1 billion. Although Plessey rejected the offer, consolidation in the European central office switch market appeared inevitable, given the high cost of developing next-generation switches and the coming 1992 unification of the European marketplace. In January 1989 the U.S. Department of Defense, in response to

concerns expressed by Plessey, ruled that the proposed hostile takeover was not a risk to national security. However, the European Economic Commission (EEC) and the British government decided to investigate the proposed merger as possibly anticompetitive. As part of its defense, Plessey tried to buy out GEC's interest in their cooperative telecommunications venture GPT, claiming that by taking on Siemens as a partner GEC was violating the terms of the GPT venture. Meanwhile, a consortium of other companies, calling itself Metsun Ltd., announced it would try to take over GEC. However, Metsun proved short-lived and quickly cancelled its plans to purchase GEC.

In other joint ventures, GEC and Compagnie General D'Electricitie (CGE) formed the joint venture GEC Alsthom. The main purpose of the venture was to combine the two companies' power generation, electricity distribution transmission, and rail transport activities to create a stronger European player in international markets.

Meanwhile, GEC announced it would enter into joint ventures with the General Electric Co. (GE) in the areas of power engineering, consumer products (mainly domestic appliances), medical equipment, and electrical distribution worth a total of $2.6 billion. GE planned to invest $580 million to establish cooperative manufacturing ventures with GEC. Once the joint ventures with GE were operational, about 40 percent of GEC's revenues would come from joint ventures. The cooperative venture was perceived as symptomatic of a global consolidation taking place among manufacturers of power generation and distribution equipment. GE had been teamed with Metsun, but dropped out to join forces with GEC.

GEC also entered into another joint venture with France's Compagnie Generale d'Electricite (CGE) involving industrial automation and controls that would have annual sales of more than $500 million worldwide. GEC placed great importance on its cooperative ventures with CGE of France and GE of the United States to position the company for the changing markets of the 1990s.

In April the EEC and the British government gave GEC and Siemens the go-ahead to acquire Plessey. In doing so, the Monopolies and Mergers Commission set three conditions. First, GEC had to give competitors the technology to make a new communications system called JTIDS, also made by Plessey. Second, the new company must be managed so as not to compromise British national security. Third, GEC could not have any part of Plessey's radar, communications, and traffic-control businesses, all of which would go to Siemens.

The takeover of Plessey was further delayed by negotiations. In August Siemens and GEC increased their offer and made a final bid of $3.3 billion for Plessey. Under the revised merger plan, outside of North America GEC would wholly own Plessey's naval systems and avionics businesses as well as its cryptography operations, while Siemens would take over Plessey's radar and defense systems. Within North America, GEC would wholly own Sippican Inc. and Leigh Instruments Ltd. in Canada and would take 75 percent of Plessey Electronic Systems Corp. in the United States. The GPT telecommunications venture was split 40–60 between Siemens and GEC, with GEC having management control. However, Plessey continued to defend itself from the hostile takeover by entering several new markets, including computers, telecommunications, and automotive electronics. Finally, on September 8, 1989, Siemens and GEC completed their takeover of Plessey.

For fiscal 1989 ending March 31, GEC reported earnings of $1.24 billion, up 13 percent over 1988, on sales of $10.39 billion, up 16 percent over 1988. The increases were attributed to acquisitions and strong performance in electronic systems and power systems. Telecommunications profits fell on growing sales due to declining margins.

During the 1990s GEC began moving away from the domestic electrical goods market and into electronics and modern technology, particularly in the defense sector. In 1990 GEC acquired parts of Ferranti, including its radar business and other gear for military aircraft. The acquisition made GEC one of Europe's main defense-electronics companies. Ferranti had recently won the highly prized $3.2 billion contract to design the radar for Europe's new fighter aircraft.

As part of its acquisition of Plessey, GEC merged its Marconi Electronic Devices unit with Plessey Semiconductors to create GEC Plessey Semiconductors. The new unit was expected to have 1990 sales of $200 million. By 1991 GEC was the fifth largest electronics firm in Europe. GEC's vision for the 1990s, as articulated by Arnold Weinstock, was to become a world force in semiconductors and telecommunications. In 1992 a single European market became a reality.

In 1994 GEC entered into a joint venture with Italian state-owned Finmeccanica SpA of Rome for civil and military radio communications, electronics, and telematic products. In 1995 GEC acquired Vickers Shipbuilding and Engineering Ltd., and Lord Weinstock retired to become chairman emeritus the following year. Under his leadership GEC had become the undisputed leader of the British electrical industry and a top European defense-electronics contractor.

Reorganization under Lord Simpson: 1995–99

In 1996, Lord George Simpson took over as managing director, bringing with him a wave of new corporate management. He initiated a major reorganization aimed at focusing the company on its key business strengths and on high-growth, high-technology business areas. Several subsidiaries were sold off, including Express Lifts, Satchwell Controls, AB Dick, the Wire and Cables Group, Marconi Instruments, and GEC Plessey Semiconductors. New acquisitions and alliances were planned as the company sought to reduce its dependence on joint ventures and focus on defense, telecommunications, and industrial electronics.

In February 1998 the firm's head office moved to One Bruton Street, London. The company eliminated some of its dependence on joint ventures by floating GEC Alstom, a $6.8 billion rail-and-power venture with Alcatel Alsthom of France, as a public company and buying Siemens' 40 percent stake in GPT. In June GEC enhanced its defense holdings by acquiring the U.S. defense-electronics company Tracor for $1.4 billion. This became part of Marconi North America, a Marconi Electronic Systems company.

Major Shifts: 1999 and Beyond

Following an announcement in early 1999 of a proposed merger of GEC's defense electronics business, Marconi Electronic Systems, with British Aerospace, GEC sold Marconi Electronic Systems to British Aerospace for $12 billion, mostly in stock. Simpson planned to use GEC's estimated $4.5 billion in cash to reposition GEC as a high-tech, high-growth, and high-margin company. GEC's remaining businesses would be in telecommunications, high technology, and a variety of industrial holdings.

The company's major divisions would be Marconi Communications, which made advanced telecommunications equipment for voice and data transmission, and Marconi Systems, which consisted of three U.S. high-tech companies: Picker, renamed Medical Systems, was a world leader in medical imaging; Gilbarco, renamed Commerce Systems, was a leading supplier of petroleum retailing equipment and systems; and Videojet, renamed Data Systems, produced coding and tracking systems for a variety of markets. Marconi Communications would account for about half of GEC's estimated $6 billion in revenues.

In April 1999 GEC acquired Reltec, a U.S. telecommunications network products company, for $2.1 billion, and announced plans to acquire Fore Systems, a U.S. Internet switching and networking equipment company, for $4.5 billion. Reltec was a world leader in next-generation broadband access equipment, and FORE Systems, Inc. reportedly made one of the best switches in the world for Internet traffic. With these two major acquisitions, GEC was confident it had the technology it needed to compete in the rapidly changing telecommunications industry, which was being transformed by the growth of the Internet and the growing volume of data transmissions. By the end of 1999 Fore System's name had been changed to Marconi Communications and its top management replaced. The Pittsburgh firm would become Marconi plc's North American headquarters.

Effective December 1, 1999, GEC was renamed Marconi plc. The company relisted itself as an IT company on the London stock exchange and planned to pursue a listing on the NASDAQ during 2000. The company launched a new print and television advertising campaign in the fall of 1999 to change its image from a secretive defense-oriented company to a global telecommunications company to rival Nortel, Lucent Technologies, and Cisco Systems. In addition to its new name, the company had a new chairman, Sir Roger Hurn, while Lord Simpson remained as Marconi's CEO.

Principal Operating Units

Marconi Communications; Marconi Services; Marconi Mobile; Marconi Systems; Marconi Capital

Principal Competitors

Siemens AG; Westinghouse Electric Corp.; General Electric Co.; Philips Electronics NV; Cisco Systems Inc.; Ericsson LM; Alcatel Alsthom Compagnie Generale d'Electricite; Nokia; Lucent Technologies Inc.; Nortel Networks Corp.

Further Reading

Berkman, Barbara N., "GEC Casts Its Global Net," *Electronic Business,* June 3, 1991, p. 39.

Berss, Marcia, "A Man to Watch," *Forbes,* December 16, 1985, p. 44.

Collier, Andrew, "GEC, Siemens Hike Offer for Plessey," *Electronic News,* August 7, 1989, p. 6.

——, "Plessey Eyes New Market Entries," *Electronic News,* August 28, 1989, p. 11.

Dorsch, Jeff, "GEC, Tracor in Merger Pact," *Electronic News,* April 27, 1998, p. 12.

Everything Electrical: A Brief History of GEC, 2nd edition. London: The General Electric Company, 1999.

Fallon, James, "DOD: Siemens, GEC Buy of Plessey is No Threat," *Electronic News,* January 9, 1989, p. 1.

——, "EEC, U.K. Probes Halt Bid for Plessey," *Electronic News,* January 16, 1989, p. 4.

——, "GEC Ends Talks to Sell Marconi Unit to Plessey," *Electronic News,* February 29, 1988, p. 26.

——, "U.K. Blocks $1.75B GEC Bid for Plessey," *Electronic News,* August 11, 1986, p. 29.

Fletcher, Peter, and Larry King, "The GEC-Plessey Duel," *Electronics,* February 1989, p. 31.

Fletcher, Peter, "GEC-Siemens Bid for Plessey May Be Realized at Last," *Electronics,* September 1989, p. 32H.

Foster, Anne, "How Bad is GEC?," *Management Today,* January 1989, p. 40.

"From Dowager to Sexy High-Tech Star?," *Business Week,* February 8, 1999, p. 110D.

"GEC, Continued: Metsun's False Dawn," *Economist,* January 21, 1989, p. 68.

Katayama, Frederick H., "GE and GEC," *Fortune,* February 13, 1989, p. 8.

Linnett, Richard, "Marconi's New Image," *Adweek Eastern Edition,* August 30, 1999, p. 4.

Lorenz, Andrew, "Time to Unpick GEC," *Management Today,* October 1996, p. 44.

"Making a Meal of Arnie's Brainchild," *Economist,* January 14, 1989, p. 21.

Morrison, Gale, "Mitel Buys GEC-Plessey," *Electronic News,* February 16, 1998, p. 1.

"Musical Chairs," *Economist,* January 27, 1990, p. 70.

"Reforming the Unreformable," *Economist,* March 1, 1997, p. 70.

Ristelhueber, Robert, "Semicon Operations Reorganized by GEC," *Electronic News,* July 30, 1990, p. 20.

Tutt, Nigel, "EC Clears Finmeccanica, GEC Venture," *Electronics,* September 26, 1994, p. 14.

Williamson, J., and C. Wilson, "Siemens, GEC Mount Major Bid for Plessey," *Telephony,* November 21, 1988, p. 10.

—David P. Bianco

MBNA Corporation

1100 North King Street
Wilmington, Delaware 19801
U.S.A.
Telephone: (302) 453-9930
Toll free: (800) 362-6255
Fax: (302) 432-3614
Web site: http://www.mbnainternational.com

Public Company
Incorporated: 1982
Employees: 22,000
Sales: $6.47 billion (1999)
Stock Exchanges: New York
Ticker Symbol: KRB
NAIC: 52221 Credit Card Issuing; 551111 Offices of
    Bank Holding Companies

Delaware-based MBNA Corporation is a bank holding company. It is the parent company of MBNA America Bank, N.A., the third largest issuer of credit cards in the world and the top issuer of affinity credit cards, issued in cooperation with professional associations, charitable organizations, and recreational groups. The firm also offers other loan and deposit products, including money market accounts and CDs, as well as insurance services. MBNA provides home equity loans through its MBNA Consumer Services subsidiary and services Canadian customers through MBNA Canada, which was formed in 1998.

An Affinity for Credit Cards: 1980s

Charles Cawley founded MBNA in 1982. The small bank, based in a Newark, Delaware supermarket, was formed as the credit card subsidiary of MNC Financial, a regional bank holding company headquartered in Baltimore. The credit card industry was growing rapidly at the time, and Cawley was eager to expand the enterprise. Rather than pursuing the same strategies as his competitors, though, Cawley was looking for a marketing strategy that would separate his product from the homogenous horde of credit card lenders that competed mostly on price.

In 1983 Cawley approached his alma mater, Georgetown University in Washington, D.C., about partnering with him. His idea was to get the Georgetown University Alumni Association to endorse a credit card that would be offered exclusively to its members and generate a royalty or percentage of all revenues derived from the cards. The enticement for cardholders was that their use of the card benefited the alma mater and that the card displayed their affiliation with Georgetown. The alumni association agreed to the project, and Cawley's first direct mailing effort was a hit. In addition to signing up an unusually large percentage of its prospects, MBNA benefited from the overall credit quality of its new customers, who were categorized generally as having relatively high income and education levels, thereby resulting in lower delinquency in charge-off levels.

As a result of his success with Georgetown, Cawley was convinced that he was on to something. By issuing ''affinity'' cards and focusing on customer service, MBNA added value to an otherwise commodity-like service. He realized that if he could duplicate the results working with other groups, he could substantially increase MBNA's profit margins by capturing a more upscale and, therefore, less risky and higher spending segment of the market. Significantly, marketing costs per account could be greatly reduced because the response rate of direct sales efforts would be much higher than the industry average. Indeed, other credit card companies at the time often resorted to mass mailings targeted to broad groups identified by zip code or income level. In contrast, MBNA's prospects were motivated to review the credit card offer simply because of their affiliation with the group sponsoring the card.

Cawley next succeeded in getting the American Dental Association to sponsor an affinity card, and he followed that program with an affinity card for the Aircraft Owners and Pilots Association. Both efforts were successful. Throughout the mid-1980s Cawley aggressively approached new partners, focusing on various clubs and associations with an upscale membership. By 1985, in fact, MBNA was managing more than $1 billion in outstanding loans, compared with just $250 million going into 1983. MBNA's net income surged to $67 million in 1986 as outstanding credit vaulted to the $2 billion mark. Revenues and profits continued to surge as MBNA added affinity

---

Company Perspectives:

MBNA is a company of people committed to: Providing the Customer with the finest products backed by consistently top-quality service. Delivering these products and services efficiently, thus ensuring fair prices to the Customer and a sound investment for the stockholder. Treating the Customer as we expect to be treated—putting the Customer first every day—and meaning it. Being leaders in innovation, quality, efficiency, and Customer satisfaction. Being known for doing the little things and the big things well. Expecting and accepting from ourselves nothing short of the best. Remembering that each of us, the people of MBNA, makes the unassailable difference.

---

cards for major groups like the Sierra Club, Association of Trial Lawyers of America, the University of Texas, and National Education Association.

MBNA sustained its swift growth rate during the middle and late 1980s by scouting out upscale groups like college alumni associations and professional societies. After it selected an organization, it would offer future royalties in exchange for the group's membership list and permission to use its name and letterhead in direct-advertising efforts. By the early 1990s some groups were generating hundreds of thousands of dollars annually as a result of credit purchases under such agreements. For example, the Sierra Club arranged to receive one half of one percent of every charge made by its group members. MBNA had succeeded in signing up 45,000 of the environmental group's members by 1994, bringing more than $400,000 to the Club's coffers annually.

Although Cawley's strategy was unique for the early 1980s, by the mid-1980s other credit card companies were employing similar tactics. Nevertheless, MBNA continued to boost market share. Steady gains were in large part the result of fruitful marketing programs. MBNA marketers regularly solicited prospective groups with phone calls and by attending trade shows. Once they had the accounts, they utilized aggressive telemarketing and direct mail techniques to constantly boost the sizes of the accounts. For example, the Penn State Alumni Association entered into an affinity card agreement during the mid-1980s with a local bank, which succeeded in signing 15,000 members to the card. MBNA took the account over in 1989 and proceeded to boost membership to more than 120,000 within four years.

MBNA maintained its high-quality customer base by relying on credit reports to identify the most affluent and responsible customers. The strength of its credit base was reflected in its extremely low percentage of uncollectible loans, which was well below the industry average. Once it got the customers, it focused on keeping them with good service. For example, MBNA was the first credit card issuer to offer 24-hour-a-day service to all of its customers, and its phones were answered by people rather than by machines. In addition, people, rather than computer software, also reviewed individual account applications.

As MBNA's accounts swelled, so did its profits. By 1987 MBNA was managing more than $3 billion in credit card loans and netting a healthy $75 million annually in income. Managed loans surpassed $4 billion and then $5 billion in 1988 and 1989, as profits ballooned to more than $100 million annually. By 1990, MBNA was managing about $8 billion in credit card loans and pulling down nearly $130 million in profit. Those figures reflected an annual growth rate of more than 17 percent between 1987 and 1990. MBNA had become the largest single issuer of gold MasterCards and the fourth biggest provider of premium Visa cards. Its gold cards, in fact, made up about 42 percent of its accounts and were responsible for nearly 60 percent of MBNA's outstanding loan balances. Going into 1991, MBNA was marketing affinity cards for about 1,400 groups, including 223 medical and 70 attorney associations.

Independence and Expansion in the Early 1990s

MBNA's rampant growth during the late 1980s mimicked the gains of its corporate parent, MNC. MNC invested heavily in real estate during the period and enjoyed solid profits. Unfortunately, the commercial real estate market collapsed before the end of the decade. By 1990, MNC, swimming in red ink, was desperate for cash. After losing more than $240 million during the first three quarters of 1990, MNC put its crown jewel, MBNA, on the auction block. Several credit card companies inquired, including Sears's Discover Card unit, but they balked at the $1.1 billion price and waited to see if the desperate MNC would go lower. Instead, MNC spun off MBNA in January of 1991 in a public stock offering that raised about $955 million. The offering took place just two weeks before MNC's deadline to pay a $271 million debt.

Among the big winners of the MBNA spin-off was Alfred Lerner, a magnate with a personal worth estimated at $600 million at the time. Lerner was a major MNC stockholder. He had sold his bank, Equitable Bancorporation, to MNC in 1990 in exchange for MNC stock. Within weeks after the sale, however, MNC was drowning in real estate losses. Lerner was called in to run the bank, and he made the decision to sell MBNA. Shortly after the public stock offering, MBNA's stock price soared, and Lerner realized more than enough profit from his MBNA shares to offset his losses from his ownership in MNC. Lerner, who still owned about ten percent of MBNA in the early 1990s, became CEO of the newly formed MBNA Corporation. Still, Cawley, as president, continued to run the company.

By the early 1990s, MBNA's work force had grown to more than 5,000. To house its thriving operations, MBNA developed new facilities, including several important new regional marketing centers in Atlanta, Dallas, Cleveland, and Maine. From those facilities, several hundred representatives would conduct direct-marketing campaigns throughout their region and also provide service and information-processing functions.

The Northeast Regional Marketing Center in Camden, Maine was representative of the marketing centers, and it also marked a tie to Cawley's past. Cawley's grandfather had once operated dress factories in Camden and adjacent Belfast, and Cawley was familiar with the area because he had summered nearby at his family's Lincolnville Beach estate. By the time the facility was completed in 1993, it was housing 250 people, and within two years MBNA had boosted that number to 600 and was planning further expansion in the area.

Key Dates:

1982: MBNA is founded as the credit card subsidiary of MNC Financial.
1983: MBNA issues its first affinity credit card.
1991: MNC Financial spins off MBNA. MBNA goes public.

Despite the U.S. economic downturn of the late 1980s and early 1990s, MBNA continued to advance throughout the early 1990s. Managed loans nearly topped the $10 million mark in 1992 as MBNA's net income clambered to an impressive $170 million. By 1992, one-third of all U.S. doctors and about 20 percent of all attorneys were carrying MBNA credit cards, and their accounts were proving to be surprisingly profitable. Indeed, some analysts had questioned the wisdom of marketing credit cards to high-income individuals, few of whom would be expected to keep a running balance at high credit card interest rates. The average annual income of MBNA's cardholders in 1992 was an industry high of $54,000. However, MBNA's typical customer kept a running balance (at an average interest rate of 17.3 percent) of $2,200, about 35 percent higher than the industry average. By 1995, the customers' average annual income had risen to $59,000 and they were carrying an average balance of $2,886 (at an average interest rate of 16.4 percent).

Furthermore, MBNA charged its customers annual card fees of $20 to $40. Despite a flurry of new competition in the credit card industry, though, MBNA's affinity strategy allowed it to continue to successfully charge fees while many competitors dropped fees or slashed interest rate charges. MBNA also profited by selling much of its receivables forward at a fixed rate, a practice that essentially allowed the company to finance its portfolio at relatively low interest rates. Although that strategy left MBNA vulnerable to rising short-term interest rates, it paid off big during the early 1990s when rates were depressed.

MBNA's strategy was to sell to people with a common interest. In addition to the organizations and financial institutions that endorsed the company's products, MBNA began looking for "created affinities." For instance, it began offering cards displaying family coats-of-arms, as well as cards picturing regional landmarks to people proud of their home towns or states. By the mid-1990s, it was marketing to fans of nearly 200 different professional sports organizations, including National Football League teams, motor sports fans, and teams in every other major sport.

Because of MBNA's efficient financing strategies, marketing tactics, and customer service, profits surged going into the mid-1990s. Managed loans jumped to $12.4 billion in 1993 as net income topped $200 million. By 1994, MBNA had issued more than 14 million cards and was partnering with more than 3,600 different organizations, including the Telephone Pioneers of America, American Legion, and more than 400 universities and colleges. Managed loans grew to nearly $19 billion by the end of 1994, and the credit quality of its accounts was still much better than the industry norm. MBNA began to augment its operations in 1993 with home equity loans offered through its

subsidiary, MBNA Consumer Services, Inc. It also launched initiatives overseas: it started in the United Kingdom with an affinity card for members of the Rolls-Royce Enthusiasts' Club.

Continued Growth in the Late 1990s

MBNA continued to strengthen operations and grow its credit card business in the latter half of the decade. The company added consumer retail loans to the list of offerings provided by MBNA Consumer Services in 1996, thus allowing customers to finance costly purchases such as computers. Also that year the firm established the MBNA Insurance Services division to offer credit-related insurance, a service the company had offered since 1987. In 1997 MBNA Insurance Services began to market property and casualty insurance, primarily auto, as well as health and life insurance products. In 1998 MBNA established MBNA Canada Bank and began marketing credit cards to Canadian consumers.

In the late 1990s MBNA grew not only through credit card growth but also through acquisitions and partnerships. In 1997 MBNA purchased the credit card operations of Fidelity Trust Company, a subsidiary of Fidelity Investments. The acquisition included about 300,000 credit card accounts and $450 million in assets. In 1998 alone MBNA completed 25 acquisitions, including the acquisition of the credit card operations of PNC Bank Corp. in December for about $2.9 billion. Ventures the following year included a partnership with CCB Financial Corp., under which MBNA bought $150 million from CCB banks located in the southeastern United States, and the acquisition of the credit card portfolio of SunTrust Banks Inc. The estimated $1.5 billion purchase included the outstanding loan balances from about 1.4 million credit card accounts.

Hoping to capitalize on the intensive growth of the Internet, MBNA brokered deals with Internet companies in the late 1990s. MBNA's agreement to issue an affinity credit card with EarthWeb, an Internet-based company that sold business supplies online, was promoted by MBNA and EarthWeb as "one of the first affinity credit card programs in the business-to-business Internet space," according to *Asset Sales Report.* MBNA also entered into a marketing partnership with Infoseek Corporation, which operated the GO Network. The GO Network included such high-profile Web sites as ABCNEWS.com, ESPN.com, NFL.com, Mrshowbiz.com, and Infoseek.com. Infoseek claimed that the GO Network had eight million members. The deal, estimated by MBNA to be worth up to $100 million, included an affinity credit card aimed at online consumers.

Net income in 1998 reached $776 million, up from $622 million in 1997. Managed loans increased 21 percent from 1997 to reach $59.6 billion. MBNA announced that it had added 9.3 million new accounts and arranged endorsements with 475 new organizations, including the Canadian Nurses Association, the University of Hawaii, the Canadian Football League, the American College of Dentists, and Miami Heat. MBNA's share of the U.S. credit card market grew to 12 percent in 1998, and its share of the credit card industry in the United Kingdom reached ten percent. The company's international operations grew rapidly to reach $4.9 billion in loan balances in 1998, an increase of 75 percent from 1997. MBNA managed to keep its loan losses low by remaining true to its proven tactic of carefully selecting responsible consumers with steady incomes; the company's characteristic customer in the late 1990s earned an average household income of $60,000 and was a homeowner.

As MBNA approached the end of the 1990s, it had successfully become a leader in the volatile and competitive credit card industry, with a solid history of increasing revenues. In 1999 MBNA acquired endorsements from 400 new groups, including the Marine Corps Association, Northwestern University, the American Automobile Association, and Carnegie Hall. Total managed loans grew $12.6 billion over 1998 to reach $72.3 billion. MBNA's net income in fiscal 1999 topped $1 billion, the best performance in the company's history.

Principal Subsidiaries

MBNA America Bank, N.A.; MBNA Consumer Services, Inc.; MBNA International Bank Limited (United Kingdom); MBNA Marketing Systems, Inc.; MBNA Canada Bank; MBNA Insurance Services; MBNA Hallmark Information Services, Inc.; MBNA Delaware.

Principal Competitors

BANK ONE Corporation; Chase Manhattan Corporation; Citigroup Inc.

Further Reading

Berss, Marcia, "The Human Touch," *Forbes,* December 21, 1992, p. 218.

Blakinger, Mary, "Two Credit-Card Giants Dominate Wilmington, Del., Landscape," *Philadelphia Inquirer,* October 2, 1999.

Bullard, Stan, "MBNA Eyes Huge Expansion," *Crain's Cleveland Business,* September 26, 1994, p. 1.

Fickenscher, Lisa, "Bally, MBNA Cobranding Upscale Card," *American Banker,* December 10, 1999, p. 15.

Hinden, Stan, "Recession Could Dim MNC's Shining Sale of Credit Card Firm," *Washington Post,* January 28, 1991, p. 27E.

Kite, Shane, "MBNA Continues Growth Via Product, Acquisitions," *Asset Sales Report,* July 12, 1999, p. 1.

Lang, Amanda, "Can MBNA Keep on Defying Gravity?," *National Post,* August 13, 1999, p. D3.

"MBNA Buys SunTrust's Credit Card Portfolio," *Atlanta Journal and Constitution,* October 16, 1999, p. C5.

"MBNA's Profits Climbed 34% in 4th Quarter," *American Banker,* January 11, 2000, p. 24.

Weber, Joseph, "How To Rope 'Em with Plastic," *Business Week,* September 26, 1994, p. 135.

—Dave Mote
—updated by Mariko Fujinaka

Meteor Industries Inc.

216 16th Street, Suite 730
Denver, Colorado 80202
U.S.A.
Telephone: (303) 572-1135
Fax: (303) 572-1803
Web site: http://www.meteorindustries.com

Public Company
Incorporated: 1993
Employees: 320
Sales: $118.4 million (1998)
Stock Exchanges: NASDAQ
Ticker Symbol: META
NAIC: 42272 Petroleum and Petroleum Products
    Wholesalers (Except Bulk Stations and Terminals);
    44719 Other Gasoline Stations

Meteor Industries Inc. is one of the fastest-growing distributors and marketers of petroleum products in the Southwestern United States. Founded in 1993 by a former accountant and a corporate attorney, Meteor focuses primarily on rural or sparsely populated areas that haven't been penetrated by the company's older and more powerful competitors. Meteor is active in almost every aspect of the petroleum industry, from wholesale dealings with small business owners to the ownership and operation of convenience stores. Meteor's growth plan is based on the acquisition of small, well-established businesses.

Meteor's Beginnings: The Acquisition of Graves Oil & Butane

Meteor was founded in 1993 by Edward J. Names and his business partner, Dennis R. Staal. Names had an undergraduate degree in Economics from the University of Colorado at Boulder and a law degree from the University of Denver. After his graduation from the latter in 1980, Names was active in both the practice of corporate law and high-profile business dealings in the Colorado area. In 1983 he became president of the Denver-based Alfa Resources, a position he held until 1995, and in

1982, after being an attorney for only two years, he became a partner at the mid-sized law firm of Schmidt, Elrod & Wills. In 1987 Names acted as special counsel to the law firm of Wills and Sawyer, a relationship he continued until 1992. Names's involvement in the business and law communities of Colorado provided contacts that proved helpful when he founded Meteor in the early 1990s.

Names's partner Staal was a Nebraska native who served as a C.P.A for Arthur Anderson and, from 1973 to 1976, as the Controller for the Health Planning Council of Omaha. In the late 1970s Staal became involved in the oil industry, becoming director of the Wulf Oil Corporation in 1977 and, two years later, that company's president, a position he kept until 1981. Staal served as a director of the Chadron Energy Corporation from 1979 to 1981 and as a director of the Saba Petroleum Company from 1986 to 1991. In the late 1980s Staal became involved with Alfa Resources, of which Names was president, and the two decided to form the partnership that resulted in Meteor.

Meteor came into being through the acquisition of a small company located in Farmington, New Mexico, called Graves Oil & Butane. Graves was engaged primarily in the wholesale marketing of propane, gasoline, diesel, and other petroleum products. While Graves made most of its revenue through its wholesale business, the company also owned and operated four gasoline stations in Farmington, one gasoline station and convenience store in Albuquerque, and three lube stations in central New Mexico.

Graves was founded in 1956 by Theron J. Graves, a prominent New Mexico businessman who owned several small companies in the area. Graves Oil was from its start focused on the distribution and marketing of petroleum products, and within a few years of its inception had struck up contracts with numerous local gas stations and service centers. At that time New Mexico was experiencing a population boom as the result of the government's expansion of military operations in the state, and the larger oil companies were rapidly expanding the number of retail gasoline stations in the area. This expansion translated into an increased customer base for Graves's wholesale division, and the company grew quickly throughout the 1960s.

Company Perspectives:

Meteor Industries Incorporated is a petroleum products marketing and distribution company that has shown exceptional growth and profitability while establishing itself as a major regional player. Since 1993 Meteor has successfully assimilated eleven acquisitions and in the process built one of the most extensive distribution networks in the Western United States. The Company's mission is to continue growing aggressively through internal expansion and earnings-accretive acquisitions in a highly fragmented industry.

Next, Graves turned its focus to the retail side of the industry, opening a series of service stations in Farmington. Because the town was small, its petroleum market had largely escaped the attention of huge national chains, allowing small, family-owned companies like Graves to get a foothold in a notoriously competitive industry.

As gasoline stations evolved to include convenience stores and mini-marts, Graves kept up with the competition. In Albuquerque the company opened a 24-hour ''super station,'' which, by the early 1990s, was generating $3 million annually and had more than 2,500 square feet of space. Graves was also quick to respond to new automation trends in the petroleum retail industry: when ''cardlock'' systems became popular with cross-country vacationers and truck drivers, Graves installed four cardlock systems at various locations. These systems allowed a customer automatic access to fuel through the utilization of a specially designed, pre-authorized card that activated the fuel pump and recorded the amount put into the vehicle. The customer was billed later. The cardlock system was useful for encouraging repeat customers, as the cards could only be used at company-owned stations.

Nevertheless, Graves's wholesale division remained the company's primary focus and was consistently responsible for about 80 percent of its revenue during its first three decades. Despite the vicissitudes of the oil industry in the 1970s and 1980s, the company's profits grew slowly and steadily, and by the early 1990s Graves was a small but solid presence in New Mexico.

1993–95: Meteor Makes Its Mark

Graves's solid reputation attracted the attention of Names and Staal when the two joined forces in the early 1990s, and the partners purchased Graves for $7.5 million. The acquisition served as the foundation for the newly formed Meteor Industries, with Names acting as CEO and Staal as CFO. Meteor continued operating some of the Graves locations under their original name, but the company's headquarters was relocated to Denver.

Meteor developed a growth strategy that continued to reflect Graves's industry focus. Wholesale distribution of petroleum products to commercial retailers as well as to oil and mining companies made up the majority of Meteor's business, while the company developed franchise agreements with Phillips Petroleum, Fina Oil, and Sun Oil to expand the company's retail

division. The acquisition of Graves was only the beginning for Meteor, which quickly began casting about for other, similar companies that could be added to its roster.

In 1994 Capco Resources Ltd., a company that owned interests in oil and gas production companies throughout the United States, Canada, South America, and Pakistan, bought a majority interest in Meteor. Capco's involvement in Meteor gave the fledgling company more financial backing than it would otherwise have had, and made it possible for Meteor to move forward with its aggressive acquisition plans. Two years after the acquisition of Graves, Meteor purchased Hillger Oil, a company with revenues of $20 million a year that operated several convenience stores in the Southwest. That same year, Meteor acquired Duke City Distributing, a company with annual revenues of about $8 million that operated one convenience store in addition to its wholesale business.

1996–99: Meteor's Rapid Rise

In 1996 Meteor acquired two more companies, American Propane LLC and Innovative Solutions Incorporated, both small companies which were rapidly absorbed into Meteor's management structure. The following year, Meteor purchased Tedken Oil, a wholesaler and retailer of oil products, with annual sales of $5 million, and Fleischli Oil, with annual revenues of about $85 million. Fleischli had marketing and distribution agreements in Colorado, Wyoming, South Dakota, Nevada, Utah, Montana, Nebraska, and Idaho.

In 1998 Meteor purchased two more small oil companies, Tri-Valley Gas and R & R Oil, with annual sales of $15 million and $11 million, respectively. R & R Oil was a particular boon to the company, as the acquisition greatly strengthened Meteor's presence in the Wyoming and Rocky Mountain Powder River Basin regions, both of which, because of their sparse populations, had open petroleum markets.

In 1999 Meteor acquired Jardine Petroleum, a distribution company with annual sales of more than $50 million. Founded in the 1930s, Jardine had a strong history in Utah and proved to be one of Meteor's most successful purchases. Jardine added eight more locations to Meteor's cardlock network, added several distribution facilities to the company's wholesale division, and increased its transportation services as well. Through the Jardine purchase, Meteor acquired the assets of Petro Express and PetroSolutions, divisions of Jardine that delivered petroleum products to the company's wholesale and retail customers. The same year Meteor strengthened its presence in northern Colorado with the acquisition of Carroll Oil, which operated five convenience stores in Northern Colorado and had two commercial cardlock systems. In February 2000, Meteor announced that it had sold its retail store subsidiary, Meteor Stores, Inc., to Capco Energy, Inc.. The deal was reportedly worth $1.5 million and was effected in order to allow Meteor to focus on expanding its wholesale and distribution operations. The company signed a five-year contract to supply the stores sold to Capco with petroleum products.

After only six years in business, Meteor had averaged two acquisitions a year, attained annual revenues of more than $100 million, and was operating 13 offices in ten states. Moreover,

Key Dates:

1956: Graves Oil & Butane founded.
1993: Graves Oil bought by Names and Staal; Meteor founded.
1995: Hillger Oil and Duke City Distributing acquired.
1997: Tedken and Fleischli Oil acquired.
1999: Jardine acquired.

despite the company's phenomenal growth, it maintained a reputation for a friendly, inclusive management style. Meteor often retained the managers and executives from the businesses it acquired, which helped to create a collaborative managerial atmosphere. Rarely, in fact, did Meteor approach a company that had not already expressed an interest in selling. Many of the companies Meteor acquired reflected a trend in the oil industry, as small, family-owned oil companies sold out as the result of either pressure from huge corporations or simple lack of interest from the next generation. Meteor stood out as a company willing to consolidate these small businesses into a powerful regional company.

Principal Subsidiaries

Meteor Marketing Inc.; Graves Oil & Butane Co., Inc.; Innovative Solutions and Technologies, Inc.; Meteor Holdings LLC (73%).

Principal Competitors

Tosco Corporation; 7-Eleven, Inc.

Further Reading

Callanan, John, "Meteoric Growth," *Journal of Petroleum Marketing*, August 1999, p. 16.

Locke, Tom, "Meteor Plans More Acquisitions, Equity Offering," *Wall Street Journal*, July 7, 1999, p. C12.

"Meteor Industries Announces Record Year-End Results," *PR Newswire*, March 30, 1999.

"Meteor Industries, Inc. Acquires Tedken Oil C. Assets and Operations," *PR Newswire*, February 13, 1997.

"Meteor Industries, Inc. Agrees to Acquire Fleischli Oil Company, Inc.," *PR Newswire*, August 13, 1997.

"Meteor Industries, Inc. Agrees to Acquire R & R Oil Company," *PR Newswire*, November 5, 1998.

—Rachel H. Martin

Métropole Télévision

89 avenue Charles de Gaulle
92200 Neuilly-sur-Seine, Cedex
France
Telephone: (+33) 1 41 92 66 66
Fax: (+33) 1 41 92 66 10
Web site: http://www.m6.fr

Public Company
Incorporated: 1986
Employees: 900
Sales: FFr 4.1 billion ($680 million) (1999)
Stock Exchanges: Paris
NAIC: 513120 Television Broadcasting Networks;
    512110 Television Show Production

Métropole Télévision is one of France's leading television broadcasters and programming producers. Métropole Télévision's flagship station is the M6 television channel, which, in 1998, captured 14.1 percent of the total French television viewing audience, and more than 19 percent of the viewing audience under the age of 50, ranking the station number two behind TF1 (Télévision Française 1). Métropole Télévision holds a joint-venture participation in the Télévision Par Satellite (TPS) television service, adding channels ''Série Club,'' ''Téva,'' ''M6 Music,'' and ''Fun TV'' to TPS and to certain cable television networks. The company's other television production interests include its Home Shopping Service, which provides programming, including ''Club Télé Achat,'' to M6 and Téva, as well as other French satellite and cable channels and to television stations in Belgium, China, and Canada. Beyond television, Métropole Télévision has placed the M6 name on a successful line of magazines, videos, and compact discs. Through subsidiaries M6 Films and Métropole Productions, the company produces and coproduces films and programs for the cinema and television markets. Advertising sales for the M6 station remain the company's chief source of revenue, topping FFr 4 billion in 1999. Métropole Télévision continues to be led by founder and CEO Jean Drucker.

''Little Station That Could'' in the 1980s

Until the early 1980s, France's television broadcasting networks remained under the tight control of the French government, which restricted the number of available stations to just three: TF1, which was privatized in 1987, and the government-owned Antenne 2 and Antenne 3. The appearance of privately owned television stations marked something of a revolution for the French television viewer. The first of the new breed of channels was Canal Plus, a subscription-based service requiring a set-top decoder, which began broadcasting in 1984. Canal Plus was soon followed by La Cinq, broadcasting on France's channel five. Plans for a sixth channel, TV6, to be operated by radio programmer NRJ and advertising agency Publicis, foundered by mid-decade.

In 1987, however, a new station joined France's airwaves. Called M6, the station quickly became known as the French version of the ''Little Engine That Could.'' Starting on a budget of just FFr 500 million per year—which represented only one-fourth of the budget for La Cinq—M6 definitely faced an uphill battle. As CEO and founder Jean Drucker told *Le Point,* ''We didn't start from zero. We started from less than zero.'' One of the station's largest hurdles was that its broadcast network remained severely limited, with reception assured in less than one-third of France, in part because of government reluctance to allow the station to expand its network of transmitters nationwide. Industry analysts were also skeptical that the French market could support a sixth television channel. Métropole Télévision's first year's balance sheet seemed to bear out the skeptics, as the company posted losses mounting to FFr 380 million.

Yet Drucker, who had previously served as president of Antenne 2 (later renamed France 2), not only had extensive experience in television, but also the deep pockets of financial backers Lyonnaise des Eaux and CLT (Compagnie Luxembourgeoise de Télédiffusion, later CLT-UFA), which each held 25 percent of Métropole Télévision. Drucker put his broadcasting experience to good use, focusing on establishing a strong identity for the new station. The company developed the M6 logo, and a ''look'' for the station that set it apart from its competitors. Standing apart was also extended to M6's broadcast schedule as well. In a country where the eight o'clock news

Key Dates:

1987:   M6 television station begins broadcasting.
1988:   Potential viewing audience reaches 18 million households.
1994:   Company is listed on Paris Stock Exchange.
1995:   Company purchases interest in Télévision Par Satellite (TPS).
1998:   Home Shopping Service and Fun TV stations are launched.
2000:   Share of national audience tops 13.5 percent.

broadcast was known as the "high mass," M6 dared to be different, offering an array of counter-programming initiatives that increasingly brought it to the attention of France's television viewers, in particular the younger viewing markets.

M6's counter-programming took on various forms, including broadcasting television series—chiefly American-made—during the traditional news time, as well as a CNN-inspired six-minute newscast presented in the time slot just before 8 p.m., when all of the other stations were still broadcasting commercials. M6's choice of programming often placed the company in difficulties with the CSA (the French television authority) and requirements that stations devote certain percentages of their broadcast time to French- and European-produced programming. American shows such as "Cagney and Lacey" and "The Cosby Show" gave M6 an increasing share of the French viewing public. M6 also developed its appeal with the youth market, devoting much of its broadcasting time to music videos.

Despite a strong showing in its urban markets, where the channel pulled in as much as 15 percent of the viewing audience, M6 remained the smallest kid on the block. With just two percent of the national audience—in a system that largely lacked local advertising—M6 remained far from its break-even point of ten percent. This situation began to change early in 1988, when the extension of the company's transmitter network allowed it to triple the number of television households it could reach. By then, with "zappers" (i.e., remote controls) in hand, more and more television viewers were tuning into M6.

Diversifying in the 1990s

By 1991, M6 had captured a nine percent share of France's viewing public. Although the station continued to rely heavily on music videos and U.S.-imported shows, Métropole Télévision had begun to show its own programming muscle. M6-produced programs included "Capital," a highly respected news magazine with an emphasis on corporate and financial matters, and "Culture Pub," a program devoted to advertising around the world, both of which began to make a mark on the French television scene. Nevertheless, the company continued to face industry criticism for its lack of French- and European-made television programming, especially from France's producer's guild, but also from many political leaders who did little to hide their interest in seeing M6 disappear altogether.

Similar pressures, and viewer disinterest, led to the demise of La Cinq by 1992, suggesting that the country indeed was not ready for six television stations. But M6's fortunes continued to rise, gaining points not only from the closing of La Cinq (which was later replaced by station Arte, a co-French-German broadcaster oriented toward cultural programming), but also from France's Big Three—TF1, France 2, and France 3. As the company neared the ten percent break-even point, it was also moving from net losses toward net profits. By 1991, with revenues of FFr 800 million, the company had cut its losses back to just FFr 140 million. Nevertheless, with the end of La Cinq, many in the industry began sounding the death knells for M6, with its total of FFr 1.4 billion in losses during its first five years of business. Métropole Télévision turned to its two largest shareholders for continued financing; in turn, Lyonnaise des Eaux and CLT both increased their shares to 34 percent.

The year 1992 proved to be M6's turning point. With its share of the television viewing audience topping ten percent for the first time, M6 became profitable, posting net profits of FFr 100 million for the year. The company's fortunes continued to rise. By 1993, as its national share of 12 percent gave it a growing percentage of the nation's total advertising expenditures—reaching 14.9 percent that year—net profits topped FFr 230 million on revenues of FFr 1.8 billion. In 1994, Métropole Télévision was ready to go public, posting just nine percent of its shares on the Paris Stock Exchange. Priced at FFr 260 per share, the listing was over-subscribed some 38 times, making it one of the year's most successful IPOs.

Métropole Télévision invested its new capital in diverse activities. The rollout of satellite television, under preparation in the mid-1990s, and the extension of cable television offered the company new programming perspectives. New channels proposed by the company included Téva, a channel featuring programming for the women's market; M6 Music, taking over the company's music video programming as M6 itself turned more and more toward programming fiction and news and entertainment magazines; and Série Club, devoted to broadcasting French and U.S.-made series. Métropole Télévision also bought into the TPS satellite network; the company's participation, together with the strong share positions of CLT and Lyonnaise, gave Métropole Télévision a leading role in TPS's operations.

By 1995, Métropole Télévision had succeeded in shedding its debts. The company continued to post steady gains in profits, despite its share of the loss-making TPS network, only slowly beginning to gain momentum. In 1996, M6 faced once again the ire of the CSA. Where M6 had enjoyed the regulatory body's lenience toward the station's disregard of its programming quotas, the company's success now forced it to toe the line, especially during the 5 p.m. to 11 p.m. time slot. The tightening of its requirements led the company to increase its own production investments. By 1998, Métropole's own productions were helping to drive the company's success, forming the majority of its top audience-generating programs.

The company's satellite television investments began to pay off in the late 1990s as well. Growing public interest in satellite broadcasting, spurred by sharp drops in the prices for satellite dish receivers and decoders, placed TPS as one of the leaders, alongside CanalSatellite, for the French market. After increasing its own participation in TPS to 25 percent, Métropole Télévision quickly made plans to create more new channels, including Fun TV, oriented toward the youth market, and the Home Shopping Service.

Métropole Télévision was also making advances on other entertainment fronts. The company's M6 Interactions subsidiary made strong inroads with its magazines, video and compact disc, and software products. Métropole Télévision also joined the big screen, providing production and financing for a number of cinema projects, including ''Quasimodo'' and ''Peut-être,'' among others. The company also began preparations for two new television channels, to be launched after the turn of the century, M6 Famille, devoted to family programming, and TV.com, featuring multimedia and computer-oriented programming. On the multimedia front, Métropole Télévision created a new subsidiary, M6 Web, grouped under its M6 Interactions subsidiary, to govern its Internet and multimedia activities. The growing importance of its multimedia activities was highlighted by M6 Interactions' growing share of the company's annual revenues: some 30 percent of 1998's FFr 3.5 billion.

In 1999, Métropole Télévision extended itself into a new arena—that of the sports arena. In May of that year, the company joined shareholder CLT-UFA in the purchase of the Girondins soccer club of Bordeaux. The purchase not only gave the company an entry into the sports market, it also gave it the possibility to include live sports broadcasting on its stations for the first time.

Métropole Télévision entered the new century with the announcement that it had gained the second place position among France's general-programming stations, with a 13.6 percent share nationwide. The ''little station that could'' had certainly proved that it could—and most likely would continue to—assert itself as a leader in the French television market.

Principal Subsidiaries

M6 Publicité SA; M6 Interactions SA; Home Shopping Service SA; Tecipress SA; M6 Droits Audiovisuels SA; TCM Droits Audiovisuels SA; TCM Gestion SA; M6 Films SA; Métropole Productions SA; C. Productions SA; Métropolest SA; M6 Thématique SA; Extension TV SA; Paris Première SA; Sedi TV SNC; Edi TV SA; Fun TV SNC; Club Téléachat SNC; M6 Numérique SNC; TPS SNC (25%).

Principal Competitors

Canal +; France Télévision; TF1; CanalSatellite; NC Numericable; France Telecom Group.

Further Reading

Aubert, Philippe, ''Une télé pas comme les autres,'' *Le Point,* January 4, 1988, pp. 74–75.
Equirou, Marine, ''Jean Drucker: M6 réalisera en 98 un bénéfice au moins égal à celui de 97,'' *Les Echos,* September 10, 1998, p. 24.
Feraud, Jean-Christophe, ''M6 brigue le deuxième rang des chaines généralistes,'' *Les Echos*, September 3, 1999, p. 16.
''M6 to Be Bound by Broadcast Quotas,'' *Tech Europe,* January 9, 1996.
Short, David, ''Small Networks Reap Big Rewards,'' *European*, October 7, 1994, p. 25.

—M.L. Cohen

Midway Airlines Corporation

300 West Morgan Street
Durham, North Carolina 27707
U.S.A.
Telephone: (919) 956-4800
Toll Free: 1-800-44-MIDWAY (1-800-446-4392)
Fax: (919) 595-6000
Web site: http://www.midwayair.com

Public Company
Incorporated: 1983 as Jet Express Inc.
Employees: 925
Sales: $217.95 million (1999)
Stock Exchanges: NASDAQ
Ticker Symbol: MDWY
NAIC: 481111 Scheduled Passenger Air Transportation;
481112 Scheduled Freight Air Transportation

Midway Airlines Corporation puts an old name on one of the youngest all-jet fleets in the United States. The original Midway Airlines flourished briefly before finally succumbing to bankruptcy in 1991. The new Midway takes a similar tack to the original, although it relocated to less crowded Raleigh-Durham, North Carolina, in 1993 after being crowded out of its Chicago home. Buoyed by the robust Research Triangle economy, Midway flies two million passengers a year to more than two dozen destinations.

Midway I: 1976–91

Midway Airport, 11 miles from downtown Chicago, had been the world's busiest before the major airlines relocated to the newer, more remote O'Hare International. Irving T. Tague founded Midway Airlines Inc. in 1976 along the lines of Southwest Airlines, the upstart that had won many hearts from its home at tiny Love Field near Dallas. Employing a staff of 200, Midway began flying on November 1, 1979, linking Chicago, Cleveland, Detroit, and Kansas City with three McDonnell Douglas DC-9 jets.

The red lips of Midway's billboards and print ads bade locals to "Kiss O'Hare good-bye"; cut-rate fares, sometimes one-third those of competitors, sweetened the offer. Midway thrived in the deregulated environment and came to totally dominate Midway Airport.

In 1984 Midway acquired bankrupt Air Florida Inc. and its three Boeing 737s. It dropped most of its routes, however, which were more geared toward leisure travelers. In Midway's "Metrolink" experiment, the carrier installed business class seating (four seats across) throughout its DC-9s. Passengers did not flock to the idea in sufficient numbers, however, and the company reverted to the industry standard, five-across rows.

Midway lost $37 million in 1984 and 1985. Chairman Arthur C. Bass was ushered out, and David Hinson was tapped as his replacement in February 1985. Hinson, a former Navy fighter pilot, had joined the airline as an investor in 1978 after a career at United Air Lines, Northwest Airlines, and Hughes Air West, under Tague. He soon restored the carrier to profitability by cutting costs and refining flight schedules, using Chicago as a hub. He also sold a couple of planes and increased daily utilization on the remaining DC-9s and 737s while reducing labor expenses.

Midway looked west for new opportunities and developed more of the low-fare, leisure traffic previous managers eschewed. The company bought commuter carrier Fischer Brothers Aviation for its feeder traffic. Cooperative agreements also were penned with Canadian Airlines, VARIG of Brazil, and Air New Zealand. Traffic grew by more than 30 percent a year in the mid-1980s. By 1986, Midway was the fourteenth largest U.S. airline with revenues of $261.4 million. Employment reached 3,000.

Originally devoted to used planes, Midway switched to new models in the name of fuel economy. Five new Boeing 737s were brought on-line in 1986 and soon after Midway ordered eight new McDonnell Douglas MD-87s. Revenues reached $412 million in 1988. Aggressive expansion (eight new cities), however, was accompanied by a drop in profits to $6.8 million.

Hinson ordered 37 MD-80 jets worth $900 million in March 1989 as Midway began flying and advertising coast-to-coast. It won a bid for assets of bankrupt Eastern Airlines—including its

Philadelphia hub, two Canadian routes, and 16 DC-9s—after government regulators blocked its sale to USAir.

Although measured growth had always been Hinson's mantra, over-expansion on the East Coast helped bring Midway to the ground. Recession, high fuel costs, and price competition with Eastern (still flying) prevented Midway from ever capitalizing on the Philadelphia hub. Hinson hired Thomas E. Schick, formerly of USAir, to help Midway survive in the summer of 1990, cutting jobs and winning concessions from suppliers. Midway sold its newly purchased slots at New York and Washington for lease back and sold its Philadelphia hub to USAir for $65 million. However, this was not enough to satisfy creditors, and the company filed bankruptcy in late May 1991. Midway had grown its fleet from three to 44 aircraft and had never had a fatal crash.

Northwest Airlines agreed to hire most of Midway's 4,300 former employees after outbidding Southwest for Midway's assets, for which it agreed to pay about $170 million. Northwest canceled the deal, however, after purchasing Midway's gate assignments, which some viewed as a defensive move to ward off competition from Southwest.

Midway finally ceased operations after Northwest dropped out of its buyout deal. Northwest blamed the deal's failure on inaccurate reporting by Midway and a newly discovered leaky fuel tank at its hangars; its defense prevailed in later lawsuits. Meanwhile, Southwest Airlines moved into the void created at Midway Airport, hiring more than 400 former Midway Airlines employees. David Hinson went on to head the Federal Aviation Administration.

Midway II: 1993 and Beyond

Jet Express, Inc., incorporated in 1983, took the name Midway Airlines Corporation in November 1993. The new investment group assembled $251 million in start-up capital. Fokker, the Holland-based aircraft manufacturer, was among the investors, and the new company's business plan rested on the wings of eight new (leased) Fokker 100 jets.

The Midway name took to the skies again on two of the Fokkers in November 1993. It was staffed by 150 employees, most alumni of the original Midway. Kenneth T. Carlson, the new president, had been one of the original Midway's founders before starting New York Air in 1980.

The company contracted with American Airlines for maintenance. Midway's relationship with American extended to frequent flier miles and access to the Sabre computer reservations

system. Initial traffic was brisk. Nevertheless, the company lost $11 million in its first year and a half of operations.

The Zell/Chilmark Fund L.P., led by Sam Zell, bought 90 percent of Midway Airlines for $25 million in July 1994. President John Selvaggio, a former American Airlines executive, was hired by new chairman Jerry Jacob, also formerly with American. In March 1995, the new management relocated the company to Raleigh-Durham Airport (RDU), in the heart of North Carolina's Research Triangle, which recently had been vacated by American Airlines. The name still fit, according to company representatives, since it was now based midway between North and South. After the transfer, Midway drew comparisons to Frontier Airlines, a West Coast airline of similar size and strategy that also had taken over an old American Airlines hub.

Although Delta Air Lines and USAir had well-established hubs in Atlanta and Charlotte, respectively, two other low-fare carriers also competed on Midway's turf: Columbia, South Carolina-based Air South (which did not survive very long) and ValuJet (later AirTran), based in Atlanta. The latter flew to two of Midway's largest markets, Boston and Orlando.

After moving to Raleigh, Midway ditched the no-frills philosophy of Southwest Airlines. The post-RDU Midway offered better amenities than other low-cost carriers but at a premium, pitching itself as an upscale carrier. Part of the gutsy play to bring Midway back into relevancy was an order for four new $45 million Airbus A320 jets, a bit larger than the Fokker 100s that made up its existing fleet, for ventures into the Caribbean.

Midway carried 1.2 million passengers in 1995. Employment increased to 1,100 since the move to RDU. The winter of 1995–96 was a trying one, however. Many pilots were furloughed and Midway had to restructure payments on its leased Fokkers. Fortunately for Midway, the bankruptcy of the Dutch manufacturer helped drive lease payments down on this model. The Caribbean gamble did not pay off, however, and Midway ended up returning all but one of the A320 jets in 1996. Nevertheless, good traffic on Cancun and Las Vegas routes justified keeping the last one. Other unprofitable routes were cut. Midway still planned to expand its offerings in the northeastern United States, however. It also sought to boost its customer service, appealing to businesswomen, for example, by designating one lavatory aboard each flight for females only.

Public in 1999

In spite of the trying winter (Midway ended up losing $8 million for the year), executives were preparing for an initial public offering. They aimed for Midway to triple in size by century's end. The company raised $20 million from two investors, allowing it to buy a few more new planes to take over the Raleigh-Atlanta route that ValuJet abandoned to Delta Air Lines after its disastrous Everglades crash.

Midway blamed its commuter partner, Midway Connection, for a sudden cessation of services related to FAA violations in 1997. Midway Airlines subsequently switched to Corporate Airlines (which operated small 19-passenger British Aerospace Jetstream 32 aircraft) as a commuter affiliate. It ordered ten Canadair Regional Jets from Bombardier in November 1997.

Key Dates:
1979: Original Midway Airlines begins flying out of Chicago's Midway Airport.
1986: Midway orders a dozen new jets to service booming traffic.
1989: David Hinson places $900 million jet order and attempts to expand into Philadelphia.
1991: The original Midway files bankruptcy, hit by tough market conditions and over-expansion.
1993: Jet Express, Inc. acquires the Midway name and attempts to start anew in Chicago.
1995: Crowded out of its home airport, Midway relocates to Raleigh-Durham.
1997: An initial public offering raises about $38 million.
1999: Investors try to take over Midway as Southwest Airlines enters its Raleigh base.

Midway went public the next month on the NASDAQ stock exchange.

Donald Burr, People Express founder, led a bid to buy Midway for $37 million. He planned to move the carrier to New York. In 1999 two investors, James H. Goodnight and John P. Sall, launched an unsuccessful takeover attempt after amassing 47 percent of company stock. They had offered $36 million for the rest of the company.

In March 1999, Southwest Airlines announced plans to serve Raleigh while US Airways (formerly USAir) provided low-cost competition in the form of its MetroJet unit. Other unpleasant news for Midway's managers came when the carrier's flight attendants became unionized.

Midway ordered 15 new Boeing 737s in June 1999 to complement its smaller Fokker 100s and Regional Jets. By this time, the airline dominated Raleigh-Durham Airport the way its namesake once had at Midway Airport. Traffic was lackluster in 1999, although it did peak at the end. Midway carried 2.1 million people during the year. Profits fell to $9.4 million from 1998's $15 million although revenues were up three percent to $218 million. The winter of 1999–2000 saw Midway increase its flight frequencies.

Principal Competitors

US Airways Group, Inc.; Delta Air Lines, Inc.; AirTran Holdings, Inc.

Further Reading

Chandler, Susan, "It's Going to Be a Bumpy Ride, Sam," *Business Week,* April 24, 1995, p. 74.

"David Hinson: Launching the Battle of Midway Airlines," *Industry Week,* August 10, 1987, pp. 51, 54.

James E. Ellis, "David Hinson Is Stretching Midway's Wings," *Business Week,* June 12, 1989, pp. 84–85.

——, "Heeding a Gospel of Measured Growth," *Business Week,* September 21, 1987, p. 62.

——, "Midway: Fogbound in Philly," *Business Week,* October 1, 1990, p. 123.

Field, David, "Chicago Airline's Resurrection Follows Airport's Rise," *Washington Times,* August 12, 1993.

——, "Midway Founder Picked to Head FAA," *Washington Times,* May 14, 1993.

——, "A Start-Up Finds Success: Triangle Niche Runs Circles Around Others," *USA Today,* March 31, 1998, p. 1B.

Fotos, Christopher P., "Ailing Midway Joins Ranks of Bankrupt US Carriers," *Aviation Week and Space Technology,* April 1, 1991, pp. 31–32.

Jaffe, Greg, "Midway Is Near Raising $200 Million," *Wall Street Journal,* August 7, 1996, p. S1.

Kelly, Kevin, Seth Payne, and Wendy Zellner, "Almost Everybody is Mad at Northwest Airlines," *Business Week,* December 2, 1991, p. 40.

Lavitt, Michael O., "Midway Plans Fast Growth to East Coast Cities," *Aviation Week & Space Technology,* November 29, 1993, pp. 40–41.

Loeffelholz, Suzanne, "Staying Power," *Financial World,* September 5, 1989, pp. 34, 37.

McCartney, Scott, "Southwest Air Plans Service to Raleigh," *Wall Street Journal,* March 4, 1999, p. A5.

McKenna, James T., "Airline Analysts Fear Big Loss Unless Fares Meet Cost Hikes," *Aviation Week & Space Technology,* October 22, 1990, pp. 30–31.

——, "Northwest Wins Approval To Buy All Midway Airlines Assets," *Aviation Week & Space Technology,* October 14, 1991, pp. 30–31.

Moorman, Robert W., "Midway Home," *Air Transport World,* June 1996, pp. 147–49.

"New Midway Emerges with Fokker 100 Fleet," *Aviation Week & Space Technology,* August 16, 1993, p. 36.

Ott, James, "Midway, First Product of Deregulation, Symbolized Era by Setting Precedents," *Aviation Week & Space Technology,* January 13, 1992, p. 45.

——, "Midway Halts Operations as Northwest Drops Buyout," *Aviation Week & Space Technology,* November 18, 1991, pp. 22–23.

Snyder, David, "Failing Up: After Midway Bust, Hinson's FAA Mess," *Crain's Chicago Business,* July 1, 1996. p. 11.

Weiner, Steven B., "A Profitable Survivor," *Forbes,* March 9, 1987, p. 106.

—Frederick C. Ingram

Minyard Food Stores, Inc.

777 Freeport Parkway
Coppell, Texas 75019
U.S.A.
Telephone: (972) 393-8700
Fax: (972) 462-9407
Web site: http://www.minyards.com

Private Company
Incorporated: 1932
Employees: 8,000
Sales: $1.08 billion (1999)
NAIC: 44511 Supermarkets and Other Grocery (Except
     Convenience) Stores; 44711 Gasoline Stations with
     Convenience Stores; 445299 All Other Specialty Food
     Stores; 23311 Land Subdivision and Land Development

Minyard Food Stores, Inc. is a privately owned and operated grocery store chain in Texas. The family-run business includes three supermarket chains: Sack 'n Save Warehouse Food Stores, Carnival Food Stores, which cater to ethnic minorities, and the traditional Minyard Food Stores. The company operates more than 80 stores, the majority of which carry the Minyard Food Store banner and are located primarily in the Dallas-Fort Worth regions. Minyard also owns a number of gas stations. The company is run by sisters Lisbeth Minyard and Gretchen Minyard Williams, descendants of the founders.

Building a Regional Presence: 1930s–70s

The time was the Depression era of the 1930s. A.W. "Eck" Minyard, an employee with the U.S. Postal Service, was concerned that his younger brothers, who had just completed high school, would have difficulty finding work. To supply jobs for his siblings, Eck bought a small store in east Dallas for $1,200. The first Minyard Food Store, which was little more than 500 square feet in size, opened on February 12, 1932. Eck operated the store with three of his brothers—H.C. "Henry" Minyard, M.T. "Buddy" Minyard, and H.J. "Hap" Minyard—as well as his sister, Fay Minyard. The store was successful enough to spawn the opening of another store and a convenience store by the end of the 1930s.

Store expansion slowed during the 1940s as the younger brothers set off to fight with the U.S. military during World War II. Eck and Fay manned the original store but temporarily closed the other stores while their brothers were away. Signs on the closed doors informed customers, "Closed. Gone to War. Be back after Hitler's funeral." After the brothers returned, Minyard grew steadily, adding three new stores in the 1940s. The following decade Minyard added six new stores. The company also expanded outside of Dallas County with the opening of a location in McKinney in 1957. In 1959 the family founded Minyard Properties Inc., which enabled the company to acquire and develop land and build shopping centers. Also at the end of the 1950s Minyard opened its largest store yet.

Growth continued in the 1960s and 1970s, and by the end of the 1960s the Minyards owned and operated 16 stores, five more than at the beginning of the decade. The 1970s marked a period of rapid growth for Minyard, and the company opened 21 new grocery stores. In addition, Minyard Properties had acquired nine shopping centers. To accommodate such expansion, the Minyard clan found the need for a central headquarters and distribution facility. In 1961 the family bought a 70,000-square-foot building complex in Dallas and moved its corporate offices and distribution operations.

Unmatched Expansion in the 1980s

Minyard Food Stores had enjoyed five decades of success, and the company intended to continue moving forward and growing operations with the needs of the communities it served in mind. Because of the company's growth in the 1970s, Minyard was forced to once again move its administrative offices and distribution center. In 1981 Minyard headquarters was established in Coppell, a town located between Dallas and Fort Worth that was a two-minute drive from the Dallas-Fort Worth International Airport. The large complex was nearly 400,000 square feet in size and sat on an 81-acre parcel of land.

In 1982 Minyard diversified from its standard grocery store format by opening its first Sack 'n Save Warehouse Food Store.

Sack 'n Save followed a warehouse format and offered products in bulk, which reduced prices. Customers also bagged their own groceries at Sack 'n Save. The new concept was considered necessary to remain competitive in the grocery industry, which faced slow growth in the mid-1980s.

Minyard's growth of the 1970s paled in comparison to its growth in 1987. In April 1987 Minyard purchased 24 stores from Safeway Stores Inc., which planned to exit the Dallas market and sell its 141 stores. At the time, Minyard operated 56 stores, and thus the acquisitions significantly boosted the company's presence in the Dallas-Fort Worth region. Minyard bought 12 stores in Dallas County, nine in Tarrant County, and three in distant counties. Minyard was able to reopen all 24 of the stores in record time—within five days. In August Minyard purchased three more stores from Safeway. By the end of the year Minyard owned and operated 62 Minyard Food Stores and ten Sack 'n Save stores. Prior to the acquisition, Minyard ranked fourth and had a market share in the Dallas area of 15 percent, according to *Supermarket News,* a trade publication. Tom Thumb-Page was the top supermarket in the Dallas market, with a share of 24 percent. Tom Thumb-Page operated 48 stores in the Dallas-Forth Worth market and had plans to buy ten of the Safeway locations. Tom Thumb-Page was followed by Kroger, with a 19 percent share. Kroger had 29 stores in the Dallas area and 16 in Tarrant County. Kroger planned to add nine of the Safeway stores. Third place went to Safeway.

Less than a year after guiding the company through its most challenging expansion endeavor, Chairman and CEO Buddy Minyard, the last of the original founders, died of a heart attack at the age of 78. Buddy had been actively involved in the day-to-day operations of the company since the opening of the first store. Strongly committed to the Dallas community, Buddy had participated in numerous service organizations and contributed to many causes, including the Scottish Rite Masonic order, the Leukemia Society of America, and the Boy Scouts. He was a founding member of the Dallas Urban League Inc., a community service organization, and was heavily involved with the grocery community as well—Buddy served as the president of the Dallas Retail Grocers Association in 1959 and served on the board of the National Retail Grocers Association. Buddy Minyard's commitment to the community was reflected in Minyard Food Stores, which had a working philosophy of responding to the shopping needs of the customers.

With Buddy Minyard's death, the Minyard leadership torch was passed along to Buddy's two daughters, Lisbeth "Liz" Minyard and Gretchen Minyard Williams. The "Minyard girls," as they were known within the local grocery community, had served as vice-presidents during their father's tenure as CEO. Other family members involved with the company were cousin Bob Minyard and Gretchen's husband, J.L. Sonny Wil-liams, who was company president. J.L. began working at Minyard as a bagger at the age of 13.

Increased Competition and Innovation in the 1990s

As Minyard Food Stores entered a new decade, it faced many new challenges, including a rapidly changing consumer environment. Taking a bold step to meet the changing needs of the community, Minyard announced in 1990 that it would open a new store format dedicated to serving the growing, and mostly underserved, population of minorities and ethnic neighborhoods. Although Minyard Food Stores carried some ethnic products, the new stores, which would operate under the name Carnival Food Stores, would offer ethnic merchandise, in addition to traditional grocery products, throughout the store, including produce and meat departments. The stores would target the needs of African American, Hispanic, or Asian consumers, depending on the neighborhood. Minyard's J.L. Williams explained in *Supermarket News,* "The Dallas-Fort Worth area is a mosaic of diverse people, communities and cultures comprising a market that is virtually untapped. . . . Predictions that the area's population mix will drastically change by the year 2000 and the growing customer demand for product variety are the two basic reasons we have developed this new store concept for our chain."

Minyard opened three Carnival Food Stores, converted from Minyard Food Stores, in Forth Worth in the summer of 1990; two catered to African Americans and one focused on Hispanic shoppers. The Hispanic-oriented stores featured signs in both English and Spanish and delicacies not commonly found in traditional grocery stores, such as beef heads. The Hispanic stores also offered bulk bins of such staples as corn, pinto beans, and rice, as well as such popular products as Mexican soft drinks and health and beauty aids. The Carnival concept performed strongly, with sales up 30 to 40 percent per store, and Minyard announced plans to open additional Carnival stores to bring the total up to seven by late 1991.

As Minyard continued to grow and diversify, it also faced increasingly aggressive competition. The Dallas market had heated up immensely, and supermarkets vied for consumer dollars by offering triple-coupon discounts and other promotions. Not only did Minyard face competition from longtime stores such as Tom Thumb-Page, which moved beyond traditional grocery offerings to offer a combined grocery and drug store, and Kroger, but the company faced new rivals as outside companies honed in on the Dallas market. North Carolina grocery chain Food Lion announced plans to open up to 50 stores in the Dallas-Fort Worth market. Food Lion CEO Tom E. Smith commented on the chain's entry into the Texas market in *Supermarket News* and said, "Our study of Dallas-Fort Worth found high prices, oversized stores and a lack of conveniently located stores." Food Lion claimed that Dallas-Fort Worth generated grocery sales of $7 billion a year and that Food Lion's entry into the market would cause food prices to drop six percent. Industry analysts stated that the 11-county region known as the Metroplex offered one of the largest and most competitive grocery store selections in the nation.

In reaction to the increased competition, and also to realize the company mission to serve the needs of the consumer, Minyard focused on improving customer service and tested new ideas in the early 1990s. For example, an upscale Minyard Food Store in Dallas provided free valet parking and offered shoe shining services inside the store. Liz Minyard explained in *Dallas Times Herald,* ''In the last 50 years, grocery stores have undergone a dramatic change—in terms of the size of the stores, the volume of the merchandise, computerization, and the range of products and services offered.... We try to make each store a little different, to appeal to the customers in the store.'' Although the company slowed expansion efforts, it continued to open new stores in strategic locations. In 1991, for instance, Minyard reentered the Plano, Texas market, which was growing more competitive, when it opened a 70,000-square-foot Sack 'n Save.

In 1992 Minyard Food Stores celebrated its 60th anniversary. To emphasize the company's local roots, Minyard launched a storewide promotion that featured a ''Made in Texas'' theme. The Texas Lone Star Jackpot promotion included a grand prize of $60,000 in addition to a host of other prizes and giveaways, including televisions, clocks, free trips, and concert tickets. The large-scale promotion was so successful that Minyard continued the concept in ensuing years. Unlike promotions offered by other grocery chains, which centered around marketing promotions by national brands, Minyard developed its own campaigns and then searched for vendors to participate. Minyard's promotions, which included such campaigns as the Great American Dream Home Sweepstakes, which had a grand prize with a value of more than $170,000, the Tour the Ballparks with the Texas Rangers campaign, and the Summer Safari Sweepstakes, provided the company with an edge over competitors as well. According to the company, total store sales jumped about 3.5 percent during major promotions.

By the mid-1990s it was clear that Minyard had weathered the storm of the early 1990s. The threat presented by incoming Food Lion failed to bear fruit, and by 1994 Food Lion announced store closures of about half of its stores in the Dallas-Fort Worth region. By 1997 the company exited Texas. Other competitors alleged to be entering the Dallas grocery market never arrived. Although Tom Thumb-Page lost its number one status to Albertson's, Minyard managed to move up to third in 1996. According to *Market Scope,* Minyard had a market share

of 15.3 percent in the Dallas region. Although competition was fierce, the growing population in the region meant an increase in the number of mouths to feed. Food store sales in Texas, reported the state comptroller's office, grew 27 percent between 1990 and 1996, reaching $34.04 billion. Minyard, too, enjoyed increased sales: in 1993 the company rang up sales of about $760 million; in 1996 Minyard had sales of $950 million.

Much of the company's success in the 1990s was attributed to the leadership of the Minyard girls. The sisters worked at the stores from an early age, receiving valuable training. ''From the time we were 13 and 16, we had on-the-job training,'' recalled Gretchen Minyard Williams in the *Fort Worth Star-Telegram.* ''We were never given an allowance. We had to work if we wanted any spending money.'' Both attended Texas Christian University and majored in business administration. Although both were expected to pursue careers, they were never pressured to join the family business. The sisters chose to follow in their father's footsteps, however, and worked their way up the executive ladder. When their father passed away, the sisters became co-chairs of the company, with Liz focused on community relations and customer service and Gretchen specializing in marketing and employee relations. The Minyard sisters made it onto *Working Woman* magazine's list of the top 50 female business owners in the United States beginning in 1992. Both acknowledged that it was sometimes difficult working within a male-dominated industry but stated that as women, they provided a unique and valuable perspective. Liz Minyard told *Progressive Grocer,* ''Many of the men who work in the industry don't even do the grocery shopping, which always surprises me.... My sister and I have always done the shopping, because we believe it gives us a customer's perspective of our stores.''

In the middle to late 1990s Minyard continued to grow and strengthen store operations. In 1997 the company added to its multitude of services by opening gasoline stations, called ''Minyard's On The Go,'' at two Minyard Food Stores. The company had plans to open up to 35 gas stations over the course of several years. In addition to expanding locations to serve the growing population, Minyard also focused on providing shopping opportunities to underserved communities. In 1995 the company opened a Minyard Food Store in the inner-city neighborhood of south Dallas. It was the first major supermarket to open in the community in about 30 years and enabled residents to shop within their community. The *Dallas Morning News* reported that Dallas Mayor Ron Kirk, who attended the grand opening, told shoppers, ''I cannot tell you how much it means to have good corporate people like the Minyards that believe in putting back what they've taken and being more a part of the community than just taking away.'' Minyard also opened a store in west Dallas, another underserved area, and in 1998 built a store in southeast Fort Worth, also a lower income region with a large minority and elderly population. As in south Dallas, the entrance of Minyard in southeast Fort Worth marked the first major grocery store opening in about 30 years. Minyard also opened a Carnival Food Store, its largest to date, in north Fort Worth, yet another severely underserved community, in 1998.

Minyard exceeded $1 billion in sales for the first time in its history in 1998 and had been a strong contender in the regional grocery store wars for decades. As the company approached the new millennium, it planned to continue building upon its tradition of serving the customer's needs. Although new competitors loomed on the horizon, including Wal-Mart Stores Inc.'s Neighborhood Markets and H.E. Butt Grocery Co., the largest supermarket chain in Texas, Minyard, accustomed to perpetual competition, remained undaunted. J.L. Williams told the *Dallas Morning News* in January 1999, "Next month is our 67th anniversary. We've been here a long time and plan on being here a long time." At the close of the 20th century, Minyard owned and operated 44 Minyard Food Stores, 20 Sack 'n Save stores, and 20 Carnival Food Stores. The company was the tenth largest private company in Dallas and the largest private company run by women.

Principal Subsidiaries

Minyard Properties Inc.

Principal Competitors

Albertson's, Inc.; The Kroger Co.; Randall's Food Markets, Inc.; Wal-Mart Stores Inc.

Further Reading

Donegan, Priscilla, "A Woman's Place: Although Women Still Dominate the Grocery Store Aisles, They're Few and Far Between in the Industry's Executive Suites. But Times Are Changing—Slowly," *Progressive Grocer,* May 1, 1989, p. 37.

Fox, Bruce, "Minyard Unveils New Format; Carnival Food Stores Target Minorities," *Chain Store Age Executive,* February 1, 1991, p. 35.

Gubbins, Teresa, "Minyard Pumps You Up," *Dallas Morning News,* January 22, 1997, p. F1.

Halkias, Maria, "Grocers Intensify Competition for Share of Lucrative D-FW Market," *Dallas Morning News,* April 11, 1998, p. F1.

——, "Grocery Chains Thriving After 'Store Wars'," *Dallas Morning News,* February 26, 1997, p. D1.

Hansard, Donna Steph, "Minyard Buying 24 Safeway Stores," *Dallas Morning News,* April 14, 1987, p. D1.

Harris, Joyce Saenz, "Gretchen Minyard Williams and Liz Minyard—Sisters Carrying on the Family Tradition," *Dallas Morning News,* January 3, 1993, p. E1.

Ingram, Bob, "At Minyard, 'Big D' Stands for Diversity," *Supermarket Business,* May 1, 1994, p. 41.

Jackson, David, "Minyard Groceries' Founder Dead at 79," *Dallas Morning News,* February 21, 1988, p. A1.

Lundy, Audrey Steinbergen, "New Minyard Fills a Void for Many in South Dallas," *Dallas Morning News,* September 16, 1995, p. A29.

Narayan, Chandrika, "Big Links in the Chain: Sisters Steer Steady Course at Minyard," *Dallas Times Herald,* January 19, 1991, p. 1.

Rodriguez, June Naylor, "The Working Life: With a Nose-to-the-Grindstone Attitude Instilled by Their Father, Success for Minyard's Grocery Women Is in the Bag," *Fort Worth Star-Telegram,* May 5, 1994, p. 1.

Smith, Jack Z., "Minyard Plans $6.5 Million Store in Southeast Fort Worth," *Fort Worth Star-Telegram,* February 11, 1997, p. 1.

Turcsik, Richard, "Food Lion To Enter Dallas; Plans 30–50 Stores in '91," *Supermarket News,* April 16, 1990, p. 1.

——, "Minyard Opens First 3 Ethnic-Oriented Stores," *Supermarket News,* August 6, 1990, p. 1.

——, "Minyard's Lone Star Jackpot Hits Home," *Supermarket News,* August 24, 1992, p. 25.

Weinstein, Steve, "Going Beyond Price," *Progressive Grocer,* September 1, 1994, p. 54.

Wren, Worth, "Minyard Adds to Line of Ethnic Food Stores," *Fort Worth Star-Telegram,* August 27, 1991, p. 1.

—Mariko Fujinaka

Le Monde S.A.

21 bis, rue Claude-Bernard
75242 Paris Cedex 05
France
Telephone: (33) 1 42 17 20 00
Fax: (33) 1 42 17 21 21
Web site: http://www.lemonde.fr

Limited Partnership
Incorporated: 1944
Sales: FFr 1.5 billion ($250 million) (1999)
NAIC: 51111 Newspaper Publishers

Producer of what many consider the most prestigious newspaper in France since the end of the World War II, Le Monde S.A. has expanded its list of publications to include a variety of monthly and other magazine formats, while launching itself into the world of multimedia through its subsidiary Le Monde Interactif. Le Monde is operated as a limited partnership, with much of its shares controlled by its editorial staff, who have long enjoyed a veto over the company's financial and management decisions. In that sense, Le Monde is perhaps unique among the world's daily newspapers, in that its chief executive is chosen by its journalists and editors. Financially, Le Monde has long proved a precarious exercise; after spending much of the 1990s in the red, however, the company has returned to profitability, posting rising revenues (forecasted to reach FFr 1.5 billion for 1999) while increasing its daily readership to more than 400,000 copies. The company has also announced its intention to invest some FFr 150 million in modernizing its printing plants in the year 2000. In addition to the daily newspaper, Le Monde publishes a series of respected specialty papers, including: the monthly *Le Monde Diplomatique,* with 180,000 copies in France and another 300,000 sold internationally; *Le Monde des Philatélists,* the company's oldest newsmagazine, with a circulation among 40,000 stamp collectors; *Le Monde de l'Education, de la Culture et de la Formation,* devoted to educational and related trends; *Le Monde Dossiers et Documents,* directed at a student audience; and *Dossiers et Documents Littéraires,* also directed toward a student audience, with in-depth treatments of literary topics. Le Monde has been led by Jean-Marie Colombani since 1994.

From the Ruins of the French Press in the 1940s

Tainted by the spectre of collaboration with the Nazi occupier during the Second World War, nearly all of France's daily newspapers—including its most prestigious paper, *Le Temps*—were banned from further publication after the Liberation. By then, however, the Free French government, led by General Charles de Gaulle in London, had already begun to encourage the formation of a new generation of news dailies. Although setting up a new newspaper was no easy task, particularly in light of the severe shortages of paper during and following the war, the new generation of newspapers was offered a loan of FFr 1 million.

De Gaulle's idea was to encourage the founding of a "serious" newspaper, along the lines of prestigious, internationally respected titles such as the *Times* of England or the *New York Times.* In 1944 the team of Hubert Beuve-Méry, René Courtin, and Christian Funck-Brentano took up De Gaulle's challenge, launching a new daily newspaper, *Le Monde* ("the world"). Born in 1902, Beuve-Méry was to have the greatest impact on Le Monde's growth, and he quickly came to be the embodiment of the newspaper himself. A journalist, acting as a correspondent in Prague for *Le Temps* before the war, Beuve-Méry quit his position after *Le Temps* gave its editorial support to the Munich treaty with Hitler in 1938. After working for the newspapers *Le Matin* and the *Petit Journal*—where he was confronted with the corruption, opportunism, and low standards of the French press of the period—Beuve-Méry joined the active Resistance. In 1944 the French minister of information recommended to De Gaulle that Beuve-Méry form a new newspaper for postwar France.

Beuve-Méry accepted, opening shop in the former *Le Temps* headquarters on Paris's rue d'Italie. Paying rent to the former owners of *Le Temps,* Le Monde was not only based in *Le Temps* offices, it also made use of the former journal's printing facility and a number of its former employees who had come through the war untainted by the stain of collaboration. The new news-

Key Dates:

1944: *Le Monde* newspaper launched.
1948: Appearance of 1,000th edition.
1954: Launch of *Le Monde Diplomatique* weekly.
1955: Circulation tops 200,000.
1968: Circulation tops 800,000 during student riots.
1973: Launch of *Le Monde Dossiers et Documents.*
1974: Launch of *Le Monde de L'Education.*
1975: Launch of *Le Bilan du Monde.*
1987: Sale of rue d'Italie office building.
1989: Construction of new printing plant.
1995: Launch of Le Monde web site.
1996: Company restructures as public limited company.
1998: Creation of subsidiary Le Monde Interactif.
1999: Circulation tops 400,000.
2000: Company announces FFr 150 million printing plant modernization program.

paper even made use of *Le Temps'* gothic-style letterhead and broadsheet format. Yet Le Monde quickly and resolutely showed its determination to create a new breed of French journalism, free of political favoritism and the courtship of big money interests. With the one million franc loan from the government, Le Monde went to press. The first issue of *Le Monde* appeared on December 18, 1944, printed on both sides of a single sheet of paper, in an edition of 147,190 copies. Beuve-Méry himself became one of the newspaper's most respected editorialists, signing his columns under the pen name of "Sirius."

Le Monde was able to repay the government loan by April 1945. The paper had met with success among the country's—particularly the Paris region's—readers. By the end of the decade, the company's average press runs neared 170,000 copies. Le Monde, which was operating nonetheless in a continuously precarious financial condition, celebrated its 1,000th edition in 1948. Shortly after, the company entered the first of many management crises.

Le Monde had originally been set up as a limited liability company, with its direction shared among a tightly closed circle of seven directors, who were forbidden to open the company's capital to outside interests. The company ran into its first management crisis as the world entered a new type of war—the Cold War. Despite the Soviet threat to western Europe, Le Monde, under Beuve-Méry, was determined to retain its neutral position, both in respect to the French government and to the world political scene. The company's co-founders, Courtin and Funck-Brentano, disagreed with this approach, however, and after a clash with Beuve-Méry, stepped down from the directors' positions in 1949. The ensuing crisis extended for the next two years. Finally, as the paper's financial health became increasingly fragile, Beuve-Méry suggested that the company be disbanded and that he be allowed to step down from his position as Le Monde's chief.

The resulting furor from the paper's editorial staff changed the nature of the company's management. The editorial staff

proclaimed its right to participate in decisions affecting the company's direction; the paper's editors and journalists also demanded that Beuve-Méry be reinstated as *Le Monde's* editor-in-chief. Following on the editorial staff's actions was support from an unusual front. The newspaper's readership, too, demanded a say in the paper's direction. Forming their own association, Les Lecteurs du Monde, the newspaper's readers, stating that they refused to be treated "as an object, a thing, a piece of merchandise," succeeded in gaining a position on the company's board of directors, alongside the editorial staff. The newly composed directorship, now composed of 280 shares, met in December 1951 and reinstated Beuve-Méry in his position. *Le Monde* became unique among the world's leading newspapers in that its readership shared a strong role in the company's direction.

By the mid-1950s, *Le Monde's* circulation had swelled to more than 200,000 copies. Yet the company continued to face a great deal of pressure, both financial and political. In 1956 a new newspaper appeared on Paris's newsstands. Called *Le Temps de Paris,* the new daily openly declared its intention to "destabilize" *Le Monde.* Instead, *Le Temps de Paris* folded just three months later. By then, however, the French government, led by Guy Mollet, took its own stab at destabilizing *Le Monde*—which remained an open and respected critic of the French political system, no matter which party held the current power. Faced with rising costs, particularly as a result of the institution of the French press distribution monopoly, Nouvelles Messageries de la Presse Parisienne (NMPP), created in 1947, *Le Monde* sought government approval to increase its prices. After the government refused its permission, *Le Monde's* readership once again came to the newspaper's rescue, buying multiple copies or simply sending the company checks to make up the sought-after difference in price.

By the time of its 20th anniversary, Le Monde had succeeded in gaining a measure of financial stability. The company had completed the purchase of the rue d'Italie offices, while also extending its printing capacity to some 150,000 copies per hour. The company's revenues topped FFr 40 million, while its readership continued to enjoy average levels of 200,000 copies. *Le Monde's* readership was to explode—if only briefly—during the student movement of 1968, which had adopted *Le Monde* as its "official" newspaper. Sales of *Le Monde* reached more than 800,000 copies. The company, however, was about to enter a new period of financial and management crisis.

Diversification for the 21st Century

Beuve-Méry retired in 1969, succeeded by Jacques Fauvet. Under Fauvet, Le Monde began a series of expansion moves to take it beyond its reliance on its single newspaper product. Although this process had already begun in the 1950s, with the appearance of the title *Le Monde des Livres,* and of the weekly *Le Monde Diplomatique,* launched in 1954, which quickly gained an international reputation for the quality of its in-depth coverage of major issues of the day, the company's expansion was approached more deliberately beginning with the 1970s. Among the new Le Monde titles created in the 1970s were *Le Monde Dossiers et Documents,* directed at a high school and university student readership, launched in 1973; *Le Bilan du Monde,* a review of the year's economic and social events, created in 1975; and the influential *Le Monde de L'Education,* launched in 1974 and later extended as *Le Monde de L'Education, de la Culture et de la Formation.*

Le Monde entered the 1970s with an average readership of 500,000. By the beginning of the 1980s, however, the newspaper was once again facing a grave crisis, as its readership slipped back to less than 250,000. The economic recession of the 1970s had lowered readers' enthusiasm for daily newspaper purchases. A new management crisis, involving the choice of a successor to Fauvet and lasting more than two years, had tarnished *Le Monde's* image. Worse, the paper had lost much of its former credibility. If *Le Monde* under Beuve-Méry had held fast to its independence—to the point where the paper grew to face the outright hostility of former benefactor De Gaulle—during the 1970s the paper had increasingly begun to support the position of the country's Socialist Party, not only while in opposition, but after the Socialists had taken over the government under Valery Giscard d'Estaing in 1974.

By the early 1980s, *Le Monde* was no longer known as the independent critic of French politics, but as a mouthpiece for the Socialist government. The taint to its image—and disappointment among its readership—led to steady losses in circulation. Meanwhile, the company, which had long enjoyed a position as publisher of France's leading daily newspaper, saw rival *Le Figaro* pass it in circulation. At the same time, new competition appeared on the French newsstands, with the launch of the daily *Libération,* which quickly established its popularity among the 15–35 year age group.

Le Monde's losses mounted and took on still greater momentum in the late 1980s and early 1990s. To rescue the company from an increasingly drastic financial position in the mid-1980s, the company's direction, now under André Fontaine, undertook a series of heavily criticized actions, including the sale of the company's rue d'Italie building, a reduction of staff, and a ten percent cut in salaries. At the same time, the company brought in new personnel for its administrative departments. Finally, in 1987, Le Monde opened its shares to outside investors. Accepting the participation of a number of institutional investors, who joined the newly created shareholding group Le Monde Entreprises, the company's shares were divided as well among its editors, journalists, and readers, under the Société des Lecteurs du Monde. At the same time, the company spun off its advertising sales division into a joint partnership with the advertising agency Publicis, creating the subsidiary Régie Press (later Le Monde Publicité), with Le Monde retaining a controlling 51 percent share.

If the company was able to stabilize its readership, its financial position was soon hit by a new recession, one that was to grip France into the middle of the 1990s. Le Monde had taken on a new debt burden, with the construction of a new, modern printing facility at Ivry-sur-Seine; while sharing the costs with publisher Hachette, which purchased 34 percent of the new subsidiary Le Monde Imprimerie, the purchase came to hurt the company as its readership was once again under pressure from the failing economic climate. The company was also about to enter yet again a protracted battle for its leadership.

By 1996, Jean-Marie Colombani had emerged as victor, taking the position as the company's chief executive. Colombani set about transforming the company, launching what quickly became known as "le nouveau Monde" ("the new world"). After changing the company's stature, from limited liability company to a public limited company, permitting it to raise more potential investments, Colombani led a redesign of the newspaper's look, increasing the number of graphics and improving readability, while adding new supplements and sections.

The "new world" quickly found success among France's readership, and the paper began making steady gains in average daily sales through the second half of the 1990s. The success of the new Monde look led the company's other publications to adopt a similar graphic styling. By 1999, Le Monde had succeeding in pulling itself out of the red, and its average readership levels topped 400,000 for the first time in 20 years. Meanwhile, Le Monde had begun to prepare for the future, making a new diversification move into the world of multimedia with the launch of subsidiary Le Monde Interactif in 1998. Created to take charge of the newspaper's web site—one of the French-speaking world's most popular—and to develop it into an important francophone "portal," Le Monde Interactif also took over development of such product areas as CDs and CD-ROMs, while beginning the process of building an electronic archive of the Le Monde newspapers going back to its 1944 beginnings. At the same time, the company prepared for the future, announcing in January 2000 its intention to invest FFr 150 million in modernizing its printing plant.

Principal Subsidiaries

Le Monde Interactif (65%); Le Monde Publicité (51%).

Principal Competitors

Le Figaro; Le Soir; The Herald Tribune; Libération.

Further Reading

Eveno, Patrick, *Le Monde, 1944–1995, histoire d'une entreprise de presse,* Paris: Le Monde Editions, 1996.
Feraud, Jean-Christophe, "*Le Monde* va développer sa filiale multimédia en partenariat avec le groupe Grolier Interactive," *Les Echos,* January 8, 1999, p. 18.
"French Daily "Le Monde" Barred," *Africa News Service,* November 15, 1999.
"Jean-Marie Colombani: 'Le Premier ministre doit se saisir du dossier NMPP,' " *Les Echos,* January 18, 2000, p. 21.
"Le Monde, France's Largest National Newspaper, Selects Unisys e-@ction Publishing Solutions," *Business Wire,* December 22, 1999.
Thibau, Jacques, *"Le Monde." Histoire d'un journal. Un journal dans l'Histoire,* Paris: Nouvelle édition, Plon, 1996.
Tuttle, Alexandra, "Lofty in Tone, Austere in Appearance," *Time International,* October 15, 1990, p. 54.

—M.L. Cohen

Morgan Stanley Dean Witter & Company

<table>
<tr><td>

1585 Broadway
New York, New York 10036
U.S.A.
Telephone: (212) 761-4000
Fax: (212) 761-0086
Web site: http://www.msdw.com

Public Company
Incorporated: 1924 as Dean Witter & Company
Employees: 52,927
Sales: $36.04 billion (1999)
Stock Exchanges: New York
Ticker Symbol: MWD
NAIC: 52311 Investment Banking and Securities Dealing;
    52312 Securities Brokerage; 52221 Credit Card
    Issuing

</td></tr>
</table>

Morgan Stanley Dean Witter & Company, formed in 1997 through the merger of Morgan Stanley Group, Inc. and Dean Witter, Discover & Co., is an investment banking and retail brokerage firm. The company is made up of three primary divisions—securities, asset management, and credit services—and is one of the top retail brokerages in the United States, with more than 450 U.S. offices. The firm also has growing international operations, with more than 30 overseas branches. In addition to asset management and securities trading, Morgan Stanley Dean Witter offers corporate finance, merchant banking, and research and advisory services. The company is a leading issuer of credit cards, particularly the Discover Card.

Early Years as a Securities Brokerage: 1920s–70s

The original Dean Witter brokerage house was founded in 1924 by Dean Witter, his brother Guy, and cousin Jean. The trio started Dean Witter & Co. as a West Coast securities firm dealing in municipal and corporate bonds. They set up shop in San Francisco and, in 1928, purchased a seat on the San Francisco Stock Exchange; that exchange was incorporated later into the Pacific Stock Exchange. The company enjoyed im-

mense success during the explosive bull market of the 1920s. In 1929, in fact, Dean Witter opened a New York office and purchased a seat on the New York Stock Exchange.

Dean Witter survived the Depression-era securities industry shakeout and even managed to post profits every year during the 1930s and into the 1940s. The company also became known as an innovator on Wall Street. For example, Dean Witter was one of the first securities firms to establish an account executive training program. The company grew rapidly during the 1950s and 1960s, establishing itself as a major U.S. brokerage house. Dean Witter died in 1969, and, the following year, Guy Witter retired, passing the top position to Jean Witter's son, William M. Witter, who became CEO of the operation. The company was taken public in 1972 with an offering of 1.5 million shares on the New York Stock Exchange. In 1977 Dean Witter purchased InterCapital Inc., an investment management firm with $200 million in assets.

At the same time that Dean Witter was rising to prominence on Wall Street, another company was making its mark on the securities brokerage business. Reynolds & Co. was started in 1931 by Richard S. Reynolds Jr., Thomas F. Stanley, and Charles H. Babcock, all members of the Reynolds family. That company also went public in the early 1970s, becoming Reynolds Securities. In 1978 Reynolds and Witter joined forces in what was then the largest merger in the history of the U.S. securities industry. Both firms were industry leaders and neither had posted a loss since they had opened their doors. The resultant company, Dean Witter Reynolds, was the fifth largest broker in the United States.

New Ownership and Diversification in the 1980s and Early 1990s

By the late 1970s, Sears, the largest retailer in the world, was facing several challenges. Its retail store operations were increasingly under fire from new competitors, particularly from discount retailers and upscale department store chains. Likewise, its well-known catalog division was threatened by a new breed of specialty catalog retailers. In short, Sears retailing strategy had become obsolete and the company was floun-

Company Perspectives:

We believe that Morgan Stanley Dean Witter clearly has demonstrated its ability to adapt, prosper and grow in a rapidly changing and often turbulent marketplace. We believe the diversity of our revenue streams and our ability to manage risk make us less subject to market volatility. Our global commitment and expertise position us to take full advantage of the continuing trend of globalization. Our capacity for innovation enables us to serve our clients in an increasingly complex financial marketplace. And as the consolidation of the financial services industry continues, we believe we have the range of products and broad distribution channels that will enable us to continue to gain market share.

dering. In an effort to overcome its problems, Sears experimented with a variety of fixes. During the early 1980s, for example, it decided to diversify into new businesses, including financial services. Toward that end, Sears acquired Dean Witter Reynolds in 1981 for about $600 million.

Sears hoped that Dean Witter would provide the foundation for a giant financial services network—the Sears Financial Services Group—that would be offered to consumers through the company's extensive chain of retail stores. The network would provide Sears customers with an easy way to purchase mutual funds, stocks, and insurance, and even allow them to obtain financing for homes and other purchases. To head Dean Witter, Sears chose Philip J. Purcell, a strategic planner at the Sears Chicago headquarters. Purcell moved to New York to run the operation from Dean Witter's office.

Sears decided early that Dean Witter should make a major shift in its strategy. Instead of serving both the retail and institutional sectors, it would shift its focus to the former, the individual consumer. Purcell believed the market would fuel growth in the financial services industry in the coming decade, and he felt that Sears offered the infrastructure to reach that group. Thus the strategy was relatively synergistic: Sears would create a sort of financial services supermarket aimed at the broad middle consumer market. A combination of heavy foot traffic and general goodwill toward Sears would lead millions to entrust their money with Dean Witter and its affiliates. "A lot of people don't trust brokers, but they do trust Sears," explained John Fallon, a Dean Witter account executive, in the December 14, 1987 *Crain's Chicago Business.*

Many critics regarded Sears's scheme as simplistic and illusory. "Do consumers really want to buy socks and stocks under the same roof?" they questioned. Similarly, stockholders wondered why Sears was involving itself with financial services, when its core business was being assaulted by Wal-Mart and other aggressive contenders. In response, Sears cited its success with Allstate, an insurance company that it had started in 1931. Sears enjoyed success with that operation and hoped to replay those gains with broader financial offerings. In addition to Dean Witter, in fact, Sears purchased Coldwell Banker, a provider of mortgage and brokerage services. Sears aimed to achieve a synergy between Allstate, Coldwell, and Dean Witter

that would allow the three to benefit from their complementary offerings.

During the early 1980s, Sears used its retail store network to open new Dean Witter and Coldwell Banker offices in areas of the country in which they had been nonexistent or poorly represented. After establishing a base in the local Sears store, satellite offices were spun off in surrounding neighborhoods. Sears invested millions of dollars into the Dean Witter operation during the early 1980s, opening 280 new offices between 1981 and 1986. Indeed, in 1983, Sears announced its intent to at least double Dean Witter's chain of 350 outlets during the 1980s and to establish it as a leading securities firm for individual investors. Sears initiated similar growth plans for Coldwell Banker as well.

Sears's aggressive efforts to turn its financial services division into a star performer had achieved lackluster results by the mid-1980s, however. Critics of the strategy sounded off after the stock market crash of 1987, which seemed to expose weaknesses in the division. Indeed, after focusing on building Dean Witter's retail sales, the financial services division was facing the possibility of a long-term bear market during which retail sales growth would undoubtedly wane. Worse yet, Dean Witter's position in the traditional investment banking and underwriting sectors had deteriorated rapidly since 1981. Many of its top executives and managers had jumped ship after the transition to retailing. Not surprisingly, Dean Witter's rank in the corporate debt and equity underwriting market had slipped from tenth to 15th, and investment banking accounted for less than ten percent of Witter's revenues by 1987.

Sears financial group posted a loss of $37 million in 1987 on sales of about $3.5 billion, while Sears earned $1.35 billion from $44 billion in sales during that year. Nevertheless, some contended that Dean Witter's performance was not as bad as it seemed. In fact, the overall financial services operations had posted healthy profits of $80 million just one year earlier. Furthermore, much of the 1987 loss was attributable to the Discover Card, a credit card introduced the year before by Sears, which sought to enter the growing $200 billion industry. Sears had invested $200 million into the project during 1986, with the expectation of losing money in the short term.

Discover Card had been set up as a division of Dean Witter, which was still under Purcell's direction. The main appeal of the card for consumers was that it was free; most other cards at the time charged annual fees ranging from $10 to $50. In addition, the card offered cashback bonuses and interest-free cash advances. The card was distinguished from Visa and Mastercard in that Sears controlled its brand image, features, service level, and pricing. Even though many retailers were initially slow to accept the card, within two years the card boasted more than 22 million subscribers and was accepted at 740,000 merchant outlets.

Discover's growth dropped off significantly during the late 1980s as credit card competition intensified. According to some analysts, Discover's profitability failed to live up to Sears's original expectations, and the concept received a generally lukewarm reception from the Visa/Mastercard-dominated credit card market. Nevertheless, Sears poured more than $1 billion into the project, and Discover turned its first profit in 1988. Discover's account base continued to increase past 25 million by the early 1990s as the total number of dispensed cards topped 40 million. In fact, Discover became the largest single issuer of general purpose credit cards. Its profitability remained well below that of many of its peers, but its sheer size allowed Discover to generate earnings of about $174 million annually by 1991.

Like Discover, Dean Witter's other operations experienced some challenges during the late 1980s. Although Dean Witter had nearly doubled in size between 1981 and 1989, it appeared as though Sears had failed to achieve the financial services synergy for which it had hoped. Sears announced plans to close about 200 of Dean Witter's 650 outlets, primarily those located in its department stores. Viewed as a failed attempt to capitalize on the individual financial services market, the barely profitable Dean Witter was frowned upon by frustrated Sears stockholders. In the early 1990s, however, the fortune of Dean Witter and its Discover Card began to turn.

Falling interest rates in the early 1990s sent many investors scurrying to the stock market in search of higher returns. As a result, Dean Witter's sales skyrocketed. Much of its gains were attributable to Dean Witter's emphasis on mutual funds. The company had begun investing heavily in its mutual fund offerings in the early 1980s, speculating that the funds would become the investment vehicle of choice for its target market. That strategy began to pay off in the early 1990s. Significantly, Dean Witter introduced a new family of proprietary funds (funds managed in-house) in 1992, giving it a steady stream of cash in the form of management fees as well as up-front fees charged to enter the funds. As cash began to pour in, Witter's mutual fund assets increased to more than $50 billion by 1992.

To the surprise of its critics, Dean Witter staged a major comeback in the early 1990s. In 1990 Witter posted profits of $109 million while the average Wall Street brokerage house saw a loss of $162 million. In 1991, moreover, net income from Dean Witter and its Discover division rose to $171 million and

$173 million, respectively, as combined sales soared to a record $3.35 billion. Then, in 1992, total net income surpassed $400 million from revenues of $3.7 billion. Although Witter's securities operations were enjoying healthy gains, its success was also the result of big advancements by Discover, which was finally beginning to bear fruit.

As its financial services division posted solid gains during the early 1990s, the performance of Sears's core retail operations waned. By 1992, the mismanaged retail giant was suffering under a massive $38 billion debt load. In an effort to pare its debt and refocus its energies on its core business, Sears announced its intentions to sell its financial services operations. Although they were going to lose their deep-pocketed parent, many Dean Witter managers welcomed the decision to spin off the operation. Indeed, some of them felt that the Sears name was not helping their image; in 1992 Sears posted the worst performance in its 108-year history, a staggering $3.9 billion loss.

On February 22, 1993, Sears spun off 20 percent of Dean Witter and Discover into an independent, publicly traded company called Dean Witter, Discover & Co. The remaining 80 percent was spun off on June 30, 1993. During its first year of operation, Dean Witter Discover revenues rose more than 20 percent to $4.6 billion as net income reached $600 million. Moreover, the company's stock soared. Gains continued in 1994 as both credit card and securities operations continued to advance, causing many of Witter's competitors to adopt the operating strategies that they had once ridiculed. Going into the mid-1990s, Dean Witter, Discover & Co. remained the largest credit card issuer in the United States, was the third largest broker, and offered a variety of related financial and transaction processing services. In 1994, moreover, the company started a new credit card, Prime Option, aimed at the Mastercard/Visa segment of the market.

Major Changes in the Late 1990s

Heading into the second half of the decade, Dean Witter was still getting a feel for its newly established independence. The independence, however, was short-lived. As early as 1994, Dean Witter began exploring the possibility of joint partnerships with Morgan Stanley Group, Inc., a well-respected investment banking firm known for working with large and influential companies worldwide. A few years later, in 1997, the two companies announced that they would merge, creating the largest asset management company and the largest securities firm, in terms of equity capital, in the United States. The deal, valued at $10.22 billion, was finalized on May 31, 1997, and the new company was named Morgan Stanley, Dean Witter, Discover & Co. Each share of Morgan Stanley stock was converted into 1.65 shares of Dean Witter.

The two companies asserted that the merger was mutually beneficial. Morgan Stanley gained access to millions of U.S. customers through Dean Witter's extensive U.S. network of sales offices, and Dean Witter's stock offerings and investment choices were expanded considerably through Morgan Stanley. Morgan Stanley also provided Dean Witter with access to international markets. Despite the companies' insistence that the merger was an ideal fit, many industry observers remained skeptical. Journalist Peter Truell commented on the merger in the *San Diego Union-Tribune:* "the new firm faces the stiff challenge of integrating Morgan Stanley's aristocratic culture ... with the meat-and-potatoes environment at Dean Witter, whose brokers ply their trade everywhere from suburban office complexes to small-town storefronts. In a way, the merger would be as if Sears and Saks Fifth Avenue decided to join together."

The combined company shortened its name to Morgan Stanley Dean Witter & Co. (MSDW) in 1998 and worked to settle into its new organization. To strengthen its core operations of securities, asset management, and credit transaction services, the company began to divest itself of noncore businesses. MSDW sold its global custody businesses, namely Morgan Stanley Trust Company and Morgan Stanley Bank Luxembourg, S.A., to Chase Manhattan Corporation. The company also sold its Correspondent Clearing operations to NationsBanc Montgomery Securities LLC. Other divestments included MSDW's Prime Option MasterCard business, which it ran with NationsBank of Delaware, N.A.; its 73 percent stake in subsidiary SPS Transaction Services, Inc.; and some credit card receivables tied to its discontinued BRAVO Card.

Although the late 1990s were volatile years for financial markets globally, MSDW performed well and began to put to rest the doubts of industry skeptics. Total revenues for fiscal 1998, which ended November 30, were $31.13 billion, compared with fiscal 1997 sales of $27.13 billion. Profits reached a record $3.3 billion, a 27 percent jump over 1997 earnings. In addition, despite continued weak economic conditions in Europe and Asia, MSDW worked to strengthen overseas operations. In 1998 the company increased its staff in Europe by 20 percent and its staff in Asia by ten percent. In early 1999 MSDW acquired AB Asesores, the largest financial services company in Spain, and also partnered with National Bank of Kuwait SAK to offer asset management services. The company also extended its global reach to India, where it formed an alliance with JM Financial to create JM Morgan Stanley. Also in 1999 MSDW opened an investment banking branch in Argentina to better serve Latin American interests and formed an alliance with Sanwa Bank to offer mutual fund and investment products to Japanese clients.

MSDW's credit card operations continued to perform strongly, and in fiscal 1998 net income from the credit card division rose 47 percent to reach $688 million. The company launched the Discover Platinum Card in late 1998 and introduced its first credit card overseas, in the United Kingdom, in 1999. Also in 1999 more than 5.4 million new credit card accounts were established, the largest increase in one year since 1987. MSDW added to its online offerings in the late 1990s as well, launching *i*choice, an online service that offered trading capabilities and broker advice, and changing the name of Discover Brokerage Direct to Morgan Stanley Dean Witter Online.

After only a few years in its new incarnation as MSDW, the company seemed to have adjusted to its new environment. MSDW reported net revenues of $22.01 billion for fiscal 1999, an increase of 34 percent over fiscal 1998. Assets under management rose from $376 billion in 1998 to $425 billion. The company's securities business, which accounted for 74 percent of total net revenues, reported record net income of $3.67

billion, a rise of 64 percent from fiscal 1998. The asset management division, which contributed ten percent of total revenues, also performed strongly, reporting net income of $455 million, an annual increase of 83 percent. Credit services enjoyed a 19 percent increase in net income over fiscal 1998, reaching a record $662 million. The global financial services leader planned to continue growing its international operations and strengthening domestic businesses in the new century, determined to live up to its goal to be "a stable force in a turbulent world."

Principal Subsidiaries

Morgan Stanley Dean Witter Online; NOVUS Financial Corporation; NOVUS Services, Inc.; Morgan Stanley Dean Witter Advisors Inc.; Morgan Stanley Dean Witter Insurance & Annuities; Morgan Stanley Dean Witter Investment Consulting Services; Morgan Stanley Dean Witter Managed Futures; Morgan Stanley Dean Witter Trust FSB; Morgan Stanley Dean Witter Unit Trust; Van Kampen Investments Inc.; Miller Anderson & Sherrerd, LLP; Morgan Stanley Asset Management Inc.

Principal Competitors

The Goldman Sachs Group, Inc.; Merrill Lynch & Co., Inc.; Salomon Smith Barney Holdings Inc.

Further Reading

Beldky, Gary, and Robert Reed, "Dean Witter Woes Spur Retrenchment," *Crain's Chicago Business,* December 14, 1987, p. 1.
Dutt, Jill, "Merger Could Mean Boon for Fund Holders," *Washington Post,* February 9, 1997, p. H3.
Elstrom, Peter J.W., "What's Next for Split-Up Sears: Discover Loses Muscle in Card Battle," *Crain's Chicago Business,* October 5, 1992.
Gleason, Mark, "Consumers Discovered Gold with Sears' Bold Credit Card," *Cincinnati Business Courier,* October 12, 1992, p. 12.
Herr, Jeff, "Job Growth on Track Despite Sears Moves," *Arizona Business Gazette,* October 1, 1992, p. 1.
Lefton, Terry, "Amid Rate, Fee and Rebate Squabbles, Sears Finds It Costs To Discover," *Brandweek,* November 9, 1992, p. 34.
Lipin, Steven, and Anita Raghavan, "Wall Street Is Surprised and Bullish," *Wall Street Journal,* February 6, 1997, p. C1.
Parker, Marcia, "Debt, Credit Rating Crucial at Dean Witter," *Crain's New York Business,* October 5, 1992, p. 1.
Roberts, William L., "Dean Witter, Discover Spinoff May Become Major Competitor," *Philadelphia Business Journal,* February 1, 1993, p. 3.
Robinson, David, "Dean Witter's Retail Focus Is Finally Paying Off," *Buffalo News,* September 20, 1992.
Sloan, Allan, "Rowing Nowhere Fast," *Newsweek,* February 17, 1997, p. 50.
Truell, Peter, "Giant Merger Links Wall St. with Main St.," *San Diego Union-Tribune,* February 6, 1997, p. A1.
Waldstein, Peter D., "Sears Stores Cut Financial Outlets," *Crain's Chicago Business,* March 13, 1989, p. 1.
Willis, Gerri, "Dean Witter Laughs Last," *Crain's New York Business,* February 7, 1994, p. 1.
Zonana, Victor F., "Trying To Become Financial Supermarket," *Los Angeles Times,* September 30, 1992, p. D1.

—Dave Mote
—updated by Mariko Fujinaka

Navy Federal Credit Union

P.O. Box 3000
Merrifield, Virginia 22119-3000
U.S.A.
Telephone: (703) 255-8000
Toll Free: (800) 656-7676
Fax: (703) 255-8741
Web site: http://www.navyfcu.org

Nonprofit Cooperative
Incorporated: 1933 as Navy Department Employees'
    Credit Union of the District of Columbia
Employees: 3,000
Total Assets: $10 billion (1999)
NAIC: 52213 Credit Unions

Navy Federal Credit Union has been the world's largest credit union since the early 1960s. With assets of more than $11 billion, it is a financial powerhouse that serves nearly two million members and symbolizes the growth of the thrift industry in the United States. Once a source of emergency savings for those unable to find credit elsewhere, Navy Federal has come to offer car loans and home mortgages, placing it in direct competition with commercial banks resentful of credit unions' privileges as nonprofit institutions.

Origins

The early 1930s were not prime years for banking. Yet, from the midst of the Great Depression grew what would become the largest credit union in the world. An informal emergency pool put together by employees of the Navy Department in Washington, D.C., led to the incorporation on January 17, 1933 of the Navy Department Employees' Credit Union of the District of Columbia (NDCU). Its "working title" was equally cumbersome: Navy Department Branch of F.E.U. No. 2, Credit Union of the District of Columbia. Membership in the Federal Employees' Union (FEU) was the "common bond" requirement for the credit union, which by law was limited to serving a specific group of persons with a united interest. Ten thousand

shares were offered at $10 each. The membership fee was 25 cents. Loans were limited to $25 each, at a maximum interest rate of one percent a month. William L. Harrison, president of the Navy Department Branch of the FEU, presided at the first NDCU meetings. The only office space the credit union could obtain at the Navy Department building was a desk next to the lobby, after hours.

The credit union concept itself was just then maturing. Washington, D.C., had only passed legislation allowing them in June 1932, against the protests of traditional bankers. NDCU started operations in February and had to shut down for the "banking holiday" Roosevelt declared the next month to stop panicking investors from closing their accounts *en masse*. In spite of the obstacles, membership crept upwards and so did the demand for loans. At the end of 1933, it had 49 members and 18 borrowers. Assets were $450. The next year, the thrift had 250 members and about $2,700 in assets. It paid its first dividend in 1936—three percent, which rose to six percent by 1940, when assets reached $80,000. By the next year, it had attracted nearly a thousand members.

Although NDCU had finally gained some credibility and the accompanying perquisites—its own office, money to hire personnel, and promotional support—World War II changed the playing field substantially. Congress introduced legislation (Regulation W) to curb access to consumer credit. The Soldiers' and Sailors' Civil Relief Act—which prevented creditors from executing judgments during wartime—and conscription combined to give the credit union a serious collections problem. Federal examiners criticized the institution for excessively lenient lending policies which led to massive writeoffs in 1943. Dividends were subsequently suspended, and membership began to wane.

The thrift was rechartered under more flexible federal rules in June 1947. Paul Boyer, formerly treasurer, became president. Now the Navy Department Employees Federal Credit Union (NDEFCU), its potential membership expanded to include military and civilian Navy personnel in the Washington area. Robust growth in assets and membership followed the reorganization. This growth, however, soon led to another delinquency crisis.

Postwar Professionalization

The board named William A. Hussong, Jr., as the credit union's first office manager in October 1951. This marked the beginning of the professionalization of the thrift. Hussong, who had helped start the Railway Employees Federal Credit Union, at first found himself in a tug-of-war with the board, who were reluctant to share power. They ultimately relented when faced with rising delinquencies and possibility of federal censure for lax bookkeeping. Fifteen percent of the bank's loans were delinquent in 1952.

Although NDEFCU introduced improvements such as a keysort card system and mail-in payment coupons, membership fell with the Korean War and the bank's inability to maintain decent dividends. Against this backdrop, in 1954 the credit union decided to extend membership beyond Washington, to all Navy employees worldwide. Payroll deductions would make this plan workable. Officers, deemed more stable and creditworthy, were the first to become eligible. The thrift changed its name to the Navy Federal Credit Union (NFCU), and the next year, moved its expanded operations into the Navy's ''N'' Building.

NFCU increased its range of services as membership, savings, and loans swelled in the last half of the decade. The membership pool now included naval aviation cadets and noncommissioned officers, and most members lived outside the Washington area. NFCU ended the decade with $10 million in assets and 23,000 members. The credit union was reorganized, and salaries and benefits brought in line with those of military employees. Most of the membership was made up of military employees by this time, and one by one high-ranking military officers began to be picked for the board of directors. After Hussong's replacement Tom Landers stepped down to enter a consulting career, in 1963 the board chose Richard Cobb, a retired Navy captain, as the next manager. Formerly head of the Navy's Procurement Policy Division, he would remain at NFCU for nearly 20 years.

As expansion and new accounting requirements multiplied NFCU's administrative workload, Hussong pushed for an investment in a new computer system. In 1960, the board fired the autocratic but influential Hussong, ostensibly over the controversy surrounding the new computer. After months of frustrating tests, the board finally settled on an IBM 1401 (with 4K of memory) in 1962. NFCU had become the world's largest credit union by this time, propelled largely by new car loans, which in a few years had come to represent a majority of its business. NFCU's headquarters were moved to Building 143 in the Navy Yard Annex in 1964, the same year enlisted personnel were offered membership privileges.

A series of mergers with other credit unions at Navy bases began in 1967 with the Washington Navy Yard Federal Credit Union. Some smaller credit unions, championed by the Credit Union National Association (CUNA) and a few politicians, protested against NFCU's growing dominance. At the same time, the thrift industry was under attack from commercial banks, resentful of their tax-exempt status. At the end of the 1960s, NFCU boasted more than 100,000 members and assets of $120 million.

New Rules in the 1970s and 1980s

The 1970s saw wildly cyclical supplies of capital and competition for savings accounts. A staff of hundreds at NFCU serviced about 20 locations each at home and abroad, including on board the USS *Little Rock*. The variety of services proliferated as well. Cobb was named to a position on the board, treasurer, in the early 1970s. Cementing the role of Navy officers on the board, Vice Admiral Vincent A. Lascara served as chairman for most of the 1970s.

NFCU moved to an impressive, spacious new headquarters in Vienna, Virginia, in 1977. A new mainframe computer system was installed to handle the records of 450,000 members. Soon after the move, new legislation allowed credit unions to begin offering mortgage loans. However, as the differences between commercial banks and thrifts became harder to distinguish, the latter found themselves subject to more banking regulations, while banks were freed to pay more competitive rates on savings. NFCU also had to contend with newly liberal bankruptcy laws of the time. To help influence the regulatory climate, NFCU rejoined CUNA, the leading thrift industry trade group, in the late 1970s.

Cobb stepped down as manager in August 1980, to be replaced by Rear Admiral Joe G. Schoggen, who had joined NFCU after serving in the Navy's Resale Systems unit. NFCU ended the year with assets of $866 million. Credit unions received their long desired deregulation in 1982. Some consolidation in the industry followed as NFCU's membership continued to grow, reaching 692,000 in 1985. NFCU's assets approached $2 billion, up from $1.6 billion in 1984. Tom Hughes became president and CEO of NFCU in 1988, as savings and loans institutions began venturing onto the turf of credit unions by offering consumer loans.

Expansion in the 1990s

NFCU ended 1990 with $4.6 billion in assets, and passed $8 billion in the mid-1990s. It operated 56 domestic branches and 26 overseas. The thrift dropped out of CUNA again after the

Key Dates:

1933: Unionized Navy Department employees incorporate their own small thrift.
1936: Navy Department Credit Union (NDCU) pays its first dividend of three percent.
1947: NDCU rechartered as a federal credit union and extends membership to all Washington area naval personnel.
1951: Professionalization of thrift begins with appointment of the first office manager.
1954: Beginning with officers, membership offered to all US Navy employees worldwide.
1962: Navy Federal Credit Union (NFCU) becomes the world's largest credit union.
1969: Membership tops 100,000.
1977: NFCU relocates to massive new headquarters building in Vienna, Virginia.
1999: Assets top $11 billion.

trade group sued the federal government over a regulation (ending shared management between corporate credit unions and trade groups). The Navy practice of loaning cash to its branches in Spain and Italy prompted an outcry over lending public money to a private institution. NFCU also operated about 200 automated teller machines (ATMs)—all of them without a surcharge. It supported the Department of Defense's efforts to ban surcharges at all ATMs on military installations.

Hughes retired in 1996, leaving command to Brian McDonnell, a 26-year NFCU veteran. NFCU spent $60 million to expand its headquarters as membership continued to grow. It approached two million in the late 1990s as assets topped $11 billion. Mortgage and equity loans doubled to $3 billion between 1997 and 1998.

At the end of the century, NFCU's extensive Y2K compliance measures caught the attention of CNN. It had begun preparing in 1991 to accommodate substandard communications infrastructure in the countries where it did business. Its solutions incorporated redundant lines of communication, including cellular telephones, to keep in touch with its many far-flung branches.

Principal Competitors

Citigroup; Wachovia Corporation; Bank of America.

Further Reading

Arndorfer, James B., "Navy Federal Threatens to Quit CUNA Unless It Drops Challenge of New Rule," *American Banker,* March 20, 1995.

Cope, Debra, Robert M. Garsson, and Linda Corman, "Choppy Water for Credit Union Admiral," *American Banker,* October 15, 1990, p. 10.

Donovan, Sharon, "Management Profile: Rear Admiral Joe G. Schoggen," *Credit Union Management,* September 1985, pp. 6ff.

Gentile, Paul, "Navy Federal Credit Union Featured on CNN Y2K Report," *Credit Union Times,* http://www.cutimes.com/y2k/1999/yr08119-4.html.

Gilpatrick, Kristin, "Worldwide Ready," *Credit Union Management,* August 1999, p. 14.

Glassman, Harvey, "Navy Federal Again Tops Credit Unions; Leads Nation in Assets, Deposits, Share Accounts," *American Banker,* May 26, 1982, p. 1.

Martin, Kenneth R., *Home Port: A History of the Navy Federal Credit Union,* Bryn Mawr, Pa.: Dorrance & Co., 1983.

Mazzolini, Joan M., "As Credit Unions Grow, Competition Heats Up with Banks, S&Ls," *American Banker,* January 21, 1988, pp. 16ff.

McAllister, Bill, "Navy Told to End Cash Advances to Four Overseas Credit Unions," *Washington Post,* February 5, 1996, p. F8.

McDonnell, Brian, "Defense CUs Are Helping Members Use Credit Wisely," *Credit Union Magazine,* July 1998, pp. 14–16.

Molvig, Dianne, "Envisioning Leadership," *Credit Union Management,* April 1996, p. 14.

"Navy Federal Keeps Delinquencies Low," *National Mortgage News,* August 23, 1999, p. 28.

Nelson, Jane Fant, "Credit Unions in Transition," *United States Banker,* May 1984, p. 55+.

O'Brien, Jeanne, "Navy Federal Credit Union Keeps Ship-Shape with Enterprise View," *Bank Systems & Technology,* January 1999, p. 52.

Patterson, Maureen, "Operating Efficiently," *Buildings,* May 1999, pp. 70–74.

Schwartz, Susana, "Navy Federal Moves to Client/Server System," *Bank Systems & Technology,* May 1999, p. 57.

Slater, Robert Bruce, "Banks' Credit Union Crusade," *Bankers Monthly,* December 1992, p. 13.

Young, Renee, "Anchors Aweigh," *Building Design & Construction,* June 1998, pp. 96–100.

—Frederick C. Ingram

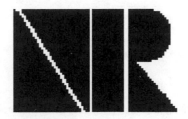

Northern Rock plc

Northern Rock House
Gosforth
Newcastle upon Tyne
NE3 4PL
England
Telephone: (44) 0191 285 7191
Fax: (44) 191 284 8470
Web site: http://www.northernrock.co.uk

Public Company
Incorporated: 1860 as Northern Counties Permanent
 Building Society
Employees: 4,700
Total Assets: £20.7 billion ($32.02 billion)(1999)
Stock Exchanges: London
Ticker Symbol: NRK
NAIC: 52211 Commercial Banking; 52231 Mortgage and
 Nonmortgage Loan Brokers

Former building society Northern Rock plc is one of the United Kingdom's largest retail banks, and the largest financial institution in its Northeast region home base. Northern Rock ranks in the top 15 of the country's retail banks. In its core product, home mortgage lending, however, Northern Rock ranks near the top, posting as much as ten percent of the total English market for home mortgages. Northern Rock's conversion from private building society to public banking entity took place in October 1997. The company is widely admired for its cost-efficient structure, emphasizing telephone- and postal-based banking over branch office banking. Northern Rock operates an extensive network of 100 branch offices, which primarily serve as sales offices for the company's products. By promoting more cost-efficient banking—including the closing of some 25 branch offices to consolidate its branch office network—Northern Rock is able to offer highly competitive interest and mortgage rates. Among the company's products are mortgage and re-mortgaging packages, including linked home mortgage and personal loan packages, such as the company's offer of mortgages exceeding property values, launched in Feb-

ruary 1999. Over half of the company's mortgage sales, however, are in the re-mortgaging bracket, leaving the company vulnerable to price competition from such mortgage industry newcomers as Prudential Egg and Standard Life. The company has parried another vulnerability—hostile takeover—with a built-in "poison pill": in its conversion to a publicly listed company, Northern Rock established the charitable Northern Rock Foundation, which receives five percent of the company's net profits but, in the event of the takeover, will receive 15 percent of any newly formed entity's shares and voting rights. Northern Rock is listed on the London Stock Exchange; its 1999 assets are said to be enough to make it eligible to join the prestigious FTSE 100, which will in turn make the company more attractive to institutional investors. Northern Rock is led by CEO Leo J. Finn, who is expected to retire soon after the turn of the century after a career spanning more than 40 years at Northern Rock.

Building Society to Bank in the 1960s

When Northern Rock Building Society converted its status from that of mutual-aid organization to publicly listed retail bank, it became one of the last of the United Kingdom's largest building societies to do so. The late 1990s thus all but ended a movement that had been largely responsible for providing homes for the people of the United Kingdom. The building society movement first appeared in the late eighteenth century, but its biggest growth coincided with the growth of the British Industrial Revolution. The changing economic and social landscape of the country—as industrialization brought more and more of the population into the United Kingdom's urban and industrial areas—created a demand for new initiatives to house the swelling ranks of a new working class.

The earliest building societies had been formed chiefly by small groups of artisans, who grouped their resources together in order to purchase lands and to build their homes. These societies were known as "terminating societies." Once homes had been built for all of a group's members—rarely more than 30 in number—the society was discontinued. By the mid-nineteenth century, however, England's booming industrial society had created vast new urban centers with increasingly large

Company Perspectives:

We will continue to introduce innovative mortgage products and steadily expand our commercial and personal finance lending activities. We are also giving active consideration to securitisation both as a funding mechanism and to provide additional volume growth. New retail savings products will be introduced both on and off shore, and we will continue to expand our sources of wholesale funding. Whilst margins will undoubtedly remain under pressure, we remain confident that our ability to innovate and our efficiency will result in the Group's continuing prosperity, meeting the aspirations of shareholders and customers.

numbers of workers finding employment in the nation's booming factories, shipyards, and mines. The building society concept quickly evolved to embrace this new population. Less affluent than the artisan class, the working class could make up for its lack of wealth in sheer numbers—the "modern" building society of the mid-nineteenth century had shed the terminating society's role as direct home builder to resemble a bank, keeping the savings of a large pool of members and making housing loans that its members were expected to repay. By the middle of the century, the housing societies had expanded beyond mere lending, becoming secured saving facilities offering interest on its members' savings.

Unlike the terminating societies, this new breed of building society was meant to remain a fixture in British economic and social life. Many building societies, in fact, touted this aspect, adding the designation "Permanent" to their names. However, not all of these building societies were entirely permanent. By the end of the nineteenth century more than 1,700 building societies were in operation, but by the end of the twentieth century, that number had been pared down to just 80 societies. And in the late 1990s, nearly all of the remaining handful of building societies chose to convert their status to that of publicly listed banking institutions.

Two of the more enduring societies were established in the 1860s. The Northern Counties Permanent Building Society was formed in 1860, and Rock Building Society was formed in 1865. Both building societies served an exclusively northeastern membership. The two building societies prospered in the later decades of the century, especially after legislation enacted in the Building Society Act of 1874 gave the building society a more solid legal footing. The building society provided a number of essential functions for the era. For one, building societies such as Rock and Northern Counties Permanent were able to provide mortgages to an industrial workforce that remained for the most part underpaid and close to poverty. For another, and perhaps most important to the survival of the building society concept into the end of the twentieth century, the building society acted as a cooperative endeavor that fitted well with the beginnings of union movements and the call for democracy in British government. The building society offered a measure of protection to its members as well, particularly during the massive economic fluctuations that marked the end of the nineteenth and beginning of the twentieth centuries. The building

society's social commitment proved even stronger than the building society itself: after going public in 1997, Northern Rock not only created the charitable Northern Rock Foundation as a means of continuing to serve the social needs of its northeastern regional base, but also continued a policy of avoiding the repossession of its mortgage-holders' homes for those falling into arrears because of economic problems.

During the twentieth century, the building society movement took on a still more solid position in the British economic landscape, as more and more building societies merged together. By the mid-1960s, the number of building societies had been greatly reduced, in favor of a smaller number of large building societies with the economic clout to compete against the United Kingdom's banks and other lending institutions. In 1965, Northern Counties Permanent Building Society and Rock Building Society joined the movement toward industry consolidation, merging to form the Northern Rock Building Society. While small by national standards, the new Northern Rock took a position as the northeast region's leading financial institution, offering, beyond its concentration on home mortgages, a variety of savings and other traditional banking products.

Banking on the Twenty-First Century

Northern Rock quickly took a leading role in the consolidation of the building society movement. From the early 1970s through the end of the century, Northern Rock acquired the assets and members of some 53 other buildings societies. Several of these largest acquisitions came in the 1990s. The home building market had collapsed in the late 1980s, after a decade of overbuilding and inflated land pricing. Many building societies found themselves struggling in the early 1990s, as a vast recession settled on the British economy. Northern Rock's tight, cost-efficient management had kept it in relatively robust shape, enabling it to make several key acquisitions at this time. In 1992, the company acquired the assets and membership of Lancastrian Building Society. The following year, Northern Rock added Surrey Building Society to its accounts. The addition of North of England Building Society, acquired in 1994, was one of Northern Rock's largest. The merger gave Northern Rock an additional 400,000 members, as well as a leading six percent of the home mortgage market, propelling Northern Rock into the top ten of the United Kingdom's building societies.

Meanwhile, the so-called "Big Bang" deregulation of the United Kingdom's banking system, enacted in 1986, had opened new markets to building societies. While Northern Rock remained close to its home mortgage lending core, it soon became a leader in the re-mortgaging market, attracting new members seeking Northern Rock's competitive interest rates. Northern Rock also branched out a bit, adding insurance products with a joint-venture formed in 1996 with Britain's Guardian Royal Exchange to sell its Guardian Insurance products through Northern Rock's branch network. Northern Rock later added life insurance products, through a distribution agreement with Legal & General, in which Northern Rock was to act as an "introducer" of Legal & General to its society members. Meanwhile, Northern Rock diversified even farther afield, entering the nursing home industry, through its Regency Care Homes Limited subsidiary, which was established in 1990. While that subsidiary remained very small part of Northern

Rock's overall business, it nonetheless saw a bit of growth in the middle of the decade, with the 1996 acquisition of Kingsclear Homes Limited. That acquisition, for £40 million, added Kingsclear's 23 nursing homes to Regency's 15 nursing homes, for a total bed count of nearly 2,000. Northern Rock also functioned as the operator of a small number of housing developments, although this activity too remained peripheral to the company's main business.

By the late 1990s, the building society movement seemed to be finally losing steam. More and more of the country's building societies, including the largest of the building societies such as Halifax and the Woolwich, were announcing their intention to convert their status from private society to that of publicly quoted bank. Northern Rock continued to assert its intention to remain as a building society into 1996. However, in April 1996 the building society announced that it too was preparing to go public, following its members' approval in October of that year. Industry analysts suspected that the move was made in part to parry a potential hostile takeover—according to British law, newly public companies are given a five-year grace period during which they are protected against hostile takeover attempts. Northern Rock encouraged its members' approval by offering one of the industry's largest share packages—500 shares to each member, regardless of the amount of their holdings, which, at the time of the public offering, was worth more than £1,500.

Northern Rock's members approved the conversion in April 1997, and the conversion itself took place in October 1997, as the building society-turned-bank changed its name, to Northern Rock plc. As part of the conversion, Northern Rock set up the Northern Rock Foundation, a charitable organization committed largely to the northeast region's social needs. Under terms of the conversion, Northern Rock Foundation began receiving five percent of Northern Rock's net income; in the event of a takeover of the company, the foundation's legacy was safeguarded with provisions to give it 15 percent of the resulting merged operation's shares and voting rights. Philanthropic considerations aside, many analysts saw this move as a highly creative poison pill defense against the threat of a hostile takeover.

The new Northern Rock quickly garnered industry approval with its tight management, highly competitive products and cost-efficient structure. In order to maintain its leadership in the home mortgage market, a position that the company had managed to raise to more than ten percent by 1998, Northern Rock worked to slash costs. In 1998, the company closed 25 of its branch offices. The company also encouraged its customers to abandon in-person transactions in favor of the company's telephone and ATM services. In this way, Northern Rock expected to be able to continue to offer the industry's most competitive rates, even as it faced new competition, as industry outsiders such as Prudential and Standard Life announced their intention to enter the home mortgage business. Since more than half of Northern Rock's new mortgage business came from the re-mortgaging market—which presumably could be easily attracted away from the company by any more competitive package—Northern Rock took steps to ensure its competitiveness.

Not all of its steps, however, met with customer approval. In 1998, Northern Rock made a major gaffe when it suddenly decided to consolidate its range of savings products from nine separate accounts to just three. Unfortunately, the company only informed its customers on the day of the conversion, and some 400,000 customers suddenly found their savings receiving much lower interest rates than their previous accounts. To compound the problem, Northern Rock maintained a withdrawal penalty if customers wished to transfer their savings to the company's new, higher-interest-bearing accounts. The result was a public relations fiasco—in the face of an Office of Fair Trading investigation, Northern Rock was forced to back down, allowing customers to transfer their savings without penalty, while paying back more than £3 million in lost interest. Many of the company's savings customers defected, withdrawing their savings altogether.

However, by 1999 Northern Rock had managed to restore its reputation. Defending its earlier move as an industry-wide practice, Northern Rock instituted a "Savers Pledge," which included, among other provisions, a promise to inform customers of any such changes, and even to inform them of new, higher interest-bearing products as they became available. In this way, Northern Rock was seen as taking a leadership role in the British banking industry's fairness policies. Meanwhile, if Northern Rock had managed to win the displeasure of some of its customers, it remained a favorite of the stock market. By early 1999, the company was eligible for a listing on the prestigious FTSE 100; such a listing would improve the company's image among large institutional investors. Northern Rock also found itself becoming more and more attractive to North American investors, and in 1999 the company was reportedly investigating the possibility of taking a listing on the New York Stock Exchange.

Principal Subsidiaries

Kingsclear Homes Limited; Northern Rock (Guernsey) Limited; Northern Rock Mortgage Indemnity Company Limited; Regency Care Homes Limited.

Principal Competitors

Abbey National; HSBC Holdings; Alliance & Leicester; Lloyds TSB; Bank of Scotland; Prudential Corporation; Barclays; Royal Bank of Scotland; Halifax; Woolwich.

Further Reading

Beugge, Charlotte, ''Change of Heart at Northern Rock,'' *Daily Telegraph*, March 7, 1998.

——, ''Northern Rock Goes over the Top to Recapture First-Time Buyers,'' *Daily Telegraph*, January 28, 1999.

Cicutti, Nic, ''Northern Rock Reveals Floatation Plans,'' *Independent*, April 4, 1996, p. 22.

Montagu-Smith, Nina, ''Anger over the Rock Shake-Up,'' *Daily Telegraph*, May 8, 1999.

''Northern Rock's New Role,'' *Economist*, April 6, 1996, p. 76.

Paterson, Leo, ''Northern Rock Pours Cold Water on Bid Rumours,'' *Independent*, January 29, 1998, p. 25.

Potter, Ben, ''Cling on to Northern Rock,'' *Daily Telegraph*, July 4, 1998.

Yates, Andrew, ''Northern Rock Stays a Solid Bet,'' *Independent*, January 29, 1998, p. 24.

—M.L. Cohen

Paxson Communications Corporation

601 Clearwater Park Road
West Palm Beach, Florida 33401
U.S.A.
Telephone: (561) 659-4122
Fax: (561) 659-4252
Web site: http://www.paxson.com

Public Company
Incorporated: 1991
Employees: 990
Sales: $248.4 million (1999)
Stock Exchanges: NASDAQ
Ticker Symbol: PAX
NAIC: 513120 Television Broadcasting; 513220 Cable
and Other Program Distribution

Paxson Communications Corporation was founded in 1991 by Lowell ''Bud'' Paxson, the man who cofounded the Home Shopping Network in the early 1980s. After building a Florida radio station empire in the early 1990s, Paxson sold that business in 1997 to Clear Channel Communications for $693 million. The company had acquired its first television station in 1994. Following passage of the Telecommunications Act of 1996, Paxson began aggressively acquiring UHF stations throughout the United States. At first the stations were part of Paxson's Infomall TV Network (inTV), which broadcast infomercials and other types of long-form paid programming. Then in 1998 Paxson launched Pax TV, the United States' seventh broadcast network, and replaced much of its infomercial programming. Toward the end of 1999 NBC purchased a 32 percent interest in the company, with an option to acquire up to 49 percent ownership in 2002 if the Federal Communications Commission (FCC) increased its limits regarding ownership of television stations.

Background and Early History to 1993

Lowell ''Bud'' Paxson bought his first radio station in 1956. In 1978 he sold electric can openers on his Pinellas County, Florida, radio station, paving the way for the St. Petersburg-based Home Shopping Network (HSN), which Paxson cofounded with attorney and real estate investor Roy Speer in the early 1980s. Paxson became president of HSN, which went public in 1986. He resigned in 1990 and founded Paxson Communications, selling 12.8 million shares of his HSN stock for $68.9 million. In 1991, Paxson's first year of operation, the company had revenue of $650,000. By 1992 revenues were $17 million and, just a year later, $32 million.

Paxson built a Florida radio empire in just a few years, starting in 1991 with the acquisition of WHPT-FM and WHNZ-AM, serving the Tampa Bay market, for $6.4 million. In 1992 Paxson acquired an AM-FM station in Miami for $14.6 million, an AM station in Orlando, and an FM station in Jacksonville. In late 1992 Paxson started the Christian Network, a nonprofit charity that aired gospel-oriented music videos, Bible discussions, and other religious programming. He continued to support the network financially, but was not active in its management.

In 1993 the company acquired another FM station in Miami for $10.9 million, an AM-FM combination in Orlando for $5.6 million, and one AM and one FM station in Jacksonville for a total of $7.2 million. It also acquired a second FM station in Tampa, another FM station in Orlando, and another AM-FM combination in Jacksonville. In 1993 Paxson held a 12.3 percent share of Florida's $260 million radio market.

Going Public, Acquiring Television Stations: 1994

In 1994 Paxson transformed itself into a public company by acquiring 55 percent of the publicly held American Network Group (ANG) for $2.5 million. At the time Paxson was valued at $107 million and owned 13 radio stations, all in Florida, and the Florida Radio Network. Paxson wanted to become a public company without having to incur costs associated with an initial public offering (IPO). Becoming a public company gave Paxson access to public capital to fuel the company's growth through acquisitions.

By April 1994 Paxson had acquired 4.4 million shares of American Network's common stock, or about 68 percent. Fol-

Company Perspectives:

PAX TV has made a promise to deliver family entertainment television that's free of senseless violence, free of explicit sex, and free of foul language. In the network's first ten months on the air, viewers have responded to that PAX promise—and to its programs. America's families have made PAX TV the fastest growing broadcast television network in history.

lowing approval of the merger by American Network Group's shareholders, who would receive one share of Paxson stock for nearly four shares of ANG stock, Paxson's shares began trading on the NASDAQ small-cap market and the Boston Stock Exchange in November 1994.

Paxson also acquired its first television station in 1994 when it purchased WPBF-TV, the ABC network affiliate in West Palm Beach, Florida. Other television stations acquired in 1994 included WTLK-TV, an independent station serving Atlanta and Rome, Georgia, and WYVN-TV in Martinsburg, West Virginia, for $1.9 million. Before the end of 1994 Paxson had also committed to buy a television station in San Bernardino, California, for $18 million, that served the Los Angeles area; a religious television station in San Jose, California; and a television station in New London, Connecticut, for $25.8 million.

At the end of 1994 Paxson declared a 50 percent stock dividend, which increased the company's shareholder equity by $33 million. For 1994 the company had revenues of $62 million, with 80 percent coming from radio. It reported a net loss of $8.1 million and had yet to turn a profit.

Developed Infomall TV Network: 1995–96

In 1995 Paxson relocated its company headquarters from Clearwater to West Palm Beach. Paxson planned to own television stations in 18 of the top 20 markets by the end of 1995. The company created a new television division, Paxson Communications TV, naming Dean Goodman, former general manager of three Miami radio stations and a television station, as president. The company's strategy was to acquire independent television stations, most of them UHF stations on the fringes of major markets, and create a television infomercial network called the Infomall TV Network, or inTV.

Paxson hoped that "must-carry" rules, which required cable systems to carry local broadcast signals, would extend the reach of the company's stations. However, the cable industry was preparing to fight the must-carry rules in court, especially regarding having to carry stations with infomercial programming. Paxson's infomercial clients included Apple Computer, Toyota, Fidelity Investments, Estée Lauder, and Time-Life. To meet public interest requirements, Paxson's stations also carried children's programming during the day as well as local public affairs, news, and event programming, with advertising coming from local merchants and professionals.

During 1995 Paxson paid $40 million to ValueVision International Inc. for two stations, WHAI-TV in Bridgeport, Con-

necticut, and ABC affiliate WAKC-TV in Akron, Ohio. When the deal closed in March, Paxson owned ten television stations. For fiscal 1995 Paxson reported a net loss of $46.8 million. Its long-term debt had risen 179 percent to $240 million.

The Telecommunications Act of 1996, passed in February 1996, changed the rules governing ownership of radio and television stations. Under the old rules, companies could not own more than two AM and two FM stations in a single market without special waivers. The new law allowed companies to own eight overlapping radio stations in a local market. The legislation also removed the 12-station cap affecting ownership of television stations.

Following passage of the Telecommunications Act, Paxson became more aggressive in acquiring radio and television stations. The company was attempting to assemble a UHF station group covering 20 of the top 30 U.S. markets for its Infomall TV Network, known as inTV. It had already bought 17 UHF stations in the past two years, some of which were run under management agreements. With the television stations acquired in 1996, Paxson's Infomall TV Network (inTV) would reach nearly 50 million households.

Paxson's strategy was to acquire underperforming television stations and replace existing programming with inTV. During 1996 it bought a station serving Burlington, North Carolina, for $5 million from TV Communications; signed a local marketing agreement to operate a television station in Athens, Georgia; and entered into a joint venture with Offshore Broadcasting Corp. to co-own a television station in Providence, Rhode Island. It acquired television stations in Minneapolis/St. Paul; Albany, New York; Gadsden/Birmingham, Alabama; Ogden/Salt Lake City, Utah; and Sacramento, California. It added another television station in a top 15 market with the purchase of KBCB in Bellingham/Seattle, Washington, giving Paxson television stations in 13 of the top 15 markets.

The company also expanded its holdings of Florida radio stations during 1996. It bought two local stations in Miami, then purchased nine radio stations in the Florida Panhandle from Southern Broadcasting Cos.—including five in Tallahassee, two in Pensacola, and two in Panama City—and WDIZ-FM in Orlando from Shamrock Communications for a total of $43.5 million. Paxson also acquired WIOD-AM, the leading English-language news/talk radio station in Miami, for $13 million from Cox Broadcasting Inc. and announced plans to acquire three Panama City stations from B. Radio and Boss Radio Group, bringing the number of radio stations Paxson would own to 38. Later in the year Paxson acquired its sixth Orlando radio station and a sixth radio station in Jacksonville.

The company also owned numerous billboard locations, which were used to promote Paxson's radio and television stations. In June 1996 Paxson acquired Cashi Signs of Orlando, which owned 72 local billboards with 169 advertising faces, for $4 million. At the time Paxson reportedly owned 333 billboards in Florida.

During fiscal 1996 Paxson registered with the Securities and Exchange Commission (SEC) to sell 150,000 shares of nonvoting stock to raise $150 million for use in acquiring more radio and television stations or entering into time brokerage agreements

Key Dates:

1991: Lowell Paxson establishes Paxson Communications Corporation in Clearwater, Florida, as a private company to acquire Florida radio stations.

1994: Paxson acquires American Network Group and becomes a public company; company acquires its first television station, WPBF-TV serving West Palm Beach, Florida.

1995: Paxson relocates company headquarters to West Palm Beach.

1996: Telecommunications Act of 1996 changes ownership rules governing radio and television stations.

1997: Paxson sells its radio stations to Clear Channel Communications for $693 million.

1998: Paxson launches the United States' seventh broadcast network, Pax TV.

1999: National Broadcasting Company, Inc. (NBC) invests $415 million in Paxson for a 32 percent interest in the company.

with them. The company's television division brought in $60.9 million in revenues, a 105 percent increase from $29.7 million in 1995. Overall, the company had $144.5 million in revenues, a 67 percent increase from 1995. It reported a net loss of $48 million, due mainly to acquisition expenses and debt repayments.

Acquiring More TV Stations, Divesting Radio Stations: 1997

Paxson had begun expanding inTV programming to include a variety of news, sports, and entertainment. Analysts speculated that Paxson and other infomercial broadcasters were diversifying their programming in anticipation of a Supreme Court review of must-carry rules, which gave local stations access to an estimated 40 million cable subscribers. When the Supreme Court upheld the must-carry rules, which were part of the Cable Act of 1992, Paxson's stock rose more than 20 percent in one day. The news was good for independent station owners, whose programming would be carried on cable systems, but bad for cable networks such as C-Span and The Golf Channel that were struggling to find a place on those systems. Following the Supreme Court ruling, Paxson received offers from at least ten major television companies—including the top four broadcast networks—interested in buying airtime on Paxson's network of stations.

In order to raise funds to acquire more Florida radio properties and independent television stations for inTV, Paxson divested its two West Palm Beach television stations, selling its ABC affiliate, WPBF-TV, to The Hearst Corporation for $85 million, and its UPN affiliate WTVX-TV to the Paramount Television Group for $34.3 million. At the time Paxson owned 43 radio stations—39 of them in Florida—and had 47 television stations affiliated with inTV that reached 54 percent of U.S. households. It also owned more than 500 Florida billboard locations.

Television acquisitions in 1997 included its fourth California station, KKAG-TV in Porterville/Fresno, for $7.96 million

in cash. The company entered the Pittsburgh market with the $35 million acquisition of WPCB-TV from Cornerstone Tele-Vision. The company also purchased television stations in St. Petersburg and Miami. However, its biggest acquisition was WINS-TV in New York, which it bought from ITT and Dow Jones for $257.5 million. Paxson changed the station's call letters to WPXN and made it the company's flagship station. It planned to replace the station's business and sports format with network programming. In June Paxson and Bloomberg Television signed an agreement for Bloomberg to provide WPXN with news and information programming from 6 a.m. to 6 p.m. for five days a week. Paxson also made its first announcement regarding a broadcast network, which it planned to launch in September 1998.

The acquisition of WINS-TV gave Paxson its 50th television station, with national coverage growing to 57 percent. The legal limit for UHF stations was 70 percent of the country, which Paxson planned to reach by the end of 1998. In other 1997 transactions Paxson acquired inactive television stations in Cedar Rapids/Dubuque, Iowa, and Batavia/Buffalo, New York. It also acquired WVVI-TV in Washington, D.C., and television stations in Raleigh, North Carolina; Charleston, West Virginia; and Tucson, Arizona. The deals gave Paxson 62 stations and coverage of more than 60 percent of all U.S. television households.

Paxson acquired The Travel Channel for $75 million in June from Landmark Communications, including $20 million in cash and $55 million in stock. In September Paxson sold a controlling 70 percent interest in The Travel Channel to The Discovery Channel for $20 million.

After 44 years in the radio industry, Lowell Paxson announced that Paxson Communications would sell its radio division for $693 million in cash to Texas-based Clear Channel Communications. The sale involved 46 radio stations, including 42 in Florida, as well as Paxson's six sports and news networks and expansion Arena Football League and American Hockey League teams. It also included Paxson's billboards. The sale left Paxson free to concentrate on its television business, and the company began announcing plans to create a seventh broadcast network.

For fiscal 1997 Paxson's revenues exceeded $88 million, a 41 percent increase over 1996 revenues of $62 million. However, operating losses grew to nearly $22 million compared to $4 million in 1996.

Launching a New Broadcast Network: 1998

Details of Paxson's proposed broadcast network began to emerge in November 1997. Originally to be called Pax Net, the network would be focused on "family values." Unable to sell Hollywood on the idea of buying airtime and assuming the risk of getting advertisers, Paxson began making offers to buy network programming.

Pax Net announced its flagship show would be "Touched by an Angel," for which it paid a reported $950,000 per episode. Scheduled to debut August 31, 1998, the network's other prime-time shows included "Promised Land"; "Dr. Quinn, Medicine Woman"; "Dave's World"; and three original shows, including a late night talk show. Infomercials were expected to occupy morning-to-afternoon slots on weekends. Religious programming would be shown after midnight. The network's target audience was women between the ages of 25 and 54.

In January 1998 Paxson bought the off-network rights at the industry convention of the National Association of Television Program Executives (NATPE) for "Diagnosis Murder" and "The Father Dowling Mysteries," and exclusively produced shows of the World Wrestling Federation (WWF). Later in the year Paxson reached an agreement with DIC Entertainment, a Walt Disney subsidiary, to provide weekend children's programming for Pax Net.

In addition to obtaining off-network and original programming for its new broadcast network, Paxson was making carriage deals with major cable operators. It sealed a nationwide cable distribution pact with Tele-Communications Inc. (TCI). Comcast Corp., the fourth largest cable company with more than 4.3 million subscribers, signed an agreement to carry Pax Net in areas where Paxson did not own a station or have an affiliate. As the August 31 launch day approached, Paxson signed carriage deals with other cable operators, including 15th-ranked TCA Cable TV and 10th-ranked Intermedia Partners, which added nearly two million cable subscribers to Pax Net's potential audience.

Paxson continued to purchase television stations in 1998, including WCFC-TV in Chicago for $120 million, which made Paxson the first television group to own stations in all top 20 markets in the United States. Other acquisitions included WFHL-TV of Champaign/Decatur, Illinois; three low-power stations in Seattle, Indianapolis, and Portland, Oregon, from ValueVision for $25 million; a second low-power station in Seattle for $10 million from ValueVision; and KBSP-TV, a full-power station serving Portland, Oregon, from Blackstar LLC. To raise funds Paxson sold WOAC-TV, a full-power station serving the Cleveland market, to Shop At Home for $23 million. It also sold its interest in Atlanta station WNGM-TV to USA Broadcasting Inc. and exercised its right to acquire WPXP-TV of West Palm Beach from Hispanic Broadcasting Inc. The company gained permits to construct full power stations in seven other markets.

The company planned to hire 600 new employees, including about 500 ad sales representatives at local stations and up to 100 new employees for the corporate headquarters in West Palm Beach. Jeff Sagansky, former president of CBS Entertainment and more recently co-president of Sony Pictures Entertainment, was named president and CEO of Paxson Communications and would oversee the launch of Pax Net. Sagansky would report to Chairman Lowell Paxson.

When Pax TV (the "Net" was quietly dropped) launched on August 31, 1998, its weekday prime-time schedule featured daily reruns of "Touched by an Angel," "Dr. Quinn, Medicine Woman," and "Diagnosis Murder." The lineup was considered fairly tame in comparison to those of two other newly launched networks, UPN and WB, which offered original prime-time shows. Unlike WB and UPN, Pax TV would broadcast 24 hours a day.

Wall Street was also not confident of Pax TV's chances for success, driving down Paxson's stock from a 52-week high in April 1998 of $13.81 to $10.18. Citing "high financial risk," Standard & Poor's had downgraded Paxson's debt rating to B from B+ just prior to the launch.

The network's audience potential was 76 percent of all U.S. television households. Paxson owned 78 of its 95 affiliates and had carriage arrangements with several cable operators. Some of Pax TV's affiliates were owned by D.P. Media Inc., which was owned by Lowell Paxson's son Devon Paxson, and his wife, Roslyck Paxson.

Paxson expected that start-up costs for the new network would result in a $90 million net loss for 1998, but it expected to break even in 1999 with a 1.0 national household rating, or about one percent of the approximately 100 million U.S. television households. That target would put Pax on a par with such cable networks as USA Network, ESPN, and TBS. Overnight ratings following the launch indicated that local ratings varied from a 3.3 household rating in New Orleans and Sacramento to no measurable viewing activity in Columbus, Ohio, and Jacksonville, Florida. In its second week on the air Pax TV's prime-time lineup drew a 1.0 household rating in 33 of 40 markets measured by Nielsen Media Research.

For fiscal 1998 Paxson reported that its working capital had shrunk to $1.8 million. Its net loss was $137.9 million, while total revenues rose 52 percent to $134.2 million.

A Partner in NBC: 1999 and Beyond

During the first half of 1999 Paxson sold three stations (located in Dayton, Ohio; Green Bay, Wisconsin; and Champaign, Illinois) to Acme Television for $40 million. In addition Paxson acquired an independent Pittsburgh station from Cornerstone Television for an estimated $30 million and agreed to assume operations of the WB affiliate in Louisville, Kentucky. The company was also searching for a larger corporate headquarters.

In August 1999 the FCC approved new rules that allowed companies to own more than one television station in the same market. The ruling was expected to increase the value of Paxson's "fringe" stations and helped Paxson's stock hit a 52-week high before closing at around $14 a share. The company also hired investment banker Salomon Smith Barney to explore the possibility of merging or selling its assets to another party. Paxson hinted that it would be interested in selling up to 32 percent of its stock to one of the big four networks in exchange for a programming alliance. At the time Paxson owned or operated 72 stations reaching 76 percent of U.S. television households.

By September Paxson had found its suitor in NBC, which invested $415 million in new Paxson stock, giving it 32 percent of Paxson's common stock. NBC's investment had to be less than 33 percent to meet existing FCC ownership rules. After February 1, 2002, NBC would have the option to acquire up to 49 percent of Paxson for $1.2 billion, but only if the FCC raised its current ownership limit. NBC saw Paxson as giving it a second path of distribution for its entertainment programming.

Prior to NBC's investment Paxson was struggling financially. Through June 1999 it had reported a negative net operating cash flow of $102.6 million and was carrying long-term debt of $382 million. It was also behind in its licensing payments for Pax TV programming. Paxson said it would use the $415 million to complete about $120 million worth of station acquisitions as well as to meet working capital needs and to expedite digital conversion of Paxson's 72 stations.

It was expected that NBC's investment in Paxson, together with Viacom's $35.9 billion purchase of CBS, would put pressure on federal regulators to change the rules affecting ownership of television stations. The rules in effect prohibited companies from owning VHF stations that reached more than 35 percent of the national audience or UHF stations that reached more than 70 percent, since UHF stations counted as half a market. The major networks were lobbying for a 50 percent cap. Those opposed to raising the limit were the National Association of Broadcasters (NAB), some individual station owners, and station groups, who feared that it would put too much power in the hands of the large networks.

When the terms of NBC's agreement with Paxson were revealed, it became clear that NBC was more of an equal partner than a minority shareholder. According to documents filed with the Securities and Exchange Commission (SEC), NBC would have approval authority over Paxson's budgets, program acquisitions, and development, and even the hiring of employees. NBC would also determine Paxson's marketing and sales strategy. For the next ten years NBC would have the right to convert any Pax TV stations in the top 50 markets to NBC affiliates. Paxson would need NBC's approval to sell any of its stations in the top 20 markets, or to sell any stations that would result in Pax TV's national coverage falling below 70 percent. NBC also had the right of first refusal to acquire any Paxson station in the top 50 markets. In return, Pax TV might be able to broadcast episodes of popular NBC shows. Paxson was also considering asking CNBC to develop financial programming targeted to its core audience of women between 25 and 54 years of age.

Following NBC's investment, Paxson acquired nine stations, including eight Pax TV affiliates, from D.P. Media for about $135 million. In January 2000 Standard & Poor's raised Paxson's debt rating from B to B+, citing the positive implications following NBC's investment in the company.

Principal Competitors

American Broadcasting Co., Inc. (ABC); Columbia Broadcasting System, Inc. (CBS); FOX Broadcasting Co.; United Paramount Network (UPN); Warner Bros. Television Network.

Further Reading

Beall, Pat, "Partner's Public Status Key to Paxson Merger," *Orlando Business Journal,* June 24, 1994, p. 16.

Boliek, Brooks, "Paxson-NBC Heats up Ownership Debate," *Back Stage,* September 24, 1999, p. 55.

Brown, Sara, "Paxson Goes 20 for 20," *Broadcasting & Cable,* February 2, 1998, p. 9.

——, "Paxson Makes Cable Connections," *Broadcasting & Cable,* August 3, 1998, p. 17.

Deggans, Eric, "Infomercial King Paxson Buying Two Florida TV Stations," *Knight-Ridder/Tribune Business News,* May 6, 1997.

Freeman, Michael, "Paxson: Beyond Infomercials," *Mediaweek,* March 3, 1997, p. 8.

——, "Paxson Pacts for Programs," *Mediaweek,* November 10, 1997, p. 5.

Goldsmith, Jill, "Paxson on Block After FCC Ruling," *Variety,* August 16, 1999, p. 22.

Gunther, Marc, "Will Uncle Bud Sell Hollywood?," *Fortune,* August 18, 1997, p. 185.

Larson, Megan, "It's Wright Time at Pax," *Mediaweek,* September 20, 1999, p. 5.

Levine, Felicia, "Radio, TV Giant Picks West Palm," *South Florida Business Journal,* December 16, 1994, p. 1A.

——, "TV's Next Frontier: Paxson Plans Infomercial Network," *South Florida Business Journal,* January 20, 1995, p. 1A.

Littleton, Cynthia, and John Dempsey, "Paxson Eyes Seventh Heaven," *Variety,* November 10, 1997, p. 21.

Lunsford, Darcie, "Network Drama: Finding a Home," *South Florida Business Journal,* May 28, 1999, p. 1A.

McClellan, Steve, "Bud Paxson Sets His Sights to Be Lucky Number 7," *Broadcasting & Cable,* June 30, 1997, p. 42.

——, "The Peacocking of Pax," *Broadcasting & Cable,* October 11, 1999, p. 68.

McClellan, Steve, and Joe Schlosser, "Paxson Goes for 7th," *Broadcasting & Cable,* October 27, 1997, p. 4.

——, "Paxson in a Family Way," *Broadcasting & Cable,* November 10, 1997, p. 10.

"New Pax Net Plans 'Wholesome' Shows," *Television Digest,* November 24, 1997, p. 2.

Ostrowski, Jeff, "Paxson Sorts Through Suitors for TV Time," *South Florida Business Journal,* May 2, 1997, p. 1.

Peers, Martin, "Paxson's Maxin' His Station Empire," *Variety,* June 23, 1997, p. 25.

Petrozzello, Donna, "Paxson Buys Travel Channel," *Broadcasting & Cable,* June 23, 1997, p. 56.

——, "Paxson Goes Public," *Broadcasting & Cable,* November 14, 1994, p. 54.

Piotrowski, Michael A., "From the Public Airwaves to the Public Markets," *Tampa Bay Business Journal,* April 29, 1994, p. 1.

Pursell, Chris, "Pax in State of Flux," *Variety,* November 1, 1999, p. M19.

Spiegel, Peter, "Thanks, Partner," *Forbes,* May 19, 1997, p. 146.

Torpey-Kemph, Anne, "Paxson Juggles Stations," *Mediaweek,* March 29, 1999, p. 24.

Whitefield, Mimi, "Paxson Communications' TV Stations May Be Network," *Knight-Ridder/Tribune Business News,* July 1, 1997.

Zbar, Jeff, "The Bud Paxson Show," *Florida Trend,* June 1995, p. 54.

Zier, Julie A., "Paxson Building Infomercial Net: HSN Co-Founder Purchasing UHF Fringe Stations, Seeking Affiliates at NATPE," *Broadcasting & Cable,* January 16, 1995, p. 102.

—David P. Bianco

Penn National Gaming, Inc.

Wyomissing Professional Center
825 Berkshire Boulevard, Suite 200
Wyomissing, Pennsylvania 19610
U.S.A.
Telephone: (610) 373-2400
Fax: (610) 376-2842
Web site: http://www.pennnational.com

Public Company
Incorporated: 1972
Employees: 1,870
Sales: $171.5 million (1999)
Stock Exchanges: NASDAQ
Ticker Symbol: PENN
NAIC: 711212 Racetracks; 713290 Other Gambling
  Industries

Penn National Gaming, Inc. is a gaming and pari-mutuel wagering company that owns and operates five horseracing tracks in Pennsylvania, West Virginia, and New Jersey, as well as ten off-track wagering facilities in Pennsylvania. The company's two Pennsylvania tracks are Penn National Race Course, a thoroughbred track located outside Harrisburg, and Pocono Downs Racetrack, a harness racetrack located outside Wilkes-Barre. Through a joint venture, Penn National owns 89 percent of the Charles Town Entertainment Complex, a Charles Town, West Virginia, facility that offers live horse racing, pari-mutuel wagering, and video gaming machines. The company owns 50 percent of two race tracks in New Jersey: Freehold Raceway in Freehold, New Jersey, and Garden State Park, in Cherry Hill. At its racetracks and off-track facilities, Penn conducts pari-mutuel wagering on both its own races and on simulcasts of races run at other tracks. The company is in the process of acquiring two casinos located in Mississippi.

1970s–80s: Off to the Races

Penn National Gaming was formed in the early 1970s, when a group of central Pennsylvania civic leaders banded together to establish and operate a thoroughbred racing track. The track, a one-mile oval, was built on approximately 225 acres of land 15 miles northeast of Harrisburg, Pennsylvania. It opened for its first day of racing on August 30, 1972, drawing a crowd of more than 10,500 spectators. During its first year of operation, Penn National had only 100 race dates, which made it difficult for the track to build up a large base of fans before season's end. The following year, however, the track added 100 more dates, establishing a year-round racing calendar. With the additional race dates, Penn National's popularity began to grow.

In 1978, Penn National expanded, opening the first turf course in Pennsylvania, a ⅞-mile oval located next to the company's existing track. The turf track, which was praised for its consistency and safety, allowed Penn to again bulk up its racing calendar.

Throughout the early 1980s, the company introduced new ways to stir interest in racing to keep wagering revenues healthy. In 1982, it began offering customers a new way to wager—via phone. Christened "Telebet," the new initiative was Pennsylvania's first telephone betting system. It allowed a bettor to open a betting account by depositing funds with Penn National. The account holder could then place bets both on Penn races and on simulcast events simply by making a phone call. Any winnings were posted to the winner's account, for withdrawal or future wagering.

In 1983, Penn found another way to reach out to its customers. The company launched its own television program— "Racing Alive"—which was broadcast at the race course and, eventually, on various Pennsylvania cable TV stations. The show aired about an hour before post time on each live racing day and included commentary about that day's race, as well as general information on betting and handicapping, featured races from other tracks, and interviews with racing personalities.

Also in the 1980s, the company began to explore intertrack simulcasting. There were two sides to simulcasting: importing and exporting. Penn National took advantage of both. It began showing imported simulcasts of other races at the track during idle time between races. It also began exporting simulcasts of its own races to various other racetracks. In both cases, racetrack patrons were able to place bets on the simulcast races. Proceeds from the wagering—less the amount paid out to winning bettors—were shared by the originating track, the track simulcasting the race, and the purse fund for horse owners. Therefore, both importing and exporting simulcasts served to increase Penn's revenues.

Early 1990s: Building an Off-Track Business

Until the end of the 1980s, Penn National had focused almost exclusively on building business at its track, attracting patrons to the race course by adding live race dates and offering more wagering opportunities through simulcasting. Although these efforts had proven successful, Penn knew that in order to continue to grow it needed to reach a broader customer base. So in the early 1990s, the company began to push outward, offering betting to customers in other areas of Pennsylvania.

The company's then-CFO, Robert Ippolito, explained Penn's reasoning in a May 1997 interview with *Investor's Business Daily:* "We decided that if we can't get people to come to the track, we ought to bring the track to the people—in areas where people won't drive 45 minutes to an hour to a racetrack on a regular basis."

Penn's vehicle for "bringing the track to the people" was the establishment of off-track wagering facilities (OTWs). Under Pennsylvania law, each racetrack in the state was authorized to operate a pre-determined number of off-track betting locations within the state. Penn National was allowed six such sites. The company opened its first OTW in May 1992 in Reading, a southeastern Pennsylvania city approximately 35 miles from Penn National Race Course. The 22,500-square foot facility provided area racing enthusiasts a comfortable place to dine, drink, and lounge, while wagering on races simulcast from all over the country.

When the Reading OTW proved a success, Penn National set about finding locations for the remaining five of its allotted sites. In 1994, the company opened a facility in Chambersburg, a mid-sized community about an hour southwest of the race course. Two more OTWs followed in 1995 and 1996. The facilities—in York and Lancaster—were both approximately 25 miles from the Penn National track.

The roll-out of the OTWs paid off in a big way for Penn. Between 1991 and 1995, the company's sales grew from $33.3 million to $57.6 million. In addition to merely boosting the company's revenues, the OTWs proved very cost-efficient and highly profitable. Because the fixed overhead at the off-track facilities was significantly lower than at the company's race track, their potential for moneymaking was far greater.

Mid-1990s: Expansion

Penn National went public in June 1994, trading on the NAS-DAQ exchange. Although the company consistently posted im-

proved earnings, its stock price showed only modest gains for the first several months of trading. In early 1996, however, Penn announced a 1995 net income of $5 million, up 92 percent over 1994's $2.6 million. As a result, the company's stock price started a steady climb that would last the remainder of the year.

As Penn approached the end of 1996, it had opened four of the six OTWs that it was allowed under state law. A fifth facility, located in Williamsport, was in the works and scheduled to open in early 1997. Once the company opened its sixth and final OTW, it would have reached a state-imposed ceiling on off-track expansion. In order to circumvent this ceiling and continue growing, Penn National looked north, to Pocono Downs Racetrack, near Wilkes-Barre Pennsylvania. Pocono Downs, one of only two harness racing tracks in the state, consisted of a ⅝-mile oval track, a 3,000-seat grandstand, and a clubhouse for dining and wagering.

Perhaps more important than the track itself, the Pocono acquisition also included the right to operate five off-track wagering facilities. Two such facilities were already established—in Allentown and Erie—when the acquisition was finalized on November 27, 1996.

Meanwhile, Penn National had another deal in the works. In early 1996, the company had entered into a joint venture with Bryant Development Company of Sterling, Virginia, which held an option to purchase the Charles Town Race Track in Charles Town, West Virginia. Penn planned to sink major money into the renovation and restoration of the 60-year-old track, which had suffered in recent years from a declining interest in racing. The plan, however, was contingent upon one key factor: before committing to the renovation, Penn wanted permission to install video gaming machines at the track.

The gaming machine decision rested in the hands of the county's voters, who just two years earlier had voted down a similar proposal. By the November 1996 elections, however, the voters had apparently had a change of heart. The referendum allowing gaming machines passed, and Penn National and Bryant went forward with the acquisition. Penn National became the majority owner of the track, with an 89 percent share.

Late 1990s: New Opportunities, New Alliances

The Charles Town acquisition was completed in January 1997, and Penn immediately began an extensive renovation of the track's clubhouse and grandstand. The $27 million project also included the addition of two new restaurants and a Hollywood-themed gaming section. After being closed several months for its facelift, the track reopened for racing in April, under the new name "Charles Town Entertainment Complex." The gaming area was completed over the ensuing summer, celebrating its grand opening in the autumn. The complex initially offered 400 video gaming machines, which simulated traditional spinning reel slot machines, along with video card games like poker and blackjack. By March 1998, Penn had added 209 more machines. By year-end, the company had 799 machines at Charles Town, with approval to install up to 1,000 total if demand dictated.

While Penn focused on ramping up its gaming operation in West Virginia, the growth of off-track facilities continued as planned in Pennsylvania. Two new OTW's opened in March

Key Dates:

1972: Penn National Race Course opens for its first race.
1978: A turf course is added to the Penn National facility.
1992: Company opens its first off-track wagering facility.
1994: Penn National goes public.
1996: Company acquires the Pocono Downs racetrack, near Wilkes-Barre, Pennsylvania.
1997: Penn National acquires 89 percent ownership of the Charles Town Race Track in West Virginia.
1999: Company acquires 50 percent ownership in two New Jersey racetracks and enters into an agreement to purchase two Mississippi casinos.

1998, bringing the company's total to nine. The new sites were in Carbondale and Hazleton, both approximately 30 miles from the Pocono Downs track. In the fall of 1998, Penn purchased an existing OTW in Johnstown, the company's second facility to be located in the western half of the state.

The early part of 1999 saw Penn National expanding into a new state. In January, the company entered into a joint venture with a New Jersey racing company in order to purchase Freehold Raceway, a 146-year-old harness half-mile harness track in central New Jersey. The joint venture, in which Penn held 50 percent ownership, also secured a long-term lease on Garden State Park, a racetrack in Cherry Hill, New Jersey. New Jersey legislature was, at that time, in the process of deciding whether to allow off-track and telephone wagering. If approval was granted, Penn and its partner planned to immediately expand their newly acquired facilities.

In April 1999, Penn formed still another strategic alliance. Through an agreement with American Digital Communications, Inc., the company became the exclusive U.S. wagering hub for TrackPower, a subscription pari-mutuel satellite service. TrackPower provided live transmissions of horse races from various tracks to its subscribers' homes throughout the United States and the Caribbean. Subscribers were able to place bets, via phone or computer, which, under the terms of the agreement, were to be handled though the Penn National wagering hub.

Meanwhile, Penn National's investment in its Charles Town facility was paying off spectacularly. The track and, more significantly, the gaming machines increased revenue by almost 50 percent in the first half of 1999, as compared to the first half of 1998. Charles Town got an added boost in April 1999, when West Virginia passed legislation approving the use of the more traditional coin-out and reel spinning slot machines, in addition to the video machines that were currently in use. Subsequently, Penn began to convert some of its video machines to coin-out machines.

The company also requested permission from the West Virginia Lottery Commission to install an additional 500 gaming machines at Charles Town, bringing the total to 1,500. Penn received the go-ahead for its additional machines in September 1999, and immediately initiated plans for expansion of the gaming area. "Additional gaming devices have been a driving force in patronage, revenue and EBITDA [earnings before interest,

taxes, depreciation and amortization] growth, and the addition of the reel-spinning, coin-out features address a common request we have had from players at Charles Town," Penn's CEO, Peter Carlino, said in a October 26, 1999 press release, adding "The significant increase in machines underscores our optimism for further growth from this facility in 2000."

Penn National finished up 1999 by laying the groundwork for further expansion. In December, the company announced plans to purchase two casinos located in Mississippi: Casino Magic and Boomtown Biloxi. Casino Magic—which was located in Bay St. Louis, approximately 45 miles east of New Orleans, Louisiana—consisted of a 39,500-square foot casino and a 201-room hotel, as well as a golf course, an RV park, and a marina. The Boomtown Biloxi property was a 33,632-square foot casino in Biloxi, Mississippi. Penn National agreed to purchase both properties for $195 million.

Betting on Future Growth

After spending the latter part of the 1990s establishing beachheads in West Virginia, New Jersey, and Mississippi, it appeared that Penn National would devote a good portion of its energies to managing and expanding those operations. The potential for adding off-track and telephone wagering to its New Jersey operation was an especially likely avenue of growth, presuming legislative approval.

It also appeared probable that Penn would continue to look to other states for expansion opportunities. Most notably, as of October 1999, the company had tentative plans to develop a harness racetrack and off-track facility near Memphis, Tennessee, pending a favorable ruling by the Supreme Court of Tennessee.

Principal Subsidiaries

Plains Co.; Mountainview Thoroughbred Racing Association; Pennsylvania National Turf Club, Inc.; Penn National Speedway, Inc.; Penn National Holding Co.; Penn National Gaming of West Virginia, Inc.; Penn National GSFR, Inc.; Sterling Aviation, Inc.; Northeast Concessions, Inc.; Downs Racing, Inc.; PNGI Pocono, Inc.; Tennessee Downs, Inc.; Backside, Inc.; Audio Video Concepts; Mill Creek Land, Inc.; Wilkes-Barre Downs, Inc.; Grantville Racing, Inc.; PNGI Charles Town Food & Beverage, LLC; Pennwood Racing, Inc. (50%).

Principal Competitors

Aztar Corporation; Churchill Downs Incorporated; International Speedway Corporation; The Pennsylvania Lottery; The Trump Organization.

Further Reading

Dochat, Tom, "Penn National's Growth is No Gamble," *Sunday Patriot-News* (Harrisburg, Penn.), June 29, 1997, p. S05.
Grugal, Robin, "The New America: Penn National Gaming Inc.," *Investor's Business Daily*, May 29, 1997, p. A3.
Heerwagen, Peter, "Charles Town Races Back on Track with Penn National," *North Valley Business Journal*, December 1, 1996, p. 1.

—Shawna Brynildssen

PeopleSoft Inc.

4660 Hacienda Drive
Pleasanton, California 94588-8618
U.S.A.
Telephone: (925) 225-3000
Fax: (925) 694-4444
Web site: http://www.peoplesoft.com

Public Company
Incorporated: 1987
Employees: 7000
Sales: $1.4 billion (1999)
Stock Exchanges: NASDAQ
Ticker Symbol: PSFT
NAIC: 51121 Software Publishers

PeopleSoft Inc. is a global leader in enterprise application software, serving more than 4,000 customers in the fields of customer relations management, human resources management, financial management, and supply chain management, along with a slew of industry-specific concerns. Clients include small- and medium-sized businesses as well as some of the largest companies in the world. After enjoying explosive growth during its first decade of existence, PeopleSoft's pace of expansion slowed over the last two years of the 20th century, as increased competition and Y2K concerns reduced demand for its products. During that period, however, the company rededicated itself to providing cutting-edge, Internet-based software applications in an effort to recapture market share and reignite growth.

The Origins of PeopleSoft

Dave Duffield and Ken Morris are the progenitors of People-Soft. Both software developers had been working at Integral Corp. before jumping ship to start their own company. In fact, Duffield had founded Integral in 1982 and served as its chief executive until 1984. Integral started out providing consulting services but later moved into the lucrative market of mainframe computer software. Duffield was credited with helping to grow Integral into a $40 million (in sales) producer of human resources applications for use on mainframes.

By the mid-1980s, after taking Integral public, Duffield had effectively lost control of the company that he had founded. That loss of authority ultimately would cause Duffield to jump ship. The conflict arose when Duffield took an interest in the burgeoning personal computer networking industry. At the time, mainframes were still the dominant platform for large and mid-sized companies, and Integral had profited handsomely by chasing that big market. But early on Duffield recognized the potential of personal computer networks (dubbed client/server systems because the PCs were linked to a server system). He believed that Integral should shift its focus away from mainframes and toward client/servers, which he viewed as the wave of the future.

Integral's board of directors disagreed with Duffield, so he decided to leave the organization. He even offered to sign a no-compete agreement with Integral in return for one year's salary, which would have kept him from competing with Integral in the human resources software industry. Integral's board foolishly rejected the offer, and Duffield started a new company that he called PeopleSoft. Duffield took fellow Integral employee Ken Morris with him, and together they began designing human resources software geared for client/server systems. In 1988 Morris and Duffield introduced the first high-end human resources software application ever designed for a client/server system.

Although PeopleSoft's first program was greeted by a willing market, the tiny firm was strapped for cash. To fund the start-up, Duffield took out a mortgage on his home; he and Morris tapped the nest egg to fund the development of their first program. That effort generated revenues of about $200,000 in 1988, the company's first year of sales. Significantly, the company scored a major coup in 1988 when it landed Eastman Kodak as its major customer. That gave a much-needed boost to PeopleSoft's bottom line.

Kodak, like many other corporations in the late 1980s, was beginning to realize the advantage of the client/server approach. A company could purchase a number of relatively inexpensive PCs, network them through a more expensive server, and have a system with capabilities similar to a mainframe. The obvious advantages were much lower costs and, in many cases, increased flexibility. At the same time, PeopleSoft's human resources software became a valuable tool for companies that were reorganizing and cutting costs during the recession of the early 1990s. Thus, as the client/server industry took off and PeopleSoft's innovative human resources program became known, sales shot up. In 1989 PeopleSoft generated an impressive $1.9 million in sales. That figure exploded to $6.1 million in 1990, about $420,000 of which was netted as income.

Funding Woes Lead to IPO

Despite big sales and profit gains, cash was short. PeopleSoft was trying to hire new staff, buy new computer systems, market its existing software, and develop new products—all on a shoestring budget. To make matters worse, Integral Corp. (where PeopleSoft's success had not gone unnoticed) was forcing PeopleSoft to spend money in court. In 1990 Integral and a San Francisco-based company called Tesseract Inc. filed separate lawsuits against PeopleSoft, claiming it had obtained proprietary trade information from them. They even sought injunctions to halt the sale of PeopleSoft products. A San Francisco judge denied the injunction requests and PeopleSoft was able to settle out of court in 1991, but only after expending significant legal fees from its tight budget.

Duffield, despite the cash drain, was not about to give up control of his company again to outside financiers, and he was able to secure a $1 million line of credit from a bank. That helped to offset some costs, but he needed more. In 1991 Duffield sold 11 percent of his company for $5 million to Norwest Partners, a venture capital firm. He used much of that cash to update the company's systems and also to help fund development of a new client/server program for financial management applications. In addition to the $5 million, PeopleSoft enjoyed net earnings in 1991 of $1.9 million from sales of $17.1 million.

By 1992 PeopleSoft was growing at a seemingly exponential pace. Its human resources applications were selling like hotcakes and it was gearing up to launch its awaited financial management programs. To fund the growth, Duffield finally decided to take the company public. In November 1992 PeopleSoft made its initial public offering, which brought $36 million into its coffers. Investor enthusiasm sent the stock's price cruising 64 percent higher than the original offer price on the same day. Six months later PeopleSoft netted a fat $50.4 million with a second offering. The wary Duffield still managed to keep about 50 percent ownership in the company. "We waited four years," Duffield said in the April 1993 issue of *Diablo Business,* adding, "We didn't want to give away a big part of the company, and we didn't."

By 1992 PeopleSoft was controlling about 40 percent of the entire high-end market for human resources programs—some of PeopleSoft's human resources applications priced out at $600,000 or more. Because a plethora of companies were hopping into the client/server game by that time, however, the enterprise was banking on its freshly introduced financial applications to help it sustain rapid growth. The financial software industry was crowded with competitors, but PeopleSoft had staffed its programming department with some heavy hitters, and it believed that its experience in the client/server industry gave it an edge. Although financial program sales contributed only a few million dollars to PeopleSoft's revenue base in 1992, company sales and profits spiraled upward to $31.6 million and $4.8 million.

Duffield had hoped that his financial programs would eventually account for as much as one-half of company sales. The software was welcomed by the market and seemed to be living up to Duffield's expectations by late 1993. The line of financial programs was expanded to include applications for general ledger accounting, asset management, and accounts payable/receivable management. When sales from that line kicked in during 1993, revenues and profits vaulted to about $58.2 million and $8.4 million. Interestingly, that sales figure approximated the 1992 revenues for Integral, the company that Duffield had started and left six years earlier; soon, PeopleSoft would leave that mainframe software company in the dust.

An interesting sidebar to the PeopleSoft story during the late 1980s and early 1990s was the Raving Daves, a rock band made up of PeopleSoft employees. Named after the company's chief executive and founder, the Raving Daves provided insight into the quirky but effective culture at PeopleSoft. PeopleSoft was loosely structured and efficient. Employees were empowered to make important decisions and nobody had a secretary or receptionist—even Duffield answered his own telephone. The environment was designed to spawn creativity and innovation, as evidenced by the formation of the Raving Daves (a group of eight musicians and singers who were full-time PeopleSoft employees). The group became the centerpiece of the company's image advertising campaign in 1995.

Expansion in the Mid-1990s

PeopleSoft's unique management formula combined with the growth in client/server systems in 1993 and 1994 and propelled the company to prominence. The client/server market mushroomed, in fact, at a much greater rate than most analysts had predicted. PeopleSoft controlled a whopping 50 percent share of the entire human resources software market by 1994. By that time a horde of former mainframe software developers began leaping head first into the client/server market. But PeopleSoft benefited from what was known as "clean technology," meaning that its applications had been written specifically for client/server and had not been converted from a mainframe environment.

By 1994 PeopleSoft's client base had broadened to include corporate giants like Hewlett-Packard, Advance Micro Devices, Rolm, and Pacific Bell, among many others. Furthermore, overseas interest in the company's programs was proliferating. Exports jumped to about $1.6 million in 1993, with customers buying from as far away as Australia, France, England, and South America. Buoyed by increasing demand at home and abroad for PeopleSoft's human resources applications and, in particular, its financial applications, Duffield began considering new markets. He planned, eventually, to lead PeopleSoft into client/server software markets in manufacturing, health care, education, and government, to name a few.

The first new market that Duffield tried to crack was the giant manufacturing sector. Specifically, PeopleSoft began chasing manufacturers of automobiles, electronics, and consumer durables in 1995. The manufacturing market offered massive growth potential for the company, as client/server software sales to that segment were then growing at a rate of 78 percent annually (compared with a still-healthy 38 percent for the financial software market). Duffield believed that success with manufacturing software would allow PeopleSoft to quadruple its revenues within two years. To meet that challenge, PeopleSoft brought on board leading manufacturing software veterans like Roger Bottarini and Chris Wong.

Because of its ambitious foray into manufacturing software, PeopleSoft again was looking for funds to fuel the growing enterprise. Rather than sell off more of the company, Duffield cleverly arranged to have the project funded externally. PeopleSoft entered into a joint venture with its old financier, Norwest Venture Capital. Norwest fronted the development capital and PeopleSoft contributed the intellectual property (such arrangements had been pioneered in the capital-intensive biotechnology industry). As a result, PeopleSoft, which owned 49 percent of the venture, was able to get the program up and running much faster at much reduced risk.

Growth Accelerates, Slows in the Mid- to Late 1990s

By the mid-1990s, PeopleSoft controlled roughly 20 percent of the U.S. client/server packaged software market and continued to enjoy tremendous growth and profitability. From a respectable $175 million in 1992, PeopleSoft's sales more than tripled to $575 million by 1994. Net income rose from $8.4 million to $14.55 million over the same period. By 1995, the company had offices throughout North America and Europe, as well as in Singapore, South Africa, Brazil, and Australia.

PeopleSoft's expansion continued in 1996, when it purchased the Red Pepper Software Company, a provider of supply chain management programs. PeopleSoft also was recognized by *Fortune* magazine that year as one of the fastest growing companies in America (as it had been in 1994 and 1995, and as it would be again in 1997). Net income for 1996 jumped to $35.9 million.

Another banner year for the company was 1997. It formed two new independent business units (IBUs)—Service Industries and Communications, Transport, and Utilities—to complement its seven pre-existing ones (which focused on financial services; health care; higher education; manufacturing; the public sector; retail; and the U.S. federal government). PeopleSoft also completed three strategic acquisitions—of Campus Solutions, Inc., Salerno Manufacturing, Inc., and TeamOne, LLC—that bolstered its Student Administrative Application suite of software. In addition, PeopleSoft launched an international version of its popular Human Resources Management Suite, as well as one of a widely used financial application suite. These offerings were capable of supporting operations in French, German, Spanish, and Japanese, and English. Most important, though, 1997 marked PeopleSoft's fledgling venture into cyberspace, when it inaugurated a pilot program to allow users to access several of the company's popular software programs over the Internet (a venue that would become increasingly essential to the company's operations in the coming years). PeopleSoft's total revenues that year exploded to nearly $816 million, and net income skyrocketed as well, to $108.2 million.

The year 1998, however, marked the end of PeopleSoft's streak of annual 80 to 90 percent growth increases that dated back virtually to the company's inception. The shock waves generated by the Asian economic crisis of 1997, coupled with heightened competition in the industry and a widespread shift in corporate procurement policies away from new software acquisition in favor of Y2K remediation measures, resulted in a comparative slackening of demand for PeopleSoft's wares (although revenues increased nearly 61 percent in real terms, to $1.3 billion). Undaunted, the company used the period as an occasion to streamline its operational structure, condensing its IBUs into three overarching divisions: the Product Industries Division, which handled the company's manufacturing, retail, communications, transportation, and utility businesses; the Services Industry Division, responsible for operations in the health care, financial services, and service industry sectors; and the Government and Higher Education Division, which dealt with the academic, public sector, and federal government markets. In addition, PeopleSoft expanded its eBusiness offerings in 1998 in anticipation of future market needs. The company also rolled out its Enterprise Performance Management product, an integrated suite of analytic business software that distinguished PeopleSoft as the first entity able to provide such a wide array of analytic tools across all industries. To cap off its busy year, the company moved into its new headquarters in Pleasanton, California.

Although many of the same factors that slowed revenue growth in 1998 persisted even more strongly in 1999 (the year even witnessed the first layoffs in company history and revenues increased a comparatively paltry 25 to 30 percent), PeopleSoft made some important advances during the course of the year. Early in the year, PeopleSoft introduced e7.5, a program designed to become the backbone of all of the company's subsequent eBusiness initiatives. This was also the first program to bring real Internet functionality to PeopleSoft's software options. A few months later, the company introduced PeopleSoft 8, software that offered 100 percent Internet-based technologies and applications. The year saw a significant change in the company's management personnel as well. In May 1999, Craig A. Conway joined the company as president and chief operating officer. In September, he was named chief executive officer, displacing company founder Duffield. Duffield, though, remained intimately involved with PeopleSoft's operations in his continued capacity as company chairman. Conway quickly led PeopleSoft in its acquisition of Vantive Corporation, a leading customer relations management (CRM) firm with a thriving Internet presence. This union positioned PeopleSoft as the only major enterprise software company able to offer both CRM products and a full range of back-office applications, all with full Internet accessibility.

In early 2000, PeopleSoft moved to extend its Internet advantage when it launched PowerTools 8, the first server-centric platform released by a major enterprise applications company. (A server-centric platform is one for which software need only be installed once on a central server to be able to run on any linked network terminals. This affords a company a greater degree of flexibility in its utilization of a software product.) With innovations such as this, PeopleSoft's prospects seemed promising as it moved into the 21st century.

Principal Competitors

Baan Company; Oracle Corporation; SAP AG.

Further Reading

Berry, Michael, "Software Supernova: After Sales Tripled in Its Third Year," *Diablo Business,* April 1993.

Burstiner, Marcy, "Software Union: If You Can't Beat 'Em, Join 'Em," *San Francisco Business Times,* January 27, 1995.

Clifford, Carlsen, "Software Maker Aims High with New Products," *San Francisco Business Times,* April 10, 1992.

Fernandez, Lorna, "PeopleSoft Buttons Up Image Under Conway's Reign," *East Bay Business Times,* November 22, 1999.

Gadbois, Ray, "PeopleSoft Inc. Announces PeopleSoft Financials Implementation Partnership Program," *Business Wire,* May 9, 1994.

Labate, John, "PeopleSoft," *Fortune,* March 7, 1994.

"PeopleSoft Inc.," *San Francisco Business Times,* November 18, 1994.

"PeopleSoft Plans E-Biz Future," *The Age,* November 30, 1999.

Rauber, Chris, "People Power Software Company: PeopleSoft Grows Beyond Human Resources Niche," *San Francisco Business Times,* April 29, 1994.

Snyder, Bill, "Band on the Run," *PC Week,* May 29, 1995.

Zecher, Linda, "E.F. Codd Joins PeopleSoft Board of Directors," *Business Wire,* September 17, 1992.

—Dave Mote
—updated by Rebecca Stanfel

Pittway Corporation

200 South Wacker Drive
Suite 700
Chicago, Illinois 60606
U.S.A.
Telephone: (312) 831-1070
Fax: (312) 831-0828
Web site: http://www.pittway.com

Public Company
Incorporated: 1950 as Pittsburgh Railway Company
Employees: 7,600
Sales: $1.327 billion (1998)
Stock Exchanges: New York
Ticker Symbol: PRY
NAIC: 33429 Other Communications Equipment
    Manufacturing

Pittway Corporation is one of the world's leading manufacturers and distributors of professional fire and burglar alarms and other security systems. In early 2000, Pittway's shareholders overwhelmingly accepted a tender offer from Honeywell to merge Pittway into Honeywell's Home and Building Control business. This new $5 billion division is poised to become the dominant global entity across the entire home and business security and surveillance industry. Founded in 1950 as the Pittsburgh Railway Company, the firm was originally a subsidiary of the Standard Gas and Electric Company, a public utility holding company formed during the mid-1920s. The Pittsburgh-based business operated numerous street railway and bus companies. In 1957 the board of directors at Standard Gas and Electric voted to dissolve and subsequently convert itself into a closed-end investment company—in accordance with the Investment Company Act of 1940—named Standard Shares. As a result of the dissolution, Pittsburgh Railways became a public company, but Standard Shares, with 42 percent ownership of its stock, retained operating control of the firm.

The Early Years

During the late 1950s, Standard Shares drew the interest of Neison Harris. A year after graduating from Yale University, Harris entered the beauty supply business. In 1944 he set up a company called Toni Co. that manufactured beauty products, such as the first home permanent wave, with his brother Irving. The success of Toni products was so great that the Harris brothers sold their company to Gillette Company in 1948 (when Neison was only 33 years old) for approximately $20 million. For the next 12 years, Neison Harris served as president of Toni and as a member of Gillette's board of directors.

Harris grew disenchanted with Gillette management when it changed Toni's operating structure and product line, and he resigned. Along with his brother Irving and sister June, he purchased stock in Standard Shares until they had a controlling interest. But purchasing Standard was only a means to an end; Harris knew that Pittsburgh Railways was the principle asset of Standard, and it was this company that garnered his interest. With the era of mass private transportation clearly in decline, Harris saw an opportunity to remake Pittsburgh Railways.

Growth and Diversification in the 1960s

Using his family's controlling interest, Harris convinced the board of directors at Standard Shares to redeploy Pittsburgh Railways' assets and diversify into areas more financially promising than bus and trolley car operation. Harris immediately went on a shopping spree and, in April 1962, acquired G. Barr & Company, a rapidly growing aerosol products packager. A year later, he purchased the Alarm Device Manufacturing Company (Ademco), a leading manufacturer and distributor of burglar and fire alarm equipment. By the time the city of Pittsburgh condemned the streetcar business in 1964, Neison also had bought Seaquist Manufacturing Corporation and the Industrial Publishing Company, a publisher of business directories and trade magazines.

In 1967 Pittsburgh Railways changed its name to Pittway because of the major changes in the direction of its business. Around the same time, company offices were relocated from

Company Perspectives:

Our strategy has been very simple. We want to have a full range of alarm and monitoring equipment. We want to achieve design, performance and manufacturing excellence in all the product markets we serve. We want to be leaders, not followers, in new technology. We want the capability to reach our worldwide customer base quickly and efficiently. Finally, we want to give our customers outstanding support and service so they can succeed with their businesses.

Pittsburgh to Chicago, where the Harris family resided and directed its operations. With Neison Harris as president of Pittway and Irving Harris as chairman of the board at Standard Shares, the two brothers collaborated in developing the core businesses of alarm systems, packaging, and publishing, and also expanded into real estate.

The company's packaging businesses, Barr and Seaquist, grew rapidly during the middle and late 1960s, in large part because of the success of pressurized aerosol products. In 1968 management wanted to develop a presence in Europe in addition to entering the growing aerosol pump business. Seaquist subsequently acquired an interest in German aerosol valve manufacturer Perfect-Ventil GmbH and, two years later, purchased the French company Valois, a leading producer of perfume and pharmaceutical valves. The success of Perfect-Ventil impressed the Harris brothers, and they decided to make it a wholly owned subsidiary of Seaquist in 1971.

Pittway continued its diversification strategy by entering the real estate business in 1968. For $2.5 million, the Harris brothers acquired a ten percent equity position in Metropolitan Structures, a high-profile real estate developer in Chicago headed by Bernard Weissbourd. Metropolitan built office buildings, apartment buildings, industrial parks, and shopping centers. Much of the company's work, especially in Chicago, was done in cooperation with renowned architect Ludwig Mies van der Rohe. During the same time, the company also purchased a 50 percent interest in a huge apartment development project on Nuns Island near Montreal.

By the end of the 1960s, Pittway's success was indisputable. The company's four main divisions—the Alarm Device Division, the Barr/Stalfort Division, the Seaquist Division, and the Industrial Publishing Division—grew from a total sales figure of $46.4 million in 1965 to $61.8 in 1968, an average annual increase of ten percent. Earnings for these same divisions grew from the 1965 figure of $3.8 million to $8.7 million in 1968, an average annual increase of 31 percent.

Continued Success in the 1970s

For Pittway, the success of the 1960s continued into the 1970s, mitigated only by minor setbacks. In 1968 Industrial Publishing acquired Patterson Publishing, and then augmented this purchase with Reinhold Publishing in 1974. These two companies published highly regarded magazines such as *Hospitality, Progressive Architecture,* and *Air Transport World.* With the acquisition of Penton in 1976, a prestigious publisher of

specialized trade magazines, Pittway's Industrial Publishing became one of the leading American magazine publishers.

Seaquist, and the entire aerosol filling industry, were hurt by the negative press that surrounded the banning of fluorocarbons and aerosols during the mid-1970s. Ecologists accused the company of making aerosol propellants that destroyed the ozone layer of the earth's atmosphere. Yet Seaquist's decision in 1976 to expand into the dispensing cap business kept it in financial health. A short time later, Seaquist Closures, one of Seaquist's subdivisions, rapidly developed into the leader of what soon became a major packaging market. Around the same time, Pittway acquired a 35 percent stake in the Pfeiffer Group, a German producer of pumps for both the pharmaceutical and perfume industries. As a result of these measures, Pittway was able to increase its market share in the aerosol filling business even though sales decreased by 17 percent.

BRK Electronics was purchased in 1970 to add ionization smoke detectors to the product line at Ademco. With the expansion of the smoke detector business in the early 1970s, BRK grew exponentially and, by 1975, had developed into a separate division at Pittway. By 1977 BRK was the largest producer of residential smoke detectors in the world, with sales peaking at $84 million and operating profits at $32 million. Ademco benefited enormously from the acquisition of BRK and the growing concern with crime prevention. In 1963, when Ademco first became part of Pittway, sales and operating profits were a mere $2 million and $800,000, respectively; by 1981 sales reached $96 million and operating profits had jumped to $22.2 million.

Troubles and Triumphs in the 1980s

The early 1980s did not look favorably on Pittway. With the onset of a recession, BRK Electronics sales fell to $44 million by 1980 and operating profits decreased to a mere $5 million. Competition in the mature residential smoke alarm business pushed the retail price of a smoke detector down from $49 to $9. In the mid-1980s, however, BRK began to make a comeback when smoke detector codes spurred the demand for residential alarm detectors. BRK also expanded its manufacturing base by designing such products as rechargeable flashlights, timers, night lights, and fire extinguishers.

The fierce competition in the retail market for alarm equipment spilled over into the commercial market, and Pittway's Ademco profits nearly disappeared along with a substantial loss of its market share. In 1984 Ademco rehauled its distribution policy to cover items manufactured by competitors as well as those produced internally. The company also expanded its network of regional warehouses by acquiring a number of regional alarm distribution companies. Management then created Ademco Distribution (ADI) to handle its distribution business. By 1988 sales of alarm equipment began once again to increase rapidly, and ADI was soon the leader in its field.

Pittway management also decided that Ademco needed to make a significant investment in advanced alarm system products; thus the company developed new product lines of control communicators, passive infrared motion sensors, short-range radio devices, and long-range radio systems. A commitment to replacing older factory equipment was implemented, and the

```
┌─────────────────────────────────────────────────┐
│                  Key Dates:                     │
│                                                 │
│  1950:  Company is founded as Pittsburgh Railway Com- │
│         pany.                                    │
│  1962:  Company buys G. Barr & Co. and enters the aerosol │
│         industry.                                │
│  1963:  Pittsburgh Railway Company buys Ademco.  │
│  1967:  Company changes name to Pittway.         │
│  1976:  Pittway acquires Penton Publishing.      │
│  1988:  Ademco Distribution Inc. is formed.      │
│  1993:  AptarGroup is formed.                    │
│  1996:  Penton Publishing is spun off as an independent │
│         company.                                 │
│  2000:  Pittway merges with Honeywell's Home and Build- │
│         ing Control division.                    │
└─────────────────────────────────────────────────┘
```

company established a maquila plant in Juarez, Mexico to provide it with relatively simple but labor-intensive alarm components. Slowly, Ademco garnered a reputation as a leading manufacturer of innovative, high-quality alarm systems and started to reclaim the market share it had lost during the early part of the decade.

The publishing division of Pittway did not suffer at all during the 1980s, nor did Seaquist. In fact, Pittway's Penton/Industrial Publishing Company kept growing and improving its standing in the national magazine specialty market. In 1985 the company (now known as Penton) purchased *Millimeter.* In 1987 *American Machinist* and *33 Metal Producing* also were acquired, along with *Electronics, Electronic Design, Electronic Design International,* and *Microwaves & RF.* Penton also developed successful magazines such as *Computer Aided Design* and *Foodservice Distributor* internally. While Penton was adding titles to its growing list of magazines, Seaquist was also busy with acquisitions. Both Bielsteiner, a German producer of dispensing closures, and SAR, a leading Italian manufacturer of aerosol pumps, were purchased during the decade, along with interests in numerous small packaging companies throughout Europe.

Restructuring Throughout the 1990s

Beginning in 1988, Pittway and Standard Shares embarked on a comprehensive restructuring strategy to focus their combined resources on businesses with the potential for solid and long-term growth. The Harris family intended to shed unrelated businesses in an attempt to strengthen the firm's financial position. Led by King Harris, Neison Harris's son, Pittway and Standard Shares merged in November 1989 to consolidate operations under the name of Pittway Corporation. In 1991 Pittway sold Bielsteiner to the Pfeiffer Group. In 1992 the company sold BRK Electronics and its consumer products, smoke detector, and fire extinguisher subdivision, First Alert, for $92.5 million to the division's management. The same year, Barr was sold to Canada's CCL Industries. In 1993 Pittway was given approval to spin off its Seaquist Packaging Group, which then merged with the Pfeiffer Group to create a new public company, AptarGroup. By 1997, AptarGroup's sales had soared to more than $650 million.

Pittway's Penton division also continued to grow and change. Throughout the early and mid-1990s, Penton continued to acquire trade publications with strong positions in their fields. Of perhaps greatest significance among these were the titles *Food Management* and *EEPN.* The company also launched new magazines, including *Wireless System Design, IW Growing Companies,* and Penton's *Embedded Systems,* and discontinued four smaller publications that were not meeting the company's goals of being first or second in their segments. During this period Penton added to its other holdings as well, acquiring three prominent trade show companies—A/E/Systems, Industrial Shows of America, and Independent Exhibitions—to bring its roster of such businesses to a total of 55.

These actions proved quite beneficial for Penton and Pittway, as the publishing division's revenues and earnings both increased dramatically. Penton's sales jumped from $165 million in 1993 to more than $205 million by 1997, while operating income exploded from $7.2 million to $25.3 million over the same period. Buoyed by this success, Pittway opted to spin Penton off into a freestanding company. To do so, Penton was merged with a non-Pittway company called Donohue-Meehan Publishing to form a new, publicly traded firm called Penton Media. The new business' sales exceeded $240 million in 1998 alone.

As a result of this protracted restructuring process, Pittway emerged in 1998 as a company focused exclusively on alarm system manufacture and distribution. Of course, this industry had remained at the core of its business plan throughout the decade, and its alarm division had grown rapidly in its own right during that time. Composed of the Pittway Security Group (which included both Ademco and ADI) and the Pittway Systems Technology Group (which included the System Sensor Division, Notifier/Fam-Lite, Notifier UK, Inertia Fire Systems, Fire Control Instruments, and Microlite), the sales generated by Pittway's alarm businesses skyrocketed from $483 million in 1993 to $1.144 billion in 1997. (After the spin-off of Penton, the alarm businesses accounted for all of the company's 1998 sales of $1.327 billion.) Over the same period, operating income generated by these groups more than tripled, from $33.4 million in 1993 to $104.4 million in 1998.

Although the Systems Technology Group expanded significantly in the 1990s, acquiring fire alarm control companies in the United States, United Kingdom, and Australia (including 1999's takeover of Silent Knight), the Security Group—led by Ademco—proved to be the major engine of growth. On top of purchasing ten companies between 1990 and 1999 (including alarm distributors in the United Kingdom, the Netherlands, Italy, and the United States, along with closed circuit television manufacturers in the United States, United Kingdom, and Canada), Ademco reaped the rewards of a strategic decision it had made in the late 1980s. At that time, the division had taken a calculated risk when it decided to devote substantial effort and capital to developing a modular series of control/communications under the VISTA brand. This gamble paid off handsomely in the 1990s, as these VISTA controls became the industry standard and were selected by most of the United States' leading alarm installation firms. Heartened by these results, Ademco soon devised a VISTA line for foreign markets, which helped the division obtain new business around the world. By 1999, the Security Group had more than 40,000 active customers and 117 distribution centers throughout the United States, Canada, Mexico, and Puerto Rico, as well as an ever-expanding European presence.

Pittway's success made it an attractive takeover target. (It had long been speculated that security giant Tyco International would launch a hostile bid for the company.) In December 1999, Honeywell, a leader in the technology and manufacturing sectors, made a tender bid for Pittway's shares. The per-share offer of $45.50 represented a significant premium over the company's trading price at the time (around $29) and was resoundingly accepted by Pittway's shareholders. Honeywell planned to incorporate Pittway into its own Home and Building Control division (a $3.4 billion unit of the $24 billion company). By combining the strengths of Honeywell and Pittway, the new $5 billion venture appeared situated to capture a dominant position in the $10 billion fire and security industry.

Principal Subsidiaries

Alarm Device Manufacturing Co.; Fire Control Instruments, Inc.; Fire-Lite Alarms, Inc./NOTIFIER; Javelin Systems.

Principal Competitors

Protection One; Tyco International Ltd.

Further Reading

D'Avesa-Williams, Tina, ''Securing New Business Opportunities,'' *Access Control and Security Systems Integration,* November 30, 1997.

''Honeywell to Purchase Pittway,'' *Chicago Sun-Times,* December 20, 1999.

Murphy, H. Lee, ''Pittway Corp.'s Deal King Strikes the Ultimate Bargain,'' *Crain's Chicago Business,* January 3, 2000.

——, ''Pittway Sounds the Alarm for Restructuring,'' *Crain's Chicago Business,* August 17, 1992.

Pledger, Marcia, ''Business Spun Off in the Right Direction,'' *Plain Dealer,* August 11, 1998.

''Smoke Detectors: Hot Item in Fall Advertising,'' *Media Decision,* September 1977.

Tarsala, Michael, ''Leaders and Success: Ademco Security's Guthart,'' *Investor's Business Daily,* May 15, 1997.

—Thomas Derdak
—updated by Rebecca Stanfel

Poliet S.A.

21-23, rue des Ardennes
75940 Paris CEDEX 19
France
Telephone: (+33) 1.40.03.32.00
Fax: (+33) 1.42.03.12.90
Web site: http://www.saint-gobain.fr

96% Owned Subsidiary of Compagnie de Saint-Gobain
Incorporated: 1901 as Etablissements Poliet et Chausson
Employees: 20,000
Sales: FFr 27.09 billion ($4.5 billion) (1998)
NAIC: 42139 Other Construction Material Wholesalers

Long-time leader in the French construction materials distribution market, Poliet S.A. is also, since 1999, a subsidiary of French industrial conglomerate Compagnie de Saint-Gobain. Poliet acts as a holding company for businesses in several areas. The company's chain of more than 700 Point P stores distributes construction materials and other products, including bathroom equipment and wall and floor tiles, chiefly to the professional craftsman and construction markets. For the do-it-yourselfer, Poliet offers its Lapeyre subsidiary's chain of 75 Lapeyre and 50 GME warehouse stores, with a specialty in joinery products such as windows, doorways, and stairways. Together, Poliet's distribution activities account for more than 50 percent of its annual sales, which reached FFr 27 billion before Poliet's acquisition by Saint-Gobain. Poliet's other activities include production of industrial mortar and related equipment, through its Weber & Broutin subsidiary; production of roofing tiles, through Industrielle de Tuiles; and production of industrial concrete, through its Stradal subsidiary. The acquisition by Saint-Gobain, for a total of more than FFr 15 billion, marks the industrial giant's largest acquisition to date and gives Saint-Gobain a strong entry into the distribution market. For traditionally France-oriented Poliet, the acquisition may mark the beginning of a strong international growth drive, building on its parent company's well-developed overseas networks. In 1999, Saint-Gobain, which posted more than FFr 100 billion in annual sales, increased its holding in Poliet to more than 96 percent.

Cementing the French Market at the Turn of the Century

If Poliet later became synonymous with building materials distribution in France, its origins lay in producing those materials itself. At the turn of the century, Paul Chausson saw his future in the production of concrete. Walking along the Saint Martin canals, Chausson predicted that concrete would become an important ingredient in building France's industry, and, as more and more of the country's population moved out of the cities, in building their homes as well. In 1901, Chausson, with the financial backing of Jules Poliet, founded his own company, Etablissements Poliet & Chausson. Poliet's presence remained, in large part, financial; Chausson himself provided the company's leadership until his death in the early 1930s.

Beginning with the production of lime, Poliet & Chausson quickly added concrete production and then plaster products as well. The company soon began to commercialize its own products, opening a number of stores. Oriented toward the professional market, the Poliet & Chausson stores sought to provide all of the materials necessary for construction, boasting its ability to supply builders everything they need from the foundation to the roof. The company also offered delivery services.

The devastation of World War I provided Poliet & Chausson with the opportunity for explosive growth. The need to reconstruct much of northern and eastern France brought about a strong demand for construction products and, especially, concrete, which was quickly replacing brick and stone as the building material of choice. From the end of the war until the start of the Depression era, Poliet & Chausson rapidly increased its production and sales. By the 1930s, the company was producing more than 1.7 million tons of cement each year, making it the country's largest manufacturer of concrete. To support these production levels, Poliet & Chausson had grown into a network of nearly 40 production facilities, a distribution network that reached across the country and its own fleet of 250 barges for transporting its lime, cement, and plaster products.

If the postwar period had marked Poliet & Chausson's greatest success, the company went into a decline during the Depression years, culminating in a near halt of activity during the Second

Key Dates:

1901: Etablissements Poliet & Chausson is founded by Paul Chausson and Jules Poliet.
1930: Production reaches 1.7 million tons.
1933: Founder Paul Chausson dies.
1940: Activities suspended during World War II.
1945: Restart of production operations.
1952: Production reaches two million tons.
1969: Takeover by Banque Paribas.
1971: Restructuring as holding company Poliet S.A.
1975: Acquisition of Lapeyre S.A.
1970s: Acquisitions of Weber & Broutin, SAMC, and 25 percent of Ciments Français.
1984: Acquisition of Vachette.
1990: Takeover of Lambert Frères S.A.
1996: Acquisition by Saint-Gobain.
1997: Sale of Vachette.
1999: Saint-Gobain increases ownership to 96.13 percent.

World War. The company was hit hard by the death of Paul Chausson in 1933, at a time when the building market, crippled by the economic crisis, was collapsing, forcing Poliet & Chausson to reduce its production as well. The vast social unrest of the time and the rising strength of the French labor movement brought on more disruption in production. The buildup to and outbreak of World War II, the loss of labor to the war effort, the requisitioning of many of Poliet & Chausson's factories for supporting France's military, and, finally, the French surrender to Germany, put a temporary end to the company's activity.

Growth in the Second Half of the 20th Century

The liberation of France in 1945 and the need to reconstruct a country once again devastated by war provided the opportunity for Poliet & Chausson's rebirth. Production of cement, plaster, and related products resumed, and the company now began boosting its distribution network. By the beginning of the 1950s, Poliet & Chausson once again ranked as a top cement producer in France. Production levels, which reached one million tons in 1946, topped two million tons in 1952. The company also began boosting its distribution activities, with an eye toward becoming France's largest distributor of materials to the construction market.

This goal was accomplished in large part by the 1960s. To achieve its objectives, Poliet & Chausson embarked on a massive acquisition drive, buying up a number of smaller, family-run businesses as well as larger competitors to complement its own network of construction material depot stores. Among the companies acquired during the period were Etablissements Toussaints; Comptoirs Industriels et Commerciaux de Matériaux; Etablissement Escallier; and the group Trouillard. At the same time, Poliet expanded its manufacturing facilities, especially for the production cement and plaster products.

The heavy investments needed to sustain its rapid growth brought Poliet & Chausson into financial trouble by the end of the 1960s. In 1969, the company was forced to turn to its bank,

Paribas, for aid. Paribas began building up its shares in the company, and by 1969 had taken over Poliet & Chausson altogether. Paribas replaced the existing Poliet & Chausson management; by the beginning of the 1970s, the new management, led by Jean-Pierre Germot, was determined to take Poliet into a new direction.

The company underwent a dramatic restructuring in 1971. Renamed Poliet, the company now became more or less a holding company, and its activities were regrouped under a number of newly created subsidiaries. In particular, Poliet's activities were divided along its two main lines, distribution and production. Breaking from the highly centralized management approach of the time, Poliet's subsidiaries took on a decentralized direction, with each subsidiary responsible for its own operations.

During the decade, the company also began to reenforce its distribution activities, now grouped under the Point P insignia. Although Poliet had succeeded in becoming France's largest distributor of building construction materials, it was more or less absent from the joinery market and, especially, sales to the consumer home improvement market. Poliet remedied that deficit with the acquisition of Lapeyre S.A. in 1975, adding that company's production facilities and retail store network.

On the production side, Poliet ended its cement and concrete production operation, turning that division over to the Société des Ciments Français, in exchange for a 25 percent share of Ciments Français and FFr 70 million. Instead, Poliet concentrated on building up its building supply business, acquiring Weber & Broutin, the French leader in mortar products, and SAMC, specialized in gypsum production, helping to boost Poliet's plaster and plaster block production operations.

Poliet continued its development during the 1980s and early 1990s, building up its network of Point P centers, while diversifying its operations into other manufacturing areas related to the building, construction, and home improvement markets. In 1984, Poliet acquired Vachette, one of France's leading lock makers. By 1989, Poliet had grown to annual revenues of more than FFr 14 billion. The company went public, listing on the Paris stock exchange, while remaining majority controlled by Banque Paribas.

Two years later, the company's revenues neared FFr 20 billion. Contributing to this jump in sales was Poliet's takeover of Lambert Frères, one of its chief rivals in building construction materials distribution. As part of this acquisition, Poliet turned more resolutely toward distribution, while also dropping its status as a holding company to become actively engaged in the direction of its distribution and manufacturing operations. The Poliet and Lambert distribution networks were regrouped under the Point P banner. The addition of the Lambert group added a new area of operations to Poliet, that of roofing tiles, through the Société Industrielle de Tuiles. At the same time, the company exited a number of areas, including selling off its share of Ciments Français and shedding its plaster production, marking a final break from its original operations. By the middle of the 1990s, Poliet had successfully restructured itself into a diversified yet centralized industrial group with sales of more than FFr 22 billion per year.

Nevertheless, Poliet remained an almost exclusively French company. To improve its international status, especially in view of the approaching single economic market among European Union countries, Poliet began to reenforce its different operations through a series of acquisitions, including the 1993 acquisition of Spanish roofing tile maker Valforsa. That same year saw the addition of another roofing tile manufacturer, Tuilerie de Périgord, in France. The company also boosted its Weber & Broutin subsidiary with the purchases of Terranova, Stahel-Keller, and Promial. In 1994, after reenforcing the Lapeyre subsidiary with the acquisition of Les Zelles, Poliet moved into Italy, acquiring Cotto Toscano, a maker of roofing tiles. Poliet continued its acquisition drive into the mid-decade, buying up a number of companies, primarily in France, including Circé; Matériaux des Chesnez; Kieffer; Yonnaise de Bétons; Bétons et Matériaux du Maine; Stradal; Brunet Matériaux; Fermat; and Sogepal. Poliet boosted its Point P subsidiary, by then posting some 60 percent of its annual sales, with the acquisitions of Millecamps et Vanderperre and of the Socimat group.

Throughout this period, Poliet not only registered consistent growth, but consistent profitability as well, despite an extended financial crisis brought on by an international recession and an overbuilt construction market. If Poliet had weathered the economic storm, however, its largest stockholder Paribas faced financial problems. In 1996, Paribas agreed to sell Poliet to Compagnie de Saint-Gobain, one of France's largest and oldest industrial conglomerates, with diversified interests around the world. With the Poliet purchase, Saint-Gobain hoped to protect itself from market cycles in its other business areas, particularly with the addition of Poliet's strong distribution division. The total purchase price of FFr 15 billion, plus an additional FFr 2 billion in debt, marked Saint-Gobain's largest acquisition ever and boosted its own revenues past FFr 100 billion. As part of the purchase arrangement, the Poliet purchase was to take place in several steps and was not completed until January 1999, when Saint Gobain increased its ownership of Poliet to more than 96 percent.

After selling off the Vachette lock manufacturing subsidiary to Sweden's Assa Abloy in 1997, Poliet and Saint-Gobain looked forward to exporting Poliet's distribution expertise overseas. Despite its interest in developing international operations in the early 1990s, Poliet distribution activities remained almost entirely focused on France. Saint-Gobain, on the other hand, had concentrated on building up its production and manufacturing expertise—until the Poliet acquisition, its distribution operations had remained limited to the United States market. With the joining of Saint-Gobain's financial clout and strong international network of operations and Poliet's century-long expertise in the production and distribution of building materials, Poliet began to make plans to become a name recognized worldwide in the 21st century.

Principal Subsidiaries

Lapeyre S.A.; Weber & Broutin; Industrielle des Tuiles; Stradal; Point P.

Principal Competitors

Berisford International plc; Boral Ltd.; Royal Group Technologies; Groupe Castorama-Dubois Investissements.

Further Reading

Bauer, Anne, "Poliet: vingt années de croissance régulière et ininterrompue," *Les Echos,* May 9, 1996, p. 6.

Cosnard, Denis, "Saint-Gobain va prendre 100% de Poliet pour 15 milliards de francs et offre à Paribas plusieurs années de plus-value," *Les Echos,* May 9, 1996, p. 6.

"Jean-Louis Beffa à l'affut dans le secteur de la distribution de produits pour le batiment," *La Tribune*, February 2, 2000.

"Saint-Gobain Holds 96.13 Percent of Poliet (Saint-Gobain detient 96.13% de Poliet)," *Le Figaro,* January 7, 1999.

—M.L. Cohen

Pomeroy Computer Resources, Inc.

1020 Petersburg Road
Hebron, Kentucky 41048
U.S.A.
Telephone: (606) 586-0600
Fax: (606) 586-4414
Web site: http://www.pomeroy.com

Public Company
Incorporated: 1992
Employees: 1,699
Sales: $756.8 million (1999)
Stock Exchanges: NASDAQ
Ticker Symbol: PMRY
NAIC: 44312 Computer and Software Stores; 541512
   Computer Systems Design Services

Pomeroy Computer Resources, Inc. is a value-added reseller of desktop computer equipment and a provider of related technology services. The company has 30 regional offices located in 14 states throughout the Southeast and Midwest. Its customer base is comprised of large and medium-sized commercial, health governmental, educational, and financial organizations.

Pomeroy operates in two industry segments: products and services. The products segment, which accounts for almost 90 percent of the company's total revenue, includes the sale, leasing, and distribution of computer hardware, software, and related products from more than 35 major technology manufacturers. The company's services segment is broken down into three categories: lifecycle services, internetworking services, and customer support services. Under the lifecycle category, Pomeroy provides repair and maintenance; installations, moves, and changes; and asset redeployment and tracking. Internetworking services includes project management; network design, integration, and management; and cabling services. The company's customer support services consist of Internet-based training, customized help desk services, and videoconferencing and teleconferencing technologies.

ComputerLand Beginnings: 1981–91

David Pomeroy was working as a finance manager for a car dealership on the outskirts of Cincinnati when he decided to become a computer dealer. Since moving to the Cincinnati area in 1970, the independent-minded Pomeroy had grown increasingly certain that he wanted to own and operate his own business, and by the late 1970s, he was ready to make his move. As it happened, his personal entrepreneurial urges coincided with the dawning of a new era in the computer industry—the age of the personal computer. Pomeroy began looking for a way to get in on the action.

Until the early 1970s, computers had been prohibitively expensive for the average individual and were used almost exclusively by businesses, universities, and government. By the mid-1970s, however, computer manufacturers were able to condense an ever-increasing amount of power on an ever-smaller microchip. These improvements in technology led to lower prices, making home computers for the first time an affordable option for average consumers. In 1975 the nation's first retail computer store opened in Santa Monica, California.

A year later, Steve Jobs and Steve Wozniak formed the Apple Computer Company and introduced the Apple II personal computer. Clever advertisements for the new computers in the *Wall Street Journal* caught the eye of David Pomeroy. Pomeroy, who was just then in the process of deciding what kind of business to start, was taken with the idea of selling Apple computers. Apple, however, turned down his request to become a dealer. Still determined to get into the computer business, Pomeroy contacted ComputerLand, a California-based chain of computer outlets. As it happened, ComputerLand was just then looking for a franchisee in the Cincinnati market. Pomeroy sent in a deposit to secure the franchise rights and, in 1981, opened Cincinnati's first ComputerLand.

Pomeroy's timing was superb. Shortly after he opened his store, industry giant IBM entered the personal computer arena with the introduction of the 5150 PC personal computer—a DOS-supported, 4.77 megahertz machine, starting at $1,565. With the introduction of its PC, IBM began using outside distributors to sell its products for the first time ever. Pomeroy jumped at

---

Company Perspectives:

Pomeroy Computer Resources, Inc. is a full-service computer integration company, providing a comprehensive assortment of professional services from consulting to procurement to configuration to asset management to ensure complete customer satisfaction and corporate sustainability. This statement serves as a guideline, ensuring that all the employees of Pomeroy Computer Resources' strategy and tactics are focused upon two critical elements—customer satisfaction and profitability. We believe that the two go hand in hand.

---

the opportunity. "I was the first dealer to sign up for IBM," he said in an April 1994 interview with the *Kentucky Post.*

Although Pomeroy entered the computer business at a time when more people were buying PCs for personal use, the majority of his sales still came from businesses and organizations. For the first several years, noncorporate customers accounted for only 20 percent of Pomeroy's sales. That percentage decreased in the early 1990s, when large electronics stores began offering personal computers—drawing individual, non-business consumers away from computer specialty stores. Faced with increased competition from these big box retailers, Pomeroy focused his attention on what was already his core customer base: businesses.

He knew that servicing corporate accounts meant more than simply selling hardware. One of the most basic demands of corporate customers was that their computer systems be configured, or customized, to meet specific requirements.

ComputerLand already offered this service, as did virtually all computer resellers. But Pomeroy's range of services went beyond mere configuration. Many of his customers at that time were businesses just on the verge of converting to computer systems. Often, their experience with computers was fairly limited. Faced with rapidly evolving technology and a multiplicity of options, these customers needed someone to hold their hand through the entire conversion process. Pomeroy filled that need by offering a wide range of services—from helping them choose the right system to installing it for them, to offering employee training to providing follow-up maintenance.

In 1990 Pomeroy won a contract with Procter & Gamble (P&G) that was to prove pivotal in his store's growth. In addition to locking in a substantial amount of business, the P&G contract—in effect, a stamp of approval from a highly respected company—enhanced Pomeroy's credibility. Within just a few years, the company had secured a whole host of major corporate clients, including Kroger, Kentucky Fried Chicken, Long John Silver's, and the Commonwealth of Kentucky.

Being Independent: 1992–94

Pomeroy had never especially wanted to be a franchisee. He disliked the associated costs and the control exerted by headquarters and had taken the ComputerLand franchise in 1981 only because it appeared to be the best way to break into the

business. By the early 1990s, however, Pomeroy was ready to free himself from ComputerLand dictates and go it alone.

In early 1992, he reorganized his business as Pomeroy Computer Resources, Inc. (PCR), an independent company providing computers sales and support to corporate customers. In conjunction with the reorganization, Pomeroy went public, selling 1.1 million shares and generating $8.8 million.

Using funds from the initial public offering (IPO), Pomeroy began pursuing expansion opportunities in markets he believed were underserved by PCR's larger competitors. The new company branched out geographically right away, making its first acquisition just months after completing the offering. The purchase was C&N Corporation, a computer products provider with locations in Knoxville, Tennessee and Jacksonville, Florida.

The years 1993 and 1994 brought still more expansion, with the acquisition of Connecting Point, a computer retailer in Louisville, and Xenas Communications Corp., a provider of communications products and services based in Cincinnati. The latter purchase was a particularly farsighted one; Pomeroy felt certain that the videoconferencing and teleconferencing services offered by Xenas would be merging with the computer industry in the coming years. He believed that having the technology already in place would put PCR ahead of the game.

The company proved remarkably adept at integrating its acquisitions, and its profits soared. In 1993 its first full year as an independent, publicly held company, PCR reported net income of $1.9 million—a 171 percent gain from 1992's $702,000. Another healthy gain in 1994 gave Pomeroy year-end profits of $2.73 million on revenues of $144.58 million.

In 1995, as business continued to grow, Pomeroy broke ground on a new 100,000-square-foot distribution center and a 40,000-square-foot corporate headquarters in Hebron, Kentucky, just outside Cincinnati. By early 1996, the company had moved into its new facilities.

Focusing on Services: 1996–97

Since his ComputerLand days, Pomeroy had understood the importance of offering a wide array of technical services, as well as computer hardware. Accordingly, he had invested substantial resources in building up the service side of the business in addition to the products side. In the mid-1990s, however, the company made a calculated shift in direction, a strategic decision to make service the *core* of its business. "We're migrating to being a systems integrator," Stephen Pomeroy, David Pomeroy's son and PCR's vice-president of marketing, said in a December 1996 interview with *Computer Reseller News.*

The decision to focus on service was followed by a flurry of appropriately service-oriented acquisitions. In March 1996, PCR purchased The Computer Supply Store, a Des Moines, Iowa computer reseller and services provider. A few months later, the company acquired AA Microsystems, of Birmingham, Alabama, a small network systems integrator. In October 1996, Pomeroy made its third acquisition of the year: Dilan Inc., a network integrator based in Hickory, North Carolina, with offices in Charlotte, Raleigh, and Winston-Salem, North Carolina, and Greenville, South Carolina. Dilan had been primarily a

Key Dates:

1981: David Pomeroy opens a ComputerLand franchise in Cincinnati, Ohio.
1990: Pomeroy wins contract with Procter & Gamble.
1992: Pomeroy severs ties with ComputerLand, reorganizes as Pomeroy Computer Resources, Inc., and completes an initial public offering (IPO).
1996: PCR makes a strategic shift in focus toward technology services.
1998: Pomeroy forms a wholly owned subsidiary, Pomeroy Select Integration Solutions, to hold its services business.
1999: Pomeroy Select Integration Solutions files registration statement for an IPO.

technology services provider since its inception in 1989, with a focus on networking—establishing large, interconnected systems of computers. Its background and expertise made it a particularly good fit for Pomeroy's new strategy.

The year 1997 saw three more acquisitions. In June, Pomeroy purchased Magic Box Inc., a network integrator located in Miami, Florida. The following month, the company acquired Micro Care, an Indianapolis-based provider of computer services. The final acquisition of the year, completed in October, was The Computer Store, a Columbia, South Carolina network integrator. Altogether, Pomeroy made six acquisitions in 1996 and 1997, expanding into nine new locations and adding a combined total of almost $96 million in annual sales.

Pomeroy's decision to focus on providing services, rather than reselling hardware, was proving a highly practical one from a financial perspective. Because profit margins in the services area were almost four times higher than in the hardware distribution business, the company's new service-related acquisitions had a very positive impact on its bottom line. In 1997, for example, more than half of Pomeroy's profits came from its services segment—even though that segment accounted for only 12 percent of total revenue.

In early 1997, Pomeroy was selected by IBM to participate in its new Authorized Assembly Program. As a member of the program, Pomeroy was allowed to purchase IBM computer components and use them to assemble computers that met customer specifications. This allowed PCR to keep inventory to a minimum and to offer customers an even broader range of customization options. Being chosen for the program also served to further boost PCR's reputation for professionalism; the company was one of only 19 IBM resellers worldwide to be designated as authorized assemblers.

Also in 1997, Pomeroy established a new business division to serve the growing number of organizations and companies that wanted to lease, rather than purchase, computer systems. Computer leasing was rapidly becoming a favored option for many organizations, as the pace of technological advancement made frequent computer upgrades or replacements a necessity. Pomeroy's new division—Technology Integration Financial Services—offered clients lease packages that included hard-ware, installation, services, maintenance, and cabling. Leasing was not new to Pomeroy. Since 1989, the company had leased a small percentage of its systems through a joint venture with a Cincinnati-based leasing company. As the interest in leasing increased, however, moving the business in-house became more economically sensible.

Pomeroy Select Integration Solutions: 1998–99

Pomeroy continued to build its service business through acquisitions in 1998. In March, the company acquired Global Combined Technologies Inc., a reseller and integrator headquartered in Oklahoma City, with additional facilities in Tulsa, Oklahoma and Dallas, Texas. Global was Pomeroy's largest purchase to date, with 120 employees and almost $80 million in annual revenues. Also in March, the company finalized the acquisition of the Richmond, Virginia-based Commercial Business Systems Inc., a much smaller systems integrator. Pomeroy made its final 1998 acquisition in December, purchasing Access Technologies, Inc., a Memphis, Tennessee telecommunications and networking provider.

Also in 1998, Pomeroy made the division between its products and services segments more formal by establishing a wholly owned subsidiary—Pomeroy Select Integration Solutions (PSIS)—to house all of its services business. A January 15, 1999 press release stated that the company formed the subsidiary to ''provide a separate identity for its IT services business, to foster the continue growth of such business, and to enable PSIS to better attract and retain technical personnel.'' Shortly after it was formed, Pomeroy Select filed a registration with the SEC for an initial public offering.

Steady expansion of the services business continued throughout 1999, via both acquisition and internal growth. In May, the company purchased Systems Atlanta Commercial Systems, Inc., a Georgia-based systems integrator and provider of technology staffing. Three months later, a second acquisition—of Acme Data Systems in Columbus, Ohio—was completed. Acme specialized in networking and large enterprise installations. Also in 1999, Pomeroy opened a new regional sales and services office in Little Rock, Arkansas. The Systems Atlanta acquisition and the opening of the Little Rock branch gave the company entry into two new states.

The year 1999 also saw the signing of several key contracts for Pomeroy. Between March and August, the company won ten one-year contracts with various organizations, including IBM and the State of Arkansas. Together, the contracts were expected to generate between $90 and $110 million for Pomeroy. The company also secured a three-year contract with Procter & Gamble, which was estimated to be worth more than $75 million.

2000 and Beyond

As Pomeroy prepared to move into the future, it appeared to be ideally positioned for more rapid growth. Demand for both computer hardware and support services was expected to remain strong, keeping the company's revenues high and allowing it to continue expanding into new geographic markets.

In the future, as in the past, Pomeroy's growth was likely to depend heavily upon acquisitions in the technology services sector. The company's expansion was expected to be fueled, in part, by funds from the planned public offering of Pomeroy Select Integration Solutions stock. No official date had been set for the offering, but company representatives expected that it would take place in 2000.

Principal Subsidiaries

Global Combined Technologies, Inc.; Pomeroy Computer Resources of South Carolina, Inc.; Pomeroy Select Integration Solutions, Inc.; Technology Integration Financial Services, Inc.; Xenas Communication Corp.

Principal Competitors

ASI Corp.; En Pointe Technologies, Inc.; European Micro Holdings, Inc.; Manchester Equipment Co., Inc.; Micros-To-Mainframes, Inc.; Multiple Zones International, Inc.

Further Reading

Head, Lauren Lawley, "Pomeroy's Profits, Sales Expand with Acquisitions," *Business Courier: Serving the Cincinnati-Northern Kentucky Region,* July 16, 1999, p. 29.

Miller, Ursula, "Big Blue Gives Pomeroy Big Boost," *Cincinnati Enquirer,* April 15, 1997.

——, "Pomeroy Division To Go Public," *Cincinnati Enquirer,* January 16, 1999.

Rosa, Jerry, "Pomeroy Buys, Seeks Status as Integrator," *Computer Reseller News,* December 9, 1996, p. 179.

Sekhri, Rally, "Technical Services Focus Boosts Pomeroy's Profits," *Business Courier: Serving the Cincinnati-Northern Kentucky Region,* May 29, 1998, p. 28.

Williams, Tom, "The Ascent of Pomeroy," *Kentucky Post,* April 12, 1994, p. 8K.

—Shawna Brynildssen

Presstek, Inc.

9 Commercial Street
Hudson, New Hampshire 03051
U.S.A.
Telephone: (603) 595-7000
Toll Free: (888) 627-6777
Fax: (603) 595-2602
Web site: http://www.presstek.com

Public Company
Incorporated: 1987
Employees: 260
Sales: $54.96 million (1999)
Stock Exchanges: NASDAQ
Ticker Symbol: PRST
NAIC: 333293 Printing Machinery and Equipment
    Manufacturing

Headquartered in Hudson, New Hampshire, Presstek, Inc. is a leading developer and international marketer of non-photographic, non-toxic, digital imaging (DI), and printing-plate technologies for the graphic arts, publishing, and printing industries. Robert and Lawrence Howard founded Presstek, Inc. in 1987 to explore new ways of making the printing press a computer peripheral able to produce color-offset printing. Presstek's products and applications incorporate its proprietary PEARL and DI technologies and use PEARL consumables for computer-to-plate and direct-to-press applications. The company's patented PEARL and DI thermal laser diode family of products enable its worldwide customers to produce high-quality, full-color lithographic printed materials more quickly and at less cost than is possible with traditional methods. Other advantages include faster turnaround time, increased productivity, and significant reduction of chemical waste effluents that damage the environment. Presstek's business development plan involves entering into strategic alliances, partnerships, licensing agreements, and joint development projects with major corporations in the graphic arts and printing industries. The company works with a worldwide network of dealers that sell, market, and support its products. Presstek is also engaged in the manufacture of products and applications that incorporate the use of its proprietary technologies, including polymer-based dry and/or wet printing plates, aluminum-based dry and/or wet printing plates, and stand-alone platesetters used for off-press imaging of printing plates. The company owns over 300 issued and/or pending patents throughout the world and has received numerous awards for the excellence of its products and its innovative impact on the printing industry.

1987–89: Pressing On After Gutenberg

In the 15th century, Johannes Gutenberg was reputedly the first European to use movable type. Five centuries later, American entrepreneur Robert Howard invented the dot-matrix printer for computers. In 1969 he founded Centronics Data Corporation to manufacture computer-related printing devices, and in 1984 he founded Howtek Inc. in Hudson, New Hampshire, to develop a color hard-copy printer based on the company's new Thermo-Jet, solid-ink-jetting technology. Howtek introduced the Pixelmaster solid-ink-jet color printer in 1986; that same year Howtek also launched the first set of products that created a new industry: the Desktop Scanning Market. Howtek developed one of the largest installed bases of desktop-drum scanners for the graphic arts market as well as scanners for the life sciences and medical X-ray markets. The public company remained an industry leader.

In 1987 Robert Howard and his son—Dr. Lawrence Howard—founded Presstek, Inc. for the purpose of designing and developing a proprietary Direct Imaging (DI) Technology capable of accepting digital files of fully composed pages from a variety of color electronic prepress and desktop publishing systems. They believed that a DI Technology could image (burn) color-separated pages directly onto waterless printing plates. This simple one-step process, they thought, would require none of the photographic processes and chemistry associated with traditional plate-imaging technologies. Thus, DI technology would simplify and eliminate many of the time-consuming and complex steps associated with printing plates and color printing—and produce no chemical wastes to pollute the environment.

In September 1988 Presstek completed its first direct-imaging press. This prototype press was based on a spark-discharge technology: at the discharge of an electric spark, data was directly imaged, or etched, onto Presstek's proprietary printing plates. This first DI press relied on a complex system of software and hardware, and in 1989 it was viable enough for Presstek to win a development agreement with Germany-based Heidelberg Druckmaschinen AG, the world's largest manufacturer and marketer of printing presses.

1990–94: Pressing to Improve an Industry

Included in the initial and subsequent Heidelberg agreements was the stipulation that Presstek would supply that company with "kits" containing all that was needed to install the DI Technology on Heidelberg's GTO press, regarded as the finest small-format printing press. Heidelberg produced the Heidelberg GTO-DI, based on Presstek's spark-discharge technology, and received the "Best of Print '91 Award" for it at the Print 1991 trade show.

Since its inception in 1987 and through most of 1991, Presstek functioned as a development-stage company, generating limited revenues. The company's activities consisted primarily of product design, development, testing and refining, market analysis, and the development of strategic alliances. Not until the fourth quarter of 1991 did the company begin to make commercial shipments of its manufactured products, such as Direct Imaging Kits and Presstek DI printing plates and inks. "In 1992, after four years as a development-stage company, Presstek successfully made the transition into a manufacturing company, with revenues of $12,558,000, yielding a net profit of $3,606,000," wrote Presstek Chairman of the Board Robert Howard in the company's 1992 annual report.

Sensitive to the market's demand for higher-quality printed materials, even in short-run markets, in 1993 Presstek continued to develop its proprietary DI technology and created *PEARL:* a direct imaging technology that used an infrared semiconductor laser instead of a spark discharge to burn away the surface of the plate material and produce graphic-arts quality color prints. Thus, with PEARL—the world's first filmless, thermal-digital printing technology available for color printing—Presstek closed the gap between prepress (electronic-page preparation) and the printing press. PEARL DI constituted a daylight-safe, filmless, chemical-free technology that eliminated photosensitive materials and their accompanying toxic by-products. PEARL's one-step exposure process, its level of quality, and its freedom from environmental damage represented an important break-through in the computer-to-plate/press market.

Presstek patented PEARL, and in September 1993 shipped to Heidelberg the kits needed to install PEARL on the GTO-DI. Presstek discontinued its spark-discharge technology and concentrated on developing PEARL, a technology not hampered by technical limitations. The cost of the changeover had a negative effect on revenues and net income but the company was able to maintain its profitability despite the resulting drop in product sales, a write-off of $1.95 million for spark-discharge assets and inventory, and start-up costs for PEARL.

In 1994 Presstek announced a five-for-four stock split and doubled its manufacturing facility in Hudson, mainly to accommodate Heidelberg's growing demand for laser-diode imaging modules, orders for new computer-to-plate systems, and expected increases in the use of Presstek's pollution-free printing plates. In February Heidelberg began full production of GTO-DI presses integrated with PEARL imaging technology and using Presstek's PEARL consumable aluminum-printing plates. Commercial printers, color service bureaus, digital on-demand print shops and corporate in-house plants—among others—responded well to the GTO-DI, which gained international customers. Presstek's revenues for fiscal 1994 totalled $16.52 million, up over 41 percent from 1993, while profits increased 92 percent to $1.84 million, compared to 1993 profits of $960,000.

1995–97: High Visibility and Profitability

At DRUPA '95, the world's largest graphic arts trade show, Heidelberg demonstrated its Quickmaster DI 46-4, the first fully automated digital offset lithographic printing press integrating PEARL DI technology and thermal ablation printing plates. (The words *thermal ablation* refer to controlled thermal detachment and/or vaporization of debris from a printing plate.) Key ingredients of the Quickmaster DI, which replaced the GTO DI, were PEARL's polyester-based waterless plate material and Presstek's automated plate-changing cylinder. A roll of the plate material capable of handling 35 separate printing jobs was loaded into the plate cylinder. At the push of a button, in less than 20 seconds, each of the four plates (one plate for each of the three process colors—cyan, magenta, yellow—and one for black) was automatically changed and imaged in exact register with each other. Within minutes the inking system was color-balanced to produce brilliant, perfect, offset lithographic images.

The Quickmaster DI could produce runs of as few as 200, or more than 20,000, sheets. The Graphic Arts Technical Foundation (GATF) awarded its InterTech Technology Award to the new press for innovative excellence. Presstek also received the National Association of Printers and Lithographers Award for contributing DI technology to the printing industry. Quickmaster DI was positioned to become a market leader.

During the trade show, one of the first manufacturers to show serious interest in acquiring Presstek's technology was Czech Republic-based Adast Adamov Company, a manufacturer of offset sheet-fed presses. A mutual agreement with Presstek led to Adast's becoming a licensee of PEARL DI technology and creating a larger-format (19 by 26 inch) multicolor press known as the 705C DI. Adast sold its presses to North Carolina-based Omnitrade Industrial, which then marketed them in North America, under the name of the Omni-Adast 705C DI series.

Key Dates:

1987: Presstek, Inc. is founded by the Howards, a father and son team.

1988: Company completes its first direct imaging press, based on spark-discharge technology.

1989: Presstek begins trading on the NASDAQ exchange.

1991: Presstek signs a master agreement with Heidelberger Druckmaschinen AG to introduce the GTO DI press, based on Presstek's spark-discharge technology.

1993: Presstek patents PEARL technology, the first film-less, thermal-digital printing technology available for color printing, and installs PEARL technology on the GTO DI.

1995: Company demonstrates the PEARLsetter, the first computer-to-plate system.

1997: Presstek introduces PEARLgold, the world's first process-free thermal printing plate designed for off-set printing presses.

1998: Robert W. Hallman is appointed CEO, succeeding Richard A. Williams, who is appointed Chairman of the Board.

Presstek gained further visibility at DRUPA by introducing the PEARLsetter computer-to-plate system, an application of the company's PEARL DI technology and consumables. The PEARLsetter was a computer-to-plate (CTP) imaging device that could image both of Presstek's wet and dry offset plates. The PEARLsetter directly accepted a PostScript file from a prepress system. PEARL technology used a high-powered semiconductor laser diodes that pulsed on and off in response to the bitmap signal defined by the raster-image processor to generate a printer's dot. The laser passed through a fibers' optic coupler to a lens assembly which then focused the energy to a fine spot for plate imaging. The imaged plates required no processing other than the wiping of debris ablated from the plates, which could then be immediately mounted and registered on the press. Thus, the PEARLsetter gave CTP users a chemical-free and daylight-safe imaging product; high quality output; easier make-ready; lower production costs; and a higher level of productivity. *Electronic Publishing*, an industry periodical, gave its Hot Product Award to Presstek in recognition of PEARLsetter's combination of leading-edge technology and industry impact.

Presstek's thermal ablation-based printing plates, the first major change in printing-plate technologies in many years, were an important ingredient in building market share for the company. The company's PEARLdryABL plate had a longer press life, was more durable and scratch resistant, and gave the press operator increased visibility between image and non-image areas. PEARLdry plates were used on the Quickmaster DI, the GTO, and the Adast 705C DI, to name but a few presses based on PEARL DI technology.

Already on the way to establishing a strong patent portfolio to protect its intellectual property, Presstek realized that proprietary manufacturing technologies were also needed to assure the lowest possible cost for its quality products. To this end, Presstek bought 90 percent of the stock of Catalina Coatings, Inc. (later renamed Delta V Technologies, Inc.), an Arizona corporation engaged in the development, manufacture, and sale of vacuum-deposition-coating equipment as well as the licensing and sublicensing of patent rights. Presstek's thermal-plate technology, combined with Delta V's advanced plate manufacturing, enabled the company to offer the graphic arts industry quality plates at a lower cost.

In July 1996 Nilpeter A/S of Denmark announced production of a high-speed rotary label printing press integrated with a special PEARL-based DI system that imaged Presstek's thermal plates directly on the press-plate cylinder. For fiscal 1996 Presstek announced record revenues of $48.63 million and net income of $7.12 million.

In May 1997 Presstek shipped its 500th Quickmaster DI 46-4 PEARL imaging kit to Heidelberg and announced a two-for-one stock split. By the end of September the company had shipped an additional 250 kits. Presstek worked with Imation Corp. to develop a new method for the production of true half-tone "dot-for dot" color-press proofs. The companies integrated a modified version of Presstek's CTP imaging system with Imation's Matchprint Laser Proof materials and created the PEARLhdp, a thermal halftone digital CTP imaging system.

During May Presstek also introduced PEARLgold, a second-generation thermal lithographic printing plate that enabled run lengths of more than 100,000 impressions. Presstek's PEARLgold plate was the world's first process-free thermal printing plate and was designed for offset printing presses equipped with dampening systems. The PEARLgold thermal printing plate was digitally imaged, placed on the press, and run. Since no additional steps or processes were needed before or after imaging, the plate functioned very efficiently and produced no toxic byproducts. PEARLgold was a major advance in digital-plate technology because it required no pre- or post-exposure processing, baking procedure, or intermediate cleaning. It was a truly process-free, commercial-quality CTP plate that could be imaged on a broad range of available thermally based computer-to-plate systems, such as the PEARLsetter product line. PEARLgold won the 1997 GATF InterTech Technology Award, the *Publish Magazine* Impact Award, and the Seybold Editors Choice Award.

Among Presstek's licensees during 1997 was Alcoa Packaging Equipment, a division of the Aluminum Company of America, which based itself on Presstek's direct-imaging technology and thermal ablation printing plates to develop a new method of printing halftone-images on beverage cans. The modified PEARLsetter, dubbed PEARLhdp, used proofing materials supplied by Imation. The halftone proofing system enabled the user to make proofs that replicated the dot structure used for imaging plates. Both Presstek and Imation worked jointly to market the product. Presstek also signed a long-range Development and Sales Agreement with Japan-based Fuji Photo Film, Ltd., one of the world's leading suppliers to the graphic communications industry.

During fiscal 1997, revenues grew 88 percent to $91.56 million, compared to $48.63 million for 1996; net income increased 102 percent to peak at $14.37 million, compared to 1996 income of $7.12 million. It was noteworthy that Presstek's proprietary consumable thermal plates accounted for 20 percent of total revenues.

1998–2000: Pressing Forward Despite Financial Setbacks

To increase its patent portfolio, in January 1998 Presstek acquired Seattle, Washington-based Heath Custom Press, Inc., a company owning many patents for the design and manufacture of custom printing presses. In a news release, Heath President Ross Peterman was quoted as saying that there were "numerous applications for specialty presses and equipment which could utilize Presstek's thermal imaging systems and plate products." Obviously, Presstek was of the same opinion.

In September 1998, Robert W. Hallman was appointed Presstek's Chief Executive Officer. He replaced former CEO Richard A. Williams, who was appointed Chairman of the Board, following the retirement of Robert Howard, Presstek Chairman Emeritus. Hallman, an established expert in plate and prepress technologies, was recognized in the industry as one of the world's top graphic-arts technologists for his work in non-silver and related environmentally safe media. He was the holder of over 30 patents. Upon the retirement of President and Chief Operating Officer Robert E. Verrando in January 1999, Hallman assumed the duties of president and chief scientific officer (CSO).

For fiscal 1998, Presstek reported revenues of $84.39 million, down eight percent from 1997, and a net loss of $2.69 million in net income. Presstek President and CSO Robert Hallman, in a 1998 press release, commented that the shortfall in revenues was due in part to a decrease of 43 percent in sales to Heidelberg. "This revenue reduction, together with the non-recurring or unusual charges," said he, "essentially accounts for most of the negative impact on operating income." He noted, however, that revenues from sources other than Heidelberg increased 136 percent in 1998 and sales of consumable plates increased 63 percent over those of 1997. "Although over-all revenues declined $7.2 million, we made good progress in broadening our revenue base in 1998," Hallman explained.

During 1999 Presstek intensified development of new products for introduction at DRUPA 2000, the international trade show to be held in May 2000. Consequently, during this "pre-DRUPA" year, development expenditures remained at elevated levels. Presstek also pursued business opportunities available all over the world. For example, with Imation Corp.—a $1.3 billion technology company with offices in 60 countries—Presstek signed a sales and marketing agreement granting Imation exclusive worldwide distribution rights to Presstek's PEARLhdp product line. The companies also signed a service-and-support agreement allowing Imation to provide worldwide service and support for the PEARLsetter and PEARLhdp. In September Presstek and Akiyama Printing Machinery Manufacturing Corp. of Tokyo announced a joint development program to create a DI version of Akiyama's J Print press, which permitted one-pass, multi-color printing on both sides of the sheet in one pass. The goal was to create the first DI press for the book-printing market.

Then, in order to focus more directly on its core products, Presstek divested its subsidiary, Delta V Technologies, Inc., which was an equipment-only business. At about the same time, Presstek granted 3M—a $15-billion global manufacturing company—a semi-exclusive license for Presstek's intellectual property relating to vacuum-deposited polymer multilayer technology (VDPML). Presstek, however, retained exclusive rights to VDPML technology applied to manufacturing printing plates. Presstek's President and CSO Robert Hallman said that VDPML technology would "provide significant cost reductions in current plate designs and offer potential for additional novel plate structures."

Although total revenues for fiscal 1999 dropped to $54.96 million, during the fourth quarter revenues grew 20 percent to $17.03 million, compared to $13.80 million for the same quarter in 1998. Presstek had returned to profitability in its core business and expected continuing revenue growth throughout 2000, according to the company's news release of February 14, 2000.

Presstek received the next confirmation of a possibly profitable future in February when it signed a non-binding Memorandum of Understanding that outlined intent to form a strategic alliance with Xerox Corporation. The integration of Xerox's DigiPath technology and Presstek's DI technology was to enable the design of products to answer the "ink-on-paper" needs of the graphic and related markets. The companies expected to launch some of their initial products at DRUPA 2000 in May.

Presstek celebrated its tenth anniversary in 1997, the year of its record revenues and net income. The following two years of financial losses did not deter the young company from the adjustments needed to establish new relationships, introduce new products of the highest quality, and continue to build up its core business: proprietary printing-plate technologies for the graphic arts, publishing, and printing industries. It is noteworthy that Presstek continuously broadened the revenue base of its core business during a transition to its goal of being a long-term provider of process-free, thermal ablation plates and products. At the beginning of a new century—judging from Presstek's ability to "Press on, and Forward"—it was likely that the company was on the way to many more years of creative innovations and profitable operation.

Principal Competitors

Agfa Gevaert N.V.; Creo Products, Inc.; Indigo N.V.; Kodak Polychrome Graphics LLC; Xeikon N.V.

Further Reading

"Presstek Eliminates Processing," *Electronic Publishing*, August 1997, p. 11.
"Presstek/Heidelberg Venture Begins," *Paperboard Packaging*, May 1994, p. 54.
Quickmaster DI Profitability Study, Heidelberg, Germany: Heidelberger Druckmaschinen AG, October 1999.

—Gloria A. Lemieux

PULASKI FURNITURE CORPORATION

Pulaski Furniture Corporation

One Pulaski Square
Pulaski, Virginia 24301
U.S.A.
Telephone: (540) 980-7330
Fax: (540) 994-5756

Public Company
Incorporated: 1955 as Pulaski Veneer and Furniture
   Company
Employees: 2,150
Sales: $198 million (1999)
Stock Exchanges: NASDAQ
Ticker Symbol: PLFC
NAIC: 337122: Furniture, Wood Household-Type, Not
   Upholstered (Except TV and Radio Housings, and
   Sewing Machine Cabinets) Manufacturing

The Pulaski Furniture Corporation manufactures mid-priced dining room and bedroom furniture, curio cabinets, occasional furniture, such as small tables, desks, and accent pieces, and grandfather, mantel, and wall clocks. The company highlights many kinds of wood in its product line, including pine, maple, oak, ash, cherry, and mahogany. Wood veneers, inlays, carvings, embossings, and other "fancy faces" are imported, acquired from local manufacturers, or produced by the Pulaski Furniture Corporation. Ornate and nostalgic furniture are the company's mainstays, particularly its line of curio cabinets.

Finding a Market Niche in
Furniture Design and Manufacturing

Fred Stanley, Sr. and C.B. Richardson founded the Pulaski Furniture Corporation in the economically depressed town of Pulaski, Virginia, in 1955. Stanley brought experience from employment at the Stanley Furniture Company in Stanleytown, Virginia, while Richardson brought experience as chief operating officer of the RCA Victor Radio Case Plant which closed in Pulaski in 1948. Bernard Wampler, then a recent graduate of North Carolina State University with experience in furniture

manufacturing, became involved as assistant supervisor. With the formation of the Pulaski Veneer and Furniture Corporation, Stanley, Richardson, and Wampler reopened the former RCA plant in downtown Pulaski to produce moderately priced bedroom furniture.

Furniture manufacturing has always been a cyclical business, and the Pulaski Veneer and Furniture Corporation endured the difficulties of the industry in its first years. When a slim cash supply required the company to write partial paychecks, hams, flour, and other such goods from the Richardson farms often satisfied the balance. After five years in business, however, the company had reached $5.5 million in sales and purchased the Morris Novelty Corporation, a producer of such novelty furniture items as small occasional tables. The acquisition included a manufacturing facility in Martinsville, Virginia, which became known as "plant #2," while several of the Morris family remained as employees. An initial public offering of stock in 1962 provided funds to further expand the company, then renamed the Pulaski Furniture Corporation (PFC).

With new manufacturing capabilities, a new supply of funds and a strong market for home furnishings, the company prospered in the early 1960s. PFC purchased 28 acres of land in Dublin, Virginia, where the company built a wood mill in 1964 to produce the veneer and cross banding used in furniture manufacturing. At this time the furniture designers embraced simple styles which facilitated the manufacture of furniture and kept prices low. As factory employees developed their skills, the company's furniture designs became more elaborate. By the mid-1960s PFC had found a market niche in bedroom and dining room furniture with ornate designs. Though only slightly more difficult to produce, the stylized furniture had an expensive look and gave PFC its identity among such well-known brands as Bassett, Broyhill, Thomasville, and Lane, as well as among small furniture manufacturers. Furniture designer Leonard Eisen came to work for the company at this time.

After serving as superintendent, vice-president of manufactures, and executive vice-president, Bernard Wampler became president and CEO of PFC in 1967. Under Wampler's leadership, the identity of PFC evolved to incorporate nostalgic furniture designs with broad customer appeal. A fall 1971 public offering of

125,000 shares of stock, at $33.00 share, prepared the company as the proceeds were used for the expansion of manufacturing and warehouse facilities. The company required a new plant to produce "case goods," dining room and bedroom furniture, and built another facility on its acreage in Dublin. In 1976 construction began at the Martinsville plant to upgrade and renovate the facility, increasing the capacity of that plant by 50 percent.

Marketing Nostalgia in the 1970s and 1980s

Renovation of the Martinsville facility enabled the company to fulfill consumer demand for its landmark Keepsake Collection, a line of nostalgic furniture initiated by Eisen along with Wampler. The product line featured late 19th century, middle-American styles in golden oak wood furniture, a sharp contrast to the ornate, synthetic items the company made at the time. The collection consisted primarily of nostalgic accent pieces, such as hall trees, washstands and shaving stands, but PFC later added dining room and bedroom furniture. Introduced at the biannual furniture market at High Point, North Carolina, in spring 1976, the Keepsake Collection established the standard for nostalgic furniture items in the furniture manufacturing industry and set a milestone as the best selling line of case goods in the furniture industry. In January 1982 PFC shipped the one millionth piece, amounting to over $300 million in retail sales when no other collection had ever sold one million units. The line of furniture helped the company withstand economic recession, as PFC enjoyed brisk sales for nearly eight years before sales declined in the mid-1980s.

As demand subsided for the Keepsake Collection, the company began to produce curio cabinets at its Martinsville plant in 1982. Curio cabinets tended to be used for personal collections of nostalgic pieces, such as dolls, statuary, china, and other items, as well as for personal memorabilia. Like the Keepsake Collection, many collectibles hearken back to seemingly less complicated eras, and curio cabinets gave customers a place to showcase them. The cabinets featured flexible shelving, mirrored backs, unobstructed viewing, and lighting appropriate to the collectible inside. For example, a doll collection required regular lights rather than the preferred halogen lights, because halogen light changed the color of the dolls' hair. PFC's marketing for the curio cabinets focused on collectors, with advertisements in collectors' magazines, rather than toward the general home decorating market. The initial seven curio models priced at $100 retail.

PFC often took a fun approach in its decisions on what kinds of occasional furniture to produce. Other collections included

such nostalgic items as player pianos and wooden telephone booths for the home; the latter sold 2,000 units each year for its first three years. In 1984 Eisen introduced a collection of accent and occasional furniture inspired by Hollywood movies. The "Casablanca" group included a World War II vintage-look console-chest, while the "Stage Coach" group spotlighted a smaller version of the Wells Fargo Wooton Organizer Desk. Made of oak, the desk featured a pull-down writing desk and organizing slots. The "Ice Cream Works" featured a marble top ice cream bar with freezer-refrigerator and bar stools, and, by coincidence, was launched in the year of the 150th anniversary of the invention of the soda fountain. Product merchandising for such specialized pieces motivated the development of the Pulaski Galleries. Set within approximately 800 retail stores, the Galleries highlighted eight to 24 accent pieces by displaying each item on its own raised platform.

The company continued to expand its manufacturing capabilities to accommodate its burgeoning business. A 1983 joint venture, Triwood, Inc., in which PFC owned 25 percent, produced particle board and improved the plywood making process. Also in 1983 PFC acquired 17.5 acres and a 815,000 square foot building adjoining the downtown Pulaski, Virginia, plant, as well as equipment, from the Coleman Furniture Corporation. Renovation of part of the plant included conversion to production of plywood, "turnings," and machined parts. Completed in 1985, the remaining space was used for a warehouse and offices. The $4 million project involved a new finishing plant, completed in 1988.

PFC supplemented its product line with the 1985 acquisition of the Gravely Furniture Corporation, the leading maker of grandfather, mantel, and wall clocks. In a stock transaction valued at $9.5 million, PFC acquired a 326,000 square foot production, warehouse, and office facility on 79.5 acres in Ridgeway, Virginia. Renamed the Ridgeway Clock Company, under the ownership of PFC the company's first major project involved the production of 1,986 commemorative, Lady Liberty grandfather clocks for the centennial of the Statue of Liberty in 1986. In addition to a solid mahogany cabinet, design elements involved fluted pilasters, beveled glass doors, polished brass, and an etching of the torch on the clock face. With a retail price of $5,000, PFC donated a portion of the profits to the Statue of Liberty-Ellis Island renovation project.

In keeping with the company's nostalgic, ornate furniture design, PFC acquired Craftique, Inc. of Mebane, North Carolina, for $5.3 million in 1988. Craftique specialized in the reproduction of antique solid mahogany furniture. In 1991 the company reproduced a mahogany block front desk from the 18th century, a $2,500 copy of an original that sold at auction in 1983 for $687,500. Also, in 1989 PFC opened an upholstery plant in Christiansburg, Virginia.

Ornate styling and nostalgia continued to be of significance to the success of PFC into the 1990s. Furniture industry trends turned toward an eclectic mix of furniture styles which reflected diverse public tastes and a more casual attitude toward home decoration. Eisen's 50-piece collection encompassed several distinct styles, such as a French Empire secretary and a Victorian *tete-a-tete* love seat with a serpentine-shaped back to keep a young woman and her suitor from getting too close. PFC introduced the popular fossil stone table in 1990, a glass-top table, available in different types, with a metal base and fossil stones from the Philippines along the edge of the table top. By 1992 the company had developed over 100 models of curio cabinets for collectibles, available in a variety of styles, including French, Italian, 18th-century American, Victorian, and modern. PFC became the largest manufacturer of curio cabinets and produced over 1,000 different furniture items as well.

The 1990s: From Fluctuating Revenues to Stable Growth

PFC experienced dramatic changes in its revenues and faced higher production costs in the 1990s. While sales increased from $115.1 million in 1988 to $131.8 million in 1989, in 1990 revenues reached only $132.5 million. During the economic recession PFC experienced a dramatic decrease in 1991, to $120.6 million in revenue. Lower priced furniture and promotional items with lower profit margins tended to sell, while production for fewer units of each piece increased the costs. A production rate of 300 units per style was less cost efficient than a production rate of 500 units per style. The company maintained earnings, but retailer bankruptcies increased, resulting in a loss of $1.2 million from bad credit. The number of credit holds grew also, as previous credit problems required the retention of a product order from shipment until payment had been received from the retailer.

PFC sought to reduce overhead and expand its growth potential through import and export activities. In 1989 the rising costs of lumber led the company to import unfinished dining room chair parts from Asia for assembly and finishing at the Pulaski facility. Led by John Wampler, the son of Bernard Wampler, PFC took advantage of the low cost of labor and materials and the lack of government mandates for safety in Far Eastern countries, especially Taiwan. Also, the Ridgeway Clock company had an export business in place when it was acquired by PFC, providing a network of business associations which facilitated growth through worldwide expansion. Export countries included Europe, Asia, Mexico, the Middle East, and Canada, with sales from export at eight percent in 1993.

A growing demand for different styles of curio cabinet led PFC to improve its production methods. Jim Stout, manager of the original Pulaski, Virginia, plant traveled around the world to study the technology available to improve flexibility, productivity, and cost efficiency. The result involved a combination of technology from Japan, Italy, Germany, and the United States applied to the needs of producing hall trees, consoles, entertainment centers, as well as curio cabinet frames. Computer technology aligned the wood and identified where to cut the board for best yield. With the new technology, wood which entered the rough mill on Monday usually left by Friday as a finished wood furniture product packaged for shipment. Computers programmed for each furniture item provided flexibility in manufacturing schedules. The process reduced the number of workers per machine from six to two, but those two positions became more highly skilled. Implementation of the technology created a total of 110 skilled, higher paying positions. PFC worked with the New River Community College and the Virginia Department of Economic Development to provide training for its employees.

In 1993 construction to expand plant #1 began in Pulaski to accommodate the technology with a new 75,000 square foot factory, bringing the company's total production, warehousing, and office space to 1.4 million square feet. After an investment of $13.6 million, full production began in May 1994, running two work shifts, rather than one, each day. With slow retail sales in 1995, however, all of the company factories operated on reduced schedules, four days a week.

With erratic customer demand in 1995 PFC needed to balance originality with caution. In 1996 the company did produce a collection of furniture for automobile racing fans, the HomeTrack Collection. The 17-piece line included a black-and-white checkered armchair or recliner with racing tire shaped arm rests, a glass-top coffee table with Goodyear tires as a base, and a curio cabinet designed for racing memorabilia and collectibles. The furniture debuted at the NASCAR Winston Cup event in Daytona Beach, Florida, in February. The merchandise was available only at Winston Cup events, through a mobile showroom managed by furniture retailer Heilig-Meyers.

In June 1996 PFC's subsidiary Craftique, was chosen to reproduce the work of Thomas Day, a free, black cabinet maker of the early 19th century, considered the best cabinet maker in North Carolina during the antebellum period. Craftique collaborated with the Thomas Day House/Union (Tavern) Restoration project and the North Carolina Department of Cultural Resources to determine which pieces to reproduce. Day's style spanned from simple to grandiose and incorporated Empire, 18th-century, and Federal design elements. The 18-piece collection comprised three pieces copied from the museum and 15 pieces copied from privately owned furniture, with each piece made to order. Craftique made the furniture from Honduran mahogany obtained from renewable tree planting programs. The reproduction procedure required detailed drawings, precise measurements, and a complex process of matching wood color, grain, and size to conserve the expensive wood.

To accommodate its $10 million import-export activities, PFC purchased an 80,000 square foot building on a ten-acre site in Pulaski which had been recently vacated. The company had been looking for a new site when the local government informed PFC that the clothing manufacturing plant had gone on sale. The town of Pulaski lent PFC $500,000 from its Urban Development Action fund to buy the building. As the second largest employer in the area, PFC created 260 jobs between 1993 and 1997, had invested $14 million in the area, and had previously repaid a development loan. PFC invested an additional $1.5 million to acquire and renovate the property. Operations began in early 1997, warehousing merchandise from Italy, Taiwan, Thailand, Singapore, Malaysia, and Indonesia.

As sales and demand continued to fluctuate in the mid-1990s, PFC sought stability by focusing on its main business, mid-priced case goods and occasional furniture. PFC and its partners sold Triwood in 1995. Craftique did not meet the company's profit goals leading to its sale in 1997. PFC also closed its upholstery seating operation, which lost money, allowing raw materials to be used on existing designs. In 1997 sales reached $158.9 million. The company balanced stability and change when, upon the retirement of Bernard Wampler in 1997, John Wampler became CEO of the company.

Acquisitions in 1998 reflected the company's ambition to enhance its core business. PFC obtained a contract to manufacture furniture for hotels and motels, as other furniture manufacturers receded from that area to concentrate on residential customers. In October PFC purchased the Dawson Furniture Company of Webb City, Missouri. Dawson specialized in pine and oak wood furniture which would complement PFC's product offerings with a different product mix and lower-priced furniture items. PFC expected the acquisition to stimulate new product development and expand its distribution network.

Marketing development, a strong retail market, and increased product demand stimulated sales in the late 1990s. In 1998 sales grew to $172.4 million, while in 1999 sales increased to $198.2 million, a 15 percent increase which included $15.2 million in sales from Dawson products. PFC's strength continued to be furniture impulse items such as clocks, curio cabinets, and occasional furniture. At the turn of the century, curio cabinets had become an essential part of the living room for many Pulaski customers. About half of the company's sales in the late 1990s came from its 175 models of curio cabinets, retail priced from $199 to $3,000.

Principal Subsidiaries

Pulaski Foreign Sales Corporation, Inc.

Principal Competitors

Bassett Furniture Industries, Inc.; Ethan Allen Interiors, Inc.; Furniture Brands International.

Further Reading

Allegrezza, Ray, "Pulaski to Buy Dawson Furniture," *Furniture-Today,* October 19, 1998, p. 2.

Brown-Kelly, Sandra, "Pulaski Furniture Picks Wampler Jr. Chief Executive," *Roanoke Times,* December 4, 1993, p. 8A.

——, "Pulaski Furniture Predicts Good Year," *Roanoke Times,* February 11, 1995, p. 4A.

Bryant, Pat, "New Designs Take Guesswork out of Today's Victorian," *Richmond Times-Dispatch,* December 22, 1991, p. 6H.

"Craftique to Produce Thomas Day Collection," *HFN The Weekly Newspaper for the Home Furnishings Network,* January 1, 1996, p. 24.

Craver, Richard, "Virginia Furniture Maker Sues Former Executive and His New Employer," *Knight-Ridder/Tribune Business News,* November 29, 1999.

Day Pashley, Beth, "Taking the Checkered Flag: The HomeTrack Collection of NASCAR-inspired Furniture Revs up Home Decor," *Roanoke Times,* April 14, 1996, p. 1.

Dellinger, Paul, "Pulaski Furniture Adds Space, Computers, 110 Jobs," *Roanoke Times,* August 13, 1993, p. 1A.

——, "Computerized Curios the Latest at Pulaski Furniture Corporation," *Roanoke Times,* June 11, 1995, p. 3NRV.

——, "Furniture Facility Dedicated: Pulaski Furniture Outgrew Its Building," *Roanoke Times,* June 28, 1997, p. 3B.

Dunne, Beverly, "Top 25 Furniture Makers Seek Growth through Exports," *Wood & Wood Products,* June 1993, p. 39.

Garret, Barbara, "A New Day for 19th C. Furniture," *Wood & Wood Products,* September 1996, p. 36.

Hamilton, William. "Collectible Craze Hits Furniture Business," *Montreal Gazette,* November 25, 1999, p. 4D.

Holiday, Ann, "Curio Cabinet Just the Thing for Collections," *Richmond Times-Dispatch,* April 24, 1992, p. 28.

——, "Name Your Style, and You Can Get It," *Richmond Times-Dispatch,* April 14, 1989, p. 21.

——, "New Furniture Blends Time and Space," *Richmond Times-Dispatch,* October 25, 1991, p. 23.

McIntosh, Jay, "Pulaski to Sell Craftique, Close U.S. UPH Operation," *Furniture-Today,* July 28, 1997, p. 2.

Milenky, Elissa, "Pulaski Furniture to Expand, Add 30 Jobs This Year," *Roanoke Times,* August 6, 1996, p. 1.

Mitchell, Gordon, "Clocking a Record," *Barrons,* March 3, 1986, pp. 53–56.

Nightengale, Cyndi Y., "Croquet, Anyone?" *Los Angeles Times,* June 3, 1995, p. 3.

Platz, Bruce, "Building a Better Factory," *FDM, Furniture Design & Manufacturing,* 1996, pp. 42–50.

"Pulaski Furniture Common," *Wall Street Journal,* September 3, 1971, p. 11.

"Pulaski Furniture Has Slow Spring," *Roanoke Times,* June 16, 1995, p. 9A.

"Pulaski Furniture's President Is Honored," *Richmond Times-Dispatch,* November, 18, 1991, p. 5B.

"Pulaski Gravely Plan to Merge," *Wall Street Journal,* June 12, 1985, p. 12.

The Pulaski Story, Pulaski, Va.: Pulaski Furniture Corporation.

"Pulaski to Test New Clean-Air Process," *Furniture-Today,* March 10, 1997, p. 2.

Schnabel, Megan, "Pulaski Furniture CEO Steps Down," *Roanoke Times,* February 15, 1997, p. 5A.

——, "Pulaski Furniture Has Been Rebuilding," *Roanoke Times,* December 19, 1998, p. 7A.

——, "Pulaski Furniture Makers Move in New Directions," *Roanoke Times,* May 3, 1998, p. 2.

——, "Pulaski Furniture Trims Its Operations: Domestic Upholstery Line to Be Dropped; Craftique Division to Be Sold," *Roanoke Times,* August 2, 1997, p. 4A.

Slaughter, Powell, "Shoemaker, Erwins to Buy Craftique from Pulaski," *Furniture-Today,* September 22, 1997, p. 2.

Stowe, Michael, "Pulaski Furniture Again Files for Trademark Infringement," *Roanoke Times,* October 28, 1994, p. 11A.

——, "Pulaski Furniture Sues; Trademark Violations Claimed," *Roanoke Times,* October 20, 1994, p. 8B.

Sturgeon, Jeff, "Furniture Maker Files Lawsuit over Design; Pulaski Furniture Says Suit 'Without Merit'" *Roanoke Times,* November 30, 1999, p. 7A.

——, "Pulaski Furniture: Growth Prospects Forecast as Strong," *Roanoke Times,* February 13, 1999, p. 5A.

Werne, Jo, "A Curio to Show Your 'Curiosities'," *Miami Herald,* July 1, 1984, p. 4H.

——, "Lady Liberty Elegant Reminder," *Miami Herald,* April 27, 1986, p. 8H.

——, "Occasional Furniture Recalls the Silver Screen," *Miami Herald,* October 30, 1983, p. 23H.

—Mary Tradii

Pyramid Breweries Inc.

91 South Royal Brougham Way
Seattle, Washington 98134
U.S.A.
Telephone: (206) 682-8322
Fax: (206) 682-8420
Web site: http://www.pyramidbrew.com

Public Company
Incorporated: 1984 as Hart Brewing, Inc.
Employees: N/A
Sales: $28.81 million (1999)
Stock Exchanges: NASDAQ
Ticker Symbol: PMID
NAIC: 31212 Breweries; 312111 Soft Drink
   Manufacturing

Pyramid Breweries, Inc. is a craft brewer of specialty beers and sodas. Its more than 20 English-style ales and German-style wheat beers are marketed under the Pyramid Ales and Thomas Kemper Brewing Company brands. In addition, the company produces a line of four specialty sodas under the Thomas Kemper Soda Company name. Pyramid brews its beers at two breweries in Seattle, Washington and Berkeley, California, both of which include attached alehouses with restaurants. The company also sells its beverages through a network of independent distributors in more than 30 states. The majority of sales, however, come from Washington, Oregon, and California.

Mid-1980s: A Tale of Two Breweries

Pyramid Breweries was formed by the union of two small craft breweries, or microbreweries, in the state of Washington. The first, Hart Brewing, Inc., was established in 1984 in the small western Washington logging town of Kalama by Beth Hartwell and her husband. Hart's inaugural beer, Pyramid Pale Ale, was one of the first microbrews to be produced in America.

The second of the breweries was The Thomas Kemper Brewery, of Bainbridge Island, just across Puget Sound from Seattle. The Thomas Kemper Brewery was formed in 1985 by

two friends—Andy Thomas and Will Kemper—who both had degrees in chemical engineering. Their operation was a small one, housed in the men's basements. Despite its size, however, the brewery's full-bodied, German-style lagers managed to attract a local following. Just a year after starting the brewing operation, Thomas and Kemper moved into a new facility, just outside the town of Poulsbo on the Washington coast.

In 1986, while The Thomas Kemper Brewery settled into its new home in Poulsbo, Hart Brewing introduced its second beer: Pyramid Wheaten Ale. The Wheaten Ale was the first year-round wheat beer produced in America since Prohibition. Three years later, in 1989, the Hartwells sold their growing brewery to five Seattle investors.

While 1989 brought a change in ownership for Hart, the year marked the beginning of an annual tradition for Thomas Kemper: that year, the brewery held its first Oktoberfest. The event, which was held at the brewing facility, was a promotional event designed to introduce the Thomas Kemper beers to area residents and visitors. Although the Oktoberfest celebration started out on a small scale, it rapidly gained in popularity, soon drawing thousands of visitors to the small town.

At one of these Oktoberfests, Thomas Kemper's brewers introduced a new beverage that was to eventually evolve into its own product line. Wanting to offer non-drinkers and children their own special beverage, the brewery created a batch of hand-crafted root beer. The root beer was an enormous hit; by some accounts, the soda actually outsold the beer. A year later, encouraged by the root beer success, Thomas and Kemper formed the Thomas Kemper Soda Company to develop and market a line of premium beverages that were more flavorful than the average soda.

Mid-1990s: Joining Forces

In 1992, with Hart Brewing and Thomas Kemper both picking up steam, the two breweries merged. Under the terms of the deal, Hart acquired the Thomas Kemper Brewery, but not the Thomas Kemper Soda Company, which remained as a stand-alone business under Thomas's and Kemper's ownership. Hart then made a second significant step toward expansion,

moving into a newly built, 11,000-square foot facility in Kalama and leaving behind its original home on the town's Main
Street.

As it happened, the Hart-Thomas Kemper merger came at an
important time for the breweries; both were on the verge of
introducing significant new products. In 1993, Thomas Kemper
introduced a German-inspired raspberry wheat beer called
Weizen Berry. Weizen Berry was an immediate success, soon
becoming the most popular fruit beer in the Northwest. Also
introduced in 1993, Hart's new Hefeweizen, a full-flavored,
unfiltered wheat beer, became an instant favorite with beer
lovers in the region.

By the middle of the 1990s, the two breweries were thriving.
Hart Brewing had become the fourth largest craft brewer in the
United States. Thomas Kemper was likewise showing amazing
growth, with 1995 year-end sales up 100 percent over 1994
sales. The Thomas Kemper brand was one of the top three
brands in the state. Encouraged by skyrocketing sales and increasing consumer demand for microbrews, in March of 1995
Hart opened a second brewery in downtown Seattle. The Seattle
facility, which was located near the city's Kingdome football
and baseball stadium, had a 250-seat adjoining alehouse.

1996–97: Expansion, Difficult Market Conditions

In late 1995, Hart went public, selling two million shares of
its stock and netting $34.2 million. The company used proceeds
from its initial public offering to expand its production capacity
in both the Seattle and Kalama breweries. By the end of 1996,
the Kalama facility's annual capacity had been extended to
95,000 barrels from its original 10,000-barrel output. The Seattle brewery's capacity was increased from 40,000 to 98,000
barrels. With the increased production ability in the Seattle
brewery, Hart decided to close the original Thomas Kemper
facility in Poulsbo and move its operations to Seattle.

Throughout the middle of the nineties, Hart's sales had
grown exponentially. By the beginning of 1996, the company's
annual revenues had climbed to $25.3 million, up from just $2.9
million three years earlier. Its three best selling brands were
Pyramid Hefeweizen, Pyramid Apricot Ale, and the original
Pyramid Pale Ale. Because the Pyramid line made up the bulk
of the company's sales and reputation, in 1996 Hart Brewing,
Inc. changed its name to Pyramid Breweries, Inc. It continued,
however, to market its Thomas Kemper products under the
Thomas Kemper name.

At the end of 1996, although it had shown tremendous
revenue growth, Pyramid was still very much a regional brewer;
the majority of its improved sales had come from an increased
market share in the states of Oregon and Washington. In early
1997, however, the company moved to broaden its geographic
presence, opening a new brewery and alehouse in Berkeley,
California, its first operation outside Washington. The new
facility was in a renovated warehouse within walking distance
of the University of California at Berkeley campus. It consisted
of 122,000 square feet, a 260-seat alehouse/restaurant and an
annual production capacity of 80,000 barrels. The large size of
the facility offered much potential for expansion; Pyramid estimated that it could ultimately extend the brewery's production
capacity to 200,000 barrels, if warranted.

The Berkeley brewery was to be a first step in a long-term
growth strategy. Pyramid planned to develop an entire network
of similar breweries in various high-traffic regional markets
across the country. The company also planned to achieve
greater geographic penetration by aggressively expanding its
distribution network. In 1996, it kicked off this initiative, adding 20 new states to its distribution territory. By the end of the
year, the company's products were available in a total of 31
states. Sales in Washington, Oregon, and California still accounted for more than 80 percent of total revenues, however.

Pyramid also diversified its product line in 1997, purchasing
The Thomas Kemper Soda Company, which had been left out
of the 1992 merger. The acquisition added two premium
sodas—root beer and cream soda—to the Thomas Kemper
brand. It also provided the small soda company with capital
needed to grow. Within a year of having been acquired by
Pyramid, Thomas Kemper Soda had introduced two new beverages: Orange Cream Soda and Black Cherry Soda.

Despite its efforts to expand, 1996 and 1997 were challenging years for Pyramid. The craft, or microbrew, market had
grown extremely rapidly, with small, independent breweries
springing into existence at a breathtaking pace. This proliferation of craft brewers, both in the Pacific Northwest and across
the nation, led to greatly heightened competition for Pyramid in
all of its markets. To make matters worse, the growing consumer interest in mircrobrews during the early 1990s had
enticed virtually all of the major domestic brewers into the fray;
such industry giants such as Anheuser-Busch, Miller Brewing,
and others had introduced full-flavored, European-style beers to
compete with the microbrews. Many had also formed alliances
with or made investments in specific craft brewers. Competition
from these national brewers was particularly damaging to Pyramid; with their much greater financial resources, influence, and
distribution networks, they were able to drive down product
prices and reduce distribution options for the smaller breweries.

Pyramid's finances began to show the effects of the adverse
market conditions in 1996. Sales flattened, increasing only two
percent over 1995, and net income plummeted. The company
took steps to trim overhead and boost profits in 1997, closing
down its Kalama, Washington brewery and redistributing production between its Seattle and Berkeley facilities. Sales for that
year improved by 13.6 percent, but Pyramid still ended up with
a $2.1 million net loss at year-end.

1998: Trying to Turn Around

The company spent part of 1998 rethinking and refocusing both its growth strategy and its marketing efforts. It suspended its earlier strategy of building a chain of breweries in various locations, deciding instead to focus efforts on its existing Northwest/West Coast markets. It also initiated a new marketing campaign, themed ''Have a good beer,'' and introduced new product packaging and promotional materials for both its Pyramid and Thomas Kemper lines.

However, 1998 financial results were no more promising than 1997. Sales decreased by 7.2 percent, and Pyramid again posted a net loss. In July, the investment firm of Sugar Mountain Capital, LLC purchased a 19.5 percent stake in the flagging company. As part of the acquisition, Sugar Mountain's managing partner, Kurt Dammeier, joined Pyramid's board of directors. The company also brought in two new top-level executives: Gary McGrath and Martin Kelly. McGrath, formerly employed by Miller Brewing Company, became Pyramid's new vice-president of sales in November 1999. Kelly, a former executive of both Miller Brewing and Coca-Cola, became the company's chief operating officer. Both men were beverage industry veterans of more than 15 years, and it was hoped that their expertise would be pivotal in the company's turnaround.

At the end of 1999, Kelly was promoted to CEO and president, replacing the company's president of more than seven years, George Hancock. At the same time, Dammeier—who had become the company's largest shareholder—became chairman of the board of directors. Meanwhile, Pyramid continued to falter. Although 1999 sales showed a slight improvement, the company posted a net loss of $4.4 million for the year. Shortly after assuming his new position, Kelly announced a reorganization of executive management and called for a strategic review of operations. As part of the reorganization, two new top-level positions were created and filled by existing Pyramid employees: Director of Brewery Operations and Director of Corporate Operations. Both positions reported directly to Kelly.

Kelly also announced the company's first quarterly cash dividend and authorized a stock buyback of up to $2 million in shares. ''Paying a cash dividend, in addition to our a stock repurchase program, reflects our confidence in Pyramid's future prospects,'' he explained in a February 24, 2000 press release. ''These actions also reflect our commitment to improve returns for Pyramid shareholders,'' he added.

Looking Ahead

As Pyramid continued its efforts to reverse the downward trend of the late 1990s, it pinned part of its hopes on its alehouse operations. This segment of the company was perhaps the most promising, posting a 16 percent revenue gain in 1999. ''We feel that our Alehouse Division has substantial opportunity to add value to the company, both by improving existing operations and achieving unit growth through acquisitions or new developments,'' Kelly said in a February 2, 2000 press release. Another potential area of growth for Pyramid lay in its soda subsidiary. Wholesale soda shipments increased 11 percent in 1999, in marked contrast to beer shipments, which increased only two percent.

Principal Subsidiaries

The Thomas Kemper Brewing Company; The Thomas Kemper Soda Company.

Principal Competitors

Redhook Ale Brewery, Inc.; Boston Beer Company.

Further Reading

Marcial, Gene G., ''Microbrews—Without the Froth,'' *Business Week*, March 16, 1998, p. 96.

''Pyramid Breweries Inc. Declares Regular Quarterly Cash Dividend,'' *Business Wire*, February 24, 2000.

''Pyramid Breweries Inc.,'' *Seattle Post-Intelligencer*, December 20, 1999, Bus. Sec.

''Pyramid, Redhook Indicate Recovery in Craft-Beer Market,'' *Seattle Post-Intelligencer*, August 6, 1999, Bus. Sec.

''TK History,'' *Thomas Kemper Soda Company Website*, http://www.tksoda.com/history.

—Shawna Brynildssen

Rabobank Group

PO Box 17100
3500 HG Utrecht
The Netherlands
Telephone: (+31) 30 216-2804
Fax: (+31) 30 216-1976
Web site: http://www.rabobankorganisatie.nl

Cooperative
Incorporated: 1972 as Coöperatieve Centrale Raiffeisen-
    Boerenleenbank (Rabobank)
Employees: 45,000
Total Assets: Nfl 550 billion ($ 261.9 billion)(1999)
NAIC: 52211 Commercial Banking

Rabobank Group, known in the Netherlands as Coöperatieve Centrale Raiffeisen-Boerenleenbank, is the third-largest provider of financial services in the Netherlands and ranks as the 32nd largest bank worldwide. Unlike its chief domestic rivals, publicly listed ABN Amro Holding N.V. and ING Groep N.V., Rabobank has clung steadfastly to its status as a private cooperative, composed of 439 independent member banks with some 1,800 branches under the Rabobank name. With a membership of more than 550,000, Rabobank supplies financial products in one form or another to some seven million customers—more than half of the population of the Netherlands. Formed in order to provide financial support to the Netherlands' farming community, Rabobank remains true to its roots and accounts for more than 85 percent of the country's food and agriculture-related financial services business. Since the mid-1980s, however, Rabobank has been engaged in an aggressive expansion drive, both within the Netherlands and on the international financial scene. Rabobank has extended its portfolio of services to include insurance, through subsidiary Interpolis; asset management and investment fund products through subsidiary Robeco Group, acquired in 1996; international wholesale banking services, targeting especially the worldwide food and agriculture markets, through subsidiary Rabobank International, with 121 branches in 35 countries; private banking and asset management through International Private Banking & Trust; domestic private banking through Schretlen & Co.; and leasing, trade finance, and vendor financing through subsidiary De Lage Landen. With assets topping Nfl 550 billion in 1999, Rabobank is also making moves to join the new single-currency market. In October 1999, Rabobank announced its intention to form an alliance with German cooperative bank Deutsche Genossengesellschaft (DG Bank). Initially planned to take the form of a joint-venture partnership, the alliance is expected to lead to full-fledged merger in the early years of the new century.

Farmers Cooperative Movement in the 19th Century

Rabobank's origins lay in the cooperative banking movement of the 19th century. In 1864, Friedrich Wilhelm Raiffeisen, of Heddesdorf in Germany, started up a local banking cooperative that was to inspire similar cooperatives worldwide. Raiffeisen's model was based on providing mutual assistance to its members, especially in the form of loans and other financial assistance, providing a sense of commitment to community that has remained a hallmark of the cooperative banking movement into the 21st century. The Raiffeisen banks operated on a local basis as part of a larger cooperative network. Administration was frugal, and all profits were reinvested in the bank. The Raiffeisen form of cooperative banking soon spread across the German border into the Netherlands, where it held a strong appeal for the country's farmers.

The first Dutch financial organization to meet the full criteria of the Raiffeisen model was the Coöperatieve Landbouwersbank en Handelsvereeniging, in Lonneker, near Enschede. Established in 1896, this bank remained in operation for nearly 70 years, and remained an independent operation until the late 1950s. The establishment of the Lonneker bank, and its emphasis on the agricultural community, inspired the startup of other farming-focused banking cooperatives. Hard hit by the economic climate, and finding little assistance from the traditional financial community, the Netherlands' farmers turned to the Raiffeisen cooperative model of mutual aid. The first of these farmer-owned cooperative banks appeared in 1897, called the Boerenleenbank (or "farmers loan bank"), in the town of Geldorp, quickly followed by similar Boerenleenbanks in Leene, Heeze, and Heeswijk. By the following year, the Boerenleenbank concept had spread through much of the Netherlands.

Company Perspectives:

We, the staff and management of the Rabobank Group, have as both point of departure and primary goal the best interests of our customers. We aim to add value by: providing those financial services considered best and most appropriate by our customers; ensuring continuity in the services provided with a view to the long-term interests of the client; commitment to our clients and their concerns and issues so that we can contribute to achieving their ambitions. We believe it is important that clients immediately recognise and personally experience the following values in all our activities: integrity: we act according to our stated aims; respect: we will interact with clients so that they experience our respect for them; expertise: we must be able to fulfill every promise we make.

In 1898, the first initiatives were taken to group together the many independently operating Boerenleenbanks under a central administration. In June of that year, a group of southern farmers' banks formed the Coöperatieve Vereeniging van Raiffeisen-Banken en Landbouwvereenigingen in Utrecht. This was followed soon after in the north by the creation of the Coöperatieve Centrale Boerenleenbank in Eindhoven. Member banks of both the northern and southern cooperatives remained independently operated, yet benefitted from a central administration. The Dutch farmers' union, the Nederlandsche Boerenbond, which had been behind the formation of the banking cooperatives, had initially intended to form a single, nationally operating central organization. Efforts were made to merge the two groups together in that same year. The two organizations, echoing traditional north-south tensions, were unable to agree on a merger, however.

By the 1920s, the farmers' banking cooperative movement had spread throughout the Netherlands, comprising more than 1,200 locally operating member banks. The combined assets of these banks gave the cooperatives a position as one of the Netherlands' largest savings and loan institutions. These farmers' cooperatives retained a near-monopoly on the agricultural community savings and loan market until the 1950s, when the Dutch banking industry began to restructure. Where banks had typically focused on single-product activities, more and more banks were beginning to offer multiple products. In 1957, for example, the country's commercial banks began offering savings accounts for the first time.

The farmers banking cooperatives quickly responded to the changing banking climate by expanding their services. In the early 1960s, the cooperatives began offering insurance services. In 1965 the cooperatives added commercial accounts and other services. In that year, the Centrale Boerenleenbank acquired Amsterdam-based private broker and bank Schretlen & Co. Two years later, the two cooperatives joined together to form the Bankgirocentrale. By the end of the decade, both cooperatives were also operating travel agency services.

At the start of the 1970s, the two cooperatives announced their intention to join forces. The actual merger took place in December 1972, forming the Coöperatieve Centrale Raiffeisen-Boerenleenbank. The new organization quickly became known as Rabobank. Comprised of more than 1,500 independent banks, which took on the Rabobank name, the new financial institution became one of the country's top three providers of banking and other financial services.

International Bank for the 21st Century

Despite diversifying its portfolio of financial products since the early 1960s, Rabobank remained focused on providing traditional retail banking products to an exclusively Dutch, and especially agricultural market. In the late 1970s, faced with increasing competition from traditional banks, the farmers' cooperative began to open outwards. In 1970s, Rabobank joined with a number of other European banking cooperatives to form the Unico Banking Group. Two years later, Rabobank dropped the membership requirement for its private depositors; only customers arranging business and professional loans were required to become Rabobank members. This change enabled Rabobank to find wider appeal among the general Netherlands population, and by the 1990s the bank was able to claim that roughly half of the country's 14 million citizens were customers of one or more of its financial products. Nevertheless, Rabobank succeeded in retaining a large membership base, which neared some 600,000 by the end of the century. At the same time, Rabobank had successfully maintained its low operating costs and strong profits, enabling the bank to achieve the coveted Triple-A rating from both Moody's and Standard & Poor.

Rabobank's future growth opportunities in the Netherlands remained limited, however. Yet increasing pressure from its capital-rich, publicly listed competitors, at a time when financial barriers among European Community member states had begun to fall—culminating with the introduction of a single European currency in 1999—forced Rabobank to look beyond the Netherlands' borders. The bank took its first international steps in 1983, when it acquired 84 percent of ADCA Bank in Germany. Also during that year, Rabobank opened its first overseas office, in London, heralding the launch of the company's global operations, Rabobank International.

Rabobank also began stepping up diversification of its product portfolio. In 1986, the bank began offering mutual funds and shareholder products, including the Rabobank Obligatiefonds and the Rabobank Andelenfonds. The bank also stepped up its activities beyond the agricultural sphere, to the extent that, by 1987, loans to the business community outpaced loans to the agricultural market for the first time. In that year, also, the banks leadership was given to Herman Wijffels. As head of Rabobank until the late 1990s, Wijffels was given much of the credit for developing Rabobank's international business and transforming it into one of the world's top financial institutions. By the beginning of the 1990s, Rabobank determined to diversify its activities in order to become a full-service financial services provider offering banking, investment, and insurance products.

While Rabobank's publicly traded counterparts were able to finance aggressive expansion and acquisition programs, Rabobank, guarding its private, cooperative status, had to look elsewhere for growth. The cooperative took a two-pronged approach. The first part involved extending its financial expertise, particularly in the high-growth food and agricultural sector,

Key Dates:

1864: A cooperative bank is founded by Friedrich Wilhelm Raiffeisen in Heddesdorf, Germany.
1897: Boerenleenbank (''farmer's loan bank'') is founded in Geldorp, Netherlands, with Raiffeisen's bank as a model.
1898: Grouping of the many bank co-ops occurs, under Coöperatieve Vereeniging van Raiffeisen-Banken en Landbouwvereenigingen in the south, and Coöperatieve Centrale Boerenleenbank in the north.
1925: Dutch farmers bank cooperative achieves national penetration.
1957: Dutch banking is deregulated.
1961: Co-ops introduce insurance services.
1965: Co-ops introduce commercial banking services.
1967: The two major co-ops form a joint-venture, Bankgirocentrale.
1969: Travel agency services are introduced.
1972: Rabobank emerges from the merging of the two major co-ops.
1986: Rabobank begins offering mutual funds.
1999: A joint-venture and merger agreement with DG Bank of Germany is planned.

to a worldwide scale. For this the company pursued an internal growth strategy, opening new branches and entering new country markets, while also seeking local partnerships and acquisitions in the agricultural banking sector, such as the 1989 purchase of Primary Industry Bank of Australia. By the middle of the decade, Rabobank International was present in more than 30 countries; by the beginning of the new century, nearly 160 Rabobank International and other subsidiary branches operated in more than 40 countries.

The second prong to Rabobank's 1990s growth strategy came through a series of strategic mergers. The first occurred in 1990, when Rabobank merged with insurance cooperative Interpolis, bringing the latter's portfolio of insurance products to Rabobank's customers. Rabobank also entered the sales promotions products category (leasing, wholesale financing, and other debt financing) for the international durable equipment manufacturing market with De Lage Landen. Both Interpolis and De Lage Landen operated primarily in the Netherlands, but with worldwide interests as well. In the early 1990s, Rabobank, which had developed a modest assets management business, began to approach Robeco, one of the world's leading assets management companies, based in Rotterdam. The cooperation between Rabobank and Robeco became a partnership when Rabobank acquired 50 percent of Robeco in 1996, with an option to acquire full ownership, and completed the acquisition in 1998. The total purchase price of around NfL 1 billion gave the privately held Robeco the much-needed capital to fund its own worldwide expansion and added Robeco's strong assets portfolio to Rabobank's list of products.

By the late 1990s, Rabobank's transformation into a diversified financial products provider had largely been completed. Yet

the bank remained a relatively small player in a market set to see explosive growth with the launch of the Eurodollar in 1999. As its publicly listed competitors moved towards an aggressive consolidation of the European financial market, mirroring a continuing worldwide consolidation, Rabobank was forced to look beyond the Netherlands borders in order to secure its position in Europe. Analysts saw the inevitability of alliances among Rabobank and its European cooperative counterparts, such as Credit Agricole of France. Instead, Rabobank turned first to Dutch insurance broker Achmea Holding NV, with the intention to form a 50–50 joint venture offering asset management, pension, life insurance and other insurance products. That deal, however, fell through.

Meanwhile, Rabobank International's ambitious expansion program—in particular its attempt to expand beyond its food and agriculture base into the health sector and other markets—had begun to cut into its parent's profits, threatening Rabobank's prized Triple-A rating. Rabobank responded with a series of job cuts and a refocusing of Rabobank International on the bank's core expertise in the food and agriculture sectors. Rabobank, meanwhile, had not yet given up in its attempt to find a suitable partner for its European growth. In October 1999, the cooperative announced its intention to form a 50–50 joint venture, with an eye toward a future merger, with fellow cooperative bank, Deutsche Genossengesellschaft, known as DG Bank. The move, greeted with approval by market analysts, suggested further partnerships and mergers within the European cooperative banking movement, still a financial force in France, Belgium, Spain, and Germany after nearly 150 years.

Principal Subsidiaries

Rabobank International; International Private Banking & Trust; Interpolis; De Lage Landen; Robeco Group; Nedship Bank; Schretlen & Co.; Glide Investment Management; Rab Vastgoed.

Principal Competitors

ABN Amro Holding N.V.; ING Groep N.V.; Fortis, Inc.; Caisse Nationale de Credit Agricole; Deutsche Bank AG; HSBC Holdings plc.

Further Reading

''Investment Banking: Against the Tide,'' *Economist*, September 5, 1998.
''Rabobank gelooft heilig in haar maatschappelijke rol,'' *De Telegraaf*, June 6, 1998.
''Rabobank International heeft nieuwe strategie,'' *De Telegraaf*, September 24, 1999.
''Rabobank stevent af op fusie met Duitse DG Bank,'' *De Telegraaf*, October 15, 1999.
Smit, Barbara, ''The Banker Who Invests in Integrity,'' *European*, May 1, 1997, p. 32.
Van der Leij, Lien, ''Rabobank Targets Leadership in Agribusiness,'' *Reuters*, September 24, 1999.
Woo, K.I., ''Dutch 'Farm' Bank Sets Long-Term Aim,'' *Nation*, March 23, 1999.

—M.L. Cohen

Raven Industries, Inc.

205 East Sixth Street
Sioux Falls, South Dakota 57117
U.S.A.
Telephone: (605) 336-2750
Fax: (605) 335-0268
Web site: http://www.ravenind.com

Public Company
Incorporated: 1956
Employees: 1,463
Sales: $152.8 million (1999)
Stock Exchanges: NASDAQ
Ticker Symbol: RAVN
NAIC: 314999 All Other Miscellaneous Textile Product
Mills; 326199 All Other Plastics Products
Manufacturing; 334514 Totalizing Fluid Meter and
Counting Device Manufacturing; 334519 Other
Measuring and Controlling Device Manufacturing

Raven Industries, Inc. is a diversified manufacturer of plastic, electronic, and special apparel products, which its sells to niche markets. Founded to make commercial and recreational balloons in 1956, the company quickly used its expertise in this area to produce an assortment of other products, ranging from massive plastic storage containers for use in agriculture and industry to ski pants. Its most profitable and steadily performing unit is its plastics division, which manufacturers polyethylene sheeting, high altitude balloons, and giant storage tanks. Raven's sewn products division makes outerwear (especially active sportswear), hot air balloons, and parade inflatables. Raven's third unit, its electronics division, constructs control systems—such as ultrasonic soil-depth control devices and sprayer controls—for agricultural and industrial customers. These high-tech devices regulate such precise tasks as determining how deeply seeds are planted in soil and how much fertilizer is applied to crops. Long a major supplier to defense contractors, Raven has been forced to adjust to leaner military budgets. Beginning in the mid-1990s, Raven has eliminated noncore operations and has striven to gain dominance in its niche markets. Raven operates several successful companies as subsidiaries, including Aerostar and Automatic Coil.

The Early Years

Raven Industries was launched in 1956 by a group of General Mills Inc. (GM) employees. Much of the impetus for founding Raven came from Ed Yost, a maverick thinker at GM's High Altitude Research Division. GM had received a contract from the U.S. Navy in the early 1950s to explore the new balloon technologies for defense and scientific purposes, and Yost took charge of the project. (While gas balloons were used sporadically at this time, they were expensive and could carry little weight.) In 1955 Yost successfully flew a tethered hot air balloon, much to the Navy's pleasure.

After receiving a $47,000 grant from the Office of Naval Research in 1956, Yost founded Raven Industries to design, build, and launch hot air balloons. Yost and his investors opted to locate the company in Sioux Falls, South Dakota, because of the favorable wind conditions there—with relatively balanced spring and fall winds, balloons tended to ascend and descend straight up and down there, which made retrieving and tracking them an easier task. In addition to earning Yost the moniker "father of hot air ballooning," Raven quickly won other classified contracts from the Navy.

Almost from its inception, Raven expanded beyond making balloons, applying the technologies it had mastered in that endeavor to new ventures. David Christensen, who joined the company in 1962, explained to *Barron's* how the seemingly disjointed directions in which Raven's early growth took the company were actually logical: "The balloons were largely made of plastic, so the company got into plastics. It learned about electronics for the research instruments carried up in the air, so we [branched] into electronics. And then, when the balloon flight was over and the recordings had been made, the data . . . had to be recovered by parachute. So the company got into sewn goods." To be sure that the company did not drift too far from its original mission, Yost formed Aerostar in 1960. That subdivision was devoted solely to producing balloons.

Even with all of its diversification, Raven continued to rely heavily on government contracts. During the late 1960s, for example, the company won a massive five-year $74 million contract to produce electronic equipment—especially radios and modules—for the armed forces. This arrangement accounted for a significant portion of the company's revenues during that period. In 1972 Christensen ascended to the positions of president and chief executive officer and guided the company as it continued to seek out new markets.

The Early 1980s

By 1983, Raven's sales had risen to $31 million. Although the United States was then mired in a recession, Raven's diversification protected it from the most turbulent vicissitudes of the period. The economic downturn certainly damaged the company's business of producing large plastic containers for agriculture and industry ("People aren't investing yet in large capital improvements," Christensen told the *Dow Jones News Service* on August 20, 1982, by way of explanation), but Raven's innovative ballutes—a fabric material that was a cross between a balloon and a parachute—was in heavy demand from the military. (Ballutes could be used to drop ammunition from aircraft.) Raven also continued to develop electronic technology. By building on the control devices it had devised for balloons, Raven was able to launch several successful products that controlled various aspects of farms and feedmills. In 1983, for instance, the company released a system that controlled the manufacture of feed pellets for cattle.

Nonetheless, government contracts remained essential to Raven's viability. In 1984 alone, defense orders accounted for more than 20 percent of the company's total sales. "The question we have to debate internally is how much defense business do we want in relation to our total business," Christensen explained to the *Dow Jones News Service* on November 25, 1983. This was particularly true because military procurement was not the only potential venue for Raven's diverse products. As the dominant paradigm of American agriculture shifted from small family farms to "agribusinesses" that operated on vast scales, Raven found new customers for its productivity-enhancing electronic control systems. For instance, the company's computerized monitoring system for the application of herbicide to fields sold quite briskly in 1985. Another key product in this sector was Raven's grain loss monitor, an electronic device used with combines to measure the amount of grain wasted in planting. To bolster its position in this industry, Raven acquired Beta 11 Inc. in 1984. This St. Louis, Missouri-based producer of electronic feed mill control systems had annual sales exceeding $2 million.

The company clearly recognized that opening up new markets would remain crucial to its continued success (as Christensen would explain later to *Barron's,* the company's aim during this period was to forge a "diverse, recession-resistant structure"). To this end, Raven acquired Glasstite, Inc. of Dunnell, Minnesota, in April 1986. This privately held company manufactured fiberglass truck tops, and the purchase afforded Raven entrance to the automotive market. Raven solidified its place in that sector in 1987, when it acquired Astoria Fibra-Steel, a utility truck body business. The company continued to develop its original product lines as well. In 1987 Raven's Aerostar was chosen to produce custom-made inflatables for Macy's annual Thanksgiving Day Parade. Moreover, Aerostar did a brisk business supplying hot air balloons to the growing recreational ballooning market.

Even with all of the changes the company underwent during the 1980s, Raven adhered to its long-standing organizational structure. Because its operations were so far-flung, the company gave the directors of each division a great deal of autonomy. Raven termed this system "intrapreneurialism" and allowed each division head to maintain his or her own sales, production, and engineering staffs. "They're almost independent entities," a company executive told the *Journal of Business Strategy.* "The idea is that the division manager knows the business best so, to some extent, let him or her run it." Raven did provide a managerial umbrella over the divisions, though, overseeing credit, accounting, data processing, and most personnel functions.

The Early 1990s

Tensions in the Persian Gulf and the United States' involvement in the Gulf War were a boon to Raven's short-term sales. After the Air Force awarded Raven a $6 million contract to produce electronic temperature control devices for the C-130 cargo transplant planes in 1989, the company won a $22 million contract from the Army in 1991 to manufacture 250,000 suits designed to protect American soldiers from possible chemical and biological warfare attacks in Iraq. Not surprisingly, sales for fiscal year 1992 (which ended January 31, 1992) rose dramatically—to $100.6 million, up from $85.5 million in 1991. In fact, the company was named one of America's fastest-growing companies by *Financial World* in 1991. Moreover, immediately after the Gulf War, Raven received orders from different military departments to restock electronic equipment that had been depleted during the campaign. Despite the revenue garnered by defense orders, though, Christensen would later rue the large contracts. "In some ways, working with the military can spoil you, in that a large contract can lull you to sleep," he noted to the *Journal of Business Strategy.*

Christensen's concerns were triggered by the rapid decrease in defense spending that occurred in the aftermath of the Gulf War. With the Cold War over and no significant threats on the horizon, the military's budget was severely curtailed. But despite the fact that 30 percent of its total sales in fiscal year 1991 were connected to defense contracts, Raven remained optimistic. With six years of record sales behind it by 1993, the company set itself the goal of becoming a $200 million company by 2000. Christensen confidently told *Barron's* that Raven could make up for losses in defense work with orders for the company's automotive products, automation controls, precision farming devices, and outerwear. In fact, the company recently

Key Dates:

1956: Raven Industries is founded by four former General Mills employees.
1986: Raven acquires Glasstite, Inc. and Poly Plastic & Design Corp.
1987: Company buys Astoria Fibra-Steel.
1993: Company purchases Automatic Coil Corp.
1995: Raven acquires A.J. Electronics Inc. and certain assets of Winzen International; sells Astoria.
1996: Company builds new factory for Glasstite in Arizona; purchases full line of products from K. Eldredge Electronics.
1997: Raven takes over Norcore Plastics, Inc.
1999: Company sells Glasstite.

had formed an alliance with major catalogue retailers Lands End and L.L. Bean to produce Gor-Tex parkas and sportswear.

The Mid-1990s

Raven continued to try to reduce its dependence on government contracts throughout the mid-1990s. To strengthen its position in the nondefense-related electronics market (in 1992, for example, the military was the end customer for more than 90 percent of the electronics division's sales), Raven acquired Automatic Coil Corp. from Designatronics in 1993 and A.J. Electronics Inc. from DDL Electronics in January 1995. The company focused on expanding other aspects of its operations as well. Also in 1995, Raven bought several assets of Winzen International that were related to high-altitude balloon manufacturing. Moreover, in January 1996, Raven acquired a full line of ultrasonic sensor controls from K. Eldredge Electronics of Australia. Intended to strengthen Raven's position in the precision farming sector, the Eldredge purchase added to Raven's product line devices, which included a sensor control that automatically regulated operating depths on air seeders and planters and an ultrasonic head height control system for combines.

It seemed initially that Raven would be able to recover quickly from the loss of defense-related revenue. Sales for fiscal year 1994 rose to $121.5 million from $111.2 million in fiscal year 1993. Raven's sales flattened in fiscal year 1995, however, reaching only $121.7 million, and dropped for the first time in more than a decade in 1996, to $120.4 million. Equally disturbing was the company's diminishing profits. Net income reached an all-time high of $7 million in fiscal year 1994, but dropped nearly 13 percent—to $6.1 million—in fiscal year 1995 and recovered only marginally—back to $6.2 million—in 1996.

Refocusing in the Late 1990s

Raven resolved to overcome these difficulties. In February 1997, the company made an important acquisition when it added Norcore Plastics, Inc. to its plastics division. Based in Tacoma, Washington, Norcore was a leader in the manufacture of large industrial storage tanks. Norcore had benefited in particular from its application of "dual laminate" technology, which produced tanks capable of handling high-purity chemicals and liquids (of

special use to the semiconductor manufacturing industry). This $3 million acquisition not only complemented Raven's existing storage tank operations, but also provided the company with a West Coast manufacturing location.

Through moves such as this one, and buoyed by the soaring U.S. economy, Raven was able to recapture its earlier momentum by the late 1990s. In fiscal year 1997, the company earned a net profit of $7.7 million on sales of $139.4 million. Sales rose to $149.6 million in fiscal 1998, and again to $152.8 million the following year. The company's continued success, however, was called into question by the underperformance of certain of its divisions, which threatened to weight down the entire company.

At the close of the decade, Christensen declared in a press release that Raven would "refocus" on core operations through a restructuring in which it intended "to redeploy or dispose of non-core assets." At the time of the announcement, the company had already shed its Astoria unit and, in October 1999, made the decision to sell its automotive business's flagship enterprise—Glasstite—for $8.5 million. Although Glasstite had returned to profitability in 1998 after two years of losses, analysts had long accused Raven of overextending itself in the automotive sector. Of special concern was the company's investment of $1.5 million to build a new 50,000-square-foot manufacturing plant for Glasstite—an outlay that Raven had not been able to recoup.

By exiting the automotive market, Raven demonstrated its commitment to concentrating on sportswear, agriculture, and plastics. Raven also would continue to compete in its original niche—ballooning. Aerostar had launched a major international marketing campaign in June 1998, seeking to boost orders for its custom-made inflatable balloons. In 1999, the company received a contract from NASA to produce a unique high-atmosphere balloon. "I'm confident you'll see this company back on a growth track," Christensen told the *Associated Press*.

Principal Divisions

Automatic Coil; Electronics Systems Division; Engineered Films Division; Flow Controls Division.

Principal Competitors

O'Sullivan Corporation; Top Air Manufacturing, Inc.

Further Reading

"CEO Interview: Raven Industries," *Wall Street Transcript,* October 24, 1994.
Meyer, Harvey, "Underdog: A Military Contractor Spreads Its Wings," *Journal of Business Strategy,* September 19, 1997.
Palmer, Jay, "Raven Industries Enjoys Ballooning Business," *Barron's,* August 17, 1992, p. 14.
"Raven Industries," *Implement and Tractor,* January 11, 1996.
"Raven Industries Acquires Norcore Plastics, Tank & Technology," *Composite News,* February 10, 1997.
"Raven Industries Outlook," *Dow Jones News Service,* August 12, 1983.
"Raven Industries Sees Net Up Strongly in 4th Quarter," *Dow Jones News Service,* November 25, 1983.
Slovak, Julianne, "Raven Industries," *Fortune,* May 21, 1990.

—Rebecca Stanfel

RDO Equipment Company

2829 South University Drive
Fargo, North Dakota 58103
U.S.A.
Telephone: (701) 237-7363
Fax: (701) 271-6328
Web site: http://www.rdoequipment.com

Public Company
Incorporated: 1968
Employees: 1,554
Sales: $578.6 million (1999)
Stock Exchanges: New York
Ticker Symbol: RDO
NAIC: 42181 Construction and Mining (Except Oil Well)
Machinery and Equipment Wholesalers; 42182 Farm
and Garden Machinery and Equipment Wholesalers

Founded by agriculture mogul Ronald D. Offutt, RDO Equipment Company is a leading retailer of new and used equipment, machinery, and heavy duty trucks. Maintaining the largest network of John Deere dealerships and Volvo truck centers in North America, RDO Equipment sells its products to the agricultural, construction, manufacturing, and transportation industries. RDO Equipment also provides parts and service for its equipment, as well as financial services. Since 1998, RDO Equipment has operated through six chief divisions: RDO Construction Equipment; RDO Used Equipment; RDO Truck Center; RDO Agricultural Equipment; RDO Material Handling; and RDO Financial Services. With 65 stores in 11 states, RDO Equipment is a major player in the ongoing restructuring and consolidation of the equipment and truck retail industries in the United States.

A Farming Background

Ronald D. Offutt, the founder of RDO Equipment Co., was the fourth generation of Great Plains farmers in his family. He grew up on a 200-acre potato farm in western Minnesota, where he worked at his father's side. The elder Offutt gave his son a great deal of responsibility at a young age. When he was only 12, Ronald Offutt was allowed to fire four farm workers.

Offutt left the family farm to attend Concordia College in Moorhead, Minnesota. After graduating in 1964 with a dual degree in business administration and history, Offutt interviewed with four insurance companies, but received no job offers. He returned to the potato farm, and shortly thereafter convinced his father to sell him half of the property for $48,000.

Founding RDO Equipment in 1968

In 1968 Offutt charted a new course. The local John Deere dealer in Casselton, North Dakota was in the process of selling his business. Offutt knew that Deere was one of the most highly regarded manufacturers of agricultural machinery and equipment, and he believed that the Deere dealership could bring his family more profits than farming alone. Offutt turned to his father for assistance and entreated him to take out a second mortgage on the farm to help buy the dealership. Although his father was dubious, he agreed. Offutt also sold a potato warehouse and borrowed an additional $10,000 from his grandmother to secure all the necessary financing. With the Deere dealership in his name, Offutt farmed in the mornings and evenings and spent his days at the store.

Offutt's instincts proved correct, and the dealership quickly turned a profit. Aided by steep inflation and soaring farmland values, the Deere dealership brought the Offutts a constant flow of revenue (as well as a source of inexpensive farm equipment for their own use). He christened his new company RDO Equipment, which stood for his own initials.

Other Ventures in the 1970s and 1980s

Despite RDO Equipment's initial success, Offutt did not give the business his full attention. In 1970 he started raising irrigated potatoes in the sandy soil of Hubbard County, Minnesota. Most observers predicted this endeavor would fail, since never before had any farmer attempted to grow potatoes in a region that required such extensive irrigation. Despite this skepticism, Offutt's experiment was an unequivocal success. By 1974, he had profitably quadrupled his acreage. Flush with this

Company Perspectives:

Our mission is to hire and promote people who grow professionally with the company, to continue strong employee achievement programs, and to be totally aware and knowledgeable of our customers' needs. Our vision consists of one strong and bold statement: "We will strive for excellence and be the premier dealer group in providing superior products and services to our customers." We will strive: to deliver quality products and services; to maintain strong partnerships based on honesty, integrity, and trust with our employees, our customers, and our suppliers; to continue pursuing innovative change; to encourage teamwork among employees; to remain financially viable through repeat business of satisfied customers; to nurture, develop, and give proper recognition to our employees.

early triumph, in 1976 Offutt bought the famed Rockefeller Ranch in Texas, which proved to be a dismal failure. Not only did the ranch's cattle become sick, but Offutt also had selected a potato seed that grew poorly in the Texas climate. After losing nearly half his net worth by 1978, he returned to Minnesota and concentrated on his ventures there.

In the 1980s, Offutt built up RDO Equipment's network of Deere dealerships. He also expanded his potato farming business, building a potato processing plant in Park Rapids, North Dakota. Operated by another Offutt company—RDO Frozen Foods—the plant cleaned, cut, fried, froze, and packaged his constantly increasing crop of tubers. His sense of timing was uncanny. Just as his processing plant (which could process 50 million pounds of potatoes a year) came up to speed, American consumption of the spud increased dramatically as fast food chains made french fries a staple side dish.

In 1989 Offutt once again returned his attention to RDO Equipment and oversaw an expansion of the company's reach. Rather than continue only to sell and repair agricultural equipment, he began to acquire or build dealerships that offered construction and other industrial equipment and machinery— such as backhoes, crawler dozers, and excavators. Like his farm equipment dealerships, Offutt's construction machinery stores specialized in Deere products, although they did carry other brands, including Vermeer, Nissan, Mustang, Sullair, and Hitachi. Offutt's decision to enter the construction equipment market was informed by his core strategy—what the *Fargo Forum* termed "the relentless diversification into related businesses." Intimately acquainted from his farming background with the periodic downturns of agricultural markets, Offutt wanted RDO Equipment to gain a foothold in a sector divorced from the wild price fluctuations of commodities markets.

Growth in the Early 1990s

In the early 1990s, Offutt added to his network of agricultural and construction dealerships. By the close of 1996, RDO Equipment owned and operated 32 dealerships in seven states: North Dakota, Minnesota, Arizona, California, South Dakota, Texas, and Washington. Although RDO Equipment simply

acquired most of the properties in its empire (which retained their original names), the company did construct a few new stores, building four between 1991 and 1996. RDO Equipment's sales kept pace with the steadily increasing number of dealerships. The company's annual revenues rose from $71.2 million in fiscal year 1992 (ending January 31, 1992) to $223.6 million for fiscal year 1996. During the same period, RDO Equipment's net income grew from $1.7 million to $4.8 million.

Rapid Expansion: 1997

Despite these impressive gains, RDO Equipment's true growth spurt did not begin until 1997, when Offutt opted to take the company public with the hope of generating capital with which to fuel future expansion. In its initial public offering, launched in January 1997, RDO Equipment sold about 42 million shares and raised $68.3 million, becoming the first corporation based in North Dakota to be listed on the New York Stock Exchange. The company immediately used $10 million of this total to retire debts and paid out another $15 million in dividends to existing shareholders. The remaining $34 million was intended "to allow us to continue to grow the company, expand our dealership numbers," Offutt explained to the *Fargo Forum*.

Offutt's plan to bulk up the RDO Equipment Network and to branch out into new markets was logical. Although its construction equipment sector was performing well—spurred by low interest rates, low inflation, and economic growth—RDO Equipment's agricultural dealerships were dealt a severe blow by the farm crises of the mid-1990s. The weather phenomenon known as El Niño had caused a tremendously wet winter in 1996–97, which wrought havoc on crop production. Compounding the situation was the fact that the Asian economic collapse of 1997 eroded export markets for American farmers. To make matters even worse, domestic commodity prices were also quite low. Not surprisingly in this environment, farmers lost confidence in their future earning potential and deferred making major capital investments—including the purchase of new equipment.

Responding to this adverse trend, RDO Equipment established a new subsidiary—RDO Rental Co.—in February 1997, with the twin goals of extending its brand and retail presence and of raising its profile in the service and repair sector. The same month it was created, RDO Rental Co. acquired Sun Valley Equipment Corp. for $8.1 million. A major construction equipment rental business, Sun Valley offered RDO Equipment a decisive entrance into this new sector and boosted the rental division's store number from five to 12.

RDO Equipment formed another new subsidiary in February 1997 as well. In an effort to complement its industrial and construction equipment operations—and thereby to protect itself further from the vicissitudes of the commodities market— RDO Equipment began to sell and service heavy-duty trucks through its RDO Mack Sales and Service division. With the acquisition of its first truck dealership—a Mack truck outlet in Fargo, North Dakota—RDO Mack Sales and Service also gained the right to purchase Mack dealerships or win Mack franchises in the sales territory encompassing North Dakota and parts of Minnesota. Capitalizing on this development, RDO

Key Dates:

1968: Ronald Offutt purchases his first John Deere agricultural equipment dealership, launching RDO Equipment.

1997: Company makes initial public stock offering; establishes its Used Equipment Division; acquires RDO Rental Co. and Sun Valley Equipment Corp.; purchases first truck dealership; establishes RDO Financial Services Co.

1998: Company reorganizes into five divisions; becomes dealer of Hyster material handling products; acquires 89 percent of Salinas Equipment Distributors, Inc.; purchases Midlands Rental and Machinery, Inc. and Midlands Material Management, Inc.

2000: RDO Equipment sells its rental division to United Rental Inc.

Mack Sales built a Mack sales and service center in Grand Forks, North Dakota, in March 1997.

At the same time, RDO Equipment continued to pursue a greater share of the construction equipment market. In May 1997, the company announced that it would acquire Kuenstler Machinery, which distributed, sold, rented, and serviced construction equipment through its stores in Austin, Laredo, and San Antonio, Texas. With 1996 sales exceeding $20 million, Kuenstler also provided RDO Equipment with a Deere sales territory of 41 Texas counties. As a result of its spate of acquisitions, RDO Equipment could claim ownership of 42 retail stores by May 1997. Paul Horn, the company's president and chief operating officer, told the *Fargo Forum* on May 31, 1997 that he was confident that RDO Equipment would grow "to a billion dollars and beyond."

But the company was not content to grow only by acquiring more stores and penetrating new markets. RDO Equipment also wanted to increase the sales generated by its existing stores. In an effort to ensure that its customers would return to the various RDO Equipment stores, the company created another subsidiary in December 1997. This new RDO Financial Services division was established to provide equipment loans and leases to customers of the dealer network, as well as to offer extended warranties, credit life insurance, and disability insurance. As Horn explained in a press release, RDO Financial Services was designed to "strengthen our relationship with customers, improve same store sales, and as a result, enhance revenues and earnings."

RDO Equipment's first year as a public company had proved successful. The number of stores in its network had grown from 32 to 50, mainly through the acquisition of existing dealerships. Of this total number, 26 were construction equipment dealerships, 16 provided agricultural machinery, and eight offered equipment rentals. Sales for 1997 rose to $302.4 million, and income grew to a record $11.1 million. RDO Equipment's year-on-year track record was even more impressive. The company's revenues had increased at an annual compound rate of 33 percent from 1992 through 1997, while its net income had

grown at a compound annual rate of 45 percent during the same period. But Offutt was not content with these gains. "Going forward we will continue to grow the business by taking advantage of industry trends toward further dealer consolidation and by leveraging our strength and expertise in acquisitions, consolidation and retail sales, service and marketing," he proclaimed in a press release on March 19, 1998.

New Markets: 1998

In accordance with this agenda, RDO Equipment made another series of acquisitions in 1998. On January 1, the company completed its purchase of John Deere construction equipment dealerships in Billings and Great Falls, Montana. On January 12, RDO Equipment agreed to acquire Hall GMC, Inc. and Hall Truck Center, heavy-duty truck dealerships in Fargo and Grand Forks, North Dakota. At the same time that it bolstered its construction and trucking markets, RDO Equipment shed its agricultural irrigation equipment business, in part because the farm industry was still mired in a slump.

In a prepared statement, Offutt announced that strengthening RDO Equipment's share of the heavy-duty truck market was his "top priority" for the middle of 1998. This goal was achieved when RDO Equipment signed a letter of intent with Volvo Trucks North America, Inc. in May, whereby RDO was granted rights to expand its ownership interest in Volvo truck dealerships.

RDO Equipment ventured into yet another new business sector in August 1998, when it was chosen by the Hyster Company to distribute, sell, service, and rent Hyster's lift trucks in the upper Midwest. A month later, RDO acquired another significant player in the material handling business, Midlands Rental & Machinery Assets (composed of Midlands Rental & Machinery Inc. and Midlands Material Management Inc.). With annual revenues of about $429.4 million, Midlands offered RDO Equipment a significant presence in this segment of the market. "Material handling is a great way to leverage our basic skill set across another platform of growth and continue our strategy of revenue diversification," Horn told *Business Wire*. That same month, RDO Equipment expanded its core operations into a new region, when it purchased an 89 percent stake in the Salinas Equipment Distributors, Inc.

To integrate all of its various acquisitions, RDO Equipment reorganized its operations into distinct divisions in October 1998—construction equipment, agriculture, trucks, used equipment, rent to rent, and materials handling. At the same time, RDO Equipment cut prices in its newly constituted agriculture division, because sales for the year had dropped about 20 percent. The company hoped that this new corporate structure would allow it to maintain closer relationships with its customers.

1999 and Beyond

RDO Equipment entered 1999 with the task of implementing its new divisional strategy. At the same time, though, the company continued to expand. In February 1999, RDO Equipment acquired a Volvo truck dealership with full-service truck centers in Dallas and Fort Worth, Texas. With this purchase, the company gained access to the second largest heavy-duty truck market in the United States.

But the company's rapid growth had left it stretched thin. With the market for its agricultural products still weak, and facing increased competition in other segments, RDO Equipment's profit margins dropped in 1999. Although the company's total sales reached $578.6 million that year, its net income fell precipitously to $1.7 million. In response, RDO Equipment sold its rental division to United Rental, Inc. in February 2000. It planned to use the proceeds of the sale to focus on its other divisions. Despite the new challenges facing the company, RDO's position was strong. With more than 65 dealerships, the company had cultivated leadership in areas far beyond its original focus on agriculture.

Principal Subsidiaries

RDO Financial Services Co.; Salinas Equipment Distributors, Inc.

Principal Divisions

RDO Construction Equipment Division; RDO Agriculture Division; RDO Used Equipment Division.

Principal Competitors

AGCO Corporation; Caterpillar Inc.; CNH Global N.V.; Ingersoll-Rand Company; Kobe Steel, Ltd.; Komatsu Ltd.

Further Reading

Conlin, Michelle, ''The Sultan of Spuds,'' *Forbes,* May 19, 1997, p. 60.

Copeland, Julie, ''RDO Announces 35 Percent Revenue Rise,'' *Grand Forks Herald,* November 20, 1998, p. B7.

Cory, Matt, ''RDO Hits Stock Market,'' *Grand Forks Herald,* January 25, 1997, p. D1.

——, ''RDO Records Banner Year,'' *Grand Forks Herald,* March 20, 1998, p. B7.

Knutson, Jonathon, ''Offutt Conducts First RDO Stockholders Meeting,'' *Fargo Forum,* May 31, 1997, p. B1.

Pates, Mikkel, ''He's Much More Than a Farmer: Diversification Keeps Offutt Going Strong,'' *Fargo Forum,* October 14, 1995, p. 1.

——, ''Offutt Says Now Is Not Time for Potato Expansion,'' *Fargo Forum,* March 22, 1997, p. B4.

Perkins, Jerry, ''The Lord of the Fries,'' *Des Moines Register,* September 25, 1994, p. 3.

Richardt-Sylskar, Hope, ''RDO Expands with Local Office,'' *Marshall (Minn.) Independent,* May 13, 1996, p. A8.

''RDO Equipment Co. Announces Results for 1998 Fiscal Year,'' *Business Wire,* March 19, 1998.

''RDO Equipment Co. Forms Finance Subsidiary,'' *Business Wire,* December 9, 1997.

—Rebecca Stanfel

Rent-Way, Inc.

One Rentway Place
Erie, Pennsylvania 16505
U.S.A.
Telephone: (814) 461-5225
Toll Free: (800) RENT-WAY
Fax: (814) 455-3267
Web site: http://www.rentway.com

Public Company
Incorporated: 1981
Employees: 944
Sales: $494.35 million (1999)
Stock Exchanges: New York
Ticker Symbol: RWY
NAIC: 532299 All Other Consumer Goods Rental

A leading operator of rental purchase stores in the United States, Rent-Way, Inc. rents such merchandise as home entertainment equipment, computers, furniture, and major appliances on a weekly or monthly basis. Since its initial public offering in 1993, the company has grown from 19 stores in three states to over 1,000 stores in 41 states. Rent-Way stores are typically located in low- to middle-income neighborhoods in high-traffic strip malls; the typical Rent-Way customer, often with limited credit or cash-on-hand, finds it easier to make weekly or monthly payments than to purchase merchandise outright. The company offers its customers rental agreements ranging from one week to several years, with an average rental agreement lasting 16 weeks. Customers also have the option to purchase merchandise at the conclusion of a rental agreement, or they can return the merchandise at any time during the agreement without penalty. The company offers free pickup and delivery of merchandise and does not charge customers for normal wear and tear. In 1998 Rent-Way made *Fortune* magazine's annual list of America's 100 fastest-growing companies. The following year, Rent-Way became second only to Rent-A-Center in the fragmented rental purchase industry, having completed a merger with industry giant Home Choice Holdings, Inc.

The First Store in 1981

Company cofounders William E. Morgenstern and Gerald A. Ryan opened their first rental-purchase store in Erie, Pennsylvania, in 1981. Morgenstern was first introduced to the industry in 1979 while he worked as a store manager and then district manager for Rent-A-Center in Fort Worth, Texas. Ryan, on the other hand, came to the new venture from a different background, having been instrumental in forming Spectrum Control, Inc., a company that produced electronic components.

Like other rental-purchase stores, Rent-Way would offer its customers merchandise via weekly or monthly agreements. Agreements could be canceled at any time without penalty, and customers were offered the option to purchase merchandise at the end of a rental agreement. The store made its profit through mark-ups on merchandise. While the majority of Rent-Way's customers had little or no credit and very little cash-on-hand and found Rent-Way a financially convenient option, some were furnishing temporary or vacation homes only a few months a year, and some wished to test electronic equipment before purchasing it. While the store offered furniture, appliances, and jewelry, the bulk of its rental agreements were for home entertainment equipment. The average customer returned merchandise after 16 weeks, and most merchandise could be rented several times during its lifetime. Rent-Way did not charge its customers for normal wear and tear and sometimes offered free repairs. The store offered free pick up and delivery of merchandise.

Morgenstern and Ryan had ambitious plans for the company. They believed bigger was better and strove to capture a significant portion of the industry's market share. Since acquired stores generated a profit more quickly than newly opened stores, the company concentrated on acquisitions. By 1993, Rent-Way had 19 stores in three states and had completed its initial public offering (IPO) on the New York Stock Exchange. After the IPO, the company set a goal: to capture between six and ten percent of the estimated $4.4 billion rental-purchase industry by the year 2000.

Rapid Expansion in the Mid-1990s

In 1994, the company acquired DAMSL Corporation, which doubled the number of stores it owned from 20 to 40. The following year, Rent-Way purchased a 45-store chain from McKenzie Leasing Corporation. The McKenzie acquisition made Rent-Way the tenth largest rental-purchase company in the United States.

Rent-Way realized that in order to succeed in the competitive rental-purchase market, it needed to offer its customers outstanding service. The company's ''Welcome, Wanted, and Important'' program was one way it strove to set itself apart from the roughly 1,500 to 2,000 independently owned mom-and-pop rental-purchase shops throughout the country. ''We think it's critical that our customers feel satisfied by the products we offer and the treatment they receive,'' explained Morgenstern in *Management Review*. He added: ''In most service industries, customers who have limited purchasing power are viewed pejoratively. Rent-Way puts all its entry-level employees through an intensive 13-week program that puts a strong emphasis on customer service.'' Customers who experienced problems in Rent-Way stores could call headquarters using a special customer hotline (1-800-RENT-WAY) that rang through to the President's office. ''Out of 26,000 customers, we average about 15 calls a week,'' Morgenstern said in *Management Review*. The company also impressed its customers with its clean, well-stocked stores.

During this time, while acquisitions were fast and furious, Rent-Way focused on making its new employees as comfortable as its customers. Whenever Rent-Way acquired a new chain, it initiated a ''pal system,'' where management from Rent-Way stores visited new stores to make new employees feel welcome. Their aim was to develop a sense of loyalty rather than risk the usual mistrust that occurred when one company took over another. Explained Morgenstern in *Management Review,* ''We want to end up with the best of both cultures and we realize each company can learn from the other.''

Rent-Way employees were also allowed to take part in problem-solving task forces made up of three to five people.

Regional managers conducted regular meetings with store managers to make upper-level management aware of problems within the company. Upper-level management then organized employee task forces to solve each problem.

Rent-Way continued its breakneck pace in 1996 and 1997. In 1996, the company purchased the 11-store Diamond Leasing Corporation, which had stores in Delaware, Maryland, and Pennsylvania. The purchase expanded Rent-Way's portfolio to 104 stores. In January 1997, the company acquired the 70 store Rental King chain. The move was a good one for Rent-Way; Rental King stores were nearly as profitable as Rent-Way stores. A Rental King store typically earned $400,000 a year as compared to the $500,000 a typical Rent-Way store earned. Also in January, Rent-Way spent $6.7 million for Bill Coleman TV's 15 Michigan-based stores. In July, the company acquired R.A. Wolford, Inc., a four-store chain in Pennsylvania. Rent-Way paid an about ten times the target company's monthly revenue for each acquisition.

Rent-Way believed the smooth integration of its new stores was paramount to its success. Using its point-of-sale software, Rent-Way was able to get an acquisition's operating systems working with its own in a short period of time. ''The key to our success has been the way we assimilate companies into our organization,'' remarked CFO Jeffrey Conway in *Investors Business Daily*. ''We don't put the Rent-Way name on it until it's operating the way we like it,'' Conway said.

Further Growth in 1998 and 1999

Rent-Way continued its tremendous growth in 1998. In January, the company added 50 more stores to its portfolio when it purchased the South Carolina-based Ace T.V. Rentals; 46 of these stores were in South Carolina and four were in California.

In February, the company acquired the Daytona-based Champion Rentals. The 145 Champion Rental stores gave Rent-Way access to new markets in Alabama, Arkansas, and Georgia. In July, the Company acquired Fast Rentals, Inc., a rental purchase chain with six stores in Alabama and two in Georgia. In September, Rent-Way purchased Cari Rentals, a 23-store chain with stores in Iowa, Missouri, Nebraska, and South Dakota.

Also that month, Rent-Way entered into its largest purchase agreement ever, signing a merger agreement with Home Choice Holdings, Inc., an enormous chain with 459 stores in 26 states. The $330 million acquisition opened new markets for Rent-Way in 11 states including 100 Home Choice stores in Texas. Rent-Way kept the Home Choice name in newly renovated stores but planned to eventually switch to a single banner. Also in September 1998, *Fortune* magazine named Rent-Way the tenth fastest growing stock in America and the nation's 56th fastest growing company.

The acquisition program continued in 1999. In June of that year, Rent-Way purchased America's Rent-to-Own Center, a 21-store chain in Arkansas, Kansas, Missouri, and Oklahoma with revenues of $18. Later in the year, Rent-Way purchased rival RentaVision for $250 million. RentaVision had 250 stores.

Reaching Goals in 2000

Since Rent-Way's IPO in August 1993, the company had more than tripled its size and had exceeded its goal of capturing six to ten percent of the industry's market share. As of 1999, it had 11 percent of the estimated $4.4 billion rental-purchase market.

In 2000, the company planned to roll out new products and services, including prepaid telephone service and computers. Toward that end, in January 2000, Rent-Way acquired a 49 percent interest in DPI Teleconnect, a privately held provider of prepaid local phone service. Rent-Way agreed to acquire an additional 21 percent interest upon receipt of regulatory approvals. DPI was licensed to offer prepaid local phone service in 21 states and had planned to expand to over 40 states by the end of 2000. DPI provided service to customers who could not afford the fees required by their local telephone service. While DPI was only one year old, it already had 14,000 customers who were paying about $50 a month for the prepaid phone service. Both DPI and Rent-Way felt the partnership was a good one: about six million households in the United Sates were wired for phone service but did not have it; a significant portion of these homes were near Rent-Way stores.

Commenting on DPI's mission, David Dorwart, company president, said in press release that "Historically individuals who for whatever reason could not meet the credit or deposit requirements of the local phone company have done without a phone. The service DPI offers provides them with access to local phone service, 911, and the Internet. Partnering with Rent-Way will allow DPI to grow more quickly and become a leader in the prepaid local phone service industry." Rent-Way would receive the benefit of extra traffic in its locations as well as ten percent commission from the sale of DPI's service. Rent-Way's investment in DPI was expected to total $7.5 million.

Around the same time, Rent-Way negotiated a deal with Compaq to rent computers to customers on a 15-month contract. Rent-Way paid $950 per Compaq computer and was hoping to negotiate a similar deal with Dell Computer. The company's computer rentals were successful from the start. "We are very optimistic about the potential of bringing computers to our customer base in a much bigger way in the months and years ahead," Conway said in a February 14, 2000 news release. Conway, who was formerly vice-president and chief financial officer of Rent-Way, was promoted to president of the company in January 2000. As it approached a new century Rent-Way looked towards increasing its annual sales to the $1 billion mark.

Principal Competitors

Rent-A-Center, Inc.; Aaron Rents, Inc.; Bestway, Inc.

Further Reading

Breskin, Ira, "Rent-Way Tackles Its Market Through Streak of Acquisitions," *Investor's Daily,* September 5, 1997.

"How a Winning Strategy Helps Pay the Rent," *Management Review,* October 1995, p. S4.

Milite, George, "Short-Term Teams Yield Long-Term Results," *Supervisory Management,* September 1995, p. 7.

Pachuta, Michael J., "Rent-Way Gobbles Up Rivals to Double Its Market Share," *Investor's Business Daily,* May 6, 1998.

"Rent-Way and Home Choice Merging," *Consumer Electronics,* September 14, 1998.

"Rent-Way Completes Acquisition of 70 Rental Purchase Stores and Issues $20 Million of Convertible Subordinated Debentures," *Business Wire,* February 6, 1977.

"Rent-Way Completes Merger with Home Choice; Enters Into New Credit Facility," *PR Newswire,* December 10, 1998, p. 7282.

"Rent-Way, Continuing Breakneck," *Television Digest,* January 12, 1998, p.17.

"Rent-Way, Inc. Acquires Twenty-One Store Chain," *PR Newswire,* June 30, 1999, p.2992.

"Rent-Way Inc. Acquires Twenty-Three Store Chain," *PR Newswire,* September 10, 1998.

"Rent-Way Stock Offering," *Television Digest,* April 29, 1996, p. 20.

—Tracey Vasil Biscontini

Roy F. Weston, Inc.

1 Weston Way
West Chester, Pennsylvania 19380
U.S.A.
Telephone: (610) 701-3000
Fax: (610) 701-3186
Web site: http://www.rfweston.com

Public Company
Incorporated: 1957
Employees: 1,650
Sales: $147.8 million (1999)
Stock Exchanges: NASDAQ
Ticker Symbol: WSTNA
NAIC: 54133 Engineering Services; 54171 Research &
    Development in the Physical, Engineering, & Life
    Sciences; 54138 Testing Laboratories

Roy F. Weston, Inc. provides a range of environmental consulting, design, engineering, and construction services designed to solve problems associated with air, water, and land pollution; hazardous material and toxic waste treatment and disposal; workplace hazards; product use; and energy conservation. Its main focus is on infrastructure redevelopment, which it defines as bringing facilities, land, buildings, and other resources that have been environmentally compromised back to profitable use. Weston's clients include private industry, federal agencies, and state, city, and county governments. The company operates through a network of 60 offices located throughout the United States, as well as offices in Europe, Latin America, and Asia.

Founding and Early Growth in the 1950s and 1960s

Roy Weston acquired an interest in the earth and its ecosystems at an early age. As a child growing up in Reedsburg, Wisconsin, the budding environmentalist spent much of his time outdoors, engaged in pursuits such as fishing and hunting. By the time he enrolled in the University of Wisconsin, he was already considering a career that would keep him involved in environmental issues. Choosing a major in civil engineering and a minor in sanitary engineering, Weston graduated from Wisconsin in 1933. He then continued his education, studying public health engineering at the University of Minnesota before completing a master's degree in civil engineering at New York University in 1939.

Fresh out of college, Weston was hired by the Philadelphia-based Atlantic Refining Co. as an industrial pollution control engineer. Because the concept of environmental responsibility was just then becoming an issue for U.S. industry, such positions were virtually unheard of. Weston was only the second industrial pollution control engineer in the nation.

Weston stayed at Atlantic Refining for 16 years. By 1949, however, he was already laying the foundation for his own business by taking on consulting work in his spare time. In 1951 he merged his sideline consulting business with that of two other environmental consultants: Wes Eckenfelder and John Hood, of Ridgewood, New Jersey.

In 1955 Weston left his position at Atlantic Refining to concentrate completely on his and his partners' consulting business. Two years later, he bought out Eckenfelder and Hood and established the consulting firm of Roy F. Weston, Inc. At that time, the company consisted of a staff of ten and had its offices in Newtown Square, Pennsylvania, just west of Philadelphia. Its main focus was on the biological treatment of industrial wastewater.

In the early 1960s, a recession put the brakes on traditional industrial wastewater business, leading Weston to expand its client base by tapping the public sector. The resulting infusion of new government clients catapulted the company into a period of rapid growth. By the mid-1960s, with 62 employees, Weston had outgrown its space in Newtown Square. It moved to a 53-acre estate in West Chester, Pennsylvania, which had been built in the 19th century by attorney and environmentalist John F. Lewis. In 1967, with revenues climbing near $2 million, Weston opened regional offices in Illinois and Georgia. By 1969, the company had a staff of almost 200 and had opened two more regional offices—in New York and Texas. That same year, Weston made its first public stock offering, generating capital for even greater expansion.

Company Perspectives:

The mission of Roy F. Weston, Inc. is to assist clients and customers in defining, anticipating, and avoiding or solving health and safety, environmental quality, and resource sustainability problems and achieving greater economic efficiency through application of the principles of natural economics and sustainable development. Be known as a leader in providing professional services and business means, that enhances value for its principal stakeholders: clients, shareholders, employees, and business providers, affiliates, and partners.

Increasing Awareness and Rapid Growth in the 1970s

The 1970s were a time of tremendous growth in the environmental consulting and engineering industries. In 1970 President Richard Nixon created the Environmental Protection Agency (EPA), charging it with the mission of protecting human health and safeguarding the natural environment—air, water, and land—upon which life depended. The EPA's role included finding ways to clean up and prevent pollution, ensuring compliance and enforcement of environmental laws, assisting states in environmental protection efforts, and raising the public's awareness and understanding of environmental issues. The formation of this new agency set the stage for sweeping changes in U.S. environmental regulation.

Throughout the 1970s, the EPA created programs and proposed legislation designed to clean up the air and the water. The decade's environmental initiatives included setting new standards for auto emissions; phasing out the use of lead in gasoline; limiting industrial water pollution; banning the use of various toxic substances in manufacturing and farming; and establishing standards for the treatment of the public drinking water supply. Under the Resource Conservation and Recovery Act of 1976, the EPA also began establishing controls over the generation, transportation, treatment, storage, and disposal of hazardous waste.

As the environmental movement picked up steam, Weston's business also grew. Although the company's original focus had been on wastewater cleanup, the growing concern over other types of pollution led the company to broaden its range of services. It rapidly moved into new fields, including air pollution controls, solid waste management, and the treatment and disposal of hazardous materials.

The decade was also a time of tremendous geographic growth for Weston. In 1970 the company established a European subsidiary, Weston Europe S.p.A., in Milan. The following year saw the opening of an office in Kobe, Japan. The company also established a research and development lab and in-plant pollution control services unit at its Pennsylvania facility.

In the mid-1970s, Weston sold its newly formed European subsidiary and focused more intently on building up its domestic business. From 1973 to 1976, the company opened facilities in seven new states: Virginia, Maryland, New Mexico, Alabama, Tennessee, California, and Louisiana. It also expanded

via the acquisition of four environmental engineering and consulting firms: Phillip Steel & Associates, Battaille Associates, Trygve Hoff & Associates, and Environmental Engineers, Inc., of Concord, New Hampshire. Weston's expansion rapidly swelled its gross earnings; between 1974 and 1976, the company's revenues grew from $10 million to $15 million.

Roy Weston, who was by then in his late 60s, had already turned the company's day-to-day operations over to a younger management team. By the end of the 1970s, however, the company was suffering from growing pains—and Weston grew dissatisfied with his managers' performance. After firing two different presidents in two years' time, the spirited founder recaptured control of his company, taking its daily operations back into his own hands. In 1979 Weston and his family bought out the company's shareholders, returning it to private ownership status.

Superfund Business in the 1980s

With the advent of the 1980s, Roy Weston began preparing again to transfer control of the company to a successor. In 1980 he appointed his two sons-in-law, A. Frederick Thompson and Thomas Swoyer, to top-level positions. Swoyer, who held a degree in air pollution control, became the company's president and chief operating officer. Thompson, with a Ph.D. in civil engineering, became executive vice-president of quality assurance and finance.

The year 1980 was also significant to the company, because it marked the passage of the federal Superfund legislation. The Superfund Act—more properly known as the Comprehensive Environmental Response, Compensation, and Liability Act—addressed the identification and remediation of hazardous waste sites. The law authorized the EPA to compel responsible parties to clean up the abandoned sites. It also provided a $1.6 billion federal fund for site remediation in the event that the responsible parties could not be identified or located or failed to act.

The establishment of this federal remediation fund meant that millions of dollars were suddenly earmarked for spending on hazardous waste disposal—providing tremendous opportunities for environmental consulting and engineering firms. Weston wasted no time taking advantage of the new legislation. In 1981 the company became one of the nation's first Superfund contractors. It would go on to win more than $500 million in EPA contracts for Superfund site cleanups by the end of the decade.

The Superfund legislation also created more nongovernment work for the company. As the EPA pressured private industry to clean up its act, more and more companies turned to firms like Weston to help them solve their waste disposal problems. By 1987, the company's client list included a full half of the Fortune 500 companies. Private sector contracts accounted for approximately 45 percent of total revenues that same year.

Part of Weston's success during this time was due to its being one of only a few companies offering such a comprehensive range of services. Whereas many pollution-control firms specialized in only certain types of pollutants or solutions, Weston's capabilities were broad and multifocal. ''We were in on this from the very beginning, and we aren't tied to any particular solution,'' Weston explained in a September 1987

Key Dates:

1939: Roy F. Weston takes job as pollution control engineer with Atlantic Refining Co.
1949: Weston begins doing environmental consulting work on the side.
1955: Weston leaves Atlantic Refining to focus on consulting full time.
1957: Roy F. Weston, Inc. is established.
1969: With offices in five states and a staff of 200, Weston goes public.
1979: Company's performance flags; Weston emerges from semi-retirement to take over; Weston family takes company private again.
1981: Weston becomes one of nation's first Superfund contractors.
1986: Company makes one million share public offering.
1991: Roy Weston retires; Frederick Thompson becomes chairman, and William Marrazzo becomes CEO.
1997: Marrazzo resigns, is replaced by William Robertson.

interview with the *Philadelphia Inquirer,* adding "We have in-depth knowledge in many fields."

Another reason for Weston's ascension was its focus on and use of new technologies. More than two-thirds of the company's employees had a background in either science or engineering, and such a technically proficient work force created a fertile environment for research and development. By the late 1980s, Weston had developed two new thermal-based systems for treating contaminated waste. The first was the Transportable Incineration System, a portable incinerator used to burn material contaminated with PCBs and other pollutants. The second was the Low-Temperature Thermal Treatment System, a patented device that used heat to drive volatile materials out of soil.

Not surprisingly, Weston's sudden influx of public and private business fueled a major growth spurt in the mid-1980s. In the years between 1982 and 1987, the company's revenues more than quadrupled, growing from $22.2 million to $98.7 million. Earnings increased from $315,000 to $2.7 million during the same time span. To accommodate the growing business, Weston expanded into new facilities in new locations, adding a dozen new offices and hundreds of employees. It also made four new acquisitions: Peer Systems, Inc., Charles R. Velzy Associates, Inc., Gulf Coast Laboratories, Illinois, and ATC Incorporated.

In the middle of its frenzied expansion, Weston went public again, making in 1986 a public offering of one million shares priced at $12.50 per share. Despite bringing new shareholders into the mix, Weston and his family retained tight control of the company. The stock offered to the public carried only one-tenth of the voting power of the regular common stock—which was owned by the company's officers and directors.

Although the late 1980s were a time of corporate success, they also marked a personal tragedy for the Weston family and a change in leadership for the company. In late 1989, Thomas Swoyer, Roy Weston's son-in-law and the company's chief operating officer, died at the age of 42. He was replaced by William Marrazzo, who had joined Weston in 1988 after serving eight years as Philadelphia's water commissioner.

The 1990s

By 1990, Weston had more than 2,500 employees, 49 offices in 25 states and the District of Columbia, and revenues of around $224 million. It was ranked as the third largest environmental consulting firm in the nation by the *Engineering News Record.* With the company seemingly poised for continued success, Roy Weston retired. His son-in-law, A. Frederick Thompson, became the company's chairman, and Marrazzo became its CEO.

Unfortunately, the change in leadership coincided with a reversal in the environmental industry. In the early 1990s, the government cut back on the enforcement of hazardous waste cleanup regulations—and the annual growth rate in environmental consulting fell from 30 percent to five percent. The overall softening of the industry sent Weston's earnings into a steady decline. The company's gross revenues fell from $330 million in 1992 to $176.5 million in 1996. Although it lowered costs by cutting jobs, Weston was unable to compensate for the precipitous drop in revenues and, in 1996, posted a net loss of $16.7 million.

The company's downturn was serious enough to bring Roy Weston out of retirement. In March 1996, the 85-year-old Weston removed his son-in-law from the chairman's seat and took over the position himself. He held the seat for only five months before resigning it again, however, saying that he wanted to focus on long-term strategy. Weston's next move was to hire Patrick McCann as the new vice-president of strategic development. McCann, who previously had worked for the hazardous waste disposal subsidiary of WMX Technologies, Inc., was charged with drafting a plan to turn the faltering company around.

The company's new plan centered around becoming less dependent upon government contract work and more focused on private industry. Implementation was slow, however, and the company continued to struggle, finishing 1996 with a net loss of $16.7 million. By spring of 1997, the Weston family, who controlled 62 percent of the company's voting power, was convinced that major changes were required to bring the company back to profitability. In early May, the family told the company's board of directors that they were unhappy with the strategy to move away from government work. They also put together a slate of opposition board candidates, in preparation for the next shareholder vote.

Before it reached the voting stage, however, Weston's five outside directors resigned their positions. The departing directors were replaced with the Weston family's earlier-chosen candidates—all of whom had close ties to Washington and to government agencies that had traditionally been Weston clients. Shortly after the Westons orchestrated the change of directors, the company's president and CEO, Marrazzo, tendered his resignation. "My decision to resign as president and CEO of the company results from my belief that, since the incoming board intends to redefine the company strategy, it is in the best interest of the company for the board to have maximum flexibility in that effort and to begin with a clean slate,'' he said in a May 1997 interview with the *Philadelphia Business Journal.* Weston's chief operating officer and chief financial officer also resigned.

Marrazzo was replaced by William Robertson, the chairman of a small Virginia-based software development company. Patrick McCann, the vice-president of strategic development who had been hired in 1996, was appointed chief operating officer. By the end of 1997, the company had revised its strategy and was ready to begin implementing it. The revamped strategy involved moving away from traditional low-growth environmental services and emphasizing new high-margin, high-growth areas. As such, the company's main focus became infrastructure redevelopment—bringing facilities, land, and other resources that had been environmentally compromised back to profitable use—for both public and private sector clients.

Weston returned to profitability in 1998, and remained profitable throughout 1999. It finished up the year with net revenues of $147.8 million, compared with $140.4 million for 1998. Profits for 1999 were $988,000—up from $858,000 for 1998.

Looking Ahead

Weston believed that its improvements in 1998 and 1999 were proof of the viability of its new direction. ''For the first time since 1995, Weston's annual net revenues increased, and for the second consecutive year, contract bookings showed steady improvement,'' Robertson said in a February 3, 2000 press release. ''This confirms our business strategy focused on the infrastructure redevelopment market is working.'' Assuming continued gains in revenues and profits, it seemed likely that the company would continue to pursue the strategy it implemented in late 1997.

Principal Subsidiaries

Weston International; Roy F. Weston of New York, Inc.

Principal Competitors

Bechtel Group, Inc.; Brown and Caldwell; Commodore Applied Technologies, Inc.; EA Engineering, Science, and Technology, Inc.; Ecology and Environment, Inc.; ECOS Group, Inc.; Harding Lawson Associates Group, Inc.; The Keith Companies, Inc.; Montgomery Watson; NSC Corporation; Sevenson Environmental Services, Inc.; Superior Services, Inc.; Tetra Tech, Inc.; TRC Companies, Inc.; United Water Resources; URS Corporation.

Further Reading

Binzen, Peter, ''Where Environmental Concern Hasn't Gone to Waste,'' *Philadelphia Inquirer,* October 29, 1990, p. D03.
Bivens, Terry, ''Roy F. Weston Inc. Turns Poisons of Environment into Blossoming Profits,'' *Philadelphia Inquirer,* p. C01.
Sczubelek, Suzanne, ''A Pioneer To Hand Over Reins: Leaving Top Post at Environmental Firm,'' *Philadelphia Inquirer,* August 18, 1991, p. C06.
Warner, Susan, and Andrea Knox, ''Founder Comes Back to Revitalize Foundering Environmental Firm,'' *Philadelphia Inquirer,* June 1, 1997, p. D1.
Weber, Maura, ''Corporate Coup Rocks Weston,'' *Philadelphia Business Journal,* May 30, 1997, p. 1.
''Weston Announces New Plans, Directors,'' *Business Wire,* November 9, 1997.

—Shawna Brynildssen

Rush Communications

530 Seventh Avenue
New York, New York 10018
U.S.A.
Telephone: (212) 840-9390
Fax: (212) 840-9390

Private Company
Incorporated: 1990
Employees: 150
Sales: $70 million (1998 est.)
NAIC: 51211 Motion Picture and Video Production;
51312 Television Broadcasting; 54181 Advertising
Agencies

Rush Communications is the most successful African American-owned media company in the United States, operating divisions in far-ranging segments of the entertainment industry, from advertising (Rush Media) to film (Def Pictures) and television (Russell Simmons Television). Rush was founded by Russell Simmons, a native of Queens, New York, and has grown in barely more than one decade to a company of national prominence, and one that not only successfully markets "hip-hop" culture to consumers, but helps to define it as well. An original founder of the phenomenally successful hip-hop label Def Jam Records, Simmons and his company are focused on the continued popularity and growth of marketable urban culture in all its forms. Although Simmons sold his ownership of Def Jam Records in 1999, his company continues to project itself as one with its antecedents firmly rooted in an African American ethos.

The Making of a Promoter:
Russell Simmons and Def Jam in the Early 1980s

Growing up in a solidly upper-middle class African American neighborhood in Queens, New York, Simmons was the son of a college professor and was not exposed to the music that would so alter his life until his freshman year at New York's City College in 1977. At that time, hip-hop had yet to be known as any sort of coherent or definable musical form, but its beginnings were already in place: the sounds of Funkadelic, James Brown, and Al

Green had popularized a new type of African American music, and small shows in which such music was played began cropping up in cities around the country. Simmons became instantly enamored with not only funk music, but the entire lifestyle—hip, edgy, and urban—such music represented, and he began frequenting New York clubs and parties to scout out new talent. As his knowledge of the music increased, Simmons recognized both an economic and artistic opportunity and began promoting small bands and shows around the New York area. Simmons proved to be a shrewd promoter, with a keen taste for what would and would not appeal, and within a couple of years he had turned to promotion full-time.

During this time Simmons became acquainted with Rick Rubin, a wealthy, young Long Island native attending New York University. Although he was not African American, Rubin had become deeply involved in the underground funk music scene and had started recording and producing local African American funk bands, using his NYU dorm as his studio. In 1979 Rubin founded Def Jam Records, using his family's money for backing, and was soon a ubiquitous presence at downtown clubs and shows. Rubin and Simmons, though from different backgrounds, were fast friends, and in 1983 Simmons joined Rubin as an equal partner in Def Jam.

Between the year in which Def Jam was created and the year Simmons joined as its partner rap music had begun to supplant the popularity of funk. Lyrics, some with a decidedly subversive, political edge, began to be spoken and rhymed instead of simply sung, and the instruments traditionally associated with popular music were usurped by record players and recording instruments that allowed a musician to splice and intersperse prerecorded tracks with his own voice. Rubin was especially quick to pick up on this trend, and he began seeking out rap acts to record for Def Jam.

Def Jam's First Successes:
The Mid-1980s to the Early 1990s

In 1985 Def Jam produced its first recording that reached rap fans across the country and helped the label reach regional and, eventually, national prominence. That year, the label produced

Curtis Blow's "Christmas Rap," which sold more than 50,000 copies, and made Def Jam a small but potentially powerful presence in the burgeoning rap industry. In addition to selling well, "Christmas Rap" caught the eye of CBS Records (a company bought a few years later by Sony Records), which, in an effort to keep current on urban, youth-oriented trends, offered to Def Jam a $600,000 distribution deal the following year. The offer was an enviable one by industry standards and gave Def Jam exclusive control over production, while CBS picked up the tab for marketing and distribution costs. The contract followed industry standards, however, in that CBS Records received all of the profits from Def Jam's efforts, with the latter receiving a set percentage of royalty payments.

In 1986 Def Jam premiered LL Cool J, an artist who was to become one of the label's most successful and ground-breaking acts. Only 17 years old at the time, LL Cool J epitomized the type of swaggering charisma and overt sexuality embraced by hip-hop artists, and within a year of signing with Def Jam he had skyrocketed to international fame. That year the label produced LL Cool J's version of the famous Aerosmith song "Walk This Way"—the video which is considered by some in the industry to be one of the best in musical history—and in doing so became a label of national recognition.

Soon after the success of LL Cool J, Def Jam began promoting the talents of three white Jewish boys from the Bronx—an incongruous trio in the world of rap—who were to become known as the Beastie Boys. The Beastie Boys' album "Licensed to Ill" created a national sensation and helped to make rap almost as popular in the white community as more traditional forms of rock.

Although the Beastie Boys and LL Cool J made free use of obscenities and, to some critics, misogynistic imagery, the two acts were fairly innocuous in their commentary on contemporary racial and economic issues. Def Jam, however, was not one to shy away from pushing the envelope, no matter who might be offended, and in 1990 began producing the controversial band Public Enemy. Led by the articulate and outspoken Chuck D., Public Enemy made headlines not only in the entertainment section of national newspapers; overtly political, and still more

overtly angry, the band grabbed the attention of politicians and community leaders and became for some a symbol of violence and racial separatism. In addition, although even African American radio stations refused to play tracks from the band's album "Apocalypse '91," the release sold more than 500,000 copies in five days, making it one of the most successful rap albums ever produced. Def Jam, like its West Coast competitor Death Row Records, had by the early 1990s turned risk-taking into profit, with the company's revenue in 1991 totaling out at upwards of $34 million.

Such profit, however, did not come without compromise: without the financial backing of CBS, Def Jam had limited influence in the music industry, and its reliance on the major label made the company inherently less autonomous, in both the development of its artists and image, than it would be had it remained independent. The issue of independence—one that became increasingly important to the hip-hop industry throughout the 1990s—eventually became an untenable problem between Simmons and his partner Rick Rubin, and by 1990 the two had parted ways, with Simmons and CBS retaining control over Def Jam.

Simmons Branches Out: The Development of Rush Communications in the Early 1990s

After proving himself as a shrewd businessman in the music industry, and one who was capable of catering to the traditional needs of the financial world while simultaneously projecting a street-wise, youthful image, Simmons turned his focus to other areas of the entertainment industry. In the early 1990s the entrepreneur began developing several projects in different areas, all of which were controlled by an umbrella company called Rush Communications. The name was so chosen because "Rush" was Simmons's nickname from childhood and well reflected the pace at which he moved.

In 1991 Simmons's company joined forces with veteran Hollywood producers Bernie Brillstein and Brad Grey, and together the three men created the wildly popular "Def Comedy Jam" for HBO. The show initially consisted of eight half hour programs, each of which highlighted a young up-and-coming African American comedian. The show, which was hosted by Martin Lawrence, was so successful that HBO renewed the program's contract the following year for an additional 22 episodes. Paid $2 million for its efforts, Rush Communications managed to produce the episodes for less than $600,000; a handsome profit indeed for a television novice's first production effort. Proving itself popular on television also established that the image and urban culture Simmons wished to market went beyond the music industry and could be developed and exhibited and, therefore, sold in a myriad of contexts.

In the early 1990s, it became increasingly evident that what was becoming known as hip-hop culture had a definite appeal in the apparel market. Young men and women in growing numbers were imitating the looks they saw during hip-hop shows and videos: suddenly baggy, low-waisted pants, tight "baby tees" with prominent logos, and loose-fitting jackets were being seen in cities around the country. Simmons was not long in turning this trend to his company's advantage and began in 1993 to produce a small line of clothing called Phat Farm.

Initially sold in one boutique in New York, Phat Farm was an immediate success. The line was kept limited, with only one designer producing a few basic pieces, each of which carried prominently the Phat Farm logo, but within its first year of operation the label brought in about $2 million. Because of Simmons's connections within the music and entertainment industry, stars from Def Jam and television alike began to wear the label to public functions, and soon Phat Farm began to gain national attention.

Only one year after Phat Farm's inception the label began to be picked up at specialty stores around the country. Soon, Phat Farm became the brand of choice for young, fashion-conscious club-goers. Initially worn primarily by men, the brand branched out into women's apparel under the name Baby Phat, producing inexpensive, body-conscious pieces that were intended for casual day and evening wear.

The middle of the decade saw many changes for Rush Communications. In 1995 the company's most prominent operation, Def Jam Records, was sold in part to Poly Gram Entertainment, leaving Rush with a 40 percent ownership. That year, too, Rush had its first real success in film production, creating four films in one year, including the Eddie Murphy hit "The Nutty Professor." Far from believing himself spread too thin, Simmons soon thereafter started another company division, called Rush Media, which focused on print and television advertisement. During the next couple of years, Rush Media produced ads for such companies as Coke, HBO, and ESPN.

Rush Communications by the middle of the 1990s had branched out into almost every facet of the media industry and was by all appearances proving itself successful in whatever it endeavored to accomplish. Simmons, with his boundless energy and seemingly endless connections, controlled personally each of Rush's new operations and possessed the uncanny ability to appear present everywhere at once. Simmons's secret to growth seemed bound up in a threefold strategy by which the entrepreneur first sought out high-powered mentors with a great amount of expertise in one segment of an industry, next used this mentor to establish contacts on both the artistic and financial end of a business, and then actively courted partners who already had clout within the industry. Simmons utilized this method in his initial involvement in the music industry, and in television, film, and media production, as well as clothing design, making Rush Communications by the late 1990s the most visible African American-owned company in the country.

Rush Takes a Gamble: The Sale of Def Jam and Further Expansion in the Late 1990s

Although in the latter part of the 1990s Rush continued to receive the majority of its profits from Def Jam Records, with the label bringing in about 60 percent of the company's revenue, Simmons was restless, eager to focus on a broader array of operations. His clothing line, which after only two years in business was being distributed nationally to department and specialty stores, was doing particularly well at the time, with 1997 sales totaling out at upward of $10 million. In addition, Simmons had begun a television show and magazine called *Oneworld,* which devoted itself to every aspect of urban youth culture, and the two were gaining in popularity. The television show was especially trendy, as it was hosted by a popular Japanese American model named Kimora Lee, who later became Simmons's wife in a high-profile ceremony in 1998.

In 1999, after months of negotiation, Rush sold its 40 percent ownership of Def Jam to Seagram's Universal Music, leaving the company—and Simmons—free to focus on its other operations. The sale caused some industry experts and Def Jam fans to speculate about Simmons's sway in the hip-hop music world, but through careful publicity and the development of other projects the company continued to maintain its reputation as an industry leader, with 1998 sales at $70 million.

Principal Competitors

EMI Group plc; Time Warner Inc.; Universal Studios, Inc.

Further Reading

Dingle, Derek, ''Lessons from the Top,'' *Black Enterprise,* May 1999, p. 101.

Muhammad, Tariq, ''The Real Lowdown on Labels,'' *Black Enterprise,* December 1995, p. 74.

Simpson, Janice, ''The Impresario of Rap,'' *Time,* May 4, 1992, p. 69.

Smith, Eric, ''Hip-hoppreneurs,'' *Black Enterprise,* December 1997, p. 66.

Vaughn, Christopher, ''Russell Simmons' Rush for Profits,'' *Black Enterprise,* December 1992, p. 66.

Webb, Veronica, ''Happy Birthday to 'Huge Hefner','' *Interview,* November 1995, p. 72.

—Rachel H. Martin

Sabena S.A./N.V.

Avenue Mounierlaan, 2
1200 Brussels
Belgium
Telephone: 32 (2) 723 31 11
Fax: 32 (2) 723 87 08
Web Site: http://www.sabena.com

State-Owned Company
Incorporated: 1923 as Société Anonyme Belge
   d'Exploitation de la Navigation Aérienne
Employees: 10,600
Sales: BFr 86.8 billion ($2.1 billion) (1998)
NAIC: 481111 Scheduled Passenger Air Transportation;
   481112 Scheduled Freight Air Transportation; 481211
   Nonscheduled Chartered Passenger Air
   Transportation; 48819 Other Support Activities for
   Air Transportation

Sabena S.A./N.V. has become Europe's fastest growing airline on the strength of speedy connections through Brussels, the "capital of Europe." Its base sees a steady stream of European diplomats and NATO emissaries. Also strong in former colonies in Africa, Sabena carries nine million passengers a year. The company is 49.5 percent owned by Swissair, with the remaining shares being held by the Belgian government and other interests. Its management structure is complicated by a power-sharing arrangement between its Flemish and French-speaking factions. Flying for more than 75 years, Sabena is one of the world's oldest airlines.

Colonial Origins

Belgian civil air transportation has its origins in SNETA, the National Society for the Study of Air Transport, founded in 1919. SNETA ferried passengers to neighboring capitals on primitive planes left over from World War I. Société Anonyme Belge d'Exploitation de la Navigation Aérienne— S.A.B.E.N.A. for short—replaced SNETA in 1923.

Sabena flew the three-engined civil transports of the day. Its first official service was to the United Kingdom via Brussels-Ostend-Lympne, and its first scheduled passenger route connected Brussels and Strasbourg in 1924. The next year, it sent pilot Edmond Thieffry on a 51 day flight (75 hours in the air) to Leopoldville (Kinshasa) in the Belgian Congo, where Sabena then began to build a local route network. In ten years, Sabena was operating scheduled flights on the Brussels-Leopoldville route.

World War II interrupted civil aviation throughout Europe. After the war, Sabena took wing under chairman Gilbert Périer. In 1947, the Brussels-New York route, flown by new DC-4s, was added to Sabena's long-haul international routes. Sabena also operated the ubiquitous Convair in the 1950s. In the next two decades, the carrier would bring in state-of-the-art jets such as the Caravelle and the Boeing 707 and 747.

Employment reached 10,000 in 1957. Overstaffed and undercapitalized, Sabena finally instituted a restructuring in 1968. In 1969, Sabena added a Vienna-Brussels-New York route in conjunction with Austrian Airlines.

The 1970s–80s

In spite of its new fiscal discipline, the oil crises of the 1970s and fierce transatlantic price competition from newly deregulated U.S. carriers hit Sabena hard. Chairman Carlos Van Rafelghem oversaw yet another restructuring. Workforce reduction and wage controls were combined with an infusion of new capital from the government. The company was also divided into subsidiaries. Sabena's balance sheet improved for a few years following these moves.

In the early 1970s, there was talk of combining Sabena with KLM and Luxair to form Benelux Airlines, but these plans were scrapped. Subsequent merger talks with Scandinavian Airlines System (SAS) were also unproductive, and Sabena remained an independent airline.

In 1989, the carrier shortened its name from Sabena Belgian World Airlines to Sabena World Airlines or SWA. It sought to

Company Perspectives:

Our mission is to serve airline customers safely, punctually and profitably from the heart of Europe. Our vision is to grow worldwide as a sustained profitable airline Group by exceeding cost effectively the needs of our customers, leveraging our partnerships and developing our people.

become identified as an airline dedicated to the European Community, and toward that end exploited its uncrowded Brussels hub, connecting underserved, secondary markets such as Bristol, Nuremberg, and Lyon.

In December 1989, KLM and British Airways (BA) announced they would each take 20 percent stakes in SWA at a cost of $55 million (£33 million) each. Sabena planned to nearly double its fleet of 35 planes within five years to meet the conditions of the pact. However, protests by British Midland and Belgian charter carrier Trans European Airways caught the ear of the European Commission and the British Monopolies and Mergers Commission. Sabena was already operating in the red, and in September 1990 management asked the Belgian government for help meeting a cash crisis. This, along with the unfavorable regulatory climate, conspired to kill the BA/KLM deal.

Crisis in the 1990s

Civil airlines worldwide were hurt by the Persian Gulf War, high fuel costs, and a global recession. At the end of 1990, Sabena's new chairman Pierre Godfroid, who came to Sabena from his position as head of Campbell Soup Co.'s European operations, had the responsibility of restructuring the company and readying it for privatization. His plan cut 2,500 of 11,000 jobs over three years. Management techniques were refined along total quality management (TQM) lines. Sabena unveiled a new corporate identity in the early 1990s, beckoning patrons to "enjoy" the company. Employees did not enjoy the austerity measures, however, resulting in a few strikes.

The carrier's search for a new investment partner finally brought it to Air France, with whom it signed a cooperative pact in April 1992. The Belgian holding company Finacta invested BFr 6 billion, including Air France's capital. The Belgian government added another BFr 9 billion, raising Sabena's total capital to 16 billion.

Although traffic rose in 1994, tough competition prevented Sabena from enjoying a profit. It lost $125.6 million on sales of $1.2 billion. Political and economic problems in Africa contributed to weaker than expected business there.

Air France withdrew its investment in 1994. Its partnership with Sabena could not stop the tide of red ink at either airline. However, in May 1995, Swissair moved to broaden its cooperation with Sabena in all areas of operations. On July 25, SAirGroup, Swissair's parent, acquired 49.5 percent of Sabena's shares for BFr 10.5 billion. Sabena group achieved turnover of BFr 59 million and a passenger count of five million in 1995. Cargo volumes swelled as well. However, both Sabena and Swissair suffered serious losses.

A pact between KLM and Northwest Airlines, given unprecedented antitrust immunity in 1992, sparked a series of alliances that would divvy up most North Atlantic traffic between four main airline groupings within a few years. Sabena partnered with Delta Air Lines on such routes, beginning with Brussels-Atlanta where two carriers jointly staffed an aircraft. The code-sharing was later extended to a few of Sabena's German destinations. Other partners in Delta's "Atlantic Excellence" program included Swissair and Austrian Airlines.

Sabena seized a couple of point-to-point opportunities from Bologna created by European deregulation. It operated charter flights through its Sobelair subsidiary while Delta Air Transport served as its regional airline. Sabena partnered with the budget carrier Virgin Express (51 percent owned by Virgin Atlantic but based in Brussels) on a Brussels-London route. It had also added code-share agreements with Tyrolean Airways and Finnair. A code share with TAP Air Portugal extended Sabena's reach to Macau. The company bought a 49.5 percent stake in Air Zaire in 1996.

Godfroid, along with two other executives, resigned abruptly in March 1996 in a period of labor turmoil. He had proposed scrapping existing labor agreements following their expiration, sparking a crippling series of strikes. Paul Reutlinger, Swissair's marketing vice-president, was immediately appointed CEO. *Air Transport World* reported the carrier's payroll accounted for 40 percent of operating costs, nearly twice that of the profit leader British Airways.

Striking pilots were brought back on-line by the threat of Swissair abandoning its $207 million investment in Sabena. The pilots had objected to raising yearly flying time from 625 hours to 650. Their strike only lasted a few hours. Otherwise, SAirGroup aimed to acquire a 62.5 percent controlling interest by 2001, if it could overcome European Union (EU) ownership restrictions, as Switzerland was not an EU member.

Sabena found a needed bargain in the fall of 1996 when it joined Swissair and Austrian Airlines in a $1 billion order for nine Airbus A330 widebody jets. All three planned to expand their alliance with Delta Air Lines to unprecedented levels of cooperation. Still, Sabena realized huge financial losses in 1996 with below-average traffic growth and load factors. Restructuring charges compounded the losses. Revenues were BFr 56.8 billion ($1.5 billion). Its 60 planes carried 5.2 million passengers and 113,000 metric tons of cargo.

Recovery in 1997

Passenger traffic and productivity increased handsomely during the first half of 1997, the beginning of a recovery. The company thinned its long-haul fleet to reduce operating costs. By 2000, it planned to unload its Boeing 747s in favor of Airbus A330s, creating the possibility of having aircrew qualified to fly more than one type, potentially saving several million dollars a year. Commonality would also lower maintenance costs. Swissair preferred Airbus as well.

Sabena planned to add more short and medium range planes. It operated Avro and Boeing aircraft on these routes, and its charter subsidiary Sobelair flew Boeing 737 and 767 jets exclusively. In addition, Sabena Technics performed third-party overhauls on Boeing 737s, raising the possibility of massive layoffs should Airbus win the contract for shorter-range planes. Other types Sabena operated in the 1990s were the British Aerospace BAe 146s and Embraer EMB-145s of Delta Air Transport.

The maintenance, repair, and overhaul (MRO) division, Sabena Technics, competed in a crowded market. The 2,000-employee unit participated in an upgrade program for the Lockheed Martin C-130H Hercules, a ubiquitous military transport plane.

To reduce payroll costs, the company planned to base its flight personnel in Switzerland, which had lower employer taxes. In fact, the pilots would not actually have to leave Belgium, just pay taxes to Switzerland.

Sabena added Brussels-Cincinnati in cooperation with Delta Air Lines in 1997. It also entered an agreement with VLM, an independent carrier based in Antwerp. Its losses for the year were reduced, and Sabena led Europe in traffic growth. Cargo shipments were also up.

Employees were retrained to improve customer service and keep passengers from thinking Sabena an acronym for "Such a Bad Experience, Never Again." Traffic continued to boom in 1998, rising 30 percent in the first quarter. Service to the United Kingdom reached 100 flights per day. Sabena expanded international routes aggressively, adding Beirut and Bangkok. Its Africa 2002 program aimed to bolster its network of 20 destinations there. The resulting rapid fleet build-up forced Sabena to import pilots. Another one-day pilots' strike came as a result of Sabena banning Virgin Express pilots from recruitment.

Sabena partnered with CityBird, a new Belgian long-haul airline in March 1998, taking an 11 percent share. It also joined the Qualiflyer Group started by Swissair, Austrian Airlines, and several other European carriers. It reduced its holdings in CityBird to less than three percent after CityBird started a Brussels-Kinshasa route in cooperation with Lignes Aériennes Congolaises. A couple of Sabena's feeder routes, Brussels-Paris and Brussels-Luxembourg, were flown by Schreiner Airways operating as Sabena Connect.

Sabena showed a profit of BFr 1.26 billion in 1998, the year of its 75th anniversary. In early 1999, Sabena revamped its colors, returning to its traditional blue and white from the dull gray that had previously dominated its livery.

After Delta Air Lines made Air France its main transatlantic partner, Swissair and Sabena both joined a competing alliance with American Airlines. However, they also remained in Delta's "Atlantic Excellence" group. Switzerland and the EU were working on an agreement that would allow SAir Group to take a majority ownership in Sabena without forfeiting Sabena's status as an EU carrier.

Principal Subsidiaries

Sobelair (60%); Delta Air Transport; Air Zaire (49.5%).

Principal Competitors

British Airways plc; KLM Royal Dutch Airlines; Deutsche Lufthansa AG; Groupe Air France.

Further Reading

Buchan, David, "International Airline Deals: Sabena's Marriage Ends Months of Speculation," *Financial Times,* June 21, 1989.

"Competition: TEA Mounts Pressure Against Sabena World Airlines," *European Report,* Business Brief, May 5, 1990, p. 1.

Feldman, Joan M., "Some Call It Oligopoly," *Air Transport World,* May 1996, pp. 45+.

Forward, David C., "About-Face at Sabena," *Airways,* November 1999, pp. 23–29.

Goldsmith, Charles, "Threat of Swissair Pullout Ends Strike by Sabena Pilots Over Savings Package," *Wall Street Journal,* November 1, 1996, p. A10.

Goldsmith, Charles, and Margaret Studer, "Swissair, Sabena, Austrian Airlines Will Buy Jets—Joint-Fleet Purchase Marks Extensive Collaboration; Delta Will Participate," *Wall Street Journal,* December 20, 1996, p. A9.

Harrison, Michael, "BA's Sabena Link in Doubt After Referral," *Independent,* March 28, 1990, Business/City Sec. p. 22.

Hill, Leonard, "Such a Bad Experience. . .," *Air Transport World,* April 1996, pp. 39+.

Michaels, Daniel, "Airline Mergers Face Unfriendly Skies—International Carriers Say Outdated Regulations Hijack Globalization," *Wall Street Journal,* November 15, 1999, pp. A34.

Oster, Patrick, "The Suitors at Sabena's Gate," *Business Week,* July 25, 1994, p. 73.

Ott, James, "Sabena Hub Will Increase Flights to Underserved Cities," *Aviation Week & Space Technology,* May 7, 1990, pp. 92–93.

Reed, Arthur, "Better Living," *Air Transport World,* July 1998, pp. 162–64.

Sparaco, Pierre, "Air France, Sabena Begin Linking Operations," *Aviation Week & Space Technology,* November 9, 1992, p. 35.

——, "European Carriers Seek More Repair Business," *Aviation Week & Space Technology,* March 11, 1996, pp. 44+.

——, "Sabena Pursues 'Ideal US Partner'," *Aviation Week & Space Technology,* September 6, 1993, pp. 33–34.

——, "Sabena Targets 1998 Financial Turnaround," *Aviation Week & Space Technology,* November 3, 1997, pp. 48+.

——, "Sabena to Keep European Focus While Cutting Costs," *Aviation Week & Space Technology,* April 25, 1994, pp. 32–33.

——, ''Sabena's Losses Imperil SAirGroup's Upturn,'' *Aviation Week & Space Technology,* April 28, 1997, pp. 41+.

——, ''Sabena's Traffic Soars; Profitability in Sight,'' *Aviation Week & Space Technology,* May 4, 1998, pp. 27+.

——, ''Troubled Sabena Appoints New Leadership,'' *Aviation Week & Space Technology,* March 11, 1996, pp. 34+.

Unsworth, Edwin, ''British Airways, KLM Each Buy 20 Percent Shares in Belgian Air Carrier,'' *Journal of Commerce,* December 14, 1989, p. 5B.

Usborne, David, ''Sabena in Plea for Cash,'' *Independent,* September 20, 1990, Business/City Sec., p. 28.

—Frederick C. Ingram

Stericycle Inc.

28161 North Keith Drive
Lake Forest, Illinois 60045
U.S.A.
Telephone: (847) 367-5910
Toll Free: (800) 355-8773
Fax: (847) 367-9493
Web site: http://www.stericycle.com

Public Company
Incorporated: 1989
Employees: 550
Sales: $270 million (1999)
Ticker Symbol: SRCL
Stock Exchanges: NASDAQ
NAIC: 562112 Hazardous Waste Collection; 562211
Hazardous Waste Treatment and Disposal

Stericycle Inc. is the largest provider of regulated medical waste management services in the United States. The definition of regulated medical waste is any waste that gives rise to or causes an infectious disease or that harbors a human pathogenic organism. Medical waste thus includes such items as disposable, single use products as needles, gloves, syringes, and laboratory and surgical room supplies that have come into contact with bodily fluids or blood; blood products; and cultures of infectious agents. Accordingly, the company provides comprehensive medical waste management services that include medical waste collection, transportation, treatment and disposal. The firm's acquisition of BFI Medical Waste Business in April 1999 catapulted it into the upper echelons of medical waste management. Yet the purchase of BFI was only the latest in a series of strategic acquisitions that have been made by management starting in 1992. Stericycle operates throughout the United States, in four Canadian provinces, and in the late 1990s implemented an aggressive expansion program into Central and South America.

Late 1980s Origins

The company was founded and incorporated in 1989 by a group of investors who had extensive experience in both hospi-

tal services and the pharmaceutical industry. The anticipated future growth of the medical waste management services industry was the prime factor in convincing these executives of the potential for establishing such a firm, with the estimated market amounting to approximately $1.5 billion by the year 2000. The early years of the company's existence focused primarily on research and development. By the end of its first full year in business, 1991, Stericycle boasted a client list of 12 and sales of $1.6 million. Abbott Laboratories executive Mark C. Miller was brought in to serve as the company's president and CEO.

One of the company's developments, perhaps the most important service the company provided during the early years of its existence, was the Electro-Thermal-Deactivation treatment process. A proprietary waste management system, ETD was the only commercially-effective system that included the six following components: 1) it eliminated human pathogens in medical waste products without producing dangerous emissions or liquid effluents; 2) it reduced the total volume of medical waste by nearly 85 percent; 3) it made medical waste unrecognizable; 4) it allowed for the recycling of plastics from medical waste products; 5) it allowed for the remaining medical waste to be used as safe landfill or useable fuel in energy production; and 6) it was a cost-effective method. Using its ETD technique as a primary marketing tool, the company was able to open its first ETD treatment facility in early 1992 in Morton, Washington, which was followed closely by additional facilities in Woonsocket, Rhode Island, Loma Linda, California, and Yorkville, Wisconsin.

The 1990s: Growth and Expansion

Stericycle was soon providing provide medical waste collection, transportation, treatment, disposal, reduction, reuse and recycling services, with additional educational and consulting services primarily in selected states across America. In addition, as part of the services provided to recycle medical waste, the company supplied medical waste plastics to a manufacturer that made new plastics products.

From its inception, management at the company focused all its efforts and resources on developing proprietary treatment and recycling processes, constructing and equipping its regulated medical waste treatment facilities, building a recycling, research, and development center, and obtaining the necessary government permits and approvals to conduct its business. This initial strategy was a direct result of management's perception of certain trends and developments within both the health care and regulated medical waste industries. During the late 1980s, the handling and disposal of medical waste generated a great deal of attention from the general public as well as from government regulatory agencies due to a incident which occurred in 1988. During that year, disposable syringes and other medical waste washed upon the shore along the coastlines of New York and New Jersey. Concerns about the possible transmission of HIV, hepatitis B, and other infectious diseases heightened awareness about the proper management of medical waste. In response, the federal government enacted the Medical Waste Tracking Act of 1988 that established a program for tracking and treating medical waste. Additionally, OSHA issued specific regulations regarding the handling of and exposure to medical waste and the exposure to bloodborne pathogens.

In light of these regulatory developments, Stericycle management believed that health care providers were going to focus on six concerns, including the reduction of on-site handling of medical waste in the attempt to reduce contact between such materials and employees, the assurance of safe transportation of regulated medical waste, the assurance of the destruction of potentially harmful infectious human pathogens, the minimization of medical waste disposal sites on the environment; and the participation in medical waste recycling programs where convenient. The company's ETD process was just one response to the above developments. The two additional commercial technologies that Stericycle focused on for treating regulated medical waste were incineration and autoclaving. Incineration burned medical waste and reduced it to ashes, thus reducing the volume of waste. Autoclaving treated medical waste with high temperature steam and pressure that kills infectious pathogens. All three of the company's principal treatment technologies were considered state-of-the-art at the time, and provided the company with a firm basis to expand its operations.

In 1993, with high expectations for industry growth, the company embarked upon an aggressive acquisitions policy.

These acquisitions included: Therm-Tec Destruction Service of Oregon, Inc., in Portland, Oregon; Recovery Corporation of Illinois, in Lombard, Illinois; Safe Way Disposal Systems, Inc., in Middletown, Connecticut; Safetech Health Care in Valencia, California; Bio-Med of Oregon, Inc., in Portland, Oregon; WMI Medical Services of New England, Inc., in Hudson, New Hampshire; Doctors Environmental Control, Inc., in Santa Ana, California; and Sharps Incinerator of Fort, Inc., in Fort Arkinson, Wisconsin. Each of the acquisitions were selected for its ability to provide the company with additional volume for its treatment facilities, as well as for a substantial new base of customers that accompanied the purchases.

This strategic acquisitions plan of Stericycle occurred during the same time that alternate care generators grew in importance. During the late 1980 and early 1990s, in response to health care containment costs and the growth of managed care, care for patients began to shift away from high-cost acute care settings as found in hospitals to less costly off-site alternative treatment locations. In fact, the total expenditures for alternative site health care locations grew from $5 billion in 1985 to nearly $22 billion by the end of 1994. The result of this development meant that such common diseases and conditions as neurological conditions, infectious diseases, digestive disorders, HIV/AIDS, and a wide variety of cancers were treated in alternative site locations rather than in hospitals. Most importantly for Stericycle, these alternative care sites began to provide a significant source of revenue for the regulated medical waste industry since they did not produce a large enough amount of medical waste to justify the capital expenditures for their own medical waste treatment facilities. In order to provide services for getting rid of the small quantities of medical waste that these alternative care sites generated, Stericycle entered into a number of strategic telemarketing agreements with such organizations as the Massachusetts Dental Society and the Sisters of Providence Health System located in the states of Oregon and Washington.

By 1993, company sales had reached $9.1 million, representing a very small share of the billion dollar industry. Moreover, the company continued to realize net losses, having invested capital in acquisitions and improving operations. However, this strategy would soon pay off; by the end of fiscal 1996, sales had increased to $24.5 million, and then they skyrocketed to $46.2 million by the end of 1997. Much of the increase in sales during this period was a result of management's strategy to focus on higher-margin alternative health care sites, and the additional revenues derived from the company's aggressive acquisitions plan. Approximately 70 percent of the firm's revenues were generated from hospitals, blood banks, and pharmaceutical companies, while 30 percent was generated from outpatient clinics, medical and dental offices, dialysis centers, laboratories, biomedical companies, schools, park districts, funeral homes, fire and police departments, municipal health departments, correctional facilities, and veterinary offices. Buoyed by its success and in need of capital to continue expanding its operations, in 1996 Stericycle made an initial public offering of its stock on the NASDAQ Exchange.

Late 1990s and Beyond

During the late 1990s, Stericycle management continued its aggressive acquisitions strategy. In 1997, the company established a joint venture firm, Medam, to build a facility that would use its proprietary Electro-Thermal Deactivation technology in order to provide services to health care sites in and around Mexico City. Stericycle also purchased Med-Tech Environment Limited, a company based in Toronto, Canada with operations throughout the provinces of Alberta, British Columbia, Ontario, and Quebec. At the same time, Stericycle entered into an agreement with Companhia Auxiliar de Viacao e Obras (CAVO), to license its ETD system for use in Brazil. In addition, the company purchase all of the outstanding stock of Waste Systems, Inc., with it primary operations in the southwestern portion of the United States. However, the more important factor in the WSI acquisition involved Stericycle's interest in positioning itself to capitalize on WSI's nascent operation in Germany. With another 12 acquisitions during 1998 alone, the company had acquired 29 firms from 1993 to the end of 1998, doubled its customer base, and increased it sales volume to $66.7 million.

Along with the aggressive acquisitions strategy that Stericycle had formed for penetrating overseas markets, management also focused on consolidating and expanding its presence in the United States. Stericycle acquired Regional Recycling, Inc. and Controlled Medical Disposal, Inc., both located in New Jersey, and Allegro Carting and Recycling, Inc in New York City. All of these purchases significantly enhanced the company's operations in the northeast portion of the United States. In the Midwest, Stericycle bought Medisin, Inc., located in Kentucky, and Superior Services of Wisconsin, Inc. In the Southeast, the company purchased 3CI Complete Compliance Corporation, while in the Southwest additional acquisitions of Mediwaste Disposal Services LLP and Arizona Hazardous Waste Disposal strengthened Stericycle's position.

The most far-reaching acquisition, however, was the company's purchase of Browning-Ferris Industries, Inc. (BFI). Stericycle entered into an agreement with Allied Waste Industries, Inc. to buy all of the medical waste operations of BFI, which were located throughout the United States, Canada, and Puerto Rico, and the entire medical waste management operation of Allied Waste itself. The BFI Medical Waste Business, at the time of the purchase in April 1999, was the largest medical management waste services firm in North America, with over 120 locations. With a fully integrated and regulated medical waste collection, transportation, transferral, treatment and disposal system in operation, the company reported revenues of approximately $198 million for fiscal 1998 and had over 1,400 full-time employees. Thus, in one carefully thought-out acquisition, Stericycle tripled its annual revenue base but, even more significantly, added over 200,000 customers to its current client list of 78,000.

Management at Stericycle were convinced they had engineered one of the most unique and important strategic acquisitions in the industry to date. Virtually overnight, Stericycle substantially expanded both the size and scope of its operations. At the same time, management believed the acquisition created significant economies of scale due to the fixed costs within the industry that were associated with the collection and treatment of medical waste. In fact, management was confident enough to project a savings of nearly $18 million within 24 months of closing the acquisition transactions. In terms of complementing Stericycle's already existent operations, the acquisition of BFI was seen as enabling the company to better serve its customers throughout North America.

Undoubtedly, Stericycle had engineered one of the most successful acquisitions in the medical waste management industry to date. As a result, the company was poised to establish itself as one of the pre-eminent leaders in the field. If management could incorporate and utilize the vast resources of personnel and equipment that BFI brought with it, the future of Stericycle seemed very bright.

Principal Subsidiaries

Med-Tech Environmental Ltd.; BFI Waste Management, Inc.; Medical Compliance Services, Inc.; Environmental Control Company, Inc.; Waste Management, Inc.; Waste Systems, Inc.

Principal Competitors

Medical Waste Management, Inc.; Scherer Healthcare, Inc.; Waste Management, Inc.

Further Reading

Comerford, Mike, "Stericycle Deal for Allied Waste Unite a 'Milestone'," *Chicago Daily Herald,* April 16, 1999, p. 1.

Marcial, Gene G., "Stericycle: A Clean Play," *Business Week,* October 19, 1998, p. 152.

Mayors, Diane, "Stericycle President & CEO Interview," *Wall Street Corporate Reporter,* February 4, 1999.

McMullen, Cheryl A., "New Industry Leader: Stericycle Quadruples Size, Buys BFI's Medical Waste Assets," *Waste News,* December 20, 1999, p. 11.

Oloroso, Arsenio, Jr., "Stericycle Aiming for Top of the Heap," *Crain's Chicago Business,* May 4, 1998, p.4.

"Stericycle Announces International Expansion," *Wall Street Journal,* October 26, 1999, p. C7(E).

"Stericycle in $440 Million Deal with Allied," *New York Times,* April 16, 1999, p. C4.

"Stericycle Inc.," *Wall Street Journal,* April 16, 1999, p. B6(E).

"Stericycle Inc.," *Waste Treatment Technology News,* December 1999.

"Stericycle Makes Acquisitions," *Wall Street Journal,* August 12, 1999, p. C11(W).

"Stericycle Reports 85% Increase in Net Income for Third Quarter, 1999," *Wall Street Journal,* November 3, 1999, p. C4(E).

—Thomas Derdak

Strouds, Inc.

780 South Nogales Street
City of Industry, California 91748
U.S.A.
Telephone: (626) 912-2866
Fax: (626) 913-4841
Web sites: http://www.strouds.com; http://
   www.linenexperts.com

Public Company
Incorporated: 1987
Employees: 1,637
Sales: \$227.6 million (1999)
Stock Exchanges: NASDAQ
Ticker Symbol: STRO
NAIC: 442299 All Other Home Furnishings Stores

Strouds, Inc., ''The Linen Experts,'' is a specialty retailer that offers a wide selection of home textiles for bed, bath, and tabletop in a large array of colors, styles, patterns, brands, and prices. The product line comprises the company's private label brands, Joyce Stroud Collection and JS Relaxed, popular brands, such as Fieldcrest, Martex, Wamsutta, Croscill, and Springmaid, and designer collections, such as Adrienne Vittadini, Laura Ashley, Fendi, Alexander Julian, Collier Campbell, and Palais Royal. Specializing in quality linens at competitive prices, Strouds also offers complementary home accessories, such as pillows, window coverings, and picture frames, and some stores sell home furnishings.

Innovation Fosters Success

Wilfred ''Bill'' Stroud began the Strouds chain of linen stores in 1979 based on his perception that a niche existed for bed and bath specialty retail stores. Experience had taught Stroud, then a divisional merchandising manager for Broadway Department Stores in California, that when a department store reduced its inventory in a particular department, specialty retailers entered the market to fulfill customer needs. As a merchandise manager at various times for records, sporting goods, and toy departments, Stroud had seen that specialty retail stores thrived when department stores trimmed inventory in those areas. After he had been asked by corporate executives to reduce the company's selection of linens, Stroud saw an opportunity for a specialty retail store to sell home textiles.

Knowing that selection attracted consumers to specialty retail stores, Stroud decided to create a store that would provide a broad assortment of bed, bath, and table linens. To fund the business Stroud accumulated \$500,000 from a second mortgage on his home, his pension plan, and friends willing to invest in his idea. With the involvement of his wife, Joyce, and his son Jeff, Stroud planned two stores in the Los Angeles area to take advantage of cluster marketing. Strouds Linen Warehouse, a 4,400-square-foot store with a basic interior and unfinished wood shelves, opened in Pasadena, northeast of central Los Angeles, in November 1979. A 6,100-square-foot store opened in Torrance, south of Los Angeles, the following month.

Finding that its customers sought high-quality merchandise, Strouds quickly adapted to serve an upscale market. The company upgraded the atmosphere in its stores and added high-end merchandise and a skilled sales staff, dubbed ''Linen Experts,'' to assist customers with selection and coordination of linens and accessories. A library of informational brochures about specific products assisted both sales staff and customers. Store-level flexibility allowed managers to offer styles appropriate to each store's customer base. At the Pasadena store customers preferred traditional styles, while the Beverly Hills store attracted customers with more progressive taste.

The pricing strategy, to offer merchandise at ''White Sale'' prices every day, made linen suppliers uneasy about selling to Bill Stroud, in part because department stores discouraged vendors from selling the same merchandise offered in their stores to retailers who sold it at a lower cost. Department stores did not offer the same array of choices, however, and the success of Strouds stores changed the attitudes of linen vendors. They liked the fact that Strouds offered a complete selection of merchandise presented in attractive ''vignettes,'' a Strouds innovation that showed how different items worked together and how decorative accessories completed the look of a room.

Visual presentation became the hallmark of Strouds linen stores, as the company adapted its product displays according to the way customers shop, by style and lifestyle rather than by brand. "Vignette" displays included full-sized beds dressed with complementary linens and accessories, regardless of brand, taking an interior decorator approach to merchandise presentation. The company used neutral colors as a background in order to emphasize the patterns and colors of the merchandise. Strouds stores also displayed towels and linens by color rather than by brand. "Cross-merchandising," which presented items as they would be used together in a room, such as the display of shower curtains near towels of complementary colors, stimulated strong average sales per transaction.

Within five years Strouds had expanded to a chain of 16 stores throughout southern California, as well as three stores in northern California and one store in Las Vegas. Sales reached $28.8 million in 1984 and continued to grow with new store openings. The company grew more slowly as the California economy slowed and capital funding diminished. Strouds opened only two stores in 1985 and no stores in 1986. Five new stores in 1987 and two stores in 1988 were all located outside of Los Angeles, in areas where the economic downturn had the least impact. Bill Stroud attained industry recognition in 1986, when *Home Furnishings Daily* recognized Stroud as one of the top ten innovators in the retail of bed, bath, and table linens, and in 1987 when the National Bed, Bath and Linen Association elected Stroud, "Chain Store Retailer of the Year."

The 1990s: Superstores, Outlet Stores, and Competition

Strouds began development of its first superstores and clearance outlet stores in the late 1980s. In December 1988 the company expanded its Northridge store in the San Fernando Valley to 11,900 square feet and in January 1989 opened a new 8,900-square-foot store in Thousand Oaks, northwest of Los Angeles. Superstores provided a wider selection of merchandise, from 25,000 to 30,000 stock-keeping units (SKUs), and allowed space for 50 to 80 vignettes, including 12 to 15 beds. With the opening of a 16,000-square-foot superstore in Pasadena in June 1989, Strouds converted the original Pasadena store into a clearance store. The company's Downey location, southeast of central Los Angeles, had been converted to a clearance store in 1985 and had proven worthwhile as an outlet for slow-moving merchandise, odd lots, discontinued styles, and low-priced brands and styles. This alternative format allowed Strouds to broaden its customer base while providing an outlet for the superstores where Strouds continually offered a fresh selection of styles and colors. By the end of 1989, three new superstores had opened in the San Francisco Bay area and an 18,600-square-foot superstore opened in Orange, in Orange County. Strouds ventured outside of California with a second store in Las Vegas, which opened in October 1989.

In the early 1990s Strouds gained momentum. In southern California, Strouds expanded eight stores into superstores, while eight new superstores opened, including the 20,600-square-foot Beverly Connection store in June 1990. Three of the new superstores replaced original stores, which were converted to outlet stores. Also, four new outlet stores opened under the name Strouds Linen Outlet. Four new superstores opened in northern California and five stores were expanded to superstores, including the San Mateo site, which was the company's largest store at the time at 25,600 square feet. Strouds expanded its original Las Vegas location to 20,900 square feet.

By the time Strouds went public in 1994, the company owned and operated 33 superstores, nine original stores, and seven outlet stores, for a total of 49 stores with $174.3 million in sales in fiscal year ending February 1995. The public offering of 3.3 million shares, at $12.50 per share, raised $37 million for debt payment and further expansion. With Wayne Selness as its new CEO, Strouds planned to enter the Midwest, opening two stores in Illinois and two in Minnesota in 1994 and 1995. Strouds also opened two superstores in Maryland, becoming the second largest retailer of home textiles in the United States, with 61 stores and $189.8 million in sales in 1995.

Increased competition in the home textiles and accessories market led Strouds to broaden its product offerings. Linens 'N Things, the largest national home textiles chain, and Bed, Bath and Beyond had entered the California market with a wider range of products, while national departments stores and West Coast chains, such as Pacific Linen and Three-D Bed and Bath, also intensified competition. Strouds began to experiment with decorative accessories that complemented its linens. The company offered metal beds, lamps, wall art, and other items that integrated well into its vignettes. A new kitchenware department introduced dinnerware, cookware, cutlery, and other kitchen items.

Strouds stores tended to be smaller than its competitors', averaging 15,000 square feet compared to its competitors' 30,000 to 45,000 square feet. New Strouds stores outside of California tended to be larger than the company norm at around 25,000 square feet. Within California Strouds responded to the competitive threat with an experimental prototype for a 50,000-square-foot home decorating store, called the "Home Compass," which opened in Irvine in December 1996.

The Home Compass concept involved a mixture of textiles, furniture, and accessories for each room of the house, displayed in an unstructured, circular pattern. In addition to bedroom and bathroom vignettes, merchandise displays included kitchens, dining rooms, and living rooms that reflected casual to formal lifestyles. Living room merchandise proved to be the company's largest addition, with a large selection of furniture as well as area rugs and window treatments in 14 different vignettes. New merchandise included an expanded line of infant and juvenile bedding, as well as cribs and dressers. The store included a demonstration and seminar room, a cafe and gourmet foods area, and a "garage sale" area for markdowns and special promotions. Services in the Home Imagination Center included luxury linens by special order, a bridal registry, two professional decorators available for consultation at a customer's home, and custom services for upholstery, carpeting, closet storage, window treatments, replacement windows, and vinyl siding.

Competition and the higher costs of the large store format sent Strouds' profitability downward, and lower sales per square foot resulted in the company's first annual loss—of $22.8 million—in 1996. The company took a pretax charge of $16.3 million for fiscal year ending February 1997 and announced a restructuring plan in April 1997. Before the plan could be implemented, CEO Wayne Selness resigned. Bill Stroud stepped in as CEO until July 1997 when the company hired Charles Chinni, a former merchandising executive for Macy's and Kmart.

Return to Basics in the Late 1990s

Under Chinni's leadership, Strouds addressed profitability. Behind the scenes the company streamlined various distribution functions, inventory management, and vendor returns of defective goods, reducing per unit supply chain costs. The company also eliminated several layers of management, including four executive positions, to streamline its staff expenses. Strouds reoriented its expansion strategy to reinforce its California market. The company suspended out-of-state expansion and, in 1997, 1998, and early 1999, closed seven unprofitable stores in Chicago, Minneapolis, Washington D.C., and Nevada, as well as two California stores. The strategy for new store openings involved market clustering near existing stores, store expansion, and relocation of stores in alignment with demographic shifts. In 1998 Strouds opened a 17,000-square-foot store in Monterey and an outlet store in San Jose.

The most significant change involved a restored focus on the company's traditional strength as a home textile retailer. Strouds reduced and revised its merchandise categories and reduced its number of product vendors from 200, who supplied 85 percent of the company's goods in 1996, to 40 vendors who supplied the same percentage in 1998. Strouds also reduced its store size appropriate to streamlined merchandise categories and economic efficiency, while upgrading visual displays. The company updated its "Linen Experts" program to provide sales staff with current information on products and fashions. A shift in marketing, from television to print advertising and direct mail, allowed Strouds to spend less on advertising while promoting the company more frequently to targeted markets.

The restructuring plan succeeded as new store openings maintained increases in yearly sales. In 1997 sales of $221.8

million still resulted in a net loss of $3.8 million, but in 1998 Strouds began to rebound with net income of $214,000 on $227.6 million in sales. Strouds attributed strong improvements in store-level sales to more frequent promotions, fewer store openings by competitors, and a strong economy. Company management was pleased that Strouds was one of three home textile retailers chosen to sell the new Guess? Home Collection.

With the company's return to profitability, Bill Stroud retired as Chairman of the Board in February 1999. In April of that year the Home Fashions Products Association and the New York Home Textiles Show honored Stroud with a Retailer of the Year Award. With 65 stores at that time, Bill and Joyce Stroud had built the third-largest bed and bath retail company in less than 20 years. Stroud was noted for fairness and integrity in dealing with vendors, as well as for sponsorship of the annual Strouds Golf and Tennis Classic, which had raised over $2 million for the American Heart Association since 1989. Mark Grand, who had held various executive positions with Strouds from 1987 to 1995, received the Outstanding Merchant Award.

In 1999 Strouds began to explore a variety of new strategies for broadening its customer base. The company launched an online mail-order program at www.linenexperts.com in May 1999. Strouds sought to reach beyond its mature, over-40 customer, whose preferences range from the moderately priced to luxury merchandise, to attract younger consumers with new styles and lower-priced merchandise. The company also explored the concept of boutiques, from 5,000 to 6,000 square feet, which would offer top-quality linens. Strouds expected to locate the boutiques in shopping malls anchored by upscale department stores such as Nordstrom or Bloomingdales.

In September 1999 a prototype for a new small-store format opened in Thousand Oaks. The 9,900-square-foot store retained Strouds' superstore selection with a more efficient, upscale, merchandise display. The format differentiated Strouds from its main competitors, who tended to focus on different merchandise categories or on different geographical markets. The Home Compass concept store would continue to be an experimental laboratory for new product categories.

In November 1999 Strouds announced plans to open four stores in the Phoenix area, which would be the company's first foray outside of California in over three years. A store planned for Paradise Valley would offer a wide selection of goods for bed and bath at low prices as well as an upscale assortment of fashion bedding and decorative accessories. Strouds planned three outlet stores, in Scottsdale, Glendale, and Phoenix. In a press release announcing the expansion into Arizona, Chinni described the company's status: "Renewed by the completion of our restructuring, we are now well positioned to compete in an industry we helped create." Chinni completed a series of executive appointments to support the company's renewal, including Robert Menar as Chief Operating Officer and Harry Brown as Executive Vice President and General Merchandising Manager.

Principal Competitors

Bed, Bath and Beyond, Inc., Home Depot Express, Linens 'n Things, Inc., Pacific Linen, Three D Bed & Bath.

Further Reading

Adler, Sam, "Eastward Ho!" *HFN The Weekly Home Furnishing Network,* February 6, 1995, p. 34.

Bermingham, Geoffrey B., "Strouds Retools Its Forces: Redefines Management, Puts Specialists in Charge," *HFD-The Weekly Home Furnishings Newspaper,* August 30, 1993, p. 42.

Boyle Schwartz, Donna, "West Coast Competition Turf Wars: Can West Coast Specialty Retailers Survive Category Killer Onslaught?" *HFN The Weekly Newspaper for the Home Furnishing Network,* July 28, 1997, p. 1.

——, "Cheers for Chinni as Strouds CEO," *HFN The Weekly Newspaper for the Home Furnishing Network,* July 14, 1997, p. 4.

——, "Dressing Up: Strouds Sells the Furnishings to Go with Its Linens," *HFN The Weekly Newspaper for the Home Furnishing Network,* May 29, 1995, p. 1.

——, "Strouds' Compass Guides Shoppers; Circular Layout Differentiates Specialty Chain," *HFN The Weekly Newspaper for the Home Furnishing Network,* December 23, 1996, p. 1.

Chirls, Stuart, "Bill Stroud to Retire," *HFN The Weekly Newspaper for the Home Furnishing Network,* February 22, 1999, p. 1.

Cole, Benjamin Mark, "Retailer Strouds to Go Public with $54 Million IPO," *Los Angeles Business Journal,* August 29, 1994, p. 1.

"Hard Lines at Strouds; Trying Housewares," *HFN The Weekly Newspaper for the Home Furnishing Network,* November 6, 1995, p. 1.

Hartnett, Michael, "Strouds Sets Sights on Midwestern Markets," *Discount Store News,* May 15, 1995, p. H13.

Herlihy, Janet, and Stuart Chirls, "1999 Retailer of the Year Awards Salute the Best," *HFN The Weekly Newspaper for the Home Furnishing Network,* April 12, 1999, p. 14.

Moore, Brenda L., "Having Gone through the Wringer, Strouds Sets Sights on Expanding," *Wall Street Journal/California,* October 6, 1999, p. 2.

"New Format Shows Strouds' Direction," *Discount Store News,* January 20, 1997, p. 3.

Scally, Robert, "Strouds Learns from Mistakes," *Discount Store News,* July 27, 1998, p. 6.

——, "Strouds Throws Back Shroud, Rolls out New Small Format," *Discount Store News,* September 6, 1999, p. 3.

Schoulberg, Warren, "Chinni Is New Strouds CEO," *Home Textiles Today,* July 14, 1997, p. 2.

Silberg, Lurie, "Specialty Retailer Strouds Back on Solid Footing," *HFN The Weekly Newspaper for the Home Furnishing Network,* May 4, 1999, p. 6.

——, "Strouds Restructures Management," *HFN The Weekly Newspaper for the Home Furnishing Network,* March 30, 1998, p. 60.

Stodder, Sato, "Man of the House: Bringing Linens Out of the Closet Turned This Retail Maverick into a Household Name," *Entrepreneur,* January 1996, p. 154.

"Strouds' New Idea," *HFN The Weekly Newspaper for the Home Furnishing Network,* December 16, 1996, p. 1.

"Strouds Online Store Open for Business," *HFN The Weekly Newspaper for the Home Furnishing Network,* May 17, 1999, p. 10.

"Strouds Starts E-Commerce," *Discount Store News,* May 24, 1999, p. 17.

"Strouds Taps Former Kmart Exec for CEO Post," *Los Angeles Times,* July 9, 1997, p. 2.

—Mary Tradii

TelePizza S.A.

Calle Azalea
1 Edificio F-Miniparc 1
El soto de la Moraleja
28109 Alcobendas, Madrid
Spain
Telephone: (+34) 91 657 9000
Fax: (+34) 91 650 9680
Web Site: http://www.telepizza.es

Public Company
Incorporated: 1987 as PizzaPhone
Employees: 8,377
Sales: Pta 67.63 billion ($419 million) (1999)
Stock Exchanges: Madrid
Ticker Symbol: Telepizza
NAIC: 722211 Limited-Service Eating Places.

Fast-growing TelePizza S.A. has helped to redefine Spain's eating habits. The Madrid-based chain of fast food restaurants and delivery services has built up a network of more than 767 stores. Approximately half of TelePizza's outlets are owned by the company. The remainder are operated under franchise agreements. Having built up the largest selling fast food chain in Spain, where it outperforms even McDonald's, TelePizza has set out to conquer the world. More than 250 of its outlets are located in the international market, especially in Chile, Portugal, Mexico, Poland, the United Kingdom, France, and Morocco. TelePizza has also branched out from its original pizza recipe, bringing the restaurant concepts TeleGrill (chicken, ribs) and TeleWorld (international food court) to the Spanish consumer. Floated on the Madrid stock exchange in 1996, TelePizza ranked as that exchange's fastest-growing stock for most of the rest of the 1990s. Uncertainty over the company's future—as founder Leopoldo Fernandez Pujals sold his 40 percent of the company in late 1999—helped to hurt TelePizza's share price, especially amid rumors of a possible merger between TelePizza and rival TeleChef. That merger, in fact, became reality when the two companies agreed to join forces in February 2000. The merger will create a mostly complementary network of restaurants featuring nearly all of the typical fast food items, from pizza to hamburgers to sandwiches and beyond.

Changing Eating Habits in the 1980s

Fast food was more or less unheard of in Spain up until the late 1980s. The country's dining habits typically revolved around long, drawn-out, family-centered meals—often featuring the Spanish specialty tapas. Foreign foods remained in large part ignored in a country that was only just emerging from some five decades of fascist rule. The death of Francisco Franco in the 1970s returned Spain to the fold of its democratic European neighbors. The country quickly and enthusiastically adapted to the new liberties of democracy, especially the liberalization of the country's economy. The result was an increasingly active lifestyle, where, for the first time, women joined the work force in massive numbers.

As in other countries, these changes led inevitably to changes in dining habits. With less time to prepare meals and, also, more leisure activities to distract the diners' attention, the country was ripe for the introduction of fast food. Among the first to recognize this shift in the country's culinary culture was Leopoldo Fernandez Pujals. In 1988 the Cuban-born, American-raised Pujals opened his first restaurant, selling pizzas delivered to the customer's door.

Pujals had come to the United States in 1960 at the age of 13, joining the first Cuban exodus following Fidel Castro's rise to power. Sent by his wealthy father, a lawyer, to Ft. Lauderdale, Florida to improve his English, Pujals soon was joined by his family, who had been forced to give up their home. Pujals spent the rest of his youth impoverished; the family's Havana home later served as the Philippines' embassy in Cuba. After finishing high school, Pujals joined the army, where he rose to the rank of captain, assigned to the officer training school in Fort Belvoir. In 1969, however, Pujals was sent to serve in Vietnam. His story might have ended there—slated to be sent on a spy mission to Cambodia, Pujals was instead assigned a desk job, through the intervention of one of the officers he had trained at Fort Belvoir. As Pujals himself told *The European:* ''I was extremely lucky

Key Dates:

1987: First PizzaPhone restaurant opened.
1988: Name changed to Telepizza.
1990: Opening of 20th restaurant.
1992: International expansion to Portugal, Mexico, Chile, and Poland.
1996: Listing on Madrid Stock Exchange.
1998: Opening of 600th restaurant; stock split 20 for 1.
1999: Acquisition of Hippo Pizza (UK); launch of TeleOriental; founder Pujals sells stock.
2000: Merger of TelePizza with TeleChef.

not to be involved in serious combat.'' Nonetheless, Pujals's military background was to benefit his later career.

After finishing his tour of duty, Pujals returned to the United States, where he took on American citizenship. Pujals graduated from Stetson University in Florida, married, and began a family. He also began his career as a salesman. For this, Pujals applied to and won a position with Procter & Gamble, to receive the benefits of that company's expertise in sales and sales training. Pujals quickly distinguished himself at P & G. Assigned to selling Camay soaps, Pujals met an entire year's sales targets in just three months. When Pujals was offered only a mere $1,000 bonus for his efforts, he quit Procter & Gamble and instead joined the sales force of Johnson & Johnson, for which he sold heart valves and other surgical supplies.

Pujals's career lasted longer with Johnson & Johnson. Fluent in both English and Spanish, Pujals was soon sent to Guatemala, and then to Spain, where he was named to run the company's sales and marketing division in that country in 1981. Nonetheless, by the late 1980s, Pujals began to look for new opportunities. Encouraged by his father, Pujals determined to set out on his own. As he told the *Independent:* ''By then I was 40 and my father told me that if you hadn't founded a business by then, it would be too late. So I decided to give it a try.''

Pujals's American background enabled him to recognize that Spain was undergoing a similar shift in work culture and dining habits as had occurred in the United States in the 1960s. With more and more women joining the work force, and people working longer hours, consumers began seeking greater convenience in their shopping and food needs. Pujals was convinced that the time was right to introduce American-style home delivery to the Spanish market. Pujals's food choice turned to pizza. Before opening his first store, Pujals spent time performing extensive market testing—offering free pizzas to his suburban Madrid neighborhood's teenagers, Pujals experimented with different dough and topping recipes, polling his teenage test audience until he found a recipe that appealed to them all. With that recipe, Pujals, now joined by brother Eduardo, opened his first outlet, called PizzaPhone, in 1987.

Fast Food Giant in the 1990s

Pujals initially stayed with his job at Johnson & Johnson, working nights at PizzaPhone. By 1988, he was convinced of the pizza delivery service's future. In that year, Pujals left Johnson & Johnson and sold his home to finance his company's growth. Pujals and brother Eduardo also managed to raise some $300,000 in outside investments. The pair went to work polishing the company's concept. Changing its name to TelePizza, Pujals looked back to the United States for inspiration. For one, the company, borrowing from McDonalds, insisted on promoting a clean image, not only in its stores, but also among its employees, who were expected to dress neatly and behave politely to customers. Fast delivery was promoted as another company plus: taking a leaf from Domino's Pizza in the United States, TelePizza began touting its own 30-minute delivery service. Madrid, and soon all of Spain, was to be crisscrossed by a fleet of specially outfitted Vespa scooters painted in what the company called ''TelePizza Red.'' For those who preferred dining out, TelePizza offered a comfortable sit-down setting, akin to that found at a Pizza Hut restaurant.

Pujals brought other elements of his military and sales background into play. Sales were monitored carefully in daily computer reports, not only store by store, but street by street. Once a store reached a certain sales volume, a new outlet was opened in a nearby location to maintain the level of service and quality. Managers were expected to book sales increases each month, or risk being taken to task. Pujals's military-inspired insistence on discipline and cleanliness was matched by intensive marketing efforts—including blanketing neighborhoods with leaflets tucked under the windshield wipers of parked cars.

In a country where fast food was rare and home delivery even rarer, TelePizza's success was instant. By 1990, the company operated 20 stores. Soon after, the company began exporting its concept internationally, touching other countries with the fast food bug, starting with Portugal and Chile, and then Poland and Mexico as well. Spain, however, remained the company's primary market. In the first half of the 1990s, TelePizza achieved dramatic growth. By 1995, the company operated more than 250 TelePizza outlets.

By then, too, a storm was growing in the company's ranks. A dispute erupted between Pujals, on one side, and brother Eduardo and the company's investors, on the other. Eduardo and the investors wanted to cash in on the company's success, taking a share of its rising profits. Pujals, however, determined to continue reinvesting profits to fuel the company's continued expansion. The rift that developed quickly saw Eduardo take control of the company away from its founder. Angered, Pujals sold part of his stake in the company to Banco de Bilbao y Vizcaya. Recognizing Pujals's importance to the company, the bank managed to calm the situation by bringing the two sides to a compromise. In 1996 Pujals agreed to float the company on the stock market, enabling Eduardo and the original investors to cash out their shares.

TelePizza's public offering counted as one of the most successful in the Madrid exchange's history. Oversubscribed some 49 times, the stock proved popular not only among the growing numbers of professional investors in Spain, but also among the company's customers. TelePizza's employees, too, were offered a chance to cash in on the company's success—in part to give them a stake in the company's continued strong growth. More than 95 percent of employees accepted TelePizza's offer of stock. The fast rise of the share price gave way to a situation in which, for some employees, their share dividends were worth more than their annual salary. In the first 18 months of trading, TelePizza's stock had multiplied by ten; in 1998 the company split its stock in a 20-for-one split to maintain a lower limit on its per-share price.

The stock offering enabled the company to step up its expansion drive. By the end of 1998, the company had grown to nearly 600 locations and had captured some 60 percent of the country's pizza market, a large enough share to force Pizza Hut to exit the Spanish market. TelePizza went on the acquisition trail, buying up rival chain Pizza World (the company's success had inspired a number of imitators) from Agrolimen, adding that chain's nearly 100 outlets. In recognition of the rising popularity of the fast food market in general, TelePizza began to diversify into other food types. In 1997 the company launched the TeleGrill concept, featuring chicken and ribs specialties. TelePizza also began developing a TeleOriental concept, featuring Chinese, Japanese, and Indian food specialties. At the same time, TelePizza began plans for its own "food court" style restaurants, borrowing from the American style of a centrally located dining area surrounded by several restaurants offering various food specialties, all of which were available for home delivery. The first of the company's prototype food courts opened in Madrid in 1998, featuring TelePizza and TeleGrill specialties.

After opening the first TeleOriental in Madrid in 1999, the company moved into a new market, buying up the United Kingdom-based Hippo Pizza chain and its 13 locations. TelePizza also jumped into northern Africa, opening its first locations in Morocco. While the company's fortunes continued to increase—by the end of 1999 the company operated more than 760 outlets, including more than 250 outlets outside of Spain—it once again ran into difficulties among its shareholders. In June 1999, Pujals, who remained the company's leading shareholder, while relinquishing the chief executive position to Carolos Lopez Casas, announced that he had sold some five percent of the company to the Ballve and Olcese families, owners of rival fast food chain TeleChef. The sale announcement touched off consternation among investors, particularly in that the sale had been made at a below-market price, and touched off rumors of a possible merger of the two companies. The resulting confusion sent TelePizza's stock plunging for the first time since its public offering.

To stabilize the situation, Pujals agreed not to pursue the sale of any more of his stock—worth 31 percent of the company—for at least 120 days. In September, however, Pujals announced that he was selling off his remaining stock, selling another 5.4 percent to the TeleChef families and the remaining 25 percent to institutional investors. Pujals, said to have pocketed some US

$320 million in the deal, then stepped down as the company's chairman. The sale once again set off merger rumors between TelePizza and TeleChef, a move criticized by analysts who were unimpressed with TeleChef's own management. Although both parties denied that a merger was being considered, such a move seemed inevitable.

That inevitability came to be in early 2000. In February of that year, the two companies announced their agreement to merge operations, with the merger expected to be completed by the end of that month. The resulting fast food group was to become the undisputed giant of the Spanish fast food landscape and a strong contender in the burgeoning European and Latin American scenes. With mostly complementary locations, the new management stated its intention to close only 20 TeleChef locations, while converting an additional 20 to a new combined TelePizza-Telechef concept. These moves helped restore confidence in TelePizza's future growth.

Principal Subsidiaries

Circol; Delivery Delta; Eydal; Fawn; Inmobiliaria Lombard (Mexico); Luxtor; Minena; Mixor; PizzaNorte (Portugal); Pizzas Del Centro (Mexico); Precocinados Naturales (Prenasa); Sedes; TelePizza Algeciras; TelePizza Chile; TelePizza Cordoba; TelePizza Fuenlabrada; TelePizza Insular; TelePizza Logrono; TelePizza Mexico; TelePizza Moratalaz; TelePizza Polonia (Poland); TelePizza Portugal; TodoPizza (Mexico); TodoPizza Limitada (Chile).

Principal Competitors

Domino's Pizza, Inc.; Pizza Hut Inc.; PizzaExpress; Whitbread plc.

Further Reading

Barghini, Tiziana, "Spain's Telepizza Promises Sizzling Shares," *Reuters,* June 30, 1999.

"Fancy a Pizza? Talk to Telepizza's New Machine," *Reuters,* March 25, 1999.

Hayley, Julia, "Telepizza Shares Plunge on Sale Report," *Reuters,* September 21, 1999.

Morais, Richard C., "Sizzler," *Forbes,* March 22, 1999.

Nash, Elizabeth, "Dateline: Madrid: The Cuban Who Conquered Spain," *Independent,* March 17, 1999, p. 2.

Navarro, Juan, "Spain's Telepizza Parts Ways with Founder," *Reuters,* October 22, 1999.

Parry, John N., "Pizza Magnate Delivers the Profits," *The European,* December 19, 1996, p. 28.

Tremlett, Giles, "Leo Rakes Up Profits from His Pizza Delivery Business," *The European,* April 20, 1998, p. 50.

—M.L. Cohen

Tennant Company

701 North Lilac Drive
Post Office Box 1452
Minneapolis, Minnesota 55440
U.S.A.
Telephone: (612) 540-1208
Toll Free: (800) 553-8033
Fax: (612) 540-1437
Web site: http://www.tennantco.com

Public Company
Incorporated: 1909
Employees: 2,241
Sales: $429.4 million (1999)
Stock Exchanges: NASDAQ
Ticker Symbol: TANT
NAIC: 333319 Other Commercial and Service Industry
    Machinery Manufacturing; 325612 Polish and Other
    Sanitation Good Manufacturing

Tennant Company is the world's foremost manufacturer of industrial floor maintenance equipment, including sweepers, scrubbers, and combination sweeper/scrubbers, in a variety of ride-on and walk-behind models. These heavy-duty floor cleaning machines, which are priced between $7,500 and $90,000, are used to maintain indoor and outdoor surfaces in factories, warehouses, stadiums, parking garages, and airports. Tennant dominates the U.S. market with an estimated 60 percent market share and holds about one-third of the world market. The company also makes smaller, less expensive ($3,000 to $8,000) machines—including sweepers, scrubbers, carpet extractors, buffers, and polishers—for commercial markets, including schools, hospitals, office buildings, and retail outlets; as well as coatings for concrete and wood floors. The company maintains manufacturing facilities in Minneapolis; Holland, Michigan; Uden, the Netherlands; and Waldhausen, Germany. It sells its products directly in eight countries and through distributors in an additional 45.

Early History

Tennant Company was founded in Minneapolis in 1870 by an Irish immigrant named George Henry Tennant. Tennant had opened a sawmill and woodshop to supply the growing number of houses with hardwood floors, wooden downspouts, and rain gutters. Over the next 30 years the woodworking shop expanded, surviving several fires, and by the turn of the century had become one of the leading manufacturers of hardwood flooring in the Upper Midwest. Many of the original G.H. Tennant hardwood floors can still be found in the stately homes along the main streets of Minneapolis and St. Paul. The company was incorporated in 1909.

The innovation that would shape Tennant's business and revolutionize floor care was a classic example of ingenuity born of frustration. In 1932 Ben Casper, a local junior high school janitor weary of laboring over floors on his hands and knees, discovered a way to dry clean his floors. Casper fashioned a scouring contraption from a coffee can wrapped in steel wool that he hooked up to an old washing machine motor. The janitor demonstrated his idea to a neighbor, who just happened to be a shop foreman at Tennant. Tennant acquired the rights to manufacture the machine, and within a few years, a variation of the janitor's model formed the backbone of the company's business.

Tennant had developed a floor finishing and treating system based on oils and sealers to be applied with a buffer. Along with the floor-care machine, the Tennant Floor Maintenance System flourished, and by 1940, over 100,00 square feet of wooden floors in bakeries, schools, and factories were maintained with its products. In the 1940s, treatment products were developed for concrete floors.

The outbreak of World War II ushered in a new era for Tennant. As defense plants sprang up, heavy-duty machines were required to keep those installations immaculate. Tennant responded with the production of the Model K, a much larger machine with a wider cleaning path. The product line was expanded to include scarifiers, a series of outdoor machines that could be used to route and loosen up the surfaces of airport ramps, bridges, and highways. Tennant also participated in the war effort by subcontracting parts for the Norden bombsight manufactured by Honeywell. During this period, sales went from $330,000 in 1938 to $1 million in 1945.

Postwar Growth

The postwar period witnessed a continuation of Tennant's explosive growth. Ongoing innovations in equipment created increased demand, and the market for scrubbers and sweepers rapidly expanded. A landmark event was the invention of the first vacuumized power sweeper in 1947 by Ralph Peabody, a Tennant Company engineer. The sweeper revolutionized industrial floor maintenance by controlling dust dispersion during sweeping. The Model 36, as it was called, formed the prototype of a long line of sweepers, scarifiers, and scrubbers. The year 1950 marked the introduction of sweepers with front wheel steering, and in 1953 Tennant launched the first mechanically raised hopper, followed by the first hydraulically driven sweeper in 1961.

As a result of Tennant's rapid expansion in the 1950s, the company outgrew its plant in Minneapolis and relocated to a larger headquarters in suburban Minneapolis in 1957. Tennant later added five other facilities in the greater suburban area of the Twin Cities. In 1969 Tennant went public with its first stock offering and made its first major acquisition with the purchase of Taylor Material Handling in Michigan.

The 1960s and 1970s were decades of prosperous growth for Tennant. In the early 1960s, Tennant took the first steps to carve out a stronger niche for the company's products in Europe by granting a license to its importer, R.S. Stokvis Company, to manufacture the company's products in Holland. By 1970, Tennant had bought out the license agreement from Stokvis in a takeover of Stokvis/De Nederlandsche Kroon Rijwiefabrieken and formed a wholly owned subsidiary, Tennant NV, based in Uden, the Netherlands.

Looking toward expansion in the Pacific, Tennant embarked upon a joint venture with Fuji Heavy Industries in Japan in 1964. In the long term, this relationship did not live up to its initial promise as Fuji was less than aggressive in promoting and distributing Tennant's products. In Australia, too, during this same period, sales failed to advance as expected under Tennant's national distributor, Clark Equipment. In the mid-1970s, Tennant phased out Clark and began selling directly. Sales increased from $750,000 in 1976 to $11 million by 1994.

In the United States, Tennant further solidified its position as an industry leader by introducing service and parts through authorized service dealers around the country. Unlike its major competitors, Tennant also maintained its own direct sales force, which actively sought out new markets and customer feedback. In this way, the sales force not only sold Tennant's products and services, but also served as a sounding board for customer concerns. Tennant's sales force promoted the company's complete product line out of three regions (western, central, and eastern), and worked in tandem with service representatives in these areas.

1979–89: Quality Improvement Campaign

A major turning point for Tennant Company took place in 1979, when the company launched an all-out quality improvement campaign after a thorough evaluation of the company's operations by quality expert Philip Crosby. While Tennant's sales were booming at the time, CEO Roger Hale and other senior managers were keenly aware that American companies were quickly losing their competitive edge in the global marketplace. At the same time, Hale was detecting warning signs about Tennant's quality as complaints came in from Japanese customers about sweepers leaking hydraulic oil. Strangely enough, U.S. customers had not bothered to protest the same leaks, which Hale took as an indication of American complacency to issues of quality. Then came the news that Toyota's lift-truck division was planning to enter the floor sweeper business. With a formidable Japanese competitor looming on Tennant's horizon, Hale and other Tennant executives moved quickly to explore dramatic quality improvements.

Tennant's extensive rework stations were the first target. These areas, where 20 of the company's top mechanics worked overtime to get faulty machines ready for shipping, took up 15 percent of assembly space, and an average of 33,000 hours was spent annually on manufacturing rework, a practice that was considered standard across U.S. industry. Resolving to do it right the first time, Hale transferred rework mechanics to assembly to catch mistakes on the line from the beginning.

Tennant's vast number of suppliers posed another problem. Supplied parts represented 65 percent of the average cost of a sweeper or scrubber, and with so many suppliers, there were inevitable inconsistencies in parts and inadequate training for assemblers. Tennant carefully weeded out its suppliers and reduced their numbers from 1,100 in 1980 to 250 in 1992. The number of defects dropped dramatically. Employees were also trained in statistical process control (SPC), a method of monitoring defects and setting goals to reduce them. According to *Training* in 1990, SPC allowed the company to cut by half the number of inspectors of parts manufacturing.

In a further effort to reduce errors, small teams of managers and workers were formed to focus on how procedures could be

Key Dates:

1870: George Henry Tennant founds a company specializing in the manufacture of wood flooring.
1909: Company is incorporated.
1932: Local janitor develops a machine to dry clean his floors; Tennant later acquires the rights to manufacture the machine.
1945: Sales reach $1 million.
1947: A company engineer invents the first vacuumized power sweeper.
1969: Company goes public.
1970: Company forms a wholly owned manufacturing subsidiary in the Netherlands.
1976: Roger Hale takes over leadership of the company.
1979: Company launches a major quality improvement campaign.
1992: Preeminence 2000 campaign is launched.
1994: Castex Inc., a maker of commercial floor and carpet cleaning equipment, is acquired.
1999: Paul Andra KG, a German maker of commercial floor maintenance equipment, is acquired; Janet M. Dolan is named CEO of the company.

improved. These small groups became a way of life at Tennant and encouraged regular employee feedback in all areas of the business. Management also relied on the team process to stay in touch with day-to-day operations. The 1993 edition of *The 100 Best Companies to Work for in America* gave Tennant high marks for management responsiveness and general working conditions. The report also highlighted the incentive programs and recognition program that have helped prompt greater employee participation in the quality improvement campaign.

Roger Hale, a great-grandson of Tennant's founder, who had led the company since 1976, embraced the quality philosophy with the fervor of a missionary. His account of how the company transformed itself, *Quest for Quality: How One Company Put Theory to Work,* published in 1989, became required reading for other companies interested in quality management. Tennant also sponsored an annual conference on quality. In addition to the extensive training introduced for company employees, a department was created to run external training programs for companies eager to emulate Tennant's approach.

Tennant's quality campaign not only produced savings for the company, but also translated into tangible benefits for its customers. Tennant's products were more reliable, and during the 1980s prices on some machines actually went down. Warranty coverage was extended. Tennant's sweepers and scrubbers were featured in *Fortune's* 1988 roundup of top-notch U.S. products in an article entitled "What America Makes Best." According to *Management Accounting* in 1992, Tennant significantly improved product quality and reduced total quality costs from 17 percent of sales in 1980 to 2.5 percent of sales in 1988.

As part of its ongoing quality improvement campaign, Tennant was investing what *Barron's* called an incredibly high level of revenues, close to five percent, in new product research and development. By the mid-1990s, the company had cut its product development cycle in half, from four to two years. Some of the more innovative products to emerge in this period were environmentally safe resurfacing coatings and a heavy-duty machine for use in airports to pick up and recycle the deicing fluids sprayed on planes before takeoff.

1990s and Beyond

Tennant weathered the recession of the early 1990s with minor layoffs and a slump in sales of its floor coatings products. Overall sales in 1991 dropped six percent to $144 million and earnings were off by approximately 25 percent. As a way to invigorate its quality efforts, Tennant launched a Preeminence 2000 campaign in 1992 to define a strategy to propel the company into the next century. The company's mission was to be the preeminent company in the industry with the goal of doubling sales by the millennium. Continued diversification and expansion of overseas sales seemed to be the key to prosperity despite a stagnant market at home.

Under Hale's leadership, Tennant had moved to expand international sales, initially concentrating on Europe. Using its base in the Netherlands as a springboard, Tennant had gradually assumed ownership of the Stokvis organizations in Germany (1978), the United Kingdom (1982), and France (1994), establishing direct sales and service operations in all four countries. A fifth direct sales office in Spain got its start in 1991 and had more than doubled in size four years later.

Tennant Australia, a wholly owned subsidiary, became a full sales, marketing, and service organization and the first to offer service 24 hours a day, seven days a week. In 1989, after ending its 25-year joint venture with Fuji Heavy Industries, Tennant formed Tennant Japan K.K. and with its master distributor, Nippon Yusoki Company, Ltd., initiated direct imports from the United States to Japan. In 1992 Tennant formed Tennant Company Japan Branch to sell commercial floor care equipment. In 1994 overseas sales accounted for $72 million, or 25 percent of revenues.

Tennant's significant inroads into the commercial market were enhanced by the acquisition in February 1994 of Castex Industries, Inc., the world leader in carpet maintenance equipment, for $26.8 million. Castex itself had widened its scope in 1989 by taking over Nobles Industries, which offered much broader established distribution channels for its line of hard floor maintenance equipment. Castex/Nobles was integrated with Tennant Trend, which had been formed in 1982, and these operations were consolidated in a new manufacturing facility in Holland, Michigan. Castex complemented Tennant's product line with a wide range of walk-behind scrubbers, sweepers, and wet/dry vacuums, as well as carpet extractors and floor polishers, appropriate for use in commercial settings such as office buildings, hospitals, and supermarkets.

Tennant's ambitious program to dominate the commercial floor equipment market was further bolstered with the purchase of Eagle Floor Care, Inc., a manufacturer of propane burnishers that same year. By the end of 1994, commercial floor maintenance equipment sales had more than tripled since the year before due to marketplace acceptance of the new acquisitions.

The year 1994 was a high point for Tennant in more ways than one. Sales of $281 million were up 27 percent over 1993, with sales in North America registering a 33 percent increase. That same year, Tennant was the first non-Fortune 500 company to receive *Purchasing* magazine's Medal of Professional Excellence. Other recipients of the award included Motorola, Hewlett Packard, Chrysler, and General Electric. *Purchasing* made special note of the company's outstanding performance in the areas of supplier relations, product teams, and quality.

The late 1990s were a period of steady growth in sales and profits for Tennant; growth fueled both by the expansion into the commercial sector and heightened new product development. In 1998 alone, the company introduced three new commercial products and five industrial products. Among the latter were two products designed for outdoor cleaning: the Model 830-II street sweeper and the 4300 All-Terrain Litter Vacuum, a riding vehicle used to pick up small pieces of garbage. Tennant products had long been used outdoors, but these models were among the company's first to be designed specifically for such use. In addition to pursuing the outdoor niche, Tennant also identified a second niche market as a key growth opportunity, that of contract cleaners. Businesses everywhere were increasingly outsourcing their floor maintenance, and Tennant aimed to supply contract cleaners with the equipment they needed.

By the late 1990s Tennant had also completed a total overhaul of its worldwide computer systems, an initiative that began in 1994. By linking all operations and customer information, the company hoped to improve customer service, sell more efficiency to its customers, and design products and services that better meet customer needs.

In April 1998 Janet M. Dolan was named president and chief operating officer at Tennant, having previously served as general counsel, head of the floor coatings division, and then head of the company's entire North American operations. One year later, Dolan became the first company CEO not descended from the founder when Roger Hale stepped down from that position after 23 years at the helm. In January 1999 Tennant made an important European acquisition when it paid almost $7 million for Paul Andra KG, a German, privately owned maker of commercial floor maintenance equipment, including single-disk machines, wet/dry vacuum cleaners, and vacuumized scrubbers. The company sold about $27 million in products on an annual basis, mainly under the Sorma brand name, with 75 percent of sales occurring in Germany and Austria. This acquisition not only provided Tennant with a strong position in the key country of Germany, it also provided a base for extending the Sorma and Tennant commercial product lines into other countries.

In October 1999 Tennant announced a restructuring intended to position the company for greater growth and profitability in the 21st century. Aiming to reduce operating costs by $5 million per year, Tennant consolidated some operations and facilities and divested certain units, including the Eagle Floor Care line of burnishing equipment. About 150 jobs were trimmed from the workforce. Tennant also began moving from a "build-to-stock" manufacturing system to a "build-to-order" manufacturing capacity—according to the company, the

first in the industry to take this ambitious step. Longer term, Tennant set financial goals for itself of annual sales increases of ten to 12 percent and an increase in its operating margin to more than ten percent. (This margin had ranged from 9.2 percent to 9.7 percent from 1995 to 1998.) In the press release announcing this restructuring, Dolan neatly summed up the history of a consistently successful firm when she said that Tennant "has prospered for 130 years by adapting to a changing world and will continue to do so."

Principal Subsidiaries

Castex Incorporated; Paul Andra KG (Germany); Tennant Holding B.V. (Netherlands); Tennant UK Limited.

Principal Competitors

Athey Corporation; Federal Signal Corporation; Minuteman International, Inc.; Nilfisk-Advance Inc.; RPM, Inc.; Toyota Motor Corporation.

Further Reading

Brammer, Rhonda, "Gleaming Prospects," *Barron's,* September 20, 1999, pp. 22, 24–25.

Carr, Lawrence, and Thomas Tyson, "Planning Quality Cost Expenditures," *Management Accounting,* October 1992, pp. 52–56.

Ewen, Beth, "Pacing Herself: Tennant's New CEO Wants Big Growth a Little at a Time," *Corporate Report-Minnesota,* June 1999, pp. 14+.

Hale, Roger L., "Tennant Company: Instilling Quality from Top to Bottom," *Management Review,* February 1989, p. 65.

Hale, Roger L., et. al., *Made in the U.S.A.: How One American Company Helps Satisfy Customer Needs Through Strategic Supplier Quality Management,* Minneapolis: Tennant Company, 1991.

Hale, Roger L., Douglas R. Hoelscher, and Ronald E. Kowal, *Quest for Quality: How One Company Put Theory to Work,* Minneapolis: Tennant Company, 1987, 148 p.

Hequet, Marc, "Selling In-House Training Outside," *Training,* September 1991, pp. 51–56.

Knowlton, Christopher, "What America Makes Best," *Fortune,* March 28, 1988, pp. 40–53.

Levering, Robert, and Milton Moskowitz, *The 100 Best Companies to Work for in America,* New York: Doubleday, 1993, pp. 447–50.

Oberle, Joseph, "Employee Involvement at Tennant," *Training,* May 1990, pp. 73–79.

Palmer, Jay, "Come the Recovery . . . and Tennant Seems Poised to Clean Up," *Barron's,* February 3, 1992, pp. 17, 36.

Peterson, Susan E., "Tennant Co. Promotes Janet Dolan to President, Chief Operating Officer," *Minneapolis Star Tribune,* April 8, 1998, p. 3D.

Porter, Anne Millen, "Does Quality Really Affect the Bottom Line?," *Purchasing,* January 16, 1992, pp. 61–64.

Raia, Ernie, "Medal of Excellence: Swept Away by Tennant," *Purchasing,* September 22, 1994, pp. 37–45.

"Sweeper Manufacturer Writes the Book on Quality," *Diesel Progress, Engines and Drives,* April 1993, p. 18.

Tennant Anniversary Book, 1870–1995, Minneapolis: Tennant Company, 1995, 38 p.

—Leslie D. Hyde
—updated by David E. Salamie

Thomas Cook Travel Inc.

American Express Company
World Financial Center
200 Vesey Street
New York, New York 10285
U.S.A.
Telephone: (212) 640-2000
Fax: (212) 619-9802
Web site: http://www.americanexpress.com

Assets Acquired by American Express in 1994 (Brand Name Not Acquired)
Incorporated: 1965
Dissolved: 1994
Employees: 4,000 (1993)
Sales: $1.9 billion (1993)

Prior to its acquisition by the American Express Company in 1994, Thomas Cook Travel Inc. was the third-largest travel agency in the United States. At the time of the takeover, Thomas Cook operated 500 offices across the country and sold one out of every 50 airline tickets in the United States. Staffed by more than 3,000 employees, the company had an impressive roster of business clients including Ford Motor Co., AT&T, and John Hancock Financial Services. Independently owned by Linda and David Paresky, Thomas Cook Travel licensed its name from the oldest travel agency in the world, The Thomas Cook Group Ltd., based in the United Kingdom.

Thomas Cook Is Founded in 1841

The Thomas Cook Group Ltd. was the eponymous creation of an industrious English entrepreneur. From a humble beginning chartering a train to a temperance rally in 1841, Cook expanded his business into one of the world's first full-service travel firms. After the resounding success of his first venture, Cook quickly expanded his operations, providing rail trips and making hotel reservations for customers for journeys all over the British Isles. Cook's excursions proved so popular that he began offering trips to Europe, North America, and—beginning in 1871—around the world. Buoyed by these successes, Cook's company was able to open 120 travel offices in the United Kingdom and abroad by 1885, and Cook himself branched out to write guidebooks. The company also remained on the cutting edge of developments in the travel industry. Thomas Cook Ltd. began offering cruise trips as early as the mid-1870s, pioneered an early form of travelers' check, and was booking air travel by 1911, a mere eight years after the Wright Brothers made history at Kitty Hawk, North Carolina.

The company also had a long history in the American market. Just months after the Civil War ended in 1865, Cook's ran its first U.S. tour, which included stops at various battlefields. Six years later, Cook formed a partnership with an American businessman that they called Cook, Son & Jenkins. This relationship subsequently dissolved acrimoniously, but by then it had helped Cook's entrench itself in the American market. To bolster its business further, the company took a pavilion at the Centennial Celebration in Philadelphia in 1876, and later expanded its offerings to include not just traditional sightseeing trips but even travel packages for immigrants coming to the United States and Canada. By 1896, Cook's American business made travel arrangements to the Klondike for gold prospectors.

Control of the company remained with the Cook family until the late 1920s. Thomas Cook himself had died in 1892, and his son and business partner did the same eight years later. His three grandsons then ran the company until the last of them retired in 1928, at which point it was sold to a Belgian travel concern, Compagnie des Wagons-Lits et des Grands Express Europeens. When Germany occupied Belgium in World War II, the company was taken over by the German Custodian of Enemy Properties, but the British government arranged for it to be re-acquired by several railway companies at the close of the war. When the railroads were nationalized in 1948, ownership of Thomas Cook Ltd. passed to the crown as well.

Although Thomas Cook had become an institution both in the United Kingdom and the United States, the company risked losing touch with younger consumers in the 1960s. As a state-run business, Thomas Cook was unable to invest the same level of funding into its operations that its private rivals could. While other travel agencies crafted new strategies to attract more cus-

Key Dates:

1845: Thomas Cook organizes his first commercial tour.
1928: Company is sold to Compagnie des Wagons-Lits et des Grands Express Europeens.
1948: Thomas Cook falls under the control of the British government.
1965: Crimson Travel is founded by David and Linda Paresky.
1974: Midland Bank acquires Thomas Cook Travel Inc.
1979: Dun & Bradstreet purchases Thomas Cook Travel.
1988: Robert Maxwell acquires the company and sells a 50 percent stake to the Pareskys.
1992: The Pareskys gain 100 percent control of Thomas Cook Travel.
1994: The Pareskys sell the business to American Express.

tomers and increase revenue, such as purchasing airlines, Thomas Cook saw its sales flatten. As a result, the British government tentatively explored selling the travel agency.

U.S. Corporate Laws Prevent New Owner of Thomas Cook from Owning U.S. Offices

Midland Bank acquired Thomas Cook in 1974. Since U.S. banking laws prohibited any national bank—such as Midland—from owning domestic travel agencies, Midland sold Thomas Cook's U.S. operations to Dun & Bradstreet in 1975. Midland did not relinquish control of the Thomas Cook name, but Dun & Bradstreet was allowed to continue to operate the U.S. travel agencies under the Cook name through a licensing agreement. Although The Thomas Cook Group Ltd. had no equity in the American operations, it did link the agencies into its travel network. More importantly, the British branch could supply the independent American offices with travelers' checks, which represented an increasing portion of The Thomas Cook Group Ltd.'s revenues. Only American Express outperformed Cook in this segment of the travel industry.

Crimson Travel Is Founded and Flourishes

At about the same time that Dun & Bradstreet made this pivotal purchase, Crimson Travel Service—the Cambridge, Massachusetts-based travel agency that would later carry the Thomas Cook American franchise—began to expand. Founded in 1965 by the husband-and-wife duo David and Linda Paresky, Crimson quickly grew through creative marketing efforts. Graced with the same gift for travel innovation as Thomas Cook, Paresky launched a number of bold initiatives. As a competitor explained in the September 18, 1994, *Boston Globe,* "Paresky saw before most of us that the masses wanted to go, and he knew where they wanted to go." Crimson chartered several immensely popular "Cruises to Nowhere," that brought the luxury of a cruise vacation to middle-class consumers. In 1968 the company forged a strategic alliance with a Western-themed television show called "Boomtown," whereby Crimson chartered mass trips for kids (guided by Trailer, the show's host) and received ample exposure in the process. The "Boomtown" trips were a huge success and continued through the

1990s. By 1969 Crimson had opened its third Boston-area branch office, and its leisure travel business soared. By 1987 the company reported billings of $150 million.

As Crimson saw its fortune rise, the travel industry as a whole experienced tectonic changes in the 1980s. The frenetic globalization of American business meant that corporate employees traveled more frequently and purchased a growing percentage of airline tickets. Since Crimson's revenues came mostly from vacationers, not business people, the company would risk its future profitability if it did not develop the corporate side of its operations. In 1988 Crimson purchased Heritage Travel, a rival Cambridge agency. Not only was Heritage equipped with cutting-edge computer technology, but it also ran a formidable corporate business.

Thomas Cook Changes Ownership in 1988

In 1988 Dun & Bradstreet put Thomas Cook up for sale in order to concentrate on its core marketing, credit risk, finance, and directory information divisions. Publishing magnate Robert Maxwell purchased Thomas Cook in 1989, and immediately renewed the licensing agreement with Midland to use the storied Cook name. At the time of Maxwell's acquisition, Thomas Cook was a sizable operation, generating sales of $365 million and operating 60 full-service locations and nine regional reservation centers. Many industry analysts speculated that Maxwell would quickly sell the company, since publishing was his primary concern. However, Maxwell pledged to expand Thomas Cook through a series of acquisitions that would make the franchise the leading American travel service firm.

But despite his protestations to the contrary, Maxwell sold a 50 percent stake in Thomas Cook to the Pareskys' Crimson/Heritage business in 1988. With Maxwell, the Pareskys presided over the third-largest agency in the country, with revenues topping $1.3 billion. David Paresky served as president, chairman, and chief executive of his new empire, and he moved Thomas Cook's corporate headquarters from New York City to Cambridge. The co-owners quickly turned to bolstering Thomas Cook's roster of corporate clients.

While the ownership of Thomas Cook changed hands in the United States, the keeper of the coveted license—The Thomas Cook Group Ltd.—went through its own shifts. In 1992 Midland sold its subsidiary to LTU Group, one of Germany's largest tour operators, and Westdeutsche Landesbanke, a German bank. Westdeutsche Landesbanke purchased 90 percent of The Thomas Cook Group Ltd.'s shares, while LTU Group controlled the remaining ten. The *Orange Country Register* was quick to point out to its readers that the sale in no way affected Thomas Cook Travel Inc. "The company licenses the name and expects to continue doing so under the new ownership," noted the paper.

The Pareskys Gain 100 Percent Control of Thomas Cook Travel

Although Thomas Cook Travel Inc. had no problems with the license, the company did endure some turbulent times in 1991 when Maxwell died suddenly. One of his privately held companies, Headington Holdings Limited, went into bankruptcy. Headington owned Maxwell Travel Inc., which in turn owned Maxwell's 50 percent share of Thomas Cook. A number of potential buyers hungrily eyed the stake in Thomas Cook, including Midland Bank, which had by then divested the bank that had prevented it from owning the chain in 1979. Paresky had right of first refusal, though, and in 1993 he and his wife purchased the Maxwell stake.

Even with complete control of Thomas Cook Travel, Paresky planned no major changes. "We're continuing with the same strategy we've had before, differentiating our service through innovation and quality," he told The *Boston Globe* on January 12, 1993. "I don't think our operating philosophy will change." 1993 sales soared to over $1.7 billion, and the company ran approximately 500 offices throughout the United States.

Paresky's efforts to bolster Thomas Cook's corporate accounts had succeeded. At the close of 1993, 84 percent of the company's sales were from businesses. Thomas Cook's list of clients was impressive. Ford Motor Co., Fidelity Investment, Hewlett-Packard, and John Hancock Mutual Life Insurance Co. all made their travel arrangements through Thomas Cook. In 1994 the company won three more substantial accounts—the British Embassy, Walsh America, and Pharmaceutical Marketing Services Inc.

Sale to American Express

Despite their success, the Pareskys approached arch-rival American Express about selling Thomas Cook. "American Express will bring more size and more strength and more ability to invest in our people," Paresky explained to *Travel Weekly* on September 15, 1994. To the *Boston Globe*, Paresky admitted that the cost of upgrading technology to better serve global business travelers was a factor in the decision to sell. American Express had much to gain from the purchase. Already gigantic—with over 1,700 travel offices in more than 120 nations—American Express would boost its annual sales an additional 33 percent with this new division. The acquisition also had significant prestige value. Although American Express had recently snapped up five other large agencies, the Cook deal was to be the largest takeover in the history of the travel industry.

The transaction was finalized in September 1994 with American Express paying $375 million for the company. Although they had relinquished their ownership interests, the Pareskys

remained involved in the business. Both were appointed vice-presidents, and in 1995, David Paresky was reported to be "in line" to become president of American Express Travel.

American Express also moved to acquire the corporate accounts of The Thomas Cook Group Ltd. (which represented about ten percent of the British company's total revenues). While this segment of the business was lucrative, The Group was willing to part with it to in order to concentrate on servicing leisure travelers and on its burgeoning financial services division. However, American Express was not able to obtain from The Group the rights to the venerable Thomas Cook name. The Pareskys' licensing agreement had been due to expire in 1999, and, according to the *Guardian*, The Thomas Cook Group Ltd. took immediate steps to secure a new licensee. As a result, all former Thomas Cook offices were to be re-christened American Express.

Further Reading

Ackerman, Jerry, "American Express to Cut about 300 Jobs," *Boston Globe*, May 23, 1995.

——, "Crimson to Cook to Gold," *Boston Globe*, September 18, 1994.

Carroll, Cathy, "American Express Buys Thomas Cook," *Travel Weekly*, September 15, 1994.

Gilpin, Kenneth, "American Express to Expand Travel Arm," *Seattle Post-Intelligencer*, September 10, 1994.

Golden, Fran, "Industry Weighs Impact of Crimson/Heritage-Thomas Cook Merger," *Travel Weekly*, December 28, 1989, pp. 17–18.

——, "Maxwell to Buy Thomas Cook Travel," *Travel Weekly*, February 16, 1989, p. 1.

——, "Thomas Cook Joins Forces with Crimson," *Travel Weekly*, December 18, 1989, p. 1.

Sit, Mary, "Executives Buy Thomas Cook Travel," *Boston Globe*, January 12, 1993.

Stone, John, "Thomas Cook Group Sold to New Owners," *Tour & Travel News*, June 15, 1992.

Swinglehurst, Edmund, *Cook's Tours: The Story of Popular Travel*, Dorset, England: Blandford Press, 1982.

——, *The Romantic Journey: The Story of Thomas Cook and Victorian Travel*, New York: Harper & Row, 1974.

"Top Officers Buy Remaining Interest in Thomas Cook," *Associated Press*, January 11, 1993.

Tran, Mark, "AmEx Set to Snap up US Travel Rival," *Guardian*, September 10, 1994.

—Wendy J. Stein
—updated by Rebecca Stanfel

Thousand Trails, Inc.

2711 LBJ Freeway, Suite 200
Dallas, Texas
U.S.A.
Telephone: (972) 243-2226
Fax: (972) 488-5008
Web site: http://www.1000trails.com

Public Company
Incorporated: 1991 as USTrails, Inc.
Employees: 839
Sales: $67.9 million (1999)
Stock Exchanges: American
Ticker Symbol: TRV
NAIC: 721211 RV (Recreational Vehicle) Parks and
    Campgrounds

Thousand Trails, Inc. operates 53 membership-based campgrounds under the Thousand Trails and NACO banners. The company's camping facilities are located in 17 states and in British Columbia, serving more than 100,000 member customers. In addition, a Thousand Trails subsidiary manages 169 public campgrounds for the U.S. Forest Service.

1970s Origins

Thousand Trails' history of financial woes began not long after founder Milt Kuolt created the first Thousand Trails campground in 1972 in Chehalis, Washington, a 90-minute drive from Seattle. Kuolt, in his mid-40s at the time, believed he could make his fortune selling campground memberships, a concept grounded on the premise that Americans would flock to secure, affordable, and well-maintained campground sites for their vacations. For the price of a single extended vacation to Hawaii, for instance, Thousand Trails customers could make a down payment on a lifetime membership, entitling them to visit a variety of locations whenever they chose. Kuolt's immediate need after establishing the first campground was to develop more sites. At each Thousand Trails campground he wanted to establish a suitable mixture of the pristine outdoors and the security and amenities of a private resort. Typically, two-thirds

of the acreage included within a campground was left untouched. The remaining third was developed for the member campers. Recreational vehicle sites were created, some with electrical and sewer hookups, sheltered from each other by curtains of trees. Clubhouses were built, serving as activity centers for the member campers, many of whom were retirees, and security measures were taken. The camping complexes were gated, patrolled 24 hours a day by guards.

Providing a controlled environment in a natural setting required considerable development money. Kuolt quickly found himself strapped for cash. In 1976, when Kuolt was in hot pursuit of building his portfolio of camping properties, an opportunity arose that revealed the company's dire need for money. Kuolt was presented with the chance to buy 199 acres of defaulted property, its mortgage held by a banker who offered to sell it to Kuolt for $1 million. Kuolt believed the acreage was worth half the amount, but the banker stipulated that if Thousand Trails acquired the property for $1 million, the bank would extend the company a $2.5 million credit line. In an April 11, 1983 interview with *Forbes* magazine, Kuolt explained that the asking price was unacceptable, but he was forced to agree to the terms because of the precarious financial state of his company: "My closest advisers pulled me right out of this room and said, 'Kuolt, we don't give a damn if you push the whole goddamn piece of land into Puget Sound. You sign that goddamn deal with this banker. You need the cash'."

Kuolt, never reticent in his use of strong language, was forced to capitulate to the banker's offer, but the $2.5 million credit line did not resolve his company's financial problems. As the expansion of Thousand Trails continued, Kuolt again found himself in need of capital. In 1979, he took Thousand Trails public, turning to an initial public offering (IPO) for a fresh supply of cash. At the time of the company's IPO, liabilities exceeded assets by more than $2 million. In his 1983 *Forbes* interview, Kuolt conceded, "We were technically bankrupt," but the $5.7 million raised from the IPO relieved the pressure only temporarily. Within a year, Thousand Trails again stood on the brink of financial failure. Marketing expenses had stripped the company of its IPO proceeds. To stay the company's collapse, Kuolt searched for an institution willing to extend Thousand Trails more credit. In 1980, First National Bank of Boston emerged as the company's savior, granting it $10 million of credit, an offer that Kuolt was forced to accept at two percent over the prime rate.

As the 1980s began, Thousand Trails was heavily in debt and suffering from a recurring problem. Escalating operating costs had hamstrung the company, forcing Kuolt to take a new approach to the problem. Instead of treatment, the company needed a cure, which led Kuolt to look at the company's operation from a more detached, objective view. As befitted his candid, no-holds-barred demeanor, Kuolt cast the finger of blame directly on himself. "You've got to pull yourself away and say, now what's wrong with the company?," he explained in his 1983 *Forbes* interview, adding "Well, the goddamn chairman, he's fouling it up." Kuolt stepped down from the chairman's office in 1981, sacrificing himself as a last resort to save Thousand Trails. Later in the year, Kuolt started a new airline company named Horizon Air, while the person he se-lected to head Thousand Trails grappled with the profound problems hobbling Thousand Trails' progress.

New Leadership for the 1980s

Jim Jensen, a self-described "new age" manager, moved into Kuolt's office in 1981. During the previous two years, Jensen had taken a hiatus from corporate life to pursue readings in metaphysics and psychology and to take a trip to Brazil, where he met with a Brazilian psychic who performed psycho-kinesis, mental telepathy, and telekinesis. Jensen's avid interest in seeking alternative methods of self-improvement dovetailed with his method of management. Before his two-year self-exploratory sojourn, Jensen had cemented his reputation as an effective leader at Grantree Furniture Rental, the principal sub-sidiary of Oregon-based Grantree Corp. Instilling what he called "whole brain" communications to his employees, Jensen spearheaded prolific growth. During his six-year term as president and chief operating officer of Grantree Furniture Rental, Jensen transformed the subsidiary from a 183-em-ployee, $6 million-in-sales operation to a $72 million-in-sales enterprise that employed 1,400 workers.

Jensen's achievements at Grantree Furniture Rental had impressed Kuolt, convincing him that he had found the person capable of resolving Thousand Trails' fundamental problem.

The company was suffering because it consistently spent more money than it collected. Lifetime memberships were priced at an average of $6,000, but the middle-income campers who purchased the memberships usually only made a down payment equal to 40 percent of the full price. The company, which recorded partial payments at the full membership price as reve-nue on its balance sheet, was spending 45 percent of sales on marketing, rendering it incapable of meeting its cash flow needs. The only way to overcome this obstacle was to borrow money or to sell portions of the company to equity investors, a tactic that could not be used in the long term.

Despite the financial crisis, Jensen pressed ahead with ex-pansion. He inherited 14 campgrounds when he took control in 1981 and over the next two years increased the number of properties to 21. To tide the company over financially, he continued to seek outside sources for infusions of cash, doing what Kuolt had done since the company's birth. When sales reached $56 million in 1982, Jensen brokered a $25 million credit line from a Phoenix-based, state-regulated savings and loan association named Western Savings. In return, Western Savings gained a 24 percent ownership stake in the company. The credit line from Western Savings was dedicated to property acquisition and development, while commercial credit lines, which amounted to another $25 million in 1983, were used to supply working capital.

Thousand Trails was falling deeper and deeper in debt, but as Jensen looked ahead from his vantage point in 1983, his forecast was optimistic. He believed that within two years, the company's ever-growing receivables would collect enough in repayments to finally pay down the company's debt. In the interim, the company was forced to finance its aggressive expansion by continuing to borrow against receivables, further deteriorating its financial health. In 1984, when the company announced a record $19.1 million in earnings, it used $52 million more cash than it pro-duced. The following year, earnings plunged 90 percent to $1.8 million after a considerable number of members dropped out of the company's system before paying for their full memberships, stripping Thousand Trails of revenue it had prematurely re-corded. Marketing expenses at this point were two times greater than down payments, saddling the company with a cash shortage of $55 million. When the first quarter results of 1986 revealed a nearly $2 million loss, expansion came shuddering to a stop. Again, company officials endeavored to reduce marketing costs. Debt by the beginning of 1986 represented 244 percent of share-holders' equity.

In 1986 and 1987, Thousand Trails lost a total of $67 million, still unable to generate positive cash flow without the help of financing. The company's financial performance moder-ately improved in the late 1980s, but by the beginning of the 1990s it stood on the verge of bankruptcy. The company oper-ated one of the largest of membership campground resort sys-tems in the nation, comprising 39 campgrounds situated in 15 states and in British Columbia, but its financial problems were grave. In 1990, the company obtained financing from only one source, NACO Finance Corp. (NFC), which itself was mired in financial problems. NFC had been created by Southmark Corp. in 1987 to finance some of its subsidiaries, which included Thousand Trails. By 1990, a Southmark subsidiary that owned

Key Dates:

1972: Milt Kuolt establishes first Thousand Trails campground.
1979: Thousand Trails completes initial public offering.
1981: Kuolt steps down as chairman of the company.
1991: Thousand Trails and NACO are acquired by USTrails, Inc.
1996: USTrails changes its name to Thousand Trails, Inc.
1999: Thousand Trails signs agreement to acquire Leisure Time Resorts of America, Inc.

68.8 percent of Thousand Trails was in Chapter 11 bankruptcy reorganization, making Thousand Trails' position that much more untenable.

Fresh Start for the 1990s

For a brief period, a familiar figure emerged as a possible savior for Thousand Trails. Milt Kuolt, who had sold Horizon Air to Alaska Airlines in 1986, had moved on to become chairman of Delta Campground Management Corp., which in November 1990 announced its intention to buy a controlling interest in Thousand Trails from Southmark's ailing subsidiary, San Jacinto Savings Association of Houston. Kuolt and his company later backed away from the deal, but another deal soon took its place. In 1991, as part of its own Chapter 11 reorganization efforts, NFC acquired National American Corporation (NACO), a manager of timeshare facilities and full service resorts, and 69 percent of Thousand Trails. The new company was named USTrails, Inc., which operated as Thousand Trails' parent company. USTrails acquired the remaining interest in Thousand Trails in 1994. Two years later, the entire organization was renamed Thousand Trails, Inc.

Against the backdrop of these significant corporate maneuvers, important changes were made in the way Thousand Trails operated. In April 1992, after years of suffering losses from rising marketing costs, the company suspended its sales program. No new campground memberships were sold, and, in fact, by the fall of 1992, the company began helping its members to sell their memberships in the secondary market. By May 1994, the company was ready to renew its marketing efforts and implemented a sales program to build up its membership base. Initially, with USTrails governing Thousand Trails' operation, memberships were sold on a limited basis, but in May 1995 the company introduced a range of new membership options. Before halting its sales program in 1992, the company sold campground memberships for prices up to $8,000, but in 1995 marketing efforts began focusing on a greater number of membership options, available for a wide range of prices. Membership packages were offered that gave customers the option of using one system, either Thousand Trails or NACO, or both, for prices ranging between $495 and $2,495. By 1996, when all of the entities operated under one corporate banner, the average price paid by members for a membership package was $779.

By 1996, after the final merger that created a multifaceted Thousand Trails, the scope of the company's operations comprised several networks of properties. Under the Thousand Trails logo, there were 35 campgrounds, complementing the 23 campgrounds operating under the NACO banner. The 58 campgrounds controlled by the company comprised 19,300 campsites, which were used by 81,000 Thousand Trails members and 47,000 NACO members. In addition, a subsidiary named UST Wilderness Management managed 35 public campgrounds for the U.S. Forest Service, a service it began providing in 1994.

By the late 1990s, after years of fitful progress, the company continued to be beleaguered by the realities of its business. By the end of the decade, the number of campgrounds controlled by Thousand Trails had been reduced to 53, scattered among 17 states and British Columbia. Sales were on the wane, as was net income, although the company had recorded ten consecutive quarters of profit by the first quarter of 2000. As Thousand Trails prepared for the future, the emphasis was on increasing its membership base. Toward this end, the company entered into a joint marketing agreement in 1997 with Fleetwood Industries, Inc., the largest U.S. manufacturer of RVs. Under the terms of the arrangement, purchasers of new Fleetwood RVs received temporary Thousand Trails memberships. In another bid to increase sales, Thousand Trails announced in December 1999 that it had signed an agreement to acquire Leisure Time Resorts of America, Inc., which owned and operated ten membership campground resorts in Oregon and Washington. The continued pursuit of property acquisitions and marketing alliances with other leisure-related companies represented the company's most likely chance to improve its financial performance in the 21st century.

Principal Subsidiaries

National American Corporation; Resort Parks International, Inc.; Thousand Trails (Canada), Inc.; UST Wilderness Management Corporation; Coast Financial Services, Inc.

Principal Competitors

Resorts USA, Inc.; Travel America, Inc.; Affinity Group Holding, Inc.; International Leisure Hosts, Ltd.; Kampgrounds of America, Inc.

Further Reading

Crider, Jeff, "Thousand Trails' Rebound: Membership Firm Is Seeing Profits with a New, No-Nonsense Business Strategy," *RV Business,* October 1998, p. 20.
McGough, Robert, "Flying High on Debt," *Forbes,* April 11, 1983, p. 93.
"Minding His Business," *Inc.,* November 1983, p. 120.
Neurath, Peter, "Leisurely Growth Spells Success for Leisure Time," *Puget Sound Business Journal,* July 22, 1991, p. 5.
——, "Thousand Trails Not Resorting to Real Estate Sales," *Puget Sound Business Journal,* June 11, 1993, p. 13.
——, "Thousand Trails Strives To Fend Off Bankruptcy," *Puget Sound Business Journal,* November 12, 1990, p. 12.
"Not-So-Happy Trails," *Forbes,* July 14, 1986, p. 13.

—Jeffrey L. Covell

The Todd-AO Corporation

900 North Seward Street
Hollywood, California 90038
U.S.A.
Telephone: (323) 962-5305
Fax: (323) 9466-2327
Web site: http://www.todd-ao.com

Public Company
Incorporated: 1952
Employees: 920
Sales: $118.5 million (1999)
Stock Exchanges: NASDAQ
Ticker Symbol: TODDA
NAIC: 512191 Teleproduction and Other Post-Production
    Services; 512240 Sound Recording Stereos

The Todd-AO Corporation is famous for providing a wide range of post production services to the motion picture, television, and commercial advertising industries. Renowned for sound engineering, the company's services include editing, narration, rerecording, digital sweetening, sound and picture synchronization, music scoring, Automated Dialogue Replacement, Foley sound effects, content transfer, and vaulting/storage. Moreover, the company's video services include editing, graphics in 2D or 3D, visual effects, color correction, film-to-video transfer (telecine), and vaulting/storage. Finally, its distribution and studio services for home video, pay television, cable, and domestic and international television companies include foreign language dubbing, subtitling, restoration, satellite downlink, Digital TV, Digital Versatile Disc (DVD) services, transmission of television channels, and format conversions. The company's employees have won more than 40 Academy and Emmy Awards; the talent and comprehensive services of Todd-AO and its subsidiaries attract such acclaimed producer/director clients as Steven Spielberg, Ron Howard, Woody Allen, and Robert Altman. The Walt Disney Company and its affiliates account for more than 15 percent of Todd-AO's revenues. Todd-AO maintains facilities worldwide, in Los Angeles, New York City, Atlanta, London, and Barcelona.

Wide Screen Motion Pictures in the 1950s

Though the Todd-AO Corporation would one day make its greatest mark in the area of sound engineering, the company originated with the creation of the Todd-AO filmmaking process for a wide screen. Renowned Broadway producer Michael Todd provided the imaginative stimulus for a wide-angle, single-lens process; the American Optical Company (AOC) provided the practical knowledge to develop it. Ever the showman, Todd addressed AOC's concerns over receiving proper recognition in development of the process by attaching the first two initials of that company's name to his last name, to form Todd-AO, knowing that curious people would ask what ''AO'' represented.

Todd's sense of the spectacular made him a natural enthusiast for a wide screen film-making process called Cinerama created by Fred Waller around 1950. While normal movie screens at that time tended to be a flat 20 feet by 16 feet, Cinerama involved a 51-foot wide by 25-foot high, deeply curved screen designed to engulf the human field of vision. The impact on the viewer and sense of viewer participation amazed Todd. Waller also incorporated the first use of stereo sound which approximated the visual source of the sound on the screen.

With Lowell Thomas, noted for his filmed expedition to Lhasa, Tibet, in 1949, Todd obtained a license to make the first Cinerama feature-length film, *This is Cinerama*. The color production consisted of travelogue clips, such as Niagara Falls from a helicopter and scenes from *Aida* at the opera house in Milan, Italy. Todd wanted to open the film with something to enthrall the audience, so he took a film crew to the Far Rockaway amusement park and had the cameras attached to the first seat of a roller coaster to give the viewer the impression of being on a roller coaster ride. Todd's exuberance proved to be too much for the board of Thomas-Todd Productions, however, and the company completed the film without him.

Cinerama had several limitations which frustrated Todd and motivated the development of the Todd-AO movie-making process. The Cinerama process required three cameras which together approximated a 145 degree view. This proved troublesome as the alignment of the cameras had to create a complete picture.

Shown on a wide screen with three projectors, the two "seams" where the three pictures met were often fuzzy, and the color often differed among the three projections. Also, the wide-angle lenses of the three cameras created distortions in the picture. As the seams and distortions precluded close-up shots, Cinerama proved inadequate for the production of narrative films.

Todd believed that a wide screen process could be invented which filmed from a single lens in a single camera, and he sought the best mind in optics to create such a camera. That turned out to be Dr. Brian O'Brien, head of the Institute of Optics at the University of Rochester. Having been contemplating a move to head research at AOC, O'Brien introduced the president of that company to Todd. While AOC considered Todd's proposal, Todd approached Richard Rogers and Oscar Hammerstein II about obtaining the film rights to their successful Broadway musical *Oklahoma!*

In anticipation of an agreement with AOC, Todd formed Magna Theater with Hollywood friends and acquaintances to produce, distribute, and show motion pictures filmed with the yet-to-be-developed cameras. The board of directors included Chairman Joe Schenck, executive head of production at Twentieth-Century Fox, and George Skouras, president of United Artist Theater Circuit, who put up a majority of funds. Preliminary filming with a 70mm camera owned by Fox (previously used in 1929 but overshadowed by the new "talkies") convinced Rodgers and Hammerstein to grant Magna the film rights to *Oklahoma!* They, along with producer Arthur Hornblow, Jr., whom they wanted for *Oklahoma!* joined the board of Magna as well. The Todd-AO Corporation formed at the end of 1952, with Magna Theater as its primary shareholder.

The first president of Todd-AO was Henry Woodbridge, vice-president of AOC, with O'Brien as head of the research team. Todd-AO hired Mitchell Camera Company to design a high speed camera, Phillips of Holland to design the projection equipment, Eastman Kodak to produce the larger size, 65mm negative, and Ampex to develop a six-track stereo sound recording system. Todd-AO crafted four lenses, a 37 degree, a 48 degree, a 64 degree as well a 128 degree lens, nicknamed the "bugeye," which came closest to the combined wide angle of the three Cinerama lenses. The "bugeye" created distortions in

filming, but O'Brien assured Todd that an optical printer would be developed to fix the distortions. Todd took a camera to Far Rockaway to film the roller coaster ride with the Todd-AO process, providing an apt comparison to Cinerama. The process also tested well for close-up shots and proved better than Cinerama in terms of mobility, for pan and dolly shots, as the Cinerama camera had to be stationary.

Todd-AO Starts Making Movies: The 1950s–60s

Filming of *Oklahoma!* began late in 1954. While Rodgers and Hammerstein had total artistic control, Todd insisted that the opening scene show actor Gordon McRae riding through a field of corn, "as high as an elephant's eye," according the opening song, "Oh, What a Beautiful Mornin'." Production of the movie involved all four of the new lenses, in contrast to the 35mm film process which used different focal lengths to create optical variety. Shot on 65mm film, *Oklahoma!* was printed on 70mm film for projection, allowing 5mm for a six-track magnetic stereo soundtrack. Todd-AO had opened a mixing, editing, and sound recording studio for Todd-AO as well as standard film processes. Todd edited a 25-minute trailer of movie clips from *Oklahoma!* to show Hollywood filmmakers in June 1955. The enthusiastic response of this critical audience stimulated active trading of Todd-AO stock which rose from about $7.00 a share to $22.50 per share. Many buyers held the stock in the expectation of increased stock value after the premier of *Oklahoma!*

Oklahoma! premiered at the Rivoli Theater in New York City on October 10, 1955. Projection of Todd-AO movies required a 52-foot wide by 26-foot high screen with a 13-foot deep curve, and conversion to such wide screen projection cost theaters $40,000. In this new type of theater, the six-track sound played through five speakers behind the screen, while one track played through speakers around the theater; the "surround" track simulated the real location of sound effects on the screen. Under Michael Todd's influence, the movie was promoted like a Broadway show to accentuate the uniqueness of the wide screen process. At a time when adult admission to a movie cost $.75, reserved seats for *Oklahoma!* ranged from $1.75 to $3.50 with a five percent royalty from admission going to Todd-AO and Magna. Like a Broadway production, no popcorn could be served in a Todd-AO theater.

While the movie itself received great acclaim, the film process did not have the impact Todd and others expected. Reasons included a scratch on the film, which the audience attributed to the filming process, and distortions in the picture as a corrective optical printer had not come to fruition. The movie did win an Academy Award for Best Sound in 1955, however, and the first run at theaters lasted over a year. A film short, *The Miracle of Todd-AO*, produced in 1956, accompanied *Oklahoma!* during the later period of its first run. The film included test footage which emphasized the more spectacular aspects of the wide screen effects, such as the roller coaster ride. Magna's partnership with United Theater Circuit assured a market for Todd-AO productions, but nationwide only 60 theaters had converted for Todd-AO by 1957.

Todd sold some of his shares in Todd-AO and Magna to fund his production of *Around the World in 80 Days*, a project he started expressly for creative autonomy in showing off the spectacular effects of the Todd-AO system. Filmed in various locations around the world, Todd used the 128 degree "bug-eye" lens for such scenes as a Spanish bullfight and bicycling through the narrow streets of London in high traffic. By the time of that movie's premier on October 17, 1956, an optical printer had been developed to eliminate distortions created by the lenses in filming. The success of *80 Days* was evidenced by the fact that it won five Academy Awards, including Best Picture and Best Color Photography. In 1957 Todd-AO received the first of several Academy Awards for Scientific/Technical Achievement.

The third movie production in Todd-AO, *South Pacific*, another Rodgers and Hammerstein musical, involved a slower film speed in order to show the film on a conventional flat screen. This allowed the movie to be shown at any movie theater but retained the high quality image and stereophonic sound of the Todd-AO process. *South Pacific* won the 1958 Academy Award for Best Sound.

In 1958 Twentieth Century-Fox Film Corporation invested $600,000 in Todd-AO through acquisition of four percent of preferred stock from Magna Theater. Magna then owned 63 percent of Todd-AO, while AOC held the balance. Fox also acquired the rights to film at least one picture a year in Todd-AO over the seven and one-half years. Several wide screen processes had emerged in the late 1950s; as the novelty of CinemaScope faded, Fox invested in Todd-AO as a better process.

Films produced by Fox using the Todd-AO system in the 1960s included *Can-Can*; *Cleopatra*; *The Sound of Music*, *The Agony and the Ecstasy*, and *Doctor Dolittle*. Other films shot with Todd-AO camera and sound technology included *The Alamo* by United Artists and *Airport* by Universal Pictures in 1970.

A Sound Engineering Company in the 1960s–70s

While filmmaking shifted to Todd-AO inspired processes, the primary direction of Todd-AO shifted to sound recording and mixing services for the motion picture and television industries. Todd-AO's sound system for the wide screen had proven high quality, and the company excelled in post-production sound mixing and editing. By the mid-1950s new sound technology had changed the approach movie directors took to post-production sound editing, allowing sound engineers to stop their machine, reverse the recording to make changes in problem areas, improve the quality of the sound mix, rehearse and

redo. Moreover, by the early 1960s "punch-in recording" allowed a director to stop, reverse, and rerecord.

While movie studios maintained their own post production facilities, Todd-AO handled studio overload, and producers and directors sought the services of Todd-AO's talented staff. Todd-AO or its employees received Academy Awards for Best Sound for *The Alamo*; *West Side Story*; *The Sound of Music*; *Cabaret*; *The Exorcist*, *E.T.—The Extra-Terrestrial*; and *Out of Africa*, and had many other nominations. Fred Hynes, a sound engineer who joined Todd-AO with the making of *Oklahoma!*, would receive the Academy's Gordon E. Sawyer Lifetime Achievement Award in 1987.

Multidirectional Expansion in the 1980s–90s

By the time Todd-AO became a public company on the Nasdaq stock exchange in 1987, United Artists Communications, Inc. (UACI) ownership in Todd-AO had reached 85 percent. Robert and Marshall Naify obtained a 52 percent majority ownership in Todd-AO stock through the public offering and subsequently sold their majority interest in UACI. (The brothers had served in executive positions at Todd-AO and, as co-chairmen of the board, oversaw the public offering of stock.) Todd-AO then undertook a series of acquisitions to expand the growth and profit potential of the company in a time of expanding opportunities in the cable, satellite, and home video markets.

In 1986 Todd-AO began to expand its capacity for sound services with the acquisition of Glen Glenn Sound for $8.9 million. Glen Glenn credits included sound production for *I Love Lucy, Bonanza, Mission: Impossible, My Three Sons*, and other popular television shows. The company has received Emmy Awards for *Hill Street Blues*, *Cheers*, and *Cagney and Lacey*. Renamed Todd-AO/Glen Glenn Studios, the company made an agreement with CBS/MTM Company to license certain facilities for recording sound for movies and television. The agreement involved the upgrade and refurbishment of four sound stages with state-of-the-art equipment including a six-track stereo studio, a combination film/video studio for stereo television, a video sweetening studio, and a studio for Foley live sound effects recording, and Automatic Dialogue Replacement. Todd-AO also upgraded its own studios with new consoles and the latest technology.

In September 1987, Todd-AO acquired the Trans/Audio sound studio in New York City, which it renamed Todd-AO Studios East. The acquisition made Todd-AO the largest independent post production sound facility in the world as well as the only sound studio with operations on both the east and west coasts. The company remodeled and renovated the east coast facilities, upgrading the studio to state-of-the-art equipment and bringing the total number of dubbing studios to 19.

Todd-AO's growth and acquisition strategy sought to offer its clients complete audio and video services within one company as well as to offset the cyclical and seasonal nature of motion picture production. In 1994 Todd-AO Video Services acquired Film Video Masters, and in February 1995 acquired from George Lucas the Skywalker Sound South studio in San Francisco. Todd-AO purchased Chrysalis Television Facilities and its satellite transmission and post production television and movie facilities from the Chrysalis Group in May 1995. In April 1996 the acquisition of Pacific Title and Art brought specialization in the production of film, title, and optical special effects as well as digital services for motion pictures into the Todd-AO fold. The acquisition of Editworks, which specialized in commercial advertising in Atlanta, expanded Todd-AO's geographic connections.

Under CEO and president, Salah M. Hassanein, who had been a director since 1962 and held several high level positions with Todd-AO and UACI, the company continued its growth strategy through acquisition into the late 1990s. A public offering of 1.5 million shares of stock at $10.50 per share in late 1996 funded further acquisitions and technology and equipment upgrades. In January 1997 Todd-AO acquired the stock of International Video Conversions in Burbank. That company's video tape services included duplication, telecine, and format conversions including High Definition Television (HDTV).

The June acquisition of Hollywood Digital Company for $26.1 million added cutting edge technology such as the "virtual network" which provided digital pre- and post-production services in the studio or on location. In addition to a talented staff, the comprehensive list of post production services included on-line digital editing, telecine, color correction, graphics, special effects, audio editing, tape duplication, music prelay, sound mixing, and video sweetening. Hollywood Digital tended to provide these services to long-format products, including feature films, preview trailers, sitcoms, episodic television shows, and mini-series. Though the advantages of this acquisition were slow to take hold due to the upgrade of much of that company's technology and equipment, the location of a new facility near advertising agencies in Santa Monica in spring 1998 aided Hollywood Digital's development.

Growth from acquisitions and increased demand for production services led to a 25.5 percent increase in revenues in 1997 over 1996 to $79 million. A rising number of independent filmmakers and television show producers, and a surge in the number of broadcast channels, served to heighten demand for production services. The increased revenue included the third year of annual growth at over ten percent at Todd-AO Video Services and record revenues at Todd-AO Studios and Todd-AO Studios West. Todd-AO Studios won two Emmy Awards during this time, for sound mixing for *Titanic* and sound editorial for *The Shining*, both for television productions.

Amidst diversification and internal and geographic growth, Todd-AO continued to reach high achievements in sound engineering. In 1997 the company received its sixth Academy Award for Scientific/Technical Achievement. Academy Awards for Best Sound were given to Todd-AO employees for *Last of the Mohicans*, *Apollo 13*, and *Saving Private Ryan*, its 20th Academy Award to date.

Growth Potential in the 21st Century

Through two 1998 acquisitions, Todd-AO anticipated significant growth in its post production services. In May Todd-AO purchased Pascal Video to address the potential market in Digital Versatile Disk (DVD) technology. Todd-AO Video Services DVD, Inc. was created for the conversion of

film and video content to DVD format in anticipation of future demand for television shows and thousands of movies on DVD. The company hired Richard Ayock, an expert on DVD, as president and chief operating officer. Todd-AO also expected global distribution and satellite channel expansion, prompting the addition of Tele-Cine Cell Group (TCCG) of the United Kingdom. Todd-AO expanded operations at TCCG, particularly the satellite transmission division with two 2.4 meter satellite dishes on the roof of the main building and a 3.7 meter dish at an adjacent facility.

Acquisitions involved geographic considerations as well as service capabilities. In June 1999 Todd-AO purchased the stock of the SoundOne Corporation in New York City. The acquisition broadened Todd-AO's post production facilities on the East Coast (where production of motion pictures had increased in recent years) and added a strategic entry into Europe. SoundOne's credits included the motion pictures *Fargo*, *You've Got Mail*, and *Men in Black*. A September 1999 agreement with 103 Estudio in Barcelona, involved the acquisition of 50 percent of that company's stock and a plan to upgrade the facility with state-of-the art digital equipment to dub foreign language movies and television programs. In 2000 the company expected to open a foreign language dubbing and audio post production facility in Munich, Germany, in a joint venture with Disney Character Voices International, Inc. Todd-AO hoped to establish similar ventures in France, Italy, and Asia.

During 1999, however, the company's stock dipped to $8 per share, down from $13 in 1998. Analysts attributed the decline in investor enthusiasm to the fact that competition in the industry had heightened and that film studios were becoming more budget-minded, noting that competitor Four Media Co. had also seen a drop in its stock value over the past couple of years. Hassanein, the company's president and CEO, stated his belief that "the current market valuation does not reflect Todd-AO's unique position and growing global reach," and announced that Todd-AO would look into the possibility of merging with, or forming a joint venture with, another company. In December 1999, Todd-AO announced that it had agreed to be acquired by Liberty Media Corporation. Under the agreement, Liberty Media would obtain 60 percent ownership in Todd-AO and 94 percent voting power. At the time Todd-AO expressed its expectations that the merger with Liberty Media (the cable television programming division of AT&T that oversaw Discovery Channel, E! Entertainment, and Black Entertainment Television), would be a merger of talent and technology as well as ownership.

Principal Divisions

Todd-AO Studios; Todd-AO Studios West; Todd-AO Scoring; Todd-AO Sitcom; Todd-AO Video Group; Todd-AO Interactive; Sound One/Todd-AO Studios East; Todd-AO Atlanta; Todd-AO London; 103 Todd-AO Estudios (Spain).

Principal Competitors

Four Media Company; Harmony Holdings, Inc.; Laser-Pacific Media Corp.; Video Services Corp.

Further Reading

Champagne, Christine, "Postcards from the Edge," *SHOOT*, May 1, 1998, p. 37.

"Chrysalis Group to Sell Chrysalis TV to Todd-AO," *Extel Examiner*, February 9, 1995.

"Director Sydney Pollack Joins Todd-AO's Board," *PR Newswire*, April 17, 1998.

Hilton, Kevin, "New Regime at Tele-Cine," *Pro Sound News Europe*, August 1998, p. 4.

Jones, Scott, "Todd-AO/Editworks: With a Little Help, Editworks Grows," *SHOOT,* May 16, 1997, p. 34.

"Liberty Media to Acquire Control of Todd-AO," *PR Newswire*, July 30, 1999, p. 2,762.

Liebs, Anthony, "Todd-AO's Next Project: Editing a Takeout Film?," *Mergers and Acquisitions Report*, June 14, 1999.

Swertlow, Frank, "Post-Production Firm Todd-AO Posts Rapid Growth," *Los Angeles Business Journal*, October 20, 1997, p. 10.

Timms, Dominic, "Todd-AO Close to an Offer for TCCG," *Broadcast*, March 20, 1998, p. 12.

Todd, Michael, Jr., and Susan McCarthy Todd, *A Valuable Property: The Life Story of Michael Todd*, New York: Arbor House, 1983.

"Todd-AO Streamlines Operations to Better Serve its Clients and Provide Operational Efficiencies," *PR Newswire*, December 14, 1999, p. 1,792.

"Twentieth Century-Fox to Buy Preferred Issue of Todd-AO for $600,000," *Wall Street Journal*, December 19, 1958, p. 4.

"United Artists Communications Offers its Shares of Todd-AO Corp.," *Business Wire*, November 7, 1986.

Ward, Phil, "Todd-AO Continues European Expansion," *Pro Sound News Europe*, November 1999, p. 3.

—Mary Tradii

Torchmark Corporation

2001 Third Avenue South
Birmingham, Alabama 35233
U.S.A.
Telephone: (205) 3254200
Fax: (205) 3254157
Web Site: http://www.torchmarkcorp.com

Public Company
Incorporated: 1929 as Liberty National Insurance
    Company
Employees: 4,260
Sales: $2.22 billion (1999)
Stock Exchanges: New York
Ticker Symbol: TMK
NAIC: 524113 Direct Life Insurance Carriers; 524114
    Direct Health and Medical Insurance Carriers; 52519
    Other Insurance Funds; 52393 Investment Advice;
    551112 Offices of Other Holding Companies

Torchmark Corporation is an insurance and diversified financial services holding company. Most of the company's history involves a single corporate entity, Liberty National Insurance Holding Co., but in the 1980s the company entered a period of aggressive acquisition. By 1993, Torchmark controlled ten principal subsidiaries, branching out into individual life and health insurance; funeral, fire, and property insurance; financial planning; mutual funds; and investment management services. After a period of consolidation in the 1990s culminating in its decision to spin off two of its subsidiaries in 1998, the company narrowed its focus to the provision of life and health insurance products along with annuities, through its various divisions. The company also planned on continuing to offer financial planning services in conjunction with one of its former subsidiaries, Waddell & Reed.

It Began As a Scam in the Early 1900s

The company's roots extend back to the turn of the 20th century, when the Heralds of Liberty was incorporated in

Huntsville, Alabama. Although the entity purported to be a fraternal benefit society, it was actually a front for another company, headquartered in Philadelphia. The fraternal charter limited the Alabama Insurance Department's ability to oversee the Heralds of Liberty, enabling the parent to circumvent state insurance regulations. The parent company's officers used a variety of schemes to embezzle funds from the fraternity. The officers sold it worthless bonds, borrowed money on insufficient collateral, and had the Heralds make "payments" to the parent. After 20 years of these illicit practices resulted in a backlog of unpaid claims, the Alabama Insurance Department took over the fraternity in June 1921.

The state agency assigned deputy insurance commissioner Robert Park Davison to the case. He proceeded to "clean house" at the Heralds of Liberty. He forced all of the fraternity's officers and directors to resign and was made "Supreme Commander" of the group. Frank Park Samford, Davison's colleague and cousin, was elected "Supreme Recorder." The unusual titles reflected the group's origins as a secret society. Davison and Samford went to the parent's headquarters in Philadelphia to begin reformation of the Heralds of Liberty. They found that the group was insolvent: unpaid claims amounted to $80,000, but the firm held only $1,410 in cash. The Heralds had no reserves, and premiums on the policies that existed were insufficient to meet financial demands. Davison and Samford discovered that the only policy the Heralds had sold was a lottery-type plan, or "Joint Life Distribution Plan." The scheme divided policyholders into classes by age. When a policyholder died, his beneficiary and the holder of the lowest certificate number in each class were both paid. Although the Heralds had tried to eliminate these policies through exchanges and introduction of new insurance plans, the parent company was dependent on this business for financial support and was compelled by the nature of the plan to continue to place new policies in the existing classes. It took the new officers until the mid-1930s to rid the company of these policies.

Liberty Goes Legit by 1929

Davison and Samford worked during the 1920s to raise premiums, sell legal life insurance policies based on an adequate reserve, pay past-due claims, and build up a team of trustworthy agents. By 1927, the year the headquarters of the reformed company moved to Birmingham, Alabama, it had 26 employees and one new officer, an assistant secretary. To build up a reserve fund, Davison and Samford made the company's first stock offering in 1929 under its new name, Liberty National Life Insurance Co. Many officers and agents borrowed money to purchase shares of the $325,000 offering. The stock offering was supplemented with an additional assessment on Heralds of Liberty policyholders. Liberty National's officers feared that many clients would cancel their policies, but by July 1929 the company appeared to have endured its transformation into a legitimate insurer.

Disaster struck again when the stock market crashed that year. Many of those who had borrowed to capitalize the new company were stuck with debts that exceeded the value of their collateral. To make matters worse, the cash generated by the initial stock issue had been deposited with the Southern Bank and Trust Company as trustee and, before Liberty National had a chance to invest, it became apparent that the money could not be withdrawn without breaking the bank. Unlike many other banks during this crisis, Southern managed to stay open, and Liberty National was able to withdraw its funds in small increments over the next few months.

Liberty National struggled over the next five years to endure the Great Depression. Income from premiums declined as customers were forced to cancel their policies, and losses were sustained when banks failed and debtors defaulted on their bonds. Cost-cutting helped the company survive losses during the depression, and Liberty National even invested $95,000 to acquire the distribution system of a failing competitor. Circumstances compelled Liberty to use creative financing to remain solvent in the early years of the decade. In 1931 the company purchased a 70 percent interest in a headquarters building, then claimed it as an asset to maintain an adequate surplus. Davison and Samford even offered to surrender some of their stock to the company in 1932 to subsidize Liberty National's surplus, but that drastic step was not necessary. In fact, Liberty National paid its first cash dividend the following year. The insurance company's officers perceived that its shareholders doubted the continued viability of Liberty National and felt that the $21,000 dividend would restore investor confidence. That

first payment started a custom that was followed every year in the company's history.

When Davison died in 1934, Samford was elected president and chief executive officer, more traditional administrative titles than "Supreme Commander." Liberty National enjoyed a period of growth and prosperity after that year and worked to build a dependable base of financial strength. Innovative policies helped the company compete successfully with its older and larger rivals. Liberty National made its first acquisition in 1944 through an interesting series of events. Late in 1943, Rufus Lackey, the principal stockholder of the Brown-Service Insurance Company, offered to sell his share of the Alabama insurer to Liberty National for $5 million, provided the transaction was completed by the end of the year. Liberty National had the will, but neither the cash nor the borrowing power to make the acquisition on such short notice. Samford and the company's general counsel secured personal loans with their Liberty National stock as collateral, purchased the stock themselves, and Brown-Service merged with Liberty National in 1944.

Brown-Service, a successful regional company, specialized in burial insurance plans. Liberty National utilized the subsidiary's large agency force to accomplish the greatest market penetration ever achieved by a life insurance company. Although Liberty National later discontinued the sale of burial insurance policies, the plan provided substantial savings to many citizens of Alabama and helped Liberty National build a highly efficient and profitable operation. In the 1960s, more than 80 percent of white Alabamans held Brown-Service policies. Even as late as the mid-1980s, almost half of the people who died in Alabama each year were insured under a Brown-Service policy.

Post-World War II Expansion

Liberty National progressed steadily after 1945. The company made several relatively minor acquisitions, expanded geographically, and introduced numerous new insurance products. Beginning in 1952, the company began recording consecutive annual increases in both earnings and dividends that went unmatched by any other member of the New York Stock Exchange.

In 1958 Liberty National altered Birmingham's skyline by placing a one-fifth-sized replica of the Statue of Liberty atop its Birmingham headquarters. During the 1950s and 1960s, the insurer grew to become America's second largest publicly owned provider of so-called industrial insurance. This type of policy was renewed weekly and had been discontinued by most other major insurers, but Liberty National was reluctant to abandon these policies, which were popular with the company's rural customers. By the end of the 1960s, it ranked eighteenth in regular coverage and had expanded its geographical service area to include Georgia, Florida, Tennessee, and California. In 1968 Liberty National sold more than $1 billion in new policies for the first time.

Frank P. Samford, Jr., replaced his father as president and chief executive officer of Liberty National in 1967. He served in that position until 1985. The younger Samford brought Liberty National's policyholders more modern coverage. In the late

1960s, for example, the company introduced an estate plan and a special program for college students. The company's agents continued to take a very personal approach to life insurance, however. In 1975 its 2,500 agents still sold monthly life insurance door to door. Other, more urban, companies had abandoned these low-premium policies, but Liberty National continued to earn profit margins of 15 percent on the old-style coverage.

Restructuring and Acquisition in the Late 1970s and 1980s

In 1979 Liberty National undertook an agenda of expansion and diversification through acquisition. Prior to that time, most of the company's investments were concentrated in mortgages, bonds, and a limited number of stocks, but by the mid-1980s, the company had grown from a regional life insurance firm into a diversified national insurance and financial services corporation. From 1980 to 1982, the company spent more than half a billion dollars to purchase several insurance and investment businesses. In 1980 the company bought Globe Life and Accident Insurance Company. Headquartered in Oklahoma City, Globe was founded in 1951 by John Singletary and Ralph Reese. Although the company was established with borrowed money, it had grown into a consistently profitable firm through the use of innovative marketing techniques such as direct mail. When Singletary died in 1977, Ronald K. Richey was elected president and CEO. In 1979 the company underwent a crisis when the executor of Singletary's estate sought to sell his 36 percent share. Liberty National purchased the company in a friendly takeover and made Richey a director of the parent. He succeeded Samford as president and CEO in 1986.

The year 1979 also saw the creation of the Liberty National Insurance Holding Company, which became the parent company of all of Liberty National's holdings following a corporate reorganization in 1980. The new entity made two major acquisitions in 1981: Continental Investment Corporation and United American Insurance Company of Dallas. Continental owned Waddell & Reed (W&R) and United Investors Life Insurance Company, two businesses that would become primary subsidiaries of Liberty National. W&R was created as a sales and distribution division for United Mutual Funds and was named for the fund's founders, Chauncey Waddell and Cameron Reed. United Funds became the first mutual fund group to be registered under the Investment Company Act of 1940, the legislation that brought funds under the jurisdiction of the Securities and Exchange Commission.

Waddell & Reed (W&R) hoped their group of mutual funds would make it easier for middle-income Americans to participate in the investing process. United Investors Life Insurance Company was created as an outgrowth of W&R in 1961. Its term insurance product soon accounted for a major part of Continental Investment Company's income. Problems in the national economy and the stock market, as well as difficulties stemming from Continental's ownership of Waddell & Reed, combined to force W&R into bankruptcy reorganization in the 1970s. The firm emerged from the crisis with new leadership and new products: financial planning seminars and services. By the early 1980s, W&R was a leading American financial planner. Liberty National purchased W&R's parent, Continental Investment Corporation, for $155 million in 1981.

The United American Insurance Company of Dallas, Liberty National's other major acquisition of 1981, was founded in 1947 by Casey Dunlap and Russ Donovan. This company had pioneered the employment of independent health insurance agents in the mid-1950s. It parlayed this new sales system into a nationwide system that extended into Canada by the time it was acquired by Liberty National for $138 million.

Liberty National's expansion into mutual funds, health insurance, and financial services rendered its formal name, Liberty National Insurance Holding Co., too limiting. The company adopted the name Torchmark Corporation in 1982. Torchmark combined the Statue of Liberty's torch and the word "hallmark" to form a unique name that drew upon the company's long history, yet reflected its new components.

While many other insurance providers were lured into the high-return, high-risk junk bond and commercial real estate markets of the 1980s, Torchmark maintained three-fourths of its invested assets in reliable, government-guaranteed securities and short-term investments. When the bottom fell out of the junk bond and real estate markets in the late 1980s, Torchmark emerged unscathed. Torchmark's conservative investment strategies earned its primary subsidiaries the industry's highest ratings. The national scandals, however, did affect the company, in the form of increased contributions to the federal guaranty fund to bail out insolvent insurers.

The 1990s

The 1990s began promisingly for Torchmark, as the 1992 marked the company's forty-first consecutive year of growth in 1992. By then, its stock price had shot up an astronomical 1,675 percent from its 1980 levels. In 1994, however, the company experienced some setbacks. In large part as a result of some poorly performing investments and the fallout from several different legal disputes in Alabama stemming from alleged misconduct by agents at Liberty National Life Insurance Company (some involving age discrimination and punitive damages claims and others relating to an exchange of Liberty's cancer policies), the company's growth streak was snapped. Revenues declined to $1.875 billion from 1993's $2.177 billion and net income dropped $31 million from 1993's results, to $269 million.

The year 1994 also saw some alterations in the company's business balance, as Torchmark made the strategic decision to focus more heavily on its life insurance operations at the expense of its health insurance ones (life insurance products tended to have higher operating margins, build better assets, and be under less year-to-year growth pressure). Buoyed by the acquisition of American Family Life Insurance Company for $552 million in November of that year, Torchmark's life insurance revenues jumped 16 percent from 1993's levels, while the health insurance sector contracted by 31.2 percent over the same period.

The restructuring of 1994 helped stanch the decline in Torchmark's revenues, as 1995 sales climbed to $2.067 billion, recouping nearly all of the 1993–94 drop. Net income, however, declined nearly 47 percent from 1994—to $143 million—as a result of poor growth in the Medicare supplemental insurance sector along with the company's litigation exposure, heavy debt burden from the American Family Life acquisition, and underperforming oil and gas investments. (The Medicare business had been slumping ever since federal legislation enacted in 1992 capped the commissions that vendors of such policies could charge.) To remedy this situation as best it could, Torchmark opted to divest itself of its holdings in the energy industry to streamline its operations and dedicate itself more effectively to its core insurance, mutual fund, and asset management businesses. In 1995, therefore, Torchmark liquidated its investments in Torch Energy Advisors, Inc. and the Black Warrior coal mine venture and sold off its holdings in Nuevo Energy Co. as well.

These maneuvers proved tremendously beneficial, as 1996 net income skyrocketed to $311 million on revenues of $2.071 billion. Life insurance operations remained the single largest growth engine, and the company's direct response business was particularly profitable. (As the name suggests, direct response relies on marketing insurance directly to customers via post, television, and other media rather than by the traditional use of agents. Torchmark's Global Life and Accident Insurance Company spearheaded this portion of the company's business.)

Torchmark's success continued in 1997. Revenues increased to $2.282 billion and net income rose to $324 million, as every sector of the company except its Medicare supplement products showed strong growth and administrative efficiencies reduced operating expenses. In March 1998, Torchmark acted further to reduce its indebtedness, when it made an initial public stock offering of 34 percent of its ownership interest in W&R. In November, Torchmark spun off the firm into a free-standing entity, though it continued to rely on its former subsidiary for some of its financial services operations. Torchmark also sold its Family Service Life subsidiary in June 1998 and used the proceeds to pay down debt and buy back some of its outstanding shares. Revenues for the year climbed to $2.158 billion, though net income dropped to $244 million in light of the company's debt restructuring and discharge.

These changes stood the company in good stead, as 1999's net income grew to $341 million. After weathering the storm of the mid-1990s, the company seemed well-positioned to meet the challenges of the 21st century.

Principal Subsidiaries

American Income Life Insurance Company; First United Life Insurance Company; Globe Life and Accident Insurance Company; Liberty National Life Insurance Company; United American Insurance Company; United Investors Life Insurance Company.

Principal Competitors

The Allstate Corporation; Citigroup Inc.; Conseco, Inc.; Liberty Mutual Insurance Companies; Metropolitan Life Insurance Company; Prudential Insurance Company of America; UN-UMProvident; USAA.

Further Reading

''A Dying Business,'' *Forbes,* April 15, 1975.
Frank, Robert, ''Torchmark To Buy American Income for $563.5 Million,'' *Wall Street Journal,* September 16, 1994.
''Industrial Insurance Profitable Line for Liberty National Life,'' *Barron's,* July 29, 1968.
Samford, Frank P., Jr., *Torchmark Corporation: History of a New Company,* Princeton, N.J.: Princeton University Press, 1985.
''Torchmark To Spin Off Waddell & Reed United Sometime in Early 1998,'' *Wall Street Journal,* November 18, 1997.

—April S. Dougal
—updated by Rebecca Stanfel

Trendwest Resorts, Inc.

9805 Willows Road
Redmond, Washington 98052
U.S.A.
Telephone: (425) 498-2500
Toll Free: (800) 722-3487
Fax: (425) 498-3050
Web site: http://www.trendwestresorts.com

Majority-Owned Subsidiary of JELD-WEN, Inc.
Incorporated: 1989 as Trendwest Resorts, Inc.
Employees: 1,064
Sales: $200.95 million (1998)
Stock Exchanges: NASDAQ
Ticker Symbol: TWRI
NAIC: 53121 Offices of Real Estate Agents and Brokers;
    52231 Mortgage and Nonmortgage Loan Brokers

Trendwest Resorts, Inc. sells timeshare ownership interests in condominiums located in Washington, Oregon, California, Arizona, Utah, Hawaii, British Columbia, Mexico, and Fiji. Trendwest acquires vacation properties and transfers ownership of the units to WorldMark, The Club, a nonprofit benefit corporation created by Trendwest to protect the rights of its member owners. The company uses a point-based system in which credits purchased by customers are used to reserve vacation accommodations. Trendwest markets its vacation product through a network of more than 20 sales offices, which are located primarily in metropolitan markets. The company serves roughly 90,000 timeshare owners, managing properties at 31 resorts that contain more than 1,600 condominium units.

Origins

Trendwest's formation came at the behest of executives working for JELD-WEN, Inc., a low-profile, privately owned company based in Klamath Falls, Oregon, with an impressive roster of assets. The company achieved considerable success manufacturing wooden doors, windows, and millwork products, eventually becoming one of the largest privately owned enterprises in the United States, as ranked by *Forbes* magazine. As

JELD-WEN's annual sales hurtled toward the $1 billion mark, it leveraged its success in doors and windows to branch out into an array of different businesses, diversifying with decided relish. The company formed or acquired a family of subsidiaries that carried the JELD-WEN name into financial services, hospitality and recreation, real estate, and retail, accumulating more than 100 subsidiaries whose geographic reach stretched across the United States and into nine foreign countries. One of the company's diversifying efforts led to the development of a golf resort in Redmond, Oregon, named Eagle Crest, which provided the link between JELD-WEN and the creation of Trendwest.

During the late 1980s, JELD-WEN executives noticed increasing timeshare sales at Eagle Crest and were intrigued. Interested in exploring the business opportunities in vacation ownership, JELD-WEN officials asked William F. Peare to create a timeshare program whose implementation would be governed by a separate JELD-WEN subsidiary. Trendwest was created in March 1989, when Peare, with the aid of Jeff Sites and Mike Moyer, began devising a new vacation ownership concept that represented an evolutional step forward in the business of timeshare sales. The trio spent eight months designing the unique system, devoting considerable energy toward canvassing potential Trendwest customers. Peare, Sites, and Moyer interviewed Eagle Crest timeshare owners to discover why they were attracted by vacation ownership and what could be done differently. Further, they asked all the people who declined to buy into Eagle Crest why they had done so, and what, if anything, would have induced them to buy a timeshare. Based on the research, Peare developed a new program that became known as WorldMark, The Club.

At the time of Peare's investigation, the vacation ownership industry had evolved from its European roots in the 1950s in a clear direction. The prevailing trend, as the industry matured, was toward increased flexibility for vacation owners. Originally, the concept of timeshare was based on fractional ownership—groups of Europeans purchased a vacation home together and divided the property's usage among the group, providing no choice of location and little flexibility in terms of selecting vacation dates. Next, cooperative ownership emerged as the prevalent timeshare model, its design predicated on the ownership of apartment buildings situated in tourist destinations. By the time the timeshare concept had migrated to the United States, cooperative ownership had become a business. Companies were formed whose sole business consisted of selling weeklong stays in hotels, providing customers with a fixed week at a fixed location. The design was far from ideal. Member owners soon tired of the rigidity of having to stay at one location during a particular week, which forced timeshare marketers to provide increased flexibility by offering a floating week during a fixed season. By the late 1980s, as Peare, Sites, and Moyer sat huddled around a table trying to address the needs of potential customers, timeshare owners could select a particular week for their vacations, but they had little choice in where to spend their vacations.

Peare, in the course of his interviews with both established and potential new customers, discovered that people wanted to vacation more often with shorter stays at a variety of locations. The research concluded that customers wanted to vacation both at destinations within driving distance from their homes and at more exotic locations overseas. Customers also wanted greater diversity in the length of their vacations. Instead of being shackled to one-week stays, customers wanted the option to schedule vacation periods ranging between two-night stays to extended, two-week vacations. In short, the research conducted in 1989 revealed a demand for greater diversity and flexibility, prompting Peare and his colleagues to develop a system that would distinguish Trendwest from all other timeshare companies.

At the heart of the new company that took shape in 1989 was a point-based system that Trendwest pioneered. Instead of purchasing a one-week block at a particular location, customers purchased what Trendwest called "Vacation Credits." After purchasing a minimum number of credits, members could use the points to reserve vacation accommodations at different time periods and at different locations. The number of credits withdrawn from an owner's account was determined by the location of the accommodations, the size of the accommodations, the season of the year, whether the stay included the weekend or not, and the length of the stay. To use their credits judiciously, owners consulted a valuation booklet. Any credits not used during the year were carried over to the next year and, if an owner wished to, credits from the upcoming year could be borrowed for use during the current year.

The Formation of WorldMark in 1989

To implement the program, Trendwest created WorldMark, The Club. Laws regulating timeshare businesses required protections against any loss of property rights stemming from the debt or financial condition of the developer. Therefore, Trendwest, as the developer, established WorldMark to be a legally and financially separate entity, free from any debt and guaranteed to always have sufficient resources to operate the properties through its own source of income from the annual dues paid by WorldMark members. WorldMark, a nonprofit benefit corporation, operated similarly to a large homeowner's association, providing protection for those who purchased Trendwest's vacation product. It was created for the specific purpose of owning, operating, and maintaining the real property purchased and developed by Trendwest. Once Trendwest had developed a vacation property, it transferred the property to WorldMark free and clear of any monetary encumbrances in exchange for the exclusive right to sell the vacation credits created by the units transferred.

In October 1989, sales of ownerships in WorldMark began in Kirkland, Washington. Trendwest, as it set out to implement its innovative marketing program, began with three employees and three condominium units, supported by one sales office. It was a modest start, particularly in light of the deep coffers of Trendwest's parent company, JELD-WEN, but growth would soon come. The company needed to add to its portfolio of vacation properties and, concurrently, establish a web of sales offices to support geographic expansion. Trendwest chose to situate some of the new offices near a particular WorldMark resort, but the majority were located in major metropolitan areas within the company's operating territory, offices that Trendwest referred to as "offsite sales." By concentrating on offsite sales offices, the company conducted its crucial marketing efforts closer to its prospective customers and thereby was able to draw upon a larger customer base.

No matter the effectiveness of its sales presentations, Trendwest could not succeed without an attractive list of vacation destinations and accommodations. Acquiring vacation properties was of paramount importance as Trendwest entered the 1990s and sought to assemble a mixture of drive-to locations and more "exotic" tourist destinations. The company's units at Eagle Crest, where WorldMark would eventually own 83 units, were complemented by 14 units at a resort named Valley Isle in Maui, Hawaii, which were transferred to WorldMark in April 1990. In August 1990, the company purchased units at Lake Chelan Shores in Chelan, Washington. In 1991, Trendwest added four new destinations to its catalogue of properties: Lake Tahoe in January; Kauai, Hawaii, in July; Long Beach, Washington, in September; and Bass Lake, California, in October. Expansion continued in 1992, as the company fleshed out its presence in Washington with the purchase of units in Sequim in January and Leavenworth in July. The year also marked Trendwest's entry into Canada with the acquisition of 72 units in Whistler, British Columbia, in February. A single acquisition was completed in 1993, the purchase of 20 units at the Beachcomber in Pismo Beach, California.

Energetic Growth Begins in 1993

After three full years of operation, Trendwest loomed as a rising force in the timeshare industry. Annual sales had swelled

Key Dates:

1989: Trendwest Resorts and WorldMark, The Club are founded.
1990: First vacation properties in Hawaii are acquired.
1992: First international destination, Sundance in Whistler, British Columbia, joins company's fold.
1994: First condominiums in Mexico are acquired.
1997: Trendwest completes its initial public offering.
1999: Fijian condominiums become available to Trendwest customers.

to $45.5 million, driven upward by expansion into Washington, California, Hawaii, and British Columbia, where the company managed properties in 12 resorts. Systemwide, by 1993, Trendwest managed 239 units, which served as a benchmark for the prolific growth to follow during the ensuing five years. Between 1993 and 1998, the company averaged 30 percent annual revenue growth, as the number of units under its control nearly quadrupled. Peare, presiding as president and chief executive officer, orchestrated the company's growth by adhering to the strategy devised in 1989. Trendwest would expand by acquiring drive-to properties within a five-hour drive of its members and complement these weekend getaway destinations with properties more suitable for extended vacations.

Trendwest widened its operating territory in 1994 by completing a foray into Mexico, acquiring units at Coral Baja in San Jose del Cabo, Mexico, in November. By the end of the year, sales had increased to $63.8 million, from which the company reported a profit of $5.3 million. Over the course of the next two years, five more acquisitions were completed, two in Washington and California in 1995 and three in California, Nevada, and Oregon in 1996, bringing the total number of Trendwest resorts to 19 by the end of 1996 and total units to 746. The company eclipsed $100 million in sales in 1996, posting $116.9 million, with $12.6 million in net income.

1997 Public Offering and Late 1990s Expansion

As Trendwest prepared to enter the late 1990s, expectations were running high. The company's point-based system had proven to be a market winner, serving as a model that other timeshare companies were emulating. To reap the full benefits of his successful innovation, Peare needed to accelerate expansion, both in terms of the company's vacation properties and its network of sales offices. Expansion meant money, prompting Peare to take the company public through an initial public offering (IPO). After adding the Klamath Falls-based Running Y Ranch in February 1997, Peare and his senior executives prepared for the company's public debut. The IPO, completed in August 1997, raised $51.8 million, giving the company the resources it needed to aggressively expand during the late 1990s. JELD-WEN retained its majority interest in the company, controlling roughly 80 percent of Trendwest's stock. Following the IPO, another resort in Hawaii was added to the company's properties, as well as the Clear Lake resort in northern California.

With 52,000 members by the end of 1997, Trendwest could count itself among the industry's elite. Sales for the year in-

creased nearly 30 percent to $151.5 million, while net income recorded a more animated leap, jumping more than 60 percent to $20.6 million. In terms of vacation ownership sales, Trendwest ranked as the fifth largest company in its industry, occupying the same tier as Disney, Marriott, Hilton, and Signature Resorts. The company attributed much of its success to its strategy of situating its sales offices in metropolitan areas, rather than relying exclusively on resort-based marketing efforts. In 1997, three new sales offices were opened, giving the company a total of 14 sales locations.

As Trendwest neared the completion of its first decade of business, there was just cause for celebration. After adding four new resorts—including the first in Utah—and 344 condominium units in 1998, sales eclipsed $200 million and net income rose to a record high $24 million. The company's network of sales offices was increased by seven during the year, highlighted by the establishment of two offices in Utah and one in Arizona that marked the company's entry into the Southwest. Also in 1998, Trendwest secured a three-year $30 million revolving line of credit, which set the stage for a period of aggressive expansion as the company pushed forward into the 21st century. In 1999, five new resorts were added to the company's catalogue of properties, with three additional resorts scheduled to be transferred to WorldMark during the first half of 2000. Of the new properties, the most noteworthy acquisition was Trendwest's entry into Fiji. By December 1999, 38 units in a timeshare resort on Denarau Island had been transferred to WorldMark, the first stage of a plan to develop 76 units in Fiji. Concurrent with the expansion into Fiji, Trendwest announced its intention to acquire and develop resort locations in Queensland, Australia. On this note, the company concluded its inaugural decade of business and prepared for a future that promised to witness the further extension of its innovative point-based system.

Principal Subsidiaries

TW Holdings, Inc.; Trendwest Funding I Inc.; Trendwest Funding II Inc.

Principal Competitors

Cendant Corporation; Sunterra Corp.; Fairfield Communities, Inc.

Further Reading

Crider, Jeff, *RV Business,* October 1998, p. 20.
McGough, Robert, ''Flying High on Debt,'' *Forbes,* April 11, 1983, p. 2.
Mehlman, William, ''Price Lull Induced Big Buys by Thousand Trails Insiders,'' *The Insiders'Chronicle,* June 21, 1982, p. 1.
Miller, Brian K., ''Roller Coaster Time-Shares,'' *Business Journal-Portland,* August 28, 1998, p. 11.
''Minding His Business,'' *Inc.,* November 1983, p. 120.
Neurath, Peter, ''Thousand Trials Not Resorting to Real Estate Sales,'' *Puget Sound Business Journal,* June 11, 1993, p. 13.
——, ''Thousand Trails Strives to Fend Off Bankruptcy,'' *Puget Sound Business Journal,* November 12, 1990, p. 12.
''Not-So-Happy Trails,'' *Forbes,* July 14, 1986, p. 13.
Peare, William F., ''Trendwest Resorts Inc.,'' *Puget Sound Business Journal,* July 16, 1999, p. 50.
''They're Baaack!,'' *Forbes,* October 20, 1997, p. 18.

—Jeffrey L. Covell

Tumbleweed, Inc.

1900 Mellwood Avenue
Louisville, Kentucky 40206
U.S.A.
Telephone: (502) 893-0323
Fax: (502) 893-6676
Web site: http://www.tumbleweedrestaurant.com

Public Company
Incorporated: 1995 as Tumbleweed LLC
Employees: 2,200
Sales: $51.3 million (1999)
Stock Exchanges: NASDAQ
Ticker Symbol: TWED
NAIC: 72211 Full-Service Restaurants; 72241 Drinking
  Places (Alcoholic Beverages)

Tumbleweed, Inc. owns, franchises, or licenses more than 50 Tumbleweed Southwest Mesquite Grill & Bar casual-dining restaurants. The restaurants are located in Kentucky, Illinois, Indiana, Ohio, Tennessee, and Wisconsin, and also in Germany, Saudi Arabia, Jordan, and Egypt. Tumbleweed's menu consists of two distinct cuisines: spicy Tex-Mex dishes, such as burritos, enchiladas, and tacos; and mesquite-grilled Southwestern dishes, such as ribs, steaks, chicken, and seafood. The price range of the menu items is fairly broad, in order to appeal to traditional casual dining customers as well as more cost-conscious patrons. The average price of a Tumbleweed meal in 1999, including beverages, was between $9 and $10.

1975–95: Founding and Early Growth

Despite its distinctly western-sounding name, Tumbleweed was actually founded east of the Mississippi—in New Albany, Indiana. It was the brainchild of George and Linda Keller, a young married couple who had grown up in the New Albany area, just across the river from Louisville.

In 1975, the Kellers decided to open a Mexican restaurant, convinced by friends in Arizona that the popularity of Mexican cuisine was on the rise. Since Mexican food was in decidedly short supply in Indiana in the mid-1970s, however, the couple

had little precedent in the way of recipes and menus. Amassing a collection of cookbooks, they began testing different recipes, using a trial-and-error approach to refine their concoctions. Eventually, they developed a complete menu for the new eatery, which opened in 1976 as Tumbleweed.

Tumbleweed was a big hit right away, with patrons lining up on the sidewalk to wait for one of the restaurant's 28 tables. The venture turned a profit its very first year and continued to do so consistently. Soon, the Kellers came to believe they could turn their single restaurant into a chain; by 1989, they had opened four more Tumbleweeds, all in the Louisville area. In addition, they had sold franchises for five other Tumbleweed locations: two in New Albany, one in Salem, Indiana, one in Lexington, Kentucky, and one in Fort Wright, Kentucky.

By the mid-1990s, the Kellers had expanded their chain to include seven company-owned and seven franchised restaurants in Kentucky, Indiana, and Wisconsin, as well as two joint-venture food-court outlets. The menu had evolved into a combination of mesquite-grilled foods and flavorful, spicy Mexican meals. This dual menu, which created a sort of hybrid between a steak house and a Mexican restaurant, was designed to appeal to a broader range of patrons than either type of restaurant alone could.

The Kellers believed there were tremendous growth opportunities for Tumbleweed. They knew, however, that to take advantage of those opportunities, the business needed an infusion of capital. "Tumbleweed is nowhere near its potential," George Keller said in an address to his employees in December 1994, as reported by the *Louisville Courier-Journal*. Keller said that reaching that potential required "financial resources greater than the current ownership is able to provide." In order to secure the capital necessary for further expansion, Keller worked with one of Tumbleweed's executives to structure a buyout.

The buyout was led by John Butorac, Jr., a long-time veteran of the restaurant business. In his 27 years as a restaurateur, Butorac had served as owner, operator, consultant, and senior operations executive for a number of chains—including Chi-Chi's, Fuddrucker, Two Pesos Mexican Cafes, and Kentucky Fried Chicken. He had joined Tumbleweed in 1991 as a consultant and had since then played a key role in the chain's growth and development.

Joining Butorac were James Mulrooney, David Roth, and David Cooper. Mulrooney was an accountant with a background in real estate development and restaurant operations. Like Butorac, he had spent several years in management positions with Chi-Chi's. Roth and Cooper were partners in a local law firm. The principles formed Tumbleweed LLC—a limited liability company established for the express purpose of purchasing the Tumbleweed chain—and set about finding more investors to put up cash for the deal. When the buyout was completed in January 1995, the investor group consisted of more than 60 individuals who, together, put up approximately $15 million. George and Linda Keller received $9.8 million for the company's assets, and an additional $1 million in exchange for signing a non-compete agreement.

Butorac took over as the company's new president and CEO, and Mulrooney served as executive vice-president and CFO. George Keller, who had retained a minority stake in the chain, held a position on its board of directors.

1995–97: Growth Through Franchising

Tumbleweed's new management group had ambitious plans for the chain's growth. Their goal was to have 114 restaurants open by the end of 1998, which would mean adding roughly 24 new restaurants each year. They planned to make no substantial alterations to the restaurants' concept, menu, staffing, or management style—merely to accelerate the pace.

By early 1996, however, Tumbleweed had managed to add only five restaurants, bringing the chain total to 19. Butorac and his team had revised the company's expansion strategy to allow for more modest goals: 40 restaurants open by the end of 1997, and up to 65 by the end of 1998. In a December 1996, interview with *Business First* of Louisville, Butorac attributed the slower-than-projected growth to the company's inability to quickly enlist qualified franchisees.

In order to attract more franchisees, the owners began to review and modify the existing franchise program. One of the first changes they made was designed to offer more flexibility in restaurant size. Up to that point, the average Tumbleweed consisted of approximately 7,000 square feet, with seating for around 275 people. Because of their size, these restaurants were economically viable only in fairly large markets, which limited the pool of potential franchise sites. Butorac realized, however, that there were many smaller markets where a scaled-down version of the restaurant could be profitable.

Soon, Tumbleweed franchisees had three restaurant sizes to choose from: the traditional "maxi," or one of two new, smaller options: the "midi" or the "mini." The midi comprised approximately 5,400 square feet and seated 225, while the 3,500-square foot mini had room for 130. The company's new franchise literature claimed that the flexible Tumbleweed concept was "adaptable for virtually any size market."

Another feature designed to make Tumbleweed attractive to potential franchisees was the company's use of a central commissary for the majority of the individual restaurants' food needs. Whenever possible, cooked food ingredients and sauces were prepared in advance at the commissary and shipped to the restaurants, leaving only the final preparation for the restaurant workers. Because the restaurant itself was not responsible for extensive cooking, it required less kitchen space than it otherwise would have. This allowed for more seating space, and hence the potential for greater income. It also greatly simplified day-to-day operations for the restaurant owners and managers, and ensured consistency in the menu items. The commissary did not operate to make a profit; franchisees were charged only slightly more than the actual cost of the food.

By late 1997, there were 29 Tumbleweed restaurants up and running. Of the 29, 17 were company-owned and 12 were franchised. Although most of its growth to that point had been geographically focused in Kentucky, Indiana, and Ohio, the company was preparing to jump into international markets. In November 1997, Tumbleweed teamed up with Terry Smith—a restaurateur in Brussels, Belgium—to put together a licensing deal.

Smith was a Chi-Chi's franchisee with 17 restaurants in ten European, Middle Eastern, and Far Eastern countries. Under the terms of the licensing deal, Smith's newly formed company—Tumbleweed International LLC—was given exclusive rights to develop Tumbleweed restaurants outside North and South America. Smith immediately began converting his 17 Chi-Chi's locations to Tumbleweeds, reopening the first in Ehrlangen, Germany, in February 1998. Restaurants in Jedda, Saudi Arabia, and Brussels soon followed. At the same time, Tumbleweed International began construction on three new locations: one in Amman, Jordan, and one in Cairo.

Because Smith's company was a licensee, rather than a franchisee, it had the ability to grant franchises of its own. Within just a few months of signing the licensing deal, Tumbleweed International had sold franchise rights to investors in Lebanon and Turkey. As of May 1998, Tumbleweed International's plans were to have 40 units operational by late 1999.

1998–99: Direct Public Offering

By the end of 1998, the Tumbleweed chain had grown to approximately 40 restaurants in six states and three foreign countries. More than half of the restaurants were corporate-owned. The company had total revenues of $42.8 million, and net income of $1.3 million.

In September 1998, Butorac received permission from the Securities and Exchange Commission to take Tumbleweed public. The company hoped to raise $12 million by selling 1.2 million shares priced at $10 each. Because $12 million was a small offering, however, the company leaders knew they would

```
┌─────────────────────────────────────────────┐
│              Key Dates:                       │
│                                               │
│ 1976:  The first Tumbleweed opens in New Albany, Indi- │
│        ana.                                   │
│ 1995:  Tumbleweed executive John Butorac leads an in- │
│        vestor group in a buyout of the company. │
│ 1998:  The first international Tumbleweed location opens │
│        in Ehrlangen, Germany; the company completes a │
│        direct public offering.                │
│ 1999:  Tumbleweed is listed on the NASDAQ exchange. │
└─────────────────────────────────────────────┘
```

have a hard time finding an underwriter to handle it. Thus the company decided to offer its shares in a direct public offering (DPO), a method that eliminated the underwriter that was used in the more common initial public offering (IPO).

Taking the DPO route meant that the company's executives had to market shares directly to investors. After distributing about 10,000 prospectuses, they managed to attract 1,186 investors, who between them purchased 776,543 shares. Most of the investors were customers or company employees, and 80 percent of them were located in the five-county area around Louisville. Although the offering fell short of its intended goal, it did generate almost $7.8 million, a very good showing, considering the difficulties of going public directly, without an underwriter. In conjunction with the offering, Tumbleweed was reorganized from a limited liability company into a corporation: Tumbleweed, Inc.

While most of the proceeds from Tumbleweed's DPO went to pay down debt, part also went to fuel further expansion and to boost advertising efforts. By the spring of 1999, the company had opened two new franchised stores, and four more sites were contracted for. Management's goal was to open a total of 15 new restaurants by the end of the year. The company also dropped $1 million into a new advertising campaign designed to increase awareness in markets outside Louisville. The campaign—with a ''Fun, Food and Friends'' theme—emphasized Tumbleweed's Southwestern-style cuisine, rather than its Mexican dishes.

When Tumbleweed went public, it did not immediately meet the minimum criteria for listing on the NASDAQ exchange. Its shares were instead traded on the less-widely followed OTC Bulletin Board. In April 1999, however, NASDAQ approved the company for listing on its National Market exchange. The NASDAQ listing was important because it gave Tumbleweed stock a far greater exposure. In an April 29, 1999 press release, Butorac called the listing a ''corporate milestone'' in the company's continuing progress. ''This listing will enhance the visibility of Tumbleweed to individual and institutional investors,'' he said, adding ''This should improve the liquidity of the holdings of our current shareholders and help us in our efforts to expand the coverage and sponsorship of the company's shares.''

During the first half of 1999, Tumbleweed's expansion rate accelerated. By August, eight new restaurants had been added, bringing the total number to 48. Of the 48 locations, 28 were corporate-owned, five were licensed to Tumbleweed International, and the remainder were franchised. Tumbleweed was also laying the groundwork for further expansion in the near future. In August, the company signed a development agreement with one of its existing franchisees to open at least 11 units in the coming five years. Moreover, in September, a new franchisee in Virginia contracted to open at least 13 new restaurants over a six year period, giving Tumbleweed entry into a new state.

The Tumbleweed of the Future

At the end of 1999, five years after Butorac's investor group acquired Tumbleweed, the company remained committed to expansion. Although it had failed to achieve the kind of explosive growth the owners originally aimed for, it had nonetheless made significant strides toward reaching its potential. In the five years since the buyout, the chain had more than tripled in size, expanding into two new states and four foreign markets, all the while remaining consistently profitable.

As Tumbleweed rolled into the new century, its management planned to continue growing the chain through the addition of both franchised and corporate-owned restaurants. The company would likely continue to seek entry into new geographic territories, while at the same focusing on increasing its presence in many of its existing markets.

Principal Competitors

Applebee's International, Inc.; Avado Brands Inc.; Brinker International, Inc.; Carlson Restaurants Worldwide Inc.; Lone Star Steakhouse & Saloon, Inc.; O'Charley's Inc.

Further Reading

Boyd, Terry, ''Louisvillians to Take Tumbleweed Around the World,'' *Business First of Louisville,* May 11, 1998.

Boyd, Terry, ''Tumbleweed Gets Approval for Direct Public Offering,'' *Business First of Louisville,* September 28, 1998.

Cooper, Ron, ''Tumbleweed Growth to be Spurred by Franchisees,'' *Business First of Louisville,* December 2, 1996.

Egerton, Judith, ''Tumbleweed Restaurant Chain to be Sold: Deal to Help Firm Expand,'' *Louisville Courier-Journal,* December 29, 1994, p. C1.

Redding, Rick, ''Tumbleweed Sets Expansion Plans after Stock Sale,'' *Business First of Louisville,* April 5, 1999.

Williams, Shirley, ''Taste for Success Spurs Couple to New Ventures,'' *Louisville Courier-Journal,* November 1, 1989, p. N1.

—Shawna Brynildssen

Ty Inc.

280 Chestnut
Westmont, Illinois 60559
U.S.A.
Telephone: (630) 920-1515
Fax: (630) 920-1980
Web site: http://www.ty.com

Private Company
Founded: 1985
Employees: 1,000
Sales: $1 billion (1998 est.)
NAIC: 339931 Doll and Stuffed Toy Manufacturing

Ty Inc. is a designer and manufacturer of stuffed toys. The company is best known for its "Beanie Babies"—a series of small, stuffed animals, each with its own name. Beanie Babies, which are produced in limited numbers, have become a favorite of collectors, and hard-to-find models often command hundreds, or even thousands, of dollars in the secondary market. Ty keeps a low profile, with virtually no advertising or promotional efforts. It distributes its products only through specialty, card, and gift stores rather than through large chain retailers.

1985–94: Floppy Cats and Beanie Babies

Ty Inc. was founded by and named after H. Ty Warner, a forty-something eccentric who wanted to build a better stuffed toy. Warner, who was raised in a suburb of Chicago, was an old hand at the toy business by the time he started his own toy company. After graduating in 1962 from Kalamazoo College in Michigan, he became a salesperson for Dakin Inc., a San Francisco-based manufacturer of stuffed toys. Warner remained at Dakin for almost 20 years, building a successful career and a reputation for being flamboyant and eccentric.

In 1980 Warner left Dakin and the toy business behind to spend a few years in Europe. When he returned to the states in the early 1980s, it was with a plan. Using a $50,000 inheritance he had received in 1983, Warner established Ty Inc. and designed his first stuffed toy—a white Himalayan cat named Angel. The cat, which retailed for around $20, was purposely under-stuffed so that it could be manipulated into different positions and poses. Warner started making the rounds of specialty stores and gift boutiques to pitch his new product and met with success. He followed up with a whole line of Himalayan cats, each bearing a different look and a different name.

By the early 1990s, the Ty catalog featured several under-stuffed, floppy animals, most in the $10 to $20 price range. But Warner was thinking smaller. He wanted to create a quality stuffed toy in the $5 range—something that a child could afford to buy with allowance money. The result was the Beanie Baby, a $5, pocket-sized toy made of polyester plush and loosely filled with PVC pellets. Warner introduced the first nine Beanie Babies at a Chicago toy trade show in 1993. Each of the nine toys came with a short poem and its own name—Spot the Dog, Squealer the Pig, Patti the Platypus, Cubbie the Bear, Chocolate the Moose, Pinchers the Lobster, Splash the Whale, Legs the Frog, and Flash the Dolphin.

1994–96: Birth of a National Craze

In January 1994 Beanie Babies quietly went on sale in Chicago. Shunning advertising campaigns and large, national chains, Ty targeted smaller specialty and gift shops, a practice he had carried over from his years at Dakin. He explained how his Dakin experience had influenced his distribution decision in an interview with *Forbes* in 1996: "That taught me that it's better selling 40,000 accounts than it is 5 accounts," he said. "It's more difficult to do, but for the longevity of the company and the profit margins, it's the better of the two."

Early sales of the toys were good, but not astonishing. In the early summer of 1994, Ty increased consumer interest slightly by introducing several new Beanie designs. It also began expanding its sales territory to include the East and West Coasts, the South, and scattered locations throughout the rest of the country. Ty brought out new Beanie characters periodically throughout the year, and young customers began to look forward to adding the new introductions to their existing collections.

By the summer of 1995, the demand for Beanies was escalating, in large part because of their scarcity. As with toy crazes of the past—like Tickle Me Elmo or Cabbage Patch Dolls—Beanie Babies became hotly desired simply because there weren't enough of them to go around. The reason there *weren't* enough to go around was that Warner himself made sure of it. He began limiting the number of Beanies that each store could buy, allowing only 36 of each character per month. When stores sold out of a particular model, customers had to wait for the next month's delivery—which sometimes arrived on time and sometimes didn't. For the Beanie aficionado who desperately needed a certain character to complete his or her collection, the anticipation was almost unbearable—and the competition from other collectors was intense. Warner was proving a master at capitalizing on the age-old principle of supply and demand.

While Warner's inventory-limiting tactic would probably have created a stir on its own, it was his decision to "retire" Beanie characters that delivered the coup de grace. In 1996, when Ty began announcing on its Web site that it would stop making certain creatures, it whipped the Beanie community into a frenzy. Collectors and dealers realized that some of the retired characters could become truly valuable. An extremely active secondary market sprang up, with buyers willing to pay outrageously inflated prices for the rarer Beanies. Some of the hardest-to-find characters commanded up to $6,000 in the aftermarket—more than 1,000 times their original selling price. Beanie fans began looking at their collections as serious investments.

The character retirements and the explosive growth of the Beanie aftermarket had an extremely positive impact on Ty's sales. Unsure of which Beanie might be retired next—and therefore become much more valuable—customers were determined to get their hands on *all* the characters. Stores that carried Beanies began to get hundreds of calls each day to find out which, if any, were available. Dozens of shoppers lined up outside on days when new shipments arrived. And stores that maintained Beanie Baby waiting lists routinely had more than 1,000 names of customers waiting to get the characters they wanted.

As Beanie fans proliferated, they built a whole network of information sources and events dedicated to their hobby. Dozens, if not hundreds, of individual Web sites were built to offer news, rumors, pictures, and descriptions of the growing number of Beanie characters. Beanie Baby fairs, swaps, and conventions held all around the nation gave devotees the chance to ooh and ahhh over each other's collections and to buy, sell, or trade the creatures. Hastily produced books and magazines appeared in bookstores, cataloging the various characters and their' estimated secondary market prices.

In the middle of all the frenzy, Warner and his company began to assume almost mythic proportions. Since Ty's inception, it had been something of a mystery. In the competitive toy business, where most companies did their best to out-advertise each other, its absence of blatant self-promotion was an anom-

aly. And the company's low profile wasn't limited to advertising. Warner kept Ty's headquarters in Oak Brook, Illinois, as insulated as possible, with no signage, no listed street address, and no listed telephone number. He rigorously avoided the media, almost never granting an interview, and forbade his employees to answer questions about him. This enigmatic approach inflamed the public's curiosity—and engendered myriad rumors and speculations about the company and its founder.

1997–98: New Products, New Distribution Channels

Ty continued to periodically introduce new Beanie characters and retire others. By early 1997, approximately 100 characters had been introduced and 25 had been retired. The company had experienced tremendous growth, quadrupling its employee count between 1995 and 1996. Although Ty was characteristically tight-lipped about finances, analysts estimated that its sales had grown from $25 million to $250 million during the same period.

In the spring of 1997, Ty made its first venture into conventional toy marketing when it teamed up with McDonalds for a Beanie Baby Happy Meal promotion. The five-week promotion, which began in April, offered one of ten Ty creations with the purchase of every McDonalds Happy Meal. The Happy Meal toys were smaller versions of the originals, and were called "Teenie Beanies." Explaining why he decided to partner with McDonalds, Warner cited the promotion's potential for reaching new markets. "We really did it to expand our product to children who wouldn't be shopping in upscale shopping malls," he said in a 1997 interview with *Reuters Business Report*. "We saw McDonalds as the best avenue to get these kids to see them."

Ty finished 1997 with an estimated $400 million in sales and a demand for Beanies that showed no signs of abating. Just to be sure, however, Warner unveiled a new initiative designed to rekindle any flagging consumer interest. In early 1998, Ty partnered with Cyrk Inc., a Massachusetts-based promotions company, to develop the "Beanie Babies Official Club." Simultaneously, Warner made a $10 million investment in Cyrk, which gave him approximately seven percent ownership in the company.

Beanie Baby mavens who wanted to join the official club had to buy a $10 membership kit at one of the specialty stores that carried Ty products. The kit included various Beanie paraphernalia, such as a character checklist, a membership card and certificate, stickers, and a newsletter. Once enrolled in the club, members were eligible to order special Beanies that were produced exclusively for the club and were not available in stores. Members also received periodic newsletters, access to password-only sections of the Ty Web site, and "top secret news and info about Beanie Babies and authorized Ty products."

In late 1998 Ty attempted to build on the success of the wildly popular toy by introducing a line of auxiliary products. The company began offering calendars, collectors' cards, card binders, and protective containers designed to store the heart-shaped "Ty" tags found on all Ty products. The new merchandise line, like the Beanie Baby Club kits, was handled by Cyrk.

Key Dates:

1985: Ty Warner founds Ty Inc.
1993: Ty exhibits Beanie Baby toys at Chicago trade show.
1994: Beanie Babies go on sale in Chicago specialty shops.
1997: McDonalds offers Ty Teenie Beanies as part of a Happy Meal Promotion.
1998: Ty starts the Beanie Baby Official Club.
1999: Ty announces that all Beanie Babies will be retired.
2000: Company decides to keep producing Beanie Babies, as well as new line of Beanie Kids.

Ty also introduced a line of nine "Beanie Buddies." The Buddies were similar in appearance to the Beanie Babies, but larger—around eighteen inches, as compared to the eight-inch Babies. They were also more expensive, retailing for around $15. Ty expanded the line of Buddies by periodically adding new characters

Meanwhile, retailers were still contending with customer stampedes every time a new shipment of Beanies was delivered, and Ty's sales were ratcheting ever higher. When total Beanie sales reached $1 billion, Warner celebrated by giving each of his employees two special-edition, autographed "Billionaire Bear" Beanies. The bears were estimated to be worth $3,500 if sold on the secondary market.

1999: The End of the Beanie Empire?

By the middle of 1999, it looked as though the Beanies' popularity was finally beginning to wane. The number of sales and the prices in the secondary market started to fall off, and the frenzied demand at the retail level began to cool. Consumers, always on the lookout for the latest thing, were turning their attentions elsewhere. This decline in consumer interest was not in itself shocking. Almost everyone—except perhaps diehard Beanie fans—expected the stuffed toys to eventually be eclipsed by the next fad. Most industry experts were only surprised that their vogue had lasted as long as it had.

As it turned out, however, Warner wanted a more dramatic send-off for his Babies. On August 31, 1999, Ty posted a brief message on its Web site, stating that all Beanies would be retired at 11:59 p.m. on December 31, 1999. The message also introduced ten new characters—the last one a black bear named "The End." The announcement sent shock waves through the Beanie community, prompting hundreds of calls to retailers from upset collectors. Ty refused to elaborate on the Web site message, leaving its customers guessing at whether the retired Beanies would be replaced by new ones or the whole line would be discontinued.

Many collectors and dealers chalked the announcement up as a marketing ploy—a way to revive dwindling consumer interest in the creatures. They believed that Ty was merely clearing the way for a whole new generation of Beanies. Others familiar with the industry, however, believed that the Beanies really were on their way out. Some applauded Warner for being shrewd enough to end Beanie-mania with a bang, rather than a slow fade.

2000 and Beyond

From the most savvy toy industry expert to the youngest Beanie fan, no one could be sure what the future held for Ty. Many predicted that the company would release a brand-new line of collectible toys in the hopes of duplicating the Beanie Baby frenzy. The company itself remained characteristically secretive about its plans. Then spokespersons announced that the company would hold a consumer vote to determine the fate of Beanie Babies. To no one's surprise, fans voted to keep Ty in production; and the company complied, introducing a new line in early 2000 as well: Beanie Kids. With Warner's knack for toy design and his genius for marketing, Ty was very well positioned for continued success.

Principal Competitors

Applause Enterprises, Inc.; The Boyds Collection, Ltd.; Hasbro, Inc.; Mattel, Inc.; Russ Berrie and Company, Inc.; Play by Play Toys & Novelties, Inc.; Vermont Teddy Bear Co., Inc.

Further Reading

Baglole, Joel, "Beanie Babies Born into Wealth," *Toronto Star*, November 11, 1998.

Faust, Fred, "Ohhhh Babies No Fee Fi Fo Fum, Just Toys after This 'Beanie' Stalk," *St. Louis Post-Dispatch*, February 24, 1997, p. 1A.

Mannix, Margaret, "Beanie Bubble," *U.S. News & World Report*, August 3, 1998, p. 53.

Palmer, Ann Therese, and Alex Tresniowski, "Up Front: Bean There, Done That," *People*, September 20, 1999, p. 72.

Precker, Michael, "Beanie Baby Boom," *Dallas Morning News*, March 8, 1997, p. 1C.

Samuels, Gary, "Mystique Marketing," *Forbes*, October 21, 1996, p. 276.

"Trends: Beanie-Mania," *People*, July 1, 1996, p. 84.

—Shawna Brynildssen

UICI

4001 McEwen Drive, Suite 200
Dallas, Texas 75244
U.S.A.
Telephone: (972) 392-6700
Fax: (972) 392-6721
Web site: http://www.uici.net

Public Company
Incorporated: 1982 as United Insurance Companies, Inc.
Employees: 4,000
Sales: $1.18 billion (1998)
Stock Exchanges: New York
Ticker Symbol: UCI
NAIC: 524114 Direct Health and Medical Insurance
   Carriers

UICI is a diversified company that offers insurance and financial services to niche consumer and institutional markets. Through its many subsidiaries, UICI operates in five key areas: life, health, property, and casualty insurance; credit cards; student loans; institutional technology; and real estate. UICI has succeeded by targeting its services to narrow markets underserved by other providers, such as by selling insurance to students and the self-employed, as well as offering credit cards to higher risk clients. The company also has a thriving business that supplies technical and administrative support service to health care payors and providers. UICI conducts most of its insurance marketing through its staff of 5,000 agents, who work on a straight commission basis. Among its subsidiaries are The MEGA Life and Health Insurance Co., The Education Finance Group (EFG), Insurdata, The National Motor Club of America, and AMLI Realty Company. Although UICI initially was involved in the insurance sector only, the company began to diversify its holdings in 1992, in anticipation of greater federal regulation of the health care industry.

Early Years: 1983–86

Ronald L. Jensen founded United Insurance Companies, Inc. in 1983. Previously, Jensen had served for 22 years as the chairman and president of another insurance company, Life

Investors. In 1981 Jensen sold a controlling interest in that business to AEGON N.V., a Dutch holding company. Although this transaction made Jensen a wealthy man, he continued to look for new professional challenges. He soon hit on the idea of selling insurance to specific niche groups that other insurers tended to overlook.

With this goal in mind, Jensen launched United Insurance. He also took over United Group Association (UGA), a small insurance agency that was ''essentially bankrupt,'' according to *Investor's Business Daily*. Although UGA became a wholly owned subsidiary of United Insurance, the two maintained separate corporate structures, and Jensen retained his closely held ownership stake in UGA. Rekindling his relationship with AEGON, Jensen devised an arrangement whereby UGA would sell insurance policies issued by the Dutch company. United Insurance's role would then be to co-insure UGA's operations. In fact, for the first three years of its existence, this was United Insurance's only business.

As a result, United Insurance did not underwrite or even administer the policies it sold. Instead, through its UGA subsidiary, it concentrated on marketing health and life insurance policies to a particular group of consumers—self-employed workers who, because they did not receive insurance through their employers (as most Americans did), had to purchase their own policies. This market was virtually untapped and offered United Insurance considerable opportunities. With more than seven million consumers classified as self-employed (defined as any person who ran a business with ten or fewer employees), United Insurance had a significant pool from which to draw. ''Within any industry there are niches that companies can capitalize on,'' Jensen told the *Dallas Business Courier*. ''The secret is in picking out the niche.'' The company built a network of agents who sold policies face-to-face and were paid on a commission basis. United Insurance grew quickly, with its earnings rising from $13.2 million in 1984 to $30.1 million in 1985.

To reach its target market, United Insurance cultivated a strong relationship with the National Network for the Self-Employed (NNSE), an organization representing the interests of self-employed workers nationwide. In a major boost to United Insurance, NNSE endorsed United Insurance as its preferred accident and health insurance provider. In return, United Insur-

Company Perspectives:

From its founding, UICI's primary direction was to choose a narrow focus in the health insurance business offering a narrow range of insurance products distributed by a dedicated field force. That direction changed in 1993. We did not abandon the Health Insurance business; rather, the overriding direction and focus was to ask the question, how does UICI diversify? While diversification has been a success story, I believe UICI should again modify its game plan and overriding direction. I believe the primary direction of UICI should now be to strengthen and expand the insurance business with particular emphasis placed on positioning and strengthening the role of the field forces.

ance agents encouraged membership in NNSE while selling policies. This alliance was crucial to United Insurance's success. Nearly 90,000 consumers belonged to NNSE, and the organization's public endorsement of the insurance company led to the ''vast majority of sales for United Insurance,'' according to the *Dallas Business Courier*.

Continued Growth and Diversification: 1986–92

In 1986 Jensen opted to take United Insurance public to expand the scope of the company's operations. Jensen's primary goals in the initial public stock offering were to put his company in a more secure financial position and to allow it to assume greater control over its operations. Instead of relying on AEGON to provide most of the services associated with United Insurance's business (and having to pay it to provide them), Jensen planned to acquire a company that could itself administer and service the policies his affiliates sold. Because such an acquisition would be costly, Jensen hoped to use the capital raised from the stock sale to fund his purchase. The offering was a success, raising about $16 million. Later in the year, United Insurance acquired the Oklahoma-based Mark Twain Life Insurance Corp. Mark Twain not only afforded United Insurance with an ample administrative base, so that that company might one day undertake its own underwriting, but it also broadened United Insurance's reach. With the acquisition, United Insurance became licensed to sell insurance in 27 additional states.

Following United Insurance's success in reaching the self-employed, the company expanded its niche-oriented strategy to include a new group in 1987, when it purchased Keystone Life Insurance Co. Keystone was a leading provider of student health, accident, and life insurance. Through Keystone, United Insurance launched its Student Insurance Division (SID) and entered the student insurance market, selling group student health programs to colleges and universities. Just as United Insurance had nurtured its relationship with NNSE, the company now used its sales force to build alliances on campuses. During its first year, SID experienced massive losses, and many analysts expected that United Insurance would quickly shed its latest subsidiary. Nevertheless, Jensen stayed the course, a decision that ultimately paid dividends for the company.

By 1989 United Insurance's total assets were valued at $244.6 million, while its net income was $32.8 million. More-

over, the company continued to add to its portfolio of subsidiaries in the late 1980s and early 1990s. As it had in the past, United Insurance expanded vertically within its selected niche markets. By far the most important of these acquisitions occurred in 1988, when United Insurance purchased Orange State Life Insurance, a Florida company specializing in small group insurance. United Insurance renamed its new subsidiary The MEGA Life and Health Insurance Co., and within a few short years, MEGA came to generate a substantial portion of United Insurance's business. In the early 1990s, United Insurance also purchased Chesapeake Life Insurance Co. and Mid-West National Life Insurance Co.

Diversification into Credit Card Services and Administration: 1992–96

United Insurance's landscape changed suddenly and dramatically in 1992, when Governor Bill Clinton campaigned for and won the presidency in large part by virtue of his vow to reform the U.S. health care system. United Insurance, which was almost wholly dependent on the health insurance market, felt quite threatened by the sorts of changes under discussion. (In 1992 alone, nearly 80 percent of United Insurance's revenues was derived from its health insurance operations, 68 percent from the Self-Employed Agency Division, and an additional ten percent from the SID. Earnings from purchased blocks of life insurance represented the remainder of the company's income.) With its core assets jeopardized by proposed health care legislation, United Insurance looked for ways to safeguard itself. It decided that the best strategy would be for the company rapidly to diversify itself outside the health care sector. As Jensen would explain later in an Annual Report, ''UICI made a very important choice at that time . . . to purchase companies that could offer employment opportunities for its employees . . . in the event [Clinton] was successful [in dramatically revamping the U.S. health care system].''

To implement this new approach, United Insurance ventured into the credit card business in 1992 when it purchased two small insurance agencies that issued credit cards to those who could not otherwise obtain them because of bad credit reports or a lack of credit history. To jump-start its new business, United Insurance initially began issuing cards to everyone who purchased its life insurance policies. After a shaky beginning in 1992, when the new credit card division lost $134,000, it struggled even more significantly in 1993, losing more than $4.2 million. After this debacle, United Insurance decided to de-link the issuance of credit cards from the sale of life insurance policies and began to promote the cards in their own right, particularly through a cable television advertising campaign. The company had reason for optimism. Despite the losses suffered by the credit card division, United Insurance's assets had risen to $814.8 million, and its net income to $32.8 million, by the close of 1993.

United Insurance's diversification program did not end with the launch of its credit card division. In 1995 it branched out into the fledgling but booming field of providing administrative services to health care insurers when it acquired a 51 percent stake in Insurdata (United Insurance purchased the remaining 49 percent of Insurdata in 1997). This Irving, Texas-based company had experience with the clerical aspects of health care—data entry, filing, and copying—and allowed United Insurance to provide these services at a lower cost to insurers seeking to outsource these time-consuming and labor-intensive tasks. Insurdata also took over the processing of United Insurance's own student insurance division. Insurdata's other clients included preferred provider organizations (PPOs), managed care organizations, assorted insurance carriers, Blue Cross/Blue Shield organizations, and third-party administrators.

The year 1996 brought even more changes to United Insurance. To signify its broad range of services, and to emphasize the fact that it was no longer exclusively an insurance provider, the company changed its name to UICI. The company continued to expand into new spheres that year as well when it acquired AMLI Realty Company, a 20 percent owner of AMLI Commercial Properties.

Despite its many forays into new arenas, however, UICI had not abandoned its lucrative and substantial insurance operations. (President Clinton's health care initiative had failed fundamentally to alter the U.S. health care market.) In 1996 UICI acquired PLF Life Insurance Co.'s Health Administration Offices, which had underwritten and serviced most of UGA's health insurance business. By purchasing this independent insurance agency, UICI gained the opportunity to underwrite more of its policies. In fact, The MEGA Life Insurance announced in April 1996 that it would begin issuing policies directly, rather than through AEGON, as it had done in the past. Moreover, Jensen sold his 100 percent ownership of UGA to UICI in 1996, bringing that company entirely within the UICI fold and allowing UICI total control over its most important sales and marketing arm. In addition, SID had become the largest provider of student health insurance in the United States by the mid-1990s. Buoyed by these successes, UICI's assets totaled $1.32 billion in 1996, and its net income grew to $69.2 million.

Offering Student Loans: 1997

UICI made perhaps its boldest move in June 1997, when it acquired the Hyannis, Massachusetts-based Education Finance Group (EFG), and thereby expanded into the complex realm of

student loans. Founded in 1992, EFG was firmly rooted in the business. Its loan volume in 1996 had exceeded $350 million, and it offered an array of student loan products and services, including federally funded loans. UICI's strategy was logical. The company had gained access to many college and university administrators through its years of marketing student health care. The company could use these contacts to grow its new loan business.

Four months after completing its acquisition of EFG, UICI announced its purchase of EduServ Technologies, Inc., which UICI planned to fold into its EFG division. Like many of UICI's prior ventures, EduServ conformed to its desire to target niche markets. EduServ had built its business by servicing school-based loan initiatives (such as the Perkins Program)—institutional loan programs administered directly through schools. In December 1997, UICI added another subsidiary to its EFG division when it bought Educational Loan Administration Group, Inc. (ELA), which also limited itself to specialized services. ELA focused on offering loans directly to parents who wished to finance their children's education.

In addition to launching its student loan venture, UICI continued to develop its credit card services. Following a stellar year for the division in 1996, in which it earned $15.1 million and increased its credit card portfolios 44 percent, UICI opened its own credit card bank, United Credit National Bank. In this way, UICI furthered its trend toward self-sufficiency. With the bank, the credit card division was no longer dependent on third-party banks to finance its operations. To increase demand for its cards, UICI committed to more television advertising, as well as a substantial direct marketing effort. Also in 1997, UICI acquired National Motor Club of America, Inc., a provider of motor club services to drivers. By year's end, UICI's assets totaled more than $1.5 billion, and net income had risen to yet another record high—$86.5 million.

Refocusing: 1998–2000

Just when it seemed that UICI's prolonged efforts to reduce dependence on its health care holdings had succeeded, the company was undermined by a difficult financial year in 1998 that caused its stock prices to plummet. Although the company's assets remained high at $2.47 billion, its net income plunged to a level below that of 1996—$58.8 million. Shocked by the downturn, Jensen stepped down as president and chief executive officer, although he remained intimately involved in the company as its chairman. He was replaced by Greg Mutz. After so many years of refocusing on new operations, UICI found that its health insurance business was still essential to the company's viability, a fact that proved problematic in 1998 when both the self-employed and student insurance divisions (long the top earners for UICI) reported significant losses. New business in the company's self-employed insurance sector dropped about 22 percent, while earnings in the student insurance division plummeted 14 percent. Company officials pledged to refocus on the insurance business, especially on the struggling self-employed area.

By recommitting to its insurance operations, however, UICI did not intend to abandon its financial services divisions. UICI did shed some of its less successful ventures, including several small companies in its health care administration sector. But the company remained fully supportive of EFG, which had experienced considerable losses in 1998 as well. UICI refinanced a portion of EFG's loans in an effort to stabilize the division and continued to focus on expanding it. Ranked the nation's fastest-growing student loan lender, EFG had a great deal of potential. In 1999 EFG acquired AMS Investment Group, Inc., which held the distinction of being the largest provider of tuition payment plans in the United States. Early in 2000, UICI restructured EFG's management in a further effort to position it for growth and profitability. In a similar fashion, UICI reorganized the management of its credit card division (christened United CreditServ in 1999), which had reported losses in 1999.

UICI also continued to expand its successful health care administration programs. In January 2000, the company announced the merger of Insurdata and HealthAxis.com, a leading online insurance marketer. Since Insurdata had emerged as one of the nation's leading providers of health care administration software, the combined entity—which would adopt the HealthAxis.com moniker—was poised to become one of the largest players in Web-related health insurance space. With all of these maneuvers, UICI hoped to prepare itself for continued strong growth.

Principal Subsidiaries

The MEGA Life and Health Insurance Company; Mid-West National Life Insurance Company of Tennessee; The Chesapeake Life Insurance Company; National Motor Club of America; United Credit National Bank; United Membership Marketing Group, LLC; Insurdata, Incorporated; Educational Finance Group, Inc.

Principal Competitors

Aon Corporation; SLM Holding Corporation; Atlantic American Corporation; Guarantee Life Insurance Company; HCC Insurance Holdings, Inc.

Further Reading

Bounds, Jeff, "Company, Shareholder Wage Court, Public Relations Battle," *Dallas Business Journal,* July 9, 1999.

Jaffe, Thomas, "United We Stand," *Forbes,* April 4, 1988.

Jones, John, "Companies in the News," *Investor's Business Daily,* May 26, 1995.

Opdyke, Jeff, "United Insurance Wins Following for Offbeat Prose, Strong Results," *Wall Street Journal,* September 29, 1993.

Paschal, Jeff, "Mark Twain Staff Increased from 30 to 50," *Journal Record,* March 17, 1987.

Schurman, Mitchell, "United Insurance Grows rapidly as It Focuses on Self-Employed Workers," *Dallas Business Courier,* May 19, 1986.

"UICI Acquires Controlling Interest in Education Finance Group," *PR Newswire,* June 12, 1997.

"United Insurance Cos. To Buy PLF Life Unit," *Best's Insurance News,* January 12, 1996.

Wichner, David, "Regulator Seeks To Sell Farm and Home's Assets," *Phoenix Gazette,* April 30, 1991.

—Rebecca Stanfel

United Jewish Communities

111 Eighth Avenue, Suite 11E
New York, New York 10016
U.S.A.
Telephone: (212) 284-6500
Fax: (212) 284-6844
Web site: http://www.ujc.org

Nonprofit Organization
Founded: 1932
Employees: 500
Sales: $1.5 billion (1998 est.)
NAIC: 81311 Religious Organizations

The United Jewish Communities (UJC) was created in 1999 through the merger of three of the largest Jewish charitable organizations in North America—the Council of Jewish Federations (CJF), the United Jewish Appeal (UJA), and the United Israel Appeal (UIA). Comprising 189 local Jewish federations, the UJC raises over one billion dollars annually. UJC's funds support such diverse causes as the resettlement of Jewish refugees in Israel, care for elderly Jews in the United States, formal and informal Jewish education, and relief programs in the former Yugoslavia. Although UJC commanded a $37 million operating budget in 1999, it faces considerable competition from private foundations that have steadily gained a greater share of Jewish Americans' charitable donations.

The Jewish Federations: 1895–39

The roots of the modern UJC date back to 1895, when various Jewish charitable organizations in Boston, Massachusetts, banded together for fund-raising purposes and formed the Federation of Jewish Charities of Boston. This federation conducted a single community-wide fund-raising campaign for Boston's many Jewish charities, ranging from the Charitable Burial Association to the Hebrew Women's Sewing Society. Individual donors gave their money to the federation, which in turn distributed it to community programs. The Boston federation's chief advantage was that it eradicated duplicative—and often competitive—fund-raising efforts. Jewish communities in

other American cities observed the Boston federation's success and followed suit.

Although numerous Jewish federations were created during the early decades of the 20th century, each federation remained independent and locally-oriented, serving the particular needs of the Jewish community it represented. In 1932, however, the CJF was launched as an umbrella organization of American and Canadian federations. The CJF did not seek to control local federations but instead strove to foster communication between them and to strengthen their combined impact.

At the same time that the CJF built the framework for a national Jewish charitable organization, other Jewish philanthropic groups were focusing on international issues. At the close of the 19th century, for instance, a coalition of Zionist and non-Zionist Jews formed the non-political United Palestine Appeal (later renamed the United Israel Appeal) to provide humanitarian assistance abroad. In a similar vein, the American Jewish Joint Distribution Committee (JDC) was established at the outset of World War I by a coalition of American Jewish groups to aid Jewish populations in war-torn Europe and Ottoman Palestine. In the 1920s and 1930s, the JDC funneled tens of millions of dollars to provide relief to Soviet Jews. Furthermore, in 1929 Chaim Weizmann and Louis Marshall launched the Jewish Agency to raise funds for the Zionist cause. (Although the Jewish Agency was short-lived in its first incarnation, the group was reconstituted in 1973. Weizmann himself became Israel's first president in 1948.)

These varied Jewish charities were prompted to join forces in the 1930s, as Adolph Hitler's National Socialist party in Germany became more virulently anti-Semitic with each passing year. The reality of Hitler's campaign of terror against German Jews was driven home to Jewish Americans in November 1938, when *Kristallnacht* (the "Night of Broken Glass") galvanized the American Jewish population to take action. In response to the widespread violence and destruction carried out against German Jews and their property that night, the leaders of three influential Jewish groups—the JDC, the United Palestine Appeal, and New York Association for New Americans—united to form the United Jewish Appeal (UJA) in January 1939.

422

Company Perspectives:

Jewish federations across North America commit themselves to the renaissance of the Jewish people in North America, in Israel, and throughout the world. Thus, we articulate, in word and deed, the mission of this new entity to: Utilize our financial and human resources to improve the quality of Jewish life worldwide—honoring the covenant that "All Jews are Responsible One for the Other," and that only through unified action can we solve our community's most pressing problems; Nurture vital experiences of Jewish life and learning in North America to create a compelling culture of shared meaning, shared responsibility, and shared values as Klal Yisrael, one people in all its diversity, with a shared commitment to its future; Join in partnership with our fellow Jews in Israel in building unity and mutual respect and solidifying Israel's central role in our Jewish identity and future; Inspire Jews to fulfill the mitzvah of Tzedakah, securing the financial and human resources necessary to achieve our mission of caring for those in need, rescuing Jews in danger, and ensuring the continuity of our people; Provide the strategic resources, assistance, and direction to help local federations fulfill their individual, regional, and collective responsibilities of Tikkun Olam, community building and Jewish renaissance; and Involve more of our fellow Jews in the work of our community and provide opportunities for a new generation of leaders to continue our sacred work of caring for one another.

United Jewish Appeal: 1939–90

UJA quickly emerged as the primary American fund-raising organization committed to Jewish causes outside the United States. From its outset, the UJA collaborated with the federations to provide relief to Jewish groups in Europe, sending abroad a portion of the revenue raised by the federations. Between January and December 1939, UJA raised $14 million to help German Jews escape the Nazis. After World War II—as American Jews confronted the tragedy of the Holocaust—UJA took a central role in bringing Jewish refugees out of Europe and resettling them in the United States. In 1946, the organization collected $100 million during one campaign alone, and in 1947, it oversaw the arrival of more than 25,000 Jewish survivors to the United States.

In 1948, UJA's focus changed dramatically with the founding of the state of Israel. Instead of bringing Jewish war and Holocaust survivors to the United States, UJA raised $200 million in 1948 to resettle them in Israel. UJA also channeled donations from individual Jewish Americans into social services programs in Israel, supporting land reclamation, hospital construction, and schools. The survival of Israel quickly became the fundamental cause and the unifying force of much of American Jewry. As the *Jewish Advocate* explained, "the establishment and well-being of Israel were paramount for American Jewish philanthropists, and Jewish federations were the funnels of that money to Israel."

In this way, Jewish federations emerged as the centerpiece of a complex web of charitable organizations. Although each federation remained independent, they all collaborated closely with UJA for the preservation of Israel. As they had for most of their history, federations conducted annual campaigns to raise funds in their communities. However, UJA partially supported these campaigns with a fund-raising effort of its own. Each federation then determined how it wanted to allocate its revenues. In the 1950s, most used about 40 percent of their funds to support local programs. The remaining 60 percent was given to UJA, which in turn allocated the money to international Jewish causes, primarily in Israel.

To accomplish this task, UJA relied on the Jewish Agency, the UIA, and the JDC. The UIA transferred UJA campaign proceeds to the Jewish Agency in Israel, and also served as the Agency's representative in the United States. The Jewish Agency distributed the massive contributions garnered from UJA to Israeli organizations of the Agency's choosing. The JDC usually received an allocation of UJA funds to aid Jewish groups experiencing hardship in foreign countries outside of Israel. The federations also received guidance from the CJF, which provided input on the allocation of annual campaign funds in the United States.

This system was an unparalleled success, making UJA one of the more illustrious charities of all time. UJA was especially effective in times of crisis, when Israel's very survival seemed at stake. As the *Baltimore Jewish Times* wryly noted, "history shows there's nothing quite like war in the Middle East to open people's hearts and pocketbooks." Together with the federations, UJA raised $175 million in the first month following the Israeli Six Day War in 1967 and a total of $308 million during the entire year. Even more impressive was the $100 million donated to UJA in the first week of the Yom Kippur War in 1973.

Just as these wars—and the threats of Arab leaders to drive the fledgling nation into the sea—prompted American Jews to increase their support of the federations and the UJA, so too did events in the late 1980s and early 1990s. The plight of Ethiopia's Jews set in motion UJA's Operation Moses, a 1987 campaign that ultimately led to a secret Israeli airlift in which 7,000 Ethiopian Jews—known as Falashas—were taken out of Ethiopia and moved to Israel. UJA also supported a number of programs that provided food, housing, and education to the relocated Falashas in Israel.

Even more compelling for most Jewish Americans was the fate of their brethren in the Soviet Union. As Communism collapsed and lost its centralizing authority in the late 1980s, anti-Semitism gained force in the Soviet Union. Attacks on synagogues and the desecration of Jewish cemeteries increased significantly. In 1989, UJA launched a special campaign to remove Jews from the Soviet Union and resettle them in Israel. Though this "Passage to Freedom" campaign fell short of its monetary goal, it still raised $50 million for the cause. In 1990, the UJA once again undertook another emergency campaign, Operation Exodus, which ultimately collected $900 million and allowed 800,000 Jews to emigrate to Israel.

Declining Donations to UJA: 1991–99

Escalating tensions in Iraq in the early 1990s had a similar effect on UJA's annual campaign. After Saddam Hussein's re-

---

Key Dates:

1932: The Council of Jewish Federations (CJF) is created to serve as an umbrella organization for local American and Canadian Jewish federations.

1939: The United Jewish Appeal (UJA) is formed through the merger of the fund-raising campaigns of the American Jewish Joint Distribution Committee (JDC), the United Palestine Appeal (later United Israel Appeal), and the New York Association for New Americans.

1946: UJA raises more than $100 million in a single campaign.

1948: State of Israel is founded.

1990: UJA launches the Operation Exodus Campaign and raises $900 million.

1997: UJA and CJF form joint operating partnership.

1998: United Israel Appeal (UIA) joins the partnership.

1999: United Jewish Communities is created through the merger of UJA, CJF, and UIA.

---

gime fired SCUD missiles at Israel in 1991, UJA and the federations had a record fund-raising year, gathering over $1.2 billion (which was more than the combined earnings of the American Cancer Society, CARE, and the March of Dimes.)

However, the massive amounts raised that year proved to be the final time in the century that UJA could so galvanize American Jewry. Cracks began to appear in the once impenetrable wall of UJA. Contributions to the federation system flattened—and then dropped—in the mid-1990s. In 1994, for example, the federations raised $797 million, well below the $820.3 million collected in 1989. More troubling were broader trends. Although about 75 percent of Jews over the age of 65 continued to support federations and the UJA, less than 35 percent of those under the age of 35 did so. Instead of donating to the federations' generic annual campaigns, younger Jews were apt to send their philanthropic dollars to a new generation of Jewish charitable foundations, which allowed donors to target certain causes or geographic regions.

Ironically, younger Jews disassociated from UJA and the federations in part because these venerable institutions had accomplished their goals. The state of Israel was prosperous and secure, and peace in the Middle East seemed a likely prospect. As a result, American Jews were less willing to fund federations, which allocated such a sizable percentage of their proceeds to the UJA—and thus Israel. Federations steadily decreased the portion of their funds going abroad, but many younger Jews felt as though the federated system was still doing little to address the issues confronting Jews in America: "assimilation, loss of Jewish identity and lack of Jewish education," according to the *Jewish Advocate*.

As a result of declining contributions, the CJF commissioned a $500,000 study to investigate the state of Jewish philanthropy in the United States and to explore the possibility of merging CJF and UJA. Tensions between the two charities escalated. UJA continued fiercely to lobby federations to allocate hefty percent-

ages of their funds to international causes. "We are the surrogates for overseas, the stand-in for the Jew in Armenia or Ashdod, who can't stand at a federation allocation meeting to represent his or her viewpoint," one UJA official proclaimed to the *Jewish Telegraphic Agency*. On the other hand, the CJF advocated that federations take care of local problems and local causes that interested community members, such as funding Jewish day schools or sending students to Israel.

A potential merger between UJA and CJF remained a topic of discussion from 1994 to 1996. "We began looking at the changing environment here and in Israel," UJA national chairman Joel Tauber told the *Baltimore Jewish Times*. "What we concluded was our current structures don't really meet the needs of the new environment." As many observers noted, what drove the conflict was a deeper question: "What's most important to American Jews about being Jewish?," as the *Wall Street Journal* asked.

In May 1997, UJA and CJF agreed to form a joint operating partnership in an attempt to bring donors back to the federations. Although each organization would maintain its own board of directors, the partnership sought to eradicate the conflicts between the two groups. Further negotiations continued with the eventual goal of formally merging the two charitable groups. One of the driving forces behind the merger was now-former UJA head Tauber, who argued that uniting the groups would diminish the layers of bureaucracy between the individual donor and the ultimate recipient of the funds. (As the *Baltimore Jewish Times* noted, "to the layperson and the giver, the list of agencies may as well constitute a new line of kosher alphabet soup"). Merging the UJA and CJF would deliver annual savings of about $3 million by eliminating overlapping efforts.

United Jewish Communities: 1999 and Beyond

After six years of discussions, UJA, CJF, and UIA (which had joined the partnership in May 1998), pledged to merge into one entity in 1999. In November of that year, this new organization named itself the United Jewish Communities (UJC). The federations emerged as the dominant players in UJC. Not only were they given legal "ownership" of the UJC (though what "owning" meant was not clearly defined either before or after the merger), but they were also given more direct control over determining the international causes to be supported by UJC. Instead of federations giving a portion of their revenue to UJA, which gave these to the Jewish Agency, which in turn decided what causes to support, UJC established a process it labeled the Overseas Needs Assessment Distribution (ONAD). In this distribution process, a committee representing 18 federations met annually to hear pitches from the Jewish Agency and the JDC about specific programs and needs. ONAD then determined which overseas services were "core" and which were "elective." The shift was a radical one. "The era of Israel putting out its hand and having Diaspora Jews fill it is over," Steve Hoffman, director of the Jewish federation of Cleveland, asserted to the *Jerusalem Post* on November 16, 1999.

At its first General Assembly, UJC elected Canadian business leader Charles Bronfman (co-chairman of the entertainment and beverage titan The Seagram Company Ltd.) as its chairman, Stephen Solender as its president, and Louise Frankel as executive vice-president and chief operating officer. By this time, the UJC had also adopted its mission statement and had established the four content areas—or "pillars"—that would guide donation decisions: Jewish Renaissance and Renewal; Human Services and Social Policy; Israel and Overseas; and Campaign/Financial Resource Development.

In its first year, UJC adopted several new initiatives that sought to increase donations to the federations. Foremost among these was the creation of a new trust that would allow donors to give to a specific cause, instead of contributing solely to the overarching annual campaigns. It was hoped that this trust would help UJC fend off competition from the more issue-specific foundations. The UJC also sponsored Generation J, a web site targeting young Jews, and instituted other unique ventures in partnership with federations that were intended to bring wealthy, young Jews into the federation fold. For instance, UJC identified over two dozen Jewish high-tech entrepreneurs who did not contribute to Jewish philanthropies and invited them to participate in a discussion about the meaning of Judaism.

Despite its many efforts, the ultimate success of UJC remained uncertain. Many specific issues had not been resolved, such as how much each federation should pay into the UJC system. "We think we're becoming something new, but we're in uncharted water," Solender told the *Wall Street Journal*. "The end game isn't so clear right now." Nevertheless, many indications were positive. The UJC's 1999 annual campaign raised $790 million, up from the 1998 total of $765 million. "More and more people now realize that the annual campaign is our most effective vehicle for responding to urgent needs at home, in Israel, and in 60 other countries," a UJC spokesperson asserted.

Further Reading

"$25 Million Increase Seen in 1999 UJA-Federation Drive; $790 Million Predicted in Fifth Consecutive Record Year," *PR Newswire*, June 25, 1999.

Feiden, Douglas, "Foundations Gaining Lead in Underwriting Innovation," *Forward*, November 17, 1995.

Gardiner, Beth, "Jewish Charities Adapting to New Trend in Giving," *Albany Time Union*, November 27, 1999.

Gitell, Seth, "Baby Boom Putting UJA in a Pickle: New Study Stirs Hope, Concerns," *Forward,* May 23, 1997.

Henry, Marilyn, "Jewish Agency Heads to Plead for Funds from U.S. Jewry," *Jerusalem Post*, November 16, 1999.

——, "GA Ends with United Body, Divisive Issues," *Jerusalem Post*, November 21, 1999.

Littman, Ruth, "Jewish Agencies May Merge by 2000," *Baltimore Jewish Times*, August 4, 1995.

Mendelsohn, Martha, " 'A Prince of the Jewish People': UJA-Federation Pays Tribute to William Rosenwald, a UJA Founder, at Memorial Service," *The Jewish Week*, December 13, 1996.

Miller, Lisa, "Can a Venerable Jewish Charity Make a Comeback?" *Wall Street Journal*, January 19, 2000.

Rabinovitz, Barbara, " 'Bleak' Future Seen for Fund-Raising by Jewish Federations: Local Consultant Says U.S. Jews Living in 'A Post-Federated World'," *The Jewish Advocate*, July 30, 1998.

Serwach, Joseph, "Tauber: Force for Unity: Local Exec Prime Mover in Charity Merger," *Crain's Detroit Business*, January 10, 2000.

Stark, Ellen, "To Curb Costs, UJA Lets Local Groups Raise Funds," *Money*, December 1, 1994.

Yudelson, Larry, "CJF Approves Study That Could Lead to Big Changes in Relationship with UJA," *Jewish Telegraphic Agency*, April 20, 1994.

—Rebecca Stanfel

United Retail Group Inc.

365 West Passaic Street
Rochelle Park, New Jersey 07662
U.S.A.
Telephone: (201) 845-0880
Fax: (201) 909-2210
Web site: http://www.unitedretail.com

Public Company
Incorporated: 1989
Employees: 4,700
Sales: $378.6 million (1999)
Stock Exchanges: NASDAQ
Ticker Symbol: URGI
NAIC: 44812 Women's Clothing Stores; 44815 Clothing
  Accessories Stores

With locations in 36 states, United Retail Group Inc. owns a growing national chain of apparel stores which cater specifically to the needs of larger sized women and teens. Tapping a market which has historically been marginalized and ignored by the retail industry, United Retail focuses exclusively on providing clothing, accessories, shoes, and cosmetics to women of size 14 and up, with fashion-conscious casual wear being the company's primary source of revenue. United Retail was previously owned and operated by fashion retailer The Limited, and is now run by former Limited executive Raphael Benaroya, a 30-year veteran of the apparel industry. Under Benaroya's guidance, the company has grown to oversee over 500 stores in 36 states, operating under two names: The Avenue and Sizes Unlimited. The Avenue is upscale in focus, with locations primarily in major shopping malls, while the Sizes Unlimited chain offers larger sized clothing at lower prices and is located mainly in strip malls. After a period of lagging sales in the mid-1990s, United Retail is a highly profitable company, with sales at decade's end of almost $400 million.

Founding of United Retail: 1987–92

In 1987 the huge national fashion chain The Limited introduced two new store concepts under the auspices of its Lane Bryant division: Sizes Unlimited and Lerner Woman. Targeting larger sized women between the ages of 18 and 50, the two stores were meant for the most part to attract a clientele similar to that of The Limited's eponymous stores: fashion conscious women who were shopping on a somewhat restricted budget.

In the 1980s The Limited had enjoyed tremendous national growth, with stores located in almost every major mall nationwide, and these had attracted a loyal customer following. The Limited's clothes were inexpensive, trendy, and body conscious, and the company's designers were quick to mimic the latest fashions from less affordable labels. Though The Limited grew to become a highly successful corporation, the company's stores appealed primarily to a restricted consumer market of younger, highly body-conscious women. Therefore, as the company grew in profitability, it looked for ways in which to appeal to a broader customer range. The introduction of Lerner Woman and Sizes Unlimited was a part of the company's overall growth strategy, and within a year the two stores had grown to 88 locations.

The Lerner Woman stores were slightly higher in price and quality than Sizes Unlimited, and were located in upscale, usually enclosed, shopping malls. Sizes Unlimited locations were focused in less expensive strip malls, and offered apparel which was not as trendy as the store's sister division. Both stores had as their main focus women's casual wear, designed for sizes 14 and higher, with Lerner Woman also offering a limited line of dressier career clothes. Prices were kept affordable, as they were at The Limited's original chain, and by 1989 the two new chains were enjoying steady growth.

At the end of the 1980s the market for fashionable apparel specifically designed for the larger consumer was on an upswing. From specially made swimsuits to lingerie, well-made, larger sized apparel was a growing niche market. In 1989, with further growth in mind, the parent division of Lane Bryant moved to consolidate the two new concept chains; they were merged together under the rubric of Lerner. To prevent loss of name recognition, Sizes Unlimited retained its store name, while administrative functions were consolidated. During this time, the head of Lane Bryant, the division which oversaw the two stores, was Raphael Benaroya, and it was he who engineered the strategy that eventually turned the chains into United Retail.

Benaroya was a veteran of the retail market and had an ambitious vision of the role he was to play in the development of the industry. A native of Israel, Benaroya received his undergraduate degree from the University of Minnesota in 1972 and immediately after graduating began a career in the management end of the apparel industry. He first went to work for General Mills, at which he became involved in the company's Izod Lacoste division. After working with Izod Lacoste on product development and sales, Benaroya took a position working with the highly popular label Jordache. From there, Benaroya moved to The Limited, where he eventually became president of that company's Lane Bryant division. By the time Lane Bryant introduced Sizes Unlimited and Lerner Woman to the public, Benaroya was well prepared to run a company of his own.

It was at Lane Bryant where the entrepreneur recognized the untapped potential of larger sized women's apparel and accessories, and when Sizes Unlimited and Lerner Woman both showed healthy sales, Benaroya moved to make the stores independent. With the help of outside investors, the Lernmark division became a company independent of The Limited, in 1989. Benaroya left Lane Bryant to become Lernmark's CEO, and that same year he changed the company's name to United Retail Group.

Benaroya's first move upon becoming head of United Retail was to change the name of the company's Lerner Woman stores to The Avenue, a decision which, while causing some confusion among consumers, was meant to distance the stores from their former parent company. Under Benaroya's leadership, United Retail initially experienced steady growth, and within two years the company was operating 153 Avenue stores and 252 Sizes Unlimited locations. While most of the company's locations were centered in the eastern and southern parts of the country, the stores were also introduced at strategically selected shopping centers and strip malls across the country.

The early 1990s saw a drastic increase in the number of new apparel companies going public. In 1992 alone two dozen clothing and accessory companies made their debut on the stock exchange, and investors were becoming increasingly willing to take risks on an industry which previously had been run by primarily private revenue. United Retail, after showing strong expansion and sales, was one of the 24 apparel companies to go public in 1992, a move which proved not entirely successful for the company during the mid-1990s. After the company's initial public offering (IPO), Benaroya retained a 20 percent ownership of United Retail, while The Limited purchased a 16 percent stake.

United Retail Flounders: 1992–98

Benaroya approached his new company with an aggressive plan for fundamentally altering the manner in which large sized women's clothing was marketed and designed. Speaking to reporter Marianne Wilson of *Chain Store Age Executive* in the fall of 1991, Benaroya noted that "With 40 percent of the American women's market in size 14 and up, we think The Avenue is a concept that is long overdue. Style and fashion is as important to a large-sized woman as it is to a smaller-sized one. The days when the large-sized shopper would settle for dowdy looking clothes and ugly stores are over."

With this idea in mind, Benaroya's company began focusing on bringing in designs which flew in the face of traditional larger sized apparel. The inventory of The Avenue and Sizes Unlimited was revamped to be even more fashion-conscious, and the stores themselves, particularly those under The Avenue rubric, were given extensive makeovers. Because The Avenue stores were intended to compete with more upscale department stores and chains, the locations were redesigned to have a more salon-like appearance, with subtle lighting and marble floors added to all the company's new locations and some of the already existing sites as well. In addition, United Retail introduced in-house credit cards under The Avenue name, with special purchasing incentives given to card holders.

The way in which Benaroya approached the operation of his company was unique too. Instead of leaving floor and sales work entirely to his non-management employees, Benaroya made it a house rule of United Retail that all upper-management employees, himself included, worked the floor of certain stores for a set amount of time every year. This way, United Retail's executives didn't lose touch with what worked—and what didn't—in the image and sales of the company. Benaroya also responded personally to many of United Retail's customer comments and complaints, and so proved himself to be not only a committed businessman, but a committed salesperson as well. "I love to sell," Benaroya told Wilson, adding "And I love to talk with customers. I think that's the only way you can stay in touch with what's really going on in the retail business."

Unfortunately for United Retail, Benaroya's enthusiasm and shrewd sense of salesmanship couldn't save the company from some dangerously difficult times in the mid-1990s. During that time, the industry's competition became tougher than ever, particularly in such niche market areas as larger sized apparel. Benaroya and his company weren't the only players in the industry to see the untapped opportunity for great profits in the plus-sized market, and competition had begun to chip away at United Retail's sales by 1993. Such fashion labels as Liz Claiborne, as well as such department stores as Saks Fifth Avenue and Dillards, had all introduced their own lines of specially sized women's apparel, making it increasingly difficult for United Retail's locations to keep up with or outpace rivals. In addition, such companies already had well established name recognition among consumers, and so were more easily able to move their new lines without hugely expensive ad campaigns.

After a flurry of growth in the early 1990s, the apparel industry in the middle of the decade took a downward turn: out of the 24 companies that went public in 1992, 17 of them saw their stock drop significantly the next year. United Retail was hit particularly hard, with the company's stock falling 44.7 percent in the first half of 1993, and with third quarter losses of

Key Dates:

1987: The Limited introduces Sizes Unlimited and Lerner Woman.
1989: The two chains are consolidated and spun off as United Retail.
1992: United Retail goes public.
1994: United Retail reports dangerously low sales.
1998: The company is revamped and stages a comeback; 300 Sizes Unlimited stores are converted to The Avenue concept.

$2.1 million. After rapid expansion at the beginning of the decade, the company was forced to begin downsizing and closed some of its less lucrative locations. By 1994, United Retail's earnings had fallen almost 70 percent, and the company was in dire need of restructuring.

The reasons for United Retail's faltering sales were myriad, and had to be responded to in numerous ways. Between the store's name change, greatly increased competition from other retailers, and the company's own aggressive expansion, United Retail had found itself in an untenable situation financially and had to make major changes if it was to survive.

The first saving strategy Benaroya and his team developed was to refocus United Retail's inventory on brand recognition. Thus far in the company's history, The Avenue and Sizes Unlimited had carried other retailer's products as well as a limited amount of the company's own Avenue label. In 1994, United Retail began giving more shelf space to its Avenue line and made a concerted marketing effort to make customers aware of The Avenue not only as a store, but as a label as well. The company began producing such items as casual and career wear under its Avenue label, and by 1995 most of the company's locations carried primarily Avenue apparel.

United Retail also responded to its lagging sales by increasing the variety of its apparel and accessories. Previously, both The Avenue and Sizes Unlimited had focused mainly on casual wear; in the mid-1990s the company began offering more choices in career wear, particularly women's suits, lingerie, and clothing for dressier occasions. To keep its stores stocked with Avenue products, United Retail purchased a 128-acre distribution center in Troy, Ohio, which had capacity to serve almost triple the amount of locations owned by the company. By 1997, after closing less profitable stores and refocusing its image,

United Retail was still in the red but was starting to make a comeback.

1998–2000: United Retail's Renewed Success

In 1997 United Retail had an operating income of $3.2 million; the next year, due to increased sales and brand recognition, the company's operating income reached $23.5 million. Within one year, Benaroya had led his company back to profitability.

Through the company's restructuring it had become apparent that The Avenue stores were more popular, and better reflected consumer trends, than the company's Sizes Unlimited locations. With that fact in mind, United Retail in 1999 converted 300 of its Sizes Unlimited stores to The Avenue name. That year, sales were at $382.6 million, and the company planned to open 25 new stores within the next two years. After a period of financial uncertainty, United Retail at decade's end had proved itself to be a viable force in the apparel industry.

Principal Subsidiaries

United Retail Inc.

Principal Operating Units

The Avenue.

Principal Competitors

Catherines Stores Corporation; Charming Shoppes, Inc.; The Limited, Inc.; Liz Claiborne, Inc.

Further Reading

Chanko, Kenneth M., "Sizes Unlimited to Exit Off-Price Biz," *Discount Store News*, August 10, 1987, p.2.
Coleman-Lochner, Lauren, "Rochelle Park, N.J. Based Retailer Reports Record Earnings," *Knight-Ridder/Tribune Business News*, August 13, 1998.
Macintosh, Jeane, "Fashion Firms Grow Shy of Public Eye," *Women's Wear Daily*, July 12, 1993, p. 12.
"United Retail Group Announces Plan to Unify ''AVENUE'' Brand, Stores, and Credit Cards," *Business Wire*, April 6, 1999, p. 1,312.
"URG Expects Net to Decline in 2nd Quarter," *Women's Wear Daily*, July 11, 1994, p. 10.
Wilson, Marianne, "The Avenue Replaces Lerner Woman; Name Change Supported by New Fashion Image and Upscale Design," *Chain Store Age Executive*, October 1991, p. 25.

—Rachel H. Martin

Universal Studios, Inc.

100 Universal City Plaza
Universal City, California 91608-1002
U.S.A.
Telephone: (818) 777-1000
Fax: (818) 866-1402
Web site: http://www.universalstudios.com

Wholly Owned Subsidiary of Seagram Company, Ltd.
Incorporated: 1912 as Universal Film Manufacturing
  Company
Employees: 14,000
Sales: $7.5 billion (1999)
NAIC: 512120 Motion Picture and Video Distribution;
  512220 Integrated Record Production/Distribution;
  513210 Cable Networks; 713110 Amusement and
  Theme Parks; 453220 Gift, Novelty, and Souvenir
  Stores

Universal Studios, Inc. is active in a variety of entertainment enterprises. Its Universal Studios Group division offers production facilities in Universal City, California, and Orlando, Florida, to independent producers of filmed entertainment and commercial advertising. The company's motion picture distribution operation includes residual video and DVD distribution. Universal also produces syndicated televisions shows and airs its archive of television shows and motion pictures on international and domestic cable networks. Much of Universal's studio facilities are open for public tours and offer attractions and rides based on motion picture and television themes. Movie theme parks are also in operation in Spain and China. Other business activities involve licensing for consumer products, such as apparel with movie and television characters, the chain of Spencer's Gifts stores (located on theme park properties and in shopping malls), online shopping and archives, and interactive electronic games. Universal Music Group, the largest music company in the world, includes over a dozen recording labels and related publishing and technology operations. A wholly owned subsidiary of Seagram Company, Ltd. since 1995, Universal has a rich history dating back to the early days of motion pictures.

Early 20th Century Origins

Carl Laemmle's entry into the motion picture production began in the industry's infancy. In 1905, while Laemmle searched for a place to open a clothing store in Chicago, he stumbled onto a line of people waiting to see a nickelodeon. Intrigued by the popularity of moving pictures, Laemmle changed careers and opened The White Front Theater. In one month Laemmle recouped his investment and opened a second theater with Robert Cochrane, a business associate. Laemmle expanded further with the Laemmle Film Service, which became the largest movie distributor in the country. By 1909 Laemmle and Cochrane were grossing $10,000 a week doing business in the Midwest and in Canada.

Laemmle and Cochrane's production of motion pictures stemmed from a dispute with the Motion Picture Patents Company, which had attained monopolistic power at the time. Finding himself with no motion pictures to exhibit, due to the rift with the patent company, Laemmle decided to make movies himself. The first effort of the Independent Motion Picture Company (IMP) involved a one-reel film entitled *Hiawatha*. Eventually, production would increase to an average of one film per week. The Universal Film Manufacturing Company was formed in 1912 when IMP merged with five other companies; Laemmle became president and Cochrane vice-president of the new concern.

Universal offered a variety of motion picture packages which allowed an exhibitor to show a different film every day. The Complete Service Plan, for example, included a two-reel comedy, a serial, and a feature film. In 1913 the company began to offer a regular newsreel titled *The Universal Animated Weekly*. Universal's first full-length feature film, *Traffic In Souls* (1913), grossed $0.5 million; the movie's real significance was in innovative editing and plot lines which gave the impression of simultaneously occurring events, a concept never before conveyed in film.

Universal expanded its movie making capacity with the opening of Universal City in 1914. Laemmle acquired the 230-acre Taylor Ranch north of the Hollywood Hills for $165,000, envisioning a studio as a city. Laemmle's promotion of the grand opening of Universal City, aimed primarily at theater owners, attracted thousands of people from the general public as well. The promotion stated that everyone should come to see how movies are made "to make the people laugh or cry or sit on the edge of their chairs the world over." The public was so fascinated with film making that Universal City offered organized tours for 25 cents apiece, which included a box lunch, and the company erected bleachers near the sets. About 500 people visited Universal City daily until the advent of sound movies required enclosed stages.

In 1915 Universal produced over 250 films, primarily two reel shows and serials, but also feature length films of over 70 minutes long. The company classified films according to budget and status. A Red Feather film and a Bluebird film received low and midrange budgets, respectively. A Jewel film involved a large budget and prestigious stars of the time, such as Harry Carey, Carmel Myers, and Rudolph Valentino, and directors such as Erich von Stroheim. John Ford helped to define the genre of American Westerns in the numerous films he directed after joining Universal in 1914.

Motion Pictures in the 1920s and 1930s

Renamed Universal Pictures Corporation in 1922, the company continued to focus on short, low budget serials, westerns, and melodramas through the 1920s and 1930s while other studios shifted to feature films. The company did produce two feature films in the 1920s, however, which became silent film classics. *The Hunchback of Notre Dame* (1923), starring Lon Chaney and directed by Wallace Worsley, achieved critical acclaim and financial success. *Phantom of the Opera* (1925) starred Chaney as well as a large cast of the studio's popular stars.

Dynamics of the film industry troubled Universal in the mid-1920s; the company did not have the advantage of affiliation with a theater chain where most first run movies in major cities were shown. Universal contracted with independent theaters which tended to be in rural areas, so movies at this time catered to rural audiences. Universal also accessed European markets where American westerns and action movies found an audience.

When Carl Laemmle, Jr., became general manager in charge of production in 1929, Universal adopted a more sophisticated approach. Laemmle, Jr., cut the studio's output by 40 percent in order to allow for longer films of higher quality. His interest in novels led to several prominent productions. For the sound motion picture *All Quiet on the Western Front*, Universal received its first award from the Academy of Motion Picture Arts and Sciences, for Best Picture, in 1930. Laemmle, Jr., was also the driving force behind the studio's production of *Dracula* (1931), starring Bela Lugosi. In fact, Universal would gain renown for its horror movies, with eight films produced be-

tween 1931 to 1935, including *Frankenstein* (1932) and *The Mummy* (1932), both starring Boris Karloff.

Most of the higher quality films that Laemmle, Jr., initiated did not engage the audiences of their day, however, and box office receipts did not compensate for the high cost of feature film production. When Laemmle, Jr.'s, production of the Broadway musical *Showboat* went over budget in 1935, his father offered his controlling interest as collateral for over $1 million in debt to fund the project. When the investors called their option in 1936, Standard Capital acquired Laemmle's interest in the company for $4.1 million, ending the Laemmle era at Universal.

Renamed New Universal, the company consolidated its resources by reducing production and closing European operations. In 1936 Universal completed two films begun before the change in ownership; *My Man Godfrey* and *Three Smart Girls,* received nine Academy Award nominations between them. Deanne Durbin, the 15-year-old soprano star of *Three Smart Girls,* became one of the studio's biggest stars, making 21 movies during her 12 years at Universal. In 1938 Durbin received a special Oscar for bringing youthfulness to the silver screen.

With the arrival of two RKO executives at Universal, Nate Blumberg as president and Clifford Work as head of production, the company hoped to entertain the masses on a lower budget. Universal recovered from its losses with the popularity of Durbin's movies as well as the success of *Destry Rides Again* (1939), starring Marlene Dietrich and James Stewart. From a net loss of $1.8 million in 1936, Universal garnered a net profit of $1.5 million in 1939.

Shifting Fortunes from World War II through the 1960s

The onset of World War II increased public demand for escape through motion pictures. Youth-oriented productions included Sherlock Holmes, Inner Sanctum mysteries, and the Bud Abbott and Bud Costello comedy team, whose debut in *One Night in the Tropics* (1940) featured the famous skit, "Who's on first?" Universal produced monster movies, low budget westerns, movie sequels, and desert dramas, also know as "sand 'n' sex" movies. War-themed movies included 13 films featuring the popular Andrew Sisters released between 1940 and 1945. Mature movies included the genre of *film noir,* which had not yet attained its appreciated status. Some of Universal's notable films included *Shadow of a Doubt* (1943), directed by Alfred Hitchcock, *The Suspect* (1944), directed by Robert Siodmark, and *Scarlet Street* (1945) by Fritz Lang. Wartime production peaked in 1945 when Universal averaged one feature length motion picture per week; from 1940 and 1945 production neared 350 movies.

Universal's 1946 merger with International Pictures stemmed from the desire to improve the quality of motion picture productions. Two new production heads, Leo Spitz and William Goetz, eliminated short serials, "programmer" westerns, and low budget movies to concentrate on feature length films. They dropped several stars but retained Abbott and Costello, Durbin, and Donald O'Connor, star of *Francis the Talking Mule* and its sequels (1955–56).

Key Dates:

1913: *Traffic in Souls*, Universal's first feature length film, is produced.
1930: Studio's first Academy Award for Best Picture for *All Quiet on the Western Front*.
1945: Wartime motion picture production reaches rate at one film per week.
1952: Decca Records acquires Universal.
1962: MCA acquires Decca Records.
1975: String of hit movies topped with release of *Jaws*.
1982: *E.T.-The Extra-Terrestrial* grosses $300 million.
1995: Seagram Co. Ltd. acquires majority interest in Universal.

Universal Pictures made several higher quality movies, but these did not bring high returns at the box office. One exception, *The Egg and I*, was the top grossing movie of 1947 at $5.75 million. Operating at a loss in the late 1940s, Universal Pictures exploited the popularity of the low budget Ma and Pa Kettle movies with ten productions.

Ownership changed again in 1952 when Decca Records acquired controlling interest in Universal Pictures. With Milton Rackmil as president and Ed Muhl as vice-president of production, gross receipts increased $7 million by 1954. Muhl sought lesser known independent producers to make movies at the studio's facilities. The company succeeded with Albert Zugsmith, known for *The Incredible Shrinking Man* (1954) and *Touch of Evil* (1958), Aaron Rosenberg, who produced *The Glenn Miller Story* (1954), and Robert Arthur, producer of *Operation Petticoat* (1959) which grossed $9.5 million.

Universal's most successful producer at this time was Ross Hunter, the so-called "King of the Weepies." Hunter collaborated with director Douglas Sirk on ten films between 1953 and 1959, including romantic dramas, such as the remake of *Imitation of Life* (1959) with Lana Turner. Hunter's production of *Pillow Talk* (1959), starring Rock Hudson and Doris Day, grossed $7.5 million and prompted a surge in the romantic comedy genre. The studio's stars at this time included Audie Murphy, Kirk Douglas, Tony Curtis, Maureen O'Hara, Charleton Heston, and Jane Wyman.

Despite the quality of movies being made, television proved quite a competitor, and movie audiences began staying home. In 1957 Universal leased 550 movies, made before 1948, to Screen Gems for airing on television. After profits of $4 million in 1956 and 1957, Universal lost $2 million in 1958, while the motion picture industry experienced a 12 percent decline in ticket sales. As a result, Decca cut production and sold Universal City to the Music Corporation of America (MCA) for $11.25 million.

In 1962 MCA acquired controlling interest in Decca, thus obtaining the Universal studios, which MCA wanted for television production. MCA renovated studio facilities and reinstituted tours of Universal City in 1964. Early movie productions under MCA included Alfred Hitchcock's *The Birds* (1962), which grossed $4.6 million, and *To Kill a Mockingbird* (1962), which won three Academy Awards, including Best Actor for

Gregory Peck. Ross Hunter continued to be the company's most successful producer with *Thoroughly Modern Millie* (1968), followed by the all-star blockbuster *Airport* (1970), which grossed $45.3 million.

The Blockbuster Years: 1970s and 1980s

The year 1973 unfolded as a high watermark year for Universal. Richard Zanuck and David Brown's production of *The Sting*, starring Robert Redford and Paul Newman, grossed $79 million at the box office and won seven Academy Award nominations, including Best Picture. In fact, Universal films competed with each other that year for the Oscars, as George Lucas's production of *American Graffiti*, which grossed $56.7 million, received four nominations. Other highly acclaimed and financially successful movies included *The Day of the Jackal* and *High Plains Drifter*. The year was also notable as Lew Wasserman became chairman and CEO of MCA, while Sheinberg, responsible for bringing Steven Spielberg to Universal, became chief operating officer and president.

Universal made its share of the succession of Hollywood blockbusters. *Jaws* (1975), produced by Zanuck and Brown and directed by Spielberg, drew the largest movie audience to date, grossing $133.4 million, only to be topped by Twentieth Century Fox's *Star Wars* two years later. While Universal suffered huge flops, such as *Gable & Lombard*, the company produced several popular films, such as *Smoky and the Bandit* (1977), *National Lampoon's Animal House* (1978), and *The Blues Brothers* (1980).

During the 1980s Universal released several award-winning movies. *Coal Miner's Daughter* (1980) grossed $38.5 million, and Sissy Spacek won an Oscar for Best Actress. *On Golden Pond* (1981) grossed $63 million and won three of ten Academy Award nominations, including Best Actor for Henry Fonda and Best Actress for Katherine Hepburn. Universal's success peaked with Spielberg's production of *E.T.-The Extra-Terrestrial*, which broke box office records within three months and grossed $300 million by the end of 1982. Among Universal's 16 Oscar nominations in 1982, *E.T.* won four of eight nominations, while Meryl Streep won Best Actress for *Sophie's Choice*. Sidney Pollack's production of *Out of Africa* (1985) won seven Academy Awards, including Best Picture and Best Director for Pollack. Other popular movies included *Back to the Future* (1985), *Dragnet* (1987), *Field of Dreams* (1989), and *Back to the Future II* (1989).

Wasserman's expansion of studio facilities, completed in 1982, included the addition of 220 acres, making Universal City the largest studio lot in Hollywood. New facilities included 36 sound stages, a Technicolor film processing laboratory, and a 14-story administration building. A 200,000 square foot office complex housed independent producers in "bungalows." When Spielberg started his own production company, Amblin Entertainment, Universal installed him in a bungalow with editing facilities, a screening room, and other facilities not typically provided.

With Tom Pollock as president of Universal Pictures in 1986, the company adopted new procedures to reduce capital outlay. For the production of *Twins* (1986), Universal contracted with the two stars, Arnold Schwarzenegger and Danny DeVito, to accept a smaller salary balanced by a percentage of the gross. The strategy succeeded as *Twins* grossed $57.2 million in domestic distribution in less than a year. Pollock's philosophy involved a mix of "A" and "B" quality movies to lower production costs. *Fried Green Tomatoes* (1991) proved a sleeper hit among the company's "B" movies. Pollock also helped Ron Howard and Brian Grazer form Imagine, whose award-winning production *Apollo 13* (1995) grossed $162 million within the first ten weeks.

In 1988, Universal Studios Florida opened in Orlando for television, motion picture, and commercial advertising production. Two years later, the facility would open for public tours. The movie theme entertainment complex, a joint venture between MCA and Cineplex Odeon Corporation, included rides and attractions. The backlot and facilities accommodated small film and television projects, and some major motion production also took place there, including Imagine's *Parenthood*. Long-term agreements involved Unitel Video's television and mobile production facilities and Century III's all-digital edit bay. Hanna-Barbera Productions opened an animation studio and an attraction based on its popular cartoon characters at Universal Studios Florida, while cable network Nickelodeon produced most of its shows at its facility, including game shows which sought contestants and audience among studio visitors.

New Owners, New Directions in the 1990s

Matsushita Electrical Industrial Company of Japan acquired MCA in November 1990. Matsushita was the largest manufacturer of home electronics in the world under the Panasonic brand and had created the VHS format. The new owners did not understand the dynamics of filmmaking, however, as they did not agree with the idea that the $40 million failure of a film like *Havana* would be compensated through successful films. During Matsushita's ownership, Universal released *Jurassic Park*, *Schindler's List*, and *We're Back! A Dinosaur's Story*. The Amblin productions grossed $548.7 million; 60 percent of Universal's movie revenues derived from three of 18 movies released in 1993.

Conflicts between Matsushita and MCA's executives over strategic expansion hampered the company's tenure of ownership. Moreover, Universal lost its top producer when Spielberg formed a new studio company, DreamWorks SKG. In 1995, Matsushita sold an 80 percent interest in MCA to Seagram Company Ltd. for $5.7 billion. The Seagram board named Frank Biondi as CEO and chairman of MCA, which they renamed Universal Studios, Inc., thus consolidating the various entertainment companies, including the music recording companies, under one name.

Edgar Bronfman, Jr., chairman of Seagram led the company through decisions which the board, Bronfman family members, and many shareholders questioned. That Seagram sold 25 percent of its stake in DuPont to acquire MCA proved to be the first of several controversial decisions. Bronfman acquired Polygram for its profitable music business but was unable to sell the film division in one piece. In September 1997 he merged USA Network with HSN, the parent of the Home Shopping Network. Though Universal still owned 46 percent of USA Network,

critics were wary when USA Chairman Barry Diller gained control of a business that generated cash for Seagram. Biondi, hired for his strengths in television, resigned as CEO after 18 months at Universal.

The Universal Studios Networks Division was created in August 1997 for the international marketing of branded televisions channels. USA Network licensed Universal's library for domestic use, while Universal distributed internationally. The division successfully launched "13th Street-The Action Suspense Channel" in France, featuring dubbed versions of such American favorites as *Miami Vice*, *Magnum PI.*, and similar shows. The station was launched in Spain and Germany in 1998, while some shows aired on USA Network Brazil and USA Network Latin America. Through eight international offices, the division attained program distribution in over 180 countries, including production of local talk shows in England and the Netherlands. Universal eventually integrated Polygram's television division and began productions of domestically syndicated shows, such as *Motown Live* and *Blind Date*. A new version of *The Woody Woodpecker Show* debuted in 1999.

While Bronfman brought a traditional business approach to Hollywood, creativity waned in movie making. Bronfman streamlined management and implemented several cost saving measures, but Universal's market share for movie tickets declined due to lower production, with only 12 films in 1997. Major failures included *Fear and Loathing in Las Vegas* (1998), which grossed $10 million. Nevertheless, Universal rebounded with the releases of *Patch Adams*, *Notting Hill*, and The *Mummy*, which together had grossed $790 million globally by mid-August 1999, while a joint release with Miramax, *Shakespeare in Love*, won box office success and seven Academy Awards. The Universal Pictures division lost $200 million despite revenues of $3.38 billion in 1999. The company expressed high hopes for Imagine's late 2000 release of a feature length version of *The Grinch Who Stole Christmas*, starring Jim Carey.

Universal Studios succeeded in other areas. In 1999 *The Mummy* garnered over $1 billion in video and Digital Versatile Discs (DVD) sales. Universal sought to expand on this success with the release of its horror classics, such as *The Invisible Man* (1933) and Alfred Hitchcock classics on DVD. Universal Music Group carried the company with strong profits. In electronic video games the company expected positive returns on the summer 2000 launch of *E.T. Interactive*.

Universal also sought to improve its profits through theme park expansion. In 1996 Universal City in California introduced Jurassic Park: The Ride, a replication of the theme park in the popular movie. Universal acquired Port Aventura in Spain, and opened The Universal Experience in Beijing. Universal Studios Florida added the Islands of Adventure theme park, featuring five islands of attractions, such as one based on the children's literature of Dr. Seuss and another on popular superheroes. Universal expected its studio theme park under construction in Osaka to open in 2001.

As the company headed toward a new century, some industry analysts speculated that Seagram might try to sell Universal. Though Seagram refused to comment on the rumors, critics suggested that board members at Seagram were pressuring

Bronfman to consider a sale, as the Universal film studios continued to lose money. Still others alleged that the fair asking price for a company the size of Universal would be prohibitive, and that perhaps the successful theme park operations might be put on the block separately. Although its future ownership, size, and scope was perhaps uncertain, the Universal name in Hollywood had survived many such changes in parent companies, and if its illustrious history were any indication, it would likely continue as an innovator in one or more of its areas of expertise—film, television, music, theme parks, home video, and consumer products.

Principal Divisions

Universal Music Group; Universal Pictures; Universal Studios Consumer Products Group; Universal Studios Home Video; Universal Studios Recreation Group; Universal Television & Networks Group; Spencer Gifts.

Principal Competitors

EMI Group plc; Sony Music Entertainments, Inc.; Time Warner, Inc.; The Walt Disney Company; Viacom, Inc.

Further Reading

Cox, Dan, "U Passing the Hat," *Variety,* January 18, 1999, p. 1.
Deckard, Linda, "Universal Hollywood Eyes 5 Mil Attendance," *Amusement Business,* June 21, 1993, p. 3.
Dennis, Laura, "At Universal, Beginning May 24, Dinosaurs Again Will Rule," *Travel Weekly,* February 22, 1996, p. 22.
Dick, Bernard F., *City of Dreams: The Making and Remaking of Universal Pictures,* Lexington: University Press of Kentucky, 1997.
Egan, Jack, "Barry Diller Wheels and Deals," *U.S. News & World Report,* November 3, 1997, p. 62.
Emmons, Natasha. "Universal Studios City Walk Hollywood Set for 93,000 Square-Foot Expansion," *Amusement Business,* December 27, 1999, p. 70.
Fitzpatrick, Eileen, "*Mummy* Shoots Universal's Sales Over $1 Bil.; Retailers Win with Sight and Sound," *Billboard,* December 25, 1999, p. 63.
Hirschhorn, Clive, *The Universal Story,* New York: Crown Publishers, Inc., 1983.
Kent, Lisa, "Nickelodeon to Produce at Universal Complex in Orlando in 1990," *Back Stage,* June 10, 1988, p. 6.
Littleton, Cynthia, "Diller Redefines USA, Eyes New Day," *Variety,* February 16, 1998, p. 37.
——, "Sale Returns U to Syndie TV Arena," *Variety,* December 14, 1998, p. 149.
Masters, Kim, "Bronfman Stirs Universal: Despite Weak Films and a Rash of Firings, the Young Boss Keeps Insisting that His Studio Will Do Just Fine," *Time,* May 4, 1998, p. 46.
McConnell, Chris, "Century III at Universal Studios," *Broadcasting & Cable,* September 12, 1994, p. 56.
Medina, Hildy, "In Need of a TV Network, Universal Turns to Europe," *Los Angeles Business Journal,* September 15, 1997, p. 13.
Miller, Richard, "Universal Studios and Hanna-Barbera Productions," *Back Stage,* June 10, 1988, p. 6.
Morden, Ethan, *The Hollywood Studios: House Style in the Golden Age of the Movies,* New York: Alfred A. Knopf, 1988.
Moshavi, Sharon D., "AMC Buys Universal Packaging," *Broadcasting,* May 20, 1991, p. 55.
"New Productions at Universal Studios Florida Keep Studios and Backlots at Capacity," *Orlando Business Journal,* December 7, 1990, p. 2A.
Parkes, Christopher, "Entertainments More Bad News to Come from Universal Studios, Company Warns," *Financial Times,* May 7, 1999, p. 30.
"Resignation of Universal Studios Head Spells Trouble for Seagram," *Knight Ridder/Tribune Business News,* November 20, 1998.
Scally, Robert, "Kmart, Universal: Licensing Classics," *Discount Store News,* November 23, 1998, p. 3.
"Seagram May Sell Universal Studios, Drinks Group Eyes Disposal of Lossmaking Film Unit: The Theme Parks Could Go Separately," *Financial Times,* February 4, 2000, p. 21.
"Seagram: Mr. Bronfman in Tinseltown," *Economist,* November 21, 1998, p. 66.
Thomas, Tony, *The Best of Universal,* New York: Vestal Press, Ltd., 1990.
"Unitel to Open Unit at Florida Universal Studios," *Back Stage,* October 9, 1987, p. 1.
"Universal Studios and Hanna-Barbera Productions," *Back Stage,* June 10, 1988, p. 6.
"Universal Studios Created," *Television Digest,* August 11, 1997, p. 6.

—Mary Tradii

Wakefern Food Corporation

600 York Street
Elizabeth, New Jersey 07207
U.S.A.
Telephone: (908) 527-3300
Fax: (908) 527-3397
Web site: http://www.shoprite.com

Member-Owned Cooperative
Founded: 1946
Employees: 3,000
Sales: $3.5 billion (1999)
NAIC: 42241 General Line Grocery Wholesalers; 311999
   All Other Miscellaneous Food Manufacturing; 44511
   Supermarkets and Other Grocery (Except
   Convenience) Stores

Wakefern Food Corporation is the wholesale purchasing and distributing cooperative for about 190 ShopRite supermarkets that operate in New Jersey (where it is the dominant grocery chain), New York, Connecticut, Pennsylvania, and Delaware. Owned by 43 independent grocers, it is the largest such co-op in the United States. To provide goods at competitive wholesale prices for its member stores, the co-op purchases foods and other items both at home and abroad and distributes them from its warehouses in New Jersey, where it maintains its corporate headquarters. Using 2.5 million square feet of warehousing, most of it located within one mile of the Port of New York docks, Wakefern distributes goods, some packaged under its own label, to its member stores. To accomplish this, it uses one of the largest private transportation fleets on the East Coast, consisting of over 400 tractors and 2,000 trailers, which provide day-to-day deliveries of its various goods throughout its fairly concentrated network of ShopRite stores. Wakefern also offers centralized services to its member stores, including advertising, group insurance, and marketing. It also has facilities for processing its own brand milk, fruit juices, and fish. All ShopRite grocery companies are Wakefern members and, regardless of the number of stores each owns, they all have an equal voice in the governance of the cooperative. Two of the member companies—Big V Supermarkets Inc. and Inserra Supermarkets, Inc.—own and operate over one quarter of the stores, but most member grocers operate fewer than five.

Starting Out with a Risky Enterprise: 1946–50

The end of World War II brought an end to food rationing and price controls in the United States, but it also created problems for independent grocers who faced quickly stiffening competition from such rapidly growing supermarket chains as A&P. The problem was that such chains were able to undercut the retail prices of the independent grocers by volume buying at the wholesale level and by utilizing more efficient marketing strategies.

In New Jersey in the summer of 1946, Ed Casson, a representative of Del Monte Foods, repeatedly heard the same complaint from independent grocers in the Newark area, that as individuals the independents had to purchase wholesale canned foods for retailing at the same prices customers at the chain stores were paying for them. Casson suggested that the independent grocers meet together to try to find a solution to the problem. Two of them, Abe Kesselman and Sam Aidekman, began doing so on a regular basis and were soon joined by five others: Al Aidekman, Dave Fern, Sam Garb, Albert Goldberg, Bill Kesselman, and Louis Weiss. The group then started experimenting, making some bulk wholesale purchases and splitting them for retail sale in their grocery stores, storing some items in their homes until they were depleted. It was a system that seemed to work well, so they formalized their cooperative venture on December 5, 1946, when each of them put up $1,000 and incorporated their association as the Wakefern Food Corporation. The Wakefern name, an acronym, was developed from the *w* from Weiss, the *a* from Aidekman, the *k* from Kesselman, and *fern* from Dave Fern. The extra *e* was added to make the name both agreeable and pronounceable.

The founding members were fully aware that other grocers had attempted to form co-ops and had failed, and they expected problems. They knew that they would have to put a lot of extra time and effort into the enterprise, rotating the responsibility of accepting deliveries at their first storage facility, a 1,000-square-

Company Perspectives:

At Wakefern, generations of families have served generations of their customers' families. Although they have grown from the small "Mom and Pop" stores of the 1940s, most of the Member companies of Wakefern are still family owned and operated businesses—many with second, third and even fourth generations involved. Many of these families are descendants of immigrants who came to America hoping to improve the lives of their families and future generations. Since the early days, the family businesses of Wakefern have helped and complemented one another by sharing ideas and information, and by perfecting the art of compromise. Compromise, interdependence and mutual respect are the threads that weave a family together—a nuclear family, a family business, or a co-op.

foot storefront on Miller Street in Newark. They used their own cars and pickup trucks to transport food to that "warehouse" and took turns paying for deliveries and keeping the company's books. They operated without any long-range plan, just trying to stay afloat and not be beaten out by the chain giants.

Their first problem was to get credit from major food manufacturers. They were considered too risky an enterprise by most large food producers because they lacked sufficient capital, but they got a break when a loyal customer's husband, who worked for Campbell's Soup Company, convinced that manufacturer to extend credit to Wakefern. Del Monte and other companies soon followed suit.

The next need was for an immediate expansion of Wakefern's membership to help improve the cooperative's wholesale buying strength. The founders all undertook the task of enlisting new members, a difficult and frustrating effort. At the time, $1,000 or more was a lot of money to put at risk for most independent grocers, but the members' persistence and the donation of their free time to help prospective members paid off. Over the first five years, growth was gradual but steady.

In 1949, the company moved into a 15,000-square-foot warehouse in Port Newark, hired a warehouse manager, and contracted the services of a trucking company for the delivery of purchased goods. It was still a marginal operation, however, not yet very efficient and rather costly. At the time it forced member grocers to sell some items at a loss in order to remain competitive with the chain supermarkets.

In the next year, 1950, membership grew to 28. Annual sales reached $2.2 million, and a full-time office staff was doing the managing and accounting work the founders had originally undertaken themselves in order get the enterprise established. The change allowed for some longer range planning, including modifications designed to improve the cooperative's efficiency and to enhance its market image.

Period of Rapid Growth and Change: 1951–60

Wakefern took the first important step the next year. On March 15, 1951, it began advertising in the *Newark Evening News* under a new name—ShopRite—a name that the co-op's members finally decided upon after careful deliberation. The $1,500 ad was a calculated risk, and only nine members were willing or able to participate in financing it. All of them, adding "ShopRite" to their stores' names, logged a significant increase in sales. They continued to advertise under the new name, and other Wakefern members, seeing the important benefits, soon joined in and changed their stores' names as well. The change also attracted other independent grocers, and within a year Wakefern's membership grew to over 50, almost doubling.

Wakefern's new advertising and merchandising program became "the cornerstone of its success." New memberships that resulted from it spurred an important increase in volume, and that resulted in some significant developments, including a move to a larger warehouse, a growth in trucking operations, and enlarged stores with a complete line of products. Also, Wakefern began marketing foods packaged under ShopRite's own, private label, a strategy that started as a promotional ploy in October 1951, when, for the Halloween season, its stores sold doughnuts packaged under the ShopRite name. It soon evolved into a whole line of ShopRite labeled foods, some processed by the cooperative itself.

The advertisements also helped the member grocers keep in touch with their customers by including biographical information about new members and announcing such events as the opening of new warehouses or the renovation or remodeling of any of its members' stores. Thus, even as their stores grew in size and number, the ShopRite owners continued a tradition of personal community involvement that characterized the "mom and pop" corner groceries from which their stores evolved.

In addition to using ads to provide information about the local store owners and their ShopRite stores, for four years, from 1952 to 1956, the co-op published and distributed a newsletter, "The ShopRite Ladies Home News." In it, a fictional character named "Sally Rite" shared tips on saving money and preparing foods.

By its tenth anniversary in 1956, Wakefern's membership had climbed to over 70, and its sales volume had reached $100 million, made possible by its bold warehouse and distribution strategies. These started in 1953, when Wakefern built the first of its large warehouses in Cranford, New Jersey, and took on additional staff members. Survival seemed certain, even though the members still had to face difficult decisions, an important one being whether or not to succumb to a major marketing trend, the issuing of trading stamps, which, by the mid-1950s, had become a national craze. In 1958, after a heated meeting, the members opted not to do so. Instead, they voted to cut their retail prices by ten percent. The decision at first caused a decline in sales, but after a few months ShopRite's "low price leader" concept took hold, and their sales started a new upward swing.

At the same time, many of the ShopRite stores were expanding in size, either remodeled or relocated to accommodate the self-service system that was replacing the older, less efficient full-service system. By 1960, some of the old stores, a few originally only 2,000 to 3,000 square feet in size, had been transformed into much larger operations up to ten times their original size.

Key Dates:

1946: Consortium of New York and New Jersey grocers form the Wakefern cooperative.

1949: Co-op moves into 15,000-square-foot warehouse in Port Newark and hires professional staff.

1951: Seeking a more competitive industry image, Wakefern begins using "ShopRite" name in its marketing and advertising and institutes the ShopRite brand of foods.

1953: Company builds first large warehouse in Cranford, New Jersey, and adds more staff members.

1956: Wakefern members elect to cut retail food prices ten percent rather than issue trading stamps.

1966: Supermarkets General Corp. forms and subsequently leaves Wakefern to form Pathmark.

1989: ShopRite institutes its Supermarket Careers training program.

1992: Wakefern member Big V Supermarkets opens PriceRite mini-warehouse club.

Increased Use of a Professional Staff and Temporary Setbacks: 1960–80

Through the 1960s and 1970s, Wakefern completed the task of turning over its management to a professional staff, freeing its members of direct involvement in any of the day-to-day operations of the co-op. The staff directed its volume buying, merchandising, warehousing, and distribution, always with an eye to improving efficiency and thereby cutting costs.

There were obstacles, including two problematic setbacks in the 1960s. The first occurred in 1962 when several smaller members sued Wakefern and what were then its two largest members: General Supermarkets and Supermarkets Operating Co. Their complaint was that the larger member companies wielded too much power and grabbed up the best store locations. Then, in 1966, the sued companies merged to form Supermarkets General Corp., which subsequently took its 65-store chain out of the cooperative and formed Pathmark, cutting Wakefern's volume in half and effectively closing its Long Island market. However, the loss prompted the remaining members to redouble their expansion efforts, opening new stores and improving their marketing and purchasing strategies. It took only three years for the changes to allow the cooperative to again reach the sales volume it had enjoyed before the withdrawal of Supermarkets General.

It was during the 1970s that Wakefern adopted the principle that each of its members would have just one vote in major decision making, regardless of the number of ShopRite stores each owned. The rule—"One Member, One Vote"—helped ensure member input in shaping policies. That attracted new members and enough financial backing to continue Wakefern's ongoing expansion, especially the addition of new warehousing facilities in the 1980s. By that time, Wakefern could confidently claim that ShopRite "had become the recognized market leader." It had also become the largest surviving retailer-owned cooperative in the nation.

Wakefern's Community Service Record and Continued Success: 1980–2000

Throughout the last two decades of the 20th century, Wakefern compiled a significant record of achievements, not just as a successful cooperative in a business sense but as an enterprise profoundly committed to helping the host communities of the ShopRite stores.

By 1996, the year in which Wakefern reached it 50th anniversary, those stores were serving over three million customers per week in a five-state network, and in sales the co-op was ranked 14th in the nation among supermarket chains. It had 36 member companies, each of which was an independent corporation. All together, they employed over 35,000 associates in retail outlets and another 3,000 in staff positions in Wakefern's purchasing, merchandising, warehousing, and distributions operations and administrative roles. To service the stores in its network, in 1997 alone, Wakefern's distribution fleet logged 23 million miles.

The ShopRite stores also reflected Wakefern's commitment to staying abreast of industry changes, to employing technological advances, and to promoting change through its own innovations, as in its Supermarket Careers program. Initiated in 1989, Supermarket Careers was created to help special needs students train for work in ShopRites or other stores. By 1999, the award-winning program was offered in the curriculum of 42 schools in five states.

In the 1990s, Wakefern adopted CGO (computer-generated ordering), fully automating the stock-replenishing process in the majority of its stores; EDI (electronic data interchange); and computer-based training for its employees. The larger ShopRite stores also began offering the full line of services and departments that typifies the chain giants' "megamarkets," including pharmacies, delis, catering, salad bars, coffee shops, and banking services. In 1992, one of its largest members, Big V Supermarkets, opened the first PriceRite mini-warehouse club, hoping to get a share of a market dominated by Sam's Wholesale Clubs.

Despite such up-sizing tendencies, Wakefern takes pride in the fact that its members have maintained an ongoing commitment to their respective communities and the continued participation of family members in their businesses. In projects like the Community Food Bank of New Jersey and the Special Olympics, ShopRites have played a very significant and highly publicized role, constant reminders that the stores are locally owned and operated by people who care about their community. Wakefern's record of assisting charities has been noteworthy throughout its history.

Principal Competitors

The Great Atlantic & Pacific Tea Company, Inc.; C&S Wholesale Grocers Inc.; Di Giorgio Corporation; Fleming Companies, Inc.; The Grand Union Company; IGA, Inc.; King Kullen Grocery Company Inc.; Pathmark Stores, Inc.; Royal Ahold N.V.; Shurfine International, Inc.; The Stop & Shop Companies, Inc. Stop & Shop; SUPERVALU INC.; Wal-Mart Stores, Inc.

Further Reading

Brookman, Faye, "The ShopRite Superstore," *WWD*, August 28, 1998, p. 9.

"Can Can Alive and Kicking," *Progressive Grocer*, September 1991, p. 28.

Duff, Mike, "At ShopeRite, They're Taking Quality on the Road," *Supermarket Business*, April 1992, p. 39.

Fensholt, Carol, and Partch, Kenneth, "ShopRite's PriceRite: For Predators Planning to Pounce, a Poison Pill?," *Supermarket Business*, December 1992, p. 28.

Garry, Michael, "Protecting Its Turf," *Progressive Grocer*, November 1995, p. 84.

"How America's Largest Retailer-Owned Cooperative Took Form 50 Years Ago," *Supermarket News*, May 13, 1996, p. 2S.

Interview with Wakefern CEO Thomas Infusino, *Supermarket News*, May 13, 1996, p. 4S.

McGintyk, Tony, "Wakefern's ShopRite Takes on All Comers in Nonfoods," *Supermarket Business*, November 1987, p. 55.

Millstein, March, Denise Zimmermann, and Chris O'Leary, "Automation's in Order at Wakefern," *Supermarket News*, December 4, 1995, p. 22.

Snyder, Glen, "Wakefern/ShopRite Thinks BIG," *Progressive Grocer*, January 1992, p. 61.

Turcsik, Richard, "MMI Hired to Handle Wakefern Store Brands," *Supermarket News*, December 26, 1994, p. 41.

Weinstein, Steve, "Wakefern: A Co-op That Works," *Progressive Grocer*, October 1991, p. 27.

——, "Wakefern Operations: Overcoming Obstacles," *Progressive Grocer*, November 1991, p. 38.

——, "Wakefern Gives More Than Money," *Progressive Grocer*, December 1991, p. 23.

—John W. Fiero

Wall Street Deli, Inc.

One Independence Plaza, Suite 100
Birmingham, Alabama 35209
U.S.A.
Telephone: (205) 870-0020
Fax: (205) 868-0860
Web site: http://www.wallstreetdeli.com

Public Company
Incorporated: 1966 as Sandwich Chef, Inc.
Employees: 779
Sales: $58.3 million (1999)
Stock Exchanges: NASDAQ
Ticker Symbol: WSDI
NAIC: 722211 Limited-Service Restaurants

Wall Street Deli, Inc. operates a chain of 118 delicatessen-style restaurants under the Wall Street Deli banner. The company's delis are located in office buildings, serving a variety of made-to-order sandwiches, soups, and salads. A majority of the locations also serve breakfast items, including bagels, muffins, and fresh fruit. The restaurants range in size from 800 square feet to 5,000 square feet, with the smaller units—called Express—offering the same menu as the larger units but without salad bars. Franchisees operate 17 Wall Street Delis.

1960s Origins

Wall Street Deli was founded in 1966 in Birmingham, Alabama, as Sandwich Chef, Inc., the entrepreneurial creation of Alan V. Kaufman. In his late 20s when he started Sandwich Chef, Kaufman set out to build a chain of delis for a specific market niche. He focused expansion in suburban markets, specifically targeting office buildings ranging in size between 150,000 square feet and 200,000 square feet. Sandwich Chef outlets were established in the lobbies of such buildings, drawing their business from the office workers working in the floors above. Benefiting from what amounted to a captive customer base, the Sandwich Chef concept flourished during its first decade of business. Kaufman established outlets throughout the Gulf states and beyond, building a chain of mid-scale delis that

stretched from the East Coast to the Rockies. After 15 years of steady, aggressive expansion, Sandwich Chef units were located in Houston, Dallas, New Orleans, Denver, Memphis, Birmingham, Chicago, and Washington, D.C., enabling the chain to collect in excess of $20 million in sales by the early 1980s. The 212 outlets composing the chain in 1982, however, represented the company's peak strength, a high point followed by a protracted downward spiral. The effort to restore the company's lost vitality and to again reach the halcyon heights of 1982 ultimately led to the emergence of Wall Street Deli, Inc.

Kaufman, who had watched Sandwich Chef flourish during the 1970s, had to endure the chain's sputtering performance during the 1980s. Although it likely provided little solace, the abrupt change in the company's fortunes was chiefly caused by forces out of Kaufman's control. Sandwich Chef maintained a strong presence in oil-producing areas such as Houston, Dallas, New Orleans, and Denver, which felt the brunt of the damage caused by the oil crunch of the early 1980s. As markets economically dependent on oil-related industries suffered, so did Sandwich Chef. In many of the office buildings where the company's delis were located, occupancy plummeted, stripping Sandwich Chef units of their customer base. The recessive economic conditions significantly reduced sales at some Sandwich Chef units and forced others to close, leading to depressed financial results for the company and to the reduction of its store count. In 1982—the company's benchmark year—Sandwich Chef earned $857,000 from its 212 stores. For years later, with 203 stores under its control, the company netted $655,000, posting a loss of $617,000 the following year because of store closures. By the end of the 1980s, the number of outlets composing the chain had fallen to 189.

Aside from the dour economic conditions during the 1980s, other factors contributed to the languid performance of Sandwich Chef. Generally, the stores were out-of-date and many were in poor condition. The décor was painfully mid-1970s, featuring brown and orange color schemes, vinyl wall coverings, and Formica counter tops, all illuminated by flat fluorescent ceiling lighting. To address these cosmetic problems and the more pernicious, fundamental flaws exposed by the oil crisis, Kaufman and his corporate lieutenant, Robert G. Barrow, a Sandwich Chef director since 1967, developed two new concepts.

First Wall Street Deli Opens in 1987

The first, introduced in July 1985, was R.C. Cooper Deli, a more upscale version of the Sandwich Chef concept. Like the Sandwich Chef stores, R.C. Cooper Deli was created for office building lobbies, but the R.C. Cooper Deli units were developed for much larger buildings than the company's flagship chain. R.C. Cooper Deli stores were targeted for buildings of at least 500,000 square feet. The company's second concept represented a more radical departure for Kaufman and Barrow, moving them away for the first time from the familiarity of office buildings. Wall Street Deli was launched in 1987, appearing at first in food courts within shopping malls, where the company hoped the new concept would benefit from the high volume of pedestrian traffic. Featuring a more expensive menu than R.C. Cooper Deli, Wall Street Deli initially received less of the resources devoted to expansion than R.C. Cooper Deli enjoyed, but both figured prominently in Kaufman's plans to steer Sandwich Chef out of the doldrums. Cosmetically, both of the new concepts demonstrated a fresh, revamped approach to deli stores. Vinyl and Formica were replaced with ceramic walls, quarry tile floors, and numerous mirrors. Wall Street Deli units contained mahogany wood trim, brass light fixtures, and vintage pictures of Wall Street and New York City, as well as sandwiches named after the five boroughs of New York City.

Aside from the much-needed changes in décor, other important alterations distinguished the Sandwich Chef units from their 1980s counterparts. Both of the newer concepts were considerably larger than Sandwich Chef, ranging in size from 2,500 square feet to 3,000 square feet, compared to the 1,500-square-feet Sandwich Chef outlets. Additionally, the sandwiches were larger at the new restaurants, five ounces compared to three ounces. Further, Wall Street Deli and R.C. Cooper Deli stores offered expanded menus, including pasta bars, a broader range of soups, and salad bars that were roughly twice the size of those found in Sandwich Chefs. Both Wall Street Deli and R.C. Cooper Deli also featured ovens in the front window, enabling the stores to prepare a greater amount of food on premises, including breads, muffins, and biscuits.

The expansion of the two new concepts occupied much of the company's attention during the latter half of the 1980s. Barrow, in a January 15, 1990 interview with *Nation's Restaurant News,* remembered the anxious years spent trying steer Sandwich Chef in a new direction, saying, ''We were certainly scrambling and trying to get our affairs in order.'' R.C. Cooper Deli, the first of the new concepts to make its debut, was treated as the primary expansion vehicle, quickly nearing the same store count as its 20-year-old sister chain, Sandwich Chef. Less attention was given to the expansion of the Wall Street Deli concept, but by the end of the 1980s the mahogany-wood, upscale deli concept would factor heavily into Kaufman's plans for the 1990s.

The end of the 1980s represented a crossroads for Sandwich Chef, Inc. The company exited the decade with a handful of store banners operating under its corporate umbrella, no longer the homogenous deli operator that had entered the 1980s. In 1989, there were 61 Sandwich Chef stores in operation, a total nearly matched by the fast-growing R.C. Cooper Deli, which had grown to 59 stores in four years. Rounding out the company's roster of retail outlets were 12 Wall Street Deli units, all situated in shopping malls, as well as ten stores operating under the Fast Stop and LaPrima banners, neither of which would prove integral to the company's future.

Leading the company's resurgence were the Wall Street Deli and R.C. Cooper stores, which were delivering encouraging financial results. Each were located in denser traffic areas than Sandwich Chefs—R.C. Cooper Delis in larger office buildings and Wall Street Delis in shopping malls—and, accordingly, were posting greater sales averages. In 1989, a Sandwich Chef unit averaged $146,500 in sales a year, a total that fell well short of the $304,000 averaged by R.C. Cooper Delis and the $404,000 averaged by Wall Street Delis. The sales figures, underpinned by greater profit margins, convinced Kaufman and Barrow that it was time to shelve the Sandwich Chef concept in favor of the two new concepts. In January 1990, the company announced that during the ensuing 18 months all Sandwich Chefs would be converted to Wall Street Delis or R.C. Cooper Delis or would be sold or closed. ''Our image is changed,'' Barrow proclaimed in the January 15, 1990 issue of *Nation's Restaurant News.* ''We just decided not to use it [Sandwich Chef] as a trade name anymore,'' he noted, adding, ''We decided a lot of these Sandwich Chefs were run down and shabby looking, and we decided to help ourselves by using a brand new name.''

Although Barrow never specified in early 1990 which deli concept—R.C. Cooper Deli or Wall Street Deli—the company would latch onto as its primary expansion vehicle, expansion plans for the immediate future pointed to one concept in particular. The company intended to open 20 to 25 new stores in 1990, 18 of which were to be Wall Street Delis. Significantly, concurrent with the decision to abandon the Sandwich Chef chain, Kaufman and Barrow decided to forego establishing Wall Street Delis in shopping malls, choosing instead to erect the stores in metropolitan-based office buildings, the traditional market for Sandwich Chef Inc. The 18 new Wall Street Delis and the remaining R.C. Cooper Delis included within 1990's expansion plans were expected to penetrate two new markets, Atlanta and southern Florida, as well as strengthen the company's presence in its existing eight-city operating territory.

Name Change in 1992

As Kaufman and Barrow pushed ahead with the transition, execution trailed expectations. Originally projecting an 18-month period to strip away the vestiges of the past, the company's senior management found the process more cumbersome than expected. Although the company remained profitable during the early 1990s, 34 months after announcing the program to convert, sell, or close all Sandwich Chef stores, there were still 12 such units in operation. In October 1992, however, the company renewed its commitment to the changeover by changing its corporate title from Sandwich Chef, Inc. to Wall Street Deli, Inc. The name change reflected the company's concerted push into a higher-end segment of the retail market and it reflected the altered composition of the company. As of June 1992, there were three LaPrima stores, all scheduled to be sold in 1993, 12 Sandwich Chefs, 64 R.C. Cooper Delis, and 43 Wall Street Delis, the size of the eponymous chain having more than tripled in two years.

Wall Street Delis had proven to be the company's strongest performer, with individual units grossing between $600,000 and $1 million in annual sales. Consequently, the successful chain served not only as the company's namesake but also figured as the exclusive focus of Kaufman's expansion plans. Looking ahead to 1993, the company planned to widen its operating territory to a 13-state region, with 15 new locations targeted for Wall Street Deli outlets. "It took us a long time," Kaufman remarked in a October 19, 1992 interview with *Nation's Restaurant News,* "but we've finally got this thing going."

As Kaufman shuttered the last dozen Sandwich Chefs and geared for the expansion of the Wall Street Deli concept, the newly-named Wall Street Deli, Inc. exited the early 1990s and the recessive economic conditions that permeated the period. Despite an upturn in the national economy and Kaufman's perception that his company had "finally got this thing going," the years immediately following the name change proved difficult. Kaufman suffered a heart attack in early 1995, which forced him to relinquish some of his control over the day-to-day operation of the company. Midway through 1995, when the company reported its financial results for fiscal 1995, a disappointing loss compounded the concern touched off by Kaufman's health problems. The company reported a $921,000 loss for the year, despite a ten percent increase in revenues to $68.2 million. The net loss was attributable to the closure of 11 underperforming stores and the elimination of the company's commissary system, which led to a $3.2 million charge against earnings. A week after announcing the financial loss, Kaufman relinquished his titles as president and chief executive officer, passing day-to-day control to Barrow. Kaufman remained chairman of Wall Street Deli, Inc.

Fitful Progress during the Late 1990s

Conditions were slow to improve during the next several years, as the company continued to struggle through an elongated period of transition. Closing the commissary system and turning to a vendor for distribution caused problems, as did the lackluster performance of particular stores, particularly the company's ten-store operation in Memphis, which was sold in late 1996. Amid modest expansion, which generally was offset by the closure of stores that did not meet the company's performance goals, Wall Street Deli, Inc. reported a series of worrisome financial results. In 1997, the company's net income amounted to a mere $63,000, which was followed by $3.8 million net loss the following year and a $2.3 million loss in 1999. As the company's profitability waned, its annual sales totals slid downward. Wall Street Deli, Inc. recorded $65.5 million in revenue in 1997, $63.8 million in 1998, and $58.3 million in 1999.

To cure the company's anemic financial performance several programs were begun, their implementation presided over by a new leader. At the end of the company's fiscal 1998 year in June 1998, Jeffrey V. Kaufman, Alan Kaufman's son, was named president and chief executive officer. Kaufman, who had joined his father's company in 1985, inherited 112 Wall Street Deli stores. In the year prior to his appointment, the company had launched a national franchise program for the Wall Street Deli concept as a means to improve financial performance. Additionally, the company introduced what it called the "Street Wraps" program, a tortilla-wrapped sandwich that debuted in 80 stores between mid-1997 and mid-1998. Although both the franchise program and the Street Wraps program were in their early stages of development at the end of the 1990s, management anticipated that eventually the programs would invigorate the company's overall financial performance.

As Wall Street Deli, Inc. exited the 1990s, its efforts to kindle a meaningful surge in revenue and profit growth were diverted by a proposed buyout of the company. Time-consuming discussions were held with two parties throughout the company's fiscal 1999 year, but both proposals were terminated, with the last round of deliberations ending in July 1999. Company officials attributed much of Wall Street Deli, Inc.'s operational and management difficulties during the year to time and effort spent analyzing the proposed buyouts. Following the end of such discussions, management hoped a clear focus on the company's operation would produce encouraging results, but more discouraging news followed. The company reported a $201,228 loss for its fiscal 2000 first quarter and a 15.7 percent decline in revenues. The results, announced in December 1999, marked the end of a troublesome decade for the company, spurring efforts to find a remedy. Kaufman hired a new vice-president of operations and a new chief financial officer to help ameliorate the company's performance, but as the company entered the 21st century there were few signs that its problems were entirely a thing of the past.

Principal Subsidiaries

Sandwich Chef of Alabama, Inc.; Downtown Food Service, Inc.; Sandwich Chef of Colorado, Inc.; Sandwich Chef of Texas, Inc. Sandwich Chef of D.C., Inc.; Sandwich Chef of Illinois, Inc.; Sandwich Chef of Louisiana, Inc.

Principal Competitors

The Quizno's Corporation; Blimpie International, Inc.; Wendy's International, Inc.; Subway; Burger King Corporation; Schlotzsky's, Inc.; McDonald's Corporation.

Further Reading

Davis, Jessica, "Wall Street Deli Taking a Bite Out of the Philly Market," *Philadelphia Business Journal,* June 14, 1993, p. 3.

Hansen, Bruce, "Memphis' Downtown Deli No Flagship for Wall Street," *Memphis Business Journal,* November 8, 1993, p. 3.

Hayes, Jack, "Trinity Acquires Wall Street Deli, Takes Sandwich Chain Private," *Nation's Restaurant News,* March 8, 1999, p. 1.

——, "Sandwich Chef Chain Converts to 'Upscale' Wall Street Deli," *Nation's Restaurant News,* October 19, 1992, p. 3.

Prewitt, Milford, "Wall Street Deli Takes Loss in '95, Shuffles Top Execs.," *Nation's Restaurant News,* September 4, 1995, p. 11.

Rubinstein, Ed, "Wall Street Deli Hopes to Reap Dividends from Sanitation System, New Products," *Nation's Restaurant News,* March 1, 1999, p. 21.

"Sandwich Chef Alters Name, Stock Symbol," *Nation's Restaurant News,* December 14, 1992, p. 14.

"Sandwich Chef's Annual Net Jumps 30%," *Nation's Restaurant News,* September 14, 1992, p. 14.

Seligman, Bob, "A Sandwich Chef by Any Other Name," *Nation's Restaurant News,* January 15, 1990, p. 38.

"Wall St. Deli Starts Fiscal 2000 with 1st-Q Loss of $201,228," *Nation's Restaurant News,* December 6, 1999, p. 12.

"Wall Street Deli Buyout Agreement Expires," *Nation's Restaurant News,* May 3, 1999, p. 3.

"Wall Street Deli Loses $3.8M for Fiscal 1998," *Nation's Restaurant News,* September 7, 1998, p. 12.

"Wall Street Deli Names Kaufman Chief Executive," *Nation's Restaurant News,* June 1, 1998, p. 4.

"Wall Street Deli Revamps as 1st-Quarter Profits Fall 96%," *Nation's Restaurant News,* December 4, 1995, p. 12.

"Wall Street Deli to Sell Memphis Operations," *Nation's Restaurant News,* October 7, 1996, p. 2.

—Jeffrey L. Covell

The Washington Companies

101 International Way
Missoula, Montana 59807
U.S.A.
Telephone: (406) 523-1300
Fax: (406) 523-1398
Web site: http://www.washcorp.com

Private Company
Incorporated: 1964 as Washington Construction
Employees: 4,400
Sales: $744 million (1998 est.)
NAIC: 48831 Port and Harbor Operations; 48833
    Navigational Services to Shipping; 483111 Deep Sea
    and Freight Transportation; 482111 Line-Haul
    Railroads; 23411 Highway and Street Construction;
    23493 Industrial Nonbuilding Structure

The Washington Companies is an association of distinct business entities owned by Dennis R. Washington. The group got its start in 1964 when Dennis Washington founded a construction firm. Since then it has steadily grown, as he acquired or launched related enterprises. The Washington Companies now operates in construction, transportation, machinery, and mining sectors. The Washington Marine Group exists as a sub-association of businesses within The Washington Companies. These businesses—which include C.H. Cates and Sons Ltd., Seaspan International Ltd., Kingcome Navigation Company, Norsk Pacific Steamship Company, Seaspan Coastal Intermodal, Vancouver Shipyards, and Victoria Shipyards—are involved in coastal and deep sea transportation, ship repair, and shipbuilding. Similarly, the Washington Rail Group—consisting of Montana Rail Link, Inc., I & M Rail Link, Inc., and Southern Railway of British Columbia Ltd.—provides rail transportation. In addition to these two major sub-associations of companies, Washington's holdings also include Envirocon, Inc. (which specializes in environmental remediation), Montana Resources, Inc. (a mining company), Morrison Knudsen Corporation (a diversified engineering and construction company), and Westran, Inc. (trucking company). Each of the Washington Companies operates individually, but can rely on the collective Companies for resources.

Humble Beginnings

Dennis Washington's childhood was often chaotic. The future founder of The Washington Companies contracted polio as a young boy, and lived with a number of different relatives after his parents divorced. After graduating from high school in Missoula, Montana, Washington set off for Alaska and found a job in heavy construction. For two years, he was part of a team that built a pulp mill. He returned to Montana soon after, and worked for King and McLaughlin, a construction company owned by his uncle. He rose through the ranks, and by the time he was 23 he oversaw Montana's largest highway construction project.

Early Years of Washington Construction: The 1960s

Despite his success at King and McLaughlin, Washington wanted the satisfaction of owning his own company. He took out a loan for $30,000 from a local Caterpillar dealer, and founded Washington Construction in 1964. His first contract was a daunting one. Commissioned by the U.S. Forest Service to build a new parking lot at the visitor's center in Glacier National Park, Washington had to work in August snows atop the Continental Divide. It was a success. For the next few years, Washington received additional contracts from the forest service, primarily to repair flooded or damaged roads in remote wooded areas.

Federal funding for the Forest Service dwindled in the late 1960s, and Washington was forced to diversify his operations to include highway construction. Although this sector of the construction industry was fiercely competitive, Washington had little choice. "It was something I had to do to stay in business," he would explain later. Luckily, the nation was in the midst of the federally funded interstate highway boom, and Washington's business grew along with the miles of asphalt. By 1969 he was the largest contractor in the state of Montana.

Diversification in the 1970s

In the early 1970s, Washington anticipated that the interstate highway system would lose funding, just as the Forest Service

Company Perspectives:

The Washington Companies, bearing the name of founder Dennis R. Washington, are a group of separate business entities sharing a common philosophy—to provide the highest quality services at the least cost. This is accomplished by maintaining concentration within a core of related industries. Resources are focused and integrated for cost containment and financial strength, creating excellence and a consistent competitive edge.

had a few years earlier. "I said to myself, 'Dennis . . . [i]f you're going to survive, you're going to have to get into something where you can use your experitse and equipment and not be totally dependent on government programs,' " Washington explained. Thus, Washington Construction branched out into new areas once again, particularly dam building and mining. In 1972, the company won a large phosphate mining contract near Soda Springs, Idaho. The revenue earned through this venture fueled additional expansion in the 1970s.

Washington Construction continued to win federal, state, and local highway projects. However, these jobs were scattered geographically, making it difficult and expensive for the company to move its heavy equipment from place to place. To remedy this problem, Washington acquired Western Transport Crane and Rigging—now known as Westran, Inc.—in 1973. The Missoula-based Western Transport provided highway truck freight brokerage, as well as contract hauling of bulk materials. Just as Washington purchased Western Transport to move his company's cumbersome equipment, he founded Equipco that same year to repair and maintain his construction equipment. Although Equipco would later offer its services to other companies, its primary function was to repair Washington's specialized machinery.

Washington continued to diversify his holdings. In 1976, he acquired Modern Machinery Co., which sold heavy equipment to the construction, mining, and logging industries. Modern Machinery also supplied parts and services. At the time Washington purchased Modern Machinery, the subsidiary consisted of a single dealership in Spokane, Washington. However, during the late 1970s Washington quickly added new dealerships in Boise and Pocatello, Idaho, as well as in Missoula and Billings, Montana.

With his roster of companies growing at a rapid rate, Washington instituted the structure that has characterized The Washington Companies for much of its history. Instead of personally overseeing each of his acquired companies' day-to-day operations, Washington ensured that the businesses had a strong president and the capacity to make individual decisions. "Always bring in the best experts around to run a business you don't understand," he told *Forbes* on May 15, 1989. However, it was necessary that he provide some sort of centralized administrative, legal, tax, business development, and real estate assistance. Washington Corporations was founded in 1979 to carry out such tasks. Headquartered in Missoula, Washington Corporations offered an array of services to The Washington Companies.

Expansion in the 1980s

A new chapter in the history of The Washington Companies opened in 1985, when Dennis Washington took a calculated risk and acquired the mining operations of the former Anaconda Mining Company (owned by Atlantic Richfield) in Butte, Montana. Although Butte's copper mines had once produced unparalleled wealth, soft commodity prices and high copper production prices in the early 1980s had led Atlantic Ritchfield to close the famed mine. It lay dormant for three years until one of The Washington Companies—Montana Resources, Inc.—bought it. Before Montana Resources reopened the mine in August 1986, Washington vowed to make the enterprise profitable. His primary strategy was to cut costs. Hiring 325 non-union workers desperate for employment in the economically depressed city of Butte (the mine had previously been run by 600 union workers), Washington mined copper around the clock. His sense of timing was perfect. Within three years, the price of copper had doubled, and he had cleared $100 million from his original investment.

Washington used his profits from the mine as a platform to expand further into new areas of business. Focusing on the transportation industry, he purchased Burlington Northern Railroad's southern Montana route in 1987. With over 1,000 miles of track extending from Huntley, Montana, to Sandpoint, Idaho, this line was a vital link in freight transportation across Montana. Washington renamed the line Montana Rail Link, which held the distinction of being the largest privately held railroad in the United States. Just as he had strived to reduce cost at the Butte mine, Washington attempted to reduce labor costs at Montana Rail Link. Although he did not end union involvement, he did reduce the number of union contracts from 14 to two. As a result, his rail line was able to compete more effectively with trucking companies for freight hauling contracts. "We've got lumber companies that haven't used the rails in 30 years," one of Washington's employees told *Forbes*.

With his holdings becoming increasingly far flung Washington sought to consolidate some of his overlapping enterprises. In 1987, he merged his original company—Washington Construction—with two of his later acquisitions—Industrial Constructors and Conda Mining—to form Washington Contractors Group, Inc.

Recognizing an opportunity in the fledgling industry of environmental cleanup, Washington founded Envirocon, Inc. in 1988. He already possessed much of the equipment and construction skills required to conduct environmental remediation and waste management. For instance, in 1987 his construction company had conducted a massive cleanup of uranium tailings in Grand Junction, Colorado, for the Department of Energy. Envirocon would carve out a niche for itself in the removal of hazardous and radioactive materials, soil excavation, decontamination, demolition, mine reclamation, and soil and groundwater reclamation. The company quickly found clients in both the public and private sectors.

Washington also continued to add industries related to the transportation sector. In 1989 he bought Coast Engine & Equipment Company, which primarily specialized in rebuilding powerplants and components for the rail and marine transportation

Key Dates:

1964: Dennis R. Washington founds Washington Construction.
1973: Company acquires heavy equipment hauler Western Transport Crane (Westran, Inc.); founds Equipco to repair and maintain construction equipment.
1979: Washington Corporations is founded to offer administrative services to the growing empire of Washington Companies.
1985: Dennis Washington enters the mining business with the purchase of Anaconda Mining Company.
1987: Rail transportation is added to the Washington fold with the acquisition of Burlington Northern Railroad's southern Montana route.
1996: Company acquires a 38 percent stake in Morrison Knudsen Corporation.

industries. More importantly, Washington ventured directly into the marine transportation market with his 1992 acquisition of C.H. Cates and Sons, a Canadian tugboat company. Founded in 1886, Cates provided ship docking services to most vessels using the Port of Vancouver. Cates also offered Washington an entrance into international markets. In 1994, Southern Railway of British Columbia was added to the roster of The Washington Companies. This short-line had run between Vancouver and Fraser Valley since 1887.

The 1990s: Continued Growth in New Spheres

In 1992, Washington attempted to take Washington Contractors Group—the consolidated enterprise that contained the first of the Washington Companies—public. However, he could not find underwriters for the $59 million offering. Instead, he oversaw the merger of Washington Contractors Group with Kasler Corporation of California. A solid company that specialized in highway and bridge construction, Kasler brought considerable revenue to the merger. Washington Construction Group, Inc. emerged from the union. A public company, Washington Construction Group quickly grew to become a leading contractor in the western United States.

Washington continued his buying spree in 1994 when he rounded out his growing marine transportation division with Seaspan International Ltd., the largest tug and barge company in Canada. Seaspan had thrived by transporting products to and from industries along the entire west coast of North America. Its most common cargo included forest products, as well as those from the petroleum, chemical, and mineral industries. By acquiring Seaspan, Washington also gained several Seaspan-owned shipyard and drydock companies. Foremost among these was Vancouver Shipyards Co. Ltd., which designed, built, maintained, and repaired all types of oceanfaring vessels—ranging from cruise ships to tugs to ice breakers. Washington's $135 million acquisition of Seaspan was fully completed in 1996.

In June 1995, Washington again bolstered his position in the marine transportation sector with his purchase of the Bahamian corporation Norsk Pacific Steamship Company, Limited for $20 million. The third largest company in the British Columbian barge market, Norsk carried newsprint and other paper products from Northwest paper and pulp mills to San Francisco, Long Beach, and San Diego, California. Moreover, Norsk also owned a substantial terminal division that ran waterfront terminals, warehouses, and transfer stations at Seattle and Long Beach's large ports.

The year 1996 brought Washington's largest acquisition, when he gained a 38 percent stake in Morrison Knudsen Corporation. With 1996 revenues topping $1.5 billion, the Boise, Idaho-based Morrison Knudsen employed over 23,000 employees and had divisions spanning the United States and 35 foreign countries. As both a diversified engineering and construction company, the publicly traded Morrison Knudsen served environmental, process, power, industrial, transportation, mining, and construction markets worldwide. Its past projects included the construction of both the Hoover Dam and the space shuttle hangar at Cape Canaveral, Florida. However, the company had been experiencing financial woes and had filed for bankruptcy before its merger with rival Washington.

Upon merging his Washington Construction Group with Morrison Knudsen, Washington gained an entrance to global markets. Ironically, Washington had worked as a young subcontractor for Morrison Knudsen, and had even met one of the company's founders. ''I looked at him with awe,'' Washington explained to *Barron's*, adding ''And now I have a chance to represent his company and restore its past glory.''

Unlike the hands-off strategy he employed in his other acquisitions, Washington chose to head Morrison Knudsen, acting as the company's president, chief executive officer, and chairman of the board. ''I want to be identified with Morrison Knudsen,'' Dennis Washington told *Barron's,* adding, ''I want to know the key players in the company so that I can have constructive input. It's pretty hard to fit in the back seat when you want to drive.'' His leadership proved effective. Soon after taking the helm, he made the bold move of committing Morrison Knudsen to fixed-cost, rather than its traditional cost-plus contracts. (Cost-plus contracts are those in which the contractor is paid for all costs incurred for the project along with an additional amount for his services. Fixed-cost contracts are those in which the contractor receives a set amount for his work, irrespective of the ultimate costs incurred. Thus a fixed-cost contract imposes a greater degree of risk on a contractor because cost overruns could erode his profit margin. At the same time, however, a contractor who is able to keep his costs down stands to reap a greater benefit.) Washington's maneuver was a resounding success. One year after the merger was completed, the price of shares in the combined companies nearly doubled.

Washington continued to develop his presence in the transportation sector as well. In 1997, he spearheaded the purchase of Kingcome Navigation. This Vancouver, British Columbia-based company operated log barges and towing vessels. The bulk of its business was in providing fiber transportation for MacMillan Bloedel Ltd. A year later, The Washington Companies rounded out its marine transit sector by purchasing the Coastal Marine Operations of Canadian Pacific Railway. Rechristened by Washington as the Seaspan Coastal Intermodal

Company, this commercial truck and ferry service to Vancouver Island was logically folded into Washington's empire.

Creating Structure in the Late 1990s

In 1998, Washington oversaw the formation of two umbrella organizations within the rubric of The Washington Companies. The Washington Marine Group was formalized to link the northwest marine companies into a cohesive network. Similarly, the Washington Rail Group was launched to develop and protect common interests among the railroad holdings. As the century drew to a close, Washington strove to ensure synchronization among his numerous and diverse companies.

The sheer number of Dennis Washington's many holdings presented the greatest challenge at the close of 1999. Nevertheless, Washington had taken care during his long spate of acquisitions to build upon core areas. Despite the vastness of his empire, The Washington Companies tended to be concentrated in four key industries: construction, mining, marine transportation, and rail transit. Moreover, Washington had ensured that each of the many companies he owned were headed by strong and competent leaders. In a sense, Washington's greatest challenge was to let each of the far-flung Washington Companies run itself.

Principal Subsidiaries

Montana Rail Link, Inc.; I & M Rail Link, Inc.; Southern Railway of British Columbia Ltd.; Seaspan International Ltd.; Cates Tugs; Kingcome Navigation; Westran, Inc.; Washington Corporations; Equipco; Modern Machinery, Inc.; Montana Resources, Inc.; Envirocon, Inc.; Coast Engine and Equipment Co.; Morrison Knudsen Corporation (38%)

Principal Operating Units

Washington Marine Group; Washington Rail Group.

Principal Competitors

Cyprus Amax Minerals Company; Granite Construction; Phelps Dodge Corporation.

Further Reading

Einhorn, Cheryl Strauss, ''Mountain Man's American Dream,'' *Barron's,* September 30, 1996.

Ludwick, Jim, ''Kasler Executives Argue Against Lopsided Merger,'' *Missoulian,* June 13, 1993.

Rigdon, Joan, ''Old-Fashioned Empire Building,'' *Rocky Mountain News,* June 23, 1998.

Schreiner, John, ''U.S. Magnate Now Buys B.C.'s Tug Master,'' *National Post,* January 11, 1996.

Smith, Ellit Blair, ''Montana Billionaire's Legacy Is Biggest Burden,'' *USA Today,* October 27, 1997.

Stern, Richard, ''Denny's Always the Low-Cost Producer,'' *Forbes,* May 15, 1989.

''U.S. Owner to Shed Canada Tugs, Barges in Anti-Trust Action,'' *Wall Street Journal,* January 15, 1997.

—Rebecca Stanfel

Weight Watchers

Weight Watchers International Inc.

175 Crossways Park West
Woodbury, New York 11797
U.S.A.
Telephone: (516) 390-1400
Toll Free: (800)333-5756
Fax: (516) 390-1302
Web site: http://www.weightwatchers.com

Wholly Owned Subsidary of Artal Luxembourg SA
Incorporated: 1963
Employees: 4,500
Sales: $400 million (1999 est.)
NAIC: 812191 Diet and Weight Reducing Centers

Weight Watchers International Inc. is the largest and most successful weight loss program in the world. The company has grown from the dream of one woman into a worldwide franchise with annual revenues of more than $400 million. Weight Watchers International has captured more than 40 percent of the weight-control market; more than a million people attend the company's weight loss classes in 30 countries around the world. In 1999 parent firm H.J. Heinz sold the company's diet center enterprise to the European investment firm Artal Luxembourg SA for $735 million. Heinz retained ownership of the Weight Watchers line of frozen foods, desserts, and breakfast products.

The Early Years

In 1961 Jean Nidetch was an overweight, 40-year-old home-maker living in Queens, New York. At 214 pounds and wearing a size 44 dress, Nidetch was always on a diet but never lost any weight. Thoroughly discouraged by dieting fads that did not help her, she attended a diet seminar offered by the City Board of Health in New York City. Although she lost 20 pounds following the advice provided, she soon discovered her motivation diminishing. Determined to stay on her diet and lose weight, she phoned a few overweight friends and asked them to come to her apartment. When her friends arrived, Nidetch confessed that she had an obsession with eating cookies. Her friends not only sympathized but also began to share their own obsessions about food. Soon

Nidetch was arranging weekly meetings for her friends in her home. The women shared stories about food and offered each other support. Most important, they all began to lose weight.

Within a short time, Nidetch was arranging meetings for more than 40 people in her small apartment. Not long afterward, she began to arrange support group meetings at other people's homes. As more and more people attended the meetings, Nidetch realized that losing weight was not merely adhering to a diet, but encouraging people to support each other and change their eating habits. One couple, Felice and Al Lippert, invited Nidetch to speak to a group of overweight friends at their house in Baldwin Harbor. After meeting every week for four months, Al lost 40 pounds and Felice lost nearly 50. Al Lippert, a merchandise manager for a women's apparel chain, began to give Nidetch advice on how to organize and expand her activities, and soon a four-person partnership was formed among Nidetch and her husband, Marty, and Al and Felice Lippert. In May 1963, Weight Watchers was incorporated and opened for business in Queens, New York.

The company's first public meeting was held in a space located over a movie theater. Although the meeting was not advertised, more than 400 people waited in line to hear Nidetch speak. Nidetch divided the crowd into groups of 50 and spent the entire day addressing the overwhelming guilt and hopeless-ness that many people felt about being overweight, as well as providing advice about shedding pounds effectively. Nidetch began to hold meetings three times a day, seven days a week. When she started to show signs of fatigue, Al Lippert suggested that she pick key people who had lost weight themselves and had strong communication skills to help her expand the pro-gram. The first 100 people chosen to run meetings throughout New York City shared their personal stories and helped people gain control over their eating habits. Nidetch's extraordinary speaking skills and Al Lippert's genius for organization helped raise Weight Watchers to the level of an evangelical movement.

Dynamic Growth in the Middle to Late 1960s

From 1963 to 1967, Lippert organized training programs, expanded the number of company locations throughout the

United States, and implemented a franchising system. By 1968, Weight Watchers had 102 franchises in the United States, Canada, Great Britain, Israel, and Puerto Rico. It was relatively easy for a person to get a franchise for Weight Watchers programs. Lippert sold the territory for a minimal fee, then charged the franchisee a royalty rate of ten percent on the gross income. The most important requirement was that the franchisee had graduated from the company's programs and kept off the weight that he or she had lost. Most of the franchisees were women from New York City who were willing to travel to establish a Weight Watchers franchise. This group was emotionally involved in the program and had a great deal of faith in its principles; as a result, their commitment to the franchise sometimes bordered on religious fervor.

The middle and late 1960s saw a boom for the company. In 1965 Lippert contracted various food companies in the United States to produce Weight Watchers food lines for supermarkets and grocery stores, including low-calorie frozen entrees and dry and dairy low-calorie foods. Lippert was also creative in other ways. He designed a billfold that held small packets of sugar substitutes, skimmed milk, and bouillon that enabled adherents of the Weight Watchers program to more easily control their diet when away from home. Lippert began to sell items for use in the Weight Watchers classroom, such as postal scales to weigh food; established a joint venture with *National Lampoon* to publish *Weight Watchers Magazine*; and opened a summer camp for children with weight problems.

One of the company's most successful ideas, created under the direction of Felice Lippert, was the publication of a Weight Watchers cookbook. Since the inception of the company, Felice Lippert had been in charge of new recipe development, nutrition, and food research. Her first Weight Watchers cookbook catapulted to the top of the bestseller lists and sold more than 1.5 million copies. In 1968 the company made its first stock offering to the public. Although some financial analysts on Wall Street were skeptical of the offering, the general public was overwhelmingly enthusiastic. The first day of trading saw Weight Watchers stock shoot up from an initial price of $11 to $30.

Changes in the 1970s

In 1973 Weight Watchers held its 15th anniversary celebration in Madison Square Garden in New York City. Host of past Republican and Democratic party presidential conventions, legendary boxing matches, and other historic national events, the Garden was filled to the rafters with admirers of the Weight Watchers program. It was a far cry from the tenth anniversary celebration held just five years earlier, which was held in a high school auditorium. Although celebrities in attendance included Bob Hope and Pearl Bailey, people had really come to see Jean Nidetch. She spoke until 1:30 a.m., with the crowd captivated by her inspiring stories.

With the company's rapid growth, in 1973 Nidetch decided to resign from her position as president of Weight Watchers to devote herself entirely to public relations. She traveled the world granting an endless number of radio, newspaper, and magazine interviews and speaking to huge audiences about the success of Weight Watchers programs. Al Lippert continued to organize the operation, hiring Dr. Richard Stuart, an expert in behavioral psychology, to help the company create a training department and design the first guides and manuals for the Weight Watchers program. Lippert also hired Carol Morton, a Weight Watchers graduate and German teacher, to begin operations in Europe. From 1974 to 1976, Lippert, along with a growing list of professional staff members in the areas of marketing, advertising, licensing, and nutrition, began to formalize a strategy for continued growth. Weight Watchers was not only an inspirational program that helped people lose weight, but a highly successful business venture. Lippert and his staff focused on the best way to attract people to Weight Watchers meetings and to sell them food, cookbooks, magazines, camps, spas, and various other weight loss products.

By the late 1970s, however, Al Lippert had experienced two heart attacks and recognized that the phenomenal growth of Weight Watchers was much too rapid for his small management group to handle. Annual revenues had grown to approximately $50 million, and it was at this point that Lippert started searching for a larger corporate partner to help Weight Watchers achieve the next level of organization and success. H.J. Heinz Company approached Lippert about purchasing Foodways National, one of Weight Watchers' frozen food licensees. Heinz initially sought to merge Foodways with Ore-Ida, its own frozen food and controlled-portion entree producer. Heinz management, however, soon realized that it was the Weight Watchers International brand name that was valuable, not its licensee. As a result, Heinz acquired Weight Watchers and Foodways National in 1978 for approximately $100 million. Lippert remained chief executive officer and chairman of the board at Weight Watchers.

Between 1978 and 1981, management at Heinz assimilated Weight Watchers into its corporate organization. Heinz divided the company into three parts: Foodways National's frozen food business was subsumed under Ore-Ida; Camargo Foods, a condiments, dry snacks, and dairy producer, and a licensee of Weight Watchers that was also purchased by Heinz, was merged with Heinz U.S.A.; and Weight Watchers' meeting service business remained Weight Watchers International. Heinz's strategy was to incorporate the food business of Weight Watchers into its own food operations, while allowing the meeting service business to continue functioning separately.

Expansion and Diversification in the 1980s

Chuck Berger, the new president of Weight Watchers International, initiated an aggressive strategy that included an innovative program for weight loss, an improved meeting service, and a plan to buy back the company's franchise territories. In 1983 Berger became CEO of Weight Watchers International and, along with Andrew Barrett and Dr. Les Parducci, laid the foundation for a brand new weight loss diet. Dubbed "Quick Start," the diet aimed to quicken the rate of weight loss during the first two weeks. Launched with a well-conceived media blitz, the new program helped to double the company's revenues within two years. Barrett, as executive vice-president, improved marketing, added new food product lines, and concentrated on the lifestyle needs of people with weight control problems. One of his most successful ideas was the "At Work Program," which organized meetings for professional women at their place of work.

Between 1982 and 1989, Weight Watchers International experienced unprecedented growth in product sales. In 1982 the Weight Watchers brand name food items switched from aluminum-tray to fiberboard packaging and introduced one of the world's first lines of microwaveable frozen food entrees. Foodways National also introduced low-calorie dessert products, and by 1988 the company's desserts had a larger market share than Sara Lee and Lean Cuisine. In 1982 *Weight Watchers Magazine* had a circulation of approximately 700,000 readers; by 1986, circulation had increased to more than one million. The magazine had changed its focus and was marketed to women committed to "self-improvement." Collaborating with Time-Life's books division, Weight Watchers International developed a series of highly successful fitness tapes for the video market and started additional projects for books, audiotapes, and videos in the areas of exercise, weight loss, and health awareness.

By 1988, each of the three separate business units of Weight Watchers was recording skyrocketing revenues. When combined, sales for the Weight Watchers businesses amounted to more than $1.2 billion. Even as these figures were released, however, the weight control business was changing dramatically. In 1989 and 1990, numerous competitors like Jenny Craig, Slim-Fast, Healthy Choice, and Nutri/System began to challenge Weight Watchers for a share of the market. During 1990 and 1991, after nearly seven years of increasing market share, the company suddenly stopped growing. Sales of Weight Watchers brand food products declined precipitously, and even the renowned support group meetings began to fall in attendance.

In 1991 Brian Ruder, a vice-president in marketing at Heinz, was hired as the president of a newly reconstituted Weight Watchers Food Company. Ruder immediately embarked on a comprehensive reorganization strategy, implementing new sales, marketing, finance, manufacturing, and research and development procedures. Within 15 months of the new company's formation, Ruder had redesigned almost half of its products. New product development time amounted to a mere 14 weeks, down from the 22-month cycle previously adhered to. One product line, low-fat, low-calorie entrees called "Smart Ones," was an immediate success. During the same time, Dr. Les Parducci was appointed by Heinz management as the head of Weight Watchers International. Parducci revamped the company's strategy for meeting services by simplifying the contents of programs, relocating meetings to more attractive surroundings, introducing more fun and interesting materials for members, and developing an entire new line of convenience food products.

Trouble in the Mid-1990s

Although these changes helped Weight Watchers stem defections to its rivals and revive its food sale business, the entire weight loss industry suffered a downturn in the mid-1990s. Many consumers had tired of feeling a perpetual need to count calories and of the perceived regimentation of diet classes. Spurred on by fitness gurus such as Susan Powter, whose rallying cry "Stop the Insanity" summed up many people's frustrations with the diet business, consumers began to look to health clubs and nutritional guides as a path to losing unwanted pounds. As an industry analyst explained to *Business Week,* "The whole industry has been under pressure. There has been a shift from dieting to general health concerns such as fat intake and general lifestyle." Moreover, a new generation of diet drugs was coming on the market, offering the hope that weight loss would become as simple as popping a pill. Weight Watchers also received some adverse publicity in 1993, when the Federal Trade Commission filed suit against it, alleging that it had engaged in misleading advertising. (The suit was eventually settled with no admission of wrongdoing in 1997.) As a result of these events, attendance at Weight Watchers classes dropped 20 percent in 1994 alone.

The company responded quickly to these events. In 1995 Weight Watchers International began to craft what *Business Week* described as a "health-first, vanity-second message." This approach stressed the health values of losing weight through Weight Watchers classes over the cosmetic effects of "looking better." To buttress this message, Weight Watchers negotiated agreements with insurance companies to give premium rebates on life insurance policies to Weight Watcher members. The company also made a more concerted effort to reach out to men, who had long been neglected by the diet industry (understandably so, however, as 95 percent of customers were female), holding male-only classes in some of its centers.

In an effort to streamline the company's operations further, Heinz sold *Weight Watchers Magazine* (whose circulation had dropped significantly from its mid-1980s peak of more than a million readers) to Southern Progress Corp., a subsidiary of Time Inc., in 1996. Although these changes were unable to return Weight Watchers to its former, robust growth levels, they did allow the company to remain profitable throughout the middle of the decade.

By 1997, the diet industry's fortunes were improving. The new class of diet drugs had not only failed to become the panacea for which many consumers had hoped, but were in fact linked to significant health problems. In addition, consumers had found that losing weight through exercise or fad diets had proved no simpler or more successful than the formula offered by Weight Watchers and its competitors. However, Weight Watchers had changed with the times as well. Recognizing that consumers still wanted to have more flexibility in the food they ate, the company unveiled its "1,2,3 Success" program. This innovative plan assigned point values to all foods, allowing dieters to eat whatever they chose, so long as they did not exceed the prescribed number of points. The company also hired the former Duchess of York, Sarah Ferguson, to be its spokesperson for the campaign. "1,2,3 Success" proved a tremendous boon to the company, driving up attendance at its classes worldwide by nearly 50 percent and boosting profits substantially.

Despite this revitalization, Heinz—in the course of a sweeping corporate reorganization—sold Weight Watchers International to the European investment firm Artal Luxembourg for $735 million in July 1999. Artal was a private investment group, which had as its sole investment advisor The Invus Group, Ltd. of New York; in an odd sort of synergy, Artal had also invested heavily in Keebler cookies and Sunshine biscuits. Discussing the sale in a press release, Heinz CEO William R. Johnson remarked, "Weight Watchers is the gold standard in the global weight control business, but its services orientation does not fit with Heinz's long-term food growth strategy, and this sale enables us to focus on Weight Watchers foods and our other global food businesses." Later in the year, Weight Watchers International repurchased its *Weight Watchers* magazine business from Southern Progress Corp., and Artal remained confident that its marketing experience could further strengthen the Weight Watchers brand. As a result, Weight Watchers International seemed well positioned to enter the 21st century.

Principal Competitors

Jenny Craig, Inc.; Slim-Fast Food Company.

Further Reading

Alexander, Keith L., "A Health Kick at Weight Watchers," *Business Week,* January 16, 1995.

Dienstag, Eleanor Foa, "The Weight Watchers Story," in *Good Company: 125 Years at the Heinz Table,* Warner Books, 1994.

Fannin, Rebecca A., "Corporate Close Up: Slimmer Pickings in U.S. Prompt Weight Watchers To Look Abroad," *Advertising Age International,* February 17, 1997.

Freeman, Sholnn, "European Firm Buys Division of H.J. Heinz Co.," *New Orleans Times-Picayune,* July 23, 1999.

Fridman, Sherman, "Weight Watchers to Shed Y2K Fat Or Maybe Not," *Newsbytes,* November 22, 1999.

The History of Weight Watchers, Jericho, N.Y.: Weight Watchers International Inc., 1995.

"H.J. Heinz Co. Sells Weight Watchers Weight Control Business to Artal," *Market News Publishing,* July 22, 1999.

Pollack, Judann, "Fed Up with Promoting Diets, Weight-Loss Rivals Branch Out," *Advertising Age,* March 29, 1999.

Sabatini, Patricia, "Slimming Down Heinz Plans to Shut 20 Plants, Sell Weight Watchers Classes," *Pittsburgh Post-Gazette,* February 18, 1999.

Schroeder, Michael, "The Diet Business Is Getting a Lot Skinnier," *Business Week,* June 24, 1991.

Spangler, Todd, "Heinz to Slim Down: Its Weight Watchers Classrooms Are Being Sold," *York Daily Record,* July 23, 1999.

—Thomas Derdak
—updated by Rebecca Stanfel

Weiner's Stores, Inc.

6005 Westview Drive
Houston, Texas 77055
U.S.A.
Telephone: (713) 688-1331
Fax: (713) 688-6976
Web site: http://www.weiners.com

Public Company
Incorporated: 1991
Employees: 3,800
Sales: $276.8 million (1999)
Stock Exchanges: NASDAQ
Ticker Symbol: WEIR
NAIC: 45299 All Other General Merchandise Stores

Houston-based Weiner's Stores, Inc. is a discount retailer with more than 130 locations in Texas, Louisiana, and Mississippi. The shops offer both name brand and private label apparel and footwear, accessories, gift items, bed and bath products, as well as toys, fragrances, and electronics. Weiner's promotes its stores, which are primarily located in urban strip malls and shopping centers, as community oriented. The company caters mostly to minority populations, and 80 percent of its clientele are African Americans and Hispanics. Weiner's Stores was a family-run business until the mid-1990s, when it filed for Chapter 11 bankruptcy protection and brought in outside management.

Building Business: The First 60 Years

Isidore Weiner opened his first Weiner's Store on Houston Avenue in Houston, Texas, in 1926. The store was a relatively small 3,000 square feet in size and was located on the outskirts of town, where the rents were lower and the competition less fierce. Unfortunately for Weiner, however, the timing of his store opening was less than opportune—the economic depression of the 1930s forced Weiner to file for bankruptcy in 1932. Weiner managed to evade ruin, however, and worked slowly to build up business once again. Eventually, Weiner was able to fully pay all creditors. After the nation emerged from the Depression, Weiner opened his second store, again in a remote locale. Although the decision to locate the store in a spot far from the increasingly popular downtown Houston area may have puzzled some, the strategy worked for Weiner, who purposely placed his stores in neighborhoods, where they could better serve the community.

Weiner's Stores grew steadily and slowly until the late 1970s, when Isidore Weiner's two sons, Sol and Leon, assumed command of the company. Although the titles of chairman or CEO were not adopted by the brothers, they were the leaders and primary owners of the business. Sol handled merchandising, while Leon took care of operations. The brothers implemented an expansion strategy for Weiner's Stores, and the company opened an average of eight to 12 new stores a year over the next decade and a half. By the late 1980s there were more than 130 locations. Although most of the stores operated within a 300-mile radius of Houston, Weiner's had expanded into the Dallas region, as well as in Louisiana. In 1988 Weiner's opened outlets in the Louisiana towns of New Iberia and Lake Charles, and a year later the company planned to open three stores in the Baton Rouge area. The stores themselves had grown since Isidore Weiner opened the first 3,000-square-foot location. By the 1980s Weiner's Stores averaged between 28,000 and 30,000 square feet and offered a wide range of value-priced clothing and accessories for the family.

By 1992 there were 151 Weiner's outlets located in Texas and Louisiana, and the company continued to grow. The company looked to the Fort Worth area in the early 1990s. Although Fort Worth had struggled economically in the late 1980s and early 1990s, Weiner's Stores felt the region presented positive opportunities for Weiner's. In 1992 Weiner's announced plans to open its first store in Tarrant County. Don Stine, Weiner's director of advertising, addressed the economic uncertainties of the area and explained in the *Fort Worth Star-Telegram,* "If you moved Saks Fifth Avenue into Fort Worth, it might have a little trouble there right now, and then again, it might not. . . . We tend to do well in good times and bad." Weiner's added a second store in Tarrant County in 1994 and hoped to have eventually a total of six to eight stores operating in the area. The company, which did not build new stores but inhabited existing open spaces instead, stated that it would continue to be on the lookout for desirable properties in the Fort Worth area.

Increased Competition and Financial Challenges in the Early to Mid-1990s

After a favorable growth period in the 1980s, Weiner's faced increasing challenges in the 1990s. As the retail industry began to enjoy high productivity in the mid-1980s following a long slump, new and aggressive competitors entered the fray. Numerous discount retailers, including such powerful businesses as T.J. Maxx, Marshall's, and Venture, entered Weiner's familiar markets, grabbing valuable market share. The popularity and increasing presence of such major discount department stores as Target, Kmart, and Wal-Mart stores also hurt Weiner's Stores. In addition, not only did Weiner's face competition in the discount retail sector, but it also struggled against traditional department stores, which waged their own battles against discounters by reducing prices and staging major sales promotions.

Coupled with the increased competition was an industrywide decline in profitability in the mid-1990s. Not only had the rise in competition created a saturated market, but the increased productivity of the late 1980s and early 1990s had led to weakened profitability as costs began to rise and cut into profit margins. According to the *Daily News Record,* more than 100,000 retailers had filed for bankruptcy protection between 1990 and 1996, a jump of 60 percent compared with the period ranging from 1984 to 1989. Hardest hit was the discount store market, in which most of the significant competitors, with the exception of the "Big Three" players—Wal-Mart, Kmart, and Target, had at some point struggled against bankruptcy. For example, Venture Stores, which had grown rapidly in the early 1990s, announced in 1995 that it would cease its expansion and remodel existing stores. Marshall's stores, suffering from sagging sales, closed more than 280 of its 330 unprofitable stores before being acquired by TJX Companies, Inc., the parent company of rival T.J. Maxx. TJX in turn planned to close about 200 underperforming locations in 1996. Michael Exstein, an analyst with PaineWebber, explained to *Bloomberg Business News,* "Off-pricers are having a hard time drawing customers. . . . The industry is a mess."

Even the "Big Three" of discount retailing, which accounted for about 80 percent of industry sales, were affected by increasing costs. Kmart, for instance, announced in 1995 that it would close 72 stores. Still, the superstores had advantages over smaller rivals, and the *Daily News Record* reported that supercenters were expected to account for nearly half of the sales in the discount store industry by the year 2000. In addition, except for growth of the supercenters, flat growth was projected for the discount store industry.

Regional retail chains felt the industrywide pinch strongly, and many struggled to remain afloat. Kurt Barnard, publisher of *Barnard's Retail Marketing Report,* told the *Houston Chronicle,* "Regional discounters are wriggling and writhing in an effort to assure themselves a continued lease on life. . . . The outcome of those efforts is very much in doubt." With competition from the dominant superstores and anticipated industry consolidation that would inevitably lead to a growing number of massive discount chains, small regional stores appeared to face a highly gloomy outlook.

In April 1995 Weiner's Stores filed for Chapter 11 bankruptcy protection. The 158-store chain was affected by the same problems and aggressive competition plaguing similar businesses, and Weiner's also blamed an unseasonably warm winter in 1994 that left store shelves filled with winter apparel that subsequently had to be sold for severely discounted prices. Weiner's was left with liabilities of $70.4 million and assets of $96.7 million. Immediately after filing, Weiner's received a $30 million line of credit from CIT Group/Business Credit, Inc., of New York. The loan allowed Weiner's Stores to continue operations while restructuring debt. The company remained confident that Weiner's Stores would pull through. Andy Weiner, grandson of founder Isidore and a vice-president at the company, told the *Houston Chronicle,* "We've been in business 69 years. . . . We're going to be in business another 69 years." Others in the local business community agreed with Weiner. Maury Aresty, president of the Houston Retail Merchants Association, said in the *Houston Chronicle,* "Weiners [sic] has always been a remarkably efficient machine. They have very low corporate overhead. . . . They have a young, bright team inheriting the business. They will be a lot stronger company when they emerge from bankruptcy."

As a first step in its restructuring, Weiner's Stores made plans to close ten unprofitable stores—five in the Houston region, three in Dallas, one in Longview, and one in Lafayette, Louisiana. In November 1995 Weiner's announced additional closures, which included the exiting of Tarrant County. By December the company had closed 20 underperforming stores. In late 1995 Weiner's made another significant move toward reorganization when it hired Herbert R. Douglas as the new president and CEO. Douglas was the first leader in Weiner's history who was not a member of the family. Douglas also was named to the company's board of directors, which would continue to be chaired by Sol and Leon Weiner. The Weiner brothers announced they would head into semiretirement and were optimistic about the new management and future of Weiner's Stores. Sol Weiner told the *Houston Chronicle,* "It's a changing of the guard. I think it's another era in the firm, you could say."

Restructuring and Regrowth: Late 1990s

Herbert Douglas, who had 32 years of experience in the retail industry, began to tackle the task of bringing the struggling retailer out of bankruptcy protection. Douglas had served most recently as the CEO of New Jersey-based Jamesway, a company that Douglas led through liquidation in December 1995. At Weiner's, Douglas assembled a management team that included several people from Jamesway—Jerome Feller as vice-president and general merchandise manager; Joseph Kassa as vice-president of sales, promotion, marketing, and real estate; John Dineen as director of merchandise for men's and children's clothing; and James Berens as vice-president of store operations.

Unfortunately for Douglas, increased competition and a warm winter were not the only reasons for slumping sales at Weiner's Stores. The new management team hired a market research firm to conduct a survey to assess customer opinions of Weiner's and learned that the stores had a poor image among customers. Weiner's Stores had neglected to keep up with modern demands, the survey indicated, and Weiner's offered a hodgepodge of close-out merchandise that was often outdated. Douglas explained in *Discount Store News,* "Most customers thought that Weiner's had old, defective, irregular merchandise of low quality. They said the stores were very difficult to shop, the sales associates were not friendly, and the return policy was not good." In addition, stores were disorganized and dirty, poorly lit, and filled with broken shelving. "There were tens of millions of square feet added to Texas' retail scene during the early 90s, and Weiner's never changed," Douglas continued. "The stores were never renovated, and there was no new technology brought into the chain. No one had control of what was going onto the sales floor, and the company was run with an enormous inventory."

One of the first items on the agenda of Weiner's new management was to liquidate $40 million worth of outdated merchandise to lower excess inventory levels. The strategy of buying close-out apparel and merchandise in mass quantities, often regardless of quality or style, was changed to a more select buying policy. Weiner's cut its vendor base from about 800 people to 400 people and worked to build closer relationships with its vendors. Stores were remodeled along a more consumer-friendly design and were modernized with new computerized systems. Weiner's also launched a major advertising campaign designed to update and reinvigorate the chain's stodgy image. Douglas outlined the need for a new marketing tactic in *Discount Store News* and said, "When we took over, we found that there was so much dislike for our company that we felt we needed something to represent us

that was extremely consumer-friendly." The resultant campaign featured a humorous superhero named Weinerman. Weinerman's cause was to fight for lower apparel prices and prevent consumers from overpaying for name-brand items. His arch rival was Needless Markup.

Weiner's Stores also adopted a new mission to serve a predominantly minority clientele. Many of the company's stores that were located in predominantly white, suburban areas were closed as Weiner's focused on lower income, urban neighborhoods. The store merchandise was altered to include more name-brand items, such as Levi's, Nike, Reebok, adidas, and Fila. Explained Douglas in *Discount Store News,* "Our customer is mostly an African-American or Hispanic inner city resident, and labels are very important to them." To better serve its clientele, Weiner's also began to carry a wider variety of sizes.

With its new structure in place, Weiner's Stores emerged from bankruptcy protection in August 1997. Since filing for Chapter 11 bankruptcy protection, Weiner's had closed 27 unprofitable stores and opened several new locations, including two in the Dallas region. By mid-1997 only one member of the Weiner family remained with the company—Michael Klaiman, son-in-law of Sol Weiner, was the director of the shoe division. Weiner's had sales of about $263.6 million for the fiscal year ended January 31, 1997.

In the late 1990s Weiner's Stores worked to adjust to its new corporate mission. The year 1998 proved to be a difficult one for a number of reasons. Ironing out the quirks of a new merchandising system affected sales during the first quarter, and during the second and third quarters the industrywide drop in demand for Levi's jeans and name-brand athletic footwear led to decreased profitability, despite positive sales growth. Also during the third quarter, many stores were adversely affected by extreme weather conditions, including floods and hurricanes. Because of these factors, Weiner's reported a net loss of $5.0 million on revenues of $260.9 million for the fiscal year ended January 30, 1999. The company reported a net income of $12.7 million during the previous year and a net loss of $17.2 million the year before that. Bankruptcy-related items, including a gain of $18.7 million during 1997 due to the discharge of debt, affected Weiner's bottom line in 1996 and 1997.

Although sales were not as strong as Weiner's had hoped during 1998, the company managed to log some positive events. Weiner's opened seven new stores and closed three and added "Bed and Bath" sections to a number of its stores, marking the company's first foray beyond apparel and footwear. By early 1999 Bed and Bath shops were in 35 stores, and during the fourth quarter that ended January 1999, Bed and Bath shops contributed about $2.7 million in sales. In the summer of 1998 Weiner's returned to the Fort Worth region and opened a second store in the area a year later. Weiner's was profitable for the first nine months of 1999, earning $463,000 during the second quarter on sales of $79.53 million. The company continued to expand geographically, opening new stores in Mississippi, and added more variety, including toys, candy, videos, and electronics, to its merchandise mix.

As Weiner's Stores greeted a new century, it had 132 store locations. Weiner's reported revenues of $276.8 million for the year ended January 29, 2000, an increase of 6.1 percent compared with the previous year. The company planned to open ten new stores during 2000, including several in a new market—Arkansas. Weiner's, which had teetered on the brink of extinction twice in its 73 years, would face future challenges as it battled rivals in the highly competitive discount retail store industry. Weiner's appeared to have a solid future, however, serving the retail needs of its preferred niche—the minority communities in Texas, Louisiana, Mississippi, and Arkansas.

Principal Competitors

Wal-Mart Stores Inc.; J.C. Penney Company, Inc.; Ross Stores, Inc.; The TJX Companies, Inc.

Further Reading

Baker, "Weiner's Plans 2nd Fort Worth Area Store," *Fort Worth Star-Telegram,* January 7, 1999, p. 2.

Boisseau, Charles, "Weiner's New CEO an Outsider," *Houston Chronicle,* December 19, 1995, p. 1.

Hassell, Greg, "Discounters Have Rough Time at the Register," *Houston Chronicle,* July 20, 1995, p. 1.

——, "Weiner's Bankruptcy Cloak Shed," *Houston Chronicle,* August 30, 1997, p. 1.

——, "Weiner's Files Chapter 11/Stores Hurt by Tough Competition, Mild Winter," *Houston Chronicle,* April 13, 1995, p. 1.

——, "Weiner's Has a Laugh on Itself," *Houston Chronicle,* August 21, 1996, p. 1.

Kaplan, Richard, "Red Hot Weiner's," *Discount Store News,* February 23, 1998, p. A10.

"Managing the Productivity Loop Paradox," *Daily News Record,* September 2, 1996, p. 5.

Mowbray, Rebecca, "Bright Future/Weiner's Works Way Back to Profitability," *Houston Chronicle,* September 11, 1999, p. 1.

Nishimura, Scott, "Weiner's Plans Store in Town Center Mall," *Fort Worth Star-Telegram,* October 26, 1992, p. 1.

——, "Weiner's Stores Expanding in Tarrant County," *Fort Worth Star-Telegram,* February 7, 1994, p. 5.

—Mariko Fujinaka

Westaff

Westaff Inc.

301 Lennon Lane
Walnut Creek, California 94598
U.S.A.
Telephone: (925) 930-5300
Fax: (925) 934-5489
Web site: http://www.westaff.com

Public Company
Incorporated: 1954 as Western Employers Service
Employees: 1,170 regular staff; 36,500 temporary
  employees
Sales: $650.75 million (1999)
Stock Exchanges: NASDAQ
Ticker Symbol: WSTF
NAIC: 56132 Temporary Help Services

Westaff Inc., based in the San Francisco Bay Area, is the oldest temporary employment company on the West Coast. The company specializes in providing so-called Essential Support Services—mainly clerical and light industrial, including such tasks as word processing, data entry, reception, customer service and telemarketing, warehouse labor, manufacturing, assembly, and lab assistance. Westaff has a network of more than 360 offices in the United States, Australia, New Zealand, and three European countries. Westaff itself owns nearly three quarters of these offices outright. About 20 percent are operated by franchisers, and about six percent are run by licensees. Westaff concentrates its American operations in suburban and rural markets. Westaff reported sales totaling $650.75 million in 1999, up more than $50 million from 1998. In a bid to attract and keep qualified temporary help, Westaff was among the first temporary employment companies to offer its temporary workers benefits packages that included health insurance, 401(k) accounts, and stock plans.

Company Beginnings in 1948

Westaff was founded in 1948 by Robert Stover. When Stover settled in San Francisco after World War II, he knew about a temporary staffing agency that had been founded in Chicago in 1929. Investigating the industry, he discovered that no such companies existed on the West Coast. With $800 in his pocket, a rented typewriter, and a tiny office in downtown San Francisco, he set up his own staffing company, which he called Western Employers Service. The first thing he did was to have 2,000 blotters printed with the name and phone number of the new company. Then, every morning, before he went to the office, Stover called on 25 potential customers, for a minute each, no longer. This was just long enough to let them know what Western did and to give them a blotter. Temp services were virtually unknown at the time, and Stover marketed Western to San Francisco businesses as a resource to be used in times of emergency, for example, when a full-time employee became ill or quit.

In the early days, Stover solicited new employees by means of the classifieds, advertising for individuals who wanted to work two to three days a week. He found a particularly fruitful source of talent among Australian war brides who had come to the United States with their American husbands. Although they were highly skilled secretaries, trained in the British system, they often had difficulty finding work, because they were foreign and because they were young married women employers believed were liable to quit abruptly because of pregnancy. They came to be valued by Western's clients, however, who started requesting one of the "Western girls" specifically. Although in less demand in the 1940s and 1950s, Western also provided male temps, the so-called "Minute Men," who did inventory work, shipping and machine operations, car washing, soda fountain boy duties, poll taking, and the like.

Growth, Development, and Expansion: 1950s–80s

By 1953, Western was catching on. It had Bank of America for a customer and had cornered the temporary employment market in San Francisco. The expense of its quick expansion put the company thousands of dollars in debt. In need of additional capital to expand, Stover approached banks about loans. Examining his books, the bankers realized that Stover was tithing—donating ten percent of all income—to his church. They suggested that he postpone the donations until the business was in sounder financial condition. Stover refused and went home for

Company Perspectives:

We are extremely focused on the largest niche of the U.S. temporary staffing market—the essential Support Services sector. Westaff has 50 years of experience in servicing this business area: expertise in recruiting and training Essential Support personnel and specialized knowledge of our customers' unique needs. We believe this 'specialization' has enabled Westaff to establish itself as a market force in the industry.

We offer our field staff a team-oriented bonus and commission package that supports and rewards collective performance. We have also implemented a staff recruitment program focused on community-based industry professionals who utilize their knowledge and experience to hire the best sales and service teams.

With the continuing enhancement of our 'technological weapons,' our company-wide information system, we believe the entire network of Westaff offices will have the necessary tools to outperform local, regional and national competitors with innovative, quality service.

the weekend, convinced the bank would turn down his loan request and he would have to close Western. The bank, however, reasoned that anyone with such unshakable religious principles had to be a good credit risk and gave Stover a $25,000 line of credit—substantially more than he had asked for.

A year later, in 1954, the company was incorporated in California with Stover as president. In 1958 it adopted a new name, Western Girl, Inc.; a new logo, a cowgirl twirling a lasso; and a new slogan, "You Can Count on a Western Girl." Western quickly spread around the Bay Area, to Oakland and San Jose, and by the end of the 1950s across the Rockies into Denver. In the mid-1960s, Western opened its first foreign branch in Denmark. Within a few years, others followed in Norway, the United Kingdom, and Australia. In 1973 the company changed its name again, becoming Western Temporary Services.

In 1963 the company had added a new division to provide temporary labor to light industries. Such labor, along with clerical and office work, eventually would form the backbone of Western's business. But in the 1970s and 1980s Western Temporary Services became famous for a completely different kind of temporary worker—Santa Claus. In December 1976, the *New York Times* reported that Western had more than 2,000 Santas in stores and was the nation's top Santa supplier. In 1979 it formed a new division specifically for its Santa Claus business.

Two Santa innovations were introduced in the 1980s. In 1985 Western began publicizing its annual "Santa Index," which showed how well or poorly Christmas retail business was doing. The idea behind the index was that when sales were falling, stores started ordering more Santas. The Santa Index became a regular holiday feature in the national media. In the mid-1980s, Western also began a school for its Santas—the only one of its kind, the company claimed. Important lessons for would-be Santas included: never promise children anything;

make sure you know the names of all the reindeer; never refer to a child's mother or father—if they are divorced or separated, the remark could inadvertently hurt the child; and, a Santa suit is extremely warm, so bathe daily and use a strong deodorant. But Santa Claus was just the tip of the iceberg; it only accounted for a mere one percent of Western's business.

By 1988, Western was the largest privately owned temporary staffing company in the United States and one of the five largest overall in the United States. It had 285 offices across the nation, 40 offices overseas, and annual revenues of more than $200 million. The company formed a Legal Services division that provided companies with temporary lawyers and paralegal help. It also had a Perfume and Cosmetics Division the primary purpose of which was to provide trained sales help to department stores in high-volume seasons.

Further Growth in the 1990s

In 1991 Western experienced a growth spurt. It was the 34th largest privately held company in the San Francisco area. It expanded into Switzerland and Sweden; it reached 350 offices in the United States. It also had expanded out of the temporary help field, forming two film and TV production subsidiaries, Western Images and Western Videotape. In the wake of the sudden expansion, founder Robert Stover gave thought to taking the company public, to raise capital to continue its aggressive program of acquisition.

By 1993, Western was becoming well focused on a core market of the clerical and light industrial workers it later termed "Essential Support." Its international network was a hybrid of company-owned offices and franchises. In 1991 it introduced a computerized system to evaluate the skills of new workers and to train them in what was then cutting-edge office technologies such as WordStar, Lotus, and the up-and-coming Windows. In spring 1993 the company launched its newest division for outsourcing, which would specialize in site-managing special projects for clients.

Western also was pursuing temporary medical services more aggressively. In 1967 it established a medical division, Western Medical Services, which provided home care assistance. In 1993 Western Medical had more than 60 offices across the nation and received Medicare certification for more than 12 of them, that year, which qualified them for Medicare, Medicaid, and Medicaid waiver programs. The company hoped to have certification for all of its offices by 1994.

By 1994 Western Temporary Services had eight divisions—Office, Light Industrial, Technical, Medical, Santa/Photo, Accounting, Marketing, and Outsourcing—and 350 offices worldwide. It had moved its headquarters out of San Francisco to the suburban community of Walnut Creek, California. Stover had abandoned his plan to go public in 1991. In October 1993, however, the company filed with the Securities and Exchange Commission its intent to sell 1.7 million shares in a public offering. But only a month and a half later it reversed course again and called off the IPO, citing adverse market conditions.

In 1994 Western Temporary Services changed its name to Western Staff Services. The new name was intended to reflect the company's new strategy being developed by a special company task force headed by company CEO Robert Stover that called for rapid expansion into high-tech staffing, in particular in the field of information technology. As part of the task force's plan for growth in the high-tech temp sector, Western acquired Technical Executive Career Services Inc. of Norcross, Georgia in August 1995.

The year 1995 was the start of a period of explosive growth at Western Staff. Between January and July, it opened 23 new offices in New York, Maryland, Michigan, Minnesota, Ohio, Iowa, Illinois, Indiana, Louisiana, Texas, Montana, and California. It opened a new U.K. office in Taunton and acquired two foreign temp firms, Ausbiz Pty. Ltd of Darwin, Australia and ABC Vikar A/S of Drammen, Norway. In October 1995, Western acquired its franchise MERBCO, Inc. Mike Phippen, MERBCO's owner, had started with a single Western office eight years earlier and built it into a chain spread across the Minneapolis-St. Paul area and parts of Wisconsin. After MERBCO was purchased, Phippen moved into Western's corporate headquarters in Walnut Creek as executive vice-president. He was given responsibility for Western's bread-and-butter clerical and light industrial Temporary Services division. Less than three months later, Phippen was made president. By the end of the decade, he was Stover's heir apparent. When, in late 1998, Stover announced that he was stepping down as CEO, Phippen was the natural choice to take over the position. Its handling of Phippen is a graphic illustration of Western Staff's commitment to retaining and exploiting the expertise of staff in the companies it acquired. It rarely let managers of acquired

businesses go; instead it promoted them into area manager or vice-president positions.

Western resurrected its IPO plans in March 1996, announcing that it would offer 1.5 million shares of common stock for $12 a share. Analysts observed that the boom times being enjoyed by staffing companies boded well for the offering. The previous fiscal year, Western had posted a profit of $7.5 million—84 cents a share. In addition, in the quarter that ended just before the announcement, Western's profits climbed 21 percent to $2.5 million, 18 cents per share. At the same time, analysts warned that the temporary staffing industry was one of the first to suffer in times of recession. It had been the recession in the early 1990s that was responsible for sinking Western's earlier IPO plan. The offering finally was made in May 1996 and was well received by investors. The stock closed its first day at $15.88 a share, well above the $12 for which Western originally had hoped.

Western's expansion continued in 1997 with acquisitions in Topeka, Kansas; San Antonio, Texas; Hartford, Connecticut; Washington, D.C.; and elsewhere. Two acquisitions in Australia and New Zealand increased its presence there to 20 offices. That same year, Western initiated a program to attract more student workers that included regular pay increases, tuition assistance awards, seasonal paid vacations, and a "Benefit Card" that provided discounts on dental care, eye care, and prescriptions.

Western Staff Services spun off its Western Medical Services division into a wholly owned subsidiary. At the time, the division had 56 offices in 20 states, with total revenues of $43 million in fiscal year 1996. In October 1997 Western sold off its Photo/Santa division to New Jersey-based Cherry Hill Photo Enterprises. Western had decided Santa did not fit with the company's core business. In January 1998 Western initiated its "Future Funds" program, which offered its qualifying temps some of the benefits normally associated with full-time employment, such as an employer matching 401(k) plan and a discounted employee stock purchase plan.

Western Staff continued to acquire other companies throughout 1998. In all, it made 15 acquisitions during the year, including the purchase of the Texas-based Personnel Connection in July 1998. With 14 offices in Texas, California, Florida, and Arizona, as well as more than $36 million in annual sales, the agency was Western's largest acquisition ever. Western's subsidiary, Western Medical Services, went on a buying spree itself, acquiring 15 home health agencies between October 1997 and July 1998. But Western Staff Services' desire to focus even more closely on its core business—office, light industrial, and technical services—led it to look for a buyer for Western Medical. Stricter Medicare rules, which caused a minor crisis in home medical services, also contributed to the decision to sell the company. One proposed sale fell through in fall 1998. Finally, in early 1999, Sparta Surgical Corporation agreed to purchase Western Medical for an undisclosed price.

Management Changes and Innovative Ideas: 1998 and Beyond

Western underwent two major changes in 1998. In July, its founder, Robert Stover, announced he would retire as CEO at the end of the year. Stover remained with Western as chairman of the board. In September, at the same time that it announced that President and COO Mike Phippen would be named the new CEO, the company also announced that it was changing its name once again, to Westaff.

Westaff's problems finding a buyer for Western Medical, together with a series of thorough-going management changes on the regional level, resulted in a substantial dip in Western's stock prices. They fell from a high of $21.67 a share in May 1998 to only $4.68 in April 1999. Paradoxically, this occurred at a time when Westaff's revenues were doubling and its earnings returns on sales were tripling. Over the next ten months, the stock never rose above $9 a share.

Western continued to approach temporary staffing with innovative ideas in 1999. In spring of that year, it inaugurated a mobile unit, a van called the Job Squad that recruited applicants in the streets of San Francisco and other Bay Area communities. Would-be temps could fill in applications and see the Westaff welcome video right on the sidewalk. The company planned to use the Job Squad in other American markets, including Washington, D.C.; Dallas, Texas; Denver, Colorado; and Pittsburgh, Pennsylvania.

Principal Subsidiaries

Western Images.

Principal Divisions

Temporary Services Division; Technical Division; Accounting Division; Marketing Division; Outsourcing Division.

Principal Competitors

Interim Services, Inc.; Kelly Services, Inc.; Manpower, Inc.; RemedyTemp, Inc.; Personnel Group of America, Inc.

Further Reading

Calbreath, Dean, "Western Temp May Let Public Share in Firm," *San Francisco Business Times,* September 6, 1991, p. 17.

Ford, George C., "Founder of California-Based Westaff Anticipates Strong Growth Past 2000," *Knight-Ridder/Tribune Business News,* October 27, 1998.

Guynn, Jessica, "Western Staff Services of Walnut Creek, Calif., Picks New Name," *Contra Costa Times,* September 25, 1998.

"North Pole Unemployment: 0%," *Time,* November 25, 1985, p. 86.

"Sparta Surgical Corporation To Acquire All of the Assets of Western Medical Services, Inc.," *PRNewswire,* March 22, 1999.

Speer, Tibbett L. "Temporary Sanity: W. Robert Stover Is Too Private To Ever Go Public. Yet His Walnut Creek Temporary Agency—First of Its Kind in the West, Now 10th-Largest in the Country—Is About To Do Just That," *Diablo Business,* January 1993.

"Walnut Creek, Calif.-Based Temporary Hire Firm Hopes Stock Rebounds," *Contra Costa Times,* April 11, 1999.

Watson, Lloyd, "Walnut Creek Company's Schools for Santas," *San Francisco Chronicle,* November 18, 1988, p. C3.

Welch, Michael, "Temporary Solutions . . . May Last Longer Than You Think," *Corporate Report-Minnesota,* June 1992, p. 61.

"Western Staff Services Acquires MERBCO, Inc.," *Business Wire,* October 23, 1995.

"Western Staff Services Celebrates 47th Year in Business; Opens 25 Offices in the U.S. and U.K.; Acquires Companies in Australia and Norway," *Business Wire,* August 7, 1995.

—Gerald E. Brennan

Wolters Kluwer NV

Stadhouderskade 1
P.O. Box 818
NL-1000 AV Amsterdam
The Netherlands
Telephone: (31) 20-6070400
Fax: (31) 20-6070490
Web site: http://www.wolterskluwer.com

Public Company
Incorporated: 1882
Employees: 16,500
Sales: EUR 3.08 billion ($6.03 billion) (1999)
Stock Exchanges: Amsterdam
Ticker Symbol: WTKWY
NAIC: 51113 Book Publishers; 51114 Database and
     Directory Publishers

Wolters Kluwer NV is one of the worldwide leaders in publishing, and the Netherlands' second largest publisher after Reed Elsevier, with US$6.03 billion in sales in 1998. Under the slogan "Creating Value for Professionals," Wolters Kluwer and its subsidiaries are primarily active in the specialized publishing markets of business, law, tax, medicine, education, science, professional training, and electronic publishing, while maintaining only a limited presence in general consumer and trade publishing. With operations in various European countries, the United States, Canada, and several Asian nations, Wolters Kluwer has pursued a growth strategy dominated by strategic acquisitions, though it has begun to focus on deriving more of its growth from the development of its existing properties.

19th-Century Roots

The modern incarnation of Wolters Kluwer of the 1990s traces its origins to four Dutch publishing families of the 19th century: Wolters, Noordhoff, Kluwer, and Samson. During that century, the Industrial Revolution, combined with constitutional and legal reforms that more closely united the formerly loose association of Dutch provinces, prompted a growing demand for educational and informational literature. Many publishers, print shops, and typographers responded to this demand, numbering some 600 by the end of the 1880s. Until the 20th century, however, publishing in the Netherlands remained the province of small-scale, often family-run businesses with fewer than ten employees. The first large publishing house, the Elsevier Bookselling and Publishing Company, appeared in Amsterdam in 1881, but remained an exception for some time to come.

J.B. Wolters founded the Schoolbook publishing house—later to be called the J.B. Wolters Publishing Company—in the provincial capital city of Groningen in 1836, providing educational and instructional materials for a country just beginning the transformation to a modern industrial economy. Wolters was childless, and upon his death in 1860, his brother-in-law, E.B. ter Horst, took over the company. Under ter Horst the company began a period of expansion, adding a printing shop and bindery to its editorial functions. Ter Horst brought his son, E.B. ter Horst, Jr., into the company in 1885, and ter Horst, Jr., was made a partner in the company eight years later. Disagreements between father and son led the senior ter Horst to leave the company soon afterwards. Ter Horst, Jr., led the company until his death in 1905. By then, the company's fortunes had fallen, to the point where the heirs to the company, ter Horst, Jr.'s half-brothers F.R. and A. ter Horst, considered closing the company. Instead, the brothers reorganized the company from a partnership into a corporation, and for the first time brought in directors from outside the family. F.R. ter Horst, formerly a banking professional, became the company's managing director, overseeing the editorial portions of its textbook and academic publishing activities from his home in The Hague. The company's production facilities remained in Groningen.

In 1915 a separate office was opened in The Hague. Two years later Dr. Anthony M.H. Schepman, who was married to a niece of F.R. ter Horst, joined the J.B. Wolters Company and was soon named a director of the company, a position he held for more than 40 years. Under the joint leadership of ter Horst and Schepman, the company continued to expand its operations. In 1920 the company opened an office in what is now known as Jakarta, Indonesia, in the Dutch East Indies, to provide books for the Dutch-speaking population there. Setbacks for the com-

458

pany came with the Depression of the 1930s, and the introduction of modern Dutch spelling, which removed many Germanisms from the Dutch grammar and spelling and rendered many of Wolters' titles obsolete. These setbacks resulted in a shutdown of its Hague offices. World War II, during which Schepman was interned as a member of the Dutch elite in a German concentration camp, added to the company's difficulties. After the war, and especially after Indonesia achieved its independence in 1949, the company enjoyed a period of enhanced prosperity. Wolters also moved into the Flemish-speaking areas of Belgium, especially with the promotion of Algemeen Beschaafd Nederlands (or ABN, a standardization of the language similar to Standard Received English) over the many Dutch and Flemish dialects still spoken throughout both countries. However, in 1954, the Republic of Indonesia moved to prohibit the importation of Indonesian-language books printed outside the country. The J.B. Wolters-Djarkata division attempted to set up printing facilities in Indonesia, but in 1959, Indonesia nationalized many of the foreign companies operating there, including J.B. Wolters-Djarkata.

Convergence in the Late 1960s and Early 1970s

By then, a postwar wave of mergers across Dutch industry had begun to affect the publishing industry as well. The era of the small family publishing house was fading. The Noordhoff publishing house, founded in 1858 by P. Noordhoff to serve the educational and vocational market, was located directly next door to Wolters' offices in Groningen, and was still managed by the Noordhoff family. Driven by the increasingly competitive nature of the Dutch publishing industry, Noordhoff approached Wolters about merging the two companies. Wolters, nearly three times the size of Noordhoff but facing the same competition from much larger publishing companies, agreed. The merger of the two houses was accomplished in 1968, literally by the breaking down of the wall that had long separated their offices. The next phase in Wolters' history followed four years later, when it merged with the Information and Communication Group, which had been formed from an earlier merger with the Samson publishing family.

Nicolaas Samson's publishing career began as an offshoot of his civil service career in the Dutch village of Hazerswoude. As the recent modernization of Dutch law was slowly reaching from the larger cities to the outlying provinces, the need arose for new administrative materials and forms, which Samson provided. Samson's operated first in an office of the town hall, but by 1883 he had moved his publishing activities, including printing shop, bindery, and warehouse, to offices next to his home in Alphen aan den Rijn. In 1886 Samson left the civil service to operate his publishing business full time. At first

Samson's business concentrated on administrative forms, but he soon added periodicals and books for the administrative market. In 1888 Samson's oldest son, Jacobus Balthus, joined the company; he was joined by his younger brothers Nicolaas and Willem in 1914 and 1915. After a brief period of financial difficulty, Samson's sons took over the company and expanded its operations.

Samson died in 1917. By then, the company had achieved a national reputation; it also maintained strong ties with the government. The company added educational materials and related forms and services to its list in 1920. Samson continued to prosper, yet always remained close to its core business. In 1970 Samson merged with the publisher A.W. Sijthoff, forming the Information and Communication Union (ICU), which merged with Wolters-Noordhoff two years later. The new company adopted the ICU name but in 1983 changed its name again, to Wolters-Samson.

The final branch of Wolters-Kluwer was founded in the 1880s in Deventer, in the eastern Netherlands, by Ebele E. Kluwer. Kluwer began as a bookseller. By 1891 he had published his first book, on arithmetic, called *The Thinker,* which was directed at the secondary school market. For many years, Kluwer concentrated on the educational and academic market, including children's books. In 1892 Kluwer published one of the first trade papers aimed at the educational market, called *De Sollicitant.* Several years later he initiated a successful series of picture books. Another of Kluwer's publications was *De Nederlandsche Jager,* a trade periodical for hunters. Within a decade, Kluwer expanded to include business information and technical works, and soon after into tax and professional publications as well. In 1909 Kluwer published *De Vakstudie* tax series, which provided purchasers with periodic supplements of updated information. By 1920 Kluwer was publishing similar works for other professional areas, by then in a more easily updated looseleaf binder form. These series were extremely profitable for the company, fueling its expansion and remaining one of its most important markets. Kluwer's sons, Evert, Nico, and Eben, joined the firm between 1914 and 1921, and his daughters and their husbands also became involved in the company. Kluwer died in 1929, leaving the company to his sons. Kluwer Publishers remained a family concern, growing to become the Netherlands' third largest publisher, with subsidiaries in the United States and elsewhere, with revenues of 966 million guilders, by 1986.

Consolidation in the 1980s

The Netherlands were largely untouched by the wave of hostile takeovers that marked the 1980s. That changed in 1987, when Elsevier, the country's largest publishing house, announced its intention to buy up Kluwer's stock. A year earlier, Elsevier had initiated talks with Kluwer to suggest a merger between the two companies. Kluwer rejected the plan, pointing to differences in corporate cultures. In June 1987, Elsevier announced a bid of 390 guilders per Kluwer share, which had been worth only 266 guilders per share two weeks before. Kluwer responded by issuing another 2.5 million common shares and beginning talks with Wolters Samson about a possible friendly merger between the two companies. Kluwer's preference for a merger with the smaller house of Wolters Samson was explained by the greater similarity between the two compa-

Key Dates:

1836: J.B. Wolters founds Schoolbook publishing house.

1858: P. Noordhoff establishes Noordhoff publishing house.

1886: Nicolaas Samson leaves civil service to run his eponymous publishing business on a full-time basis.

1891: Ebele E. Kluwer publishes his first textbook.

1968: Schoolbook (now known as J.B. Wolters Publishing Company) and Noordhoff merge.

1970: Samson publishing merges with A.W. Sijthoff to form the Information and Communications Union (ICU).

1972: Wolters-Noordhoff merges with ICU and takes its name.

1983: ICU changes its name to Wolters-Samson.

1987: Kluwer merges with Wolters-Samson to fend off hostile takeover bid by Elsevier; the new entity is called Wolters Kluwer.

1990: Company purchases J.B. Lippincott and Company from HarperCollins.

1996: Wolters Kluwer spends $1.9 billion for tax and business materials publisher CCH, Inc.

nies' corporate cultures, and in the similarity in their publishing focus. Shortly thereafter, Kluwer issued an additional two million shares of preferential stock to Wolters Samson, vowing to do whatever necessary to stop Elsevier's takeover bid. By August 3rd, however, Elsevier had won control of 48.2 percent of Kluwer's stock, spending 25 million guilders in the final days to acquire it. However, by August 14, Wolters Samson was able to announce that it had acquired 50.9 percent of Kluwer's outstanding common stock, effecting the merger of their two companies. The new company, called Wolters Kluwer NV, moved its headquarters to Amsterdam. In the final count, Elsevier retained approximately 33 percent of the new company's shares; in 1990 it announced its intention to sell these shares, surrendering, for the time being, the idea of a merger between the two companies. Analysts, however, continued to predict that the firms would eventually join forces.

Growth of a Giant

With the merger, Wolters Kluwer became the Netherlands' second largest publisher. With international holdings including the U.S. subsidiaries Kluwer Law Book Publishing Company, Raven Press, Aspen Systems, and others, Wolters Kluwer entered a period of foreign acquisitions. Over the next two years the company extended into France, West Germany, and Spain. By 1989, roughly 44 percent of its revenues were earned in foreign markets. The pending formation of the European market opened a lucrative arena for the company's well-developed tax and legal publishing arms. The company increased its focus on these areas, dropping several of its Dutch trade and consumer publishers, including Bert Bakker and Martinus Nijhoff International. Its acquisitions continued, with purchases of the IPSOA Editore of Italy, Kieser Verlag of Germany, Tecnipublicaciones of Spain, and Tele Consulte of France. In 1990 the company moved to strengthen its share of the U.S. medical market,

completing the US$250 million purchase of the 200-year-old J.B. Lippincott and Company from HarperCollins. By that year, Wolters Kluwer included nearly 100 companies, posting annual revenues of more than two billion guilders.

Lippincott had been founded in 1836, when Joshua B. Lippincott opened J.B. Lippincott & Co. in Philadelphia; Lippincott's 1849 purchase of Grigg, Elliot & Co., then the world's largest book distributor, allowed him to extend his company's anniversary to the other company's 1792 founding date. The company grew quickly, with medical publications featuring prominently among its titles. After overseeing the incorporation of his company in 1885, Lippincott died the following year, leaving the firm to his three sons. By the end of the century, Lippincott was one of the three largest U.S. publishers. In addition to its medical list, it published for the educational market; however, it was best known for its trade books, which accounted for approximately 50 percent of its business. In the 1950s, however, the company reasserted its interest in other markets, particularly in medical and nursing books and journals. It also expanded its educational and college offerings, placing less and less emphasis on trade books. A major event occurred in 1972, when, finding itself undercapitalized, the company was forced to go public, with the Lippincott family retaining majority ownership. The new corporation launched a period of aggressive expansion, entering new markets and extending its established divisions. By 1977, however, rising costs and other factors had increased the company's debt-to-equity ratio to two to one. The following year, Lippincott was purchased by Harper & Row. Lippincott's activities were pared down to a core focused around medical and nursing books and journals. This formula proved successful; by the time Lippincott was purchased by Wolters Kluwer, its revenues had risen by 500 percent.

The opening of European borders in 1992 meant increasing numbers of new laws and regulations that would need to be translated into many languages. Wolters Kluwer stepped up the internationalization of its activities, concentrating on the most highly developed countries of the European Union. By 1993 its international sales represented 62 percent of its yearly revenues. Its European sales outside of the Netherlands accounted for 45 percent of its total revenues, the United States for 11 percent, and the Netherlands for 37 percent. Wolters Kluwer continued acquiring companies, including Liber in Sweden in 1993. The company established its first Eastern European subsidiary, IURA Edition, in Bratislava, Slovakia, and announced intentions for further Eastern European expansion. Electronic media, including computer diskettes, CD-ROMs, and CD-I technology, had become another growing area for Wolters Kluwer, accounting for six percent of its sales in 1994.

Continued Expansion to Close Out the 20th Century

The year 1995 proved to be another busy one for the company, as it acquired a slew of businesses, including Jugend & Volk (Austria); Dalian (France); Fateco Fîrlag and Juristfîrlaget (Sweden); Deutscher Kommunal-Verlag Dr. Naujoks & Behrendt (Germany); and Colex Data (Spain). The same year, Lippincott and Raven Press, a medical publisher, were merged to form Lippincott-Raven Publishers. By now, the firm operated in 16 countries and had over 8,000 employees. Yet it was still not done growing. In 1996, Wolters Kluwer completed a significant purchase when it spent US$1.9 billion to take over a prominent U.S. publisher of tax and business materials, CCH, Inc. This acquisition greatly strengthened Wolters Kluwer's position in that segment of the U.S. publishing market. To build on this achievement, the company bought several other businesses over the next few years (including Bankers Systems, Inc. and two divisions of the West Group's Information America unit) and rolled them into CCH's operations. This division also came to play a prominent role in Wolters Kluwer's operations in Asia, as CCH arms did business in Australia, New Zealand, Japan, Singapore, and Hong Kong.

The company enjoyed continued success in 1997. Total sales and net income both rose 21 percent over 1996 levels, thanks mainly to strategic acquisitions. Wolters Kluwer's operations in Germany, France, the United Kingdom, and the United States were particularly profitable. Despite these gains, speculation remained rife that Wolters Kluwer would be taken over by Elsevier (now Reed Elsevier, after the latter's merger with another publishing powerhouse, Reed International, PLC). These predictions were nearly borne out when the firms announced a proposed merger in October 1997. The deal fell through in March 1998, however, when Wolters Kluwer decided that the divestments that would be required to secure regulatory approval for the transaction were too high a price to pay.

In the wake of this incident, Wolters Kluwer convened a working group of managers from its operations around the world to devise a plan for the next phase of the company's growth and development. The resulting ''Strategic Agenda 2002'' led the company to decide to refocus its business on several core competencies. Specifically, Wolters Kluwer opted to concentrate on its operations in the legal and tax publishing, business publishing, medical/scientific publishing, and educational publishing/professional training realms. To achieve this goal, the company continued to acquire firms that could bolster its efforts in these areas, and to divest itself of holdings that fell outside them. For example, in August 1999, Wolters Kluwer sold its Wayland Publishers unit, because that division published children's books—a field in which the company no longer wished to compete. On the other hand, the company made three acquisitions in 1998 that dramatically heightened its profile in the medical/scientific publishing industry, bringing Waverly, Inc., Ovid Technologies, Inc., and Plenum Publishing Corporation into its fold.

''Strategic Agenda 2002'' also identified the growing importance that electronic and online media would have in the publishing world. Wolters Kluwer was acutely aware of the risk that its traditional paper offering could be rendered obsolete if it failed to stay abreast of the technological developments cascading through the industry. As a result, the company rededicated itself to integrating new media into its traditional methods of presentation (electronic publishing had provided nearly 19 percent of the firm's revenues as far back as 1996, a figure the company expected to grow significantly in subsequent years). To this end, the company's Kluwers Academic Publishers division joined a 12-firm consortium in November 1999 that was striving to revamp the way scientists use the Internet to conduct research. The aim of this partnership was to bridge gaps between otherwise independent and disconnected databases (the databases' proprietary owners remained free to set the terms of access, however). Moreover, Wolters Kluwer stepped up its efforts to provide high-level customer service and to develop innovative hardware and software in order to expand the range of options its customers had at their disposal to access the breadth of the company's information sources. With its newly streamlined organization and a clear view of both the challenges and opportunities before it, Wolters Kluwer appeared poised to flourish in the 21st century.

Principal Subsidiaries

CCH, Inc.; Aspen Publishers; Ovid Technologies, Inc.; Kluwer Academic Publishers; Lippincott-Raven Publishers; Stanley Thornes.

Principal Competitors

Reed Elsevier; Thomson Corporation; VNU N.V.

Further Reading

de Vries, Johan, *Four Windows of Opportunity: A Study in Publishing,* Amsterdam: Wolters Kluwer, 1995.

duBois, Martin, ''Reed Elsevier and Wolters Kluwer End Merger Plans After Concerns at EU,'' *Wall Street Journal,* March 10, 1998.

Feldman, Gayle, ''Going Dutch,'' *Publishers Weekly,* June 21, 1991.

Hagerty, Bob, ''Esoteric Publisher Avoids the Obvious,'' *Wall Street Journal (Europe),* April 25, 1990.

''John Wiley and Sons: Reference Linking Service Announces Name,'' *M2 Presswire,* December 10, 1999.

Milliot, Jim, ''Wolters Kluwer to Buy Waverly,'' *Publishers Weekly,* February 16, 1998.

Scott, Robert W., ''With $1.9 Billion Sale, CCH Gains Dutch Uncle,'' *Accounting Today,* December 11, 1995.

''Wolters Kluwer Bolsters Healthcare Unit with $200 Million Ovid Buy,'' *Electronic Information Report,* October 16, 1998.

—M.L. Cohen
—updated by Rebecca Stanfel

World Bank Group

1818 H Street, North West
Washington, District of Columbia 20433
U.S.A.
Telephone: (202) 477-1234
Fax: (202) 477-6391
Web Site: http://www.worldbank.org

Private Institution
Incorporated: 1946 as the International Bank for
    Reconstruction and Development
Employees: 9,000
Total Assets: $23 billion (1999)
NAIC: 522293 International Trade Financing; 52211
    Commercial Banking

The World Bank Group, created towards the end of World War II, provides loans, soft loans, and guarantees for development projects around the world. A multilateral institution, it calls five billion people its clients; most of them live on less than two dollars a day. Its mix of financial support and advice is credited, for example, with saving India's agriculture system after World War II. The World Bank derives its support from 180 member nations and pitches bond offerings to the world's capital markets. Critics question the necessity of its leagues of highly-paid advisers and the social and environmental responsibility of some of its development projects. At the beginning of the millennium, the group was concentrating on harmonizing its private and public sector efforts into comprehensive "Country Assistance Strategies."

World War II Origins

The International Bank for Reconstruction and Development was the first "Multilateral Development Bank." Before World War II had ended, Harry Dexter White, assistant secretary of the U.S. Treasury, and the eminent British economist John Maynard Keynes had been among those conceptualizing an international institution to stabilize exchange rates and provide a source of financing for reconstruction and development among countries ravaged by the war.

Forty-four countries sent representatives to Bretton Woods, New Hampshire, to discuss the bank in July 1944. The bank's sister institution, the International Monetary Fund (IMF) was also created at Bretton Woods. The new bank received most of its funds from the New York investment community. However, at United States insistence, the bank was headquartered in Washington, D.C. The United States also insisted that executive directors have full-time, competitively salaried positions. The United States dominated the multilateral institution from the beginning: it provided one-third of the start-up capital.

Thirty-eight countries were members of the bank, which had an initial staff of 72. The U.S. government picked Eugene Meyer, a 70-year-old retired investment banker, to lead the new institution, which officially opened on June 25, 1946. Meyer had previously been involved in European famine relief and had extensive government experience. However, he resigned six months later after a dispute with U.S. executive director Emilio Collada, who was pressing for a stronger board. New York lawyer John J. McCloy succeeded Meyer as president. He emasculated the board and staffed management with New York cronies, like Chase Bank's Eugene Black, who replaced Collada.

The bank made its first, general reconstruction loans to France, the Netherlands, Denmark, and Luxembourg in 1947. The French loan of $250 million was the largest it would ever make, in real terms. As the U.S. government shouldered more of the burden for reconstruction under the Marshall Plan, launched in June 1947, the IBRD looked towards lending development funds to Third World countries. Physical infrastructure accounted for most of its lending in this area. The IRBD's bond issues began showing consistent profits in 1948, earning the bank an outstanding credit rating. That year also marked the first loan to a developing country—$13.5 million for a hydroelectric project in Chile.

When McCloy left the bank after two years to accept an ambassador's post in Germany, Black was named president. Robert Garner, whom McCloy had recruited from General Foods, remained vice-president. Under Black, the bank specialized in more focused project lending. It was then lending about $400 million a year.

The bank's first bond offering abroad, worth £5 million, came in London in 1951. That year, the bank negotiated with the British and Iranian governments over oil issues. Later, it helped resolve the Indus water dispute between India and Pakistan. It also unsuccessfully attempted to secure Western funding for the Aswan Dam project in Egypt. This type of involvement led to the creation of the International Center for the Settlement of International Disputes (ICSID) in 1966.

The bank was reorganized on geographical lines in 1952. Three years later, it founded the Economic Development Institute, a staff college. By this time the bank had 500 employees.

Although the IBRD's managers sought to promote private enterprise, they needed to obtain government guarantees of any loans they made to the private sector. The International Finance Corporation (IFC) was created in 1956 specifically to make private sector loans. Robert Garner served as its first president.

Soft Loans in the 1960s

The "World Bank Group" first came into being in the 1960s. Although the success of the IBRD allowed it to more than double its authorized capital to $25 billion in 1959, its services were out of reach of the many developing nations unable to pay commercial rates. The International Development Association (IDA) was established in 1960 specifically to handle assistance to such high-risk borrowers. This program of concessional lending had been brewing for several years before Senator Mike Monroney was able to sell the Eisenhower administration on it. It gave its first credit to Honduras for highway construction. (The IDA's funds are periodically replenished by more than 30 of the richest nations and by World Bank profits.)

George Woods, another New York banker, became president in January 1963. His prime interest was macroeconomics, and he favored intervention in the politics of recipient nations. However, agricultural (land ownership) reform was a touchy subject among such newly-established governments, and remained a stumbling block in efforts to reduce poverty in the mostly rural Third World. Under Woods, the IFC became responsible for industrial loans. He also led the IFC to cooperate with United Nations agricultural and educational agencies as never before.

Robert McNamara—the former auto executive who had helped shaped U.S. policy during the Vietnam War—took over the IBRD presidency on April 1, 1968. He greatly increased the rate of the bank's lending and focused efforts on finding ways to help owners of small farms become more productive; such agricultural improvements proved more successful in Asia than in Africa. McNamara also boosted the bank's search for capital beyond the U.S. market and increased support for research activities. An early 1970s reorganization was also on McNamara's agenda.

Oil Crises in the 1970s

With the Yom Kippur War and the corresponding quadrupling of oil prices by the Organization of Petroleum Exporting Countries (OPEC), 1973 was a year that shaped economic policies around the world. OPEC nations, newly flush with cash, set up their own sources of development financing. Further, the World Bank felt impelled to take measures to offset higher fuel prices in oil-importing developing countries while the Ford administration capped its loans at $5.8 billion.

Population control and pollution control were two new areas of funding in the early 1970s. In the last half of the decade, the bank became more involved in urban development. It also softened its reluctance to deal with government-owned businesses, instead evaluating the independence of management as a criterion for investment.

However, by this time, the People's Republic of China had become involved in World Bank programs. The bank's low-key approach produced much success in that country, which used IDA loans for agriculture and education projects while oil wells were financed with IBRD loans. Nations eligible for IDA loans were those with per capita incomes of less than $750 per year (the majority of this population was concentrated in China and India). Agricultural loans, called "the key to improving the living standards of the bulk of the poor," accounted for a third of IBRD/IDA loans. Unfortunately, inflation reduced the real value of IDA loans by nearly 25 percent in 1977.

After another round of oil price increases, interest rates rose dramatically at the end of 1979, trapping the bank in fixed rates set when credit was relatively inexpensive. The bank moved to issue loans with floating interest rates in 1982. Otherwise, its terms remained inflexible, fortified with cross-default clauses. The bank began to press for more reforms among borrowing nations through structural adjustment loans (SALs), mostly in Africa and Latin America.

Debt Crisis in the 1980s

The Reagan years were ones of heavy defense buildup and deficit spending. Commercial banker A.W. Clausen succeeded McNamara upon his retirement in 1981. He was soon confronted with the Latin American debt crisis. A few years later, former U.S. Senator Barber Conable became the first professional politician to lead the World Bank in 1986. One of his first tasks was to trim the budget and streamline the staff somewhat. However, managers were then freed to hire their subordinates right back. Some 300 workers received "golden handshakes" in an exercise that cost the bank $200 million. In spite of the uncertainty these measures produced, Conable won the support of both employees and shareholders: in 1988, the IBRD landed its largest ever general capital increase (GCI) from the U.S. government.

Conable attempted to shift the bank's focus from infrastructure to business ventures. One area of concern was the relatively low levels of private sector investment of IFC-financed projects. China increased pressure on foreign investors in the mid-1980s and Yugoslavia, the IFC's largest borrower, saw its private sector production collapse. The *Wall Street Journal* reported that many borrowers that the IFC had reported as privately-owned in fact had substantial government ownership.

Poverty per se again became a leading part of the bank's agenda, as defined by such measurements as daily caloric intake. Broadly-defined environmental concerns also became increasingly important as the bank struggled to harmonize its efforts with nongovernmental organizations (NGOs). However these were difficult to square with development enterprises such as those in Thailand that critics alleged produced deforestation.

The Multinational Investment Guarantee Agency (MIGA) was established in 1988 to encourage private investment in the Third World by attenuating some of the risks of operating in politically and economically unstable environments. Although its charter stated it should be "apolitical," by this time the question of "governance" issues dominated World Bank thinking about lending in Africa, and work in China was suspended

following the Tiananmen Square massacre. The IBRD made nominally its largest ever loan to Mexico in 1990: $1.26 billion to support debt reduction. The debt crisis had finally subsided by this time, helped in part by falling interest rates.

Competing in the 1990s

Conable stepped down in 1991. His successor, Lewis Preston, was an eminent commercial banker. Upon taking over, Preston set up a management structure similar to the one at J.P. Morgan. By this time, the bank had begun lending to newly-liberated Eastern Europe and Russia itself.

As the bank approached its golden anniversary, a new headquarters was under construction. Meanwhile, pundits rallied under the slogan "Fifty years is enough." The Wapenhans Report in 1992 criticized the bank's bias towards project lending, while two years later a team of outside observers criticized one of the bank's dam projects on India's Narmada River. Many believed the World Bank was simply too rich and too bloated. It employed 6,000 high-paid staff (at $150,000 a head, according to *The Economist*) and 1,000 consultants, only a fraction of them based inside poor countries. By 1995, the World Bank had more than 9,000 employees and a $1 billion payroll. While administrative expenses grew 60 percent in the mid-1990s, loan disbursements were flat.

The United States considered changing the articles of the IBRD to allow it to lend directly to the private sector to help the group as a whole meet a target of making half its loans in the private sector, which was becoming more important in the post-Communist world. However, many at the World Bank were uneasy about making the institution's top credit rating susceptible to the additional commercial risks of lending to private enterprises. The IFC, led by Sir William Ryrie, was then calling for an additional $1.3 billion in capital to maintain its annual growth rate.

South Korea became the first country to progress from IDA borrowing all the way to becoming a donor. Emerging markets as a whole were attracting unprecedented amounts of private capital, $244 billion in 1996 versus 1990's $44 billion. This entrepreneurial interest in development provided some competition to the World Bank itself, which saw its market share fall from 50 percent to ten percent in just a few years.

The U.S. Congress resisted the IDA's requests for capital replenishment. Other rich countries followed suit, claiming hard times of their own. The political risk insurance of MIGA proved very popular, and that agency also strained for additional capital to meet demand. The IFC, however, saw its total financing nearly double to $8 billion between 1994 and 1996. It had a harder time obtaining sovereign guarantees on infrastructure projects as local governments were taking over more of them.

Savvy Australian-born investment banker James D. Wolfensohn became the bank's president in June 1995. He inherited a slew of challenges. At least one former World Bank executive criticized the institution for diluting its strengths in infrastructure development in favor of "boutique" investments. By the late 1990s, the emerging markets investment bonanza was over, making private capital prohibitively expensive again for World Bank clientele.

Principal Operating Units

International Bank for Reconstruction and Development; International Development Association; International Finance Corporation; Multilateral Investment Guarantee Agency; International Centre for Settlement of Investment Disputes.

Principal Competitors

European Bank for Reconstruction and Development; J.P. Morgan & Co.; Salomon Brothers International; CS First Boston; Emerging Markets Partnerships; Darby Overseas Investments.

Further Reading

Adkisson, Richard V., Review of *Bankers with a Mission: The Presidents of the World Bank, 1946–91,* by Jochen Kraske, William H. Becker, William Diamond, and Louis Galambos, *Journal of Economic Issues,* March 1998, pp. 256–57.

Bovard, James, "World Bank Unit's Lip Service to Private Sector," *Wall Street Journal,* June 21, 1988, p. 1.

Bray, Nicholas, "World Bank Arm's New General Seeks to Deploy All Assets—Peter Woicke Will Leverage Expertise, Prestige, Funds of International Finance," *Wall Street Journal,* October 12, 1998, p. 16A.

Crane, David, "New World Bank Head Not an Ordinary Banker," *Toronto Star,* October 12, 1995, p. 2D.

Fidler, Stephen, "U.S. Seeks to Raise World Bank's Private Profile," *Financial Times,* May 1, 1991.

Fitzgerald, Peter F., "Money for Power," *China Business Review,* November/December 1993, p. 30.

Gopinath, Deepak, "Identity Crisis," *Infrastructure Finance,* September 1997, pp. 27–34.

Harris, Anthony, "World Bank Strives for Agility in the Markets," *Financial Times,* April 14, 1988.

"A Job for Atlas and Hercules Combined," *The Economist,* March 30, 1991, p. 71.

Kapur, Devesh, John P. Lewis, and Richard Webb, eds., *The World Bank: Its First Half Century,* 2 vols., Washington, D.C.: Brookings Institution, 1997.

Keefe, Victoria M., "The World Bank Group as Private-Sector Catalyst," *Journal of Project Finance,* Winter 1996, pp. 46–52.

Kraske, Jochen, et al., *Bankers with a Mission: The Presidents of the World Bank, 1946–1991,* Oxford: Oxford University Press, World Bank, 1996.

Lawrence, Richard, "World Bank Eases Access for Business," *Journal of Commerce,* August 14, 1996, p. 1A.

Mendelsohn, M.S., "Changes at the World Bank," *Banker,* August 1982, p. 35ff.

——, "IDA: Gift-Giver of the World Bank; Cut in U.S. Aid to Soft-Loan Affiliate Could Hurt Poor Nations," *American Banker,* September 28, 1983, p. 1.

Millner-Adams, Michelle, *The World Bank: New Agendas in a Changing World,* London and New York: Routledge, 1999.

Murphy, Craig N., Review of *The World Bank Group: A Guide to Information Sources,* by Carol R. Wilson, *Business History Review,* Winter 1992, p. 827.

Owen, Henry, "The World Bank: Is Fifty Years Enough?" *Foreign Affairs,* September/October 1994, p. 97.

Rowen, Hobart, "World Bank to Widen Role—With Blessings from Carter," *Washington Post,* September 19, 1977, p. 14D.

Rowley, Anthony, "Urgently Needed: New Financial Architecture," *Banker,* October 1998, pp. 28–30.

Sankaran, Sundaram, "The Humane Conversion of Barber Conable," *Asian Finance,* September 15, 1991, p. 56.

"U.S. versus the World Bank," *Financial Times,* May 13, 1991.

Wolfensohn, James D., "We Must Have Sustainable Prosperity: The Challenge of Inclusion," *Vital Speeches of the Day,* October 15, 1997, pp. 5–9.

"World Bank—Footing the Progress Bill," *Far Eastern Economic Review,* September 24, 1992, p. 50.

"World Bank Group at Bay," *Financial Times,* September 26, 1994, p. 19.

The World Bank: Knowledge and Resources for Development, Washington, D.C.: The World Bank, September 1999.

Wuliger, Robert, "A World Economy: Paradigms Lost and Found," *Challenge,* January/February 1992, p. 4.

—Frederick C. Ingram

Wynn's International, Inc.

500 North State College Boulevard, Suite 700
Orange, California 92868
U.S.A.
Telephone: (714) 938-3700
Fax: (714) 938-3739

Public Company
Incorporated: 1947
Employees: 2,121
Sales: $360.3 million (1999)
Stock Exchanges: New York
Ticker Symbol: WN
NAIC: 324191 Petroleum Lubricating Oil and Grease
    Manufacturing; 325612 Automobile Polishes and
    Cleaners Manufacturing; 326291 Rubber Product
    Manufacturing for Mechanical Use; 339991 Gasket,
    Packing, and Sealing Device Manufacturing; 422690
    Other Chemical and Allied Products Wholesalers

Wynn's International, Inc. manufactures a variety of petro-chemical, rubber, and plastic products for the consumer and industrial markets through three primary subsidiaries. Wynn Oil Company produces and sells chemicals and equipment for automotive repairs to do-it-yourself and professional markets worldwide. This subsidiary also produces industrial lubricants, solvents, coolants, and greases for manufacturing, farming, mining, and aerospace uses. With divisions in more than 14 countries, Wynn Oil products are marketed in more than 100 countries through independent distributors and sales representatives. Wynn's-Precision produces injection and composite molded O-rings, composite gaskets and seals, and several other plastic and rubber products for automotive, aerospace, and industrial manufacturing. The company also provides custom engineered seals and O-rings and is a leader in the industry for engineering these products for transportation fuel systems. Finally, Wynn's Robert Skeels & Company subsidiary provides builders' hardware and locksmith supplies to retail outlets, industrial plants, hospitals, hotels, and government agencies in California, Arizona, and Nevada.

From Garage-Based Production to International Conglomeration

Wynn's International began in Chestein Wynn's dilapidated one-car garage in San Gabriel, California, where the 70-year-old retired attorney concocted a product to reduce engine wear by reducing friction. In 1939 Wynn started giving bottles of his "friction proofing" oil to friends and, eventually, began to distribute his product to local gas service stations. Resource shortages during World War II prevented Wynn from producing and marketing his invention, but he continued to research and improve on the formula. In 1945 production resumed in Wynn's garage; with his son Carl, Wynn incorporated the company as Wynn Oil Company in 1947.

Wynn's Friction Proofing Oil gained acceptance and acclaim through Carl Wynn's penchant for sensational demonstrations of the product's value. In one instance he submerged two outboard motors in the ocean harbor at San Pedro for 14 days. The motor treated with Wynn's Friction Proofing oil, undamaged by salt water, started immediately in front of an audience of stunned engineers. In another display Carl Wynn lubricated an airplane engine with the product and then flew the plane for seven minutes without oil in the crankcase. In 1950 Johnny Parsons won the Indianapolis 500 automobile race in the "Friction Proofing Special" race car. Carl Wynn succeeded his father as president of Wynn Oil in 1950.

With sales at $1 million in 1950, Wynn's was prepared to expand. The company had opened a production facility in Azusa, California, after the garage burned down in 1948, and three years later Wynn's initiated international distribution. Foreign manufacturing at St. Niklas, Belgium, near Antwerp, was established in 1958. The company also became more serious about testing its product. In a 1954 50,000-mile test supervised by independent consultants, the car with Wynn's Friction Proofing oil attained a ten percent increase in gas mileage, 44 percent less bearing damage, and 21 percent less starting friction. To enhance research and development of new products, the company opened Wynn's Research Center at its plant in Azusa in 1962.

Under the leadership of Wesley E. Bellwood as president in 1965, and with Carl Wynn as chairman, Wynn's expanded and

Key Dates:

1939: Wynn distributes "friction proofing" oil from his garage.
1948: Production facility opens.
1951: International distribution begins.
1969: Initial public offering of stock.
1977: Company achieves $100 million in sales.
1985: Acquisition of Precision Rubber Products, Inc.
1991: Introduction of Wynn's Emission Control fuel additive.
1999: 95th consecutive cash dividend in last quarter.

diversified. The company acquired Robert Skeels & Company, a lock and locksmith supply company in southern California. Although hardware supply never became central to company activities, Roberts Skeels proved a steady profit-maker.

In 1969 an initial public offering of 305,000 shares of stock at $17.50 per share provided capital for further expansion. The company constructed an office building and improved production at the Azusa plant, while a new 42,000-square-foot plant in Cincinnati initiated production of automotive and industrial petrochemicals. In 1971 Wynn's expanded its plant in Belgium.

Wynn's strategy of diversification involved the acquisition of innovative companies with national brand identity. In March 1971 the company acquired two subsidiaries of Roy Richter Industries: Cragar Industries, Inc. and Bell Helmets, Inc. Cragar designed, produced, and marketed specialty and high-performance wheels and automotive accessories, while Bell Helmets produced safety helmets and other motorsport accessories. Wynn's also acquired Peat Manufacturing Company, a die-casting company that supported operations at Cragar. These companies did well in the Wynn's fold in the 1970s. Sales at Cragar almost tripled with its top-selling "mag" wheel styles. In 1973 Wynn's reincorporated and adopted a new name that better reflected its diversified and overseas business activities. Wynn's International, Inc. became the holding company for Wynn Oil Company and the other subsidiaries.

Diversification and New Products in the 1970s–80s

Several acquisitions furthered diversification of reincorporation. Wynn's purchased Dualmatic Manufacturing, manufacturer of four-wheel drive accessories in Longmont, Colorado. Dualmatic made its mark with a locking wheel hub that allowed the driver of a four-wheel drive vehicle to disengage the front wheel drive for reduced wear and better gas mileage on the highway. In 1975 Wynn's purchased sporting goods manufacturer Riddell Inc. of Des Plaines, Iowa. The 1978 acquisition of Lone Star Manufacturing, which operated under the newly formed Wynn's Climate Systems, took Wynn's into the business of producing air conditioning units for the automotive aftermarket, primarily for dealer installation and Japanese imports. Lone Star had grown substantially since 1971 and survived the economic recession in Detroit by selling to Japanese automakers. In 1981 Lone Star obtained a $2.5 million contract to produce 105,000 air conditioner units for Toyo Kogyo Com-

pany, manufacturer of the Mazda brand of automobiles. The U.S. government had been encouraging Japanese companies to purchase more automotive parts in the United States to alleviate conflict over the trade imbalance.

As annual sales surpassed $100 million in 1977, Wynn's found opportunity in the energy crisis of the late 1970s. Two products introduced at this time enhanced fuel efficiency. A fuel system cleaner added to the gas tank, named "1 in 10," saved as much as a gallon of gas for every ten gallons used. A similar product, Wynn's X-tend Engine Treatment, saved up to one gallon of gas for every eight gallons when added to the oil crankcase. Both products attracted an international customer base. With more than 20 chemists at its research facilities in Azusa, Paris, and St. Niklas, the company expected to meet demand for similar products. Bell Helmets also benefited from the oil shortage, as increased motorcycle and bicycle transportation resulted in increased helmet sales in 1979; sales of motorcycle helmets increased 38 percent.

Industrial products introduced by Wynn Oil at this time included the first aluminum forging compound designed to meet new Environmental Protection Agency (EPA) standards for lead-free petrochemical products. With growing worldwide concerns about reducing pollution, the product was on backorder internationally as soon as it became available. Another new product, a mold releasing agent for the production of glass bottles, eased release of the glass containers from the mold in which they were shaped.

A steady increase in sales and profits in the late 1970s allowed Wynn's to boost its production capacity. In addition to a manufacturing and warehousing facility in Johannesburg, South Africa, a 113,000-square-foot facility in Azusa, built in 1979, expanded production of automotive and industrial petrochemicals. A new facility for the production of polymer, the essential ingredient in oil additives, went on line in October 1981. Two more plants, including one overseas, followed over the next two years, supporting the introduction of six new car care products by the Petrochemical Specialty Division in 1982.

Wynn's divested some operations in a restructuring program to seek opportunities with growth potential and high profit margins. Although Riddell produced a profitable line of football helmets, with a high profit margin, Wynn's sustained some losses with the discontinuation of the company's shoe line and sold the company in 1980. The company disposed of Cragar Industries and Peat Manufacturing two years later. Wynn's acquired Bestop Manufacturing in Boulder, Colorado, manufacturer of convertible tops for jeeps and cars, and merged it with Dualmatic, forming Wynn's Automotive Products, Inc. in 1982. In 1984 the company purchased Starlite Industries, Inc., a manufacturer of automotive seat covers, seat cushions, floor mats, car covers, and other automotive accessories with facilities in Los Angeles and in Fremont, Ohio. Wynn's eventually consolidated the sales, manufacturing, warehousing, and financial administration of the company into its Automotive Products.

A joint venture with Diesel Kiki of Tokyo, named Wynn-Kiki, manufactured heat exchangers for air conditioners for new car production as well as for the automotive aftermarket. Wynn's contributed Lone Star's Texas facilities to the venture.

Customers included Chrysler (Lone Star's largest), American Motors, Nissan, Honda, and others. Chrysler changed contractors, however, obtaining its air conditioners through its new partner Mitsubishi.

In 1985 the company acquired Fluid Recycling Services, which produced coolant and oil recycling equipment designed to save manufacturers the costs of hazardous waste disposal. Wynn soon found, however, that the company had inherited the cash flow problem that the previous owners had sold the company to resolve and began to liquidate assets. The subsidiary's president had ideas on how to operate the company and purchased Fluid Recycling Services from Wynn's in 1990.

Wynn's completed the acquisition of Precision Rubber Products Corporation of Lebanon, Tennessee, in November 1985. Renamed Wynn's-Precision, the company produced O-rings, seals, and other molded rubber products for the automotive, aerospace, and hydraulic industries, including such clients as General Motors, Ford, Chrysler, and Cummins Engine Company. Wynn's-Precision provided development, engineering, durability testing, and manufacturing for the special needs of its clients. The company and its three subsidiaries maintained eight factories, including one in Canada, as well as a Service Center network for regional warehousing and customer support.

Fluctuating Fortunes in the Late 1980s and Early 1990s

In 1988 James Carroll, president of Wynn's-Precision, succeeded John Lillicrop as president and CEO of Wynn's International. The appointment followed a struggle between Lillicrop and Carroll to gain control of the company, then for sale, and take it private. Stock value reached $30 per share until the October 1987 stock market crash. When the board announced a halt on the move to sell the following January, Wynn's stock dipped to below $20 a share, but rebounded to around $26 a year later. With three companies holding a large percentage of shares, Wynn's adopted a shareholder rights plan to deter a hostile takeover.

In 1991 Wynn Oil patented a fuel additive designed to lower particulate exhaust emissions and improve fuel efficiency. The peroxide-based formula provided the ancillary benefit of a better combustion performance, which improved gas mileage and horsepower. Two years of field research on Wynn's Emission Control included two major truck fleets and a transit system. Swift Transportation Company of Phoenix tested the product over five months and 3.3 million miles. The research team of four Swift employees and three Wynn's employees found that fuel economy improved 6.99 percent on 107 diesel trucks and emission reduction reached 40 percent. To control the results the team used a placebo additive on 19 trucks and the drivers did not know if their truck had Wynn's fuel additive or the placebo. Swift expected to save $1 million year with use of the product. California Milk Producers of Artesia, California tested Wynn's Emission Control on its 67-truck fleet with similar results and expected to save $100,000 a year. The City of Phoenix Transit System used the additive in high-performance Jet A fuel and gained a 5.8 percent improvement in fuel efficiency, as well as substantially reduced particulate emissions, tested at different operating velocities.

After earlier efforts fell short of expectations, Wynn's Climate Systems (WCS) perfected its automotive antifreeze/coolant recycling system. Introduced in 1990, the system removed and recycled air conditioner refrigerant in accordance with the Clean Air Act, which restricted venting CFC-containing air conditioner refrigerant. In 1992 Wynn's received a landmark endorsement by General Motors (GM) for its new X-Tend Antifreeze Recycling System for individual cars, a self-contained, drain and refill, chemical and filtration recycling process. As automotive repair professionals found the system to be effective and easy to use, GM gave its approval for use of the environmentally responsible process on all GM vehicles. The new Du-All Power Drain and Fill Bulk Recycler allowed for recycling a quantity of the fluid at a later time. Wynn Oil developed the accompanying chemical product, Mark X Power Flush. Similar applications for other car systems, such as the fuel system, followed.

Wynn's experienced several financial fluctuations in the late 1980s and early 1990s. The acquisition of Precision Rubber helped Wynn's rebound from a $1.9 million loss in 1985, adding $53 million in sales in 1986. Including the sale of Wynn's Automotive Products for $1.7 million, profit in 1986 reached $6.5 million. With two-thirds of the company's business in overseas markets, in more than 80 countries, a weaker U.S. dollar in foreign currency exchange improved Wynn's balance sheet in 1986, but by 1989 the reverse occurred. All of the company's divisions were hurt by a slow economy and slow car sales in 1989 and 1990, resulting in an overall decline of 3.9 percent in sales in 1990. Despite a loss of $11.2 million in 1991 due to a $14.9 million restructuring charge at WCS, the company still paid its 67th consecutive dividend since 1975 in the last quarter of 1991.

Wynn's took a number of profit-stimulating measures in all of its divisions. WCS continued to struggle, leading to plant closures and the layoff of more than half of the work force. New manufacturing equipment reduced production costs for WCS and Wynn Oil. Wynn Oil focused on strategic growth in international markets, particularly Japan, Canada, Australia, and New Zealand. The subsidiary expanded existing operations in France with two acquisitions in 1989 and 1990 and expanded into Germany and Mexico in late 1992. Wynn's also consolidated the marketing departments of the company's four divisions into one office. Wynn's-Precision increased revenues despite slow automotive production rates and planned to enter new markets with new product programs, new service centers, and development of the custom-engineered product program. By 1992 Wynn's returned to profitability with $7.2 million net income and experienced a 32 percent increase in profit to $11.8 million in 1994.

The fortunes of WCS continued to change. After WCS fulfilled a $1.5 million contract for Range Rover sport utility vehicles, the division benefited from conversion to the manufacture of air conditioner components that met new environmental standards. The retrofit kit featured new aluminum condensers that allowed air conditioners designed to run on Freon to operate on R-134a, a CFC-free refrigerant. Wynn's was the first to accommodate the EPA's ban on CFC-containing Freon, effective December 1995, but it provided WCS with a higher profit margin than its products had experienced in the past. The struggling division showed no sign of permanent improvement, however, as factory installed air conditioning became the norm and thus reduced aftermarket demand for air conditioners. In May 1996 Wynn's sold WCS to Moog Automotive for $25 million, thus eliminating the Automotive Parts Division.

Financially and organizationally Wynn's stability continued in the late 1990s. In December 1996, the board of directors elected James Carroll as chairman of Wynn's International, with John Huber as president and COO. After a three-for-two stock split in December 1995, and again in December 1996, the board initiated a tender offer stock repurchase of up to 1.1 million shares in early 1997. As revenue grew 13 percent each year from 1993 to 1997, and while net income continued to grow as well, the company paid its 95th consecutive quarterly dividend since 1975 for the last quarter of 1998. With no debt and a cash-on-hand at $40 million Wynn sought entry into the European market for seals through an acquisition or joint venture.

Focus on Wynn's-Precision in the Late 1990s

Although Wynn Oil had been eclipsed by STP in the fuel additives market, the company maintained its position as a major supplier of petrochemicals to the professional auto repair industry as well as to manufacturing industries. Wynn Oil continued to introduce new consumer products and supported them with new marketing programs. In 1998 Wynn's supplemented existing car repair warranty programs with the launch of the Extended Care Service Contract. The program offered a warranty protection for repairs to new and late model used vehicles, as well as towing, car rental, and toll free Roadside Assistance. Internationally, Wynn Oil faced economic instability in Asia, the Pacific Rim, and Brazil, as well as a decline of up to 25 percent of sales in Asia and Eastern Europe due to a strong U.S. dollar. France and Belgium continued to provide a solid base for expansion to Germany, Italy, and the United Kingdom, while consumer products continued to provide sound opportunities for growth in France, Spain, Canada, South Africa, and Australia, where awareness of the Wynn's brand remained strong.

Acquisition, reorganization, and expansion at Wynn's-Precision marked Wynn's approach to growth in the late 1990s. In October 1996 Wynn's-Precision purchased Lawson Mardon Wheaton, Inc., of Springfield, Kentucky, an automotive plastics company. Lawson was the major supplier of components, constant-velocity joints (CVJ), boots, and rack-and-pinion bellows to automakers. Wynn's-Precision consolidated all plastics manufacturing at the 90,000 square foot facility in Springfield.

In May 1997 the company made investments in major growth areas of Wynn's-Precision. Reorganization involved a $10 million investment to concentrate production of custom engineered seals, which experienced a 20 percent growth rate in 1996, in one of the Lebanon facilities. In Lynchburg, Virginia, Wynn's-Precision added one-third more floor space for the production of composite gaskets to accommodate a 20 percent growth rate for three years in a row. The purchase of a 26-acre site adjacent to the facility anticipated future growth.

By summer 1998 Wynn's-Precision required even further expansion. A new O-ring plant in Livingston, Tennessee, involved all new equipment for the manufacture of compression

and injection moldings of O-rings for transportation fuel systems. The Livingston facility accommodated new contracts for fuel injector seals and a $15 million contract for leakless transmission pan gaskets of rubber-on-plastic. To support the higher demand for rubber, Wynn's-Precision began construction on a new 30,000-square-foot rubber mixing facility to supplement an existing facility in Lebanon. At a cost of $8 million, the updated plant incorporated new computer-controlled equipment. Wynn's-Precision temporarily outsourced some of its contracts until the project was completed in spring 2000.

Wynn's-Precision expanded through the acquisition of Goshen Rubber Companies in October 1999. The transaction for $85 million included $45 million in cash and the balance in assumed debt. The Indiana-based manufacturer of O-rings, gaskets, and rubber seals antivibration mounts, grommets, tips, bumpers, and elastomeric balls generated $172 million in revenue in 1998. Goshen Rubber added 21 manufacturing plants and 2,200 employees to Wynn's-Precision's nine plants and 1,120 employees.

Principal Subsidiaries

Wynn Oil Company; Wynn's-Precision, Inc.; Robert Skeels & Company.

Principal Competitors

Burmah Castrol plc; Goodyear Tire & Rubber Company; U.S. Industries, Inc.

Further Reading

Begin, Sherri, ''Growth in the Mix: Wynn's Precision Launches Expansion,'' *Rubber & Plastics News,* August 30, 1999, p. 3.
——, ''Wynn's Seeks Acquisitions in Both U.S. and Overseas,'' *Rubber & Plastics News,* June 28, 1999, p. 3.
Berkman, Leslie, ''Wynn Oil Moves Quarters to Azusa,'' *Los Angeles Times,* April 24, 1990, p. D6.
Boyd, Justin, ''Auto Supplier Wynn's to Buy Goshen Rubber,'' *Plastics News,* November 8, 1999, p. 27.
''Car Parts Supplier Is Buoyed by Japan,'' *New York Times,* June 14, 1982, p. 1D.
Christian, Susan, ''Wynn's to Market Auto Air-Condition Converters,'' *Los Angeles Times,* May 21, 1993, p. 6D.
''Deal Valued at About $31 Million; Wynn's Completes Buy of Rubber Firm,'' *Los Angeles Times,* November 24, 1985, p. 7B.
''Fluid Recycling: Helping Industry Reuse Instead of Lose,'' *California Business,* May 1990, p. 107.
Gordon, Mitchell, ''Back in Gear: After an Earnings Stall in '80, Wynn's Again Picks Up Speed,'' *Barron's,* July 20, 1981, p. 36.
——, ''Cool Customers: They're Keeping, Wynn's a Maker of Air Conditioners,'' *Barron's,* January 28, 1985, p. 45.
——, ''Loading Up: New-Car Extras Spell Good News for Wynn's International,'' *Barron's,* January 23, 1984, p. 53.
Johnson, Ted, ''1992 a Winning Year for Wynn's International Inc.,'' *Los Angeles Times,* January 29, 1993, p. 5D.
Jones, John A., ''Wynn's International Recovers from a Bad Slump in 1991,'' *Investor's Business Daily,* July 20, 1992, p. 34.
——, ''Wynn's Set to Accelerate After Dropping Air Conditioners,'' *Investor's Business Daily,* July 15, 1996, p. 14B.
''Manufacturers: Wynn's Changes Senior Managers, Splits Stock,'' *Autoparts Report,* January 2, 1997.
Miller, Joe, ''Wynn's-Precision Invests in Seal, Gasket Plants,'' *Rubber & Plastics News II,* May 12, 1997, p. 1.

——, "Wynn's Seeks European Sites," *European Rubber Journal,* May 1998, p. 6.

O'Dell, John, "Wynn's Blames Restructuring Costs for '91 Loss," *Los Angeles Times,* January 31, 1992, p. 5D.

——, "Wynn's Buys Automotive Plastics Business," *Los Angeles Times,* October 1, 1996, p. 10D.

——, "Wynn's International Reports Record '94 Profit," *Los Angeles Times,* January 31, 1995, p. 6D.

"Orange-Based Wynn's Agrees to Buy Goshen, Assume Debt," *Los Angeles Times,* October 22, 1999, p. 3C.

Rowe, Jeff, "Wynn's Sells Auto Products Unit in Restructure Move," *Los Angeles Times,* September 6, 1986, p. 7B.

Tighe, John Charles, "Stock Watch: Investment Group Puts Its 20.8% Stake in Wynn's International Up for Sale," *Los Angeles Times,* February 19, 1989, p. 8.

"To Make Air Conditioners in Texas," *Japan Economic Journal,* September 18, 1984, p. 10.

"Wynn Oil Combination Sold," *Wall Street Journal,* April 16, 1969, p. 30.

"Wynn Oil Seeks Name Change," *Wall Street Journal,* April 5, 1973, 1969, p. 16.

"Wynn's CEO Carroll Takes Over as Chairman," *Los Angeles Times,* December 12, 1996, p. 8D.

"Wynn's, Chronos Team Up," *Rubber & Plastics News,* July 19, 1999, p. 5.

"Wynn's Names Bellwood Chairman; Founder Retires," *Wall Street Journal,* February 25, 1970, p. 33.

"Wynn's to Consolidate," *Dallas Business Journal,* November 23, 1990, p. 27.

"Wynn's X-tend Du-All Recycling System: Two Steps Ahead of the Competition," *PR Newswire,* September 10, 1992.

—Mary Tradii

Zion's Cooperative Mercantile Institution

2200 South 900 West
Salt Lake City, Utah 84137
U.S.A.
Telephone: (801) 579-6000
Web site: http://www.zcmi.com

*Wholly Owned Subsidiary of The May Department Stores
Company*
Incorporated: 1870
Employees: 4,000
Sales: $247.5 million (1999)
NAIC: 45211 Department Stores

Organized in 1868, Zion's Cooperative Mercantile Institution (ZCMI) claims the distinction of being the first full-line department store in the United States. ZCMI was also likely the only department store to be owned by a church, namely The Church of Jesus Christ of Latter-Day Saints (LDS), until it was sold in 1999 to The May Department Stores Company. ZCMI operates 13 retail stores in Salt Lake City, Ogden, West Valley City, Murray, Orem, Sandy, Logan, Layton, and St. George, Utah, as well as stores in Idaho Falls and Chubbuck, Idaho. According to a 1999 study, ZCMI is the 18th largest department store chain in the United States and is the only major chain based in the Intermountain West.

Origins: ZCMI, a Mormon Defense Against Gentiles

In the 1830s, the LDS church moved its base from New York State, where it had been organized, to Ohio, then to Missouri, and next to Nauvoo, Illinois, and finally to the Salt Lake Valley in 1847. The move had been prompted in an effort to escape persecution from non-Mormons or Gentiles, but in the Utah Territory the church continued to face considerable opposition, such as the 1857 Utah War when the federal government sent an army to confront the church and its President Brigham Young. Still, the Mormons remained relatively isolated in the Intermountain West until the first transcontinental railroad was completed in 1869 north of Salt Lake City.

"To Brigham Young and other leaders of the LDS Church," wrote historian Martha Bradley, "the railroad and the increased contact that it brought with national markets and the world outside presented a most serious threat to the cohesiveness and solidarity of the Saints. Because he anticipated trouble, confusion, and the inevitable cultural and social diversity that accompanied the railroad, Brigham Young planned what amounted to a frontal attack."

At the October 1868 LDS General Conference, President Brigham Young and other church leaders urged the members to cooperate economically. Later in the month LDS businessmen from around the territory met in Salt Lake City to organize a wholesale cooperative store. Brigham Young was elected president of the "People's Store" or ZCMI. Its initial directors were also church leaders. The store's goal was to offer lower prices than the enemy Gentile businesses while promoting church unity.

Not all LDS merchants joined the new institution at first. In fact, some of ZCMI's early opponents were excommunicated and began the forerunner of *The Salt Lake Tribune*, illustrating that little separation of church, state, and business existed in that pioneer era. In 1869 ZCMI's main store, the Eagle Emporium on 200 South Main Street, opened its doors for business, with clothing, dry goods, hats, caps, boots, and shoes for sale. Soon a second wholesale store opened, with groceries, farm tools, stoves, and hardware available. From that time until 1924, ZCMI had eight departments, each with a retail and wholesale division: dry goods, grocery, hardware, chinaware, shoes, rugs, meats, and men's clothing.

ZCMI was formally incorporated in 1870 after the territorial legislature passed its first incorporation laws. By that time, some 150 cooperatives had been established not only in the Utah Territory, but also in Wyoming, Idaho, Nevada, and even South Dakota. Such coops depended on ZCMI Wholesale for many products and were also supplied with locally made items. Brigham Young strongly encouraged home manufacturing and cooperative ventures to make the Mormons as self-sufficient as possible.

ZCMI was financially successful in its early years. By 1873 its annual sales were $4.5 million, and within just four years the

---

Company Perspectives:

ZCMI, one of the most respected names in retailing, is the department store leader in its markets—providing an exceptional combination of merchandise selection and customer service.

Mormons enjoyed dividends of over $500,000 on their initial investment of $280,000. ZCMI expanded in the 1870s and early 1880s. New ZCMI stores were opened in Logan, Utah, in 1873 and Ogden, Utah, in 1881. Moreover, ZCMI bought the Deseret Tanning and Manufacturing Association in 1879.

However, the church's political troubles soon engulfed ZCMI. Because of federal laws outlawing polygamy, church leaders were forced to hide from government authorities seeking to arrest them. Also, in the face of threatened government actions against the church, it sold all of its ZCMI shares to private individuals. Ironically, during the so-called "underground" years, ZCMI expanded its operations. For example, by around 1890 its Salt Lake City clothing factory employed 300 men, women, and children and was the largest factory west of Chicago.

1890–1930: An Americanized and Commercialized Store

Following the 1890 LDS Manifesto banning polygamy among church members in the United States, ZCMI began to separate itself at least partially from its parent church. In 1891, it ended the practice of sending ten percent of its cash dividends to the church. Also, for the first time, non-Mormons were allowed to buy ZCMI stock, as long as the church or its leaders retained stock control. Finally, the church ended sanctions against those who shopped with ZCMI competitors. Individual choice and capitalistic competition had triumphed over group values and enforced cooperation. Although some Mormons remained defensive against outsiders, LDS church members were allowed to make their own economic and political choices. Following these developments, Utah finally gained statehood in 1896 after decades of failed attempts.

As Utah's population doubled between 1890 and 1920, ZCMI began appealing to all residents, not just church members. For example, after 1920 the sign proclaiming "Holiness to the Lord" was relegated to church buildings only and thus discontinued at ZCMI. All store employees began receiving their wages in cash, rather than in store goods as they had in the pioneer era.

The system of cooperatives that existed earlier ended in the early 1900s, and the Provo, Logan, and Ogden stores were sold by 1906, leaving ZCMI to operate on a centralized basis from its main Salt Lake City store, with local warehouses in several locations in Idaho and Utah.

Meanwhile, ZCMI sales continued to increase, from $3.2 million in 1896 to $5.3 million in 1906, $7.7 million in 1916, and $9.9 million in 1917. In fact, sales rose until 1921, when ZCMI business declined 27 percent; Utah in 1920 suffered through a depression, while most of the nation enjoyed prosperity.

Although leaders of the LDS church remained in control of ZCMI, the company began in the early 20th century to hire more managers who had college training and considerable professional work experience in marketing and business management. Church standards were expected of all ZCMI workers and managers, but an increasing number no longer had close personal or family ties to church leaders.

Modernization: 1930–60

During the Great Depression, Utah received a great deal of aid from the federal government. For example, New Deal farm subsidies added over $10 million to the state's economy. This stimulated consumer spending, and ZCMI sales started to recover from their downturn in the 1920s.

After the 1935 Wagner Act strengthened labor unions, ZCMI's wholesale division organized the Wholesale Employees Association in 1937. This occurred in spite of the LDS church's opposition to unions.

During wartime, the nation was finally rid of its depressed economic picture. ZCMI sales doubled during this time, reaching $22 million in 1945. The company supported the war effort by offering bonds as sales incentives and promoting salvage and conservation programs.

In 1946 Harold H. Bennett was chosen as the new ZCMI general manager. He modernized ZCMI with the help of managers recruited from Macy's and Marshall Field and Company. In 1946 ZCMI added an escalator, the first in a store in the western United States, and in 1954 the company constructed Salt Lake City's first store-side parking terrace. Bennett also began a long-term involvement with the National Retail Merchants Association in 1945, and in the early 1960s twice served as that group's president. In 1958 Bennett became the first ZCMI president who was not also president of the LDS church.

In the 1950s ZCMI realized that its wholesale operations, which produced 40 percent of ZCMI's sales but only 13.5 percent of its profits, were basically obsolete. So in 1960 it decided to completely end its wholesale business and use the extra money to build its retail operations.

ZCMI Expands: 1962 to the 1990s

In 1962 ZCMI opened a large new store in the Cottonwood Mall, located in the Salt Lake City suburban neighborhood of Holladay. Part of a nationwide trend as the nation's suburbs expanded with the growing families of the "baby boom" generation, the Cottonwood Mall was the state's "first complete suburban shopping center," according to the October 16, 1999 *Salt Lake Tribune*.

In addition to the downtown Salt Lake City store and the Cottonwood Mall store, ZCMI had added several other large department stores by the 1990s. The new Utah stores were located in the Ogden City Mall, Layton Hills Mall in Layton, Cache Valley Mall in Logan, University Mall in Orem, Valley Fair Mall in West Valley City, Southtowne Center in Sandy, Red Cliffs Mall in St. George, Fashion Place in Murray, and Foothill Village Mall in suburban Salt Lake City. Two new

Key Dates:

1870: ZCMI is incorporated.
1873: A branch store in Logan, Utah, opens.
1876: ZCMI outlets are consolidated into the "Mercantile Palace" in downtown Salt Lake City.
1886: LDS church sells all its ZCMI stock during polygamy conflict.
1891: Non-Mormons are allowed to buy ZCMI stock, and ZCMI quits paying tithes to church.
1901: Rexburg store converted to warehouse.
1958: Harold H. Bennett becomes first ZCMI president who is not president of the LDS church.
1960: Wholesale division is closed to allow expansion of retail business.
1962: New store is opened in Holladay's Cottonwood Mall.
1973: ZCMI Service Center is opened to consolidate corporate offices and service departments.
1999: ZCMI is sold to The May Department Stores Company.

Idaho stores operated in the Grand Teton Mall in Idaho Falls and the Pine Ridge Mall in Chubbuck near Pocatello.

Efforts to expand also included plans to break into the Southwest. In 1990 ZCMI opened four new stores in Arizona (Phoenix, Scottsdale, and two in Mesa), as well as a new store in Las Vegas, Nevada. However, all five these stores were eventually closed.

In 1993 ZCMI celebrated its 125th anniversary with a hefty newspaper insert that combined ads for some of its major name brands and historical photos and text. The firm also hosted a gala evening of music by the Utah Symphony and a fashion show with styles from the past. However, ZCMI's good times were about to end.

The LDS Church's Sale of ZCMI

In spite of optimistic statements from its leaders, ZCMI in reality lost a great deal of money in the late 1990s. Its flagship store in downtown Salt Lake City suffered as the central business district declined. Extensive construction for a new light-rail system and renovation of Interstate 15, Utah's major north-south highway, hurt many downtown businesses, including ZCMI. Construction of a new mall in southern Provo prompted ZCMI to renovate its store in nearby Orem's University Mall. Begun in the major retailing season in fall 1998, that expensive remodeling hurt sales of ZCMI's most profitable unit.

In addition, ZCMI faced intense competition from mass merchandisers, discount stores, catalog sales, and even electronic commerce in the 1990s. Just as Sears had shuttered its general catalog in the face of a boom in specialized catalog sales, ZCMI's general retailing declined while specialized retail chains prospered. The bottom line was that ZCMI's net income declined from $1.8 million in fiscal 1996 to just $209,410 in 1997 and to a net loss of $8.5 million in 1998.

The LDS church, owners of 51 percent of ZCMI stock, decided finally that it had to sell its historic department store. The church was growing rapidly all over the world and simply could not afford to keep losing so much money. According to Jeff Stinson, a Midwest Research securities analyst, several companies expressed an interest in buying ZCMI. "When you look at the high-quality regional chains, ZCMI was one of the last ones," said Stinson in the December 15, 1999 *Salt Lake Tribune*.

After rejecting a bid by Cincinnati's Federated Department Stores, the country's largest department store chain, ZCMI directors reluctantly chose another buyer. Shareholders of both ZCMI and The May Department Stores Company approved a merger, effective December 31, 1999, in which ZCMI became one of May's wholly-owned subsidiaries. Based in St. Louis, May operated 409 department stores in 34 states and the District of Columbia.

May agreed to let ZCMI operate under its historic name for two years, during which time ZCMI stores would not be forced to open on Sunday. After two years, ZCMI would become part of May's Meier & Frank chain. The agreement also stipulated that after two years, rights to use the ZCMI name would revert back to the LDS church.

New ownership led ZCMI to conduct massive sales, especially in departments that were scheduled for elimination. For example, ZCMI, one of the few department stores that still sold electronics, was directed to close that department due to the competition from large chain stores such as Circuit City and Ultimate Electronics. The toy and book departments also were targeted for closing.

While May Department Stores acquired ZCMI, the church, through its company Zions Securities, retained ownership of the ZCMI Center, a downtown mall that housed numerous businesses. In 2000 the ZCMI Center's owners hired a consultant to look at a possible name change.

Although the LDS church sold its hospital system, which became Intermountain Health Care, and its interest in Zion's Bank, it remained an economic powerhouse not only in the Intermountain West, but also in many other states and even to a smaller extent overseas. It owned the largest cattle ranch in the United States, the Deseret Book Company, insurance companies, real estate, several television and radio stations through its Bonneville International Corporation, Brigham Young University and other academic institutions, and of course its rapidly growing number of chapels and temples all over the world. The authors of *Mormon America* detailed some of the church's business interests and the growing role of prominent Mormons in politics, business, sports, and other secular fields. Thus, in spite of being forced to sell ZCMI, the LDS church, with about ten million members and an estimated $25 billion in assets, continued to be a major player on the world stage.

Principal Competitors

Wal-Mart Stores, Inc.; Nordstrom, Inc.; Dillard Department Stores, Inc.; Sears, Roebuck and Co.; J.C. Penney Company, Inc.

Further Reading

Arrington, Leonard J., *Great Basin Kingdom: Economic History of the Latter-Day Saints,* Lincoln: University of Nebraska Press, 1958.

Bradley, Martha Sonntag, *ZCMI: America's First Department Store,* Salt Lake City: ZCMI, 1991.

Oberbeck, Steven, "With ZCMI Sold, What Next?," *Salt Lake Tribune,* October 16, 1999, pp. D5–D6.

Ostling, Richard N., and Joan K. Ostling, *Mormon America: The Power and The Promise,* New York: HarperSanFrancisco, 1999.

Sahm, Phil, "As Expected, May Buys ZCMI," *Salt Lake Tribune,* October 16, 1999, pp. A1, A5.

——, "LDS Church Held Up Sale of Struggling ZCMI," *Salt Lake Tribune,* December 15, 1999, pp. F1–F2.

——, "Owners Ponder a Name Change for ZCMI Center," *Salt Lake: Tribune,* February 19, 2000, p. A1.

——, "Tis a Sign of Change at ZCMI," *Salt Lake Tribune,* December 22, 1999, pp. F1, F6.

—David M. Walden

INDEX TO COMPANIES

Index to Companies

Listings in this index are arranged in alphabetical order under the company name. Company names beginning with a letter or proper name such as Eli Lilly & Co. will be found under the first letter of the company name. Definite articles (The, Le, La) are ignored for alphabetical purposes as are forms of incorporation that precede the company name (AB, NV). Company names printed in bold type have full, historical essays on the page numbers appearing in bold. Updates to entries that appeared in earlier volumes are signified by the notation (upd.). Company names in light type are references within an essay to that company, not full historical essays. This index is cumulative with volume numbers printed in bold type.

INDEX TO INDUSTRIES

Index to Industries

CONSTRUCTION

ENGINEERING & MANAGEMENT SERVICES

ENTERTAINMENT & LEISURE

FINANCIAL SERVICES: BANKS

FINANCIAL SERVICES: NON-BANKS

FOOD PRODUCTS

FOOD SERVICES & RETAILERS

INFORMATION TECHNOLOGY

MATERIALS

PERSONAL SERVICES

PETROLEUM

PUBLISHING & PRINTING

REAL ESTATE

RUBBER & TIRE

TELECOMMUNICATIONS

WASTE SERVICES

NOTES ON CONTRIBUTORS

Notes on Contributors

BIANCO, David. Freelance writer, editor, and publishing consultant.

BISCONTINI, Tracey Vasil. Pennsylvania-based freelance writer, editor, and columnist.

BRENNAN, Gerald E. Freelance writer based in California.

BRYNILDSSEN, Shawna. Freelance writer and editor based in Bloomington, Indiana.

COHEN, M. L. Novelist and freelance writer living in Paris.

COVELL, Jeffrey L. Freelance writer and corporate history contractor.

DERDAK, Thomas. Freelance writer and adjunct professor of philosophy at Loyola University of Chicago.

FIERO, John. Freelance writer, researcher, and consultant.

FUJINAKA, Mariko. Freelance writer and editor based in California.

HAUSER, Evelyn. Freelance writer and marketing specialist based in Northern California.

INGRAM, Frederick C. South Carolina-based business writer who has contributed to *GSA Business, Appalachian Trailway News,* the *Encyclopedia of Business,* the *Encyclopedia of Global Industries,* the *Encyclopedia of Consumer Brands,* and other regional and trade publications.

LEMIEUX, Gloria A. Freelance writer and editor living in Nashua, New Hampshire.

MARTIN, Rachel. Denver-based freelance writer.

ROTHBURD, Carrie. Freelance technical writer and editor, specializing in corporate profiles, academic texts, and academic journal articles.

STANFEL, Rebecca. Freelance writer and editor based in Montana.

TRADII, Mary. Freelance writer based in Denver, Colorado.

WALDEN, David M. Freelance writer and historian in Salt Lake City; adjunct history instructor at Salt Lake City Community College.

WERNICK, Ellen. Freelance writer and editor.